Mental Health Act Manual

MENTAL HEALTH ACT MANUAL

Twenty-Sixth Edition

RICHARD M. JONES M.A. (Kent and Brunel), Solicitor, C.Q.S.W.
Consultant, Blake Morgan LLP, Solicitors
Honorary Visiting Professor of Law, Cardiff University

SWEET & MAXWELL

THOMSON REUTERS

Published in 2023 by Thomson Reuters, trading as Sweet & Maxwell.
Thomson Reuters is registered in England & Wales, Company No. 1679046.
Registered office and address for service:
5 Canada Square, Canary Wharf, London E14 5AQ.

For further information on our products and services, visit *http:// www.sweetandmaxwell.co.uk.*

Computerset by Sweet & Maxwell.
Printed and bound by CPI Group (UK) Ltd, Croydon, CR0 4YY
A CIP catalogue record of this book is available from the British Library.

ISBN (print): 978-0-414-11580-4

ISBN (e-book): 978-0-414-11582-8

ISBN (print and e-book): 978-0-414-11581-1

Appendix D is reproduced with kind permission of The Law Society and may also be found at the following web address: *https:// www.lawsociety.org.uk/topics/private-client/ representation-before-mental-health-tribunals*

PREFACE

A "Draft Mental Health Bill" was published by the Government in June 2022. The draft Bill was then submitted for pre-legislative scrutiny by a joint committee of the House of Commons and House of Lords which published its report in January 2023. Although the joint committee welcomed the draft Bill and said that they "would like to see it introduced in this Session of Parliament" (para.23) they also concluded that the draft Bill "should not be the end - or even a pause - in the process of reform of mental health legislation" (para.24). In the preface to the 25th edition of this Manual I said that if "the draft Bill is enacted in anything like its present form, it will continue the process started by the [Mental Health (Amendment) Act 1982] of adding a patchwork of ad hoc amendments to the framework of legislation established in [the Mental Health Act 1959]". Neither the draft Bill nor the Independent Review of the Mental Health Act, chaired by Professor Sir Simon Wessely, that preceded it were met with anything like universal acclaim, and it is highly unlikely that the Bill will be introduced in this session of Parliament. It is therefore to be hoped that the Government will use this pause to consider whether the direction of travel set out in the draft Bill is appropriate. It is surely time for the piecemeal approach that has been taken to mental health law reform since the 1959 Act to be abandoned and a root and branch review of the legislation to be undertaken. Support for this approach can be found in the report of the joint committee which stated that "there was a view among some of our witnesses, survey responses and at the roundtable with service users that more fundamental reform of the Mental Health Act is required or would be desirable" (para.20).

The new material incorporated in this edition includes:

Guidance

- Government guidance on section 17 leave of absence and on discharges granted under s.42 of the Act.

Cases

- In *R. (on the application of Worcestershire CC) v Secretary of State for Health and Social Care* [2023] UKSC 31, the Supreme Court held that if a patient who was being provided with after-care services under s.117 was discharged from detention and was subsequently detained in the area of another local authority, that local authority became responsible for providing services under s.117 as long as the patient was ordinarily resident there.
- A seminal judgment on the relationship between the Mental Health Act and the Mental Capacity Act is given by HHJ Burrows in *Manchester University Hospitals NHS Foundation Trust v JS and Manchester City* [2023] EWCOP 12. In this case, Judge Burrows had to consider "an area of the law that is extremely complicated, in fact unduly so in view of the vulnerable circumstances of the people to whom it applies and the need for it to be used by busy clinicians in their daily work. This is the issue of ineligibility under the Mental Capacity Act 2005 (MCA) and, in particular, Schedule 1A and Case E" (para.5). Case E is concerned with patients who

are "within the scope" of the Mental Health Act but are not subject to it. An appeal against this decision was dismissed ([2023] EWCOP 33).

- *Blackpool Borough Council v HT (A Minor)* [2022] EWHC 1480 (Fam) where Macdonald J. addressed the extra hurdles that must be overcome if a child or young person is the be admitted under the Act to a Tier 4 Child and Adolescent Mental Health Services bed.

- *R. v Walker* [2023] EWCA Crim 548 where Dingemans L.J. considered when it would be appropriate for a court to sentence a mentally disordered offender to a section 45A "Hybrid Order".

- *R. v Wellington (Francis Junior)* [2022] M.H.L.R. 15, a case where the Court of Appeal considered the impact of a mentally disordered offender's culpability on sentencing.

- In *Norfolk and Suffolk NHS Foundation Trust v HJ* [2023] EWFC 92, David Lock KC, sitting as a Deputy High Court Judge, identified the principles that apply to an assessment as to whether medical treatment provided to someone in lawful detention amounts to a further deprivation of their liberty. This case also considered whether a patient's gastrointestinal illness came within the scope of s.63 of the Act.

- In *R. (on the application of Maher) v First-tier Tribunal (Mental Health)* [2023] EWHC 34 (Admin), Stacey J. considered the relationship between the presumption of privacy in cases involving the mental health of a patient and the open justice principle. The judge held that the Deputy Chamber President had acted unlawfully when she decided not to provide a victim with the reasons for the tribunal's decision to order the conditional discharge of the patient.

Legislation

Reference is made to a new legal framework introduced by the Police, Crime, Sentencing and Courts Act 2022 which allows for the remote access by non-participants to proceedings, including tribunal proceedings, that are to be held in public.

I have attempted to state the law based on material that was available to me on August 14, 2023.

Richard Jones

TABLE OF CONTENTS

PART 4

PART 5

PART 6

APPENDICES

TABLE OF CASES

PART 1: MENTAL HEALTH ACT 1983

MENTAL HEALTH ACT 1983

(1983 c.20)

ARRANGEMENT OF SECTIONS

[3]

[5]

[7]

An Act to consolidate the law relating to mentally disordered persons.

[May 9, 1983]

General Note

1-001   The origins of modern mental health legislation lie with the Mental Health Act 1959 which repealed all existing legislation dealing with mental illness and mental deficiency. It was based on the *Report of the Royal Commission on the Law Relating to Mental Illness* (Cmnd. 169) and incorporated the principles that no one should be admitted to hospital if care in the community would be more appropriate, and that where admission to hospital required compulsion, which was to be a medical instead of a judicial matter, this should if possible be avoided. In January 1975, the Labour Government announced its intention to review the 1959 Act in the light of the many changes which had taken place in treatment and care, in the patterns of services for the mentally disordered, and in public attitudes. An interdepartmental committee of civil servants was set up to undertake the review and it considered a number of suggestions for amending the Act including comprehensive reviews which had been carried out by the Royal College of Psychiatrists and by MIND in Vol. 1 of its publication, *A Human Condition.* It also considered that part of the *"Report of the Committee on Mentally Abnormal Offenders"* (Cmnd. 6244) (The Butler Report) which reviewed Pt V of the 1959 Act which is concerned with offender patients. The interdepartmental committee's suggestions were set out in a consultative document, "*A Review of the Mental Health Act 1959*" (HMSO, 1976), and comments were invited from interested bodies and individuals. Following the publication of the consultative document, two further major contributions to the debate came in the form of the second volume of MIND's *A Human Condition* on offender patients and the British Association of Social Workers' document, *"Mental Health Crisis Services—A New Philosophy"*.

In 1978, the Government published its response to the consultative exercise in a White Paper, "*The Review of the Mental Health Act 1959*" (Cmnd. 7320). Some of the proposals in the White Paper were set out in a tentative form because they were either not put forward in the consultative document or were not fully developed at that time. Comments on these proposals were invited but before the Government could translate its proposals into an amending Bill a change of government took place. Further consultations then took place and the Conservative Government's conclusions were embodied in a Bill which was published in November 1981, together with an accompanying White Paper, "*Reform of Mental Health Legislation*" (Cmnd. 8405). The Bill, which was scrutinised by a Special Standing Committee of the House of Commons, was enacted in October 1982 as the Mental Health (Amendment) Act 1982. It made substantial amendments to the 1959 Act as well as introducing new powers relating to the treatment and discharge of mentally disordered patients. In Cmnd. 8405, the Government announced its intention to introduce a consolidation measure soon after the Royal Assent had been given to the 1982 Act and a Consolidation Bill was introduced in the House of Lords on January 20, 1983. This was referred to the Joint Committee on Consolidation Bills which reported on February 9, 1983 (HL 81, HC 193). The Bill was enacted as the Mental Health Act 1983 on May 9, 1983.

In October 1998, the Labour Government appointed a group of experts (the "Committee") to advise on the degree to which the 1983 Act needed updating "to support effective delivery of modern patterns of clinical and social care for people with mental disorder and to ensure that there is a proper balance between safety (both of individuals and the wider community) and the rights of individual patients" (*Review of the Mental Health Act 1983*, 1999, App.A). The Parliamentary Under-Secretary of State made it clear to the Committee at its first meeting that the Government would not accept any recommendation that would enable a patient who was subject to compulsory powers to be non-compliant with medication when "appropriate care in appropriate settings is in place" (*Review of the Mental Health Act 1983*, 1999, App.C, para.11). The Committee published its report in November 1999. Fundamental to the Committee's approach was a desire for new legislation to promote the principle of non-discrimination on the grounds of mental health. This inevitably led the Committee to emphasise the notion of patient autonomy. As the Committee stated, "in the context of physical health a patient with capacity is free to choose whether or not to accept treatment: his or her autonomy is respected". The Committee adopted a pragmatic approach in its recommendations. Although the Committee accepted that the safety of the public must be allowed to outweigh the individual autonomy of a capacitated mentally disordered person "where the risk is great", it provided no adequate explanation as to why the principle of patient autonomy should not lead to such a person being dealt with through the justice system. The Committee divided on whether a capacitated mentally disordered person should have the same "right" as a capacitated physically disordered person to self-harm or whether such patients should be protected from themselves through mental health legislation. The Committee concluded that the choice between the two approaches was a "moral" one that should be taken by politicians and not the Committee.

1-002

Given the nature of the Committee's approach to patient autonomy, it was hardly surprising that when the Government published its response to the Committee's proposals in the form of a Green Paper (*Reform of the Mental Health Act 1983: Proposals for Consultation*, Cm. 4480) it rejected the introduction of a notion of capacity into the criteria for compulsory intervention. The Government's view was that it "is the *degree of risk* that patients with mental disorders pose, to themselves or others, that is crucial to [the decision on whether a patient should be made subject to a compulsory order]. In the presence of such risk, questions of capacity—while still relevant to the plan of care and treatment—may be largely irrelevant to the question of whether or not a compulsory order should be made" (p.32).

The Green Paper was followed in December 2000 by a White Paper, "*Reforming the Mental Health Act*" (Cm. 5016). This confirmed the Government's emphasis on risk: "Concerns of risk will always take precedence, but care and treatment provided under formal powers should otherwise reflect the best interests of the patient" (para.2.16). The theme of risk was further emphasised by the Government's concern that existing legislation had "failed to provide adequate public protection from those whose risk to others arises from severe personality disorder" (Foreword, p.1).

A Draft Bill was published in June 2002 (Cm. 5538). The Bill was scrutinised by the Joint Committee of the Houses of Commons and Lords on Human Rights, which reported in November 2002 (HL

Paper 181; HC 1294). The Draft Bill did not cover everything that was intended to be in the final version of the Bill to be introduced in Parliament but was accompanied by a consultation document seeking views about a number of policy areas. Following the consultation process, the Government published a new version of the Bill in September 2004 (Cm. 6305). The revised draft Bill was subject to pre-legislative scrutiny from a Joint Committee of the House of Commons and House of Lords. Having considered a great deal of evidence, much of it hostile to the Government's proposals, the Committee reached the view that "the Government should proceed with the Bill, but only with significant amendments, as proposed in our report" (HL Paper 79-1; HC 95-1, p.5). The Government published its response to the Joint Committee's report in July 2005 (Cm. 6624). On March 23, 2006, the Secretary of State for Health announced that the Government had abandoned its plans to proceed with the draft Bill and would instead proceed to "introduce a shorter, streamlined Bill that amends the [1983] Act".

The Mental Health Bill, which was given its first reading in the House of Lords on November 16, 2006, was scrutinised by the Joint Committee on Human Rights which published its report in February 2007 (HL Paper 40; HC 288). A progress report was published by the Joint Committee in June 2007 (HL Paper 112; HC 555). The main innovation in the Bill was the introduction of community treatment orders. The Parliamentary debates on the Bill, especially those in the House of Lords, largely focused on the Government's response to amendments proposed by Conservatives, Liberal Democrats and crossbenchers who were advocating on behalf of the Mental Health Alliance, an organisation which stated that it "is a coalition of 79 organisations working together to secure humane and effective mental health legislation" (the Alliance lost five of its members in May 2007 over the issue of which professional groups should have the power to renew the detention and supervised community treatment of patients). Opinions regarding both the alleged inadequacy of the current state of the law and the Government's proposals were forcibly expressed. A disinterested observer would have been surprised to learn that although the 1983 Act was clearly in need of reform, it was generally thought to have provided a legislative structure which worked reasonably well in practice by striking an appropriate balance between the interests of patients and the public. The Mental Health Act 2007 received the Royal Assent on July 19, 2007.

In the Queen's Speech delivered on June 21, 2017, it was announced that the "Government will reform mental health legislation and ensure that mental health is prioritised in the National Health Service in England". The Government subsequently said that it had asked Sir Simon Wessely, past President of the Royal College of Psychiatrists, to chair an independent review into the Mental Health Act. The report of the review, "*Modernising the Mental Health Act*" (December 2018), can be accessed at: *www.gov.uk/government/groups/independent-review-of-the-mental-health-act*. The aim of the review's 154 recommendations was to "shift the dial" in the legislation in favour of "greater respect for wishes, choices and preferences" (p.12). Only a relatively small number of recommendations in the review required amendments to the Act. On December 6, 2018, the government announced that it would introduce a new Mental Health Bill, and that it had accepted two of the report's recommendations: (1) those detained under the Act will be allowed to nominate a person of their choice to be involved in decisions about their care; and (2), people will be able to express their preferences for care and treatment and have these listed in statutory "advance choice" documents (*www.gov.uk/government/news/government-commits-to-reform-the-mental-health-act*). The government subsequently published a White Paper, "*Reforming the Mental Health Act*", on January 13, 2021, which can be accessed at: *https://www.gov.uk/government/consultations/reforming-the-mental-health-act/reforming-the-mental-health-act*. Under the heading "Next Steps", the White Paper states:

"As a next step, and in the spirit of co-production established by the review, we will consult widely to gather the views of everyone who may be impacted by the planned reforms, including service users, their families and carers, mental health clinicians and professionals, and experts in mental health and mental capacity legislation, to ensure the reforms work for everyone. We will use the evidence and views from this consultation to make final policy decisions and to draft a revised Mental Health Bill, which we will introduce when Parliamentary time allows."

A Draft Bill (CP 699) was published on June 27, 2022 as part of that consultation process. It can be accessed at: *https://assets.publishing.service.gov.uk/government/uploads/system/uploads/attachment_ data/file/1093555/draft-mental-health-bill-web-accessible.pdf*. The draft Bill was considered by a joint committee of the House of Lords and House of Commons which published its report (HC 696; HL Paper 128) on January 19, 2023: see *https://committees.parliament.uk/publications/33599/documents/182904/ default*. The report states that the "draft Bill amends the Mental Health Act (MHA) 1983, primarily to implement recommendations of the 2018 Independent Review. It also includes some other measures that were not recommended by the Review, such as the removal of learning disability and autism as potential grounds for detention under Section 3 of the MHA" (para.16).

For fuller accounts of the convoluted process that led to the passing of the 2007 Act, see Paul Bowen,

Blackstone's Guide to the Mental Health Act 2007 (2007) pp.6–18 and Phil Fennell, *Mental Health: the New Law* (2007) pp.2–12. The history of mental health legislation up to and including the 1983 Act is considered by Paul Unsworth in *The Politics of Mental Health Legislation* (1987) and by Phil Fennell in Ch.1 of *Principles of Mental Health Law and Policy* (2010).

Coronavirus Pandemic

A fourth version of "Legal guidance for services supporting people of all ages during the coronavirus pandemic: Mental health, learning disability and autism, specialised commissioning" was published by NHSE and NHSI, on January 25, 2021. It is referred to throughout the text as the "NHS Guidance" and can be accessed at: *www.england.nhs.uk/coronavirus/wp-content/uploads/sites/52/2020/03/C1075-legal-guidance-for-mh-ld-autism-specialised-commissioning-services-v4-25-jan-21.pdf*.
Mental Health Law Online has a Coronavirus resources page which can be accessed at: *www.mhlo.uk/bh*. **1-003**

The Mental Health Act in Wales

Subject to a number of exceptions that are noted in the annotations to the relevant sections, the functions of the Secretary of State under the Act were transferred to the National Assembly for Wales by the National Assembly for Wales (Transfer of Functions) Order 1999 (SI 1999/672, art.2 Sch.1) (as amended by SI 2000/253, art.4 Sch.3). These functions are now exercised by the Welsh Ministers by virtue of the Government of Wales Act 2006 s.162, Sch.11 para.30. References to regulations that have been made under the Act by the Welsh Ministers are made throughout this work. The Mental Health (Wales) Measure 2010, a Measure of the National Assembly of Wales, received Royal Approval on December 15, 2010. Amongst its provisions is the enactment of ss.130E to 130L of the Act which are concerned with the provision of independent mental health advocacy services for Welsh qualifying patients. Wales has its own mental Health Review Tribunal: see s.65. A second edition of a Code of Practice for Wales on the Act was published by the Wales Assembly Government in 2016. It can be accessed at: *https://gov.wales/mental-health-act-1983-code-practice*. **1-004**

Policy of the Act

According to the Court of Appeal, the "policy and objects" of the Act (prior to its amendment by the 2007 Act) are "to regulate the circumstances in which the liberty of persons who are mentally disordered may be restricted and, where there is conflict, to balance their interests against those of public policy" (*R. v Secretary of State for the Home Department Ex p. K* [1990] 3 All E.R. 562, 570, per McCowan L.J.). In *Secretary of State for Justice v RB* [2011] EWCA Civ 1608; [2012] M.H.L.R. 131, paras 25, 26, the court said that the policy of the Act is treatment not containment.
In *R. (on the application of B) v Dr SS (Responsible Medical Officer)* [2006] EWCA Civ 28; [2006] M.H.L.R. 131, Lord Phillips CJ said at para.43: **1-005**

"The MHA is primarily concerned with the compulsory detention of patients suffering from mental disorders in order that they may receive treatment for those disorders. The compulsory detention is justified because it is necessary in order to ensure that the patient receives the treatment. Ensuring that the patient receives the treatment is justified because this is necessary for the health or safety of the patient or for the protection of others."

The distinction between the policy of this Act and that of the Mental Capacity Act 2005 was explained by UT Judge Jacobs in *MC v Sygnet Behavioural Health Ltd* [2020] UKUT 230 (AAC); [2021] M.H.L.R. 157 at para.10:

"There are two regimes, governed by the 1983 Act and the 2005 Act. They deal with different things, but they are related. The mental health regime is concerned with detention on the basis of a mental disorder, a need to protect the patient or the public, and the availability of treatment in hospital. The mental capacity regime is concerned with the best interests of a person who lacks capacity to make decisions. Those are separate matters but they can interrelate. The mental health regime will involve a deprivation of liberty, and the mental capacity regime may do so."

Judicial interpretation

In *R. v Hallstrom Ex p. W (No.2)* [1986] 2 All E.R. 306 at 314, McCullough J. said: **1-006**

"There is … no canon of construction which presumes that Parliament intended that people should, against their will, be subjected to treatment which others, however professionally competent, perceive, however sincerely and however correctly, to be in their best interests. What there is is a canon of construction that Parliament is presumed not to enact legislation which interferes with the liberty of the subject without making it clear that this was its intention. It goes without saying that, unless clear statutory authority to the contrary exists, no one is to be detained in hospital or to undergo medical treatment or even to submit himself to a medical examination without his consent. That is as true of a mentally disordered person as of anyone else."

This passage was cited with approval by the Court of Appeal in *St George's Healthcare NHS Trust v S* [1998] 3 All E.R. 673 at 692–693.
Also see *R. v Secretary of State for the Home Department, Ex p. Simms* [2000] 2 A.C. 115, 131, where Lord Hoffmann said that fundamental rights "cannot be overridden by general or ambiguous words".

Allocation of resources to detained patients

1-007   The fact that a patient is detained under the Act does not provide the patient's responsible clinician (RC) with the power to demand that the NHS gives priority to the care of that patient: see *R. (on the application of F) v Oxfordshire Mental Health Healthcare NHS Trust and Oxfordshire NHS Health Authority* [2001] EWHC Admin 535; [2001] M.H.L.R 140 where Sullivan J. said at paras 64, 66:

"Treatment is provided to all patients in the real world where the availability of facilities is constrained by resources. By way of example, the [RC] may well consider that it would be beneficial for a particular Part II or Part III patient if he/she was given better facilities whilst in hospital: more privacy, more spacious accommodation, access to particular therapy, more attention by the nursing staff, etc. There is nothing in the 1983 Act to suggest that the Health Authority must then provide those facilities. In so far as the 1983 Act confers additional powers on the [RCs], it does so vis-à-vis the [RC's] patient, not the Health Authority ... In simple terms, since resources are limited, there is bound to be a queue of patients seeking treatment. I do not accept the proposition that the [RC's] position under the 1983 Act is such as to propel his or her Part II or III patients to the head of the queue."

In *R. (on the application of K) v West London Mental Health NHS Trust* [2006] EWCA Civ 118; [2006] M.H.L.R. 89, the question before the Court of Appeal was whether the NHS Trust was obliged to pay the costs of a detained patient's treatment in an independent hospital where leave of absence under s.17 had been granted by the patient's RC for the purpose of enabling the patient to be admitted to that hospital. In answering the question in the negative, the court held that:

1.   The decision whether or not any particular services should be provided under s.3 of the National Health Service Act 1977 is one for the Secretary of State (or his delegate) and not one for the RC. Section 3, so far as is material, provides: "It is the Secretary of State's duty to provide throughout England and Wales, to such extent as he considers necessary to meet all reasonable requirements—(a) hospital accommodation ..." (now see s.3 of the National Health Service Act 2006).

2.   When performing his functions under s.3, the Secretary of State (or his delegate) is not bound to accept and act on the clinical judgment of the RC. A decision as to whether to devote resources to a particular treatment depended on many considerations, including the seriousness of the condition, the likely success of the proposed treatment, the cost of the treatment and the competing needs of other patients.

3.   A RC has no power to give directions as to how others are to discharge their functions and s.17 cannot be construed as conferring such a power.

4.   The Secretary of State (or his delegate) is not obliged to use his best endeavours to give effect to a decision of a RC under s.17.

The Court further held that *F*, above, had been correctly decided.

Injunctions to support an authority's performance of its duties under the Act

1-008   In *Broadmoor Hospital Authority v R.* [2000] 2 All E.R. 727, the issue before the Court of Appeal was whether a statutory body is entitled to be granted an injunction in civil proceedings to support its performance of its statutory duties. It was held that:

1.   If a public body is given a statutory responsibility which it is required to perform in the public interest, then, in the absence of an implication to the contrary in the statute, it has standing to apply to the court for an injunction to prevent interference with its performance of its public

responsibilities and the court should grant such an application when it appears to the court to be just and convenient to do so; and

2. Conduct outside a hospital can affect what happens within the hospital and if this is so jurisdiction exists in the court to provide protection by injunction. However there would need to be a substantial risk to the hospital's powers being prejudiced for the court to exercise its discretion to issue an injunction. Lord Woolf MR said at 736:

> "If for example an individual was causing interference with the discipline of a [high security] hospital by writing letters to the patients then notwithstanding the ability of the authority to censor correspondence, in the appropriate situation an injunction against the individual could be granted to reduce the risk of discipline being undermined and treatment interfered with."

Mental Capacity Act 2005

Paragraph 7.8 of the *Code of Practice* states: **1-009**

> "It is good practice, where practicable, for clinicians and others involved in the assessment or treatment of patients under the Act to try to find out whether the person has an attorney or deputy and to establish effective means of communication to ensure that the attorney or deputy is informed and, where relevant, consulted about the patient's care. Information regarding the appointment of any registered LPA, attorney or deputy can be obtained through a search of the registers maintained by the Office of the Public Guardian."

The effect of certain decisions taken by donees of LPAs and deputies is considered at para.7.6 of the Code:

> "In certain cases, conditions can be imposed on patients subject to the Act in relation to leave of absence from hospital, community treatment orders (CTOs) or conditional discharge. If an attorney or deputy takes a decision on the patient's behalf which goes against one of these conditions, the patient will be taken to have gone against the condition. In CTO and conditional discharge cases, this might result in the patient's recall to hospital being considered."

The interaction between this Act and the 2005 Act is discussed in the following passage from the judgment of HH Judge Burrows in *PH v A Clinical Commissioning Group* [2022] EWCOP 12:

> "18. The interaction between the Mental Capacity Act (MCA)/Court of Protection and the MHA is a difficult area of law. The MHA is mainly concerned with the detention and treatment of mentally disordered patients in hospital. In respect of those patients, the MCA largely defers to the MHA. This is explicitly so in s.28 of the MCA and Schedule 1A. Indeed, once a patient is detained under the MHA, decisions about medical treatment for mental disorder including the manifestations of the mental disorder are, for all intents and purposes outside the reach of the MCA/COP.
>
> 19. The position is different once a MHA patient who lacks the relevant capacity is discharged into the community and made subject to one of the community orders under that Act: a community treatment order (CTO)(s.17A MHA), guardianship (s.7 MHA) or (in the case of a restricted patient) by way of a conditional discharge. Then the two regimes may have to work together. This is particularly so where the patient is subject to restrictions that amount to a deprivation of his liberty – something the MHA cannot authorise, save in the very limited circumstances of a condition attached to leave of absence (s.17(3) MHA).
>
> 20. The use of the MCA and COP becomes relevant where the detained patient is moving towards a discharge where there will be a need for orders from that Court to enable discharge to take effect. There is a rich and complex jurisprudence in this area. There are COP decisions dealing with conditionally discharged patients living in the community under MCA Orders: see for instance *Birmingham City Council v SR*, Lancashire County Council v JTA [2019] EWCOP 28 (Lieven, J.). Then there is the relationship between standard authorisations and guardianship: see *C (by his litigation friend, the OS) v A Borough Council* [2012] COPLR 350 (Peter Jackson, J.). Finally, the Birmingham case confirms the decision of the Upper Tribunal in *DN v Northumberland, Tyne and Wear NHS Foundation Trust* [2011] UKUT 327 (UTJ Jacobs) and in *AM v South London & Maudsley NHS Foundation Trust* [2013] COPLR 510 (Charles, J.) namely that there is nothing wrong in principle for the COP to make best interests declarations, and to authorise deprivation of liberty where P is detained

under the MHA, but where the COP order will take effect only at the point of his discharge – that order indeed enabling the discharge to take effect.

...

22.   There is no doubt that in many cases the involvement of the COP is essential where a patient under the MHA is approaching discharge ... . The previous Vice President, who was also the President of the Upper Tribunal dealing with appeals from the First-tier Tribunal, Mr Justice Charles grappled with these procedural issues in a number of cases, most notably in *Secretary of State for Justice v KC & C Partnership NHS Foundation Trust* [2015] UKUT 376 (AAC)."

In this case, His Honour reached the following conclusion:

"24. I am unable to see how this Court has any useful and proper function in this process at this stage. Overseeing the statutory bodies in the discharge of their duties by the periodic ordering of statements, assessments and reports is a very costly and inefficient way of proceeding. That is from the viewpoint of those statutory bodies. However, it is equally so from the Court's point of view. I must look at this from the perspective of the overriding objective in COPR 2017 r.1.1. The proceedings at this stage will be expensive and lengthy. They will not be considering decisions that Peter would be making if he had the capacity to do so until there is a discharge plan readily available to be chosen and approved. In those circumstances, allotting any of the Court's time to the application at the moment is inappropriate."

Inherent jurisdiction

1-010   In *A Local Authority v LD, RD* [2023] EWHC 1258 (Fam) (para.1), Mostyn J. said that the reference in his judgment to "'The inherent jurisdiction' is to the inherent power of the High Court, devolved to it from the Crown following the constitutional settlement enacted by the Act of Settlement 1701, to protect vulnerable, but nevertheless capacitous, adults."

In *Wakefield MDC & Wakefield CCG v DN* [2019] EWHC 2306 (Fam), Cobb J. said, obiter, that the Court's inherent jurisdiction cannot be deployed to deprive a capacitous adult of their liberty. In this case, his Lordship recognised that he differed "from the approach of Gwynneth Knowles J. in her judgment in the case of *Hertfordshire County Council v AB* [2018] EWHC 3103 (Fam)" (para.49). In *Cumbria, Northumberland Tyne & Wear NHS Foundation Trust v EG* [2021] EWHC 2990 (Fam), Leiven J. preferred the reasoning of Cobb J. on this issue (para.88). Here Ladyship said at paras 90 and 92:

"In my view the inherent jurisdiction does not extend to depriving a person with capacity of their liberty for two fundamental reasons. Firstly, whether under Article 5 or the common law, the right to liberty is jealously protected and should only be removed in carefully understood and constrained circumstances. This has recently been reflected by the Grand Chamber in *Ilnseher v Germany (Application No 10211/12)* [2019] MHLR 278, drawing together dicta from earlier decisions of the court, stated (at para 129):

'the permissible grounds for deprivation of liberty listed in article 5(1) are to be interpreted narrowly. A mental condition has to be of a certain severity in order to be considered as a 'true' mental disorder for the purposes of sub-paragraph (e)'

...

A further reason for rejecting the argument that EG can be deprived of his liberty under the inherent jurisdiction is that the domestic caselaw, principally stemming from [*A Local Authority v DL* [2012] 3 All ER 1064], shows that the use of the inherent jurisdiction in respect of vulnerable adults is a facilitative rather than a dictatorial one. It is to be used to allow the vulnerable person to have the space, away from the factor which is overbearing their capacitous will, to make a fully free decision. An order which deprives that person of their liberty is a dictatorial order which severely constrains their freedom, however well meant, rather than allowing them the space to reach a freely made decision."

Court orders granted against mentally incapable persons

1-011   In *Wookey v Wookey* [1991] 3 All E.R. 365, the Court of Appeal held that an injunction ought not to be granted against a person who is incapable of understanding what he is doing or that it is wrong, because such a person is incapable of complying with it. The appropriate way of dealing with the problem behaviour of a mentally incapable person is the use of the powers under this Act. However, an interlocutory injunction might be appropriate if the court considers that the mental condition of the person against whom the injunction is sought should be investigated. In such cases the Official Solicitor should be approached for advice as to whether or not he would wish to act for the person who was liable to have an injunction made against him. *Wookey* was applied by Cobb J. in *Redcar & Cleveland Borough Council v PR* [2019] EWHC 2305 (Fam), where his Lordship said at para.46:

> "Insofar as lessons may be learned from the difficulties which arose in this case, it may usefully be suggested that before a local authority makes an application under the court's inherent jurisdiction which is designed to regulate the conduct of the subject by way of injunction, particularly where mental illness or vulnerability is an issue, it should be able to demonstrate (and support with evidence) that it has appropriately considered:
>
> i)   whether X is likely to understand the purpose of the injunction;
> ii) will receive knowledge of the injunction; and
> iii) will appreciate the effect of breach of that injunction.
>
> If the answer to any of these questions is in the negative, the injunction is likely to be ineffectual, and should not be applied for or granted as no consequences can truly flow from the breach."

If, in a borderline case, the judge concludes that the person concerned possesses the required level of capacity to enable an order to be made against him, the person's legal advisers should monitor the situation and if the position deteriorates return to the court with an application to discontinue the order (*Harris v Harris, CA, April 22, 1999*).

In *Cooke v Director of Public Prosecutions* [2008] EWHC 2703 (Admin); [2008] M.H.L.R. 348, the Divisional Court held that an anti-social behaviour order (ASBO) should not be made against a person who, by reason of mental ill health, would not have the capacity to understand or comply with the order. Lord Dyson said at para.13:

> "A Defendant who suffers from a personality disorder may on that account be liable to disobey an ASBO. In my judgment, however, that is not a sufficient reason for holding that an order, which is otherwise necessary to protect the public from a Defendant's anti-social behaviour, is not necessary for that purpose, or that the court should not exercise its discretion to make an order."

This approach was subsequently adopted and endorsed by the Divisional Court in *Fairweather v Commissioner of Police for the Metropolis* [2008] EWHC 3073 (Admin) at paras 29 to 31. Note that ASBOs have been replaced by civil injunctions, Community Protection Notices (CPN) or Criminal Behaviour Orders (CBO).

The degree of capacity which an individual must have in order to be subject to the contempt jurisdiction was considered by the Court of Appeal in *P v P (Contempt of Court: Mental Capacity)* [1999] 2 F.L.R. 897 where it was held that it was not necessary for the person to comprehend the meaning or significance of courts or of the legal process. What was required was that a potential contemnor should understand that an order has been made forbidding him to do certain things and that if he did them he may very well be punished.

Voting

In order to vote, a person must be on the electoral register. Section 3A of the Representation of the **1-012** People Act 1983 essentially excludes the following categories of patients who have been detained in psychiatric hospitals as a consequence of criminal activity from voting in parliamentary and local government elections: any person in respect of whom an order or direction has been made or given under s.37, 38, 44, 45A, 46, 47 or 51(5) of this Act; any person in respect of whom an order has been made under s.5(2)(a) of the Criminal Procedure (Insanity) Act 1964; and any person in respect of whom the Court of Appeal has made an order under either s.6(2)(a) or 14(2)(a) of the Criminal Appeal Act 1968. Other patients, both detained and informal, are entitled to be registered to vote pursuant to either s.7 or s.7A of the 1983 Act. Section 35 of the Electoral Administration Act 2006 amends Sch.4 to the Representation of the People Act 2000 so that mental health patients who are detained under Pt II of this Act are no longer prevented from voting in person if they are granted leave of absence under s.17. The amended Sch.4 also enables such patients to vote by post or by proxy if registered to do so.

Section 73(1) of the 2006 Act abolished any "rule of the common law which provides that a person is subject to a legal incapacity to vote by reason of his mental state". It is therefore the case that a person cannot be prevented from voting on capacity related grounds.

Section 29 of the Mental Capacity Act 2005 prevents a person from voting on behalf of a mentally incapacitated person.

Registering a hospital patient to vote has no impact on identifying the responsible after-care bodies under s.117 because under s.7(2) of the Representation of the People Act 1983, a patient is regarded as being resident in the hospital only for the purposes of entitlement to be registered to vote.

The blanket disenfranchisement of patients who are subject to orders made by a court under Pt III of the Act breaches art.3 of Protocol No.1 to the European Convention on Human Rights: see *Hirst v United Kingdom (No.2)* (2006) 42 E.H.R.R. 41, and the note on Protocol No.1 in Pt 5. The Government's response to this judgment is set out at p.28 of *"Responding to Human Rights judgments: Report to the Joint Committee on Human Rights on the Government's response to Human Rights judgments 2016–17"*, Cm 9535, December 2017:

> "In a statement to Parliament on 2 November 2017, the Secretary of State for Justice set out the Government's proposals to make administrative changes to address the *Hirst* judgment, while maintaining the bar on convicted prisoners in custody from voting. First, the Government will make it clear to criminals when they are sentenced that while they are in prison this means they will lose the right to vote. Second, the Government will amend Prison Service guidance to address an anomaly in the current system, where offenders who are released back in the community on licence using an electronic tag under the Home Detention Curfew scheme can vote, but those who are in the community on Temporary Licence cannot.
>
> On 7 December 2017, the Committee of Ministers noted with satisfaction the Government's proposed measures, encouraged the UK to implement them as soon as possible and asked the UK to provide an update on implementation by 1 September 2018."

The following statement can be found at p.23 of *"Report of the Joint Committee on Human Rights on the Government's response to Human Rights judgments 2017–2018"* (Cm 9728, November 2018):

> "Operational guidance has now been amended to address an anomaly in the current system, where offenders who are released early back in the community before the end of the custodial part of their sentence under the home detention curfew scheme can vote, but prisoners in the community released on temporary licence cannot vote. The Government has also made clear to criminals when they are sentenced that while they are in prison they will lose the right to vote. This is intended to address a specific concern of the *Hirst* judgment that there was not sufficient clarity in confirming to convicted offenders that they cannot vote in prison.
>
> The Government considers that all necessary measures have now been taken. An Action Report was submitted to the Committee of Ministers on 1 September 2018."

On December 6, 2018, the Committee of Ministers of the Council of Europe agreed that the UK had complied with the *Hirst* judgment and declared its examination closed.

Marriage

1-013   The marriage of patients detained under the Act is provided for under s.1 of the Marriage Act 1983. Anyone, including the doctor in charge of the patient's treatment, who does not believe that the patient is capable of giving a valid consent to the marriage may enter a caveat with the Superintendent Registrar before the ceremony. The caveat can be in the form of a letter which sets out the grounds for contending that the patient lacks the required capacity. A patient is capable of entering into a marriage if he is capable of understanding the nature of the contract of marriage, which includes an understanding of the nature of sexual intercourse and its foreseeable consequences: see *A Local Authority v AK* [2012] EWHC B29 (COP) where Bodey J. made the following comment on the role of Registrars at para.53:

> "This case has thrown up the role of Registrars and of the registration service when a borderline-incapacitated individual presents wanting to marry. It is not a Registrar's job to assess mental capacity and plainly he or she would be wholly unqualified to do so. If there is doubt in the Registrar's mind when an individual responds to the standard questions put at the notice-attestation meeting, then the procedure is for the doubt to be referred upwards, first to the local Superintendent Registrar and thereafter, if necessary, to the Office of the Registrar General. In a really tricky case, this could end up with a decision to call for a psychiatric report into capacity. That said, the standard handbook provided to Registrars presently says nothing about the need for mental capacity to contract a marriage and does not mention the Mental Capacity Act 2005."

The Superintendent Registrar will give the person who gave notice of marriage an opportunity to answer the objection and to produce evidence in rebuttal of the grounds alleged. If the Superintendent Registrar is in doubt whether or not the caveat ought to obstruct the issue of a certificate for marriage, he may refer the matter to the Registrar General. There is a right of appeal to the Registrar General against a Superintendent Registrar's refusal to issue his certificate for marriage by reason of a caveat.

Section 12(1)(d) of the Matrimonial Causes Act 1973 provides that a marriage is voidable (as distinct from void ab initio) on the ground "that at the time of the marriage either party, though capable of giving a valid consent, was suffering (whether continuously or intermittently) from mental disorder within the meaning of [the Mental Health Act 1983] of such a kind or to such an extent as to be unfitted for marriage".

The impact of the Human Rights Act 1998 on the marital rights of detained patients is considered in the note on art.12 of the European Convention on Human Rights: see Part 5.

Civil Partnerships

Under s.13 of the Civil Partnership Act 2004, any person may object to a proposed civil partnership. **1-014** The notice of objection, which must be sent to the registration authority, has to state the objector's place of residence and the ground of objection. If the registration authority refuses to register the civil partnership because of the objection, either of the proposed civil partners may appeal to the Registrar General (Civil Partnership Act 2004 s.15).

If two people wish to register as civil partners of each other at the place where one of them is detained under the Act (otherwise than by virtue of s.2, 4, 5, 35, 36, or 136), the notice of the proposed civil partnership must be accompanied by a supporting statement made by the hospital managers which (a) identifies the hospital where the person is detained, and (b) states that the managers have no objection to that hospital being specified in a notice of proposed civil partnership as the place at which the person is to register as a civil partner (Civil Partnership Act 2004 s.19). The statement must be in the form prescribed by the Civil Partnership (Registration Provisions) Regulations 2005 (SI 2005/3176) reg.4(2).

Among the grounds set out in s.50 of the 2004 Act under which a civil partnership is voidable are:

(i)   either partner did not validly consent to its formation as a result of unsoundness of mind, and

(ii)   at the time of its formation either of the partners, although capable of giving a valid consent, was suffering (whether continuously or intermittently) from mental disorder of such a kind or to such an extent as to be unfitted for civil partnership.

The right of a detained patient to pay for treatment

In *Coombs v Dorset NHS Primary Care Trust* [2013] EWCA Civ 471, the Court of Appeal held that **1-015** a patient who is detained under the Act can pay for his care or treatment as long as this does not conflict with recommendations made by his responsible clinician. Rix L.J. said at para.34:

"[T]here is nothing inherent in the structure or wording of the Mental Health Act 1983 or the [National Health Service Act 2006], and nothing by way of public policy, to exclude absolutely the possibilities of detained patients (or their family or others holding responsibility for looking after their assets) paying for or contributing in part to the cost of their treatment or care. Presumably, private patients detained in a private hospital do exactly that. Detained patients who are being looked after by an NHS authority will have most, if not all, of their costs funded by the state: but even in their case, it may be possible, as in the case of any patient within the NHS system, to purchase private accommodation or other top-up care facilities available within the applicable Guidance. Of course, it will not be possible to provide for care or treatment which is in conflict with the recommendations of the responsible clinician. Nor may it always or perhaps even often be possible within the NHS system to purchase additional care or treatment facilities without running into the principle of free provision and the limitations upon the exceptions to that principle. However, the cases cited above show that responsible clinicians may recommend treatment or care which the NHS is not under a duty to provide, because it goes beyond its statutory duty. There seems to me no reason in statute or public policy why there should be an absolute bar on the provision of facilities, recommended by or consistent with the recommendations of the responsible clinician, which may be available at a price, within or without the NHS system."

NHS England has published guidance on "*Choice in Mental Health Care*" which can be accessed at: *www.england.nhs.uk/mental-health/about/choice*.

The rights of victims of serious violent and sexual offences

1-016   This topic is considered in Ch.40 of the *Code of Practice*. Also see the General Note to the Tribunal Rules under the heading "victims".

Risks to prominent people or locations

1-017   Regulation 13 of the NHS Commissioning Board and Clinical Commissioning Groups (Responsibilities and Standing Rules) Regulations 2012 (SI 2012/2996), which is headed "Fixated threat assessment services", states:

"(1)   [NHS England] must arrange, to such extent as it considers necessary to meet all reasonable requirements, for the provision as part of the health service of specialised clinical risk assessment and management services for people with mental health problems who may present a risk to prominent people or locations.

(2)   The arrangements to be made by [NHS England] under paragraph (1) must include—

(a)   the provision of funding for mental health staff to provide the services referred to in paragraph (1); and

(b)   such provision for partnership working with other persons or health services as is considered necessary to facilitate the effective delivery of those services."

The Fixated Threat Assessment Centre (FTAC) was established in 2006. Its role is described on its website:

"FTAC is the first joint NHS/police unit in the United Kingdom. Its purpose is to assess and manage the risks from lone individuals who harass, stalk or threaten public figures. Many such people are suffering from serious mental illnesses and have fallen through the care net.

FTAC helps such people get the care they need and, by doing so, decreases any risk they might pose, not just to prominent people, but to the individuals' families and to those around them.

FTAC is a unit within the Metropolitan Police Service (MPS). It has a national remit."

Inquests with a jury

1-018   Section 7(2)(a) of the Coroners and Justice Act 2009 states:

"(2)   An inquest into a death must be held with a jury if the senior coroner has reason to suspect—

(a)   that the deceased died while in custody or otherwise in state detention, and that either—

(i)   the death was a violent or unnatural one, or (ii) the cause of death is unknown,
..."

The phrase "otherwise in state detention" in para.(a) covers patients detained under this Act. Paragraph 31 of the report by INQUEST, noted below, states:

"Under the new legal framework in force from July 2013, coroners now have a duty to make reports to a person, organisation, local authority or government department or agency where the coroner believes that action should be taken to prevent future deaths. These Reports to Prevent Future Deaths (PFDs) replaced Coroner's Rule 43 reports."

Investigations into the deaths of detained patients

1-019   In November 2015, the Department of Health published "Article 2 of the European Convention on Human Rights and the investigation of serious incidents in mental health services" which provides advice to NHS organisations on the factors to be taken into account when deciding whether an independent investigation needs to be carried out to satisfy the State's obligations under Article 2 of the European Convention on Human Rights. The guidance can be accessed at: *www.gov.uk/government/uploads/ system/uploads/attachment_data/file/474020/Article_2_advice_acc.pdf.*
    Deaths in Mental Health Detention: An investigation framework fit for purpose? (2015) is a report by INQUEST into deaths in mental health settings where the patient is detained under this Act. The report, which can be accessed at: INQUEST's website (*www.inquest.org.uk/*), identified a lack of (i) an

independent system of pre-inquest investigation as compared to other deaths in detention and (ii) a robust mechanism for ensuring post-death accountability and learning.

Riots

Section 1(6)(b) of the Riot Compensation Act 2016 provides an exemption for the relevant policing **1-020** body from liability to pay compensation where a riot has occurred in "a hospital where persons are detained under Parts 2 or 3 of the Mental Health Act 1983". This is on the basis that another party has responsibility for maintaining order in such a hospital.

Diplomatic immunity

By virtue of the Diplomatic Privileges Act 1964 s.2, Sch.1 art.29, "the person of a diplomatic agent **1-021** shall be inviolate. He shall not be liable to any form of arrest or detention. The receiving State shall treat him with due respect and shall take all appropriate steps to prevent any attack on his person, freedom or dignity". Article 1(e) defines a "diplomatic agent" as "the head of the mission or a member of the diplomatic staff of the mission" and art.37 extends the provisions of art.29 to "the members of the family of a diplomatic agent forming part of his household" who are not nationals of the receiving state. Diplomats and their families should not therefore be made subject to the provisions of the Act unless the inviolability afforded by the 1964 Act has been lifted.

According to Dr David Pariente, the legal department of the Foreign and Commonwealth Office has advised that such inviolability:

"can only be lifted by the State which the diplomat represents; in normal circumstances the State's consent must be obtained from the appropriate Head of Mission, usually an Ambassador, with whose agreement the provisions of the Mental Health Act can then be exercised. Irreversible and hazardous treatments would require his consent. In cases of extreme emergency, where immediate detention of the diplomat is the only way to protect human safety, such action would be justifiable on the basis of the inherent right of self-defence, or the duty to protect human life. In such a case the Foreign and Commonwealth Office should be informed immediately."

Dr Pariente further reports that the Medical Defence Union has "advised that the consent of the Head of Mission should be sought in writing; and that the issue of breach of confidentiality should not present a problem to a doctor who was clearly acting in the best interests of the patient" ("Diplomatic immunity and the Mental Health Act 1983" (1991) *Psychiatric Bulletin* 15 at 207–209).

An approved mental health professional faced with the possibility of making an application in respect of a person who is covered by the 1964 Act should contact the Foreign and Commonwealth Office— Diplomatic Missions and International Organisations Unit, Protocol Directorate who will be able to confirm the person's diplomatic status and, if necessary, request the relevant Head of Mission to provide the necessary consent.

Foreign travel

Apart from the provisions noted under *Extent*, below, the reach of the Act is limited to England and **1-022** Wales. The Foreign and Commonwealth Office has published "*Foreign travel advice for people with mental health issues*" (2013) which can be accessed at: *www.gov.uk/foreign-travel-advice-for-people-with-mental-health-issues*.

Equality Act 2010

Paragraph 3.7 of the *Code of Practice* states: **1-023**

"The Equality Act makes it unlawful to discriminate (directly or indirectly) against a person on the basis of a protected characteristic or combination of protected characteristics. Protected characteristics under this Act include age, disability, gender reassignment, marriage and civil partnership, pregnancy and maternity, race, religion or belief, sex and sexual orientation. The protected characteristic of disability includes a mental impairment that has a substantial and long-term adverse effect on the person's ability to carry out normal day-to-day activities."

International

1-024   International human rights law is built on the fundamental principle that all people should be protected equally under the law. Article 1 of the Universal Declaration of Human Rights (UDHR), adopted by the United Nations in 1948, provides that "all people are free and equal in rights and dignity". The UN subsequently drafted two binding international human rights conventions to promote the implementation of, and expand upon the rights established in the UDHR. They are the International Covenant on Civil and Political Rights (ICCPR) and the International Covenant on Economic, Social, and Cultural Rights (ICESR). Both conventions entered into force in 1976. Together with the UDHR and the UN Charter, they make up what is known as the "International Bill of Human Rights". The UK has ratified both conventions and is therefore under an obligation, under international law, to ensure that its policies do not conflict with the rights established therein. The ICCPR is particularly relevant to patients who are subject to compulsory powers under the Act and a number of its articles are mirrored in the European Convention on Human Rights (EHCR). In 1991, the UK ratified the Convention on the Rights of the Child (CRC) which is relevant to patients who are under 18. Although the rights under the ICCPR and the CRC are not directly enforceable in England and Wales, they can be used as an aid to interpreting the rights under the ECHR. In *Smith v Secretary of State for Work and Pensions* [2006] UKHL 35; [2006] All E.R. 907, para.78, Lady Hale cited the CRC, and said obiter:

> "Even if an international treaty has not been incorporated into domestic law, our domestic legislation has to be construed so far as possible so as to comply with the international obligations which we have undertaken."

1-025   The ECHR is not the only relevant human rights instrument emanating from Europe. The Charter of Fundamental Rights of the European Union was proclaimed at Nice in December 2000. The rights set out in the Charter, which are partly based on the rights recognised by the ECHR, are divided into six sections: dignity, freedoms, equality, solidarity, citizen's rights and justice. Article 3(2) is of particular relevance to the Act:

> "In the fields of medicine and biology, the following must be respected in particular:— the free and informed consent of the person concerned according to the procedure laid down by law."

The status of the Charter was explained by Munby J. in *R. (on the application of A,B,X and Y) v East Sussex County Council (No.2)* [2003] EWHC 167 (Admin) at para.73:

> "The Charter is not at present legally binding in our domestic law and is therefore not a source of law in the strict sense. But it can, in my judgment, properly be consulted insofar as it proclaims, reaffirms, or elucidates the content of those human rights that are generally recognised throughout the European family of nations, in particular the nature and scope of those fundamental rights that are guaranteed by the [ECHR]."

On February 23, 1999, the Committee of Ministers of the Council of Europe adopted "Principles concerning the legal protection of incapable adults", Recommendation R (99) 4. The European Court of Human Rights has said that although "these principles have no force in law for this Court, they may define a common European standard in this area" (*Shtukaturov v Russia* (2012) 54 E.H.R.R. 27; [2008] M.H.L.R. 238, para.95).

The United Nations Convention on the Rights of Persons with Disabilities (CRPD) was adopted by the General Assembly on December 13, 2006 and was ratified by the UK Government on June 8, 2009. The European Union ratified the Convention on December 23, 2010. As an unincorporated international treaty the Convention does not have direct effect in UK law and is therefore not justiciable in UK courts and tribunals.

In *AH v West London MHT* [2011] UKUT 74 (AAC) the Upper Tribunal, presided over by Carnwath L.J., said at para.16:

> "The CRPD provides the framework for Member States to address the rights of persons with disabilities. It is a legally binding international treaty that comprehensively clarifies the human rights of persons with disabilities as well as corresponding obligations on state parties. By ratifying a Convention, a state undertakes that wherever possible its laws will conform to the norms and values that the Convention enshrines."

This approach was approved by the Court of Appeal in *Burnip v Birmingham City Council* [2012]

EWCA Civ 629, where Maurice Kay L.J. said that the Convention has "the potential to illuminate our approach to both discrimination and justification" (para.22). In *Assange v Swedish Prosecution Authority* [2012] UKSC 22, Lord Dyson noted that "there is a 'strong presumption' in favour of interpreting an English statute in a way which does not place the United Kingdom in breach of its international obligations" (para.122). However, this approach operates only where the court is dealing with an ambiguous legal provision (*R. (on the application of SG) v Secretary of State for Work and Pensions* [2015] UKSC 16, per Lord Kerr at paras 239 and 241).

In *R. (on the application of SC) v Secretary of State for Work and Pensions* [2021] UKSC 26, Lord Reed said:

> "There is … no basis in the case law of the European court, as taken into account under the Human Rights Act, for any departure from the rule that our domestic courts cannot determine whether this country has violated its obligations under unincorporated international treaties" (para.84).

Among those covered by the CRPD are people "who have long term … mental [or] intellectual … impairments which in interaction with various barriers may hinder their full and effective participation in society on an equal basis with others" (art.1). Article 14 of the Convention, which is headed "Liberty and security of the person", states:

> "1. States Parties shall ensure that persons with disabilities, on an equal basis with others:
>   (a) Enjoy the right to liberty and security of person;
>   (b) Are not deprived of their liberty unlawfully or arbitrarily, and that any deprivation of liberty is in conformity with the law, and that the existence of a disability shall in no case justify a deprivation of liberty.
> 2. States Parties shall ensure that if persons with disabilities are deprived of their liberty through any process, they are, on an equal basis with others, entitled to guarantees in accordance with international human rights law and shall be treated in compliance with the objectives and principles of this Convention, including by provision of reasonable accommodation."

The implications of the final phrase of para.1(b) are profound in that, unless it could be argued that the phrase should be interpreted as meaning that the existence of a disability should not be the sole ground for justifying a deprivation of liberty, the Act contravenes the Convention. It is noteworthy that the United Nations High Commissioner for Human Rights in his 2009 *Thematic study — on the enhancing awareness and understanding of the Convention on the Rights of Persons with Disabilities* states, at para.48, that proposals made during the drafting of the Convention to limit the prohibition of detention to cases "solely" determined by disability were rejected. And in a "*Statement on article 14 of the Convention on the Rights of Persons with Disabilities*" made by the Committee on the Rights of Persons with Disabilities in September 2014 it is said that legislation "in which persons may be detained on the grounds of their actual or perceived disability, provided there are other reasons for their detention, including that they are dangerous to themselves or to others" is incompatible with art.14. It follows that, in order to be compliant with the Convention, legislation that allows for the detention of persons must be de-linked from the disability so as to apply to all persons on an equal basis. This approach is impossible to reconcile with art.5(1)(e) of the ECHR which permits detention on the ground of unsoundness of mind. It is therefore not possible for the UK Government, which has incorporated the ECHR into domestic law through the Human Rights Act 1998, to legislate to implement art.14. In *Rooman v Belgium* [2020] M.H.L.R. 1, the European Court of Human Rights confirmed that "Article 5, as currently interpreted, does not contain a prohibition on detention on the basis of impairment, in contrast to what is proposed by the UN Committee on the Rights of Persons with Disabilities in points 6–9 of its 2015 Guidelines concerning Article 14 of the CRPD" (para.205).

The Convention is considered by Phil Fennell and Urfan Khaliq in "Conflicting or complementary obligations? The UN Disability Rights Convention on Human Rights and English Law", E.H.R.L.R. 2011, 6, 662–674 and by Peter Bartlett in "The United Nations Convention on the Rights of Persons with Disabilities and Mental Health Law", (2012) 75(5) M.L.R. 752–778. A survey of UN reports undertaken by the Essex Autonomy Project found that there "is no unified UN position on the question of whether involuntary placement and treatment [for mental health conditions] can be lawful under UN human rights standards; different positions have been taken in different reports": see "*Is Involuntary Placement and Non-Consensual Treatment Ever Compliant with UN Human Rights Standards?*" (January 2018), p.3, which can be accessed at: *https://autonomy.essex.ac.uk/wp-content/uploads/2018/01/EAP-UN-Survey.pdf*.

The only international instrument against which UK mental health law can be judicially tested is the ECHR. The rights set out in the Convention are derived essentially from the UDHR. The Human Rights Act 1998 incorporates articles from the ECHR into UK law. Four of the articles incorporated are particularly relevant to the operation of mental health legislation: arts 3, 5, 6 and 8. In *R. (on the application of SC) v Mental Health Review Tribunal* [2005] EWHC 17 (Admin); [2005] M.H.L.R. 31 at para.54, Munby J. said that the exercise by state authorities of compulsory powers in relation to persons suffering from mental disorder calls for increased vigilance in reviewing whether the ECHR has been complied with. In *R. (on the application of B) v Dr SS (Responsible Medical Officer)* [2006] EWCA Civ 28; [2006] M.H.L.R.131, Lord Phillips CJ said at para.41 that "the overall scheme of the MHA" is not incompatible with the ECHR.

International human rights law applicable to those who suffer from a mental disorder has been extensively reviewed by Lawrence O. Gostin and Lance Gable in "The human rights of persons with mental disabilities: a global perspective on the application of human rights principles to mental health" (2004) 10 *Maryland Law Review* 1, 20–121 and by Kris Gledhill in Ch.27 of *Principles of Mental Health Law and Policy* (2010).

Most of the materials mentioned above can be accessed on the website of the Human Rights Library of the University of Minnesota (*www1.umn.edu/humanrts/*).

Transitional provisions

1-026 Detailed transitional provisions are set out in Sch.5. Transitional provisions that relate to the implementation of the Mental Health Act 2007 are contained in Sch.10 to that Act. They stipulate the extent to which an amendment to the Act by the 2007 Act applies to or has an impact on a patient who is subject to the Act when the amendments come into force. Further transitional provisions are contained in the Mental Health Act 2007 (Commencement No.6 and After-care under Supervision: Savings, Modifications and Transitional Provisions) Order 2008 (SI 2008/1210); the Mental Health Act 2007 (Commencement No.7 and Transitional Provisions) Order 2008 (SI 2008/1900); and the Mental Health Act (Commencement No.8 and Transitional Provisions) Order 2008 (SI 2008/2561). The Department of Health published "*Implementation of the Mental Health Act 2007: Transitional Arrangements*" (July 31, 2008).

Extent

1-027 The Act applies to Scotland and Northern Ireland only to the extent provided for in ss.146 and 147, respectively. The whole of the Act was extended to the Isles of Scilly on March 12, 1985, by the Isles of Scilly (Mental Health) Order 1985 (SI 1985/149) with the modification that the expression "local social services authority" in the Act shall, in relation to the Isles, mean the Council of the Isles constituted under the Isles of Scilly Order 1978 (SI 1978/1844).

Abbreviations

1-028 In the annotations, the following abbreviations are used:

Aarvold Committee: *Report on the Review of Procedures for the Discharge and Supervision of Psychiatric Patients subject to Special Restrictions* (Cmnd. 5191).

Butler Committee: *Report of the Committee on Mentally Abnormal Offenders* (Cmnd. 6244).

Code of Practice: The *Code of Practice* published under s.118(4) of this Act.

Joint Committee: House of Lords and House of Commons Joint Committee on Human Rights.

Mental Health Bill: the Mental Health Bill introduced to Parliament on November 16, 2006.

Public Bill Committee: Public Bill Committee—Mental Health Bill (Lords).

The Reed Committee: Review of Health and Social Services for Mentally Disordered Offenders and others requiring similar services, Chairman: Dr John Reed, HMSO, 1992.

Reference Guide: *Reference Guide to the Mental Health Act 1983* (2015).

Royal Commission: *Report of the Royal Commission on the Law Relating to Mental Illness and Mental Deficiency 1954–1957*, Chairman—Lord Percy (Cmnd. 169).

Special Standing Committee: The special Standing Committee which considered the Mental Health (Amendment) Bill.

the Tribunal Rules: the Tribunal Procedure (First-tier Tribunal) (Health, Education and Social Care Chamber) Rules 2008 (SI 2008/2699).

the 1982 Act: the Mental Health (Amendment) Act 1982.

the 2007 Act: the Mental Health Act 2007.

tribunal: the First-tier Tribunal (Mental Health) or the Mental Health Review Tribunal for Wales.

the English Regulations: Mental Health (Hospital, Guardianship and Treatment) (England) Regulations 2008 (SI 2008/1184).

the Welsh Regulations: the Mental Health (Hospital, Guardianship, Community Treatment and Consent to Treatment) (Wales) Regulations 2008 (SI 2008/2439) (W.212).

the Welsh Rules: the Mental Health Review Tribunal for Wales Rules 2008 (SI 2008/2705) (L.17).

Part I Application of Act

Application of Act: "mental disorder"

The provisions of this Act shall have effect with respect to the reception, care and **1-029** treatment of mentally disordered patients, the management of their property and other related matters.

(2)   In this Act—

["mental disorder" means any disorder or disability of the mind; and
"mentally disordered" shall be construed accordingly;]
[…]

and other expressions shall have the meanings assigned to them in section 145 below.

[(2A)   But a person with learning disability shall not be considered by reason of that disability to be—

(a)   suffering from mental disorder for the purposes of the provisions mentioned in subsection (2B) below; or

(b)   requiring treatment in hospital for mental disorder for the purposes of sections 17E and 50 to 53 below,

unless that disability is associated with abnormally aggressive or seriously ir-responsible conduct on his part.

(2B)   The provisions are—

(a)   sections 3, 7, 17A, 20 and 20A below;

(b)   sections 35 to 38, 45A, 47, 48 and 51 below; and

(c)   section 72(1)(b) and (c) and (4) below.]

[(3)   Dependence on alcohol or drugs is not considered to be a disorder or dis-ability of the mind for the purposes of subsection (2) above.]

[(4)   In subsection (2A) above, "learning disability" means a state of arrested or incomplete development of the mind which includes significant impairment of intelligence and social functioning.]

Amendments

The amendments to this section were made by the Mental Health Act 2007 ss.1, 55, Sch.11 Pt 1.

Definition

patient: s.145(1).   **1-030**
hospital: s.145(1).

General Note

Apart from indicating the extent of the Act, this section defines the term "mental disorder", excludes   **1-031**
dependence on alcohol or drugs from the definition, and makes special provision for patients who have a learning disability.

Code of Practice

Guidance on the definition of mental disorder for the purposes of the Act is contained in Ch.2. Is-   **1-032**
sues of particular relevance to patients with learning disabilities and autistic spectrum disorders are considered in Ch.20. Chapter 21 considers issues relating to patients with personality disorders.
Paragraph 2.4 of the Code states that relevant professionals "should determine whether a patient has a disorder or disability of the mind in accordance with good clinical practice and accepted standards of what constitutes such a disorder or disability".

The Code, at para.2.5, provides the following non-exhaustive list of "recognised conditions" which could fall within the definition:

- Affective disorders, such as depression and bipolar disorder;
- Schizophrenia and delusional disorders;
- Neurotic, stress-related and somatoform disorders, such as anxiety, phobic disorders, obsessive compulsive disorders, post-traumatic stress disorder and hypochondriacal disorders;
- Organic mental disorders such as dementia and delirium (however caused);
- Personality and behavioural changes caused by brain injury or damage (however acquired);
- Personality disorders;
- Mental and behavioural disorders caused by psychoactive substance use;
- Eating disorders, non-organic sleep disorders and non-organic sexual disorders;
- Learning disabilities;
- Autistic spectrum disorders (including Asperger's syndrome);
- Behavioural and emotional disorders of children and young people.

The Explanatory Notes to the 2007 Act state at para.17:

"Disorders or disabilities of the brain are not regarded as mental disorders unless (and only to the extent that) they give rise to a disability or disorder of the mind as well."

The definition also includes some disorders of "sexual preference" such as "paraphilias like fetishism or paedophilia" (ibid., para.24).

Paragraph 2.8 of the Code states:

"Difference should not be confused with disorder. No-one may be considered to be mentally disordered solely because of their political, religious or cultural beliefs, values or opinions, unless there are proper clinical grounds to believe that they are the symptoms or manifestations of a disability or disorder of the mind. The same is true of a person's involvement, or likely involvement, in illegal, anti-social or 'immoral' behaviour. Beliefs, behaviours or actions which do not result from a disorder or disability of the mind are not a basis for compulsory measures under the Act, even if they appear unusual or cause other people alarm, distress or danger."

Human Rights Act 1998

1-033   See Pt 5 under "Persons of unsound mind" in art.5(1).

Subsection (1)

1-034   **Management of their Property**   Given the repeal of Pt VII of the Act by the Mental Capacity Act 2005, this phrase is otiose.

Subsection (2)

1-035   **Mental disorder**   The definition of mental disorder, which acts as the gateway to the powers available under the Act, is consistent with the interpretation that the European Court of Human Rights has given to the phrase "persons of unsound mind" in art.5(1)(e) of the European Convention on Human Rights (ECHR). In *Winterwerp v Netherlands* (1979) E.H.R.R. 387, para.37, the Court held that this phrase is:

"not one that can be given a definitive interpretation ... it is a term whose meaning is constantly evolving as research in psychiatry progresses, an increasing flexibility in treatment is developing and society's attitude to mental illness changes, in particular so that a greater understanding of the problems of mental patients is becoming widespread. In any event, Art.5(1)(e) obviously cannot be taken as permitting the detention of a person simply because his views or behaviour deviate from the norms prevailing in a particular society."

With respect to the assessment of a mental disorder in a child, para.19.5 of the *Code of Practice* cautions as follows:

"...[T]he developmental process from childhood to adulthood, particularly during adolescence, involves significant changes in a wide range of areas, such as physical, emotional and cognitive development – these factors need to be taken into account, in addition to the child and young person's personal circumstances, when assessing whether a child or young person has a mental disorder…"

The definition provides clinicians with a very wide discretion in identifying which - conditions come within its scope. This is, perhaps, worrying given the propensity of some in the psychiatric profession to medicalise normality: see Joel Paris, *Overdiagnosis in Psychiatry: How Modern Psychiatry Lost Its Way While Creating a Diagnosis for Almost All of Life's Misfortunes* (2015). In the context of a criminal trial where the appellant claimed that he failed to appreciate what he was doing was wrong because he was suffering from "avoidant personality disorder", the Court of Appeal said that the courts should "resist the temptation to medicalise normality" (*R. v Deighton* [2005] EWCA Crim 3131 para.14 per Longmore L.J.).

In *DL-H v West London Mental Health Trust* [2017] UKUT 387 (AAC); [2017] M.H.L.R. 372, UT Judge Jacobs said that the "borderline between religious beliefs and mental disorder can be a fine one and one that is difficult to draw. It is right that evidence from both sides of the divide should be admissible to help the tribunal make a soundly-reasoned decision" (para.10).

Although the two internationally recognised diagnostic manuals which are widely used by British psychiatrists, the ICD-11 (World Health Organisation) and the DSM-5 (American Psychiatric Association), provide classifications of mental disorder, it "cannot be said that something that is not in any classification is not a mental disorder" (Public Bill Committee, col.16, per the Minister of State). Judge Jacobs made reference to the use of the diagnostic manuals in DL-H *Devon Partnership NHS Trust* [2010] UKHT 102 (AAC); [2010] M.H.L.R. 162 at para.24:

"It is important to understand the purpose for which the criteria were devised. The specific criteria in ICD-10 are labelled as diagnostic criteria *for research* and the introduction to … DSM-IV (4th edition) contains this warning:

'… In most situations, the clinical diagnosis of a DSM-IV mental disorder is not sufficient to establish the existence for legal purposes of a "mental disorder", "mental disability", "mental disease" or "mental defect".'

That leaves open the question of how a patient's mental state is to be clarified for the purposes of the Mental Health Act. The answer cannot depend on the manual that happens to be used. This is an issue that will have to be considered by the Upper Tribunal in an appropriate case. There must be an answer that provides protection for patients from vague or differing definitions while ensuring that those who present a danger are not left free to harm themselves or others for failing to meet over-prescriptive criteria."

In this case, Judge Jacobs held that "there is no prohibition in principle on a tribunal substituting its diagnosis for that of the experts whose evidence was before the tribunal. It must, of course, have reasons for doing so and it must allow the patient's representative a chance to deal with its view before making a decision" (para.20). In *R. (on the application of Khela) v Brandon Mental Health Unit* [2010] EWHC 3313 (Admin), Judge Thornton QC said that there is no remedy currently available that "enables the court to order that the diagnosis of [the responsible clinician] should be changed and corrected" (para.6).

Patients who are being treated in a general hospital can suffer from a mental disorder which requires their detention under the Act, but which does not come within the clinical experience of most psychiatrists. Dr Eleanor Feldman describes how she:

"encountered a situation where a patient had an acute and severe but reversible brain disorder, in this case limbic encephalitis, and its treatment involved steroids and other very toxic drugs used in immunotherapy. The patient was grossly disorientated and lacked mental capacity to make a decision about his treatment or the need to remain in hospital. Moreover, his behaviour was very disturbed requiring strong and prolonged measures over a matter of up to two weeks to restrain and sedate him, to administer treatment and keep him on the neurology unit." ("The use of the Mental Health Act and common law in non-consenting patients in the general hospital" (2006) *Psychiatry* 5(3): 107–9).

In *St George's Healthcare NHS Trust v S* [1998] 3 All E.R. 673, 696, Judge L.J. said that the court did not doubt "that reactive depression (not merely a transient sense of being 'a little down' or 'fed up with everything') is capable of amounting to a mental disorder". His Lordship also said, at 957, that a person cannot be characterised as being mentally disordered "merely because her thinking process is unusual, even apparently bizarre and irrational, and contrary to the views of the overwhelming majority of the community at large".

The difficulties of drawing a distinction between mental distress and symptoms amounting to a recognisable psychiatric illness were identified by Judge P. in *R v D* [2006] EWCA Crim 1139 at para.30:

"As the Law Commission reports [in *Liability for Psychiatric Illness*, No.249 (1998) HC 525], the distinction 'is not clear', quoting one medical consultee who suggested that the 'overlap between mental health and illness is so large a grey area that it is not suitable for the legal purpose to which the diagnosis is being put'. The classification in DSM-IV and ICD-10 were not themselves always sufficient 'to distinguish those with the greatest impairment of functioning', and several of the consultees commented that it would be unjust to relay on the criteria in these classifications to distinguish psychiatric illness from 'mere mental distress'. It was suggested that some did not 'reflect the complexities of the psychological impact of trauma', and current categorisation might exclude some diagnoses which were generally acceptable. Observations like these confirm that current understanding of the workings of the mind is less than complete".

Also of relevance in this context are Hobhouse L.J.'s observations in *R. v Chan-Fook* [1994] 2 All E.R. 552 at 559 on the decision of the Court of Appeal in *Attia v British Gas* [1988] Q.B. 304 regarding the position at civil law:

"[T]he Court of Appeal discussed whether the borderline should be drawn between on the one hand the emotions and distress and grief, and on the other hand some actual psychiatric illness such as anxiety neurosis or a reactive depression. The authorities recognise that there is a line to be drawn and whether any given case falls on one side or the other is a matter for expert evidence."

A similar approach was taken by the House of Lords in *R. v Ireland; R. v Burstow* [1997] 4 All E.R. 225 at 231, a case under the Offences against the Person Act 1861, where Lord Steyn said that neuroses "must be distinguished from simple states of fear, or problems in coping with everyday life. Where the line is to be drawn must be a matter of psychiatric judgment". Also see *Nottinghamshire County Council v LH* [2021] EWHC 2584 (Fam) where the court received evidence from a psychiatrist that a 12 year old girl was not detainable as she did not have a psychiatric condition. The psychiatrist advised the court that the girl's extreme degree of distress was due to her social circumstances and her presentation "must be viewed in the context of serious safeguarding concerns within the family home, exacerbated by parental difficulty in maintaining safety" (para.9).

In earlier times, Bowen L.J. said that "the state of a man's mind is as much a fact as the state of his digestion" (*Edgington v Fitzmaurice* (1885) 29 Ch.D 459 at 483).

Mind   In the context of the *McNaghten* rules, which set out the test for insanity, Devlin J. said that the term "mind" should be "used in the ordinary sense of the mental faculties of reason, memory and understanding" (*R. v Kemp* [1957] 1 Q.B. 399 at 407). This statement was approved by Lord Diplock in *R. v Sullivan* [1983] 2 All E.R. 673 HL at 677. Lord Diplock's judgment in *Sullivan* suggests that if a disorder severely impairs these faculties it can be categorised as a disorder of mind, irrespective of the aetiology of the disorder.

Subsections (2A), (2B)

1-036   These subsections (which do not apply to autistic spectrum disorders (*Code of Practice*, para.2.17)), together with subs.(4), preserve the way the Act works with regard to people with a learning disability. They provide that for certain purposes of the Act a person may not be considered to be suffering from a mental disorder simply as a result of having a learning disability: the disability must be "associated with abnormally aggressive or seriously irresponsible conduct" on the part of the person concerned. This is a matter for recommending doctors to determine.

The preservation of the status quo by the 2007 Act has little to commend it. The Minister of State responded to an expression of puzzlement about the rationale for the approach adopted by explaining that "there has been a historic attachment to saying that learning disability should be included in the Bill in this way, and I am afraid that there is no getting away from that" (Public Bill Committee, col.43).

Is associated with   This phrase denotes an association which may not be the result of causation (*P v Mental Health Review Tribunal and Rampton Hospital* [2001] EWHC Admin 876; [2002] M.H.L.R. 250 para.26). The association must be with the learning disability and not with an unrelated physical disorder or condition. Lord Adebowale gave the following example of a case where an association with learning disability was absent:

"Mr S, who has a severe learning difficulty, autism and communication difficulties, lives in a residential setting. He was detained under the 1983 Act because he was becoming increasingly agitated and exhibited aggressive behaviour, banging his head against a wall. It was later discovered—this is shocking but true—that Mr S had a small twig in his ear, which was causing him distress, as it would most people, and which he expressed in his agitated behaviour. This scenario shows how the distress of a person with a learning disability can be automatically attributed to a mental disorder without paying sufficient attention to physical factors. This is about not just lazy diagnosis but making false assumptions" (*Hansard*, HL Vol.668, col.66).

The *Code of Practice* states:

"20.10 It is important to establish whether a person's learning disability is associated with conduct that could be categorised as abnormally aggressive, not simply aggressive. Relevant factors when assessing this include:

- when such aggressive behaviour has been observed, and how persistent and severe it has been
- whether it has occurred without a specific trigger or seemed disproportionate to the circumstances that triggered it
- whether, and to what degree, it has resulted in harm or distress to other people, or actual damage to property
- how likely it is to recur, and
- how common similar behaviour is in the population generally.

20.11 Similarly, in assessing whether a person's learning disability is associated with conduct that is not only irresponsible but seriously irresponsible, relevant factors may include:

- whether behaviour has been observed that suggests a disregard or an inadequate regard for its serious or dangerous consequences
- how recently such behaviour has been observed and, when it has been observed, how persistent it has been
- how seriously detrimental to the individual, or to other people, the consequences of the behaviour were or might have been
- whether, and to what degree, the behaviour has actually resulted in harm to the person or the person's interests, or in harm to other people or to damage to property, and
- how likely it is to recur.

20.12 Bizarre or unusual behaviour is not the same as abnormally aggressive or seriously irresponsible behaviour."

Abnormally aggressive or seriously irresponsible conduct   The origin of this phrase, which is taken from the definition of psychopathy in the Mental Health Act 1959, was recounted by Lord Rix:

"These words are very familiar to me because they arrived in the 1983 Act after a long three-way process of negotiation on the telephone between the the then Minister, the noble Lord Elton, myself, then in the capacity as secretary general of Mencap, and a copy of *Roget's Thesaurus*. It was the best compromise we could then reach between the Government's position that people with a learning disability should come under the scope of the Act, and my position that people with a learning disability are not ill and should not be treated as if they were" (*Hansard*, HL Vol.687, col.662).

The *Code of Practice* states at para.20.09:

"Neither term is defined in the Act, and it is not possible to define exactly what kind of behaviour would fall into either category. Inevitably, it will depend on the nature of the behaviour and the circumstances in which it is exhibited, and also on the extent to which it gives rise to a serious risk to the health or safety of the person or others, or both."

What is "abnormally aggressive" or "irresponsible conduct" must, to a certain extent, depend upon the cultural and social context within which the behaviour occurs. In *R. v Trent Mental Health Review Tribunal Ex p. Ryan* [1992] C.O.D. 157, Nolan L.J. said:

"No doubt whether the conduct is the result of the disorder ... is a medical question. Whether it amounts to seriously irresponsible or abnormally aggressive behaviour seems to me ... to raise questions other than of a purely clinical nature".

In *Re F (Mental Health Act: Guardianship)* [2000] 1 F.L.R. 192, the Court of Appeal adopted a restrictive construction of the phrase "seriously irresponsible conduct" by holding that a 17-year-old patient's natural desires to return home, albeit to an inadequate home where she had been exposed to chronic neglect and possible sexual exploitation, could not be categorised as irresponsible conduct. Thorpe L.J. said at 198:

> "The urge to return [home] is almost universal ... The deficiencies of the home are more apparent to other adults than to the young who have known no other. Furthermore, any measure of irresponsibility must depend on an evaluation of the consequences of return ... Clearly each case must depend on its particular facts and we would not wish to be taken as offering any general guideline."

Although his Lordship emphasised that the court had reached its conclusions "on the special facts of a difficult and unusual case", the court's finding is significant because the urge to return home is not the only "almost universal" urge that might affect a patient. The desire to be member of a family group would also fall into this category. When determining whether a person's conduct falls into the category of "seriously irresponsible conduct", the clinician should pay special attention to the consequences of the conduct (or potential conduct) for the person and/or others. The clinician should refrain from categorising conduct as being seriously irresponsible in the absence of a clear opinion based on reliable evidence that the conduct is likely to pose a significant risk to the person's health or safety or to the health or safety of others. It is doubtful whether the term "conduct" covers the passive endurance by a patient of the irresponsible behaviour of others.

In *Newham LBC v BS* [2003] EWHC 1909 (Fam), Wall J. applied *Re F* and held, rather surprisingly, that a person's total lack of road sense and a tendency to rush into the road without looking did not amount to "seriously irresponsible conduct". However, in *GC v Managers of the Kingswood Centre of Central and North West London NHS Foundation Trust* (CO/7784/2008) King J. said that it is not arguable that the *Newham* decision sets down a general proposition of law that a tendency to rush into the road could never amount to seriously irresponsible conduct. This case concerned a patient with obsessive compulsive disorder which manifested itself as a compulsion to pick up litter, even if that litter was in the road. The patient had been knocked down by vehicles but considered himself invincible. King J. held that the hospital managers were entitled to conclude that such conduct could be categorised as being "seriously irresponsible". I am grateful to Alexander Ruck Keene, barrister, for drawing my attention to this case.

There is no requirement for the person to be *currently* engaging in abnormally aggressive or seriously irresponsible conduct. It is enough that the learning disability caused such conduct in the past and that there is a real risk that, if treatment in hospital is discontinued, it will do so in the future: see *Lewis v Gibson* [2005] EWCA Civ 587; [2005] M.H.L.R. 309, where Thorpe L.J. said at para.31:

> "To make a balanced assessment of the patient's present state some regard must be had to the past history and the future propensity. A conclusion based only on the recent past, which might represent a transient phase of quiescence, would be superficial."

That conduct need not have occurred in the recent past is illustrated by *R. (on the application of P) v Mental Health Review Tribunal for the East Midlands and North East Regions* [2002] EWCA Civ 697, a case where the conduct had not been exhibited by the patient for several years. Although this case involved a patient who was suffering from a psychopathic disorder, the same terminology that appears in this provision was considered by the court.

Subsection (3)

1-037   This provision prevents a dependence on alcohol or drugs alone from being treated as a mental disorder for the purposes of the Act. In some respects this is an odd exclusion because alcohol and drug dependency are recognised as treatable mental disorders in both ICD-11 and DSM-5, and such dependency may be a ground for detention under art.5(1)(e) of the ECHR. The rationale for the exclusion as contained in the Mental Health (Amendment) Act 1982 was explained by the Government in Cmnd 7320 at para.1.29:

> "Government advisory bodies have ... pointed out that that it is incompatible with current thinking on the nature of drug dependence and drinking problems to regard them as mental disorders. These conditions are increasingly seen as social and behavioural problems, manifested in varying degrees of habit and dependency. However it is recognised that alcohol or drug dependency can be associated with certain forms of mental disorder."

The exclusion does not prevent a person being categorised as mentally disordered if, as well as being dependent on alcohol or drugs, he is suffering from:

(i)   an unrelated mental disorder, or

(ii)   a mental disorder which arises from, or is suspected to arise from, alcohol or drug dependence or from the withdrawal of alcohol or drugs (*Secretary of State for Justice v MP* [2013] UKUT 025 (AAC) at para.15).

Therefore, a person who is suffering from a drug or alcohol induced psychosis or from delirium associated with alcohol withdrawal would not be excluded by this provision. It is also the case that a person's alcohol or drug dependency could be treated under the authority of s.63 if the dependency is categorised as being a consequence of the patient's diagnosed mental disorder, is interfering with the treatment of the disorder, or is exacerbating the symptoms of the disorder (*B v Croydon Health Authority* [1995] 1 All E.R. 683 CA). However, detention is not lawful if its sole purpose is to address the patient's drug taking and chaotic lifestyle (*CM v Derbyshire Healthcare NHS Foundation Trust* [2011] UKUT 129 (AAC); [2011] M.H.L.R. 153). A person who is not dependent on alcohol or drugs but who is acutely intoxicated following the administration of alcohol or drugs would not be excluded from the definition of mental disorder by this provision.

In his "*Review of Homicides by Patients with Severe Mental Illness*" (March 2006), Professor Tony Maden states at p.63:

"Substance misuse in the context of serious mental illness and violence may greatly increase risk, yet there is little sign within [the cases studied] of it being considered as an indication for use of compulsory powers. The 1983 Act does not allow detention for substance use alone but it is an important indicator of the nature and extent of mental illness, and the associated risk to others, so it should be included in any assessment for possible detention."

Drugs   This term includes medicines and illicit drugs and "may be taken to include solvents and similar substances with a psychoactive effect" (*Code of Practice*, para.2.10).

Subsection (4)

This provision defines "learning disability" for the purposes of subs.(2A). The definition requires an **1-038** impairment of both intelligence *and* social functioning (*R. v McDonagh* [2008] NICA 6; [2008] M.H.L.R. 219 (CA, Northern Ireland)). Guidance on the definition is given in Ch.20 of the *Code of Practice*.

"*Valuing People: a new strategy for learning disability for the 21st Century*", Department of Health, 2001, para.1.5, states that:

"Learning disability includes the presence of:

- A significantly reduced ability to understand new or complex information, to learn new skills (impaired intelligence), with;
- A reduced ability to cope independently (impaired social functioning);
- which started before adulthood, with a lasting effect on development."

Arrested or incomplete development of mind   This phrase excludes persons whose learning disability derives from accident, injury or illness occurring after the mind has fully developed. Although examining the relationship between the mind and the brain is beyond the scope of this Manual, it is instructive to note that in *N McM v Secretary of State for Work and Pensions (DLA)* [2014] UKUT 0312, UT Judge Wikeley, on interpreting the phrase "a state of arrested development or incomplete physical development of the brain" for the purposes of the social security legislation, accepted the evidence of Professor Sarah-Jayne Blakemore that neuroscience research carried out in the past 15 years "indicates that the human brain undergoes protracted development until at least the third decade of life" and that "the brain will have ceased developing, in terms of experience-expectant changes in grey matter and white matter, by the thirties or early forties in most people" (para.31). Professor Blakemore also advised that "the phrase 'arrested development' is 'arguably unhelpful and misleading' and so is not commonly used either clinically or in neuroscience these days, as it implies that no recovery of function can take place" (para.48).

Includes   What follows is not an exclusive list of attributes associated with the disability.

Significant impairment of intelligence and social functioning   Whether the impairment is considered to be "significant" is a matter for clinical judgment. In *AM (Zimbabwe) v Secretary of State for the Home Department* [2020] UKSC 17, at para.31, Lord Wilson said:

"Like the skin of a chameleon, the adjective [significant] takes a different colour so as to suit a different context."

In *Meggary v Chief Adjudications Officer The Times*, November 11, 1999, the Court of Appeal held that a high IQ was not conclusive in determining the existence of a "severe impairment of intelligence and social functioning" for the purposes of determining an autistic child's entitlement to disability living allowance. Simon Brown L.J. said:

"In most cases, no doubt, the measurement of IQ will be the best available method of measuring intelligence. But among the dictionary definitions of intelligence one finds the reference not merely to the functions of understanding and intellect but also to the qualities of insight and sagacity. It seems to me that in the case if an autistic child those qualities may well be lacking and to the extent that they are there will be a functional impairment which overlaps both limbs of the regulation, i.e. both intelligence and social functioning."

The significance of the impairment must be measured against the standard of normal persons, not other people with learning disabilities (*R. v Hall (John Hamilton)* (1998) 86 Cr. App. R. 159).

PART II COMPULSORY ADMISSION TO HOSPITAL AND GUARDIANSHIP

General Note

1-039   The principles that underpin this Part were identified by Sir Thomas Bingham M.R. in the following extract from his judgment in *Re S-C (Mental Patient: Habeas Corpus)* [1996] 1 All E.R. 532 CA at 534, 535:

"[N]o adult citizen of the United Kingdom is liable to be confined in any institution against his will, save by the authority of law. That is a fundamental constitutional principle, traceable back to Ch.29 of Magna Carta 1297 (25 Edw. 1 c. 1), and before that to Ch.39 of Magna Carta (1215). There are, of course, situations in which the law sanctions detention. The most obvious is in the case of those suspected or convicted of crime. Powers then exist to arrest and detain. But the conditions in which those powers may be exercised are very closely prescribed by statute and the common law... . [Mental patients] present a special problem since they may be liable, as a result of mental illness, to cause injury either to themselves or to others. But the very illness which is the source of the danger may deprive the sufferer of the insight necessary to ensure access to proper medical care, whether the proper medical care consists of assessment or treatment, and, if treatment, whether in-patient or out-patient treatment.

Powers therefore exist to ensure that those who suffer from mental illness may, in appropriate circumstances, be involuntarily admitted to mental hospitals and detained. But, and it is a very important but, the circumstances in which the mentally ill may be detained are very carefully prescribed by statute. Action may only be taken if there is clear evidence that the medical condition of a patient justifies such action, and there are detailed rules prescribing the classes of person who may apply to a hospital to admit and detain a mentally disordered person. The legislation recognises that action may be necessary at short notice and also recognises that it will be impracticable for a hospital to investigate the background facts to ensure that all the requirements of the Act are satisfied if they appear to be so. Thus we find in the statute a panoply of powers combined with detailed safeguards for the protection of the patient."

In *St George's Healthcare NHS Trust v S* [1998] 3 All E.R. 673, the Court of Appeal held that the Act cannot be deployed to achieve the detention of individuals against their will merely because their thinking process is unusual, even apparently bizarre and irrational, and contrary to the views of the overwhelming majority of the community at large. It could only be used to justify the detention of a mentally disordered person who fell within the prescribed conditions.

A patient who is detained under the Act retains all civil rights which are not taken away expressly or by necessary implication by his detention (*Raymond v Honey* [1982] 1 All E.R. 756 HL).

A child can be detained under this Part (an eight-year-old child has been detained under s.2: see Victoria Thomas et al, *BJPsych Bulletin* (2015) 302–304). Section 25 of the Children Act 1989, which sets restrictions on the use of secure accommodation for children, does not apply to a child who is detained under any provision of the Act (Children (Secure Accommodation) Regulations 1991 (SI 1991/1505) reg.5).

In the "*Report by the Committee for Privileges on Parliamentary Privilege and the Mental Health Act*" June 18, 1984, HL (254), the Committee for Privileges was of the view that the provisions of the Act override any previously existing privilege of Parliament or peerage so far as it conflicts with the liability of mentally disordered peers to compulsory detention in hospital under ss.2 to 6.

Powers, other than those contained in the Act, that are available to individuals to control and detain patients are set out in Appendix A.

The detention of compliant mentally incapable patients

The *Code of Practice* is incorrect when it states that a "person with a learning disability or autism **1-040** cannot be informally admitted [to hospital] if they do not have capacity to consent to or refuse that admission and treatment" (para.20.30). The correct legal position is that the informal admission to hospital and the subsequent medical treatment of any compliant mentally incapacitated patient can be provided under the Mental Capacity Act 2005 (MCA) if he is not being deprived of his liberty in the hospital. An assessment should be undertaken if it is thought that a patient is being deprived of his liberty because a failure either to detain the patient under this Act or to authorise the deprivation under Sch.A1 of the MCA if the patient is being deprived of his liberty would violate the patient's right under art.5 of the European Convention on Human Rights (*HL v United Kingdom* (2005) 40 E.H.R.R. 32; [2004] M.H.L.R. 236). The nature of a deprivation of liberty is considered in Part 6.

In *AM v South London & Maudsley NHS Foundation Trust* [2013] UKUT 365 (AAC); [2014] M.H.L.R. 181, para.34, Charles J. held that with regard to a compliant mentally incapacitated patient who needs to be detained in hospital, decision-makers have to consider whether the patient should be detained under this Act, or whether the assessment or treatment in the proposed circumstances should be founded on the MCA and any deprivation of liberty it involves should be authorised under the deprivation of liberty safeguards (DOLS). His Lordship said that to do that, the decision-makers have to consider whether the MCA and DOLS alternative are applicable and available and, if so, whether and when they should be used. Given the demand that exists for assessments for DOL authorisations, decision-makers should also consider whether it would be possible to obtain a DOL authorisation within a reasonable timescale. In making their decision, the decision-makers have to consider which alternative best achieves the objective of ensuring the patient's assessment or treatment in the least restrictive way. If the patient is not compliant to either being admitted to hospital or to being treated there for his mental disorder, this Act should be invoked. *AM* is further considered in Part 6.

The *Code of Practice* offers guidance on the choice of legal regime in the following paragraphs:

"13.58 The choice of legal regime should never be based on a general preference for one regime or the other, or because one regime is more familiar to the decision-maker than the other. Such considerations are not legally relevant and lead to arbitrary decision-making. In addition decision-makers should not proceed on the basis that one regime is generally less restrictive than the other. Both regimes are based on the need to impose as few restrictions on the liberty and autonomy of patients as possible. In the particular circumstances of an individual case, it may be apparent that one regime is likely to prove less restrictive. If so, this should be balanced against any potential benefits associated with the other regime.

13.59 Both regimes provide appropriate procedural safeguards to ensure the rights of the person concerned are protected during their detention. Decision-makers should not therefore proceed on the basis that one regime generally provides greater safeguards than the other. However, the nature of the safeguards provided under the two regimes are different and decision-makers will wish to exercise their professional judgement in determining which safeguards are more likely to best protect the interests of the patient in the particular circumstances of each individual case."

It is difficult to identify from these paragraphs which criteria decision-makers should adopt when deciding between the two regimes. The Code's failure to provide helpful guidance on this issue is evidence by what is stated at para.13.60:

"In the relatively small number of cases where detention under the Act and a DoLS authorisation or Court of Protection order are available, this *Code of Practice* does not seek to preferentially orientate the decision-maker in any given direction. Such a decision should always be made depending on the unique circumstances of each case."

Decision-makers could address the question of the choice of regime as follows:

1. As both detention under this Act and an authorisation under the DOL safeguards have the same effect of sanctioning the deprivation of a person's liberty, it is not possible to claim that one regime is less restrictive than the other.
2. From the patient's perspective, the restrictions placed on him by the care plan will be of particular importance. Those restrictions will be the same whichever statutory regime is being used to implement the restrictions.
3. The only variable is the safeguards that are provided under both regimes. Despite the statement in the *Code of Practice* that decision-makers should not proceed "on the basis that one regime generally provides greater safeguards than the other" (see para.13.58, quoted above), decision-makers are likely to consider that the safeguards provided to the patient by this Act, in particular timely access to a tribunal, the consent to treatment provisions contained in Part IV, and the availability of after-care services under s.117 for those detained under s.3, offer far greater protection to the patient than those provided by the DOL regime.

Although such an approach is consistent with the statement in the Code that decision-makers should take into account "which safeguards are more likely to best protect the interests of the patient" at para.13.59, it is unlikely to have been in the minds of either Charles J. or the authors of the Code as it would inevitably lead to the decision-makers opting to use this Act. Having said that, it is difficult to identify an alternative principled approach that decision-makers could use to identify the "the least restrictive way" in the particular circumstances of each individual case. Perhaps all that can be said is that decision-makers should exercise their professional judgment in a pragmatic manner which takes into account: (i) the patient's best interests; (ii) the comparative impact of the two regimes on the patient; (iii) the availability of a DOL authorisation; (iv) whether the patient's capacity is fluctuating; and (v) the likelihood of the patient's continuing compliance: see *AM* at para.73.

Paragraph 13.69 of the Code states:

"In the rare cases where neither the Act nor a DoLS authorisation nor a Court of Protection order is appropriate, then to avoid an unlawful deprivation of liberty it may be necessary to make an application to the High Court to use its inherent jurisdiction to authorise the deprivation of liberty."

For an example of the use of the inherent jurisdiction in this situation, see *An NHS Trust v Dr A* [2013] EWHC 2442 (COP).

The power to control the activities of detained patients

1-041   See the notes on s.139 under this heading.

PROCEDURE FOR HOSPITAL ADMISSION

Admission for assessment

1-042   **2.**—(1)   A patient may be admitted to a hospital and detained there for the period allowed by subsection (4) below in pursuance of an application (in this Act referred to as "an application for admission for assessment") made in accordance with subsections (2) and (3) below.

(2)   An application for admission for assessment may be made in respect of a patient on the grounds that—

(a)   he is suffering from mental disorder of a nature or degree which warrants the detention of the patient in a hospital for assessment (or for assessment followed by medical treatment) for at least a limited period; and

(b)   he ought to be so detained in the interests of his own health or safety or with a view to the protection of other persons.

(3)   An application for admission for assessment shall be founded on the written recommendations in the prescribed form of two registered medical practitioners, including in each case a statement that in the opinion of the practitioner the conditions set out in subsection (2) above are complied with.

(4)   Subject to the provisions of section 29(4) below, a patient admitted to

hospital in pursuance of an application for admission for assessment may be detained for a period not exceeding 28 days beginning with the day on which he is admitted, but shall not be detained after the expiration of that period unless before it has expired he has become liable to be detained by virtue of a subsequent application, order or direction under the following provisions of this Act.

Definitions

patient: s.145(1).
hospital: ss.34(2), 145(1).
mental disorder: ss.1, 145(1).
medical treatment: s.145(1), (4).

1-043

General Note

This section authorises the compulsory admission of a patient to hospital for assessment (or for assessment followed by medical treatment), and for detention for this purpose for up to 28 days. Contrary to the assumption made by UT Judge Jacobs in *MS v North East London Foundation Trust* [2013] UKUT 92 (AAC); [2013] M.H.L.R. 158, at para.9, its effect is not confined to proving professionals with a power to assess the patient: see subs.(2)(a). Given the very wide definition of "medical treatment" in s.145(1), the treatment of the patient, which need not be confined to treatment which is an inherent part of the assessment process, will commence on his admission. As the assessment of a patient's mental disorder and his response to being treated is an on-going process and as the power to treat the patient under this section is identical to the power to treat contained in s.3, this section can be regarded as a short-term treatment section. Patients detained under this section are subject to the consent to treatment provisions contained in Pt IV (s.56(3)).

1-044

If the applicant is an AMHP, she must take such steps as are practicable to inform the patient's nearest relative that the application either is to be or has been made (s.11(3)).

If, after 28 days have elapsed the patient is to remain in hospital, he must do so either as an informal patient or be detained under s.3 if the conditions of that section are satisfied. It is not possible to use either the common law or the holding powers contained in s.5 to extend the 28 day period (see the *Williamson* case, below).

In *R. (on the application of Sessay) v South London and Maudsley NHS Foundation Trust)* [2011] EWHC 2617 (QB); [2012] M.H.L.R. 94, the Divisional Court held that the Act provides a complete statutory code for the detention of non-compliant mentally incapacitated patients and that the common law doctrine of necessity does not apply during the period when a patient is being assessed for detention under the Act. However, the court said at para.57:

> "[I]n our view it is unlikely in the ordinary case that there will be a false imprisonment at common law or deprivation of liberty for the purposes of Article 5(1) [of the European Convention on Human Rights] if there is no undue delay during the processing of an application under ss.2 or 4 MHA for admission."

It is therefore the case that if, following an assessment of the patient, the potential applicant and recommending doctors agree that an application to detain the patient should be made, the patient may be held during the time that it takes to process the application as long as the process is not unduly delayed; also see the note on "duly completed" in s.6(1).

In *R. v Wilson Ex p. Williamson* [1996] C.O.D. 42, Tucker J. held that an application made under this section:

> "is only intended to be of short duration for a limited purpose—assessment of the patient's condition with a view to ascertaining whether it is a case which would respond to treatment, and whether an [application] under s.3 would be appropriate. It was intended that the assessment should take place within 28 days, without any extension of time unless it was necessary for the purpose of replacing the nearest relative. Although there is nothing to suggest that s.2 is a once and for all procedure, there is nothing in the Act which justifies successive or back to back, applications under this section. ... The powers under s.2 can only be used for the limited purpose for which they were intended, and cannot be utilised for the purpose of further detaining a patient for the purposes of assessment beyond the 28-day period, or used as a stop-gap procedure."

The *Williamson* case provides authority for the proposition that an application under s.2 cannot be used for an improper purpose. Tucker J. identified two examples of such a purpose: (1) using a second application under s.2 in order to extend the 28-day assessment period (subs.(4) prevents a second application being made under this section during the currency of an existing section); and (2) using an application under s.2 as a "stop-gap" procedure in circumstances where it is not possible to proceed with a s.3 application because of a nearest relative objection (see s.11(4)). The fact that a second use of s.2 was involved in the *Williamson* case is not relevant to (2) as the rationale for finding the use of the section to be improper is that those who had made the decision to use s.3 as the initial detaining section must have reached the conclusion that the patient does not require detention for assessment.

In *C v South London and Maudsley Hospital National Health Service Trust* [2001] M.H.L.R. 269, McCombe J., on refusing an application for leave under s.139, said that an application under this section could be made "where at least one of the doctors may have thought informally that s.3 admission might in the long run be desirable". In this case, a preliminary decision was made to admit the patient under s.3 but this was aborted when the approved social worker (now the approved mental health professional (AMHP)) reported that the patient's nearest relative would object to the application. An application under this section was made three days later by a different AMHP, who "may well have known" that an application under s.3 would not be possible. This application was supported by a medical recommendation from one of the doctors who had made the original decision to proceed under s.3. It is clear from the judgment in this case that McCombe J. considered that the fact that medical recommendations had not been made to support a possible application under s.3 was of particular significance: also see the note on "Section 2 or section 3 as the initial detaining section?", below.

An application for a second s.2 can be made in close proximity to the first s.2 if a significant change in the patient's situation, such as a deterioration in the patient's mental state, can be said to justify the need for a reassessment. This happened in *R. (on the application of Morahan) v His Majesty's Assistant Coroner for West London* [2022] EWCA Civ 1410, where Lord Burnett C.J. recounted, without comment, at paras 17 and 18 that a patient had been detained under s.2 on five occasions during 2017. It was only on the last occasion that the s.2 was followed by an application under s.3.

An application under this section should be the usual method of detaining a patient who requires to be assessed. An emergency application under s.4 should only be used where the need for the patient's admission is so urgent that it is not practicable to obtain the second medical recommendation that is required for an admission under this section.

An AMHP may not lawfully apply for the admission of a patient whose discharge has been ordered by the decision of the First-tier Tribunal, the Mental Health Review for Wales or a Hospital Managers' panel of which the AMHP is aware unless the AMHP has formed a reasonable and bona fide opinion that she has information not known to the tribunal or panel which puts a significantly different complexion on the case as compared with that which was before the tribunal or panel: see *R. v East London and City Mental Health NHS Trust Ex p. Brandenburg*, which is considered in the General Note to s.3 under the heading "The detention of a patient subsequent to a discharge by the First-tier Tribunal (Mental Health), the Mental Health Review Tribunal for Wales or a Hospital Managers' panel".

An order for the patient's discharge from this section can be made at any time prior to the expiration of the 28-day period by his responsible clinician, the hospital managers or, subject to s.25, his nearest relative (s.23(2)(a)). A discharge cannot be effected by implication, e.g. by an assessment for detention under s.3 concluding that the patient should not be detained under that section.

There is nothing to prevent a patient who has been detained under this section from being arrested in respect of a criminal offence.

Must a bed be identified for the patient at the hospital named in the application?

1-045   There is no requirement in either the Act or the Regulations for the potential admitting hospital to have confirmed that a bed is available for the patient before the application is signed. It would clearly be wise for confirmation to be sought from the hospital that they would be willing to admit the patient either when the applicant thought it appropriate to initiate the admission or when a bed became available for the patient.

If the patient has not been admitted to the hospital identified in the application within 14 days of the time when he was last medically examined prior to the recommendations required by subs.(3) being made, the application will lapse (s.6(1)(a)).

Section 2 or section 3 as the initial detaining section?

1-046   The responsibility for deciding which section to use is that of the applicant: "It is the [AMHP] who makes the application, not the doctors" (*R. v East London and the City Mental Health Trust Ex p. Brandenburg* [2003] UKHL 58, per Lord Bingham at para.12). The role of the recommending doctors is to support the application which is "founded" on the recommendations (s.11(7)).

The advice contained in the 1999 edition of the *Code of Practice* was frequently interpreted as requiring s.3 to be used as the initial detaining section for patients who are "well known" to the mental health service and who have a care plan. This interpretation was reinforced by concern expressed by the Mental Health Commission (MHAC) over the "misuse" of s.2 where s.3 would have been more appropriate to admit such patients (see, for example, para.3.1 of the *MHAC's Sixth Biennial Report*, 1993–1995) and the widely held but totally erroneous view expressed by some practitioners that treatment under Pt IV cannot be given to patients detained under s.2. The MHAC subsequently modified its view on this issue and became supportive of the approach adopted here: see para.4.39 of the *MHAC's Twelfth Biennial Report*, 2005–2007. The question of whether s.2 or s.3 should be used to admit a patient is considered in the following paragraphs of the *Code of Practice*:

"14.27 Section 2 should only be used if:

- the full extent of the nature and degree of a patient's condition is unclear
- there is a need to carry out an initial in-patient assessment in order to formulate a treatment plan, or to reach a judgement about whether the patient will accept treatment on a voluntary basis following admission, or
- there is a need to carry out a new in-patient assessment in order to re-formulate a treatment plan, or to reach a judgement about whether the patient will accept treatment on a voluntary basis.

14.28 Section 3 should be used if:

- the patient is already detained under section 2 (detention under section 2 cannot be renewed by a new section 2 application), or
- the nature and current degree of the patient's mental disorder, the essential elements of the treatment plan to be followed and the likelihood of the patient accepting treatment as an informal patient are already sufficiently established to make it unnecessary to undertake a new assessment under section 2."

This Part of the Act provides two routes which can be used to detain and treat patients: s.2 which provides for the assessment and treatment of patients for a non-renewable period of up to 28 days, and s.3 which provides for the patient's detention and treatment for a potentially unlimited period. A patient whose current mental health and circumstances require him to be subject to the very significant procedure of compulsory detention surely needs to be assessed however well known he might be to the mental health service. Something has happened in that patient's life to justify intervention under the Act and it is the factors that precipitated the detention and their impact on the patient that need to be assessed. The extent of any prior knowledge that might exist about the patient does not deflect from the need to assess the patient's *current* situation, including the state of his physical health: see, for example, the following coroner's reg.28 report: *www.judiciary.uk/wp-content/uploads/2019/11/Maureen-Jarvis-2019-0357_Redacted.pdf*. When a patient is admitted to hospital for treatment for a physical disorder, he is subject to a full assessment on admission even if he has had multiple previous admissions. Why should a patient who is admitted for treatment for a mental disorder be treated differently? It is submitted that Parliament's intention was for s.2 to be used as the initial section to detain patients because that section specifically provides for the patient's assessment, and that an application under s.3 be made if the assessment leads the clinical team to conclude that the patient needs a further period of treatment whilst being detained. Other factors which support the approach advocated here are:

(i)   the fact that s.3(2)(c) states that an application under s.3 should be made if the necessary treatment can *only* be provided under that section suggests that such an application should not be made unless the patient has been assessed under s.2 as needing treatment under detained powers for a period longer than 28 days. This is because both sections provide clinicians with identical powers to treat the patient;

(ii)   the finding of Tucker J. in *R. v Wilson Ex p. Williamson*, above, that one of the purposes of s.2 is to ascertain whether an application under s.3 would be appropriate;

(iii)   dicta in a number of cases where the judges have assumed that s.2 can be used to admit a well known patient; see for example, *R. v Bournewood Community and Mental Health NHS Trust Ex p. L* [1998] 1 All E.R. 634, 641, CA, where Lord Woolf M.R. said that it would have been possible to use s.2 to admit the patient who had been in very close contact with the mental health services for most of his life, and *R. v East London and City Mental Health NHS Trust Ex p. Brandenburg*, above, where the Court of Appeal assumed that it could be appropriate to detain a patient under s.2 subsequent to his discharge by a tribunal;

(iv)   section 29(4) allows for the extension of the patient's detention under s.2 if a displacement application is made to the county court before the s.2 expires on the ground that the patient's nearest relative has "unreasonably objected" to a s.3 application being made. This provision, and the absence of any equivalent remedy to an applicant who uses s.3 as an initial detaining section and is then faced with an objection from the nearest relative, is a clear indication that the Act was drafted on the assumption that an application under s.2 would precede an application under s.3; and

(v)   the fact that it is not possible to convert an application under s.4 into an application under s.3 in respect of a well known patient (see s.4(4)).

Those who advocate the use of s.3 as the initial detaining section for patients who are already well known to the mental health service fail to identify the action that an AMHP applicant should take when faced with a s.11(4) objection made by the nearest relative of a patient who has been assessed as being either actively suicidal, as posing an immediate and serious risk to the safety of others, or at risk of a serious and imminent deterioration of his mental health. In the experience of the author, this is a dilemma which has been experienced by practitioners on a regular basis. An application under s.2 cannot be made in these circumstances (see the *Williamson* case, above) and although the AMHP would have the option of applying to the county court under s.29 for an interim order displacing the nearest relative on the ground that the objection was unreasonable, the granting of the order may be too late to avoid catastrophic consequences for the patient and/or others. The *Code of Practice* does not offer any guidance on how an AMHP should act in such a situation.

The deteriorating patient

1-047   See the note under this heading in the General Note to s.3.

The detention of compliant mentally incapable patients

1-048   The question of whether such patients should be detained under this Act or be made the subject of a deprivation of liberty authorisation under the Mental Capacity Act 2005 is considered in the General Note to this Part under this heading.

Human Rights Act 1998

1-049   See the note on s.3 under this heading.
    In *MH v United Kingdom* (2014) 58 E.H.R.R. 965, the European Court of Human Rights held that the failure to provide the means for a mentally incapacitated patient to bring proceedings to challenge a detention under this section constituted a violation of art.5(4) of the European Convention on Human Rights. This case, together with the Government's response to it, is considered in the General Note to s.68 under this heading.

Applications to the First-tier Tribunal (Mental Health) or the Mental Health Review Tribunal for Wales

1-050   The patient may make an application within 14 days of his admission under this section (s.66(1)(a), (2)(a)). However, if the tribunal office is closed during the whole of the 14th day, the application will be validly received if it arrives at that office at any time during the first succeeding day on which the office is open (i.e. the next business day) (*R. (on the application of Modaresi) v Secretary of State for Health* [2011] EWCA Civ 1359; [2011] M.H.L.R. 311). Also see the note on the Human Rights Act 1998, above.
    If a nearest relative's discharge of the patient from detention under this section is barred by the patient's responsible clinician by using her power under s.25, the nearest relative does not acquire a right to apply to the tribunal.

Code of Practice

1-051   The roles of mental health professionals when undertaking assessments that might lead to an application for admission to hospital and the criteria for detention under this section are considered in Ch.14. Conflicts of interests that might arise in the assessment process are considered in Ch.39. Guidance on the transport of patients can be found in Ch.17.

Subsection (1)

An application under this section can be made by either the patient's nearest relative (NR) or by an **1-052** AMHP (s.11(1)). The applicant must use Form AI (for NRs) or Form A2 (for AMHPs) (in Wales, Form H01 (for NRs) or Form H02 (for AMHPs)): see reg.4(1) of the English and Welsh Regulations. The application will be addressed to the managers of the hospital to which admission is sought (s.11(2)). If the applicant is an AMHP, she must take such steps as are practicable to inform the patient's NR that the application either is to be or has been made (s.11(3)). The NR cannot prevent an AMHP from making an application. In deciding whether to make an application, an AMHP is required to have regard to any wishes expressed by relatives of the patient (s.13(1)). This does not mean that the AMHP is placed under a legal obligation to consult with the patient's relatives before she makes an application. The applicant must have seen the patient within the previous 14 days (s.11(5)) and an AMHP applicant must interview the patient before the application is made (s.13(2)). The patient has to be admitted to hospital within 14 days of the time when he was last medically examined prior to the recommendations required by subs.(3) being made (s.6(1)(a)). It is possible to make an application in respect of a person who is already receiving hospital treatment as an in-patient on an informal basis (s.5(1)). An application for the admission of a ward of court cannot be made without the leave of the High Court (s.33(1)).

The question of whether a bed must be identified for the patient at the hospital named in the application before the application is signed is considered above under the heading *Must a bed be identified for the patient at the hospital named in the application?*.

The effect of an application for admission for assessment is set out in s.6. The hospital named in the application is not placed under a legal obligation to admit the patient: see the note on "to hospital" in s.6(1).

Detained there   The patient can be granted leave of absence from the detaining hospital under s.17, but only after the patient has received a period of in-patient treatment at that hospital: see the *Hallstrom* case noted in the General Note to s.3 under the heading *"Is a period of in-patient treatment a requirement if a patient is detained under this section?"*. Making an application in respect of a patient where the intention is to grant the patient immediate leave of absence to enable the patient to be treated at another hospital is unlawful because the application provides authority for the patient to be detained in the hospital named in the application (see s.6(2)), which is where the initial assessment must take place.

Subsection (2)

Although informal admission should be the preferred mode of admission, compulsion should be used **1-053** on a patient who is willing to be admitted informally if its absence would place the patient's safety and/or the safety of others at risk: see the General Note to s.131.

Paragraph (a)

Is suffering   A patient whose symptoms of mental disorder are being controlled by medication still **1-054** suffers from that disorder: see the note on *The deteriorating patient* in the General Note to s.3.

In *R. v Kirklees MBC Ex p. C* [1993] 2 F.L.R. 187 CA, Lloyd L.J., speaking obiter, said at 190 that:

"having regard to the definition of patient in s.145 there is, in my view, power to admit a patient for assessment under s.2, if he or she appears to be suffering from mental disorder, on the ground that he or she is so suffering, even though it turns out on assessment that [he or] she is not. Any other construction would unnecessarily emasculate the beneficial power under s.2 and confine assessment to choice of treatment"."

This approach was confirmed in *St George's Healthcare NHS Trust v S* [1998] 3 All E.R. 673, where the Court of Appeal held that the identification of the presence of mental disorder for the purposes of this section cannot be a final concluded diagnosis; the final diagnosis may or may not confirm that provisional view.

Mental disorder   There is no requirement for a diagnosis of the nature of the patient's mental disorder to have been made (*JP v South London and Maudsley NHS Foundation Trust* [2012] UKUT 486 (AAC); [2013] M.H.L.R. 148, para.13). Also see *Griffiths v Chief Constable of Suffolk Police* [2018] EWHC 2538 (QB), where Ousley J. said at para.268: "Dr Stagias agreed that what was required was an illness or disorder which warranted detention for assessment; this did not require diagnosis itself, nor did it need a major illness or disorder".

Unlike the position under s.3, it is possible for a learning disabled person whose condition is not associated with "abnormally aggressive or seriously irresponsible conduct" to be the subject of an application under this section. The CQC is therefore incorrect when it states that "[u]nder the MHA, people with a learning disability have to show 'abnormally aggressive or seriously irresponsible conduct' to be admitted to hospital" (*Monitoring the Mental Health Act in 2020/21*, p.54).

Nature or Degree   The meaning of this phrase is considered in the note on s.3(2)(a).

Which warrants the detention of the patient in a hospital   This requirement assumes that an initial assessment has concluded that the patient's need for assessment and treatment cannot be met without recourse to this section by, for example, applying for guardianship: see further para.14.7 of the *Code of Practice* and *AM v South London & Maudsley NHS Foundation Trust*, which is noted in the General Note to this Part under *The detention of compliant mentally incapacitated patients*. In *AM*, Charles J. said at para.15:

"[This section has] to be applied on the basis that for detention in hospital to be 'warranted' it has to be 'necessary' in the sense that the objective set out in the relevant statutory test cannot be achieved by less restrictive measures."

The patient must need a period of detention as a hospital *in-patient*: see the note on "detained there" in subs.(1). The detention must be related to or linked with the patient's mental disorder; the patient's need for treatment for an unrelated physical disorder does not provide the necessary warrant (*St George's Healthcare NHS Trust v S*, above). In the *St George's* case, the Court of Appeal declared an admission under this section to be unlawful because the grounds prescribed in this paragraph were not established. Judge L.J. said at 697:

"The contemporaneous documents themselves demonstrate that those involved in the decision to make an application for admission failed to maintain the distinction between the urgent need of [the patient] for treatment arising from her pregnancy, and the separate question whether her mental disorder (in the form of depression) warranted her detention in hospital. From the reasoning to be found in them, the conclusion that the detention was believed to be warranted in order that adequate provision could be made to deal with [the patient's] pregnancy and the safety of her unborn child is unavoidable."

Assessment   The patient's detention under this section does not automatically lapse on the completion of the assessment because: (1) the authority to detain can only end either on the expiration of the 28-day period, an order of discharge being made by a tribunal, or an order for discharge being made under s.23; and (2) this section authorises the detention of the patient for assessment "or for assessment followed by medical treatment".

Paragraph (b)

1-055   There is no requirement for the two recommending doctors to agree on the nature of the risk justifying detention under this section.

According to para.14.9 of the *Code of Practice* the "factors to be considered in deciding whether patients should be detained for their own health or safety include:
the evidence suggesting that patients are at risk of:

- suicide
- self-harm
- self-neglect or being unable to look after their own health or safety
- jeopardising their own health or safety accidentally, recklessly or unintentionally, or
- that their mental disorder is otherwise putting their health or safety at risk
- any evidence suggesting that the patient's mental health will deteriorate if they do not receive treatment, including the views of the patient or carers, relatives or close friends (especially those living with the patient) about the likely course of the disorder
- the patient's own skills and experience in managing their condition
- the patient's capacity to consent to or refuse admission and treatment (and the availability of the deprivation of liberty safeguards (DoLS))
- whether the patient objects to treatment for mental disorder – or is likely to
- the reliability of such evidence, including what is known of the history of the patient's mental disorder and the possibility of their condition improving

- the potential benefits of treatment, which should be weighed against any adverse effects that being detained might have on the patient's wellbeing, and
- whether other methods of managing the risk are available."

Health   The patient's mental as well as physical health is covered by this term. This interpretation was adopted by the Mental Health Act Commission in its *Second Biennial Report*, 1985–1987, at para.11.3. The opinion that is sometimes heard from practitioners that an application under this section can only be made if the patient is either a danger to himself or others or is engaging in seriously disruptive behaviour is incorrect. Also see the note on *The deteriorating patient* in the General Note to s.3.

Safety   With the patient being exposed to the risk of being harmed, either through his own acts or omissions or through the acts or omissions of others.

Predicting risk of suicide is extremely problematic, even for patients who are considered to be at high risk of suicide: see the research examined by M. Rahman and N. Wolferstan in "A human right to be detained? Mental healthcare after 'Savage' and 'Rabone'", *The Psychiatrist* (2013), 37, 294–296.

Protection of other persons   See the note on s.72(1)(b)(ii) under this heading. Paragraph 14.10 of the *Code of Practice* states:

"In considering whether detention is necessary for the protection of other people, the factors to consider are the nature of the risk to other people arising from the patient's mental disorder, the likelihood that harm will result and the severity of any potential harm, taking into account:

- that it is not always possible to differentiate risk of harm to the patient from the risk of harm to others
- the reliability of the available evidence, including any relevant details of the patient's clinical history and past behaviour, such as contact with other agencies and (where relevant) criminal convictions and cautions
- the willingness and ability of those who live with the patient and those who provide care and support to the patient to cope with and manage the risk
- whether other methods of managing the risk are available, and
- harm to other people including psychological as well as physical harm."

The *Code of Practice* considers the sharing of information to manage risk in the following paragraphs:

"10.15 Although information may be disclosed only in line with the law, professionals and agencies may need to share information to manage any serious risks which certain patients pose to others.

10.16 Where the issue is the management of the risk of serious harm, the judgement required is normally a balance between the public interest in disclosure, including the need to prevent harm to others, and both the rights of the individual concerned and the public interest in maintaining trust in a confidential service.

10.17 Whether there is an overriding public interest in disclosing confidential patient information may vary according to the type of information. Even in cases where there is no overriding public interest in disclosing detailed clinical information about a patient's state of health there may, nonetheless, be an overriding public interest in sharing more limited information about the patient's current, and past status under the Act, if that will help ensure properly informed risk management by the relevant authorities, families and carers."

In *R. v North West London Mental Health NHS Trust Ex p. Stewart* (1996) 39 B.M.L.R. 105, Harrison J. said:

"The protection of 'other persons' does not necessarily mean the public at large because it could simply relate to an individual person or persons rather than to the public at large, nor is there the requirement that such persons should be protected 'from serious harm.'"

Although the matter is not free from doubt, it is likely that this phrase covers both protection from physical harm and protection from serious emotional harm: see para.14.10 of the *Code of Practice*, above. The protection of the mental health of the main carer of the patient could therefore be the predominant trigger for "sectioning" the patient. Even though this provision does not make reference to the protection of a person's property, actual or threatened damage to a person's property could cause that person serious emotional harm.

Although an unborn child is not a "person" in need of protection (*The Attorney General's Reference*

(No.3 of 1994) [1998] A.C. 245 at 254), the "health or safety" of the potential mother can be assessed on the basis that she is heavily pregnant: see *St George's Healthcare NHS Trust v S*, above, where Judge L.J. said at 696:

> "Those responsible have to deal in realities, and [the patient] was dangerously ill [with preeclampsia]. Although the risks were caused by her pregnancy, the potential damage could have fallen within s.2(2)(b)."

It is therefore permissible to detain a pregnant patient whose mental disorder requires assessment in circumstances where a major concern is the likely impact on the mother's physical and/or mental health of an unsupervised birth. Also see the note on Human Rights Act 1998 in s.3.

Subsection (3)

1-056   The medical recommendations, which may be made either separately or jointly, should be perused by the applicant before the application is signed. They must comply with the provisions of s.12 and the regulations made under s.12A. A medical recommendation which is signed after the date of the application is invalid; also see the note on "on or before the date of the application" in s.12(1)).

The fact that an application has had to be aborted because, for example, the offer of a bed at the hospital named in the application has been withdrawn does not effect the validity of the medical recommendations that were made in support of the application. As long as the time limit set out in s.6(1)(a) is not contravened, the medical recommendations can be used to support a fresh application addressed to a different hospital.

Registered medical practitioner   Means "a fully registered person within the meaning of the Medical Act 1983 who holds a licence to practise under that Act" (Interpretation Act 1978, Sch.1).

Subsection (4)

1-057   **Not exceeding 28 days**   The 28-day period can be extended if an application is made to the county court on specified grounds for an acting nearest relative to be appointed (s.29(4)) or if the patient has gone absent without leave and has been returned to the hospital before the section expires (see the note on "a patient" in s.21(1)).

Beginning with   The day on which the patient was admitted is counted as the first day when calculating the 28 day period (*Zoan v Rouamba* [2000] 2 All E.R. 620 CA). The authority to detain the patient will expire at midnight on the twenty-eighth day.

The day on which he is admitted   This is either the day on which the patient was admitted to the hospital from the community whilst subject to an application under this section, or the day on which the patient who was in hospital informally was made subject to such an application. In both cases, admission only takes effect for the purposes of this provision when the application has been accepted by a person who has been authorised by the hospital managers to accept it: see reg.3(2) of the English and Welsh Regulations. The time and date of the admission should be recorded on Form H3 (in Wales, Form HO14).

Under the following provisions of this Act   The use of the term "following" prohibits a further application under this section being made during the currency of an existing s.2 application (*R. v Wilson Ex p. Williamson* [1996] C.O.D. 42).

Admission for treatment

1-058   **3.**—(1)   A patient may be admitted to a hospital and detained there for the period allowed by the following provisions of this Act in pursuance of an application (in this Act referred to as "an application for admission for treatment") made in accordance with this section.

(2)   An application for admission for treatment may be made in respect of a patient on the grounds that—

(a) he is suffering from [mental disorder] of a nature or degree which makes it appropriate for him to receive medical treatment in a hospital; and

(b) [...]

(c) it is necessary for the health or safety of the patient or for the protection of other persons that he should receive such treatment and it cannot be provided unless he is detained under this section[; and

(d) appropriate medical treatment is available for him.]

(3) An application for admission for treatment shall be founded on the written recommendations in the prescribed form of two registered medical practitioners, including in each case a statement that in the opinion of the practitioner the conditions set out in subsection (2) above are complied with; and each such recommendation shall include—

(a) such particulars as may be prescribed of the grounds for that opinion so far as it relates to the conditions set out in paragraphs (a) and [(d)] of that subsection; and

(b) a statement of the reasons for that opinion so far as it relates to the conditions set out in paragraph (c) of that subsection, specifying whether other methods of dealing with the patient are available and, if so, why they are not appropriate.

[(4) In this Act, references to appropriate medical treatment, in relation to a person suffering from mental disorder, are references to medical treatment which is appropriate in his case, taking into account the nature and degree of the mental disorder and all other circumstances of his case.]

Amendments

The amendments to this section were made by the Mental Health Act 2007 ss.1(4), 4(2), (3), 55, Sch.11 Pt 2.

Definitions

patient: s.145(1).
hospital: ss.34(2), 145(1).
mental disorder: ss.1, 145(1).
medical treatment: s.145(1), (4).

General Note

This section provides for the compulsory admission of a patient to hospital for treatment and for his subsequent detention, which can last for an initial period of up to six months (s.20(1)). The authority to detain a patient under this section can be renewed (s.20(2)). Patients admitted under this section are subject to the consent to treatment provisions contained in Pt IV (s.56(3)). There is no legal rule which prevents: (a) an application under this section from being made subsequent to the patient's admission under s.4 (*Re Makin* [2000] M.H.L.R. 41), or (b) a patient who has been detained under this section from being subsequently detained under s.2: see further the General Note to s.2 under the heading *Section 2 or section 3 as the initial detaining section?*.

For the power to restrain the patient if, following an assessment, the potential applicant and recommending doctors agree that an application under this section should be made, see *R. (on the application of Sessay) v South London and Maudsley NHS Foundation Trust* which is considered in the General Note to s.2.

A patient who had been detained under this section after having been released from prison on licence part way through a sentence should not, upon absconding from the detaining hospital, have been returned to prison by the Home Secretary (now the Secretary of State for Justice) using his recall power without

1-059

reference to or consultation with the hospital doctors. Normally the s.3 would take precedence over a recall *(R. (on the application of S) v Secretary of State for the Home Department* [2002] EWHC Admin 2424; [2003] M.H.L.R. 114).

Where a patient is admitted to hospital under this section, any previous application that had been made in respect of him under this Part (i.e. an application under s.2 or 4 or a guardianship application under s.7) is automatically cancelled (s.6(4)).

An order for the patient's discharge from this section can be made by his responsible clinician, the hospital managers or, subject to s.25, his nearest relative (s.23(2)(a)). If the patient is subject to a community treatment order (CTO), the CTO will cease to have effect on his discharge from this section: see s.17C(c).

There is nothing to prevent a patient who has been detained under this section from being arrested in respect of a criminal offence. If the patient is subsequently remanded into custody or sentenced under the criminal law, the provisions of s.22 will apply.

Where a patient who has been detained under this section ceases to be so detained and leaves hospital, he has an entitlement to after-care services (s.117).

Is a period of in-patient treatment a requirement if a patient is detained under this section?

1-060   In *R. v Hallstrom Ex p. W* [1986] 2 All E.R. 306, McCullough J. held that admission under this section only covered those whose mental condition was believed to require a period of in-patient treatment in the hospital named in the application. (This finding was approved by the Court of Appeal in *R. v Barking Havering and Brentwood Community Healthcare NHS Trust* [1999] 1 F.L.R. 106.) His Lordship said at 315:

> "In my judgment, the key to the construction of section 3 lies in the phrase 'admission for treatment'. It stretches the concept of 'admission for treatment' too far to say that it covers admission for only so long as it is necessary to enable leave of absence to be granted [under section 17], after which the necessary treatment will begin. 'Admission for treatment' under section 3 is intended for those whose condition is believed to require a period of treatment as an in-patient. It may be that such patients will also be thought to require a period of out-patient treatment thereafter, but the concept of 'admission for treatment' has no applicability to those whom it is intended to admit and detain for a purely nominal period during which no necessary treatment will be given."

The phrase "and his mental disorder . . . makes it appropriate for him to receive treatment in a hospital" in s.3(2)(a) also leads to the conclusion that the section is concerned with those whose mental condition requires in-patient treatment. Treatment in a hospital does not mean treatment at a hospital as [leading counsel for the defendants], in effect contends. If his construction were correct there would be a distinction between the patient who could appropriately be treated at home and the patient who could appropriately treated at the out-patients' department of a hospital. Such a distinction would be without reason. When it is remembered that the section authorises compulsory detention in a hospital it is at once clear why a distinction should be made between those whom it is appropriate to treat in a hospital (i.e. as in-patients) and those whom it is appropriate to treat otherwise (whether at the out-patient department of the hospital or at home or elsewhere)."

These remarks, which equate "treatment in a hospital" with "in-patient treatment", were described as being obiter and were rejected by Wilson J. in *R. (on the application of DR) v Mersey Care NHS Trust* [2002] EWHC 1810 (Admin); [2002] M.H.L.R. 386, which is considered in the note on s.20(4)(c). His Lordship held that the phrase "medical treatment in a hospital" in s.20(4)(a) incorporated treatment at a hospital and that the lawfulness of the renewal of the patient's detention did not depend upon a plan to put the patient at times in a hospital bed. His Lordship concluded his judgment as follows:

> "Unless and until [the reform of the Mental Health Act] is enacted, the law will remain (if my interpretation of it be sound) that the compulsory administration of medication to a patient can be secured only by making him liable to be detained or renewing such liability; that such may be achieved only if a significant component of the plan is for treatment in hospital; and that, in such an enquiry, the difference between in-patient and out-patient treatment is irrelevant" (para.34).

Although his Lordship was correct in equating the tests in ss.3(2)(a) and 20(4)(a), his judgment in so far as it relates to s.3(2)(a) is obiter and therefore not binding as a precedent. The following factors suggest that it should not be applied to applications for the initial detention of a patient:

1. The sub-heading to ss.2 to 6 of the Act is "Procedure for hospital admission". In order to be admitted to a hospital, a person must become an in-patient of that hospital.

2. The effect of a duly completed application is to provide authority for the patient to be conveyed to the named hospital, to be admitted to that hospital (s.6(1)(2)) and to be detained there (s.3(1)).

3. An approved mental health professional (AMHP) can only make an application if she is satisfied that "detention in a hospital" is the most appropriate way of providing for the patient's mental health needs (s.13(2)). In *Hallstrom* McCullough J. said at 316: "Parliament must have been directing the social worker's attention to the patient's need for in-patient treatment".

4. On an application under s.3, the recommending doctors are required to state why "other methods of treatment or care" such as "out-patient treatment" are not appropriate (see Forms A7 and A8).

It is submitted that the correct interpretation of this section is that an application for the detention of a patient under this section can only be made if the patient is assessed as requiring a period of hospital in-patient treatment for his mental disorder.

The "nominal period" in *Hallstrom* was an overnight admission. In *Re Shearon* [1996] C.O.D. 223, the Divisional Court held that whilst an admission for one week is a relatively small part of the initial six-month period of detention authorised by this section, there was no possible reason for stigmatising a genuine initial one week's intended in-patient treatment as "a purely nominal period during which no necessary treatment will be given". The court further held that the fact that the application was made simultaneously with the institution of a parallel Care Plan did not invalidate the admission and render it unlawful.

Must a bed be identified for the patient at the hospital named in the application?

There is no requirement in either the Act or the Regulations for the potential admitting hospital to **1-061** have confirmed that a bed is available for the patient before the application is signed. The doctors providing the medical recommendations to support the application must certify that appropriate medical treatment is available to the patient in the hospital(s) named in the recommendations: see Forms A7 and A8. It would clearly be wise for confirmation to be sought from the hospital named in the application that they would be willing to admit the patient either when the applicant thought it appropriate to initiate the admission or when a bed became available for the patient.

If the patient has not been admitted to the hospital identified in the application within 14 days of the time when he was last medically examined prior to the recommendations required by subs.(3) being made, the application will lapse (s.6(1)(a)).

The detention of compliant mentally incapable patients

The question of whether such patients should be detained under this Act or be made the subject of a **1-062** deprivation of liberty authorisation under the Mental Capacity Act 2005 is considered in the General Note to this Part under this heading.

The re-sectioning of a patient subsequent to a discharge by the First-tier Tribunal (Mental Health), the Mental Health Review Tribunal for Wales or a Hospital Managers' panel

In *R. v East London and The City Mental Health Trust Ex p. Brandenburg* [2003] UKHL 58; [2004] **1-063** M.H.L.R. 44, the House of Lords considered the following question: when a tribunal has ordered the discharge of a patient, is it lawful to re-admit him under s.2 or s.3 of the Mental Health Act when it cannot be demonstrated that there has been a relevant change of circumstances?

The only speech of substance was given by Lord Bingham who identified the following "overriding principles" at paras 6 to 8:

1. The common law respects and protects the personal freedom of the individual, which may not be curtailed save for a reason and in circumstances sanctioned by the law of the land. This principle is reflected in, but does not depend on, art.5(1) of the European Convention on Human Rights (ECHR). It can be traced back to Chapter 29 of Magna Carta 1297 and before that to Chapter 39 of Magna Carta 1215.

2. The law may properly provide for the compulsory detention in hospital of those who suffer from mental disorder if detention is judged to be necessary for the health or safety of the patient or for the protection of others. The necessity for such detention in appropriate cases is recognised by art.5(1)(e) of the ECHR and has long been given effect in domestic law.

3.   A person compulsorily detained on mental health grounds should have the right to take proceedings by which the lawfulness of his detention may be decided by a court and his release ordered if the detention is not lawful. This right is expressed in art.5(4) of the ECHR.

4.   The rule of law requires that effect should be loyally given to the decisions of legally constituted tribunals in accordance with what is decided. It follows that no one may knowingly act in a way which has the object of nullifying or setting at nought the decision of a tribunal. It is not therefore open to the nearest relative of a patient or an AMHP to apply for the admission of the patient, even with the support of the required medical recommendations, simply because he or she or they disagree with a tribunal's decision to discharge. That would make a mockery of the decision.

Lord Bingham continued by stating at para.9 that in applying these principles, account must be taken of certain important considerations:

1.   While doctors may be expected to exercise their best professional judgment in diagnosing the condition and assessing the cases of those suffering from mental disorder, and prescribing treatment, their conclusions will rarely be capable of scientific verification. There will often be room for bona fide differences of professional opinion.

2.   The condition of many of those suffering from mental disorder will not be static. Episodes of acute illness may be followed by episodes of remission. Thus it does not follow that a tribunal decision, however sound when made, will remain so. Other things being equal, the longer the period since the decision was made the greater the chance that the patient's mental condition may have altered whether for better or worse.

3.   The focus of the tribunal's inquiry into the mental health of the patient is on whether he is "then suffering" from mental disorder. "Then" refers to the time of the tribunal's review and the tribunal has no power to consider the validity of the admission that gave rise to the liability to be detained. Although the tribunal cannot ignore the foreseeable future consequences of discharge, it is not called upon to make an assessment which will remain accurate indefinitely or for any given period of time.

4.   A conscientious doctor whose opinion has not been accepted by the tribunal will doubtless ask himself whether the tribunal's view is to be preferred and whether his own opinion should be revised. But if, having done so, he adheres to his original opinion he cannot be obliged to suppress or alter it. His professional duty to his patient, and his wider duty to the public, requires him to form, and if called upon express, the best professional judgment he can, whether or not that coincides with the judgment of the tribunal.

5.   It is plainly of importance that the AMHP is subject to the statutory duty under s.13 to apply for the admission of a patient where he is satisfied that such an application ought to be made and is of the opinion specified in that section.

Lord Bingham, in applying the principles set out above, rejected a change of circumstances test and held at para.10 that an AMHP may not lawfully apply for the admission of a patient whose discharge has been ordered by the decision of a tribunal of which the AMHP is aware unless the AMHP has formed a reasonable and bona fide opinion that he has information not known to the tribunal which puts a significantly different complexion on the case as compared with that which was before the tribunal. His Lordship gave three hypothetical examples to illustrate the situations where re-sectioning the patient would be justified:

(a)   The issue at the tribunal is whether the patient, if discharged, might cause harm to himself. The tribunal, on the evidence presented, discounts that possibility and directs the discharge of the patient. After the hearing, the AMHP learns of a fact previously unknown to him, the doctors attending the patient and the tribunal: that the patient had at an earlier date made a determined attempt on his life. Having taken medical advice, the AMHP judges that this information significantly alters the risk as assessed by the tribunal.

(b)   At the tribunal hearing the patient's mental condition is said to have been stabilised by the taking of appropriate medication. The continuing stability of the patient's mental condition is said to depend on his willingness to take that medication. The patient assures the tribunal of his willingness to continue to take the medication and, on the basis of that assurance the tribunal directs the discharge of the patient. Before or after discharge the patient refuses to take the medication or communicates his intention to refuse. Having taken medical advice, the AMHP perceives a real risk to the patient or others if the medication is not taken.

(c)   After the tribunal hearing, and whether before or after discharge, the patient's mental condition significantly deteriorates so as to present a degree of risk or treatment or supervision not evident at the hearing.

The following findings were also made at paras 10 to 12:

1. The position of the patient's nearest relative does not in principle differ from that of the AMHP, although the nearest relative could not in many cases be expected to be familiar with the evidence or appreciate the grounds on which the tribunal had based its decision.
2. An AMHP may well learn of the existence of an earlier tribunal hearing when performing his functions under s.13(2) and will then wish to know the reasons for it. However, if no such information comes to light the law does not place on the AMHP (or a nearest relative applicant) a duty to make reasonable enquiries to establish whether any decision has been made by any tribunal and, if so, the grounds upon which it was based.
3. If an AMHP makes an application to section the patient subsequent to a decision of the tribunal to discharge him, he should be informed why the decision of the tribunal to discharge him is not thought to govern his case if the application is inconsistent in effect with that decision. As the disclosure of such reasons could be potentially harmful to the patient or to others, it may be necessary for the AMHP to give them in very general terms.
4. In terms of there being a duty to give reasons for taking a different view from the tribunal, while it would doubtless be helpful if a medical recommendation identified any new information on which it was based, a recommending doctor is not required to do more than express her best professional opinion.

In *South Staffordshire and Shropshire Healthcare NHS Foundation Trust v The Hospital Managers of St George's Hospital* [2016] EWHC 1196 (Admin), Cranston J. held at para.30 that the principle established in *Brandenburg* also applies to a decision of a panel of the hospital managers exercising their power to discharge a patient under s.23. His Lordship said that "the Parliamentary intention is that a panel appointed under section 23 of the Act has equal standing when ordering discharge to that of a Tribunal operating under section 72".

The AMHP who is considering making an application might not have attended the tribunal hearing or hospital managers panel hearing which led to the discharge of the patient. In such a situation, the AMHP should use her best endeavours to establish the factual basis upon which the tribunal or panel reached its decision. Where it is practical, this could include an examination of the written reports that were submitted to the tribunal or panel, contacting those who gave evidence to the tribunal or panel and a consideration of the written reasons that the tribunal or panel gave for its decision.

In *R. (on the application of Care Principles Ltd) v Mental Health Review Tribunal* [2006] EWHC 3194 (Admin); [2006] M.H.L.R. 365, Collins J. held that:

1. The "new information" test established in *Brandenburg* covers not only what might have happened subsequent to the tribunal's decision, but also material which had not been taken into account by the tribunal, if such material were discovered (para.43).
2. Section 6(3) enables the hospital managers to act on an application that appears to be "duly made". The extent of their obligations under that provision must depend on the facts of a particular case. If they are aware of the existence of a previous tribunal decision ordering the discharge of the patient, it requires a critical consideration of the justification for the detention in the light of that decision. It is not "sufficient for them simply to say: we were satisfied that the [AMHP] had properly considered it and discussed it, although it is not specifically explained in the application" (para.45).

With regard to point 2, if the hospital managers are aware of the existence of a decision of a tribunal or panel to discharge the patient they should only accept the application if they are satisfied that the "new information" test has been met. The applicant should inform the managers of the existence of a tribunal or panel discharge known to her.

The effect of the *Brandenburg* judgment is that if there is simply a disagreement between the tribunal or panel and the mental health professionals about the interpretation of the evidence presented to the tribunal or panel, the decision of the tribunal or panel, assuming that it is lawful (see the *Ashworth Hospital Authority* case, below), must be allowed to stand.

In *R. (on the application of H) v Oxfordshire Mental Healthcare NHS Trust* [2002] EWHC Admin 465; [2002] M.H.L.R. 282, a case which was decided before *Brandenburg*, Sullivan J. upheld the re-detention of the patient subsequent to his deferred discharge by a tribunal in circumstances where:

(i)   the patient had refused to co-operate with the arrangements that were being made for his discharge from the hospital;
(ii) where, in any event, no suitable arrangements had been identified;

(iii)   the patient was, in consequence, "becoming increasingly agitated, stressed and disturbed as the prospect of release drew closer, to the extent of refusing to discuss the matter with his social workers and doctors and, indeed, throwing a table at the social workers" (para.65); and

(iv)   those involved in the re-sectioning had given "careful thought" to the decision of the tribunal (para.63).

His Lordship said that in directing discharge "the tribunal could not have proceeded upon the basis that the [patient's] symptoms would deteriorate to such a marked degree as has in fact occurred" (para.67). This decision is consistent with the principle established in *Brandenburg*.

In *R. (on the application of H) v Ashworth Hospital Authority* [2002] EWCA Civ 923; [2001] M.H.L.R. 314, the Court of Appeal addressed the question of what steps are open to mental health professionals and the hospital managers if they are faced with a tribunal decision for discharge which they honestly and reasonably believe is perverse or arguably perverse. The Court held that:

1.   In the absence of material circumstances [now new information: see the *Brandenburg* case, above] of which the tribunal is not aware when it orders discharge, it is not open to the professionals to re-section the patient even if they have been legally advised that there are substantial grounds for saying that the tribunal's decision is arguably unlawful.

2.   The appropriate action for the authorities to take in this situation is to apply to the Administrative Court for a stay of the tribunal's decision where there was a grant of permission to apply for judicial review [now see below]. This is the case even if the decision of the tribunal has been fully implemented by the patient being released from the hospital. The effect of a stay is to suspend the tribunal's order, and temporarily to treat it as being of no effect. The grant of an injunction under s.37 of the Senior Courts Act 1981 would be inappropriate in these circumstances.

3.   The grant of permission to apply for judicial review is not a sufficient condition of a stay. The court should usually refuse to grant a stay unless satisfied that there is a strong, and not merely an arguable, case that the tribunal's decision was unlawful. Even in such a case, the court should not grant a stay in the absence of cogent evidence of risk and dangerousness.

4.   In a case where a stay is ordered, it is essential that the validity of the tribunal's decision be determined by the court in a judicial review with the degree of speed that is appropriate and usual where a detained person seeks habeas corpus (i.e. if at all possible, within days of the order of stay).

5.   If the patient refuses to return to the hospital following the grant of a stay, the machinery of the Act can be mobilised to see that he does.

Where the patient's discharge has been ordered by a tribunal, rather than making an application to the Administrative Court for a stay, an applicant should now apply to the tribunal itself to stay the proceedings or to suspend the effect of its own decision pending a determination by the tribunal or the Upper Tribunal of an application for permission to appeal against that decision: see r.5(3)(j)(l) of the Tribunal Rules and r.5(2)(g)(h) of the Welsh Rules.

The deteriorating patient

1-065   The "Committee of Inquiry into the events leading up to and surrounding the fatal incident at the Edith Morgan Centre, Torbay, on September 1, 1993" examined the issue of the "sectionability" of a patient whose mental health is likely to deteriorate: see *The Falling Shadow: One Patient's Mental Health Care 1978–1993* (1995), pp.153–169. The Committee disagreed with the view expressed by the *Internal Review of Legal Powers on the Care of Mentally Ill People in Community* that a patient could not be admitted under compulsory powers "simply on the grounds that his or her past medical history suggests that he or she will relapse in the future" (Department of Health, 1993, para.3.2). The conclusion that the Committee reached was that "there is probably no legal impediment to the readmission of a ['revolving door'] patient ... at the point of loss of insight when he refuse[s] further medication" (p.160). In fact this conclusion does not conflict with the statement made by the Internal Review as a patient who has lost insight would not be detained "simply" on the ground of his medical history.

The Committee found the case of *Devon CC v Hawkins* [1967] 2 Q.B. 26, to be "highly pertinent" to the issue. The question before the court was whether a person who was taking drugs which successfully controlled his epilepsy could be said to be "suffering from" that disease. The answer given by the Lord Chief Justice, Lord Parker, was in the affirmative. His Lordship said that "so long as drugs are necessary to prevent the manifestation of disease, the disease in my judgment remains". In other words, so the Committee stated, what the patient "was 'suffering from' rested on a prognosis of what would occur in the future if medication was withdrawn" (p.155).

Although it might be the case that a person with a history of mental disorder who is being successfully medicated for that disorder can be said to be "suffering from" that disorder, it does not follow that merely because that person stops taking his medication the disorder becomes one of a "nature or degree which makes it appropriate for him to receive medical treatment in a hospital" (s.3(2)(a)) or one of a "nature or degree which warrants the detention of the patient in a hospital for assessment" (s.2(2)(a)). While a patient whose symptoms are being well controlled by medication cannot be said to be suffering from a "degree" of mental disorder sufficient to justify detention, can that patient be detained because of the "nature" of his disorder? The meaning of "nature or degree" was considered by Popplewell J. in *R. v The Mental Health Review, Tribunal for the South Thames Region Ex p. Smith*, which is noted under subs.(2)(a).

The course of a patient's mental disorder is never entirely predictable and the Act requires the professionals involved in assessing a patient for possible compulsory admission to exercise their judgment to determine whether the patient's condition and situation at the time of the assessment meet the statutory criteria for admission. If it is the case that a mere failure to continue with medication would always be sufficient to satisfy the statutory criteria with respect to a patient who has a history of admissions subsequent to previous failures to continue with medication, this would result in the personal examination of the patient by the recommending doctors under s.12(1) being an empty exercise. One of the objectives of the examinations and interview of such a patient would be to identify whether there is any evidence (apart from the cessation of medication) to suggest that it is likely that history will repeat itself in that the symptoms of the patient's mental disorder will reappear. If there is such evidence, the "nature" of the patient's mental disorder could lead professionals to conclude that detention in hospital is either "appropriate" or "warranted" even though there is either no current manifestation of the disorder (the "degree"). The same conclusion could be reached if the symptoms of the mental disorder are present, but not yet acute.

It is suggested that the following approach should be taken by those involved in the assessment of a "revolving door" patient who has ceased to take medication for his mental disorder:

(i)   a withdrawal from medication is a significant, but not a determining factor in the assessment;

(ii)   the role of the professionals involved in the assessment is to assess the patient's response to the withdrawal and to identify the reasons for the decision to cease taking medication;

(iii) the "nature" test can be satisfied even though there is no evidence that the patient's mental health has begun to deteriorate: see *Smirek v Williams*, which is noted under "of a nature or degree" in subs.(2)(a); and

(iv)   although it would not be possible to determine that the provisions of either ss.2(2)(a) or 3(2)(a) are satisfied solely on the ground that the patient has ceased to take medication, an evaluation of the patient's history and, in particular, of his reaction to withdrawal from medication in the past, could lead to a decision that the "nature" of the mental disorder justifies an application being made.

Section 2 or section 3 as the initial detaining section?

The question whether it is appropriate to detain a patient under this section or under s.2 is considered in the General Note to s.2 under this heading.   **1-066**

Human Rights Act 1998

In *Winterwerp v Netherlands* (1979) 2 E.H.R.R. 387, the European Court of Human Rights (ECtHR)   **1-067**
held that in order for the detention of a person of unsound mind to be lawful the mental disorder from which the patient is suffering must be of a kind or degree warranting compulsory confinement. This finding is reflected in the phrase "nature or degree" in subs.(2)(a). *Winterwerp* also confirmed that in order to achieve compliance with art.5 of the European Convention on Human Rights (ECHR), detention under the Act must be a necessary and proportionate response to the patient's situation. In *Pleso v Hungary* [2014] M.H.L.R. 72, para.66, the ECtHR said:

"The Court is of the view that where, as in this case, the issue is not whether there is an imminent danger to the person's health but rather whether medical treatment would improve his condition or the absence of such treatment would lead to a deterioration in that condition, it is incumbent on the authorities to strike a fair balance between the competing interests emanating, on the one hand, from society's responsibility to secure the best possible health care for those with diminished faculties (for example, because of lack of insight into their condition) and, on the other hand, from the individual's inalienable right to self-determination (including the right to refusal of hospitalisation or medical treatment, that is, his or her 'right to be ill'). In other words, it is imperative to apply the principle of proportionality inherent in the structure of the provisions enshrining those Convention rights that are susceptible to restrictions".

The requirement of proportionality is reflected in the terms of subs.(2)(c). Other less severe measures must have been considered and found to be insufficient to safeguard the individual or public interest, leaving no alternative to detention (*Withold Litwa v Poland* (2001) 33 E.H.R.R. 53). In *JD v West London Mental Health NHS Trust* [2016] UKUT 496 (AAC), UT Judge Jacobs said at para.29:

"... I seldom encounter an argument on Article 5 that could not equally have been put on the relevant provisions of the Mental Health Act 1983 using normal domestic principles of interpretation. Those provisions are structured around a proportionality analysis that favours the patient's liberty unless all of the conditions that justify detention are met."

The question whether the continued detention of an asymptomatic patient contravenes art.5 was considered by the Court of Appeal in *R. (on the application of H) v Mental Health Review Tribunal, North and North East London Region* [2001] EWCA Civ 415; [2001] M.H.L.R. 48, where Lord Phillips M.R. said at para.33:

"The circumstances of the present case ... are not uncommon. A patient is detained who is unquestionably suffering from schizophrenia. While in the controlled environment of the hospital he is taking medication, and as a result of the medication is in remission. So long as he continues to take the medication he will pose no danger to himself or to others. The nature of the illness is such, however, that if he ceases to take the medication he will relapse and pose a danger to himself or to others. The professionals may be uncertain whether, if he is discharged into the community, he will continue to take the medication. We do not believe that Article 5 requires that the patient must always be discharged in such circumstances. The appropriate response should depend upon the result of weighing the interests of the patient against those of the public having regard to the particular facts. Continued detention can be justified if, but only if, it is a proportionate response having regard to the risks that would be involved in discharge."

The ECtHR has confirmed that the detention of a patient under art.5 may be justified on the ground of protecting the public (*Witold Litwa v Poland*, above) in a situation where the patient needs control and supervision rather than clinical treatment (*Reid v United Kingdom* (2003) 37 E.H.R.R. 9, para.51).

The finding of the Court of Appeal in *St George's Healthcare NHS Trust v S* [1998] 3 All E.R. 673, that a unborn child is not a "person" in need of protection for the purposes of ss.2(2)(b) and 3(2)(c) could possibly be challenged on the ground that a failure to protect the unborn child constitutes a violation of the child's right to life under art.2 of the ECHR. Although the ECtHR has found in the context of abortion and fertility treatment that an unborn child does not have a right to life and is not a "person" within the meaning of art.2, it has not ruled out that, in certain circumstances, safeguards may be extended to the unborn child (*Vo v France* (2005) 40 E.H.R.R. 12, para.80).

Although art.5 is not concerned with the suitability of the treatment that the detained patient receives or the conditions of his detention, subject to the requirement that he be detained in a hospital, clinic or other appropriate institution (*Ashingdane v United Kingdom* (1985) 7 E.H.R.R. 528 para.44), the medical treatment of a patient can constitute "inhuman or degrading treatment" under art.3 of the ECHR if it reaches a minimum level of severity. Subsequent to the Ashingdane decision, the ECtHR has developed its approach for the need for the detained person to receive appropriate therapy. In *Rooman v Belgium* [2020] M.H.L.R. 1, which is noted in Part 5 under art.5(1)(e), the Court held that an obligation is placed on the authorities to ensure that appropriate and individualised therapy is provided.

If a patient has been assessed as either needing a particular treatment or requiring a specialist opinion, an excessive delay in providing that treatment or opinion could give rise to a claim under art.8(1) of the ECHR if the delay has a serious impact on the patient's health (*Passannante v Italy* (1998) 26 E.H.R.R. CD 153).

A failure or refusal to provide treatment that is discriminatory will be unlawful, either under art.14 of the ECHR or the Equality Act 2010.

Applications to the First-tier Tribunal (Mental Health) or the Mental Health Review Tribunal for Wales

1-068   The patient may make an application within six months of admission (s.66(1)(b), (2)(b)) and during each subsequent renewal period (ss.66(1)(f), (2)(f), 20(2)). Section 66(2A) disapplies s.66(1)(b) for recalled community patients. A reference to the tribunal by the hospital managers will be made in the circumstances set out in s.68. The patient's nearest relative may make an application within 28 days of receiving notification that an order for discharge has been barred under s.25 (s.66(1)(g), (2)(d)).

Code of Practice

The roles of mental health professionals when undertaking assessments that might lead to an applica-   **1-069**
tion for admission to hospital and the criteria for detention under this section are considered in Ch.14.
Guidance on the application of the "appropriate treatment" test set out in subs.(3)(d) can be found in
Ch.23. Conflicts of interests that might arise in the assessment process are considered in Ch.39. Guidance on the transport of patients can be found in Ch.17.

Subsection (1)

An application under this section can be made by either the patient's nearest relative (NR) or by an   **1-070**
AMHP (s.11(1)). The local authority with responsibility for providing the AMHP as the potential applicant is identified in s.13(1B) and (1C). The applicant must use Form A5 (for NRs) or Form A6 (for
AMHPs) (in Wales, Form H05 (for NRs) or Form H06 (for AMHPs)): see reg.4(1) of the English and
Welsh Regulations. The application will be addressed to the managers of the hospital to which admission is sought (s.11(2)). If an AMHP makes the application, she must consult with the patient's NR if
this is practicable and the application cannot proceed if the NR objects (s.11(4)). The positive consent
of the NR to the application is not required. The applicant must have seen the patient within the previous 14 days (s.11(5)) and an AMHP applicant must interview the patient before the application is made
(s.13(2)). The patient must be admitted to hospital within 14 days of the time when he was last medically examined prior to the recommendations required by subs.(3) being made (s.6(1)(a)). It is possible
to make an application in respect of a person who is already receiving hospital treatment as an in-
patient on an informal basis (s.5(1)). An application for the admission of a ward of court cannot be made
without the leave of the High Court (s.33(1)).

The question of whether a bed must be identified for the patient at the hospital named in the application before the application is signed is considered above under the heading *Must a bed be identified for
the patient at the hospital named in the application?*.

The effect of an application made under this section is set out in s.6. The hospital named in the application is not placed under a legal obligation to admit the patient: see the note on "to hospital" in s.6(1).

Detained there   The patient can be granted leave of absence from the detaining hospital under s.17,
but only after the patient has received a period of in-patient treatment at that hospital (*R. v Hallstrom
Ex p. W* [1986] 2 All E.R. 41). Making an application in respect of a patient where the intention is to
grant the patient immediate leave of absence to enable the patient to be treated at another hospital is
unlawful because the application provides authority for the patient to be detained in the hospital named
in the application (see s.6(2)), which is where the initial in-patient treatment must take place. It would
also be unlawful for an application to be made under this section if the motive for making the application was to enable an application for a community treatment order to be made in respect of a patient who
did not require in-patient treatment. Also see the note on "*Is a period of in-patient treatment a requirement if a patient is detained under this section?*", above.

The period allowed   The patient may be detained for an initial period of six months renewable for a
further six months and thereafter renewable at yearly intervals (s.20(1), (2)).

Subsection (2)

Although informal admission should be the preferred mode of admission, compulsion could be used   **1-071**
on a patient who is willing to be admitted informally if its absence would place the patient's safety and/or
the safety of others at risk: see the General Note to s.131.

Paragraph (a)

Suffering from   A patient whose symptoms of mental disorder are being controlled by medication still   **1-072**
suffers from that disorder: see the note on "*The deteriorating patient*", above.

Mental Disorder   A patient with a learning disability who suffers from no other form of mental
disorder can only be made subject to an application under this section if the disability is associated with
abnormally aggressive or seriously irresponsible conduct on his part (s.1(2A), (2B)).

It is lawful for a person to be detained under this section even though it has not been possible to
identify the diagnostic category of his mental disorder: see the note on s.2(2)(a) under this heading.

Of a Nature or Degree   The meaning of this phrase is also considered in the note on s.72(1)(b)(i). In

R. v Mental Health Review Tribunal for the South Thames Region Ex p. Smith (1999) 47 B.M.L.R. 104 Popplewell J. held that:

(i)	although the wording of this phrase is disjunctive, in very many cases the nature and degree of the patient's mental disorder will be inevitably bound up so that it matters not whether the issue is dealt with under nature or degree;
(ii)	the word "nature" refers to the particular mental disorder from which the patient suffers, its chronicity, its prognosis, and the patient's previous response to receiving treatment for the disorder. In making this finding, his Lordship rejected a submission made by counsel for the patient that the "nature" of a patient's mental disorder is a static condition; and
(iii)	the word "degree" refers to the current manifestation of the patient's disorder.

This criterion can therefore be satisfied in respect of a well-known asymptomatic patient who has ceased to take medication for his mental disorder and who has a history of a significant deterioration in his mental health after ceasing to take such medication. This interpretation is supported by the following comment made by Hale L.J. in *Smirek v Williams* [2000] M.H.L.R. 38 at para.19:

"There are, of course, mental illnesses which come and go, but where there is a chronic condition, where there is evidence that it will soon deteriorate if medication is not taken, I find it impossible to accept that that is not a mental illness of a nature or degree which makes it appropriate for the patient to be liable to be detained in hospital for medical treatment if the evidence is that, without being detained in hospital, the patient will not take that treatment."

And in *R. (on the application of MM) v Home Secretary* [2007] EWCA Civ 687; [2007] M.H.L.R. 304, Toulson L.J. said at para.48:

"I can see no reason in law why it could not be appropriate for a person in MM's position to be detained for treatment before reaching the stage stipulated by [MM's counsel] (that is, when psychotic symptoms either had recurred or were certain to be on the point of recurring); but determining the point at which the risks are such as to make detention for treatment appropriate may involve a difficult judgment on the facts of a particular case."

Although it might be lawful to make an application in respect of a patient before the reappearance of the symptoms of mental disorder, whether making such an application would be a proportionate response to the patient's situation is a separate question. The requirement of proportionality is reflected in the necessity ground in subs.(2)(c). It is submitted that the crucial factor in determining whether an application should be made in respect of an asymptomatic patient is the assessment of the risk to the patient and/or others following the cessation of medication. This issue is considered in the note on *The deteriorating patient*, above.

Appropriate for him to receive medical treatment in a hospital   It is submitted that this provision can only be satisfied if the patient requires treatment for his mental disorder as a hospital in-patient: see the comment on *R. (on the application of DR) v Mersey Care NHS Trust* in the General Note to this section.

An assessment of the patient's response to being treated can be a part of the medical treatment that the patient receives (*B v Barking Havering and Brentwood Community Healthcare NHS Trust* [1999] 1 F.L.R. 106 CA).

Paragraph (c)

1-073   There is no requirement for the two recommending doctors to agree on the nature of the risk which justifies detention under this section.

Necessary   The necessity must relate to both compulsion and treatment. In *Reid v Secretary of State for Scotland* [1999] 1 All E.R. 481, 504, Lord Clyde said that the test is "one of necessity, not desirability".

Health   See the note on s.2(2).

Safety   See the note on s.2(2).

Protection of other persons   See the note on s.2(2) and on s.72(1)(b)(ii) under this heading.

And that it cannot be provided By, for example, an informal admission or an admission under s.2.

Unless he is detained under this section See the General Note to s.2 under the heading *Section 2 or section 3 as the initial detaining section.*

Paragraph (d)

This paragraph, which was inserted by the 2007 Act, should be read with subs.(4) and s.145(4). It **1-074** replaces the requirement that the treatment of certain categories of patients detained under this section must be "likely to alleviate or prevent a deterioration of his condition" (the "treatability test") with a requirement that "appropriate treatment" be available to all patients. The 10th edition of this work stated, at para.1-051, that the interpretation in case law of the treatability test was so broad that "it is difficult to imagine the circumstances that would cause a patient to fail it". A similar comment can be made of the appropriate treatment test, given that it will almost always be appropriate to provide the patient with either specialist nursing or care for the purpose of either alleviating or preventing a worsening of the patient's mental disorder or one or more of its symptoms or manifestations so as to satisfy the terms of s.145(4). The *Code of Practice* recognises, at para.23.17, that there "may be patients whose particular circumstances mean that treatment may be appropriate even though it consists only of nursing and specialist day-to-day care under the clinical supervision of an approved clinician in a safe and secure therapeutic environment with a structured regime". With regard to patients with a personality disorder, the Code states at para.21.11:

> "People with personality disorders may take time to engage and develop motivation for such longer-term treatment. But even patients who are not engaged in that kind of treatment may need other forms of treatment, including nurse and specialist care, to manage the continuing risks posed by their disorders, and this may constitute appropriate medical treatment."

Those who opposed the change brought about by the 2007 Act were concerned that the new test provides for the possibility of a person being detained simply for preventive purposes without any medical benefit. One of the proponents of this argument, Lord Carlile, called in aid the following extract from the evidence that Professor Nigel Eastman gave to Joint Committee on the Draft Mental Health Bill:

> "Therapeutic benefit to the individual is of crucial importance in terms of protecting the boundary of what is the business of mental health professionals. I am not at all against protecting the public, of course not, but it must be in conjunction with some benefit to the individual that goes beyond simply stopping them offending. If you adopt a definition of treatability which is simply the reduction of risk or the avoidance of offending, that means that locking somebody up is treating them" (*Hansard*, HL Vol.688, col.304).

As medicine is the "science and art concerned with the cure, alleviation and prevention of disease, and with the restoration and preservation of health" (Shorter Oxford English Dictionary), it is difficult to see how medical treatment could ever be described as being "appropriate" for the patient if a view had been taken that there was no possibility of the patient ever gaining any therapeutic benefit from it, apart than the benefit that arises from preventing offending in the community. Further, it is unlikely that a doctor could be said to be acting ethically if she was involved in the admission of a patient to hospital in the knowledge that the patient would receive no therapeutic benefit from the treatment that was going to be provided. In any event, the concern about the absence of any reference to therapeutic benefit has been partly allayed by the inclusion of s.145(4) by the 2007 Act. In *SLL v Priory Heath Care and Secretary of State for Justice* [2019] UKUT 323 (AAC); [2020] M.H.L.R. 178, UT Judge Church said at para.47:

> "The Mental Health Act 2007 replaced the 'treatability test' with the 'appropriate treatment test', and the MHA definition of 'medical treatment' hinges on the purpose for which it is administered rather than its effect. In written submissions to the Tribunal the Secretary of State opposed discharge on the basis that while the clinical opinion was that the appellant's mental disorder was untreatable the proper test did not require an assessment of the efficacy of the treatment available or of the appellant's willingness to participate in it. However, it is difficult to see how a form of medical treatment which is not believed to have any realistic prospect of achieving any therapeutic benefit to a patient whatsoever could properly be considered 'appropriate' for him even if it fell within the MHA definition of 'medical treatment'".

Although it was claimed in Parliament that the new test might not be compliant with the European

Convention on Human Rights, the Joint Committee considered that "in terms of the Convention, there would appear to be no obstacle to replacing 'treatability' with 'availability of appropriate treatment' as a condition of detention" (para.20). The European Court of Human Rights Court has held that an obligation is placed on the authorities to ensure that appropriate and individualised therapy is provided to detained patients: see *Rooman v Belgium* [2020] M.H.L.R. 1, which is noted in Part 5 under art.5(1)(e). In *Reid v United Kingdom* (2003) 37 E.H.R.R. 9 para.51, the Court held that confinement under art.5(1)(e) "may be necessary not only where a person needs therapy, medication of other clinical treatment to cure or alleviate his condition, but also where the person needs control and supervision to prevent him, for example, causing harm to himself and other persons".

The recommending doctors must state on either Form A7 or A8 in which hospital(s) the appropriate treatment will be available to the patient. If the hospital named by both doctors is not the hospital that accepts the application, the application is fundamentally defective and incapable of rectification under s.15. There is no requirement on either Form for the recommending doctors to specify the nature of the appropriate treatment.

1-075   **Appropriate**   See the definition in subs.(4). In *Re Ian Brady*, December 11, 2013, the First-tier Tribunal (Mental Health) accepted as being helpful the evidence of one of the witnesses, Professor Eastman, who "had divided the treatment of patients with mental health problems into three different forms, which had been referred to during the case as limbs one, two and three" (para.227). The tribunal went on to describe these "limbs":

> "Limb one is treatment of the patient's core disorder; limb two is seeking to give the patient the skills necessary to cope with situations that they had previously found difficult or stressful but without attempting to change the core disorder; limb three is management focused on managing the patient's environment so that conflict in situations is minimised. This includes management in the hospital when the patient is on leave from the hospital and when the patient is in the community; 'this neither alters the core disorder nor gives skills to the patient'" (para.228).

The treatment, which must be actually available to the patient (*Code of Practice*, para.23.14) but need not be continuous (*R. (on the application of Epsom and St Helier NHS Trust) v Mental Health Review Tribunal* [2001] EWHC 101, para.47), need not necessarily be the most appropriate treatment that could be provided, although "wherever possible" this should be provided (*Code of Practice*, para.23.13). The treatment must be available in the hospital where the patient is to be detained (*WH v Llanarth Court Hospital* [2015] UKUT 695; [2016] M.H.L.R. 245 para.47). However, visits by the patient to a hospital to which he might be transferred was "rehabilitative planning" that came within the scope of the definition of medical treatment in s.145(1) (WH at para.53). What constitutes appropriate treatment for the patient, which is a matter of clinical judgment, may change over time. Paragraph 23.16 of the *Code of Practice* states:

> "Medical treatment which aims merely to prevent a disorder worsening is unlikely, in general, to be appropriate in cases where normal treatment approaches would aim (and be expected) to alleviate the patient's condition significantly. However, for some patients with persistent and severe mental disorders, management of the undesirable effects of their disorder may be the most that can realistically be hoped for."

Treatment can be both available and appropriate even if the patient objects to it. In *SH v Cornwall Partnership NHS Trust* [2012] UKUT 290 (AAC); [2012] M.H.L.R. 383, UT Judge Jacobs said at para.14:

> "The delivery of treatment, and the related issue of consent, is practically and conceptually distinct from the issue whether it is appropriate and available. Treatment may be appropriate, whether or not the patient consents. And it may be available, whether or not the patient is willing to receive it. Appropriateness and availability are issues that arise prior to the decision whether to give the treatment. It is only at that later stage that the patient's consent arises."

Even if the treatment is both appropriate and available, it must also satisfy the necessity test set out in para.(c).

The risk that the patient poses can be relevant to the satisfaction of the appropriate treatment test. In *MD v Mersey Care NHS Trust* [2013] UKUT 0127 (AAC), Judge Jacobs said at para.9:

"The treatment that is appropriate for a particular patient is determined by the patient's medical condition and the risk a patient presents is a consequence or feature of that condition. Risk is as relevant to treatment as any other feature of the disorder."

Patient engagement

In *MD*, Judge Jacobs approved of the approach that had been taken by the First-tier Tribunal to risk **1-076** and to the patient's lack of engagement in treatment. In its reasons for its decision not to discharge the patient the tribunal said:

"In our view, when assessing how long it is reasonable or appropriate to wait for a patient to engage with treatment, or to what extent relatively small indications of progress along the road to eventual motivation or engagement are sufficient to overcome the argument that continued detention amounts to mere containment, the likelihood of harm occurring and the potential severity of the harm, especially when taken together, will be highly relevant factors to consider, along with the patient's ability to weigh up their options and the likely outcomes for themselves and for others, and their potential ability to choose to engage at some point in the future."

Judge Jacobs returned to the issue of a patient's engagement with treatment in *DL-H v Partnerships in Care and the Secretary of State* [2013] UKUT 500 (AAC); [2014] M.H.L.R. 241, where it was held that:

1. Treatment that is otherwise available and appropriate does not cease to be so merely because the patient refuses to engage or cooperate with it (para.18).
2. A patient's refusal to engage with therapy is not decisive, although it is potentially a relevant factor that has to be taken into consideration (para.26).
3. Although s.145 defines treatment widely, there is a common thread that runs through all the elements: its purpose must be to confer some benefit on the patient, if only to the extent of preventing the patient's condition getting worse. However, the definition is so broad that it may not be difficult to identify something that will, at the least, prevent a worsening (paras 24 and 40).
4. Precision of fact-finding focused on the terms of the definition and the particular treatment that the hospital says is available will help to ensure that patients are only detained in accordance with the legislation (para.38).
5. If the tribunal finds that the patient is not prepared to engage and will never be brought to engage, that will not necessarily be decisive. This is because the definition of treatment is so broad that it includes much that does not require the patient's engagement in formal therapy (para.42).

The *Code of Practice* considers patient engagement in the following paragraphs:

"23.19 A patient's attitude towards the proposed treatment may be relevant in determining whether the appropriate medical treatment test is met. An indication of unwillingness to co-operate with treatment generally, or with a specific aspect of treatment, does not make such treatment inappropriate.
23.20 In particular, psychological therapies and other forms of medical treatments which, to be effective, require the patient's co-operation are not automatically inappropriate simply because a patient does not currently wish to engage with them. Such treatments can potentially remain appropriate and available as long as it continues to be clinically suitable to offer them and they would be provided if the patient agreed to engage."

Treatment or containment?

In *MD v Nottinghamshire Health Care NHS Trust* [2010] UKUT 59 (AAC); [2010] M.H.L.R. 93, **1-077** para.31, Judge Jacobs said: "It may be that medical treatment is still available for a patient but, because of the circumstances of a particular case, it is no longer appropriate". In this case, the Upper Tribunal rejected a submission that detention without the possibility of reduction of the risk posed by the patient was containment not treatment ("treatment has to be appropriate, but need not reduce the risk" (para.34)) and confirmed the decision of the First-tier Tribunal that appropriate medical treatment was available because there was the *potential* for milieu therapy to benefit the patient (para.35). The latter finding begs the question of how to distinguish milieu therapy from mere containment: see further, J. Phull and P. Bartlett, "'Appropriate' medical treatment: what's in a word?", Med Sci Law 2012: 1–4.

In *Re Ian Brady*, above, the tribunal, on rejecting a submission that the way in which Ashworth Hospital was providing for the patient amounted to no more than containment, said at para.280:

"The Care Team has tailored a carefully considered environment in which it seeks to maintain the level of stability in Mr Brady's mental disorder which enables him to cope with its symptoms."

In *WH v Llanarth Court Hospital* [2015] UKUT 695; [2016] M.H.L.R. 245 UT Judge Knowles said:

"If the purpose of the treatment the patient receives is to prevent a worsening of the symptoms or manifestations of his mental disorder [as required by s.145(4)], it is likely to constitute appropriate treatment even though the outcome of such treatment may have little or no beneficial effect on the patient" (para.56)."

There has been no reported case where a tribunal has found that a patient's treatment in hospital constituted mere containment.

Tribunal hearings

1-078   With regard to the approach that the tribunal should adopt when considering the appropriate treatment test, UT Judge Jacobs said in *DL-H v Devon Partnership NHS Trust* [2010] UKUT 102; [2010] M.H.L.R. 162 at para.33:

"The tribunal must investigate behind assertions, generalisations and standard phrases. By focusing on specific questions, it will ensure that it makes an individualised assessment for the particular patient. What precisely is the treatment that can be provided? What discernible benefit may it have on this patient? Is that benefit related to the patient's mental disorder or to some unrelated problem? Is the patient truly resistant to engagement?"

In *WH v Llanarth Court Hospital*, above, Judge Knowles said at para.58 that the following approach articulated by Sullivan J. in *R. (on the application of Epsom and St Helier NHS Trust v Mental Health Review Tribunal* [2001] EWHC Admin 101 at para.52 "has much to recommend it to tribunals troubled by the issue of appropriate treatment for detained patients":

"The matter has to be looked at in the round, including the prospect of future in-patient treatment, but there will come a time when, even though it is certain that treatment will be required at some stage in the future, the timing of that treatment is so uncertain that it is no longer 'appropriate' for the patient to continue to be liable to detention. It is the tribunal's function to use its expertise to decide whether the certainty, or the possibility, of the need for in-patient treatment at some future date makes it 'appropriate' that the patient's liability to detention shall continue."

Subsection (3)

1-079   See the notes to s.2(3).

Written recommendations   If an application to hospital A is not accepted due to the lack of a hospital bed, the recommendations can be used to support an application to hospital B as long as the recommendations state that appropriate treatment for the patient is available at that hospital.

Subsection (4)

1-080   Note the circularity of the definition contained in this provision. The final phrase indicates that social factors can be taken into account.

All other circumstances   "All the patient's circumstances must be looked at, including their age and gender, where they live, where their family and social contacts are, and their cultural background" (*Hansard*, HL Vol.688, col.320, per the Minister of State).

Admission for assessment in cases of emergency

1-081   **4.**—(1)   In any case of urgent necessity, an application for admission for assessment may be made in respect of a patient in accordance with the following provisions of this section, and any application so made is in this Act referred to as "an emergency application".

(2)   An emergency application may be made either by an [approved mental

health professional] or by the nearest relative of the patient; and every such application shall include a statement that it is of urgent necessity for the patient to be admitted and detained under section 2 above, and that compliance with the provisions of this Part of this Act relating to applications under that section would involve undesirable delay.

(3)   An emergency application shall be sufficient in the first instance if founded on one of the medical recommendations required by section 2 above, given, if practicable, by a practitioner who has previous acquaintance with the patient and otherwise complying with the requirements of section 12 below so far as applicable to a single recommendation, and verifying the statement referred to in subsection (2) above.

(4)   An emergency application shall cease to have effect on the expiration of a period of 72 hours from the time when the patient is admitted to the hospital unless—

(a)   the second medical recommendation required by section 2 above is given and received by the managers within that period; and

(b)   that recommendation and the recommendation referred to in subsection (3) above together comply with all the requirements of section 12 below (other than the requirement as to the time of signature of the second recommendation).

(5)   In relation to an emergency application, section 11 below shall have effect as if in subsection (5) of that section for the words "the period of 14 days ending with the date of the application" there were substituted the words "the previous 24 hours".

Amendment

The words in square brackets in subs.(1) were substituted by the Mental Health Act 2007 s.21, Sch.2 para.2.

Definitions

application for admission for assessment: ss.2, 145(1).   **1-082**
patient: s.145(1).
approved mental health professional: s.145(1), (1AC).
nearest relative: ss.26(3), 145(1).
the managers, s.145(1).
hospital: ss.34(2), 145(1).

General Note

This section provides for the compulsory admission of a person to hospital for assessment for a period   **1-083**
of up to 72 hours based on the medical recommendation of one doctor who, if practicable, should have previous acquaintance with the patient. The grounds for detention under this section are the same as for s.2, with the addition that both the applicant and the recommending doctor must certify that "it is of urgent necessity for the patient to be admitted and detained under section 2" and that "compliance with the provisions ... relating to applications under that section would involve undesirable delay".
Paragraph 15.8 of the *Code of Practice* states:

"An emergency may arise where the patient's mental state or behaviour presents problems which those involved cannot reasonably be expected to manage while waiting for a second doctor. To be satisfied that an emergency has arisen, the person making the application and the doctor making the supporting recommendation should have evidence of:

•   an immediate and significant risk of mental or physical harm to the patient or to others
•   danger of serious harm to property, or

- a need for the use of restrictive interventions on a patient (see chapter 26)."

Under the Mental Health Act 1959, the equivalent procedure (s.29 of that Act) was misused and became the most widely used form of compulsory admission. Subsequent to the implementation of the Act, pressure from the Mental Health Act Commission was largely responsible for a decrease in both the number and proportion of applications made under this section. The desire to avoid applications being made under this section has occasionally led to situations where applications have not been made in circumstances where the criteria set out in subs.(2) have been satisfied; see, for example, the Coroner's "Regulation 28 report to prevent future deaths" in the case of Nigel Abbott which can be accessed at: *www.judiciary.uk/wp-content/uploads/2019/10/Nigel-Abbott-2019-02842.pdf.* The following on-going matter of concern was listed by the Coroner: "Whilst section 4 is available to be used, it is not used".

Paragraph 15.7 of the *Code of Practice* states:

"Section 4 should never be used for administrative convenience. So, for example, patients should not be admitted under section 4 merely because it is more convenient for the second doctor to examine the patient in, rather than outside, hospital." Paragraph 15.10 of the *Code of Practice* states:

"If AMHPs find themselves having to consider making emergency applications because of difficulties in securing a second doctor, they should report that to the local authority on whose behalf they are acting (or in accordance with other agreed arrangements, if they are different). The local authority should review this issue promptly with the relevant NHS commissioner (see paragraph 14.80 on locally agreed policies)".

In *R. (on the application of Sessay) v South London and Maudsley NHS Foundation Trust)* [2011] EWHC 2617 (QB); [2012] M.H.L.R. 94, the Divisional Court held that the Act provides a complete statutory code for the detention on non-compliant mentally incapacitated patients and that the common law doctrine of necessity does not apply during the period when a patient is being assessed for detention under the Act. However, the court said at para.57:

"[I]n our view it is unlikely in the ordinary case that there will be a false imprisonment at common law or deprivation of liberty for the purposes of Article 5(1) [European Convention on Human Rights] if there is no undue delay during the processing of an application under ss.2 or 4 MHA for admission."

It is therefore the case that if, following an assessment of the patient, the potential applicant and recommending doctor agree that an application to detain the patient should be made, the patient may be held during the time that it takes to process the application as long as the process is not unduly delayed; also see the note on "duly completed" in 6(1).

An application under this section cannot be renewed at the end of the 72 hour period. If compulsory detention is to be continued, the application must either be "converted" into a s.2 application under subs.(4), in which case the patient can be detained for 28 days beginning with the date of his admission under this section, or an application for treatment should be made under s.3. The Act does not contain a procedure under which a s.4 application can be converted into a s.3 application by the addition of a second medical recommendation.

An application under this section can be made if a patient who has been detained in a general hospital under s.5(2) needs to be transferred to a psychiatric hospital urgently.

As, under s.25, the nearest relative of a detained patient has to give not less than 72 hours' notice of his or her intention to discharge the patient, only the responsible clinician (RC) and the hospital managers have the power to order the discharge of a patient detained under this section: see s.23.

Patients admitted under this section are *not* subject to the consent to treatment provisions contained in Pt IV (s.56(3)(a)). If the patient is mentally capable of making a decision about treatment, the common law enables him to refuse to be treated for either a physical or mental disorder. However, if the patient is assessed as being mentally incapable of making a decision about treatment, the treatment can be provided under the Mental Capacity Act 2005 if it is deemed to be in his best interests.

Applications to the First-tier Tribunal (Mental Health) or the Mental Health Review Tribunal for Wales

1-084   The patient may make an application, but if the second medical recommendation provided for in subs.(4) is not forthcoming it will lapse (s.66(1)(a), (2)(a)).

Code of Practice

Guidance on the making of applications under this section is contained in Ch.15.   **1-085**

Subsection (1)

Application   An application under this section can be made by either the patient's nearest relative (NR)   **1-086**
or by an AMHP (s.11(1)). Paragraph 15.4 of the *Code of Practice* states:

> "If the application is made by an AMHP, the nearest relative should be informed at the same time,
> or within a reasonable time afterwards, unless the patient requests otherwise (or does not have a near-
> est relative). The circumstances detailed in paragraph 14.62 should be considered in deciding whether
> to inform the nearest relative against the patient's wishes."

Paragraph 14.62 of the *Code* is reproduced in the notes on s.11(4)(b) under the heading "Not reasonably practicable". The duty of the AMHP under s.11(3) to inform the NR of an application under s.2 is
triggered if the application under this section is "converted" to a s.2 by virtue of subs.(4) (*Re GM* [2000]
M.H.L.R. 41, para.28).
   The applicant must use Form A9 (for NRs) or Form A10 (for AMHPs) (in Wales, Form HO9 (for
NRs) or Form HO10 (for AMHPs)): see reg.4(1) of the English and Welsh Regulations. The applicant
must have seen the patient within the previous 24 hours (s.11(5)) and the patient must be admitted to
hospital within 24 hours beginning from the time when he was medically examined or when the ap-
plication was made, whichever is the earlier (s.6(1)(b)). These time limits were introduced by the 1982
Act to help "to prevent [this section] being used for cases other than those of real emergency" (Cmnd.
7320, para.2.6).
   An application for the admission of a ward of court cannot be made without the leave of the High
Court (s.33(1)).
   The effect of an application made under this section is set out in s.6. The hospital named in the ap-
plication is not placed under a legal obligation to admit the patient: see the note on "to hospital" in s.6(1).

Subsection (2)

Approved mental health professional   An AMHP applicant must comply with the requirements of   **1-087**
s.13.

Urgent necessity ... undesirable delay   See para.15.8 of the *Code of Practice* which states:

> "An emergency may arise where the patient's mental state or behaviour presents problems which
> those involved cannot reasonably be expected to manage while waiting for a second doctor. To be
> satisfied that an emergency has arisen, the person making the application and the doctor making the
> supporting recommendation should have evidence of:
>
> •   an immediate and significant risk of mental or physical harm to the patient or to others
> •   danger of serious harm to property, or
> •   a need for the use of restrictive interventions on a patient (see chapter 26)."

Both the "urgent necessity" and the "undesirable delay" tests have to be met before an application can
be made under this section. The applicant has to confirm that this is the case on Form A9 (for NRs) or
A10 (for AMHPs). The recommending doctor must also state that the tests are satisfied on Form A11.

Subsection (3)

One of the medical recommendations   Which must be completed on Form A11 (in Wales, Form   **1-088**
HO11): see reg.4(1) of the English and Welsh Regulations. A medical recommendation provided under
this section cannot be used to support a subsequent application made under s.3. There is no requirement for the recommending doctor to be approved under s.12.

Subsection (4)

1-089 **Period of 72 hours**   If the application is "converted" into a s.2 application under this subsection, the 28 days period provided for in s.2 will run from the time of the patient's admission to hospital under this section. An AMHP or a nearest relative applicant should not complete an application form for an admission under s.2 if a "conversion" is effected.

Second medical recommendation ... is given   A second doctor who, bearing in mind the status of the first recommending doctor, complies with the provisions of s.12 should examine the patient as soon as possible after admission to decide whether the patient should be detained under s.2: see para.15.13 of the *Code of Practice*. If a second medical recommendation is given, a record should be made in Part 2 of Form H3 (in Wales, Form HO14).

　　If it is decided that the patient should not be detained under s.2, this does not have the effect of automatically discharging the section as a discharge prior to the expiration of the 72 hours can only be effected by a decision to discharge being made by either the patient's responsible clinician or the hospital managers under s.23.

Hospital   Local social services authorities must be informed of those hospitals where arrangements are in force for the reception, in cases of special urgency, of patients requiring treatment for mental disorder (s.140).

Application in respect of patient already in hospital

1-090 　　**5.**—(1)   An application for the admission of a patient to a hospital may be made under this Part of this Act notwithstanding that the patient is already an in-patient in that hospital or, in the case of an application for admission for treatment that the patient is for the time being liable to be detained in the hospital in pursuance of an application for admission for assessment; and where an application is so made the patient shall be treated for the purposes of this Part of this Act as if he had been admitted to the hospital at the time when that application was received by the managers.

　　(2)   If, in the case of a patient who is an in-patient in a hospital, it appears to the registered medical practitioner [or approved clinician] in charge of the treatment of the patient that an application ought to be made under this Part of this Act for the admission of the patient to hospital, he may furnish to the managers a report in writing to that effect; and in any such case the patient may be detained in the hospital for a period of 72 hours from the time when the report is so furnished.

　　[(3)   The registered medical practitioner or approved clinician in charge of the treatment of a patient in a hospital may nominate one (but not more than one) person to act for him under subsection (2) above in his absence.

　　(3A)   For the purposes of subsection (3) above—

　　　　(a)   the registered medical practitioner may nominate another registered medical practitioner, or an approved clinician, on the staff of the hospital; and

　　　　(b)   the approved clinician may nominate another approved clinician, or a registered medical practitioner, on the staff of the hospital.]

　　(4)   If, in the case of a patient who is receiving treatment for mental disorder as an in-patient in a hospital, it appears to a nurse of the prescribed class—

　　　　(a)   that the patient is suffering from mental disorder to such a degree that it is necessary for his health or safety or for the protection of others for him to be immediately restrained from leaving the hospital; and

　　　　(b)   that it is not practicable to secure the immediate attendance of a practitioner [or clinician] for the purpose of furnishing a report under subsection (2) above,

[58]

the nurse may record that fact in writing; and in that event the patient may be detained in the hospital for a period of six hours from the time when that fact is so recorded or until the earlier arrival at the place where the patient is detained of a practitioner [or clinician] having power to furnish a report under that subsection.

(5) A record made under subsection (4) above shall be delivered by the nurse (or by a person authorised by the nurse in that behalf) to the managers of the hospital as soon as possible after it is made; and where a record is made under that subsection the period mentioned in subsection (2) above shall begin at the time when it is made.

(6) The reference in subsection (1) above to an in-patient does not include an in-patient who is liable to be detained in pursuance of an application under this Part of this Act [or a community patient] and the references in subsections (2) and (4) above do not include an in-patient who is liable to be detained in a hospital under this Part of this Act [or a community patient].

(7) In subsection (4) above "prescribed" means prescribed by an order made by the Secretary of State.

Amendments

The amendments to this section were made by the Mental Health Act 2007 ss.9(2), 32, Sch.3 para.2.

Definitions

1-091

patient: s.145(1).
hospital: ss.34(2), 145(1).
application for admission for treatment: ss.3, 145(1).
application for admission for assessment: ss.2, 145(1).
the managers: s.145(1).
mental disorder: s.145(1).
approved clinician: s.145(1).
community patient: ss.17A(7), 145(1).

General Note

1-092

This section provides for applications for compulsory detention under s.2 or 3 to be made in respect of mentally disordered patients who are already receiving treatment in hospital as informal patients. It also sets out the procedures, the "holding powers", that can be used if it is considered that an informal patient might leave the hospital before there is time to complete an application under either s.2 or s.3. The holding powers, one for doctors and approved clinicians (subs.(2)) and the other for nurses (subs.(4)), cannot be used to prolong the detention of a patient whose section is about to expire or in respect of a community patient (subs.(6)). While it is permissible for staff to attempt to dissuade an informal in-patient from leaving the hospital, he cannot be physically prevented from leaving in the absence a holding power being invoked. In the Irish Court of Appeal case *P.L. v The Clinical Director of St. Patrick's University Hospital* [2018] IECA 29, Hogan J. said at para.39:

> "While I do not doubt that hospital personnel could lawfully attempt to persuade a patient not to leave, this must involve persuasion and not restraint. Just as a host might lawfully attempt to persuade a reluctant guest to stay for dinner, he could not lawfully restrain the guest from leaving. The same holds true in the present case: the applicant was a voluntary patient and he was therefore free in principle to leave at any time."

Although detention under subss.(2) or (4) cannot be renewed, "that does not prevent it being used again on a future occasion if necessary" (*Code of Practice*, para.18.38). Hospital managers must ensure that patients detained under under subss.(2) or (4) are given information about their position and their rights as required by s.132.

Patients who are detained under the provisions of subs.(2) or (4) are not subject to the consent to treatment provisions contained in Pt IV (s.56(3)(b)). If the patient is mentally capable of making a decision about treatment, the common law enables him to refuse to be treated for either a physical or mental disorder. However, if the patient is assessed as being mentally incapable of making a decision about treatment, the treatment can be provided under the Mental Capacity Act 2005 if it is deemed to be in his best interests.

By virtue of s.8(1) of the Health and Social Care Act 2008 and reg.3 and Sch.1, para.5 to SI 2014/2936, a hospital which provides for the assessment or medical treatment (other than surgical procedures) of patients detained under the Act (with the exception of s.135 or 136) must be registered for that activity by the Care Quality Commission (CQC). As the powers contained in subs.(2) and (4) can be invoked in any hospital in England or Wales, it is clearly impracticable for a hospital to seek registration with the CQC on the ground that such powers might be invoked at some point in the future. In *Assessment or medical treatment for persons detained under the Mental Health Act 1983* (updated February 5, 2019), the CQC states:

"This regulated activity includes the use of short term, emergency holding powers under Section 5 of the Mental Health Act. It therefore also applies to hospital services other than specialist mental health inpatient services, such as acute hospitals, where the Mental Health Act could be used to detain patients for short periods under temporary arrangements."

Although the CQC has encouraged general hospitals to register to assess and treat detained patients, it is understood that the CQC turns a "blind eye" to occasions when the holding powers are used in a general hospital that is not so registered.

A person who has been detained under either subs.(2) or subs.(4) may be retaken if he absents himself from the hospital without leave as long as the 72 hour (for subs.(2)) or six-hour (for subs.(4)) period has not expired (s.18(5)).

An account of further powers that are available to restrain and/or detain mentally disordered persons is contained in Appendix A.

Transfers to other hospitals

1-093   A patient who is detained under subss.(2) or (4) cannot be transferred to another hospital under reg.7 of the English Regulations or reg.23 of the Welsh Regulations because such a person is not "liable to be detained in a hospital by virtue of an application" under this Part (see s.19(1)(a), (2)(a)).

If a mentally capable patient who has been detained by subs.(2) needs to be taken to another hospital (the "receiving hospital") for urgent treatment or for security reasons, the transfer can be made if the patient consents to it. However, the s.5(2) will automatically lapse when the patient is moved from the hospital named on the Form H1 because the holding power only provides authority for the patient to be detained in "the hospital", i.e. the hospital that was providing in-patient treatment to the patient at the time when the Form was signed. It is submitted that the Form H1 would be reactivated if the patient returned to that hospital with his consent within the 72-hour period. Consideration would have to be given to invoking either subs.(2) or subs.(4) if the patient made an attempt to leave the receiving hospital.

If the patient either does not consent to the transfer, or is mentally incapable and is resisting being transferred, and the urgency of the situation is such that there is not sufficient time to comply with the formalities of an application under s.2, an application under s.4 can be made and the transfer effected under s.19. Alternatively, the application under s.4 could be made out to the receiving hospital. If the patient is mentally incapable and is not resisting being transferred, the transfer can be effected under the Mental Capacity Act 2005 if the transfer is assessed as being in his best interests: also see paras 18.42–18.45 of the *Code of Practice.*

Code of Practice

1-094   Guidance on the use of the "holding powers" is contained in Ch.18.

Human Rights Act 1998

1-095   The powers contained in subss.(2) and (4) do not violate the European Convention on Human Rights (ECHR) because the procedural safeguards established under Convention case law do not apply to emergency situations (*Winterwerp v Netherlands* (1979) 2 E.H.R.R. 387, para.39). The use by staff of common law powers to detain and control patients in emergency situations whilst awaiting the presence of either a doctor or a specialist nurse who has the power to act under either subss.(2) or (4) is also allowable under the ECHR: see Appendix A. However, such powers should only be used as a "safety net" to cover situations where it is not possible to immediately invoke the statutory powers. In other words, to be consistent with the ECHR, common law powers should not be used as an alternative to the powers contained in the Act.

Doctors and nurses who use the holding powers are exercising "functions of a public nature" and are therefore "public authorities" for the purposes of s.6 of the Human Rights Act (s.6(3)(b)).

Subsection (1)

In-patient   The combined effect of this subsection and subs.(6) is that: **1-096**

   (i)   an application for compulsory admission to hospital can be made in respect of an informal patient notwithstanding that he is already an in-patient in hospital;

   (ii)   an application for compulsory admission cannot be made in respect of community patients or patients who are already in hospital under compulsory powers except that an application under s.3 can be made in respect of a patient detained under s.2;

   (iii)   where an application is made in respect of a patient who is already in hospital, it is treated for the purposes of this Part of the Act as if the patient were admitted to the hospital at the time when that application was received by the managers; and

   (iv)   the holding powers contained in subss.(2) and (4) cannot be used in respect of either a detained or a community patient.

At the time when that application was received by the managers   The application will be served by delivering it personally to an officer of the managers who is authorised to receive it, or electronically to the managers: see reg.3(2) of the English and Welsh Regulations.

Subsection (2)

This subsection enables an informal patient, including a patient who is subject to a deprivation of   **1-097**
liberty authorisation under the Mental Capacity Act 2005 but excluding a community patient (subs.(6)), to be detained for up to 72 hours if the doctor or approved clinician (AC) who is in charge of the patient's treatment reports that an application under s.2 or 3 ought to be made. The power can be exercised in any hospital and the doctor or AC need not be a psychiatrist. As the power comes into effect as soon as Form H1 is furnished to the hospital managers (see below) and as the hospital managers do not have the ability to discharge the power, the Form cannot be declared invalid on the ground that the reasons given on the Form for the need for an application to be made are deemed to be insufficient.

Unlike the power contained in subs.(4), this subsection can be invoked even though the patient is not attempting to leave the hospital. The power cannot be used to prolong the detention of a patient whose section is about to expire (subs.(6)) or to provide time for an application to be made to the county court pursuant to s.29(4) to displace a nearest relative after the expiration of the 28-day period of detention provided for under s.2 (*McDougall v Sefton Area Health Authority*, April 9, 1987, McNeill J., cited in *L. Gostin, Mental Health Services—Law and Practice*, 1986, at para.10.04). The Mental Health Act Commission (MHAC) reported that it advised a NHS trust "that consecutive applications of s.5(2) are uncommon and hardly ever necessary if assessments are carried out promptly" (*Seventh Biennial Report*, 1995–1997, para.3.2). It is submitted that, following the decision in *R. v Wilson Ex p. Williamson* [1996] C.O.D. 42, noted in the General Note to s.2, this practice is unlawful.

The purpose of the power is to prevent a patient from discharging himself from hospital before there is time to arrange for an application under s.2 or s.3 to be made. The patient need not have been admitted to the hospital for treatment for a mental disorder. As soon as the power is invoked, arrangements should be made for the patient to be assessed by a potential applicant and potential recommending doctors. The responsibility for providing the approved mental health professional (AMHP) as the potential applicant is that of the local authority for the area where the hospital is located (s.13(1)). Paragraph 18.8 of the *Code of Practice* states that patients "should not be admitted informally with the sole intention of then using the holding power". For the transfer of patients who are detained under this provision, see the note on Transfers to other hospitals, above.

The "Inquiry into the Care and Treatment of Gilbert Kopernik-Steckel" recommended that the MHAC should produce advice on the use of statements in a patient's file such as "For section 5(2) if he tries to leave". Although statements which fetter the discretion of the section 5(2) clinician should be avoided, there is nothing objectionable in the doctor or AC who is in charge of the patient's treatment making a record to the effect that "section 5(2) should be considered if the patient makes an attempt to leave". Paragraph 18.18 of the *Code of Practice* states:

"Doctors and approved clinicians may leave instructions with ward staff to contact them (or their nominated deputy) if a particular patient wants or tries to leave. But they may not leave instructions for their nominated deputy to use section 5, nor may they complete a section 5 report in advance to be used in their absence. The deputy must exercise their own professional judgment."

In *R. v Wilson Ex p. Williamson*, above, the court declared that the patient's detention under s.2 was unlawful. Counsel for the hospital managers argued that this provision would not be available following the court's decision because it was "designed for the patient who had been a voluntary patient" and that to use the provision in respect of a patient who had been detained in the hospital unlawfully would be to "take advantage of unlawful status" and would make the hospital managers vulnerable to judicial review on the ground that they were "using it for improper purposes". Although counsel's points have some substance, the correctness of his opinion must be doubted because a patient who has been unlawfully detained is clearly an "in-patient", and it surely cannot be "improper" for the patient's consultant to utilise the only provision that is available to her to prevent a patient, who might have been diagnosed as being either dangerous or suicidal, from being discharged from the hospital: also see para.35.13 of the *Code of Practice*, which is reproduced in the General Note to s.6, and para.31.21 of the Reference Guide. In *R. v Birmingham Mental Health Trust Ex p. Phillips*, May 25, 1995, the fact that the patient had been made the subject of this provision immediately after it was discovered that the application under s.2 that had been made in respect of her was invalid was accepted by Tucker J. without comment. However, the use of s.5(2) in this situation would only be lawful if the invalid section had been discharged by either the hospital managers or the patient's RC: see subs.(6).

There is no procedure for discharging the patient from the holding power. The power will automatically lapse if:

(i)   the result of the assessment is a decision not to make an application under s.2 or 3; or
(ii)   the power is invoked by a doctor or an AC who has been nominated under subs.(3) and the clinician in charge of the patient's treatment subsequently decides that no assessment for possible detention needs to be carried out; or
(iii)   an application under s.2 or 3 is made; or
(iv)   the 72 hours period expires without an assessment having taken place.

Where this power has been invoked by the doctor or AC nominated under subs.(3), there is no need to involve a potential applicant in the assessment if the clinician in charge of the patient's treatment subsequently examines the patient and concludes that an application should not be made.

If an AMHP concludes at the assessment that an application in respect of the patient is not required and the assessing doctor holds a contrary view, there is nothing in this provision that prevents the assessment from being prolonged to enable the patient's nearest relative to consider whether he or she wishes to make an application.

This power should not be used merely to justify the intervention of staff in an emergency to respond to an informal patient's disturbed behaviour as such intervention can be justified under the powers outlined in Appendix A.

The emergency detention of persons who are not in-patients

1-098   If a person who is not an in-patient is on hospital premises and is acting in a manner which suggests that an assessment for an application under the Act is urgently required, action could be taken to prevent the person from leaving the hospital in order for the assessment to take place. Such action should be for the shortest possible period and must be proportionate to the identified risk: see *R. (on the application of Sessay) v South London and Maudsley NHS Foundation Trust* [2001] EWHC 2617 (QB); [2012] M.H.L.R. 94 and the powers outlined in Appendix A. Given the need to act swiftly, consideration should be given to invoking s.4. An alternative course of action would be for the hospital to contact the police with a request that the person be detained under s.136. Hospital staff could prevent the person from leaving the hospital for a short period while waiting for the arrival of the police.

1-099   **In-patient in a hospital**   The patient could be receiving treatment in a general hospital for a physical condition. In *Great Western Hospitals NHS Foundation Trust v AA* [2014] EWHC 132 (Fam) this provision was invoked in respect of a pregnant patient who was being treated in a labour suite. The patient's caesarean section and the potential use of restraint on her were authorised under the court's inherent jurisdiction. Paragraph 18.11 of the *Code of Practice* states:

"Sometimes a report under section 5(2) may be made in relation to a patient who is not at the time under the care of a psychiatrist or an approved clinician. In such cases, the doctor invoking the power should make immediate contact with a psychiatrist or an approved clinician to obtain confirmation of their opinion that the patient needs to be detained so that an application can be made. If possible, the doctor should seek such advice before using the power."

A patient who is being treated in an out-patient department, in a day hospital or as a day patient cannot be detained under this provision. The second edition of the *Code of Practice* at para.8.4 offered the following definition of "in-patient": "one who has understood and accepted the offer of a bed, and who has freely appeared on the ward and who has co-operated in the admission procedure". In *R. (on the application of DR) v Mersey Care NHS Trust* [2002] EWHC 1810 (Admin); [2002] M.H.L.R. 386 para.27, Wilson J. said that the word in-patient "suggests the allocation and use of a hospital bed". His Lordship made no reference in his judgment to the *Code of Practice* definition. A suggested definition of a mentally incapable informal in-patient is: a compliant patient who has arrived at the ward where his allocated bed is located and who has not provided any evidence of resistance (either verbal or physical) to the admission procedure. In both cases, the availability of a bed for the patient is a pre-condition to attaining in-patient status. The current edition of the *Code of Practice* merely states that, in the context of this section, "a hospital in-patient means any person who is receiving in-patient treatment in a hospital" (para.18.7). If this provision is invoked in a situation where the patient is not a hospital in-patient, the patient could claim damages for the unlawful detention: see, for example, *PB v Priory Group Ltd* [2018] MHLO 74.

As the power contained in this subsection only applies if the patient is an informal in-patient, it is necessary to identify how a patient can divest himself of his in-patient status. For example, can an in-patient avoid being held under this provision by the simple expedient of saying to the clinician who is about to invoke the power, "I discharge myself?". It is highly unlikely that the courts would find that a patient could end his in-patient status in this manner as such a finding would have the effect of totally subverting Parliament's intention in enacting this provision. It is submitted that a patient does not lose his in-patient status until he has physically removed himself from the hospital (which includes the hospital grounds). This approach was endorsed by the Court of Appeal, Northern Ireland in *Re McGee* [2007] NICA 38; [2008] M.H.L.R. 216, where it was held that a patient did not cease to be an in-patient for the purposes of the equivalent provision in the Northern Irish legislation when he expressed his desire to leave the hospital an hour after being told of the decision of the tribunal to discharge him from detention. Girvan L.J. said at para.12: "He did not physically remove himself from the hospital [and his] bed was still available to him".

Registered medical practitioner or approved clinician in charge   A registered medical practitioner   **1-100**
means "a fully registered person within the meaning of the Medical Act 1983 who holds a licence to practise under that Act" (Interpretation Act 1978, Sch.1).

In Charge   Determining the person "in charge" of the patient's medical treatment is a question of fact. The *Code of Practice* states:

"18.4 The identity of the person in charge of a patient's medical treatment at any time will depend on the particular circumstances. A professional who is treating the patient under the direction of another professional should not be considered to be in charge.
    18.5 There may be more than one person who could reasonably be said to be in charge of a patient's treatment, eg where a patient is already receiving treatment for both a physical and a mental disorder. In a case of that kind, the psychiatrist or approved clinician in charge of the patient's treatment for the mental disorder is the preferred person to use the power in section 5, if necessary."

According to the *Code of Practice* at para.18.10, the person in charge should only exercise the power after having personally examined the patient. Surprisingly, the Act does not require the patient to be examined.

An application ought to be made   Although the most frequent circumstance leading to the use of this power is an attempt by the patient to leave the hospital, this ground enables a patient to be detained in the absence of such behaviour. For example, the patient could be detained in a situation where he had recently returned to the hospital after having left contrary to professional advice and the clinician in charge of the patient's treatment believed that it was likely that the patient would absent himself again in the near future.

If an application is made during the 72-hour period, the application will commence from the time when it was accepted by the hospital managers and not from the time when this provision was invoked. The responsibility for deciding whether to make an application under s.2 or s.3 is that of the applicant, not the recommending doctors. The application need not be addressed to the hospital which is holding the patient under this provison.

Report   Using Form H1 (in Wales, Form HO12): see reg.4(1) of the English and Welsh Regulations. The power takes effect as soon as the Form is furnished to the hospital managers: see below.

1-101   **Detained in the hospital**   Although this provision is silent on the point, it is submitted that the patient is detained by the hospital managers. If the patient is an in-patient of a hospital which is managed by more than one set of hospital managers, the patient can be detained in any part of the hospital that is managed by the hospital managers of the ward where the patient is an in-patient. There is, it is submitted, no authority to detain the patient in a part of the hospital that is managed by different hospital managers.

72 hours   This is the maximum period during which a patient can be detained. The authority to detain under this provision is not renewable. However, circumstances could arise where a change in the patient's situation could lead to a second use of this provision being contemplated soon after its first use.

If a patient who has been detained under this provision absconds, he cannot be retaken once the 72-hour period has expired (s.18(5)).

Time when the report is ... furnished   In the Scottish case of *Milborrow, Applicant*, 1996 S.C.L.R. 315 Sh. Ct, it was held that a report is "furnished" to the hospital managers when it is committed to the internal mail system operated by those managers. The period of detention therefore starts at that point or when the report is handed over to a member of staff who is authorised to receive it, which could include a member of the nursing staff: see Form H1 (or HO12) and para.18.6 of the *Code of Practice*.

If the patient is intent on leaving the hospital immediately, the powers outlined in Appendix A will provide authority for the patient to be detained for the short period that is required to complete Form H1. Once Form H1 has been completed and committed to the hospital's internal mail system or handed to the authorised member of staff, the patient can be detained even though he might have left the ward area. However, if the patient has left the hospital and its grounds before the completion of Form H1, the hospital managers cannot subsequently detain him and return him to hospital on the authority of that form. This is because by leaving hospital the patient relinquishes his in-patient status which is an essential pre-condition to the use of this subsection. As a patient who is not "liable to be detained", he could not be returned to hospital under the auspices of s.18.

Subsection (3)

1-102   This subsection, which should be read with subs.(3A), is aimed at lessening pressure on clinicians to contravene the provisions of subs.(2) by, for example, allowing persons other than the "medical practitioner or approved clinician in charge" to sign Form H1 or by blank forms being signed for use when emergencies occur.

May nominate   The nominated clinician, who could be a junior doctor in a general hospital, should exercise her own judgment when exercising the power under subs.(2). She can be advised, but not required to consult with a senior colleague before exercising the power.

Good practice dictates that the nomination should be put in writing and conveyed to all relevant staff. It is the doctor or AC in charge of the patient's treatment and not the hospital managers who must make the nomination. The nominee should be a doctor or AC who has been assessed as having the knowledge and experience that qualifies her to perform the onerous task of deciding whether patients should be deprived of their liberty.

Paragraph 18.14 of the *Code of Practice* states:

"Doctors should not be nominated as a deputy unless they are competent to perform the role. If nominated deputies are not approved clinicians (or doctors approved under section 12 of the Act), they should wherever possible seek advice from the person for whom they are deputising, or from someone else who is an approved clinician or section 12 approved doctor, before using section 5(2). Hospital managers should see that arrangements are in place to allow nominated deputies to do this."

The doctor or AC in charge of the patient's treatment should only nominate a class of doctors, such as "the duty doctor", if "there is only one nominated deputy for any patient at any time and it can be determined with certainty who that nominated deputy is" (*Code of Practice*, para.18.16). The nominated doctor or AC cannot delegate to another because of the legal principle *delegatus non potest delegare*.

Only one doctor or AC may be nominated to act during any particular period. A nomination "to Dr A or, in Dr A's absence, to Dr B" would be unlawful.

On the staff of that hospital   The doctor or AC must be employed or contracted to undertake clinical responsibilities at the hospital. A medical practitioner nominee must be fully registered person within the meaning of the Medical Act 1983 (Interpretation Act 1978, Sch.1).

Subsection (3A)

For the purpose of making a nomination under subs.(3), a doctor who is in charge of the patient's **1-103** treatment can nominate either another doctor or an AC (who need not be a doctor), while an AC who is in charge of the patient's treatment can nominate either another AC or a doctor. The nominee has to be "on the staff" of the relevant hospital.

Subsection (4)

This subsection provides for nurses of a prescribed class (see subs.(7)) to invoke a "holding power" **1-104** in respect of an informal patient, including a patient who is subject to a deprivation of liberty authorisation under the Mental Capacity Act 2005 but excluding a community patient (subs.(6)), for a period of not more than six hours. During this period the "medical practitioner or approved clinician in charge" or her nominated deputy should examine the patient with a view to making a report under subs.(2). The power to detain the patient takes effect at the time when the nurse makes her report. It can only be used if the patient is indicating either verbally or otherwise that he wishes to leave the hospital. A nurse invoking this provision is entitled to use the minimum force necessary to prevent the patient from leaving hospital. Where a patient requires restraint but is not showing any inclination to leave the hospital, nurses have to rely on the powers outlined in Appendix A. The nurse who makes the report does not have to detain the patient personally (Reference Guide, para.8.84).

This power can only be used in respect of patients who are receiving hospital treatment for mental disorder; it is not sufficient for the patient to be merely suffering from a mental disorder. Although the power can be invoked in any hospital where the patient is receiving treatment for mental disorder, it is unlikely that a non-psychiatric ward will be staffed with nurses of the "prescribed class". In an emergency, a nurse who is not of the prescribed class may use the powers set out in Appendix A to restrain a patient who might be a danger to self or others from leaving hospital for a short period until a practitioner who has the power to invoke either this provision or subs.(2) attends.

Exercising the holding power is the personal decision of the nurse who cannot be instructed to exercise it by anyone else.

Degree   The patient cannot be made subject to this power if he is not exhibiting any manifestations of mental disorder: see the note on "of a nature or degree" in s.3(2)(a).

Restrained from leaving the hospital   The patient can be restrained from leaving any part of the hospital, including its grounds.

Immediate attendance of a practitioner   It is submitted that the nurses' holding power need not be invoked if either the clinician who is in charge of the patient's treatment or her nominee is in the hospital building and can attend at the ward within a few minutes of the crises occurring. A combination of the powers outlined in Appendix A and the legal maxim *de minimis non curat lex* (the error is too trivial to be of any consequence) would enable the patient to be held during this brief period. Paragraph 18.29 of the *Code of Practice* states that, before using this power "nurses should assess:

- the likely arrival time of the doctor or approved clinician, as against the likely intention of the patient to leave. It may be possible to persuade the patient to wait until a doctor or approved clinician arrives to discuss it further, and
- the consequences of a patient leaving the hospital before the doctor or approved clinician arrives – in other words, the harm that might occur to the patient or others."

Six hours   This is the maximum and non-renewable period during which a patient can be detained. If a patient who has been detained under this provision absconds, he cannot be retaken once the six hour period has elapsed (s.18(5)).

From the time when that fact is so recorded   On Form H2 or, in Wales, HO13. Although neither Form requires the nurse to give reasons for invoking the power, the *Code of Practice*, at para.18.33, states that these should be recorded in the patient's notes. The power will end six hours later or on the earlier arrival of one of the clinicians entitled to make a report under subs.(2). If a decision is made not to exercise the powers under subs.(2), the patient can either leave the hospital or remain as an informal patient.

Subsection (5)

1-105   This subsection provides that where the "holding power" provided for in subs.(4) is followed by a report made under subs.(2), the period of 72 hours provided for in subs.(2) runs from the time when the record required by subs.(4) is made.

Subsection (6)

1-106   With the exception of a patient who is detained under s.2 being made subject to an application under s.3, this provision prevents an application for detention being made if the patient is already detained under the Act. It also prevents the subs.(2) and (4) holding powers of being invoked with respect to a detained patient or a patient who is subject to a CTO.

Subsection (7)

1-107   **Prescribed**   Regulation 2 of the Mental Health (Nurses) (England) Order 2008 (SI 2008/1207) states:

> "(1)   For the purposes of section 5(4) of the Mental Health Act 1983 (power to detain patient in hospital for maximum of 6 hours) a nurse of the prescribed class is a nurse registered in either Sub-Part 1 or 2 of the register maintained under article 5 of the Nursing and Midwifery Order 2001, whose registration includes an entry specified in paragraph (2).
>
> (2)   An entry in the register referred to in paragraph (1) is an entry indicating that the nurse's field of practice is either—
>
> > (a)   mental health nursing, or
> >
> > (b)   learning disabilities nursing."

A nurse of the prescribed class can invoke the holding power with regard to both mentally ill and learning disabled patients.

Secretary of State   The functions of the Minister, so far as exercisable in relation to Wales, are exercised by the Welsh Ministers (see the General Note to the Act) who have made a similar order: see SI 2008/2441 (W.214).

Effect of application for admission

1-108   **6.**—(1)   An application for the admission of a patient to a hospital under this Part of this Act, duly completed in accordance with the provisions of this Part of this Act, shall be sufficient authority for the applicant, or any person authorised by the applicant, to take the patient and convey him to the hospital at any time within the following period, that is to say—

> (a)   in the case of an application other than an emergency application, the period of 14 days beginning with the date on which the patient was last examined by a registered medical practitioner before giving a medical recommendation for the purposes of the application;
>
> (b)   in the case of an emergency application, the period of 24 hours beginning at the time when the patient was examined by the practitioner giving the medical recommendation which is referred to in s.4(3) above, or at the time when the application is made, whichever is the earlier.

(2)   Where a patient is admitted within the said period to the hospital specified in such an application as is mentioned in subs.(1) above, or, being within that hospital, is treated by virtue of s.5 above as if he had been so admitted, the application shall be sufficient authority for the managers to detain the patient in the hospital in accordance with the provisions of this Act.

(3)   Any application for the admission of a patient under this Part of this Act

which appears to be duly made and to be founded on the necessary medical recommendations may be acted upon without further proof of the signature or qualification of the person by whom the application or any such medical recommendation is made or given or of any matter of fact or opinion stated in it.

(4) Where a patient is admitted to a hospital in pursuance of an application for admission for treatment, any previous application under this Part of this Act by virtue of which he was liable to be detained in a hospital or subject to guardianship shall cease to have effect.

Definitions

patient: s.145(1).   **1-109**
hospital: ss.34(2), 145(1).
the managers: s.145(1).
application for admission for treatment: ss.3, 145(1).

General Note

This section authorises: (1) the applicant for the patient's detention or anyone authorised by her to **1-110** take and convey the patient to the hospital named in the application within specified periods (subs.(1)); and (2) the hospital managers to detain the patient once he has been admitted to that hospital (subs.(2)). It also enables the hospital managers to act on statutory documents that appear to be valid (subs.(3)) and provides for the termination of existing applications subsequent to a patient's admission for treatment under s.3 (subs.(4)). The courts have held that the power to detain necessarily carries with it a power of control: see the note on "to detain the patient" in subs.(2).

Local authorities have a duty under s.47 of the Care Act 2014 to take reasonable steps prevent loss or damage to the moveable property (including pets) of an adult who has been admitted to hospital if no suitable arrangements have been or are being made. The local authority can recover its reasonable expenses from the adult.

The legality of the patient's detention

The legality of a patient's detention in circumstances where the requirements of the Act relating to **1-111** applications have not been fulfilled was considered in the following passage from the judgment of Laws J. in *R. v Managers of South Western Hospital Ex p. M* [1994] 1 All E.R. 161 at 176:

"Section 6(1) and (2) confer authority to convey or detain the patient in hospital where the application is 'duly completed in accordance with the provisions of this Part of this Act.' In my judgment this is an objective requirement and means that the application must not only *state* that the relevant provisions (which include the requirements of section 11(4)) have been fulfilled, but also that it be the case that they have actually been fulfilled. Here they were not; section 11(4) was not complied with. It follows, in my judgment, that the managers were not authorised to detain the applicant unless they were entitled to act upon [the approved mental health professional's] application by virtue of section 6(3).The contrast between section 6(1) and section 6(3) is of course between the words 'duly completed' and 'appears to be made.' In my judgment, where an application on its face sets out all the facts which, if true, constitute compliance with the relevant provisions of Part 2 of the Act (again, including section 11(4)) it is an application which 'appears to be duly made' within section 6(3). If any of the facts thus stated are not true, then although the application *appears* to be duly made, it is not duly completed for the purposes of section 6(1) and 6(2). Here, [the approved mental health professional's] application did state all the facts which, if true, constituted compliance with the relevant statutory provisions. Accordingly it was an application which appeared to be duly made. It follows that, although the managers were not authorised to detain the patient by section 6(2) standing alone, they were entitled to act upon the application, and thus to detain the patient, by virtue of section 6(3). Accordingly, the applicant's detention is not unlawful."

In *Re S-C (Mental Patient: Habeas Corpus)* [1996] 1 All E.R. 532, CA, Sir Thomas Bingham M.R. said, at 542, 543, that he:

"would accept almost everything in [the passage quoted above] as correct with the exception of the last sentence. The judge goes straight from a finding that the hospital managers were entitled to act upon an apparently valid application to the conclusion that the applicant's detention was therefore not unlawful. That is, in my judgment, a non sequitur. It is perfectly possible that the hospital managers were entitled to act on an apparently valid application, but that the detention was in fact unlawful. If that were not so the implications would, in my judgment, be horrifying. It would mean that an application which appeared to be in order would render the detention of a citizen lawful even though it was shown or admitted that the [approved mental health professional] purporting to make the application was not an [approved mental health professional], that the registered medical practitioners whose recommendations founded the application were not registered medical practitioners or had not signed the recommendations, and that the [approved mental health professional] had not consulted the patient's nearest relative or had consulted the patient's nearest relative and that relative had objected. In other words, it would mean that the detention was lawful even though every statutory safeguard built into the procedure was shown to have been ignored or violated. Bearing in mind what is at stake, I find that conclusion wholly unacceptable."

The other members of the Court of Appeal agreed with this finding. It should be noted that the decision in *Re S-C* applies to an administrative decision and not to an order of the court (*R. (on the application of A Claimant) v Harrow Crown Court* [2003] EWHC 2020 (Admin), para.24). An irregular order of the court made under the Act is effective and must be obeyed until set aside by the High Court (*South West Yorkshire Mental Health NHS Trust v Bradford Crown Court* [2003] EWHC 640 (Admin)).

In *R. v Central London County Court Ex p. London* [1999] 3 All E.R. 991 CA para.32, Stuart-Smith L.J., in giving the leading judgment, said, obiter, that he understood the Court of Appeal in *Re S-C* to have interpreted the phrase used by Laws J. which they had criticised as meaning that the patient's *continued* detention is not unlawful, rather than the original detention was not unlawful. These observations were not followed by the Court of Appeal in *TTM v London Borough of Hackney* [2011] EWCA Civ 4; [2011] 3 All E.R. 529 which confirmed that the decision in *Re S-C* was that the detention was unlawful from the point when the patient was admitted under the defective application.

1-112   The following propositions can be said to represent the law on this issue:

(1)   An application for admission made by an approved mental health professional (AMHP) or a nearest relative setting out all the relevant facts which, if true, constituted compliance with the relevant provisions of this Part of the Act, is an application which "appears to be duly made" for the purposes of subs.(3).

Note that there is judicial authority for the proposition that a patient may be detained before the application is completed: see in *R. (on the application of Sessay) v South London and Maudsley NHS Foundation Trust* which is noted under "Duly completed" in subs.(1).

(2)   After having carefully checked (per Neill L.J. in *Re S-C* at 544 and see para.35.9 of the *Code of Practice*) the documentation for obvious errors, the hospital managers are entitled to act on the application without further proof of the facts stated therein. In *Re S-C* Sir Thomas Bingham M.R. said at 537:

> "[Section 6] provides protection for a hospital to which a patient is admitted or in which a patient is detained. Such a hospital is not at risk of liability for false imprisonment if it turns out that the [approved mental health professional] does not meet the definition in section 145(1), or if the recommendations which purport to be signed by registered medical practitioners are in truth not signed by such, although appearing to be so. That is obviously good sense. A mental hospital is not obliged to act like a private detective; it can take documents at face value. Provided they appear to conform with the requirements of the statute, the hospital is entitled to act on them."

(3)   If, subsequent to having accepted an application, the hospital managers discover that the application is fundamentally defective (e.g. a s.3 application which was made despite the fact that the patient's nearest relative objected to it), this has the effect of rendering the detention of the patient unlawful. In these circumstances the hospital managers should:

(a)   inform the patient of the situation and of the need for him to obtain legal advice;

(b)   make an appropriate note on the patient's file; and

(c)   if the patient is not re-detained under s.3 (which has the effect of discharging any previous application (subs.(4)), the managers should exercise their power under s.23 to discharge the patient from his liability to be detained if the patient's responsible clinician (RC) has not already exercised her power of discharge. That the detention should be "brought to an end" was confirmed by Collins J. in *TTM* at first instance: see the note on subs.(3). If the patient is not discharged from detention, habeas corpus and/or judicial review proceedings could be brought. With regard to the latter, the patient could issue a claim for false imprisonment and/or compensation under art.5 of the European Convention on Human Rights (ECHR) against the local authority for the period starting with the date of his initial detention. This would be the case even if the AMHP had acted in good faith (*TTM v London Borough of Hackney*, above).

(4)   A decision to re-detain the patient could be preceded by the use of the holding powers contained in s.5 if the relevant criteria are satisfied: see the Reference Guide at para.31.21.

The advice set out in (3) and (4) is confirmed in the *Code of Practice* which states at para.35.13:

"If admission documents reveal a defect which fundamentally invalidates the application and which cannot, therefore, be rectified under section 15 of the Act, the patient can no longer be detained on the basis of the application. Authority for the patient's detention can be obtained only through a new application (or, in the interim, by the use of the holding powers under section 5 if the patient has already been admitted to the hospital). Unless that authority is to be sought, the hospital managers should use their power under section 23 to discharge the patient. The patient should be informed both orally and in writing, and in an accessible format for the patient."

For the action to be taken where, subsequent to the patient's admission, it is discovered that the AMHP made an honest mistake when identifying the patient's nearest relative, see the note on "appearing to be the nearest relative" in s.11(4)(b).

Admission to a Tier 4 CAMS bed

This issue was addressed by MacDonald J. in *Blackpool BC v HT (A Minor)* [2022] EWHC 1480 (Fam). His Lordship said: **1-113**

"43. It is plain on a proper analysis of the mental health legislation and guidance that, even where an application for admission for assessment is certified by two qualified medical professionals as meeting the criteria under s.2 of the Mental Health Act 1983, the provision of the Tier 4 CAMHS bed remains subject to the outcome of a referral that complies with the National Referral and Access Process, which includes the completion of an Access Assessment undertaken by reference to the criteria contained in the service specification for the Tier 4 CAMHS Service.

44. With respect to the role of the court where the Access Assessment has concluded that an admission to a Tier 4 CAMHS Service is not appropriate notwithstanding the certification of an assessment application by two qualified medical professionals, that role is necessarily limited. The court will not ordinarily entertain a claim for judicial review in respect of a decision not to allocate medical resources to a particular case, here the relevant decision being not to admit a child or young person to a Tier 4 CAMHS bed following an Access Assessment (see *R v Central Birmingham Health Authority ex parte Collier*, Unreported 6 January 1988 and *R v Cambridge Health Authority Ex p. B* [1995] 1 WLR 898). The court may, and in cases such as this one often does, join NHS England (and sometimes the relevant Clinical Commissioning Group [now the Integrated Care Board]) where the circumstances are such that the court may wish to invite reconsideration by the NHS Trust of the decision not to make Tier 4 inpatient provision for the subject child. By way of example, this step was taken by Sir James Munby in *Re X* [2017] EWHC 2036 (Fam). Alternatively, the court may consider directing a direct a single joint expert qualified in Tier 4 CAMHS to provide a second opinion, albeit that the efficacy of this approach is likely to be limited by the fact that upon receipt of the report the court's powers to give effect to an expert recommendation contrary to the position taken by NHS England are limited for the reasons I have already described."

Tier 4 beds are commissioned by NHS England. If an application is made for the patient's admission to a Tier 4 bed and the application is rejected, there is nothing to prevent a fresh application being made for admission to a non-Tier 4 bed.

Damages for an unlawful detention

In *Bostridge v Oxleas NHS Foundation Trust* [2015] EWCA Civ 79; [2015] M.H.L.R. 127 the patient had been unlawfully detained for 442 days because he had been recalled to hospital on the basis of an invalid community treatment order (CTO). His case was reviewed twice by a tribunal, where no-one identified the illegality, and on both occasions the tribunal found that his condition warranted continued detention in the hospital. The single issue before the Court of Appeal was whether the patient "is entitled   **1-114** to substantial damages instead of the nominal damages awarded by the judge, in circumstances where he would anyway have been detained lawfully had the defendant NHS trust been aware of the unlawfulness" (para.1). Vos L.J. said at para.20 that the "tort of false imprisonment is compensated in the same way as other torts such as to put the claimant in the position he would have been in had the tort not been committed. Thus if the position is that, had the tort not been committed, the claimant would in fact have been in exactly the same position, he will not normally be entitled to anything more than nominal damages". As the patient had suffered no loss because he would have been lawfully detained under s.3 throughout the period concerned had the lack of authority to make a CTO been drawn to the Trust's attention, the Court held that patient was only entitled to nominal damages. Substantial damages were not required "either to reflect the loss of liberty or the loss of the procedural and substantive protections afforded by a lawful detention" (para.30). At first instance, the judge anticipated that the award of damages would be £1. The approach taken by the Court of Appeal in *Bostridge* was followed by the Supreme Court in *R. (on the application of O) v Secretary of State for the Home Department* [2016] UKSC 19.

Guidance on the amount of compensation to be awarded in a case where a prisoner had suffered loss by being unlawfully detained contrary to art.5(4) of the European Convention on Human Rights was given by the Supreme Court in *R. (on the application of Faulkner) v Secretary of State for Justice* [2013] UKSC 23. The Court held that at the present stage of the development of the remedy of damages under s.8 of the Human Rights Act 1998, courts should be guided, following *R. (Greenfield) v Secretary of State for the Home Department* [2005] 1 W.L.R. 673, primarily by any clear and consistent practice of the European court. In particular, the quantum of awards under s.8 should broadly reflect the level of awards made by the European court in comparable cases brought by applicants from the UK or other countries with a similar cost of living. The court awarded compensation of £6,500 for an unlawful detention that lasted 10 months. Also see *TW v Enfield Borough Council* which is noted in s.11(4) under "not reasonably practicable" and *R.(on the application of Faulkner) v Director of Legal Aid Caseworker* [2016] EWHC 717, which is noted under art.5(5) of the European Convention on Human Rights in Part 5. Case law on the awarding of damages under s.8 was reviewed by Green J. in *DSD and NBV v Commissioner of Police for the Metropolis* [2014] EWHC 2493 (QB).

Disputes regarding compliance with the Act

1-115   If there is a genuine dispute about whether a provision of the Act has been complied with (e.g. the patient's nearest relative disputes the AMHP's assertion on the application form that the consultation required by s.11(4) took place), the hospital managers should not attempt to resolve the dispute but should leave the patient to consider challenging the detention. In *Re S-C*, above, Turner J., speaking at first instance, said: "There is, in my judgment, no means by which managers can investigate the truth or otherwise of assertions that the form has not been duly made, let alone is there any guidance as to the manner in which they should adjudicate on such issue and come to a conclusion contrary to that which appears on the face of the application form" ([1996] C.O.D. 221). These comments are consistent with the judgments delivered in the Court of Appeal.

Defective Court Orders

1-116   See the note under this heading in the General Note to Part III.

Delay in finding a hospital bed for a patient who has been assessed under the Act

1-117   Any failure by an AMHP to complete an application under this Act due to the failure to identify a hospital which is willing to admit the patient within a reasonable time constitutes a serious incident. Such incidents should be logged and transmitted to senior management within the local authority. This information should also be shared with the relevant NHS Trust.

If there is a delay in finding a hospital bed for a patient who would have been the subject of an application had a bed been available and, due to that delay, the patient remains at his home, responsibility for providing professional support to the patient at his home is that of the local mental health service bearing in mind the respective legislative responsibilities of the local authority and the NHS Trust. It follows from this that the local authority and the NHS Trust should have in place a joint operational policy which specifies the action that should be taken to support AMHPs when there is a significant delay in accessing a hospital bed after a decision has been made to detain the patient. The policy should indicate the support that will be made available to AMHPs and the patient in both the short and medium term, taking into account the duty owed to AMHPs under s.2 of Health and Safety at Work etc Act 1974. For an example of the tragic consequences that resulted from a failure to provide such support, see the coroner's Regulation 28 report into the death of Elena Wells dated November 23, 2020 (*https://www.judiciary.uk/publications/elena-wells*).

It is lawful to admit a patient to a hospital where it is anticipated that a bed would become available for him within a reasonable time. The integrated care board's s.140 policy should indicate which hospital(s) would be available to admit a patient in cases of special urgency. These could include private hospitals which have commissioned by the ICB to admit patients in such circumstances.

Although there is no authority under the Act to detain the patient at his home or elsewhere during the course of an assessment, the case of *R. (on the application of Sessay) v South London and Maudsley NHS Foundation Trust)*, which is noted in subs.(1) under "duly completed", is authority for the proposition that the patient may be held for a short period while a decision that has been made to make an application in respect of the patient is processed.

Once an application has been completed, there is no power to detain the patient while awaiting transportation to hospital. The only power to detain is that of the hospital named in the application. However, it is likely that a court would apply *Sessay* by finding that there would be no unlawful detention as long as the patient's transportation to hospital is not unduly delayed. The patient is in legal custody while being transported to hospital: see s.137. It is the AMHP's responsibility to ensure that all the necessary arrangements are made for the patient to be transported to hospital: see para.17.9 of the *Code of Practice* which is noted under "convey him" in subs.(1).

Local arrangements for responding to delays in placing patients are considered in the *Code of Practice* at para.14.86 which states:

"Local recording and reporting mechanisms should be in place to ensure the details of any delays in placing patients, and the impacts on patients, their carers, provider staff and other professionals are reported to commissioning and local authority senior leads. These details should feed into local demand planning. AMHPs should be supported by their local authority in these circumstances and should not be expected by commissioners and providers to address the delay themselves. In the meantime, commissioners should, in partnership with providers, ensure that alternative arrangements to meet the person's needs pending the availability of a bed are accessible, eg crisis houses, and should communicate those arrangements to the local authority. The local authority should ensure that AMHPs are aware of these arrangements."

Treatment in an A and E department en route to the hospital named in the application

If a patient who has been made the subject of an application requires emergency treatment for a physical injury or disorder he could be taken to and treated in an A and E department under common law powers or, if he was mentally incapacitated, under the Mental Capacity Act 2005 before being transported to the hospital named in the application: see the note on "Convey him" in subs.(1).   **1-118**

In *Webley v St George's Hospital NHS Trust* [2014] EWHC 299 (QB), an AMHP applicant had delegated to the police the power to convey the patient to the hospital named in the application. Before he could be admitted, the patient's physical health deteriorated and he was taken to another hospital's A and E department for treatment. After having been detained in the A and E department for two hours, the patient evaded the attention of security guards and was seriously injured in a fall after he left the department. Bean J. held that the police owed a common law duty of care to the patient which "involved a duty to take reasonable steps to ensure that he did not come to physical harm while in their custody; a duty to take reasonable care only to release him into a safe environment; and a duty to provide relevant information to those into whose care he was transferred" (para.41). The "relevant information" included the fact that the patient had been assessed as being at risk of absconding. It was further held that the staff of the A and E department also owed a duty of care to the patient which included the duty to take reasonable steps to ensure his safety. A point that was not taken in this case was whether the patient, when he was being treated at the A and E department, was still in the process of being conveyed to the hospital named in the application and, if he was, whether the security staff at the department had been authorised to convey him and, therefore, to keep him in custody (see s.137). It is suggested that: (1) a court would find that the patient was still involved in an, albeit interrupted, conveyance to the hospital; and (2) the doctrine of delegatus non potest delegare would prevent the police from further delegating their power of conveyance to the security staff.

Treatment in a general hospital

If a patient who has been made the subject of an application requires an immediate period of in-patient treatment for a physical injury or disorder, it is unlawful for the patient to be admitted directly to the general hospital after having been given a "notional" leave of absence from the psychiatric hospital named in the application. If the patient is mentally competent, he could be admitted directly to the general hospital with his agreement and then taken to the psychiatric hospital before the expiry of the   **1-119**

14-day period provided for in para.(a). If the patient is unwilling to be admitted to the general hospital, he could be admitted to that hospital under the Act although any treatment for his physical condition could only proceed with his consent if he had the required mental capacity. In this situation, the general hospital would be the hospital named in the application and the patient's responsible clinician would be the psychiatrist who is in charge of the treatment of the patient's mental disorder at that hospital. To cater for this situation, it would be advisable for the psychiatric hospital to enter into a service level agreement with the general hospital for the provision of psychiatric treatment and Mental Health Act administration services at that hospital. To enable the managers of the general hospital to deal appropriately with any application for discharge that the patient might make, it is suggested that the managers should attempt to appoint the committee that has been established by the managers of the psychiatric hospital to hear such applications on their behalf.

Human Rights Act 1998

1-120   The approach adopted in *Re S-C* to defective applications was implicitly endorsed by the European Court of Human Rights in *Mooren v Germany* (2010) 50 E.H.R.R. 23, where it was held that defects in a detention order did not necessarily render the underlying detention unlawful for the purposes of art.5(1) of the ECHR unless they amounted to "a gross and obvious irregularity".

In *Munjaz v United Kingdom* [2012] M.H.L.R. 351, the European Court of Human Rights held that in certain circumstances the seclusion of a detained patient could amount to a further deprivation of his liberty under art.5 of the ECHR: see the note on *Residual deprivation of liberty* in the General Note to s.118 and the summary of the *Munjaz* case in the note on "detention" under art.5(1)(e) in Part 5.

Code of Practice

1-121   The transport of patients is covered in Ch.17.

Subsection (1)

1-122   If an application is not accepted by the hospital managers within the period set out in either para.(a) or (b), it will cease to have effect.

An Application   Comprises the application form and the medical recommendation form(s).

Duly completed   An application is duly completed when all of the relevant statutory forms have been completed and signed. Until the application is duly completed, the patient is not subject to the Act's powers. However, in *R. (on the application of Sessay) v South London and Maudsley NHS Foundation Trust)* [2011] EWHC 2617 (QB); [2012] M.H.L.R. 94, the Divisional Court said at para.57:

> "[I]n our view it is unlikely in the ordinary case that there will be a false imprisonment at common law or deprivation of liberty for the purposes of Article 5(1) [of the ECHR] if there is no undue delay during the processing of an application under ss.2 or 4 MHA for admission."

It is therefore the case that if, following an assessment of the patient, the potential applicant and recommending doctor(s) agree that an application to detain the patient should be made, the patient may be held during the time that it takes to process the application as long as the process is not unduly delayed. If there is a delay in finding a bed for the patient, see *Delay in finding a hospital bed for a patient who has been assessed under the Act*, above.

If those who are assessing the patient are asked to leave the patient's home before a decision to make an application to detain him has been made they would be trespassers if they remained and the householder would be entitled to use reasonable force in ejecting them (*Townley v Rushworth*, 62 L.G.R. 95, DC). The professionals would not become trespassers if one co-owner gave them permission to stay, despite the fact that the other co-owner requested that they leave: see the note on "enter and inspect" in s.115.

A duly completed application does not provide authority for the applicant to force entry into the patient's home. If force is required to gain entry after the application has been completed, an application should be made for a warrant under s.135(2). If the AMHP or the person authorised under this subsection have access to the patient in his home after the application has been completed, there is no requirement for a warrant to be obtained as this section provides sufficient legal authority for an objecting patient to be conveyed to hospital.

If, having signed the application form, an AMHP applicant discovers a minor and rectifiable error on one of the medical recommendations and it is not possible to contact the relevant doctor to right the error, it is permissible for the patient to be conveyed to the hospital on the authority of the application and for the error to be rectified within the 14-day period permitted by s.15.

Applicant   Who will be either the patient's nearest relative or an AMHP (ss.4(2), 11(1)).

Any person authorised by the applicant   Such as the police or ambulance services. The delegation can be either to the service generally or to a named member of the service (Interpretation Act 1978 s.5, Sch.1). There is nothing to prevent an AMHP from delegating the power of conveyance to a member of the patient's family as long as the decision to delegate is preceded by a risk assessment. The AMHP should provide written authority to the authorised person if the patient is likely to be unwilling to be moved (*Code of Practice*, para.17.13). The AMHP is not provided with a power to direct another person to convey the patient. Where delegation takes place, the AMHP retains ultimate responsibility to ensure that the patient is conveyed in a lawful and humane manner (*Code of Practice*, para.17.18).

If it is not practicable for the AMHP to attend at the hospital named in the application, or where "the applicant is not travelling in the same vehicle as the patient, the application form and medical recommendations should be given to the person authorised to transport the patient, with instructions for them to be presented to the member of hospital staff receiving the patient" (*Code of Practice*, para.17.21).

"Guidance on the electronic communication of statutory forms under the Mental Health Act", DHSC, 2020, para.2 states:

"Where an AMHP submits an application for detention electronically and then delegates conveyance of the patient, for example to ambulance staff, a paper copy of the form is not needed to indicate that conveyance is lawful so long as the AMHP can provide evidence of a completed application supported by the necessary medical recommendations. In line with paragraph 17.26 of the Code of Practice, agencies should agree local policies and procedures regarding the nature of authorisation given by AMHPs (and others) when authorising people to transport patients on their behalf.

This should be the case whether a form is submitted electronically or in hard copy. In accordance with sections 2, 3 and 6 of the MHA, an application for detention submitted by an AMHP must be founded on the necessary medical recommendations. As such, it's the responsibility of the AMHP to support their application with 2 accompanying medical recommendations. It's vital that these statutory documents are retained and sent to the receiving hospital as a package."

Convey him   Paragraph 17.9 of the *Code of Practice* states:

"Where the AMHP is the applicant, they have a professional responsibility to ensure that all the necessary arrangements are made for the patient to be transported to hospital. All relevant agencies should co-operate fully with the AMHP to ensure safe transport to hospital."

The power to convey is only triggered when the application is "duly completed". The exercise of the power can either be delayed subject to the maximum periods specified in subs.(1) or not exercised at all if, subsequent to the application being completed, the AMHP forms the opinion that there is no need to use it.

Either the applicant or the person delegated by the applicant (including ambulance staff) can use such force as is reasonably necessary to achieve the objective of conveying the patient to the hospital named in the application (s.137(2)). Paragraph 17.18 of the *Code of Practice* states: "People authorised by the applicant to transport patients act in their own right and not as the agent of the applicant. They may act on their own initiative to restrain patients and prevent them absconding, if absolutely necessary". If the patient is likely to be violent or dangerous, police assistance should be requested (*Code of Practice*, para.17.14). It follows that police assistance should not be sought on a mere refusal of the patient to be conveyed to hospital.

A patient who is being conveyed to hospital is deemed to be in legal custody (s.137(1)) and if he escapes he may be retaken within 14 days after the last medical examination for the purposes of a medical recommendation for s.2 or 3 patients, or within 24 hours from the medical examination or the time when the application was made, whichever is the earlier for a s.4 patient (s.138). The persons who are authorised to retake a patient who absconds are identified in s.138(1)(a).

To hospital   Paragraph 14.89 of the *Code of Practice* states:

"Applications for detention must be addressed to the managers of the hospital where the patient is to be detained. An application must state a specific hospital. An application cannot, for example, be made to a multi-site provider without specifying which of the provider's sites the patient is to be admitted to. Providers should identify a bed manager or other single point of contact who will be responsible for finding a suitable bed as soon as possible and telling the applicant the name of the site at which it is situated. Effective systems of bed management including discharge planning, possible alternatives to admission and demand planning should be in place. The bed manager should work closely with commissioners to proactively identify local need, and with assessing doctors and AMHPs to secure a bed. AMHPs should be adequately supported by their local authority in establishing working partnerships with other local agencies listed at paragraph 14.80."

The other local agencies listed in para.14.80 are local authorities, providers, NHS commissioners, police forces and ambulance services.

The application is addressed to the hospital, not to a particular unit or ward of that hospital. It is therefore lawful for a patient to be admitted, for example, to a s.136 suite or a designated "holding area" if the hospital has confirmed that a bed will be made available for the patient within a reasonable period. The patient is "admitted" at the time when he arrives at the hospital and either the application for detention is handed to an authorised person who accepts the application or it is sent to the hospital managers electronically (reg.3(2) of the English Regulations). The time and date of the admission should by recorded on Form H3 (in Wales, Form HO 14): see reg.4(4) of the English Regulations and the note on "sufficient authority for the managers" in subs.(2).

It is unlawful to convey a patient to hospital on the authority of an application which does not state the name of the potential admitting hospital. It is also unlawful to take the patient to a hospital that is not the hospital named on the application even though the hospital named on the application and the hospital to which the patient is taken come under the control of the same hospital managers. Although the named hospital is not under a legal obligation to admit the patient, it should only refuse to admit the patient on reasonable grounds, e.g. a suitable bed is not available or there are good clinical reasons to refuse admission.

In its *Eighth Biennial Report*, 1997–1999, para.4.45, the Mental Health Act Commission suggested that if a patient cannot be admitted to hospital in an emergency for want of a bed "the [AMHP] should complete the application, making it out to a hospital specified to the relevant health authority in the notice required to be given under s.140 of the Act, and convey the patient to that hospital". This advice is subject to the criticism that the managers of the hospital specified in the s.140 notice are not legally obliged to admit the patient and, in any event, it might be clinically inappropriate for the patient to be admitted to that hospital. The MHAC returned to this theme in its *Ninth Biennial Report*, 1999–2001 where a "Good Practice Example" is set out at para.2.50. The example states that if no bed is available at the hospital named in the application, the patient can be formally admitted to the hospital by being held in a "holding area" and that if it proves impossible to identify a bed within the hospital, the patient should be granted leave of absence under s.17 to a "temporary bed" in another hospital. The practice commended by the MHAC of "admitting" the patient in a situation where no commitment has been made by the hospital to make a bed available for him is both potentially dangerous and of doubtful legality for the reasons set out below. Holding a patient who might be acutely ill in a non-clinical area of a hospital for what might turn out to be a considerable amount of time can be neither in the interests of the patient nor of staff. Assuming that an approved clinician has been found who is willing to become the patient's responsible clinician (RC), it is at the very least extremely bad practice for the risk assessment that must precede a s.17 leave to be conducted in such an environment. It is also difficult to see how the hospital managers can adequately comply with their duties under s.132 in these circumstances.

The purpose of both ss.2 and 3 is for the patient to be admitted to the hospital named in the application and for him to be "detained there" (ss.2(1), 3(1)), i.e. at the hospital named in the application. To secure this aim one of the responsibilities of the recommending doctor is to ensure that, where there is to be an application for admission, a hospital bed will be available for the patient unless it has been agreed locally that AMHPs will do that (*Code of Practice*, para.14.77). It is suggested that although it would be legally possible to "hold" a patient in a waiting area of the admitting hospital while a bed that has been identified for the patient is being made available, a patient cannot be said to have been admitted to a hospital if there is no prospect of a bed becoming available at that hospital within a reasonable period. It is therefore arguably unlawful for an AMHP to make an application to detain a patient and to convey him to the hospital named in the application if it is known that no bed will become available for the patient at that hospital within a reasonable period.

Can it be said that the patient has been "admitted" to the hospital for the purposes of s.6(2) if no bed has been allocated to him? If the patient has not been legally "admitted", the hospital managers have no power to detain him and he cannot be granted leave of absence. Even if it could be successfully argued that the patient who is being kept in a "holding area" of a hospital without the prospect of a bed being made available for him within a reasonable period has been admitted to that hospital, McCullough J. said in *R. v Hallstrom Ex p. W* [1986] Q.B. 1090 that the term "detention" in s.13 "cannot realistically include a purely nominal period before leave of absence is given, after which the treatment which the patient stands in need is to begin". Although the decision in *Hallstrom* was made in the context of a patient who had been granted leave of absence into the community, the finding of McCullough J. is equally applicable to a patient who has been granted immediate leave of absence to another hospital. In both cases, the detention at the hospital named in the application would be a sham.

The *Code of Practice* at para.14.91, states that patients who have been made subject to an application should not be moved unless it is known that the hospital named in the application is willing to accept them and, at para.14.99, considers the action to be taken if, on arrival at the hospital named in the application, a bed is no longer available for the patient. Paragraphs 14.91 and 14.99 are reproduced in the notes on s.11(2).

The guidance given in the *Code of Practice* on this issue should be followed.

Paragraph (a)

14 days   This period may be used to test out whether detention is the most appropriate option for the   **1-123**
patient. Paragraph 14.87 of the *Code of Practice* states that there "may be cases where AMHPs conclude that they should delay taking a final decision in order to see whether the patient's condition changes, or whether successful alternatives to detention can be put in place in the interim". The period can also be used where a bed is not immediately available for the patient.

Beginning with the date   Including the date on which the patient was last examined (*Zoan v Rouamba* [2000] 2 All E.R. 620 CA).

Last examined by a registered medical practitioner   The relevant date is that of the last medical examination, not the day on which the medical recommendation form was signed by the doctor. If the medical practitioners examined the patient separately, not more than five days must have elapsed between the respective examinations (s.12(1)). A registered medical practitioner means "a fully registered person within the meaning of the Medical Act 1983 who holds a licence to practise under that Act" (Interpretation Act 1978, Sch.1).

Paragraph (b)

Whichever is the earlier   As an emergency application must be "founded on" the medical recom-   **1-124**
mendation (s.4(3); also see Form A10), it should not be signed until the medical recommendation has been received by the applicant.

Subsection (2)

In *D'Souza v Director of Public Prosecutions* [1992] 4 All E.R. 545 at 553–554, Lord Lowry said: **1-125**

"A person who is detained in hospital under section 6(2) is lawfully detained. If he goes absent without leave, he is then at large ..., and, since he ought not to be at large and is, by virtue of section 18(1), liable to be taken into custody and returned to the hospital, he would inevitably appear to be *unlawfully* at large [within section 17(1)(d) of the Police and Criminal Evidence Act 1984] until he is taken into custody."

The *D'Souza* case is considered in the General Note to s.135.

Sufficient authority for the managers   The application will be served by delivering it personally to an officer of the managers who is authorised to receive it, or electronically to the managers: see reg.3(2) of the English and Welsh Regulations. That officer will check the documents for obvious errors and decide whether or not to accept the application. The application should only be accepted if it "appears to be duly made" and is "founded on the necessary medical recommendations" (subs.(3)). Even if the application has been properly completed, there is no obligation placed on the managers by the Act to accept the application and detain the patient. There is nothing objectionable in the managers making enquiries as to the circumstances of the application to enable the appropriate officer to be put in a position to make an informed decision on whether to accept the application. If the application is accepted on behalf of the managers, the documents should be passed to an officer who has been authorised under reg.4(3) of the English Regulations (reg.4(2) of the Welsh Regulations) to scrutinise them for the purposes of possible rectification under s.15.

Once the application has been accepted, a record of admission shall be made by the managers in the form set out in Form H3: see reg.4(4) of the English Regulations (Form HO14 in Wales: see reg.4(3) of the Welsh Regulations). The Form is an administrative record; it does not provide authority for the patient's detention.

To detain the patient   The authority to detain the patient commences from the date and time entered paragraph (a) or (b) on Form H3, and not from the date entered on the application form for the patient's detention.

The courts have held that the express power to detain a patient for treatment necessarily implies a power to control that patient which includes the power to place him in seclusion: see the notes on s.139 under the heading "The power to control the activities of detained patients".

Subsection (3)

1-126   The effect of this provision is explained in the Reference Guide:

> "8.91 The managers do not have to seek further proof that the signatories are who they say they are or that they have the qualification to make the application which they have signed to say they have. Nor do they need to seek further proof for any factual statement or opinion contained in the document.
> 8.92 For example, the managers do not need to check that signatories who state they are registered medical practitioners are in fact, registered, or seek independent verification of the time when the patient was last examined or that there was sufficient urgency to justify the making of an emergency application."

In *TTM v London Borough of Hackney* [2011] EWCA Civ 4; [2011] 3 All E.R. 529, the Court of Appeal confirmed that this provision does not have the effect of making lawful an application for admission which is fundamentally defective. Toulson L.J. made the following observations on the purpose of this provision at para.37:

> "It is intended to enable hospital managers, possibly at short notice, to admit for treatment someone who they have reasonable cause to believe is in immediate need of such admission for the health and safety of himself or for the protection of the public, and, with this end in view, Parliament has considered it reasonable for the hospital managers to be able to rely on an application which appears to have been completed in accordance with the requirements of the Act. Since the section empowers hospital managers to admit a patient in respect of whom an application for his admission appears to have been duly made, it follows that they have a defence against any claim which might otherwise have been made against them for acting on an invalid application."

His Lordship further stated at para.68:

> "It is in the public interest that a hospital trust should act promptly on receipt of an application for admission which appears to be in proper form, and that it should not think it necessary for its own legal protection to incur time and expense in checking the accuracy of the various matters which s 6(3) entitles it to accept as correct."

At first instance ([2010] EWHC 1349 (Admin), para.29), Collins J. made reference to para.13.9 of the 2008 edition of the *Code of Practice* and said that it was apparent from that paragraph "that the obligation to scrutinise arises after the admission based check that the documents appear to amount to an application that has been duly made. If, following such scrutiny, it is apparent that there was a defect which cannot be rectified under s.15 because it is fundamental, the detention should be brought to an end": also see the General Note to this section.

In *R. (on the application of Care Principles Ltd) v Mental Health Review Tribunal* [2006] EWHC 3194 (Admin); [2006] M.H.L.R. 365, Collins J. held that the extent of the hospital managers obligations to scrutinise the application must depend on the facts of a particular case. If they are aware of the existence of a previous tribunal decision ordering the discharge of the patient, it requires a critical consideration of the justification for the detention in the light of that decision: see the note on this case under the heading *The re-sectioning of a patient subsequent to a discharge made by the First-tier Tribunal (Mental Health), the Mental Health Review Tribunal for Wales or a Hospital Managers' Panel* in the General Note to s.3.

Subsection (4)

1-127   The Reference Guide states at para.8.98:

> "Because an application for admission for treatment automatically ends any previous application for

admission, it would also bring to an end a patient's CTO, if before going onto the CTO, the patient had been detained under section 3. In that case, a new CTO would have to be made for the patient when they no longer needed to be detained in hospital."

In *R. (on the application of M) v Hospital Managers of Queen Mary's Hospital* [2008] EWHC 1959 (Admin) para.18, Underhill J. considered this provision and said, without deciding the point, that an ineffective application under s.3 which is subsequently found to be unlawful would not undermine the s.2 application that preceded it, and that the s.2 application would remain in force, or be revived, until it expired.

A similar provision relating to the making of a hospital order or a guardianship order by a court under s.37 can be found in s.40(5). For the effect that reception into guardianship has on existing applications, see s.8(5).

Application for admission for treatment   But not an application for assessment under s.2.

GUARDIANSHIP

Application for guardianship

7.—(1)   A patient who has attained the age of 16 years may be received into   **1-128** guardianship, for the period allowed by the following provisions of this Act, in pursuance of an application (in this Act referred to as "a guardianship application") made in accordance with this section.

(2)   A guardianship application may be made in respect of a patient on the grounds that—

(a)   he is suffering from mental disorder […] of a nature or degree which warrants his reception into guardianship under this section; and

(b)   it is necessary in the interests of the welfare of the patient or for the protection of other persons that the patient should be so received.

(3)   A guardianship application shall be founded on the written recommendations in the prescribed form of two registered medical practitioners, including in each case a statement that in the opinion of the practitioner the conditions set out in subsection (2) above are complied with; and each such recommendation shall include—

(a)   such particulars as may be prescribed of the grounds for that opinion so far as it relates to the conditions set out in paragraph (a) of that subsection; and

(b)   a statement of the reasons for that opinion so far as it relates to the conditions set out in paragraph (b) of that subsection.

(4)   A guardianship application shall state the age of the patient or, if his exact age is not known to the applicant, shall state (if it be the fact) that the patient is believed to have attained the age of 16 years.

(5)   The person named as guardian in a guardianship application may be either a local social services authority or any other person (including the applicant himself); but a guardianship application in which a person other than a local social services authority is named as guardian shall be of no effect unless it is accepted on behalf of that person by the local social services authority for the area in which he resides, and shall be accompanied by a statement in writing by that person that he is willing to act as guardian.

Amendment

In subs.(2)(a), the words omitted were repealed by the Mental Health Act 2007 s.55, Sch.11 Pt 1.

Definitions

1-129 patient: s.145(1).
mental disorder: ss.1, 145(1).
local social services authority: s.145(1).

General Note

1-130 The White Paper that preceded the Act stated that guardianship powers are needed for "a very small number of mentally disordered people who do not require treatment in hospital, either formally or informally, [but who] nevertheless need close supervision and some control in the community as a consequence of their mental disorder. These include people who are able to cope provided that they take their medication regularly, but who fail to do so, and those who neglect themselves to the point of seriously endangering their health" (Cmnd. 8405, para.43).

According to the *Code of Practice*, the "purpose of guardianship is to enable patients to receive care outside hospital when it cannot be provided without the use of compulsory powers. Such care may, or may not, include specialist medical treatment for mental disorder" (para.30.2). It "provides an authoritative framework for working with a patient, with a minimum of constraint, to achieve as independent a life as possible within the community. Where it is used, it should be part of the patient's overall care plan" (para.30.4). The Code suggests that guardianship "is most likely to be appropriate where:

- the patient is thought to be likely to respond well to the authority and attention of a guardian and so be more willing to comply with necessary treatment and care for their mental disorder, and
- there is a particular need for someone to have the authority to decide where the patient should live or to insist that doctors, AMHPs or other people be given access to the patient" (para.30.9).

There is no requirement for guardianship to be preceded by a period of detention. Guardianship is used infrequently. As at March 31, 2018, 300 people in England were subject to guardianship: see *https ://digital.nhs.uk/data-and-information/publications/statistical/guardianship-under-the-mental-health-act-1983/england-2016-17-and-2017-18-national-statistic.*

Sections 5 and 6 of the Mental Capacity Act 2005 provide social care professionals who are caring for mentally incapacitated persons with protection against civil and criminal liability for certain acts done in connection with the care of such persons. The powers that staff have under that Act, which include the power to use restraint which does not constitute a deprivation of liberty, will usually be sufficient to ensure that the best interests of a mentally incapacitated person are satisfied. However, the *Code of Practice* on the 2005 Act, at para.13.20, provides the following examples of situations where staff might feel that a guardianship application would be appropriate:

- "they think it important that one person or authority should be in charge of making decisions about where the person should live (for example, where there have been long-running or difficult disagreements about where the person should live);
- they think the person will probably respond well to the authority and attention of a guardian, and so be more prepared to accept treatment for the mental disorder (whether they are able to consent to it or it is being provided for them under the Mental Capacity Act); or
- they need authority to return the person to the place they are to live (for example, a care home) if they were to go absent."

The reception of a patient into guardianship does not carry with it resource implications for the local authority (apart from associated administrative costs) because the fact that a patient is subject to guardianship does not provide that patient with an entitlement to receive services under either s.117 or the Care Act 2014.

In cases where there is a significant dispute between the local authority and a mentally incapacitated patient and/or his carers about how best to meet the patient's needs, an application to the Court of Protection might be a more appropriate option than guardianship: see *C v Blackburn and Darwen Borough Council* which is noted under s.8(1)(a).

This section specifies the circumstances whereby a patient aged 16 or over may be received into the guardianship of a local social services authority or a person who is acceptable to the authority. A patient shall cease to be subject to guardianship if an order for his discharge is made by the tribunal (s.72(4)), his responsible clinician (RC), by the responsible local social services authority or by his nearest relative (s.23(2)(b)). A discharge by the nearest relative cannot be barred under the provisions of s.25.

The powers of the guardian are set out in s.8. A local social services authority (LSSA) has a duty to ensure that patients received into guardianship are visited: see reg.23 of the English Regulations and reg.10 of the Welsh Regulations. If the patient is hospitalised or placed in a care home the local authority has visiting and other duties placed upon it by s.116. As a patient under guardianship is not "liable to be detained" for the purposes of s.56(3), he is not subject to the consent to treatment provisions contained in Pt IV.

Upon a patient being received into guardianship, the LSSA must take such steps as are practicable to inform the patient and the patient's nearest relative (unless the patient has requested otherwise) of the rights set out in reg.26(3), (4) of the English Regulations and reg.15 of the Welsh Regulations. The LSSA must also take steps to have a patient and the patient's nearest relative (unless the patient has requested otherwise) informed about independent mental health advocacy (s.130D). There is also a duty placed on the LSSA to inform a patient when his guardianship is renewed (s.20(6); also see reg.26(1)(n) of the English Regulations and reg.15(4) of the Welsh Regulations).

Reception into guardianship extinguishes any previous application made under this Part by virtue of which the patient was subject to guardianship or liable to be detained in hospital (s.8(5)). It is therefore the case that if the patient was subject to a community treatment order (CTO) at the time of his reception into guardianship, the CTO will cease to have effect by virtue of s.17C(c). However the CTO would not cease to have effect if the patient was subject to an order or direction made under Part III at the time when he was placed on the CTO: see para.26.136 of the Reference Guide.

There is nothing to prevent a guardianship patient from being the subject of an application for admission to hospital. If the application is for admission for treatment under s.3, the guardianship ends (s.6(4)).

Under s.19 and regs 7, 8, and 11 of the English Regulations and regs 23, 24 and 27 of the Welsh Regulations detained patients and patients who are subject to guardianship may be transferred between hospitals and guardians or between detention in hospital and guardianship: see the notes to s.19.

If a patient who has been made the subject of an application under this section is remanded into custody or sentenced under the criminal law, the provisions of s.22 will apply.

It is an offence under the Act to neglect or ill-treat a patient who is under guardianship (s.127(2)).

Children

An application for guardianship cannot be made in respect of a person who is either aged under 16 **1-131** (subs.(1)) or a ward of court (s.33(3)). In *Re F (Mental Health Act: Guardianship)* [2000] 1 F.L.R. 192, the Court of Appeal held that wardship should not have been rejected by the judge as a more appropriate remedy than guardianship for a seventeen year old patient. An immediate consequence of wardship would have been the appointment of the Official Solicitor as her guardian ad litem, thereby securing the benefit of separate representation for the child. Thorpe L.J. said at 199: "[Guardianship] is not a child-centred jurisdiction and the child lacks the benefit of independent representation".

Proceedings under s.31 and Sch.3, para.5 of the Children Act 1989 could be brought in respect of a child under 16 who requires supervision and control in the community as a consequence of mental disorder. A child is not a privately fostered child for the purposes of Pt IX of the 1989 Act while he is subject to guardianship (Children Act 1989 Sch.8, para.4).

The use of guardianship to authorise the deprivation of a person's liberty

See the note under this heading in s.8. **1-132**

Dealing with hoarding disorder, domestic squalor and/or dangerous premises

People who live in domestic squalor may be suffering from hoarding disorder which has been **1-133** recognised as a standalone diagnosis in DSM-5. The action that a local authority can take when satisfied that premises are either (a) in such a filthy or unwholesome condition as to be prejudicial to health, or (b) are verminous is set out in ss.83 to 85 of the Public Health Act 1936. Part III of the Environmental Protection Act 1990 provides powers for local authorities to require the abatement of a range of problems including "any premises in such a state as to be prejudicial to health or a nuisance" and "any accumulation or deposit" which meets the same test. "Premises" includes open land such as a garden. These powers are considered in *Professional Practice Note: Hoarding and how to approach it – guidance for Environmental Heath Officers and others, Chartered Institute of Environmental Health*, June 2015. Information on "Hoarding disorder" produced by the NHS can be accessed at: *www.nhs.uk/conditions/hoarding-disorder*. Useful information can also be found on the website of "Help for hoarders". Local authorities also have extensive powers under the Care Act 2014 to respond to the needs of adults who are experiencing neglect.

If the person concerned is mentally incapacitated, it might be possible to take action under the Mental Capacity Act 2005. In *"When protection matters"*, N.L.J., 15&22 April 2011, pp.537, 538, Robert

Eckford describes how the Court of Protection made orders to allow a local authority to undertake works on a property for the sole purpose of allowing the tenant (P) to maintain his tenancy. P was suffering from a paranoid delusional disorder which led him to refuse permission to the local authority landlord to undertake annual gas inspections, thus placing himself, his neighbours and the property at risk. The order made by the court authorised contractors to enter the property and to undertake works, required P to reside at a care home for seven days, and permitted the local authority to use reasonable and proportionate force, if necessary, to effect P's removal to the care home. Similar use of the court's power could be used in a situation where P is living in domestic squalor. The relevant law was examined in *Re AC (Capacity: Hoarding: Best Interests)* [2022] EWCOP 39 where the court ordered a trial of care at home of a patient who suffered from hoarding disorder and who was currently residing at a care home. It would also be possible to use the power in s.8(1)(a) to require a guardianship patient to take up temporary residence in a care home while necessary works were carried out at the patient's residence.

Applications to the First-tier Tribunal (Mental Health) or the Mental Health Review Tribunal for Wales

1-134   The patient may make an application within six months his reception into guardianship (s.66(1)(c), (2)(c)) and during each period of renewal (ss.66(1)(f), (2)(f), 20(2)). There is no automatic reference of guardianship cases to the tribunal.

Code of Practice

1-135   Guidance on guardianship is contained in Ch.30. Advice on deciding between guardianship, leave of absence and supervised community treatment can be found in Ch.31.
     With regard to the provision of information for guardianship patients, the Code states at para.4.52:

"Responsible local authorities are required to take steps to ensure that guardianship patients understand their rights to apply to a Tribunal and the rights of their nearest relatives. The same information also must normally be given to nearest relatives. More generally, local authorities (and private guardians) should do what they can to ensure that patients understand why they are subject to guardianship and what it means for them."

Guardianship (Missing Persons) Act 2017

1-136   The 2017 Act provides for an application to be made to a court for a guardianship order appointing a guardian in respect of some or all of a missing person's property and financial affairs. It should not be confused with the guardianship provisions of this Act.

Subsection (1)

1-137   An application for guardianship, which may be made by either the patient's nearest relative or by an AMHP (s.11(1)), must be in the form set out in Form G1 (for a nearest relative applicant) or Form G2 (for an approved mental health professional (AMHP) applicant) (in Wales, Form GU1 (for a NR applicant) or Form GU2 (for an AMHP applicant)): see reg.5 of the English Regulations and reg.9 of the Welsh Regulations. The application must either be sent to the LSSA named as guardian or to the LSSA for the area in which the individual named as guardian resides (s.11(2)). It has to be supported by two medical recommendations (subs.(3)) and it must be received by the LSSA within 14 days of the second medical examination (s.8(2)). There is no time limit within which an application must be accepted and there is no requirement for the patient to consent to the application being made. The applicant must have personally seen the patient within 14 days of making the application (s.11(5)). An AMHP, who is subject to the duty set out in s.13(1A), cannot make an application if the nearest relative objects (s.11(4)). The power of the nearest relative to object to a guardianship application can cause difficulty as:

"often social workers are concerned not that the patient may act irresponsibly, but that the relatives may act irresponsibly towards the patient. Where there is a caring relative, guardianship may not be needed. It is where there is a nearest relative who is neglectful, exploitive, or unable to care, that guardianship may well be required, but the relative has a power of veto which can only be overridden by the county court in the limited circumstances [set out in section 29]" (Phil Fennell, "The Beverley Lewis Case: was the law to blame?" *New Law Journal*, November 17, 1989, pp.1557–1558)."

Attained the age   At the commencement of his sixteenth birthday (Family Law Reform Act 1969 s.9(1)). Where on September 30, 1983, a person who was not by then 16 years old was subject to guardianship, the authority for guardianship terminated on that day (s.148(1), Sch.5 para.8(1)).

Period allowed   A patient may be kept under guardianship for an initial period of up to six months from the day on which the application was accepted (s.20(1)). The authority for guardianship may be renewed for a further period of six months, and then for yearly periods (s.20(2)).

Subsection (2)

Paragraph (a)

Mental disorder   There is no requirement for the patient to be mentally incapacitated. A patient with a learning disability who suffers from no other form of mental disorder can only be made subject to an application under this section if the disability is associated with abnormally aggressive or seriously ir-responsible conduct on his part: see the notes on s.1(2A), (2B).   **1-138**

Nature or degree   The meaning of this phrase is considered in the note on s.3(2)(a).

Paragraph (b)

Interests of the welfare of the patient   All factors which might affect the well-being of the patient are covered by this phrase, including the patient's need to be protected from exploitation. The wording is wide enough to encompass the need to prevent the patient's welfare being prejudiced at some time in the future. If the concern relates to possible future harm, the recommending doctors would need to be satisfied that there is a real risk of such an eventuality occurring, e.g. an attempt by a relative to remove a mentally incompetent patient from a care setting to accommodation where the patient's welfare might be seriously prejudiced.   **1-139**

Protection of other persons   It is submitted that "protection" is not limited to protection from physical harm, but could include protection from serious emotional harm: see the notes on s.2(2)(b).

Subsection (3)

Written recommendations   Made either separately or jointly (s.11(7)) using either Form G3 (joint recommendation) or G4 (in Wales, Form GU3 (joint recommendation) or Form GU4): see reg.5(1)(c) of the English Regulations and reg.9(1)(c) of the Welsh Regulations.   **1-140**

Two registered medical practitioners   Complying with the provisions of s.12 and the regulations made under s.12A.
    A registered medical practitioner means "a fully registered person within the meaning of the Medical Act 1983 who holds a licence to practise under that Act" (Interpretation Act 1978, Sch.1).

Subsection (5)

This subsection provides for the guardian to be either a LSSA or a person who is accepted by the LSSA to act in that capacity. Neither the authority nor the individual is placed under any legal obligation to accept the duties of guardian. The guardian owes a common law duty of care to the patient. In the overwhelming majority of cases, the guardian is a local authority.   **1-141**

Local social services authority   This does not have to be the authority for the area where the patient lives. If the application is accepted, the authority will become "the responsible local social services authority" (s.34(3)). Although a local authority may decline any guardianship proposal, there is a requirement to take over the role of guardian where a private guardianship arrangement has broken down in the circumstances set out in s.10.
    Although the relevant social services authority will be named as the guardian, the authority's scheme of delegation will identify an officer who will formally undertake the guardian's legal functions. This officer will usually be the Director of Adult Social Services. She will then identify an employee, invariably a social worker, who will perform casework functions in relation to the patient. It is this person who should represent the authority at tribunal hearings. The only function that cannot be delegated to an officer is the power to discharge the patient from guardianship: see s.23(2), (4).

Or any other person   Paragraph 30.24 of the *Code of Practice* states:

"A private guardian should be a person who can appreciate any special disabilities and needs of a mentally disordered person and who will look after the patient in an appropriate and sympathetic way. The guardian should display an interest in promoting the patient's physical and mental health and in providing for their occupation, training, employment, recreation and general welfare in a suitable way. The local authority must satisfy itself that a proposed private guardian is capable of carrying out their functions and it should assist them with advice and other forms of support."

A private guardian is required to appoint a doctor as the patient's nominated medical attendant: see the note on "The nominated medical attendant" in s.34(1).

If an AMHP considers that a private guardian has performed his or her functions negligently or in any manner contrary to the interests of the welfare of the patient, an application can be made to the county court under s.10(3) for the guardianship to be transferred to another person or to the LSSA.

A private guardian does not have the power to discharge the patient from guardianship.

Accepted   The time limits for accepting an application for a patient's admission to hospital set out in s.6 do not apply to guardianship applications. The acceptance should be recorded on Form G5 (in Wales, Form GU5): see reg.5(2) of the English Regulations and reg.9(3) of the Welsh Regulations.

The area   i.e. the area where the person named as guardian resides.

Resides   In *R. (on the application of Sunderland City Council) v South Tyneside Council* [2012] EWCA Civ 1232, para.25, Lloyd L.J. said that "in general, when considering any case in which there is doubt as to the place of person's residence, the question is not only that of physical presence, and that it may be relevant to consider why the person is where he or she is, and to what extent his or her presence there is voluntary. Thus, if a person has a home, the fact that he or she is not there on a given date or for a particular period does not mean that he or she is not still resident there, if the absence is accounted for by, for example, a holiday, a business trip, or having to spend time in hospital, whether following an injury, an operation or some other form of treatment, possibly over a prolonged period, or, for that matter, a period of imprisonment following a criminal conviction".

As the terms "resides" and "ordinarily resides" are both used in legislation and as there appears to be little to distinguish them, reference should be made to the notes on "ordinarily resides" in s.26(4).

Willing to act as guardian   The statement that the person is willing to act as guardian must be in the form set out in either Form G1 or G2 (in Wales, Form GU1 or GU2). The duties of private guardians are set out in reg.22 of the English Regulations and reg.11 of the Welsh Regulations.

Effect of guardianship application, etc.

1-142   **8.**—(1)   Where a guardianship application, duly made under the provisions of this Part of this Act and forwarded to the local social services authority within the period allowed by subsection (2) below is accepted by that authority, the application shall, subject to regulations made by the Secretary of State, confer on the authority or person named in the application as guardian, to the exclusion of any other person—

    (a)   the power to require the patient to reside at a place specified by the authority or person named as guardian;

    (b)   the power to require the patient to attend at places and times so specified for the purpose of medical treatment, occupation, education or training;

    (c)   the power to require access to the patient to be given, at any place where the patient is residing, to any registered medical practitioner, [approved mental health professional] or other person so specified.

(2)   The period within which a guardianship application is required for the purposes of this section to be forwarded to the local social services authority is the period of 14 days beginning with the date on which the patient was last examined by a registered medical practitioner before giving a medical recommendation for the purposes of the application.

(3) A guardianship application which appears to be duly made and to be founded on the necessary medical recommendations may be acted upon without further proof of the signature or qualification of the person by whom the application or any such medical recommendation is made or given, or of any matter of fact or opinion stated in the application.

(4) If within the period of 14 days beginning with the day on which a guardianship application has been accepted by the local social services authority the application, or any medical recommendation given for the purposes of the application, is found to be in any respect incorrect or defective, the application or recommendation may, within that period and with the consent of that authority, be amended by the person by whom it was signed; and upon such amendment being made the application or recommendation shall have effect and shall be deemed to have had effect as if it had been originally made as so amended.

(5) Where a patient is received into guardianship in pursuance of a guardianship application, any previous application under this Part of this Act by virtue of which he was subject to guardianship or liable to be detained in a hospital shall cease to have effect.

Amendment

The words in square brackets in subs.(1)(c) were substituted by the Mental Health Act 2007 s.21, Sch.2 para.2.

Definitions

local social services authority: s.145(1).   **1-143**
medical treatment: s.145(1).
patient: s.145(1).
approved mental health professional: s.145(1), (1AC).
hospital: ss.34(2), 145(1).

General Note

The Mental Health Act 1959 gave the guardian the power that a father has over a child of 14. These   **1-144** powers were therefore very wide, as well as being somewhat ill-defined, and it was felt that they were out of keeping, in their paternalistic approach, with modern attitudes to the care of the mentally disordered. Subsection (1) replaced these general powers with specific powers limited to interfering with the autonomy of the person under guardianship only to the extent necessary to ensure that various forms of treatment, social support, training, education or occupation are undertaken. This section also specifies that the guardianship application must be forwarded to the local authority within 14 days of the date when the patient was last medically examined for the purpose of the application (subs.(2)), confirms that an application which appears to be duly made and to be founded on the necessary medical recommendations can be acted upon (subs.(3)), provides for the rectification of the statutory documents within 14 days of the acceptance of the application (subs.(4)) and states that the reception of the patient into guardianship automatically ends any previous application made in respect of the patient (subs.(5)).

The patient's guardian, who is subject to the duties laid down in Pt III of the English and Welsh Regulations, does not have any power to use or dispose of the patient's property or to carry out any financial transactions on the patient's behalf.

In *R. (on the application of S) v Plymouth City Council and C* [2002] EWCA Civ 388, the Court of Appeal was concerned with how the interest of a guardianship patient in preserving the confidentiality of personal information about himself is to be reconciled with his mother's interest, as his nearest relative, in having access to enough information about him to exercise her statutory functions under the Act. The Court held that:

1. Both at common law and under the Human Rights Act 1998, a balance must be struck between the public and private interests in maintaining the confidentiality of information about the patient and the public and private interests in permitting, indeed requiring, its disclosure for certain purposes.

2.   Striking the balance would not lead in every case to the disclosure of all the information a nearest relative might possibly want, still less to a fishing exercise amongst the local authority's files. But in most cases it would lead to the disclosure of the basic statutory guardianship documentation. In this case it would also lead to the disclosure of relevant social services records. Hale L.J. said at para.50:

> "There is no suggestion of any risk to [the patient's] health and welfare arising from this. The mother and her advisers have sought access to the information which her own psychiatric and social work experts need in order properly to advise her. That limits both the context and the content of disclosure in a way which strikes a proper balance between the competing interests."

If a local authority concludes that the powers set out in this section are insufficient to enable it to manage the case of a mentally incapacitated person appropriately, it should consider making an application under the Mental Capacity Act 2005 to the Court of Protection for an appropriate order (*Lewis v Gibson* [2005] EWCA Civ 587; [2005] M.H.L.R. 309 para.29).

Human Rights Act 1998

1-145   Guardianship proceedings must comply with the standards of art.6(1) of the European Convention on Human Rights (ECHR) because such proceedings involve the determination of a civil right. The fact that the initial determination of the guardianship application is made by an administrative body (the local authority) does not contravene art.6(1) provided that there is a right of appeal to a court (the First-tier Tribunal (Mental Health) or the Mental Health Review Tribunal for Wales) which provides the guarantees of that article (see for example, *Le Compte, Van Leuven and De Meyer v Belgium* (1981) 4 E.H.R.R. 1 para.51). The state must ensure that the appeal is heard within a reasonable time (*Buchholz v Germany* (1981) 3 E.H.R.R. 1 para.50).

As the patient's guardian is likely to exercise powers which will involve an interference with the patient's right to respect for private and family life under art.8(1) of the ECHR, a justification for the interference, which must be a proportionate response to the identified risk, will need to be found in art.8(2). In order to justify the proportionality of the power exercised, the guardian should have identified and assessed the potential effectiveness of alternatives to the use of that power.

It has been argued that the charging of those subject to guardianship who are required to reside in accommodation provided by a local authority breaches art.8: see *R. (on the application of Johnson) v Secretary of State for Health* [2006] EWHC 288 (Admin). Judicial comments made in this case suggest that it is unlikely that such an argument would succeed if the issue proceeded to trial.

The patient's private or local authority guardian is exercising functions of a public nature in respect of the patient and is therefore a "public authority" for the purposes of s.6 of the 1998 Act.

The use of guardianship to authorise the deprivation of a person's liberty

1-146   If a mentally incapacitated patient who is required under guardianship to reside at a specified place satisfies the "acid test" for a deprivation of liberty identified in *P v Cheshire West and Chester Council* [2014] UKSC 19, a deprivation of liberty authorisation (if the patient resides in a care home) or an order of the Court of Protection (if the patient resides elsewhere) under the Mental Capacity Act 2005 should be sought (*KD v A Borough Council* [2015] UKUT 251 (AAC); [2015] M.H.L.R. 358, para.39). The mere presence of guardianship with a condition of residence does not of itself amount to a deprivation of liberty, though it must be recognised that it is a very significant restriction of liberty (*A Local Authority v AB* [2020] EWCOP 39, para.12).

In *GW v Gloucestershire County Council* [2016] UKUT 499 (AAC); [2017] M.H.L.R. 80, at para.22, UT Judge Jacobs upheld a tribunal decision which found that the powers of the guardian under this section were a valuable addition to the powers granted by a standard authorisation made under the 2005 Act. It is therefore the case that the two regimes are capable of complementing each other. The power of the guardian to return an absconding patient to his place of residence was a crucial factor in favour of guardianship in *NM v Kent County Council* [2015] UKUT 125 (noted under s.72(4)) where Judge Jacobs held that although a deprivation of liberty authorisation allowed the home to prevent P from leaving, it did not deal with the possibility that he might abscond.

In *Lancashire and South Cumbria NHS Foundation Trust v AH* [2023] EWCOP 1, H.H. Judge Burrows said at para.37:

> "At one stage during the final hearing, I repeated an observation I had made at an earlier hearing, that maybe the ideal legal regime for AH would be something along the lines of guardianship under

ss. 7 and 8 of the MHA, albeit modified and implemented under the MCA. That would mean she would have to reside in a particular place (her home), but be required to attend a place for treatment, or to allow a clinician to attend her home to administer treatment. In addition, and unlike guardianship, this Court could authorise those responsible for AH's care to use reasonable force to ensure that she receives treatment and attends at a place for that treatment and monitoring."

In *NL v Hampshire County Council* [2014] UKUT 475 (AAC); [2015] M.H.L.R. 338 Judge Jacobs, in applying the decision of the Supreme Court in the *Cheshire West* case said that it "is possible for guardianship to be set up in a way that does involve a deprivation, but guardianship of itself does not necessarily involve a deprivation of liberty", and that he found "it difficult to imagine a case that could realistically arise in which [the] basic powers [set out in subs.(1)(a) to (c)] could be used in a way that would satisfy the conditions for deprivation of liberty" (para.16). Judge Jacobs further stated at para.17:

"[An] application for guardianship should be accompanied by a comprehensive care plan ....It is in the details of that plan that the potential for restriction, supervision and control sufficient to amount to a deprivation of liberty lies".

In *PJ v A Local Health Board* [2015] UKUT 480 (AAC) at para.130, Charles J. said obiter that he did not agree with Judge Jacob's conclusion in NL that guardianship, alone, cannot create a deprivation of liberty. In his Lordship's opinion, Judge Jacob's analysis "is wrong because what matters is the position on the ground caused by the implementation of the care regime which the MHA decision maker has to take into account". In fact, there appears to be little difference in the approaches taken by Charles J. and Judge Jacobs in that both consider that the implementation of the conditions attached to a guardianship application can give rise to a deprivation of liberty.

The powers that can be exercised over a guardianship patient, which are not confined to those set out subs.(1), include:

1. A power to take the patient to the place specified by the guardian, using force if necessary (subs.(1) and ss.18(3), (7) and 137).
2. A power to require the patient to reside at the specified place (subs.(1)(a)).
3. A power to prevent the patient from leaving the specified place without the leave of the guardian (subs.(1) and s.18(3)).
4. A power to return the patient to the specified place if he leaves without having obtained leave, using force if necessary (ss.18(3) and 137).

It follows that a patient who is subject to such powers can be forced to leave his home to go to a place where he does not want to go, can be required to remain there, and can be returned to that place if he leaves without being given permission to do so. Although the patient might not satisfy the "acid test" for a deprivation of liberty established by the Supreme Court in the *Cheshire West* case, surely nobody using ordinary language would describe a patient who is the subject of such powers as being someone who is not being deprived of his liberty. Cheshire West and the "acid test" are considered in Part 6.

The Government's view that guardianship cannot be used to deprive a person of his liberty is evidenced by the fact that Parliament did not reverse the burden of proof in guardianship cases when it enacted the Mental Health Act 1983 (Remedial Order) 2001 (SI 2001/3712) (see the note on s.72(4)).

Admission to hospital of patients under guardianship

If a patient under guardianship is admitted to hospital for psychiatric treatment as an informal patient he will remain subject to guardianship unless he is either discharged from it (s.23) or transferred to hospital under the procedure set out in reg.8 of the English Regulations or reg.24 of the Welsh Regulations. The guardianship will also remain in force if the patient is admitted for assessment under ss.2 or 4, but it will cease to have effect if the patient is admitted for treatment under s.3 (s.6(4)). If the patient is admitted informally he could be made subject to the holding powers provided for in s.5(2) and (4). **1-147**

Subsection (1)

The guardian may exercise powers over the patient in addition to the specific powers contained in this provision. In *R. v Kent County Council Ex p. Marston* (CO/1819/96), July 9, 1997, Owen J. said that he could "find no difficulty in accepting that section 7 of necessity implies a statutory duty to act for the welfare of the patient". His Lordship further stated that: **1-148**

"the extent and consequences of that duty are not so clear. An example, of no relevance here, would be seen if a patient were to be given a sexually provocative magazine. I would have no difficulty in accepting that the guardian would have a duty to monitor the effects and if necessary to remove the magazine."

This finding was endorsed by Simon Brown L.J. who said, in refusing leave to appeal on September 5, 1997, that it is implicit in s.7:

"that the guardian is entitled in certain respects to act so as to promote the welfare of the patient. Owen J. recognised, as I would too, that the precise extent and consequence of such an implicit duty to act for the welfare of the patient is not clear. I envisage that that may well need clarification at some future date. For example, if there were good reason to suppose that an authority was acting in some totalitarian fashion or was not properly having regard to the interests of its patients, then it seems to me clear that someone would have the standing, would have a sufficient interest to bring the case before the court so that the matter could be properly investigated and the true extent of the authority's discretion be clarified".

In *Marston*, Owen J. upheld the decision of the local authority, acting as the patient's guardian, to refuse to disclose to the patient's former foster brother where the patient was living. The foster brother was ultimately intent on taking over the care of the patient and the local authority had received medical advice that this would be contrary to the patient's interests. The patient, who was mentally incapable, had expressed no interest in seeing his former foster brother. His Lordship said that as the patient needed protection, the guardian had a right to see letters addressed to him by the foster brother and that whether "the guardian would be entitled to censor them would depend what was in them". However, as the patient was unable to read, the right to see the letters would not have to be exercised. *Marston* was not cited in *Re F (Mental Health Act: Guardianship)* [2000] 1 F.L.R. 192 where Thorpe L.J. stated, obiter, that he doubted the legality of the restrictions that the local authority, acting as guardian, has placed on the patient's contact with her parents.

A local authority guardian may delegate its functions under this provision to any committee, officer or other body or person to whom they can normally delegate functions under the Local Government Act 1972 (or the Local Government Act 2000, if relevant): see reg.21 of the English Regulations and the note thereto.

Secretary of State   The functions of the Minister, so far as exercisable in relation to Wales, are exercised by the Welsh Ministers (see the General Note to the Act).

To the exclusion of any other person   This provision prevents a person from taking a decision, including a decision made under the Mental Capacity Act 2005, on the matters covered by paras (a) to (c) which conflicts with a decision made by the guardian. The prohibition covers a deputy appointed by the Court of Protection, the donee of a lasting power of attorney, and a lay or professional carer purporting to act under the protection granted by s.5 of the 2005 Act. In *C v Blackburn and Darwen Borough Council* [2011] EWHC 3321 (COP); [2012] M.H.L.R. 202, at para.39, Peter Jackson J. held that the prohibition contained in this provision applies to public bodies, including the Court of Protection.

Paragraph (a)

1-149   **Require the patient to reside at a place**   Which, for example, could be a care home, supported accommodation or a private residence. There is no power to require that the patient resides with a particular person. Guardianship has been used to require the patient to reside in his own home in a situation where the power to require the patient to provide access to health and social care professions was needed in order to provide support to the patient. The patient can be required to change his place of residence. The designated place of residence and other requirements should be recorded in the patient's care plan and communicated to the patient both orally and in writing.

The guardian has the exclusive right to decide where the patient lives. It is therefore not lawful for another person to use the Mental Capacity Act 2005 to arrange for the person to live elsewhere.

The power to take the patient to the place specified by the guardian is contained in s.18(7). The person taking the patient can use force if this is required (s.137). If the patient leaves the place where he is required to reside without his guardian's consent, he can be taken into custody and returned to that place (s.18(3)) within the period specified in s.18(4).

Paragraph 28.7 of the *Code of Practice* states:

"Guardianship patients who are AWOL from the place they are required to live may be taken into custody by any member of the staff of a local authority, any person authorised in writing by the local authority or the private guardian (if there is one), or a police officer."

An application could be made to a magistrate under s.135(2) if it is not possible to obtain access to the place where the patient is staying. Anyone obstructing a person authorised by s.18(3) to return the patient would be guilty of an offence under s.129. It is an offence under s.128 to induce or knowingly to assist a person under guardianship to absent himself without leave of the guardian.

In *KD v A Borough Council* [2015] UKUT 251 (AAC); [2015] M.H.L.R. 358 Charles J. said that the power of the guardian to return the person to his place of residence under s.18(3) "has the effect of a requirement or an injunction preventing [that person] from leaving" (para.30) and that the power is a "more readily available, effective and sensible means" of ensuring that the person lives in a particular place than an injunction against that person from the Court of Protection (para.31). Although in *C v Blackburn with Darwen Borough Council* [2011] EWHC 3321; [2012] M.H.L.R. 202, Peter Jackson J. said that "there is no power given to the guardian to prevent the person from leaving: MCA *Code of Practice* 13.16" (para.30), it is submitted that the opinion of Charles J. is to be preferred as the power of the guardian to "require" the patient to reside at a particular place would be rendered meaningless if the patient could ignore the requirement by leaving that place. Also see *NM v Kent County Council* which is noted under *The use of guardianship to authorise the deprivation of a person's liberty*, above.

In *C v Blackburn with Darwen Borough Council* [2011] EWHC 3321 (COP), para.39, Peter Jackson J. held that the Court of Protection lacks jurisdiction to determine the place of residence of a mentally incapacitated person who is subject to guardianship while a residence requirement made under this provision remains in effect: also see the note on "to the exclusion of any other person", above and *KD v A Borough Council*, above, at paras 45–54. However, his Lordship said at para.37:

> "[I]t is not in my view appropriate for genuinely contested issues about the place of residence of a resisting incapacitated person to be determined either under the guardianship regime or by means of a standard authorisation under the DOLS regime. Substantial decisions of that kind ought properly to be made by the Court of Protection, using its power to make welfare decisions under s.16 [of the Mental Capacity Act]."

The person in control of the premises where the patient is required to reside has the power "under general law … to control who is allowed to be there and in what circumstances"; per Hale J. in *Cambridgeshire County Council v R (an Adult)* [1995] 1 F.L.R. 50 at 55. Any restrictions placed on a person having access to the patient would need to be justified under art.8(2) of the ECHR.

Although McCullough J. made the obiter comment in *R. v Hallstrom Ex p. W* [1986] 2 All E.R. 306, 312 that "there is nothing in [the Mental Health Act 1983] which appears to prevent a guardian from requiring his patient to reside in a hospital", this practice is contrary to the intention of the Act if the patient is likely to require long term hospital care: see the General Note to s.7. Also see para.30.35 of the *Code of Practice* which states that "guardianship should not be used to require a patient to reside in a hospital except where it is necessary for a very short time in order to provide shelter while accommodation in the community is being arranged".

There is no prohibition on charging a person who is subject to guardianship for the accommodation in which he is required to reside, as long as the accommodation is not being provided as an after-care service under s.117. Also see *R. (on the application of Johnson) v Secretary of State for Health* which is noted under Human Rights Act 1998, above.

There is nothing to prevent a patient who is subject to guardianship from being admitted to hospital for treatment for either a physical or a psychiatric disorder. In the event of such an admission taking place a local authority acting as the guardian of a patient is required to comply with s.116. See the note on *Admission to hospital of patients under guardianship*, above, for the legal consequences of a patient being admitted to hospital for psychiatric treatment under compulsory powers.

Paragraph (b)

Require the patient to attend   If the patient refuses to attend, guardianship does not provide authority for force to be used to secure attendance (*Code of Practice*, para.30.3).   **1-150**

For the purposes of medical treatment   Neither the guardian, the patient's nearest relative nor any other adult can consent to treatment on the patient's behalf. In *T v T* [1988] 1 All E.R. 613 at 617, Wood J. said:

> "The wording of section 8 will be seen to be much more restricted than the wider powers of the guardian under section 34 of the [Mental Health Act 1959]. One important effect is to remove the

guardian's implicit power to consent to treatment on behalf of the patient. In my judgment there is no power to consent to [an abortion] to be found in section 8 ..., and indeed, on a construction of the statute as a whole I am satisfied that medical treatment means psychiatric treatment."

A patient under guardianship is not subject to the consent to treatment provisions contained in Pt IV (s.56(3)). If the patient is mentally capable of making a decision about medical treatment, the common law enables him to refuse to be treated for either a physical or mental disorder. However, if the patient is assessed as being mentally incapable of making a decision about treatment, the treatment can be provided under the Mental Capacity Act 2005 if it is deemed to be in his best interests. If a patient's psychiatric condition is deteriorating because a refusal to accept treatment, consideration should be given to admitting the patient to hospital under s.2 (with the guardianship order remaining in force) or to transferring the patient to hospital under reg.8 of the English Regulations and reg.24 of the Welsh Regulations (with the guardianship order ceasing to have effect).

Although guardianship does not provide authority for a mentally capable patient to be treated in the absence of his consent, the existence of guardianship can have the effect of influencing the patient to co-operate with treatment. For an example, see L. Blom-Cooper et al., *The Falling Shadow*, 1995, p.90.

The responsible social services authority must arrange for an approved clinician or a s.12 doctor to visit the patient at least once a year: see reg.23 of the English Regulations and reg.10 of the Welsh Regulations.

Paragraph (c)

1-151   **Require access to the patient**   This provision, which could be used to ensure that the patient did not neglect himself, does not include a power to force entry if this is denied. If entry is denied consideration should be given to utilising the procedure set out in s.135(1). A refusal to permit a person authorised under s.135 to have access to the patient is an offence under s.129.

Registered medical practitioner   Means "a fully registered person within the meaning of the Medical Act 1983 who holds a licence to practise under that Act" (Interpretation Act 1978, Sch.1).

Subsection (2)

1-152   The application must be sent to the LSSA within the 14 day period specified in this provision. There is no timescale within which the LSSA must accept the application.

Beginning with   Including the date on which the patient was last examined by a medical practitioner (*Zoan v Rouamba* [2000] 2 All E.R. 620 CA).

Subsection (3)

1-153   **Appears to be duly made**   An incorrect or defective application can be amended under subs.(4).

Subsection (4)

1-154   This provision provides a means of righting accidental mistakes that were made when the statutory documentation was completed; it is not a device for overcoming a fundamental defect in the application: see the notes to s.15. The amended application must comply with the requirements for making an application. The Reference Guide states:

"28.61 An application or recommendation which is found to be incorrect or defective may be amended by the person who signed it, with the consent of the local authority. In practice, if the local authority is content for the document to be amended, it should be returned to the person who signed it for amendment. Consent to the amendment should then formally be given by the local authority. The consent should be recorded in writing and can take the form of an endorsement on the document itself. If this is all done within a period of 14 days starting with the day on which the application was accepted the documents are deemed to have had effect as though originally made as amended.

28.62 If more than 14 days have elapsed from the day the application was accepted a minor mistake would not invalidate an application (a 'de minimis' mistake). If there is a fundamental error, the application should be discharged and, if appropriate, a new application made.

28.63 Unlike applications for admission to hospital, there is no procedure for obtaining a new medical recommendation if the ones that come with the application originally prove insufficient. In that case, a new application would have to be made."

For minor mistakes, see *Re E (Mental Health: Habeas Corpus)* which is noted in the General Note to s.15. An application which contains a fundamentally defective error should be discharged under s.23 as soon as the error is discovered.

Accepted by the local social services authority   The authority may authorise an officer or class of officer to consent to any amendment of a guardianship application which it has accepted or any medical recommendation given for the purposes of that application: see reg.21 of the English Regulations and reg.37 of the Welsh Regulations.

Incorrect or defective   The meaning of these terms is considered in the notes on s.15.

By whom it was signed   An unsigned application or medical recommendation cannot be remedied under this provision.

Subsection (5)

As the patient's reception into guardianship has the effect of ending any pre-existing s.3 application, it also automatically brings to an end any community treatment order that had been made in respect of the patient (s.17C(c)).   **1-155**

Regulations as to guardianship

9.—(1)   Subject to the provisions of this Part of this Act, the Secretary of State may make regulations—   **1-156**

(a)   for regulating the exercise by the guardians of patients received into guardianship under this Part of the Act of their powers as such; and

(b)   for imposing on such guardians, and upon local social services authorities in the case of patients under the guardianship of persons other than local social services authorities, such duties as he considers necessary or expedient in the interest of the patients.

(2)   Regulations under this section may in particular make provision for requiring the patients to be visited, on such occasions or at such intervals as may be prescribed by the regulations, on behalf of such local social services authorities as may be so prescribed, and shall provide for the appointment, in the case of every patient subject to the guardianship of a person other than a local social services authority, of a registered medical practitioner to act as the nominated medical attendant of the patient.

Definitions

patients: s.145(1).   **1-157**
local social services authority: s.145(1).
nominated medical assistant: s.34(1).

General Note

This section, which gives power to the Secretary of State (or, in relation to Wales, the Welsh Ministers: see the General Note to the Act) to make regulations for regulating guardianship, applies to patients who have been placed on a guardianship order made by a court under s.37 (Sch.1 Pt I para.1).   **1-158**
The Mental Health (Hospital, Guardianship and Treatment) (England) Regulations 2008 (SI 2008/1184) and the Mental Health (Hospital, Guardianship, Community Treatment and Consent to Treatment) (Wales) Regulations 2008 (SI 2008/2439) (W.212) have been made under this section.

Transfer of guardianship in case of death, incapacity, etc. of guardian

10.—(1)   If any person (other than a local social services authority) who is the guardian of a patient received into guardianship under this Part of this Act—   **1-159**

(a)   dies; or

(b)   gives notice in writing to the local social services authority that he desires to relinquish the functions of guardian,

the guardianship of the patient shall thereupon vest in the local social services authority, but without prejudice to any power to transfer the patient into the guardianship of another person in pursuance of regulations under section 19 below.

(2)   If any such person, not having given notice under subsection (1)(b) above, is incapacitated by illness or any other cause from performing the functions of guardian of the patient, those functions may, during his incapacity, be performed on his behalf by the local social services authority or by any other person approved for the purposes by that authority.

(3)   If it appears to the county court, upon application made by an [approved mental health professional acting on behalf of the local social services authority], that any person other than a local social services authority having the guardianship of a patient received into guardianship under this Part of this Act has performed his functions negligently or in a manner contrary to the interests of the welfare of the patient, the court may order that the guardianship of the patient be transferred to the local social services authority or to any other person approved for the purpose by that authority.

(4)   Where the guardianship of a patient is transferred to a local social services authority or other person by or under this section, subsection (2)(c) of section 19 below shall apply as if the patient had been transferred into the guardianship of that authority or person in pursuance of regulations under that section.

[[(5)   In this section "the local social services authority", in relation to a person (other than a local social services authority) who is the guardian of a patient, means the local social services authority for the area in which that person resides (or resided immediately before his death).]

Amendments

The amendments to this section were made by the Mental Health Act 2007 s.21, Sch.2 para.3.

Definitions

1-160   local social services authority: s.145(1) and subs.(5) of this section.
patient: s.145(1).
approved mental health professional: s.145(1), (1AC).

General Note

1-161   This section provides for the transfer of guardianship in circumstances where the private guardian of a patient dies, becomes incapacitated, wishes to relinquish his functions, or is found to be performing his functions negligently. It applies to patients who have been placed on guardianship orders made by a court under s.37 (Sch.1 Pt I para.1).

For the responsibility to inform the patient's nearest relative of a transfer of guardianship under this section, see reg.26(1)(k) of the English Regulations and reg.31 of the Welsh Regulations.

It is also possible for a patient to be transferred from one guardian to another under s.19.

Subsection (1)

1-162   This subsection provides for the automatic transfer of guardianship from a private guardian to a local social services authority if the guardian either dies or gives a notice of relinquishment to the authority. The authority, as identified in subs.(5), cannot resist a notice of relinquishment. Guardianship could subsequently be transferred to another local social services authority or to a person under reg.8 of the English Regulations or reg.4(2) of the Welsh Regulations.

Subsection (2)

This subsection allows the local social services authority, or a person authorised by the authority, to act temporarily on behalf of a guardian who is ill or is otherwise incapacitated. The Reference Guide states at para.28.134: **1-163**

"The authority or person temporarily acting as guardian in these cases acts as an agent for the permanent guardian and may not go against any wishes or instructions the permanent guardian may express."

Subsection (3)

This subsection empowers an approved mental health professional to apply to the county court for an order transferring the guardianship of the patient to a local social services authority or to a person approved by that authority. **1-164**

GENERAL PROVISIONS AS TO APPLICATIONS AND RECOMMENDATIONS

General provisions as to applications

11.—(1)   Subject to the provisions of this section, an application for admission for assessment, an application for admission for treatment and a guardianship application may be made either by the nearest relative of the patient or by an [approved mental health professional]; and every such application shall specify the qualification of the applicant to make the application. **1-165**

[(1A)   No application mentioned in subsection (1) above shall be made by an approved mental health professional if the circumstances are such that there would be a potential conflict of interest for the purposes of regulations under section 12A below.]

(2)   Every application for admission shall be addressed to the managers of the hospital to which admission is sought and every guardianship application shall be forwarded to the local social services authority named in the application as guardian, or, as the case may be, to the local social services authority for the area in which the person so named resides.

(3)   Before or within a reasonable time after an application for the admission of a patient for assessment is made by an [approved mental health professional, that professional] shall take such steps as are practicable to inform the person (if any) appearing to be the nearest relative of the patient that the application is to be or has been made and of the power of the nearest relative under section 23(2)(a) below.

[(4)   An approved mental health professional may not make an application for admission for treatment or a guardianship application in respect of a patient in either of the following cases—

    (a)   the nearest relative of the patient has notified that professional, or the local social services authority on whose behalf the professional is acting, that he objects to the application being made; or

    (b)   that professional has not consulted the person (if any) appearing to be the nearest relative of the patient, but the requirement to consult that person does not apply if it appears to the professional that in the circumstances such consultation is not reasonably practicable or would involve unreasonable delay.]

(5)   None of the applications mentioned in subsection (1) above shall be made

by any person in respect of a patient unless that person has personally seen the patient within the period of 14 days ending with the date of the application.

(6) [...]

(7) Each of the applications mentioned in subsection (1) above shall be sufficient if the recommendations on which it is founded are given either as separate recommendations, each signed by a registered medical practitioner, or as a joint recommendation signed by two such practitioners.

Amendments

The amendments to this section were made by the Mental Health Act 2007 ss.21, 22(2), 55, Sch.2 para.4, Sch.11 Pt 1.

Definitions

1-166
application for admission for assessment: s.145(1).
application for admission for treatment: s.145(1).
nearest relative: ss.26(3), 145(1).
approved mental health professional: s.145(1), (1AC).
the managers: s.145(1).
hospital: ss.34(2), 145(1).
local social services authority: s.145(1).
patient: s.145(1).
mental disorder: ss.1, 145(1).

General Note

1-167
    This section contains general provisions relating to applications for admission for assessment, applications for admission for treatment, and guardianship applications. If there is a difference of opinion between professionals involved in a patient's assessment, see the following paragraphs of the *Code of Practice*:

"14.109 Sometimes there will be differences of opinion between professionals involved in the assessment. There is nothing wrong with disagreements: handled properly these offer an opportunity to safeguard the interests of the patient by widening the discussion about the best way of meeting their needs. Doctors and AMHPs should be ready to consult other professionals, especially care co-ordinators and others involved with the patient's current care, and to consult carers and family, while retaining for themselves the final responsibility for their decision. Where disagreements do occur, professionals should ensure that they discuss these with each other.
    14.110 Where there is an unresolved dispute about an application for detention, it is essential that the professionals do not abandon the patient. Instead, they should explore and agree an alternative plan – if necessary on a temporary basis. Such a plan should include a risk assessment and identification of the arrangements for managing the risks. The alternative plan should be recorded in writing, as should the arrangements for reviewing it. Copies should be made available to all those who need it (subject to the normal considerations of patient confidentiality)."

Although primary responsibility for checking that the statutory forms have been completed correctly rests with the applicant, hospital managers and local social services authorities should each designate an officer to scrutinise the documents as soon as they have been received and to take any necessary action if they have been improperly completed: see reg.4(3) of the English Regulations and reg.4(2) of the Welsh Regulations.

Human Rights Act 1998

1-168
    The European Court of Human Rights has held that there are positive obligations that are placed on public authorities which are inherent in an effective respect for family life under art.8(1) of the European Convention on Human Rights (ECHR) (*Osman v United Kingdom* (2000) 29 E.H.R.R. 245). In particular, the European Commission of Human Rights recognised that public authorities might have to take particular steps to protect the mentally disordered in order to fulfil their obligations under that

article (*X & Y v Netherlands* (8978/80): *Y v Netherlands (A91)* (1986) 8 E.H.R.R.). If a mentally disordered person is denied the care and treatment that he is assessed as needing by virtue of a nearest relative exercising the right to object to an application under subs.(4), it is arguable that the State is failing in its positive obligation under art.8 to protect that person if an application is not made under s.29(3)(c) to displace the relative.

Code of Practice

Guidance on "Applications for detention in hospital" is provided in Ch.14.   **1-169**

Subsection (1)

If it has not been possible to identify the name of the patient by the time the application is made, it   **1-170**
is suggested that the phrase "the patient known by the name of John [or Mary] Smith" be entered in the patient name space on the application form. A note of the real name of the patient should be attached to the application as soon as it is discovered. A similar note should be made if it is discovered that the patient gave a false name at the time of his admission. If the address of the patient is unknown, or if the patient appears to be homeless, the current location of the patient preceded by the c/o abbreviation should be entered in the address space of the application form.

It is for the AMHP to determine which section of the Act to invoke: "It is the [AMHP] who makes the application, not the doctors" (*R. v East London and the City Mental Health Trust Ex p. Brandenburg* [2003] UKHL 58; [2004] 1 All E.R. 400, per Lord Bingham at para.12).

Application   By virtue of reg.4(1) of the English Regulations, the following forms must be used: applications for assessment—Form A1 (for NRs) or A2 (for AMHPs); applications for treatment—Form A5 (for NRs) or A6 (for AMHPs); emergency applications—Form A9 (for NRs) or Form A10 (for AMHPs); and for guardianship application—Form G1 (for NRs) or G2 for AMHPs). Applications to hospitals in Wales must use the forms set out in the Welsh Regulations which are: applications for assessment—Form HO1 (for NRs) or HO2 (for AMHPs); applications for treatment— Form HO5 (for NRs) or HO6 (for AMHPs); emergency applications—Form HO9 (for NRs) or Form HO10 (for AMHPs) and for guardianship application—Form GUI (for NRs) or GU2 (for AMHPs).

An application which is addressed to a Welsh hospital must be in the form set out in the Welsh Regulations: see para.8.64 of the Reference Guide. An application in respect of a ward of court cannot be made without the leave of the High Court (s.33(1)).

May be made either by   Given her professional training and knowledge of the legislation and local resources, the approved mental health professional (AMHP) acting on behalf of a local authority is "usually a more appropriate applicant than the patient's nearest relative" (*Code of Practice*, para.14.30). The Royal Commission that preceded the 1959 Act considered the nearest relative to be a more appropriate applicant than a social worker: "Ideally, in our view, the application should be made by a relative of the patient on medical recommendation, with a mental welfare officer available to explain the procedure and provide the application form and to transport the patient to hospital if necessary" (para.403). In practice, applications by nearest relatives are very rare. Neither the AMHP nor the nearest relative can prevent the other from making an application. An application which is signed by a person who is neither an AMHP nor the patient's nearest relative is invalid and incapable of being rectified under s.15.

Nearest relative   Or an acting nearest relative appointed by the court under s.29. It is possible for a nearest relative to authorise some other person to act for him under reg.24 of the English Regulations or reg.33 of the Welsh Regulations.

Subsection (1A)

Regulations under section 12a   See the Mental Health (Conflicts of Interest) (England) Regulations   **1-171**
2008 which are reproduced in Pt 2. The equivalent Welsh Regulations are SI 2008/2440 (W.213).

Subsection (2)

The managers   Who are the detaining authority (*R. v South Western Hospital Managers Ex p. M* [1994]   **1-172**
1 All E.R. 161). The application, which must be addressed to a specific hospital or unit (*Code of Practice*, paras 14.89 and 14.90) is served when it is handed to an authorised person or it is sent to the hospital managers electronically: see reg.3(2) of the English and Welsh Regulations. Hospital managers are not

obliged to admit patients in respect of whom applications under Pt II have been made. In Volume 2 of his *A Human Condition* (1977) at pp.53, 59, Larry Gostin refers to the opinion that Sir Geoffrey Howe QC, M.P. gave to the North West Thames Regional Health Authority in 1974 on the role of hospital managers in respect of hospital admissions. Sir Geoffrey concluded that a hospital consultant had no right to admit a patient, except with the authority of the hospital managers.

Hospital   As the application does not authorise the applicant to take the patient to a hospital other than the hospital specified in the application, the name of the hospital should not be written on the application form until a recommending doctor has confirmed that a hospital bed has been arranged for the patient. The Mental Health Act Commission suggested that if a patient cannot be admitted to hospital in an emergency for want of a bed, the AMHP should complete an application, making it out to the hospital which has been the subject of a notification under s.140, and convey the patient to that hospital. For a criticism of this approach, see the note on "to hospital" in s.6(1). The *Code of Practice* states at para.14.91:

"Once an application has been completed, the patient should be transported to hospital as soon as possible, if they are not already in the hospital. However, patients should not be moved until it is known that the hospital is willing to accept them."

Paragraph 14.99 of the Code states:

"In exceptional circumstances, if patients are transported to a hospital which has agreed to accept them, but there is no longer a bed available, the managers and staff of that hospital should assist in finding a suitable alternative for the patient. This may involve making a new application to a different hospital. If the application is under section 3, new medical recommendations will be required, unless the original recommendations already state that appropriate medical treatment is available in the proposed new-hospital. The hospital to which the original application was made should assist in securing new medical recommendations if they are needed. A situation of this sort should be considered a serious failure and should be recorded and investigated accordingly."

Local social services authority   A guardianship application does not take effect until it is accepted by the authority. If it is accepted, the authority will become the "responsible local social services authority" (s.34(3)).

Resides   See the note on this term in s.7(5).

1-173   **Subsection (3)**   This subsection, which applies to applications made under both s.2 and s.4 (*Re GM* [2000] M.H.L.R. 41, para.28), requires an AMHP who makes an application for admission for assessment under s.2 to take such steps as are practicable to inform the patient's nearest relative that the application is either about to be or has been made and of his or her power to discharge the patient. The information could be given either orally or in writing.

If the AMHP considers that it might not be practicable to inform the nearest relative of the application on the ground that knowledge that the nearest relative had been contacted might cause the patient significant emotional distress, the AMHP should adopt the approach identified in *TW v Enfield Borough Council* [2014] EWCA Civ 362; [2014] M.H.L.R. 415 in order to reach a decision: see the notes to "not reasonably practicable" in subs.(4).

Within a reasonable time   Given that an application deprives patients of their liberty, it is unlikely that a court would consider a delay of more than 24 hours to be reasonable in the absence of circumstances that make contacting the nearest relative problematic.

Such steps as are practicable   The steps taken could include telephoning to inform a nearest relative who resides at some distance from the admitting hospital or asking a social worker from the area where the nearest relative resides to inform him or her of the application. The actual giving of the information need not necessarily be undertaken by the AMHP who made the application (*R. v Managers of South Western Hospital Ex p. M* [1994] 1 All E.R. 161).

Appearing to be the nearest relative   This section does not impose a duty of reasonable enquiry on the AMHP in deciding who is the patient's nearest relative: see the note under this heading in subs.(4). If the AMHP makes a genuine mistake and informs a person who is not the patient's nearest relative, that mistake does not have the effect of invalidating the application: see *R. v Birmingham Mental Health Trust*

Ex p. Phillips (CO/1501/95), May 25, 1995, where Tucker J. refused applications for habeas corpus and judicial review that had been made on behalf of a patient who had been detained under s.2 in circumstances where the patient's mother had been incorrectly identified as the patient's nearest relative. His Lordship said that a subsequent application that had been made to the county court under s.29 of the Act had also not been invalidated by the mistake. As soon as the mistake is discovered, the AMHP should comply with this provision by informing the correct nearest relative (if this is practicable) of the admission and of his or her power of discharge.

The power ... under section 23(2)(a)   Of the nearest relative to order the patients discharge from hospital. It is suggested that the AMHP should also inform the nearest relative of the power of the patient's responsible clinician to prevent the discharge from taking place: see s.25(1).

Subsection (4)   This subsection, which does not apply to a ward of court (s.33(1)), provides that: (1) **1-174** an application by an AMHP for admission for treatment under s.3 or for guardianship under s.7 must be preceded by a consultation with the person appearing to be the patient's nearest relative unless this is impracticable or would involve unreasonable delay, and (2) the application cannot proceed if the patient's nearest relative objects to the application being made.

In *R. (on the application of GP) v Derby City Council* [2012] EWHC 1451 (Admin); [2012] M.H.L.R. 252, para.36, Judge Pelling, sitting as a judge of the High Court, said that this section "provides constitutional protection for those that are faced with detention under the Mental Health Act. Compliance with the requirements of section 11(4) is therefore the price which is paid for the ability of those charged with the treatment of those with mental illnesses and disabilities to detain people without immediate recourse to a court and in a way which is compliant with Article 5 [of the ECHR]. Thus there is a heavy duty on those who carry out these tasks to ensure that those statutory provisions are complied with".

If the nearest relative of a patient who is detained under s.2 objects to an application being made under s.3, the patient can continue to be detained beyond the 28-day period provided for in s.2 if an AMHP applies during the currency of the s.2 to the county court for the nearest relative to be displaced under ground (c) or (d) of s.29(3) (s.29(4)).

Paragraph (a)

Objects   For the State's positive obligation if an objection is made, see the Human Rights Act 1998, **1-175** above.

In *TTM v London Borough of Hackney* [2011] EWCA Civ 4; [2011] M.H.L.R. 171, the Court of Appeal held that:

1. If an AMHP acts in contravention of this section by signing an application despite the fact that the patient's nearest relative has objected to it, the patient's detention would be unlawful from the outset, both as a matter of domestic law and within art.5 of the ECHR. Toulson L.J. said at para.54, that the fact the hospital managers acted lawfully under s.6(3) in accepting the application "did not clothe the conduct of the AMHP with lawfulness".
2. Article 5(5) provided the patient with an enforceable right to compensation against the local authority on whose behalf the AMHP acted as that authority had directly caused the unlawful detention.

The objection does not have to be made in any particular form. At an earlier hearing of the *TTM* case, it was held that AMHP must have formed an objectively reasonable belief that there was an objection to the application. In forming an opinion on this issue, the AMHP must consider whether the nearest relative had previously objected to the patient's detention by, for example, exercising his or her power to discharge the patient from detention. The nearer in time the previous events are, the more relevant they become, particularly if they show a state of mind of the nearest relative which is unlikely to be changed (*Re M* [2009] M.H.L.R. 154). However, the lawfulness of detention does not depend on whether the AMHP reasonably believes that there is no objection but on whether in fact there was no objection (*TTM v London Borough of Hackney*, above). In *GD v Edgware Community Hospital* [2008] M.H.L.R. 282 para.27, it was accepted that objection was something that might be gleaned from the totality of what was said, including the way in which it was said. In this case, Burnett J. confirmed that the objection does not have to be either reasonable or sensible. The AMHP should provide the nearest relative with sufficient information to enable him or her to form an opinion (*Re Whitbread (Mental Patient: Habeas Corpus)* (1998) 38 B.M.L.R. 94). The AMHP can proceed if the relative either does not object to the application or adopts a "neutral position (i.e. where the nearest relative neither consents nor objects but perhaps wishes to sit on the fence)" (*R. (on the application of G) v Ealing LBC* [2002] EWHC Admin.

1112, para.10, per Scott Baker J.) or if the nearest relative, having been provided with all relevant information, feels unable to come to a decision about whether to object or not.

It is not necessary for the AMHP to ask the nearest relative the specific question of whether there is an objection to the application being made (*Re GM (Patient: Consultation)* [2000] M.H.L.R. 41). However, in cases where the AMHP is unsure whether the nearest relative is objecting, the specific question should be asked (*Re M* [2009] M.H.L.R. 154). In order to avoid confusion, it is suggested that in all cases the AMHP should ask the nearest relative whether he or she objects to the application being made. The nearest relative is not placed under any obligation to consent to the application.

If a nearest relative objects to an application being made but subsequently withdraws that objection, it is advisable for the AMHP to obtain a signed written statement to that effect (*Re Shearon* [1996] C.O.D. 223 DC). A withdrawal of an objection must be full and effective and it will be vitiated by the AMHP providing the nearest relative with incorrect and misleading advice, such as informing the nearest relative that she would have to be represented by a solicitor at a displacement hearing. The provision of such advice would render the withdrawal ineffective: see *CX v A Local* Authority which is considered under "Consulted", below.

In *GD v Edgware Community Hospital*, above, para.33, Burnett J. said, obiter, that as an application under s.3 is "not made until it is given to the hospital staff", the nearest relative has a right to signify an objection up to that point. A counter argument, which is consistent with the remarks of Phillips L.J. in *Re Whitbread*, above, and the terms of s.6(1), is that as an application is "duly completed" under s.6 when it is signed by the applicant, the nearest relative's right to object under this provision ends at that point.

Once formal steps have been taken to make an application under s.3, it is not possible for an AMHP to overcome a nearest relative's objection by making an application under s.2 in respect of the patient (*R. v Wilson Ex p. Williamson*, noted in the General Note to s.2).

Unreasonable objection by a nearest relative to an application is one of the grounds in s.29(3) which enables a county court to transfer the powers of the nearest relative to an "acting nearest relative".

Paragraph (b)

1-176 **Consulted**   In his "Report on an investigation into Complaint No. 97/B/2696 against Suffolk County Council" the Local Government Ombudsman said that there is a statutory duty placed upon an AMHP to consult with the patient's nearest relative "before deciding whether to apply for a Section 3 admission" (para.58). Given the explanation of the purpose of the consultation given by Phillips L.J. in *Re Whitbread*, below, this statement is correct. It is therefore the case that the consultation can precede the obtaining of the medical recommendations.

The process of consultation might involve the AMHP in divulging confidential information about the patient to the nearest relative. In order to comply with art.8 of the ECHR, the transmission of such information should only be to the extent necessary to provide the nearest relative with a genuine opportunity to object to the application.

The AMHP cannot avoid consulting the nearest relative because of a belief that the nearest relative would not object to the application (*R. (on the application of V) v South London and Maudsley NHS Foundation Trust* [2010] EWHC 742 (Admin); [2010] M.H.L.R. 83).

In *B v Cygnet Healthcare* [2008] EWHC 1259 (Admin); [2008] M.H.L.R. 106, King J. held that:

1. The burden of showing that proper consultation has taken place falls on the AMHP.
2. As a matter of law, there is no obligation for the nearest relative to expressly lodge an objection under this provision. An intermediary who had been nominated by the nearest relative could be used if an appropriate consultation is undertaken with that person.

In the *Cygnet* case, the patient's father, as his nearest relative, told the AMHP to talk to the patient's sister because of his difficulties with English. It is suggested that it is not good practice to consult via an intermediary as the AMHP will have no means of knowing whether the views being expressed are actually those of the nearest relative.

In *Re Whitbread (Mental Patient: Habeas Corpus)* (1998) 39 B.M.L.R. 94, the Court of Appeal held that the consultation with the nearest relative can take place before the applicant has seen the patient in accordance with subs.(5). Phillips L.J. said:

"No express provision is made as to when [the] consultation should take place. Counsel for the respondents conceded that a nexus must exist between the consultation and the application that is subsequently made. The consultation must relate to that application. It must place the nearest relative in a position, if so minded, to object to that application ... Provided that the [AMHP] explains to the nearest relative that he or she is considering making an application and why, the nearest relative will be afforded the opportunity for objecting to the application that the Act requires."

His Lordship also said: "The consultation will have two objectives. The first will be to provide information to the [AMPH] to assist with the decision of whether to apply for admission. The second will be to put the nearest relative in a position to object to an application". Merely informing the nearest relative of the proposed application will not suffice (*Re Briscoe* [1998] EWHC 771 (Admin)).

In order for there to be a sufficiently informed consultation, the AMHP must inform the nearest relative of his or her rights under the Act: see para.14.64 of the *Code of Practice*. Such information would include the right to stop the application by saying "I object", the right to challenge a displacement application made under s.29 by, if necessary, being represented in court, the procedure under s.29(4) for extending the length of a s.2 application if this is relevant, and the right of discharge under s.23: see *CX v A Local Authority* [2011] EWHC 1918 (Admin); [2011] M.H.L.R. 339 where Spencer J. said that it would have been advisable for the AMHP to have made a contemporaneous record of her consultation with the nearest relative and for her to have been able to provide the nearest relative with a leaflet explaining his or her rights and the nature of a displacement application.

In *GD v Edgware Community Hospital* [2008] M.H.L.R. 282, consultation was held by Burnett J. not to have taken place where the [AMHP] and the other professionals involved in the patient's assessment did no more than nod in the direction of consultation by setting in motion:

"a course of events which was designed to leave consultation with [the nearest relative] to the very last moment, and thus seriously inhibit the chances of his having any effective input into the process and the chances of his having an opportunity to make an objection. In those circumstances, what in my judgment they contemplated, could not properly be considered consultation at all" (para.52).

In *R. v Managers of South Western Hospital* [1994] 1 all E.R. 161, Laws J. said at 175, 176, that the AMHP is not prevented in suitable circumstances from carrying out the duty to consult through the medium of another. His Lordship developed this point by stating:

"[O]rdinarily, it will clearly be desirable for the consultation to be carried out directly by the [AMHP]. But there may be circumstances in which that will be difficult, or even well-nigh impossible. What is important is that the consultation be full and effective, to ensure that the nearest relative has the opportunity to play his full part in the process.... . I do not suggest that an [AMHP] has a wholly free hand to appoint, as it were, a delegate for the purposes of consultation. It remains throughout the [AMHP's] responsibility".

As an AMHP will have the knowledge and experience to engage in a "full and effective" consultation with the nearest relative, an attempt should be made to consult through the medium of another AMHP.

Although there appears to be no legal reason to prevent an AMHP undertaking the consultation through correspondence or email, this practice is unlikely to result in the "full and effective" consultation advocated by Laws J.

(If any) The application can proceed without consultation having taken place if it appears to the AMHP that the patient has no nearest relative. Reasonable steps must be taken by the AMHP in an attempt to ascertain the identity of the patient's nearest relative.

Appearing to be the nearest relative These words "cannot in my judgment, embrace a situation **1-177** where, on the facts known to the [AMHP], the person in question is legally incapable of being the statutory nearest relative having regard to the terms of section 26" (*R. v Managers of South Western Hospital*, above, per Laws J. at 175).

This section does not impose a duty of reasonable inquiry on the AMHP applicant when identifying the patient's nearest relative; there is no requirement for the AMHP "to don the mantle of Sherlock Holmes" (see *WC*, below, para.28). The test is subjective; a court will not interfere with the AMHP's decision, save on well-recognised public law grounds (*GD*, above, para.42). A court cannot inquire into the reasonableness of the AMHP's decision, it can only inquire into the honesty of his assertion that it appeared that that relative was the nearest relative (*Re D (Mental Patient: Habeas Corpus)* [2000] 2 F.L.R. 848 CA). *Re D* was cited by Scott Baker J. in *R. (on the application of WC) v South London & Maudsley NHS Trust* [2001] EWHC Admin 1025; [2001] M.H.L.R. 187, para.27, where his Lordship said that the court will not interfere with the AMHP's conclusion under this provision unless she failed to apply the test in s.26 or acted in bad faith, or in some way reached a conclusion that was plainly wrong. *WC* was applied in *GD v Edgware Community Hospital* [2008] M.H.L.R. 282 where it was held that an additional ground for interfering with the decision of an AMHP is misuse of power.

A consequence of cases cited above is that the legality of the patient's detention will not be invalidated if, subsequent to the application being accepted by the hospital managers, the AMHP either learns of the existence of a previously unknown relative who is the patient's actual nearest relative or is appraised of previously unknown facts about the patient's situation which leads to the identification of a different nearest relative. The "new" nearest relative should be informed of the application and of his or her power of discharge under s.23 and an appropriate entry made in the patient's case record: see also the note on s.15(1).

In the absence of action being taken under s.29 to displace the nearest relative or of the nearest relative agreeing to transfer his or her functions to another under reg.24 of the English Regulations or reg.33 of the Welsh Regulations, the AMHP should consult with the person who she has identified as being the patient's nearest relative using the formula set out in s.26, even though, from a professional perspective, it might be inappropriate for that person to be consulted. However, the consultation need not take place if the AMHP considers that it is not "reasonably practicable" to undertake the consultation: see below.

Appears to the professional that in the circumstances   The "circumstances" are those known to the AMHP or believed by her to exist (*R. (on the application of V) v South London and Maudsley NHS Foundation Trust* [2010] EWHC 742 (Admin); [2010] M.H.L.R. 83, para.33).

Not reasonably practicable   The duty to consult is considered in the following paragraphs of the *Code of Practice*:

"14.60 Circumstances in which the nearest relative need not be informed or consulted include those where:

- it is not practicable for the AMHP to obtain sufficient information to establish the identity or location of the nearest relative or where to do so would require an excessive amount of investigation involving unreasonable delay, and
- consultation is not possible because of the nearest relative's own health or mental incapacity.

14.61 There may also be cases where, although physically possible, it would not be reasonably practicable to inform or consult the nearest relative because the detrimental impact of this on the patient would interfere with the patient's right to respect for their privacy and family life under article 8 of the European Convention on Human Rights to an extent that would not be justified and proportionate in the particular circumstances of the case. Detrimental impact may include cases where patients are likely to suffer emotional distress, deterioration in their mental health, physical harm, or financial or other exploitation as a result of the consultation. Consultation with the nearest relative that interferes with the patient's Article 8 rights may be justified to protect the patient's article 5 right to liberty.

14.62 Consulting and notifying the nearest relative is a significant safeguard for patients. Therefore decisions not to do so on these grounds should not be taken lightly. AMHPs should consider all the circumstances of the case, including:

- the benefit to the patient of the involvement of their nearest relative, including to protect the patient's article 5 rights
- the patient's wishes including taking into account whether they have the capacity to decide whether they would want their nearest relative involved and any statement of their wishes they have made in advance. However, a patient's wishes will not be determinative of whether it is reasonably practicable to consult the nearest relative
- any detrimental effect that involving the nearest relative would have on the patient's health and wellbeing, and
- whether there is any good reason to think that the patient's objection may be intended to prevent information relevant to the assessment being discovered.

14.63 If they do not consult or inform the nearest relative, AMHPs should record their reasons. Consultation must not be avoided purely because it is thought that the nearest relative might object to the application.

14.64 When consulting nearest relatives AMHPs should, where possible:

- ascertain the nearest relative's views about both the patient's needs and the nearest relative's own needs in relation to the patient
- inform the nearest relative of the reasons for considering an application for detention and what the effects of such an application would be, and
- inform the nearest relative of their role and rights under the Act.

14.65 If the nearest relative objects to an application being made for admission for treatment under section 3, the application cannot be made. If it is thought necessary to proceed with the application to ensure the patient's safety or that of others and the nearest relative cannot be persuaded to agree, the AMHP will need to consider applying to the county court for the nearest relative's displacement under section 29 of the Act (see paragraphs 5.7 and 5.11 – 5.24)."

The correct construction of this phrase was considered by the Court of Appeal in *TW v Enfield Borough Council* [2014] EWCA Civ 362; [2014] M.H.L.R. 415. The court held that there are two aspects to the construction: the domestic law aspect and the Human Rights Act aspect. With regard to the former, the court held, at para.45, that:

(i)   the word "practicable" means more than whether it is physically "possible" to consult the nearest relative;

(ii)   in considering what is "reasonably practicable", it is legitimate to look at what might be the result of the proposed action; and

(iii)   the word "practicable" must have sufficient elasticity to take account of the circumstances in which the powers of the mental health professionals have to be exercised.

With regard to the Human Rights Act aspect, the court held that when an AMHP is considering whether it is "reasonably practicable" to consult the nearest relative before making an application to admit a patient, the section imposes on the AMHP an obligation to strike a balance between the patient's art.5 right not to be detained unless that is done by a procedure that is in accordance with the law, which includes the duty under this provision, and the patient's art.8(1) right to respect for her private life, which includes her right to confidentiality (para.50). In other words, the AMHP has to decide which ECHR right of the patient should take priority.

Aikens L.J., who gave the lead judgment in *TW*, said that in a case where an AMHP's statutory obligation to consult the nearest relative under this provision would constitute an interference with the patient's art.8(1) rights, the decision of an AMHP as to whether it is "reasonably practicable" to consult the nearest relative will depend on whether that is justified and proportionate to do so in the particular circumstances of the case. Normally, proportionality is not assessed by reference simply to the subjective conclusion of the person making the judgment. However, a court will accord a decision-maker a wide margin of judgment as to what is proportional in a particular case (para.51). This finding is significant given that the AMHP's responsibility to strike a balance between the patient's art.5 and art.8 rights will, in some circumstances, be a difficult exercise (para.52). The court held, at para.52, that as a matter of construction of this provision:

(i)   a patient's assertion, even if founded on fact and even if reasonable, that consultation with the nearest relative would lead to an infringement of her art.8(1) rights cannot, as a matter of law, lead automatically to the conclusion that it is "not reasonably practicable" to consult;

(ii)   an AMHP's conclusion that such consultation would lead to an infringement of the patient's art.8(1) rights is not enough, in law, to lead to the decision that there should be no such consultation; and

(iii)   it is wrong in law for an AMHP to conclude that because consultation with the patient's nearest relative would require disclosure of details of the patient's case and that would therefore constitute an interference with the patient's art.8(1) rights, that must necessarily lead to the conclusion that it was "not reasonably practicable" to consult.

The patient's art.8(1) rights are likely to take priority in the circumstances identified by the *Code of Practice* at para.4.36:

"[O]ccasionally there will be cases where ... disclosing information about the patient to the nearest relative cannot be considered practicable, on the grounds that it would have a detrimental impact on the patient that is disproportionate to any advantage to be gained from informing the nearest relative. This would therefore be a breach of the patient's right to privacy under article 8 of the European Convention on Human Rights (ECHR). The risk of this is greatest where the nearest relative is someone whom the patient would not have chosen themselves. Before disclosing information to nearest relatives without a patient's consent, the person concerned must consider whether the disclosure would be likely to:

•   put the patient at risk of physical harm or financial or other exploitation

•   cause the patient emotional distress or lead to a deterioration in their mental health, or

•   have any other detrimental effect on their health or wellbeing and, if so, whether the advantages to the patient and the public interest of the disclosure outweigh the disadvantages to the patient, in the light of all the circumstances of the case.""

AMHPs should fully record their reasons for concluding that their decision regarding consultation was "justified and proportionate" in the circumstances of the case.

In *DP v South Tyneside District Council, July 14, 2011,* unreported, the patient had made allegations that her family, including her father, had tried to force her to marry against her will and that she had been at risk of being killed. She subsequently went to live in a women's refuge, and had not had recent contact with her father who was her nearest relative. When making an application under s.3, the AMHP decided not to consult with the patient's father under this provision, as he was concerned that if he disclosed the patient's whereabouts her father might compromise her safety and wellbeing. Mitting J. held that it was unrealistic, in the context in which the obligation to consult was set, that the AMHP could have had a frank consultation with the father without disclosing the patient's whereabouts. If the father had objected to the application and an application for displacement was made, the father would then have discovered the patient's whereabouts. Faced with a difficult dilemma, the AMHP had reached the reasonable conclusion that it was not practicable to consult the father.

If, subsequent to the patient's detention, the nearest relative disputes the decision of the AMHP applicant that it had not been practicable to consult, the hospital managers should not attempt to resolve the dispute: see the General Note to s.6. The appropriate remedy would be for the nearest relative to seek to challenge the legality of the patient's detention by making an application for judicial review.

Undesirable delay Given the circumstances of most guardianship applications and applications for treatment, it is unlikely that this situation would often obtain. It could occur if tracing the whereabouts of the nearest relative would involve an excessive amount of investigative work on the part of the AMHP.

In *R. (on the application of V) v South London and Maudsley NHS Foundation Trust* [2010] EWHC 742 (Admin); [2010] M.H.L.R. 83 at paras 36, 37, Wyn Williams J. held that, on the facts of the case, the AMHP had been "plainly wrong" to conclude that consulting with the nearest relative would involve an unreasonable delay in a situation where no adequate reason was given why a delay was unreasonable in the light of the fact that the patient's detention under s.5(2) would not expire for several hours. A similar conclusion was reached by Judge Pelling in *R. (on the application of GP) v Derby City Council* [2012] EWHC 1451 (Admin); [2012] M.H.L.R. 252, a case where a s.3 application was made without a consultation taking place even though the s.2 application had over seven hours to run and the AMHP, who had failed to reach the nearest relative on her mobile phone, had the time to contact her at her home.

Subsection (5)

1-178 **Personally seen** This phrase requires the physical presence of the AMHP or the nearest relative applicant. Seeing the patient cannot be achieved by the use of remote technology (*Devon Partnership NHS Trust v Secretary of State for Health and Social Care* [2021] EWHC 101 (Admin); [2021] M.H.L.R. 248). The applicant cannot use an intermediary (*R. v Managers of South Western Hospital* [1994] 1 All E.R. 161, per Laws J. at 175).

The relationship between this provision and s.13(2), which requires an AMHP to interview the patient before making an application, was examined in the following obiter passage of Phillips L.J.'s judgment in *Re Whitbread (Mental Patient: Habeas Corpus)* (1998) 39 B.M.L.R. 94:

> "In my judgment section 11(5) and section 13(2) do not necessarily refer to the same event. The precondition to an application imposed by s.11(5) applies whether the application is made by the nearest relative or by the [AMHP] and thus must be appropriate to either. It seems to me that the object of section 11(5) is to ensure that the view of an applicant that an application is desirable is informed by recent face to face contact with the patient. So far as the [AMHP] is concerned, this may or may not be the occasion upon which the interview required by section 13(2) takes place. I consider that the Act permits an application to follow from an interview that takes place more than 14 days before the application, provided that the [AMHP] has confirmed his conclusion that an application is desirable by face to face contact with the patient within 14 days of the application."

14 days ending with the date of the application With the exception of an emergency application, once an application has been completed the patient must be taken to the hospital named in the application within 14 days of the second medical examination of the patient being made (s.6(1)(a)).

Subsection (7)

1-179 **Registered medical practitioner** Means "a fully registered person within the meaning of the Medical Act 1983 who holds a licence to practise under that Act" (Interpretation Act 1978, Sch.1).

General provisions as to medical recommendations

12.—(1)   The recommendations required for the purposes of an application for   **1-180**
the admission of a patient under this Part of this Act [or a guardianship applica-
tion] (in this Act referred to as "medical recommendations") shall be signed on or
before the date of the application, and shall be given by practitioners who have
personally examined the patient either together or separately, but where they have
examined the patient separately not more than five days must have elapsed between
the days on which the separate examinations took place.

(2)   Of the medical recommendations given for the purposes of any such application, one shall be given by a practitioner approved for the purposes of this section by the Secretary of State as having special experience in the diagnosis or treatment of mental disorder; and unless that practitioner has previous acquaintance with
the patient, the other such recommendation shall, if practicable, be given by a
registered medical practitioner who has such previous acquaintance.

[(2A)   A registered medical practitioner who is an approved clinician shall be
treated as also approved for the purposes of this section under subsection (2) above
as having special experience as mentioned there.]

[(3)   No medical recommendation shall be given for the purposes of an application mentioned in subsection (1) above if the circumstances are such that there
would be a potential conflict of interest for the purposes of regulations under section 12A below.]

Amendments

The amendments to this section were made by the Mental Health Act 2007 ss.16, 22(3), (4).

Definitions

patient: s.145(1).   **1-181**
mental disorder: ss.1, 145(1).
approved clinician: s.145(1).

General Note

This section specifies the requirements that apply to medical recommendations which are made to   **1-182**
support applications for the detention of patients and guardianship applications. A recommendation may
not be given if a potential conflict of interest arises (subs.(3)).

If a doctor who has been approached with a view to making a medical recommendation decides not
to do so on the ground that the statutory criteria are not satisfied, there is nothing to prevent an AMHP
from taking steps to see whether another doctor might be willing to provide the recommendation (*TTM
v London Borough of Hackney* [2011] EWCA Civ 4; [2011] 3 All E.R. 529, para.79). In some
circumstances, it might be possible to seek judicial review of a doctor's decision not to complete a medical recommendation (*Surrey County Council v MB* [2007] EWHC 3085 (Fam), para.49).

A doctor who completes a medical recommendation on a form prescribed by the English or Welsh
Regulations is acting in a clinical capacity, often in circumstances of considerable stress and urgency.
The doctor is not "obliged to do any more than complete the form according to his or her professional
judgment in the prescribed manner". It would be "wholly inappropriate" to treat that part of the form
which requires the doctor to state the reasons why detention is required in the same way as a reasoned
determination following a tribunal hearing (*R. (on the application of H) v Oxfordshire Mental Healthcare
NHS Trust* [2002] EWHC Admin 465; [2002] M.H.L.R. 282, paras 70, 71, per Sullivan J.). In *Re RS's
Application for Judicial Review* [2015] NICA 30, the Court of Appeal in Northern Ireland said that the
Oxfordshire decision is authority for the proposition that the "statutory prescribed forms envisage the
provision of summary reasons" (para.36). The adequacy of the reasons given by doctors on the medi-
cal recommendation forms to support their opinions should be judged in the light of this case law.

A conscientious doctor whose opinion has not been accepted by a tribunal or a hospital managers'
panel exercising its power to discharge under s.23 will doubtless ask herself whether the tribunal's or

panel's view is to be preferred and whether her own opinion should be revised. But if, having done so, she adheres to her original opinion she cannot be obliged to suppress or alter it. Her professional duty to her patient, and her wider duty to the public, requires her to form, and if called upon express, the best professional judgment she can, whether or not that coincides with the judgment of the tribunal or panel (*R. v East London and The City Mental Health Trust Ex p. Brandenburg, HL*, which is noted in the General Note to s.3).

There is no provision in the Act which allows for the withdrawal of a valid medical recommendation subsequent to the completion of the application. In a case known to the author, a request for the return of a recommendation was made subsequent to the recommending doctor being subjected to pressure from members of the patient's family. An attempt to withdraw a recommendation would be a factor that the potential applicant would take into account when making a decision about the appropriateness of making an application.

Wales

1-183   Regulation 4(2) of the Mental Health (Conflicts of Interest) (Wales) Regulations 2008 (SI 2008/2440) states:

"Where the application is for the admission of the patient to a hospital which is not a registered establishment, one (but not more than one) of the medical recommendations may be given by a registered medical practitioner who is on the staff of that hospital or who receives or has an interest in the receipt of any payments made on account of the maintenance of the patient."

Code of Practice

1-184   Paragraph 14.77 of the Code states:

"If the doctors reach the opinion that the patient needs to be admitted to hospital, it is their responsibility to take the necessary steps to secure a suitable hospital bed; it is not the responsibility of the applicant. In some cases, it could be agreed locally between the local authority and the relevant NHS bodies and communicated to the AMHP that this will be done by any AMHP involved in the assessment."

Mental Health (Approval Functions) Act 2012

1-185   In 2012, it was discovered that four Strategic Health Authorities had unlawfully delegated their function of approving doctors under subs.(2) of this section, and clinicians under s.145(1), to other bodies. This error meant that there was a legal doubt about the legal validity of the detention of patients where doctors who had not been properly approved had provided medical recommendations to support the detention. In order to respond to this situation, the Government introduced emergency retrospective legislation to remove any doubt about the legality of the detentions. Section 1 of the 2012 Act validates retrospectively any approval of a doctor or an approved clinician given before the Bill received Royal Assent on October 31, 2012. This means that approvals given by bodies which had no power to perform such a function are treated as if they had always been legally granted. The Act extends to the whole of the UK.

Human Rights Act 1998

1-186   A doctor who makes medical recommendations under the Act is exercising "functions of a public nature" and is therefore a "public authority" for the purposes of the 1998 Act: see s.6(3)(b) of that Act and *R. (on the application of Wilkinson) v The Responsible Medical Officer Broadmoor Hospital* [2001] EWCA Civ 1545, per Hale L.J. speaking obiter at para.61. The effect of this is that it is unlawful for a recommending doctor to act in a way which is incompatible with a patient's rights under the European Convention on Human Rights (Human Rights Act 1998 s.6(1)). No objection to a general practitioner providing a medical recommendation was raised in *Schuurs v the Netherlands* 41 D. & R. 186, 188–189.

In an urgent case, if there is difficulty in accessing a "section 12 doctor", consideration should be given to applying for the patient's detention under s.4.

The medical assessment must be based on the actual state of mental health of the person concerned and not solely on past events (*Varbanov v Bulgaria* [2000] M.H.L.R. 263 para.47).

Duty of care owed by recommending doctors

In *M (A Minor) v Newham LBC* [1995] 3 All E.R. 353, HL, the local authority, in exercising func- **1-187**
tions under the child care legislation, arranged for a child whom they suspected was being sexually
abused to be interviewed by a social worker and a child psychiatrist. The House of Lords held that the
social worker and the psychiatrist:

> "did not, by accepting the instructions of the local authority, assume any general professional duty
> of care to the [child]. The professionals were employed or retained to advise the local authority in
> relation to the well-being of the [child] but not to advise or treat [the child]"; per Lord Browne-
> Wilkinson at 384.

As reference was made in both the Court of Appeal and in the House of Lords to *Everett v Griffiths*
[1920] 3 K.B. 163 CA; [1921] 1 A.C. 631, a case decided under the Lunacy Act 1890 where the House
of Lords assumed, without deciding the point, that a recommending doctor owed a duty of care to the
patient, it could be argued that the decision in the *Newham* case determines the liability of doctors and
approved mental health professionals (AMHPs) undertaking assessments under this Act. The legal position of professionals performing functions under the child care legislation and under this Act is, however,
quite different.

AMHPs and doctors who undertake assessments under this Act are not involved in either reporting
to or advising their employer or any other body. The AMHP is undertaking an independent legal function when determining whether to make an application and the role of the recommending doctors is to
examine the patient and support the application if it is considered that the statutory criteria are satisfied.
It is submitted that the assumption made by the House of Lords in *Everett v Griffiths*, an assumption
shared by Lord Atkinson in *Harnett v Fisher* [1927] A.C. 573 at 596 where the House of Lords left the
matter open, is correct and that the AMHP and the recommending doctors have assumed personal
responsibility towards the patient to take reasonable care to avoid an inappropriate and/or unlawful
detention. It follows that an action for negligence could be brought where the professional fails to
exercise such care. It was assumed by the Court of Appeal in *TTM v London Borough of Hackney* [2011]
EWCA Civ 4; [2011] 3 All E.R. 529, at para.97, that an AMHP owes a duty of care to the patient when
completing an application for detention. Leave for negligence actions to be pursued was given in *Winch
v Jones* [1986] Q.B. 296 and *Buxton v Jayne* [1960] 1 W.L.R. 783. As Atkin L.J. pointed out in the Court
of Appeal in *Everett* at 212, s.330 of the Lunacy Act 1890 (now to be found in an amended form in s.139
of this Act) assumes that professionals performing functions under the Act consider themselves bound
to exercise reasonable care.

Atkin L.J.'s judgment in *Everett* included the following noteworthy passage:

> "[I]t is just as it is convenient that the law should impose a duty to take reasonable care that such
> persons, if sane, should not suffer the unspeakable torment of having their sanity condemned and their
> liberty restricted; and I am glad to record my opinion, ineffectual though it may be, that for such an
> injury the English law provides a remedy" (at 233).

At the House of Lords, Lord Haldane described Atkin L.J.'s judgment as a "powerful piece of reasoning displaying anxiety to guard against a possible miscarriage of justice" ([1921] 1 A.C. 631 at 652).

In *Clunis v Camden and Islington Health Authority* [1998] 3 All E.R. 180, 192, the Court of Appeal
said that "the question whether a doctor owes a duty of care to a patient in certifying that a patient is fit
to be detained under the Mental Health Act was left undecided in *Everett v Griffiths* and still remains
open for decision in an appropriate case".

The approach to be taken in determining a public authority's common law duty of care against a
background of a statutory duty or power was set out by Lambert J. in *DFX v Coventry City Council*
[2021] EWHC 1382 (QB) at paras 165 and following.

Approved Clinicians owe a duty of care to the patient whenever they propose or administer treatment under the Act (*R. (on the application of Wilkinson) v Responsible Medical Officer Broadmoor
Hospital* [2001] EWCA 1545, para.68).

Subsection (1)

This subsection provides that medical recommendations must be signed on or before the date of the **1-188**
application by doctors who have personally examined the patient and that where the two doctors examine
the patient separately not more than five days must have elapsed between the days on which the separate
examinations took place. There is no legal duty placed on the doctors to consult each other.

A joint medical recommendation form may be completed by both doctors if they wish to provide a joint opinion. There is no requirement that such a form can only be completed where the doctors have examined the patient at the same time.

Paragraph 8.63 of the Reference Guide states:

"If doctors making recommendations have examined the patient in Wales they must use the equivalent Welsh form on which to make their recommendations. If doctors are making a joint recommendation, and one of them examined the patient in England and one in Wales, then they may use either the English or Welsh form": also see reg.4(2) of the English Regulations.

The detention of a patient under either s.2 or s.3 can take place within 14 days of the date of the second medical examination of the patient (s.6(1)(a)). Although the medical recommendations remain valid during this period, good practice suggests that fresh examinations of the patient should take place if there has been a significant change in the patient's circumstances subsequent to the date of the original examinations. Section 6 does not apply to guardianship applications.

Recommendations   Incorrect or defective recommendations can be rectified under s.15. Recommendations must be in the forms prescribed by reg.4(1) of the English Regulations, i.e. Form A3 (joint recommendation) or A4 for applications under s.2, Form A7 (joint application) or A8 for applications under s.3 and Form A11 for applications under s.4. The equivalent forms under reg.4(1) of the Welsh Regulations are: Form HO3 (joint recommendation) or HO4 for applications under s.2, Form HO7 (joint applications) or HO8 for applications under s.3 and Form HO11 for applications under s.4.

On or before the date of the application   An applicant should not sign an application and then try to obtain the medical recommendation to support it.

Personally examined   This phrase requires the physical presence of the examining doctor. Examining the patient cannot be undertaken by the use of remote technology (*Devon Partnership NHS Trust v Secretary of State for Health and Social Care* [2021] EWHC 101 (Admin); [2021] M.H.L.R. 248). There would appear to be nothing to prevent an examination taking place if there was at some point during the examination a physical barrier, such as a door, between the doctor and an uncooperative and/or potentially violent patient.

The medical examination of the patient is considered in the *Code of Practice* at para.14.71 which states:

"A medical examination must involve:

* direct personal examination of the patient and their mental state, and
* consideration of all available relevant clinical information, including that in the possession of others, professional or non-professional."

The examination should be accompanied by such further enquiries as are necessary (*Hall v Semple* (1862) 3 F. & F. 337 at 354 per Crompton J.).

A personal examination of the patient must always precede the making of a medical recommendation, even though the patient might be well known to the doctor. A doctor can examine a patient for the purposes of this provision by observing his conduct over a sufficient period of time, even if he refuses, for example, to answer questions or to submit to a physical examination or is otherwise hostile and uncooperative (*M. v South West London & St George's Mental Health NHS Trust* [2008] EWHC 1959 (Admin); [2008] M.H.L.R. 303 para.12; approved by the Court of Appeal at [2008] EWCA Civ 1112; [2008] M.H.L.R. 306 para.25 where it was said, at para.26, that there is no set time that must be taken for an examination to qualify under this provision; what is required is a matter for the professional judgment of the doctor). Also of relevance are the following observations of Egan J. delivering the majority judgment of the Irish Supreme Court in *O'Reilly v Moroney* unreported, November 16, 1993:

"There is no definition of the word 'examine' ... and the fact that Dr. Moroney himself agreed that there was no physical examination or interview does not conclude the matter. Here was a case where the doctor had evidence which he considered to be reliable to the effect that the plaintiff had threatened suicide and needed treatment so urgently that it might be unsafe to leave it until the following day. This was followed by what he actually saw outside the plaintiff's house where she was shouting and screaming, kicking out at her husband. This observation having regard to what he had been told constituted a form of 'examination' in my opinion and justified the doctor in pursuing the course which he did."

An examination of an unconscious or highly intoxicated patient would not enable the doctor to ascertain whether the criteria for admission under the Act were established. Such a patient could be admitted to hospital and treated under the authority of the Mental Capacity Act 2005.

Five days   i.e. five clear days between the days on which the medical examinations took place. Therefore if, for example, the first examination took place on January 1 the second can take place no later than January 7. The relevant dates are the dates when the examinations took place and not the dates when the medical recommendations were signed.

Subsection (2)

This subsection requires the approval by the Secretary of State or the Welsh Ministers of one of the doctors who provides a recommendation in support of an application for the admission of a patient to hospital or a guardianship application. If that doctor does not have previous acquaintance with the patient, the other recommending doctor shall, if practicable, have such previous acquaintance. The Care Quality Commission is incorrect when it states that the Act "contains an expectation that the two doctors making ... recommendations will be s.12 approved unless one of them has 'previous acquaintance' with the patient" (*Monitoring the use of the Mental Health Act in 2009/10*, p.31).

1-189

A doctor can be approved under this provision without having been approved as an approved clinician (AC). A doctor who is an AC is automatically treated as being approved under this provision (subs.(2A)). See s.142A for the mutual recognition of approvals in England and Wales.

The quality of the training provided to doctors under this provision has been criticised by D. Rigby and L. McAlpine: see BJ Psych Bulletin (2019) 43, 251-254. For a report which presents the findings of a study which explored the reasons for and nature of reported difficulties in accessing s.12(2) doctors, see "The availability of section 12 doctors for Mental Health Act assessments: interview perceptions and analysis of the national MHA Approvals Register Database", NIHR Policy Research Unit in Health and Social Care Workforce, The Policy Institute, King's College London, which can be accessed at: *www.kcl.ac.uk/research/availability-of-section-12-approved-doctors*.

Secretary of state   Section 12ZA enables the Secretary of State to enter into an agreement with another person or body under which an approval function is to be exercised by that person or body. For these purposes "approval function" is defined as the function of approving doctors under this provision and that of approving approved clinicians. An agreement can cover one or both functions.

The functions of the Minister, so far as exercisable in relation to Wales, are exercised by the Welsh Ministers: see the General Note to the Act. The Welsh Ministers have transferred this function to Local Health Boards (SI 2003/150 and SI 2003/813). The Mental Health (Mutual Recognition) Regulations 2008 (SI 2008/1204), which are reproduced in Part 2, provide that doctors approved in Wales for these purposes are treated as if approved in England as well (and vice versa).

Special experience in the diagnosis or treatment of mental disorder   In *R. v Trent Regional Health Authority Ex p. Somaratne (No.1)* (1994) 31 B.M.L.R. 140, the Court of Appeal held that "special experience" is the sole criterion for approving a doctor and that having "special experience" requires examination of the doctor's current knowledge and skills in the diagnosis and treatment of mental disorder. The approval body has to consider the doctor's qualifications and experience and not her overall suitability for appointment. Following this decision the doctor in question made a fresh application for approval to the approval body and this application was refused. An application for a judicial review of the decision was made and judgment was given by Latham J. ([1996] C.O.D. 138). In dismissing the application, his Lordship held that:

1.   The approval body was entitled to take into account the doctor's age because that issue was only considered in the context of the length of the approval that might be granted.
2.   The approval body was entitled to issue guidance to members of its Mental Health Approval Panel taking into account the number of psychiatrists in any given area and adjusting the standard to be applied in considering "special experience", provided that this was applied generally and that the adjustment was directed to consideration of experience only. In this case there was no shortage of approved doctors in the relevant areas which would justify departing from what would otherwise be considered an appropriate standard of experience.

The other such recommendation   The recipients of a survey undertaken by E. K. Ung questioned the "independence" of the second medical opinion ("Who should act as the second medical recommendation for sections 2 and 3 of the Mental Health Act", *Psychiatric Bulletin* (1993), 17, 466–468).

If the doctor who provides the second opinion is neither approved under this provision nor knows the patient, it is difficult to identify the added value that such an opinion brings to the assessment.

Shall, if practicable   In *TTM v London Borough of Hackney* [2011] EWCA Civ 4; [2011] 3 All E.R. 529, para.81, Toulson L.J. said:

"I do not think that it would be wise for the court to attempt to give a comprehensive definition of the word 'practicable' in the present context. However, Parliament must have foreseen that decisions about making applications for admission under s.3 may have to be made in circumstances of urgency. And it must have intended that the professionals involved in the process would discharge their responsibilities in a professional way with proper regard for the interests of the patient and of society. The word 'practicable' must have sufficient elasticity to accommodate these considerations, consistently with the intention of Parliament."

The Court of Appeal upheld the decision of Collins J. at first instance ([2010] EWHC 1349 (Admin)) where there had been a disagreement between the psychiatrists who had been treating the patient as to whether he satisfied the criteria for detention. In those circumstances, the hospital trust decided that it would be fairer to approach two forensic psychiatrists both of whom were approved under s.12 and neither of whom had previous acquaintance with the patient. One was from within, the other from outside the trust. Collins J., on holding that this arrangement did not breech this provision, said at para.33:

"Thus I think that the decision to use two professionals who came afresh and who, of course, had access to all hospital notes and could question nurses or other doctors was reasonable and a proper exercise of judgment of what was in the [patient's] best interests."

At the Court of Appeal, Toulson L.J. said at para.95, without deciding the point, that he would "be surprised if the application had been invalid merely because it was not supported by a written recommendation in prescribed form by a clinician who had previous acquaintance with [the patient], when his responsible clinician (who had such acquaintance) had expressed his opinion that M's admission was necessary. In these circumstances there was no breach of the underlying purpose behind s.12(2), even if there was a failure to comply with the letter of the law. In referring to the underlying purpose, I find it hard to think that Parliament would have intended in such circumstances to have discouraged the AMHP from obtaining fresh medical assessments, when the responsible clinicians believed this to be in the interests of the patient and the public".

Judgments about practicability might also have to be made in the following situations:

(i)   is it practicable to involve a doctor with previous acquaintance with the patient given the time that it will take for that doctor to attend upon the patient; and

(ii)   is it practicable to involve such a doctor given the patient's need for a specialist assessment (e.g. the AMHP might conclude that the patient's disturbed behaviour and violent fantasies require an assessment from both a general and a forensic psychiatrist, neither of whom were previously acquainted with the patient.)

If it is not possible to obtain a recommendation from a doctor who has had previous acquaintance with the patient, the applicant must explain on the relevant application form why this was the case. Although the *Code of Practice* states, at para.14.74, that it is preferable that a doctor who does not have previous acquaintance with the patient be approved under this section, this is not a legal requirement. As the key purpose of the medical recommendations is to confirm that the statutory grounds for either detention or guardianship are present and as there is no absolute requirement for one of the medical recommendations to be given by a doctor who has had previous acquaintance with the patient, it is submitted that a failure by the applicant to provide an explanation would not constitute a fundamental defect which would render the application unlawful.

Previous acquaintance   In *AR v Bronglais Hospital and Pembrokeshire and Derwen NHS Trust* [2001] EWHC Admin. 792; [2001] M.H.L.R. 175, Scott Baker J. held that this phrase did not require the doctor to have had a previous personal acquaintance with the patient. His Lordship said that the requirement is for the doctor to:

"have some previous knowledge of the patient and must not be coming to him or her cold, as it were. There is no indication as to the extent of the previous acquaintance that is necessary, and in my judgment the words 'previous acquaintance' are ordinary English words which have to be interpreted according to the circumstances of the particular case" (para.11).

In this case, his Lordship held that a doctor who (1) had attended a case conference where she learnt a good deal about the background circumstances of the patient; (2) saw the patient for the first time for about five minutes subsequent to that meeting; and (3) had scanned the patient's recently received medical notes immediately before she made her medical recommendation, did have "previous acquaintance" with the patient. A doctor who had provided a medical recommendation in respect of the patient on a previous occasion would come within this category. Also see para.14.73 of the *Code of Practice* which states that it "is sufficient for the doctor [with previous acquaintance] to have had some previous knowledge of the patient's case".

In circumstances where general practitioners have organised themselves into large rotas or co-operatives to provide emergency out-of-hours services, the Department of Health advised the Mental Health Act Commission that the deputising doctor cannot be considered "to have prior knowledge of the patient simply because he has access to the patient's records" and that the G.P.s deputising/answering service should contact the actual G.P. if it appears from the telephone call that a mental health assessment is likely (MHAC, *Sixth Biennial Report*, 1993–1995, para.8.1).

Subsection (2A)

This provides that a doctor who has been approved as an AC is automatically approved for the purposes of this section. **1-190**

Registered medical practitioner   Means "a fully registered person within the meaning of the Medical Act 1983 who holds a licence to practise under that Act" (Interpretation Act 1978, Sch.1).

Subsection (3)

See the notes on s.12A and the Mental Health (Conflicts of Interest) (England) Regulations 2008 (SI 2008/1205) which are reproduced in Part 2. Only one medical recommendation in support of an application for admission to an independent hospital may be made by a doctor on the staff of that hospital (English Regulations, reg.4(2)). In Wales, neither recommendation may be given by such a doctor (Welsh Regulations, reg.4(3)). **1-191**

[Agreement for exercise of approval function: England

12ZA.—(1)   The Secretary of State may enter into an agreement with another person for an approval function of the Secretary of State to be exercisable by the Secretary of State concurrently— **1-192**

(a)   with that other person, and

(b)   if a requirement under section 12ZB has effect, with the other person by whom the function is exercisable under that requirement.

(2)   In this section and sections 12ZB and 12ZC, "approval function" means—

(a)   the function under section 12(2), or

(b)   the function of approving persons as approved clinicians.

(3)   An agreement under this section may, in particular, provide for an approval function to be exercisable by the other party—

(a)   in all circumstances or only in specified circumstances;

(b)   in all areas or only in specified areas.

(4)   An agreement under this section may provide for an approval function to be exercisable by the other party—

(a)   for a period specified in the agreement, or

(b)   for a period determined in accordance with the agreement.

(5)   The other party to an agreement under this section must comply with such instructions as the Secretary of State may give with respect to the exercise of the approval function.

(6)   An instruction under subsection (5) may require the other party to cease to exercise the function to such extent as the instruction specifies.

(7)   The agreement may provide for the Secretary of State to pay compensation to the other party in the event of an instruction such as is mentioned in subsection (6) being given.

(8)   An instruction under subsection (5) may be given in such form as the Secretary of State may determine.

(9)   The Secretary of State must publish instructions under subsection (5) in such form as the Secretary of State may determine; but that does not apply to an instruction such as is mentioned in subsection (6).

(10)   An agreement under this section may provide for the Secretary of State to make payments to the other party; and the Secretary of State may make payments to other persons in connection with the exercise of an approval function by virtue of this section.]

Amendment

This section was inserted by the Health and Social Care Act 2012 s.38(1).

Definition

1-193   approved clinician: s.145(1).

General Note

1-194   The effect of this section, and ss.12ZB and 12ZC is explained at paras 431 to 440 of the Explanatory Notes to the Health and Social Care Act 2012. By virtue of the Health and Care Act 2022 Sch.1 para.1, references to the NHS Commissioning Board should be read as references to NHS England.

"New section 12ZA allows the Secretary of State to arrange for one or both of the approval functions [relating to s.12 doctors and approved clinicians] to be exercised by anyone else who is willing to enter into an agreement to do so. Such an agreement may cover the approval function in general, or only to a more limited extent. For example, there may be agreements with different people in relation to different parts of the country, or (for approved clinicians) in relation to the approval of people from different professions.

An agreement may be for a fixed period, or may specify how decisions about the termination of the agreement will be made. However, it will not be possible for the agreement to give the other party a contractual right to go on exercising the approval function against the Secretary of State's wishes. The Secretary of State may at any time to issue an instruction requiring the other party to stop approving people (either at all, or to a specified extent). The agreement may include provision for the Secretary of State to pay the other party compensation if this were to happen.

The other party has to comply with other instructions given by the Secretary of State. It is for the Secretary of State to decide how these other instructions should be given, but they have to be published. In practice, at least for approved clinicians, these instructions may include rules about things such as the professions from which approved clinicians may be drawn, the competencies they must possess, and the training they must undertake before being approved. Previously, these matters were dealt with in directions to SHAs.

Agreements under the new section 12ZA may include arrangements for Secretary of State to make payments to the other party. The Secretary of State may also make payments to other people in connection with the exercise of approval functions under the agreement. For example, the Secretary of State may agree to meet the costs of another body exercising the approval function, but also directly pay a third party to give expert advice to that body.

While the new section 12ZA allows for other people to exercise the approval functions by agreement, the new section 12ZB enables the Secretary of State to require the NHS Commissioning Board or any Special Health Authority to exercise those functions. The Secretary of State may require the NHS Commissioning Board or a Special Health Authority to exercise one or both of the approval functions, and (as in section 12ZA) that may apply to the function generally, or to a more limited extent.

It is also possible for approval functions to be exercised concurrently both by the NHS Commissioning Board or a Special Health Authority under section 12ZB and by another person under section 12ZA.

Like a party to an agreement under section 12ZA, the NHS Commissioning Board or Special Health Authority will have to comply with instructions given by the Secretary of State. The Secretary of State will have to publish those instructions. The Secretary of State will be able to end (or vary) the requirement on the NHS Commissioning Board or Special Health Authority at any time, which would in turn end (or vary) the Board or authority's power to approve people.

Where the Secretary of State requires the NHS Commissioning Board or a Special Health Authority to exercise an approval function, that function will be treated as a function under the NHS Act. That means, for example, that the Secretary of State will have to take that function into account when allocating funding to the NHS Commissioning Board or the authority. As in section 12ZA, the Secretary of State may also make payments to a third party in connection with the exercise of the approval function by the NHS Commissioning Board or a Special Health Authority.

New section 12ZC gives the Secretary of State and people exercising approval functions under sections 12ZA and 12ZB the power to disclose information in connection with those functions, whether or not they would otherwise have a power to do so. In addition, it allows information to be shared between those people (although not with third parties) even if that would not normally be allowed under the common law of confidentiality. Provided other legal requirements (such as data protection legislation) were complied with, this may, for example, allow one approving body to pass on to another approving body information it has received from, or about, an applicant, without having to obtain that applicant's consent.

Although sections 12ZA and 12ZB give the Secretary of State new ways in which to arrange for these approval functions to be exercised, there is nothing to prevent the Secretary of State deciding to exercise them directly through the Department of Health."

Subsection (1)

Person   Or a corporate body (Interpretation Act 1978 s.5, Sch.1).   **1-195**

Subsection (5)

Instructions   See the "Mental Health Act 1983—Instructions with respect to the exercise of an approval function in relation to section 12 doctors 2015" and the "Mental Health Act 1983–Instructions with respect to the exercise of an approval function in relation to approved clinicians 2015". Both documents can be accessed at: *www.gov.uk/government/publications/mental-health-act-exercise-of-approval-instructions-2013*. These instructions are subject to supplementary instructions dated April 8, 2020 relating to both s.12 doctors and approved clinicians. Both sets of supplementary instructions state at para.3:   **1-196**

"An approving body may extend the period of approval in paragraph 4 of the Instructions for a period of 12 months where the applicant has not completed a training course as required by paragraph 3(4) [for s.12 doctors or para.3(5) for approved clinicians] of the Instructions because the necessary training course is not available."

[Requirement to exercise approval functions: England

12ZB.—(1)   The Secretary of State may impose a requirement on [NHS England] or a Special Health Authority for an approval function of the Secretary of State to be exercisable by the Secretary of State concurrently—   **1-197**

(a)   with [NHS England] or (as the case may be) Special Health Authority, and

(b)   if an agreement under section 12ZA has effect, with the other person by whom the function is exercisable under that agreement.

(2)   The Secretary of State may, in particular, require the body concerned to exercise an approval function—

(a)   in all circumstances or only in specified circumstances;

(b)   in all areas or only in specified areas.

(3)   The Secretary of State may require the body concerned to exercise an approval function—

(a)   for a period specified in the requirement, or

(b)   for a period determined in accordance with the requirement.

(4)   Where a requirement under subsection (1) is imposed, [NHS England] or (as the case may be) Special Health Authority must comply with such instructions as the Secretary of State may give with respect to the exercise of the approval function.

(5)   An instruction under subsection (4) may be given in such form as the Secretary of State may determine.

(6)   The Secretary of State must publish instructions under subsection (4) in such form as the Secretary of State may determine.

(7)   Where [NHS England] or a Special Health Authority has an approval function by virtue of this section, the function is to be treated for the purposes of the National Health Service Act 2006 as a function that it has under that Act.

(8)   The Secretary of State may make payments in connection with the exercise of an approval function by virtue of this section.]

Amendment

This section was inserted by the Health and Social Care Act 2012 s.38(1). The amendments to it were made by the Health and Care Act 2022 Sch.1 para.1.

Definitions

1-198   Special Health Authority: s.145(1).
approval function: s.12ZA(2).

General Note

1-199   See the General Note to s.12ZA.

[Provision of information for the purposes of section 12ZA or 12ZB

1-200   **12ZC.**—(1)   A relevant person may provide another person with such information as the relevant person considers necessary or appropriate for or in connection with—

(a)   the exercise of an approval function; or

(b)   the exercise by the Secretary of State of the power—

    (i)   to enter into an agreement under section 12ZA;

    (ii)   to impose a requirement under section 12ZB; or

    (iii)   to give an instruction under section 12ZA(5) or 12ZB(4).

(2)   The relevant persons are—

(a)   the Secretary of State;

(b)   a person who is a party to an agreement under section 12ZA; or

(c)   if the Secretary of State imposes a requirement under section 12ZB on the [NHS England] or a Special Health Authority, the Board or (as the case may be) Special Health Authority.

(3)   This section, in so far as it authorises the provision of information by one relevant person to another relevant person, has effect notwithstanding any rule of common law which would otherwise prohibit or restrict the provision.

(4)   In this section, "information" includes documents and records.]

Amendment

This section was inserted by the Health and Social Care Act 2012 s.38(1). The amendment to it was made by the Health and Care Act 2022 Sch.1 para.1.

Definitions

1-201   Special Health Authority: s.145(1).
approval function: s.12ZA(2).

See the General Note to s.12ZA.   **1-202**

[**Conflicts of interest**
12A.—(1)   The appropriate national authority may make regulations as to the   **1-203**
circumstances in which there would be a potential conflict of interest such that—
  (a)   an approved mental health professional shall not make an application
        mentioned in section 11(1) above;
  (b)   a registered medical practitioner shall not give a recommendation for
        the purposes of an application mentioned in section 12(1) above.
  (2)   Regulations under subsection (1) above may make—
  (a)   provision for the prohibitions in paragraphs (a) and (b) of that subsec-
        tion to be subject to specified exceptions;
  (b)   different provision for different cases; and
  (c)   transitional, consequential, incidental or supplemental provision.
  (3)   In subsection (1) above, "the appropriate national authority" means—
  (a)   in relation to applications in which admission is sought to a hospital
        in England or to guardianship applications in respect of which the area
        of the relevant local social services authority is in England, the
        Secretary of State;
  (b)   in relation to applications in which admission is sought to a hospital
        in Wales or to guardianship applications in respect of which the area
        of the relevant local social services authority is in Wales, the Welsh
        Ministers.
  (4)   References in this section to the relevant local social services authority, in
relation to a guardianship application, are references to the local social services
authority named in the application as guardian or (as the case may be) the local
social services authority for the area in which the person so named resides.]

Amendment

This section was inserted by the Mental Health Act 2007 s.22(5).

Definitions

approved mental health professional: s.145(1), (1AC).   **1-204**
hospital: s.145(1).
local social services authority: s.145(1).

General Note

The Mental Health Act 2007 repealed s.12(3) to (7) of the Act which set out the circumstances under   **1-205**
which a medical practitioner was disqualified from making a medical recommendation in support of an
application. The Government accepted that the subsections were "complex provisions and that placing
them in secondary legislation would allow more flexibility to ensure provision keeps pace with changes
in practice over time" (*Hansard*, HL Vol.688, col.539, per Baroness Royall). This section therefore
introduces a power to enable regulations to be made by the Secretary of State (in respect of England)
and the Welsh Ministers (in respect of Wales) setting out when, because of a conflict of interest:

  (i)   an AMHP may not make an application for admission or a guardianship application; and
  (ii)   a medical practitioner may not provide a medical recommendation supporting such an
         application.

The Mental Health (Conflicts of Interest) (England) Regulations 2008 (SI 2008/1205), which are
reproduced in Part 2, have been made under this section. Regulations in respect of Wales have been made

by the Welsh Ministers: see SI 2008/2440 (W.213). It is submitted that an application that is completed in breach of these Regulations is fundamentally defective and is therefore incapable of rectification under s.15.

This section does not apply to the renewal of a patient's detention or guardianship.

Code of Practice

1-206   The circumstances in which applications by AMHPs or the provision of medical recommendations by doctors should not be made because of conflicts of interest are examined in Ch.39.

[Duty of approved mental health professionals to make applications for admission or guardianship]

1-207   **13.**—[(1)   If a local social services authority have reason to think that an application for admission to hospital or a guardianship application may need to be made in respect of a patient within their area, they shall make arrangements for an approved mental health professional to consider the patient's case on their behalf.

(1A)   If that professional is—

(a)   satisfied that such an application ought to be made in respect of the patient; and

(b)   of the opinion, having regard to any wishes expressed by relatives of the patient or any other relevant circumstances, that it is necessary or proper for the application to be made by him, he shall make the application.

(1B)   Subsection (1C) below applies where—

(a)   a local social services authority makes arrangements under subsection (1) above in respect of a patient;

(b)   an application for admission for assessment is made under subsection (1A) above in respect of the patient;

(c)   while the patient is liable to be detained in pursuance of that application, the authority have reason to think that an application for admission for treatment may need to be made in respect of the patient; and

(d)   the patient is not within the area of the authority.

(1C)   Where this subsection applies, subsection (1) above shall be construed as requiring the authority to make arrangements under that subsection in place of the authority mentioned there.]

(2)   Before making an application for the admission of a patient to hospital an [approved mental health professional] shall interview the patient in a suitable manner and satisfy himself that detention in a hospital is in all the circumstances of the case the most appropriate way of providing the care and medical treatment of which the patient stands in need.

[(3)   An application under subsection (1A) above may be made outside the area of the local social services authority on whose behalf the approved mental health professional is considering the patient's case.]

(4)   It shall be the duty of a local social services authority, if so required by the nearest relative of a patient residing in their area, to [make arrangements under subsection (1) above for an approved mental health professional to consider the patient's case] with a view to making an application for his admission to hospital; and if in any such case [that professional] decides not to make an application he shall inform the nearest relative of his reasons in writing.

(5)   Nothing in this section shall be construed as authorising or requiring an application to be made by an [approved mental health professional] in contravention

of the provisions of section 11(4) above [or of regulations under section 12A above], or as restricting the power of [a local social services authority to make arrangements with an approved mental health professional to consider a patient's case or of] an [approved mental health professional] to make any application under this Act.

Amendments

The amendments to this section were made by the Mental Health Act 2007 ss.21, 22(6), Sch.2 para.5.

Definitions

approved mental health professional: s.145(1), (1AC).   **1-208**
hospital: ss.34(2), 145(1).
patient: s.145(1).
local social services authority: s.145(1), (4).
relatives: s.26(1).
medical treatment: s.145(1).
nearest relative: ss.26(3), 145(1).

General Note

This section, which does not apply to applications made by nearest relatives, places a local social   **1-209**
services authority (LASSA) under a duty to arrange for an approved mental health professional (AMHP) to consider a patient's case on their behalf if:

(i)   the authority has reason to think that an application for admission to hospital or a guardianship application may need to be made in respect of the patient; and
(ii)   the patient is within their area (subs.(1)).

If a patient has been detained for assessment under s.2, and the LASSA that arranged for an AMHP to consider that admission under subs.(1) has reason to think that an application for treatment under s.3 may be needed, subss.(1B) and (1C) place a duty on that LSSA (rather than the one for the area in which the patient is, or where the patient lives) to arrange for an AMHP to consider the patient's case on their behalf. This duty does not arise if the s.2 lapses before the assessment for a possible s.3 application is commenced. The duties under subss.(1), (1B) and (1C) do not prevent another LSSA from exercising its power to arrange for an AMHP to consider a patient's case if this is felt by both of the authorities to be appropriate (subs.(5)). Paragraph 14.37 of the *Code of Practice* states:

"If a patient is already detained under section 2 as the result of an application made by an AMHP, the local authority on whose behalf that AMHP was acting is responsible for arranging for an AMHP to consider the patient's case again if the local authority has reason to believe that an application under section 3 may be necessary. This applies even if the patient has been detained outside that local authority's area. These duties do not prevent any other local authority from arranging for an AMHP to consider a patient's case if that is more appropriate."

The NHS Guidance states at p.33:

"In view of the Government's advice to avoid all non-essential travel, during the [coronavirus] pandemic, it should be an AMHP from the local authority where the patient is under section who makes the application. This should be agreed between local authorities."

The AMHP is placed under a duty to make an application in respect of the patient if she considers that an application ought to be made and, having considered any wishes expressed by relatives of the patient or any other relevant circumstances, that it is both necessary and proper for the application to made by her (subs.(1A)). This is the case even if the application is made outside the area of the LSSA on whose behalf the AMHP is considering the patient's case (subs.(3)). The role of the AMHP is to "arrange and co-ordinate the assessment, taking into account all factors to determine if detention in hospital is the best option for the patient or if there is a less restrictive alternative" (Explanatory Notes, para.71). Obstructing an AMHP in the exercise of her duties under this section could constitute an offence under either s.129(1)(b) or (d). It is submitted that an AMHP owes a duty of care to those who are assessed for possible admissions under the Act: see the note on "Duty of care owed by recommending doctors" in the General Note to s.12. In some circumstances, it might be possible to seek judicial review of an AMHP's decision not to make an application (*Surrey County Council v MB* [2007] EWHC 3085 (Fam), para.49).

When an application is "duly completed", the patient is in legal custody and the applicant will not be a trespasser if she refuses a request by the patient to leave: see ss.6(1), 137(1). The applicant will also not be a trespasser if, following an assessment of the patient, those assessing the patient have agreed that an application to detain the patient should be made. In this situation, the patient may be held during the time that it takes to process the application as long as the process is not unduly delayed: see *R. (on the application of Sessay) v South London and Maudsley NHS Foundation Trust* which is noted under "duly completed" in s.6(1).

It is not the AMHP's role to locate a bed for the patient. Eady J. said in *DD v Durham County Council* [2012] EWHC 1053 (QB), at para.12:

"It is for the medical practitioners to decide on clinical grounds whether the person concerned requires clinical assessment in a hospital environment and/or treatment. If so, it is for them also to determine whether there is a suitable bed available: see the *Code of Practice*, at paragraph 4.75 [now see para.14.77 of the 2015 edition of the Code which is set out in subs.(2) under "hospital"]."

If a doctor who has been approached with a view to making a medical recommendation decides not to do so on the ground that the statutory criteria are not satisfied, there is nothing to prevent an AMHP from taking steps to see whether another doctor might be willing to provide the recommendation (*TTM v London Borough of Hackney* [2011] EWCA Civ 4; [2011] 3 All E.R. 529, para.79).

There is no requirement for an AMHP to identify a change in the patient's circumstances before proceeding to make an application under ss.2 or 3 in respect of a patient who has been discharged by a tribunal or a hospital manager's panel. However, an AMHP may not lawfully apply for the admission of a patient whose discharge has been ordered by the decision of a tribunal or a panel of which the AMHP is aware unless the AMHP has formed a reasonable and bona fide opinion that he has information not known to the tribunal or panel which puts a significantly different complexion on the case as compared with that which was before the tribunal or panel. An AMHP may well learn of the existence of a decision of the tribunal or panel to discharge the patient when performing her functions under this section and will then wish to know the reasons for it. However, if no such information comes to light the law does not place on the AMHP (or a nearest relative applicant) a duty to make reasonable enquiries to establish whether any decision has been made by any tribunal or hospital manager's panel and, if so, the grounds upon which it was based (*R. v East London and The City Mental Health Trust Ex p. Brandenburg*, HL, noted in the General Note to s.3).

When making a decision about making an application, the AMHP should consider whether a potential conflict of interest arises under the Mental Health (Conflict of Interest) (England) Regulations 2008 (SI 2008/1205) from her involvement.

For the approval of AMHPs by LSSAs, see s.114.

A decision by an AMHP not to make an application

1-210   There is no legal obligation placed upon an AMHP to inform the patient's nearest relative of his or her right to make an application if the AMHP has concluded that the compulsory admission of the patient or an application for guardianship is not justified. However, the *Code of Practice* states at para.14.101:

"An AMHP should, when informing the nearest relative that they not do intend to make an application, advise the nearest relative of their right to do so instead. If the nearest relative wishes to pursue this, the AMHP should suggest that they consult with the doctors to see if they would be prepared to provide recommendations" (also see para.14.95 of the *Code of Practice for Wales*).

As a Code of Practice cannot create a legal obligation (*An NHS Trust v Y* [2018] UKSC 46, para.97) and as there is no provision in the Act which requires an AMHP to inform a nearest relative of his or her power to make an application, the imparting of confidential information about the patient's situation to the nearest relative, or any other person, without the patient's consent would be a breach of the patient's right to respect for his private life under art.8(1) of the European Convention on Human Rights (ECHR), as well as being a breach of the patient's common law right to confidentiality. "Confidentiality and information sharing" is considered at Ch.10 of the *Code of Practice*. Paragraph 10.12 states:

"Apart from information which must be given to nearest relatives, the Act does not create any exceptions to the general law about disclosing confidential patient information to carers, relatives or friends."

In *Griffiths v Chief Constable of Suffolk Police* [2018] EWHC 2538 (QB) at para.233, Ousley J. held that an AMHP was not negligent when deciding not to contact the patient's nearest relative (his estranged wife) in a situation where a decision had been taken not to make an application under s.2 in respect of the patient who went on to commit murder.

If an AMHP decides not to make an application, it is submitted that the common law duty of fairness requires her to record her reasons for taking that decision: see the judgment of Hickinbottom L.J in *R. (on the applicant of Help Refugees Ltd) v Secretary of State for the Home Department* [2018] EWCA Civ 2098 at para.122. Also note para.14.104 of the *Code of Practice* which states:

> "Where AMHPs decide not to apply for a patient's detention they should record the reasons for their decision. The decision should be supported, where necessary, by an alternative framework of care or treatment (or both). AMHPs should decide how to pursue any actions which their assessment indicates are necessary to meet the needs of the patient. That might include, for example, referring the patient to social, health or other services."

Partnership arrangements

There is nothing to prevent LASSAs from entering into agreements under s.75 of the National Health **1-211** Service Act 2006 for NHS Trusts to exercise functions under this section on their behalf: see NHS Bodies and Local Authorities Partnership Arrangements Regulations 2000 (SI 2000/617) reg.6. This allows for AMHPs to be deployed in services that are jointly run with NHS Trusts. SI 2000/617 has effect as if made under s.75, by virtue of the National Health Service (Consequential Provisions) Act 2006 s.4, Sch.2 Pt 1 para.1.

Use of statutory documentation in England and Wales

Applications to hospitals in Wales must be made in accordance with the Welsh Regulations i.e. a **1-212** Welsh application form must be used (Welsh Regulations, reg.4(1)). Welsh medical recommendation forms must be used if the patient is examined in Wales, even if the patient is admitted to a hospital in England (English Regulations, reg.4(2)). If the patient is medically examined in Wales and admitted to a hospital in England, an English application form must be used (English Regulations, reg.4(1)).

As the English and Welsh statutory forms reproduce the relevant statutory criteria in identical terms, it is submitted the completion of the wrong form would not constitute a fundamental defect that would render the application unlawful.

Human Rights Act 1998

An AMHP who is performing functions under the Act is exercising "functions of a public nature" **1-213** and is therefore a "public authority" for the purposes of the 1998 Act (s.6(3)(b)). The effect of this is that it is unlawful for an AMHP to act in a way which is incompatible with a patient's rights under the ECHR (Human Rights Act 1998 s.6(1)).

If an AMHP acts in an arbitrary fashion by, for example, resorting to making an application for detention in bad faith or making an application in circumstances where such action is a disproportionate response to the patient's situation, she will have violated art.5(1) of the ECHR: see *Tsirlis and Kouloumpas v Greece* (1997) 25 E.H.R.R. 198 para.56. In *Litwa v Poland* (2001) 33 E.H.R.R. 53 para.78 the European Court of Human Rights, in reiterating that a necessary element of the "lawfulness" of a detention within the meaning of art.5(1)(e) is the absence of arbitrariness, said that "the detention of an individual is such a serious measure that it is only justified where other, less severe measures have been considered and found to be insufficient to safeguard the individual or public interest which might require that the person concerned be detained. That means that it does not suffice that the deprivation of liberty is executed in conformity with national law but it must also be necessary in the circumstances". The requirement for the patient's detention to be a proportionate response to the circumstances is reflected in duty placed on the AMHP by subs.(2).

The giving of "reasons" to a nearest relative for a decision not to make an application in respect of the patient (see subs.(4)) could constitute an interference with the patient's right to respect for his private life under art.8(1) of the ECHR if the reasons contained information that was confidential to the patient. Either the reasons should be drafted in a manner which would not constitute such a violation or a justification for the violation must be found in art.8(2): see Part 5.

Code of Practice

1-214   Guidance on the role of AMHPs when making applications is set out in the following paragraphs:

"14.50 Once an AMHP has decided that an application should be made, they must then decide whether it is necessary or proper for them (rather than the nearest relative) to make the application. If, having considered any views expressed by the patient's relatives and all the other relevant circumstances, they decide that it is, the AMHP must make the application.

14.51 At the start of an assessment, AMHPs should identify themselves to the person being assessed, members of the family, carers or friends and the other professionals present. AMHPs should ensure that the purpose of the visit, their role and that of the other professionals is explained. They should carry documents with them at all times which identify them as AMHPs and which specify both the local authority which approved them and the local authority on whose behalf they are acting.

14.52 Although AMHPs act on behalf of a local authority, they cannot be told by the local authority or anyone else whether or not to make an application. They must exercise their own judgement, based on social and medical evidence, when deciding whether to apply for a patient to be detained under the Act. The role of AMHPs is to provide an independent decision about whether or not there are alternatives to detention under the Act, bringing a social perspective to bear on their decision, and taking account of the least restrictive option and maximising independence guiding principle.

14.53 If a patient wants someone else (eg a familiar person or an advocate) to be present during the assessment and any subsequent action that may be taken, then ordinarily AMHPs should assist in securing that person's attendance, unless the urgency of the case makes it inappropriate to do so. Patients may feel safer or more confident with a friend or other person they know well in attendance. Equally, an advocate can help to reassure patients. Some patients may already be receiving help from an advocate and, if this is the case, the advocate should also be present.

14.54 Patients should usually be given the opportunity of speaking to the AMHP alone. If an AMHP has reason to fear physical harm, they should insist that another professional is present.

14.55 It is not desirable for patients to be interviewed through a closed door or window, and this should be considered only where other people are at serious risk. Where direct access to the patient is not possible, but there is no immediate risk of physical danger to the patient or to anyone else, AMHPs should consider applying for a warrant under section 135 of the Act allowing the police to enter the premises (see chapter 16).

14.56 Where patients are subject to the short-term effects of alcohol or drugs (whether prescribed or self-administered) which make interviewing them difficult, the AMHP should either wait until the effects have abated before interviewing the patient or arrange to return later. If it is not realistic to wait because of the patient's disturbed behaviour and the urgency of the case, the assessment will have to be based on whatever information the AMHP can obtain from reliable sources. This should be made clear in the AMHP's record of the assessment."

Paragraph 39.18 states:

"The Act requires an AMHP to take an independent decision about whether or not to make an application under the Act. If an AMHP believes that they are being placed under undue pressure to make, or not make, an application, they should raise this through the appropriate channels. Local arrangements should be in place to deal with such circumstances."

For the assessment of a child or young person for detention under the Act, see paras 19.73 and 19.74. The circumstances in which applications by AMHPs should not be made because of a conflict of interest are examined in Ch.39.

Subsection (1)

1-215   This provision places an obligation on a LSSA to arrange for an AMHP to "consider the patient's case on their behalf" if the authority has reason to think that a mentally disordered person who is in their area might need to be made subject to an application for detention or guardianship. Having a "reason to think" that an application "may" need to be made provides a low threshold for triggering an AMHP's involvement. The referral to the LSSA can be made by any concerned individual such as a relative or friend of the mentally disordered person or by the police or the patient's GP. It does not matter whether the person lives in the area of the LSSA: see *R. (on the application of Sunderland City Council) v South Tyneside Council*, noted below under "Patient within their area". It is for the AMHP to decide how to proceed.

Although the AMHP is acting on behalf of the LSSA, she acts independently when performing functions under the Act: see the note on subs.(1A). As an AMHP may be approved by one LSSA but may be authorised to act on behalf of others (see the General Note to s.114), this duty can be performed either by an AMHP approved by the LASSA that has the duty under this provision and who has been authorised by that authority to act on its behalf, or by another AMHP if that AMHP has been authorised to act on its behalf by that LSSA. Subsection (5) enables (but does not oblige) another LSSA to perform the function under this provision if that is felt to be appropriate.

Patient within their area   In *R. (on the application of Sunderland City Council) v South Tyneside Council* [2012] EWCA Civ 1232, para.25, Lloyd L.J. said that the test in this provision "is one of physical presence, which may be temporary or even fortuitous. It is not at all the same as residence". It follows that if a patient who resides in the area of LSSA A is admitted to a hospital as an informal patient in the area of LSSA B and then requires assessment under the Act, LSSA B has the obligation to arrange the AMHP assessment.

Subsection (1A)

The responsibilities under this provision are placed on the AMHP and not on the employing authority (*Nottingham City Council v Unison* [2004] EWHC 893 para.18). However, as an AMHP acts on behalf of the local authority (s.145(1AC)), that authority will be vicariously liable for any lack of care or bad faith on behalf of the AMHP (*TTM v London Borough of Hackney* [2010] EWHC 1349 (Admin), para.35; affirmed by the Court of Appeal at [2011] EWCA Civ 4), even though the authority might not be the AMHP's employer (*DD v Durham County Council* [2012] EWHC 1053 (QB); [2012] M.H.L.R. 245, para.21). The AMHP should exercise her own judgment, based upon social and medical evidence, and not act at the behest of her employer, medical practitioners or other persons who might be involved with the patient's care: also see para.14.52 of the *Code of Practice*, which is set out above, and the note on s.114(10). In *St George's Healthcare NHS Trust v S* [1998] 3 All E.R. 673 at 694 CA, Judge L.J. said:

1-216

> "[The provisions of s.13] make clear that the social worker must exercise her own independent judgment on the basis of all the available material, including her interview and assessment of the 'patient', and personally make the appropriate decision. When doing so she is required to take account of the recommendations made by the medical practitioners".

Speaking of the role of the AMHP's precursor, Devlin L.J., said: "It is the business of the duly authorised officer, rather than that of the doctor, to see that statutory powers are not used for the purpose [of hospital treatment] unless the circumstances warrant it" (*Buxton v Jayne* [1960] 1 W.L.R. 783 at 784).
    The duty placed on the AMHP by this section does not affect the provisions as to consultation with nearest relatives set out in s.11(4) (subs.(5)).

An application   In *Manchester University Hospitals NHS Foundation Trust v JS* [2023] EWCOP 12, H.H. Judge Burrows said at para.65:

> "The AMHP has a very important role [in the 'sectioning' process]. It is his/her judgment, based upon the overall circumstances of the case, including the medical recommendations, the results of consultations with the patient and her nearest relative, but also an evaluation of risk and the availability of alternative care and treatment that determines whether the application is made. They are a critical MHA decision maker."

If the AMHP makes an application, the reasons for taking such action should be recorded. This was the approach taken by the Local Ombudsman in his investigation into complaint 87/B/1308 where a failure by AMHPs to make adequate records of the circumstances of the compulsory admission of a patient was sufficient for the Ombudsman to find that the employing local authority was guilty of maladministration. There is a legal obligation placed on the AMHP to give reasons to the patient if the application is inconsistent in effect with a decision of the tribunal or a hospital manager's panel to discharge him (*R. v East London and The City Mental Health Trust Ex p. Brandenburg* HL, below).
    In "An independent investigation into the care and treatment of a mental health service user (Mr.E.F.) provided by Barnet, Enfield and Haringey NHS Trust", a patient had committed a homicide following a decision by an AMHP not to follow the recommendations of two doctors that an application should be made on the ground that such action was not the "least restrictive option". The inquiry team endorsed a recommendation of the internal inquiry panel that "any reasoning for non-implementation of medical recommendations must be fully documented by the AMHP" (paras 5.42 to 5.44).
    The AMHP is obliged, as far as she is able, to ensure that the medical recommendations upon which

the application is founded comply with the provisions of s.12 and the regulations made under s.12A. The AMHP should not make an application and then look for the medical recommendations to support it because the application is "founded" on the medical recommendations (s.11(7)).

The AMHP should not challenge the diagnosis set out in the medical recommendations but, because mental disorder alone does not render a person liable to detention or guardianship, she is entitled to take the view that it is not appropriate to make an application. The view of the Royal Commission was that "medical and non-medical opinions should supplement each other; each person should be expected to contribute to the final decision only what is appropriate to his own knowledge or experience or to his relationship with the patient" (para.390).

It is for the AMHP to determine which section of the Act to invoke: "It is the [AMHP] who makes the application, not the doctors" (*R. v East London and the City Mental Health Trust Ex p. Brandenburg* [2003] UKHL 58; [2004] 1 All E.R. 400, per Lord Bingham at para.12).

Ought to be made   In the case of an application for admission to hospital, the AMHP can only be satisfied that an application ought to be made if the requirements of subs.(2) have been met.

Having regard to   For a dramatic illustration of the need for AMHPs and other professionals to listen to, and to take account of, the views of family members and others with close knowledge of the patient, see Ch.17 of L. Blom-Cooper et al., *The Falling Shadow*, 1995. The patient's nearest relative will usually be involved in applications under s.2 (see s.11(3)) and s.3 (see s.11(4)) and with guardianship applications (see s.11(4)).

Necessary or proper   Generally speaking, it would not be "necessary or proper" to make an application in respect of a patient who is willing to be admitted informally: see the General note to s.131. Neither would it be "necessary or proper" for an AMHP to make an application in respect of a mentally incapable patient who is compliant to being in hospital and to being treated for his mental disorder if the patient is not being deprived of his liberty (see the note on *The detention of compliant mentally incapable patients* in the General Note to Pt II).

In *St George's Healthcare NHS Trust v S*, above, Judge L.J. said at 695: "In deciding whether it is 'necessary or proper' to make an application under section 2, the AMHP has to approach the individual 'patient' as she is, or at any rate as on the best analysis she can make at the time, the patient appears to be". In this case, the Court of Appeal held that the fact that the patient was heavily pregnant and adamantly refusing treatment for her pre-eclampsia were, at least potentially, of compelling importance to the AMHP who had to make an informed judgment under this provision. To require the AMHP to make such a judgment by ignoring the reality of the patient's situation "would be absurd". However, the patient's illness associated with her pregnancy was not sufficient on its own to bring the provisions of this section into play.

If the AMHP decides not to make an application, it would be improper for that decision to be reviewed by another AMHP in the absence of any change in circumstances, fresh evidence or concern that the AMHP had acted unprofessionally. However, if the decision not to make an application was made by an AMHP with little knowledge of the patient, there should be no objection to that decision being reviewed by an AMHP who has an extensive knowledge of the patient's history and current situation. A procedure which allowed for the automatic review of a decision of an AMHP not to make an application would undermine the independent nature of the AMHP's role. For a contrary view, see "Disagreements between psychiatrists and social workers over compulsory admissions under the Mental Health Act", R. G. Sammut and H. Sergeant, *Psychiatric Bulletin* (1993), 17, 462–465.

By him   The use of the phrase "necessary or proper for the application to be made *by him*" enables the AMHP to conclude that although an application ought to be made, it would be more appropriate for the application to be made by another AMHP.

Subsections (1B), (1C)

1-217   See the General Note to this section.

Subsection (2)

1-218   This subsection does not apply to guardianship applications.

It is possible to have a single interview under this provision doubling as a s.4/2 interview in the first instance, followed without further interview by a s.3 application: see *Re GM (Patient: Consultation)* [2000] M.H.L.R. 41, where Burton J. said at paras 69, 70:

"It seems to me entirely possible, provided that a necessary and suitable interview is carried out, for the [AMHP] to have acquired the necessary knowledge, either retaining it in her memory or if necessary reflecting back on any notes, so that there is sufficient to justify an initial section 2 or 4 application, but subsequently, when it comes to a section 3 application, for her to be able to draw on that same knowledge when she comes to consider section 3 ... In those circumstances there is nothing which prevents the use, for the purposes of a subsequent section 3 admission, of any proper information available on an earlier section 2/4 admission, just as there is no prohibition upon the [AMHP] using acquired knowledge prior to the interview for the purposes of the interview itself ..."

In this case, the patient was the subject of an application under s.3 whilst he was being detained under s.4. A fresh interview would be required if the patient attained informal status subsequent to the expiry or discharge of the initial detaining section and before the need for a further period of detention arose. This is because the attaining of informal status should trigger a fresh enquiry, via an interview, as to the appropriateness of a further period of detention.

During the interview, there is no need for the AMHP to indicate under which section of the Act she is operating. What is required is for the role of the AMHP and the purpose the visit to be explained to the patient (*Re GM*, above, para.71).

Where a person requests an AMHP to undertake a mental health assessment in respect of a member of that person's family, and the AMHP concludes that an assessment for possible admission under the Act is required, the person who made the request should be informed as to the possible outcomes of the assessment: see the report of the Local Government Ombudsman into complaint No.97/A/2239. In his report into complaint No.97/A/1082, the Ombudsman found maladministration in a case where: (1) a family had been given inadequate notice of a planned assessment of a patient for possible admission under this Act; and (2) no less than three home care staff were present when the assessment took place.

Before making an application   The interview required by this provision can take place more than 14 days before the application, provided that the AMHP has confirmed that an application is necessary by having face to face contact with the patient within 14 days of the application as required by s.11(5): see *Re Whitbread (Mental Patient: Habeas Corpus)* (1998) 39 B.M.L.R. 94 CA, which is considered in the notes to s.11(4)(5).

Hospital   A recommending doctor has responsibility for ensuring that a hospital bed is available for the patient: see para.14.77 of the *Code of Practice* which states:

"If the doctors reach the opinion that the patient needs to be admitted to hospital, it is their responsibility to take the necessary steps to secure a suitable hospital bed; it is not the responsibility of the applicant. In some cases, it could be agreed locally between the local authority and the relevant NHS bodies and communicated to the AMHP that this will be done by any AMHP involved in the assessment."

Interview   The AMHP should explain the purpose of the interview to the patient who should ordinarily be given the opportunity of speaking to the AMHP alone (*Code of Practice*, para.14.54). In *M. v South West London & St George's Mental Health NHC Trust* [2008] EWHC 1959 (Admin); [2008] M.H.L.R. 303 para.14, Underhill J. said that the purpose of the interview is "achieved in [a] case where the [AMHP] attempts to communicate with the patient but she fails to respond, or responds inappropriately, in a manner suggesting that she does indeed require treatment". His Lordship's statement that the requirement that the interview be conducted in a "suitable" manner gave a degree of flexibility to those involved was approved by the Court of Appeal at [2008] EWCA Civ 1112; [2008] M.H.L.R. 306 para.25. Richards L.J. said, at para.26, that there is no set time that must be taken for an interview to qualify under this provision; what is required is a matter for the professional judgment of the AMHP.

If a patient has been admitted to hospital informally and has subsequently been heavily tranquilised following a violent incident, it is submitted that an attempt to interview the patient would be sufficient and that there would be no need for the AMHP to wait for the effect of the tranquilliser to be completely eliminated, with the patient becoming potentially violent again: see further para.14.56 of the *Code of Practice* which states:

"Where patients are subject to the short-term effects of alcohol or drugs (whether prescribed or self-administered) which make interviewing them difficult, the AMHP should either wait until the effects have abated before interviewing the patient or arrange to return later. If it is not realistic to wait because of the patient's disturbed behaviour and the urgency of the case, the assessment will have to be based on whatever information the AMHP can obtain from reliable sources. This should be made clear in the AMHP's record of the assessment."

An interview cannot take place with a highly intoxicated patient. In these circumstances the doctor could use the powers contained in the Mental Capacity Act 2005 to treat the patient, with the AMHP intervening only when the patient is capable of being interviewed. If an unconscious patient requires immediate hospital treatment, he could be taken to hospital under the authority of the 2005 Act.

If the AMHP is unable to gain access to premises in order to interview the person, she cannot force entry but should consider making an application to a magistrate under s.135(1).

Suitable manner   These words were added to this section as a result of an amendment moved at the Special Standing Committee by Mr Tom Benyon MP who stressed the need for those who are involved in the management of deaf psychiatric patients having either the use of an interpreter or a fluency in British Sign Language. He drew the Committee's attention to a number of cases where patients had been compulsorily detained under the 1959 Act in circumstances where a lack of speech had been mistakenly attributed to mental disorder. Other MPs were concerned that applicants should be sensitive to the difficulties faced by members of ethnic minorities who might not speak English or who might not speak it well. The words "suitable manner" should direct the AMHP's attention to the particular needs of all groups, including children, who might have difficulties in communicating effectively.

Paragraph 14.42 of the *Code of Practice* states:

"Given the importance of good communication, it is essential that those professionals who assess patients are able to communicate with the patient effectively and reliably to prevent potential misunderstandings. AMHPs should establish, as far as possible, whether patients have particular communication needs or difficulties and take steps to meet these, by arranging, for example a signer or a professional interpreter. AMHPs should also be in a position, where appropriate, to supply appropriate equipment to make communication easier with patients who have impaired hearing, but who do not have their own hearing aid."

See paras 14.115–14.119 of the Code for specific guidance in relation to the assessment of people who are deaf and paras 14.120–14.125 for people with dementia.

The Code considers the use of interpreters at para.4.6:

"Where an interpreter is needed, every effort should be made to identify an interpreter who is appropriate to the patient, given the patient's sex, religion or belief, dialect, cultural background and age. Interpreters need to be skilled and experienced in medical or health-related interpreting. Using the patient's relatives and friends as intermediaries or interpreters is not good practice, and should only exceptionally be used, including when the patient is a child or a young person. Interpreters (both professional and non-professional) must respect the confidentiality of any personal information they learn about the patient through their involvement."

All the circumstances of the case   In practice, these "might include the past history of the patient's mental disorder, the patient's present condition and the social, familial, and personal factors bearing on it, the other options available for supporting the patient, the wishes of the patient and the patient's relatives and carers, and the opinion of other professionals involved in caring for the patient" (Reference Guide, para.8.32). This phrase also includes "medical considerations" such as the "immediate and catastrophic consequences of self neglect" (*GJ v Foundation Trust* [2009] EWHC 2972 (Fam), para.117(a)).

The duty to consider "all the circumstances of the case" does not place the AMHP under an obligation to investigate the proposed place of detention, the location where the patient will be kept while there and the regime to which he will be subject, or to go back and research the views expressed by other psychiatrists who had been in the past involved with the patient's care. It is not for the AMHP to second guess the current medical advice (*DD v Durham County Council* [2012] EWHC 1053 (QB); [2012] M.H.L.R. 245, per Eady J. speaking obiter at paras 14 and 15).

The most appropriate way   The AMHP is placed under an obligation to be satisfied as to the appropriateness of detention in the light of her knowledge of the alternative forms of intervention that would be available for the patient: see the note on "All the circumstances of the case", above. This provision reflects the requirement under art.5(1) of the ECHR that detention must be a proportionate response to the circumstances: see *Litwa v Poland*, which is noted under "Human Rights Act 1998", above. AMHPs are not placed under an obligation to actively seek out alternatives before making an application.

A comprehensive knowledge of local resources available for the mentally disordered is essential if an informed judgment is to be made. The AMHP's view as to why there was no alternative to compulsory hospitalisation should be recorded in the client's case notes: see the Local Ombudsman's investigation into Complaint 87/B/1308, noted under subs. (1), above.

Care and medical treatment   This means care and medical treatment for the patient's mental disorder, and not for a medical disorder which is unconnected with her mental condition (*St George's Healthcare NHS Trust v S* [1998] 3 All E.R. 673 CA). It is therefore unlawful for an application to be made in circumstances where there is no intention either to assess or treat the patient's mental disorder. Despite the confirmation of the legal position given in the *St George's* case, it is the author's experience that the Act has been used to "authorise" the removal of mentally incompetent non-compliant patients from their homes where the sole cause of concern is the patient's need for hospitalisation to treat a physical disorder.

Subsection (3)

This subsection, which should be read with subs.(5), provides that although an AMHP can only be **1-219** approved by one LSSA, she can perform AMHP functions in the area of another LSSA (or LSSAs) if that authority has authorised the AMHP to perform such functions. An AMHP cannot be required to act on behalf of another LSSA.

Subsection (4)

This provision, which does not apply to a nearest relative who wants a guardianship application to **1-220** be made, does not require the AMHP to inform the nearest relative that he or she has the power to make an application under the Act. However, the transmission of such information by the AMHP might be considered to be good practice.

The requirement "to consider the patient's case" does not necessarily mean that the AMHP undertakes an assessment of the patient or even interviews the patient. The effect of a nearest relative's request under this provision is to require an AMHP to consider whether an application should be made in respect of the patient. The extent and nature of the inquiries made by the AMHP would depend upon the knowledge that the local mental health service has about the patient. If the patient has been the subject of a recent mental health assessment, the AMHP's obligation would be confined to identifying whether there has been a change in the patient's situation that would justify a reassessment. If the patient is not known, the patient's general practitioner should be contacted to ascertain whether the patient is mentally disordered as the obligation under this section only arises if this is the case: see the note on "patient", below. It could be that the nearest relative is the mentally disordered member of the "patient's" family.

The communication from the nearest relative can be either written or verbal. It might not always be clear whether a communication from a nearest relative amounts to a request to a local authority to act under the provisions of this subsection. It is submitted that if a nearest relative indicates concern about the patient by saying, for example, that the patient "ought to be in hospital" or that "something ought to be done" about the patient, the nearest relative should be informed of the power under this subsection and asked whether he or she wishes to exercise it.

Nearest relative   Or acting nearest relative appointed by the court under s.29. It is submitted that this provision should apply if the approach to the local authority is made by someone acting on behalf of the nearest relative, e.g. a general practitioner.

Patient   The patient could be receiving hospital treatment for a mental disorder as an informal patient.

If the LSSA considers that the person concerned is not "a person suffering or appearing to be suffering from mental disorder", which is the definition of "patient" in s.145(1), this subsection will not apply.

Inform the nearest relative   The AMHP should write to the nearest relative immediately after the decision not to make an application has been made. Note that it is the AMHP, and not the LSSA who has to inform the nearest relative. If the AMHP decides not to make an application, the nearest relative could proceed to make an application him or herself if the required medical recommendation(s) had been made. If the nearest relative's application is made under either s.2 or 3, an AMHP would be required to provide the hospital managers with a social circumstances report under s.14.

Reasons   Giving reasons need not necessarily involve the AMHP in revealing a significant degree of confidential information because statements of a general nature such as "I took medical advice and was informed that Mr X is not mentally disordered within the meaning of the Mental Health Act 1983", or "Mr X agreed to enter hospital as an informal patient", or "in my opinion it is appropriate for Mr X to continue to receive treatment at home", would constitute a reason for the purposes of this subsection. Also see the note on *The Human Rights Act*, above.

1-221   This provision confirms that nothing in this section (i) effects an AMHP's obligations under s.11(4) and the regulations made under s.12A; (ii) prevents a LSSA other than the LSSA that has duties under subss.(1), (1B) and (1C) from arranging for an AMHP to assess the patient; or (iii) can be construed as restricting an AMHP's power to make an application.

Social reports

1-222   **14.**   Where a patient is admitted to a hospital in pursuance of an application (other than an emergency application) made under this Part of this Act by his nearest relative, the managers of the hospital shall as soon as practicable give notice of that fact to the local social services authority for the area in which the patient resided immediately before his admission; and that authority shall as soon as practicable arrange for [an approved mental health professional] [...] to interview the patient and provide the managers with a report on his social circumstances.

Amendments

The words in square brackets were substituted by the Mental Health Act 2007 s.21, Sch.2 para.6. The words omitted were repealed by the Children Act 2004 s.64, Sch.5 Pt 4.

Definitions

1-223   patient: s.145(1).
hospital: ss.34(2), 145(1).
emergency application: s.4(1).
nearest relative: ss.26(3), 145(1).
the managers: s.145(1).
local social services authority: s.145(1).
approved mental health professional: s.145(1), (1AC).

General Note

1-224   This section places a duty on social services authorities to arrange for an AMHP to provide hospital managers with a report on a patient's social circumstances if the patient has been admitted to an NHS or private hospital pursuant to an application made by his nearest relative, or acting nearest relative appointed by a county court under s.29, under either s.2 or 3. It is presumably assumed that an AMHP applicant would automatically provide the hospital with the information that would be contained in a social circumstances report. The social circumstances report could include an account of the patient's family and social relationships (including the attitude of carers), history of mental disorder, previous contact with mental health services, access to community resources, employment record, financial situation and accommodation. The report should also contain an account of the circumstances of the admission. If the nearest relatives' application was made after an AMHP had refused to make one, the AMHP's report should include an account of the reasons for her decision.

A refusal to grant the AMHP access to the patient would constitute an offence under s.129(1)(b).

Other than an emergency application

It is unclear whether this section requires a social circumstances report to be made where an emergency application has been converted into a 28-day detention by the addition of the second medical recommendation required by s.2 (s.4(4)). Good practice suggests that it should be.

Area in which the patient resided

This need not necessarily be the place where the patient was staying immediately prior to his admission, as temporary absences from the place where a person lives does not affect residence, as long as there is an intention to return: see the note on "resides" in s.7(5).

Rectification of applications and recommendations

15.—(1) If within the period of 14 days beginning with the day on which a   **1-225**
patient has been admitted to a hospital in pursuance of an application for admission for assessment or for treatment the application, or any medical recommendation given for the purposes of the application, is found to be in any respect incorrect or defective, the application or recommendation may, within that period and with the consent of the managers of the hospital, be amended by the person by whom it was signed; and upon such amendment being made the application or recommendation shall have effect and shall be deemed to have had effect as if it had been originally made as so amended.

(2) Without prejudice to subsection (1) above, if within the period mentioned in that subsection it appears to the managers of the hospital that one of the two medical recommendations on which an application for the admission of a patient is founded is insufficient to warrant the detention of the patient in pursuance of the application, they may, within that period, give notice in writing to that effect to the applicant; and where any such notice is given in respect of a medical recommendation, that recommendation shall be disregarded, but the application shall be, and shall be deemed always to have been, sufficient if—

(a) a fresh medical recommendation complying with the relevant provisions of this Part of this Act (other than the provisions relating to the time of signature and the interval between examinations) is furnished to the managers within that period; and

(b) that recommendation, and the other recommendation on which the application is founded, together comply with those provisions.

(3) Where the medical recommendations upon which an application for admission is founded are, taken together, insufficient to warrant the detention of the patient in pursuance of the application, a notice under subsection (2) above may be given in respect of either of those recommendations […]

(4) Nothing in this section shall be construed as authorising the giving of notice in respect of an application made as an emergency application, or the detention of a patient admitted in pursuance of such an application, after the period of 72 hours referred to in section 4(4) above, unless the conditions set out in paragraphs (a) and (b) of that section are complied with or would be complied with apart from any error or defect to which this section applies.

Amendment

In subs.(3), the words omitted were repealed by the Mental Health Act 2007 s.55, Sch.11 Pt 1.

Definitions

patient: s.145(1).   **1-226**
hospital: ss.34(2), 145(1).
application for admission for assessment: ss.2, 145(1).
application for admission for treatment: ss.3, 145(1).
the managers: s.145(1).
emergency application: s.4(1).

General Note

This section, which does not apply to documents issued by a court, documents given in support of a   **1-227**
patient's transfer under s.19, documents relating to the renewal of the patient's detention under s.20, or to the use of the "holding powers" contained in s.5(2) and (4), or to documents relating to guardianship

or community treatment orders, provides for admission documents which are found to be incorrect or defective to be rectified within 14 days of the patient's admission. Similar provision in respect of guardianship applications is made in s.8(4). A rectified document is treated as if it had been correctly completed at the time when it was signed.

If a document which contains a minor error such as an obvious slip of the pen or an accidental omission is not rectified under subs.(1), the application is not invalidated by virtue of the de minimis principle, i.e. the error is too trivial to be of any consequence (*Re E (Mental Health: Habeas Corpus)*, unreported, December 10, 1966). For example, if there are minor differences in the way in which the patient's name is described in the admission documents, this would not affect the validity of the application as long as it is clear that those who completed the documents were referring to the same person. In *R. v Soneji* [2005] UKHL 49; [2005] 4 All E.R. 321, the House of Lords held, in a different context, that in deciding what was the legal effect of a failure to comply with a statutory requirement, a court should examine the consequences of the failure and ask whether Parliament intended that the failure should invalidate the act. Also see *M v Ukraine*, noted under *Human Rights Act 1998*, below.

Rectification is primarily concerned with dealing with inaccurate recording. It cannot be used to enable "a fundamentally defective application to be retrospectively validated" (per Sir Thomas Bingham M.R. in *Re S-C (Mental Patient: Habeas Corpus)* [1996] 1 All E.R. 532 at 537, CA) or to "cure a defect which arises because a necessary event in the procedural chain leading to the detention has simply not taken place at all. It is essentially concerned with correction of errors on the face of the document" (per Laws J. in *R. v South Western Hospital Managers Ex p. M* [1994] 1 All E.R. 161 at 177). If an admission document reveals a fundamental breach of law or procedure which is incapable of rectification under this section, either the hospital managers or the patient's responsible clinician should exercise their power under s.23 to discharge the patient from the section: see *TTM v London Borough of Hackney* [2010] EWHC 1349 (Admin) noted under s.6(3). This action is required because, once an application has been accepted by the hospital managers, only the courts can adjudicate upon the lawfulness of the application. If the patient is discharged from the section, he could be made the subject of a report under either s.5(2) or (4) and prevented from leaving hospital if it was considered that the appropriate requirements were satisfied: see the note on "in-patient in a hospital" in s.5(2). This advice is reproduced in an extended form in the General Note to s.6.

If an application is found to be fundamentally defective, authority for the patient's detention can only be obtained through a fresh application: see para.35.13 of the *Code of Practice* which states:

"If admission documents reveal a defect which fundamentally invalidates the application and which cannot, therefore, be rectified under section 15 of the Act, the patient can no longer be detained on the basis of the application. Authority for the patient's detention can be obtained only through a new application (or, in the interim, by the use of the holding powers under section 5 if the patient has already been admitted to the hospital). Unless that authority is to be sought, the hospital managers should use their power under section 23 to discharge the patient. The patient should be informed both orally and in writing, and in an accessible format for the patient."

The Care Quality Commission published guidance on "Scrutinising and Rectifying Statutory Forms for Admission under the Mental Health Act". Paragraph 5 of this document states that because "the lawfulness of an application or order is a matter for the courts, Mental Health Act Commissioners must be cautious about expressing an opinion as to the validity of an application. In particular, they may not suggest that a particular patient is entitled to be released forthwith, even if there has been a clear and fundamental breach".

The hospital managers should nominate an officer to undertake the task of scrutinising admission documents when the patient is admitted or, if the patient is already in hospital, as soon as practicable after the documents have been received: see reg.4(3) of the English Regulations and reg.4(2) of the Welsh Regulations. The *Code of Practice*, at para.35.6, distinguishes between receiving documents and scrutinising them:

"[R]eceipt involves physically receiving documents and checking that they appear to amount to an application that has been duly made (since that is sufficient to give the managers the power to detain the patient). Scrutiny involves more detailed checking for omissions, errors and other defects and, where permitted, taking action to have the documents rectified after they have already been acted on."

"Guidance on the electronic communication of statutory forms under the Mental Health Act", DHSC, 2020, para.4 states:

"Where rectifications to forms are made, including those under section 15 of the MHA, a transparent audit trail must be maintained that shows who edited the form, when they made the edit and what was added and/or omitted. All electronically completed forms should include the author's (secure) email address, alongside the postal address, in the relevant section of the statutory form so that the author can be easily contacted in case rectifications are required."

If both hard copy and electronic versions of a form exist, rectification of either form would satisfy the requirements of this section.

As to the use of obsolete or defective forms, see the General Note to Sch.1 to the English Regulations.

A person who wilfully makes a false entry or statement in an application commits an offence under s.126(4).

Human Rights Act 1998

In *M v Ukraine* [2013] M.H.L.R. 255, para.56, the European Court of Human Rights held that **1-228** although the lawfulness of detention depends on conformity with the procedural and substantive aspects of domestic law, not every fault discovered in a detention order renders the underlying detention unlawful for the purposes of art.5(1) of the European Convention on Human Rights. However, a detention order will be considered invalid if the flaw in the order amounted to a "gross and obvious irregularity" (*Mooren v Germany* (2010) 50 E.H.R.R. 23).

Electronic signatures

See the General Note to Sch.1 of the English Regulations under this heading. **1-229**

Defective Court Orders

See the note under this heading in the General Note to Part III. **1-230**

Code of Practice

Guidance on the receipt and scrutiny of documents prescribed under this Act is contained in Ch.35. **1-231**

Subsection (1)

It is submitted that: **1-232**

(1) The naming of a person who is not the patient's nearest relative on an application form is an error that can be rectified under this section if, on the information available to her, and after having made the appropriate enquiries, the approved mental health professional (AMHP) made an honest mistake because, for example, she was not aware of the existence of a close relative of the patient. The error would not be rectifiable if, on the information available to her, the person identified could not have been the patient's nearest relative. In other words, the AMHP made an error of law by misinterpreting s.26: see *Re S-C* and *R. v South Western Hospital Managers Ex p. M*, above, and *R. v Birmingham Mental Health Trust Ex p. Phillips*, noted under s.11(3), above.

(2) An honest mistake made by the AMHP regarding the identification of the patient's nearest relative which is discovered after the rectification period has expired will not render the application unlawful if the actual nearest relative is informed of his or her status and powers at the earliest opportunity.

(3) An application that is made in breach of the conflict of interest regulations made under s.12A is fundamentally defective and is not capable of being rectified.

Paragraph 31.26 of the Reference Guide states:

"In practice, any document found to contain [an error which is rectifiable under subs. (1)] should be returned to the person who signed it for amendment. When the amended document is returned to the hospital it should again be scrutinised to check that it is now in the proper form, following which consent can be given by the hospital managers (managers may authorise officers to consent to amendments on their behalf). The consent should be recorded in writing and can take the form of an endorsement on the document itself."

Beginning with   Including the day on which the patient was admitted to hospital (*Zoan v Rouamba* [2000] 2 All E.R. 620 CA).

Incorrect In that, had the facts been correctly stated, the admission would have been justified, e.g. mis-stating dates, names or places. Rectification can only be used to ensure that the relevant form reflects the factual situation that obtained when the form was completed.

Defective Probably means that incomplete information has been provided, e.g. leaving a space blank, omitting to insert a date or failing to delete one or more alternatives in places where only one can be correct. It does not mean that a completed form which accurately reflects the factual situation can be altered to provide legal justification for detention.

By whom it was signed An unsigned application or medical recommendation cannot be remedied under this section. An application or medical recommendation which is signed by a person who is not empowered to do so under this Act is also incapable of rectification. A check therefore needs to be made to confirm that the application is signed by someone who appears to be an AMHP, a nearest relative or an acting nearest relative and that the medical recommendations are signed by practitioners who are not excluded by s.12 or the regulations made under s.12A. When performing this task the scrutinising officer can take certain statements at face value: see the note on "Without further proof" in reg.3(8) of the English Regulations.

Subsection (2)

1-233   This subsection provides a remedy if *one* of the medical recommendations required under s.2 or 3 is found to be insufficient to warrant the detention of the patient. It could be used if, for example, a doctor who gives a medical recommendation for admission for treatment on Form A8 fails to convince the scrutineer that she has considered other methods of care or treatment. The hospital managers must notify the applicant in writing and if a fresh medical recommendation, not necessarily by the same doctor, is received within 14 days of the patient's admission, the application is treated as if it had been validly made from the date when it was completed. The requirement in s.12(1) that no more than five days must elapse between the two medical examinations made by the recommending doctors does not apply if a fresh medical recommendation is made under this provision. A copy of the notification to the applicant should be placed with the detention papers.
     A doctor who completes a medical recommendation on a form prescribed by the English or Welsh Regulations is acting in a clinical capacity, often in circumstances of considerable stress and urgency. The doctor is not "obliged to do any more than complete the form according to his or her professional judgment in the prescribed manner". It would be "wholly inappropriate" to treat that part of the form which requires the doctor to state the reasons why detention is required in the same way as a reasoned determination following a tribunal hearing (*R. (on the application of H) v Oxfordshire Mental Healthcare NHS Trust* [2002] EWHC Admin 465; [2002] M.H.L.R. 282, paras 70, 71, per Sullivan J.). In *Re RS's Application for Judicial Review* [2015] NICA 30, the Court of Appeal in Northern Ireland said that the *Oxfordshire* decision is authority for the proposition that the "statutory prescribed forms envisage the provision of summary reasons" (para.36).

One of the two medical recommendations A joint medical recommendation can be rectified under subs.(1) if it is "incorrect or defective". However, although a single medical recommendation can be replaced with a fresh one under this provision if it is "insufficient", this option is not available for a joint medical recommendation because both this subsection and subs.(3) are drafted on the assumption that separate recommendations have been made. There is nothing to prevent minor errors on either a joint or a single medical recommendation from being corrected: see the de minimis principle discussed in the General Note, above.

Insufficient The Reference Guide, at para.31.30, states that a "medical recommendation may be insufficient because:

- it has been signed after the date on which the application was made, or
- the doctor's reasons in the form do not appear to be sufficient to support the conclusions stated in it (but do not suggest that the conclusions are wrong or have no proper basis)"

As a document that is signed by a person who is disqualified from making a recommendation by reason of s.12 or the regulations made under s.12A does not constitute a "recommendation", it is submitted that it cannot be rectified under this provision.

The applicant   And not to the doctor who signed the recommendation. The Reference Guide, at para.31.33, recommends that the doctor should be informed of the action taken.

Subsection (3)

This subsection allows for the procedure set out in subs.(2) to be used when both recommendations   **1-234**
are good in themselves but taken together are insufficient because, for example, neither recommending doctor is "approved", under s.12 or if the examinations were too far apart. The fresh recommendation, which must be received within 14 days of the patient's admission, and the old one taken together must comply with all the requirements of the Act (subs.(2)(b)), except the requirements about the interval between recommendations and the time of the signature (subs.(2)(a)).

Subsection (4)

This subsection provides that this section cannot be used to rectify an emergency application after it   **1-235**
has expired unless it has been "converted" under the provisions of s.4(4).

POSITION OF PATIENTS SUBJECT TO DETENTION OR GUARDIANSHIP

Reclassification of patients

16.   *[Repealed by the Mental Health Act 2007 s.55, Sch.11 Pt 1]*   **1-236**

Leave of absence from hospital

17.—(1)   The [responsible clinician] may grant to any patient who is for the   **1-237**
time being liable to be detained in a hospital under this Part of this Act leave to be absent from the hospital subject to such conditions (if any) as [that clinician] considers necessary in the interests of the patient or for the protection of other persons.

(2)   Leave of absence may be granted to a patient under this section either indefinitely or on specified occasions or for any specified period; and where leave is so granted for a specified period, that period may be extended by further leave granted in the absence of the patient.

[(2A)   But longer-term leave may not be granted to a patient unless the responsible clinician first considers whether the patient should be dealt with under section 17A instead.

(2B)   For these purposes, longer-term leave is granted to a patient if—

(a)   leave of absence is granted to him under this section either indefinitely or for a specified period of more than seven consecutive days; or

(b)   a specified period is extended under this section such that the total period for which leave of absence will have been granted to him under this section exceeds seven consecutive days.]

(3)   Where it appears to the [responsible clinician] that it is necessary so to do in the interests of the patient or for the protection of other persons, he may, upon granting leave of absence under this section, direct that the patient remain in custody during his absence; and where leave of absence is so granted the patient may be kept in the custody of any officer on the staff of the hospital, or of any other person authorised in writing by the managers of the hospital or, if the patient is required in accordance with conditions imposed on the grant of leave of absence to reside in another hospital, of any officer on the staff of that other hospital.

(4)   In any case where a patient is absent from a hospital in pursuance of leave of absence granted under this section, and it appears to the [responsible clinician] that it is necessary so to do in the interests of the patient's health or safety or for the protection of other persons, [that clinician] may, subject to subsection (5) below,

by notice in writing given to the patient or to the person for the time being in charge of the patient, revoke the leave of absence and recall the patient to the hospital.

(5) A patient to whom leave of absence is granted under this section shall not be recalled under subsection (4) above after he has ceased to be liable to be detained under this Part of this Act; [...].

[(6) Subsection (7) below applies to a person who is granted leave by or by virtue of a provision—

    (a) in force in Scotland, Northern Ireland, any of the Channel Islands or the Isle of Man; and

    (b) corresponding to subsection (1) above.

(7) For the purpose of giving effect to a direction or condition imposed by virtue of a provision corresponding to subsection (3) above, the person may be conveyed to a place in, or kept in custody or detained at a place of safety in, England and Wales by a person authorised in that behalf by the direction or condition.]

Amendments

The amendments to this section were made by the Mental Health Act 2007 ss.9(3), 33(2), 39(1) and the Mental Health (Patients in the Community) Act 1995 s.3(1).

Definitions

1-238
patient: s.145(1).
hospital: ss.34(2), 145(1).
absent without leave: ss.18(6), 145(1).
responsible clinician: s.34(1).
the managers: s.145(1).

General Note

1-239
    This section provides for the responsible clinician (RC) of a patient to grant that patient leave of absence from the hospital in which he is liable to be detained for a specified or for an indefinite period and subject to such conditions as are considered to be necessary. The period of leave may be extended without the patient having to return to hospital. Longer-term leave of absence (i.e. leave for more than seven consecutive days) can only be granted if the patient's RC first considers whether the patient should be made subject to a community treatment order (CTO) (subss.(2A), (2B)). The leave of absence of a restricted patient for both community and medical leave is subject to the agreement of the Secretary of State: see below and the notes on s.41(3)(c) under "Leave of Absence".
    The RC should weigh up and record the potential benefits and risks before making a decision about leave of absence (*G v Central and North West London Mental Health NHS Trust* [2007] EWHC 3086 (QB); [2008] M.H.L.R. 24, para.152). It is unlawful to grant leave of absence to a patient who has been admitted to hospital for a purely nominal period: see the note on "any patient who is ... liable to be detained" in subs.(1). There is no legal obligation to obtain the patient's consent to the leave, and a combination of ss.18(7) and 137 provides authority for the use of force to ensure that the patient is taken to the place where he is required to be. The RC has no power to grant leave of absence to patients who have been remanded to hospital by a court under ss.35 or 36, or who are subject to an interim hospital made under s.38. Any patient who is granted leave of absence can kept in custody under the procedure set out in subs.(3).
    Paragraph 27.22 of the *Code of Practice* states:

"Hospital managers should establish a standardised system by which responsible clinicians can record the leave they authorise and specify the conditions attached to it. Copies of the authorisation should be given to the patient and to any carers, professionals and other people in the community who need to know. A copy should also be kept in the patient's notes. In case they fail to return from leave, an up-to-date description of the patient should be available in their notes. A photograph of the patient should also be included in their notes, if necessary with the patient's consent (or if the patient lacks capacity to decide whether to consent, a photograph is taken in accordance with the Mental Capacity Act (MCA))."

A "section 17 leave form" is not a statutory document and should not be treated as such.

A patient who has been granted leave of absence under this section continues to be "liable to be detained" and is therefore subject to the consent to treatment provisions in Pt IV (s.56(3)). Although there is nothing in the Act that prevents staff from using force to ensure that a patient on s.17 leave in a non-clinical setting receives medication provided under the authority of Pt IV, this practice could be unsafe for both patient and staff and, in the absence of an emergency, it would be better for the forcible administration of medication to take place after the patient has been recalled to hospital. Paragraph 27.25 of the *Code of Practice* states:

"A patient who is granted leave under section 17 remains liable to be detained, and the rules in part 4 of the Act about their medical treatment continue to apply (see chapter 24). If it becomes necessary to administer treatment without the patient's consent, consideration should be given to whether it would be more appropriate to recall the patient to hospital (see paragraphs 27.32 – 27.36), although recall is not a legal requirement."

A patient can be recalled to the detaining hospital from leave of absence if the RC considers it necessary to do so in the interests of the patient's health or safety or for the protection of others (subs.(4)).

A s.3 patient who has been granted leave under this section can have his detention renewed under s.20 if the patient's RC considers that hospital inpatient or outpatient treatment constitutes a significant part of the patient's treatment plan: see the note on s.20(4)(c)).

In *R. (on the application of K) v West London Mental Health NHS Trust* [2006] EWCA Civ 118; [2006] M.H.L.R. 89, the Court of Appeal held that:

1. A RC has no power to give directions as to how others are to discharge their functions and this section cannot be construed as conferring such a power.
2. The Secretary of State (or his delegate) is not obliged to use his best endeavours to give effect to a decision of a RC under this section.

This case is considered in the General Note to the Act under *Allocation of resources to detained patients*.

Further provisions relating to ground access, leave of absence and the escorting of patients from high security hospitals can be found at Appendix C.

A patient who has been granted leave of absence to reside in the community has been discharged *from the hospital* for the purposes of the social security legislation, although he has not been discharged *from the section* that provides the authority for his continued liability to be detained. There is no requirement for the hospital to keep a bed open for the patient while he is on long-term leave of absence.

The duty to provide aftercare services applies to a s.3 patient on leave of absence (see the note on "cease to be detained" in s.117(1)).

It is an offence to induce or help a patient absent himself without leave or to harbour or prevent a patient being returned to hospital (s.128).

This section applies without modification to patients who have been made subject to hospital or guardianship orders by a court under s.37 (Sch.1 Pt 1 para.1). It also applies, with subss.(1), (4) and (5) modified as set out below and subss.(2A) and (2B) omitted, to restricted patients (Sch.1 Pt II paras 2, 3):

"(1)   The [responsible clinician] may [with the consent of the Secretary of State] grant to any patient who is for the time being liable to be detained in a hospital under this Part of this Act leave to be absent from the hospital subject to such conditions (if any) as [that clinician] considers necessary in the interests of the patient or for the protection of other persons."

"(4)   In any case where a patient is absent from a hospital in pursuance of leave of absence granted under this section, and it appears to the [the responsible clinician] [or the Secretary of State] that it is necessary so to do in the interests of the patient's health or safety or for the protection of other persons, [that clinician] [or the Secretary of State] may, subject to subsection (5) below, by notice in writing given to the patient or to the person for the time being in charge of the patient, revoke the leave of absence and recall the patient to the hospital."

"(5)   A patient to whom leave of absence is granted under this section shall not be recalled [by the [responsible clinician]] under subs.(4) above after [the expiration of the period of [12] months beginning with the first day of his absence on leave]."

Leave of absence for restricted patients

See above and the notes to s.41(3)(c).   **1-240**

Leave of absence and deprivations of liberty

1-241   In *Welsh Ministers v PJ* [2018] UKSC 66; [2018] M.H.L.R. 411, the Supreme Court held that there is no implied power to impose conditions in a community treatment order which have the effect of depriving a patient of his liberty. It is submitted that the logical implication of this decision is that, apart from the express power contained in subs.(3) to deprive a patient of his liberty, no such power exist under this section. If the implementation of the care plan of a mentally incapacitated patient has the effect of depriving him of his liberty, the deprivation may be authorised under either the deprivation of liberty procedure set out in Sch.A1 to the Mental Capacity Act 2005 or an order of the Court of Protection made under s.16(2)(a) of that Act. If it is possible for the procedure under Sch.A1 to be used, an application should not be made to the Court of Protection for authorisation (*A Local Authority v PB* [2011] EWCOP 2675, para.64(iii)). An authorisation can only be granted under the 2005 Act if there is no conflict between it and a condition of the patient's leave: see Sch.1A, Case B.

In *A Hospital Trust v CD* [2015] EWCOP 74, Mostyn J. held that if a mentally incapacitated patient who is detained under this Act is granted leave of absence to be treated in another hospital for a physical disorder and is deprived of his liberty there, the patient will be eligible for the purposes of the deprivation of liberty procedure under the 2005 Act. However, note that in *R. (on the application of Ferreira) v HM Senior Coroner for Inner South London* [2017] EWCA Civ 31, the Court of Appeal held the patient was not deprived of her liberty because she was being treated for a physical illness and her treatment was that which it appeared to all intents would have been administered to a person who did not have her mental impairment. The patient was "physically restricted in her movements by her physical infirmities and by the treatment she received (which for example included sedation) but the root cause of any loss of liberty was her physical condition, not any restrictions imposed by the hospital" (para.10).

The 2005 Act procedures are not required to authorise the transport a mentally incapacitated patient to his intended place of residence as authority for conveying the patient is contained in ss.18(7) and 137. As the patient is liable to be detained during the conveyance, his rights under art.5 of the European Convention on Human Rights are protected: see the note on *Human Rights Act 1998*, below.

Leave of absence to another hospital

1-242   It is lawful to use this section to grant a patient "trial leave" to a hospital other than the one in which he is formally detained and for the patient to be kept in the custody of the staff of that hospital (subs.(3)). Such leave can be useful step in a patient's rehabilitation programme. In these circumstances, the approved clinician (AC) who is in charge of the patient's treatment at the base hospital continues to be the patient's RC. Although day-to-day functions relating to the care of the patient can be delegated to an AC at the second hospital, the responsibilities of the RC to renew the patient's detention and to issue certificates under Pt IV cannot be delegated. If the trial leave is successful, the patient could be transferred to the second hospital under s.19.

If the patient has been granted leave of absence to be a patient at another hospital, the conditions of the leave could enable: (i) the patient to have periods of leave for specified purposes from that hospital; and (ii) the patient's AC at the other hospital to have discretion to determine when such leave should be taken.

Guidance on "Leave to reside in other hospitals" is given in the following paragraphs of the *Code of Practice*:

"27.30 Responsible clinicians may require patients, as a condition of leave, to reside at another hospital in England and Wales, and they may then be kept in the custody of staff of that hospital. Before authorising leave on this basis, responsible clinicians should consider whether it would be more appropriate to transfer the patient to the other hospital instead (see chapter 37).

27.31 Where a patient is granted leave of absence to another hospital, the responsible clinician at the first hospital should remain in overall charge of the patient's case. If it is thought that a clinician at the other hospital should become the responsible clinician, the patient should instead be transferred to that hospital. An approved clinician in charge of any particular aspect of the patient's treatment may be from either hospital (for further guidance on allocating responsible clinicians see chapter 36)."

Leave of absence to Scotland, Northern Ireland, the Channel Islands or the Isle of Man

1-243   A patient who is granted escorted leave of absence to travel to Scotland will be subject to the Mental Health (Cross-border Visits) (Scotland) Regulations 2008 (SSI 2008/181) which provide that where patients have been granted leave of absence to travel to Scotland, they may be kept in charge of a person who is authorised for that purpose in relation to the leave. In addition, the Regulations make provision for such escorts to have the power to restrain and retake such patients in the event that they abscond.

Paragraph 25.7 of the Reference Guide states:

"Escorted leave to Scotland, Northern Ireland, the Channel Islands or the Isle of Man can only be granted if the law in the jurisdiction in question allows the patient to be kept in custody once there. At the time of publication, this applies only in Scotland."

Contradictory guidance regarding the position in Northern Ireland is given at para.27.28 of the *Code of Practice* which states:

"Escorted leave to Northern Ireland is permitted under the Act – patients may be held in lawful custody by a constable or a person authorised in writing by the managers of the hospital. In Scotland, the Isle of Man or any of the Channel Islands escorted leave can only be granted if the local legislation allows such patients to be kept in custody while in that jurisdiction. If this is contemplated for a restricted patient seek advice from the Mental Health Casework Section of the Ministry of Justice."

The reason for the stance taken by the Code can be found in a case where the patient wished to be granted escorted leave to travel to Northern Ireland (personal communication). After initially defending the case, the Secretary of State for Justice submitted the following statement to the Court accepting that such leave was in fact possible:

"(1)   A person who is granted leave of absence from hospital in England & Wales ("the hospital") under s.17(1) of the Mental Health Act 1983 ("the Act"), subject to a direction under s.17(3) of the Act that he remain in custody during his absence, may be held in lawful custody whilst in Northern Ireland by a constable or by a person authorised in writing by the managers of the hospital, under ss. 137 and 147 of the Act.

(2)   If such a person escapes from lawful custody, whether in England & Wales or in Northern Ireland, he may be taken into custody in, and returned to England & Wales from, Northern Ireland under ss. 88, 138 and 147 of the Act."

Human Rights Act 1998

A patient who has been granted leave of absence under this section continues to be "detained" for   **1-244**
the purposes of art.5 of the Convention on Human Rights (ECHR): see *L v Sweden*, App.No.10801/84, noted under the heading "detention" in the note on art.5(1)(e). In this case, the European Commission on Human Rights held that the granting of leave of absence with a condition that the patient accepts medication will not contravene the ECHR if one of the grounds in art.8(2) is satisfied. In order to satisfy one of the grounds in art.8(2) to justify the violation, the patient must be informed of both the nature of the conditions and the likely consequence of breaching the conditions (*Lambert v France* (2000) 30 E.H.R.R. 346). Also see the note on "conditions" in subs.(1).

Applications to the First-tier Tribunal (Mental Health) or the Mental Health Review Tribunal for Wales

Patients on leave of absence may make an application to a tribunal as if they were still detained in   **1-245**
hospital.

Code of Practice

Guidance on the use of this section is contained in Ch.27. Advice on deciding between guardian-   **1-246**
ship, leave of absence and supervised community treatment can be found in Ch.31.

Subsection (1)

The responsible clinician may grant   Neither the hospital managers nor hospital management can   **1-247**
restrict the exercise of the RC's discretion under this provision. The permission of the Secretary of State for Justice is required for restricted patients: see the notes on s.41(3)(c). It is lawful for the Secretary of State to decline permission unless suitable conditions are imposed by the RC (*R. (on the application of RA) v Secretary of State for the Home Department* [2002] EWHC 1618 (Admin); [2003] M.H.L.R. 54, para.41).

The RC can grant a patient leave of absence over the telephone in urgent cases. The RC does not have the power to delegate functions under this section (although the power can be exercised by another AC acting as RC in the absence of the patient's usual RC): also see the note on *Leave of absence to another hospital*, above. Paragraph 27.14 of the *Code of Practice* states:

"Hospital managers cannot overrule a responsible clinician's decision to grant leave. The fact that a responsible clinician grants leave subject to certain conditions, eg residence at a hostel, does not oblige the hospital managers, or anyone else, to arrange or fund the particular placement or services the clinician has in mind. Responsible clinicians should not grant leave on such a basis without first taking steps to establish that the necessary services or accommodation (or both) are available and will be funded." RCs "may decide to authorise short-term local leave, which may be managed by other staff. For example, patients may be given leave for a shopping trip of two hours every week to a specific destination, with the decision on which particular two hours to be left to the discretion of the responsible nursing staff" (*Code of Practice*, para.27.15). The patient's RC "may instruct nursing staff not to implement any authorised leave on medical grounds at their discretion" (MHAC, *Sixth Biennial Report*, para.9.4).

If a detained patient needs to be moved to a general hospital as a matter of urgency for treatment for a physical disorder or injury, legal authority for the move is present if either (1) leave of absence for such a move has been granted by the RC in anticipation of such an eventuality occurring; or (2) the RC has granted leave of absence over the telephone at the time of the emergency. Authority for treating the patient for the disorder or injury must be found in the common law or the Mental Capacity Act 2005 if the disorder or injury is not related to the patient's mental disorder: see the note on "medical treatment ... for the mental disorder" in s.63. If the urgency of the situation is such that there is no time to contact the RC and anticipatory leave has not been granted, the 2005 Act will provide authority for a mentally incapacitated patient to be moved to the general hospital. A mentally capable patient can be moved to the hospital with his consent. In both cases, the RC should grant the patient leave of absence under this section at the earliest opportunity as the patient is technically absent without leave. Given that an urgent need for a patient to be transferred to a general hospital for treatment is unpredictable, anticipatory leave to cover such a situation should be granted as a matter of routine.

A general hospital that receives a patient under this section for treatment for a physical disorder of injury need not be registered with the CQC to treat patients who are detained under this Act: see the note on "hospital" in s.145(1).

Any patient who is ... liable to be detained   Including a patient who has been detained under s.2 or s.4. In order to be granted leave of absence, the patient must have become an in-patient of the hospital named in the application (see the note on "in-patient" in s.5(2)) and the hospital must have accepted the application (see the note on "sufficient authority for the Managers" in s.6(2)). It is unlawful to grant leave of absence to a patient who has been admitted and detained in hospital for a purely nominal period during which no necessary treatment has been given (*R. v Hallstrom Ex p. W* [1986] 2 All E.R. 306).

A patient who has been detained under s.5(2) cannot be granted leave of absence because such a patient does not have a RC: see the definition of RC in s.34(1).

From the hospital   Which is the hospital named in the application or order which provides authority for the patient's detention. Every absence from hospital, however brief, requires leave to be given under this section. With the exception of a restricted patient who is detained in a named hospital unit (see the General Note to s.41) and a patient who moves between high security psychiatric services and other services provided at the same hospital (s.145(1AA)), leave is not required for the patient to move from one hospital building to another or to have access to the grounds of the hospital. A decision to allow the patient to leave the ward area, but not the hospital, is a clinical decision that should be made following a risk assessment. Paragraph 27.5 of the *Code of Practice* states:

"Except for certain restricted patients (see paragraphs 27.39 – 27.42 and 22.53 – 22.60) no formal procedure is required to allow patients to move within a hospital or its grounds. Such 'ground leave' within a hospital may be encouraged or, where necessary, restricted, as part of each patient's care plan."

A particular difficulty has arisen where a single hospital site contains a psychiatric and a general facility and the two facilities are administered by different NHS Trusts. In this situation, should a detained patient who needs treatment for a physical disorder at the general facility be sent to that facility under the authority of s.17 leave? Paragraph 27.7 of the *Code of Practice* answers this question by confirming that leave of absence under this section should be granted:

"What constitutes a particular hospital for the purpose of leave is a matter of fact which can be determined only in the light of the particular case. Where one building, or set of buildings, includes accommodation under the management of different bodies (eg two different NHS trusts), the accommodation used by each body should be treated as forming separate hospitals. Facilities and grounds shared by both can be regarded as part of both hospitals."

Conditions   There are no mandatory conditions that must be imposed by the RC. Conditions could, for example, require the patient to live with a particular person or at a specified place, to be a patient at another hospital, to maintain contact with the care co-ordinator, to abstain from substance misuse or to accept prescribed medication. Conditions of this nature constitute interferences with the patient's right to respect for family life under art.8(1) of the ECHR and a justification for the interference would have to be found in art.8(2): see the note on *Human Rights Act 1998*, above.

Authority for conveying the patient to a hospital or other place specified in the leave of absence is contained in ss.18(7) and 137.

Subsection (2)

Specified occasions   Such as visits to the patient's home or shopping expeditions. The RC should   **1-248**
consider whether a condition that the patient be escorted should be attached to such leave (*Code of Practice*, para.27.27).

Subsections (2A), 2(B)

These subsections do not apply to restricted patients: see the General Note, above. The *Code of*   **1-249**
Practice states:

"27.11 Leave should normally be of short duration and not normally more than seven days. When considering whether to grant leave of absence for more than seven consecutive days, or extending leave so that the total period is more than seven consecutive days, responsible clinicians should also consider whether the patient should go onto a community treatment order (CTO) instead and, if required, consult any local agencies concerned with public protection. This does not apply to restricted patients, nor, in practice, to patients detained for assessment under section 2 of the Act, as they are not eligible to be placed on a CTO.

27.12 The option of using a CTO does not mean that the responsible clinician cannot use longer-term leave if that is the more suitable option, but the responsible clinician will need to be able to show that both options have been duly considered. Decisions should be explained to the patient and fully documented, including why the patient is not considered suitable for a CTO, and also guardianship or discharge." Paragraph 31.5 of the Code contains the following guidance:

"Leave of absence may be useful in the longer term (more than seven consecutive days) where the clinical team wish to see how the patient manages outside hospital before making the decision to discharge. Leave for a longer period should also be for a specific purpose or a fixed period, and not normally more than one month. For most patients who are able to live in the community, a CTO should be considered a better option than longer-term leave for the ongoing management of their care."

The guidance that leave should not normally be more than seven days (para.27.11) or a month (para.31.5) is unduly restrictive. Patients have been successfully granted lengthy periods of s.17 leave, in some cases for a number of years, because such leave is considered to be a more suitable option than a CTO (see below).

Placing the patient on a CTO is an alternative to the practice of providing the patient with extended s.17 leave. Extended s.17 leave allows for the detention of a patient who has been placed in the community on leave of absence to be renewed under s.20 if a significant component of the patient's care plan is treatment at a hospital: see *R. (on the application of DR) v Mersey Care NHS Trust* [2002] EWHC 1810 (Admin); [2002] M.H.L.R. 386 and *R. (on the application of CS) v Mental Health Review Tribunal* [2004] EWHC 2958 (Admin); [2004] M.H.R.R. 355 which are noted under s.20(4)(c). Although these cases pre-date the introduction of CTOs, they continue to have effect (*KL v Somerset Partnership NHS Foundation Trust* [2011] UKUT 233 (AAC); [2011] M.H.L.R. 194, para.11).

Subsection (2A) uses the term "considers" without qualification. It does not state that the RC should consider a CTO and go down that route unless she has good reason not to do so. The RC is therefore obliged to examine the respective merits of a CTO and extended s.17 leave and reach a conclusion as to which is the better option for a particular patient. The Act does not provide any guidance to the RC on the criteria that should be used when coming to such a decision. RCs might prefer to use the leave option if, for example, there is a need to test out the patient's response to being on leave of absence for a period of longer than seven days before moving on to a CTO, if the patient needs to be detained in his placement (see subs.(3)), if it is anticipated that the patient might need to be recalled to hospital for more than the 72-hour period provided for in s.17F(6) or if the patient's needs could be better met by the greater flexibility provided for by s.17. A patient's antagonism to being on a CTO might also be a factor in favour of using the s.17 regime. Both options provide the RC with a power of recall.

Subsection (3)

1-250   This subsection, which authorises a deprivation of the patient's liberty (*PH v A Clinical Commissioning Group* [2022] EWCOP 12, para.19), states that the RC may direct that the patient must remain in custody during his leave if it is necessary in the interest of the patient or for the protection of other persons. Such a patient is in "legal custody" for the purposes of s.137. Patients may be kept in the custody of any officer on the staff of the hospital or any person authorised in writing by the hospital managers. If the patient is sent on leave to a care home or other non-hospital setting, the staff there must be given written authorisation by the hospital managers if they are to keep the patient in custody. The hospital managers remain legally responsible for the patient during the leave. A patient who has been granted leave under this provision can have his detention renewed under s.20 if the patient's RC considers that hospital inpatient or outpatient treatment constitutes a significant part of the patient's treatment plan: see the note on s.20(4)(c)).

The purpose of this provision is to provide those who are caring for a patient during a period of leave with an immediate power to restrain the patient should he make an attempt to abscond. Its effect is that the patient may be detained in the named hospital or care home during the period of leave and he may be escorted at all times. This power can be used to put in place security measures for patients who pose a risk to themselves or to others and to patients whose mental disorder requires that significant restrictions be placed on their movements.

Where a mentally incapacitated patient's arrangements on leave will amount to a deprivation of liberty, the RC should consider whether it is possible for that deprivation of liberty to be authorised through the use of this provision. Only if that is not appropriate should consideration be given to using a deprivation of liberty authorisation under the Mental Capacity Act 2005.

With regard to restricted patients, para.3 of "Guidance: Discharge conditions that amount to deprivation of liberty", which is reproduced in Part 4, states:

"If a patient is being considered for discharge and the responsible clinician considers that they no longer require treatment in hospital, but are not yet suitable for discharge without constant supervision, the Secretary of State can consider providing his consent to a long-term escorted leave of absence, under section 17(3) MHA."

If the leave is being used to test out whether a mentally incapacitated restricted patient can be conditionally discharged to the placement, see para.6.1 of the guidance.

A patient who escapes from custody can be re-captured immediately using the power contained in s.18; there is no need to wait for him to fail to return to the "base" hospital or for the leave to be revoked under subs.(4). For provisions relating to the powers of the person having custody of the patient, see ss.137 and 138.

Authorised in writing by the managers of the hospital   See reg.19 of the English Regulations and reg.35 of the Welsh Regulations.

Officer on the staff of the hospital   "Officer" is not defined in the Act and could include an employee who is neither a nurse nor a doctor. If the patient is to be escorted by a friend or relative, see para.27.29 of the *Code of Practice* which states:

"While it may often be appropriate to authorise leave subject to the condition that a patient is accompanied by a friend or relative (eg on a pre-arranged day out from the hospital), responsible clinicians should specify that the patient is to be in the legal custody of a friend or relative only if it is appropriate for that person to be legally responsible for the patient, and if that person understands and accepts the consequent responsibility."

Subsection (4)

This subsection provides for the revocation of leave of absence and the return of the patient to the hospital where he is liable to be detained. There is no power to recall the patient to a different hospital. Subsequent to the recall, the patient could be transferred to another hospital under s.19. It is submitted that the patient can be returned to hospital as an outpatient. Paragraph 29.59 of the Code allows for this option for CTO patients and *R. (on the application of DR) v Mersey Care NHS Trust* [2002] M.H.L.R. 386 is supportive of such an approach. **1-251**

Before issuing a recall notice the RC should "consider what effect being recalled would have on the patient" (*Code of Practice*, para.27.32). Leave of absence may only be revoked when it is necessary in the interests of the patient's health or safety or for the protection of other persons that he be returned to the hospital. Paragraph 27.32 of the *Code of Practice* states that a "refusal to take medication would not on its own be a reason for revocation, although it would almost always be a reason to consider revocation". It is unlawful to recall a patient to hospital merely to facilitate the renewal of the patient's detention under s.20 (*R. v Hallstrom Ex p. W* [1986] 2 All E.R. 306). There is no mechanism in the Act that provides for the review of a decision to recall.

Paragraph 4.18 of the *Code of Practice* states that where a patient is to be recalled to hospital, "the responsible clinician should give (or arrange for the patient to be given) oral reasons for the decision before the recall. The patient may nominate another person who they wish to be notified of the decision".

In the absence of an emergency, a patient's leave of absence should not be revoked without up to date medical evidence to demonstrate that he remains mentally disordered (*Kay v United Kingdom* (1998) 40 B.M.L.R. 20 ECtHR).

A patient who refuses to return to the hospital becomes a patient absent without leave (s.18(1)(b)) and may be taken into custody and returned to the hospital by the categories of persons set out in s.18(1).

Notice in writing   Paragraph 27.33 of the *Code of Practice* states:

"The responsible clinician must arrange for a notice in writing revoking the leave to be served on the patient or on the person who is for the time being in charge of the patient. Hospitals should always know the address of patients who are on leave of absence and of anyone with responsibility for them whilst on leave."

The Mental Welfare Commission for Scotland made the following comment on an equivalent provision in the Mental Health (Scotland) Act 1984: "In practical terms, particularly in emergency situations where the patient's condition has rapidly deteriorated, the staff who are returning the patient may have to deliver the letter of recall at the time they are taking him into custody" (Annual Report 1999–2000, p.23).

Subsection (5)

This subsection provides that an unrestricted patient cannot be recalled once the power to detain him has lapsed. A restriction order patient can be recalled by his RC at any time up to 12 months from the first day of his absence on leave. The Secretary of State can recall such a patient at any time (see the General Note to this section). **1-252**

Subsections (6), (7)

The effect of these provisions is explained in the Reference Guide: **1-253**

"11.21 A patient can be kept in custody, conveyed to a particular place or detained in a place of safety in England or Wales, if that is a condition of leave of absence from hospital granted under equivalent legislation in Scotland, Northern Ireland, the Isle of Man or any of the Channel Islands.

11.22 In each case, section 137 means they are deemed to be in legal custody while being escorted, conveyed or detained in England and Wales. As a result, if they abscond while in England or Wales, they may be retaken, under section 138, by the person authorised to keep the patient in custody in England, by a police officer, or other constable, or by an AMHP, for as long as they could be retaken under the legislation in the jurisdiction from which they are on leave."

[Community treatment orders

17A.—(1)   The responsible clinician may by order in writing discharge a detained patient from hospital subject to his being liable to recall in accordance with section 17E below. **1-254**

(2)   A detained patient is a patient who is liable to be detained in a hospital in pursuance of an application for admission for treatment.

(3)   An order under subsection (1) above is referred to in this Act as a "community treatment order".

(4)   The responsible clinician may not make a community treatment order unless—

    (a)   in his opinion, the relevant criteria are met; and

    (b)   an approved mental health professional states in writing—

        (i)   that he agrees with that opinion; and

        (ii)   that it is appropriate to make the order.

(5)   The relevant criteria are—

    (a)   the patient is suffering from mental disorder of a nature or degree which makes it appropriate for him to receive medical treatment;

    (b)   it is necessary for his health or safety or for the protection of other persons that he should receive such treatment;

    (c)   subject to his being liable to be recalled as mentioned in paragraph (d) below, such treatment can be provided without his continuing to be detained in a hospital;

    (d)   it is necessary that the responsible clinician should be able to exercise the power under section 17E(1) below to recall the patient to hospital; and

    (e)   appropriate medical treatment is available for him.

(6)   In determining whether the criterion in subsection (5)(d) above is met, the responsible clinician shall, in particular, consider, having regard to the patient's history of mental disorder and any other relevant factors, what risk there would be of a deterioration of the patient's condition if he were not detained in a hospital (as a result, for example, of his refusing or neglecting to receive the medical treatment he requires for his mental disorder).

(7)   In this Act—

    "community patient" means a patient in respect of whom a community treatment order is in force;

    "the community treatment order", in relation to such a patient, means the community treatment order in force in respect of him; and

    "the responsible hospital", in relation to such a patient, means the hospital in which he was liable to be detained immediately before the community treatment order was made, subject to section 19A below.]

Amendment

This section was inserted by the Mental Health Act 2007 s.32(2).

Definitions

1-255   responsible clinician: s.34(1).
patient: s.145(1).
application for admission for treatment: s.145(1).
approved mental health professional: s.145(1), (1AC).
mental disorder: ss.1, 145(1).
medical treatment: s.145(1).
hospital: ss.34(2), 145(1).

General Note

An overview of supervised community treatment, a term that is not to be found in the Act, is set out at para.107 of the Explanatory Notes to the 2007 Act: **1-256**

"The supervised community treatment (SCT) provisions will allow some patients with a mental disorder to live in the community whilst still being subject to powers under the 1983 Act. Only those patients who are detained in hospital for treatment will be eligible to be considered for SCT. In order for a patient to be placed on SCT, various criteria need to be met. An AMHP also needs to agree that SCT is appropriate. Patients who are on SCT will be subject to conditions whilst living in the community. Most conditions will depend on individual circumstances but must be for the purpose of ensuring the patient receives medical treatment, or to prevent risk of harm to the patient or others. Such conditions will form part of the patient's community treatment order (CTO) which is made by the RC. Patients on SCT may be recalled to hospital for treatment should this become necessary. Afterwards they may then resume living in the community or, if they need to be treated as an in-patient again, their RC may revoke the CTO and the patient will remain in hospital for the time being."

The following description of the CTO regime is taken from the judgment of the Court of Appeal in *Secretary of State for Justice v MM; Welsh Ministers v PJ* [2017] EWCA Civ 194; [2017] M.H.L.R. 282. The deletions made to the extracts, which were made by UT Judge Ward in *LW v Cornwall Partnership NHS Trust* [2018] UKUT 408; [2019] M.H.L.R. 6 at para.11, are concerned with specific issues that arose in the *PJ* case:

"47. The CTO scheme is set out in sections 17A to 17E, inclusive, of the MHA. The powers of tribunals in respect of patients under the scheme are set out in section 72 .... It is necessary to appreciate the roles and responsibilities of those involved in the CTO scheme in the context of the overall statutory framework in order to interpret that framework in a way that is consistent with the fundamental features of the legislation.

48. ... [T]he authority for the detention of a patient who is subject to a CTO ('a community patient') is suspended during the CTO by reason of section 17D(2)(a). A community patient is not liable to be detained in hospital although he may be recalled for treatment under section 17E. The exercise of the power of recall, which rests solely with the responsible clinician, is not dependent upon any compliance with or alleged breach of the CTO conditions.....

49. Sections 17A and 17B MHA provide the lawful authority for a responsible clinician to make a CTO. Section 17B(2) is the source of the power for the responsible clinician to make conditions that are necessary and appropriate for one or more of three defined purposes: a) ensuring that the patient receives medical treatment, b) preventing risk of harm to the patient's health or safety, and c) protecting other persons. Those purposes have to be read in conjunction with the power granted to the responsible clinician to make a CTO. That power is constrained so that a CTO may not be made unless the relevant criteria are met. The criteria are set out in section 17A(5). They include the continuing necessity for medical treatment for the patient's health and safety or the protection of other persons, the necessity of the retention of the power of recall to hospital and that appropriate medical treatment is available and can be provided for the patient without his continuing detention in a hospital.

50. The terms of the power are wide. It is clear from the nature and extent of the CTO scheme that the object of the power is to provide a balance between the protection of the patient and the public and the receipt by him of medical treatment without his continuing detention in hospital, where that is appropriate....
...

The safeguards:
54. The CTO scheme is provided for in a statutory framework that is a procedure prescribed by law. The criteria for the imposition of conditions that may deprive a patient of his liberty are specified in sections 17A(4) to (5) and 17B(2) MHA. They are limited to the purposes of the legislation, for example, for medical treatment. They are time limited by section 17C and they are subject to regular rights of review by sections 20A and 66 which are equivalent to the rights enjoyed by a patient detained in hospital so that there is no incoherence or lack of equivalence in the safeguards provided by the scheme. The conditions in a CTO have to be in writing: see, for example sections 17A(1) and 17B(4). The responsible clinician has the power of recall (sections 17E(1) and (2)) and the powers of suspension and variation (sections 17B(4) and (5))...."

The purpose of a CTO is set out at para.29.5 of the *Code of Practice*:

"The purpose of a CTO is to allow suitable patients to be safely treated in the community rather than under detention in hospital, and to provide a way to help prevent relapse and any harm – to the patient or to others – that this might cause. It is intended to help patients to maintain stable mental health outside hospital and to promote recovery. The principles, in particular, treating patients using the least restrictive option and maximising their independence; and purpose and effectiveness should always be considered when considering CTOs."

During the passage of the 2007 Act through Parliament, an amendment that tried to restrict CTOs to people who had been detained more than once was not made. It is therefore the case that the use of CTOs is not restricted to patients who have a history of non-compliance with medication, i.e. "revolving door patients".

A patient who is subject to a CTO is referred to throughout the Act as a community patient (s.17A(7)). The patient will be subject to the after-care provisions of s.117 as long as he is a community patient (s.117(2)). Part IVA provides for the regulation of treatment for the patient's mental disorder whilst in the community. Unlike guardianship, a CTO is not limited to patients who are over the age of 16.

Making a patient subject to a CTO is an alternative to granting the patient long-term leave of absence under s.17 and before an RC places a patient on such leave, she must "consider" whether the patient should be dealt with under this section: see the note on s.17(2A), (2B). For an account of the use of CTOs, see "Community treatment orders in England: review of usage from national data", S. Gupta et al, *BJPsych Bulletin* (2018) 42, 119–122.

Procedure

1-257   This section enables a CTO to be made by the patient's RC if she is satisfied that all of the criteria set out in subs.(5) are satisfied (subs.(4)(a)), and an AMHP agrees that the criteria are met and that an order is appropriate (subs.(4)(b)). The AMHP and the RC could be members of the same clinical team. There are no time limits that regulate the lapse of time that may take place between the AMHP's agreement and the signing of Form CTO 1 by the RC. It is submitted that the RC has an implied power to cancel a Form CTO 1 before the date and time when the CTO is stated to come into effect: see Part 3 of Form CTO1. Unlike an application for detention, there is no requirement for a Form CTO 1 to be accepted by the hospital managers before the CTO comes into force.

Patients can only be placed on a CTO if they have been either detained under s.3 or made subject to an order under Pt III without restrictions (or is treated as such after transfer from another jurisdiction): see the note to subs.(2). It is not possible for a CTO patient also to be subject to guardianship: see ss.6(4) and 8(5). The CTO must be made subject to certain conditions (s.17B) and the RC is empowered to order the patient's recall to hospital (s.17E). The duration of the CTO is specified in s.17C. Responsibility for a community patient may be assigned to another hospital under reg.17 of the English Regulations or reg.25 of the Welsh Regulations.

Although the patient's consent to the making of a CTO is not a legal requirement, "in practice patients will need to be involved in decisions about the treatment to be provided in the community and how and where it is to be given, and be prepared to co-operate with treatment" (*Code of Practice*, para.29.17). Although the patient's nearest relative cannot prevent a CTO being made, he or she can discharge the order (s.23(2)(c)).

Section 132A requires the relevant hospital managers to give information to community patients and, unless the patient objects, their nearest relatives about the effect of the CTO and their right to make an application to a tribunal. For the responsibility to inform the patient's nearest relative of the assignment of the patient to another hospital, see reg.26(1)(h) of the English Regulations and reg.32(b) of the Welsh Regulations.

Under s.130D, the:

"managers of the responsible hospital must take steps to give CTO patients information about the availability of independent mental health advocates (IMHA). Unless the patient requests otherwise, or does not have a nearest relative, the managers must also take whatever steps are practicable to give this information to the person they think is the patient's nearest relative. This must be done as soon as practicable after the CTO is made" (Reference Guide, para.26.30).

Although there is no provision in the Act for the documents relating to CTOs to be rectified, appropriate arrangements should be put in place to check that such documents have been properly completed: see the following paragraphs of the *Code of Practice*:

"35.16 There are no provisions in the Act for community treatment orders (CTOs) and related documents to be rectified once made. Hospital managers should nonetheless ensure that arrangements are in place to check that documents have been properly -completed. Significant errors or inadequacies may render patients' CTOs invalid, and errors in recall notices or revocations may invalidate hospital managers' authority to detain.

35.17 To avoid errors being made, hospital managers should ensure that responsible clinicians have access to advice about how the relevant forms should be completed and the opportunity (where practicable) to have them checked in advance by someone else familiar with what the Act requires."

Minor errors and or slips of the pen may be corrected and initialled without affecting the validity of the CTO.

This section applies without modification to patients who have been made subject to hospital or guardianship orders by a court under s.37 (Sch.1 Pt 1 para.1). A CTO cannot be made in respect of a restricted patient (s.41(3)(aa)).

Domestic Violence, Crime and Victims Act 2004

In order that hospital managers can meet their obligations under the 2004 Act to invite representa-   **1-258**
tions from victims, RCs must tell the managers if they are considering discharging the following categories of patients by making a CTO:

"[P]atients subject to unrestricted hospital orders, hospital directions whose associated limitation direction is no longer in force, and unrestricted transfer directions (including hospital orders and transfer directions which were originally restricted, but where the restriction order or direction has since ended or been lifted)" ("Guidance on the extension of victims' rights under the Domestic Violence, Crime and Victims Act 2004", Department of Health, 2008, para.1.10).

Human Rights Act 1998

If a CTO is made in the interests of the patient's health or to protect the rights and freedoms of oth-   **1-259**
ers, there would be no interference with the patient's rights under art.8 of the European Convention on Human Rights provided that the making of the order is necessary in a democratic society and is done in accordance with the law (*L v Sweden*, App. No.10801/84). Similar considerations would apply to art.11 which provides for a right "to freedom of association with others".

For conditions of a CTO that might amount to a deprivation of the patient's liberty, see the discussion under the heading *Leave of absence and deprivations of liberty* in the General Note to s.17; also see the notes on s.17B(2) (3).

Applications to the First-tier Tribunal (Mental Health) or the Mental Health Review Tribunal for Wales

Paragraphs 147 and 148 of the Explanatory Notes state: **1-260**

"A community patient may apply to the [First-tier Tribunal (Mental Health) or the Mental Health Review Tribunal for Wales], under amended s.66 ..., when a CTO is made, when it is revoked, when it is extended after six months or a year (as appropriate) and when an order is extended after the patient has been absent without leave for more than 28 days. A NR may also apply to the [tribunal under s.66] if the NR makes a discharge order which is not put into effect because the RC reports that the patient would be likely to act in a dangerous manner if discharged; or if he or she is displaced by a court order as allowed under s.29(1)(c) or (d) ....The hospital managers must refer a patient to the [tribunal] if a CTO is revoked [or if an application to the tribunal has not been made within the relevant period: see s.68(7)].

In the case of community patients who were under a hospital order before being made subject to a CTO, the power under s.66 ... to apply to a Tribunal when a CTO is made or revoked cannot be exercised until six months after the date of the hospital order. The NR of such a patient may apply to the [tribunal] whenever the patient has a right to apply [(s.69(1)(a))]. The Secretary of State can refer a case of a community patient to the [tribunal], in the same way as for detained patients [: see s.67(1)]."

The rights of community patients and their nearest relatives to make tribunal applications are also set out in figures 21 and 22 of Ch.6 of the Reference Guide.

The power of the tribunal to discharge a community patient is set out in s.72(1)(c),(1A). The tribunal also has the power to recommend that a detained patient be discharged subject to a CTO (s.72(3A)). There is no power for the tribunal to vary or discharge the conditions of a CTO.

Code of Practice

1-261   Guidance on CTOs is contained in Ch.29. Advice on deciding between guardianship, leave of absence and CTOs can be found in Ch.31.

Subsection (1)

1-262   **By order in writing**   The order, which is Form CTO1 (see reg.6(1)(a) of the English Regulations), is called a "Community Treatment Order" (subs.(3)). In Wales, the form is Form CP1: see reg.16 of the Welsh Regulations.

It is submitted that Part 3 of Form CTO1 should not be signed until Parts 1 and 2 have been completed. The CQC considers that Parts 1 and 3 of the Form can be completed by different responsible clinicians if there has been a change in the identity of the responsible clinician since the completion of Part 1 ("*Monitoring the Mental Health Act in 2011/12*", p.80).

A Form CTO 1 which is found to be fundamentally defective because, for example, Part 3 of the form was not signed does not affect the legality of either the s.3 application or the Part III order.

A detained patient   Of any age. If a child patient is a ward of court, see s.33(4).

Subsection (2)

1-263   **Liable to be detained**   A CTO can be made in respect of a patient who has been granted leave of absence under s.17.

Application for admission for treatment   Which is suspended during the currency of the CTO (s.17D(2)(a)), apart from when the patient is recalled to hospital when it is reinstated (s.17E(6)). A CTO can also be made in respect of patients who are subject to hospital orders (without a restriction order) and transfer directions (without a restriction direction): see Sch.1 Pt 1 and s.47(3). If the application, order or direction ceases to have effect, the CTO automatically ends (s.17C).

Subsection (4)

1-264   As neither the Responsible Clinician nor the Approved Mental Health Professional are placed under a legal obligation either to "examine" or "personally see" the patient before he is placed on a CTO, the decision in *Devon Partnership NHS Trust v Secretary of State for Health and Social Care* (noted under s.11(5)) does not apply to this provision.

Responsible clinician   Although there is no legal obligation placed on the RC either to examine or see the patient prior to placing him on a CTO, the RC must have up to date information on the patient to enable her to be satisfied that the criteria set out in subs.(5) are satisfied.

An approved mental health professional ... agrees   There is no obligation placed on the AMHP under this section either to see the patient or to consult the patient's nearest relative prior to signing the statement. However, the *Code of Practice* states that the "AMHP should meet with the patient before deciding whether to agree that the CTO should be made" (para.29.22). By virtue of the decision of the House of Lords in *R. (on the application of Munjaz) v Mersey Care National Health Service Trust*, noted under s.118, the AMHP should have a cogent reason for not having this meeting, which could be conducted remotely. Paragraph 29.24 of the *Code of Practice* states:

"The Act does not specify who this AMHP should be. It may (but need not) be an AMHP who is already involved in the patient's care and treatment as part of the multi-disciplinary team. It can be an AMHP acting on behalf of any willing local authority, and local authorities may agree with each other and with hospital managers the arrangements that are likely to be most convenient and best for patients. But if no other local authority is willing, responsibility for ensuring that an AMHP considers the case should lie with the local authority which would become responsible under section 117 for the patient's after-care if the patient were discharged."

Depending on the circumstances, it might be more appropriate for the default position to be for an AMHP of the local authority for the area where the patient is currently located to perform the role. This approach would be consistent with the duty placed on local authorities by s.13(1).

Contrary to what is stated at p.45 of the Care Quality Commission's "*Monitoring the Mental Health Act in 2012/13*", there is no requirement placed on the AMHP to state the reasoning for her decision.

Although the *Code of Practice*, at para.29.25, states that if the agreement of the AMHP is not forthcoming the RC "should not approach another AMHP for an alternative view", such an approach would not be unlawful. Indeed, it could be argued that the RC has a professional duty to make such an approach in an attempt to achieve an objective that she believes is in the patient's best interests. In any event, if the RC fails to obtain the agreement of an AMHP she could discharge the patient on leave of absence under s.17.

Subsection (5)

The criteria set out in this subsection essentially state that the patient continues to be detainable under s.3 (including the requirement that a patient's learning disability continues to be associated with abnormally aggressive or seriously irresponsible conduct), but can be treated in the community if he is subject to a power of recall. When determining whether the RC should be able to exercise the power of recall, the factors set out in subs. (6) should be considered.   **1-265**

Paragraph 29.16 of the *Code of Practice* states:

"A risk that the patient's condition will deteriorate is a significant consideration, but does not necessarily mean that the patient should be discharged onto a CTO rather than discharged. The responsible clinician must be satisfied that the risk of harm arising from the patient's disorder is sufficiently serious to justify having the power to recall the patient to hospital for treatment. CTOs should only be used when there is reasonable evidence to suggest that there will be benefits to the individual. Such evidence may include:

- a clear link between non concordance with medication and relapse sufficient to have a significant impact on wellbeing requiring treatment in hospital
- clear evidence that there is a positive response to medication without an undue burden of side effects
- evidence that the CTO will promote recovery, and
- evidence that recall may be necessary (rather than informal admission or reassessment under the Act)."

Paragraphs (a), (b), (e)

See the notes to s.3(2)(a),(c) and (d).   **1-266**

Paragraph (b)

This provision requires a risk assessment to be undertaken (*Traylor v Kent and Medway NHS Social Care Partnership Trust* [2022] EWHC 260 (QB), para.85(1)).   **1-267**

Paragraph (d)

The necessity of the RC having a recall power is to avoid subjecting the patient to a further assessment for detention. The recall provisions are set out in s.17E.   **1-268**

Subsection (6)

This provision requires the RC to "in particular" consider the risk of the patient's condition deteriorating in the community when deciding whether it is necessary to be able to exercise the power to recall the patient to hospital. Apart from considering the patient's history of mental disorder, it "is important that a clinician can consider all relevant factors, an obvious example being the patient's current mental state. Other relevant factors might include the degree of recovery of symptoms, any suicidal ideas or feelings of hopelessness, which will be important predictors of likely risk. In addition, a patient's insight and attitude to their treatment, and the protective circumstances into which a patient would be discharged, might be relevant" (per the Parliamentary Under-Secretary of State, *Hansard*, HL Vol.693, cols 847, 848).   **1-269**

The *Code of Practice* considers the sharing of information to manage risk at paras 10.15–10.17, which are reproduced in the notes on s.2(2)(b) under "protection of other persons".

[**Conditions**

1-270   **17B.**—(1)   A community treatment order shall specify conditions to which the patient is to be subject while the order remains in force.

(2)   But, subject to subsection (3) below, the order may specify conditions only if the responsible clinician, with the agreement of the approved mental health professional mentioned in section 17A(4)(b) above, thinks them necessary or appropriate for one or more of the following purposes—

(a)   ensuring that the patient receives medical treatment;

(b)   preventing risk of harm to the patient's health or safety;

(c)   protecting other persons.

(3)   The order shall specify—

(a)   a condition that the patient make himself available for examination under section 20A below; and

(b)   a condition that, if it is proposed to give a certificate under Part 4A of this Act [that falls within section 64C(4) below] in his case, he make himself available for examination so as to enable the certificate to be given.

(4)   The responsible clinician may from time to time by order in writing vary the conditions specified in a community treatment order.

(5)   He may also suspend any conditions specified in a community treatment order.

(6)   If a community patient fails to comply with a condition specified in the community treatment order by virtue of subsection (2) above, that fact may be taken into account for the purposes of exercising the power of recall under section 17E(1) below.

(7)   But nothing in this section restricts the exercise of that power to cases where there is such a failure.]

Amendments

This section was inserted by the Mental Health Act 2007 s.32(2). The words in square brackets in subs.(3)(b) were inserted by the Health and Social Care Act 2012 s.299(6).

Definitions

1-271   community treatment order: ss.17A(7), 145(1).
community patient: ss.17A(7), 145(1).
responsible clinician: s.34(1).
approved mental health professional: s.145(1), (1AC).
medical treatment: s.145(1), (4).

General Note

1-272   This section requires that a CTO specifies the conditions to which a community patient will be subject. There is no requirement that the patient consents to the conditions. It is not possible for a CTO not to have any conditions attached to it (subs.(1)). Although the RC and the AMHP must agree the conditions (subs.(2)), only the RC has the power to vary or suspend them (subss.(4),(5)). The mandatory conditions set out in subs.(3) are directly enforceable by recall to hospital (s.17E(2)). If the patient (or a donee or deputy taking a decision on a mentally incapacitated patient's behalf: see para.7.6 of the *Code of Practice*) fails to comply with any other condition, the RC may take that into account when considering whether it is necessary to exercise the power of recall under s.17E (subs.(6)). If the criteria for recall are met, the power can be exercised even if the patient is complying with the conditions (subs.(7)).

A patient has no right to seek the review of the conditions imposed on a CTO before a tribunal; conditions can only be challenged by judicial review. The Government's view is that for SCT to work, a patient must accept and be ready to co-operate with the conditions of a CTO; see, for example, *Hansard*, HL Vol.693, col.848 and para.29.33 of the *Code of Practice* which states:

> "The reasons for any condition should be explained to the patient and others, as appropriate, (eg the patient's independent mental health advocate (IMHA), family and carers and, in the case of a child or young person, the person(s) with parental responsibility, see chapters 4, 5, 6 and 19 on children and young people) and recorded in the patient's notes. It will be important, if the CTO is to be successful, that the patient agrees to keep to the conditions, or to try to do so, and that patients have access to the help they need to be able to comply. It is helpful if families can have access to support so they can help the patient to comply. The patient should have a discharge CPA meeting and a copy of the care plan before they are discharged from hospital onto the CTO (see paragraphs 34.13 – 34.14 and 34.19)."

This section applies without modification to patients who have been made subject to hospital orders by a court under s.37 (Sch.1 Pt 1 para.1).

Domestic Violence, Crime and Victims Act 2004

Before an AMHP agrees to the imposition of a condition or an RC either decides to impose or vary a condition, they must consider any representations from victims and the RC must inform the hospital managers if the patient comes within the scope of the 2004 Act: see the General Note to s.17A under this heading and "Guidance on the extension of victims' rights under the Domestic Violence, Crime and Victims Act 2004", Department of Health, 2008, paras 3.1 to 3.8. **1-273**

Code of Practice

Guidance on this section is contained in Ch.29 at paras 29.27 and following. **1-274**

Subsections (2), (3)

Subsection (3) does not contain an exhaustive list of conditions that can be attached to the CTO. The RC, with the agreement of the AMHP, may agree to specify other conditions as long as they are "necessary or appropriate" for one or more of the purposes set out in subs.(2). This gives a considerable amount of discretion to the RC regarding the nature of the conditions that can be imposed. They "might cover matters such as: **1-275**

- where and when the patient is to receive treatment in the community
- where the patient is to live, and
- avoidance of known risk factors or high-risk situations relevant to the patient's mental disorder" (*Code of Practice*, para.29.32).

A patient should be recalled to hospital under s.17E if he refuses to accept medical treatment for his mental disorder and he satisfies the criteria in subs.(1) of that section. It is not possible for a condition to be used to compel a patient to receive such treatment.

With regard to the mandatory condition contained in subs.(3) for the patient to make himself available for examination by a SOAD it should be noted that there is no legal requirement for a SOAD to examine the patient prior to issuing a certificate under Part IVA.

There is no power to take an objecting community patient to the place where he is required to be as a condition of the CTO: see the notes on s.18(7).

In *Welsh Ministers v PJ* [2018] UKSC 66; [2018] M.H.L.R. 411, the Supreme Court held that this Act does not give the RC power to impose conditions on a CTO which have the concrete effect of depriving a patient of his liberty within the meaning of art.5 of the European Convention on Human Rights. However, if no such conditions have been imposed but the provisions of the patient's care plan amount to a deprivation of liberty, it is submitted that a capacious patient has the right to either consent to or refuse to abide by such provisions.

If it is considered that a mentally incapacitated CTO patient would be deprived of his liberty on his discharge from hospital, either the deprivation of liberty procedure set out in Sch.A1 to the Mental

Capacity Act 2005 should be invoked or an order of the Court of Protection under s.16(2)(a) of the 2005 Act authorising the deprivation should be sought. In *Birmingham City Council v SR; Lancashire County Council v JTA* [2019] EWCOP 28, Lieven J. authorised the deprivation of liberty in the community of a mentally incapacitated CTO patient. Her Ladyship said at para.44:

> "The case-law establishes that the Court of Protection may make declarations and orders concerning best interests, including deprivation of liberty, in advance of any discharge under the MHA, see *DN v Northumberland, Tyne & Wear NHS Foundation Trust* [2011] UKUT 327 (AAC). In a case such as SR it is appropriate that this should happen, so that the FTT and the Secretary of State can be confident that SR will be deprived of his liberty to a proportionate degree when he is discharged into the community."

Also see an unreported case determined on July 5, 2019, which is considered in the July 2019 issue of 39 Essex Chambers "*Mental Capacity Report*" at p.25. In that case, Hayden J took the view that there was no jurisdictional bar to the Court of Protection authorising the deprivation of liberty of a person on a CTO lacking the material decision-making capacity, so long as the conditions on the face of the CTO did not give rise to a confinement. The editors state that "Hayden J has given permission for the relevant recital to the order to be published, and it is reproduced below:

> "AND UPON the Court being satisfied that neither the decision in *Secretary of State for Justice v MM* [2018] UKSC 60, nor that in *Welsh Ministers v PJ* [2018] UKSC 66, prevents the Court of Protection making an order under s.16(2)(a) Mental Capacity Act 2005 authorising (by s.4A(3)) the deprivation of liberty in the community of an individual lacking the material decision-making capacity who is subject to a Community Treatment Order, so long as that Community Treatment Order does not contain conditions that on their face give rise to the confinement of the individual."

An authorisation can only be granted if there is no conflict between it and a condition specified under this section: see Sch.1A, Case C of the 2005 Act. If it is possible for the procedure under Sch.A1 to be used, an application should not be made to the Court of Protection for authorisation (*A Local Authority v PB* [2011] EWCOP 2675 (Fam), para.64(iii)). The meaning of a deprivation of liberty is considered in Part 6.

Subsections (4), (5)

1-276   The power to vary or suspend a condition enables the RC to respond to changes in the patient's circumstances. It could be exercised as a result of a request made by the patient or the patient's carer. The agreement of an AMHP to the variation or suspension is not required.

An order varying a condition must be made on Form CTO2: see reg.6(2)(b) of the English Regulations (in Wales, Form CP2: see reg.16(2) of the Welsh Regulations).

[Duration of community treatment order

1-277   **17C.**   A community treatment order shall remain in force until—

  (a)   the period mentioned in section 20A(1) below (as extended under any provision of this Act) expires, but this is subject to sections 21 and 22 below;

  (b)   the patient is discharged in pursuance of an order under section 23 below or a direction under section 72 below;

  (c)   the application for admission for treatment in respect of the patient otherwise ceases to have effect; or

  (d)   the order is revoked under section 17F below, whichever occurs first.]

Amendment

This section was inserted by the Mental Health Act 2007 s.32(2).

Definitions

community treatment order: ss.17A(7), 145(1).   **1-278**
application for admission for treatment: s.145(1).

General Note

This section specifies that a CTO will end: **1-279**

1. When the period of the CTO runs out and the CTO is not extended under the provisions contained in s.20A (s.20B).
2. If the patient is discharged from the powers of the Act by virtue of an order made under s.23 by the RC, the hospital managers or the patient's nearest relative (for Pt II patients), or a direction made by a tribunal under s.72. Discharging the patient from a CTO has the automatic effect of also discharging the underlying application or order s.23(1A)). The patient is also discharged if the application under s.3 (or order under Part III) otherwise ceases to have effect.
3. If the RC revokes the CTO following the patients recall to hospital under s.17F. Revocation does not end the underlying liability to detention (s.17G).

The CTO, and the underlying liability to detention, will also end if the patient is received into guardianship (s.8(5)), on the patient being detained under s.3 if the patient was subject to s.3 before going onto SCT, but not if the patient was subject to an order or direction made under Pt III at that time (see s.6(4) and para.26.136 of the Reference Guide), and if the patient has been "detained in custody" for more than six months (s.22).

The CTO will not end if the patient is admitted to a hospital either informally or subject to s.2, is detained under s.135 or 136, or is arrested and charged for a criminal offence.

This section applies without modification to patients who have been made subject to hospital orders (Sch.1 Pt 1 para.1).

Paragraph (b)

If the patient is made subject to a CTO during a period of deferred discharge granted by the tribunal   **1-280**
under s.72(3), the CTO will end on the discharge taking effect. Placing the patient on a CTO in this situation would therefore be a pointless exercise.

[Effect of community treatment order

17D.—(1)   The application for admission for treatment in respect of a patient   **1-281**
shall not cease to have effect by virtue of his becoming a community patient.

(2)   But while he remains a community patient—

    (a)   the authority of the managers to detain him under section 6(2) above in pursuance of that application shall be suspended; and

    (b)   reference (however expressed) in this or any other Act, or in any subordinate legislation (within the meaning of the Interpretation Act 1978), to patients liable to be detained, or detained, under this Act shall not include him.

(3)   And section 20 below shall not apply to him while he remains a community patient.

(4)   Accordingly, authority for his detention shall not expire during any period in which that authority is suspended by virtue of subsection (2)(a) above.]

Amendment

This section was inserted by the Mental Health Act 2007 s.32(2).

Definitions

1-282   application for admission for treatment: s.145(1).
community patient: ss.17A(7), 145(1).
the managers: s.145(1).

General Note

1-283   This section sets out the effect of a CTO on certain provisions of the Act. They are:

1.   Although the application for admission for treatment (or its equivalent: see the note on s.17A(2)) that was made in respect of the patient remains in force during the currency of the CTO, the hospital managers' authority to detain the patient under s.6(2) is suspended.

2.   Where the Act, any other Act or any subordinate legislation, refers to patients who are "detained" or "liable to be detained", this does not include community patients. One of the effects of this is that the authority to treat the patient under Pt IV is suspended, although the three month period provided for in s.58(1)(b) continues to run.

3.   The renewal provisions contained in s.20 do not apply to the patient while he is a community patient. This means that the authority to detain the patient does not expire during the time when that authority is suspended.

The CTO will come into effect from the date and time specified in Pt 3 of Form CTO 1 (or, in Wales, Form CP1). The patient does not have to leave hospital immediately after the CTO comes into effect; he could remain in hospital as an informal patient: see para.26.22 of the Reference Guide. This option could be used if the patient is awaiting suitable accommodation.

The provisions of s.133 apply to a patient who is to be discharged from hospital subject to a CTO (s.133(1A)).

See s.22 for the effect of the patient's imprisonment on the CTO.

This section applies to patients who have been made subject to hospital orders with the modification set out in para.2A of Sch.1 (Sch.1 Pt 1 para.2).

[Power to recall to hospital

1-284   **17E.**—(1)   The responsible clinician may recall a community patient to hospital if in his opinion—

    (a)   the patient requires medical treatment in hospital for his mental disorder; and

    (b)   there would be a risk of harm to the health or safety of the patient or to other persons if the patient were not recalled to hospital for that purpose.

(2)   The responsible clinician may also recall a community patient to hospital if the patient fails to comply with a condition specified under section 17B(3) above.

(3)   The hospital to which a patient is recalled need not be the responsible hospital.

(4)   Nothing in this section prevents a patient from being recalled to a hospital even though he is already in the hospital at the time when the power of recall is exercised; references to recalling him shall be construed accordingly.

(5)   The power of recall under subsections (1) and (2) above shall be exercisable by notice in writing to the patient.

(6)   A notice under this section recalling a patient to hospital shall be sufficient authority for the managers of that hospital to detain the patient there in accordance with the provisions of this Act.]

Amendment

This section was inserted by the Mental Health Act 2007 s.32(2).

Definitions

responsible clinician: s.34(1). **1-285**
community patient; ss.17A(7), 145(1).
medical treatment: s.145(1), (4).
hospital: ss.34(2), 145(1).
responsible hospital; ss.17A(7), 145(1).
the managers: s.145(1).
mental disorder: ss.1, 135(1).

General Note

This section gives an exclusive power to the patient's RC, who could be the RC providing cover for **1-286**
the patient's usual RC, to recall a community patient to hospital in the following circumstances:

1. Where the RC decides that the patient needs to receive treatment for his mental disorder in
    hospital and that, without such treatment, there would be a risk of harm to the health or safety
    of the patient, or to other people (subs.(1)). It is submitted that the risk of harm need not be
    immediate in the sense that the patient is exhibiting symptoms of relapse, and that a recall can
    be triggered if there was concern about a predicted relapse in the near future, for example, a
    risk associated with the patient's decision to stop taking medication where the decision would
    be likely to trigger an assessment for detention (cf s.17A(6)). While a patient can be recalled
    even though he is complying with the conditions of the CTO imposed under s.17B (*Secretary
    of State for Justice v MM; Welsh Ministers v PJ* [2017] EWCA Civ 194; [2017] M.H.L.R. 282,
    para.48), a patient's refusal of medical treatment for mental disorder is not in itself sufficient
    ground to trigger a recall. Paragraph 25.26 of the *Code of Practice* states:

    "Refusal to consent to treatment in itself does not justify a recall to hospital and fuller
    consideration of the patient's presentation and circumstances is required when consider-
    ing whether a recall to hospital is warranted (see chapter 29)."

2. Where the patient fails to comply with the mandatory conditions imposed under s.17B(3)
    (subs.(2)).

A RC need not examine the patient before issuing a notice of recall; she can act on reports received
which provide an account of the patient's current behaviour and situation. Paragraph 29.45 of the *Code
of Practice* states:

"The recall power is intended to provide a means to respond to evidence of relapse or high-risk
behaviour relating to mental disorder before the situation becomes critical and leads to the patient
or other people being harmed. The need for recall might arise as a result of relapse, or by a change
in the patient's circumstances giving rise to increased risk. The responsible clinician does not have
to interview or examine the patient in person before deciding to recall them."

Unless locally it has been agreed otherwise, the RC has responsibility for co-ordinating the recall
process (*Code of Practice*, para.29.52). A patient's recall must be effected by notifying the patient in
writing (subs.(5)). The task of delivering the notice of recall is usually that of the patient's care co-
ordinator.
The patient need not be recalled to the hospital where he had been detained immediately before the
CTO was made (subs.(3)). If the patient is recalled to a different hospital, a formal transfer could
subsequently be made under s.17F(2). Patients should not be recalled to a particular hospital unless it
has been established that the hospital will accept the patient as hospitals are not obliged to admit patients
just because a recall notice has been issued. A copy of the notice of recall, which provides the authority
to detain the patient, should be sent to the managers of the hospital to which the patient is being recalled
(*Code of Practice*, para.29.60). If the patient refuses to accept the recall notice or if the patient cannot
be found, the notice should be delivered to the patient's usual or last known address (*Code of Practice*,
para.29.53).
A recall notice reinstates the power of the hospital managers to detain the patient (subs. (6)) and, if
the patient has been served with the notice (or it is considered served), he may be taken into custody
and returned to hospital (s.18(2A)). A patient who fails to respond to a recall notice becomes a patient
who is absent from the hospital without leave and the provisions of ss.18, 21, 21A and 21B will apply.
If access to the patient is denied, an application for a warrant under s.135(2) could be made once the

recall notice is considered served. The 72 hour period referred to in s.17F(6) starts on the patient's arrival at the hospital. The powers which apply to the patient on recall are set out in s.17F.

If, subsequent to the issuing of a recall notice but before it is actioned, the patient agrees to accept medication, there is no procedure which allows for the cancellation of the recall notice. In this situation, if the RC considers that there is no need for the patient to be returned to hospital, she should inform the patient and relevant professions that the notice will not be actioned. The RC should record her decision.

A CTO patient can agree to being admitted informally to a hospital without a recall procedure being used. The treatment of the mental disorder of such patients is governed by Part IVA. The holding powers set out in s.5 cannot be used in respect of a community patient (s.5(6)). However, a recall notice may be issued even if the patient is in hospital informally at that time (subs.(4)). This would cover the situation of a hospitalised patient who, by refusing treatment, places themselves or others at risk.

If a child community patient is a ward of court, the usual rule relating to the need to act in conformity with any order made by the court in the exercise of its wardship jurisdiction does not apply during a period of recall under this section (s.33(4)).

The hospital managers must take steps to inform the patient of the effect of the recall: see reg.6(7) of the English Regulations and reg.22(1) of the Welsh Regulations.

This section applies without modification to patients who have been made subject to hospital orders (Sch.1 Pt 1 para.1).

Code of Practice

1-287   Guidance on the recall of patients is given in Ch.29 at para.29.45.

Transport

1-288   Paragraph 17.35 of the *Code of Practice* states:

"A patient subject to a CTO who has been recalled can be transported by any officer on the staff of the hospital to which the patient is recalled, any police officer, any AMHP or any other person authorised in writing by the responsible clinician or the managers of that hospital. The identity of the most appropriate person to transport the patient will depend on the individual circumstances."

Subsection (1)(a)

1-289   The *Code of Practice* mistakenly identifies paragraphs (a) and (b) as alternatives at para.29.46.

Medical treatment in hospital   The hospital to which the patient is recalled need not be the hospital that discharged the patient subject to the CTO: see above. The recall could be to a hospital out-patient department: see para.29.59 of the *Code of Practice* and *R. (on the application of DR) v Mersey Care NHS Trust* [2002] M.H.L.R. 386. The patient can be transferred to units within the hospital named in Form CTO3 during the recall period. It should be noted that this section does not use the term "admission". If the patient is not admitted to the hospital, no further legal action needs to be taken and a file note should be made.

A recall to a general hospital would be appropriate if the patient was to receive treatment for a physical condition which constituted an ancillary treatment for the patient's mental disorder: see *B v Croydon Health Authority*, which is noted under s.63.

As a community patient who has been recalled to hospital is not "liable to be detained" (s.17D(2)(b)), he cannot be granted leave of absence under s.17.

For his mental disorder   The treatment will be for the patient's current mental disorder which might differ from the disorder that resulted in the patient being made subject to the CTO.

Subsection (2)

1-290   The power to recall a community patient for examination with a view to a Pt IVA certificate being given only applies to a SOAD certificate.

Subsection (3)

If this provision applies, the patient's RC will be "the approved clinician with overall responsibility   **1-291**
for the patient's case": see s.34(1) and the note thereto.

Subsection (5)

Notice in writing   Using Form CTO3: see reg.6(3)(a) of the English Regulations (in Wales, Form CP5:   **1-292**
see reg.19(1)(a) of the Welsh Regulations). For service of the notice of recall, see reg.6(5),(6)
(reg.19(4),(5) of the Welsh Regulations). A notice of recall, properly completed by the RC and served
on the patient in accordance with the regulations, provides the authority to transport a patient subject
to a CTO to hospital compulsorily, if necessary (*Code of Practice*, para.17.33). The hospital managers
must record the time and date of the patient's detention pursuant to such notice on Form CTO4
(reg.6(3)(d)) (in Wales, Form CP6: see reg.19(1)(d) of the Welsh Regulations).
   The Reference Guide states at para.26.39:

> "If the patient's responsible hospital is in Wales, recall must be done in accordance with the equivalent
> Welsh regulations, even if the patient is to be recalled to a hospital in England. That will involve us-
> ing a Welsh statutory form [Form CP 5], rather than CTO3, to give the patient notice of the recall."

Subsection (6)   As the notice provides the authority to detain the patient, a copy should be sent to the   **1-293**
hospital to which the patient is being recalled.

[Powers in respect of recalled patients

17F.—(1)   This section applies to a community patient who is detained in a   **1-294**
hospital by virtue of a notice recalling him there under section 17E above.

(2)   The patient may be transferred to another hospital in such circumstances
and subject to such conditions as may be prescribed in regulations made by the
Secretary of State (if the hospital in which the patient is detained is in England) or
the Welsh Ministers (if that hospital is in Wales).

(3)   If he is so transferred to another hospital, he shall be treated for the purposes
of this section (and section 17E above) as if the notice under that section were a
notice recalling him to that other hospital and as if he had been detained there from
the time when his detention in hospital by virtue of the notice first began.

(4)   The responsible clinician may by order in writing revoke the community
treatment order if—

    (a)   in his opinion, the conditions mentioned in section 3(2) above are satis-
fied in respect of the patient; and

    (b)   an approved mental health professional states in writing—

        (i)   that he agrees with that opinion; and

        (ii)   that it is appropriate to revoke the order.

(5)   The responsible clinician may at any time release the patient under this section, but not after the community treatment order has been revoked.

(6)   If the patient has not been released, nor the community treatment order
revoked, by the end of the period of 72 hours, he shall then be released.

(7)   But a patient who is released under this section remains subject to the community treatment order.

(8)   In this section—

    (a)   "the period of 72 hours" means the period of 72 hours beginning with
the time when the patient's detention in hospital by virtue of the notice
under section 17E above begins; and

(b)   references to being released shall be construed as references to being released from that detention (and accordingly from being recalled to hospital).]

Amendment

This section was inserted by the Mental Health Act 2007 s.32(2).

Definitions

1-295   community patient: ss.17A(7), 145(1).
hospital: s.145(1).
responsible clinician: s.34(1).
community treatment order: ss.17A(7), 145(1).
approved mental health professional: s.145(1), (1AC).

General Note

1-296   This section identifies the powers that apply to a community patient who has been recalled to hospital for a maximum period of 72 hours (subs.(6)) under s.17E. They are:

1.   The patient may be transferred to another hospital under reg.9 of the English Regulations or reg.26 of the Welsh Regulations (s.19A) by a person specified in reg.12 (for England) or reg.27 (for Wales). If such a transfer takes place, the patient is to be treated as if he had been recalled to, and detained in, that other hospital (subss.(2),(3)). A transfer between hospitals while a patient is recalled does not change the identity of the responsible hospital. Such a change can be effected under reg.17 of the English Regulations or reg.25 of the Welsh Regulations.

2.   If the RC decides that the patient meets the criteria for detention as set out in s.3(2) and requires inpatient treatment for longer than 72 hours, the RC may, subject to an AMHP's agreement, revoke the CTO (subs.(4)). The requirement to obtain the agreement of an AMHP is unfortunate because, in the absence of such agreement, the patient will continue to be subject to a CTO which the RC no longer considers to be an appropriate response to the patient's situation. Although the *Code of Practice*, at para.29.67, which is set out below, states that if the agreement of the AMHP is not forthcoming it "would not be appropriate" for the RC to approach another AMHP for an alternative view, such an approach would not be unlawful. Indeed, it could be argued that the RC has a professional duty to make such an approach in an attempt to achieve an objective that she considers is in the patient's best interests. The effect of a revocation is set out in s.17G.

3.   The RC may release the patient from detention within the period of 72 hours of the patient's recall to hospital, provided that the CTO has not been revoked (subss. (5),(8)). If by the end of the 72 hour period the patient has not been released, nor the CTO revoked, he shall then be released (subs.(6)). On release, the patient continues to be subject to the CTO (subs.(7)). Release means release from detention (subs.(8) (b)); there is nothing to prevent the released patient from remaining in hospital informally.

4.   The patient's RC also has the option of using her power under s.23 to discharge the patient from the CTO. This has the automatic effect of also discharging the underlying application for treatment.

By virtue of s.17D(2)(b), an RC does not have the power to grant a recalled patient leave of absence under s.17.

A recalled patient can be treated for his mental disorder without consent subject to the safeguards set out in either Part IV or Part IVA: see s.62A.

A recalled patient who absconds is absent without leave and the provisions of ss.18, 21, 21A and 21B will apply. In particular, if a patient is absent without leave on the day when the 72-hour period would expire, the period will start again on the patient's return to the hospital either voluntarily or under compulsion: see s.21(4).

This section applies without modification to patients who have been made subject to hospital orders (Sch.1 Pt 1 para.1).

Domestic Violence, Crime and Victims Act 2004

If the RC decides to revoke the CTO, she must inform the hospital managers if the patient comes **1-297** within the scope of the 2004 Act: see the General Note to s.17A under this heading and "Guidance on the extension of victims' rights under the Domestic Violence, Crime and Victims Act 2004", Department of Health, 2008, paras 3.1 to 3.7.

Code of Practice

Guidance on revoking the CTO is given in the following paragraphs: **1-298**

"29.63 If the patient requires inpatient treatment for longer than 72 hours after arrival at the hospital, the responsible clinician should consider revoking the CTO. The effect of revoking the CTO is that the patient will again be detained under the powers of the Act. The responsible clinician and an AMHP should reassess the patient before revoking their CTO. They must do so if necessary to satisfy themselves that the patient again needs to be admitted to hospital for medical treatment under the Act.

29.64 The CTO may be revoked if:

- the responsible clinician considers that the patient again needs to be admitted to hospital for medical treatment under the Act, or
- an AMHP agrees with that assessment, and also believes that it is appropriate to revoke the CTO.

29.65 In making the decision as to whether it is appropriate to revoke a CTO, the AMHP should consider the wider social context for the person concerned, in the same way as when making decisions about applications for admissions under the Act (see chapter 14).

29.66 As before, the AMHP carrying out this role may (but need not) be already involved in the patient's care and treatment, or can be an AMHP acting on behalf of any willing local authority. If no other local authority is willing, responsibility for ensuring that an AMHP considers the case should lie with the local authority which has been responsible for the patient's after-care.

29.67 If the AMHP does not agree that the CTO should be revoked, then the patient cannot be detained in hospital after the end of the maximum recall period of 72 hours. The patient will therefore remain on a CTO. A record of the AMHP's decision and the full reasons for it should be kept in the patient's notes. It would not be appropriate for the responsible clinician to approach another AMHP for an alternative view.

29.68 If the responsible clinician and the AMHP agree that the CTO should be revoked, they must complete the relevant statutory form for the revocation to take legal effect, and send it to the hospital managers. The responsible clinician or the AMHP must give the patient (or arrange for the patient to be given) oral reasons for revoking the CTO before it is revoked. The patient is then detained again under the powers of the Act exactly as before going onto a CTO, except that a new detention period of six months begins for the purposes of review and applications to the Tribunal (see also paragraph 25.36). Written reasons for the revocation should also be given to the patient and (where appropriate) their nearest relative. Hospital managers should notify the patient and (where appropriate) their nearest relative when they have referred the patient's case to the Tribunal (see paragraph 29.72)."

Subsection (2)

Prescribed in regulations Form CTO6 provides authority for the patient's transfer: see reg.9 of the **1-299** English Regulations. The managers of the new hospital should be given a copy of Form CTO 4 or, in Wales, Form CP6 (see the note to subs.(6)). Transfers from hospitals in Wales to hospitals in England must be done in accordance with the equivalent Welsh regulations using Welsh Form TC 6: see reg.26 of the Welsh Regulations.

For the responsibility to inform the patient's nearest relative of the assignment of the patient to another hospital which assumes responsibility for that patient as a community patient, see reg.26(1)(h) of the English Regulations and reg.32(b) of the Welsh Regulations.

Subsection (4)

1-300   A CTO can only be revoked when the patient is detained in hospital as a result of recall under this section. A decision to revoke can only be made subsequent to a risk assessment being undertaken (*Traylor v Kent and Medway NHS Social Care Partnership Trust* [2022] EWHC 260 (QB), para.85(1)).

Order in writing   On Form CTO5: see reg.6(8)(a) of the English Regulations (in Wales, Form CP7: see reg.20 of the Welsh Regulations).

Approved Mental Health Professional   The Act does not specify which local authority is responsible for ensuring that an AMHP is made available to consider the possible revocation of the CTO. Paragraph 29.66 of the *Code of Practice*, which is set out above, states that the default position for determining the responsibility for ensuring that an AMHP considers the case should lie with the local authority which has been responsible for the patient's after-care. Depending on the circumstances, it might be more appropriate for the default position to be for an AMHP of the local authority for the area where the patient is currently located to perform the role. This approach would be consistent with the duty placed on local authorities by s.13(1).

The AMHP is not required to interview the patient before reaching her decision.

Subsection (6)

1-301   **By the end of the period of 72 hours**   The start of this period must be recorded on Form CTO 4 (in Wales, Form CP6). The 72-hour period starts from the time when the patient is admitted to the hospital as a result of the recall notice and not from the time when the recall notice was issued. If the patient is absent without leave at the end of that period, see the General Note, above.

Once 72 hours have elapsed, the patient must be allowed to leave if the RC has not revoked the CTO. On leaving hospital the patient will remain on the CTO as before: see para.29.61 of the *Code of Practice* which states:

> "When the patient arrives at hospital after recall, the clinical team will need to assess the patient's condition, provide the necessary treatment and determine the next steps. The patient may be well enough to return to the community once treatment has been given, or may need a longer period of assessment or treatment in hospital. The patient may be detained in hospital for a maximum of 72 hours after recall to allow the responsible clinician to determine what should happen next. During this period the patient remains a CTO patient, even if they remain in hospital for one or more nights. The responsible clinician may allow the patient to leave the hospital at any time within the 72-hour period. Once 72 hours from the time of admission have elapsed, the patient must be allowed to leave if the responsible clinician has not revoked the CTO (see paragraphs 29.63 – 29.68 below). On leaving hospital the patient will remain on the CTO as before. Section 5(2) cannot be used to extend the 72-hour period."

The 72-hour period cannot be extended by the issue of a second recall notice.

[Effect of revoking community treatment order

1-302   **17G.**—(1)   This section applies if a community treatment order is revoked under section 17F above in respect of a patient.

(2)   Section 6(2) above shall have effect as if the patient had never been discharged from hospital by virtue of the community treatment order.

(3)   The provisions of this or any other Act relating to patients liable to be detained (or detained) in pursuance of an application for admission for treatment shall apply to the patient as they did before the community treatment order was made, unless otherwise provided.

(4)   If, when the order is revoked, the patient is being detained in a hospital other than the responsible hospital, the provisions of this Part of this Act shall have effect as if—

(a)   the application for admission for treatment in respect of him were an application for admission to that other hospital; and

(b)   he had been admitted to that other hospital at the time when he was originally admitted in pursuance of the application.

(5)   But, in any case, section 20 below shall have effect as if the patient had been admitted to hospital in pursuance of the application for admission for treatment on the day on which the order is revoked.]

Amendment

This section was inserted by the Mental Health Act 2007 s.32(2).

Definitions

community treatment order: ss.17A(7), 145(1).   **1-303**
hospital: s.145(1).
application for admission for treatment: s.145(1).
responsible hospital: ss.17A(7), 145(1).

General Note

This section provides that if a patient's CTO is revoked, the authority to detain the patient under s.6(2) **1-304** applies as if the patient had never been a community patient (subs.(2)). In addition, all of the provisions of the Act relating to patients who are liable to be detained (or detained) under s.3 apply to the patient as they did before the CTO was made, unless the Act provides otherwise (subs.(3)). The patient's nearest relative has no right to prevent the reinstatement of the s.3 by objecting to it. If, at the time when the CTO is revoked, the patient is detained in a hospital other than the one where he was detained when the CTO was made, the Act will apply as if he had been detained in that other hospital at the time when the CTO was made (subs.(4)). The "hospital managers of the new hospital must send a copy of the revocation form to the managers of the original hospital" (*Code of Practice*, para.29.71). For the purposes of calculating the renewal periods under s.20 and for applications to a tribunal, the patient is to be treated as if he had been admitted under s.3 on the day when the CTO is revoked (subs.(5)). The revocation does not effect the calculation of the three month period set out in s.58(1)(b) (s.62A(2)), i.e. the three month period does not start afresh.

Hospital managers must refer the cases of patients whose CTOs are revoked to the tribunal as soon as possible after the revocation (s.68(7)). This duty rests on the hospital managers of the hospital in which the patient is now detained, even if it was not previously the patient's responsible hospital. The tribunal does not have the power to discharge the patient during the 72-hour recall period.

This section applies to patients who have been made subject to hospital orders with the modification set out in para.2B of Sch.1 (Sch.1 Pt 1 para.2).

Return and readmission of patients absent without leave

18.—(1)   Where a patient who is for the time being liable to be detained under **1-305** this Part of this Act in a hospital—

(a)   absents himself from the hospital without leave granted under section 17 above; or

(b)   fails to return to the hospital on any occasion on which, or at the expiration of any period for which, leave of absence was granted to him under that section, or upon being recalled under that section; or

(c)   absents himself without permission from any place where he is required to reside in accordance with conditions imposed on the grant of leave of absence under that section,

he may, subject to the provisions of this section, be taken into custody and returned to the hospital or place by any [approved mental health professional], by any officer on the staff of the hospital, by any constable, or by any person authorised in writing by the managers of the hospital.

(2) Where the place referred to in paragraph (c) of subsection (1) above is a hospital other than the one in which the patient is for the time being liable to be detained, the references in that subsection to an officer on the staff of the hospital and the managers of the hospital shall respectively include references to an officer on the staff of the first-mentioned hospital and the managers of that hospital.

[(2A) Where a community patient is at any time absent from a hospital to which he is recalled under section 17E above, he may, subject to the provisions of this section, be taken into custody and returned to the hospital by any approved mental health professional, by any officer on the staff of the hospital, by any constable, or by any person authorised in writing by the responsible clinician or the managers of the hospital.]

(3) Where a patient who is for the time being subject to guardianship under this Part of this Act absents himself without the leave of the guardian from the place at which he is required by the guardian to reside, he may, subject to the provisions of this section, be taken into custody and returned to that place by any officer on the staff of a local social services authority, by any constable, or by any person authorised in writing by the guardian or a local social services authority.

[(4) A patient shall not be taken into custody under this section after the later of—

(a) the end of the period of six months beginning with the first day of his absence without leave; and

(b) the end of the period for which (apart from section 21 below) he is liable to be detained or subject to guardianship [or, in the case of a community patient, the community treatment order is in force] [...]].

[(4A) In determining for the purposes of subsection (4)(b) above or any other provision of this Act whether a person who is or has been absent without leave is at any time liable to be detained or subject to guardianship, a report furnished under section 20 or 21B below before the first day of his absence without leave shall not be taken to have renewed the authority for his detention or guardianship unless the period of renewal began before that day.

(4B) Similarly, in determining for those purposes whether a community treatment order is at any time in force in respect of a person who is or has been absent without leave, a report furnished under section 20A or 21B below before the first day of his absence without leave shall not be taken to have extended the community treatment period unless the extension began before that day.]

(5) A patient shall not be taken into custody under this section if the period for which he is liable to be detained is that specified in section 2(4), 4(4) or 5(2) or (4) above and that period has expired.

(6) In this Act "absent without leave" means absent from any hospital or other place and liable to be taken into custody and returned under this section, and related expressions shall be construed accordingly.

[(7) In relation to a patient who has yet to comply with a requirement imposed by virtue of this Act to be in a hospital or place, references in this Act to his liability to be returned to the hospital or place shall include his liability to be taken to that hospital or place; and related expressions shall be construed accordingly.]

Amendments

The amendments to this section were made by the Mental Health (Patients in the Community) Act 1995 s.2(1) and the Mental Health Act 2007 ss.21, 32(4), 55, Sch.2 para.7, Sch.3 para.3, Sch.11 Pt 5.

Definitions

patient: s.145(1).

1-306

hospital: ss.34(2), 145(1).
approved mental health professional: s.145(1) (1AC).
the managers: s.145(1).
local social services authority: s.145(1).
responsible clinician: s.34(1).
community patient: s.17A(7), 145(1).
community treatment order: ss.17A(7), 145(1).

General Note

This section, which should be read with ss.21, 21A and 21B, identifies the action that can be taken **1-307** when a detained patient, a community patient or a patient subject to guardianship absents himself without leave. It applies to patients who are absent from England and who are found in Wales, and vice versa. Provisions relating to the removal and return of patients elsewhere within the UK are contained in Pt VI. There is no power under the Act to require the return of a patient who has left the UK without authority.

This section does not apply to a patient who has been made subject to an application for detention and who escapes while being conveyed to the hospital named in the application. Once he has been located, the patient can be taken to hospital under the authority of s.6(1) if the relevant time limit set out in that provision has not expired. Reasonable force can be used when taking the patient to the hospital if required (s.137). If the patient is located in premises and access to him is denied, an application for a warrant under s.135(2) should be made: see below. For a patient who is the subject of a guardianship application and who escapes before arriving at the place specified in the application, the authority to take him to that place is found in subs.(7). If they are relevant, ss.137 and 135(2) also apply to such a patient.

By virtue of the Care Quality Commission (Registration) Regulations 2009 (SI 2009/3112), reg.17 (as amended by SI 2012/921, reg.4), the Care Quality Commission requires all service providers to notify it of any absence without leave of a person who is liable to be detained under the Act in a location used to provide secure psychiatric services under a contract with an English NHS body or the Secretary of State and also of the return of that person. The reference to a person who is "liable to be detained" includes a community patient who has been recalled to hospital in accordance with s.17E of the 1983 Act, but does not include a patient who has been conditionally discharged and not recalled to hospital in accordance with s.42, 73 or 74 (reg.17(3)(a)). A form that must be used for this purpose may be downloaded from the Commission's website (*www.cqc.org.uk*). There is no such requirement if the patient is subject to guardianship. Under reg.18(2)(f), a separate notification is required in respect of "any incident which is reported to, or investigated by, the police".

A patient who has been admitted for treatment under s.3 or received into guardianship under s.7 can be taken into custody at any time up to six months from the date on which he absconded or, if later, the end of the existing authority for detention in hospital or guardianship. A community patient cannot be taken into custody after the community treatment order (CTO) ceases to be in force, or six months have elapsed since the patient was first absent without leave, whichever is the later (subs.4). A patient who has been detained under one of the short term provisions of the Act cannot be taken into custody after the authority to detain has expired (subs.(5)).

Subsection (1)(a) of this section can be used to return a patient to the detaining hospital following the granting of a stay in proceedings to appeal the lawfulness of the decision of a tribunal to discharge the patient (*R. (on the application of H) v Ashworth Hospital Authority* [2002] EWCA Civ 923; [2002] M.H.L.R. 314, noted in the General Note to s.3 under the heading *The re-sectioning of a patient subsequent to a discharge by the First-tier Tribunal (Mental Health) or the Mental Health Review Tribunal for Wales*).

Those persons who have the power under subs.(1) to return the absconder to hospital are not provided with a power to force entry onto premises where the absconder is staying. If a power of entry is needed, an application should be made under s.135(2) for a warrant authorising a policeman to enter the premises to remove the patient or, alternatively, the police might be able to use their powers under s.17(1) of the Police and Criminal Evidence Act 1984: see the General Note to s.135. It is sensible for a hospital's absconsion policy not to require that a request for police assistance be made where this is not necessary (*Dunn v South Tyneside Health Care NHS Trust* [2003] EWCA Civ 878; [2004] M.H.L.R. 74, para.71). Regarding requesting the police for assistance, the Code states:

"28.14 The police should be asked to assist in returning a patient to hospital only if necessary. If the patient's location is known, the role of the police should, wherever possible, only be to assist a suitably qualified and experienced mental health professional in returning the patient to hospital.

28.15 The police should always be informed immediately if a patient is missing who is:

- considered to be particularly vulnerable
- considered to be dangerous, and/or
- subject to restrictions under part 3 of the Act (restricted patients) (see paragraphs 22.53 – 22.60)."

The *Code of Practice* states that whenever "the police are asked for help in returning a patient, they must be informed of the time limit for taking them into custody" (para.28.17).

It is an offence under s.128 for a person to induce or knowingly to assist a detained patient to absent himself without leave, knowingly to harbour the patient whilst he is at large, or to help the patient to avoid being retaken. A patient who is absent without leave does not thereby commit an offence (*R. v Criminal Injuries Compensation Board Ex p. Lawton* [1972] 3 All E.R. 582 at 584).

A hospital order patient, with or without restrictions, who is absent without leave may be arrested if a warrant for his arrest had been obtained from a magistrate (Criminal Justice Act 1967 s.72).

This section applies to patients who have been placed under hospital or guardianship orders by a court under s.37 with the modification that subs.(5) shall be omitted (Sch.1 Pt 1 paras 2, 4). For restricted patients subss.(3), (4) and (5) shall be omitted and in subs.(1) the words "subject to the provisions of this section" shall be omitted (Sch.1 Pt II paras 2, 4). The effect of this is that restricted patients may be retaken at any time while their restrictions remain in force. This section also applies to patients who have been sentenced and who remain liable to be detained by virtue of s.22 (s.22(1)(b)).

The National Mental Health Development Unit has published "*Strategies to Reduce Missing Patients: A Practical Workbook*" (2009).

Transport

1-308 The *Code of Practice* states:

"17.30 Where a patient who is absent without leave from a hospital is taken into custody by someone working for another agency, the managers of the hospital from which the patient is absent are responsible for making sure that any necessary transport arrangements are put in place for the patient's return.

17.31 The agency which temporarily has custody of the patient is responsible for them in the interim and should assist in ensuring that the patient is returned in a timely and safe manner.

17.32 When making arrangements for the return of patients temporarily held in police custody, hospital managers should bear in mind that police transport to return them to hospital will not normally be appropriate. Decisions about the kind of transport to be used should be taken in the same way as for patients being detained in hospital for the first time."

Patients who abscond to Scotland

1-309 The Mental Health (Absconding Patients From Other Jurisdictions) (Scotland) Regulations 2008 (SSI 2008/333) make provision for the taking into custody of a person who is subject to compulsory measures (including community-based orders) under mental health legislation in England and Wales and who is found in Scotland, as a result of their having absconded, or otherwise having failed to comply with the requirements of the order or other measure to which they are subject. It makes such provision by applying to such persons (with some appropriate modification), the sections of the Mental Health (Care and Treatment) (Scotland) Act 2003 (ss.301 to 303) which provide for the taking into custody of absconding patients who are subject to civil compulsory mental health measures in Scotland. These Regulations, along with the Mental Health (Cross-border Visits) (Scotland) Regulations 2008 (SSI 2008/181) (which is noted under s.17), are intended to bring provision dealing with persons in Scotland who abscond or otherwise fail to comply with requirements imposed under mental health measures applicable in England and Wales within the scope of the Scottish mental health legislation.

Patients who abscond from Scotland

A patient who absconds from hospital whilst being detained under the Mental Health (Care and Treatment) (Scotland) Act 2003 may be taken into custody in England or Wales and returned to Scotland: see art.8 of the Mental Health (Care and Treatment) (Scotland) Act 2003 (Consequential Provisions) Order 2005 (SI 2005/2078) which is reproduced in Part 2. As the patient will not be liable to be detained under this Act, he will not be subject to the consent to treatment provisions contained in Part 4. If compulsory treatment may be required before the patient's return can be effected, consideration should be given to making an application under Part 2. **1-310**

Human Rights Act 1998

Although it could be argued that, apart from emergency cases or cases where the patient is returned to hospital within a short period of the unauthorised absence, the return of an absconding patient to hospital would constitute a violation of art.5(1) of the European Convention of Human Rights in the absence of an up to date medical report which confirmed that he was suffering from a mental disorder (see *Kay v United Kingdom* (1998) 40 B.M.L.R. 20, noted under s.42(3)), it is likely that the procedure for the return of such patients is Convention compliant by virtue of the provisions contained in s.21B. **1-311**

Code of Practice

Guidance on this section is contained in Ch.28. The transport of patients is considered in Ch.17. **1-312**

Subsection (1)

This subsection and subs.(2) identify the action that can be taken when a detained patient goes absent without leave. Reasonable force may be used to secure the return of the patient to the hospital or the place where he is required to reside (s.137). Although there is no power to take the patient to any other place, he can initially be taken to another hospital and detained there with the written authority of the detaining hospital while arrangements are made to the patient's return. The *Code of Practice* states: **1-313**

> "28.4 Detained patients who are AWOL may be taken into custody and returned by an approved mental health professional (AMHP), any member of the hospital staff, any police officer, or anyone authorised in writing by the hospital managers.
> 28.5 A patient who has been required to reside in another hospital as a condition of leave of absence can also be taken into custody by any member of that hospital's staff or by any person authorised by that hospital's managers.
> 28.6 Otherwise, responsibility for the safe return of patients rests with the detaining hospital. If the absconding patient is initially taken to another hospital, that hospital may, with the written authorisation of the managers of the detaining hospital, detain the patient while arrangements are made for their return. In these (and similar) cases people may take a faxed or scanned copy of a written authorisation as evidence that they have the necessary authority without waiting for the original."

The patient may be taken into custody in, and returned to England or Wales from Northern Ireland (s.88).

Officer on the staff of the hospital   See the notes on s.17(3).

Any Constable   The power to arrest under this section was specifically preserved by s.26 and Sch.2 of the Police and Criminal Evidence Act 1984 (PACE). This means that the arresting policeman has a power under s.32 of PACE to search the patient at a place other than a police station.

Subsection (2)

This subsection provides that if a patient has been granted leave of absence on condition that he resides in a hospital other than the one in which he is formally liable to be detained, he can be taken into custody by an officer on the staff of the hospital where he is on leave, or by a person authorised by the managers of that hospital. **1-314**

Subsection (2A)

1-315   This provision identifies the action that can be taken when a community patient fails to respond to a recall notice or absconds from the hospital after having been recalled. If access to the patient is denied, consideration will have to be given to obtaining a warrant under s.135(2).

Subsection (3)

1-316   This provision identifies the action that can be taken when a patient who is subject to guardianship absents himself from the place where he is required to reside by the guardian. If access to the patient is denied, consideration will have to be given to obtaining a warrant under s.135(2).

Subsection (4)

1-317   This subsection, which is subject to subss.(4A) and (4B), establishes the time limit within which patients who do not come within the scope of subs.(5) and who are absent without leave can be returned to the relevant hospital or place of residence. Its effect is that the authority to take the patient into custody will last until at least six months after the first day of absence. A patient who is subject to restrictions can be retaken at any time: see the General Note to this section.

Beginning with the first day of his absence without leave   Including the first day of the patient's absence without leave (*Zoan v Rouamba* [2000] 2 All E.R. 620 CA).

Subsections (4A), (4B)

1-318   These subsections provide that if a patient's section, guardianship or CTO is renewed or extended before the first day of the patient's absence without leave, the renewal or extension is deemed not to have taken effect unless the period of renewal or extension began before that day. This means that the period during which the patient can be taken into custody is not extended by the renewal or extension.

Subsection (5)

1-319   This subsection provides that a patient cannot be taken into custody under this section if the period of his detention under one of the following powers has expired: admission for assessment (s.2(4)), emergency admission (s.4(4)), or the detention of an in-patient by a doctor or AC (s.5(2)) or nurse (s.5(4)).

Subsection (7)

1-320   This subsection provides a power to take a patient who is subject to guardianship or a detained patient who has been granted leave of absence under s.17 to the hospital or place where he is required to be. Reasonable force may be used to ensure that the patient is taken to that hospital or place (s.137).

Although there is a power in subs.(2A) to take a community patient to the hospital to which he has been recalled, there is no power to take such a patient to a place where he is required to be as a condition of the CTO because there is no power to return the patient to that place.

Regulations as to transfer of patients

1-321   **19.**—(1)   In such circumstances and subject to such conditions as may be prescribed by regulations made by the Secretary of State—

    (a)   a patient who is for the time being liable to be detained in a hospital by virtue of an application under this Part of this Act may be transferred to another hospital or into the guardianship of a local social services authority or of any person approved by such an authority;

    (b)   a patient who is for the time being subject to the guardianship of a local social services authority or other person by virtue of an application under this Part of this Act may be transferred into the guardianship of another local social services authority or person, or be transferred to a hospital.

(2) Where a patient is transferred in pursuance of regulations under this section, the provisions of this Part of this Act (including this subsection) shall apply to him as follows, that is to say—

(a) in the case of a patient who is liable to be detained in a hospital by virtue of an application for admission for assessment or for treatment and is transferred to another hospital, as if the application were an application for admission to that other hospital and as if the patient had been admitted to that other hospital at the time when he was originally admitted in pursuance of the application;

(b) in the case of a patient who is liable to be detained in a hospital by virtue of such an application and is transferred into guardianship, as if the application were a guardianship application duly accepted at the said time;

(c) in the case of a patient who is subject to guardianship by virtue of a guardianship application and is transferred into the guardianship of another authority or person, as if the application were for his reception into the guardianship of that authority or person and had been accepted at the time when it was originally accepted;

(d) in the case of a patient who is subject to guardianship by virtue of a guardianship application and is transferred to a hospital, as if the guardianship application were an application for admission to that hospital for treatment and as if the patient had been admitted to the hospital at the time when the application was originally accepted.

(3) Without prejudice to subsections (1) and (2) above, any patient, who is for the time being liable to be detained under this Part of this Act in a -hospital vested in the Secretary of State for the purposes of his functions under the [National Health Service Act 2006, in a hospital vested in the Welsh Ministers for the purposes of their functions under the National Health Service (Wales) Act 2006, in any accommodation used under either of those Acts] by the managers of such a hospital [or in a hospital vested in a National Health Service trust] [, NHS foundation trust or] [, Local Health Board] [...], may at any time be removed to any other such hospital or accommodation [which is managed by the managers of, or is vested in the National Health Service trust[, NHS foundation trust or] [, Local Health Board] [...] for, the first-mentioned hospital]; and paragraph (a) of subsection (2) above shall apply in relation to a patient so removed as it applies in relation to a patient transferred in pursuance of regulations made under this section.

(4) Regulations made under this section may make provision for regulating the conveyance to their destination of patients authorised to be transferred or removed in pursuance of the regulations or under subsection (3) above.

Amendments

In subs.(3) the words in square brackets were inserted and substituted by the National Health Service and Community Care Act 1990 s.66(1), Sch.9 para.24(2), the Health and Social Care (Community Health and Standards) Act 2003 s.34, Sch.4 para.52, the Health Act 1999 (Supplementary, Consequential, etc., Provisions) Order 2000 (SI 2000/90) Sch.1 para.16(3), the National Health Service (Consequential Provisions) Act 2006 s.2, Sch.1 para.64, the Mental Health Act 2007 s.46(2) and the Health and Social Care Act 2012 Sch.5 para.25.

Definitions

1-322   patient: s.145(1).
hospital: ss.34(2), 145(1).
local social services authority: s.145(1).
application for admission for assessment: ss.2, 145(1).
application for admission for treatment: ss.3, 145(1).
guardianship application: s.7(1).
Local Health Board: s.145(1).
the managers: s.145(1).

General Note

1-323   This section empowers the Secretary of State (or, in relation to Wales, the Welsh Ministers) to regulate the circumstances in which detained patients and patients who are subject to guardianship may be transferred between hospitals or guardians or between detention in hospital and guardianship. It only applies to transfers within England and Wales. The Mental Health (Hospital, Guardianship and Treatment) (England) Regulations 2008 (SI 2008/1184) and the Mental Health (Hospital, Guardianship, Community Treatment and Consent to Treatment) (Wales) Regulations 2008 (SI 2008/2439 (W.212)) have been made under this section. The transfer of a restricted patient between hospitals is subject to the agreement of the Secretary of State: see below and the notes on s.41(3)(c).

Those who are required to decide whether the risk posed by a patient is low enough to make it appropriate for him to be accommodated in medium rather than high security are the persons upon whom the statutory powers have been vested by Parliament. It is not for the court to substitute its judgment for the statutory decision-maker. The court's role is the secondary one of determining whether the decision-making process has been a proper one and whether the judgment reached is one reasonably open on the evidence (*R. (on the application of P) v Mersey NHS Trust* [2003] EWHC 994 (Admin), Richards J.; followed and affirmed by Munby J. in *R. (on the application of IR) v Shetty* [2003] EWHC 3022 (Admin)). The approach taken in these cases and in *L*, below, was affirmed by the Court of Appeal in *R. (on the application of YZ) v Oxleas NHS Foundation Trust* [2017] EWCA Civ 203; [2017] M.H.L.R. 293, a case involving the transfer of a transgender patient to a high security hospital, where Lord Thomas C.J. said that the "court will pay the highest regard to the bona fide professional judgement of the responsible clinician.... [S]uch judgement would generally be sufficient evidence on which a court could determine the lawfulness of the decision to transfer, absent compelling evidence to the contrary" (para.88). It followed that applications for judicial review of decisions to transfer in such cases should be "very rare indeed" (para.89).

In *R. (on the application of L) v West London Mental Health NHS Trust* [2014] EWCA Civ 47; [2014] M.H.L.R. 361, the Court of Appeal held that the requirements of the common law principles of procedural fairness applied to cases where a detained patient is being considered for transfer from conditions of medium security to conditions of high security. The court further held that:

1.   Where, as in this case, the decision in question is largely a clinically-based decision with an added rationing aspect because of the scarcity of high security beds, there is a need for circumspection as to what procedure is required (para.8).

2.   Procedural fairness can be satisfied by the "gist" of the letter of reference to the high security hospital by the hospital that wishes to transfer the patient and the assessment by the clinician from the high security hospital being provided to the patient and/or his or her representative. This procedure need not be followed in cases of urgency, where there is a clinical reason precluding such notification, or where there is some other reason such as the exposure of other patients or staff to the risk of harm (para.99).

3.   The "gist" can be provided by enclosing them with a largely pro forma communication informing the patient and/or his representatives that, if they disagree with the factual or clinical triggers for the reference or assessment, they can make submissions in writing which will be considered by the admissions panel of the high security hospital. This does not preclude the hospital providing copies of the letter of reference and the assessment rather than the "gist" of those documents, but that is not a requirement of fairness in this context (para.99).

4.   It is not necessary for the patient to be given an opportunity to make representations to the putative transferring hospital before the reference is made (para.100).

The guidance given by the Court of Appeal in this case is reflected in the *Code of Practice* at para.37.22.

In order to comply with the empowerment and involvement principle set out at para.1.7 of the *Code of Practice* and the requirements of art.8 of the European Convention of Human Rights (ECHR), patients should be involved, as far as is both practicable and proportionate, in the process leading to all transfer decisions.

In (*R. (on the application of T) v Chief Executive of Nottinghamshire Healthcare NHS Trust* [2006] EWHC 800 (Admin); [2006] M.H.L.R. 103, the patient failed in his attempt to challenge his transfer from one high security hospital to another, which was based on a policy decision of the Department of Health that, if certain criteria are met, patients should be transferred to the high security hospital closest to their postal address.

For the responsibility to inform the patient's nearest relative of a transfer under this section, see reg.26(1)(a) or (i) of the English Regulations and reg.30 of the Welsh Regulations.

This section applies to patients who are subject to hospital or guardianship orders made by a court under s.37, with the modification that subs.(2) shall read as follows:

"(2) Where a patient is transferred in pursuance of regulations under this section, the provisions of this Part of this Act (including this subsection) shall apply to him [as if the order or direction under Part III of this Act by virtue of which he was liable to be detained or subject to guardianship before being transferred were an order or direction for his admission or removal to the hospital to which he is transferred, or placing him under the guardianship of the authority or person into whose guardianship he is transferred, as the case may be]." (Sch.1, Pt 1, paras 2, 5.)

For restricted patients subs.(1), (2) and (3) shall read as follows:

"(1) In such circumstances and subject to such conditions as may be prescribed by regulations made by the Secretary of State—
   (a) a patient who is for the time being liable to be detained in a hospital by virtue of an application under this Part of this Act may [with the consent of the Secretary of State] be transferred to another hospital [...]
(2) Where a patient is transferred in pursuance of regulations under this section, the provisions of this Part of this Act (including this sub-section) shall apply to him [as if the order or direction under Part III of this Act by virtue of which he was liable to be detained before being transferred were an order or direction for his admission or removal to the hospital to which he is transferred].
(3) Without prejudice to subsections (1) and (2) above, any patient, who is for the time being liable to be detained under this Part of this Act in a hospital vested in the Secretary of State for the purposes of his functions under the [National Health Service Act 2006, in a hospital vested in the Welsh Ministers for the purposes of their functions under the National Health Service (Wales) Act 2006, in any accommodation used under either of those Acts] by the managers of such a hospital [or in a hospital vested in a National Health Service trust][, NHS foundation trust or][Local Health Board] [...], may at any time [, with the consent of the Secretary of State,] be removed to any other such hospital or accommodation [which is managed by the managers of, or is vested in the National Health Service trust[, NHS foundation trust or][Local Health Board] which is managed by the managers of, or is vested in the National Health Service Trust [...] for, the first-mentioned hospital]; and para.(a) of subs.(2) above shall apply in relation to a patient so removed as it applies in relation to a patient transferred in pursuance of regulations made under this section." (Sch.1, Pt II, paras 2, 5.)

The effect of these provisions is that any transfer of a restricted patient between hospitals, even where the hospitals are administered by the same managers, is subject to the agreement of the Secretary of State: also see the notes on s.41(3)(c).

Named hospital units

If a restricted patient is detained in a named hospital unit (see the General Note to s.41), the agreement of the Secretary of State is needed for movement out of that unit. **1-324**

Human Rights Act 1998

While art.8 contains no explicit procedural requirements, the decision-making process leading to **1-325**
measures of interference must be fair and such as to afford due respect to the interests safeguarded by that article: see *R. (on the application of L) v West London Mental Health NHS Trust*, above, at para.77. Also see para.37.18 of the *Code of Practice* which states:

"People authorising transfers on the hospital managers' behalf should ensure that there are good reasons for the transfer and that the needs and interests of the patient have been considered. Transfers are potentially an interference with a patient's right to respect for privacy and family life under article 8 of the European Convention on Human Rights (ECHR), and care should be taken to act compatibly with the ECHR when deciding whether to authorise a transfer."

Applications to the First-tier Tribunal (Mental Health) or the Mental Health Review Tribunal for Wales

1-326   The patient may make an application within 6 months of a transfer from guardianship to hospital (s.66(1)(e), (2)(e)) and once in every period for which the detention is renewed. If this right is not exercised within six months of the transfer, the hospital managers will refer the case to the tribunal (s.68(1)). A patient who is transferred from hospital to guardianship has the same right to make an application as a guardianship patient who is made subject to a guardianship application on the day that the transfer takes effect (subs.(2)(b)).

In *R. (on the application of L) v West London Mental Health NHS Trust* [2012] EWHC 3200 (Admin); [2013] M.H.L.R. 297, Stadlen J. said at para.184:

"[I]f a patient ... who has been detained pursuant to a hospital order and who has been transferred against his will from a medium security hospital to a high security hospital does not seek a direction for his discharge from detention under the 1983 Act but only a transfer back to a medium secure hospital, there is in theory nothing to stop him from applying to the Tribunal for a recommendation that he be transferred ...."

Code of Practice

1-327   Guidance on this section is contained in Ch.37 at para.37.16.

The transfer of documents

1-328   Paragraph 37.27 of the *Code of Practice* states:

"When a patient is transferred, the documents authorising detention, including the authority for transfer, any original AMHP reports, risk reports, Tribunal information, care plans and other relevant information should be sent to the hospital to which the patient is transferred. The transferring hospital should retain copies of these documents."

Subsection (1)

1-329   **Regulations**   See regs 7, 8, 10 and 11 of the English Regulations and regs 23, 24 and 27 of the Welsh Regulations.

Paragraph (a)

1-330   **Patient**   In order to be transferred under this provision, the patient must have been admitted to the hospital named in the application (see the phrase "originally admitted" in subs.(2)(a)) and the hospital must have accepted the application (see the note on "sufficient authority for the Managers" in s.6(2)). The patient must be admitted to the hospital to which he is being transferred: see reg.7(2)(b) of the English Regulations (reg.23(2)(b) of the Welsh Regulations). There is no need for an admission to the hospital to which he is being transferred to take place if the transfer is effected under subs.(3), i.e. the hospitals concerned are managed by the same hospital managers (ibid. reg.7(1)(a) and reg.23(1)(a) respectively).

A transfer under this provision can be effected at a time when the patient has been placed on leave of absence under s.17 at the hospital to which he is being transferred in which case the transfer takes place when the managers of the new hospital complete Part 2 of Form H4 (in Wales Part 2 of Form TC2).

By virtue of an application   Including a patient who has been detained under ss.2 or 4. Patients who have been made subject to hospital orders or guardianship orders by a court are also included: see the General Note, above. Patients who are detained in hospital but who have not been made subject to an application are excluded, i.e. patients detained under ss.5(2), (4), 35, 36, 38, 135 and 136 or who are detained in a place of safety under s.37(4).

Transferred to another hospital   Including a high security hospital. The transfer to another hospital of patients who are subject to s.5(2) or (4) is considered in the General Note to s.5 under the heading "Transfers to other hospitals".

Paragraph (b)

Transferred into the guardianship of another person   Transfer from one guardian to another can, in certain circumstances, also take place under s.10.   **1-331**

At the said time   Which is the time when the patient was originally admitted in pursuance of the application: see para.(a).

Subsection (2)

Paragraph (a)   The application for the detention of a patient who is transferred to another hospital under this provision is to be treated as if it is an application for the detention of the patient at that other hospital made at the time when he was originally admitted under that application.   **1-332**

Transferred   Using the procedure set out in reg.7(2) and Form H4 of the English Regulations and reg.23(1),(2),(3) and Form TC1 of the Welsh Regulations. Transfer to another hospital managed by the same managers is allowed for without formality under subs.(3).

Hospital   Or registered establishment (s.34(2)). The transfer of a patient between registered establishments where both establishments are under the same management is governed by reg.7(5) of the English Regulations and reg.23(6) of the Welsh Regulations.

Paragraph (b)   The application for the detention of a patient who is transferred into guardianship under this provision is to be treated as if the application was a guardianship application made at the time when he was admitted to hospital under the application for detention. If an unrestricted s.37 patient is transferred into guardianship, the transfer is to a civil s.7 guardianship.   **1-333**

Transferred into guardianship   Using the procedure set out in reg.7(4) and Form G6 of the English Regulations and reg.23(4),(5) and Form TC2 of the Welsh Regulations. Restricted patients may not be transferred into guardianship: see the General Note to this section.
Paragraph 10.37 of the Reference Guide states:

> "An authorisation for transfer to guardianship does not give anyone any authority to convey the patient in question anywhere. If the patient did not go to the place, if any, the new guardian requires them to live, they would be considered AWOL and so could be taken to that place in accordance with section 18."

Although the patient's nearest relative has no statutory right to object to such a transfer, he or she can discharge the patient from guardianship (s.23(2)(b)).

As if the application were a guardianship application   The original application will have either been for assessment under s.2 or for treatment under s.3 (subs.(2)(a)). Any outstanding tribunal application must proceed using guardianship criteria set out in s.72(4).

Paragraph (c)   The guardianship application of a patient who is transferred into the guardianship of another local authority under this provision is to be treated as if it is an application for the reception of the patient into the guardianship of that other authority made at the time when the patient was originally received into guardianship.   **1-334**

Transferred   Using the procedure set out in reg.8(1) and Form G7 of the English Regulations and reg.24(1),(2),(3) and Form TC3 of the Welsh Regulations.

Paragraph (d)   The guardianship application of a patient who is transferred to hospital under this provision is to be treated as if it is an application for admission for treatment of the patient made at the time when the guardianship application was accepted. The guardian should ensure that this date is communicated to the hospital managers.   **1-335**
If a patient is transferred under this paragraph, it would appear that the three-month period relating

to the administration of medicine specified in s.58(1)(b) would commence from the first occasion when medicine was administered to the patient during the period when he was subject to guardianship.

Transferred   Using the procedure set out in reg.8(2) and Form G8 of the English Regulations and reg.24(4),(5) and Form TC4 of the Welsh Regulations.

Subsection (3)

1-336   This subsection, which applies to NHS hospitals, enables a patient to be transferred to another hospital, or other accommodation managed by the same managers without any special procedure being followed. A similar provision for independent hospitals is contained in reg.7(5) of the English Regulations and reg.23(6) of the Welsh Regulations. A patient who is transferred under this provision is treated as if he had been admitted to the hospital to which he has been transferred at the time of the original application.

This subsection does not apply to patients who have been detained in hospital under s.5(2) or (4). If, following the use of these powers, the assessment of the patient concludes that an application ought to be made in respect of him, the application can be addressed to a different hospital.

Vested in the secretary of state   Or in the Welsh Ministers for the purposes of their functions under the National Health Service (Wales) Act 2006 (SI 2000/253, Sch.3; also see the General Note to this Act).

[Regulations as to assignment of responsibility for community patients

1-337   **19A.**—(1)   Responsibility for a community patient may be assigned to another hospital in such circumstances and subject to such conditions as may be prescribed by regulations made by the Secretary of State (if the responsible hospital is in England) or the Welsh Ministers (if that hospital is in Wales).

(2)   If responsibility for a community patient is assigned to another hospital—

(a)   the application for admission for treatment in respect of the patient shall have effect (subject to section 17D above) as if it had always specified that other hospital;

(b)   the patient shall be treated as if he had been admitted to that other hospital at the time when he was originally admitted in pursuance of the application (and as if he had subsequently been discharged under section 17A above from there); and

(c)   that other hospital shall become "the responsible hospital" in relation to the patient for the purposes of this Act.]

Amendment

This section was inserted by the Mental Health Act 2007 s.32(4), Sch.3 para.4.

Definitions

1-338   community patient: ss.17A(7), 145(1).
responsible hospital: ss.17A(7), 145(1).
application for admission for treatment: s.145(1).

General Note

1-339   This section enables the Secretary of State (in respect of a hospital in England) or the Welsh Ministers (in respect of a hospital in Wales) to make regulations which transfer the responsibility for a community patient to a new responsible hospital. If responsibility is transferred, the patient is to be treated as if he had been originally admitted to the new responsible hospital.

This section applies to patients who have been made subject to hospital orders with the modification that subs.(2)(b) shall be omitted (Sch.1 Pt 1 paras 2, 5A).

Subsection (1)

Prescribed by regulations   See reg.17 of the English Regulations and reg.25 of the Welsh   **1-340**
Regulations. Authority for the assignment must be given on Form CTO10 (in Wales, Form TC5).

[DURATION OF AUTHORITY AND DISCHARGE]

Duration of authority

20.—(1)   Subject to the following provisions of this Part of this Act, a patient   **1-341**
admitted to hospital in pursuance of an application for admission for treatment, and
a patient placed under guardianship in pursuance of a guardianship application, may
be detained in a hospital or kept under guardianship for a period not exceeding six
months beginning with the day on which he was so admitted, or the day on which
the guardianship application was accepted, as the case may be, but shall not be so
detained or kept for any longer period unless the authority for his detention or
guardianship is renewed under this section.

(2)   Authority for the detention or guardianship of a patient may, unless the
patient has previously been discharged [under section 23 below], be renewed—
   (a)   from the expiration of the period referred to in subsection (1) above,
         for a further period of six months;
   (b)   from the expiration of any period of renewal under paragraph (a)
         above, for a further period of one year,
and so on for periods of one year at a time.

(3)   Within the period of two months ending on the day on which a patient who
is liable to be detained in pursuance of an application for admission for treatment
would cease under this section to be so liable in default of the renewal of the authority for his detention, it shall be the duty of the [responsible clinician]—
   (a)   to examine the patient; and
   (b)   if it appears to him that the conditions set out in subsection (4) below
         are satisfied, to furnish to the managers of the hospital where the
         patient is detained a report to that effect in the prescribed form;
and where such a report is furnished in respect of a patient the managers shall, unless they discharge the patient [under section 23 below], cause him to be informed.

(4)   The conditions referred to in subsection (3) above are that—
   (a)   the patient is suffering from [mental disorder] of a nature or degree
         which makes it appropriate for him to receive medical treatment in a
         hospital; and
   (b)   […]
   (c)   it is necessary for the health or safety of the patient or for the protec-
         tion of other persons that he should receive such treatment and that it
         cannot be provided unless he continues to be detained; [and
   (d)   appropriate medical treatment is available to him.]
[…]

(5)   Before furnishing a report under subsection (3) above the [responsible clini-
cian] shall consult one or more other persons who have been professionally
concerned with the patient's medical treatment.

[(5A)   But the responsible clinician may not furnish a report under subsection
(3) above unless a person—
   (a)   who has been professionally concerned with the patient's medical treat-
         ment; but
   (b)   who belongs to a profession other than that to which the responsible

[165]

clinician belongs, states in writing that he agrees that the conditions set out in subsection (4) above are satisfied.]

(6)   Within the period of two months ending with the day on which a patient who is subject to guardianship under this Part of this Act would cease under this section to be so liable in default of the renewal of the authority for his guardianship, it shall be the duty of the [appropriate practitioner]—

(a)   to examine the patient; and

(b)   if it appears to him that the conditions set out in subsection (7) below are satisfied, to furnish to the guardian and, where the guardian is a person other than a local social services authority, to the responsible local social services authority a report to that effect in the prescribed form;

and where such a report is furnished in respect of a patient, the local social services authority shall, unless they discharge the patient [under section 23 below], cause him to be informed.

(7)   The conditions referred to in subsection (6) above are that—

(a)   the patient is suffering from [mental disorder] of a nature or degree which warrants his reception into guardianship; and

(b)   it is necessary in the interests of the welfare of the patient or for the protection of other persons that the patient should remain under guardianship.

(8)   Where a report is duly furnished under subsection (3) or (6) above, the authority for the detention or guardianship of the patient shall be thereby renewed for the period prescribed in that case by subsection (2) above.

(9)   [...]

(10)   [...]

Amendments

The amendments to this section were made by the Mental Health Act 2007 ss.1(4), 4(4), 9(4), 32(4), 55, Sch.3 para.5, Sch.11 Pts 1, 2 and 3. The cross-heading was amended by s.32(3).

Definitions

1-342   patient: s.145(1).
hospital: ss.34(2), 145(1).
application for admission for treatment: ss.3, 145(1).
appropriate medical treatment: ss.3(4), 145(1AB).
the managers: s.145(1).
mental disorder: ss.1, 145(1).
medical treatment: s.145(1), (4).
guardianship application: s.7(1).
local social services authority: s.145(1).
responsible clinician: s.34(1).
appropriate clinician: s.145(1).
appropriate practitioner: s.34(1).
responsible local social services authority: s.34(1).

General Note

1-343   This section provides for patients who have been detained for treatment under s.3 or placed under guardianship under s.7 to be detained or kept under guardianship for an initial period of up to six months. It also sets out the criteria that have to be satisfied if the authority to detain a patient or keep him in guardianship is to be renewed. Renewal, which can be for one further period of six months and subsequently for periods of one year at a time, cannot cure any illegality in the original application, order

[166]

or direction (*R. (on the application of SP) v Secretary of State for Justice* [2010] EWHC 1124 (Admin), para.4).

As a restricted patient whose restriction order has ceased to have effect is treated as if he had been admitted to hospital as an unrestricted patient on the date when the restriction order ceased to have effect (s.41(5)), the start date for renewals for such patients under this section is that date.

The finding of McCullough J. in *R. v Hallstrom Ex p. W* [1986] 2 All E.R. 306, that a decision to renew the authority to detain a patient cannot be made at a time when the patient is on leave of absence was overruled by the Court of Appeal in *R. v Barking Havering and Brentwood Community Healthcare NHS Trust* [1999] 1 F.L.R. 106. A renewal can be made while the patient is on leave of absence if hospital treatment comprises a significant component of the patient's treatment plan: see the notes on subs.(4).

For the responsibility to inform the patient's nearest relative of the patient's renewal of detention or guardianship under this section, see reg.26(1)(b) or (l) of the English Regulations and regs 8 and 15 of the Welsh Regulations.

This section applies to patients who are subject to an unrestricted hospital order or a guardianship order made by a court under s.37, with the modification that subs.(1) shall read as follows:

"(1) Subject to the following provisions of this Part of this Act, a patient admitted to hospital in pursuance of an application for admission for treatment, and a patient placed under guardianship in pursuance of a guardianship application, may be detained in a hospital or kept under guardianship for a period not exceeding six months beginning with the [date of the relevant order or direction under Part III of this Act] but shall not be so detained or kept for any longer period unless the authority for his detention or guardianship is renewed under this section" (Sch.1, Pt 1, para.6).

Human Rights Act 1998

The question whether the continued detention of an asymptomatic patient contravenes art.5 of the European Convention of Human Rights (ECHR) is considered in the General Note to s.3 under this heading. A finding by a RC that the patient is no longer suffering from a mental disorder (see subs.(4)(a)) does not require the patient's immediate release from detention if that patient poses a risk to the public: see the note on s.23 under this heading. **1-344**

It is has been argued that the lack of any involvement of the hospital managers as detaining authority in the decision to renew the patient's detention (see the *Warlingham Park Hospital* case, noted under subs.(3)) might constitute a violation of art.5(1) of the ECHR as interpreted by the European Court of Human Rights (ECtHR) in *Winterwerp v Netherlands* (1979) 2 E.H.R.R. 387: see Phil Fennell, "The Third Way in Mental Health Policy: Negative Rights, Positive Rights and the Convention", (1999) 26 *Journal of Law and Society*, 103-127.

Among the functions that a responsible clinician (RC) has is the decision whether to renew the detention of the patient under this section. In *Winterwerp v Netherlands*, above, the ECtHR held that that in order for a detention on the ground of unsoundness of mind to be lawful it must be established by objective medical expertise that the person concerned suffers from a true mental disorder. During the passage of the 2007 Act through Parliament, the Joint Committee argued that if initial detention must be based on medical expertise to be compatible with art.5, there is an argument, following *Winterwerp*, that the same should apply to the renewal of detention. In support of this argument, the Joint Committee relied on *Varbanov v Bulgaria* [2000] M.H.L.R. 263 where the court held that it would be a breach of art.5 if a person were detained on the basis that they were of unsound mind without first obtaining the opinion of a medical expert. The Joint Committee argued that this case made it clear that that the opinion of a medical expert who is a psychiatrist is necessary and that renewal of detention by a RC who is not a psychiatrist would contravene art.5. The Government, in not agreeing that *Varbanov* requires the necessary medical expertise to be provided every time by a psychiatrist, countered by claiming that: (a) there is no caselaw specifically on what is meant by medical expertise; (b) *Winterwerp* was not seeking to lay down which sort of qualifications available in a national system which would be acceptable and which would not; (c) the ECHR is a "living instrument" that must be interpreted in the light of present day conditions; and (d) within a modern workforce, it is appropriate for Mental Health Act functions to be allocated to those who are competent to perform them. In the light of these considerations, the Government's view is that *Winterwerp* must be broadly interpreted and that what was required is a person who is able to make a decision as to whether or not the person in question is of unsound mind. As the competencies that must be satisfied before a person can become an Approved Clinician include the ability to identify the presence and severity of mental disorder, the Government argued that such a person will have the objective medical expertise required by art.5. It is likely that the ECtHR court would support the Government's contention that it is for national authorities to decide which professionals possess the required expertise to perform functions under the Act as this is a matter which is likely to come within the "margin of appreciation" that the ECtHR allows national authorities to have when applying the ECHR. However, it should be noted that the ECtHR has recently indicated that in some circumstances psychiatric expertise is necessary (*Ilnseher v Germany* [2019] M.H.L.R. 278, para.130). This issue is considered at paras 21 to 29 of the Joint Committee's Report and at paras 24 to 34 of the Government's response to the Report, Department of Health, April 13, 2007.

Applications to the First-tier Tribunal (Mental Health) or the Mental Health Review Tribunal for Wales

1-345   The patient's right to apply to a tribunal arises from the date of the renewal of the detention or guardianship (s.66(1)(f),(2)(f)).

Code of Practice

1-346   Guidance on the renewal of a patient's detention is given in Ch.32.

Subsection (1)

1-347 **Six months**   A month means a calendar month (Interpretation Act 1978 s.5, Sch.1).

Beginning with   Including the day on which the patient was admitted to hospital or the day on which the guardianship application was accepted by the local social services authority (*Zoan v Rouamba* [2000] 2 All E.R. 620 CA). This means that if the patient was admitted on March 3, the six month period would expire at midnight on September 2.

The day on which he was so admitted   This is either the day on which the patient was admitted to the hospital from the community whilst subject to an application under s.3, or the day on which the patient who was in hospital either informally or subject to an application made under s.2 was made subject to such an application. In both cases, admission only takes effect when the s.3 application has either been handed to an authorised person or it has been sent to the hospital managers electronically (reg.3(2) of the English Regulations). The time and date of the admission should be recorded on Form H3 (in Wales, Form HO14).

Subsection (3)

1-348   This subsection requires the RC to examine a patient detained for treatment during the two months preceding the day on which the authority for his detention is due to expire. The period of detention can be extended if the patient is absent without leave: see s.21 and following. If the RC considers that the conditions set out in subs.(4) are satisfied, the authority to detain the patient is renewed when Form H5 (in Wales, Form HO15) has been completed and furnished to the hospital managers: see reg.13(1),(2),(3) of the English Regulations and reg.5 of the Welsh Regulations and the note on "furnish" below. The RC's duty under this section cannot be delegated. Before furnishing the report to the hospital managers, the RC must have consulted with a professional who has been concerned with the patient's medical treatment (subs.(5)) and received confirmation from such a person (not coming from the same profession as the RC) that the conditions for renewal are satisfied (subs.(5A)).

This section does not require that the RC's report should have been considered by the managers before renewal can take place, although it is good practice for this to happen. In *R. v Managers of Warlingham Park Hospital Ex p. B* (1994) 22 B.M.L.R. 1 CA Sir Thomas Bingham M.R. said at 11:

"In my judgment it is essential to distinguish between the authority to detain, which section 20 makes dependent on the due furnishing of a report, and the decision whether or not to discharge, assuming that there was a continued authority to detain, which is plainly entrusted, as section 23 makes plain, to the managers".

ending on the day   Given that the period of detention begins with the day on which the patient was admitted (subs.(1)), it will cease at the end of the preceding day: see the note on "beginning with" above.

Two months   This time limit applies to the examination of the patient by the RC, the forming of the RC's opinion and the furnishing of the report to the managers of the hospital where the patient is detained.

Responsible clinician   The guidance contained in para.39.17 of the *Code of Practice* that a person involved in making the decision whether to renew the detention of a patient "should not have any financial interest in the outcome of the decision" should not be followed in so far as it applies to the RC who is the only person who can trigger a renewal.

Examine the patient   Given the finding of the Divisional Court in *Devon Partnership NHS Trust v Secretary of State for Health and Social Care* [2021] EWHC 101 (Admin) (noted under s.11(5)), it is likely that a court would find that the physical presence of the examining doctor is required and that examining the patient cannot be undertaken by the use of remote technology. If a patient refuses to be examined or is assessed as being either too ill or too disturbed to be examined, the RC's examination of the patient could comprise: (1) her observations of the patient; (2) a consideration of the patient's medical history and prognosis; and (3) an evaluation of the patient's current condition in a multi-disciplinary case conference.

The examination could take place on an out-patient basis if the patient is on s.17 leave: see the note on subs.(4)(c).

Furnish   In the Scottish case of *Milborrow, Applicant*, 1996 S.C.L.R. 315 Sh.Ct, it was held that a report is "furnished" to the hospital managers when it is committed to the internal mailing system operated by those managers: see reg.3(7) of the English and Welsh Regulations. An alternative method of furnishing the report is to hand it to a member of staff authorised by the hospital managers to receive it.

The furnishing of the RC's report (Form H5 or, for Wales, Form HO15) gives authority for the continued detention of the patient: see subs.(8) and *R. v Managers of Warlingham Park Hospital*, noted above, where Sir Thomas Bingham M.R. said at 11: "If the authorised period of detention expires without there being a report duly furnished …, any detention after the expiry date will plainly be unlawful and render the managers at risk of successful action".

Managers of the hospital where the patient is detained   If, subsequent to the furnishing of a report under this section but before the hospital managers have had an opportunity to consider it, the patient is transferred to another hospital under s.19, the managers of that hospital should consider the report (s.19(2)(a)).

A report   The report, which should be kept with the patient's admission documents, requires the hospital managers to consider whether they should exercise their power of discharge in respect of the patient.

Forms H5 and HO15 provide for the patient's RC to state her reasons why it is not appropriate for the patient to revert to informal status. The fact that a Mental Health Act Administrator might consider the reasons given by the RC to be inadequate would not effect the validity of the renewal. The purpose of the requirement to give reasons is to assist the managers in their task of considering whether they should exercise their power under s.23 to discharge the patient. Unlike an application for detention, there is no requirement for the renewal to be accepted by the managers before it comes into force.

If the patient's situation changes, it is lawful for the RC to discharge him from detention after Pt I of the Form H5 (or Form HO15) has been signed, but before the hospital managers have had an opportunity to consider whether they should exercise their power of discharge. Where this occurs, the Form should be endorsed with a statement confirming that the RC's power of discharge was exercised on the date in question.

The fact that Part 4 of Form H5 (or Form HO 15) might not be completed until after the section has expired does not invalidate the renewal as it is the Form furnished by the patient's RC that renews the section. The furnishing of the Form must take place before the section expires.

A Form H5 or Form HO15 which is defective because of a minor error or slip of the pen would not render the renewal unlawful. Such errors may be corrected and initialled even though the rectification procedure in s.15 does not apply to this section. If the form is fundamentally defective in some way, for example it was signed by a person who is not the patient's RC or it was completed after the authority for the patient's detention had expired, the renewal would be unlawful: see *Re S-C (Mental Patient: Habeas Corpus)* [1996] 1 All E.R. 532, CA.

The date of the renewal is the date on which the authority to detain was due to expire and not the date of the report.

Unless they discharge the patient   In order to consider whether they should exercise their power of discharge under s.23(2)(a), the managers must consider the RC's report as a panel of at least three members (s.23(4)). The wording of this provision after para.(b) suggests that the managers should consider exercising their power of discharge prior to the patient being informed of the renewal. It is the conditions for renewal set out in subs.(4), rather than the conditions for the initial admission for treatment set out in s.3(2), that the managers should address: per Wilson J. speaking obiter in *R. (on the application of DR) v Mersey Care NHS Trust*, below, at para.19. Even if the conditions for renewal are met, the managers have a discretion under s.23(2) to order the patient's discharge (*R. v Riverside Mental Health Trust Ex p. Huzzey* (1998) 43 B.M.L.R. 167).

Subsection (4)

1-349   This subsection specifies the conditions which have to be satisfied if the authority to detain a patient who has been admitted for treatment is to be renewed.

It is not possible to renew the detention of a patient if there is no longer a need for the patient's treatment plan to contain an element of hospital treatment. In *R. v Barking Havering and Brentwood Community Healthcare NHS Trust* [1999] 1 F.L.R. 106, the patient had been granted leave of absence under s.17. At the time of the renewal of her detention under this section the patient was on leave of absence. The patient challenged the legality of the renewal on the ground that it contravened the ruling of McCullough J. in *R. v Hallstrom Ex p. W.* [1986] 2 All E.R. 306, that a patient's detention could not be renewed whilst she was "liable to be detained" during a period of leave of absence. In overruling McCullough J. on this point, the Court of Appeal held that as long as the patient's medical treatment viewed as a whole involved treatment in a hospital, the requirements of this section could be met. The fact that the patient happened to be away from hospital at the time of renewal did not mean that she was no longer "detained" for treatment. Further, a renewal would be lawful even if the periods of hospital care could be classified as being for the purposes of assessment and the monitoring of progress, rather than actual treatment.

The *Barking* case was applied by Sullivan J. in *R. (on the application of Epsom and St Helier NHS Trust) v The Mental Health Review Tribunal* [2001] EWHC Admin 101; [2001] M.H.L.R. 8, a case where the Trust challenged the decision of the Mental Health Review Tribunal to discharge the patient. The tribunal's decision was made on the ground that as the patient, who was residing in a nursing home on s.17 leave, was not receiving hospital treatment it was not "appropriate for her to be liable to be detained in hospital for medical treatment" for the purposes of s.72(1)(b)(i). His Lordship held that it would be inconsistent with the scheme of the Act if the mere prospect, that at some unspecified future time in-patient treatment would or might be required, compelled a tribunal to reject a patient's application for discharge. This case, which, it is submitted, also applies to the provision of hospital treatment under this section, is considered in the note on s.72(1)(b)(i).

Although Lord Woolf M.R. in *Barking* made an obiter distinction between out-patient and in-patient treatment by stating that if the treatment of the patient viewed as a whole "involves treatment as an *in-patient* the requirements of [this] section can be met" (at 113H; emphasis added), in *R. (on the application of DR) v Mersey Care NHS Trust* [2002] EWHC 1810 (Admin); [2002] M.H.L.R. 386 Wilson J. held that: (1) the test laid down in this subsection was whether the treatment plan provided for a patient to receive medical treatment in a hospital; (2) any distinction between treatment *at* a hospital and *in* a hospital was too subtle; (3) the hospital treatment must form a significant component of the patient's treatment plan, which can include specialist rehabilitation (s.145(1)); and (4) it would be an impermissible and illogical gloss on the Act to make the lawfulness of renewal dependent upon a plan to put the patient at times in a hospital bed. With regard to point (2), his Lordship did not follow the obiter remarks of McCullough J. in the *Hallstrom* case which are reproduced in the General Note to s.3. In *DR*, the treatment plan provided that the patient should attend occupational therapy at the hospital once a week, that she should receive medication for her mental disorder by injection at her home at fortnightly intervals and that she should attend the ward round at the hospital at weekly intervals. The object of the third requirement was to provide for occasions for "attempted dialogue; for monitoring; for assessment; and for review". Wilson J. held that it followed from this that a significant component of the patient's care plan was treatment in a hospital and that the conditions for renewal had been satisfied.

Given the definition of hospital in the National Health Service Act 2006, clinical contact with the patient could take place at a clinic or out-patient department maintained in connection with the institution such as a "local Community Mental Health Treatment Base": see *KL v Somerset Partnership NHS Foundation Trust* [2011] UKUT 233 (AAC); [2011] M.H.L.R. 194, at para.9 and the note on "hospital" in s.145(1). It is submitted that there must be a clear clinical rationale for the treatment to take place at the hospital rather than at some other location. For example, medical treatment such an injection of anti-psychotic medication that could be appropriately undertaken at the patient's home would not qualify as "treatment in a hospital" for the purposes of this provision. However, a requirement for the patient to attend the ward round at appropriate intervals for assessment and monitoring by staff would meet the test established by this subsection if the assessment and monitoring comprised a significant component of the patient's treatment plan. In *KL v Somerset Partnership NHS Foundation Trust* at para.9, UT Judge

Rowland accepted a submission that *DR* "shows that reviews may be part of a patient's 'medical treatment' …".

DR was applied in *R. (on the application of CS) v Mental Health Review Tribunal* [2004] EWHC 2958 (Admin); [2004] M.H.L.R. 355, where Pitchford J. upheld the decision of a tribunal not to discharge a patient from detention under s.3 where the patient had been granted leave of absence under s.17 to reside at her home subject to the condition that she attended the hospital as an outpatient for weekly sessions with a psychologist, and forward round reviews at monthly intervals. The purpose of the ward round reviews were to: (1) discuss with the patient how her leave was progressing, how her medication was suiting her and whether any adjustments were necessary to the dose of her medication; and (2) provide the patient with supportive and motivational interviewing to help her to move out of the hospital-based model of care to community-based care under the Assertive Outreach Service. His Lordship held that viewed as a whole, the course of treatment should be seen as a continuing responsive programme during which the need for treatment at the hospital and on leave was being constantly reassessed depending upon the circumstances, including the patient's response to the Assertive Outreach Service and the ward round. Until such time as the transition was complete, the element of treatment at hospital remained a significant part of the whole (para.44). His Lordship said at para.46:

"It is clear to me that the [RC] was engaged in a delicate balancing exercise by which she was, with as light a touch as she could, encouraging progress to discharge. Her purpose was to break the persistent historical cycle of admission, serious relapse and readmission. It may be in the closing stages of the treatment in hospital her grasp on the [patient] was gossamer thin, but to view that grasp as insignificant is, in my view, to misunderstand the evidence."

His Lordship commented that the patient's "knowledge of the [RC's] powers was a significant element in her willingness to accept the treatment plan" (para.48).

In *DB v Betsi Cadwaladr UHB* [2021] UKUT 53 (AAC); [2021] M.H.L.R. 335, a patient who had been on leave under s.17 since October 2019 applied to a tribunal for his discharge. He had not set foot in the hospital since that date (i.e. for 11 months). His "virtual bed", as his solicitor put it, was at two different sites during his leave. Throughout that time, DB had been living in a care home with supervised leave in the community.

UT Judge Jacobs held that:

1. It is not sufficient for the tribunal to find that that the administration of medication in a care home was a significant component of the patient's care plan; the tribunal must also find that a significant component of that plan was being provided in hospital (para.11).
2. Liability to detention under s.17 is not a fallback when other options, such as a CTO, are unsuitable or unavailable: if the statutory conditions for detention are not met, the tribunal must direct discharge (para.13).

The *Epsom*, *DR*, *DB* and *CS* cases are also considered in the notes on s.72(1)(b)(i) under "Appropriate for him to be liable to be detained in a hospital for medical treatment".

Paragraph (a)

Mental disorder   A patient's learning disability must be associated with abnormally aggressive or seriously irresponsible conduct (s.1(2A), (2B)).   **1-350**

Appropriate for him to receive medical treatment in a hospital   See (*R. (on the application of DR) v Mersey Care Trust*, above. As this provision refers to *a* hospital rather than *the* hospital, this provision can be satisfied where the patient is receiving treatment for a mental disorder at a hospital where he is required to be as a condition of leave of absence.

Paragraph (c)

Health or safety of the patient or for the protection of other persons   See the notes on s.3(2)(c).   **1-351**

Unless he continues to be detained   This term means "unless he continues to be liable to be detained" and not "unless he continues actually to be detained". This ground can therefore be satisfied in respect of a patient who has been granted leave of absence under s.17: see the *Barking* case, above.

This ground could be satisfied in relation to a potentially dangerous patient who is compliant with medication and who is willing to remain in hospital as an informal patient. This is because an essential element of the patient's treatment is his preparation for eventual discharge from the hospital. A key element of such preparation is the granting of leave of absence to the patient. Given that the patient would pose a potential risk to the public, it would not be appropriate to allow the patient to leave the hospital in the absence of a mechanism that would enable staff to require the patient to return to the hospital should he exhibit a reluctance to do so. Section 17 provides such a mechanism. This ground is therefore satisfied because an essential element of the patient's treatment programme, the testing out of his readiness for discharge, can only be put in place if he were a detained patient who could be granted leave under s.17.

Paragraph (d)

1-352   See the note on s.3(2)(d).

Subsection (5)

1-353   **One or more other persons**   Who could belong to the same profession as the RC.

Professionally concerned   In respect of a patient who is being treated in hospital, it is not sufficient for the consultee merely to be working on the ward where the patient is being treated; a particular involvement with the patient's treatment is required.

Subsection (5A)

1-354   This subsection requires the RC who is renewing the detention of the patient to obtain a written statement from a person from another profession who has been professionally concerned with the patient's treatment that states that she agrees that the conditions of renewal are satisfied. The statement must be in the form set out in Pt 2 of Form H5: see reg.13(2) of the English Regulations (in Wales, Part 2 of Form HO15: see reg.5 of the Welsh Regulations). Subsection (5) requires the RC to consult at least one other person from the multidisciplinary team before she furnishes the renewal report and it is likely that this person will also provide the written statement as long as she comes from a different professional group from the RC. However, there is nothing to prevent the consulted person named on Part 1 of Form H5 not being the same person who signs Part 2 of that Form. The opening statement in Part 2 refers to "a professional" completing that part of the Form, not "the professional". The *Code of Practice* states:

"32.6 … [S]econd professionals should:

- have sufficient experience and expertise to decide whether the patient's continued detention is necessary and lawful, but need not be approved clinicians (nor be qualified to be one)
- have been actively involved in the planning, management or delivery of the patient's treatment, and
- have had sufficient recent contact with the patient to be able to make an informed judgement about the patient's case.

32.7 Second professionals should satisfy themselves, in line with the local policies, that they have sufficient information on which to make the decision. Whether that requires a separate clinical interview or examination of the patient will depend on the nature of the contact that the second professional already has with the patient and on the other circumstances of the case. Responsible clinicians should ensure that the second professional is given enough notice to be able to interview or examine the patient if appropriate.

32.8 Before examining patients to decide whether to make a renewal report, responsible clinicians should identify and record who the second professional is to be. Hospital managers' policies may, if the hospital mangers wish, say that the identity of the second professional is to be decided or agreed by a third party – such as a senior clinician or manager – but the Act does not require that.

32.9 Unless there are exceptional circumstances, the decision of the identified second professional should be accepted, even if the responsible clinician does not agree with it, and documented in the patient's notes including the reasons for the disagreement. If, in exceptional circumstances, it is decided that the agreement of a different second professional should be sought, this should be fully documented and the decision should be drawn to the attention of the hospital managers if, as a result, a renewal report is made."

Paragraphs 32.9 does not reflect the wording of this subsection and it is submitted that in the event of the second professional deciding that the grounds for renewal are not satisfied, the agreement of another second professional could be sought even if there are no "exceptional circumstances".

Subsection (6)

This subsection, together with subss.(7) and (8), provide for the patient's appropriate practitioner to renew the authority for guardianship. "Appropriate practitioner" is defined in s.34(1). The period of guardianship can be extended under s.21. Paragraph 30.25 of the *Code of Practice* states:

1-355

"Regulations require private guardians to appoint a doctor as the patient's nominated medical attendant. It is the nominated medical attendant who must examine the patient during the last two months of each period of guardianship and decide whether to make a report extending the patient's guardianship. (Where the patient's guardian is the local authority itself, this is done by the responsible clinician authorised by the local authority.)"

It is submitted that a local authority guardian has a duty to consider the contents of the appropriate practitioner's report at a hearing in order to decide whether to exercise their power of discharge: see the note on "unless they discharge the patient", below.

appropriate practitioner   The guidance contained in para.39.17 of the *Code of Practice* that a person involved in making the decision whether to renew the guardianship of a patient "should not have any financial interest in the outcome of the decision" should not be followed in so far as it applies to the appropriate practitioner who is the only person who can trigger a renewal.

Examine the patient   See the note on this phrase in subs.(3).

A report   See reg.13 and Form G9 of the English Regulations and reg.12 and Form GU6 of the Welsh Regulations. Minor errors in the report can be corrected: see the note on "report" in subs.(3).

Unless they discharge the patient   In order to consider whether they should exercise their power of discharge under s.23(2)(b), the local authority must meet as a panel of at least three members (s.23(4)). It is the conditions for renewal set out in subs. (7) that the local authority should address. Even if the conditions for renewal are met, the local authority has a discretion under s.23(2) to order the patient's discharge: see *R. v Riverside Mental Health Trust Ex p. Huzzey* (1998) 43 B.M.L.R. 167.

The local authority should require the care professional who has lead responsibility for the patient's welfare to provide a report on the patient's response to being subject to guardianship.

Community treatment period

[**20A.**—(1)   Subject to the provisions of this Part of this Act, a community treatment order shall cease to be in force on expiry of the period of six months beginning with the day on which it was made.

1-356

(2)   That period is referred to in this Act as "the community treatment period".

(3)   The community treatment period may, unless the order has previously ceased to be in force, be extended—

(a)   from its expiration for a period of six months;

(b)   from the expiration of any period of extension under paragraph (a) above for a further period of one year, and so on for periods of one year at a time.

(4)   Within the period of two months ending on the day on which the order would cease to be in force in default of an extension under this section, it shall be the duty of the responsible clinician—

(a)   to examine the patient; and

(b)   if it appears to him that the conditions set out in subsection (6) below are satisfied and if a statement under subsection (8) below is made, to furnish to the managers of the responsible hospital a report to that effect in the prescribed form.

(5)   Where such a report is furnished in respect of the patient, the managers shall, unless they discharge him under section 23 below, cause him to be informed.

(6)   The conditions referred to in subsection (4) above are that—

(a)   the patient is suffering from mental disorder of a nature or degree which makes it appropriate for him to receive medical treatment;

(b)   it is necessary for his health or safety or for the protection of other persons that he should receive such treatment;

(c)   subject to his continuing to be liable to be recalled as mentioned in paragraph (d) below, such treatment can be provided without his being detained in a hospital;

(d)   it is necessary that the responsible clinician should continue to be able to exercise the power under section 17E(1) above to recall the patient to hospital; and

(e)   appropriate medical treatment is available for him.

(7)   In determining whether the criterion in subsection (6)(d) above is met, the responsible clinician shall, in particular, consider, having regard to the patient's history of mental disorder and any other relevant factors, what risk there would be of a deterioration of the patient's condition if he were to continue not to be detained in a hospital (as a result, for example, of his refusing or neglecting to receive the medical treatment he requires for his mental disorder).

(8)   The statement referred to in subsection (4) above is a statement in writing by an approved mental health professional—

(a)   that it appears to him that the conditions set out in subsection (6) above are satisfied; and

(b)   that it is appropriate to extend the community treatment period.

(9)   Before furnishing a report under subsection (4) above the responsible clinician shall consult one or more other persons who have been professionally concerned with the patient's medical treatment.

(10)   Where a report is duly furnished under subsection (4) above, the community treatment period shall be thereby extended for the period prescribed in that case by subsection (3) above.]

Amendment

This section was inserted by the Mental Health Act 2007 s.20(3).

Definitions

1-357   community treatment order: ss.17A(7), 145(1).
responsible clinician: s.34(1).
the managers: s.145(1).
appropriate medical treatment: ss.3(4), 145(1AB).
hospital: ss.34(2), 145(1).
responsible hospital: ss.17A(7), 145(1).
mental disorder: ss.1, 145(1).
medical treatment: s.145(1), (4).
approved mental health practitioner: s.145(1), (1AC).

General Note

1-358   This section provides that a community treatment order (CTO) lasts for an initial period of six months from the date when the order was made (subs.(1)). This period is referred to as "the community treatment period" (subs.(2)). The community treatment period can be extended for a further period of six months and, following that, it can be extended for further periods of one year at a time (subs.(3)). The community period is extended from the date when it would otherwise expire, and not from the date of the report furnished under subs.(4)(b). If the community treatment period is not extended, the CTO shall cease to have effect (s.20B).

In order to renew the community treatment period, the patient's responsible clinician (RC) must examine the patient in the two months preceding the expiry date, and send a report to the hospital managers confirming that the conditions set out in subs.(6) are satisfied (subs.(4)). If the patient does not attend for examination voluntarily, the RC may recall him to hospital for this purpose: see ss.17B(3)(a) and 17E(2). Prior to sending the report, the RC must obtain a written statement from an AMHP confirming that (a) the conditions set out in subs.(6) are satisfied, and (b) it is appropriate to extend the community treatment period (subs.(8)). Before the report is sent, the RC must have consulted with one or more people who have been professionally concerned with the patient's medical treatment (subs. (9)). On receiving the report, the hospital managers must consider whether they should exercise their power under s.23 to discharge the patient from the CTO. If they decide not to discharge the patient, he must be informed that the CTO has been extended for the relevant period (subs.(5)). For the responsibility to inform the patient's nearest relative if the patient's period of community treatment is extended under this section, see reg.26(1)(e) of the English Regulations and reg.22(1)(a) of the Welsh Regulations.

This section applies without modification to patients who have been made subject to hospital orders (Sch.1 Pt 1 para.1).

Domestic Violence, Crime and Victims Act 2004

If the RC decides not to renew the CTO, she must inform the hospital managers if the patient comes within the scope of the 2004 Act: see the General Note to s.17A under this heading and "Guidance on the extension of victims' rights under the Domestic Violence, Crime and Victims Act 2004", Department of Health, 2008, paras 3.1 to 3.7. **1-359**

Applications to the First-tier Tribunal (Mental Health) or the Mental Health Review Tribunal for Wales

The patient's right to apply to a tribunal arises from the date of the renewal of the CTO (s.66(1)(fza), (2)(fza)). **1-360**

Code of Practice

Guidance on the extension of the community treatment period is contained in the following paragraphs: **1-361**

"32.11 All decisions should be taken in line with the least restrictive option and maximum independence principle, with guardianship or discharge being fully considered. Only responsible clinicians may extend the period of the CTO. To do so, responsible clinicians must examine their patient and decide, during the two months leading up to the day on which the patient's CTO is due to expire, whether the criteria for extending the CTO under section 20A of the Act are met. They must also consult one or more other people who have been professionally concerned with the patient's medical treatment.

32.12 The responsible clinician should also consult the wider multi-disciplinary team (MDT). Where appropriate, this should include the patient, nearest relative, the independent mental health advocate (IMHA) and/or other representative, family and carers, the local authority and clinical commissioning group [now the integrated care board] responsible for the patient's after-care (chapter 33); and any other key service providers. Consultation should take place during a care programme approach (CPA) assessment and before the responsible clinician decides whether or not to extend the CTO.

32.13 When deciding whether to extend the period of a CTO the responsible clinician, second professional and AMHP should all consider carefully whether or not the criteria for extending the CTO are met and, if so, whether an extension is appropriate. For example, the longer patients have been on a CTO without the need to exercise the power to recall them to hospital, the more important it will become to question whether that criterion is still satisfied.

32.14 Where responsible clinicians are satisfied that the criteria for extending the patient's CTO are met, they must submit a report to that effect to the managers of the responsible hospital, clearly stating their reasons.

32.15 Before responsible clinicians can submit that report they must obtain the written agreement of an approved mental health professional (AMHP). Responsible clinicians should ensure that the AMHP is given enough notice to be able to interview the patient if appropriate.

32.16 This does not have to be the same AMHP who originally agreed that the patient should become a CTO patient. It may (but need not) be an AMHP who is already involved in the patient's care and treatment. It can be an AMHP acting on behalf of any willing local authority. If no other local authority is willing, responsibility for ensuring that an AMHP considers the case should lie with the local authority which is responsible under section 117 for the patient's after-care."

Subsection (1)

1-362   **Beginning with**   Means "including" (*Zoan v Rouamba* [2000] 2 All E.R. 620 CA).

Day on which it was made   When the patient's RC signs and dates Part 3 of Form CTO1, the RC is asserting that she is exercising powers under s.17A to make a CTO and that the CTO will be effective from a specified date. When is the CTO "made" for the purposes of the Act? Is it the date of the RC's signature or the date when the CTO becomes effective? It is suggested that the *Code of Practice* is correct when it states, at para.29.26, that the relevant date is the date when the order becomes effective.

Subsection (4)

1-363   The RC's report provides authority for the patient's continued period on a CTO, even if the hospital managers have not yet considered the report: see para.38.14 of the *Code of Practice*.

Examine the patient   See the note on this phrase in s.20(3).

Prescribed form   Form CTO7: see reg.13 of the English Regulations (in Wales, Form CP3: see reg.17 of the Welsh Regulations). A Form CTO7 or Form CP3 which is defective because of a minor error or slip of the pen would not render the renewal unlawful and such errors may be corrected and initialled even though the rectification procedure in s.15 does not apply to this section. If the form is fundamentally defective in some way, for example it was signed by a person who is not the patient's RC, the renewal would be invalid and the patient would no longer be subject to the CTO.

Subsection (5)

1-364   In order to consider whether they should exercise their power of discharge under s.23(2) (a), the managers must meet as a panel of at least three members (s.23(4)).

Subsection (6)

1-365   These criteria essentially state that the patient continues to be detainable under s.3 (including the requirement that a patient's learning disability continues to be associated with abnormally aggressive or seriously irresponsible conduct), but can be treated in the community if he is subject to a power of recall. When determining whether RC should be able to exercise the power of recall, the factors set out in subs.(7) should be considered.

If during a review of the CTO, the RC concludes that the conditions for extending the CTO do not apply, the RC should use the power under s.23 to discharge the CTO.

Paragraphs (a), (b), (e)

1-366   See the notes to s.3(2)(a), (c) and (d).

Subsection (7)

1-367   See the note on s.17A(6).

Subsection (8)

1-368   Paragraph 32.19 of the *Code of Practice* states:

"[The AMHP who provides the statement] does not have to be the same AMHP who originally agreed that the patient should become a CTO patient. It may (but need not) be an AMHP who is already involved in the patient's care and treatment. It can be an AMHP acting on behalf of any willing local authority. If no other local authority is willing, responsibility for ensuring that an AMHP considers the case should lie with the local authority which is responsible under section 117 for the patient's after-care."

Depending on the circumstances, it might be more appropriate for the default position to be for an AMHP of the local authority for the area where the patient is currently located to perform the role. This approach would be consistent with the duty placed on local authorities by s.13(1).

There is no requirement for the AMHP to interview the patient prior to signing the statement which is made in Part 2 of Form CTO7 or, in Wales, Form CP3.

Subsection (9)

Other persons   It is submitted that the intention of Parliament is that the AMHP who provided the **1-369** statement required by subs.(8) cannot be the consultee under this provision because the consultation would be a pointless exercise in that the AMHP will have already stated that the renewal is "appropriate" (subs.8(b)). In any event, the AMHP cannot be the consultee unless she has been professionally concerned with the patient's medical treatment.

Effect of expiry of community treatment order

[20B.—(1)   A community patient shall be deemed to be discharged absolutely **1-370** from liability to recall under this Part of this Act, and the application for admission for treatment cease to have effect, on expiry of the community treatment order, if the order has not previously ceased to be in force.

(2)   For the purposes of subsection (1) above, a community treatment order expires on expiry of the community treatment period as extended under this Part of this Act, but this is subject to sections 21 and 22 below.]

Amendment

This section was inserted by the Mental Health Act 2007 s.20(3).

Definitions

application for admission for treatment: ss.3(1), 145(1). **1-371**
community patient: ss.17A(7), 145(1).
community treatment order: ss.17A(7), 145(1).
community treatment period: ss.20A(1),(2), 145(1).

General Note

If a CTO expires, this section provides that: (1) the patient is no longer subject to the power of recall; **1-372** and (2) the application for admission for treatment (or its equivalent under Part III) ceases to have effect. In determining whether the CTO has expired, account must be taken of the fact that the community treatment period might have been extended by the provisions of s.21, which apply to patients who are absent without leave, or of s.22, which apply if the patient has been sentenced, or committed or remanded to custody by a court.

The hospital managers should ensure that the patient and, unless he has indicated otherwise, his nearest relative are informed of the ending of the CTO.

This section applies to patients who have been made subject to hospital orders with the modification set out in para.6A of Sch.1 (Sch.1 Pt 1 para.2).

[Special provisions as to patients absent without leave

1-373   **21.**—(1)   Where a patient is absent without leave—

(a)   on the day on which (apart from this section) he would cease to be liable to be detained or subject to guardianship under this Part of this Act [or, in the case of a community patient, the community treatment order would cease to be in force]; or

(b)   within the period of one week ending with that day,

he shall not cease to be so liable or subject [, or the order shall not cease to be in force,] until the relevant time.

(2)   For the purposes of subsection (1) above the relevant time—

(a)   where the patient is taken into custody under section 18 above, is the end of the period of one week beginning with the day on which he is returned to the hospital or place where he ought to be;

(b)   where the patient returns himself to the hospital or place where he ought to be within the period during which he can be taken into custody under section 18 above, is the end of the period of one week beginning with the day on which he so returns himself; and

(c)   otherwise, is the end of the period during which he can be taken into custody under section 18 above.]

[(3)   Where a patient is absent without leave on the day on which (apart from this section) the managers would be required under section 68 below to refer the patient's case to [the appropriate tribunal], that requirement shall not apply unless and until—

(a)   the patient is taken into custody under section 18 above and returned to the hospital where he ought to be; or

(b)   the patient returns himself to the hospital where he ought to be within the period during which he can be taken into custody under section 18 above.]

[(4)   Where a community patient is absent without leave on the day on which (apart from this section) the 72-hour period mentioned in section 17F above would expire, that period shall not expire until the end of the period of 72 hours beginning with the time when—

(a)   the patient is taken into custody under section 18 above and returned to the hospital where he ought to be; or

(b)   the patient returns himself to the hospital where he ought to be within the period during which he can be taken into custody under section 18 above.

(5)   Any reference in this section, or in sections 21A to 22 below, to the time when a community treatment order would cease, or would have ceased, to be in force shall be construed as a reference to the time when it would cease, or would have ceased, to be in force by reason only of the passage of time.]

Amendments

This section was substituted by the Mental Health (Patients in the Community) Act 1995 s.2(2). The amendments to it were made by the Mental Health Act 2007 ss.32(4), 37(2), Sch.3 para.6. The reference to the appropriate tribunal in subs.(3) was substituted by SI 2008/2883 art.9, Sch.3 para.40.

Definitions

patient: s.145(1).
absent without leave: ss.18(6), 145(1).
hospital: ss.34(2), 145(1).
appropriate practitioner: s.34(1).
community patient: ss.17A(7), 145(1).
community treatment order: ss.17A(7), 145(1).
the managers: s.145(1).
the appropriate tribunal: ss.66(4), 145(1).

1-374

General Note

This section, in subss.(1), (2) and (5), extends the authority for detention, guardianship or supervised community treatment of a patient who is absent without leave when or during the week before the detention or guardianship expires or the community treatment order (CTO) would cease to be in force. The detention or guardianship is extended, or the CTO will not cease to be in force, for up to one week after the patient's return to hospital or place where he ought to be. This period enables the patient to be examined and a renewal report made if appropriate. If the patient is returned within 28 days of absconding, s.21A applies for the purposes of a renewal. Section 21B applies if the patient is returned more than 28 days after absconding. If patients have not been taken into custody, or have not come voluntarily to the hospital or place where they ought to be, before the end of the period during which they can be taken into custody under s.18, no renewal can take place.

1-375

This section also postpones the requirement for hospital managers to refer a patient's case to the tribunal if the patient is absent without leave (subs.(3)) and extends the 72 hour period mentioned in s.17F if the patient is absent without leave at the end of that period (subs.(4)).

This section applies to patients who have been placed under hospital or guardianship orders by a court (Sch.1 para.1).

Subsection (1)

A patient   Although it has been said that this section does not apply to patients who are detained under s.2, the wording of this subsection does not have such an effect. It is therefore the case that if a s.2 patient is absent without leave during the final week of detention, the authority to detain can be extended for a week beginning with the day of recapture if he is recaptured before the expiration of the 28 day period provided for in s.2(4).

1-376

The community treatment order would cease to be in force   See subs.(5).

Subsection (2)

Relevant time   This allows for the patient's appropriate practitioner to examine the patient and decide whether she wishes to make a report renewing the detention or guardianship under s.20(3) or 20(6), or extending the CTO under s.20A(4). The making of such a report is authorised by s.21A(2) (or s.21A(4) for a CTO) and the date of the renewal is provided for in s.21A(3) (or s.21A(5) for a CTO). This provision also allows time for professionals to consider the appropriateness of making an application under s.3 in respect of a patient who has been detained under s.2.

1-377

Taken into custody under section 18   Although a s.2 patient cannot be taken into custody after the section expires (s.18(5)), a s.3 or guardianship patient can be taken into custody long after the detention or guardianship has expired (s.18(4)).

Subsection (3)

If the hospital managers are due to refer the patient to a tribunal under s.68 at the time when he is absent without leave, this provision requires the managers to postpone the referral until the patient either returns or is returned to the hospital where he ought to be.

1-378

Subsection (4)

1-379   If a CTO patient is absent without leave on the day when the 72-hour period provided for in s.17F would expire, the period will start again on the patient's return to the hospital either voluntarily or under compulsion.

[Patients who are taken into custody or return within 28 days

1-380   **21A.**—(1)   This section applies where a patient who is absent without leave is taken into custody under section 18 above, or returns himself to the hospital or place where he ought to be, not later than the end of the period of 28 days beginning with the first day of his absence without leave.

(2)   Where the period for which the patient is liable to be detained or subject to guardianship is extended by section 21 above, any examination and report to be made and furnished in respect of the patient under section 20(3) or (6) above may be made and furnished within the period as so extended.

(3)   Where the authority for the detention or guardianship of the patient is renewed by virtue of subsection (2) above after the day on which (apart from section 21 above) that authority would have expired, the renewal shall take effect as from that day.]

[(4)   In the case of a community patient, where the period for which the community treatment order is in force is extended by section 21 above, any examination and report to be made and furnished in respect of the patient under section 20A(4) above may be made and furnished within the period as so extended.

(5)   Where the community treatment period is extended by virtue of subsection (4) above after the day on which (apart from section 21 above) the order would have ceased to be in force, the extension shall take effect as from that day.]

Amendments

This section was substituted by the Mental Health (Patients in the Community) Act 1995 s.2(2). Subsections (4) and (5) were inserted by the Mental Health Act 2007 s.32(4), Sch.3 para.7.

Definitions

1-381   patient: s.145(1).
absent without leave: s.18(6), 145(1).
hospital: ss.34(2), 145(1).
appropriate practitioner: s.34(1).
community patient: ss.17A(7), 145(1).
community treatment order: ss.17A(7), 145(1).
community treatment period: ss.20A(1) (2), 145(1).

General Note

1-382   If a s.3 or guardianship patient who has absconded returns to the hospital or place where he is required to be not more than 28 days after absconding, or is taken into custody during that period, subss.(1) to (3) enable the patient's responsible clinician (RC) or appropriate practitioner to renew the detention or guardianship under s.20 without further formality. If the provisions of s.21 apply, the authority to detain the patient (or the authority for guardianship) is extended for up to a week from the date of his return to enable the formalities of renewal to be completed.

If a community patient who has gone absent without leave returns, or is returned, to the hospital to which he has been recalled under s.17E within 28 days of the first day of his absence, subss.(4) and (5) give the patient's RC a week after the patient's return to carry out the examination required by s.20A(4) and make her report for the extension of the CTO, if the CTO would have otherwise expired. If a patient is absent without leave on the day when the 72-hour period provided for in s.17F(6) would expire, the period will start again on the patient's return to the hospital either voluntarily or under compulsion: see s.21(4).

If the patient returns or is returned to the hospital or to the place where he ought to be more than 28 days after the date of the absconding, the provisions of s.21B apply.

This section applies without modification to patients who have been made subject to hospital or guardianship orders by a court under s.37 (Sch.1 Pt 1 para.1).

Subsection (1)

Beginning with   Including the first day of his absence without leave (*Zoan v Rouamba* [2000] 2 All   **1-383**
E.R. 620 CA).

Subsection (3)

Renewal   The renewal has effect from the date when the authority for detention or guardianship would   **1-384**
have expired if it had not been extended by s.21.

Subsection (5)

Under this provision, a CTO which has been extended under subs.(4) takes effect from the day when   **1-385**
it would have ceased to be in force if it has not been extended by s.21.

Ceased to be in force   See s.21(5).

[Patients who are taken into custody or return after more than 28 days

21B.—(1)   This section applies where a patient who is absent without leave is   **1-386**
taken into custody under section 18 above, or returns himself to the hospital or place where he ought to be, later than the end of the period of 28 days beginning with the first day of his absence without leave.

(2)   It shall be the duty of the [appropriate practitioner], within the period of one week beginning with the day on which the patient is returned or returns himself to the hospital or place where he ought to be [(his "return day")]—

(a)   to examine the patient; and

(b)   if it appears to him that the relevant conditions are satisfied, to furnish to the appropriate body a report to that effect in the prescribed form;

and where such a report is furnished in respect of the patient the appropriate body shall cause him to be informed.

(3)   Where the patient is liable to be detained [or is a community patient] (as opposed to subject to guardianship), the [appropriate practitioner] shall, before furnishing a report under subsection (2) above, consult—

(a)   one or more other persons who have been professionally concerned with the patient's medical treatment; and

(b)   an [approved mental health professional].

[(4)   Where—

(a)   the patient would (apart from any renewal of the authority for his detention or guardianship on or after his return day) be liable to be detained or subject to guardianship after the end of the period of one week beginning with that day; or

(b)   in the case of a community patient, the community treatment order would (apart from any extension of the community treatment period on or after that day) be in force after the end of that period,

he shall cease to be so liable or subject, or the community treatment period shall be deemed to expire, at the end of that period unless a report is duly furnished in respect of him under subsection (2) above.]

[(4A)   If, in the case of a community patient, the community treatment order is revoked under section 17F above during the period of one week beginning with his return day—

(a)   subsections (2) and (4) above shall not apply; and

(b)   any report already furnished in respect of him under subsection (2) above shall be of no effect.]

(5)   Where the patient would (apart from section 21 above) have ceased to be liable to be detained or subject to guardianship on or before the day on which a report is duly furnished in respect of him under subsection (2) above, the report shall renew the authority for his detention or guardianship for the period prescribed in that case by section 20(2) above.

(6)   Where the authority for the detention or guardianship of the patient is renewed by virtue of subsection (5) above—

(a)   the renewal shall take effect as from the day on which (apart from section 21 above and that subsection) the authority would have expired; and

(b)   if (apart from this paragraph) the renewed authority would expire on or before the day on which the report is furnished, the report shall further renew the authority, as from the day on which it would expire, for the period prescribed in that case by section 20(2) above.

[(6A)   In the case of a community patient, where the community treatment order would (apart from section 21 above) have ceased to be in force on or before the day on which a report is duly furnished in respect of him under subsection (2) above, the report shall extend the community treatment period for the period prescribed in that case by section 20A(3) above.

(6B)   Where the community treatment period is extended by virtue of subsection (6A) above—

(a)   the extension shall take effect as from the day on which (apart from section 21 above and that subsection) the order would have ceased to be in force; and

(b)   if (apart from this paragraph) the period as so extended would expire on or before the day on which the report is furnished, the report shall further extend that period, as from the day on which it would expire, for the period prescribed in that case by section 20A(3) above.]

(7)   Where the authority for the detention or guardianship of the patient would expire within the period of two months beginning with the day on which a report is duly furnished in respect of him under subsection (2) above, the report shall, if it so provides, have effect also as a report duly furnished under section 20(3) or (6) above; and the reference in this subsection to authority includes any authority renewed under subsection (5) above by the report.

[(7A)   In the case of a community patient, where the community treatment order would (taking account of any extension under subsection (6A) above) cease to be in force within the period of two months beginning with the day on which a report is duly furnished in respect of him under subsection (2) above, the report shall, if it so provides, have effect also as a report duly furnished under section 20A(4) above.]

(8)   [...]

(9)   [...]

(10)   In this section—

[...]

["the appropriate body" means—

(a)   in relation to a patient who is liable to be detained in a hospital, the managers of the hospital;

(b)   in relation to a patient who is subject to guardianship, the responsible local social services authority;

(c)   in relation to a community patient, the managers of the responsible hospital; and

["the relevant conditions" means—

(a)   in relation to a patient who is liable to be detained in a hospital, the conditions set out in subsection (4) of section 20 above;

(b)   in relation to a patient who is subject to guardianship, the conditions set out in subsection (7) of that section;

(c)   in relation to a community patient, the conditions set out in section 20A(6) above.]]]

Amendments

This section was substituted by the Mental Health (Patients in the Community) Act 1995 s.2(2). The amendments to it were made by the Mental Health Act 2007 ss.9(5), 21, 32(4), 55, Sch.2 para.7, Sch.3 para.8, Sch.11 Pts 1 and 3.

Definitions

patient: s.145(1).   **1-387**
absent without leave: ss.18(6), 145(1).
hospital: ss.34(2), 145(1).
community patient: ss.17A(7), 145(1).
approved mental health professional: s.145(1), (1AC).
community treatment order: ss.17A(7), 145(1).
community treatment period: ss.20A(1),(2), 145(1).
responsible hospital: ss.17A, 145(1).
responsible local social services authority: s.34(3).
local social services authority: s.145(1).
appropriate practitioner: s.34(1).

General Note

If patients have not been taken into custody, or have not come voluntarily to the hospital or place   **1-388**
where they ought to be, before the end of the period during which they can be taken into custody under s.18, no renewal can take place under this section.

If a s.3 or guardianship patient who has absconded is taken into custody, or returns to the hospital or place where he is required to be, later than 28 days after absconding, the patient's responsible clinician (RC) or appropriate practitioner must comply with the provisions of this section by examining the patient and reporting to the hospital or local social services authority within a week beginning with the date of the patient's return (the "return date") if the patient's detention or guardianship is to be renewed under s.20 (subss. (2)). This must be done however long remains until the patient's detention next needs to be renewed (Reference Guide, para.25.42). A failure by the practitioner to complete the relevant statutory form within that week will result in the automatic expiry of the detention or guardianship. If the provisions of s.21 apply, the authority to detain the patient (or the authority for guardianship) is extended for up to a week from the return date. The renewal takes effect from the day specified in subs.(6). If the patient's detention or guardianship would expire within two months of the subs.(2) report being furnished, the provisions of subs.(7) apply: see the notes on subss.(5) to (7).

If a community patient who has been absent without leave returns, or is returned, to the hospital to which he has been recalled under s.17E more than 28 days after the patient was first absent without leave, this section provides the patient's RC with a week after the day of patient's return (the "return date") to examine the patient, and, if the RC decides that the patient meets the criteria for a community treatment order (CTO), prepare for the hospital managers a report extending the CTO (subs.(2)). However, if the CTO is revoked under s.17F during that week, the report will have no effect (subs. (4A)). A failure by the RC to complete the relevant statutory form within a week of the patient's return will result in the automatic expiry of the CTO. If the CTO expired during the patient's absence, or had less than seven days to run on his return, s.21 extends it for up to a week from the return date. If the patient is absent without leave on the day when the 72-hour period provided for in s.17F(6) would expire, the period will start again on the patient's return to the hospital either voluntarily or under compulsion: see s.21(4).

Where the patient is liable to be detained or is a community patient, the RC must undertake the consultation process identified in subs.(3) before furnishing the report under subs. (2) to the hospital managers.

If a patient's detention or guardianship would remain in force a week after the return date, the detention or guardianship will lapse in the absence of a report being furnished under subs.(2). The same applies to a CTO which would be in force at the end of that period (subs.(4)).

Where a CTO would (apart from s.21) have expired before the day on which a report is furnished under subs.(2), the report will extend the community treatment period prescribed in s.20A(2) (subs.(6A). The extension will take effect from the day when order would have expired (subs.(6B)(a)), but if that period would have expired before the subs.(2) report is furnished, there shall be a further extension of the relevant s.20A(3) period (subs.(6B)(b)). If the CTO would expire (taking into account any extension under subs.(6A)) within two months of the furnishing of the report under subs.(2), the report shall also be treated as a s.20A(4) report (subs.(7A)). This avoids the need for two reports, one under subs.(2) and the other under s.20A(4), extending the CTO.

For the responsibility to inform the patient's nearest relative if the patient's detention or guardianship is renewed under subs.(7), or is renewed retrospectively under subss.(5) and (6), or if the patient's period of community treatment is extended under subs.(7A), or is extended retrospectively under subss.(6A) and (6B), see reg.26 of the English Regulations and regs 8, 15 and 22 of the Welsh Regulations.

This section applies without modification to patients who have been made subject to hospital or guardianship orders by a court under s.37 (Sch.1 Pt 1 para.1). It does not apply to restricted patients (ibid, Pt II).

Applications to the First-tier Tribunal (Mental Health) or the Mental Health Review Tribunal for Wales

1-389   The patient's right to apply to a tribunal arises from the date of the renewal of the detention, guardianship or the CTO (s.66(1)(fa) (faa), (2)(f) (fza)).

Human Rights Act 1998

1-390   See the note on s.18 under this heading.

Subsection (1)

1-391   **Beginning with**   See the note on s.21(1).

Subsection (2)

1-392   **Examine the patient**   Given the decision of the Divisional Court in *Devon Partnership NHS Trust v Secretary of State for Health and Social Care* [2021] EWHC 101 (Admin) (noted under s.11(5)), it is likely that a court would find that the physical presence of the examining doctor is required and that examining the patient cannot be undertaken by the use of remote technology.

Relevant conditions, appropriate body   See subs.(10).

Furnish to the appropriate body   Even if the unexpired period of detention or guardianship is longer than the one week provided for in this subsection.

In the Scottish case of *Milborrow, Applicant*, 1996 S.C.L.R. 315, Sh. Ct, it was held that a report is "furnished" to the hospital managers when it is committed to the internal mailing system operated by those managers: see the note on s.5(2).

Prescribed form   Form H6 for a patient who is liable to be detained, Form G10 for a patient who is subject to guardianship and Form CTO8 for a community patient: see reg.14 of the English Regulations. In Wales, the forms are: Form CP4 for a patient who is liable to be detained, Form GU7 for a patient who is subject to guardianship and Form CP4 for a community patient: see regs 13 and 18 of the Welsh Regulations.

Subsection (3)

Although the appropriate practitioner, as defined in s.34(1), must take the views expressed by the professionals into account before making a report under subs.(2), she is not obliged to obtain their agreement to this action.   **1-393**

Professional concerned with patient's medical treatment   The professional could be concerned with the patient's medical treatment in the community.

Subsection (4A)   Although there is a period of a week within which the patient's CTO can be renewed, the period during which the patient can be detained in the hospital is limited to the 72 hour period provided for in s.17F(6).   **1-394**

Subsection (5)

If a patient's liability to be detained or to be subject to guardianship would have expired before the end of the one week period provided for in subs.(2), and a report is furnished under that provision, the period of renewal shall be the period provided for in s.20(2). The date of the renewal is established by subs.(6).   **1-395**

Subsection (6)

This subsection provides that where the authority for detention or guardianship of a patient has been renewed in the circumstances set out in subs.(5), the renewal has effect from the day on which the detention or guardianship would have expired. If this renewed authority is due to expire before the day on which the report under subs.(2) is made, a further period of renewal for the prescribed period is authorised by the subs.(2) report.   **1-396**

Subsection (6A)

Ceased to be in force   See s.21(5).   **1-397**

Subsection (7)

This provision avoids the need for two reports renewing a patient's detention or guardianship, one under subs.(2) and the other under subs.20(3) or (6), if the authority for the patient's detention or guardianship would expire within two months of the report being made under subs.(2).   **1-398**

[Special provisions as to patients sentenced to imprisonment, etc

22.—(1)   If—   **1-399**
    (a)   a qualifying patient is detained in custody in pursuance of any sentence or order passed or made by a court in the United Kingdom (including an order committing or remanding him in custody); and
    (b)   he is so detained for a period exceeding, or for successive periods exceeding in the aggregate, six months, the relevant application shall cease to have effect on expiry of that period.
  (2)   A patient is a qualifying patient for the purposes of this section if—
    (a)   he is liable to be detained by virtue of an application for admission for treatment;

    (b)   he is subject to guardianship by virtue of a guardianship application; or

    (c)   he is a community patient.

(3)   "The relevant application", in relation to a qualifying patient, means—

    (a)   in the case of a patient who is subject to guardianship, the guardianship application in respect of him;

    (b)   in any other case, the application for admission for treatment in respect of him.

(4)   The remaining subsections of this section shall apply if a qualifying patient is detained in custody as mentioned in subsection (1)(a) above but for a period not exceeding, or for successive periods not exceeding in the aggregate, six months.

(5)   If apart from this subsection—

    (a)   the patient would have ceased to be liable to be detained or subject to guardianship by virtue of the relevant application on or before the day on which he is discharged from custody; or

    (b)   in the case of a community patient, the community treatment order would have ceased to be in force on or before that day, he shall not cease and shall be deemed not to have ceased to be so liable or subject, or the order shall not cease and shall be deemed not to have ceased to be in force, until the end of that day.

(6)   In any case (except as provided in subsection (8) below), sections 18, 21 and 21A above shall apply in relation to the patient as if he had absented himself without leave on that day.

(7)   In its application by virtue of subsection (6) above section 18 above shall have effect as if—

    (a)   in subsection (4) for the words from "later of" to the end there were substituted "end of the period of 28 days beginning with the first day of his absence without leave"; and

    (b)   subsections (4A) and (4B) were omitted.

(8)   In relation to a community patient who was not recalled to hospital under section 17E above at the time when his detention in custody began—

    (a)   section 18 above shall not apply; but

    (b)   sections 21 and 21A above shall apply as if he had absented himself without leave on the day on which he is discharged from custody and had returned himself as provided in those sections on the last day of the period of 28 days beginning with that day.]

Amendment

This section was substituted by the Mental Health Act 2007 s.32(4), Sch.3 para.9.

Definitions

1-400   patient: s.145(1).
application for admission for treatment: ss.3, 145(1).
guardianship application: s.7(1).
community patient: ss.17A(7), 145(1).
community treatment order: ss.17A(7), 145(1).
absent without leave: ss.18(6), 145(1).
hospital: s.145(1).

General Note

1-401   This section provides that if a patient who is the subject of an application for treatment, a guardianship application or a community treatment order (CTO) is sentenced, or committed or remanded to custody by a court, the application will cease to have effect if the period spent in custody lasts for more than six months. The CTO will end due to the fact that the s.3 application has ceased to have effect (s.17C(c)). If the patient is detained in custody for less than six months and would, in the ordinary course of events, have ceased to be liable to be detained for treatment or subject to guardianship or to a CTO prior to his discharge from custody, subss.(4) to (8) provide that he does not cease to be so liable or subject until end of the day on which he is discharged, and for the purposes of ss.18, 21 and 21A of the Act he will be treated as if he had absconded himself without leave on that day, i.e. the patient can be taken into custody within 28 days of his release (s.18(4), as amended by subs.(7) of this section) and there are seven days during which the application can be renewed (s.21) if it is due for renewal at that time. Subs.(8) applies to community patients who have not been recalled to hospital.

If the renewal report is furnished after the expiration of the previous period of detention, guardianship or CTO, the report is deemed to have been furnished on the final day of that period (s.21A). The patient's RC can exercise the power of discharge under s.23 while the patient is in custody.

As this section is not listed in paras (a) to (c) of s.56(3), the consent to treatment provisions contained in Pt IV will continue to apply to the patient during the six-month period spent in custody. This interpretation is confirmed at para.24.11 of the *Code of Practice*. Although it could be argued that the use of the term "patient" in s.56 indicates that Pt IV would not apply to persons detained in custody, "patient" is defined very broadly in s.145(1) as "a person suffering or appearing to suffer from mental disorder". It is also the case that s.56 does not require the patient to be detained in a hospital in order for the provision of Pt IV to apply: it requires the patient to be "liable to be detained". An interpretation that does not exclude the operation of the Act from prisons is consistent with the decision in *R. (on the application of the Howard League for Penal Reform) v Secretary of State for the Home Department* [2002] EWHC 2497 (Admin), where Munby J. held that the powers and duties which a local authority would otherwise owe to a child under the Children Act 1989 do not cease to be owed merely because the child is currently detained in a Young Offender Institution. His Lordship further held that the exercise of a local authority's functions under the 1989 Act take effect and operate subject to the necessary requirements of imprisonment. A Young Offender Institution is subject to the Secretary of State's control under the Prison Act 1952.

This section applies to patients who have been placed under hospital or guardianship orders by a court under s.37, with the modification that for references to an application for admission or a guardianship application there shall be substituted references to the order or direction under Pt III by virtue of which the patient is liable to be detained or subject to guardianship (Sch.1 Pt I paras 2, 7). For restricted patients the section applies with the modification that subss.(1) and (5) shall be omitted (Sch.1 Pt II paras 2, 6), i.e. the restriction order will not cease if the patient is detained in custody for more than six months.

Subsection (1)

Qualifying patient   See subs.(2).   **1-402**

United kingdom   This means Great Britain and Northern Ireland (Interpretation Act 1978 s.5, Sch.1).

Relevant application   See subs.(3).

Subsection (7)

The effect of this subsection was explained by the Parliamentary Under-Secretary of State for Health, **1-403** Baroness Cumberlege, during the passage of the Mental Health (Patients in the Community) Act 1995 (*Hansard*, HL, Vol.564, col.174):

"At present, section 22 of the Mental Health Act 1983 states that when a patient who has been subject to imprisonment is released, he should be treated as though he were absent without leave under section 18 of the 1983 Act. This is a legal device to provide a period of 28 days in which such patients could be returned to detention in hospital. However, as your Lordships know, clause 2 of this Bill [now s.18(4)] extends the period of time in which an absconding patient can be returned to hospital from 28 days to at least six months. An unintentional consequence of this is to extend the period of time within which a released prisoner could be returned to detention under the 1983 Act. I am sure your Lordships will agree that this is undesirable … The effect of the amendment, therefore, is to retain for the purposes of section 22 the period of 28 days within which a person who has been released from prison may be returned to hospital. This is followed by a period of seven days during which the responsible medical officer must examine the patient and determine whether his liability to detention should be renewed."

Subsections (7), (8)

1-404   **Beginning with**   Means "including" (*Zoan v Rouamba* [2000] 2 All E.R. 620 CA).

Discharge of patients

1-405   **23.**—(1)   Subject to the provisions of this section and section 25 below, a patient who is for the time being liable to be detained or subject to guardianship under this Part of this Act shall cease to be so liable or subject if an order in writing discharging him [absolutely from detention or guardianship is made in accordance with this section].

[(1A)   Subject to the provisions of this section and section 25 below, a community patient shall cease to be liable to recall under this Part of this Act, and the application for admission for treatment cease to have effect, if an order in writing discharging him from such liability is made in accordance with this section.

(1B)   An order under subsection (1) or (1A) above shall be referred to in this Act as "an order for discharge".]

(2)   An order for discharge may be made in respect of a patient—

   (a)   where the patient is liable to be detained in a hospital in pursuance of an application for admission for assessment or for treatment by the [responsible clinician], by the managers or by the nearest relative of the patient;

   (b)   where the patient is subject to guardianship, by the [responsible clinician], by the responsible local social services authority or by the nearest relative of the patient;

   [(c)   where the patient is a community patient, by the responsible clinician, by the managers of the responsible hospital or by the nearest relative of the patient.]

(3)   [...]

[(3A)   [...]]

(4)   The powers conferred by this section on any authority, [trust] [, board] [(other than an NHS foundation trust)] [, board] or body of persons may be exercised [subject to subsection (5) below] by any three or more members of that authority [trust] [, board] or body authorised by them in that behalf or by three or more members of a committee or sub-committee of that authority [trust] [, board] or body which has been authorised by them in that behalf.

[(5)   The reference in subsection (4) above to the members of an authority, trust[, board] or body or the members of a committee or sub-committee of an authority, trust[, board] or body,—

   (a)   in the case of [a [[Local Health Board] [or Special Health Authority] [...] or a committee or sub-committee of [a [[Local Health Board] [or Special Health Authority] [...]], is a reference only to the chairman of the authority[[...] or board] and [such members (of the authority [...] board, committee or sub-committee], as the case may be) as are not also officers of the authority[[...] or board], within the meaning of [the National Health Service Act 2006 or the National Health Service (Wales) Act 2006]; and

   (b)   in the case of a National Health Service trust or a committee or sub-committee of such a trust, is a reference only to the chairman of the trust and such directors or (in the case of a committee or sub-committee) members as are not also employees of the trust.]

[(6)   The powers conferred by this section on any NHS foundation trust may be exercised by any three or more [persons authorised by the board of the trust in that behalf each of whom is neither an executive director of the board nor an employee of the trust.]

Amendments

The amendments to this section were made by the National Health Service and Community Care Act 1990 s.66(1), Sch.9 para.24(3), the Health Authorities Act 1995 s.2(1), Sch.1 para.107(2), the Health Act 1999 (Supplementary, Consequential, etc. Provisions) Order 2000 (SI 2000/90) Sch.1 para.13(4), the Care Standards Act 2000 s.116, Sch.4 para.9(2), the Health and Social Care (Community Health and Standards) Act 2003 s.34, Sch.4 para.53, the National Health Service (Consequential Provisions) Act 2006 s.2, Sch.1 para.65, the Mental Health Act 2007 ss.9(6), 32(4), 45(1), Sch.3 para.10, SI 2007/961 art.3, Sch. para.13(2), the Health and Social Care Act 2012 s.39, and the Health and Social Care Act 2012 Sch.5 para.26.

Definitions

patient: s.145(1).   **1-406**
community patient: ss.17A(7), 145(1).
application for admission for treatment: ss.3, 145(1).
the responsible hospital: ss.17A(7), 145(1).
hospital: ss.34(2), 145(1).
application for admission for assessment: ss.2, 145(1).
the managers: s.145(1).
nearest relative: ss.26(3), 145(1).
local social services authority: s.145(1).
responsible local social services authority: s.34(3).
registered establishment: ss.34(1), 145(1).
application for admission for treatment: ss.3, 145(1).
responsible clinician: s.34(1).
Local Health Board: s.145(1).
Special Health Authority: s.145(1).

General Note

This section provides for the absolute discharge of detained patients, patients who are subject to   **1-407**
guardianship and community patients to be ordered by the patient's responsible clinician (RC), the hospital managers (or the responsible local social services authority for guardianship patients) or the patient's nearest relative. It does not apply to patients who have been remanded to hospital by a court under ss.35 or 36, or who have been made subject to an interim hospital order under s.38. In this section, the term "discharge" means discharge from detention, guardianship or from a community treatment order (CTO), not discharge from hospital.

A patient's discharge must be ordered: it cannot be effected by implication. It is therefore the case that if an application is found to be fundamentally defective it must be discharged under this section: see the judgment of Collins J. in *TTM v London Borough of Hackney* [2010] EWHC 1349 (Admin) noted under s.6(3).

The provisions of s.133, which is concerned with the duty of hospital managers to inform nearest relatives of patient discharges, apply to a patient who is to be discharged under this section.

This section applies to patients who have been placed under hospital or guardianship orders made under s.37 with the modification that subs.(2) shall read as follows:

"(2)   An order for discharge may be made in respect of a patient—
    (a)   where the patient is liable to be detained in a hospital in pursuance of an application for admission [...] for treatment by the [responsible clinician], by the managers [...],
    (b)   where the patient is subject to guardianship, by the [responsible clinician], by the responsible local social services authority [...],
    (c)   where the patient is a community patient, by the responsible clinician, by the managers of the responsible hospital [...]" (Sch.1 Pt I para.8)."

The effect of Sch.1, Pt 1 is that both the hospital managers and the RC have the power to discharge a hospital order patient during the first six months of his detention even though the patient cannot make an application to a tribunal during that period. The patient's nearest relative, who does not have the power to discharge a hospital order, can make an application to the tribunal under s.69(1).

This section also applies to restricted patients with the modification that subss.(1) and (2) shall read as follows:

"(1) Subject to the provisions of this section and section 25 below, a patient who is for the time being liable to be detained [...] under this Part of this Act shall cease to be so liable [...] if an order in writing discharging him from detention [...] (in this Act referred to as "an order for discharge") is made [with the consent of the Secretary of State] in accordance with this section.

(2) An order for discharge may be made in respect of a patient—
   (a) where the patient is liable to be detained in a hospital in pursuance of an application for admission [...] for treatment by the [responsible clinician], by the managers [...];
   (b) [...]." (Sch.1 Pt II paras 2, 7.)

The Secretary of State has his own powers to discharge restricted patients under s.42(2).

Domestic Violence, Crime and Victims Act 2004

1-408   Under Chapter 2 of Part 3 of the 2004 Act, the victims of offenders who have committed specified sexual or violent offences have certain rights if those offenders become patients subject to specific provisions of the 1983 Act ("Chapter 2 patients"). These rights include the right to ask to be informed if the patient is to be discharged. In order that hospital managers can meet their obligations under the 2004 Act to invite representations from victims, RCs must tell the managers if they are considering discharging the following categories of patients:

"[P]atients subject to unrestricted hospital orders, hospital directions whose associated limitation direction is no longer in force, and unrestricted transfer directions (including hospital orders and transfer directions which were originally restricted, but where the restriction order or direction has since ended or been lifted). It includes patients who have been discharged from such an order or direction onto SCT" ("Guidance on the extension of victims' rights under the Domestic Violence, Crime and Victims Act 2004", Department of Health, 2008, para.1.10)."

Human Rights Act 1998

1-409   In *Winterwerp v Netherlands* (1979) 2 E.H.R.R. 387, the European Court of Human Rights held that the validity of the continued confinement of a mentally disordered person depends upon the persistence of such a disorder. In a subsequent decision of the Court, it was held that it does not automatically follow that a finding by an expert authority that the mental disorder which justified a patient's compulsory confinement no longer persists compels his immediate and unconditional release into the community (*Johnson v United Kingdom* (1999) 27 E.H.R.R. 296). It is therefore the case that if a patient who is deemed to pose a risk to the public is found no longer to be mentally disordered, discharge from detention can be delayed for a limited period until such time as appropriate after-care facilities are put in place. In *Johnson*, the Court said that the authority "should be able to retain some measure of supervision over the progress of the person once he is released into the community and to that end make his discharge subject to conditions" (para.63).

The question whether a decision not to discharge a patient because of a failure to put in place appropriate after-care facilities in the community violates art.5 of the European Convention on Human Rights (ECHR) is considered in the General Note to s.117 under this heading.

In *MA v Secretary of State for Health* [2012] UKUT 474 (AAC), UT Judge Levenson held that the right of discharge conferred on a patient's nearest relative is a civil right for the purposes of art.6 of the ECHR.

When exercising their power to review the detention of a patient, the hospital managers are not a "court" for the purposes of art.5(4) of the ECHR. This is because the managers are one of the parties to the review (*De Wilde, Ooms and Versyp v Belgium (No.1)* (1979–80) 1 E.H.R.R. 373). The tribunal is the expert body established under the Act to consider applications made by patients for their discharge. It is the right to make an application to the tribunal, not the hospital managers, that satisfies the Government's obligation under art.5(4) to enable a patient to challenge the lawfulness of his detention.

The persons and bodies who have the power to discharge the patient under this provision are "public authorities" for the purposes of s.6 of the 1998 Act.

Code of Practice

Guidance on the use of the RC's power of discharge is contained in Ch.32 at paras 32.17 to 32.19. **1-410**
The exercise of the hospital managers' power of discharge is considered in Ch.38.

Subsection (1)

Patient Although an order for the discharge of a restricted patient may be made under this section, **1-411**
the discharge can only take place if the consent of the Secretary of State has been obtained: see
s.41(3)(c)(iii).

Order in writing See reg.18 of the English Regulations and reg.7 of the Welsh Regulations. Although
there is no statutory discharge form for England, there is for Wales (Form HO17).

Discharging him absolutely This provision does not contain a power to order the conditional
discharge of the patient. The 2008 edition of the *Code of Practice*, at para.31.38, stated that it would be
lawful for the hospital managers to order that the patient's unconditional discharge takes effect on a
specified date in the near future. The accuracy of this statement is open to doubt for two reasons:

(i)   a deferred discharge is not an absolute discharge. If a patient is discharged absolutely, he has
        a right to leave hospital immediately; a patient who is given a deferred discharge has no such
        right; and
(ii)   the tribunal is provided with a specific power to order the deferred discharge in s.72(3). If
        Parliament was of the opinion that hospital managers have an implied power to order such a
        discharge, why was it felt necessary to provide the tribunal with a specific power?

If the hospital managers are concerned about the adequacy of the after-care services that will be available to the patient on discharge, they should adjourn the hearing and reconvene to a date when the
relevant information should be available. If the hospital managers had the to defer the patient's discharge
to a particular date, the patient would have to be discharged on that date even though the anticipated
arrangements for his discharge had not been put in place. The current edition of the Code, which does
not reproduce para.31.38 of the 2008 edition, adopts the approach advocated here at para.38.40.

Subsection (1A)

It is submitted that, in the absence of a specific power authorising it, there is no power under this **1-412**
provision to defer the discharge of a community patient to a future date.
Discharging the patient from a CTO has the automatic effect of also discharging the underlying application or order.

Subsection (2)

In *R. v Riverside Mental Health Trust Ex p. Huzzey* (1998) 43 B.M.L.R. 167, Latham J. identified **1-413**
the criteria that hospital managers must use when considering the continued detention of a s.3 patient
where the nearest relative's application for discharge had been subject to a "barring report" made under
s.25. His Lordship said:

"[S]ection 23 provides, inter alia, a general discretion in the managers to discharge a patient. No
criteria are set out as to what should or should not be taken into account by managers when considering decision as to whether or not to discharge. The question of what are the relevant considerations
has to be answered by looking at the general scheme of the Act. Clearly the criteria set out in section 3 are of fundamental importance. If the criteria for admission no longer exist, I cannot see how
any decision by managers not to discharge could be other than perverse ... Section 23 implicitly
recognises that managers have a discretion to discharge even if those criteria have been met. Where
... a nearest relative has sought to obtain a discharge order but has been confronted by a barring report
[made under s.25], those facts must equally be relevant and material considerations. In my view, the
managers are not only entitled to, but must, consider whether or not they are persuaded by the barring report that the patient, if discharged, would be likely to act in a manner dangerous to other
persons or to himself. For if they are not so persuaded, they will have reached the position that the

nearest relative would have been entitled to an order for discharge if the [RC] had not come to what they have decided was an erroneous conclusion as to the danger presented by the patient. That cannot be anything other than a relevant and material consideration, and would be likely, in almost all circumstances, to mean that discharge should be ordered."

In this case, Latham J. held that the failure of the managers to apply their minds to the question of the patient's dangerousness meant that their decision not to order discharge was irrational and had to be quashed. *Huzzey* was applied by Jackson J. in *R. (on the application of SR) v Huntercombe Maidenhead Hospital* [2005] EWHC 2361 (Admin); [2005] M.H.L.R. 379 at para.19, where his Lordship said that "if the managers override the [RC's] report certifying dangerousness, this is a strong pointer in favour of discharge. It is not however an inflexible rule that in every case the managers must discharge if they overturn the finding of dangerousness. Mr Justice Latham in *Huzzey* acknowledged that there may be exceptions. Furthermore, para.23.12 of the [1999 edition of the *Code of Practice*] also acknowledges that there may be exceptions".

In *SR*, the ordering of the patient's discharge by the hospital managers subsequent to their decision to override the RC's report was quashed partly on the ground that the managers failed to consider whether to exercise their residual discretion not to order discharge. Hospital managers must therefore consider whether to exercise their residual power not to discharge the patient if they have decided to override the RC's certificate. The exercise of this residual power must be considered by the hospital managers "in all cases" (*Code of Practice*, para.38.23). It is submitted that the residual power should only be exercised if the grounds for continued detention are satisfied and there is evidence to suggest that the patient's health would be significantly compromised if he were to be discharged. The *Code of Practice*, at para.38.22, states that the residual power should be invoked if there are "exceptional reasons why the patient should not be discharged". The law on this issue contrasts with that which applies to the tribunal: see the notes on s.72(1)(b)(iii).

Although the *Huzzey* case was concerned with the power of hospital managers, the approach taken by Latham J. is equally applicable to the RC's power to order discharge. In *South West London and St George's Mental Health NHS Trust v W* [2002] EWHC 1770 (Admin); [2002] M.H.L.R. 392, Crane J. said at para.81: "Section 23 of the Act does not specifically guide the [RC] or the managers in exercising their power of discharge, but plainly it would appropriate for them to consider the same matters as the [tribunal]". These matters are set out at para.38.15 of the *Code of Practice*. If the nearest relative's order for the patient's discharge has been confronted by a barring report, the hospital managers must, in addition to considering the admission criteria, also ask themselves whether the patient would be likely to act in a manner dangerous to other persons or to himself if he were to be discharged (*Huzzey*, noted above). This "question provides a more stringent test for continuing the detention or the CTO" (*Code of Practice*, para.38.21).

Paragraph (a)

1-414   Application for admission for assessment. This includes an emergency application made under s.4 because such an application is "an application for admission for assessment" (see s.4(1)) which is founded on a single medical recommendation.

Responsible clinician   The RC has a duty to discharge a patient from detention if the medical conditions that justified admission cease to be met (*R. v Drew* [2003] UKHL 25; [2003] 4 All E.R. 557 para.10). A decision to discharge has immediate effect. If discharge is ordered, the RC must comply with the notification requirements of reg.18 of the English Regulations and reg.7 of the Welsh Regulations. The hospital managers have no power to prevent the RC from exercising the power of discharge. The RC, who has a continuing duty to consider whether the admission conditions remain satisfied (*R. (on the application of C) v Mental Health Review Tribunal London South and South West Region* [2000] M.H.L.R. 220, para.20), can discharge the patient at any time. If RCs "conclude that the criteria which would justify renewing a patient's detention or extending the patient's CTO (as the case may be) are not met, they should exercise their power of discharge. They should not wait until the patient's detention or CTO is due to expire" (*Code of Practice*, para.32.18). In *R. (on the application of Wirral Health Authority and Wirral Borough Council) v Dr Finnegan and D.E.* [2001] EWHC Admin 312; [2001] M.H.L.R. 66, Scott Baker J. said at para.68: "There are no statutory criteria governing the exercise of this power. Its exercise is wholly within the [RC's] discretion subject, in my judgment, to the usual restrictions of lawfulness and so forth. [I]f it is exercised for reasons based on error of law it is susceptible to challenge by judicial review".

The managers   The *Code of Practice* states:

"38.12 Hospital managers:

- may undertake a review of whether or not a patient should be discharged at any time at their discretion
- must undertake a review if the patient's responsible clinician submits a report to them under section 20 of the Act renewing detention or under section 20A extending the CTO
- should consider holding a review when they receive a request from a patient (who may be supported by their independent mental health advocate (IMHA) (see chapter 6), independent mental capacity advocate (IMCA), attorney or deputy (see chapter 7) or a carer, and
- should consider holding a review when the responsible clinician makes a report to them under section 25 barring an order by the nearest relative to discharge a patient.

38.13 In the last two cases, when deciding whether to consider the case, hospital managers are entitled to take into account whether the Tribunal has recently considered the patient's case or is due to do so in the near future. The decision should be recorded in writing and if the decision is taken not to consider the case the reasons documented."

In the last two cases, hospital managers could delegate their power to officers.

In *South Staffordshire and Shropshire Healthcare NHS Foundation Trust v The Hospital Managers of St George's Hospital* [2016] EWHC 1196 (Admin); [2016] M.H.L.R. 273, Cranston J. held that:

1. A panel of hospital managers appointed under this section has equal standing when ordering a patient's discharge to that of a tribunal operating under s.72 (para.30).
2. A tribunal's previous decision not to discharge the patient was not a relevant consideration such that the hospital managers' panel had to take it into account when considering whether to discharge the patient. His Lordship said that he could not "see anything in the 1983 Act or *Code of Practice* making a Tribunal's decision something so obviously material that not to take it into account would mean that the decision of an NHS foundation trust or its panel is flawed" (para.39).
3. A panel of the hospital managers exercising powers under this section was sufficiently separate from and independent of the Trust that appointed it to enable the Trust "in quite exceptional circumstances" to bring a judicial review challenge to its decision (paras 26 and 27). No guidance on what would constitute "quite exceptional circumstances" was given by the court. A mere disagreement with a decision of the managers to discharge a patient would clearly not fall into this category.

As there is no appeal from a panel's decision, the only legal recourse available to a patient who wishes to challenge a decision is to make an application to the High Court for the judicial review of the decision.

As the decisions of the panel are legally decisions of the Trust (they are not recommendations to the Trust), members of the panel are not personally liable for decisions taken to discharge a patient. Liability rests with the Trust as a body: see NHS Management Executive letter TEL (94) 2.

Chapter 38 of the *Code of Practice*, which contains guidance on the procedure that should be adopted by the managers when conducting reviews, provides the following specific guidance at para.38.36:

"Unless, exceptionally, it is considered too unsafe, patients should always be offered the opportunity of speaking to the panel alone (with or without their representative and anyone else they have asked to attend to support them at the hearing)."

When offering this opportunity to patients, the managers should explain that they cannot provide the patient with a guarantee of confidentiality. For example, if the patient discloses information that is relevant to the issue that the managers will be determining, the rules of natural justice and art.6 of the ECHR require that such information be shared with the hospital's representative.

Paragraph 38.28 of the *Code of Practice* states:

"The patient should be provided with copies of the reports as soon as they are available, unless (in the light of any recommendation made by their authors) panels are of the opinion that disclosing the information would be likely to cause serious harm to the physical or mental health of the patient or any other individual. The patient's legal or other representative (such as their donee or deputy), including their IMHA, and, if the patient agrees, their nearest relative and, if different, carer should receive copies of these reports."

The managers can delegate their power of discharge under subs.(4). The patient's RC has no power to prevent the managers from exercising their powers of discharge, even if she considers that the patient is dangerous.

A patient can make an application to the managers for discharge as often as he likes during a period of detention. No formal procedure is laid down for the hearing of a patient's application. In fact, there is no explicit requirement that a hearing should take place at all although the managers have a duty to consider a report made by the patient's RC under either s.20(3) or s.20A(4). Having a full hearing is not always the most appropriate mechanism for managers to use when exercising their review function. A limited hearing, involving (1) a consideration of written reports from relevant professionals, and (2) interviewing the patient, could take place in the following circumstances:

1.   Where a patient makes frequent requests for discharge from detention in the absence of any relevant change of circumstances.
2.   If the patient does not wish to contest the renewal of his detention or CTO.
3.   The patient makes an application for discharge immediately after an unsuccessful application to a tribunal in the absence of any relevant change of circumstances.

The following guidance on "uncontested renewals" is provided by the *Code of Practice*:

"38.45 Hospital managers may consider the case based on the papers, if they wish (sometimes referred to as a 'paper review'). They should hold a full hearing if they have reason to suspect that the patient may, in fact, want to contest, or there are prima facie grounds to think that the statutory grounds to renew detention or extend the CTO are not met. This is particularly important if the patient lacks capacity. The fact that patients have not said they object to the renewal or extension should not be taken as evidence that they agree with it, or that it is the correct decision.

38.46 In deciding whether or not to review the case on the papers, hospital managers should consider if previous reviews during the current period of compulsory powers have been 'paper reviews'."

If a patient makes a request for a review, and a tribunal hearing in respect of the patient is imminent, the review should be adjourned until after the hearing; also see para.38.13 of the *Code of Practice*, above. The lawfulness of not convening a managers' hearing in the light of the proximity of a tribunal hearing was confirmed in *R. (on the application of Zhang) v Whittington Hospital* [2013] EWHC 358 (Admin); [2014] M.H.L.R. 127. The managers should hold a limited hearing if the patient is not discharged by the tribunal and the patient persists with his request. If a relevant change in the patient's circumstances is identified at that hearing, either a full managers' hearing could take place or the Secretary of State could be requested to make a reference to the tribunal.

In order to avoid duplication of effort, a managers' hearing should not take place during the currency of the patient's detention under s.2 if the patient has made an application to the tribunal. However, a full hearing should take place if the patient makes an application to the managers after missing the deadline for submitting an application to the tribunal.

Although the managers have the power to order the discharge of restricted patients (including patients who have been conditionally discharged who continue to be "liable to be detained": see s.73(6)), the power is exercisable only with the consent of the Secretary of State (s.41(3)(c)(iii)). Such patients are therefore entitled to request that the managers consider conducting a review of their detention.

Subject to the exceptions noted below, it is not possible for a request for a review to be made on behalf of a patient who lacks the mental capacity to make such a request. Under the Mental Capacity Act 2005, a mentally capable person (the "donor") can execute a lasting power of attorney (LPA) which empowers another person (the "donee") to act in his stead, either generally or for specific purposes. An act done by a donee can be treated as an act done by the donor. A personal welfare LPA can only take effect after the donor has lost the mental capacity to make the decision in question. A donee could therefore make a request to the hospital managers on the patient's behalf if:

(i)   the welfare LPA either gives a general power to the donee or the power to make such a request has been specified by the donor; and
(ii) the patient does not possess the mental capacity to make the request.

A deputy appointed by the Court of Protection under the 2005 Act to make personal welfare decisions on behalf of the patient can also make a request to the hospital managers on the patient's behalf if such a power has been conferred on the deputy by the court and the patient does not have the mental capacity to make the request: also see para.7.7 of the *Code of Practice* which states:

"Attorneys and deputies are able to exercise a patient's rights under the Act on their behalf, if they have the relevant authority under the LPA or the order of the court appointing them and the patient concerned lacks the capacity to do so themselves. In particular, personal welfare attorneys and deputies may be able to exercise the patient's various rights to apply to the Tribunal for discharge from detention, guardianship or a CTO."

As managers, when exercising their power under this section, are acting in a quasijudicial capacity they must abide by the rules of natural justice which require decision makers to act fairly, in good faith and without bias and to afford each party the opportunity to adequately state his case. The managers are also placed under a common law duty to give reasons for their decision: see *R. (on the application of O) v West London Mental Health NHS Trust* [2005] EWHC 604 (Admin); [2005] M.H.L.R. 187 where Collins J. held that this duty arises at the time the decision is made. His Lordship further held that a legal defect which will arise if the original reasons were inadequate cannot be cured by the managers subsequently supplementing their reasons with a proper explanation.

Although the managers' power under this section is confined to either granting or not granting the patient's absolute discharge (subs.(1)), the managers could adjourn their consideration of the patient's case if, for example, an important piece of information about the patient had not been provided to them; also see the note on "Discharging him absolutely" in subs.(1).

Nearest relative   Who does not have the power to order the discharge of a patient who is subject to a hospital order (with or without restrictions) or to a guardianship order made by a court under Pt III: see the General Note to this section. For service of the order of discharge, see reg.3(3) of the English and Welsh Regulations.

Under the provisions of s.25, 72 hours' notice of the nearest relative's intention to order the patient's discharge must be given to the hospital managers. The patient's RC can nullify the discharge if a report is made to the managers during the 72-hour period specifying that in her opinion the patient would be dangerous if discharged (s.25(1)). A nearest relative can be displaced by the court if he or she has exercised or is likely to exercise the power under this provision "without due regard to the welfare of the patient or the interests of the public" (s.29(3)(d)).

For the disclosure of documentation to enable the nearest relative to consider exercising the power of discharge: see *R. (on the application of S) v Plymouth City Council and C* [2002] EWCA Civ 388; [2002] M.H.L.R. 118, which is noted under s.8. A doctor may visit and examine the patient for the purpose of advising a nearest relative on the exercise of the power (s.24(1)(2)).

Paragraph (b)

Guardianship   The RC must send her written order discharging the patient to the guardian (*Reference Guide*, para.28.124). There is no statutory form. Neither a private guardian nor a nominated medical attendant have the power to discharge the patient from guardianship. The RC has no power to prevent a nearest relative obtaining the discharge of a patient who is subject to guardianship. The nearest relative could be displaced if the discharge was either contrary to the welfare of the patient or to the interests of the public (s.29(3)(d)).   **1-415**

Responsible local social services authority   Is defined in s.34(3). Local authorities may consider discharging patients from guardianship at any time, but must consider doing so when they receive a report from the patient's appropriate practitioner renewing their guardianship under s.20: see the notes on s.20(6). The power of discharge can be exercised by the local authority itself, by three or more members of the local social services authority or by three or more members of a committee or sub-committee of the authority (subs.(4)). An officer (i.e. an employee) of a local authority cannot be a member of the committee or sub-committee. Where decisions are taken by three or more local authority members (or a committee or sub-committee), all three people (or at least three of them, if there are more) must agree (Code of Practice, para.30.18 and see the note on subs.(4)). Delegation of the power of discharge to an officer is not permitted: see reg.21(2) of the English Regulations and reg.37(2) of the Welsh Regulations.

Paragraph (c)

In Wales, the discharge of a community patient by the RC or the hospital managers must be in the form set out in Form CP8: see reg.21 of the Welsh Regulations.   **1-416**

Subsection (4)

Neither this subsection nor subs.(5) shall apply to the exercise by the Welsh Ministers of the powers conferred by this section (SI 2000/253 Sch.3; also see the General Note to the Act).   **1-417**

Three or more members of that authority trust or body   The reference to "three" is not only for the creation of a quorum: it is a requirement that each of the three members shall support the order for discharge. In the unlikely event of seven members being appointed to the panel and three being in favour of discharge there should be implied into this provision that the "three or more" should not be a minority of those appointed (*R. (on the application of Tagoe-Thompson) v The Hospital Managers of the Park Royal Centre* [2003] EWCA Civ 330; [2003] M.H.L.R. 326).

Subsection (5)

1-418   This subsection prevents an "officer" (i.e. an employee) of an NHS body from being a member of the body's committee that has the power to order the discharge of a detained patient under this section. There is no equivalent legislative provision that relates to independent hospitals, although the following guidance is given at para.38.7 of the *Code of Practice*: "In independent hospitals, managers' panels should not include people who are on the staff of the hospital or who have a financial interest in it".

The payment of fees to a member of the committee (frequently referred to as an "associate hospital manager") for attending meetings of the committee does not necessarily mean that that person is disqualified from performing functions under this section by virtue of becoming an employee (*Code of Practice*, para.38.6).

In *Ready Mixed Concrete (South East) Ltd v Minister of Pensions and National Insurance* (1963) 2 Q.B. 497, the court found that an employment contract exists if three conditions are met:

1.   The worker agrees that he will provide his work and skill in performance of some service for the employer, in return for remuneration.
2.   The worker agrees, expressly or impliedly, that in performing that work he will be subject to the employer's control in a sufficient degree to make him an employee.
3.   The other provisions of the contract between them are consistent with it being a contract of employment, as opposed to a contract for services.

With regard to 2, it is unlikely that a court would find that a NHS body exercises the level of control over an associate hospital manager that would be required for the manager to be regarded as an employee. The Employment Rights Act 1996 s.230(1) defines an employee as an individual "who has entered into or works under ... a contract of employment".

Members of the committee are not personally liable for decisions taken to discharge a patient. Liability rests with the detaining authority as a body (NHS Management Executive letter TEL (94)2).

Subsection (6)

1-419   This provision enables the board of an NHS foundation trust to delegate its power of discharge to three or more people who are neither executive directors of the board or employees of the trust. The constitution of the trust cannot permit delegation of the power of discharge to executive directors (s.142B).

Visiting and examination of patients

1-420   **24.**—(1)   For the purpose of advising as to the exercise by the nearest relative of a patient who is liable to be detained or subject to guardianship under this Part of this Act[, or who is a community patient,] of any power to order his discharge, any registered medical practitioner [or approved clinician] authorised by or on behalf of the nearest relative of the patient may, at any reasonable time, visit the patient and examine him in private.

(2)   Any registered medical practitioner [or approved clinician] authorised for the purposes of subsection (1) above to visit and examine a patient may require the production of and inspect any records relating to the detention or treatment of the patient in any hospital [or to any after-care services provided for the patient under section 117 below].

(3)   [...]

(4)   [...]

Amendments

The amendments to this section were made by the Mental Health (Patients in the Community) Act 1995 s.1(2), Sch.1 para.1, the Mental Health Act 2007 ss.9(7), 32(4), Sch.3 para.11, SI 2007/961 art.3, Sch. para.13(3), SI 2010/813 art.5 and the Health and Social Care Act 2012 s.39.

Definitions

nearest relative: ss.26(3), 145(1).   **1-421**
patient: s.145(1).
approved clinician: s.145(1).
community patient: ss.17A(7), 145(1).
hospital: ss.34(2), 145(1).

General Note

This section provides for the visiting and examination of patients and for the production of docu-   **1-422**
ments to a doctor or approved clinician for the purpose of advising the patient's nearest relative, or acting nearest relative appointed by a county court under s.29, as to the exercise of his or her power under
s.23(2) to order the discharge of a patient from detention, guardianship or a community treatment order.
    A person who fails to allow the visiting, interviewing or examination of a patient or who refuses to
produce any document for inspection commits an offence under s.129.

Subsection (1)

There is no power to require a social work assessment to be undertaken in respect of a patient who   **1-423**
is subject to guardianship.

registered medical practitioner   Means "a fully registered person within the meaning of the Medical Act 1983 who holds a licence to practise under that Act" (Interpretation Act 1978, Sch.1).

Subsection (2)

This provision does not provide for the records of a patient who is subject to guardianship to be made   **1-424**
available to the doctor, unless the patient is subject to s.117 after-care.

Restrictions on discharge by nearest relative

25.—(1)   An order for the discharge of a patient who is liable to be detained in   **1-425**
a hospital shall not be made [under section 23 above] by his nearest relative except
after giving not less than 72 hours' notice in writing to the managers of the hospital;
and if, within 72 hours after such notice has been given, the [responsible clini-
cian] furnishes to the managers a report certifying that in the opinion of [that clini-
cian] the patient, if discharged, would be likely to act in a manner dangerous to other
persons or to himself—
    (a)   any order for the discharge of the patient made by that relative in
            pursuance of the notice shall be of no effect; and
    (b)   no further order for the discharge of the patient shall be made by that—
            relative during the period of six months beginning with the date of the
            report.
    [(1A)   Subsection (1) above shall apply to an order for the discharge of a com-
munity patient as it applies to an order for the discharge of a patient who is liable
to be detained in a hospital, but with the reference to the managers of the hospital
being read as a reference to the managers of the responsible hospital.]
    (2)   In any case where a report under subsection (1) above is furnished in respect
of a patient who is liable to be detained in pursuance of an application for admis-

sion for treatment [, or in respect of a community patient,] the managers shall cause the nearest relative of the patient to be informed.

Amendments

The words in square brackets were substituted and inserted by the Mental Health Act 2007 ss.9(8), 32(4), Sch.3 para.12.

Definitions

1-426

patient: s.145(1).
hospital: ss.34(2), 145(1).
nearest relative: ss.26(3), 145(1).
the managers: s.145(1).
application for admission for treatment: ss.3, 145(1).
responsible clinician: s.34(1).
community patient: ss.17A(7), 145(1).
the responsible hospital: ss.17A(7), 145(1).

General Note

1-427

This section, which does not apply to hospital order patients (see the General Note to s.23), states that a patient's nearest relative, or acting nearest relative appointed by a county court under s.29, must give 72 hours' notice to the hospital managers of his or her intention to order the discharge of the patient from detention or from a community treatment order (CTO) (but not from guardianship) and that the order for discharge, when made, will have no effect if in the meantime the responsible clinician (RC) has reported to the managers that, in her opinion, the patient, if discharged, would be likely to act in a manner dangerous to other persons or to himself. If the RC makes such a report (a "barring report"), it will have the effect of preventing the nearest relative from exercising the powers of discharge for the next six months (subs.(1)(b)). It is submitted that this prohibition would also apply to any person authorised by the nearest relative subsequent to the receipt of the barring report to perform the functions of nearest relative under reg.24 of the English Regulations or reg.33 of the Welsh Regulations as the person authorised acts on the nearest relative's behalf. If the barring order is issued in respect of a patient who is detained under s.3 or is subject to a CTO, the nearest relative must be informed (subs.(2)).

In *Re GK (Patient: Habeas Corpus)* [1999] M.H.L.R. 128, Sedley L.J. said at para.6:

> "[T]he power which is vested in the nearest relative and in others is there essentially to ensure that nobody who is entitled to their discharge is prevented by bureaucracy or inertia or error in a hospital's administration from gaining their freedom. But the barring order is there to ensure that the mere desire of, in particular, a closest relative to have a patient out [of hospital] does not defeat the purpose of the Act which, both in the interests of the patient and in the interests of the public, has ultimate regard to the patient's mental state."

These observations were approved by the Court of Appeal in *K v Hospital Managers of the Kingswood Centre* [2014] EWCA Civ 1332; [2015] M.H.L.R. 75.

The wording of subs.(1) is ambiguous as to when the nearest relative's order of discharge is actually made. It could be argued the phrase "after giving not less than 72 hours notice" implies that there are two stages in the discharge process, namely:

(i)   notification of the intention by the nearest relative to order discharge; and
(ii)   the ordering of the discharge in the event of the patient's RC not issuing a report barring discharge within the 72 hour period.

However, the wording of para.(a), in particular the use of the term "made", suggests that the order for discharge can be made before the RC issues a report. In order to comply with the interpretive requirement in s.3 of the Human Rights Act 1998, it is suggested that the following interpretation is compatible with the rights of both patient and nearest relative under art.8 of the European Convention on Human Rights:

(i)   the notice of intention to discharge and the notice of discharge are subsumed into one event [NB This interpretation is endorsed by the *Code of Practice* at para.32.24 and by the *Reference Guide* at para.27.13: see the note on "72 hours' notice" in subs.(1)];

[198]

(ii)   the implementation of the notice of discharge is postponed for 72 hours in order to provide the RC with time to consider issuing a report barring discharge; and

(iii)   the nearest relative can withdraw the order of discharge within the 72 hour period in the event of the RC not issuing a barring report. It would be advisable to request the nearest relative to put his or her decision to withdraw in writing.

It follows that if the patient's RC has not issued a barring report in respect of the patient's nearest relative during the previous six months, the patient's discharge takes effect at the end of the 72-hour period. This will be the case whether or not arrangements have been made for the patient's after-care. The RC can discharge the patient under s.23 during this period. Although the patient's RC could place the patient on a CTO during the 72-hour period, the order would cease to have effect when the period expires. This is because the s.3 application that underpins the order would then be discharged: see s.17C(c).

It is submitted that a change in the identity of the patient's nearest relative after the notice of discharge has been submitted does not affect the validity of the notice, and that the new nearest relative has the power to withdraw the notice.

In *TTM v Hackney LBC* [2010] EWHC 1349 (Admin), Collins J. said that hospital managers had been correct to treat a post-admission allegation by the patient's nearest relative that, contrary to what had been stated by the approved mental health practitioner, he had objected to the patient's admission under s.3, as notice of his intention to discharge the patient.

The hospital managers should consider holding a review of the patient's detention if the RC makes a report under this provision (*Code of Practice*, para.38.12). The criteria that hospital managers must use when reviewing the detention of a patient subsequent to such a report being made were identified in *R. v Riverside Mental Health Trust Ex p. Huzzey* (1998) 43 B.M.L.R. 167 and *R. (on the application of SR) v Huntercombe Maidenhead Hospital* [2005] EWHC 2361 (Admin); [2005] M.H.L.R. 379. These cases are considered in the note on s.23(2).

Under s.29(3)(d), an application can be made to the county court to displace the patient's nearest relative on the ground that he or she "has exercised without due regard to the welfare of the patient or the interests of the public his power to discharge the patient from hospital … under this Part of this Act, or is likely to do so".

A study on patient discharges failed to demonstrate any significant difference in the clinical outcome of patients discharged by their nearest relative and those discharged by a psychiatrist (P. Shaw et al., "In relative danger? The outcome of patients discharged by their nearest relative from sections 2 and 3 of the Mental Health Act", *Psychiatric Bulletin* (2003), 27(2), 50–54).

Applications to the First-tier Tribunal (Mental Health) or the Mental Health Review Tribunal for Wales

In the case of a patient detained for treatment or a community patient, the patient's nearest relative **1-428** has a right to apply to the tribunal within 28 days of the patient's RC issuing a barring report under subs.(1) (s.66(1)(g), (2)(d)).

Code of Practice

Guidance on this section can be found in Ch.32 at paras 32.20 to 32.25.   **1-429**

Subsection (1)

Order for the discharge   Under s.23(2)(a). For service of the order, see reg.3(3) of the English and **1-430** Welsh Regulations. For case law on the method of service, see the notes on "served" in para.3(b)(i) of the English Regulations.

72 hours' notice   Paragraph 27.13 of the Reference Guide states:

"Although in theory the order should not be served until 72 hours after the notice has been given, in practice it is appropriate for hospital managers to accept a discharge order without prior notice as being both notice of intention to discharge the patient after 72 hours and the actual order to do so." Paragraph 32.25 of the *Code of Practice* contains the following illustrative standard letter of discharge for nearest relatives to use:

"To the managers of [insert name and address of hospital in which the patient is detained, or (for a patient on a community treatment order) the responsible hospital.]

Order for discharge under section 23 of the Mental Health Act 1983

My name is [give your name] and my address is [give your address]

[Complete A, B or C below]

A. To the best of my knowledge and belief, I am the nearest relative (within the meaning of the Mental Health Act 1983) of [name of patient].

or

B. I have been authorised to exercise the functions of the nearest relative of [name of patient] by the county court.

or

C. I have been authorised to exercise the functions of the nearest relative of [name of patient] by that person's nearest relative.

I give you notice of my intention to discharge the person named above, and I order their discharge from [say when you want the patient discharged from detention or a community treatment order].

[Please note: you must leave at least 72 hours between when the hospital managers get this letter and when you want the patient discharged.

The time when:

- the notice is received by the hospital manager or an authorised person; or
- if the notice is sent by pre-paid post, the day service is deemed to have taken place [for first class post, service is deemed on the second business day following posting, and for second class post, service is deemed on the fourth business day following posting; or
- the notice is put into the internal mail system; and
- the time when you want the patient discharged.]

Signed. .... Date. ...."

Furnishes to the managers a report The RC's report must be in the form set out in Pt 1 of Form M2: see 25 of the English Regulations (in Wales, Form NR1: see reg.34 of the Welsh Regulations). There is no requirement for the RC to examine the patient prior to completing the form.

Likely to act In *R. (on the application of Advinia Health Care Ltd) v Care Quality Commission* [2022] EWHC 965 (Admin), the case law on meaning of "likely" was extensively reviewed by Butcher J. who held that, in the context of the Care Act 2014 which established a framework designed to respond to the risk of failure of care providers, it meant a "more likely than not" (para.50). It is submitted that a similar finding would be made under this provision. See also in *Re JR 45* [2011] NIQB 17; [2014] M.H.L.R. 17, and para.32.23 of the *Code of Practice*, noted below.

Dangerous This is the sole reason for preventing discharge. In the context of a person being dangerous to others, the *Butler Committee* equated "dangerousness with a propensity to cause serious physical injury or lasting psychological harm" (para.4.10). As the danger can relate to the patient, this term encompasses the danger of self harm. There is no requirement for the risk of dangerousness to be an immediate risk. A patient with a history of becoming dangerous some time after ceasing to take medication would therefore be covered. In *Re Whitbread* [1999] C.O.D. 370, David Pannick QC, sitting as a deputy judge of the High Court, upheld the decision of hospital managers who had concluded that the dangerousness test was satisfied in a case where there was a "very high level of probability that lasting psychological harm could be caused to others if the barring order were to be lifted". It is submitted that the dangerousness test would also be satisfied if it was considered that it would be likely that the patient, if discharged, would suffer serious harm to his physical and/or mental health through self neglect or the neglect of others. Paragraph 32.23 of the *Code of Practice* states:

"[The dangerousness] question focuses on the probability of dangerous acts, such as causing serious physical injury or lasting psychological harm, not merely on the patient's general need for safety and others' general need for protection."

In *Rakevich v Russia* [2004] M.H.L.R. 37 para.32, the European Court of Human Rights said that "it is not necessary for the lawmaker exhaustively to interpret the term 'danger', as it is hardly possible to embrace in the law the whole diversity of conditions which involve psychiatric hazards". Some of the problems in defining dangerousness are identified by J. Atkinson and L. Patterson in *Review of Literature Relating to Mental Health Legislation* (2001) at para.2.11:

"Inherent in the problem of defining dangerousness is the difficulty of using the same word to describe harm to others and harm to self. This includes whether it is reasonable to describe 'self-neglect' as 'dangerous' as well as concerns about whether different levels of dangerousness should apply to the risk of the individual harming him/herself or others. Dangerousness is also usually situation-specific and may require complicated formulae to determine risk, for example when the likelihood of danger is high but in a rare situation."

During the period of six months The disqualification from ordering the patient's discharge is not affected by any change in the patient's legal status. Therefore a nearest relative who has been made the subject of a RC's report under this section subsequent to ordering the discharge of a patient who has been detained under s.2 is barred from ordering the discharge of the patient for the full six month period even though the s.2 is immediately followed by an application under s.3 (although the nearest relative could object to such an application (s.11(4))) or if the patient is discharged from the hospital and the section only to be re-admitted under a fresh application shortly thereafter.

Subsection (2)

Cause the nearest relative to be informed So that the nearest relative of a patient who has been   **1-431**
detained for treatment or who is a community patient could consider applying to a tribunal. The nearest relative of a patient who has been detained for assessment does not have an equivalent right.

AFTER-CARE UNDER SUPERVISION

[Sections 25A to 25J were repealed by the Mental Health Act 2007 s.55, Sch.11   **1-432**
Pt 5]

FUNCTIONS OF RELATIVES OF PATIENTS

Definition of "relative" and "nearest relative"

26.—(1) In this Part of this Act "relative" means any of the following   **1-433**
persons:—
  (a) husband or wife [or civil partner];
  (b) son or daughter;
  (c) father or mother;
  (d) brother or sister;
  (e) grandparent;
  (f) grandchild;
  (g) uncle or aunt;
  (h) nephew or niece.
  (2) In deducing relationships for the purposes of this section, any relationship of the half-blood shall be treated as a relationship of the whole blood, and an illegitimate person shall be treated as the legitimate child of
  [(a) his mother, and
  (b) if his father has parental responsibility for him within the meaning of section 3 of the Children Act 1989, his father.]
  (3) In this Part of this Act, subject to the provisions of this section and to the following provisions of this Part of this Act, the "nearest relative" means the person first described in subsection (1) above who is for the time being surviving, relatives of the whole blood being preferred to relatives of the same description of the half-blood and the elder or eldest of two or more relatives described in any paragraph of that subsection being preferred to the other or others of those relatives, regardless of sex.

(4)   Subject to the provisions of this section and to the following provisions of this Part of this Act, where the patient ordinarily resides with or is cared for by one or more of his relatives (or, if he is for the time being an in-patient in a hospital, he last ordinarily resided with or was cared for by one or more of his relatives) his nearest relative shall be determined—

(a)   by giving preference to that relative or those relatives over the other or others; and

(b)   as between two or more such relatives, in accordance with subsection (3) above.

(5)   Where the person who, under subsection (3) or (4) above, would be the nearest relative of a patient—

(a)   in the case of a patient ordinarily resident in the United Kingdom, the Channel Islands or the Isle of Man, is not so resident; or

(b)   is the husband or wife [or civil partner] of the patient, but is permanently separated from the patient, either by agreement or under an order of a court, or has deserted or has been deserted by the patient for a period which has not come to an end; or

(c)   is a person other than the husband, wife, [civil partner,] father or mother of the patient, and is for the time being under 18 years of age;

(d)   [...]

the nearest relative of the patient shall be ascertained as if that person were dead.

(6)   In this section "husband" [, "wife" and "civil partner" include a person who is living with the patient as the patient's husband or wife or as if they were civil partners], as the case may be (or, if the patient is for the time being an in-patient in a hospital, was so living until the patient was admitted), and has been or had been so living for a period of not less than six months; but a person shall not be treated by virtue of this subsection as the nearest relative of a married patient [or a patient in a civil partnership unless the husband, wife or civil partner] of the patient is disregarded by virtue of paragraph (b) of subsection (5) above.

(7)   A person, other than a relative, with whom the patient ordinarily resides (or, if the patient is for the time being an in-patient in a hospital, last ordinarily resided before he was admitted), and with whom he has or had been ordinarily residing for a period of not less than five years, shall be treated for the purposes of this Part of this Act as if he were a relative but—

(a)   shall be treated for the purposes of subsection (3) above as if mentioned last in subsection (1) above; and

(b)   shall not be treated by virtue of this subsection as the nearest relative of a married patient [or a patient in a civil partnership unless the husband, wife or civil partner] of the patient is disregarded by virtue of paragraph (b) of subsection (5) above.

Amendments

The amendments to this section were made by the Children Act 1989 (Consequential Amendment of Enactments) Order 1991 (SI 1991/1881) art.3, the Children Act 1989 s.108(7), Sch.15, and the Mental Health Act 2007 s.26(2)–(5).

Definitions

1-434   hospital: ss.34(2), 145(1).
patient: s.145(1).

General Note

This section defines "relative" and "nearest relative" for the purposes of Pt II of the Act. The follow-   **1-435**
ing patients who are subject to orders and remands under Pt III do not have nearest relatives for the
purposes of the Act: restricted patients (including conditionally discharged patients), patients remanded
to hospital under s.35 or s.36 and patients subject to interim hospital orders under s.38. Other patients
who are detained under Pt III and who are not restricted patients and patients who have been made
subject to guardianship orders by a court have nearest relatives by virtue of Sch.1 Pt 1 para.1.

The role of the nearest relative in respect of detained patients was identified by Maurice Kay J. in *R.
(on the application of M) v Secretary of State for Health* [2003] EWHC 1094 (Admin); [2003] M.H.L.R.
348 at paras 4 and 5 (words in square brackets inserted by the author):

> "The nearest relative plays an important part in the scheme of the Act. He may make an application
> for assessment (section 2), an emergency application for admission for assessment (section 4) and
> an application for admission for treatment (section 3). No application for admission or treatment
> under section 3 may be made by an [approved mental health professional (AMHP)] without first
> consulting with the nearest relative unless the [AMHP] considers that such consultation is not reason-
> ably practicable or would involve unreasonable delay (section 11(4)). [Unless the patient objects, the
> managers] of a psychiatric institution in which a patient is detained [have] to inform the nearest rela-
> tive in writing about, amongst other things, the right to apply to a tribunal, the right to be discharged,
> the right to receive and send correspondence and the right to consent to or refuse treatment (section
> 132(4)). A nearest relative may order the discharge of a patient who is detained under [section 2 and]
> section 3 (section 23). Prior to exercising this important power the nearest relative can appoint a medi-
> cal practitioner to examine the patient and the appointed practitioner can require the production of
> records relating to the detention or treatment of the patient (section 24). The right to order discharge
> under section 23 is limited when the [responsible clinician] certifies that the patient would, if released,
> be likely to be a danger to himself or others (section 25). Where a patient to be discharged other than
> by the order of the nearest relative, the detaining authority is required to notify the nearest relative
> of the forthcoming discharge unless the patient requests that no such information is supplied (sec-
> tion 133(2)).
>
> In addition to the power to order a discharge under section 23 the nearest relative may apply to
> [a tribunal in certain circumstances] for the discharge of the patient pursuant to section 66 … Where
> the nearest relative is the applicant to the Tribunal he may appoint a registered medical practitioner
> to visit and examine the patient and that practitioner may require production of and inspect any
> records relating to the detention and treatment of the patient (section 76(1))."

A person who has been identified as the patient's nearest relative has an absolute discretion as to how
he or she exercises the powers granted to the nearest relative. It follows that he or she is not placed under
a legal obligation to exercise those powers. The nearest relative can authorise any person (other than
the patient or a person disqualified under subs.(5)) to perform the functions of nearest relative. The
authority can be revoked at any time. Both the authority and the revocation must be in writing: see reg.24
of the English Regulations and reg.33 of the Welsh Regulations. A person who has been identified as
the patient's "next of kin" has no powers under the Act unless he or she is also the patient's nearest
relative.

In *R. (on the application of S) v Plymouth City Council and C* [2002] EWCA Civ 388; [2002]
M.H.L.R. 118, the Court of Appeal was concerned with how the interest of a mentally incapacitated
guardianship patient in preserving the confidentiality of personal information about himself is to be
reconciled with his mother's interest, as his nearest relative, in having access to enough information
about him to exercise her statutory functions under the Act. This case is considered in the General Note
to s.8 and in the note on the Civil Procedure Rules 1998 in Pt 3.

The leave of the court is required before the nearest relative of a ward of court exercises his or her
functions under the Act (s.33(2)).

Mental Capacity Act 2005

As this section does not provide a patient with a right to nominate his nearest relative, a condition   **1-436**
in a personal welfare lasting power of attorney made by the patient nominating the donee of the power
to be the patient's nearest relative would be ineffective. A donee or a deputy appointed by the Court of
Protection or a relevant person's representative under the deprivation of liberty safeguards may only
exercise the powers of the nearest relative if they are patient's nearest relative as defined in this sec-

tion, have been nominated to perform the function of the nearest relative under reg.24 or reg.33 (see above), or have been appointed by the county court as acting nearest relative under s.29.

Human Rights Act 1998

1-437   The patient's nearest relative, as a person who has the power to exercise "functions of a public nature", is a "public authority" for the purposes of s.6 of the 1998 Act (s.6(3)(b)).

In *MA v Secretary of State for Health* [2012] UKUT 474 (AAC), UT Judge Levenson held that the bundle of rights conferred on the nearest relative, in particular the right of discharge, are civil rights for the purposes of art.6 of the European Convention on Human Rights.

Code of Practice

1-438   Guidance on the identification, appointment and displacement of nearest relatives is given in Ch.5 which states at para.5.2:

> "Section 26 of the Act defines 'relative' and 'nearest relative' for the purposes of the Act. It is important to remember that the nearest relative for the purposes of the Act may not be the same person as the patient's 'next of kin'. The identity of the nearest relative may change with the passage of time – eg if the patient enters into a marriage or civil partnership. The nearest relative may be the patient's carer and it is important that they are recognised, particularly as they may have the most relevant information to share with professionals with regard to the patient's care and interests. If the nearest relative is not the carer, professionals should also involve the carer."

Paragraph 5.6 states:

> "Where an approved mental health professional (AMHP) discovers, when assessing a patient for possible detention or guardianship under the Act (or at any other time), that the patient appears to have no nearest relative, the AMHP should advise the patient of their right to apply to the county court for the appointment of a person to act as their nearest relative. If the patient lacks capacity to decide to apply themselves, the AMHP should apply to the county court."

It is submitted that the final phrase of this extract should read: "the AMHP should consider making an application to the county court": see para.5.12 where the term "consider" is used in respect of such applications, and the note on s.29(3)(a).

Subsection (1)

1-439   The definition of relative includes relationships established through adoption (*Reference Guide*, para.2.8). It is submitted that, apart from a husband or wife or civil partner and an adopted child, a non-blood relative is not to be counted as a relative for the purposes of this section. This is because there is no reference to non-blood relatives in the section, and if non-blood relatives were to be included, Parliament could have said so. This was done with the Children Act 1989 where "relative" is defined in s.105(1) as:

> ""Relative", in relation to a child, means a grandparent, brother, sister, uncle or aunt (whether of the full blood or half blood or by marriage or civil partnership) or stepparent."

For the occasions when relatives are to be disregarded for the purposes of ascertaining the patient's "nearest relative", see subs.(5). The remaining notes on this subsection are concerned with the definitions of relative as they affect the identification of the patient's nearest relative.

Husband or wife or civil partner   This includes the marital partner of a marriage of a same sex couple (Marriage (Same Sex Couples) Act 2013 s.11, Sch.3 para.1(c)). Changes made to the Gender Recognition Act 2004 by the 2013 Act enable couples to remain married when one or both parties obtains a full gender recognition certificate, and to remain in a civil partnership when both parties obtain a full gender recognition certificate: see SI 2015/50.

A person comes within the scope of this provision even if the marital or civil partner is under the age of 18 (subs.(5)(c)). If the patient is unmarried or has not entered into a civil partnership or if the marital or civil partner can be disregarded under subs.(5)(b), a person who had been living with the patient as the patient's husband or wife or civil partner for at least six months will be treated as if he or she were the patient's husband or wife or civil partner (subs.(6)).

Son or daughter An adopted child is treated as the child of the adoptive parents (Adoption and Children Act 2002 s.46(2)). Once an adoption has taken place, the child's natural parents and other birth relatives no longer have any legal connection with the child, including when the child becomes an adult.

An unmarried mother's child is treated as the child of the mother (subs.(2)) and, if he has parental responsibility for the child, his father. To become the patient's nearest relative, the child must be over the age of 18 (subs.(5)(c)). A step-child is not a relative for the purposes of this provision but could become a nearest relative under the provisions of subs.(7), by being appointed as an acting nearest relative under s.29, or by being authorised to act as such under reg.24 of the English Regulations or reg.33 of the Welsh Regulations.

Paragraph 113 of the Explanatory Notes to the Marriage (Same Sex Couples) Act 2013 refers to the position of a child of woman who is married to a person of the same sex:

"Paragraph 2 [of Schedule 4] makes clear that the common law presumption, that a child born to a woman during her marriage is also the child of her husband (often referred to as 'the presumption of legitimacy'), is not extended to marriages of same sex couples by section 11. Therefore, where two women are married to each other and one of the parties to that marriage gives birth to a child, the other party will not be presumed to be the parent of that child by virtue of the common law presumption. There may be other ways in which the party to the marriage who does not give birth to the child is treated in law as the parent (for example, if that woman is treated as a parent as a result of the amendment made by paragraph 40 of Schedule 7 to this Act to section 42 of the Human Fertilisation and Embryology Act 2008), but in all such cases it is not the common law presumption that treats her as the parent of that child."

Father or mother Even if the parent is under the age of 18 (subs.(5)(c)). A stepparent is not a relative for the purposes of this section, apart from where either the parents have entered into an agreement under s.4A of the Children Act 1989 or a court has made an order under that section.

An unmarried father is to be disregarded unless he has (not had) parental responsibility for the child: see subs.(2) which is concerned with deducing relationships "for the purposes of this section". This state of affairs is an exception to the general rule of construction established by s.1(1) of the Family Law Reform Act 1969 which provides that "unless the contrary intention" appears in a statute, any relationship between two persons "shall be construed without regard to whether or not the father and mother of either of them ... have or had been married to each other at any time". The "contrary intention" is contained in subs.(2). Brenda Hale comments that it "is surprising that the opportunity was not taken to correct [this exception to the general rule] in the 2007 amendments" (*Mental Health Law*, 6th edn, p.95).

In cases where a child is in the care of a local authority by virtue of a care order or where a guardian for the child has been appointed or where a residence order has been made in respect of the child, the local authority (s.27), guardian (s.28) or person named in the residence order (s.28) is deemed to be the child's nearest relative.

Subsection (2)

Relationship of the half-blood A person has a whole blood relationship with another if they are both **1-440** descended from the same pair of ancestors, e.g. two brothers who have the same parents. A person has a half blood relationship with another if they are descended from one common ancestor only, e.g. two brothers who have the same father but different mothers. In order to determine whether a relationship exists for the purposes of this section, if a patient has both a full-blood relative and a half-blood relative, they are both treated as full-blood relatives. Whole blood relatives are preferred to half-blood relatives for the purposes of determining the patient's nearest relative under subs.(3).

Parental responsibility Also see the note on "Father or Mother", above. Parental responsibility means "all the rights, duties, powers, responsibilities and authority which by law a parent of a child has in relation to the child and his property" (Children Act 1989 s.3). These responsibilities are not absolute but subject to the principle that the child's welfare is the paramount consideration (*Gillick v West Norfolk and Wisbech AHA* [1986] A.C. 112). A parental right has been described as: "a dwindling right which the courts will hesitate to enforce against the wishes of the child, and the more so the older he is.

It starts with the right of control and ends with little more than advice" (*Hewer v Bryant* [1970] 1 Q.B. 357 at 369 per Lord Denning). Parental responsibility ceases when a child passes 18 years of age (Children Act 1989 ss.2, 3, 105(1)).

The effect of para.(b) is that an unmarried father who does not currently have parental responsibility for his child is not a relative for the purposes of this section. It follows that a father who loses parental responsibility on the child reaching eighteen years of age cannot be the child's nearest relative by virtue of para.(b) (a contrary view is taken by David Hewitt in the Solicitors Journal, June 25, 2013). An unmarried father without parental responsibility can only become the child's nearest relative through the operation of subs.(7), by being appointed under s.29 as the child's acting nearest relative, or by virtue of the operation of reg.24 of the English Regulations or reg.33 of the Welsh Regulations: see the General Note to this section.

An unmarried father can acquire parental responsibility for his child under the following provisions of the Children Act 1989: by obtaining a child arrangements order (s.12(1)); by virtue of an order of the court (s.4(1)(c)); by making a parental responsibility agreement with the mother (s.4(1)(b)); by being appointed the child's guardian by the court (s.5(1)); or by being appointed as the child's guardian by the mother or another guardian (s.5(3),(4)). The appointment as guardian will not take effect while the mother is alive (s.5(8)).

By virtue of amendments made to s.4 of the 1989 Act by s.111 of the Adoption and Children Act 2002, unmarried fathers registered as such on the child's birth certificate under the terms of the Births and Deaths Registration Act 1953 will have parental responsibility for that child. Parental responsibility can only be acquired in this way in respect of births registered on or after December 1, 2003, which was the commencement date for s.111 (SI 2003/3079): see s.111(7) of the 2002 Act. It is possible to re-register the child's birth to include the father on the birth certificate if the formalities required by s.10A of the 1953 Act are complied with. By doing so, parental responsibility is gained from the date of registration. The registration may relate to a child who was born before December 1, 2003.

Agreements and orders made under ss.4 (which includes child arrangements orders), 4ZA (see below), 4A, and 5 of the 1989 Act continue in force until the child reaches the age of eighteen, unless they are brought to an end earlier (s.91(7), (8) of the 1989 Act). An unmarried father's parental responsibility for his child will also end if the child is adopted (s.46(2) of the 2002 Act).

If an unmarried father subsequently marries the mother of the child, both parents will from that date have parental responsibility for the child (Legitimacy Act 1976 s.2). An unmarried father will also acquire parental responsibility if he adopts the child (s.46 of the 2002 Act). Parents do not lose parental responsibility if they divorce.

Paragraph 19.10 of the *Code of Practice* states:

"Where a special guardianship order is in place, the special guardian will share parental responsibility with the child or young person's parents. However, except for certain purposes specified in the Children Act 1989, the special guardian is entitled to exercise parental responsibility to the exclusion of any other person with parental responsibility for the child (apart from another special guardian) (see section 14C of the Children Act 1989)."

In certain circumstances it is possible for a second female parent to acquire parental responsibility if an order is made under s.4ZA of the 1989 Act which governs situations where a child has a parent by virtue of s.43 of the Human Fertilisation and Embryology Act 2008.

Subsection (3)

1-441   **Nearest relative**   This subsection states that the general rule for determining the patient's nearest relative is to take whoever comes first on the list of relatives set out in subs.(1), with preference being given to relatives of the whole blood, and that if there is more than one relative coming within the same category the elder or eldest is to take priority regardless of the sex of the relative, subject to preference being given to the relative who either lives with or cares for the patient (subs.(4)).

The patient cannot choose his nearest relative who must be identified by applying subss.(3) to (6) to the patient's family and social situation. The fact that a relative is either mentally disordered, mentally incapable, or detained under the Act or is otherwise being held in custody does not disqualify him or her from being a nearest relative, although there could be grounds for removal under s.29(3)(b). The fact that a person has been sentenced to a period of imprisonment does not disqualify that person from being a nearest relative.

It is possible for a nearest relative to authorise another person to perform the functions of nearest relative on his behalf: see the General Note to this section.

Elder or eldest   Thus the elder or eldest wife of a polygamous marriage would normally become her husband's nearest relative.

Subsection (4)

This subsection provides that if the patient is either living with or being cared for by a relative, that **1-442** relative becomes the patient's nearest relative. If the patient either resides with more than one relative or is cared for by more than one relative, or lives with one relative and is cared for by another, the nearest relative becomes either the elder or eldest relative if both relatives come within the same category, or the relative who comes first on the list set out in subs.(1) if they do not.

Ordinarily resides   The leading modern authority on the meaning of "ordinarily resides" is *R. v Barnet LBC, Ex p. Shah* [1983] 2 A.C. 309 where Lord Scarman said in a different statutory context:

"Unless, therefore, it can be shown that the statutory framework or the legal context in which the words are used requires a different meaning, I unhesitatingly subscribe to the view that 'ordinarily resident' refers to a man's abode in a particular place or country which he has adopted voluntarily and for settled purposes as part of the regular order of his life for the time being, whether of short or of long duration" (p.343).

With regard to the need for a degree of settled purpose, his Lordship said:

"This is not to say that the [person] intends to stay where he is indefinitely; indeed his purpose, while settled, may be for a limited period... . All that is necessary is that the purpose of living where one does has a sufficient degree of continuity to be properly described as settled" (p.344).

His Lordship said that there is one important exception to his judgment:

"If a man's presence in a particular place or country is unlawful, e.g. in breach of the immigration laws, he cannot rely on his unlawful residence as constituting ordinary" (p.343).

The decision in *Shah* is based on the assumption that the person has the mental capacity to decide where to live. In *R. (on the application of Cornwall County Council) v Secretary of State for Health* [2015] UKSC 46; [2016] M.H.L.R. 164, a case decided under the National Assistance Act 1948 and the Children Act 1989, Lord Carnwath, who gave the judgment of the majority, said that if a mentally incapable person who is unable to make decisions about residence herself comes to live with her parents for a short period before being placed in residential care, the single question to be answered is "whether her period of actual residence with her parents was sufficiently 'settled' to amount to ordinary residence" (para.47). In the case before it, the Supreme Court ruled that a disabled young man's brief periods of staying with his parents at holiday times could not amount to ordinary residence.

In *R. (on the application of Worcestershire CC) v Secretary of State for Health and Social Care* [2023] UKSC 31 the court said at para.58:

"The test articulated in *Shah* requires adaptation where the person concerned is someone ... who lacks the mental capacity to decide where to live for herself. It seems to us that in principle in such a case the mental aspects of the test must be supplied by considering the state of mind of whoever has the power to make relevant decisions on behalf of the person concerned. Under the Mental Capacity Act 2005 that power will lie with any person who has a lasting power of attorney or with a deputy appointed by the Court of Protection or with the court itself."

The approach to identifying the ordinary residence of a mentally incapacitated adult taking into account the *Cornwall* decision is set out at para.19.32 of the Department of Health's "Care and Support Statutory Guidance":

"[W]ith regard to establishing the ordinary residence of adults who lack capacity, local authorities should adopt the Shah approach, but place no regard to the fact that the adult, by reason of their lack of capacity cannot be expected to be living there voluntarily. This involves considering all the facts, such as the place of the person's physical presence, their purpose for living there, the person's connection with the area, their duration of residence there and the person's views, wishes and feelings (insofar as these are ascertainable and relevant) to establish whether the purpose of the residence has a sufficient degree of continuity to be described as settled, whether of long or short duration."

In the Northern Irish case *The Western Health and Social Care Trust for Judicial Review v Secretary of State for Health* [2018] NIQB 67, McClosky J. said that "the decision in *Cornwall* makes clear that in the particular case of a person of mental incapacity, the Shah test is stripped of subjectivity" (para.30).

In *Mohamed v Hammersmith and Fulham London BC* [2002] 1 All E.R. 176, Lord Slynn said at para.18:

> "It is clear that words like 'ordinary residence' and 'normal residence' may take their precise meaning from the context of the legislation in which they appear but it seems to me that the prima facie meaning of normal residence is a place where at the relevant time the person in fact resides. That therefore is the question to be asked and it is not appropriate to consider whether in a general or abstract sense such a place would be considered an ordinary or normal residence. So long as that place where he eats and sleeps is voluntarily accepted by him, the reason why he is there rather than somewhere else does not prevent that place from being his normal residence. He may not like it, he may prefer some other place, but that place is for the relevant time the place where he normally resides. If a person, having no other accommodation, takes his few belongings and moves into a barn for a period to work on a farm that is where during that period he is normally resident, however much he might prefer some more permanent or better accommodation."

In the *Sunderland* case, below, which is concerned with the meaning of residence in s.117, Lloyd L.J. found the guidance in Mohamed to be a "good deal more helpful and relevant" than that provided in *Shah* (para.47).

In *R. (on the application of Sunderland City Council) v South Tyneside Council* [2012] EWCA Civ 1232; [2013] 1 All E.R. 394, Lloyd L.J. said at para.31:

> "I agree with the comment made in other cases that, in general, when considering any case in which there is doubt as to the place of a person's residence, the question is not only that of physical presence and that it may be relevant to consider why the person is where he or she is, and to what extent his or her presence there is voluntary, Thus, if a person has a home, the fact that he or she is not there on a given date or for a particular period does not mean that he or she is not resident there, if the absence is accounted for by, for example, a holiday, a business trip or having to spend time in hospital, whether following an injury, an operation or some other form of treatment, possibly over a long period, or, for that matter a period of imprisonment following a criminal conviction."

Each case has to be judged on its own facts and the fact that a person has left his home does not necessarily mean that he has established an ordinary residence elsewhere. McCullough J. examined this issue in *R. v Liverpool CC Ex p. F* (CO 2744/96) April 16, 1997, a case where the patient had left the parental home in acrimonious circumstances and had gone to live with his grandmother, as well as staying at a number of other places. His Lordship said that those who were charged with the task of identifying the identity of the patient's nearest relative should have considered:

> "not just the choice between whether he was ordinarily resident with his mother or with his grandmother. They should have considered also the possibility that he may not have been ordinarily resident anywhere and should have specifically asked themselves— bearing in mind his itinerant lifestyle, his lack of stability and the condition of his mental health—whether he really had settled down sufficiently at his grandmother's for her home to be regarded as his place of ordinary residence."

It follows that at person who engages in "sofa surfing" is not likely to have an ordinary residence.

If a patient leaves home, but takes up no other place of ordinary residence and no relative is caring for him, his nearest relative can be identified by applying the general rule set out in subs.(3).

The Local Government Association has published "Ordinary residence guide: determining local authority responsibilities under the Care Act and the Mental Health Act" which can be accessed at: *www.local.gov.uk/ordinary-residence-guide-determining-local-authority-responsibilities-under-care-act-and-mental.*

Cared for   A person can clearly "care about" a patient without providing "care for" that patient. In *Re D (Mental patient: habeas corpus)* [2000] 2 F.L.R. 848, the Court of Appeal held that (a) the words "ordinarily" qualifies "resided with" but not "cared for"; and (b) although the words "cared for" are not defined in the Act, they are clear and everyday words set in a context where the AMHP applicant has to act in a pragmatic and common sense manner in a situation which is fraught with emotion and difficulty. In order to justify a finding that the relative is caring for the patient, the services provided by the relative must be more than minimal and they need not have been provided over the long term. In this case, the court was asked to consider the situation of a relative who assisted the patient in managing his financial affairs, checked whether he was eating appropriately and took away and cleaned his soiled clothing and bed clothes. In finding that the relative was caring for the patient the court said that there "was more than sufficient evidence to pass the 'cared for' test, wherever one sets the threshold of services amounting to 'cared for'. In other words, the services were not merely minimal. They were services which were substantial and sustained".

The patient may be "cared for" by a relative even if they do not share a residence. In *R. v Liverpool CC*, above, McCullough J. held that the quality of regularity is important when considering whether there has been a change in the identity of the person who is to be regarded as caring for the patient. His Lordship said: "In such a case it will be necessary to take into account the duration, continuity and quality of the care afforded by the relative under consideration as having assumed the role ... and also the intention of the patient himself".

Section 10(11) of the Care Act 2014, which is headed "Assessment of a carer's need for support", states that "care" includes "practical or emotional support". In a care home setting, it is submitted that the practical and emotional support that can be provided by a relative of a resident could enable that relative to be categorised as a relative who "cared for" the resident under this provision. This could occur if, for example, the relative visited the resident regularly, attended review meetings where the needs of the resident were discussed, was the first point of contact for the care home, ensured that the resident had appropriate clothing, and provided treats for the resident.

Annex J to the Department of Health and Social Care's "Care and support statutory guidance" defines as carer as:

"Somebody who provides support or who looks after a family member, partner or friend who needs help because of their age, physical or mental illness, or disability. This would not usually include someone paid or employed to carry out that role, or someone who is a volunteer."

Subsection (5)

This subsection, which disqualifies certain persons from acting as a patient's nearest relative, is applied to persons who have been deemed to be the patient's nearest relative by virtue of s.28 (s.28(2)).   **1-443**

Paragraph (a); ordinarily resident in the united kingdom   "United Kingdom" means Great Britain and Northern Ireland (Interpretation Act 1978 s.5, Sch.1). It is easier for a person to lose their ordinary/habitual residence in a country than to acquire it. The concepts of "ordinary residence" and "habitual residence" are broadly synonymous (*Re M (A Child) (Foreign Care Proceedings Transfer)* [2013] EWHC 646 Fam, per Cobb J at para.17). In *C v S (A Minor) (Abduction)* [1990] 2 F.L.R. 442 at 454 HL Lord Brandon said:

"[T]he question whether a person is or is not habitually resident in a specified country is a question of fact to be decided by reference to all the circumstances of any particular case ... . A person may cease to be habitually resident in country A in a single day if he or she leaves it with a settled intention not to return to it but to take up long term residence in country B instead. Such a person cannot, however, become habitually resident in country B in a single day. An appreciable period of time and a settled intention will be necessary to enable him or her to become so. During that appreciable period of time the person will have ceased to be habitually resident in country A but not yet have become habitually resident in country B."

Not so resident   The effect of this provision is that:

1.   If the patient is ordinarily resident in the United Kingdom, the Channel Islands or the Isle of Man and the person who would normally be identified as the patient's nearest relative is not so resident, that person cannot be the patient's nearest relative. However, if that person has gone abroad temporarily, for example on business or on holiday, he or she will be the patient's nearest relative.
2.   If the patient is not ordinarily resident in the United Kingdom, the Channel Islands or the Isle of Man, the nearest relative of the patient can be a person who is also not so resident.

Paragraph (b); Separated   In the absence of a court order, the spouses or civil partners must have agreed that their separation is permanent; the mere fact that the couple live at different places is not sufficient to constitute separation. If one spouse or civil partner is uncertain as to whether the separation is permanent, this provision is not satisfied.

Both separation and desertion require that the couple be factually separated. It is possible for a separation to be established in a situation where both parties continue to live in the same premises if it can be said that two separate households have been established. If there continues to be a sharing of a common life by, for example, taking meals together or sharing common living areas, the parties are not separated for the purposes of the Divorce Reform Act 1969. In *Le Brocq v Le Brocq* [1964] 1 W.L.R. 1085, the wife had excluded her husband from the matrimonial bedroom by bolting the door on the inside. There was no avoidable communication between them, but the wife continued to cook meals for her husband, although he was never allowed to take meals with her, and he paid her a weekly sum for housekeeping. The court held that the necessary factual separation had not been established: there was, as Harman L.J. put it, "separation of bedrooms, separation of hearts, separation of speaking: but one household was carried on ...".

Deserted   Under matrimonial law, the main elements of desertion are the fact of separation and the intention to desert. The intention to desert involves: (a) lack of consent to the separation by the spouse who has been deserted; (b) lack of any justification for the separation; and (c) the deserting spouse having the mental capacity to form the intent: see *Cretney Principles of Family Law* (2015) at paras 10.027 at seq. A person who has been disqualified from being a patient's nearest relative under this provision can resume that role as soon as the desertion comes to an end.

Paragraph (c); under 18 years of age   Means before the commencement of his eighteenth birthday (Family Law Reform Act 1969 s.9(1)).

Subsection (6)

1-444   **Living with the patient as the patient's husband or wife or as if they were civil partners**   Under this provision, an individual who has been living with the patient as the patient's husband or wife or as if they were civil partners for at least six months shall be treated as the patient's nearest relative. The status of nearest relative is not relinquished if the cohabitation is subsequently interrupted by, for example, one of the partners being admitted to a care home. This rule is subject to the exception that the cohabitee of a married patient or a patient who is in a civil partnership cannot be the nearest relative of that patient unless the patient's spouse or civil partner can be disregarded under subs.(5)(b) on the ground of permanent separation or desertion.

It is not sufficient for the couple to be living together; they must be living together in a settled relationship as if they were husband or wife or civil partners. In *Mummery v Mummery* [1942] P. 107, a case on desertion, Lord Merriman P. doubted that it was possible to "give a completely exhaustive definition of cohabitation". This statement was cited in *Kimber v Kimber* [2000] 1 F.L.R. 383, where Judge Tyrer identified the following factors as being relevant to the question of determining whether a man and a woman are living together as husband and wife:

(a)   are the parties living together in the same household;
(b)   do they share daily tasks and duties;
(c)   is there stability and a degree of permanence in the relationship;
(d)   is the way in which financial matters are being handled an indication of the cohabitation;
(e)   do the parties have a sexual relationship with each other;
(f)   are there children of the relationship;
(g)   what is the intention and motivation of the parties; and
(h)   would a reasonable person of normal perceptions consider that the parties were cohabiting.

Judge Tyrer said that these factors "cannot be complete nor comprehensive".

Was so living until the patient was admitted

The six-month period of cohabitation must have occurred prior to the patient's admission.

Period of not less than six months   In the unreported case of *R. (on the application of Robinson) v The Hospital Managers of Park Royal Hospital*, November 26, 2007, the cohabiting partner of a detained patient purported to discharge him under s.23 on the ground that she, and not the patient's aunt, was the patient's nearest relative. The hospital declined to discharge him on the ground that the partner was not the patient's nearest relative as she did not qualify under this provision. In dismissing an application for habeas corpus and judicial review of the hospital's decision, Stanley Burnton J. said that in calculating the six-month period, a hospital should take into account periods spent apart, including time spent abroad, and/or detention in a hospital or prison (notwithstanding that such absences are under compulsion). As such periods of detention would be recorded, it would not be impracticable for a hospital to make such calculations. Although it might be difficult to identify when a period of cohabitation began, a hospital was obliged to try, as it had a duty to investigate whether a six month cohabitation period had altered the identity of the patient's nearest relative. Whether or not a period apart would bring a cohabitation period to an end for the purposes of this provision would depend on the nature and duration of the relationship when the interruption took place (This case is considered by counsel for the claimant, Laura Davidson, in "Nearest Relative Consultation and the Avoidant Approved Mental Health Professional", J.M.H.L., Spring 2009, 70–80).

With regard to the nature and duration of the relationship, the imprisonment of a patient who had been cohabiting with his partner for a number of years would be unlikely to bring the cohabitation to an end. However, if the imprisonment occurred a few days after the couple had begun to live together, it would be difficult to claim after six months that they had cohabited.

Subsection (7)

This subsection, which was enacted to respond to the position of same sex couples, provides that a **1-445** person who has been living with the patient for five years or more shall be treated as if he or she were a relative who came last on the hierarchy of relatives set out in subs.(1). By virtue of subs.(4), with the exception of someone who comes within the scope of para.(b), that person, as a relative who "ordinarily resides" with the patient, becomes the patient's nearest relative unless a relative who came higher in the hierarchy is either living with or caring for the patient. The author has been informed that this interpretation, which is also adopted by Lady Hale (Brenda Hale, *Mental Health Law*, 6th edn (2017), p.96v), was not followed by a judge in the course of displacement proceedings under s.29 in the county court. The judge apparently ruled that where there is a family member who features on the subs.(1) list, that person should always be preferred to a care home resident regardless of the fact that the patient may have lived in that care home with that resident for five years or more. It is submitted that the judge's interpretation, which would result in the "five year person" hardly ever becoming the patient's nearest relative, cannot be right as it would make para.(b), which prevents the "five year person" taking precedence over a married patient or a patient in a civil partnership in certain circumstances, redundant. Subsection (7) provides that the "five year person" is to be treated as a relative "for the purposes of this Part of this Act". Subsection (4) relates to a patient who either lives with or is cared for "by one or more of his relatives" which, by virtue of subs.(7), includes a "five year person". There is nothing in this Act which suggests that the normal rules of statutory interpretation should be disregarded in the manner adopted by the judge.

There is no requirement for the patient and the person with whom he has resided for five years or more to regard each other as being married or in a civil partnership, or to be in a relationship, or even to be friends.

There may be difficulties in identifying the patient's nearest relative in cases where the patient has been residing with a number of people who are not relatives for five years or more in a communal living situation. This could occur where, for example, the patient is a member of a religious community or if he lives in a group home. In this situation the provisions of subs.(3) would apply and the eldest person who had become a "relative" under this subsection would become the patient's nearest relative.

A particular difficulty has arisen with the identification of the nearest relative of an elderly patient who is the resident of a care home. Although the question of whether a person ordinarily resides with others is a question of fact and degree which must be determined in each case (see the note on "ordinarily resides" in subs.(4)), it would be difficult to argue that the residents of many such homes do not "ordinarily reside" with each other in that they will usually eat together, use common facilities and generally live a communal life. In other words, the residents share a common home. Such a finding would not be appropriate in a case where the residents lived in self-contained units within the home and only had occasional contact with each other for social purposes. If the patient is found to have ordinarily resided with a number of fellow residents for more than five years, the combined effect of subss.(3) and (4) is to identify the eldest of these residents as the patient's nearest relative. The fact that residents might not possess the mental capacity to consent to their admission to a care home or to them being there does not mean that they are not ordinarily resident at the home as long as they are settled there: see the *Cornwall* case noted under subs.(4). If the identified nearest relative does not wish to act in that role he or she could be asked to use the simple procedure set out in reg.24 of the English Regulations or reg.33 of the Welsh Regulations to nominate some other person to take over the responsibilities of nearest relative. If the identified nearest relative is mentally incapacitated, it will not be practicable for that person to be consulted with for the purposes of s.11(4). In this situation an application could be made to the court for an acting nearest relative to be appointed under s.29(3)(b).

In exceptional circumstances, if a relative or a spouse or civil partner of a patient who has been living in a communal situation has had a substantial and sustained contact with the patient by, for example, taking the patient out of the institution for recreational purposes, assisting with feeding the patient or entertaining the patient at his or her home, it might be possible to argue that that person was caring for the patient for the purposes of subs.(4). In these circumstances that person would take precedence over the "five year" person, who remains last on the subs.(1) list (subs.(7)(a), by virtue of subs.(3).

This provision covers the situation where an adult mentally disordered ex-patient has been "fostered" to carers under an adult placement scheme. It seems inappropriate that carers have to wait for five years before one of them is entitled to exercise the functions of nearest relative. It also appears to cover the situation of a child who has been placed with foster parents under either Pt III or Pt IX of the Children Act 1989. If the child remains at that home on reaching adulthood, the period when the child was fostered should be included in the calculation of the five-year period.

It is submitted that a landlord and tenant can only be considered as "ordinarily residing" with each other if they live in the same accommodation and there is a substantial sharing of household facilities and functions.

Ordinarily resides   See the note in subs.(4) under this heading.

Five years   Temporary separations resulting, for example, from separate holidays being taken should be disregarded in calculating this period.

Married patient or a patient in a civil partnership   The "five year" person cannot be the nearest relative of a married patient or a patient in a civil partnership unless the patient's spouse or civil partner can be disregarded because of permanent separation or desertion.

[Children and young persons in care

1-446   **27.** Where—

(a)   a patient who is a child or young person is in the care of a local authority by virtue of a care order within the meaning of the Children Act 1989; or—

(b)   the rights and powers of a parent of a patient who is a child or young person are vested in a local authority by virtue of section 16 of the Social Work (Scotland) Act 1968,

the authority shall be deemed to be the nearest relative of the patient in preference to any person except the patient's husband or wife [or civil partner] (if any).]

Amendment

This section was substituted by the Children Act 1989 s.108(5), Sch.13, para.48(1). The words in square brackets were inserted by the Mental Health Act 2007 s.26(6).

Definitions

1-447   patient: s.145(1).
nearest relative: ss.26(3), 145(1).

General Note

1-448   If an unmarried child or a child who is not in a civil partnership is in the care of a local authority by virtue of a care order (in England or Wales) or if parental rights and powers in respect of a child have been vested in a local authority (in Scotland), this section identifies that authority as the child's nearest relative. It would clearly be appropriate for the local authority to delegate its functions under this provision to an officer.

The local authority in England or Wales must comply with its duties under s.116.

This section applies to children who have been placed under hospital or guardianship orders by a court under s.37 (Sch.1 Pt 1 para.1).

Child

Is defined in the Children Act 1989 as a person under the age of eighteen (s.105(1)).

Care order

A care order is defined in s.31(11) of the Children Act 1989 to include an interim care order made under s.38 of that Act.

Nearest relative of minor under guardianship, etc

28.—[(1)   Where   **1-449**

    (a)   a guardian has been appointed for a person who has not attained the age of eighteen years; or

    (b)   a [person is named in child arrangements] order (as defined by section 8 of the Children Act 1989) [as a person with whom a person who has not attained the age of eighteen years is to live],

the guardian (or guardians, where there is more than one) or the person [so named (or the persons so named, where there is more than one)] shall, to the exclusion of any other person, be deemed to be his nearest relative.]]

(2)   Subsection (5) of section 26 above shall apply in relation to a person who is, or who is one of the persons, deemed to be the nearest relative of a patient by virtue of this section as it applies in relation to a person who would be the nearest relative under subsection (3) of that section.

[(3)   In this section "guardian" [includes a special guardian (within the meaning of the Children Act 1989), but] does not include a guardian under this Part of this Act.]

(4)   In this section "court" includes a court in Scotland or Northern Ireland, and "enactment" includes an enactment of the Parliament of Northern Ireland, a Measure of the Northern Ireland Assembly and an Order in Council under Schedule 1 of the Northern Ireland Act 1974.

Amendments

The amendments to this section were made by the Children Act 1989 s.108(5), Sch.13 para.48, the Adoption and Children Act 2002 s.139, Sch.3 para.41 and the Children and Families Act 2014 Sch.14 Pt 2 para.46.

Definition

patient: s.145(1).   **1-450**

General Note

This section provides for a person who has been appointed as a child's guardian (other than under   **1-451**
this Act), a child's special guardian or a person who is named in a child arrangements order which has been made in respect of a child, to be that child's nearest relative. It applies to children who have been placed under hospital or guardianship orders by a court under s.37 (Sch.1 Pt 1 para.1).

Subsection (1)

Attained the age   At the commencement of his or her eighteenth birthday (Family Law Reform Act   **1-452**
1969 s.9(1)).

Guardian   A guardian can only be appointed under s.5 of the Children Act 1989 (ibid., subs.(13)).

Guardians, where there is more than one   Thus two persons, as co-guardians, could have equal powers as the patient's nearest relative. Compare this with s.26(3) where only a sole nearest relative is contemplated.

Child Arrangements Order   Formerly known as a residence order. If more than one person is named in the order, those named will have equal powers as the patient's nearest relative.

Subsection (2)

1-453   This provides that s.26(5), which disqualifies certain persons from acting as a patient's nearest relative, applies to the person or persons deemed to be the patient's nearest relative by virtue of subs.(1).

Subsection (3)

1-454   **Special guardian**   See s.14A of the Children Act 1989.

Guardian under this part of this Act   Such a person could become a patient's nearest relative if, apart from guardianship responsibilities under the Act, he or she would be nearest relative by virtue of either being the person named or appointed under subs.(1) or by being identified as nearest relative under s.26.

Subsection (4)

1-455   This provision should be construed in accordance with Sch.12, paras 1 to 11 of the Northern Ireland Act 1998.

Appointment by court of acting nearest relative

1-456   **29.**—(1)   The county court may, upon application made in accordance with the provisions of this section in respect of a patient, by order direct that the functions of the nearest relative of the patient under this Part of this Act and sections 66 and 69 below shall, during the continuance in force of the order, be exercisable by [the person specified in the order].

[(1A)   If the court decides to make an order on an application under subsection (1) above, the following rules have effect for the purposes of specifying a person in the order—

   (a)   if a person is nominated in the application to act as the patient's nearest relative and that person is, in the opinion of the court, a suitable person to act as such and is willing to do so, the court shall specify that person (or, if there are two or more such persons, such one of them as the court thinks fit);

   (b)   otherwise, the court shall specify such person as is, in its opinion, a suitable person to act as the patient's nearest relative and is willing to do so.]

  (2)   An order under this section may be made on the application of—

   [(za)   the patient;]

   (a)   any relative of the patient;

   (b)   any other person with whom the patient is residing (or, if the patient is then an in-patient in a hospital, was last residing before he was admitted); or

   (c)   an [approved mental health professional];

[...]

  (3)   An application for an order under this section may be made upon any of the following grounds, that is to say—

   (a)   that the patient has no nearest relative within the meaning of this Act, or that it is not reasonably practicable to ascertain whether he has such a relative, or who that relative is;

  (b) that the nearest relative of the patient is incapable of acting as such by reason of mental disorder or other illness;

  (c) that the nearest relative of the patient unreasonably objects to the making of an application for admission for treatment or a guardianship application in respect of the patient; [...]

  (d) that the nearest relative of the patient has exercised without due regard to the welfare of the patient or the interests of the public his power to discharge the patient [...] under this Part of this Act, or is likely to do so[; or

  (e) that the nearest relative of the patient is otherwise not a suitable person to act as such.]

(4) If, immediately before the expiration of the period for which a patient is liable to be detained by virtue of an application for admission for assessment, an application under this section, which is an application made on the ground specified in subsection (3)(c) or (d) above, is pending in respect of the patient, that period shall be extended—

  (a) in any case, until the application under this section has been finally disposed of; and

  (b) if an order is made in pursuance of the application under this section, for a further period of seven days;

and for the purposes of this subsection an application under this section shall be deemed to have been finally disposed of at the expiration of the time allowed for appealing from the decision of the court or, if notice of appeal has been given within that time, when the appeal has been heard or withdrawn, and "pending" shall be construed accordingly.

(5) An order made on the ground specified in subsection [(3)(a), (b) or (e)] above may specify a period for which it is to continue in force unless previously discharged under section 30 below.

(6) While an order made under this section is in force, the provisions of this Part of this Act (other than this section and section 30 below) and sections 66, 69, 132(4) and 133 below shall apply in relation to the patient as if for any reference to the nearest relative of the patient there were substituted a reference to the person having the functions of that relative and (without prejudice to section 30 below) shall so apply notwithstanding that the person who was the patient's nearest relative when the order was made is no longer his nearest relative; but this subsection shall not apply to section 66 below in the case mentioned in paragraph (h) of subsection (1) of that section.

Amendments

The amendments to this section were made by the Mental Health Act 2007 ss.21, 23, 55, Sch.2 para.7, Sch.11 Pts 4 and 5.

Definitions

1-457   patient: s.145(1).
nearest relative: ss.26(3), 145(1).
hospital: ss.34(2), 145(1).
approved mental health professional: s.145(1), (1AC).
local social services authority: s.145(1).
mental disorder: ss.1, 145(1).
application for admission for treatment: ss.3, 145(1).
application for admission for assessment: ss.2, 145(1).
guardianship application: s.7(1).

General Note

1-458   The section gives the county court power to make an order directing that the functions of the patient's nearest relative (NR) shall be exercised by another person. The effect of an order is to displace the person who would otherwise be the patient's nearest relative. The applicant for the order can nominate a person to act as the patient's NR. Where the nominated person is, in the court's opinion, not "suitable" or there is no nomination, the court can appoint any suitable person to act as the patient's NR if he or she is willing to do so (subs.(1A)). An application to the court can be made concurrently with, or subsequent to, an application under s.3: see s.30(4) and *R. v Central London County Court Ex p. London* [1999] 3 All E.R. 991 CA. An applicant can only rely on the grounds set out in subs.(3). In order to succeed on an application the applicant must demonstrate that the statutory criteria are made out both at the date of the application and at the date of the hearing (*Lewis v Gibson* [2005] EWCA Civ 587; [2005] M.H.L.R. 309 para.38). If the court makes an order under this section, it has no further legal role to play in respect of any subsequent application for treatment or guardianship that is made in respect of the patient.

It is lawful to make an application under s.3, including in a situation where s.2 has been extended under subs.(4), before the proceedings under this section have been resolved (*R. (on the application of M) v Homerton University Hospital* noted under Interim and without notice orders, below).

If the acting nearest relative dies, "no-one can exercise the rights of the nearest relative while the order remains in force, until the court discharges it, or varies it to appoint a new acting nearest relative" (Reference Guide, para.2.57).

In *Surrey County Council Social Services v McMurray*, November 11, 1994, CA, Hale J., in dismissing an appeal by a nearest relative against an order that had been made under this section, said that "the displacement of a person as nearest relative in no way takes away his legitimate interest in the welfare of his daughter, which should always be paid proper respect by the authorities in making decisions about and arrangements for her care".

In *R. (on the application of S) v Plymouth City Council and C* [2002] EWCA Civ 388; [2002] 1 W.L.R. 2582, the Court of Appeal was concerned with how the interest of a mentally incapacitated guardianship patient in preserving the confidentiality of personal information about himself is to be reconciled with his mother's interest, as his nearest relative, in having access to enough information about him to defend a possible displacement application made under this section. This case is considered in the General Note to s.8 and in the note on the Civil Procedure Rules 1998 in Pt 3.

Section 30 gives the county court power to discharge or vary an order made under this section, and also specifies the duration of such an order if the duration has not been established under subs.(5) of this section. An order made under this section does not expire on the transfer of the patient under s.19.

It is prima facie a contempt of court to publish information relating to proceedings brought under this section where the county court is sitting in private: see s.12 of the Administration of Justice Act 1960 and *Pickering v Liverpool Daily Post and Echo Newspapers Plc* [1991] 1 All E.R. 622 HL.

County Court Procedure

1-459   For the procedure on an application to the county court, see s.31 and the Civil Procedure Rules 1998 (SI 1998/3132) Pt 8 and Practice Direction 49E—Alternative Procedure for Claims which are reproduced in Pt 3. That applications are brought under Part 8 of the Civil Procedure Rules was confirmed in *Massie v H* [2011] EWCA Civ 115; [2011] M.H.L.R. 288. A Part 8 claim form must be used by the applicant. This can be accessed at: *www.gov.uk/government/publications/form-n208-claim-form-cpr-part-8*. The court has the power to make an interim order when considering an application: see below.

Applications under this section are "have to be dealt with quickly" (*R. (on the application of S) v Plymouth City Council*, above, per Hale L.J. at para.39). In *Derbyshire CC v Maude*, July 5, 1999, CA (unreported), Sedley L.J. described a delay of a year for an application to come to the county court as "at lowest, alarming".

An application cannot be made in respect of a person who is not suffering from a mental disorder even if it is thought that the person would be likely to develop a mental disorder at some time in the future.

Interim and without notice orders   Section 38 of the County Courts Act 1984 provides the county **1-460** court with the power to make an interim order when considering an application under this section. A decision of the hospital managers to rely on such an order for the purposes of the admission and detention of a patient is lawful: see *R. v Central London County Court*, above, where Stuart-Smith L.J. said at para.24: "unless there are cogent reasons to the contrary, it is preferable that questions under s.29(3)(c) should be finally determined before an application is made under s.3, and the machinery of extension of detention under section afforded by s.29(4) should be used". This statement was considered in *R. (on the application of M) v Homerton University Hospital* [2008] EWCA Civ 197; [2008] M.H.L.R. 92, where the Court of Appeal considered the patient's claim for judicial review on the basis that, where the machinery for extended detention under subs.(4) existed, it was unlawful, in the absence of exceptional circumstances, to detain her under s.3 so that she became subject to concurrent detention regimes. In dismissing the claim, the court held that:

(i)   although in might be desirable in some cases to follow the approach advocated by Stuart-Smith L.J., there was nothing in the Act or in the case law to suggest that if a hospital chooses to go down the s.29 route to try to displace the unreasonable relative, they are then bound to conclude those proceedings before taking action under s.3; and

(ii)   there is no requirement that "exceptional circumstances" must exist before the s.29 and s.3 regimes may run in tandem.

In order for a s.3 application to be made in these circumstances, the court would have had to have made an interim order displacing the nearest relative. The Court of Appeal did not address the question of how a recommending doctor can certify that, given the patient is subject to an extended s.2, the requirement in s.3(2)(c) that the patient's treatment "cannot be provided unless he is detained under [s.3]" is satisfied. It is submitted that, as the powers of a patient's responsible clinician to treat the patient under s.2 and s.3 are identical, the requirement cannot be satisfied until the lapsing of the extended s.2 is imminent. The making of the s.3 application will enable the patient to make an application to the tribunal.

In *R. v Uxbridge County Court Ex p. Binns* [2000] M.H.L.R. 179, the court made a without notice interim order appointing the local authority as the acting nearest relative of the patient. Two hours' notice of the application was given to the nearest relative, who was not served with any papers. The displaced nearest relative was given permission to apply to the court, after giving notice to the local authority, to vary or discharge the order. On an application for judicial review of the order Hidden J. held that:

1.   Section 38 of the 1984 Act is broad enough to encompass a temporary order which was both interlocutory and conditional and was not for a specified period.

2.   There is nothing in Ord.49 r.12 of the County Court Rules (now see CPR Pt 8 and Practice Direction 49E—Alternative Procedure for Claims) which is inconsistent with the general provisions of Pt 23 of the Civil Procedure Rules which, inter alia, entitle a person against whom an order is made without notice to apply to set aside or vary it (para.23.10(1)); require the order to contain a statement of the right to make an application to set aside or vary it (para.23.9(3)); and provide a power in the court to re-list an application where an order had been made in the absence of a respondent either at the application of that person or of the court's own motion (para.23.11(2)). His Lordship said, at para.30, that the court should be slow to conclude that a practice consistent with the Civil Procedure Rules was precluded by the terms of the 1983 Act.

3.   Since the 1983 Act does not set out a complete code governing the making of orders displacing the nearest relative of a patient (for example, it does not mention interim orders), then the submission that the granting of permission to apply would necessarily be ultra vires s.30 is an incorrect one.

4.   The order made by the court was proportionate.

Binns was applied in *R. (on the application of Holloway) v Oxfordshire County Council* [2007] EWHC 776 (Admin); [2007] M.H.L.R. 225, where Beatson J. upheld an interim displacement order where the nearest relative had not been given notice of the proceedings. The conduct of the local authority in not giving notice was described as falling "far below what is required of a public authority in the exercise of its responsibilities to persons with mental illness and the nearest relatives of such person" (para.33). His Lordship held that:

1.   Order 49, r.12 (now CPR Pt 8 and Practice Direction 49E) did not assist the nearest relative as the words of that provision do not preclude an application being made without notice.

2.   What the principles of natural justice require at the preliminary stage of a process is different from what they require where a binding decision is to be made.

3. Applications which are not determinative, such as applications for interim relief, are not subject to the guarantees set out in art.6 of the European Convention on Human Rights (ECHR) unless they cause irreversible prejudice to a party's interests. An interim displacement does not fall into this category as there are sufficient safeguards in the Act for the patient and for his nearest relative.
4. An application for an interim order made without notice to the person affected should only be made where it is necessary to act urgently.
5. It is good practice for a judge hearing a without notice application to make enquiries as to whether it was practicable to have given notice to the nearest relative and to consider whether it would be possible to adjourn the hearing for such notice to be given. Those making the application should apprise the judge of all the relevant facts, including those that may be adverse to the application.

An applicant who makes a without notice application to the court has a duty to investigate the facts and to make a full and fair disclosure of all the crucial points for and against the application. It is no excuse for an applicant to say that he was not aware of the importance of matters he has omitted to state (*Marc Rich & Co Holding GmbH v Krasner* [1999] EWCA Civ 581). Judicial guidance on the procedure applicable to without notice applications was considered and expanded upon by Theis J. in *KY v DD* [2011] EWHC 1277 (Fam) at paras 13 to 16. Without notice applications are governed by Pt 23.9 and 10 of the Civil Procedure Rules.

1-461 **Human Rights Act 1998** In *R. (on the application of MH) v Secretary of State for Health* [2005] UKHL 60; [2005] M.H.L.R 302, it was contended on behalf of the patient that the Act fails to comply with art.5(4) of the ECHR, which is designed to procure the speedy release of someone who should not in fact have been detained in the first place or should not be detained any longer, in that it does not provide a right of review at reasonable intervals for a patient who finds herself detained by virtue of s.29(4) and is thus deprived of the right which a patient newly detained under s.3 would have. The House of Lords held that as the system provided for by s.29(4) is *capable* of acting compatibly with art.5(4), it could not be said to be incompatible with art.5(4) although action or inaction by the authorities under it may be so. The preferable means of achieving compatibility is for the Secretary of State to use her power under s.67(1) to refer the case to the tribunal. As the Secretary of State is under a duty to act compatibly with the patient's Convention rights, she would be well advised to make such a reference as soon as the position is drawn to her attention by the patient's lawyers. Should the Secretary of State decline to exercise this power, judicial review would be swiftly available to oblige her to do so. It would also be possible for the hospital managers or the local social services authority to notify the Secretary of State whenever an application is made under s.29 so that she can consider the position. Although judicial review and/or habeas corpus may be one way of securing compliance, this would be much more satisfactorily achieved either through a speedy determination of the county court proceedings or by a Secretary of State's reference under s.67. This case was considered by the European Court of Human Rights in *MH v United Kingdom* (2014) 58 E.H.R.R. 35; [2014] M.H.L.R. 249, where the Court held that the approach adopted by the House of Lords was compatible with art.5(4). The Court declined to consider the hypothetical situation "had the applicant not had a relative willing and able, through solicitors, to bring her situation to the attention of the Secretary of State" (para.95).

In *MA v Secretary of State for Health* [2012] UKUT 474 (AAC), UT Judge Levenson held that the fact that the patient's nearest relative does not have a right to make an application to a tribunal in respect of a patient who has been detained for assessment and whose detention has been extended by virtue of the operation of s.29(4), does not violate art.6 of the ECHR as the availability of judicial review to challenge the lawfulness of the patient's detention is an adequate remedy.

1-462 **Applications to the First-tier Tribunal (Mental Health) or the Mental Health Review Tribunal for Wales** A patient's nearest relative who has been supplanted by an order made under subs.(3)(c) or (d) of this section can apply to a tribunal within 12 months of the order being made and during any subsequent 12 month period while the order is in force: see subs.(6) and s.66(1)(h),(2)(g). An acting nearest relative who has been appointed under this section has a separate power to make an application: see the note on "Nearest relative" in s.66(1).

1-463 *Code of Practice* The displacement of the nearest relative is considered in Ch.5. With regard to the support that should be provided to patients, the Code states:

"5.21 If the patient has any concerns that any information given to the court on their views on the suitability of the nearest relative may have implications for their own safety, an application can be made to the court seeking its permission not to make the current nearest relative a party to the proceedings. The reasons for the patient's concerns should be set out clearly in the application.

5.22 Hospital managers should provide support to detained patients to enable them to attend the court, if they wish, subject to the patient being granted leave under section 17 for this purpose.

5.23 If, exceptionally, the court decides to interview the patient (as the applicant), the court has the discretion to decide where and how this interview takes place and whether it should take place in the presence of, or separate from, other parties. The patient should be fully supported in this, including through the use of an advocate to support them."

Subsection (1)   The judge has a discretion as to whether or not to make an order displacing the near-   **1-464**
est relative notwithstanding that one of the grounds set out in subs.(3) has been satisfied (*Barnet LBC v Robin* (1999) 2 C.C.L.R. 454, CA).

County Court   In *A Local Authority v SE* [2021] EWCOP 44, Lieven J., sitting in the Court of Protection, made an order displacing a nearest relative under subs.(3)(e).

Functions of the nearest relative   The nearest relative retains the power of discharge under s.23 during the currency of an application. If the nearest relative has exercised the power under reg.24 of the English Regulations or reg.33 of the Welsh Regulations to delegate his or her functions to another person, action under this section must be directed against the nearest relative and not the delegate.

In *R. v Birmingham Mental Health Trust Ex p. Phillips* (CO/1501/95), May 25, 1995, Tucker J. refused applications for habeas corpus and judicial review that had been made in respect of a patient who had been detained under s.2 and whose nearest relative had been wrongly identified for the purposes of s.11(3). His Lordship held that an application that was subsequently made under this section to displace that relative was not invalidated by the mistake.

Sections 66 and 69   Which are concerned with applications to the First-tier Tribunal (Mental Health) or the Mental Health Review Tribunal for Wales.

Subsection (1A)   If an order is made under this section, the patient's acting nearest relative will either   **1-465**
be:

(i)   the person nominated in the application to perform the role if that person is willing to do so and the court considers that person to be suitable; or

(ii)   otherwise, the person that the court specifies as being suitable to perform the role if that person is willing to do so.

With regard to (i), there is no requirement for the applicant to make a nomination.

The person appointed need not be related to the patient or otherwise qualified to be the patient's nearest relative under s.26. With regard to (i), if the application is made by an Approved Mental Health Professional (AMHP), para.5.19 of the *Code of Practice* states:

"AMHPs should nominate someone to become the acting nearest relative in the event that application is successful. Wherever practicable, they should first consult the patient about the patient's own preferences and any concerns they have about the person the AMHP proposes to nominate. AMHPs should also seek the agreement of the proposed nominee prior to an application being made, although this is not a legal requirement."

By virtue of Sch.1 to the Interpretation Act 1978, which defines a person as including a corporation, a local authority can be appointed as acting nearest relative; also see para. 2.38 of the Reference Guide. It would clearly be appropriate for the function to be delegated to a named officer and, in order to avoid the appearance of a conflict of interest, for that officer not to be an AMHP. The authority must comply with its duties under s.116.

Subsection (2)

The patient   Who is a person suffering or appearing to be suffering from mental disorder (s.145(1)).   **1-466**
The patient need not be a patient who is subject to either an application or an order made under the Act.

Relative of the patient   Is defined in s.26(1).

Residing   It is not necessary for the applicant to be ordinarily residing with the patient.

Approved mental health professional   An AMHP applicant acts in a personal capacity and is not therefore bound to follow the advice of her managers. The AMHP should receive the legal advice and support that an employer would normally provide to an employee who is involved in legal proceedings by virtue of the nature of their employment.

Paragraph 5.13 of the *Code of Practice* states that "AMHPs should bear in mind that some patients may wish to apply to displace their nearest relative but may be deterred from doing so by the need to apply to the county court". Paragraph 5.16 of the Code states:

"Before making an application for displacement, AMHPs should consider other ways of achieving the same end, including:

- whether the nearest relative will agree to delegate their role as the patient's nearest relative to someone else, or
- providing or arranging support to the patient (or someone else) to make an application themselves. This could include support from an independent mental health advocate (IMHA)."

1-467 **Subsection (3)** There is no requirement to make an application in any of the situations specified in this provision. The list of grounds is exhaustive.

Paragraph (a)

1-468 AMHPs should consider acting on this ground if the patient is likely to be subject to the provisions of the Act for more than a short period, or if a suitable person comes forward who is willing to perform the functions of the nearest relative.

Paragraph (b)

1-469 If an application is being made on the ground that the nearest relative is incapable of acting as nearest relative by reason of mental disorder, CPR Pt 21 applies and a litigation friend should be appointed if the individual lacks capacity within the terms of CPR r.21.1(2), i.e. a person who "lacks capacity within the meaning of the [Mental Capacity Act 2005]". Normally the Official Solicitor agrees to act as litigation friend and consents to the application on the basis of the medical evidence supplied. The Official Solicitor prefers the medical evidence to be provided by a doctor who will not be involved in the potential detention of the patient.

Incapable This ground is only available if the person concerned is unable to perform the functions of nearest relative. It does not cover the situation of a nearest relative who exercises his or her functions in an irresponsible manner.

If an AMHP concludes that it is not practicable to consult with the patient's nearest relative under s.11(4) because of that person's mental incapacity, an application under s.3 can proceed without an application being made to the court under this provision.

Paragraph (c)

1-470 **Unreasonably objects** Both at the date of the application and at the date of hearing (*Lewis v Gibson* [2005] EWCA Civ 587; [2005] M.H.L.R. 309). In *W v L* [1974] Q.B. 711 the Court of Appeal held that the proper test for the county court to apply is an objective one: the court should ask what an objectively reasonable person would do in all the circumstances, and not ask whether the actual nearest relative involved in the case was behaving reasonably from his or her own subjective point of view. The court stated that this test is similar to the test in adoption cases in which the House of Lords approved the following statement:

"... in considering whether she is reasonable or unreasonable we must take into account the welfare of the child. A reasonable mother surely gives great weight to what is better for the child. Her anguish of mind is quite understandable: but still it may be unreasonable for her to withhold consent" (*Re W (An Infant)* [1971] 2 All E.R. 49 at 55 per Lord Hailsham L.C. citing Lord Denning M.R. in *Re L (An Infant)* (1962) 106 Sol. Jo. 611)."

In *Re W*, the court held that two reasonable parents can perfectly reasonably come to opposite conclusions on the same set of facts without forfeiting their title to be regarded as reasonable. The question before a court hearing an application under this provision is therefore whether a nearest relative's objection comes within the band of possible reasonable decisions and not whether it is right or mistaken. Lord Hailsham said at 56:

> "Not every reasonable exercise of judgment is right, and not every mistaken exercise of judgment is unreasonable. There is a band of decisions within which no court should seek to replace the individuals judgment with his own."

In *Smirek v Williams* [2000] M.H.L.R. 38 CA Hale L.J. said that, in her view,

> "it cannot possibly be outside that band of reasonable decisions for the [nearest relative] to agree with, and rely upon, a recent decision of a [tribunal] unless there has since been a change in the circumstances leading to that decision".

As the nearest relative is objecting to an application being made and as an AMHP applicant is required by s.13(1A) to consider "relevant circumstances", it would seem that a reasonable nearest relative is entitled to consider all the circumstances of the case and not just the medical evidence.

The obiter comment of Lawton L.J. in *B(A) v B(L) (Mental Health Patient)* [1980] 1 W.L.R. 116, CA, that "the judge must have some evidence that compulsory admission to hospital and detention is necessary" suggests that a court hearing an application under this paragraph should consider the merits for detaining the patient by reference to the statutory criteria before moving on to considering the reasonableness of the nearest relative's decision. The judge should not be concerned to establish whether the technical requirements of the Act relating to applications for detention or guardianship have been satisfied. In the words of Lawton L.J. at 121:

> "The object of an application under [this paragraph] is to enable the provisions of [s.3] to be brought into operation, and until an application has been dealt with under [this section the AMHP] is not in a position to make an application under [s.3]. It follows, so it seems to me, that if there were any defects for the purposes of [s.3] in the form of the reports tendered to the county court judge they were irrelevant for the purposes of ... the application. The county court judge had to look at the reports for their medical content; he was not concerned with their statutory form."

Paragraph (d)

Without due regard   The test is an objective one (*Surrey County Council Social Services v McMurray*, November 11, 1994, CA).   **1-471**

Power to discharge the patient   From detention, guardianship or a community treatment order using the power contained in s.23. When considering an application under this paragraph, the judge should consider not only the history of the matter but also the situation with which he is faced at the date of the hearing (*Lewis v Gibson*, above).

Or is likely to do so   It is possible to make an application under this provision before the patient is made subject to the provisions of the Act.

Paragraph (e)   This paragraph, which addresses the incompatibility identified by the European Commission of Human Rights in *JT v United Kingdom* (2000) 30 E.H.R.R. C.D. 77, provides an applicant with a right to apply to the county court for an order displacing his or her NR on the ground that the NR is unsuitable to act as such. The Minister of State outlined the Government's thinking on this ground: **1-472**

> "We have in mind situations where a NR's occupation of that role and its powers under the Act pose a real and present danger to the health or well-being of the patient. Where a NR has abused the patient, for instance, he should not be allowed to exercise the rights of the NR. It is not important how recently the abuse took place. If the patient or others who know or are close to the patient have a genuine fear that the abuse may be repeated – or even that a relationship with a formally abusive NR may cause the patient distress – we intend that such a person should be considered unsuitable to act as the NR of the patient. These applications will be heard, as they now are, in the county court. The court will not be asked to sit in judgment of any of the past actions or deeds of the NR. Their role will be to determine whether the NR is otherwise suitable to act as such.
>   The opinions and views of the patient will be very important and we fully expect that they will form part of the court's deliberations. However, we do not wish the court to feel that it is prevented from displacing a NR it deems unsuitable, even where the patient would wish that person to remain

as their NR. I would instance cases where the victim of an abuser actually acts to protect the abuser, either out of fear of the abuser or through a form of identification with him. We do not wish the court to feel constrained in such circumstances in displacing a NR it finds unsuitable" (*Hansard*, HL Vol.688, col.672)."

The Government also (i) confirmed that the term "suitable" is intended to "include, but not be so narrow as to be limited to, NRs who have a history of abusing or potential to abuse the patient" (*Hansard*, HL Vol.689, col.1404, per Baroness Royall), and (ii) said that it "intends that a person is not suitable to be the NR where that person has no relationship with – and intends to have no further relationship with – the patient. In addition, it is intended that a person is not suitable to be the NR where the risk posed to the patient is by virtue of a third party and the NR exposes the patient to that risk" (The Government's response to the report of the Joint Committee on Human Rights, Department of Health, April 13, 2007, para.40).

Paragraph 5.14 of the *Code of Practice* states:

"It is entirely a matter for the court to decide what constitutes 'suitability' of a person to be a nearest relative. Factors which an AMHP might wish to consider when deciding whether to make an application to displace a nearest relative on those grounds, and when providing evidence in connection with an application, could include:

- any reason to think that the patient has suffered, or is suspected to have suffered, abuse at the hands of the nearest relative (or someone with whom the nearest relative is in a relationship), or is at risk of suffering such abuse
- whether the patient is afraid of the nearest relative or seriously distressed by the possibility of the nearest relative being involved in their life or their care, or
- whether the patient and nearest relative are unknown to each other, there is only a distant relationship, or their relationship has broken down irretrievably.
- This is not an exhaustive list."

Otherwise An application under this ground should not be brought where the facts of the case would enable an application to be made under ground (b), (c) or (d).

1-473 **Subsection (4)** This subsection provides that if the patient is detained for assessment and an application is made to the county court on ground (c) or (d) of subs.(3) before the 28 days provided for in s.2 expire, the period for which the patient may be detained is extended until the application is finally disposed of and, if an order is made, for a further period of seven days to enable the formalities of a s.3 application to be complied with. The provisions of Pt II, including the power to grant the patient leave of absence under s.17, will continue to apply during the extended period. A copy of the application to the court should be placed with the patient's statutory documentation as this provides the hospital managers with continued authority for the patient's detention.

If a patient who has had his detention extended by virtue of this provision has not applied to a tribunal within the first 14 days of the detention, there is no opportunity for the patient to make an application to the tribunal for the s.2 to be discharged even if the extended period is lengthy. For the action that should be taken in such a situation, see *R. (on the application of MH) v Secretary of State for Health*, noted under Human Rights Act 1998, above. It is submitted that it would not be compatible with the patient's rights under art.5(4) of the ECHR for the hospital managers to delay taking action until the patient is referred to the tribunal after the expiration of the six month period provided for in s.68.

There is nothing to prevent the court from making an interim displacement order during the 28-day period: see the cases noted under *Interim and without notice orders*, above.

A fresh assessment of the patient under the Act should be undertaken prior to the court hearing in order to determine whether the requirements of s.3 continue to be satisfied. It is lawful to make an application under s.3 before the proceedings under this section have been resolved (*R. (on the application of M) v Homerton University Hospital* noted under *Interim and without notice orders*, above).

A nearest relative is not deprived of his or her power of discharge under s.23 during the period of the extended s.2. The patient's RC could prevent such a discharge taking effect if the provisions of s.25 apply. The hospital managers and the RC also retain their power of discharge during this period.

Immediately before the expiration of the period for which a patient is liable to be detained Where a tribunal has ordered the discharge of the patient from s.2 and has exercised its power under s.72(3) to delay the discharge to a specified future date, the provisions of this subsection will apply if an application under this section is made to the county court before that date (*Re W* [1999] M.H.L.R. 1).

Is pending   It is submitted that an application is pending after it has been received by the court.

Paragraph (a); finally disposed of   The detention continues during the period for lodging an appeal, and if an appeal is lodged, the time taken to determine it.

If an application has been made under para.(c) and the nearest relative subsequently withdraws his or her objection, the application will be finally disposed of when it is formally withdrawn from the court by the applicant.

Subsection (5)

This subsection provides that an order made on the grounds specified in subs.(3)(a), (b) or (e) may specify a period for which the order will remain in force, unless it is discharged. One example of a way in which a court might use this power would be to specify that the order should cease on the date when the eldest child of the patient reached 18, so that he or she could then take on the role of nearest relative. Further provision relating to the duration of orders made under these paragraphs is made in s.30(4B).   **1-474**

Subsection (6)

This subsection specifies the functions of an acting nearest relative. Apart from the exceptions noted, the nearest relative's functions are exercisable by the acting nearest relative during the period of the appointment. Such functions include the power to delegate the functions to another person: see the General Note to s.26. It also provides that an order made under this section remains in force notwithstanding that the person who was the patient's nearest relative when the order was made is no longer his nearest relative, for example as a result of the death of that person. If the acting nearest relative dies, no-one can exercise the rights of the nearest relative unless the order is either discharged or varied: see s.30(3)(b).   **1-475**

Shall not apply ... in the case mentioned in paragraph (h)   See the note on *Applications to the First-tier Tribunal (Mental Health) or the Mental Health Review Tribunal for Wales*, above.

Discharge and variation of orders under s.29

30.—(1)   An order made under section 29 above in respect of a patient may be discharged by the county court upon application made—   **1-476**

    (a)   in any case, by [the patient or] the person having the functions of the nearest relative of the patient by virtue of the order;

    (b)   where the order was made on the ground specified in paragraph (a) [, (b) or (e)] of section 29(3) above, or where the person who was the nearest relative of the patient when the order was made has ceased to be his nearest relative, on the application of the nearest relative of the patient.

[(1A)   But, in the case of an order made on the ground specified in paragraph (e) of section 29(3) above, an application may not be made under subsection (1)(b) above by the person who was the nearest relative of the patient when the order was made except with leave of the county court.]]

(2)   An order made under section 29 above in respect of a patient may be varied by the county court, on the application of the person having the functions of the nearest relative by virtue of the order or on the application of [the patient or of] an [approved mental health professional], by substituting [another person for the person having those functions].

[(2A)   If the court decides to vary an order on an application under subsection (2) above, the following rules have effect for the purposes of substituting another person—

    (a)   if a person is nominated in the application to act as the patient's nearest relative and that person is, in the opinion of the court, a suitable person to act as such and is willing to do so, the court shall specify that person (or, if there are two or more such persons, such one of them as the court thinks fit);

(b) otherwise, the court shall specify such person as is, in its opinion, a suitable person to act as the patient's nearest relative and is willing to do so.]

(3) If the person having the functions of the nearest relative of a patient by virtue of an order under section 29 above dies—

(a) subsections (1) and (2) above shall apply as if for any reference to that person there were substituted a reference to any relative of the patient, and

(b) until the order is discharged or varied under those provisions the functions of the nearest relative under this Part of this Act and sections 66 and 69 below shall not be exercisable by any person.

(4) [An order made on the ground specified in paragraph (c) or (d) of section 29(3) above shall, unless previously discharged under subsection (1) above, cease to have effect as follows]—

[(a) if—

(i) on the date of the order the patient was liable to be detained or subject to guardianship by virtue of a relevant application, order or direction; or

(ii) he becomes so liable or subject within the period of three months beginning with that date; or

(iii) he was a community patient on the date of the order, it shall cease to have effect when he is discharged under section 23 above or 72 below or the relevant application, order or direction otherwise ceases to have effect (except as a result of his being transferred in pursuance of regulations under section 19 above);

(b) otherwise, it shall cease to have effect at the end of the period of three months beginning with the date of the order.]

[(4A) In subsection (4) above, reference to a relevant application, order or direction is to any of the following—

(a) an application for admission for treatment;

(b) a guardianship application;

(c) an order or direction under Part 3 of this Act (other than under section 35, 36 or 38).]

[(4B) An order made on the ground specified in paragraph (a), (b) or (e) of section 29(3) above shall—

(a) if a period was specified under section 29(5) above, cease to have effect on expiry of that period, unless previously discharged under subsection (1) above;

(b) if no such period was specified, remain in force until it is discharged under subsection (1) above.]

(5) The discharge or variation under this section of an order made under section 29 above shall not affect the validity of anything previously done in pursuance of the order.

Amendments

The amendments to this section were made by the Mental Health Act 2007 ss.21, 24, 32(4), Sch.2 para.7, Sch.3 para.14.

Definitions

patient: s.145(1).   **1-477**
nearest relative: ss.26(3), 145(1).
approved mental health professional: s.145(1), (1AC).
application for admission for treatment: ss.3, 145(1).
community patient: ss.17A(7), 145(1).
guardianship application: s.7(1).

General Note

This section provides for the discharge or variation of an order made by a county court under s.29   **1-478**
for the appointment of an acting nearest relative. It also, in subss.(4), (4A) and (4B), specifies the duration of an order.

Subsection (1)

Paragraph (a), (b) or (e)   A nearest relative who has been displaced under s.29(3)(e) cannot make   **1-479**
an application for the order to be discharged without leave of the county court (subs.(1A)). A nearest relative who is displaced under s.29(3)(c) or (d) cannot apply for the order to be discharged.

Subsection (2)

This subsection provides for an application to be made to the county court for the variation of the   **1-480**
order appointing the acting nearest relative.

Subsection (3)

If the person appointed as acting nearest relative dies, this subsection provides that (i) any applica-   **1-481**
tions that could have been made by that person under subss.(1) and (2) can be made by any relative of the patient, and (ii) no one can exercise the functions of nearest relative until the order that appointed the acting nearest relative is discharged or varied.

Subsections (4), (4A)

These subsections determine when an order appointing an acting nearest relative has been made on   **1-482**
the grounds specified in s.29(3)(c) or (d) ceases to have effect. Their effect is that the order will either expire: (i) after three months; or (ii) if the patient was detained or subject to guardianship at the time of the order, or within three months of it, at the time when the application, order or direction authorising the patient's detention or guardianship is either discharged or otherwise ceases to have effect. The order will not end if the patient is placed on a community treatment order or is made subject to a transfer under s.19. An application can be made under subs.(1) to discharge the order.

Subsection (4B)

This subsection determines when an order appointing an acting nearest relative has been made on   **1-483**
the grounds specified in s.29(3)(a), (b) or (e) ceases to have effect. Its effect is that the order will either last for the period stated in it (if any) or will last indefinitely. In both cases, the order will end if it is discharged under subs.(1).

SUPPLEMENTAL

Procedure on applications to county court

1-484   **31.** [Rules of court] which relate to applications authorised by this Part of this Act to be made to [the county court] may make provision—

   (a)   for the hearing and determination of such applications otherwise than in open court;

   (b)   for the admission on the hearing of such applications of evidence of such descriptions as may be specified in the rules notwithstanding anything to the contrary in any enactment or rule of law relating to the admissibility of evidence:

   (c)   for the visiting and interviewing of patients in private by or under the directions of the court.

Amendments

The amendments to this section were made by the Crime and Courts Act 2013 Sch.9, paras 52(1)(b) and 112.

Definition

1-485   patient: s.145(1).

General Note

1-486   This section is applied to patients who have been placed under hospital or guardianship orders by a court under s.37 (Sch.1 Pt I para.1).

Rules of court

See the Civil Procedure Rules 1998 (SI 1998/3132) Pt 8 and Practice Direction 49E—Alternative Procedure for Claims which are reproduced in Pt 3.

Otherwise than in open court

The publication of information relating to proceedings brought under the Act before a county court sitting in private is prima facie a contempt of court: see s.12 of the Administration of Justice Act 1960 and *Pickering v Liverpool Daily Post and Echo Newspapers Plc* [1991] 1 All E.R. 622 HL.

Regulations for purposes of Part II

1-487   **32.**—(1)   The Secretary of State may make regulations for prescribing anything which, under this Part of this Act, is required or authorised to be prescribed, and otherwise for carrying this Part of this Act into full effect.

   (2)   Regulations under this section may in particular make provision—

   (a)   for prescribing the form of any application, recommendation, report, order, notice or other document to be made or given under this Part of this Act;

   (b)   for prescribing the manner in which any such application, recommendation, report, order, notice or other document may be proved, and for regulating the service of any such application, report, order or notice;

   (c)   for requiring [such bodies as may be prescribed by the regulations] to keep such registers or other records as may be [so prescribed] in respect of patients liable to be detained or subject to guardianship [...] under supervision] under this Part of this Act [or community patients], and to furnish or make available to those patients, and their relatives, such written statements of their rights and powers under this Act as may be so prescribed;

(d) for the determination in accordance with the regulations of the age of any person whose exact age cannot be ascertained by reference to the registers kept under the Births and Deaths Registration Act 1953; and

(e) for enabling the functions under this Part of this Act of the nearest relative of a patient to be performed, in such circumstances and subject to such conditions (if any) as may be prescribed by the regulations, by any person authorised in that behalf by that relative;

and for the purposes of this Part of this Act any application, report or notice the service of which is regulated under paragraph (b) above shall be deemed to have been received by or furnished to the authority or person to whom it is authorised or required to be furnished, addressed or given if it is duly served in accordance with the regulations.

(3) Without prejudice to subsections (1) and (2) above, but subject to section 23(4) [and (6)] above, regulations under this section may determine the manner in which functions under this Part of this Act of the managers of hospitals, local social services authorities, [[Local Health Board], Special Health Authorities [...] [, National Health Service trusts or NHS foundation trusts] are to be exercised, and such regulations may in particular specify the circumstances in which, and the conditions subject to which, any such functions may be performed by officers of or other persons acting on behalf of those managers[, boards,] and [authorities and trusts].

Amendments

The amendments to this section were made by the Health Authorities Act 1995 s.2(1), Sch.1 para.107(4), the Mental Health (Patients in the Community) Act 1995 s.2(1), Sch.1 para.2, the Health Act 1999 (Supplementary, Consequential, etc. Provisions) Order 2000 (SI 2000/90) Sch.1 para.16(6), the NHS and Community Care Act 1990 s.66(1), Sch.9 para.24(5), the Health and Social Care (Community Health and Standards) Act 2003 s.34, Sch.4 para.55, the Mental Health Act 2007 ss.32(4), 45(2), 55, Sch.3 para.15, Sch.11 Pt 5, SI 2007/961 art.3, Sch. para.13(7) and the Health and Social Care Act 2012 Sch.5 para.27.

Definitions

community patient: ss.17A(7), 145(1).   **1-488**
the managers: s.145(1).
hospital: ss.34(2), 145(1).
local social services authority: s.145(1).
patient: s.145(1).
nearest relative: ss.26(3), 145(1).
Health Authority: s.145(1).
Local Health Board: s.145(1).
Special Health Authority: s.145(1).

General Note

This section applies to patients who have been placed under hospital, restriction or guardianship   **1-489**
orders by a court under ss.37 or 41 (Sch.1 Pt I para.1, Pt II para.1).

Subsection (1)

1-490   **Secretary of state**   The functions of the Minister, so far as exercisable in relation to Wales, are exercised by the Welsh Ministers (see the General Note to the Act and SI 1999/672 art.2, Sch.1).

Special provisions as to wards of court

1-491   **33.**—(1)   An application for the admission to hospital of a minor who is a ward of court may be made under this Part of this Act with the leave of the court; and section 11(4) above shall not apply in relation to an application so made.

(2)   Where a minor who is a ward of court is liable to be detained in a hospital by virtue of an application for admission under this Part of this Act [or is a community patient], any power exercisable under this Part of this Act or under section 66 below in relation to the patient by his nearest relative shall be exercisable by or with the leave of the court.

(3)   Nothing in this Part of this Act shall be construed as authorising the making of a guardianship application in respect of a minor who is a ward of court, or the transfer into guardianship of any such minor.

[(4)   Where a community treatment order has been made in respect of a minor who is a ward of court, the provisions of this Part of this Act relating to community treatment orders and community patients have effect in relation to the minor subject to any order which the court makes in the exercise of its wardship jurisdiction; but this does not apply as regards any period when the minor is recalled to hospital under section 17E above.]

Amendments

The words in square brackets in subs.(2) were inserted, and subs.(4) was substituted by the Mental Health Act 2007 s.32(4), Sch.3 para.16.

Definitions

1-492   hospital: ss.34(2), 145(1).
nearest relative: ss.26(3), 145(1).
community patient: ss.17A(7), 145(1).
community treatment order: ss.17A(7), 145(1).
guardianship application: s.7(1).

General Note

1-493   This section provides that the leave of the court must be obtained before a ward of court can be compulsorily detained in hospital (subs.(1)), and before the ward's nearest relative exercises his or her powers (subs.(2)). It also prohibits the reception or transfer of a ward of court into guardianship (subs.(3)) and makes any power or duty exercisable in respect of a ward who is subject to a community treatment order subject to the wardship court's jurisdiction (apart from a period when the child has been recalled to hospital) (subs.(4)).

Subsection (1)

1-494   **Section 11(4) … shall not apply**   An AMHP should not consult the nearest relative about an application to admit a ward of court under s.3 nor may the nearest relative block the application by objecting to it.

Interpretation of Part II

34.—(1)   In this Part of this Act—   1-495

["the appropriate practitioner" means—

(a)   in the case of a patient who is subject to the guardianship of a person other than a local social services authority, the nominated medical attendant of the patient; and

(b)   in any other case, the responsible clinician;]

[...]

"the nominated medical attendant", in relation to a patient who is subject to the guardianship of a person other than a local social services authority, means the person appointed in pursuance of regulations made under section 9(2) above to act as the medical attendant of the patient;

["registered establishment" means an establishment which would not, apart from subsection (2) below, be a hospital for the purposes of this Part and which—

(a)   in England, is a hospital as defined by section 275 of the National Health Service Act 2006 that is used for the carrying on of a regulated activity, within the meaning of Part 1 of the Health and Social Care Act 2008, which relates to the assessment or medical treatment of mental disorder and in respect of which a person is registered under Chapter 2 of that Part; and

(b)   in Wales, is an establishment in respect of which a person is registered under Part 2 of the Care Standards Act 2000 as an independent hospital in which treatment or nursing (or both) are provided for persons liable to be detained under this Act;]

["the responsible clinician" means—

(a)   in relation to a patient liable to be detained by virtue of an application for admission for assessment or an application for admission for treatment, or a community patient, the approved clinician with overall responsibility for the patient's case;

(b)   in relation to a patient subject to guardianship, the approved clinician authorised by the responsible local social services authority to act (either generally or in any particular case or for any particular purpose) as the responsible clinician;]

[...]

[(1A)   [...]

(2)   Except where otherwise expressly provided, this Part of this Act applies in relation to [a registered establishment], as it applies in relation to a hospital, and references in this Part of this Act to a hospital, and any reference in this Act to a hospital to which this Part of this Act applies, shall be construed accordingly.

(3)   In relation to a patient who is subject to guardianship in pursuance of a guardianship application, any reference in this Part of this Act to the responsible local social services authority is a reference—

(a)   where the patient is subject to the guardianship of a local social services authority, to that authority;

(b)   where the patient is subject to the guardianship of a person other than a local social services authority, to the local social services authority for the area in which that person resides.

Amendments

The amendments to this section were made by the Care Standards Act 2000 s.116, Sch.4 para.9(4); Health and Social Care Act 2008 (Consequential Amendments No.2) Order (SI 2010/813), art.5(3); and the Mental Health Act 2007 ss.9(9),(10), 55, Sch.11 Pt 5.

Definitions

1-496   patient: s.145(1).
local social services authority: s.145(1).
application for admission for assessment: ss.2, 145(1).
application for admission for treatment: ss.3, 145(1).
hospital: s.145(1) and subss.2 of this section.
approved clinician: s.145(1).
community patient: ss.17A(7), 145(1).
mental disorder: ss.1, 145(1).
independent hospital: s.145(1).

General Note

1-497   This section, which defines key terms in Part II of the Act, applies to patients who have been placed under hospital or guardianship orders made by a court under s.37 (Sch.1 Pt I para.1), and to restricted patients with the modification that in subs.(1) the definition of "the nominated medical attendant" and subs.(3) shall be omitted (Sch.1 Pt II paras 2, 8).

Human Rights Act 1998

1-498   The appropriate practitioner, the nominated medical attendant and the responsible clinician (RC) are exercising "functions of a public nature" and are therefore public authorities for the purposes of s.6 of the 1998 Act (s.6(3)(b)).
Decisions made by a private hospital relating to the care or treatment of detained patients are decisions of a public nature. The hospital therefore becomes a public authority for the purposes of s.6 and its decisions are susceptible to judicial review (*R. (on the application of A) v Partnership in Care Ltd* [2002] EWHC 529 (Admin); [2002] 1 W.L.R. 2610).

Subsection (1)

1-499   **The nominated medical attendant**   Is appointed by a private guardian under reg.22(a) of the English Regulations and reg.11(a) of the Welsh Regulations. Paragraph 30.26 of the *Code of Practice* states:

"It is for private guardians themselves to decide whom to appoint as the nominated medical attendant, but they should first consult the local authority. The nominated medical attendant may be the patient's GP, if the GP agrees."

Registered establishment   See the note on Human Rights Act 1998, above.
If a registered establishment (i.e. an independent hospital) loses its registration it is no longer a hospital for the purposes of the Act. The authority to detain patients at that establishment therefore ends. Also see the definition of "the managers" in s.145(1).

Responsible clinician   Guidance on changing a RC is contained in para.36.5 of the *Code of Practice* which states:

"The selection of the appropriate responsible clinician should be based on the individual needs of the patient concerned. For example, where psychological therapies are central to the patient's treatment, it may be appropriate for a professional with particular expertise in this area to act as the responsible clinician."

The RC must be an approved clinician (AC). It follows that if a patient is detained in a general hospital where he is receiving treatment for a physical disorder and the doctor in charge of the treatment is not an AC, an AC from a mental health facility should take responsibility for the treatment of the patient's mental disorder as such treatment must be given by or under the direction of an AC (s.63).

Although the responsibilities of the RC are not delegable, "the role may be occupied on a temporary basis in the absence of the usual [RC]" (Reference Guide, para.9.29). Hospitals should therefore have protocols to "ensure that cover arrangements are in place when the responsible clinician is not available (e.g. during nonworking hours, annual leave etc)" (*Code of Practice*, para.36.3). Any AC can be the temporary RC, irrespective of status. Determining the clinician who has "overall responsibility for the patient's case" for the patient is a question of fact. Note the use of the broad term "case", rather than "medical treatment". Any dispute about the identification the RC of a detained or community patient would need to be resolved by the hospital management.

With regard to the situation where the patient is receiving a range of treatments, the *Code of Practice* states:

"36.10 There may be circumstances where the responsible clinician is qualified with respect to the patient's main assessment and treatment needs but is not appropriately qualified to be in charge of a subsidiary treatment needed by the patient (eg medication which the responsible clinician is not qualified to prescribe). In such situations, the responsible clinician will maintain their overarching responsibility for the patient's case, but another appropriately qualified professional will take responsibility for a specific treatment or intervention.

36.11 Where the person in charge of a particular treatment is not the patient's responsible clinician, the person in charge of the treatment should ensure that the responsible clinician is kept informed about the treatment and that treatment decisions are discussed with the responsible clinician in the context of the patient's overall case. Guidance should be available locally on the procedures to follow, including when to seek a second opinion, if there are unresolved differences of opinion."

Subsequent to a patient being granted leave of absence under s.17 or being made subject to a community treatment order, the responsibilities of the RC could be transferred to a community based AC. The responsibilities would then be transferred back to the hospital based AC on the patient's readmission to hospital. A patient has no right to determine the identity of his RC.

The powers given to the RC under the Act do not enable that clinician to require the relevant integrated care board to give priority to the care of a detained patient: see the General Note to the Act under *Allocation of resources to detained parents*.

Although it will normally be the patient's RC who will decide whether a patient can be interviewed and under what conditions, she cannot be the final arbiter when issues arise in relation to national security. The detaining hospital can therefore impose conditions relating to security concerns which the RC may consider to be unnecessary (*R (on the application of A) v Home Secretary* [2003] EWHC 2846 (Admin); [2004] M.H.L.R. 98 para.26).

The RC of a guardianship patient does not have "overall responsibility for the patient's case". If a guardianship patient:

"happens to be living, or receiving medical treatment for mental disorder, in Wales, the local authority may appoint a person who is approved by the Welsh Ministers as an approved clinician in Wales, even if that person is not also approved as an approved clinician in England. Otherwise, the responsible clinician must be approved as an approved clinician in England" (Reference Guide, para.28.79; also see the Mental Health (Mutual Recognition) Regulations 2008 which are reproduced in Part 2).

Subsection (3)

Responsible local social services authority   Renewal reports must be addressed to this authority   **1-500**
which has the power to discharge the patient from guardianship by virtue of s.23(2)(b).

Resides   See the note on this term in s.7(5).

Part III Patients Concerned in Criminal Proceedings or Under Sentence

General Note

This Part deals with the circumstances in which patients may be admitted to and detained in hospital   **1-501**
or received into guardianship on the order of a court, or may be transferred to hospital or guardianship from penal institutions on the direction of the Secretary of State for Justice.

Home Office Circular No.66/90 (as supplemented by Home Office Circular No.12/95) draws the attention of the courts and those services responsible for dealing with mentally disordered people who come into contact with the criminal justice system to the legal powers that exist and to the desirability of ensuring effective co-operation between agencies.

The functions of the Secretary of State for Justice

1-502   The functions of the Secretary of State with regard to the management of restricted patients are undertaken on his behalf by the:

Mental Health Casework Section
9th Floor, 1 Ruskin Square
Dingwall Road
Croydon
CR0 2WF
Tel: 078 1276 0248
email: mhcsmailbox@justice.gov.uk

In cases of emergency outside office hours: 0300 303 2079. The National Offender Management Service has published guidance on "*Contacting the Ministry of Justice Mental Health Casework Section 'Out of Hours' Service – Guidance for Professionals*" (2021). This document can be accessed at: *https://assets.publishing.service.gov.uk/government/uploads/system/uploads/attachment_data/file/1035562/Mental_health_casework_out-of-hours_service_.pdf.*

The website of the Ministry of Justice setting out guidance and forms for those working with restricted patients is: *www.gov.uk/government/collections/mentally-disordered-offenders.*

The functions of the Secretary of State in relation to Wales

1-503   Through inadvertence, the functions of the Home Secretary (now the Secretary of State for Justice) under this Part, in so far as they are exercisable in relation to Wales, were transferred to the National Assembly for Wales under the National Assembly for Wales (Transfer of Functions) Order 1999 (SI 1999/672) art.2, Sch.1. These functions (subject to a number of exceptions that are noted in the appropriate sections) were transferred back to the Home Secretary by a means of a variation to the Order by the National Assembly of Wales (Transfer of Functions) Order 2000 (SI 2000/253) art.4, Sch.3. The period between the two transfer orders was covered by arrangements being put in place under s.41 of the Government of Wales Act 1998 enabling Home Office officials to exercise the functions on behalf of the Assembly.

Sentencing guideline

1-504   A guideline for sentencing offenders with mental disorders, developmental disorders and neurological impairments has been published by the Sentencing Council. The guideline came into force on October 1, 2020. It can be accessed at the Council's website: *www.sentencingcouncil.org.uk.*

In *R. v Francis Junior Wellington (AG's Reference No 1 of 2021 under s36 Criminal Justice Act 1988)* [2022] M.H.L.R. 15, the Court of Appeal said at para.35:

"[The] guideline explains how sentencing the mentally ill requires the court to consider whether the impairment or disorder reduces culpability. That will only be the case if there is sufficient connection between the impairment etc and the offending. 'Useful questions', as the guideline puts it (para 15), include whether the offender had impaired ability to exercise judgement, to make rational choices or to understand the nature or consequences of his or her actions. In short, there may be offending of which mental illness was a significant cause and otherwise where the mental illness was incidental to the offence in question. Sometimes, the mental impairment or disorder will substantially reduce culpability, sometimes not. If it does, there will be an impact of the sentence and often a significant one; but even if it does not, mental illness may be relevant, not least because of the impact of a custodial sentence on an offender (as to which see, para 22 of the guideline)."

Medical Reports prior to disposal

1-505   In *PS v R* [2019] EWCA Crim 2286; [2020] M.H.L.R. 203, at para.19, Lord Burnett C.J. said:

"The court will be assisted by a pre-sentence report and by appropriate psychiatric or psychological reports. It is important, when such reports are commissioned, that the issues to which they are relevant should be clearly identified. For example, a report directed to the issue of dangerousness may provide only limited assistance on the issue of culpability; and vice versa. It follows that, as with all matters of case preparation, early identification of the real issues is important."

If an offender is or appears to be suffering from a mental disorder, s.232 of the Sentencing Act 2020 requires the court to obtain a medical report made by a s.12 approved doctor before passing a custodial sentence other than one fixed by law. Before passing such a sentence, the court must consider any information before it which relates to the offender's mental condition and the likely effect of such a sentence on that condition and on any treatment which may be available for it.

Sentencing options

In *PS v R*, above, the Court of Appeal considered the "proper approach to sentencing offenders who suffer from autism or other mental health conditions or disorders" (para.1). Lord Burnett C.J. said at para.17:

1-506

"It will be apparent from all of the above that sentencing an offender who suffers from a mental disorder or learning disability necessarily requires a close focus on the mental health of the individual offender (both at the time of the offence and at the time of sentence) as well as on the facts and circumstances of the specific offence. In some cases, his mental health may not materially have reduced his culpability; in others, his culpability may have been significantly reduced. In some cases, he may be as capable as most other offenders of coping with the type of sentence which the court finds appropriate; in others, his mental health may mean that the impact of the sentence on him is far greater than it would be on most other offenders."

The sentencing options available to the Crown Court where an offender suffers from a mental disorder are identified in the Crown Court Compendium Part II, December 2019, Judicial College 6–9:

"(1)   if the court is satisfied that the offender is suffering from a mental condition which is such that it may be appropriate to make a hospital order, it can make an interim hospital order under s.38 whilst that appropriateness is being considered.

(2)   the court may make a hospital order under s.37 with or without a restriction order under s.41 if it considers that it is, 'the most suitable method of disposing of the case'. Where a restriction order is made under s.41, the First-tier Tribunal (Mental Health Chamber) ('the FtT') decides when the offender should be released from the hospital order, either conditionally or unconditionally.

(3)   the court may impose a determinate or indeterminate sentence of imprisonment and leave it to the Secretary of State to exercise their administrative power under s.47 to transfer the prisoner to a hospital if they consider that (i) the prisoner is suffering from a mental disorder; (ii) the mental disorder is of a nature and/or degree that it is appropriate for him/her to be detained in hospital for medical treatment; and (iii) appropriate treatment is available. Whether such a direction is made is entirely in the hands of the Secretary of State.

(4)   the court may impose a 'hybrid order' under s.45A if, when considering a hospital order under s.37 (i) the court is satisfied that the offender is suffering from a mental disorder; (ii) that mental disorder makes it appropriate for him/her to be detained in a hospital for medical treatment; and (iii) appropriate medical treatment is available. The effect of this is that instead of being removed to and detained in a prison (the hospital direction), the offender is removed to and detained in a hospital and is subject to the special restrictions set out in s.41 (the limitation direction).

(5)   where an indeterminate sentence is imposed with a s.45A 'hybrid order' and the responsible clinician or the FtT notifies the Secretary of State that the offender no longer requires treatment in hospital or that no effective treatment for his disorder can be given at the hospital to which he has been removed, the Secretary of State will normally simply remit the offender to the prison estate under s.51, unless his minimum term has expired. Where the tariff has expired, the Secretary of State may notify the FtT that he/she should be conditionally discharged, in which case he/she is subject to mental health supervision and recall in the usual way; but the Secretary of State can, and in practice usually does, refer the offender to the Parole Board as with any other post-tariff indeterminate sentence prisoner (*Fisher* ([2019] EWCA Crim 1066)."

It should be noted that the option of making a Guardianship order, which is considered in the General Note to s.37, is not identified.

Transporting patients subject to Part 3 of the Act

1-507   The *Code of Practice* states:

"22.32 Patients who are detained under part 3 of the Act transported between secure units, courts or prison are the responsibility of the unit or prison sending the patient unless other arrangements negotiated. In certain circumstances (eg an emergency situation) a clinical commissioning group [now an integrated care board] commissioned ambulance with appropriate escort may be required to transport the patient. Secure hospitals that hold patients under part 3 of the Act and prisons should have their own security protocols for transfer of patients subject to part 3 of the Act. All agencies involved in the transportation of patients should be mindful of the need to implement reasonable adjustments in arrangements to cater for the individual needs of the patient. Further information on the transport of patients generally is included at chapter 17.

22.33 A child or young person subject to part 3 should be transferred under local escort and bed watch policies. They should be transported in 'usual transport' (eg a car) unless in an emergency or otherwise agreed when an ambulance should be used.

22.34 It may be necessary for patients subject to part 3 of the Act to be subject to mechanical restraint for the purposes of ensuring a safe transfer (see paragraphs 26.88–26.90)."

The power to control the activities of detained patients

1-508   See the note on s.139 under this heading.

Defective Court Orders

1-509   An order made under the Act in excess of jurisdiction is irregular and can, on such ground, be set aside. Until it has been set aside it is effective and must be obeyed (*South West Yorkshire Mental Health NHS Trust v Bradford Crown Court* [2003] EWHC 640 (Admin); [2004] M.H.L.R. 137). The appropriate remedy in such a case is by way of judicial review: see *R. (on the application of A) v Harrow Crown Court* [2003] EWHC 2020 (Admin), where the court held that the detention of a patient on the authority of an order mistakenly made by the Crown Court does not involve a violation of the patient's rights under art.5 of the European Convention on Human Rights.

If the order announced by the judge is within the court's jurisdiction but an incorrect order is subsequently signed by the court clerk, a fresh order can be signed to correct the error.

In *M v Ukraine* [2013] M.H.L.R. 255, the European Court of Human Rights said at para.56:

"A period of detention is, in principle, 'lawful' if it is based on a court order. For the assessment of compliance with art.5(1) of the Convention a basic distinction has to be made between ex facie invalid detention orders – for example, given by a court in excess of jurisdiction or where the interested party did not have proper notice of the hearing – and detention orders which are prima facie valid and effective unless and until they have been overturned by a higher court. A detention order must be considered as ex facie invalid if the flaw in the order amounted to a "gross and obvious irregularity" in the exceptional sense indicated by the Court's case-law (see *Mooren v. Germany* (2010) 50 E.H.R.R. 23 at paras 74 and 75)."

A challenge to an order made by a magistrates' court should be made by either an appeal under s.108 of the Magistrates' Courts Act 1980 or to the High Court by way of case stated. In the absence of special circumstances, where there is a choice between the case stated procedure and judicial review, the former is the appropriate route of challenge: see *R. (on the application of LS) v Brent Magistrates' Court* unreported, July 14, 2009 where Laws L.J. said in a permission hearing that "the hospital is entitled to take documents dealing with admission, including apparent orders under Section 37 or Section 38, at their face value" and that s.40(1) provides the hospital managers with sufficient authority to admit the patient. His Lordship went on to say:

"It does seem to me to be right that it would be unreal and counter productive for the law to require the hospital managers, in effect, to take what may amount to sophisticated legal advice as to the validity of hospital orders. ... Of course I accept that the hospital must carefully ascertain that the documentation is in order and appropriate statutory orders are in place. But it is not their role to conduct an investigation, as it were, below the surface of the validity of the order".

Criminal Procedure (Insanity) Act 1964

If an accused person is found to be either not guilty by reason of insanity or unfit to plead, the Crown Court can make a hospital order (with or without a restriction order under s.41) under ss.5 and 5A of the 1964 Act. The other options available to the court are the making of a supervision order or an order for the absolute discharge of the accused. There is no power to make a guardianship order. The Reference Guide states: **1-510**

"22.8 Patients admitted to hospital when found unfit to be tried have not received a full criminal trial, and may be sent back for trial by the prosecuting authority if that authority is satisfied, after consulting their responsible clinician, that they can now properly be tried. The Secretary of State may also do this, if the patient concerned is still subject to a restriction order and still detained in hospital. This includes patients on leave of absence from hospital, but not those who have been conditionally discharged and not recalled to hospital. Before doing so, the Secretary of State must consult the patient's responsible clinician.

22.9 The general principle observed by the Secretary of State is that people who have been accused of an offence ought, if possible, to be brought to trial so that they may have an opportunity of having their guilt or innocence determined by a court. In practice, the Secretary of State will consult the responsible clinician about a relevant patient's fitness for trial during the first six months of their detention and regularly thereafter.

22.10 If sending patients back for trial, the Secretary of State may remit them either directly to the court or to prison to await trial. The patient's hospital order (and restriction order) ceases to apply on their arrival at the court or prison."

Also see Home Office Circular 24/2005 and the General Note to s.41 under *Fitness to plead under the Criminal Procedure (Insanity) Act 1964*.

DNA Profiling

The Criminal Evidence (Amendment) Act 1997, which came into force on March 19, 1997, enables the police to take non-intimate samples without consent, for DNA profiling purposes, from persons who were convicted before April 10, 1995 of one of the offences listed in Sch.1 to the Act (broadly sex, violent and burglary offences) and who are serving a sentence of imprisonment, or are detained under this Part of the Act, in respect of such an offence at the time when it is sought to take a sample. The Act also enables non-intimate samples to be taken without consent from persons detained under this Part who have been acquitted on grounds of insanity or found unfit to plead. Guidance on the Act is contained in Home Office Circular 27/1997. **1-511**

The Multi-Agency Public Protection Arrangements

The multi-agency public protection arrangements (MAPPA) grew out of the closer working relationships which developed between the police and probation (and latterly other agencies) in the late 1990s. The purpose of MAPPA is to minimise the risk to the public posed by those who may reoffend, either violently or sexually. The latest MAPPA guidance can be accessed on its website. The *Code of Practice* considers the MAPPA arrangements at paras 22.87 to 22.92. **1-512**

Code of Practice

Guidance on this Part is contained in Ch.22. **1-513**

REMANDS TO HOSPITAL

Remand to hospital for report on accused's mental condition

35.—(1) Subject to the provisions of this section, the Crown Court or a magistrates' court may remand an accused person to a hospital specified by the court for a report on his mental condition. **1-514**

(2) For the purposes of this section an accused person is—

    (a)   in relation to the Crown Court, any person who is awaiting trial before the court for an offence punishable with imprisonment or who has been arraigned before the court for such an offence and has not yet been sentenced or otherwise dealt with for the offence on which he has been arraigned;

    (b)   in relation to a magistrates' court, any person who has been convicted by the court of an offence punishable on summary conviction with imprisonment and any person charged with such an offence if the court is satisfied that he did the act or made the omission charged or he has consented to the exercise by the court of the powers conferred by this section.

(3)   Subject to subsection (4) below, the powers conferred by this section may be exercised if—

    (a)   the court is satisfied, on the written or oral evidence of a registered medical practitioner, that there is reason to suspect that the accused person is suffering from [mental disorder]; and

    (b)   the court is of the opinion that it would be impracticable for a report on his mental condition to be made if he were remanded on bail;

but those powers shall not be exercised by the Crown Court in respect of a person who has been convicted before the court if the sentence for the offence of which he has been convicted is fixed by law.

(4)   The court shall not remand an accused person to a hospital under this section unless satisfied, on the written or oral evidence of the [approved clinician] who would be responsible for making the report or of some other person representing the managers of the hospital, that arrangements have been made for his admission to that hospital and for his admission to it within the period of seven days beginning with the date of the remand; and if the court is so satisfied it may, pending his admission, give directions for his conveyance to and detention in a place of safety.

(5)   Where a court has remanded an accused person under this section it may further remand him if it appears to the court, on the written or oral evidence of the [approved clinician] responsible for making the report, that a further remand is necessary for completing the assessment of the accused person's mental condition.

(6)   The power of further remanding an accused person under this section may be exercised by the court without his being brought before the court if he is represented by [an authorised person who] is given an opportunity of being heard.

(7)   An accused person shall not be remanded or further remanded under this section for more than 28 days at a time or for more than 12 weeks in all; and the court may at any time terminate the remand if it appears to the court that it is appropriate to do so.

(8)   An accused person remanded to hospital under this section shall be entitled to obtain at his own expense an independent report on his mental condition from a registered medical practitioner [or approved clinician] chosen by him and to apply to the court on the basis of it for his remand to be terminated under subsection (7) above.

(9)   Where an accused person is remanded under this section—

    (a)   a constable or any other person directed to do so by the court shall convey the accused person to the hospital specified by the court within the period mentioned in subsection (4) above; and

    (b)   the managers of the hospital shall admit him within that period and thereafter detain him in accordance with the provisions of this section.

(10) If an accused person absconds from a hospital to which he has been remanded under this section, or while being conveyed to or from that hospital, he may be arrested without warrant by any constable and shall, after being arrested, be brought as soon as practicable before the court that remanded him; and the court may thereupon terminate the remand and deal with him in any way in which it could have dealt with him if he has not been remanded under this section.

Amendments

The amendments to this section were made by the Mental Health Act 2007 ss.1(4), 10(2), Sch.1 para.5 and the Legal Services Act 2007 s.208, Sch.21 para.54.

Definitions

hospital: ss.55(5), 145(1).   **1-515**
mental disorder: ss.1, 145(1).
approved clinician: s.145(1).
the managers: s.145(1).
place of safety: s.55(1).
authorised person: s.55(1).

General Note

This section gives effect to the recommendation of the Butler Committee that courts should have the   **1-516** option of remanding an accused person to hospital as an in-patient for the preparation of a report on his mental condition. Magistrates' courts and the Crown Court have this power if the requirements of either para.(a) (for the Crown Court) or para.(b) (for the magistrates' court) of subs.(2) are met and they are satisfied, on medical evidence, that there is reason to suspect that the accused person is suffering from mental disorder and that it would be impracticable for a report on his mental condition to be made if he were remanded on bail (subs.(3)). The remand, which can last for a maximum of 12 weeks (subss.(7)), cannot be made unless the court is also satisfied, on hearing evidence from an approved clinician, that arrangements have been made for the accused's admission to hospital (subs.(4)). If the accused person either absconds from the hospital to which he has been remanded, or absconds while being conveyed to and from that hospital, he may be arrested without warrant by any constable and brought back before the court that remanded him (subs.(10)) which may decide on some alternative approach to his case. The provisions in the Act relating to patients who are absent without leave do not apply to patients remanded under this section. The court may terminate the remand at any time.

The Law Commission Report on "*Unfitness to Plead*" (Law Com No.364) states at para.4.102:

"The section 35 MHA remand reaches its maximum extension at 12 weeks. Then, where the defendant still requires treatment, the court has to rely on agreeing with the Ministry of Justice for a section 48 MHA transfer on the basis that the defendant is in 'urgent need of treatment' to avoid the defendant inevitably being remanded in custody. The only alternative is to grant the defendant bail and rely on his continued detention in hospital under a civil sectioning order. But in the latter circumstance the court would lose all control over the release of the defendant."

The effect of subss.(3) and (4) of this section:

"is expected to be that the initiative for a remand to hospital will generally come either from the defendant's legal representative (who may already have taken steps to obtain the necessary evidence from an approved [clinician] before suggesting to the court that remand to hospital might be appropriate) or from the medical officer of the prison to which the defendant has been remanded in custody at an earlier court appearance. Prison medical officers are being asked to explore the possibility of a remand to hospital in appropriate cases. Prison medical officers will of course continue to comply to the best of their ability with requests from the courts for medical reports on prisoners remanded in custody for that purpose. If the court itself is considering the suitability of a remand to hospital and no prior arrangements with a hospital have been made, it will generally be necessary to adjourn the case so that the necessary medical recommendation can be sought and arrangements made for the defendant to be admitted to a hospital" (Home Office Circular No. 71/1984, Annex, paras 24, 25).

A remand under this section:

"does not automatically affect any existing liability for detention for assessment or treatment on any other basis, nor bring a community treatment order (CTO) or guardianship to an end. But nor does it prevent them expiring or being discharged in the normal way" (Reference Guide, para.14.23).

The purpose of a remand under this section is to inform the court about issues relating to fitness to plead and disposal; not for the purpose of obtaining evidence relevant to an issue at trial. Such an order cannot therefore be used to enable the Crown to obtain evidence that the accused had the intention, or the capacity to form the intention, to commit an offence (*R. (on the application of M) v Kingston Crown Court* [2014] EWHC 2702 (Admin); [2015] M.H.L.R. 79).

This section does not provide the remanding court with a power to either grant the patient leave of absence under s.17 from the hospital to which he has been remanded or to transfer the patient to another hospital under s.19 (although the court could further remand the patient to a different hospital: see the note on subs.(5)). If the patient needs to leave the hospital to receive, for example, emergency medical treatment at an Accident and Emergency department, the patient should be taken there and the remanding court informed of the action that has been taken. The common law (for mentally capable consenting patients) or the Mental Capacity Act 2005 (for mentally incapacitated patients) would provide authority for the patient to be treated. Appropriate security arrangements should be put in place by the remanding hospital.

A person remanded under this section is not subject to the consent to treatment provisions contained in Pt IV (s.56(3)(b)). This has led to the practice of using either s.2 or s.3 to bring the patient within the scope of Pt IV. Although this practice had been regarded by legal commentators as being legally questionable, the decision in *R. v North West London Mental Health NHS Trust Ex p. Stewart* [1997] 4 All E.R. 871 CA, where the court held that the powers under Pt II and Pt III can co-exist and operate independently of each other, confirmed that either s.2 or s.3 can be used during the currency of a s.35. This was a pragmatic decision of the Court of Appeal that does not sit easily with the scheme of the Act for the reasons set out in the 14th edition of this Manual at para.1-439. It is unlikely that a claim that a patient's dual detention amounts to a disproportionate and unjustified interference with his rights under art.8 of the European Convention on Human Rights would succeed: see *R. (on the application of M) v Homerton University Hospital* [2008] EWCA Civ 197 at paras 22 and 24.

The *Code of Practice* states:

"22.40 Where a patient remanded under section 35 is thought to be in need of medical treatment for mental disorder which cannot otherwise be given, the patient should be referred back to court by the clinician in charge of their care as soon as possible, with an appropriate recommendation and with an assessment of whether they are in a fit state to attend court.

22.41 If there is a delay in securing a court date, consideration should be given to whether the patient meets the criteria for detention under part 2 of the Act to enable compulsory treatment to be given. This will be concurrent with, and not a replacement for, the remand made by the court."

Patients who are remanded under this section do not have a nearest relative for the purposes of the Act.

Procedure

1-517   See the Criminal Procedure Rules 2020 (2020/759) rr.3.10, 28.8 and 28.9.

Criminal Procedure (Insanity) Act 1964

1-518   In a case where s.5 of the 1964 Act applies (persons not guilty by reason of insanity or unfit to plead) but the court have yet to make a disposal, the Crown Court can remand the accused under this section (as modified by the 1964 Act s.5A(2)(a),(c)).

Applications to the First-tier Tribunal (Mental Health) or the Mental Health Review Tribunal for Wales

1-519   A patient who has been remanded under this section has no right to apply to a tribunal.

Orders made in other proceedings

In certain circumstances, an order under this section can be made under the Contempt of Court Act **1-520**
1981 s.14(4A), the Family Law Act 1996 ss.48 and 63L, the Housing Act 1996 s.156, the Police and
Justice Act 2006 s.27 and the Armed Forces Act 2006 s.169 and Sch.4 para.3.

Transport to and from court

The *Code of Practice* states: **1-521**

"22.35 For patients remanded to hospital under sections 35 or 36 of the Act, or subject to a hospital
order or an interim hospital order, the court has the power to direct who is to be responsible for
transporting the defendant from the court to the receiving hospital. This direction should be based
on individual need and there should be contingency planning and measurable outcomes in place to
ensure that people do not have to return to the holding prison. Monitoring of this process should be
logged. In practice, when remand orders are first made, patients are usually returned to the holding
prison briefly using the escort provision commissioned for court to prison journeys, and arrangements are then made to admit them and make arrangements for transporting them to hospital within
the statutory period. Secure hospitals that hold patients under part 3 of the Act and prisons should
have their own security protocols for transfer of patients subject to part 3 of the Act.
   22.36 When a patient has been admitted on remand or is subject to an interim hospital order under
section 38 of the Act, it is the responsibility of the hospital to return the patient to court as required.
The court should give adequate notice of hearings. The hospital should liaise with the court in plenty
of time to confirm the arrangements for escorting the patient to and from the court. The hospital will
be responsible for providing a suitable escort for the patient when travelling from the hospital to the
court and should plan for the provision of appropriately qualified staff to do this taking into account
the age of the patient and any disability. The assistance of the police may be requested, if necessary.
If possible, and having regard to the needs of the patient, medical or nursing staff should remain with
the patient on court premises, even though legal accountability while the patient is detained for hearings, remains with the court. For restricted patients attendance at court will require the consent of
the Secretary of State for Justice. For those patients who have been transferred under section 48 of
the Act, permission to attend court will be provided in writing on initial admission. For other patients
who are required to attend court, prior approval must be sought.
   22.37 It may be possible in some circumstances, and with permission from the Tribunal or the
Court, for a patient to attend a hearing by live video link. Clinical teams should seek advice from
the relevant tribunal or court to establish whether this might be available."

Subsection (1)

This subsection "provides an alternative to remanding the accused person in custody for a medical **1-522**
report, in circumstances where it would not be practicable to obtain the report if he were remanded on
bail (for instance, if he decided to break a condition of bail that he should reside at a hospital, the hospital
would be unable to prevent him from discharging himself)" (Home Office Circular No.71/1984, Annex para.1).

Subsection (2)

Paragraph (a)

Offence punishable with imprisonment   This section applies to a person who has been accused, but not **1-523**
convicted of murder (subs.(3)).

Paragraph (b)

Magistrates' court   If a person is remanded under this section by the magistrates' court and the case **1-524**
is subsequently committed to the Crown Court, the jurisdiction of the magistrates to make a further
remand ends.

Offence punishable on summary conviction with imprisonment   The offence could have been committed by a person under the age of 21 (s.55(2)).

Satisfied that he did the act   The power to remand for reports under this section applies to someone in respect of whom s.37(3) applies (*Bartram v Southend Magistrates' Court* [2004] EWHC 2691 (QB); [2004] M.H.L.R. 319 para.6).

Consented   The consent relates to the making of the order and not to the extension of the order under subs.(5). A withdrawal of consent is therefore not relevant to the question of renewal.

Subsection (3)

1-525   **Paragraph (a); evidence**   For general provisions as to medical evidence, see s.54. The court can call a doctor who has provided a written report to give oral evidence (s.54(2A)).

Registered medical practitioner   Who must have been approved by the Secretary of State or the Welsh Ministers under s.12, or by another person by virtue of s.12ZA or 12ZB (s.54(1)). A registered medical practitioner means "a fully registered person within the meaning of the Medical Act 1983 who holds a licence to practise under that Act" (Interpretation Act 1978 Sch.1).

Reason to suspect   The diagnostic threshold under this section is not high.

Mental disorder   If the person has a learning disability, the disability must be associated with abnormally aggressive or seriously irresponsible conduct (s.1(2A), (2B)). A learning disabled person might also suffer from another form of mental disorder.

Paragraph (b); impracticable   This presumably refers to the impracticability of preparing a sufficiently thorough report if the accused were to be granted bail.

Fixed by law   Although the power to remand to hospital is not available in respect of a person who has been *convicted* of murder who must be sentenced to life imprisonment (Murder (Abolition of Death Penalty) Act 1965 s.1(1)), a remand under this section can be made in a murder trial before conviction. A person who charged with murder can be bailed to a hospital to enable psychiatric reports to be prepared (Bail Act 1976 s.3(6A)).

Subsection (4)

1-526   An order under this section which has been made without this subsection being complied with is ultra vires. If there is doubt as to whether the hospital place would be funded, the court should adjourn for a short period to enable enquiries to be made, and if necessary, to hear evidence and/or representations from the relevant funding body (*R. (on the application of Bitcon) v West Allerdale Magistrates' Court* [2003] EWHC 2460 (Admin); [2003] M.H.L.R. 399). If, subsequent to an offer of a bed having been made, circumstances arise which prevent the hospital from admitting the patient, the case should be returned to the court as a matter of urgency.

Or of some other person   Who need not be an approved clinician.

Seven days   The court does not have the power either to renew or extend this period.

Beginning with   Including the date of the remand (*Zoan v Rouamba* [2000] 2 All E.R. 620 CA).

Place of safety   As defined by s.135(6),(7).

Subsection (5)

1-527   See the note on "consented" in subs.(2).

Further remand him   The new period of remand starts from the expiry date of the previous period of remand. The total period spent on remand cannot exceed 12 weeks in all (subs.(7)). It is submitted that a further remand can only be made to a different hospital if the requirements of subs.(4) are satisfied in respect of the person's admission to that hospital.

Subsection (7)

At any time "It will be open to the [responsible clinician] in every case to inform the court if the object of the remand is achieved before the expiry of the stipulated time, so that the adjourned hearing may be brought forward accordingly or if necessary an alternative form of remand, either in custody or on bail, may be substituted" (Butler Committee, para.12.9). An application could also be made to terminate the order if the patient proves to be unmanageable at the hospital.

1-528

Subsection (8)

This provision was successfully moved during the passage of the Mental Health (Amendment) Act 1982 against Government advice. The Government view was that it would be unlikely to be of great benefit to the accused person, firstly because he already has the right to commission his own private clinical report and, secondly, because the court is unlikely to end his remand on the basis of such a report.

1-529

Once the accused has received the private clinical report, he has the right to apply to the court to seek an end to the remand even if the reports that the court has asked for are not available.

The *Code of Practice* states under the heading "Independent medical assessment":

"22.16 A patient who is remanded to hospital for a report (section 35) or for treatment (section 36) is entitled to obtain, at their own expense, or where applicable through legal aid, an independent report on their mental condition from a doctor or other clinician of their choosing, for the purpose of applying to court for the termination of the remand. Hospital managers should help in the exercise of this right by enabling the patient to contact a suitably qualified and experienced solicitor or other legal adviser.

22.17 Where the court refers the patient for assessment or treatment under sections 35 or 36, the initial report that has been requested by the court would be remunerated from central funds and not by the legal aid agency. If, however, the patient wishes to obtain a report to challenge the report produced for the court, providing that the merits criteria are satisfied, this could be remunerated under the patient's criminal legal aid. Additionally, the patient would need to satisfy the financial eligibility criteria specified by either the magistrates' court or Crown Court. The patient's representative could also consider making an application to the legal aid agency for prior authority to commission a report to challenge the report produced by the clinical staff."

Subsection (9)

Convey See the General Note to this section under *Transport to and from court*. For general provisions regarding conveyance, see s.137.

1-530

Shall admit him The hospital managers are placed under an obligation to admit the patient.

Subsection (10)

The absconder must be brought before the court that remanded him. There is no time limit on a recapture under this provision or under s.36(8).

1-531

Arrested The power to arrest under this section was specifically preserved by s.26 and Sch.2 of the Police and Criminal Evidence Act 1984 (PACE). This means that the arresting policeman has a power to search the patient under s.32 of PACE at a place other than a police station.

Remand of accused person to hospital for treatment

36.—(1) Subject to the provisions of this section, the Crown Court may, instead of remanding an accused person in custody, remand him to a hospital specified by the court if satisfied, on the written or oral evidence of two registered medical practitioners, that,

1-532

    [(a) he is suffering from mental disorder of a nature or degree which makes it appropriate for him to be detained in a hospital for medical treatment;] [and

    (b) the appropriate medical treatment is available for him.]

  (2) For the purposes of this section an accused person is any person who is in

custody awaiting trial before the Crown Court for an offence punishable with imprisonment (other than an offence the sentence for which is fixed by law) or who at any time before sentence is in custody in the course of a trial before that court for such an offence.

(3) The court shall not remand an accused person under this section to a hospital unless it is satisfied, on the written or oral evidence of the [approved clinician who would have overall responsibility for his case] or of some other person representing the managers of the hospital, that arrangements have been made for his admission to that hospital and for his admission to it within the period of seven days beginning with the date of the remand; and if the court is so satisfied it may, pending his admission, give directions for his conveyance to and detention in a place of safety.

(4) Where a court has remanded an accused person under this section it may further remand him if it appears to the court, on the written or oral evidence of the [responsible clinician], that a further remand is warranted.

(5) The power of further remanding an accused person under this section may be exercised by the court without his being brought before the court if he is represented by [an authorised person who] is given an opportunity of being heard.

(6) An accused person shall not be remanded or further remanded under this section for more than 28 days at a time or for more than 12 weeks in all; and the court may at any time terminate the remand if it appears to the court that it is appropriate to do so.

(7) An accused person remanded to hospital under this section shall be entitled to obtain at his own expense an independent report on his mental condition from a registered medical practitioner [or approved clinician] chosen by him and to apply to the court on the basis of it for his remand to be terminated under subsection (6) above.

(8) Subsections (9) and (10) of section 35 above shall have effect in relation to a remand under this section as they have effect in relation to a remand under that section.

Amendments

The amendments to this section were made by the Mental Health Act 2007 ss.1(4), 5(2), 10(3), Sch.1 para.6 and the Legal Services Act 2007 s.208, Sch.21 para.55.

Definitions

1-533
hospital: ss.55(5), 145(1).
mental disorder: ss.1, 145(1).
the managers: s.145(1).
responsible clinician: s.55(1).
approved clinician: s.145(1).
place of safety: s.55(1).
authorised person: s.55(1).
approved medical treatment: ss.3(4), 145(1AB).
medical treatment: s.145(3), (4).

General Note

1-534
This section empowers the Crown Court to remand an accused person (see subs.(2)), who is in custody either awaiting trial or during the course of a trial and who is suffering from mental disorder, to hospital for treatment for a maximum of 12 weeks. It provides an alternative to the Secretary of State's power under s.48 to transfer unsentenced prisoners to hospital. Where the accused person is in urgent

need of treatment and is not due to appear before the Crown Court in the immediate future, the procedure under s.48 is to be preferred. Paragraph 36 of Home Office Circular No.71/1984 states:

"Section 36 provides the Crown Court with an alternative to the procedure laid down by the Criminal Procedure (Insanity) Act 1964 of finding a defendant under disability ('unfit to plead'). The power in s.36 can be used in cases in which if the defendant could receive treatment in hospital for a period it might be possible to proceed with the full trial. The Crown Court may prefer in appropriate cases to proceed in this way rather than under the Criminal Procedure (Insanity) Act, under which the defendant would thereafter have to be detained as a restricted patient (which may not be appropriate in relation to the nature of the alleged offence)."

In the magistrates' court there is provision in s.37(3) to make a hospital order in respect of a defendant who has not been convicted.

A remand under this section "does not automatically affect any existing liability for detention for assessment or treatment on any other basis, nor bring a community treatment order (CTO) or guardianship to an end. But nor does it prevent them expiring or being discharged in the normal way" (Reference Guide, para.14.23).

As the Act does not provide for the application of Pt II to a patient who has been remanded under this section, there is no power to grant the patient leave of absence under s.17 or transfer the patient to another hospital under s.19 (although the court could further remand the patient to a different hospital: see the note on subs.(4)).

A person remanded under this section as a "patient liable to be detained under this Act" is subject to the consent to treatment provisions contained in Pt IV (s.56(3)).

If the remanded person absconds, the provisions in the Act relating to patients who are absent without leave do not apply. If the accused person either absconds from the hospital to which he has been remanded, or absconds while being conveyed to and from that hospital, he may be arrested and brought back before the court that remanded him (subs.(8)).

If it is anticipated that the patient will cease to be an accused person due to the case against him collapsing, an application under Part II could be prepared by completing the statutory documentation with the exception of the signature on the application form. This could be added when the patient ceased to be an accused person.

Patients who are remanded under this section do not have a nearest relative for the purposes of the Act.

Procedure

See the Criminal Procedure Rules 2020 (2020/759) rr.3.10, 28.8 and 28.9.   **1-535**

Applications to the First-tier Tribunal (Mental Health) or the Mental Health Review Tribunal for Wales

A patient who has been remanded under this section has no right to apply to a tribunal.   **1-536**

Orders made in other proceedings

In certain circumstances, an order under this section can be made under the Armed Forces Act 2006 s.169 and Sch.4 para.4.   **1-537**

Transport to and from court

See the General Note to s.35 under this heading.   **1-538**

Subsection (1)

Crown Court   But not the magistrates' court. However, such courts have the alternative, under s.37(3), of making a hospital order in respect of a defendant charged but unconvicted.   **1-539**

Hospital   Or a registered establishment (ss.34(2), 55(5)).

Evidence   For general provisions relating to medical evidence, see s.54. The court can call a doctor who has provided a written report to give oral evidence (s.54(2A)).

Two registered medical practitioners   At least one of whom must have been approved by the Secretary of State or the Welsh Ministers under s.12, or another person by virtue of s.12ZA or 12ZB (s.54(1)). There is no prohibition on both of the doctors being on the staff of the same hospital. A registered medical practitioner means "a fully registered person within the meaning of the Medical Act 1983 who holds a licence to practise under that Act" (Interpretation Act 1978, Sch.1).

Mental disorder   If the person has a learning disability, the disability must be associated with abnormally aggressive or seriously irresponsible conduct (s.1(2A), (2B)). A learning disabled person might also suffer from another form of mental disorder.

Nature or degree   See the note on s.3(2)(a).

Appropriate medical treatment   See the note on s.3(2)(d).

Subsection (2)

1-540   **Fixed by law**   Unlike s.35, this section does not apply to a person who has been charged with murder. If such a person is in need of urgent treatment, he could be removed to hospital under s.48 if he is awaiting trial having been remanded in custody by a magistrates' court. A person who charged with murder can be bailed to a hospital to enable psychiatric reports to be prepared (Bail Act 1976 s.3(6A)).

Subsection (3)

1-541   **Or of some other person**   Who need not be a clinician.

Beginning with   Including the date of the remand (*Zoan v Rouamba* [2000] 2 All E.R. 620 CA).

Subsection (4)

1-542   **A further remand is warranted**   Because the criteria set out in subs.(1) still apply. It is submitted that a further remand can only be made to a different hospital if the requirements of subs.(3) are satisfied in respect of the patient's admission to that hospital.

Subsection (7)

1-543   See the notes on s.35(8).

Subsection (8)

1-544   See the notes on s.35(9) and (10).

HOSPITAL AND GUARDIANSHIP ORDERS

Powers of courts to order hospital admission or guardianship

1-545   **37.**—(1)   Where a person is convicted before the Crown Court of an offence punishable with imprisonment other than an offence the sentence for which is fixed by law [...], or is convicted by a magistrates' court of an offence punishable on summary conviction with imprisonment, and the conditions mentioned in subsection (2) below are satisfied, the court may by order authorise his admission to and detention in such hospital as may be specified in the order or, as the case may be, place him under the guardianship of a local social services authority or of such other person approved by a local social services authority as may be so specified.

[(1A)   In the case of an offence the sentence for which would otherwise fall to be [imposed under [section 258, 258A, 268A, 273, 274, 274A, 282A, 283, 285 or 285A] of the Sentencing Code or under Chapter 7 of Part 10 of that Code, nothing] in those provisions shall prevent a court from making an order under subsection (1) above for the admission of the offender to a hospital.

[(1B) For the purposes of subsection (1A) above—

(a) a sentence falls to be imposed under [section 258 or 258A] of the Sentencing Code if the court is obliged by that section to pass a sentence of detention for life under section 250 of that Code;

[(aa) a sentence falls to be imposed under section 268A or 282A of that Code if it is required by section 282B(2) of that Code and the court is not of the opinion there mentioned;]

(b) a sentence falls to be imposed under [section 273, 274 or 274A] of that Code if the court is obliged by that section to pass a sentence of custody for life;

(c) a sentence falls to be imposed under [section 283, 285 or 285A] of that Code if the court is obliged by that section to pass a sentence of imprisonment for life;

(d) a sentence falls to be imposed under Chapter 7 of Part 10 of that Code if it is required by [section 311(2), 312(2A), 313(2A), 314(2A) or 315(2A)] of that Code and the court is not of the opinion there mentioned.]

(2) The conditions referred to in subsection (1) above are that—

(a) the court is satisfied, on the written or oral evidence of two registered medical practitioners, that the offender is suffering from [mental disorder] and that either—

(i) the mental disorder from which the offender is suffering is of a nature or degree which makes it appropriate for him to be detained in a hospital for medical treatment and [appropriate medical treatment is available for him]; or

(ii) in the case of an offender who has attained the age of 16 years, the mental disorder is of a nature or degree which warrants his reception into guardianship under this Act; and

(b) the court is of the opinion, having regard to all the circumstances including the nature of the offence and the character and antecedents of the offender, and to the other available methods of dealing with him, that the most suitable method of disposing of the case is by means of an order under this section.

(3) Where a person is charged before a magistrates' court with any act or omission as an offence and the court would have power, on convicting him of that offence, to make an order under subsection (1) above in his case [...], then, if the court is satisfied that the accused did the act or made the omission charged, the court may, if it thinks fit, make such an order without convicting him.

(4) An order for the admission of an offender to a hospital (in this Act referred to as "a hospital order") shall not be made under this section unless the court is satisfied on the written or oral evidence of the [approved clinician who would have overall responsibility for his case] or of some other person representing the managers of the hospital that arrangements have been made for his admission to that hospital [...], and for his admission to it within the period of 28 days beginning with the date of the making of such an order; and the court may, pending his admission within that period, give such directions as it thinks fit for his conveyance to and detention in a place of safety.

(5) If within the said period of 28 days it appears to the Secretary of State that

by reason of an emergency or other special circumstances it is not practicable for the patient to be received into the hospital specified in the order, he may give directions for the admission of the patient to such other hospital as appears to be appropriate instead of the hospital so specified; and where such directions are given—

    (a)   the Secretary of State shall cause the person having the custody of the patient to be informed, and

    (b)   the hospital order shall have effect as if the hospital specified in the directions were substituted for the hospital specified in the order.

(6)   An order placing an offender under the guardianship of a local social services authority or of any other person (in this Act referred to as "a guardianship order") shall not be made under this section unless the court is satisfied that that authority or person is willing to receive the offender into guardianship.

(7)   [...]

(8)   Where an order is made under this section, the court [shall not:

    (a)   pass sentence of imprisonment or impose a fine or make a [community order (within [the meaning given by section 200 of the Sentencing Code]] [or a youth rehabilitation order (within [the meaning given by section 173 of that Code]] in respect of the offence,

    (b)   if the order under this section is a hospital order, make a referral order (within [the meaning given by section 83 of that Code]) in respect of the offence, or

    (c)   make in respect of the offender [...] an order under [section 376 of that Code] (binding over of parent or guardian),]

but the court may make any other order which it] has power to make apart from this section; and for the purposes of this subsection "sentence of imprisonment" includes any sentence or order for detention.

Amendments

The amendments to this section were made by the Criminal Justice Act 2003 s.304, Sch.32 para.38, the Criminal Justice and Immigration Act 2008 s.148, Sch.26 para.8, the Mental Health Act 2007 ss.1(4), 4(5), 10(4), 55, Sch.1 para.7, Sch.11 Pt 1, the Violent Crime Reduction Act 2006 ss.49, 65, Sch.1 para.2, Sch.5, the Crime (Sentences) Act 1997 s.56(2), Sch.6, the Youth Justice and Criminal Evidence Act 1999 s.67, Sch.4 para.11, the Criminal Justice Act 2003 s.304, Sch.32 para.38, the Powers of Criminal Courts (Sentencing) Act 2000 s.165, Sch.9 para.90, Criminal Justice and Immigration Act 2008 ss.6, 149, Sch.4 para.30, Sch.28 Pt 1, the Legal Aid, Sentencing and Punishment of Offenders Act 2012 ss.122, 142, Sch.19 para.1 and Sch.26 para.2, the Criminal Justice and Courts Act 2015 Sch.5 para.1, the Sentencing Act 2020 Sch.24, Pt 1 para.73, the Counter-Terrorism and Sentencing Act 2021 s.46, Sch.13 para.8 and the Police, Crime, Sentencing and Courts Act 2022 s.3(16).

Definitions

1-546
hospital: ss.55(5), 145(1).
local social services authority: s.145(1).
mental disorder: ss.1, 145(1).
approved clinician: s.145(1).
appropriate medical treatment: ss.3(4), 145(1AB).
medical treatment: s.145(1), (4).
patient: s.145(1).
the managers: s.145(1).
place of safety: s.55(1).

General Note

1-547
This section empowers a Crown Court or magistrates' court to make a hospital or guardianship order as an alternative to a penal disposal for offenders who are found to be suffering from mental disorder

at the time of sentencing such as to warrant their detention in hospital or reception into guardianship. The effect of hospital and guardianship orders are set out below and in s.40. An offender's nearest relative has no role to play in the making by the court of a hospital or guardianship order (s.40(4)). When a person is made subject to a hospital or guardianship order under this section, any previous application or order made in respect of that person ceases to have effect (s.40(5)).

Procedure

See the Criminal Procedure Rules 2020 (2020/759), rr.3.10, 24.3, 28.8, 28.9 and 39.13.   **1-548**

Hospital orders

The purpose and effect of a hospital order are explained in the following passage from the judg-   **1-549**
ment of Mustill L.J. in *R. v Birch* (1989) 11 Cr. App. R.(S.) 202 at 210:

"Once the offender is admitted to hospital pursuant to a hospital order or transfer order without restriction on discharge, his position is almost exactly the same as if he were a civil patient. In effect he passes out of the penal system and into the hospital regime. Neither the court nor the Secretary of State has any say in his disposal....
In general the offender is dealt with in a manner which appears, and is intended to be, humane by comparison with a custodial sentence. A hospital order is not a punishment. Questions of retribution and deterrence, whether personal or general, are immaterial. The offender who has become a patient is not kept on any kind of leash by the court ... The sole purpose of the order is to ensure that the offender receives the medical care and attention which he needs in the hope and expectation of course that the result will be to avoid the commission by the offender of further criminal acts."

A patient who has been placed under a hospital order is subject to the consent to treatment provisions in Pt IV (s.56(3)). As a hospital order is not a punishment, the offender will not come within the parole process.
This section "does not allow a court to override clinical judgment, including an assessment of (i) whether a particular patient can and should be treated at a particular hospital and (ii) the prioritisation of beds" (*R. (on the application of ASK) v Secretary of State for the Home Department* [2019] EWCA Civ 1239, per Hickinbottom L.J. at para.27).
In *R. v Vowles* [2015] EWCA Crim 45; [2016] M.H.L.R. 66, Lord Thomas CJ, who gave the judgment of the Court, reviewed the jurisprudence on the sentencing of mentally disordered offenders. His Lordship referred to the following passage from Mustill L.J.'s judgment in *R. v Birch* which made clear that before the powers under this section were invoked, the judge had to consider the connection between the defendant's mental disorder and the offending conduct:

"Where the sentencer considers that, notwithstanding the offender's mental disorder, there was an element of culpability in the offence which merits punishment. This may happen where there is no connection between the mental disorder and the offence, or where the defendant's responsibility for the offence is 'diminished' but not wholly extinguished....
In the absence of any question of culpability and punishment, the judge should not impose a sentence of imprisonment simply to ensure that if the Review Tribunal finds that the conditions under section 73 are satisfied and is therefore constrained to order a discharge, the offender will return to prison rather than be set free: *Howell* (1985) 7 Cr.App.R. (S.) 360 and *Cockburn* (1967) 52 Cr.App.R. 134."

Lord Thomas said at para.47 that this "passage underlined the importance of the observations which Lord Lane CJ had made in *Castro* (1985) 7 Cr App R(S) 68 where he stressed that the sentence had to be looked at, not only from the point of view of the offender but also from the point of view of the public". His Lordship continued at para.48:

"More recently this court has emphasised the need to examine the issues with great care and to take into account not merely the psychiatric evidence but also broader issues such as the extent of the culpability attributable to the mental disorder, the need to protect the public and the regime on release."

Lord Thomas also said that the "fact of mental illness enables the sentencing court to consider an alternative to immediate imprisonment, but is *not* a passport to a medical disposal as many of the psychiatric opinions we have considered in this case appear to presume" (para.196).

Having reviewed the case law, his Lordship provided the following guidance on the approach to be adopted to sentencing (although the guidance is primarily directed to indeterminate sentences, it is also in large part applicable to all determinate sentences (para.5)):

"51. It is important to emphasise that the judge must carefully consider all the evidence in each case and not, as some of the early cases have suggested, feel circumscribed by the psychiatric opinions. A judge must therefore consider, where the conditions in s.37(2)(a) are met, what is the appropriate disposal. In considering that wider question the matters to which a judge will invariably have to have regard to include (1) the extent to which the offender needs treatment for the mental disorder from which the offender suffers, (2) the extent to which the offending is attributable to the mental disorder, (3) the extent to which punishment is required and (4) the protection of the public including the regime for deciding release and the regime after release. There must always be sound reasons for departing from the usual course of imposing a penal sentence and the judge must set these out.

52. As to the fourth of the considerations to which we have referred, Lord Bingham at paragraph 23 of his judgment in *Drew* [[2003] UKHL 25], which was decided prior to the amendment of s.45A, accepted that there was force in the submission of the Secretary of State that where the medical criteria were met, judges had given less than adequate weight to the conditions governing release. He was, at that time, unpersuaded that a change in practice was desirable. In the light of the amendments to s.45A, the observations of Hughes LJ [in *AG's reference No. 54 of 2011* [2012] 1 Cr App R(S) 106] which we have referred at paragraph 48(ii) and the general evidence before us, we consider that a judge when sentencing must now pay very careful attention to the different effect in each case of the conditions applicable to and after release. As is shown by the case of *Teasdale* [[2012] EWCA Crim 2071] to which we have referred at paragraph 48(iv), this consideration may be one matter leading to the imposition of a hospital order under s.37/41.

53. The fact that two psychiatrists are of the opinion that a hospital order with restrictions under s.37/41 is the right disposal is therefore never a reason on its own to make such an order. The judge must first consider all the relevant circumstances, including the four issues we have set out in the preceding paragraphs and then consider the alternatives in the order in which we set them out in the next paragraph.

54. Therefore, in the light of the arguments addressed to us and the matters to which we have referred, a court should, in a case where (1) the evidence of medical practitioners suggests that the offender is suffering from a mental disorder, (2) that the offending is wholly or in significant part attributable to that disorder, (3) treatment is available, and it considers in the light of all the circumstances to which we have referred, that a hospital order (with or without a restriction) may be an appropriate way of dealing with the case, consider the matters in the following order:

(i)   As the terms of s.45A(1) of the MHA require, before a hospital order is made under s.37/ 41, whether or not with a restriction order, a judge should consider whether the mental disorder can appropriately be dealt with by a hospital and limitation direction under s.45A.

(ii)   If it can, then the judge should make such a direction under s.45A(1). This consideration will not apply to a person under the age of 21 at the time of conviction as there is no power to make such an order in the case of such a person as we have set out at paragraph 19 above.

(iii)   If such a direction is not appropriate the court must then consider, before going further, whether, if the medical evidence satisfies the condition in s.37(2)(a) (that the mental disorder is such that it would be appropriate for the offender to be detained in a hospital and treatment is available), the conditions set out in s.37(2)(b) would make that the most suitable method of disposal. It is essential that a judge gives detailed consideration to all the factors encompassed within s.37(2)(b). For example, in a case where the court is considering a life sentence under the Criminal Justice Act 2003 as amended in 2012 (following the guidance given in *Attorney General's Reference (No.27 of 2013), R v Burinskas* [2014] 1 WLR 4209), if (1) the mental disorder is treatable, (2) once treated there is no evidence he would be in any way dangerous, and (3) the offending is entirely due to that mental disorder, a hospital order under s.37/41 is likely to be the correct disposal.

(iv)   We have set out the general circumstances to which a court should have regard but, as the language of s.37(2)(b) makes clear, the court must also have regard to the question of whether other methods of dealing with him are available. This includes consideration of whether the powers under s.47 for transfer to prison for treatment would, taking into account all the other circumstances, be appropriate.

55. If the court, after considering the matters set out in s.37(2)(b), considers that a hospital order is the most suitable method, then it will generally be desirable to make such an order without

consideration of an interim order under s.38 unless there is very clear evidence that such an order is necessary."

Lord Thomas said, at para.12, that "the primary importance of the determination by the sentencing judge in a case where the option is either to impose an indeterminate sentence or to make a hospital order under s.37/s.41 is the release regime that will apply to the offender". In *R. v Rendell* [2019] EWCA Crim 621; [2020] M.H.L.R. 60 at para.45, Thirlwall L.J. said:

"The regime for release on life licence is different from the regime for release on a hospital order/ restriction order. The focus for the parole board is broad; it considers the likelihood of reoffending and the risk to the public resulting from it. Under the section 37/41 regime the focus is entirely on the appellant's mental health although, as Dr Lally explained, the risk to the public and the risk of deterioration of the appellant's mental health are closely linked, the former being greater if there is a deterioration in the latter."

Her Ladyship confirmed, at para.52, that the "question of whether the section 37/41 regime or section 45A (or the section 47/49) regime best protects the public is a matter of fact in each case"; also see *R. v Edwards*, below at para.34vii, *R. v Fisher* [2019] EWCA Crim 1066; [2020] M.H.L.R. 103 at para.39 and *R. v Sowerby* [2020] EWCA Crim 898 at para.55.

In *R. v Edwards* [2018] EWCA Crim 595; [2018] M.H.L.R. 105, the Court of Appeal said that a "level of misunderstanding of the guidance offered in *Vowles* appears to have arisen as to the order in which a sentencing judge should approach the making of a s.37 or a s.45A order and the precedence allegedly given in *Vowles* to a s.45A order. In our view, s.45A itself could have been better drafted but the position is clear. Section 45A and the judgment in *Vowles* do not provide a 'default' setting of imprisonment, as some have assumed" (para.12). In order to assist those representing and sentencing offenders with mental health problems that may justify a hospital order, a finding of dangerousness and/or a s.45A order, the court summarised, at para.34, the following principles that it had "extracted from the statutory framework and the case law.

i. The first step is to consider whether a hospital order may be appropriate.
ii. If so, the judge should then consider all his sentencing options including a s.45A order.
iii. In deciding on the most suitable disposal the judge should remind him or herself of the importance of the penal element in a sentence.
iv. To decide whether a penal element to the sentence is necessary the judge should assess (as best he or she can) the offender's culpability and the harm caused by the offence. The fact that an offender would not have committed the offence but for their mental illness does not necessarily relieve them of all responsibility for their actions.
v. A failure to take prescribed medication is not necessarily a culpable omission; it may be attributable in whole or in part to the offender's mental illness.
vi. If the judge decides to impose a hospital order under s.37/41, he or she must explain why a penal element is not appropriate.
vii. The regimes on release of an offender on licence from a s.45A order and for an offender subject to s.37/41 orders are different but the latter do not necessarily offer a greater protection to the public, as may have been assumed in *Ahmed* [[2016] EWCA Crim 670; [2016] M.H.L.R. 282] and/or or by the parties in the cases before us. Each case turns on its own facts.
viii. If an offender wishes to call fresh psychiatric evidence in his appeal against sentence to support a challenge to a hospital order, a finding of dangerousness or a s.45A order he or she should lodge a s.23 application. If the evidence is the same as was called before the sentencing judge the court is unlikely to receive it.
ix. Grounds of appeal should identify with care each of the grounds the offender wishes to advance. If an applicant or appellant wishes to add grounds not considered by the single judge an application to vary should be made".

The court said at para.12: "... the graver the offence and the greater the risk to the public on release of the offender, the greater emphasis the judge must place upon the protection of the public and the release regime". The court recognised that "sound reasons" not to impose a penal element to the sentence may include "the nature of the offence and the limited nature of any penal element (if imposed) and the fact that the offending was very substantially (albeit not wholly) attributable to the offender's illness."

Consideration of the practical differences between, and advantages and disadvantages of an order made under s.45A and a restriction order made under ss.37/41 can be found in *R. v Nelson* [2020] EWCA

Crim 1615; [2021] M.H.L.R. 219 at paras 31 to 39 and in *R. v Nash* [2022] EWCA Crim 67, at paras 15 to 18. Also see *R. v Walker* [2023] EWCA Crim 548 which is noted under s.45A.

The finding in *R. v Birch*, above, that a custodial term could be imposed on a mentally disordered defendant where a hospital order was not found to be the most suitable method of disposing of the case, was approved by the House of Lords in *R. v Drew* [2003] UKHL 25; [2003] M.H.L.R. 282 where it was held that under both national law and the jurisprudence of the European Court of Human Rights a sentence of imprisonment could be passed on a mentally disordered defendant who was criminally responsible and fit to be tried.

The commencement date of a hospital order is the date when the order was made by the court, not the date of the patient's admission to the hospital: see the note to s.40(4). A court may request information about the availability of hospital places under s.39. The offender can be admitted to a hospital which is not situated in the locality where he is normally resident (*R. v Marsden (Practice Note)* [1968] 1 W.L.R. 785).

The hospital order will cease to have effect if the offender is not admitted to the hospital named in the order within 28 days of the making of the order: see *R. (on the application of DB) v Nottinghamshire Healthcare NHS Trust*, noted under subs.(4).

In *R. v Galfetti* [2002] EWCA Crim 1916; [2002] M.H.L.R. 418, the sentencing of a mentally disordered offender had been subject to repeated adjournments whilst attempts were made to secure a hospital bed for him. A hospital order was eventually made nine months after conviction. May L.J. giving the judgment of the court said at para.51:

"Whenever a hospital place is not available within a reasonable time for an offender for whom a hospital order is the appropriate disposal, the court is disabled from affording justice in the way which Parliament has provided".

His Lordship identified, at para.52, the following possibilities which are available to the sentencing court in these circumstances, none of which is "wholly satisfactory":

1. The judge can and should make every effort to persuade the hospital authorities to find a suitable place.
2. There may come a time in an individual case when, by reason of delay, a sentence other than a hospital order should be considered. However, it could scarcely ever be satisfactory, if a court is constrained to pass a different sentence simply because an appropriate hospital place is not available.
3. The court will take delay into account in deciding the eventual disposal. His Lordship said at para.48: "[I]n so far as it is necessary to characterise the process as providing a remedy under Article 6(1) [of the European Convention on Human Rights], it lies in taking the delay and its consequences into account in determining the disposal".

His Lordship said, at para.53, that the court would "draw attention in appropriate quarters to our profound disquiet" at the situation that it had encountered and to "the possible lacuna which this case illustrates, that there may be no route by which a defendant convicted in the Crown Court can appeal an order adjourning his sentence".

The court cannot defer sentence on the basis of the offender undertaking to undergo treatment at a psychiatric hospital (*R. v Skelton* [1983] Crim.L.R. 686).

The Court of Appeal has said that where a court is considering making a hospital order the defendant should, except in the rarest circumstances, be represented by counsel (*R. v Blackwood* (1974) 59 Cr. App. R. 170).

The court can make a hospital order in the case of an offender who is subject to an interim hospital order made under s.38, without his being brought before the court (s.38(2)).

Where the Crown Court makes a hospital order, it may also make an order under s.41, restricting the discharge of the offender from hospital, if it considers that it is necessary for the protection of the public from serious harm so to do.

Health Bodies and local social services authorities have a duty to provide after-care services for hospital order patients who cease to be liable to be detained and leave hospital (s.117).

Malingering

1-550 In their article "Malingered Mental Health: Legal Review and Clinical Challenges in English and Welsh Law" (*International Journal of Mental Health and Capacity Law* No.28 (2021) at p.39), Peter Beazley and Charlotte Emmett say:

"As noted earlier, one of the most obvious 'external incentives' for malingering might be to gain a

Hospital Order disposal instead of a custodial sentence. The ability to gain a Hospital Order, has, however, been reduced somewhat by the judgment in *R v Vowles* which has required clinicians and judges to take a more rigorous approach to assessing the links between the mental disorder and offending behaviour."

Applications to the First-tier Tribunal (Mental Health) or the Mental Health Review Tribunal for Wales

Either the patient or the patient's nearest relative can apply to a tribunal in the period between six **1-551** and 12 months after the making of the hospital order and in any subsequent period of one year (ss.66(1)(f), (2)(f), 40(4), 69(1)(a), Sch.1 Pt 1 paras 2, 6, 9). References to the tribunal are governed by s.68. The lack of a right to make an application during the first six months of the patient's detention does not violate art.5(4) of the European Convention on Human Rights (*De Wilde, Ooms and Versyp* (1971) E.H.R.R. 373, para.76).

Named hospital units

If a hospital order is made together with a restriction order made under s.41, the court has the power **1-552** to order that the patient be admitted to and detained in a named hospital unit: see the note to s.41 under this heading.

Guardianship orders

Little use has been made of guardianship orders by the courts even though, in the view of the Butler **1-553** Committee, they "offer a useful form of control of some mentally disordered offenders who do not require hospital treatment [and are] particularly suited to the needs of offenders [with learning disabilities] including those inadequate offenders who require help in managing their affairs" (para.15.8).

Paragraph 8(iv)(c) of Home Office Circular No.66/90 states:

"[T]he purpose of guardianship is primarily to ensure that the offender receives care and protection rather than medical treatment, although the guardian does have powers to require the offender to attend for medical treatment. The effect of a guardianship order is to give the guardian power to require the offender to live at a specific place (this may be used to discourage the offender from sleeping rough or living with people who may exploit or mistreat him, or ensure that he resides at a particular hostel), to attend specific places at specified times for medical treatment, occupation, education, or training, and to require access to the offender to be given at the place where the offender is living to any doctor, approved [mental health professional], or other person specified by the guardian. This power could be used, for example, to ensure the offender did not neglect himself."

The effect of a guardianship order made by a court is similar to that of civil guardianship, except that the patient's nearest relative has no power of discharge (s.40(2) (4), Sch.1 Pt I paras 2, 8).

The offender must be over the age of 16 at the time when the order is made (subs.(2)(a) (ii)) and the guardian must be willing to receive the offender into guardianship (subs.(6)). Section 39A can be used to ascertain the attitude of a potential guardian. The powers of the guardian and the effect of the guardianship order are set out in s.40. Section 18(7) provides a power to convey the offender to the place where he is required to reside under the order. There is no provision for returning the offender to court on any subsequent failure by the offender to comply with the provisions of the guardianship order.

The first day of the patient's guardianship is the date of the order (s.40(4)).

A guardianship order made under this section should not be confused with a guardianship order made under the Guardianship (Missing Persons) Act 2017 which provides for an application to be made to a court to appoint a guardian in respect of some or all of a missing person's property and financial affairs.

Applications to the First-tier Tribunal (Mental Health) or the Mental Health Review Tribunal for Wales

A patient who has been made subject to a guardianship order can apply to a tribunal within the first **1-554** six months of the order (s.69(1)(b)), and during each renewal period (ss.66(1)(f), 2(f), 40(4), Sch.1 Pt 1 paras 2, 6, 9). The patient's nearest relative can apply within the first 12 months of the order and in any subsequent 12-month period (s.69(1)(b)(ii)).

Period spent subject to a hospital order made under the Criminal Procedure (Insanity) Act 1964 counting toward a sentence

1-555   In *R. v Rooney* [2020] EWCA Crim 1132, at paras 23 and 25, the Court of Appeal held that the provisions in ss.240A, 240ZA, 241 and 242 of the Criminal Justice Act 2003 make no provision for any period as a consequence of a hospital order under this section, with or without a restriction order, automatically to count towards a sentence in a way that a remand in custody, or a remand, admission or removal to a hospital under ss.35, 36, 38 or 48 of the Act would.

Appeals

1-556   A hospital order is a form of sentence and is therefore appealable to the Court of Appeal (Criminal Appeal Act 1968 ss.9(1), 50(1)). Section 11(3) of the 1968 Act provides that the Court of Appeal can quash a sentence if they consider that the appellant should be sentenced differently for an offence for which he was dealt with by the court below and in place of it pass such sentence or make such order as the court below had power to pass or make when dealing with him for the offence. The subsection "is sufficiently wide to permit the court to re-sentence the appellant on information placed before it which was not put before the sentencing judge ... Such an approach clearly allows the Court of Appeal to substitute a sentence on the basis of psychiatric and other evidence coming to light after the sentence was passed" (*R. v Beatty* [2006] EWCA Crim 2359; [2006] M.H.L.R. 333 para.51). In *R. v Crerand* [2022] EWCA Crim 962, at para.34, Cutts J. said:

> "[I]f the mental disorder is treatable, once treated there is no evidence he would be in any way dangerous and the offending is entirely due to that mental disorder, a hospital order under s.37 /41 is likely to be the correct disposal."

In *R. v Miller* [2021] EWCA Crim 1955, Holroyde L.J, on quashing a sentence of life imprisonment and replacing it with a hospital and restriction orders, noted that the "Parole Board would not be able to impose a requirement of compliance with medication, which is the key to risk management."

An appeal will not be allowed where the real purpose of the appeal "was to move the appellant from the release regime consequent upon a life sentence to the regime consequent on a hospital order. That is not a proper basis for an appeal if the original sentence was not wrong in principle. There are some, relatively few, cases where medical evidence obtained years after sentence convincingly demonstrates that the sentencing court proceeded on the wrong basis because of an error by an expert—see e.g. *R v Ahmed* [2016] EWCA Crim 670. On analysis that is not this case. The sentence was not wrong in principle" (*R. v Bala* [2017] EWCA Crim 1460; [2017] M.H.L.R. 375 per Thirwall L.J. at para.47).

A hospital order can be substituted for a custodial sentence even if the medical criteria for the making of such an order were met at the time of the sentence: see *R. v O* [2011] EWCA Crim 376; [2011] M.H.L.R. 106, where the substitution was made 13 years after sentencing when a hospital bed was not available for the offender. Also see *R. v Hempston* [2006] EWCA Crim 2869; [2011] M.H.L.R. 99, where the substitution was made 28 years after sentence on the ground that the medical evidence received by the Court of Appeal confirmed that the appellant's mental disorder had reduced his culpability for his crimes to the extent that a hospital order with restrictions was the appropriate disposal.

If the Court of Appeal substitutes a custodial sentence with a hospital order, the order will usually run from the day it is made, although it is possible for the court to backdate it: see s.29(4) of the 1968 Act.

The power of the court under s.11 of the 1968 Act must not be exercised in such a way so that an appellant is more severely dealt with on appeal than she was dealt with in the court below: see s.11(3) and *R. v Thompson* [2018] EWCA Crim 639 where the Court of Appeal reviewed the case law on s.11(3). A hospital order cannot be regarded as more severe than a sentence of imprisonment, even though it may involve detention for a longer period of time (*R. v Bennett* (1968) 52 Cr. App. R. 514), or if the term of imprisonment imposed by the sentencing court is about to expire (*R. v Searles* [2012] EWCA Crim 2685). In *R. v Lavender* [2012] EWCA Crim 1179, para.10, the court said that the cases of "*Bennett* 52 Cr.App.R 514 and ... *Crozier* [1990] 12 Cr.App.R (S) 206, [make] it clear that where the assistance and help for the future which is the purpose of a hospital order replaces punishment, such disposal is not to be considered punitive albeit that, when analysed in terms of its potential for detention, it could be so regarded".

Fresh psychiatric evidence can be received by the court under s.23 of the Criminal Appeal Act 1968. The written reasons given by a Mental Health Tribunal for its decision are not evidence of the kind contemplated by s.23 (*R. v Miller* [2021] EWCA Crim 1955). The general principles relating to the application of s.23 were considered by the Court of Appeal in *R. v Rogers* [2016] EWCA Crim 801. In *R.*

v Fort [2013] EWCA Crim 2332; [2014] M.H.L.R. 334 at paras 66 and 67, Aikens L.J. said:

"In the context of conviction appeals, this court has emphasised that fresh expert evidence, (which in many cases concerns the mental state of the appellant) will not automatically be received by the court pursuant to section 23 ...: see *R v Erskine; R v Williams* [2010] 1 WLR 183. Reception will depend on the facts and circumstances of the particular case. Whilst the court must have regard to the matters set out in section 23(2), ultimately the test is the broad one set out in section 23(1), viz. whether this court thinks it 'necessary or expedient in the interests of justice' to receive the proposed 'fresh' evidence.

Similar flexibility must be appropriate on sentence appeals which concern the mental state of the appellant at the time of the original sentence. Thus we note that in *R v Charles de Silva* (1994) 15 Cr App R(S) 296, this court received fresh medical evidence on the mental condition of the appellant. It was argued, successfully, that the fresh evidence demonstrated conclusively that the previous medical view that there was no connection between the appellant's mental illness and his offence, was wrong."

In *R. v O* [2011] EWCA Crim 376, the court observed:

"Any case involving as it does reliance on evidence of mental condition not adduced at the time of the original court appearances must require the most careful scrutiny".

In *R. v Cleland* [2020] EWCA 906, para.48, the court confirmed that:

"... following the admission of fresh evidence as to the offender's mental health at the time of sentence, the court has the power to substitute the sentence which it considers is (and, as the evidence now shows, always was) appropriate."

The court went on to say at para.49, that if fresh evidence shows the offender's mental state at the time of sentence:

"... was otherwise than the judge believed it to be, the court has power to quash the original sentence if it considers that the appellant 'should be sentenced differently', and to impose such sentence as it considers appropriate."

Fresh medical evidence should not be admitted where such evidence is concerned with the applicant's present condition, not her condition at the time of sentence, and does not seek to suggest that the opinions expressed by the psychiatrists at the time of sentencing were wrong (*R. v Yusuf* [2013] EWCA Crim 2077; [2014] M.H.L.R. 288).

If fresh medical evidence supports the contention that a hospital order should have been made in respect of an offender who was sentenced to a term of imprisonment, the nature of the Court of Appeal's powers under the Act are statutorily circumscribed and, in particular, a hospital order cannot be made if there is no bed available for the offender or if the offender does not then suffer from a mental disorder of a nature or degree which makes it appropriate for him to be detained in hospital (*R. v Lomey* [2004] EWCA Crim 3014; [2004] M.H.L.R. 316).

The Court of Appeal has allowed appeals against the imposition of restriction orders because it differed with the trial judge's assessment on the question of the risk of future harm: see, for example, *R. v Goucher* [2012] M.H.L.R. 107. The court has also allowed such appeals because of the progress that the patient had made at the psychiatric hospital since the trial; see, for, example, *R. v Daniels* [2014] EWCA Crim 2009; [2015] M.H.L.R. 91. However, the court has not been consistent in its approach. In *R. v Shah* [2011] EWCA Crim 2333; [2012] M.H.L.R 92 at para.12, the court said that such action will only be taken in "exceptional cases". And in *R. v Ruby* [2013] EWCA Crim 1653; [2014] M.H.L.R. 205 at para.37, Pitchford L.J. said:

"We make it plain that this court will not interfere with a sentence that was appropriate at the time it was imposed merely because the offender has made progress during his service of that sentence. We may only interfere if the sentence was unlawful, wrong in principle or manifestly excessive."

In *R. v Griffith* [2002] EWCA Crim 1838; [2002] M.H.L.R. 427, the Court of Appeal said that a submission that a medical report made subsequent to the trial indicated that the restriction order was no longer necessary would be best directed at the tribunal who would review the appellant's case and should not be the subject of a decision by the court. In this context, it should be noted that s.73 does not provide the tribunal with a power to change a patient's status from a restricted to a non-restricted patient. The Secretary of State has such a power under s.42(1).

It is fundamental to the trial process that a defendant must advance all aspects of his case at trial and a court will not admit fresh evidence to enable a defendant to run a different case if that case could have been run first time round (*R. v Ahluwalia* (1993) 96 Cr. App. R. 133).

Defective Court Orders

1-557   See the General Note to this Part.

Orders made in other proceedings

1-558   In certain circumstances, a hospital order or a guardianship order can be made under the Contempt of Court Act 1981 s.14(4),(4A), the Family Law Act 1996 s.51 and the Armed Forces Act 2006 s.169 and Sch.4 para.1. A restriction order can also be made under the 2006 Act: see Sch.4 para.2. It is also possible for such orders to be made under the terms of the Colonial Prisoners Removal Act 1884 and the Repatriation of Prisoners Act 1984.

Transport to and from court

1-559   See the General Note to s.35 under this heading.

Domestic Violence, Crime and Victims Act 2004

1-560   The 2004 Act, which is considered in Ch.40 of the *Code of Practice*, applies to patients who have been made subject to unrestricted hospital orders (s.36(3)), although no conditions can be placed on the patient on his discharge, apart from conditions attached to a CTO (s.36(5)).

The Ministry of Justice has published "Duties to victims under the Domestic Violence, Crime and Victims Act 2004: Guidance for Clinicians" which can be accessed at: *https:// assets.publishing.service.gov.uk/government/uploads/system/uploads/attachment_data/file/614535/ guidance-dvcv-act.pdf.*

Human Rights Act 1998

1-561   If an offender satisfies the criteria for a hospital order set out in subs.(2) but is not made the subject of such an order because of an inability to identify a hospital that would be willing to accept him (see subs.(4)), he could claim that his rights under art.5(1) of the European Convention on Human Rights (ECHR) had been breached if he was subsequently incarcerated in a non-therapeutic environment to the detriment of his mental health (*Aerts v Belgium* (2000) 29 E.H.R.R. 50; also see *Drew v United Kingdom* (2006) 43 E.H.R.R. SE2; [2006] M.H.L.R. 203, para.40).

In *Brand v Netherlands* [2001] M.H.L.R. 275, the European Court of Human Rights declared inadmissible an application that a lengthy detention of a mentally disordered person in prison pending a place being found in a secure psychiatric institution constituted a breach of art.3 of the ECHR on the ground that there was no evidence that the applicant's mental health or the possibilities of treatment had suffered on account of the time spent in prison. In *Drew v United Kingdom*, above, para.43, the Court said it did not consider that "the detention of the applicant on a prison medical wing for eight days without access to effective medication [for his mental disorder] reached the threshold of art.3".

Determining whether the accused "did the act or made the omission charged" for the purposes of subs.(3) is not a criminal trial and the accused's rights under art.6 of the ECHR are not engaged (*Director of Public Prosecutions v P* [2007] EWHC 946 (Admin); [2007] 4 All E.R. 628, paras 55, 61).

Also see note on s.3 under this heading.

Subsection (1)

1-562   **Convicted**   Under s.51(5) (6) the court can make a hospital order (with or without a restriction order) in respect of a mentally disordered transfer direction patient in his absence and, if he is awaiting trial, without convicting him.

Fixed by law   This section does not apply to persons who have been convicted of murder who must be sentenced to life imprisonment (Murder (Abolition of Death Penalty) Act 1965 s.1(1)).

Magistrates' court   Although a magistrates' court does not have the power to attach a restriction order under s.41 to a hospital order made under this section, it may, instead of making a hospital order or other disposition, commit him to the Crown Court for sentencing under s.43 with a view to a hospital order with restrictions being made.

Offence punishable on summary conviction with imprisonment   For young offenders, see s.55(2).

Hospital   Or a registered establishment (ss.34(2), 55(5)).

Subsections (1A), 1(B)   These subsections, which were brought into force on April 4, 2005, do not apply to pre-commencement offences. Their effect is that the mandatory sentencing requirements contained in the provisions listed in paras (a) to (d) of subs.(1A) do not prevent the court from making a hospital order under subs.(1).   **1-563**

Subsection (2)   The fact that the conditions in this subsection are satisfied does not compel the making of a hospital order or indeed give rise to a presumption that one will be made: see *R. v Vowles* [2015] EWCA Crim 45; [2016] M.H.L.R. 66.   **1-564**

Paragraph (a)   This provision does not contain criteria equivalent to those contained in s.3(2)(c).   **1-565**

Evidence   For general requirements as to medical evidence, see s.54. The court can call a doctor who has provided a written report to give oral evidence (s.54(2A)). The doctors should prepare an up-to-date assessment of a defendant so that the court may be satisfied as to his current mental condition at the time of sentencing, and as to his susceptibility to treatment at the time of sentencing (*R. v Preston* [2003] EWCA Crim 2086 para.6). When preparing their evidence from sources, doctors are not bound by the rules of evidence. They have to look at the whole picture. But they have to exercise judgment over material which is of first, second or even third hand hearsay as to the weight that can be attached to it (*Kiernan v Harrow Crown Court*, below, para.28).

Where there are significant differences in the evidence of the doctors giving evidence to the court, the judge should explain in his sentencing remarks why he accepted one set of evidence and rejected the other (*Kiernan v Harrow Crown Court* [2003] EWCA Crim 1052 para.19). During the course of his judgment, Scott Baker J. said, at para.25, that he could see no reason in ordinary circumstances why it would be appropriate for a doctor who was to give evidence "to begin making his own investigations by contacting the victim, or someone else in a similar situation, for his own account of events, especially if, as happened in this case, it was not possible for the applicant to give him the other side of the story".

In *R. v Tudor* [2012] EWCA Crim 1507 the Court of Appeal held that it would be rare for a judge to be found to have acted wrongly in principle in refusing to adjourn to allow the preparation of a second medical report as to whether to impose a hospital order when a full and thorough report had concluded that such a disposal was not appropriate. An example of such a course being adopted is "where the reporting expert had been provided with patently wrong or incomplete information upon which an otherwise conclusive opinion had been based" (para.15). The court agreed with counsel's concession that shopping around for a favourable medical report, particularly at public expense, is a practice which is not to be encouraged. Also note that in *R. v Ahmed* [2012] EWCA Crim 99, para.33, Elias L.J. said if "a judge has made a determination not to make a hospital order when he was empowered to do so, it plainly is not legitimate for an appellant to obtain two further reports from two further expert medical witnesses and to seek to rely on those to secure a change in the sentencing outcome".

In *R. v Crozier* (1990–91) 12 Cr. App. R.(S.) 206, the Court of Appeal applied *W v Egdell* [1990] 1 All E.R. 835 CA (noted under s.76) by holding that, given the particular circumstances of the case, a psychiatrist who had prepared a medical report for the defence had acted responsibly and reasonably when he handed a copy of his report to counsel for the prosecution. This was a case where the strong public interest in the disclosure of the psychiatrist's opinion overrode his duty of confidence to his client. The psychiatrist was "firmly of the view that the appellant suffers from psychopathic disorder, continues to be a danger to the public and should be kept in a secure hospital without limit of time. He held this opinion so strongly that he felt impelled to ensure that the court became aware of it" (per Watkins L.J. at 213).

Two registered medical practitioners   One of whom must be approved by the Secretary of State or the Welsh Ministers under s.12, or by another person by virtue of s.12ZA or 12ZB (s.54(1)). A registered medical practitioner means "a fully registered person within the meaning of the Medical Act 1983 who holds a licence to practise under that Act" (Interpretation Act 1978, Sch.1).

Unlike the situation that obtains when applications are made under Pt II, this section does not place any constraints on the timing of the medical examinations of the offender. As the doctors are providing evidence to the court, not medical recommendations, the Mental Health (Conflict of Interest) (England) Regulations 2008 do not apply. This means, inter alia, that both doctors could be on the staff of the admitting hospital and could have a financial interest in the matter.

The Court of Appeal has advised that the trial judge should hear evidence from the doctor who will be treating the offender (*R. v Blackwood* (1974) 59 Cr. App. R. 170).

Suffering from The Court of Appeal has said that the offender's mental condition could have developed since the date of the offence (*R. v Smith* [2001] EWCA Crim 743; [2001] M.H.L.R. 146).

Mental disorder If the person has a learning disability, the disability must be associated with abnormally aggressive or seriously irresponsible conduct (s.1(2A), (2B)). A learning disabled person might also suffer from another form of mental disorder.

Nature or degree The meaning of this phrase is considered in the note on s.3(2)(a).

Appropriate medical treatment See the note on s.3(2)(d).

Attained the age At the commencement of his sixteenth birthday (Family Law Reform Act 1969 s.9(1)). Also see s.55(7).

Warrants his reception into guardianship Compare with the criteria set out in s.7(2) for guardianship applications made under Pt II.

Paragraph (b)

1-566 *Nature of the offence* "Although hospital orders are frequently made in cases involving grave offences of violence, the gravity of the offences is not an important consideration in making a hospital order (except in so far as it indicates a need for detention in secure conditions). Hospital orders have been upheld or imposed on appeal on offenders whose offences would not have justified a substantial term of imprisonment" (D.A. Thomas, *Principles of Sentencing* (2nd edn, 1979) p.299).

Most suitable method of disposing of the case Note subs.(8) and *R. v Vowles*, which is considered above. In *R. v Birch* (1989) 11 Cr. App. R(S.) 202 at 215, the Court of Appeal pointed out that prison might be chosen as an alternative to hospital either because the offender was dangerous and no suitable secure hospital accommodation was available or because there was an element of culpability in the offence which merited punishment, as might happen where there was no connection between the mental disorder and the offence or where the offender's responsibility for the offence was reduced but not wholly extinguished. As was pointed out in *R. v Drew* [2003] UKHL 25; [2003] 4 All E.R. 557 at para.17, there is no divergence in this respect between national law and Strasbourg jurisprudence. In *X v United Kingdom* (App.No.5229/71, October 5, 1972) the European Commission on Human Rights rejected as manifestly inadmissible a complaint by a mentally disordered defendant that he should be held in a psychiatric hospital and not in prison.

1-567 **Subsection (3)** This provision, which empowers a magistrates' court (including a youth court: see *R. (on the application of P (a minor)) v Barking Youth Court* [2002] EWHC 734 (Admin); [2002] M.H.L.R. 304) to make a hospital or guardianship order without proceeding to conviction where the defendant is suffering from mental disorder, applies only where the court, having heard the evidence required by subs.(4), is satisfied that the defendant did the act or made the omission charged. It does not apply to non-imprisonable offences. Magistrates do not have the power to commit the defendant to the Crown Court for a restriction order to be considered where they proceed under this provision. The Butler Committee said at para.10.34: "In trivial cases the magistrates may properly have recourse to the expedient of adjourning the proceedings sine die or of simply not proceeding". Section 11 of the Powers of Criminal Courts (Sentencing) Act 2000 (remand by magistrates' court for medical examination) can apply where a magistrates' court is considering whether to make an order under this provision.

An order under this provision can be made even though the court has not proceeded to trial. It can therefore be made in cases where the defendant is unable by virtue of his mental disorder to give his consent as to the mode of trial. In *R. v Lincolnshire (Kesteven) Justices Ex p. O'Connor* [1983] 1 W.L.R. 335 DC, the accused's mental disorder was such that he was unable to understand what it meant to consent to summary trial. The magistrates decided that as they were unable to try the case, it followed that they had no power to make a hospital order under this provision. The Divisional Court held that the magistrates could have made a hospital order without holding a trial. Lord Lane C.J. said at 338:

"In our judgment the words of [s.37(3)] are clear. It gives the justices power in an appropriate case to make a hospital order without convicting the accused. No trial is therefore called for. The circumstances in which it will be appropriate to exercise this unusual power are bound to be very rare and will usually require ... the consent of those acting for the accused if he is under a disability so that he cannot be tried."

O'Connor was considered by the Divisional Court in *R. v Ramsgate Justices Ex p. Kazmarek* (1985) 80 Cr.App.R. 366 and in *R. v Chippenham Magistrates' Court Ex p. Thompson* (1996) 32 B.M.L.R. 69. In *Kazmarek* it was held that in the case of an offence triable either summarily or on indictment where the accused elects trial by jury, this subsection can apply because the magistrates "would have power, on convicting him of that offence" to make a hospital order. *Kazmarek* was distinguished in *Thompson* where the court held that this subsection cannot apply in the case of an offence triable *only* on indictment in the Crown Court because in such a case the magistrates could not convict the offender of that offence.

In *R. (on the application of Singh) v Stratford Magistrates' Court* [2007] EWHC 1582 (Admin); [2007] 4 All E.R. 407, the Divisional Court was concerned with the meaning and ambit of this provision when an accused in the magistrates' court contends that he is insane at the time of the events charged. It was held that:

1. Insanity can be relied upon as a common law defence to a summary charge in the magistrates' court. If established by the accused in a case to which it is relevant, it prevents conviction.
2. The accused has no right to a trial on the issue of insanity. The magistrates can either:
    (a) try the issue of insanity and pronounce its conclusions upon it, without convicting or acquitting the accused, provided that the conditions for making a hospital or guardianship order under this provision are met; or
    (b) if satisfied that there is no purpose in resolving the issue of insanity, and if an order under this provision is going to be made, the court can deal with the case without trying that issue.

    If it is clear that no order under this provision is going to be possible on the medical evidence, then in the absence of some other compelling factor the case must proceed to trial, so that if the accused was insane, he is acquitted, and if he was not, he is convicted.
3. Before embarking on a case to which this provision may be applied, magistrates should make it clear that it is a possibility and should invite submissions upon the course to be adopted. In particular, careful consideration must be given to any reason advanced why the issue of insanity should be tried. Such an application should be resolved having regard to the interests of justice, which include, but are not limited to, the justice of the accused.

In the *Barking* case, above, the court said that the procedure for determining whether a person is fit to plead in the magistrates' court is specifically provided for by this provision when read in conjunction with s.11(1) of the Powers of Criminal Courts (Sentencing) Act 2000. Section 11(1) reads as follows:

"(1) If, on the trial by a magistrates' court of an offence punishable on summary conviction with imprisonment, the court—
    (a) is satisfied that the accused did the act or made the omission charged, but
    (b) is of the opinion that an inquiry ought to be made into his physical or mental condition before the method of dealing with him is determined,
the court shall adjourn the case to enable a medical examination and report to be made, and shall remand him."

Further guidance was given by Goldring L.J. in *R. (on the application of Blouet) v Bath and Wansdyke Magistrates' Court* [2009] EWHC 759 (Admin); [2009] M.H.L.R. 71, at para.9:

"The approach which the district judge should follow is this. First, there should be up-to-date—and I emphasise the words 'up-to-date'—medical evidence before him. If there is a possibility of a s37(3) order being made, he will then try the issue in accordance with s11(1) of the Act. If thereafter there arises the obligation to adjourn for further reports then that is what must happen. It may of course be that – given the up-to-date reports which he will then have – only a very short adjournment will be needed or, if everyone agrees that in the circumstances it is not, the matter can proceed under s37(3) if that be appropriate."

In *Crown Prosecution Service v P* [2007] EWHC 946 (Admin); [2007] 4 All E.R. 628, Smith L.J. said, at para.16, that s.11(1) of the 2000 Act and this provision "do not provide the solution to all of the problems which may confront a youth court before which a young person of doubtful capacity appears".

The court held that:

1. Before criminal proceedings are commenced, appropriate consideration should be given to the question of whether civil proceedings under the Children Act are more appropriate.
2. If, in criminal proceedings, the defence raises an issue relating to the capacity of the young person before any evidence is heard, the court should use its inherent jurisdiction to order the stay of the proceedings if it appears that the person charged cannot, by reason of incapacity, have a fair trial in only exceptional cases.
3. In most cases, the medical evidence concerning capacity should be considered as part of the evidence in the case and not as the sole evidence in a freestanding application.
4. The court has a duty to keep under continuing review the question of whether the criminal trial ought to continue. If at any stage the court concludes that the child is unable to participate effectively in the trial, it may decide to call a halt. If the trial is halted on this ground, the court should then consider whether to switch to a consideration of whether the young person has done the acts alleged (the fact finding process), under the procedure referred to in the *Barking* case.
5. The fact that the young person cannot take an effective part in the fact finding process does not infringe his rights under art.6 of the ECHR.

Smith L.J. said at para.56:

"The decision as to whether or not to switch to fact finding is one for the discretion of the court. The court will wish to consider the possibility that (either on the basis of existing medical evidence or further medical evidence) it might be appropriate to make a hospital order. If that possibility exists, the court should usually find on the facts. But even if a hospital order seems unlikely, there may be other advantages in continuing to complete the fact-finding process. If the court finds that the child did the acts alleged, it may be appropriate to alert the local authority to the position with a view to consideration of care proceedings. Although the youth court's findings may not be binding in the context of care proceedings, the fact that those findings have been made might result in the simplification of care proceedings. I consider that proceedings should be stayed as an abuse of process before fact-finding only if no useful purpose at all could be served by the finding of facts."

Did the act or made the omission charged   In *Singh*, above, Hughes L.J. said at para.33:

"[In] all cases where an order under s.37(3) is a possibility, the court should first determine the fact-finding exercise. That may be concluded, as here, on admissions, or it may involve hearing evidence. If the court is not satisfied that the act/omission was done/made, an unqualified acquittal must follow, whatever the anxieties may be about the accused's state of health."

This fact-finding exercise is not a criminal trial (*Director of Public Prosecution v P*, above). In determining the issue, the prosecution is only required to prove the ingredients which comprise the actus reus of the offence, not the mens rea (*R. v Antoine* [2000] 2 All E.R. 208 HL).

Without convicting him   The person has the same right of appeal against the order as if it had been made on his conviction (s.45). Although a person dealt with under this provision is not convicted, the order is a "conviction" for the purposes of the Rehabilitation of Offenders Act 1974 s.1(4), because it includes a finding that the person did the act or made the omission charged. A criminal records entry will therefore be made.

A person who is made subject to a hospital order under this provision is an "offender" for the purposes of s.142 of the Magistrates' Courts Act 1980. Under s.142: "A magistrates' court may vary or rescind ... [an] order ... made by it when dealing with an offender ..." There were sound practical reasons for treating a defendant, made subject to a hospital order, as an offender for the purposes of s.142. If having made a hospital order the magistrates discovered information which suggested that the defendant might not suffer from mental disorder, or might not have done the acts complained of, or, as in the present case, that arrangements could not in fact be made for his admission to hospital, it was highly desirable that there should be a procedural means by which the magistrates could rectify the error (*R. v Thames Magistrates' Court Ex p. Ramadan* [1999] 1 Cr. App. R. 386). *Ramadan* was applied in *Bartram v Southend Magistrates' Court* [2004] EWHC 2691 (QB); [2004] M.H.L.R. 319, para.19, where Collins J. said that:

"there might be a case where it would be in the interests of the accused to have the matter reopened because whilst he was unable to give instructions and was unfit to plead, the evidence which established that he had done the act could not be challenged. When his mental state recovered sufficiently to enable him to give proper instructions, it might be that it became apparent that he did indeed have a defence to the charge which was laid against him. Thus in such a case he might want the charge to be tried because he expected that he would be acquitted of it".

Subsection (4)

In *R. (on the application of DB) v Nottinghamshire Healthcare NHS Trust* [2008] EWCA Civ 1354; **1-568** [2009] M.H.L.R. 376, the Court of Appeal held that a hospital order, including a hospital order which is made subject to the restrictions contained in s.41, ceases to have effect if the offender who is the subject of the order is not admitted to the hospital named in the order within the period of 28 days from the date of the making of the order. It follows that after the 28 days have expired there is no authority either to convey the offender to the hospital or to detain him there. In this situation, "no doubt consideration can rapidly be given to the question whether the defendant can be compulsorily admitted to a hospital pursuant to Pt II of the Act rather than Pt III"; per Stanley Burnton L.J. at para.30. His Lordship said at paras 25, 26:

"It would I think be preferable for the standard form of order to specify the date when the 28 day period expires. In addition, it would be sensible for orders made under section 37 to include a direction or recommendation (for it has no statutory force) on the lines of that set out in [Circular 66/1980]. All parties should bear in mind the power of the sentencing court under [section 385 of the Sentencing Act 2020] to vary or, if necessary, to rescind an order. If an order is rescinded, a hospital order may be made subsequently; but the court should consider rescission of an order as a last resort, since the consequence will usually be to prolong a patient's detention in prison.

In the present case the orders made by the Crown Court did not make provision for the detention of the Appellant pending his transfer to hospital: the direction 'that pending admission to a hospital within the 28 day period, the defendant should be conveyed to and detained in a place of safety, namely …' had been, in each case, deleted. The result was that there was no lawful authority for his detention during that period. The exercise by the sentencing court of the power conferred on by the last part of section 37(4) to direct conveyance to and detention in a place of safety pending admission to hospital is not automatic or mandatory. Unless the offender is to be immediately conveyed from the court to the hospital, the court must ensure that the power is expressly exercised."

In *R. v Ellerton* [2022] EWCA Crim 194 the Crown Court had made a hospital order without regard to the express provision of this subsection. Macur L.J. said:

"16. The case was re-listed before the judge in the Crown Court on 23 March 2021. The judge refused to intervene, considering that the time limit of 28 days specified in section 155(1) of the Powers of Criminal Courts (Sentencing) Act 2000 as amended, precluded him from varying the sentence under the so called 'slip rule.' He indicated that the case should instead be referred to this Court, or the Divisional Court.

17. Whilst we did not hear argument on the point, we are satisfied that what should have been made clear to the judge was that this was a request to vary the form and not substance of the sentence, which is permissible outside the time limits. (See *Saville* (1980) 2 Cr.App.R.(S), 26 and *Norman* [2006] EWCA Crim 1792. That is, although the judge could not have rescinded the invalid sentence and sentenced afresh, he was still in a position to regularise the sentence by requesting information from the regional health authority with respect to hospitals at which arrangements could be made for the admission of the offender; see section 39(1) of the Act."

This subsection applies both to orders made following conviction under subs.(1) and to orders made under subs.(3) (*R. v Thames Magistrates' Court Ex p. Ramadan*, above).

Approved clinician   Who could be one of the doctors giving evidence under subs. (2)(a). "Where evidence is given that a bed will be made available within that timescale, the hospital managers must ensure that the commitment is met" ("Mental Health Act 2007: Guidance for the courts on remand and sentencing powers for mentally disordered offenders", Ministry of Justice, March 2008, para.4.20). But see subs.(5).

Some other person   Who need not be a clinician.

28 days   Any time that the patient is unlawfully at large is disregarded when calculating this period (s.138(5)). The Secretary of State has been given the power to reduce this period under s.54A. In Wales, this power is exercised by the Welsh Ministers (see the General Note to the Act).

Beginning with   Including the date of the making of the order (*Zoan v Rouamba* [2000] 2 All E.R. 620 CA).

Conveyance ... and detention   See the General Note to s.35 under the heading Transport to and from court. General provisions relating to conveyance and detention are set out in s.137.

Place of safety   Is defined in s.55(1). There are no provisions for discharge or leave of absence from a place of safety. If a patient escapes from a place of safety, s.138 allows for him or her to be retaken. This power is subject to the time limits set out in s.18(4). A restriction order patient may be retaken at any time.

 A patient who is detained in a place of safety under this provision is not subject to the consent to treatment provisions contained in Pt IV (s.56(3)(b)). However, following the decision by the Court of Appeal in *R. v North West London Mental Health NHS Trust Ex p. Stewart* [1997] 4 All E.R. 871, it seems that a patient who has been detained in a place of safety which is a hospital could be brought within the scope of Pt IV if he was made the subject of an application under Part II: see the General Note to s.35.

Subsection (5)

1-569   "This provision is intended to meet the case of a hospital which has agreed to accept the patient being unavoidably unable to do so, e.g. because of a fire or an epidemic; but in practice it is generally easier for the patient to be returned to court for a further order to be made so as to give a further 28-day period in which a bed may become available. The Crown Court hospital order form 5034 is designed to facilitate this procedure" (Home Office Circular No. 69/1983 para.5).

 If it proves impossible to find a bed for the offender, the Crown Court has power under s.155 of the Powers of Criminal Courts (Sentencing) Act 2000 [now see s.385 of the Sentencing Act 2020] to vary or rescind the sentence: see *R. (on the application of DB) v Nottinghamshire Healthcare NHS Trust*, which is noted under subs.(4). An analogous power for magistrates' courts is contained in s.142 of the Magistrates' Courts Act 1980.

Secretary of State   Or, in relation to Wales, the Welsh Ministers (see the General Note to this Act).

28 days   See the note on subs.(4) above.

Subsection (6)

1-570   This subsection provides that the court cannot make a guardianship order without the consent of the potential guardian. The consent of the offender is not required.

 In *R. (on the application of Bukowicki) v Northamptonshire CC* [2007] EWHC 310 (Admin); [2007] M.H.L.R. 121, Mole J. held that that subs.(2)(b), read with this provision, makes it clear that that the judge's judgement about the suitability of making a guardianship order must be subordinate to the willingness of the local authority to accept the guardianship. The authority has a wide discretion as to the factors that they are able to take into account in deciding if they are willing to accept an offender into guardianship. When exercising that discretion, the authority should take into account every material consideration relevant to their ability to manage him under the order. The authority should also take into account the relevant chapter of the *Code of Practice* (Ch.30) and its own policy on guardianship.

Subsection (8)

1-571   This subsection "clearly contemplates the ability of the court to make orders over and above the hospital order itself. It specifically precludes the making of a sentence of imprisonment or a community order, or, in relation to young people, referral orders or attempts to bind over parents or guardians. But it preserves the powers of the courts to make other orders and so thought was given as to whether there were other orders that could be made which could secure the prevention of the appellant from simply leaving the jurisdiction as and when he chose to do so" (*R. v Chowdhury* [2011] EWCA Crim 936; [2011] M.H.L.R. 157, para.17). It is concerned with the powers of the court in sentencing and it has no application to transfers ordered by the Secretary of State for Justice under s.47 (*R. (on the application of Miah) v Secretary of State for the Home Department* [2004] EWHC 2569 (Admin); [2004] M.H.L.R. 302 para.23).

 Although it is lawful for a court to impose a custodial sentence and a hospital order on the same occasion but for different offences, it is a matter of obvious impracticability for a hospital order and a sentence of custody to be simultaneously carried out. A sentence of custody takes effect from the day on which it is passed, and that clearly, in practical terms, is inconsistent with the terms of the order which is that the defendant should be admitted to a psychiatric hospital forthwith (*R. v Rogerson* [2004] EWCA Crim 2099; [2006] M.H.L.R. 175).

Any other order   For example, a compensation order or an order disqualifying the offender from driving.

Interim hospital orders

38.—(1)   Where a person is convicted before the Crown Court of an offence   **1-572** punishable with imprisonment (other than an offence the sentence for which is fixed by law) or is convicted by a magistrates' court of an offence punishable on summary conviction with imprisonment and the court before or by which he is convicted is satisfied, on the written or oral evidence of two registered medical practitioners—

(a)   that the offender is suffering from [mental disorder]; and

(b)   that there is reason to suppose that the mental disorder from which the offender is suffering is such that it may be appropriate for a hospital order to be made in his case,

the court may, before making a hospital order or dealing with him in some other way, make an order (in this Act referred to as "an interim hospital order") authorising his admission to such hospital as may be specified in the order and his detention there in accordance with this section.

(2)   In the case of an offender who is subject to an interim hospital order the court may make a hospital order without his being brought before the court if he is represented by [an authorised person who] is given an opportunity of being heard.

(3)   At least one of the registered medical practitioners whose evidence is taken into account under subsection (1) above shall be employed at the hospital which is to be specified in the order.

(4)   An interim hospital order shall not be made for admission of an offender to a hospital unless the court is satisfied, on the written or oral evidence of the [approved clinician who would have overall responsibility for his case] or of some other person representing the managers of the hospital, that arrangements have been made for his admission to that hospital and for his admission to it within the period of 28 days beginning with the date of the order; and if the court is so satisfied the court may, pending his admission, give directions for his conveyance to and detention in a place of safety.

(5)   An interim hospital order—

(a)   shall be in force for such period, not exceeding 12 weeks; as the court may specify when making the order; but

(b)   may be renewed for further periods of not more than 28 days at a time if it appears to the court, on the written or oral evidence of the [responsible clinician], that the continuation of the order is warranted;

but no such order shall continue in force for more than [twelve months] in all and the court shall terminate the order if it makes a hospital order in respect of the offender or decides after considering the written or oral evidence of the [responsible clinician] to deal with the offender in some other way.

(6)   The power of renewing an interim hospital order may be exercised without the offender being brought before the court if he is represented by counsel or a solicitor and his counsel or solicitor is given an opportunity of being heard.

(7)   If an offender absconds from a hospital in which he is detained in pursu-

ance of an interim hospital order, or while being conveyed to or from such a hospital, he may be arrested without warrant by a constable and shall, after being arrested, be brought as soon as practicable before the court that made the order; and the court may thereupon terminate the order and deal with him in any way in which it could have dealt with him if no such order had been made.

Amendments

The amendments to this section were made by the Mental Health Act 2007 ss.1(4), 10(5), Sch.1 para.8, the Legal Services Act 2007 s.208, Sch.21 para.56 and the Crime (Sentences) Act 1997 s.49(1).

Definitions

1-573
mental disorder: ss.1, 145(1).
hospital: ss.55(5), 145(1).
hospital order: ss.37, 145(1).
the managers: s.145(1).
responsible clinician: s.55(1).
approved clinician: s.145)(1).
authorised person: s.55(1).
place of safety: s.55(1).

General Note

1-574
The Butler Committee "gained the impression that many doctors found it difficult to decide whether to recommend that a hospital order should be made where they have been able to examine the patient only briefly in a prison hospital under the pressure of impending court proceedings, since it was often impossible to know how he would react subsequently to the psychiatric hospital regime" (para.12.5). This section responds to this concern by empowering a Crown Court or magistrates' court to send a convicted offender to hospital for up to twelve months to enable an assessment to be made on the appropriateness of making a hospital order or direction in respect of him. An order can be made by the youth court if the offender is under 18 years of age. The court cannot make an interim hospital order in respect of an unconvicted person.

If the court makes an interim hospital order under this section, "the offender's response in hospital can be evaluated without any irrevocable commitment on either side to this method of dealing with the offender if it should prove unsuitable" (Home Office Circular No.71/1984, Annex, para.15). The purpose of the order is "not to hold the position until a place in an appropriate hospital is available for an offender for whom a hospital order is known to be appropriate" (*R. v Galfetti* [2002] EWCA Crim 1916; [2002] M.H.L.R. 418 per May L.J. at para.7).

In *R. (on the application of LS) v Brent Magistrates' Court* unreported, July 14, 2009, the court held in a permission hearing that an offender's presence in court is not required for the making of an order under this section by reason of the terms of subs.(2). Neither need the offender be present if the order is renewed (subs.(6)) or if the court makes a hospital order (subs.(2)).

In *R. v Vowles* [2015] EWCA Crim 45; [2016] M.H.L.R. 66 at paras 55 and 56, Lord Thomas CJ cautioned against the use of this section "unless there is very clear evidence that such an order is necessary":

"[A] judge should pause long and hard before making ... an interim order. Although, as was the evidence before us, there are now a number of private providers to the NHS who have facilities at which offenders who are the subject of interim orders can now be held, the making of such an order has the consequence that as regards the victim of the crime there is no closure until the final order is made, there are significant costs to the general administration of justice in bringing a case back to court and there is acute pressure on the availability of secure beds."

An offender who is placed under an interim hospital order is subject to the consent to treatment provisions contained in Pt IV (ss.40(4), 56(3)). Otherwise, the legal position of a patient subject to such an order differs markedly from that of a patient subject to a hospital order: see the note on s.40(3).

An offender who absconds when subject to an interim hospital order may be arrested without warrant by any constable and brought before the court that made the order, which may decide on an alternative way of dealing with him.

Patients who are subject to orders made under this section do not have a nearest relative for the purposes of the Act.

Procedure

See the Criminal Procedure Rules 2020 (2020/759) rr.3.10, 28.8 and 28.9. **1-575**

Applications to the First-tier Tribunal (Mental Health) or the Mental Health Review Tribunal for Wales

The patient does not have a right to make an application to the tribunal: see the note on s.40(3). If, when the case returns to court for sentencing, the court makes a hospital order under s.37, the patient will be unable to make an application to a tribunal during the first six months of the order: see the note to s.37 under this heading. **1-576**

Appeals

An interim hospital order is a form of sentence and is therefore appealable to the Court of Appeal (Criminal Appeal Act 1968 ss.9(1), 50(1)). Under s.11(3) of that Act, such an order may only be made by the Court of Appeal if it first quashes the trial judge's sentence. The Court of Appeal has described this state of affairs as being "obviously unsatisfactory" (*R. v Cooper* [2001] EWCA Crim 57; [2001] M.H.L.R. 2 per Hooper J. at para.18). **1-577**

A court that has made an order under this section may end it and make its final sentencing decision despite the fact that an appeal against the order is outstanding: see s.11(5) of the 1968 Act.

Orders made in other proceedings

In certain circumstances, an interim hospital order may be made under the Contempt of Court Act 1981 s.14(4),(4A), the Family Law Act 1996 s.51 and the Armed Forces Act 2006 s.169 and Sch.4 para.5. **1-578**

Transport to and from court

See the note on s.35 under this heading. For general provisions relating to conveyance and detention, see s.137. **1-579**

Subsection (1)

Offence punishable with imprisonment   This is construed in accordance with s.47(5) (s.55(6)). **1-580**

Fixed by law   This section does not apply to persons who have been convicted of murder.

Offence punishable on summary conviction with imprisonment   See s.55(2).

Evidence   For general requirements as to medical evidence, see s.54. The court can call a doctor who has provided a written report to give oral evidence (s.54(2A)).

Two registered medical practitioners   One of whom must be approved by the Secretary of State or the Welsh Ministers under s.12, or by another person by virtue of s.12ZA or 12ZB (s.54(1)). A registered medical practitioner means "a fully registered person within the meaning of the Medical Act 1983 who holds a licence to practise under that Act" (Interpretation Act 1978 Sch.1). Also note subs.(3).

Is suffering from mental disorder   It is not sufficient that the doctors have a mere reason to suspect that the offender is suffering from mental disorder. If the person has a learning disability, the disability must be associated with abnormally aggressive or seriously irresponsible conduct (s.1(2A), (2B)). A learning disabled person might also suffer from another form of mental disorder.

Hospital order   Or a hospital direction and a limitation direction (s.45A(8)).

Hospital   Or a registered establishment (ss.34(2), 55(5)). A court may request information about the availability of hospital places under s.39.

Subsection (3)

1-581   The requirement of this provision does not apply to an order made under s.37.

Subsection (4)

1-582   In *R. (on the application of DB) v Nottinghamshire Healthcare NHS Trust*, noted under s.37(4), the Court of Appeal held that a hospital order ceases to have effect if the offender who is the subject of the order is not admitted to the hospital named in the order within the period of 28 days from the date of the making of the order, as stipulated by it. It is submitted that this finding applies to an order made under this section.

Approved clinician   Who could be the doctor referred to in subs.(3).

Some other person   Who need not be a clinician.

28 days   The Secretary of State and the Welsh Ministers have been given the power to reduce this period (s.54A).

Beginning with the date of the order   Including the date of the order (*Zoan v Rouamba* [2002] 2 All E.R. 620 CA).

Place of safety   See the note on s.37(4). A significant difference between a patient who is in a place of safety under s.37(4) and a patient who is in a place of safety under this provision is that the latter is subject to the consent to treatment provisions contained in Pt IV (s.56(3)).

Subsection (5)

1-583   This provides that if doubts remain as to the appropriateness of a hospital order (or a hospital direction and a limitation direction (s.45A(8)) after three months, the interim hospital order can be renewed at monthly intervals up to an overall total of 12 months.

Renewed   It is submitted that the order can be renewed in respect of a different hospital if the requirements of subs.(4) are satisfied in respect of the patient's admission to that hospital.

The continuation of the order is warranted   The continuation of the order would not be warranted in a situation where the assessment has been completed, the assessment has concluded that a hospital order would be warranted, but there is a delay in identifying a suitable hospital that would be willing to accept the patient: see *R. v Galfetti* [2002] EWCA Crim 1916; [2002] M.H.L.R. 418.

Subsection (7)

1-584   The absconder must be brought before the court that made the order. There is no time limit on a recapture under this provision.

Arrested   The power to arrest under this section was specifically preserved by s.26 and Sch.2 of the Police and Criminal Evidence Act 1984 (PACE). This means that the arresting policeman has a power to search the patient under s.32 of PACE at a place other than a police station. Section 72 of the Criminal Justice Act 1967 also provides for a power of arrest under this provision, but only if a warrant of arrest has been issued by a magistrate.

Information as to hospitals

1-585   **39.**—(1)   Where a court is minded to make a hospital order or interim hospital order in respect of any person it may request—

   (a)   the [integrated care board or] [Local Health Board] for [the area] in which that person resides or last resided; or

(b) [NHS England] [the National Assembly for Wales or any other] [integrated care board or] [Local Health Board] that appears to the court to be appropriate,

to furnish the court with such information as [that [integrated care board or] [Local Health Board] [or [[NHS England] or the] National Assembly for Wales] have] or can reasonably obtain with respect to the hospital or hospitals (if any) in [their area] or elsewhere at which arrangements could be made for the admission of that person in pursuance of the order, and [that [integrated care board or] [Local Health Board] [or [[NHS England] or the] National Assembly for Wales] shall] comply with any such request.

[(1ZA) A request under this section to [NHS England] may relate only to services or facilities the provision of which [NHS England] arranges.]

[(1A) In relation to a person who has not attained the age of 18 years, subsection (1) above shall have effect as if the reference to the making of a hospital order included a reference to a remand under section 35 or 36 above or the making of an order under section 44 below.

(1B) Where the person concerned has not attained the age of 18 years, the information which may be requested under subsection (1) above includes, in particular, information about the availability of accommodation or facilities designed so as to be specially suitable for patients who have not attained the age of 18 years.]

(2) [...]

Amendments

The amendments to this section were made by the Health Authorities Act 1995 ss.2(1), 5(1), Sch.1 para.107(5), Sch.3, the National Health Service Reform and Health Care Professions Act 2002 s.2(5), Sch.1 para.46, SI 2007/961 art.3, Sch. para.13(8), the Mental Health Act 2007 s.31(2), the Health and Social Care Act 2012 Sch.5 para.28 and the Health and Care Act 2022 Sch.1 para.1, Sch.4 para.15.

Definition

hospital order: ss.37, 145(1).   **1-586**
interim hospital order: ss.38, 145(1).
hospital: ss.55(5), 145(1).
Local Health Board: s.145(1).

General Note

This section provides that whenever a court is considering making a hospital order, a hospital and a   **1-587**
limitation direction (s.45A(8)) or an interim hospital order it may ask the appropriate integrated care board, Local Health Board, NHS England or the National Assembly for Wales to provide information as to the availability of suitable hospital places for the person in question (subs.(1)). It also enables the court to request information about the availability of hospital places for child offenders in respect of whom the court is considering a remand under ss.35 or 36 or, in respect of a magistrates' court, a committal to hospital under s.44 (subs.(1B)). The information that may be requested includes information about the "availability of accommodation designed so as to be specially suitable" for child patients (subs.(1C)). Paragraph 105 of the Explanatory Notes states: "The purpose of [subs.(1C)] is to ensure that courts do not place a child in a prison setting when a suitable hospital bed would be a more appropriate option".

Local Health Boards and integrated care boards are required by s.140 to notify relevant social services authorities of those hospitals where patients can be treated in cases of special urgency.

Procedure

1-588   See the Criminal Procedure Rules 2020 (SI 2020/759), rr.3.10 and 28.8.

Subsection (1)

1-589   **Resides**   See the note on this term in s.7(5).

Hospital   Or registered establishment (ss.34(2), 55(5)).

[Information to facilitate guardianship orders

1-590   **39A.**   Where a court is minded to make a guardianship order in respect of any offender, it may request the local social services authority for the area in which the offender resides or last resided, or any other local social services authority that appears to the court to be appropriate—

    (a)   to inform the court whether it or any other person approved by it is willing to receive the offender into guardianship; and

    (b)   if so, to give such information as it reasonably can about how it or the other person could be expected to exercise in relation to the offender the powers conferred by section 40(2) below;

and that authority shall comply with any such request.]

Amendment

This section was inserted by the Criminal Justice Act 1991 s.27(1).

Definitions

1-591   local social services authority: s.145(1).
guardianship order: ss.37, 145(1).

General Note

1-592   This section enables the court to find out whether the relevant local social services authority or a private guardian approved by the authority is willing to receive the offender into guardianship and, if this were to happen, how the authority or guardian might exercise their guardianship powers in relation to the offender.

Code of Practice

1-593   Paragraph 22.8 of the Code states that local authorities "should appoint a named person to respond to requests from the courts about mental health services available in the community including under guardianship".

Effect of hospital orders, guardianship orders and interim hospital orders

1-594   **40.**—(1)   A hospital order shall be sufficient authority—

    (a)   for a constable, an [approved mental health professional] or any other person directed to do so by the court to convey the patient to the hospital specified in the order within a period of 28 days; and

    (b)   for the managers of the hospital to admit him at any time within that period and thereafter detain him in accordance with the provisions of this Act.

(2)   A guardianship order shall confer on the authority or person named in the order as guardian the same powers as a guardianship application made and accepted under Part II of this Act.

(3)   Where an interim hospital order is made in respect of an offender—

   (a)   a constable or any other person directed to do so by the court shall convey the offender to the hospital specified in the order within the period mentioned in section 38(4) above; and

   (b)   the managers of the hospital shall admit him within that period and thereafter detain him in accordance with the provisions of section 38 above.

(4)   A patient who is admitted to a hospital in pursuance of a hospital order, or placed under guardianship by a guardianship order, shall, subject to the provisions of this subsection, be treated for the purposes of the provisions of this Act mentioned in Part I of Schedule 1 to this Act as if he had been so admitted or placed on the date of the order in pursuance of an application for admission for treatment or a guardianship application, as the case may be, duly made under Part II of this Act, but subject to any modifications of those provisions specified in that Part of that Schedule.

(5)   Where a patient is admitted to a hospital in pursuance of a hospital order, or placed under guardianship by a guardianship order, any previous application, hospital order or guardianship order by virtue of which he was liable to be detained in a hospital or subject to guardianship shall cease to have effect; but if the firstmentioned order, or the conviction on which it was made, is quashed on appeal, this subsection shall not apply and section 22 above shall have effect as if during any period for which the patient was liable to be detained or subject to -guardianship under the order, he had been detained in custody as mentioned in that section.

[(6)   Where—

   (a)   a patient admitted to a hospital in pursuance of a hospital order is absent without leave;

   (b)   a warrant to arrest him has been issued under section 72 of the Criminal Justice Act 1967; and

   (c)   he is held pursuant to the warrant in any country or territory other than the United Kingdom, any of the Channel Islands and the Isle of Man,

he shall be treated as having been taken into custody under section 18 above on first being so held.]

Amendments

The amendments to this section were made by the Mental Health Act 2007 s.21, Sch.2 para.7 and the Mental Health (Patients in the Community) Act 1995 s.2(4).

Definitions

hospital order: ss.37, 145(1).   **1-595**
approved mental health professional: s.145(1), (1AC).
the managers: s.145(1).
hospital: ss.55(5), 145(1).
hospital order: s.55(4).
guardianship order: ss.37, 55(4), 145(1).
guardian: s.55(1).
absent without leave: ss.18(6), 145(1).
interim hospital order: ss.38, 145(1).
patient: s.145(1).
application for admission for treatment: ss.3, 145(1).

General Note

This section provides that, with very few exceptions, a patient who is admitted to hospital under a   **1-596**
hospital order without restrictions or placed under guardianship by a guardianship order is treated the

same as a patient who has been admitted to hospital or placed under guardianship under Pt II of the Act. The necessary modifications to the provisions of Pt II are made by Pt I of Sch.I and are noted in subs.(4). The effect of an interim hospital order is set out in subs.(3). Subsection (5) provides for the cessation of previous applications or orders.

Any reference to hospital orders and guardianship orders in subs.(2), (4) or (5) of this section shall be construed as including a reference to any order or directions under this Part having the same effect as a hospital or guardianship order (s.55(4)).

The court documents should be carefully checked by the hospital managers: see the note on *Defective Court Orders* in the General Note to this Part.

Subsection (1)

Paragraph (a)

1-597   *Constable*   Means the office of constable, and not the rank of constable (Police Act 1996 s.29, Sch.4).

Convey the patient to hospital   For general provisions relating to conveyance, see s.137. Before proceeding to convey the patient to hospital, the authorised person should confirm with the hospital that it is still willing to accept the patient because this section does not give authority to convey the patient *from* hospital if admission is refused.

Within a period of 28 days   Any time that the patient is unlawfully at large is disregarded when calculating this period (s.138(5)). Once this period has expired, the hospital order ceases to provide authority for the offender's conveyance to hospital or his detention there: see *R. (on the application of DB) v Nottinghamshire Healthcare NHS Trust*, noted under s.37(4).

Subsection (2)

1-598   **Same powers**   As contained in s.8(1). A patient placed under a guardianship order is not subject to the consent to treatment provisions contained in Pt IV because he is not a patient who is "liable to be detained": see s.56(3).

Subsection (3)

1-599   This subsection sets out the effect of an interim hospital order made under s.38. Apart from coming within the scope of Pt IV, an interim hospital order patient is treated very differently from a hospital order patient. This is because an interim hospital order patient is not to be treated as if he had been admitted in pursuance of an application for admission for treatment; he is detained "in accordance with the provisions of s.38". The consequences of this are that neither the patient nor his nearest relative can apply to a tribunal, no-one has the right to discharge the patient, and the patient may not be granted leave of absence or be transferred to another hospital. Although applications have been made to the court for authority to either grant the patient leave of absence or to transfer the patient, the Act does not provide the court with an express power to make such orders.

Convey the offender to the hospital   See the General Note to s.35 under the heading *Transport to and from court*. For general provisions relating to conveyance and detention, see s.137.

Within the period mentioned in s.38(4)   28 days beginning with the date of the order.

Shall admit him   The hospital specified in an interim hospital order cannot subsequently withdraw its agreement to accept the offender. However, if circumstances arise which prevent the hospital from admitting the patient, the case should be returned to the court as a matter of urgency.

Subsection (4)

1-600   **Hospital order**   With three substantive exceptions, the effect of this subsection is to place a patient who has been placed under a hospital order in the same legal position as a patient who has been admitted to hospital for treatment under s.3. The exceptions are: (1) the nearest relative of a hospital order patient cannot order his discharge under s.23 (Sch.1 paras 2, 8); (2) unlike a s.3 patient, the hospital order patient cannot apply to a tribunal within the first six months of his detention (Sch.1 paras 2, 9); and (3) the initial six month maximum period of detention runs from the day that the hospital order is made by the court, not the patient's admission to the hospital (Sch.1 paras 2, 6).

If the medical conditions which justified the making of the hospital order cease to be met at any time, the duty of the patient's responsible clinician, exercising a medical judgment, is to discharge the offender from the hospital order (*R. v Drew* [2003] UKHL 25; [2003] M.H.L.R. 282 para.10).

Guardianship order The effect of a guardianship order made under s.37 is essentially the same as if the patient had been made the subject of a guardianship application under s.7. The major difference between the two is that with a guardianship order the power of the nearest relative to discharge the patient from guardianship does not apply (Sch.1 paras 2, 8).

Subsection (5)

Guardianship order Made by a court under Part 3.

Cease to have effect A previous hospital order (or a transfer direction (ss.47(3), 55(4))) will not cease **1-601** to have effect if a restriction order made in respect of the patient under s.41 is in force at the material time: see s.41(4) and the note thereto. The ending of the previous order or application does not effect the continuity of the three-month period provided for in s.58(1)(b). The imposition of the subsequent order provides the patient with a fresh opportunity to make an application to a tribunal during the second six months of his detention under that order.

An interim hospital order is not specified in this provision (see s.38(1)). If the patient is subject to a s.3 application when such an order is made by the court, the application should either be discharged under s.23 or allowed to continue during the currency of the interim order, in which case it will be reinstated (if it has not expired in the meantime) once the interim order is terminated. If the court proceeds to make a hospital or guardianship order in respect of the patient, this provision will terminate the s.3.

Subsection (6)

This subsection is concerned with the taking into custody of absconding patients who have gone **1-602** abroad. Paragraph 11.20 of the Reference Guide states:

"The Act does not permit patients to be retaken outside the UK, the Isle of Man or the Channel Islands. In certain cases, under the Extradition Act 2003, patients who are convicted offenders or accused of a crime may be extradited back to England, if the necessary warrants have been issued. The effect of section 40(6) is that if a patient subject to a restricted hospital order is detained overseas under extradition arrangements, the patient is treated as having been taken into custody under section 18 when first held on the basis of the extradition warrant in the country in question, rather than when returned to the UK. If the patient's restriction order is for a fixed period (see paragraph 21.15), that may affect whether it is still in force when the patient returns to England or Wales."

RESTRICTION ORDERS

Power of higher courts to restrict discharge from hospital

41.—(1)   Where a hospital order is made in respect of an offender by the Crown **1-603** Court, and it appears to the court, having regard to the nature of the offence, the antecedents of the offender and the risk of his committing further offences if set at large, that it is necessary for the protection of the public from serious harm so to do, the court may, subject to the provisions of this section, further order that the offender shall be subject to the special restrictions set out in this section, […] and an order under this section shall be known as "a restriction order".

(2)   A restriction order shall not be made in the case of any person unless at least one of the registered medical practitioners whose evidence is taken into account by the court under section 37(2)(a) above has given evidence orally before the court.

(3)   The special restrictions applicable to a patient in respect of whom a restriction order is in force are as follows—

(a) none of the provisions of Part II of this Act relating to the duration, renewal and expiration of authority for the detention of patients shall apply, and the patient shall continue to be liable to be detained by virtue of the relevant hospital order until he is duly discharged under the said Part II or absolutely discharged under section 42, 73, 74 or 75 below;

[(aa): none of the provisions of Part II of this Act relating to [community treatment orders and community patients] shall apply;]

(b) no application shall be made to [the appropriate tribunal] in respect of a patient under section 66 or 69(1) below;

(c) the following powers shall be exercisable only with the consent of the Secretary of State, namely—

    (i) power to grant leave of absence to the patient under section 17 above;

    (ii) power to transfer the patient in pursuance of regulations under section 19 above [or in pursuance of subsection (3) of that section]; and

    (iii) power to order the discharge of the patient under section 23 above; and if leave of absence is granted under the said section 17 power to recall the patient under that section shall vest in the Secretary of State as well as the [responsible clinician]; and

(d) the power of the Secretary of State to recall the patient under the said section 17 and power to take the patient into custody and return him under section 18 above may be exercised at any time;

and in relation to any such patient section 40(4) above shall have effect as if it referred to Part II of Schedule 1 to this Act instead of Part I of that Schedule.

(4) A hospital order shall not cease to have effect under section 40(5) above if a restriction order in respect of the patient is in force at the material time.

(5) Where a restriction order in respect of a patient ceases to have effect while the relevant hospital order continues in force, the provisions of section 40 above and Part I of Schedule 1 to this Act shall apply to the patient as if he had been admitted to the hospital in pursuance of a hospital order (without a restriction order) made on the date on which the restriction order ceased to have effect.

(6) While a person is subject to a restriction order the [responsible clinician] shall at such intervals (not exceeding one year) as the Secretary of State may direct examine and report to the Secretary of State on that person; and every report shall contain such particulars as the Secretary of State may require.

Amendments

The amendments to this section were made by the Mental Health (Patients in the Community) Act 1995 s.2(1), Sch.1 para.5, the Mental Health Act 2007 ss.10(6), 32, 55, Sch.3 para.17, Sch.11 Pt 8, the Crime (Sentences) Act 1997 s.49(2) and by SI 2008/2883 art.9, Sch.3 para.41.

Definitions

1-604   hospital order: ss.37, 55(4), 145(1).
patient: s.145(1).
hospital: ss.55(5), 145(1).
community treatment order: ss.17A(7), 145(1).
community patient: ss.17A(7), 145(1).
responsible clinician: s.55(1).
the appropriate tribunal: ss.66(4), 145(1).

General Note

This section empowers the Crown Court, having made a hospital order under s.37, to make a further **1-605** order (a "restriction order") restricting the patient's discharge, transfer or leave of absence from hospital without the consent of the Secretary of State. Such a patient is a restricted patient (s.79). Magistrates' courts may only commit a convicted offender to the Crown Court with a view to a restriction order being made (s.43(1)).

A restriction order, which can only be made where it is necessary to protect the public from serious harm (subs.(1)), does not require renewal to prevent it from lapsing, but remains in force until it is discharged by the patient's responsible clinician with the agreement of the Secretary of State under s.23, by the Secretary of State under s.42, or by the tribunal under s.73. The patient's nearest relative does not have the power to discharge the patient (s.40(4), Sch.1 Pt II paras 2, 7).

Paragraph 22.85 of the *Code of Practice* states:

"In exceptional circumstances, the Secretary of State for Justice may 'direct' a restricted patient's admission into hospital, outside the NHS commissioning arrangements. This is usually where it is critical that the patient receive treatment and identifying a suitable bed is difficult."

The nature of a restriction order was considered by Mustill L.J. in *R. v Birch* (1989) 11 Cr. App. R.(S.) 202 at 211–212:

"A restriction order has no existence independently of the hospital order to which it relates; it is not a separate means of disposal. Nevertheless, it fundamentally affects the circumstances in which the patient is detained. No longer is the offender regarded simply as a patient whose interests are paramount. No longer is the control of him handed over unconditionally to the hospital authorities. Instead the interests of public safety are regarded by transferring the responsibility for discharge from the [responsible clinician] and the hospital to [...] the Secretary of State and the [tribunal]. A patient who has been subject to a restriction order is likely to be detained for much longer in hospital than one who is not, and will have fewer opportunities for leave of absence."

His Lordship made the following observations at 213–215 on the principles to be observed in deciding whether a restriction order is appropriate:

"[The judge] is required to choose between an order without restrictions, which may enable the author of a serious act of violence to be at liberty only a matter of months after he appears in court, and a restriction order which may lead the offender to be detained for a long time: longer in some cases than the period which he would serve if sent to prison: see *Haynes* (1981) 3 Cr. App. R. (S.) 330. It is moreover a choice which depends on a prognosis, the ultimate responsibility for which is left with the judge.

This responsibility may be hard to discharge, since the judge will often have nothing on which to base his decision, if he feels reservations about the medical evidence, apart from the considerations stated by the statute, namely the nature of the offence and the antecedents of the offender: which will often consist only of a single episode of fatal violence and a blank criminal record. Where there is a trial the judge can form an impression of [the] defendant as the case unfolds which may enable him to make his own assessment of his dangerousness. But in the more usual case where a plea of guilty to manslaughter on the grounds of diminished responsibility is accepted by the prosecution and the court, this opportunity is largely absent, and did not exist at all in the present case, where the appellant was too distressed to remain for the hearing in the Crown Court ....

Nevertheless, section 41(1) is there and the judge must apply it. Quite plainly the addition of the words 'from serious harm' has greatly curtailed the former jurisdiction to make a restriction order: most particularly because the word 'serious' qualifies 'harm' rather than 'risk.' Thus the court is required to assess not the seriousness of the risk that the defendant will re-offend, but the risk that if he does so the public will suffer serious harm. The harm in question need not, in our view, be limited to personal injury. Nor need it relate to the public in general, for it would in our judgment suffice if a category of persons, or even a single person, were adjudged to be at risk: although the category of persons so protected would no doubt exclude the offender himself. Nevertheless the potential harm must be serious, and a high possibility of a recurrence of minor offences will no longer be sufficient [...]

It would [...] be a mistake to equate the seriousness of the offence with the probability that a restriction order will be made. This is only one of the factors which section 41(1) requires to be taken into account. A minor offence by a man who proves to be mentally disordered and dangerous may properly leave him subject to a restriction. In theory the converse is also true. *Courtney* (1987) 9 Cr.

App. R.(S.) 404 shows that a serious offence committed by someone who is adjudged to have a very low risk of reoffending may lead to an unrestricted hospital order.

Nevertheless, the court will need to be very sure of its ground in such a case, and we consider that there is nothing in the 1983 Act to derogate from the following statement of principle by Lord Parker C.J., in *Gardiner* (1967) 51 Cr. App. R. 187:

'Thus, for example, in the case of crimes of violence, and of the more serious sexual offences, particularly if the prisoner has a record of such offences, or if there is a history of mental disorder involving violent behaviour, it is suggested that there must be compelling reasons to explain why a restriction order should not be made.'

Finally we would make [a further point] on section 41. [The] sentencer should not impose a restriction order simply to mark the gravity of the offence (although this is an element in the assessment of risk), nor as a means of punishment: for a restriction order merely qualifies a hospital order and a hospital order is not a mode of punishment."

In *R. v Salmon* [2022] EWCA Crim 1116, the offender appealed against the imposition of a restriction order. His RC gave evidence that the order "is unlikely to provide any additional safeguards as compared to those provided by a CTO" (para.26). The Court of Appeal agreed that the procedure for recall would follow a similar route whether or not a restriction order was made, but noted that a restriction order "would place an additional restriction on discharge from hospital" and therefore "focuses on precautionary measures before discharge rather than the procedure to be adopted after the appellant has been discharged" (para.35). The appeal was dismissed.

In the context of the criminal law, the Court of Appeal has said:

"The prevalence of (even minor) offending may cause serious harm to society, but that does not mean that an individual offence considered in isolation has done so. Shoplifting, for example, may be a significant social problem, causing serious economic harm and distress to the owner of a modest corner shop; and a thief who steals a single item of low value may contribute to that harm, but it cannot realistically be said that such a thief caused serious harm himself, either to the owner or to society in general" (*R. (on the application of Mahmood) v Upper Tribunal* [2020] EWCA Civ 717, para.39).

The current approach to the sentencing of mentally disordered offenders which takes into account the amendments made to the Act by the Mental Health Act 2007 was set out by the Court of Appeal in *R. v Vowles* [2015] EWCA Crim 45 which is considered in the General Note to s.37.

It is the duty of a judge hearing a case who has formed a clear provisional view on the material presented that a restriction order should be made, to inform the parties that this is so, so that, by way of evidence and argument they will be able to deal with it (*R. v Goode* [2002] EWCA Crim 1698 at para.36). If a court is considering making an order under this section the defendant should be represented by counsel (*R. v Blackwood* (1974) 59 Cr. App. R. 170).

A restriction order remains in force even if the patient is subsequently imprisoned for an offence committed after his conditional discharge (*R. v Mersey Mental Health Review Tribunal Ex p. K* [1990] 1 All E.R. 694 CA), and the patient may be recalled to hospital on the expiry of his prison sentence (*R. v Secretary of State for the Home Department Ex p. K* [1990] 1 All E.R. 703).

In subss.(3) to (5) of this section any reference to a hospital order, a guardianship order or a restriction order are to be construed as including a reference to any order or direction under this Part having the same effect as such orders (s.55(4)).

Named hospital units

1-606   Section 47 of the Crime (Sentences) Act 1997 provides that where a court makes a restriction order it has the power to order that the patient be admitted to and detained in a named hospital unit. Paragraph 22.26 of the *Code of Practice* states:

"A named hospital unit can be any part of a hospital which is treated as a separate unit. The hospital managers of the hospital will define the boundaries of the hospital however it will be for the court (or the Secretary of State for Justice, as the case may be) to confirm the unit or hospital covered by the detention authority in each case where it makes use of the power. When transferring a prisoner to hospital with a restriction direction attached, the Secretary of State for Justice may direct that the patient be detained in a specific hospital unit. This will normally be to a named ward to prevent patients being moved to lower levels of security within a hospital without the Secretary of State for Justice's agreement. Admission to a named unit will mean that the consent of the Secretary of State for Justice will be required for any leave of absence or transfer from the named unit, even if the transfer is to the same level of security, or transfer is to another part of the same hospital or to another hospital. If however, the transfer involves no change to either the named unit or hospital prior agreement from the Secretary of State for Justice is not required. For example, if the detention authority covers a named hospital, to move patients between units within that hospital will not require Secretary of State for Justice permission. The mental health casework section (MHCS) should be informed of the move."

Applications to the First-tier Tribunal (Mental Health) or the Mental Health Review Tribunal for Wales

A patient who is subject to a restriction order may apply to a tribunal in the period between six and 12 months of the order and in any subsequent period of one year (s.70) and the Secretary of State may, and in some circumstances must refer such patients to a tribunal (s.71). The patient's nearest relative has no power to apply to a tribunal. The powers of a tribunal when considering the case of a restricted patient are set out in s.73.   **1-607**

If the patient becomes subject to a "notional hospital order" by virtue of the restriction order ceasing to have effect (subs.(5)), the patient is given the same powers to apply to a tribunal as those enjoyed by a s.3 patient (s.69(2)). These powers are also enjoyed by the patient's nearest relative (s.69(1)).

Appeals

See the note on s.37 under this heading.   **1-608**

Guidance on the restricted patient system

The Ministry of Justice and HM Prison and Probation Service have published guidance which **1-609** "provides stakeholders (including patients and their families, victims, Responsible Clinicians and other report writers and multi-disciplinary team members) with an overview of the restricted patient system in England and Wales and the role of the Secretary of State for Justice and the Mental Health Casework Section (MHCS) in Her Majesty's Prison and Probation Service (HMPPS)" (para.1). The guidance can be accessed at: *www.gov.uk/government/publications/mentally-disordered-offenders-the-restricted-patient-system.*

"*The Designation and Management of High Profile Restricted Patients*" (HM Prison and Probations Service, 2019) sets out what criteria are considered when designating a restricted patient "high profile" and what effects that has on the management of that patient whilst detained in a hospital or in the community, following a conditional discharge. It can be accessed at: *www.gov.uk/government/publications/the-designation-management-of-high-profile-restricted-patients.*

Multi-Agency Public Protection Arrangements

For a document which sets out information for MHCS staff and those working directly with restricted **1-610** patients to outline Multi-Agency Public Protection Arrangements (MAPPA) requirements see: *www.gov.uk/government/publications/multi-agency-public-protection-arrangements-mappa-and-the-restricted-patient-system.* Also see chapter 26 of the MAPPA arrangements on "Mentally Disordered Offenders" which can be accessed on the MAPPA website.

Domestic Violence, Crime and Victims Act 2004

The Ministry of Justice has published "*Duties to victims under the Domestic Violence, Crime and* **1-611** *Victims Act 2004: Guidance for Clinicians*" (March 2009) which can be accessed at: *www.gov.uk/government/publications/domestic-violence-crime-and-victims-act-2004-rights-of-victims.* A letter dated April 22, 2014 from the Head of Mental Health Casework Section at the Ministry of Justice states:

"As a result of a Ministerial commitment, as of 22 April 2014, victims of restricted mentally disordered offenders, who have opted in to the Victim Contact Scheme, will be told if permission for community leave is granted by the Secretary of State unless there are exceptional reasons why they should not be told. Exceptional reasons will include risk to the patient, so any concerns about this must be flagged up to MHCS in the application for community leave."

See also Ch.40 of the *Code of Practice.*

Fitness to plead under the Criminal Procedure (Insanity) Act 1964

1-612   "Resuming a Prosecution when a patient becomes fit to plead" is guidance which explains the powers and responsibilities of the Secretary of State for Justice, the Crown Prosecution Service and Her Majesty's Courts and Tribunal Service when a restricted patient becomes fit to plead and sets out the procedure to be followed when a prosecution is resumed. Paragraphs 8 and 9 of the guidance state:

> "The Mental Health Casework Section (MHCS) will keep the issue of a patient's fitness to plead under review and will obtain the opinion of the responsible clinician at least once a year. The Secretary of State for Justice will notify the CPS when the responsible clinician has determined that a restricted patient is now fit to plead. The MHCS will also provide the CPS with the responsible clinician's report which will address, so far as possible, those factors relevant to the decision to resume proceedings set out below. MHCS is of the view that for the general administration of justice, including obligations towards the prosecution of offenders, the clinical report can lawfully be shared with the CPS to enable the administration of justice process take its course, pursuant to Article 6(1)(c) of the General Data Protection Regulations 2018 (GDPR) because the 'processing is necessary for compliance with a legal obligation to which the controller is subject.'
>
> MHCS will also ensure that where the CPS is not going to resume a prosecution, the responsible clinician has considered, and where appropriate put in place, suitable arrangements for the lawful ongoing detention and treatment of the patient under Part II of the Mental Health Act 1983 powers, once the case has been remitted to court and a final disposal made."

The detaining hospital is responsible for securing the attendance of the patient at court (para.21). The guidance can be accessed at: *www.gov.uk/government/publications/resume-a-prosecution-when-a-patient-becomes-fit-to-plead*. The 1964 Act is considered briefly in the General Note to this Part.

Period spent subject to a hospital order made under the Criminal Procedure (Insanity) Act 1964 counting toward a sentence

1-613   See the General Note to s.37 under this heading.

Subsection (1)

1-614   **Hospital order is made**   The offender must therefore have satisfied the conditions of s.37(2). Although this section implies that the offender will be kept in secure accommodation, this will not be necessary in all cases. The Butler Committee, at para.14.21, gave the following example of a restricted patient who might not need to be accommodated in secure accommodation:

> "[T]he persistent molester of small children may need the continuing supervision after discharge which a restriction order allows, and should not be permitted simply to walk out of hospital whenever he wishes, but is unlikely to need the secure containment of bolts and bars".

Crown court   A Crown Court has jurisdiction to make a restriction order in respect of an offence which only became triable by that court under the provisions of s.40 of the Criminal Justice Act 1988 (*R. v Avbunudje* [1999] 2 Cr. App. R.(S.) 189 CA). Section 40 enables a summary only offence to be included in an indictment in certain specified circumstances. Although a magistrates' court cannot make a restriction order, it does have the power to commit the offender to the Crown Court with a view to such an order being made by that court (s.43(1)).

Antecedents   It has been reported that this term is

> "construed by the judges to include not just previous convictions, but also accounts of previous unprosecuted dangerous behaviour made in psychiatric reports (subject to any objection by defence counsel), and some [judges] said that evidence of failure of previous treatment might also be significant. A history of violence would cause particular concern, especially if it appeared that the violence was escalating in seriousness" (*The Restricted Hospital Order: From Court to Community*, Home Office Research Study 186, 1998, p.40).

The public   The public does not include an unborn child who, when born, could be protected by the provisions of the Children Act 1989 (*R. v Jones* [2000] M.H.L.R. 12 CA).

In *Anderson v Scottish Ministers* [2001] UKPC D 5; [2001] M.H.L.R. 192, para.37, Lord Hope said:

"The word 'public' and the phrase 'in order to protect the public from serious harm' in each of the various amendments included in section 1 of the [Mental Health (Public Safety and Appeals) (Scotland) Act 1999] is capable of meaning either the public in general or a section of the public, as the context requires. In Doherty's case there is no question of his coming into contact with the public in general as he would be remitted to prison in the event of his discharge from hospital. But the persons with whom he would be liable to come into contact in a prison may be regarded as a section of the public. They include prison officers, other inmates and a variety of persons who visit prisons for religious, educational, social work or other purposes. Read in this way, the effect of the amendments introduced by section 1 of the 1999 Act is to require the sheriff or the Scottish Ministers, as the case may be, to be satisfied in Doherty's case that it is necessary for him to be detained in a hospital to protect that section of the public from serious harm ..."

Serious harm   The insertion of this phrase into the 1982 Act gave effect to recommendation of the Butler Committee which proposed that the equivalent section in the 1959 Act should be revised to make it clear that the intention of a restriction order is to protect the public from serious harm. The Committee wished to ensure that a court would not impose restrictions on "the petty recidivist because of the virtual certainty that he will persist in similar offences in the future" (para.14.24).

In *R. v Salmon* [2022] EWCA Crim 1116, the Court said at para.24:

"The 1983 Act does not itself contain a definition for this purpose of 'serious harm'. In the context of the sentencing of dangerous offenders, section 306 of the Sentencing Act 2020 defines "serious harm" as meaning 'death or serious personal injury whether physical or psychological'. We are not immediately persuaded that that test can be read directly across to the different context of the Mental Health Act , not least because in well-established case law such as *R v Birch* (1990) 90 Cr App R(S) 78, it was held that the harm 'need not be limited to personal injury'. We need not however explore that question further, because we accept that where, as here, the harm foreseen is in the category of physical or psychological injury, the court should apply the test of the risk of death or serious injury."

The court should expressly address the question whether the order is necessary for the protection of the public from serious harm (*R. v Czarnota* [2002] EWCA Crim 785; [2002] M.H.L.R. 144). In doing so, it must undertake an assessment of risk (*R. v Cooper* [2009] EWCA Crim 2646). The index offence itself need not be serious: see, for e.g., *R. v Kamara*, below.

"Serious harm" refers to possible serious harm to the public in the future rather than to proven serious harm to the public in the past and an offender who has no history of serious violence but who, on the medical evidence, has a potentiality for causing serious harm could be made the subject of an order under this section (*R. v Kamara* [2000] M.H.L.R. 9 CA). It is not necessary that the harm should be purely physical: a risk of serious psychological harm will suffice (*R. v Melbourne* [2000] M.H.L.R. 2 CA). Indirect harm can suffice such as downloading material which perpetuates a market that leads to further abuse of children (*R. v Brooks* [2019] EWCA Crim 2004, para.48). A risk to one person of serious harm can be sufficient (*R. v Macrow* [2004] EWCA Crim 1159 para.16), but not a risk of self-harm (*R. v Osker* [2010] EWCA Crim 955; [2010] M.H.L.R. 115). The word "serious" qualifies "harm" rather than "risk". Thus the court is required "not to assess the seriousness of the risk that the defendant will re-offend, but the risk that if he does so the public will suffer serious harm" (*R. v Birch* (1989) 11 Cr. App. R.(S.) 202). In *R. v Cox* [1999] M.H.L.R. 30 the Court of Appeal said that risk of serious harm to the public must be real, rather than fanciful or remote.

The imposition of a restriction order was confirmed in *R. v Golding* [2006] EWCA Crim 1965; [2006] M.H.L.R. 272, where the court found that the appellant, who had multiple convictions for burglary but had never acted violently, satisfied the "serious harm" criterion because his psychosis was not controlled and his predilection to drugs and alcohol could well lead him to behave violently if he was confronted by a householder. The court rejected counsel's submission that if "the evidence and material before the court in this case is sufficient to make a restriction order, it is difficult to consider any case where a defendant suffers from paranoid schizophrenia where he will not be susceptible to a section 41 order" on the ground that the decisions to be made as to such orders "are very much fact specific decisions" (paras 10, 11). *Golding* is consistent with the decisions of the Court of Appeal in *Kamara*, above, and the Divisional Court in *R. (on the application of Jones) v Isleworth Crown Court* [2005] EWHC 662 (Admin) where the court emphasised that in deciding whether an offender posed a future risk of serious harm the judge was not bound to determine that risk by reference to the nature of past violence. Moses J. said at para.19:

"Of course the evidence as to what had happened in the past provides a guide to the future; but it does not determine the nature of the risk, particularly in the context of an escalation of violence by one who suffers from paranoid schizophrenia and hears commands to harm other people."

When making a judgment about "serious harm" the court can take into account the risk to the offender from failing to take appropriate treatment to restrain his symptoms: see *Narey v Her Majesty's Customs and Excise* [2005] EWHC 784 (Admin); [2005] M.H.L.R.194 at para.19 where the court said that the importation of kilos of cocaine inevitably leads to a risk of serious harm to those to whom it is sold for consumption. In *R. v Beaumont* (98/02694 Y2) July 28, 1998, CA, Moses J. said that "setting fire to premises, even if it is difficult for them to ignite successfully, is likely to cause, in our judgment serious harm to others who may be affected by [the] fire".

Subsection (2)

1-615   **One of the registered medical practitioners**   Who need not necessarily be approved under s.12. A registered medical practitioner means "a fully registered person within the meaning of the Medical Act 1983 who holds a licence to practise under that Act" (Interpretation Act 1978, Sch.1). In *R. v Blackwood* (1974) Cr. App. R. 170, the Court of Appeal stressed the desirability of the doctor who gives oral evidence being on the staff of the admitting hospital.

Evidence   It is of the utmost importance that when medical practitioners are considering whether to recommend a restriction order, they should expressly address the question whether such an order is necessary for the protection of the public from serious harm (*R. v Chalk* [2002] EWCA Crim 2435; [2002] M.H.L.R. 430 para.34).

In *R. v Birch*, above, the Court of Appeal, at 212, gave the following answer to the question whether a Crown Court judge had jurisdiction to make a restriction order in circumstances where those doctors who expressed an opinion on the matter were unanimous that the patient was not dangerous:

"It is in our judgment quite clear that the answer is 'yes'. There is a contrast between the language of sections 37(2) and 41(1) and (2). Before a hospital order can be made, the Court must be satisfied of the stated conditions 'on the written or oral evidence of two practitioners'. But where a restriction order is in question, section 41(2) requires no more than that the Court shall hear the oral evidence of one of the medical practitioners. It need not follow the course which he recommends. Section 41(1) makes the assessment of the risk, in the light of the factors there identified, one for the court. In our judgment *R. v Blackwood* (1974) 59 Cr. App. R. 170 and *R. v Royse* (1981) 3 Cr. App. R.(S.) 58 are just as good law under the 1983 Act as they were under the earlier statute."

The finding in *Birch* was applied in *R. v Crookes* [1999] M.H.L.R. 45, where the Court of Appeal said that the judge was right to impose a restriction order in a case where the medical evidence was unanimous in recommending that such an order was not necessary. In this case, the judge felt that none of the doctors was able to explain to his satisfaction why a young man with no record of violence, and not seen as in any way to be dangerous, could suddenly react with an outburst of potentially lethal ferocity.

In *R. v Ristic* [2002] EWCA Crim 165; [2002] M.H.L.R. 129 at para.10, Goldring J., in giving the judgment of the court, said that the fact that none of the doctors who had prepared reports or who had given evidence had suggested a restriction order "did not mean that the judge could not impose it, after consideration of the evidence and the requirements of the section". However, the power and discretion of the judge to impose a restriction order in these circumstances should only be exercised after careful consideration and with some caution (*R. v Roberts* [2003] EWCA Crim 858, para.12). If a judge does not accept the unanimous recommendations of psychiatrists that a restriction order is not necessary, better reasons should be given in justification than the mere citing of the levels violence exhibited by the offender in the past (*R. v Haile* [2009] EWCA Crim 1996; [2009] M.H.L.R. 300; also see *R. v Hurst* [2007] EWCA Crim 3436; [2008] M.H.L.R. 43). Where the doctors giving evidence to the court are not unanimous about the appropriateness of a hospital disposal, sentencing is a matter for the judge to resolve in the light of the evidence and all the circumstances of the case (*R. v Reid* [2005] EWCA Crim 392; [2006] M.H.L.R. 180).

Orally   Evidence cannot be given to the court over the telephone (*R. v Clark* [2015] EWCA Crim 2192; [2016] M.H.L.R. 219).

Subsection (3)

1-616   This subsection specifies the restrictions that are placed upon patients who are subject to restriction orders. They are: (1) there is no periodic review of the authority to detain under s.20; (2) the patient cannot be discharged, transferred to another hospital (even if managed by the same hospital managers) or granted leave of absence without the consent of the Secretary of State; (3) the patient cannot be made subject to a community treatment order; and (4) the authority to detain lasts as long as the restriction order is in force and the patient cannot obtain his discharge under the provisions of ss.17(5) or 18(4).

Paragraph (b)

No application shall be made   This paragraph only refers to a patient in his capacity as a restricted   **1-617**
patient detained, or liable to be detained, pursuant to the hospital order. It does not apply to the patient's detention under s.3, if such an application has been made in respect of him. A patient so detained therefore has a right to apply to a tribunal under s.66(1)(b) (*R. v North West London Mental Health NHS Trust Ex p. Stewart, The Times,* August 15, 1996, per Harrison J., whose decision on the ability of Pts II and III of this Act to coexist and operate independently of each other was affirmed by the Court of Appeal at [1997] 4 All E.R. 871).

Paragraph (c)

On a day-to-day basis, the powers of the Secretary of State under this provision are managed by the   **1-618**
Mental Health Casework Section (MHCS) at the Ministry of Justice: see the General Note to this Part.
The principles that the Secretary of State should apply when exercising his functions under this provision were set out by Lightman J. in *R. v Secretary of State for the Home Department, Ex p. Harry* [1998] 3 All E.R. 360, a case where the Secretary of State had refused to consent to the transfer of a restricted patient from Broadmoor Hospital to a regional secure unit, as recommended by a tribunal. His Lordship said at 369:

"In short, as it seems to me, the scheme of the 1983 Act places on the [Secretary of State] the responsibility in the case of a restricted patient to balance the patient's claim to liberty against the interests of everyone else to be safeguarded against the risks to which such liberty may give rise. For his performance of these duties the [Secretary of State] is politically accountable to Parliament. His obligation is fully to satisfy himself as to the propriety of any decision before he makes it because of the serious impact of such decision, and if the finding or recommendation of the tribunal leaves him in doubt, he is not only entitled but bound to look further afield for guidance: the finding and recommendation of the tribunal may assist him to fulfil this obligation, but cannot dilute it or impede its fulfilment or obviate the need for the exercise by him of an informed judgment whether consent should be forthcoming."

Harry was applied by Silber J. in *R. (on the application of OS) v Secretary of State for the Home Department* [2006] EWHC 1903 (Admin); [2006] M.H.L.R. 275, where his Lordship said that it was common ground that the Secretary of State

"is entitled in making his assessment of risk to consider the risk that the patient will not return after being granted leave [of absence]. This is important because the [Secretary of State] will be able to take into account factors, which the [tribunal] would not or could not consider, such as the immigration status of the patient and whether this or any other factor might lead him or her not to return to their hospital after their leave has expired" (para.22).

In *R. (on the application of P) v Secretary of State for Justice* [2009] EWHC 2464 (Admin); [2009] M.H.L.R. 236, para.62, Keith Lindblom QC, sitting as a Deputy Judge of the High Court, said that the Secretary of State is not bound by the opinion of professionals even if that opinion was unequivocal and unanimous, and is not required to seek a second clinical opinion to substantiate his own judgment on the question of risk. The Secretary of State "has to exercise a judgment of his own". In *R. (on the application of X) v Secretary of State for Justice* [2009] EWHC 2465 (Admin); [2009] M.H.L.R. 250, para.55, Mr Lindblom said that if the Secretary of State rejects a request for leave, he must give a rational explanation for doing so which properly bears on the protection of the public.

Leave of Absence   In *R. (on the application of A) v Secretary of State for the Home Department* [2002] EWHC 1618; [2003] M.H.L.R. 54, Crane J. rejected a submission that conditions cannot be attached to the Secretary of State's consent to a grant of leave of absence under s.17. His Lordship said at para.41:

"It is true that neither section 17 nor section 41(3) provides in terms for such conditions to the consent. However, section 17 enables conditions to be imposed by the [RC] on the patient. I can see no reason why the Secretary of State cannot in law decline to give consent unless suitable conditions are imposed. He can obviously refuse consent to leave for a particular period. And since the Secretary of State has a power to recall under section 41(3)(c), there is every reason why he should be able to insist upon conditions that have the effect of providing the necessary information to him. The power of recall would then be no less effective than under section 42(2)".

His Lordship said that the operation of the provisions of ss.17 and 41(3)(c) should ensure that there is "no unreasonable delay to the implementation of a tribunal's decision" to defer the conditional discharge of the patient (para.58) and that the Secretary of State should "follow recommendations made by a tribunal in the absence of sound reasons or new circumstances" (para.59). His Lordship left open the question whether conditions, such as the provision of reports, can be imposed on the RC.

In *R. (on the application of C) v Secretary of State for Justice* [2014] EWHC 167 (Admin), Cranston J. upheld a decision of the Secretary of State not to consent to a s.47/49 restricted patient having unescorted community leave in the face of a decision of the First-tier Tribunal that the patient be granted a conditional discharge. Also see s.74(5A).

In *R. (on the application of Hurlock) v Dr Page and the Secretary of State for the Home Department)* [2001] EWHC Admin 380 at para.22, Ouseley J. said that s.17 and this provision cannot argu-ably be read as imposing an obligation to grant a patient unescorted leave of absence as an alternative to a conditional discharge granted by a tribunal where those conditions are not yet fulfilled.

HM Prison and Probation Service have published guidance on *"Section 17–Leave of Absence"* (2020)and on *"Medical Leave for Restricted Patients"* (2021). Both documents are reproduced in Part 4. A leave application form for restricted patients can be accessed at: *https://www.gov.uk/government/publications/leave-application-for-restricted-patients*.

With regard to "community leave", the *Code of Practice* states:

"22.58 The Secretary of State for Justice will often consent to programmes of leave which give responsible clinicians discretion as to leave arrangements. The expectation however is that the leave will be designed and conducted in such a way as to preserve public safety and, where appropriate, respect the feelings and fears of victims and others who may have been affected by the offences.

22.59 Leave request forms are provided on the Ministry of Justice website which outlines the information required, however the attachment of leave plans may also be useful. In the event that consent for leave is given, responsible clinicians should be aware that the Ministry of Justice may request additional reports on the restricted patient as considered necessary.

22.60 Should there be any concerns or doubts about the leave being taken, it should be suspended and MHCS informed."

The Ministry of Justice and HM Prison & Probation Service have published guidance on *"Medical Leave for Restricted Patients"*. The Guidance, which is reproduced in Part 4, can be accessed at: *www.gov.uk/government/publications/leave-application-for-restricted-patients*.

Paragraph 27.41 of the *Code of Practice* states:

"For routine medical appointments or treatment, the Secretary of State's permission will be required. It is accepted that there will be times of acute medical emergency such as heart attack, stroke or penetrative wounds or burns where the patient requires emergency treatment. There may also be acute situations which, while not life threatening still require urgent treatment, eg fractures. In these situations, the responsible clinician may use their discretion, having due regard to the emergency or urgency being presented and the management of any risks, to have the patient taken to hospital. The Secretary of State should be informed as soon as possible that the patient has been taken to hospital, what risk management arrangements are in place, be kept informed of developments and notified when the patient has been returned to the secure hospital."

Further provisions relating to ground access, leave of absence and the escorting of patients from Ashworth, Broadmoor and Rampton Hospitals can be found in the High Security Psychiatric Services (Arrangements for Safety and Security) Directions 2019 which are reproduced at Appendix C.

Transfer the patient The MHCS of the Ministry of Justice has published guidance on "Transfers between Hospitals in England and Wales" (undated). To help responsible clinicians (RCs) provide all the information required to enable the Secretary of State to properly risk assess transfer proposals, a form is provided with this guidance at: *www.gov.uk/government/collections/mentally-disordered-offenders*.

The policy of the Secretary of State on transfers for restricted patients is set out at para.3 of the guidance:

"The Secretary of State recognises the importance of patients being placed in appropriate levels of security at all stages of their detention, and that the ultimate goal, where possible, is the patient's safe rehabilitation back into the community. The Secretary of State's role is to ensure that transfers between hospitals preserve public safety, and, where appropriate, respect the feelings and fears of victims and others who may have been affected by the offences. The Secretary of State will not agree to a transfer unless he is satisfied that the move will not put the public or victims at risk."

The issue of trial leave is considered in the guidance at para.10:

"In situations in which a period of testing in another hospital is considered necessary to ensure that the patient can be managed appropriately in the proposed hospital, the Secretary of State will give permission for 'trial leave' as a precursor to consent for transfer under s19. Trial leave is effected by means of granting permission for s17 leave for the sole purpose of temporary transfer to the proposed hospital. A trial transfer is the default arrangement for movement out of high secure hospitals as it leaves responsibility for the patient with the responsible clinician in the high secure hospital. It also leaves the responsible clinician free to revoke the transfer instantly in the event that it is seen not to be working until such time as the Secretary of State has given consent to the s19 transfer. The RC should specify the duration of the trial leave sought and in most cases 6 months should be sufficient to determine whether a full transfer is appropriate. MHCS will agree to extensions, not usually exceeding 12 months in total, to enable further testing to take place."

The *Code of Practice* states at para.22.63:

"It is useful for the MHCS forms accessed via the website to be used when requesting that a restricted patient be transferred between hospitals. In urgent situations, it may be sufficient for the transferring and receiving clinicians to provide confirmation of their assessments and the availability of appropriate treatment in writing to MHCS. Situations where an urgent transfer may be required include those where there is a serious risk of self-harm or harm to others which cannot be safely management [sic] in the current hospital or unit. Where the clinical team have concerns, contact with the casework manager should be made in the first instance."

It is submitted that the Secretary of State does not have the power under s.47 of the Crime (Sentences) Act 1997 to require that the patient be treated in a named hospital unit on his transfer even if one was specified by the court in the original order.

Subsection (4)

The effect of this provision is that a hospital order coupled with a restriction order continues to have effect on the making of a subsequent hospital order and that subsequent hospital orders should be disregarded for the purposes of renewal when the restriction order ceases to have effect.   **1-619**

If a second restriction order is made, both orders will be in force. As the existence of parallel restriction orders is undesirable, the Secretary of State should consider exercising his power under s.42(2) to order the absolute discharge of one of them.

Subsection (5)

This subsection provides that when a restriction order ceases to have effect, the patient is to be treated as if he had been admitted to hospital under a hospital order without restrictions made on the date on which the restriction order ceased to have effect. If the patient has been conditionally discharged from hospital before the restrictions end, he will cease to be liable to be detained (s.42(5)).   **1-620**

Subsection (6)

This subsection, which was enacted in response to recommendation 114 of the Butler Committee, is aimed at preventing restricted patients being detained for unjustifiably long periods. As a patient who has been conditionally discharged from a restriction order remains subject to that order (see s.42(2)), it is submitted that this provision applies to such patients. If the Secretary of State, having considered the RC's report and having weighed all the other evidence about the patients medical condition that is available to him is satisfied that the patient is no longer suffering from mental disorder, he should discharge him: see the note to s.42(2).   **1-621**

Powers of Secretary of State in respect of patients subject to restriction orders

42.—(1)   If the Secretary of State is satisfied that in the case of any patient a restriction order is no longer required for the protection of the public from serious   **1-622**

harm, he may direct that the patient shall cease to be subject to the special restrictions set out in section 41(3) above; and where the Secretary of State so directs, the restriction order shall cease to have effect, and section 41(5) above shall apply accordingly.

(2) At any time while a restriction order is in force in respect of a patient, the Secretary of State may, if he thinks fit, by warrant discharge the patient from hospital, either absolutely or subject to conditions; and where a person is absolutely discharged under this subsection, he shall thereupon cease to be liable to be detained by virtue of the relevant hospital order, and the restriction order shall cease to have effect accordingly.

(3) The Secretary of State may at any time during the continuance in force of a restriction order in respect of a patient who has been conditionally discharged under subsection (2) above by warrant recall the patient to such hospital as may be specified in the warrant.

(4) Where a patient is recalled as mentioned in subsection (3) above—

    (a) if the hospital specified in the warrant is not the hospital from which the patient was conditionally discharged, the hospital order and the restriction order shall have effect as if the hospital specified in the warrant were substituted for the hospital specified in the hospital order;

    (b) in any case, the patient shall be treated for the purposes of section 18 above as if he had absented himself without leave from the hospital specified in the warrant […].

(5) If a restriction order in respect of a patient ceases to have effect after the patient has been conditionally discharged under this section, the patient shall, unless previously recalled under subsection (3) above, be deemed to be absolutely discharged on the date when the order ceases to have effect, and shall cease to be liable to be detained by virtue of the relevant hospital order accordingly.

(6) The Secretary of State may, if satisfied that the attendance at any place in Great Britain of a patient who is subject to a restriction order is desirable in the interests of justice or for the purposes of any public inquiry, direct him to be taken to that place; and where a patient is directed under this subsection to be taken to any place he shall, unless the Secretary of State otherwise directs, be kept in custody while being so taken, while at that place and while being taken back to the hospital in which he is liable to be detained.

Amendment

The words omitted in subs.(4)(b) were repealed by the Mental Health Act 2007 s.55, Sch.11 Pt 8.

Definitions

1-623   patient: s.145.
restriction order: ss.41, 55(4), 145(1).
hospital: ss.55(5), 145(1).
hospital order: ss.37, 55(4), 145(1).
absent without leave: ss.18(6), 145(1).

General Note

1-624   This section empowers the Secretary of State to take the following action in respect of patients who have been placed on restriction orders: (1) to direct that the order shall cease to have effect; (2) to discharge the patient from hospital absolutely; and (3) to discharge the patient from hospital subject to conditions.

A restriction order cannot cease to have effect by inference or implication: see *R. v Secretary of State for the Home Department Ex p. Didlick* (1993) 16 B.M.L.R. 71 DC where Rougier J. said at 75:

"In my opinion subsection (1) and (2) [of section 42] indicate clearly that before a restriction order can be brought to an end, the Secretary of State must either make a declaration to that effect or must discharge the patient absolutely. Each of these is a positive act. There is no room, in my opinion, for the situation whereby a restriction order ceases to have effect by inference or implication. It follows, therefore, that, by merely allowing the conditions under which the applicant was discharged to lapse, the Secretary of State did not thereby bring to an end the operation of the restriction order."

Any reference in this section to a hospital order, a guardianship order or a restriction order shall be construed as including a reference to any other order or direction under this Part having the same effect as such orders (s.55(4)).

Human Rights Act 1998

A patient who is assessed as posing no risk to the public should not be denied a conditional discharge **1-625** solely on the ground that the inhabitants of a particular locality feared that he might be dangerous if released (*Stojanovski v The Former Yugoslav Republic of Macedonia* [2010] M.H.L.R. 292, para.35).

The exercise by the Secretary of State of his power of recall under subs.(3) will, except in emergency cases, constitute a violation of art.5(1) of the ECHR in the absence of an up to date report on the patient's medical condition (see the notes on subs.(3) and art.5).

One of the consequences of the decision of the Court of Appeal in *R. v North West London Mental Health NHS Trust Ex p. Stewart*, noted under subs.(3), is that a conditionally discharged patient who is brought back to hospital under either s.2 or s.3 can be discharged from that section by a tribunal but be liable to be re-detained by the Secretary of State using his recall power under subs.(3). It is questionable whether it could be successfully claimed that the tribunal in such a case has the power to order the discharge of the patient as required by art.5(4) of the ECHR if the order can be immediately overridden by the Secretary of State.

Applications to the First-tier Tribunal (Mental Health) or the Mental Health Review Tribunal for Wales

A patient whose restrictions have been lifted under subs.(1) may apply to a tribunal as if he had been **1-626** admitted to hospital under a hospital order (ss.40(4), 41(5)).

A conditionally discharged patient has a right to apply to a tribunal for an absolute discharge between 12 months and two years after the conditional discharge and during each subsequent two-year period (s.75(2)).

The case of a conditionally discharged patient who has been recalled to hospital must be referred to a tribunal by the Secretary of State within a month of his return to hospital (s.75(1)(a)). The patient may apply to the tribunal between six and 12 months after the recall and during each subsequent 12-month period (ss.70, 75(1)(b)). There is no duty placed on the Secretary of State to periodically refer the case of a conditionally discharged patient to the tribunal.

Guidance on the restricted patient system

The Ministry of Justice and HM Prison and Probation Service have published guidance on the **1-627** restricted patient system which "provides stakeholders (including patients and their families, victims, Responsible Clinicians and other report writers and multi-disciplinary team members) with an overview of the restricted patient system in England and Wales and the role of the Secretary of State for Justice and the Mental Health Casework Section (MHCS) in Her Majesty's Prison and Probation Service (HMPPS)" (para.1). The guidance can be accessed at: *www.gov.uk/government/publications/mentally-disordered-offenders-the-restricted-patient-system*.

Subsection (1)

This subsection enables the Secretary of State to lift the restrictions from a patient who is subject to **1-628** a restriction order if he considers that they are no longer necessary to protect the public from serious harm. If the restrictions are lifted, the patient will continue to be detained as if he had been admitted to hospital under a hospital order made without restrictions (s.41(5)). The Secretary of State, who in practice acts through the Mental Health Casework Section (MHCS) of the Ministry of Justice (see the General Note to this Part), rarely exercises this power.

Paragraph 5 of "*Lifting of special restrictions by the Secretary of State under the Mental Health Act 1983*" (2016) states:

"The powers contained in section 42(1) apply to all restricted patients. Although possible, it is unlikely that the Secretary of State would lift restrictions under section 42(1) for those patients who are transferred prisoners under section 47 or 48 or those with hospital directions under section 45A of the MHA. In these cases, the restrictions are in place because the patient would otherwise be serving a custodial sentence in prison as imposed by the court. For those with determinate sentences, the restrictions will cease automatically on the prisoner's earliest release date."

Protection of the public   In *R. v Parole Board Ex p. Bradley* [1990] 3 All E.R. 828 at 836, DC, Stuart-Smith L.J., on examining this provision said that "the precise level of risk is not (surely cannot be) spelt out".

Subsection (2)

1-629   This subsection enables the Secretary of State to order the absolute or conditional discharge of a restricted patient. Guidance which sets out the Secretary of State's approach to applications for discharge under this provision is reproduced in Part 4. The tribunal has a similar power to that of the Secretary of State under s.73. The vast majority of discharge decisions are made by the tribunal.

If the Secretary of State, after having weighed all the evidence about a patient's mental condition, is satisfied that the patient is no longer suffering from mental disorder, he should discharge the patient: see the obiter observations of Lawton L.J. in *Kynaston v Secretary of State for Home Affairs* (1981) 73 Cr. App. R. 281 CA. This course of action is required by the ECHR: see art.5(1) and the decision of the European Court of Human Rights in *Winterwerp v The Netherlands* (1979) 2 E.H.R.R. 387. The patient's discharge need not be absolute (*R. v Merseyside Mental Health Review Tribunal Ex p. K* [1990] 1 All E.R. 694 CA and *Johnson v United Kingdom* (1997) 27 E.H.R.R. 296).

The Secretary of State is not bound by any statutory criteria when exercising his judgment under this provision. This contrasts with the power of the tribunal under s.73. Regular reports on the patient, prepared by his RC, will be submitted to the Secretary of State under s.41(6).

Absolutely   An absolute discharge has the effect of extinguishing both the hospital order and the restriction order. The patient is therefore no longer "liable to be detained" (subs.(2)). In *R. (on the application of L) v West London Mental Health NHS Trust* [2012] EWHC 3200 (Admin); [2013] M.H.L.R. 297 Stadlen J. said at para.266:

"Discharge directly from a high security hospital like Broadmoor is extremely rare. A staged discharge involving normally at least a period in a medium security hospital is much more usual. There are reasons unconnected with the severity or nature of a patient's mental disorder which make it likely that a patient who is transferred to a high security hospital will experience a longer passage of time before he is ultimately discharged than would be the case if he were not so transferred."

In *Secretary of State for the Home Department v KE (Nigeria)* [2017] EWCA Civ 1382 Hickinbottom L.J. said that "it is common for orders never to be absolutely discharged because, even if an offender is conditionally discharged into the community, the risk of a recurrence of the mental disorder or its symptoms – and thus of danger to the public – remains" (para.5).

Subject to conditions   As a conditionally discharged patient is "liable to be detained" in a hospital (*Secretary of State for Justice v MM* [2018] UKSC 60; [2018] M.H.L.R. 392, para.18), he has a responsible clinician (subs.(5) and s.55(1)).

The *Code of Practice* states:

"22.79 Conditionally discharged restricted patients will in most cases be subject to community supervision and be monitored by a clinical supervisor and a social supervisor, both of whom are required to submit reports, generally quarterly, to the Ministry of Justice detailing the patient's progress, current presentation and any concerns. These reports should be comprehensive including defining clearly any risks being presented by the patient either to themselves or others. They should also record unusual occurrences such as interactions with the police and where necessary these events should be investigated further by the appropriate supervisor and information shared with other relevant parties. Although there is a requirement for regular reports, if at any time clinical teams become concerned over a patient's behaviour or presentation, they should investigate those concerns and contact the Ministry of Justice straightaway. Similarly these reports will be closely scrutinised by the Ministry of Justice and where necessary, concerns will be raised with the relevant parties involved. See paragraphs 22.87 – 22.92 below in respect of restricted part 3 patients convicted of serious offences.

22.80 The Ministry of Justice does not stipulate the professionals who can undertake the role of social supervisor. Social supervisors should have received adequate professional development, be resourced to be able to produce prompt, accurate reports and raise any concerns with regard to the patient's behaviour in the community. Social supervisors will be allocated by local authorities, who will determine that their agreed social supervisors have the correct knowledge, expertise and skills to undertake this role, in line with the efficiency and equity principle."

The Ministry of Justice has published guidance on the role of social supervisors of conditionally discharged patients (July 2019). It is understood that the view of the Secretary of State is that the local authority for the area where the patient resides is responsible for providing the social supervisor. The Butler Committee agreed with the recommendation of the Aarvold Committee (Cmnd. 5191) that "supervision should be undertaken by the person who can bring most to the case in the way of knowledge, expertise and resources in the particular circumstances of the case. The arrangements may need to take particular account of the needs of public safety" (para.8.7).

If a condition of a patient's discharge interferes with the patient's right to respect for his private and family life, it must be justified under art.8(2) of the European Convention on Human Rights (ECHR). In *R. (on the application of Craven) v Secretary of State for the Home Department* [2001] EWHC Admin 850, Stanley Burnton J. rejected a prisoner's claim that a condition of his parole not to enter an area of Newcastle where the family of his victim lived constituted a disproportionate and therefore unlawful interference with his art.8 rights. His Lordship held that distress to the victim's family was a consideration that could lawfully be taken into account by the Parole Board and by the Secretary of State. A patient who has been conditionally discharged under this provision is not subject to the consent to treatment provisions contained in Pt IV (s.56(3)(c)). In *MM*, below, Lady Hale said at para.13:

"It is usually a condition that the patient 'shall comply with treatment as directed by the clinical supervisor' (para 23 of the [previous edition of the] Guidance for clinical supervisors). However, the power to impose treatment without consent upon hospital patients, by force if need be, contained in section 63 of the MHA, does not apply to conditionally discharged restricted patients (section 56(3)(c), as substituted by section 34(2) of the 2007 Act). A patient is entitled to refuse treatment unless he lacks the capacity to make the decision, in which case the Mental Capacity Act 2005 (MCA) may permit treatment which is in his best interests, but will only permit coercion in order to impose treatment in very limited circumstances (MCA, sections 5 and 6). Hence, in *R (SH) v Mental Health Review Tribunal* [2007] EWHC 884 (Admin); (2007) 10 CCLR 306, Holman J rejected a challenge to the legality of a condition to comply with treatment as being contrary both to the common law right to choose what medical treatment to have and to the right to respect for private life in article 8 of the ECHR. Although the condition said 'shall comply', the patient remained free to choose whether or not to have the treatment at each and every time when he was required to do so. That refusal would not, by itself, necessarily lead to his recall to hospital."

The decision of the Court of Appeal in *R. (on the application of H) v Secretary of State for the Home Department* [2002] EWCA Civ 646; [2002] M.H.L.R. 87 that where a tribunal is considering ordering a conditional discharge, a Health Authority was not under an absolute obligation to procure compliance with the tribunal's conditions was affirmed by the House of Lords ([2003] UKHL 59) where it was held that the obligation is for the authority to use its best endeavours to secure compliance. The tribunal has "no power to require any psychiatrist to act in a way which conflicted with the conscientious professional judgment of that psychiatrist" (per Lord Bingham at para.29; also see *R. v Camden and Islington Health Authority Ex p. K* [2001] EWCA Civ 240 CA, noted in the General Note to s.117). It is submitted that this ruling also applies to conditions proposed by the Secretary of State.

Force cannot be used to require a patient to comply with a condition (*R. (on the application of SH v Mental Health Review Tribunal* [2007] EWHC 884 (Admin); [2007] M.H.L.R. 234).

The Secretary of State has the power to vary any condition imposed by the tribunal or by him and can impose a new condition subsequent to the patient's discharge (s.73(4)(b) (5) and *MM*, below, para.7). A patient does not commit an offence by breeching a condition of his discharge.

Conditions which result in a deprivation of the patient's liberty

In *Secretary of State for Justice v MM* [2018] UKSC 60; [2018] M.H.L.R. 392, the issue to be **1-630** resolved by the Supreme Court was whether the conditions imposed on a conditional discharge can, if the patient consents, be so restrictive as to amount to a deprivation of liberty within the meaning of art.5 of the European Convention on Human Rights. Lady Hale, who gave the main judgment, held that the word "discharge" in this subsection, when referring to the conditional discharge of restricted patients, must mean actual discharge from the hospital in which the patient is currently detained, as he remains liable to be detained (para.20). Although her Ladyship said that there is nothing in this Act which expressly prohibits a condition which amounts to a detention or deprivation of liberty in another setting, there were compelling reasons not to construe this subsection in this way. The most compelling reason is that such a power would be contrary to the whole scheme of this Act, which provides in detail for only two forms of detention (in a place of safety for up to 36 hours, or in a hospital), each with associated specific powers to convey a patient there, to detain him and to retake him if he absents himself from such detention without leave. There is no equivalent express power to convey a conditionally discharged restricted patient to the place where he is required to live or to detain him there, nor is he liable to be taken into custody and returned anywhere unless and until he is recalled to hospital by the Secretary of State (paras 33–36). The fact that a conditionally discharged restricted patient can apply far less frequently than a hospital patient to the tribunal for his release indicates that Parliament did not consider that such patients might be subject to conditions which required the same degree of protection as those deprived of their liberty (para.37). Accordingly, Lady Hale held that this Act does not permit the Secretary of State to impose conditions amounting to detention or a deprivation of liberty upon a conditionally discharged restricted patient (para.38). The Supreme Court did not make a finding on MM's argument that his valid consent to his confinement meant that the subjective element of a deprivation of liberty was not present (see Part 6), However, a strong hint that such a consent would not be valid was given by Lady Hale who said that it "is clear from decisions, such as *Buzadji v Moldova (Application No 23755/07), Grand Chamber Judgment of* 5 July 2016, that consent given in circumstances where the choice is between greater and lesser forms of deprivation of liberty – there between detention in prison and detention under house arrest – may be no real consent at all" (para.23).

In *MM*, Lady Hale said:

"Whether the Court of Protection could authorise a future deprivation, once the First-tier Tribunal has granted a conditional discharge, and whether the First-tier Tribunal could defer its decision for this purpose, are not issues which it would be appropriate for this court to decide at this stage in these proceedings" (para.27).

These issues were addressed in *MC v Sygnet Behavioural Health Ltd* [2020] UKUT 230 (AAC); [2021] M.H.L.R. 157 where UT Judge Jacobs, having reviewed the relevant case law, including *MM*, held that the First-tier tribunal has the power to co-ordinate its decision to discharge a patient on a conditional discharge with the provision of authority under the Mental Capacity Act 2005 to deprive him of his liberty. The finding in this case is further considered in the notes on s.73(4)(b).

The decision in MM was considered in the context of a discharge by the tribunal in *Cumbria, Northumberland Tyne & Wear NHS Foundation Trust v EG* [2021] EWHC 2990 (Fam) which is noted under s.72(1)(b)(i).

Subsection (3)

1-631   **The Secretary of State may recall the patient**   In *R. (on the application of MM) v The Secretary of State for the Home Department* [2007] EWCA Civ 687; [2007] M.H.L.R. 304, the Court of Appeal dismissed an appeal against the decision of Mitting J. to uphold the decision of the Secretary of State to recall the patient under this provision. Toulson L.J said at para.50:

"For the Secretary of State to recall a patient who has been conditionally discharged by [a tribunal], he has to believe on reasonable grounds that something has happened *since the decision of the tribunal*, or information has emerged *which was not available to the tribunal*, of sufficient significance to justify recalling the patient. As I have said, it is not in dispute that he must have up-to-date medical evidence about the patient's mental health."

[The italicised words were added to this formulation by Bean J. in *IT v Secretary of State for Justice* [2008] EWHC 1707 (Admin); [2008] M.H.L.R. 290 para.13, in order to make it consistent with the decision of the House of Lords in *R. (on the application of von Brandenburg) v East London and the City Mental Health NHS Trust* [2003] UKHL 58.]

The test established by the Court of Appeal in *MM* was considered by Burnett J. in *R. (on the application of Munday) v Secretary of State for the Home Department* [2009] EWHC 3638 (Admin); [2009] M.H.L.R. 401. His Lordship said, at para.28, that the following formulation of the test, which was made by counsel for the Secretary of State at para.44 of the judgment, is correct:

"… the [Secretary of State] should ask himself whether there had been such a material change of circumstances since the Tribunal's previous decision that he could reasonably form the view that the detention criteria were now satisfied."

Although a breach of a condition imposed on the patient may be "powerful evidence of, for example, relapse and the need for a recall" (*Secretary of State for Justice v KC* [2015] UKUT 376 (AAC), para.53, per Charles J.), in *MM*, the court held that a beach of a condition imposed on the patient was not a free-standing ground for the patient's recall. The question is whether the breach has the effect of enabling the Secretary of State to form a proper judgment (i.e. one that was not unreasonable in the public law sense) on the medical evidence that the statutory criteria for detention were established. The court further held that the language of the first statutory criterion ("of a nature or degree which makes it appropriate for him to be detained") would be unduly circumscribed if there had to be either psychotic symptoms or the certainty of psychotic symptoms in the imminent future before detention for treatment could be considered appropriate. It is therefore the case that a recall does not require any evidence of deterioration in the patient's mental state. At first instance, Mitting J. said that in the generality of cases, it is impracticable for the Secretary of State, prior to the issue of the recall warrant, to convene an assessment at which the patient is entitled to make representations of fact ([2006] EWHC 3056 (Admin); [2006] M.H.L.R. 358 para.49). In confirming the decision of the Secretary of State to recall a patient due to concerns about deterioration of his mental health associated with illicit drug use, his Lordship said at para.47:

"The Secretary of State is entitled to have at the forefront of his mind not just the health and safety of the patient, but also the safety of members of the public, including the patient's own family. The Secretary of State is not obliged to put the interests of people at significant risk by staying his hand in circumstances where he has medical evidence that the taking of illicit drugs would be likely to cause imminently a severe deterioration in his mental condition".

In *Munday*, above, at para.30, Burnett J. said that the second statutory criterion (the "necessity" test) is concerned with risk and that although "psychiatrists or other medical health professionals or social supervisors with their knowledge of a person might be in a position to express a view about risk, it is by its nature an exercise of evaluation which does not necessarily call for expert medical input". In this case, his Lordship held that given the patient's history of arson, a mere allegation and arrest for arson was sufficient justification for recall.

In *Kay v United Kingdom* (1998) 40 B.M.L.R. 20, the European Commission of Human Rights held that, in the absence of an emergency, there had been a breach of art.5(1) of the ECHR when a patient had been recalled under this provision without up to date medical evidence to demonstrate that he was suffering from a true mental disorder of a kind or degree warranting compulsory confinement. Although in *MM* Mitting J. accepted that the Secretary of State must have before him medical evidence which justifies the decision to recall, that medical evidence "need not be a report freshly prepared upon the precise condition recently obtaining". Where, as in *MM*'s case:

"there is abundant medical evidence to the effect that [he] suffers from paranoid schizophrenia and that his condition is likely to deteriorate imminently and significantly if he takes illicit drugs, then that evidence suffices to justify recall unless there is good reason for believing that it is no longer currently valid" (para.41).

In *R. (on the application of B) v Mental Health Review Tribunal* [2002] EWHC 1553 (Admin); [2003] M.H.L.R. 19 para.31, Scott Baker J. said obiter that the medical evidence must show that the criteria for detention are met.

The Reference Guide states at para.27.45:

"In urgent cases, a direction recalling a patient may be given verbally outside office hours by a duty officer of the Ministry of Justice's Mental Health Casework Section on behalf of the Secretary of State. In practice, the warrant would then normally be provided on the next working day".

The *Code of Practice* states:

"22.82 A patient will be recalled where it is necessary to protect the public from the actual or potential risk posed by that patient and that the risk is linked to the patient's mental disorder. It is not possible to specify all the circumstances when recall may be appropriate and public safety will always be the most important factor. Key points include:

- the decision on whether to recall will largely depend on the degree of danger posed by the patient, the gravity of the potential or actual risk and how imminent the risk is

- recall does not necessarily require any evidence of deterioration in the patient's mental state, but evidence is required that a 'change' has occurred since the discharge decision. This is so that the Secretary of State for Justice can be satisfied that recall is a proportionate and lawful action. Other than in an emergency, medical evidence will be required that the patient is currently mentally disordered
- recall will not be used to deal with anti-social or offending behaviour that is unconnected with the patient's mental disorder
- recall decisions always give precedence to public safety considerations. This may mean that the Secretary of State for Justice will decide to recall on public safety grounds even if the supervisors (see paragraphs 22.79 – 22.80) are of the view that recall would be counter-therapeutic for the patient
- recall will be considered to protect others from harm because of a combination of the patient's mental disorder and behaviour, including potential behaviour where there is evidence that indicates the imminent likelihood of risk behaviours
- in an emergency the Secretary of State for Justice may recall for assessment in the absence of fresh evidence as regards mental disorder
- the support for recall from the patient's social supervisor is important but not determinative and the Secretary of State for Justice can, satisfied that recall is necessary, make the decision to recall in the absence of any recommendation
- where however recall is recommended by at least one supervisor, then the expectation is that the patient should be recalled unless there are compelling reasons not to recall, and
- admission under sections 2 or 3 – if a restricted patient requires compulsory detention in hospital under the Act then recall will almost invariably be appropriate.

The only circumstances where recall may not be indicated would be where discharge was imminent (within days rather than weeks), or where the admission is solely due to self-harm or suicide issues and the admission is likely to last less than a month.

22.83 Should recall be indicated, the clinical team should initially discuss their concerns with MHCS and identify a suitable bed at an appropriate security level for the patient to be admitted to. Once the arrangements are confirmed, MHCS will issue a Secretary of State for Justice warrant for the recall of a patient to a named hospital or unit."

The policy of the MHCS on recalls is set out at para.5 of "*The recall of conditionally discharged restricted patients*" (2009), which is reproduced in Part 4 and can be accessed at: *www.gov.uk/government/publications/recall-of-conditionally-discharged-restricted-patients*.

Once a decision to recall has been made, it is the responsibility of the supervisor to identify an appropriate bed and to make the practicable arrangements for admission to hospital. The consent to treatment provisions contained in Pt IV apply to the patient from the date of the recall (s.56(3)(c)).

A recall warrant has immediate effect. If the patient will not return to hospital willingly on being told of the recall, then the police should be asked to assist. In non-urgent cases, the police should be provided with a copy of the recall warrant. Once recalled, and until they are readmitted to hospital, patients are treated as if they were absent without leave and can therefore be taken into custody and taken to the hospital specified in the warrant. There is no power of entry attached to a recall warrant. If it is not possible to gain access to a patient who has been recalled, an application may be made to a magistrate under s.135(2).

A three-way procedure for informing restricted patients of the reasons for their recall is set out in the Annex to Department of Health Circular No. HSG(93)20 (also see Circular LAC(93)9 addressed to local authorities in similar terms):

" *Stage 1:* The person returning the patient to hospital should inform him/her in simple terms that he/she is being recalled to hospital by the [Secretary of State] under section 42(3) of the Mental Health Act 1983 and that, to the extent that this is possible, a further explanation will be given later. The reason(s) for recalling the patient should be explained to the nearest relative, if one is available, within 72 hours.

Stage 2: An explanation should be given to the patient of the reason(s) for his/her recall as soon as possible after re-admission to hospital and in any event within 72 hours. This should be done by the [RC] or deputy, an [AMHP], or an appropriate administrator representing the hospital managers. The person giving the explanation should ensure, so far as the patient's mental condition allows, that the patient understands the reason(s).

Stage 3: A written explanation of the reason(s) for recall should be provided for the patient within 72 hours of being re-admitted to hospital. Written information on the reason(s) should also be given to the patient's nearest relative (subject to the patient's consent)."

Para.1.2 of the Annex states:

"The [RC] should inform the patient's supervising officer (social worker or probation officer) in the community, the key worker attached to the patient under the Care Programme Approach and a member of the patient's family who accepts responsibility (or a legal representative) of the reason(s) for recall. In the interests of co-ordination and longer-term care programme planning (HC(90)23), it may also be necessary to inform (or otherwise involve) other agencies who are concerned with patients care."

The references to the patient's nearest relative in stages 1 and 3 of the procedure is an error as a restricted patient does not have a nearest relative for the purposes of the Act.

In *R. (on the application of Lee-Hirons) v Secretary of State for Justice* [2016] UKSC 46; [2017] M.H.L.R. 57 the Supreme Court held that:

1. The brief oral explanation provided to the patient at the time of his recall (i.e. that it was because of his deteriorating mental health) satisfied stage 1 of the policy set out in HSG(93)20. It also complied with the Minister's common law duty to provide reasons. As art.5(2) of the ECHR does not in this respect extend beyond the demands of the common law, there was no violation of that article.

2. The failure of the Secretary of State to comply with stages 2 and 3 of the policy between the 3rd and 15th days following the patient's recall did not render the patient's detention during that period unlawful as there was "no link, let alone a direct link, between, on the one hand, the Minister's wrongful failure for 12 days to provide to the [patient] an adequate explanation for his recall and, on the other, the lawfulness of his detention" (per Lord Wilson applying *R. (on the application of Lumba) v Secretary of State for the Home Department* [2011] UKSC 12 and *R. (on the application of Kambadzi) v Secretary of State for the Home Department* [2011] UKSC 23 at para.39).

3. The patient was not entitled to damages for the breach of his common law right to receive an adequate explanation for his recall within the time set out by the policy. The breach did not amount to a tort and there was nothing to suggest that damages would have been available in an ordinary action against the Minister. The conclusion was the same in relation to the violation of art.5(2); the patient had failed to establish that the effects of the breach were sufficiently grave.

Paragraph 4.19 of the *Code of Practice* states:

"Where a conditionally discharged patient is to be recalled to hospital, a brief verbal explanation of the Secretary of State's reasons for recall must be provided to the patient at the time of recall unless there are exceptional reasons why this is not possible, eg the patient is violent or too distressed. The Secretary of State's warrant will detail the reasons. The patient should also receive a full explanation of the reasons for his or her recall within 72 hours after admission, and both written and oral explanations should be provided."

As "recall" must be understood as authorising not only the physical recall of the patient, but also the reinstatement of a regime of control in respect of the patient, the Secretary of State may issue a warrant for the recall of a patient to a hospital in which the patient is already detained under ss.2 or 3 (*Dlodlo v South Thames Mental Health Review Tribunal* (1996) 36 B.M.L.R. 145 CA). In *Dlodlo*, a restriction order patient was transferred to a local hospital. The patient was subsequently given a conditional discharge by a tribunal, but, on becoming ill, he was re-admitted to the local hospital under s.3. The re-admission was followed by the issue of a warrant for the patients recall. The legality of using s.3 to detain a restriction order patient who had been conditionally discharged was confirmed by the Court of Appeal in *R. v North West London Mental Health NHS Trust Ex p. Stewart* [1997] 4 All E.R. 871.

1-632

The policy of the MHCS is to consider recall where there is any admission to a psychiatric hospital. If an informal admission is being considered, the professional dealing with the patient should contact MHCS to discuss the case (Mental Health Casework Section Newsletter, January 2011). The July 2011 issue of the *MHCS Newsletter* states:

"Where admission is voluntary and the patient remains co-operative with treatment in hospital, the Ministry of Justice will not normally recall if medical advice is that only a brief period of in-patient treatment is necessary for observation or stabilisation. However, it is generally inappropriate for a conditionally discharged patient to remain in hospital for more than a few weeks time voluntarily. If the use of civil powers is necessary to detain a patient or enable compulsory treatment to be given, immediate recall will almost invariably be appropriate to regularise the restricted patient's status under the Act. If a patient remains on voluntary admission, MHCS will require weekly updates."

There is nothing to prevent the holding powers contained in s.5(2) and (4) from being used on a conditionally discharged patient who is being treated in a psychiatric hospital informally. MHCS should be informed if this occurs.

The contact numbers of the MHCS at the Ministry of Justice are 0781 276 0248 and 0300 303 2079 (outside office hours).

Hospital   Or registered establishment (s.34(2)). The recall can be to any hospital in England or Wales. The legality of recalling a patient to a hospital other than the hospital named in the restriction order was confirmed in the *Dlodlo* case, above.

In "The recall of conditionally discharged restricted patients", above, para.4, the Ministry of Justice states:

"There is no statutory requirement for the Justice Secretary to obtain the agreement of the hospital doctors to re-admit a recalled patient. The Justice Secretary is entitled to take a different view to that of the supervising psychiatrist, provided there are sufficient grounds/evidence to justify this and satisfy the Secretary of State that the criteria for detention under the Mental Health Act are met."

Subsection (4)

1-633   **Paragraph (b)**   This paragraph provides that a recalled patient can be taken into custody and conveyed to the specified hospital by any AMHP, officer on the staff of the hospital or any other person authorised by the hospital managers.

Subsection (5)

1-634   This subsection provides that if a restriction order ceases to have effect while the patient is on conditional discharge from hospital he will cease to be liable to be detained.

Subsection (6)

1-635   **Great britain**   England, Wales and Scotland (Union with Scotland Act 1706, preamble, art.1).

Taken to that place   See s.137 for general provisions relating to custody, conveyance and detention.

Power of magistrates' courts to commit for restriction order

1-636   **43.**—(1)   If in the case of a person of or over the age of 14 years who is convicted by a magistrates' court of an offence punishable on summary conviction with imprisonment—

    (a)   the conditions which under section 37(1) above are required to be satisfied for the making of a hospital order are satisfied in respect of the offender; but

    (b)   it appears to the court, having regard to the nature of the offence, the antecedents of the offender and the risk of his committing further offences if set at large, that if a hospital order is made a restriction order should also be made,

the court may, instead of making a hospital order or dealing with him in any other manner, commit him in custody to the Crown Court to be dealt with in respect of the offence.

(2)   Where an offender is committed to the Crown Court under this section, the Crown Court shall inquire into the circumstances of the case and may—

    (a)   if that court would have power so to do under the foregoing provisions of this Part of this Act upon the conviction of the offender before that court of such an offence as is described in section 37(1) above, make a hospital order in his case, with or without a restriction order;

    (b)   if the court does not make such an order, deal with the offender in any other manner in which the magistrates' court might have dealt with him.

(3) The Crown Court shall have the same power to make orders under sections 35, 36 and 38 above in the case of a person committed to the court under this section as the Crown Court has under those sections in the case of an accused person within the meaning of section 35 or 36 above or of a person convicted before that court as mentioned in section 38 above.

[(4) The powers of a magistrates' court under [section 14[, 16 or 16A] of the Sentencing Code] (which enable such a court to commit an offender to the Crown Court where the court is of the opinion, or it appears to the court, as mentioned in the section in question) shall also be exercisable by a magistrates' court where it is of that opinion (or it so appears to it) unless a hospital order is made in the offender's case with a restriction order.]

(5) The power of the Crown Court to make a hospital order, with or without a restriction order, in the case of a person convicted before that court of an offence may, in the same circumstances and subject to the same conditions, be exercised by such a court in the case of a person committed to the court under section 5 of the Vagrancy Act 1824 (which provides for the committal to the Crown Court of persons who are incorrigible rogues within the meaning of that section).

Amendment

Subsection (4) was substituted by s.41, Sch.3 para.55(2) to the Criminal Justice Act 2003. It was amended by the Sentencing Act 2020 Sch.24, Pt. 1, para.74 and the Counter-Terrorism and Sentencing Act 2021 Sch.13 para.15.

Definitions

hospital order: ss.37, 145(1).   **1-637**
restriction order: ss.41, 145(1).

General Note

A magistrates' court has no power to make a restriction order. If the court is satisfied that the conditions   **1-638**
exist in which it could make a hospital order, but also feels that a restriction order should be made in addition, it may commit an offender (if over 14 years of age) to the Crown Court under this section. The court does not need to be satisfied as to the "serious harm" test set out in s.41(1). The magistrates may direct that the offender be detained in a hospital, pending the hearing of the case by the Crown Court (s.44). If the Crown Court decides not to make a hospital order, it can deal with the offender in any way in which the magistrates' court could have dealt with him (subs.(2)) or it can remand him under s.35 or 36 or it can make an interim hospital order in respect of him (subs.(3)).

For the power of the committing court to deal with the offender in respect of another offence, see s.20 of the Sentencing Act 2020.

Appeals

In *Kiernan v Harrow Crown Court* [2003] EWCA Crim 1052; [2005] M.H.L.R. 1, the Court of Appeal, having considered ss.9 and 10 of the Criminal Appeal Act 1968, concluded that it had no jurisdiction to hear an appeal from a hospital order imposed by the Crown Court subsequent to a committal having been made under this section. In these circumstances, the court felt it appropriate to reconstitute itself as a Divisional Court of the Administrative Court and to consider the issue by way of a deemed application for judicial review of the decision of the Crown Court. Having quashed the decision of the Crown Court and having no power in judicial review proceedings to impose any separate penalty, the court remitted the case to a Crown Court judge.   **1-639**

Procedure

See the Criminal Procedure Rules 2020 (SI 2020/759) r.28.10.   **1-640**

Subsection (1)

1-641 **Age** See s.55(7). A person attains the age of 14 at the commencement of his fourteenth birthday (Family Law Reform Act 1969 s.9(1)).

Convicted The magistrates must have convicted the offender. In *R. v Horseferry Road Magistrates' Court Ex p. K* [1996] 3 All E.R. 719 at 735 DC, Forbes J. said:

"[The Act] makes *no* provision for committal to the Crown Court by the magistrates for imposition of a restriction order under s.41 upon a person who has been acquitted of an offence by reason of insanity. The magistrates only have such a power to commit to the Crown Court for that purpose in the case of a person *convicted* of an imprisonable offence, whether indictable or summary only".

His Lordship said that this state of affairs represented an "obvious legislative lacuna".

Magistrates' court Or youth court for those under the age of 18.

Offence punishable on summary conviction with imprisonment For young offenders, see s.55(2).

Commit him in custody Or order him to be admitted to a hospital if the conditions of s.44 are satisfied. The Secretary of State has power to transfer a mentally disordered offender from custody to hospital under s.48(2)(b).

Committal to hospital under s.43

1-642 **44.**—(1) Where an offender is committed under section 43(1) above and the magistrates' court by which he is committed is satisfied on written or oral evidence that arrangements have been made for the admission of the offender to a hospital in the event of an order being made under this section, the court may, instead of committing him in custody, by order direct him to be admitted to that hospital, specifying it, and to be detained there until the case is disposed of by the Crown Court, and may give such directions as it thinks fit for his production from the hospital to attend the Crown Court by which his case is to be dealt with.

(2) The evidence required by subsection (1) above shall be given by the [approved clinician who would have overall responsibility for the offender's case] or by some other person representing the managers of the hospital in question.

(3) The power to give directions under section 37(4) above, section 37(5) above and section 40(1) above shall apply in relation to an order under this section as they apply in relation to a hospital order, but as if references to the period of 28 days mentioned in section 40(1) above were omitted; and subject as aforesaid an order under this section shall, until the offender's case is disposed of by the Crown Court, have the same effect as a hospital order together with a restriction order [...].

Amendments

The amendments to this section were made by the Mental Health Act 2007 ss.10(7), s.55, Sch.11 Pt 8.

Definitions

1-643 hospital: ss.55(5), 145(1).
hospital order: ss.37, 145(1).
restriction order: ss.41, 145(1).
approved clinician: s.145(1).
the managers: s.145(1).

General Note

If a magistrates' court on committing an offender to the Crown Court under s.43 is satisfied that arrangements have been made for the admission of the offender to a hospital, it may direct him to be admitted to that hospital until the case is disposed of by the Crown Court. If it is impracticable or inappropriate to bring the offender before the court, the Crown Court may either adjourn the case or make a hospital order without convicting him and in his absence under s.51(5).   **1-644**

A patient who is admitted to a hospital under this section is subject to the consent to treatment provisions contained in Part IV (s.56).

Transitional provision

The repeal of the reference to restriction orders made for a specified period in subs.(3) shall have no effect in respect of—   **1-645**

(a)   a restriction order for a specified period made before October 1, 2007, or
(b)   an order made outside England and Wales which is treated under the 1983 Act as if it were a restriction order for a specified period (Mental Health Act 2007 s.40(7) and SI 2007/2798 art.2(d)).

Procedure

See the Criminal Procedure Rules 2020 (SI 2020/759) r.28.9.   **1-646**

Subsection (1)

Magistrates' court   Or youth court for those under the age of 18.   **1-647**

Admitted to that hospital   Which will normally be the hospital which had already agreed to admit the patient in the event of the magistrates' court itself making a hospital order. Once the offender has been admitted to the hospital, subss.(5) and (6) of s.51 shall apply to him as if he were a person subject to a transfer direction made under s.47 (s.51(3)).

Directions as it thinks fit for his production from the hospital   It will be the hospital's duty to arrange for the offenders attendance at the court with an appropriate escort. It is not necessary to obtain the Secretary of State's consent to leave of absence from the hospital for this purpose.

Subsection (2)

Some other person   Who need not be a clinician.   **1-648**

Subsection (3)

This subsection provides that the magistrates' court can direct that the offender be detained in a place of safety pending his admission to hospital. It also authorises a constable, approved mental health professional or any other person directed to do so by the court to convey the offender to hospital at any time and not within the 28-day period provided for by s.40(1). Subject to this exception, an order under this section has the same effect as a restriction order.   **1-649**

Appeals from magistrates' courts

45.—(1)   Where on the trial of an information charging a person with an offence a magistrates' court makes a hospital order or guardianship order in respect of him without convicting him, he shall have the same right of appeal against the order as if it had been made on his conviction; and on any such appeal the Crown Court shall have the same powers as if the appeal had been against both conviction and sentence.   **1-650**

(2)   An appeal by a child or young person with respect to whom any such order has been made, whether the appeal is against the order or against the finding upon

which the order was made, may be brought by him or by his parent or guardian on his behalf.

Definitions

1-651   hospital order: ss.37, 145(1).
guardianship order: ss.37, 145(1).
child: s.55(1).
young person: s.55(1).
guardian: s.55(1).

General Note

1-652   This section provides a right of appeal for a person who has been made the subject of a hospital order or a guardianship order made by a magistrates' court under s.37(3).

Paragraph 15.22 of the Reference Guide states:

"Appeals in respect of children or young people given hospital orders by magistrates' courts without being convicted may be brought on their behalf by their parents or guardians. This applies to appeals against the order itself and against the finding that the child or young person had done the act in question."

Procedure

1-653   See the Criminal Procedure Rules 2020 (SI 2020/759) rr.34.1 and 45.6.

[HOSPITAL AND LIMITATION DIRECTIONS

Power of higher courts to direct hospital admission

1-654   **45A.**—(1)   This section applies where, in the case of a person convicted before the Crown Court of an offence the sentence for which is not fixed by law—

(a)   the conditions mentioned in subsection (2) below are fulfilled; and

(b)   […], the court considers making a hospital order in respect of him before deciding to impose a sentence of imprisonment ("the relevant sentence") in respect of the offence.

(2)   The conditions referred to in subsection (1) above are that the court is satisfied, on the written or oral evidence of two registered medical practitioners—

(a)   that the offender is suffering from [mental disorder];

(b)   that the mental disorder from which the offender is suffering is of a nature or degree which makes it appropriate for him to be detained in a hospital for medical treatment; and

[(c)   that appropriate medical treatment is available for him.]

(3)   The court may give both of the following directions, namely—

(a)   a direction that, instead of being removed to and detained in a prison, the offender be removed to and detained in such hospital as may be specified in the direction (in this Act referred to as a "hospital direction"); and

(b)   a direction that the offender be subject to the special restrictions set out in section 41 above (in this Act referred to as a "limitation direction").

(4)   A hospital direction and a limitation direction shall not be given in relation to an offender unless at least one of the medical practitioners whose evidence is taken into account by the court under subsection (2) above has given evidence orally before the court.

(5)   A hospital direction and a limitation direction shall not be given in rela-

tion to an offender unless the court is satisfied on the written or oral evidence of the [approved clinician who would have overall responsibility for his case], or of some other person representing the managers of the hospital that arrangements have been made—

    (a)   for his admission to that hospital; and

    (b)   for his admission to it within the period of 28 days beginning with the day of the giving of such directions;

and the court may, pending his admission within that period, give such directions as it thinks fit for his conveyance to and detention in a place of safety.

(6)   If within the said period of 28 days it appears to the Secretary of State that by reason of an emergency or other special circumstances it is not practicable for the patient to be received into the hospital specified in the hospital direction, he may give instructions for the admission of the patient to such other hospital as appears to be appropriate instead of the hospital so specified.

(7)   Where such instructions are given—

    (a)   the Secretary of State shall cause the person having the custody of the patient to be informed, and

    (b)   the hospital direction shall have effect as if the hospital specified in the instructions were substituted for the hospital specified in the hospital direction.

(8)   Section 38(1) and (5) and section 39 above shall have effect as if any reference to the making of a hospital order included a reference to the giving of a hospital direction and a limitation direction.

(9)   A hospital direction and a limitation direction given in relation to an offender shall have effect not only as regards the relevant sentence but also (so far as applicable) as regards any other sentence of imprisonment imposed on the same or a previous occasion.

(10)   […]

(11)   […]

Amendments

This section was inserted by the Crime (Sentences) Act 1997 s.46. The amendments to it were made by the Criminal Justice Act 2003 s.332, Sch.37 Pt 7 and the Mental Health Act 2007 ss.1(4), 4(6), 10(8), 55, Sch.1 para.9, Sch.11 Pt 1.

Definitions

mental disorder: ss.1, 145(1).   **1-655**
hospital: ss.55(5), 145(1).
medical treatment: s.145(1), (4).
approved medical treatment: ss.3(4), 145(1AB).
approved clinician: s.145(1).
managers: s.145(1).
place of safety: s.55.

General Note

This section empowers the Crown Court, when imposing a fixed-term prison sentence on a mentally   **1-656** disordered offender convicted of an offence other than one of which the sentence is fixed by law, to give a direction for the offender's immediate admission to and detention in a specified hospital (a "hospital direction"), together with a direction that the offender be subject to the special restrictions set out in s.41 (a "limitation direction"). The offender then becomes a restricted patient (s.79). If the offender's mental health improves to the extent that he no longer needs treatment in hospital, the Secretary of State may remit him to prison under s.50(1). The power is designed to provide an appropriate disposal for a mentally disordered offender where there is an element of culpability in the offence which merits punishment. The court, which must have considered making a hospital order before imposing a sentence of imprisonment and attaching a hospital direction (subs.(1) (b)), cannot make a hospital direction without a limitation direction (subs.(3) and *R. v Poole* [2014] EWCA Crim 1641; [2015] M.H.L.R. 84). An order made under this section is not dependent on advance notification that a hospital bed is available (*R. v Finnerty* [2016] EWCA Crim 1513, para.30). The effect of hospital and limitation directions is set out in s.45B.

The *Code of Practice* states at para.22.74:

"A hospital and limitation direction may be imposed where it is considered that the offender, although suffering from a mental disorder, can be considered to be responsible, to a degree, for the offence. Generally, courts have adopted the test that there has to be a 'significant degree' of culpability for a hospital direction to be appropriate, although this test is not always applied."

In *R. v Vowles* [2015] EWCA Crim 45; [2016] M.H.L.R. 66 at para.21, Lord Thomas C.J. said that the advantage of making an order under this section "in an appropriate case is that an offender sentenced to an indeterminate or long determinate sentence can immediately be directed to have treatment in hospital, but the timing of his release is subject to the decision of the Parole Board which has to take a much wider view of the risks to the public than the [First-tier Tribunal]". Due to a level of misunderstanding of the sentencing guidance offered in *Vowles* that had arisen, the Court of Appeal in *R. v Edwards* [2018] EWCA Crim 595; [2018] M.H.L.R. 105 summarised the principles that apply when sentencing offenders with mental health problems. *Vowles* and Edwards are considered in the General Note to s.37 under the heading *Hospital orders*.

The nature of the s.45A regime was summarised in the following passage from the judgment of Dingemans L.J. in *R. v Walker* [2023] EWCA Crim 548, at paras 29 and 30:

"Section 45A of the Mental Health Act permits in effect the combination of sentences of imprisonment with Hospital Orders, which is why they are referred to as 'Hybrid Orders'. Section 45A Orders are particularly appropriate in two situations. First, where notwithstanding the existence of the mental disorder, a penal element to the sentence is appropriate and the second was where the offender had a mental disorder but there were real doubts that he would comply with any treatment requirements in hospital, meaning that the [hospital] would be looking after an offender who would be dangerous, who was not being treated. Evidence in other cases has shown one practical disadvantage of returning to prison an offender who has been treated for a delusional disorder in hospital and who is required to take antipsychotic medicine. This was that many such offenders ceased to take medication on return to prison. This was because, from their point of view, there was no obvious advantage in taking the medication. They were no longer in hospital and also because a side effect of taking the medication was that awareness of people and circumstances and surroundings were suppressed, which some prisoners considered made them very vulnerable to attack in a prison environment. Stopping taking medication causes the offender to relapse and require further treatment. This was a point identified in *R v Rendell* [2019] EWCA Crim 621; [2020] MHLR 60. Evidence given in other cases has also shown that illegal drugs were more likely to be available in prisons than hospitals, all of which could lead to a deterioration of a mental disorder of such an offender by a return to hospital. Any court considering whether to impose a section 45A Mental Health Act Hybrid Order would need to make a careful assessment of culpability notwithstanding the presence of the mental disorder in accordance with guidance given in *Vowles* and *Edwards*.

30. If there is a determinate sentence to be served under section 45 Hybrid Order, the prisoner will serve that before being released on licence. Any release on licence will be supervised by the probation officer. It is apparent that the supervision will not be as regular as supervision by a Community Mental Health Team. If there is an indeterminate sentence to be served, such as a sentence of life imprisonment which was imposed on this appellant, release would only occur once agreed by the Parole Board. Once a release has taken place, supervision will be by a probation officer, and it is important to record that once released the effect of section 50 of the Mental Health Act is 'further provisions as to prisoners under sentence' is that, by subsection (2) 'a restriction direction, in the case of a person serving a sentence of imprisonment, shall cease to have effect if it has not previously done so on his release date'. This means that the supervision of the released offender will be carried out only by the probation officer. Evidence from previous cases showed that the Parole Board did not impose conditions such as the requirement to take antipsychotic medicine and that a probation officer was unlikely to be able to intervene in the event of a subtle deterioration of mental state. Such an intervention would only take place in the event of commission of further offences by which time serious damage might have been caused to members of the public. Similar risks were identified in *Rendell* at paragraph 53."

In *R. v Yuel* [2019] EWCA Crim 1693; [2020] M.H.L.R. 171, Simon L.J. said that it "is clear that in some cases where an order is made under section 45A, the dangerousness of an offender will be such that the additional level of protection for the public afforded by an extended sentence will be necessary" (para.46).

The Court of Appeal can substitute an order under this section for a prison sentence despite the Crown Court not having been referred at the time of sentence to the possibility of such an order being made (*R. v Stead* [2012] EWCA Crim 92; [2012] M.H.L.R. 58). However, the Court of Appeal cannot impose an order under this section if such an order was not available to the original sentencing court (*R. v Stredwick* [2020] EWCA Crim 650, para.38).

As an order under this section can only be made in respect of offenders who can be sentenced to imprisonment, that is to offenders over the age of 21, an order cannot be made in respect of a person under that age at the time of conviction (*Attorney General's Reference (No.54 of 2011)* [2011] EWCA Crim 2276; [2012] M.H.L.R. 87, para.22; also see *R. v Fort* [2013] EWCA Crim 2332; [2014] M.H.L.R. 334 which is noted under s.55(6)).

Appeals

A hospital direction and a limitation direction is a form of sentence and is therefore appealable to the Court of Appeal (Criminal Appeal Act 1968 ss.9(1), 50(1)).   **1-657**

Welfare benefits and transferred prisoners

See the General Note to s.47 under this heading.   **1-658**

Named hospital units

If a hospital and limitation direction is made, the court has the power to order that the patient be admitted to and detained in a named hospital unit: see the note to s.41 under this heading.   **1-659**

Applications to the First-tier Tribunal (Mental Health) or the Mental Health Review Tribunal for Wales

A patient who is subject to directions made under this section has the same right to apply to a tribunal as a restricted patient: see the note on s.41 under this heading. The procedure to be adopted on such an application being made is set out in s.74.   **1-660**

Domestic Violence, Crime and Victims Act 2004

See Ch.40 of the *Code of Practice*. The Department of Health has published *"Mental Health Act 2007: Guidance on the extension of victims' rights under the Domestic Violence, Crime and Victims Act"* (2008).   **1-661**

Subsection (1)

Convicted   The sentence of the court can be either determinate or indeterminate.   **1-662**

Fixed by law   This section does not apply to persons who have been convicted of murder who must be sentenced to life imprisonment (Murder (Abolition of Death Penalty) Act 1965 s.1).

Subsection (2)

Evidence   For general requirements as to medical evidence, see s.54. The court can call a doctor who has provided a written report to give oral evidence (s.54(2A)).   **1-663**

Two registered medical practitioners   One of whom must be approved by the Secretary of State or the Welsh Ministers under s.12, or by another person by virtue of s.12ZA or 12ZB (s.54(1)). A registered medical practitioner means "a fully registered person within the meaning of the Medical Act 1983 who holds a licence to practise under that Act" (Interpretation Act 1978 Sch.1).

Mental disorder   If the person has a learning disability, the disability must be associated with abnormally aggressive or seriously irresponsible conduct (s.1(2A), (2B)). A learning disabled person might also suffer from another form of mental disorder.

Nature or degree   See the note on s.3(2)(a).

Appropriate medical treatment   See the note on s.3(2)(d).

Subsection (3)

1-664   **Limitation direction**   In *R. v Poole* [2014] EWCA Crim 1641, the court rejected counsel's argument that this subsection, in referring to the restrictions set out in s.41, must thereby incorporate into the court's consideration for making a limitation direction those conditions set out in s.41(1) as a prerequisite for the making of a restriction order. Macur L.J. said that there "is good reason to differentiate the pre-requirements for a restriction order against those required for a limitation direction" (para.26).

Subsection (5)

1-665   A patient who is detained in a place of safety under this provision is not subject to the consent to treatment provisions contained in Pt IV (s.56(3)(b)). However, following the decision by the Court of Appeal in *R. v North West London Mental Health NHS Trust Ex p. Stewart* [1997] 4 All E.R. 871, it seems that a patient who has been detained in a place of safety which is a hospital could be brought within the scope of Pt IV if he was made the subject of an application under Part II: see the General Note to s.35.

In *R. (on the application of DB) v Nottinghamshire Healthcare NHS Trust* [2008] EWCA Civ 1354; [2009] 2 All E.R. 792, noted under s.37(4), the Court of Appeal held that a hospital order ceases to have effect if the offender who is the subject of the order is not admitted to the hospital named in the order within the period of 28 days from the date of the making of the order, as stipulated by it. It is submitted that this finding applies to directions made under this section.

Beginning with   Including the day on which the directions were given (*Zoan v Rouamba* [2000] 2 All E.R. 620 CA).

Subsections (6), (7)

1-666   **Secretary of State**   The functions of the Secretary of State under these provisions, so far as exercisable in relation to Wales, are exercised by the Welsh Ministers: see the General Note to the Act and SI 1999/672 art.2, Sch.1, as varied by SI 2000/253 art.4, Sch.3.

Subsection (8)

1-667   This provides that ss.38(1) and (5) and 39 apply in respect of the giving of a hospital and a limitation direction as they do to the making of a hospital order. Those sections enable respectively the making of an interim hospital order and the acquisition of information from health authorities on the availability of facilities.

Subsection (9)

1-668   This provides that where a hospital and a limitation direction are made, they apply to all existing prison sentences passed on the offender.

[Effect of hospital and limitation directions

1-669   **45B.**—(1)   A hospital direction and a limitation direction shall be sufficient authority—

    (a)   for a constable or any other person directed to do so by the court to convey the patient to the hospital specified in the hospital direction within a period of 28 days; and

    (b)   for the managers of the hospital to admit him at any time within that period and thereafter detain him in accordance with the provisions of this Act.

  (2)   With respect to any person—

(a)   a hospital direction shall have effect as a transfer direction; and

(b)   a limitation direction shall have effect as a restriction direction.

(3)   While a person is subject to a hospital direction and a limitation direction the [responsible clinician] shall at such intervals (not exceeding one year) as the Secretary of State may direct examine and report to the Secretary of State on that person; and every report shall contain such particulars as the Secretary of State may require.]

Amendments

This section was inserted by the Crime (Sentences) Act 1997 s.46. The words in square brackets in subs.(3) were inserted by the Mental Health Act 2007 s.10(9).

Definitions

hospital direction: ss.45A(3)(a), 145(1).   **1-670**
limitation direction: ss.45A(3)(b), 145(1).
patient: s.145(1).
hospital: ss.55(5), 145(1).
managers: s.145(1).
transfer direction: ss.47, 145(1).
restriction direction: ss.49, 145(1).
responsible clinician: s.55(1).

General Note

The effect of hospital and limitation directions is set out at para.5.2 of the Government guidance on   **1-671**
restricted patients noted under s.41:

"A patient who is subject to a s45A hospital and limitation direction may serve his entire sentence in hospital if he continues to meet the criteria for detention under the MHA. While in hospital the patient will be managed as if he had been transferred from prison under s47 (see below). The limitation direction ceases to have effect on the patient's sentence release date, but the hospital direction continues in force until he is discharged. Therefore, if the patient continues to meet the criteria under the MHA for detention in hospital, they may remain detained in hospital beyond the date on which they would have been released from their sentence, but will no longer be subject to the restrictions.

If a patient subject to a s45A was sentenced to an indeterminate sentence (indeterminate sentence for public protection or a discretionary life sentence), the limitation direction remains in effect for the duration of their detention in hospital, even past the minimum term or tariff period. The release date for such sentences is not fixed and is determined by a direction to release by the Parole Board. The Parole Board cannot consider release until the tariff expiry date and the case will not be referred to the Parole Board while the patient remains detained under the MHA, until such time as the Tribunal has decided that, but for the limitation direction, they would be suitable for discharge.

If during the period of the sentence the offender's health improves such that they no longer meet the criteria for detention in hospital, the offender may be transferred to prison to serve the remainder of their sentence. At this point, the hospital and limitation direction no longer has any effect. Should the offender's mental health deteriorate while continuing to serve their prison sentence, they may be transferred back to hospital as a serving prisoner, under ss47/49."

Although the limitation direction ends on the patient's release date, the hospital direction does not. This means that if the patient is being treated in hospital subject to the hospital direction on the release date, the patient remains in hospital as if he were subject to an unrestricted hospital order. If the patient is transferred to prison, both the hospital direction and the limitation direction end (s.50(1), (2), (3) and (5)).

If the Secretary of State is informed by the patient's responsible clinician or the tribunal that the patient no longer requires treatment in hospital or that no effective treatment can be given in the hospital to which he has been removed, he may exercise his power of direction under s.50.

A patient who is subject to an order under s.45A comes within the after-care provisions of s.117.

Paragraph 16.22 of the Reference Guide states:

> "In practice, the Secretary of State for Justice expects clinical staff from the hospital and prison to meet to plan the patient's future care (a 'section 117 meeting') before directing the patient's removal to prison."

Leave of absence

1-672   The leave of absence of a patient who is detained under this section for both community and medical leave is subject to the agreement of the Secretary of State: see the notes on s.41(3)(c) under "Leave of Absence".

Subsection (1)

1-673   **Convey the patient**   If the patient absconds, he may be retaken under s.138. Paragraph 16.18 of the Reference Guide states:

> "Hospital and limitation direction patients who are absent without leave, or are otherwise liable to be taken into custody, under the Act are also treated as being unlawfully at large from custody for the purposes of section 49(2) of the Prison Act 1952. This may affect their release date."

DETENTION DURING HER MAJESTY'S PLEASURE

Persons ordered to be kept in custody during Her Majesty's pleasure

1-674   **46.**   *[Repealed by the Armed Forces Act 1996 s.35(2), Sch.7 Pt III.]*

TRANSFERS TO HOSPITAL OF PRISONERS, ETC.

Removal to hospital of persons serving sentences of imprisonment, etc.

1-675   **47.**—(1)   If in the case of a person serving a sentence of imprisonment the Secretary of State is satisfied, by reports from at least two registered medical practitioners—

(a)   that the said person is suffering from [mental disorder]; and

(b)   that the mental disorder from which that person is suffering is of a nature or degree which makes it appropriate for him to be detained in a hospital for medical treatment[; and

(c)   that appropriate medical treatment is available for him.]

the Secretary of State may, if he is of the opinion having regard to the public interest and all the circumstances that it is expedient so to do, by warrant direct that that person be removed to and detained in such hospital [...] as may be specified in the direction; and a direction under this section shall be known as "a transfer direction".

(2)   A transfer direction shall cease to have effect at the expiration of the period of 14 days beginning with the date on which it is given unless within that period the person with respect to whom it was given has been received into the hospital specified in the direction.

(3)   A transfer direction with respect to any person shall have the same effect as a hospital order made in his case.

(4)   [...]

(5)   References in this Part of this Act to a person serving a sentence of imprisonment include references—

(a)   to a person detained in pursuance of any sentence or order for detention made by a court in criminal proceedings [or service disciplinary proceedings] (other than an order [made in consequence of a finding of insanity or unfitness to stand trial [or a sentence of service deten-tion within the meaning of the Armed Forces Act 2006]]);

(b) to a person committed to custody under section 115(3) of the Magistrates' Courts Act 1980 (which relates to persons who fail to comply with an order to enter into recognisances to keep the peace or be of good behaviour); and

(c) to a person committed by a court to a prison or other institution to which the Prison Act 1952 applies in default of payment of any sum adjudged to be paid on his conviction.

[(6) in subsection (5)(a) "service disciplinary proceedings" means proceed-ings in respect of a service offence within the meaning of the Armed Forces Act 2006.]

Amendments

The amendments to this section were made by the Crime (Sentences) Act 1997 s.56(2), Sch.6, the Mental Health Act 2007 ss.1(4), 4(7), 55, Sch.1 para.10, Sch.11 Pt 1, the Domestic Violence, Crime and Victims Act 2004 s.58(1), Sch.10 para.18 and the Armed Forces Act 2006 s.378, Sch.16 para.97(2),(3).

Definitions

mental disorder: ss.1, 145(1).   **1-676**
hospital: ss.55(5), 145(1).
medical treatment: s.145(1), (4).
appropriate medical treatment: ss.3(4), 145(1AB).
hospital order: ss.37, 145(1).

General Note

This section enables the Secretary of State (in practice, the Mental Health Casework Section at the   **1-677** Ministry of Justice (MHCS)) to direct that a person serving a sentence of imprisonment or other deten-tion be removed to and detained in a hospital for treatment of his mental disorder. Such transfers (a "transfer direction") can only be made on medical grounds. Paragraph 22.42 of the *Code of Practice* states:

"The need for inpatient treatment for a prisoner should be identified and acted upon quickly, and prison healthcare staff should make contact immediately with the NHS Commissioning Board [now NHS England]. Responsible NHS commissioners should aim to ensure that transfers of prisoners with mental disorders are carried out within a timeframe equivalent to levels of care experienced by patients who are admitted to mental healthcare services from the community. Any unacceptable delays in transfer after identification of need should be actively monitored and investigated by the NHS Commissioning Board [now NHS England]."

In order for the Secretary of State to make a transfer direction, the following are required:

(i)   agreement on the part of two medical practitioners, expressed in their reports to the Secretary of State:
    (i)   that the person is mentally disordered; and
    (ii)   that the requirements for detention in subs.(1)(b) and (c) are satisfied;
(ii)   a hospital in which the patient may be appropriately treated; and
(iii)   a place at that hospital that is available within 14 days.

It is possible for the Secretary of State to issue a transfer direction on the same day that a court sentences the offender ("*Guidance on Restricted Patients and the Mental Health Act*", The Parole Board (2020) para.1.7).

In *R.(on the application of DK) v Secretary of State for the Home Department* [2010] EWHC 82 (Admin); [2010] M.H.L.R. 64, Collins J. said at para.33:

"One does not want to be over pedantic in these matters, but, as I have said, the court must bear in mind that it is dealing with liberty, and that therefore it is of the utmost importance that all the necessary preconditions for transfer leading to detention are properly seen through."

A transfer direction has the same effect as a hospital order made without restrictions under s.37 (subs.(3)), subject to the exception that the patient may apply to a tribunal within six months of his transfer (s.69(2)(b)). A patient who has been made subject to a transfer direction can therefore be discharged at any time by his responsible clinician (RC) or the hospital managers, can be transferred under the provisions of s.19 and will be subject to the consent to treatment provisions contained in Pt IV (s.56(3)). The renewal timetable under s.20 is calculated from the transfer direction itself: see the General Note to s.20. Although the patient's discharge from detention in hospital can take place before the expiration of his sentence, the making of a transfer direction can result in the patient remaining in hospital under compulsory powers long after the day on which he would have been released from prison had such a direction not been made. There is no power under this section for the patient to be transferred back to prison.

When giving a transfer direction the Secretary of State will in most cases also impose the restrictions provided for under s.49 (a "restriction direction") which means the patient cannot be transferred to another hospital, sent on leave or discharged by the RC without the Secretary of State's consent. In practice, the only occasion when a restriction direction will not be made is if the prisoner is very close to his earliest date of release: see below and *R. (on the application of T) v Secretary of State for the Home Department*, noted in the General Note to s.49. The Secretary of State must make a restriction direction in respect of certain prisoners: see s.49(1).

Although a person who is subject to an unrestricted order under this section cannot be recalled to prison to complete his sentence, the sentence and accordingly any licence period and conditions as would normally be imposed under the Criminal Justice Act procedure, including the prospect of recall to prison on a breach of a licence condition, continue to run notwithstanding his transfer to hospital (*R. (on the application of Miah) v Secretary of State for the Home Department* [2004] EWHC 2569 (Admin); [2004] M.H.L.R. 302).

In *R. (on the application of D) v Secretary of State for the Home Department and National Assembly for Wales* [2004] EWHC 2857 (Admin); [2005] M.H.L.R. 17 para.33, Stanley Burnton J. held that once the prison service have reasonable grounds to believe that a prisoner requires treatment in a mental hospital in which he may be detained, the Secretary of State is under a duty expeditiously to take reasonable steps to obtain appropriate medical advice, and if that advice confirms the need for transfer to a hospital, to take reasonable steps within a reasonable time to effect that transfer. In many cases, the medical advice as to the appropriateness of transfer will serve as the reports required by s.47. The steps that are reasonable will depend on the circumstances, including the apparent risk to the health of the prisoner if no transfer is effected. Inappropriate retention of a prisoner in a prison or YOI may infringe his rights under art.8 of the European Convention on Human Rights (ECHR). If the consequences for the prisoner are sufficiently severe, his inappropriate retention in a prison may go so far as to bring about a breach of art.3 of the ECHR, in which case the state is under an absolute duty to prevent or bring to an end his inhumane treatment.

His Lordship made the following comment on the position of a prisoner who has been remanded in custody:

"If there is good reason to believe that a psychiatric assessment is appropriate, it needs to be obtained before sentence, not after what is liable to be (on what on this hypothesis is the incomplete information available to the sentencing judge) an inappropriate sentence. If, before sentence, it becomes clear that detention in a hospital under the Mental Health Act 1983 is appropriate, although transfer under s.47 is not available, I do not see why arrangements cannot be made for a prisoner to be detained under that Act while being formally remanded on bail" (para.45).

1-678 In *R. v Drew* [2003] UKHL 25; [2003] 4 All E.R. 557 HL at para.19, Lord Bingham said that if:

"it were shown that a mentally disordered defendant was held in prison, that he was there denied medical treatment, available in hospital, which his mental condition required and that he was suffering serious consequences as a result of such denial, he would have grounds for seeking judicial review of the [Secretary of State's] failure to direct his transfer to hospital under [this section]; (*Keenan v United Kingdom* (2001) 33 E.H.R.R. 38)".

In judicial review proceedings, the High Court has jurisdiction to direct the Secretary of State to make an order under this section if the necessary medical reports had been completed (*R. (on the application of D) v Secretary of State for the Home Office* [2003] EWHC 2529 (Admin)). This section "does not allow a court to override clinical judgment, including an assessment of (i) whether a particular patient can and should be treated at a particular hospital and (ii) the prioritisation of beds" (*R. (on the application of ASK) v Secretary of State for the Home Department* [2019] EWCA Civ 1239, per Hickinbottom L.J. at para.27).

A decision to transfer a prisoner to hospital at the end of his sentence heightens the scrutiny which should be applied both by the Secretary of State as to the evidence on which that decision should be taken, and heightens the scrutiny which the court must apply to the decision of the Secretary of State: see *R. (on the application of TF) v Secretary of State for Justice* [2008] EWCA Civ 1457; [2008] M.H.L.R. 370, where Waller L.J. said at para.31:

"Where section 47 is proposed to be used at the very end of the sentence, and hopefully that will only be in very exceptional cases, the onus must be on the Secretary of State to show that the mind of the decision maker has focused on each of the criteria which it is necessary to satisfy if there is to be power to issue a warrant directing transfer to a hospital."

The NHS has published *"Transfer and remission of adult prisoners under the MHA: Good practice guidance"* (2021) which can be accessed at: *https://www.england.nhs.uk/publication/guidance-for-the-transfer-and-remission-of-adult-prisoners-and-immigration-removal-centre-detainees-under-the-mental-health-act-1983*. The "guidance sets out the timeframe for completing the assessment, transfer and remission of individuals detained under the MHA to and from [inpatient mental health, learning disability and/or autism] services and prisons. It applies to adult and youth detainees (sentenced, un-sentenced or on remand) aged 18 and over in the prison estate, including private prisons. There is separate guidance for children and young people in secure settings" (para.1).

Paragraph 3.6 of the guidance states:

"The timing of applications for a Secretary of State for Justice direction to transfer is crucial, particularly where the prisoner's sentence is short, or the prisoner is close to their automatic release date (ARD). Following judicial reviews of prison transfers, the High Court has clarified the legal position on applications made late in a sentence.

The Secretary of State is required to ensure the following conditions are met before he can agree to a transfer late in sentence:

- Admission to hospital is an urgent necessity
- It is necessary for the prisoner's own health and/or safety and
- The urgency of need is such that it is not safe to wait until the release date for admission to hospital.

In such circumstances, the prison mental health team should contact MHCS as soon as possible to discuss the case."

Under s.117, health bodies and local social services authorities have a duty to provide after-care services for patients who cease to be liable to be detained and leave hospital after having been transferred by the Secretary of State under this section. The responsibility for holding a "section 117 meeting" applies if the prisoner is discharged back to prison.

For the supervision in the community of a patient who has been transferred under this section and has been made the subject of a restriction direction under s.49, see the note on s.50(1)(b).

Responsibility for prison health care was fully transferred from HM Prison Service to the NHS in April 2006: see the notes to the definition of "hospital" in s.145(1).

Notional hospital orders

See the General Note to s.49 under this heading. **1-679**

Named hospital units

If the Secretary of State makes a direction under this section coupled with a restriction direction made **1-680** under s.49, he has the power to order that the patient be admitted to and detained in a named hospital unit: see the note to s.41 under this heading.

Transfers of children

Procedure for the referral for assessment, and transfer to and from hospital (under Part III of the **1-681** *Mental Health Act 1983) of a child held in custody in England*, NHS, 2021, provides guidance on the procedure for transferring to and from hospital under the Act any child who is sentenced to custody (in England) or who has been remanded to custody. The procedure covers the duties of secure estate settings in relation to the identification and transfer of children and the procedures that should be followed by the other agencies involved where detention subject to Part III is considered appropriate. The guidance can be accessed at: *www.england.nhs.uk/wp-content/uploads/2021/11/B0721_iv_Children-and-young-persons-Mental-Health-Act-transfers-guidance-part-III-justice-protocol.pdf.*

The transfer of prisoners under Schedule 1 of the Crime (Sentences) Act 1997

1-682   Schedule 1 of the Crime (Sentences) Act 1997, in conjunction with Sch.1 of the Transfer of Prisoners (Restricted Transfers) (Channel Islands and Isle of Man) Order 1998 (SI 1998/2798), deals with the transfer of prisoners between the various parts of the UK and the Channel Islands, and between those parts and the Isle of Man. They enable the Secretary of State to issue a warrant which has the effect that the transferred prisoner can be held in an English prison on a "restricted" basis which means the prisoner is subject to the English penal regime. However, the prisoner's place of origin retains jurisdiction over the court action that the prisoner is involved in. Such a transfer can be effected as a paper exercise with the prisoner remaining in an English prison while the "transfer" takes place. Once the warrant is issued, the Secretary of State can issue a warrant under ss.48 and 49 to transfer the prisoner from prison to hospital.

Human Rights Act 1998

1-683   To subject an offender requiring admission to hospital to unnecessary suffering, humiliation, distress and deterioration of his mental condition in prison could properly be regarded as inhumane or degrading treatment or punishment contrary to art.3 of the European Convention on Human Rights (*R. v Drew* [2003] UKHL 25 para.18. It could also constitute an interference with his mental and physical integrity contrary to art.8 (*R. (on the application of D) v Secretary of State for the Home Department and National Assembly for Wales*, above).

In *Pankiewicz v Poland, February 12, 2008 (App.No.34151/04)*, the European Court of Human Rights held that a delay of two months and twenty five days in transferring a mentally disordered prisoner to hospital, as recommended by two psychiatrists, violated art.5(1) of the Convention. The Court said at paras 44, 45:

> "The Court accepts the Government's arguments that it would be unrealistic and too rigid an approach to expect the authorities to ensure that a place is immediately available in a selected psychiatric hospital. However, a reasonable balance must be struck between the competing interests involved. Having regard to the balancing of interests the Court attaches weight to the fact that the applicant was held in a regular detention centre without adequate medical facilities. The delay in admission to a psychiatric hospital and thus the beginning of the treatment was obviously harmful to the applicant, in view of the expert's opinions recommending him for psychiatric treatment. In addition, the Court notes that the Government failed to advance any detailed explanation for the delay in the applicant's admission to the hospital.
>
> The Court cannot find that, in the circumstances of the present case, a reasonable balance was struck. The Court is of the opinion that even though the delay of two months and twenty five days in the admission of the applicant to a psychiatric hospital may not at first glance seem particularly excessive, it cannot be regarded as acceptable (see *Morsink v the Netherlands*, no. 48865/99, §§ 61–70, 11 May 2004; *Brand v the Netherlands*, no. 49902/99, §§ 58-67 11 May 2004; and *Mocarska*, cited above, § 48). To hold otherwise would entail a serious weakening of the fundamental right to liberty to the detriment of the person concerned and thus impair the very essence of the right protected by Article 5 of the Convention."

In *Morley v United Kingdom* (2005) 40 E.H.R.R. SE8; [2005] M.H.L.R. 174, the Court declared inadmissible the applicant's complaint that art.5 required the decision to transfer a prisoner to hospital to be made by the tribunal.

Welfare benefits and transferred prisoners

1-684   In *SS v United Kingdom, April 21, 2015 (App.No.4036/10)*, patients subject to ss.47/49 and s.45A argued that denying them the social security benefits that are paid to other detained patients was contrary to art.14 of the European Convention on Human Rights, taken with art.1 of Protocol No 1. The European Court of Human Rights rejected the applications as being manifestly unfounded. The Court said that "it is not without significance that time spent in hospital counts towards service of the sentence of imprisonment" (para.40).

Applications to the First-tier Tribunal (Mental Health) or the Mental Health Review Tribunal for Wales

By virtue of subs.(3), the patient may make an application to a tribunal within six months of the date of the direction, once during the following six months, and at yearly intervals thereafter (ss.69(2), 70). The patient's nearest relative has similar rights to make an application (s.69(1) as applied by s.55(4)). Any application, hospital order or guardianship order that was in place prior to the making of the transfer direction will cease to have effect (s.40(5)).   **1-685**

Subsection (1)

Sentence of imprisonment   See subs.(5).   **1-686**

Reports   Although this provision does not require that the report be in writing, it is obviously important that there should be a written report (*R. (on the application of DK) v Secretary of State for the Home Department* [2010] EWHC 82 (Admin); [2010] M.H.L.R. 64, para.19). In *R. v Secretary of State for the Home Office Ex p. Gilkes* [1999] EWHC 47 (Admin); [1999] M.H.L.R. 7, para.12, Dyson J. said:

"If the reports are manifestly unreliable, then the Secretary of State cannot reasonably be satisfied that the ... conditions [of this section] are met on the basis of the reports, and a decision to rely on them in such circumstances will be capable of successful challenge by judicial review. A medical report may be unreliable for a number of reasons. It may on its face not address the relevant statutory criteria. It may be based on an assessment which is so out of date that the mere fact of a lapse of time will be sufficient to render it unreliable. It may be unreliable to rely on a report based on an assessment conducted an appreciable, but not inordinate, time before the decision to transfer where the mental disorder is a fluctuating and unstable condition and/or where there has been a change of circumstances since the assessment was made. In each case, it will be for the Secretary of State to consider whether in his judgment the medical report is one on which he can safely and properly rely so as to be satisfied that the conditions set out in paragraphs (a) and (b) ... are met. One of the considerations that will be uppermost in his mind is whether the assessment on which the report is based is sufficiently recent to provide reliable evidence of the patient's current mental condition."

In this case, Dyson J. said that although it is incorrect to say that it can never be reasonable for the Secretary of State, when considering whether to make a transfer direction, to rely on a medical report made for the purposes of s.37, the Secretary of State should be slow to conclude that such a report can be safely relied on.

The judgment of Dyson J. in *Gilkes*, which was approved by the Court of Appeal in *TF v Secretary of State for Justice* [2008] EWCA Civ 1457, was applied by the Court of Appeal in *R. (on the application of SP) v Secretary of State for Justice* [2010] EWCA Civ 1590; [2011] M.H.L.R. 65, a case where one of the reporting doctors used an obsolete form. In upholding the legality of the transfer, Arden L.J. said at paras 23 and 27:

"Section 47 does not contain any express provision as to any particular level of reasoning. Not unnaturally, that is left to the general law but it is necessary to have regard to the context. The reports of the medical practitioners are written by those who are expert in medical practice and they are addressed to the Secretary of State and his officials, who are lay persons. The Secretary of State and his officials are not concerned to pursue medical reasoning. In my judgment, in principle the decision maker is only concerned to see whether the medical practitioners have given some reasons which they consider adequate and which, on what they have said, do not fail to take account of material issues or matters and do not conflict with the facts known to the Secretary of State or the statutory requirements....

I fully accept that the Secretary of State cannot write in reasons which are not there. However, at the same time in my judgment the Secretary of State is entitled to give the reports a sensible meaning and is not required to go back to the medical practitioner to ask them to articulate in words matters which are there by necessary implication."

There is no statutory time limit between the date of the report and the date of the decision of the Secretary of State. However, to achieve compliance with art.5(1)(e) of the European Convention on Human Rights the medical opinion cannot be seen as sufficient to justify deprivation of liberty under that provision if a significant period has elapsed since the preparation of the report (*Varbanov v Bulgaria* [2002] M.H.L.R. 263 at para.47).

Two registered medical practitioners   One of whom must be approved by the Secretary of State or the Welsh Ministers under s.12, or by another person by virtue of s.12ZA or s.12ZB (s.54(1)). A registered medical practitioner means "a fully registered person within the meaning of the Medical Act 1983 who holds a licence to practise under that Act" (Interpretation Act 1978 Sch.1). There is no requirement for either doctor to be an approved clinician. "In practice, the [Secretary of State] will normally want at least one of the two doctors to be practicing at the hospital named in the proposed transfer direction, so as to ensure that there is agreement as to the hospital's reception of the patient and as to his diagnosis, treatability and detention", per Stanley Burnton J. in *R. (on the application of D) v Secretary of State for the Home Department and National Assembly for Wales* [2004] EWHC 2857; [2005] M.H.L.R. 17 at para.21. The Secretary of State is not "required to shop around until he finds psychiatrists prepared to sign section 47 reports: it is his duty to obtain the reliable opinions of psychiatrists as to the transfer of a prisoner to a hospital with a vacancy that can offer appropriate care" (para.49).

It is acceptable for the doctors not to have seen the patient for some time prior to the completion of their reports if the patient's mental disorder is an enduring rather than a fluctuating condition, and the patient has refused to see them and to be examined by them for the purposes of such reports (*R. (on the application of F) v Secretary of State for the Home Department* [2008] EWHC 2912 (Admin); [2008] M.H.L.R. 361, para.30). This was described as "appropriate advice" at the Court of Appeal (*R. (on the application of TF) v Secretary of State for Justice*, above, para.29).

Paragraph (a)

1-687 **Mental disorder**   If the person has a learning disability, the disability must be associated with abnormally aggressive or seriously irresponsible conduct (s.1(2A), (2B)). A learning disabled person might also suffer from another form of mental disorder.

Paragraph (b)

1-688 **Appropriate for him to be detained … for medical treatment**   In *South West London and St George's Mental Health NHS Trust v W* [2002] EWHC 1770 (Admin); [2002] M.H.L.R. 392, Crane J. confirmed, at para.77, that this provision does not cover transfers for assessment, but said, at para.79, that he did "not consider that detention becomes unlawful immediately a particular form of treatment is suspended if there is a period of assessment in relation to another form of possible treatment and the process of monitoring under nursing, medical and psychological supervision continues". In this case, a mentally disordered prisoner who had been convicted of a serious and unprovoked assault on a stranger was transferred to hospital under this section. The question before the judge was whether the transfer, which was aimed at securing the staged discharge of the patient from the hospital, was lawful. The plan devised for the patient was that he would be admitted to hospital for several months. He would be given increasing leave from the hospital linked to occupational and other therapy. An attempt would then be made to find a place for him in a hostel and there would be liaison between the hostel staff and the hospital team. The patient would gradually spend increasing periods out of hospital and then progress to overnight stays at the hostel. In holding that the transfer was lawful, Crane J. held, at para.62, that although s.47 cannot be used simply to postpone release, "transfer to hospital involving admission, nursing, medical, and here psychological supervision, and staged discharge under medical supervision, is capable of amounting to 'treatment' …".

Paragraph (c)

1-689 **Appropriate medical treatment**   See the note on s.3(2)(d) and *South West London and St George's Mental Health NHC Trust v W*, noted under para.(b).

Hospital   Or registered establishment (ss.34(2), 55(5)). In *R. (on the application of D) v Secretary of State for the Home Department and National Assembly for Wales*, above, Stanley Burnton J. suggested, at para.60, that the difficulties that are sometimes encountered in finding a suitable hospital for a potential transfer direction patient could be ameliorated by the establishment of a national database that could be maintained within the Ministry of Justice, or the Department of Health, and which might be accessible (to authorised persons only) on the internet.

Subsection (2)

14 days   After which a fresh direction will be necessary if the patient has not been admitted to the hospital.   **1-690**

Beginning with   Including the day on which the transfer direction is given (*Zoan v Rouamba* [2000] 2 All E.R. 620 CA).

Received into the hospital   Although the agreement of the hospital to which the patient is to be transferred is not a pre-condition of a transfer direction, practical considerations will normally dictate that its agreement is necessary (*R. (on the application of D) v Secretary of State for the Home Department and National Assembly for Wales*, above, para.30). In *D*, the court was informed by a Home Office official that approximately six transfers take place each year without the agreement of the admitting hospital, and that about 650 transfers take place each year.

Subsection (3)

The only effect of this provision is to apply s.40 to a transfer direction (*R. (on the application of Miah) v Secretary of State for the Home Department* [2004] EWHC 2569 (Admin); [2004] M.H.L.R. 302, para.23).   **1-691**

Same effect as a hospital order   The patient can therefore be discharged by his responsible clinician or by the hospital managers. For the purpose of renewal, the start date of the transfer direction is the date of the direction, not the date when the patient was admitted to hospital (s.40(4)). An application for a community treatment order can be made in respect of the patient (Sch.1 Pt.1).

Subsection (5)

Any sentence or order for detention made by a court in criminal proceedings   These words are wide enough to cover detention during Her Majesty's pleasure (*R. v Secretary of State for the Home Department Ex p. Hickey (No.1)* [1995] 1 All E.R. 479, per Rose L.J. at 488).   **1-692**

Removal to hospital of other prisoners

48.—(1)   If in the case of a person to whom this section applies the Secretary of State is satisfied by the same reports as are required for the purposes of section 47 above that—   **1-693**

[(a)   that person is suffering from mental disorder of a nature or degree which makes it appropriate for him to be detained in a hospital for medical treatment; and

(b)   he is in urgent need of such treatment;] [and

(c)   appropriate medical treatment is available for him;]

the Secretary of State shall have the same power of giving a transfer direction in respect of him under that section as if he were serving a sentence of imprisonment.

(2)   This section applies to the following persons, that is to say—

(a)   persons detained in a prison or remand centre, not being persons serving a sentence of imprisonment or persons falling within the following paragraphs of this subsection;

(b)   persons remanded in custody by a magistrates' court;

(c)   civil prisoners, that is to say, persons committed by a court to prison for a limited term [...], who are not persons falling to be dealt with under section 47 above;

    (d)   persons detained under the Immigration Act 1971 [or under section 62 of the Nationality, Immigration and Asylum Act 2002 (detention by the Secretary of State)].

(3)   Subsections (2) [and (3)] of section 47 above shall apply for the purposes of this section and of any transfer direction given by virtue of this section as they apply for the purposes of that section and of any transfer direction under that section.

Amendments

The amendments to this section were made by the Statute Law (Repeals) Act 2004 Sch.1 Pt 17 Group 8, the Nationality, Immigration and Asylum Act 2002 s.62(10) and the Mental Health Act 2007 ss.1(4), 5(3), Sch.1 para.11.

Definitions

1-694   mental disorder: ss.1, 145(1).
hospital: ss.55(5), 145(1).
medical treatment: s.145(1), (4).
appropriate medical treatment: ss.3(4), 145(1AB).
transfer direction: ss.47, 145(1).
civil prisoner: s.55(1).

General Note

1-695   This section empowers the Secretary of State to direct the removal from prison to hospital of certain categories of *unsentenced* mentally disordered prisoners. By virtue of subs.(3), a person removed to hospital under this section is placed in the same position as a person who has been made the subject of a transfer direction under s.47 which, among other things, means that he becomes subject to the consent to treatment provisions contained in Part IV: see the note on s.47(3). The NHS has published *"Transfer and remission of adult prisoners under the MHA: Good practice guidance"* (2021) and *"The transfer and remission of immigration removal centre detainees under the Mental Health Act 1983: Good practice guidance"* (2021). Both documents can be accessed at: *https://www.england.nhs.uk/publication/guidance-for-the-transfer-and-remission-of-adult-prisoners-and-immigration-removal-centre-detainees-under-the-mental-health-act-1983*.

A transfer direction made in respect of persons coming within categories (a) or (b) of subs.(2) *must* be made subject to the restrictions provided for in s.49 (s.49(1)). The Secretary of State has a discretion to direct that persons coming within categories (c) or (d) be made subject to such restrictions. In practice, the Secretary of State will always apply restrictions to a transfer under this section (*Mental Health Unit Bulletin*, March 2008).

It is submitted that the requirements placed on the Secretary of State in relation to s.47 transfers which were identified by Stanley Burnton J. in *R. (on the application of D) v Secretary of State for the Home Department and National Assembly for Wales* [2004] EWHC 2857 (Admin); [2005] M.H.L.R. 17 also apply to this section: see the General Note to s.47.

A particular hospital must be specified in a transfer direction made under this section (*R. (on the application of ASK) v Secretary of State for the Home Department* [2019] EWCA Civ 1239, per Hickinbottom L.J. at para.27).

"Restricted Patients Detained in Special Hospitals: Information for the Special Hospitals Service Authority", Home Office, undated, states at para.5.11:

"It is important for responsible [clinicians] to bear in mind that prisoners transferred to hospital under [this section] will, in most cases, not have been tried and convicted, and consequentially they should be returned to court as soon as possible. If the responsible [clinician] believes the patient is not fit to return to court, there is provision under section 51(5) for the court to make a hospital order in the patient's absence and without convicting him."

L. Birmingham states that the

"main disadvantage of section 48 as a diversion mechanism is that if for any reason the subject ceases to be a prisoner on remand (for example, is bailed or the case collapses) the powers conveyed under section 48 cease with immediate effect. If there is a real risk of this happening a concurrent civil order (section 3 of the MHA) can be imposed" ("Diversion from custody" (2001) *Advances in Psychiatric Treatment*, 7, 198–207)."

The use of a concurrent s.3 in this situation is of doubtful legality because, unlike the situation that obtained in *R. v North West London Mental Health NHS Trust, Ex p. Stewart* which is noted under s.35, the application is not being made to provide professionals with powers which are immediately needed; it is being made as a contingency. The safer option would be either to prepare for a possible application under s.3 by completing the statutory documentation with the exception of the signature on the application form which could be added when the patient ceased to be a prisoner on remand or to use the holding powers contained in s.5 when the patient ceased to be a prisoner on remand.

Under s.117, health bodies and local social services authorities have a duty to provide after-care services for patients who have ceased to be liable to be detained and leave hospital after having been transferred under this section.

Code of Practice

The Code states:

1-696

"22.66 Section 48 empowers the Secretary of State for Justice by warrant to direct the removal to and detention in hospital for treatment of certain offenders such as those on remand, civil prisoners and immigration detainees. Restrictions may also be added under section 49. Subsequent attendance at court will require Secretary of State for Justice consent and will usually be given at the time of admission. Should the patient be subsequently acquitted by the court or the legal proceedings discontinued, the section 48/49 restricted transfer direction will cease and the responsible clinician in charge of the patient's care must either discharge or consider detention under part 2 of the Act.

22.67 Professionals should be aware that immigration detainees may be particularly vulnerable and may need additional support, including reasonable adjustments. Examples include the use of interpreters and an understanding of their culture, ethnicity or religion. Staff supporting these patients should be culturally competent.

22.68 Should a transfer request be made for a prisoner under sections 47 and 49 who is near the end of his or her sentence, the Secretary of State for Justice will apply heightened scrutiny to such a request to ensure that the criteria for transfer under the Act is satisfied and taking into account the potential lengthening of detention.

22.69 In exceptional circumstances, the Secretary of State for Justice may 'direct' a restricted patient's admission into hospital, outside of NHS commissioning arrangements. This is usually where it is critical that the patient receive treatment and identifying a suitable bed is difficult."

Transfers of children

See the note to s.47 under this heading.

1-697

Applications to the First-tier Tribunal (Mental Health) or the Mental Health Review Tribunal for Wales

See subs.(3) and the note on s.47 under this heading.

1-698

Subsection (1)

Reports   See the notes on "reports" and "two registered medical practitioners" in s.47(1).

1-699

Mental disorder   See the note on s.47(1)(a).

Appropriate for him to be detained … for medical treatment   But not for assessment.

Urgent need of such treatment   "Urgency" is a relative concept (*R. (on the application of ASK) v Secretary of State for the Home Department* [2019] EWCA Civ 1239, per Hickinbottom L.J. at para.227(vii)).

The Home Office informed the Butler Committee that the procedure under this section is adopted only where a prisoner's condition is such that immediate removal to a hospital is necessary and that normally when he is well enough he is either produced at court from hospital or returned to prison to await trial (ibid., para.3.38). The Reed Committee was "concerned ... that the requirement under section 48 that the need for treatment should be 'urgent' is often interpreted narrowly". The Committee concluded that this section "should be applied where a doctor would recommend in-patient treatment if a person were seen as an out-patient in the community" (*Final Summary Report*, above, para.9.6(iv). This approach has been adopted by the Government: see the "*Procedure for the transfer of prisoners to and from hospital under sections 47 and 48 of the Mental Health Act (1983)*" (2007) p.8.

Nature or degree   See the note on s.3(2)(a).

Appropriate medical treatment   See the note on s.3(2)(d).

Transfer direction   Which will cease to have effect unless the prisoner is admitted to hospital within 14 days of it being given (s.47(2)).

Subsection (2)

1-700   A direction made under this section would terminate if the criminal proceedings are dropped or if the person concerned ceases to be subject to detention by, for example, being granted bail.

Paragraph (a)   Persons coming within this category, who will be awaiting trial or sentence in the Crown Court, are subject to the further provisions contained in s.51.
The April 2011 edition of the Ministry of Justice Mental Health Casework Section Newsletter states:

"In the last edition we advised of concerns that a person remanded in custody by the Crown Court to a Young Offender Institution is not covered by the wording of s.48(2)(a) and that the Secretary of State therefore has no power to direct their transfer to hospital. Having taken further legal advice this is not correct.
    Legally no court can remand a person 'to a YOI'. For 17-20 year olds the court can only remand to prison. However a YOI (whether as a whole or a particular cell) can be designated by NOMS as a prison. It follows that s.48(2)(a) does empower the Secretary of State to transfer to hospital a young offender remanded by the Crown Court and placed in a YOI even if it does not look like (s)he is detained in prison. This is the case only for 17-20 year olds (and certain 14-16 year old males) and only if the YOI or cell has been designated as a prison.
    Except for a category of 14-16 year old males who may be remanded to prison, 10-16 year olds cannot be remanded to prison. They are remanded to local authority accommodation. If remanded by a Crown Court, the Secretary of State has no powers under s.48(2)(a) to direct their transfer to hospital. Such persons who need treatment in hospital can be remanded by the Crown Court, using its own powers, or admitted using civil powers.
    Young people remanded by a magistrates' court may be transferred from wherever they are remanded to under s.48(2)(b)."

Paragraph (b)   Persons coming within this category are subject to the further provisions contained in s.52.
Paragraph 5.9 of "Procedure for the Transfer from Custody of Children and Young People to and from Hospital under the Mental Health Act 1983 in England", Department of Health, 2011 states:

"For those children and young people remanded in custody by a magistrates' court and made subject to a transfer direction under section 48(2)(b) of the Act, the transfer direction will cease to have effect at the expiry of the period of remand unless the child or young person is then committed in custody to the Crown Court. However, if the magistrates' court further remands the child or young person under section 52(3) of the Act, the direction will not expire. Alternatively, if the court is satisfied that the child or young person no longer requires treatment in hospital, it may direct that the transfer direction ceases to have effect."

Paragraphs (c) and (d)   Persons coming within these categories are subject to the further provisions contained in s.53.

Paragraph (d)   Although the scope of this paragraph does not extend to those who are detained under the provisions of the UK Borders Act 2007, the principle of law identified by Stanley Burnton J. in *R. (on the application of D) v Secretary of State for the Home Department and National Assembly for Wales*, which is considered in the General Note to s.47, is equally applicable in the context of Immigration Removal Centres, including detention under the 2007 Act (*R.(on the application of HA (Nigeria) v Secretary of State for the Home Department* [2012] EWHC 979 (Admin), paras 127, 169).

In *R. (on the application of BA) v Secretary of State for the Home Department* [2011] EWHC 2748 (Admin), para.125, Elisabeth Laing QC, sitting as a Deputy Judge of the High Court, considered whether, on the expiry of his sentence, BA was simply detained pursuant to this section, or whether he was subject to "dual detention"; in other words, detention in hospital pursuant this section, and, at the same time, immigration detention under para.2(1) of Sch.3 to the Immigration Act 1971. Her Ladyship held that, "BA must have been subject to dual detention. I say this because, on the view I take of paragraph 2(1) ..., it requires detention from the end of a prisoner's custodial term.... A 'hospital' as defined in the 1983 Act is one of the places in which immigration detention may occur".

Restriction on discharge of prisoners removed to hospital

49.—(1)   Where a transfer direction is given in respect of any person, the   **1-701** Secretary of State, if he thinks fit, may by warrant further direct that that person shall be subject to the special restrictions set out in section 41 above; and where the Secretary of State gives a transfer direction in respect of any such person as is described in paragraph (a) or (b) of section 48(2) above, he shall also give a direction under this section applying those restrictions to him.

(2)   A direction under this section shall have the same effect as a restriction order made under section 41 above and shall be known as "a restriction direction".

(3)   While a person is subject to a restriction direction the [responsible clinician] shall at such intervals (not exceeding one year) as the Secretary of State may direct examine and report to the Secretary of State on that person; and every report shall contain such particulars as the Secretary of State may require.

Amendment

The words in square brackets in subs.(3) were inserted by the Mental Health Act 2007 s.10(9).

Definitions

transfer direction: ss.47, 145(1).   **1-702**
responsible clinician: s.55(1).

General Note

This section provides that the Secretary of State may, and in respect of certain prisoners must, add   **1-703** an order restricting the patient's discharge from hospital (a "restriction direction") to a transfer direction made under s.47. The patient then becomes a restricted patient (s.79). The effect of a restriction direction is explained in the following passage from the judgment of the Court of Appeal in *R. v Birch* (1989) 11 Cr. App. R.(S.) 202 at 212:

"If the transfer direction under section 47 is coupled with a restriction direction by the Home Secretary under section 49 (as in practice it usually is), the offender's position is in many ways the same as if he had been sent straight to hospital with order under sections 37 and 41, but the following special provisions apply: (1) Where the offender was sentenced to a fixed term of imprisonment, the restriction will automatically lift on the expiry of his sentence (allowing for remission) [the "release date"]: section 50(2). (2) Where the responsible clinician or the [tribunal] concludes that the offender no longer requires treatment in hospital for mental disorder or that no effective treatment for his disorder can be given, the Secretary of State may: (a) release him on [licence or discharge him under supervision], (b) return him to prison to serve out his sentence, or (c) take no action [: section 50(1)]."

If the Secretary of State is informed by the patient's responsible clinician (RC) or the tribunal that the patient no longer requires treatment in hospital or that no effective treatment can be given in the hospital to which he has been removed, he may exercise his power of direction under s.50.

In *R. (on the application of T) v Secretary of State for the Home Department* [2003] EWHC 538 (Admin); [2003] M.H.L.R. 239, an official in the Mental Health Unit wrote to the patient's RC declining to lift the restriction direction that had been made in respect of the patient and referred to the policy of the Secretary of State in the following terms:

> "Our normal policy is always to make a restriction direction unless it is proposed to transfer the prisoner to hospital within days of his release date and the nature of the offence suggests that restrictions are unnecessary for the protection of the public from serious harm over that short period."

The patient's challenge to this policy on the ground that a restriction order should only be imposed where there is a need for public protection was rejected by Maurice Kay J. His Lordship said that the analogy that had been made with an order made by a court under s.37 was wrong, as when making orders under this section, the Secretary of State did not stand in the shoes of the sentencing court. Rather, the Secretary of State is concerned with a person who has already been sentenced to a term of imprisonment by a court, which has not yet been fully served. Without a restriction direction a person properly sentenced to a term of imprisonment would pass wholly into the hands of the medical authorities so far as the regaining of liberty was concerned: also see the General Note to s.47.

Notional hospital orders

1-704   A patient who ceases to be subject to a restriction direction because his sentence has expired is sometimes referred to as being subject to a "notional hospital order". This term, which is not found in the Act, is used to signify that on the expiry of the sentence the patient is still subject to the s.47 transfer direction which has the same legal effect as a hospital order made under s.37. A restricted patient whose restriction order has ceased to have effect is treated as if he had been admitted to hospital as an unrestricted patient on the date when the restriction order ceased to have effect (s.41(5)). Paragraph 22.77 of the *Code of Practice* states:

> "When a transferred offender becomes unrestricted, there is still a period when, if released, they will be subject to licence conditions and management by the National Probation Service. Hospitals should remain in contact with the offender manager and victim liaison officer therefore until the end of sentence."

Named hospital units

1-705   Section 47 of the Crime (Sentences) Act 1997 provides that where the Secretary of State makes an order under this section he has the power to order that the patient be admitted to and detained in a named hospital unit. A named hospital unit can be any part of a hospital which is treated as a separate unit. The effect of this power is considered in the General Note to s.41 under this heading.

Guidance on the restricted patient system

1-706   The Ministry of Justice and HM Prison and Probation Service have published guidance which "provides stakeholders (including patients and their families, victims, Responsible Clinicians and other report writers and multi-disciplinary team members) with an overview of the restricted patient system in England and Wales and the role of the Secretary of State for Justice and the Mental Health Casework Section (MHCS) in Her Majesty's Prison and Probation Service (HMPPS)" (para.1). The guidance can be accessed at: *www.gov.uk/government/publications/mentally-disordered-offenders-the-restricted-patient-system*.The guidance states at para.5.3:

> "If a patient subject to a s47/49 transfer was sentenced to an indeterminate sentence (indeterminate sentence for public protection or a discretionary life sentence), the restriction direction remains in effect for the duration of their detention in hospital, even past the minimum term or tariff period. The release date for such sentences is not fixed and is determined by a direction to release by the Parole Board. The Parole Board cannot consider release until the tariff expiry date and the case will not be referred to the Parole Board while the patient remains detained under the MHA, until such time as the Tribunal has decided that, but for the restriction direction, they would be suitable for discharge.
>   Determinate or fixed term sentences

Where the prisoner remains in hospital, the restrictions will expire at the point of the automatic release date and they will then be managed solely by doctors with no input from the Secretary of State as an unrestricted patient. Patients in this situation are sometimes referred to as 'notional s37s'.
Indeterminate sentences
Restrictions will remain in place for so long as the patient remains detained in hospital."

Applications to the First-tier Tribunal (Mental Health) or the Mental Health Review Tribunal for Wales

A patient who is subject to a restriction direction may apply to a tribunal within six months of the **1-707** date of the direction, once during the following six months, and at yearly intervals thereafter (ss.69(2), 70). The tribunal has no power to direct the patient's discharge: see s.74.

Remissions to Prison

The March 2008 issue of the *Mental Health Unit Bulletin* contains the following statement: **1-708**

"The Secretary of State can remit to prison any patient transferred under sections 47/49 (or sections 48/49 provided he is not remanded to appear at a Magistrates' Court) to hospital if the [RC] advises that it is no longer necessary for the patient to receive treatment in hospital, or if the patient presents as untreatable. In these circumstances, the [RC] should write to the [MHCS] recommending a return to prison. The [RC] should also source the prison to which the patient should return, most often the prison from which they came. If this is not possible, however, that prison must find an alternative establishment. Once a section 117 meeting has been held and both parties (hospital and prison) have confirmed that they are content for the remission to take place, [MHCS] will issue a remission warrant. Further details … can be found in Prison Service Instruction 50/2007."

Domestic Violence, Crime and Victims Act 2004

See Ch.40 of the *Code of Practice*. The Department of Health has published "Mental Health Act **1-709** 2007: Guidance on the extension of victims' rights under the Domestic Violence, Crime and Victims Act" (2008).

Human Rights Act 1998

See the note on *technical lifer*, below. **1-710**

Technical lifer

A "technical lifer" is a person who, although sentenced to life imprisonment (whether discretionary **1-711** or mandatory) will in certain circumstances be treated as though he had originally been made the subject of a hospital order and a restriction order made under ss.37 and 41. "Technical lifer" is a non-statutory status, based on an administrative process entirely within the discretion of the Secretary of State. In *R. (on the application of IR) v Dr G Shetty and the Secretary of State for the Home Department* [2003] EWHC 3152 (Admin); [2004] M.H.L.R. 130, Munby J. rejected a claim that the procedure for attaining "technical lifer" status was a "sentencing exercise" which breached art.6 of the European Convention on Human Rights (ECHR). His Lordship commented, at para.10, that from the claimant's perspective "technical lifer" was "a desirable status because (a) he cannot in any circumstances be returned to prison, (b) he becomes entitled under art.5(4) of [the ECHR] to periodic reviews of the lawfulness of his detention even if his tariff period has not expired (see *Van Droogenbroeck v Belgium* (1982) 4 E.H.R.R. 443 and *Benjamin and Wilson v United Kingdom* (2003) 36 E.H.R.R. 1) and (c) in practice (see *Benjamin and Wilson v United Kingdom*, paras 28, 30) he will be entitled to his liberty if [a tribunal] so recommends".
In *R. v Secretary of State for the Home Department Ex p. Williams*, June 21, 1994, unreported, the court said:

"The effect of being classified as a 'technical lifer' is that the patient is treated, for the purposes of discharge, as though a hospital order under section 37 and a restriction order under section 41 of the 1983 Act had been made instead of the imposition of a sentence of imprisonment. He is treated with a view to rehabilitation and eventual release direct from hospital into the community. His case will not be referred to the Parole Board and he will not be released on life licence."

In *R. v Beatty* [2006] EWCA Crim 2359, para.53, Scott Baker L.J. said that if "the decision is made that a transferred prisoner should be treated as a 'technical lifer', the Home Office [now the Ministry of Justice] guarantees:

(i)	that the 'technical lifer' will not return to prison when he is well enough to leave hospital;
(ii)	that his tariff date will no longer be taken into consideration in deciding whether he is entitled to be discharged into the community; and
(iii)	that when he leaves hospital, [he] will go out on absolute or conditional discharge under the Mental Health Act rather than on life licence."

In *Williams*, above, the court was informed that the Home Office [now the Ministry of Justice] has an equivalent system for determinate sentence prisoners:

"... the Home Office does in fact recognise that there may be exceptional circumstances in which a determinate sentence prisoner should be rehabilitated through the hospital system and not returned to prison, even though his earliest date of release is someway ahead. This would be justifiable in cases where there was clear evidence that the sentencing Court did not dispose of the case by means of a hospital order for the kind of reason which influences the Home Office in conferring 'technical lifer' status on a transferred life sentence prisoner."

A "technical lifer" can be discharged from hospital in three possible ways. Each can be initiated only by the Secretary of State. They are:

1. A conditional or absolute discharge made under s.42(2).
2. A discharge made under s.50(1)(b).
3. Through the operation of s.74(2).

In *Benjamin and Wilson v United Kingdom* (2003) 36 E.H.R.R. 1, the European Court of Human Rights held that s.74(2) violates art.5(4) of the ECHR because the power of discharge rests with the Secretary of State rather than the tribunal. This decision prompted the Parliamentary Under-Secretary of State for the Home Department to make the following Written Ministerial Statement (*House of Commons Hansard*, January 24, 2005):

"From 2 April 2005, life sentence prisoners who have been transferred to psychiatric hospitals for treatment will no longer be considered for technical lifer status. All life sentence prisoners will have their future release determined by the Parole Board and be subject to life licence on release. This decision has been taken in the light of the judgment in the case of *Benjamin and Wilson v the United Kingdom*, which found that technical lifer policy was in breach of Art.5(4) of the European Convention on Human Rights. This will not affect those who have already been granted technical lifer status, or the consideration of any pending applications. No new applications, however, will be considered after 2 April 2005."

Those who were preparing to seek "technical lifer" status at the time when the above announcement was made had no entitlement to continue, nor had they a legitimate expectation to be consulted over the change of policy (*R. (on the application of Donaldson and Barker) v Home Secretary* [2006] EWHC 1107 (Admin); [2006] M.H.L.R. 100).

In *R. v Beatty*, above at para.59, the court said that the Criminal Cases Review Commission had pointed out that while the effect of a patient's "technical lifer" status may be identical to a hospital order there are potential benefits for the patient and the criminal justice system for a life sentence to be replaced with a hospital order. These are:

(i)	the unequivocal placement of someone who is mentally disordered into a regime of expert medical care from which he can progress, if it becomes appropriate, into a less secure regime under proper supervision and safeguards; and
(ii)	the substitution would reflect the change of approach signalled by the decision in *Benjamin and Wilson* and contained in the Home Office decision to make no further use of "technical lifer" status.

The court said, at paras 61, 62:

"Bearing in mind the criteria for granting 'technical lifer' status we think it very difficult to envisage circumstances where, 'technical lifer' status having been granted, the court would not substitute a hospital order with a restriction order for a life sentence. 'Technical lifer' status is only afforded if the prisoner is treatable.

It is obviously important, perhaps even more so now that 'technical lifer' status is no longer granted, that those who should have been the subject of a hospital order under sections 37/41 rather than life imprisonment should have the position rectified on appeal. That said, however, the court will always scrutinise with great care cases in which an appellant seeks to rely on psychiatric evidence directed to his mental state at the date of sentence that was not advanced at the time. Each case is likely to be decided on its own specific facts."

Subsection (1)

If he thinks fit   The Secretary of State is not bound by any statutory criteria when exercising his judg-   **1-712**
ment under this provision.

Subsection (2)

While a restriction direction is in force, the transfer direction also remains in force and does not need   **1-713**
to be renewed. For further provisions, see s.50. The Secretary of State does not have the power to make
a time limited restriction direction.

Subsection (3)

Report   See the note on s.41(6).   **1-714**

Further provisions as to prisoners under sentence

50.—(1)   Where a transfer direction and a restriction direction have been given   **1-715**
in respect of a person serving a sentence of imprisonment and before [his release
date] the Secretary of State is notified by the [responsible clinician], any other [ap-
proved clinician] or [the appropriate tribunal] that that person no longer requires
treatment in hospital for mental disorder or that no effective treatment for his
disorder can be given in the hospital to which he has been removed, the Secretary
of State may—
   (a)   by warrant direct that he be remitted to any prison or other institution
         in which he might have been detained if he had not been removed to
         hospital, there to be dealt with as if he had not been so removed; or
   (b)   exercise any power of releasing him on licence or discharging him
         under supervision which would have been exercisable if he had been
         remitted to such a prison or institution as aforesaid,
and on his arrival in the prison or other institution or, as the case may be, his release
or discharge as aforesaid, the transfer direction and the restriction direction shall
cease to have effect.

[(2)   A restriction direction in the case of a person serving a sentence of
imprisonment shall cease to have effect, if it has not previously done so, on his
release date.

(3)   In this section, references to a person's release date are to the day (if any)
on which he would be entitled to be released (whether unconditionally or on
licence) from any prison or other institution in which he might have been detained
if the transfer direction had not been given; and in determining that day there shall
be disregarded—
   (a)   any powers that would be exercisable by the Parole Board if he were
         detained in such a prison or other institution, and
   (b)   any practice of the Secretary of State in relation to the early release
         under discretionary powers of persons detained in such a prison or
         other institution.]

(4) For the purposes of section 49(2) of the Prison Act 1952 (which provides for discounting from the sentences of certain prisoners periods while they are unlawfully at large) a patient who, having been transferred in pursuance of a transfer direction from any such institution as is referred to in that section, is at large in circumstances in which he is liable to be taken into custody under any provision of this Act, shall be treated as unlawfully at large and absent from that institution.

[(5) The preceding provisions of this section shall have effect as if—

(a) the reference in subsection (1) to a transfer direction and a restriction direction having been given in respect of a person serving a sentence of imprisonment included a reference to a hospital direction and a limitation direction having been given in respect of a person sentenced to imprisonment;

(b) the reference in subsection (2) to a restriction direction included a reference to a limitation direction; and

(c) references in subsections (3) and (4) to a transfer direction included references to a hospital direction.]

Amendments

The amendments to this section were made by the Criminal Justice Act 2003 s.294, the Mental Health Act 2007 s.11(2), SI 2008/2883 art.9, Sch.3 para.42 and the Crime (Sentences) Act 1997 s.55, Sch.4 para.12(4) (5).

Definitions

1-716   transfer direction: ss.47, 145(1).
restriction direction: ss.49, 145(1).
hospital: ss.55(5), 145(1).
mental disorder: ss.1, 145(1).
patient: s.145(1).
responsible clinician: s.55(1).
approved clinician: s.145(1).
the appropriate tribunal: ss.66(4), 145(1).
hospital direction: s.145(1).
limitation direction: s.145(1).

General Note

1-717   This section provides that if the Secretary of State is informed that a patient who has been placed on a restriction direction or a hospital and limitation direction no longer requires treatment in hospital for mental disorder or that no effective treatment for his disorder can be given in the hospital to which he has been removed, he may either direct that the patient be returned to prison to serve the remainder of his sentence or release him from hospital on the same terms on which he could be released from prison. In both instances, the transfer direction and the restriction direction cease to have effect (subs.(1)). This section also provides for a restriction direction in the case of a person serving a sentence of imprisonment to cease to have effect on the day when he would be entitled to be released from prison (subss.(2),(3)).

If a patient subject to a restriction direction is in hospital when the restrictions cease to have effect, he will remain in hospital as a detained patient subject to a hospital order made under s.37 on the day when the restriction order ceased to have effect (s.41(5)). Such a patient is often referred to as being the subject of a "notional hospital order": see the General Note to s.49.

In *R. (on the application of Pendlebury) v Secretary of State for Justice* [2013] EWHC 3613 (Admin); [2014] M.H.L.R. 234, Recorder Fordham QC said that the judgment of Munby J. in IR, noted under Human Rights Act 1998 below, contained "a helpful description of three key questions which arise in the context of s.50". They are firstly the "s.50(1) question: does the claimant any longer require treatment in hospital for mental disorder? Or: is there any longer effective treatment for his disorder that can be given in hospital? Question 2: does the claimant's mental condition continue to be such as to warrant his compulsory confinement in a suitable therapeutic environment other than a prison? The article 5 question. Question 3: if the claimant is remitted to prison, is it more likely than not that he will suffer treatment at the hands of the prison authorities so damaging to him as to amount to inhuman or degrading treatment within the meaning of Article 3? The Article 3 question". In *Pendlebury*, the patient failed in his claim that the Secretary of State has acted unlawfully when issuing a warrant under this section on being notified by the patient's responsible clinician (RC) that the statutory criteria were satisfied on the ground that she had not accepted a finding of the first-tier tribunal that it was necessary for the patient to remain in hospital and to be treated there. The claim failed because the judge found that the RC had conscientiously re-evaluated and confirmed his opinion that the patient should be remitted to prison in the light of the tribunal's determination. The Secretary of State therefore had objective justification for the conclusion that the patient no longer required treatment in hospital.

The Secretary of State "also has the power, under s.42(2), on his own motion at any time, and under s.74(2), to authorise the [tribunal] to arrange for the discharge of a prisoner who has been transferred to a mental hospital"; per Rose L.J. in *R. v Secretary of State for the Home Department Ex p. Hickey (No.1)* [1995] 1 All E.R. 479 CA at 483.

Human Rights Act 1998

In the *Morley* case, noted under subs.(1), the applicant contended that his right to respect for his privacy under art.8 of the European Convention on Human Rights (ECHR) had been breached by virtue of his transfer from hospital to prison. The Court of Appeal dismissed this argument for the following reason: **1-718**

"In the absence of a breach of another article or articles, the convention does not render unlawful that interference with private life which inevitably follows from a lawfully imposed custodial sentence. Transfer from prison to hospital and hospital back to prison, as a part of a high-security custodial regime, cannot in present circumstances be said to be breach the article notwithstanding the differences in medical treatment which may occur" (para.49).

The patient's complaint to the European Court of Human Rights was declared inadmissible (*Morley v United Kingdom* (2005) 40 E.H.R.R. SE8; [2005] M.H.L.R. 174). The Court said at para.47:

"Even assuming, however, that the difference in regimes between the hospital and prison could be considered by itself as affecting the applicant's private life, the Court considers such interference may be regarded as complying with the second paragraph of Art.8 namely as a measure 'in accordance with the law', pursuing the aims of the prevention of disorder and crime and protection of the rights of others, as well as being 'necessary in a democratic society' for those aims."

Any argument that there are breaches of rights under the ECHR concerned with the operation of this section should be raised against the Secretary of State rather than the patient's RC, who is exercising only a clinical judgment and cannot be challenged on Convention grounds (*R. (on the application of IR) v Dr G Shetty and the Home Secretary* [2003] EWHC 3022 (Admin); [2004] M.H.L.R. 111 para.39).

Also see the note on s.74 under this heading.

Subsection (1)

In *R. (on the application of Morley) v Nottinghamshire Health Care NHS Trust* [2002] EWCA Civ 1728; [2003] 1 All E.R. 784, the Court of Appeal held that: **1-719**

1. The issue under this provision is treatability and the Secretary of State's decision necessarily turns upon a clinical judgment, that of the RC, and if that judgment was fairly and rationally made, a duty in the Secretary of State to permit and consider representations from the patient does not arise.
2. There will be cases in which circumstances, including information available to the Secretary of State, either in the documents by which the notification is given, or from other sources, create a duty in the Secretary of State to make further inquiries or take further action or both.
3. The duty upon a RC before giving a notification to the Secretary of State is to make full and fair enquiries within the hospital as to whether the treatability test is satisfied and to consider views expressed, as well as his own first hand knowledge and experience, before making a recommendation. He is not placed under a duty to disclose reports on individual components of the patient's medical regime or to present to the Secretary of State contrary views which may have been expressed by some members of the inter-disciplinary team. The extent of

enquiry and of disclosure of information will depend upon the circumstances of the particular case and will normally be judged as at the moment of decision.

In *R. (on the application of W) v Larkin and the Secretary of State for Justice* [2012] EWHC 556 (Admin); [2012] M.H.L.R. 161, Ouseley J., in a permission hearing, held that the two limbs of the test for a transfer back to prison under this section are not mutually exclusive. It is therefore not unlawful for an RC to tick both the "no longer requires treatment in hospital for mental disorder" and the "no effective treatment for his disorder can be given in the hospital to which he has been removed" boxes on the proforma that is used when a notification is made to the Secretary of State. His Lordship said at para.38:

"[I]n circumstances where it may be appropriate, but not required, for someone to receive treatment for a disorder in a hospital, notwithstanding its availability to a considerable degree in the prison estate, but, where it is not available to the hospital where he is currently detained, both boxes can sensibly be ticked 'no', as was done here."

Confirmation that a patient can be remitted to prison in a situation where treatment was not required within a hospital but it could be provided there was given in *R. (on the application of RW) v Secretary of State for Justice* [2012] EWHC 2082 (Admin); [2012] M.H.L.R. 288, para.20.

If the Secretary of State accepts the RC's advice that the patient no longer requires treatment in hospital for a mental disorder, he has a wide and unfettered discretion as to what to do with the patient; a discretion which entitles him to take into account a wide range of facts, some no doubt referable to the patient himself but others referable to wider considerations of the public interest and in any event extending far beyond the purely clinical (*R. (on the application of IR) v Dr G Shetty and the Home Secretary*, above, para.26).

Transfer direction and a restriction direction   See subs.(5)(a).

Serving a sentence of imprisonment   See s.55(6).

Release date   See subs.(3).

Notified by the responsible clinician   The RC should notify the Mental Health Casework section at the Ministry of Justice at once in writing if she considers that a patient meets the criteria set out in this subsection.

Any other approved clinician   In the *Morley* case, above, Burton J., sitting at first instance, was informed by counsel for the Secretary of State that notification from this clinician is, in practice, restricted to a situation in which such a clinician "is for some reason standing in for the [RC], and if it were any other medical practitioner plainly any such recommendation would have to be looked at carefully indeed by the [Secretary of State] to see whether it was appropriate to act on it" ([2003] M.H.L.R. 88 at para.29).

Effective treatment   This probably means treatment that will benefit the patient: see s.145(4).

May   It is not possible to construe this provision so as to impose a duty on the Secretary of State (*R. (on the application of D) v Secretary of State for the Home Department* [2002] EWHC 2805 (Admin); [2003] 1 W.L.R. 1315 at para.29).

Paragraph (a)

1-720   Once a life sentenced patient no longer requires treatment in hospital, the normal course is for the Secretary of State to remit him to prison under this paragraph where he would be eligible for a Parole Board hearing as appropriate in the normal manner.

By warrant   There is no provision for a time limit to be attached to the warrant.

Paragraph (b)

1-721   In 1985, the Home Secretary made the following policy statement on life sentence prisoners in response to a Parliamentary Question:

"When life sentence prisoners transferred to hospital under the Mental Health Act 1983 are to be released, it has hitherto been the practice to discharge such persons on a warrant of conditional discharge under section 42(3) of the Act. I now intend to use the powers available to me under section 50(1)(b) of the Act, which enables me to release such persons under the same arrangements as those they would have been subject to had they remained in, or been returned to, prison. This means that, in future, such persons will normally be released on life licences under the provisions of section 61 of the Criminal Justice Act 1967 [now see section 28 of the Crime (Sentences) Act 1997] in accordance with the sentencing Courts' intention, i.e. on the recommendation of the Parole Board and after consultation with the Lord Chief Justice and, if available, the trial judge. In exceptional cases, where the Lord Chief Justice and the trial judge so recommend, I will be prepared to consider whether it would be more appropriate to authorise discharge under section 42(2) of the 1983 Act.

Under the new procedure, a life sentence prisoner who has been transferred to hospital, can be released on life licence without having to return to prison before release. Persons released on life licence under these arrangements will be subject to recall to prison under the provisions of section 62 of the 1967 Act [now see s.254 of the Criminal Justice Act 2003]. Should their mental condition be such that they are recommended for transfer to hospital this could very quickly be effected under the provisions of section 47 of the 1983 Act."

This policy was challenged in *R. v Secretary of State for the Home Department Ex p. Stroud* [1993] C.O.D. 75. The applicant stated that a life prisoner released from prison on licence remains subject to supervision for the rest of his life whereas release under ss.42(2) or 74(2) allowed for the possibility of an eventual absolute discharge either by the Secretary of State or by a tribunal. He contended that the normal rule of practice set out in the policy statement deprived life sentence prisoners of the potential benefit of absolute discharge and thus the Secretary of State had fettered his discretion unlawfully. Henry J. held, in refusing the application for judicial review, that there was no illegality in the policy which had been adopted for legitimate reasons to ensure consistency of treatment between all those sentenced to life imprisonment.

In *R. v Secretary of State for the Home Department Ex p. Hickey (No.1)* [1995] 1 All E.R. 479, the principal question before the Court of Appeal was whether a prisoner sentenced either to a discretionary life term or to be detained during Her Majesty's pleasure, transferred subsequently to a hospital by the Secretary of State under ss.47 and 49 and who has served the tariff part of his sentence, can require the Secretary of State so to act that his case is considered by the Parole Board, notwithstanding that he is still in hospital needing, and receiving, treatment. The court held that a person who had been made the subject of such a transfer was governed by the regime laid down in the Mental Health Act and had no right to have his case referred to the Parole Board.

In *R. v Vowles* [2015] EWCA Crim 45; [2016] M.H.L.R. 66, the Court of Appeal held at para.31 that if a prisoner is sentenced to an indeterminate sentence of imprisonment and then transferred to hospital under ss.47 and 49, the ECHR did not require the lawfulness of his detention to be reviewed by a single body, exercising the functions of both tribunal and the Parole Board; also see *R. (on the application of P) v Secretary of State for the Home Department* [2003] EWHC 2953 (Admin); [2004] M.H.L.R. 64.

Life prisoners who have been transferred to hospital under the Act, and whom it is not appropriate to remit to prison even though they no longer require, or can effectively be given, hospital treatment will be referred by the Secretary of State to the Parole Board, while they remain in hospital, in the same way as if they had been remitted to prison (245 HC Official Report (6th series) written answers, col.9, 20 June 1994 and *Hickey*, above, at 485, 486).

Subsection (2)

Restriction direction   See subs.(5)(b).

1-722

Cease to have effect   The patient is to be treated as if he had been admitted to hospital under a hospital order without restrictions on the day when the restriction direction ceased to have effect (ss.49(2), 41(5)).

Unsurprisingly, a life sentence ceases to have effect on the death of the person concerned (*R. (on the application of D) v Secretary of State for the Home Department* [2002] EWHC Admin 2805 at para.30).

Release date   See subss.(3) and (4).

Subsection (3)

Transfer direction   Or hospital direction (subs.(5)(c)).

1-723

Subsection (4)

1-724   "The effect of subsection (4), and the clear intention behind it, is that if an individual absconds from the mental hospital to which he is transferred that will be treated as him being unlawfully at large, as if the hospital were the prison from which he absconded", per Collins J. in *R. (on the application of Miah) v Secretary of State for the Home Department* [2004] EWHC 2569 (Admin); [2004] M.H.L.R. 302 at para.30.

In *R. (on the application of S) v Secretary of State for the Home Department* [2003] EWCA Civ 426; [2003] M.H.L.R. 264 at para.22, the court accepted as correct the following submission made by counsel for the Secretary of State:

"Section 50(4) of the 1983 Act places those transferred from prison to hospital under sections 47 and 48 on the same footing as those still in prison: it ensures that anyone absconding from either will be treated in the same way. But section 50(4) deals only with abscondees from hospital transferred 'from any such institution as is referred to in [section 49(2)]', that is from prisons and the like, and it dictates that they be 'treated as unlawfully at large and absent from that institution'. It says nothing about those detained in hospital otherwise than pursuant to a transfer direction (under section 47 or section 48) with the result that patients detained under other provisions of the 1983 Act, notably sections 2 and 3, are to be regarded as at large irrespective of whether they are in fact in hospital or have absconded from hospital and are liable to be taken back in custody under section 18".

The court was informed that the problem that arose in this case is unlikely to recur as the Prison Service is being instructed that when the revocation of a license is requested and the offender is already sectioned under the Act, a s.47 transfer direction (which would supersede the s.2 or s.3 (ss.40(5), 55(4))) is to be sought at the same time as the revocation request is being dealt with. This is to ensure that any revocation and transfer would operate simultaneously and so avoid the recall of an offender still subject to the s.2 or s.3 (para.32).

Transfer direction   Or hospital direction (subs.(5)(c)).

Further provisions as to detained persons

1-725   **51.**—(1)   This section has effect where a transfer direction has been given in respect of any such person as is described in paragraph (a) of section 48(2) above and that person is in this section referred to as "the detainee".

(2)   The transfer direction shall cease to have effect when the detainee's case is disposed of by the court having jurisdiction to try or otherwise deal with him, but without prejudice to any power of that court to make a hospital order or other order under this Part of this Act in his case.

(3)   If the Secretary of State is notified by the [responsible clinician], any other [approved clinician] or [the appropriate tribunal] at any time before the detainee's case is disposed of by that court—

(a)   that the detainee no longer requires treatment in hospital for mental disorder; or

(b)   that no effective treatment for his disorder can be given at the hospital to which he has been removed,

the Secretary of State may by warrant direct that he be remitted to any place where he might have been detained if he had not been removed to hospital, there to be dealt with as if he had not been so removed, and on his arrival at the place to which he is so remitted the transfer direction shall cease to have effect.

(4)   If (no direction having been given under subsection (3) above) the court having jurisdiction to try or otherwise deal with the detainee is satisfied on the written or oral evidence of the [responsible clinician]—

(a)   that the detainee no longer requires treatment in hospital for mental disorder; or

(b)   that no effective treatment for his disorder can be given at the hospital to which he has been removed,

[318]

the court may order him to be remitted to any such place as is mentioned in subsection (3) above or[, subject to section 25 of the Criminal Justice and Public Order Act 1994,] released on bail and on his arrival at that place or, as the case may be, his release on bail the transfer direction shall cease to have effect.

(5)   If (no direction or order having been given or made under subsection (3) or (4) above) it appears to the court having jurisdiction to try or otherwise deal with the detainee—

    (a)   that it is impracticable or inappropriate to bring the detainee before the court; and

    (b)   that the conditions set out in subsection (6) below are satisfied,

the court may make a hospital order (with or without a restriction order) in his case in his absence and, in the case of a person awaiting trial, without convicting him.

(6)   A hospital order may be made in respect of a person under subsection (5) above if the court—

    (a)   is satisfied, on the written or oral evidence of at least two registered medical practitioners, that:

        (i)   the detainee is suffering from mental disorder of a nature or degree which makes it appropriate for the patient to be detained in a hospital for medical treatment;] [and

        (ii)   appropriate medical treatment is available for him; and]

    (b)   is of the opinion, after considering any depositions or other documents required to be sent to the proper officer of the court, that it is proper to make such an order.

(7)   Where a person committed to the Crown Court to be dealt with under section 43 above is admitted to a hospital in pursuance of an order under section 44 above, subsections (5) and (6) above shall apply as if he were a person subject to a transfer direction.

Amendments

The amendments to this section were made by SI 2008/2883 art.9, Sch.3 para.43, the Criminal Justice and Public Order Act 1994 s.168(2), Sch.10 para.51 and the Mental Health Act 2007 ss.1(4), 5(4), 10(3), Sch.1 para.12.

Definitions

transfer direction: ss.47, 145(1).   **1-726**
hospital order: ss.37, 145(1).
responsible clinician: s.55(1).
approved clinician: s.145(1).
the appropriate tribunal: ss.66(4), 145(1).
hospital: ss.55(5), 145(1).
mental disorder: ss.1, 145(1).
appropriate medical treatment: ss.3(4), 145(1AB).
restriction order: ss.41, 145(1).
medical treatment: s.145(1), (4).

General Note

This section provides that a transfer direction made in respect of remanded prisoner shall cease to   **1-727**
have effect when the case has been finally dealt with by the appropriate court (subs.(2)). The linked restriction direction will also cease to have effect at that time. In the meanwhile the Secretary of State has power to direct the patient's return to prison (subs. (3)). If the Secretary of State does not exercise this power, the court can, on receiving the requisite evidence, either order the patient to be returned to prison or released on bail (subs.(4)). The transfer direction will cease to have effect if the Secretary of

State or court exercise their powers under subss.(3) and (4). If the patient has not been sent back to prison or released on bail, the court can make a hospital order in respect of a mentally disordered patient in his absence and without convicting him (subss.(5), (6)).

Human Rights Act 1998

I-728   The power of the court under subss.(5) and (6) to make a hospital order in the absence of a conviction or a finding that the person concerned "did the act or made the omission charged" (as required by, for example, s.37(3)), would appear to be a breach of art.6 of the European Convention on Human Rights in that the court has passed sentence in the absence of a trial.

Subsection (3)

I-729   **Notified by the responsible clinician**   See the note on s.50(1).

No effective treatment   A stronger test than the "appropriate treatment" test required by s.3(2)(d).

Subsection (4)

I-730   **Written or oral evidence**   For general requirements as to medical evidence, see s.54.

Subsection (5)

I-731   This provision, together with subs.(6), enables the court to make a hospital order (with or without restrictions) in respect of a mentally disordered accused person who is awaiting trial without bringing that person before the court.

In *R. (on the application of Kenneally) v Snaresbrook Crown Court* [2001] EWHC Admin. 968; [2002] M.H.L.R. 53 DC para.35, Pill L.J. said that to "pass sentence, even a sentence one of the objects of which is to assist the defendant, without first convicting him is a drastic step, one that should be taken only in exceptional circumstances". In this case, the court held that it was not clear whether the power to make an order under this provision was an exercise of the Crown Court's jurisdiction in matters relating to trial on indictment within the meaning of s.29(3) of the Senior Courts Act 1981, which precludes any jurisdiction in the High Court to quash the order. The High Court did, however, have the power to quash the order if the Crown Court made a relevant jurisdictional error. Tomlinson J. said at para.52: "[I]t seems to me anomalous that the Crown Court should have and should exercise a jurisdiction affecting the liberty of the subject which apparently admits of no direct right of appeal or review". Also see the note on "without convicting him", below.

Inappropriate   In *Kenneally*, Pill L.J. said that this word,

"must be construed restrictively. [Section 51(5)] must not be used as a routine and easy way of avoiding a potentially troublesome trial. To construe it as 'sparing a defendant a trial' is superficially attractive, especially when the outcome of the trial is readily predictable, but there is a public interest as well as that of the defendant himself in the resolution of issues, and especially when the failure to resolve them ... may have difficult and long term implications. I would not necessarily restrict the word 'inappropriate' so as to mean 'physically impossible' but a high degree of disablement or relevant disorder must be present. The section does not apply in a situation in which all that is involved is possible inconvenience for the Court and inevitable distress for the defendant and others likely to be concerned in a trial, if a trial is held" (para.32).

Hospital order (with or without a restriction order)   A judge, prior to the imposition of a restriction order under s.41, following the making of a hospital order under this provision, is not obliged to resolve any factual dispute between the Crown case and the defence case before he makes a finding that the "serious harm" criterion in s.41(1) is satisfied (*R. v Kingston Crown Court Ex p. Mason*, July 27, 1998, CA).

Person awaiting trial   Once the trial has commenced, any question relating to the mental fitness of the accused to be tried must be determined under s.4 of the Criminal Procedure (Insanity) Act 1964 and not under this provision (*R. v Griffiths* [2002] EWCA Crim 1762; [2002] M.H.L.R. 407). In *Griffiths*, the court made reference to the following obiter comment on the meaning of this phrase made by Tomlinson J. in *Kenneally*, at para.48: "It seems to me likely that the word 'trial' is ... intended to refer

... to the more immediately recognisable features of a criminal trial, beginning, broadly, with the swearing-in of the jury".

Without convicting him   As there has been no conviction, there is no right of appeal to the Court of Appeal (Criminal Appeal Act 1968, s.9 and *R. v Griffiths*, above).

Subsection (6)

Two registered medical practitioners   One of whom must be approved by the Secretary of State or   **1-732**
the Welsh Ministers under s.12, or by another person by virtue of s.12ZA or 12ZB (s.54(1)). A registered medical practitioner means "a fully registered person within the meaning of the Medical Act 1983 who holds a licence to practise under that Act" (Interpretation Act 1978, Sch.1).

Mental disorder   If the person has a learning disability, the disability must be associated with abnormally aggressive or seriously irresponsible conduct (s.1(2A), (2B)). A learning disabled person might also suffer from another form of mental disorder.

Nature or degree   See the note on s.3(2)(a).

Detained in a hospital for medical treatment   But not for assessment.

Appropriate medical treatment   See the note on s.3(2)(d).

Depositions   The Court is entitled to have regard to the evidence in the case in deciding whether to make an order (*Kenneally*, above, at para.34).

Further provisions as to persons remanded by magistrates' courts

52.—(1)   This section has effect where a transfer direction has been given in   **1-733**
respect of any such person as is described in paragraph (b) of section 48(2) above; and that person is in this section referred to as "the accused".

(2)   Subject to subsection (5) below, the transfer direction shall cease to have effect on the expiration of the period of remand unless the accused is [sent] in custody to the Crown Court for trial or to be otherwise dealt with.

(3)   Subject to subsection (4) below, the power of further remanding the accused under section 128 of the Magistrates' Courts Act 1980 may be exercised by the court without his being brought before the court; and if the court further remands the accused in custody (whether or not he is brought before the court) the period of remand shall, for the purposes of this section, be deemed not to have expired.

(4)   The court shall not under subsection (3) above further remand the accused in his absence unless he has appeared before the court within the previous six months.

(5)   If the magistrates' court is satisfied, on the written or oral evidence of the [responsible clinician]—

   (a)   that the accused no longer requires treatment in hospital for mental disorder; or
   (b)   that no effective treatment for his disorder can be given in the hospital to which he has been removed,

the court may direct that the transfer direction shall cease to have effect notwithstanding that the period of remand has not expired or that the accused is [sent] to the Crown Court as mentioned in subsection (2) above.

(6)   If the accused is [sent] to the Crown Court as mentioned in subsection (2) above and the transfer direction has not ceased to have effect under subsection (5) above, section 51 above shall apply as if the transfer direction given in his case were a direction given in respect of a person falling within that section.

(7)   The magistrates' court may, in the absence of the accused, [send him to the Crown Court for trial under section 51 or 51A of the Crime and Disorder Act 1998]

(a)   the court is satisfied, on the written or oral evidence of the [responsible clinician], that the accused is unfit to take part in the proceedings; and

(b)   [...], the accused is represented by [an authorised person].

Amendments

The amendments to this section were made by the Criminal Justice Act 2003 s.41, Sch.3 para.55(1),(3), the Mental Health Act 2007 s.11(4) and the Legal Services Act 2007 s.208, Sch.21 para.57.

Definitions

1-734   transfer direction: ss.47, 145(1).
responsible clinician: s.55(1).
hospital: ss.55(5), 145(1).
mental disorder: ss.1, 145(1).
authorised person: s.55(1).

General Note

1-735   This section provides that a transfer direction made in respect of a person who has been remanded in custody by a magistrates' court ceases to have effect at the expiration of the period of remand unless the accused is then sent in custody to the Crown Court (subs.(2)). However, if the magistrates' court further remands the accused under subs.(3) the direction will not expire. Alternatively, if the court is satisfied, on receiving the requisite evidence, that the accused no longer requires treatment in hospital it may direct that the transfer direction shall cease to have effect (subs.(5)). The court also has power to send the accused to the Crown Court for trial in his absence if it is satisfied that he is unfit to take part in the proceedings (subs.(7)).

Subsection (4)

1-736   **Months**   Means calendar months (Interpretation Act s.5, Sch.1).

Subsection (5)

1-737   **Written or oral evidence**   See s.54.

Further provisions as to civil prisoners and persons detained under the [Immigration Acts]

1-738   **53.**—(1)   Subject to subsection (2) below, a transfer direction given in respect of any such person as is described in paragraph (c) or (d) of section 48(2) above shall cease to have effect on the expiration of the period during which he would, but for his removal to hospital, be liable to be detained in the place from which he was removed.

(2)   Where a transfer direction and a restriction direction have been given in respect of any such person as is mentioned in subsection (1) above, then, if the Secretary of State is notified by the [responsible clinician], any other [approved clinician] or [the appropriate tribunal] at any time before the expiration of the period there mentioned—

(a)   that that person no longer requires treatment in hospital for mental disorder; or

(b)   that no effective treatment for his disorder can be given in the hospital to which he has been removed,

the Secretary of State may by warrant direct that he be remitted to any place where

[322]

he might have been detained if he had not been removed to hospital, and on his arrival at the place to which he is so remitted the transfer direction and the restriction direction shall cease to have effect.

Amendments

The amendments to this section were made by the Nationality, Immigration and Asylum Act 2002 s.62(10), the Mental Health Act 2007 s.11(5) and by SI 2008/2883 art.9, Sch.3 para.44.

Definitions

transfer direction: ss.47, 145(1).   **1-739**
hospital: ss.55(5), 145(1).
restriction direction: ss.49, 145(1).
responsible clinician: s.55(1).
approved clinician: s.145(1).
mental disorder: ss.1, 145(1).
the appropriate tribunal: ss.66(4), 145(1).

General Note

This section provides that a transfer direction made in respect of a civil prisoner or a person detained   **1-740**
under the Immigration Acts ceases to have effect on the expiration of the period of detention that would
have occurred had the removal to hospital not taken place (subs.(1)). Where a transfer direction *and* a
restriction direction have been made the Secretary of State has power to direct that the patient be returned
to prison, and on his arrival there both the transfer direction and the restriction direction shall cease to
have effect (subs.(2)).

SUPPLEMENTAL

Requirements as to medical evidence

54.—(1) The registered medical practitioner whose evidence is taken into ac-   **1-741**
count under section 35(3)(a) above and at least one of the registered medical
practitioners whose evidence is taken into account under sections 36(1), 37(2)(a),
38(1)[, 45A(2)] and 51(6)(a) above and whose reports are taken into account under
sections 47(1) and 48(1) above shall be a practitioner approved for the purposes of
section 12 above by the Secretary of State[, or by another person by virtue of section 12ZA or 12ZB above] as having special experience in the diagnosis or treatment of mental disorder.

[(2) For the purposes of any provision of this Part of this Act under which a
court may act on the written evidence of any person, a report in writing purporting
to be signed by that person may, subject to the provisions of this section, be received
in evidence without proof of the following—

(a) the signature of the person; or

(b) his having the requisite qualifications or approval or authority or being of the requisite description to give the report.

(2A) But the court may require the signatory of any such report to be called to
give oral evidence.]

(3) Where, in pursuance of a direction of the court, any such report is tendered
in evidence otherwise than by or on behalf of the person who is the subject of the
report, then—

(a) if that person is represented by [an authorised person], a copy of the
report shall be given to [that authorised person];

(b) if that person is not so represented, the substance of the report shall be

[323]

disclosed to him or, where he is a child or young person, to his parent or guardian if present in court; and

(c) except where the report relates only to arrangements for his admission to a hospital, that person may require the signatory of the report to be called to give oral evidence, and evidence to rebut the evidence contained in the report may be called by or on behalf of that person.

Amendments

The amendments to this section were made by the Crime (Sentences) Act 1997 s.55, Sch.4 para.12(6), the Mental Health Act 2007 s.11(6), the Legal Services Act 2007 s.208, Sch.21 para.58 and the Health and Social Care Act 2012 s.38(2).

Definitions

1-742
mental disorder: ss.1, 145(1).
the managers: s.145(1).
hospital: ss.55(5), 145(1).
child: s.55(1).
young person: s.55(1).
guardian: s.55(1).
authorised person: s.55(1).

General Note

1-743
This section specifies when medical evidence in proceedings under this Part of the Act must be given by a doctor who has been approved by the Secretary of State or the Welsh Ministers under s.12, or by another person by virtue of s.12ZA or 12ZB, and provides for the circumstances when written evidence by a doctor or a person representing the managers of a hospital may be accepted by a court. There is no requirement for the doctor to be an approved clinician.

A doctor who has been approved under s.12 is also approved for the purposes of s.4 of the Criminal Procedure (Insanity) Act 1964 (*R. v Ghulam* [2009] EWCA Crim 2285, para.1.19).

Code of Practice

1-744
Under the heading "Assessment by a doctor", the Code states:

"22.9 A doctor who is asked to provide evidence in relation to a possible admission under part 3 of the Act should bear in mind that the request is not for a general report on the defendant's condition but for advice on whether or not the patient should be diverted from prison by way of a hospital order, or a hospital direction (or a community order with a mental health treatment requirement under criminal justice legislation).

22.10 Doctors should:

- identify themselves to the person being assessed, explain who has requested the report and make clear the limits of confidentiality in relation to the report. They should explain that any information disclosed, and the medical opinion, could be relevant not only to medical disposal by the court but also to the imposition of a punitive sentence, or to its length, and
- request relevant pre-sentence reports, the inmate medical record and previous psychiatric reports, as well as relevant documentation regarding the alleged offence. If any of this information is not available, the doctor's report should say so clearly.

22.11 The doctor, or one of them if two doctors are preparing reports, should have access to a bed or take responsibility for referring the case to another clinician who does if they propose to recommend admission to hospital within the period of 28 days beginning with the date of the making of the order under section 37, section 38 or section 45A of the Act. If the court is making an order under the Criminal Procedure (Insanity) Act 1964, the Court does not need a 'bed offer' as it does for other court orders but it is good practice for any doctor providing a recommendation of a hospital disposal under Domestic Violence, Crime and Victims Act 2004 (DVCVA)2 to contact the anticipated named hospital in the order.

22.12 The doctor should, identify and access other independent sources of information about the person's previous history (including convictions). This should include information from GP records, previous psychiatric treatment and patterns of behaviour."

Subsection (1)

Registered medical practitioner   Means "a fully registered person within the meaning of the Medical Act 1983 who holds a licence to practise under that Act" (Interpretation Act 1978, Sch.1).   **1-745**

Subsection (3)

This subsection has been enacted because medical reports "may contain facts or comments which might cause distress not only to the accused but also to his relatives. If the accused wishes, however, he may insist that the medical practitioner should give oral evidence, and he may then call evidence in rebuttal" (Home Office Circular No. 69/1983, para.44).   **1-746**

[Reduction of period for making hospital orders

54A.—(1)   The Secretary of State may by order reduce the length of the periods   **1-747**
mentioned in sections 37(4) and (5) and 38(4) above.

(2)   An order under subsection (1) above may make such consequential amendments of sections 40(1) and 44(3) above as appear to the Secretary of State to be necessary or expedient.]

Amendment

This section was inserted by the Criminal Justice Act 1991 s.27(2).

General Note

This section enables the Secretary of State to reduce, by statutory instrument, the time periods for   **1-748**
the admission of mentally disordered offenders to hospital.

Secretary of State

Or, in relation to Wales, the Welsh Ministers (see the General Note to the Act).

Interpretation of Part III

55.—(1)   In this Part of this Act—   **1-749**

["authorised person" means a person who, for the purposes of the Legal Services Act 2007, is an authorised person in relation to an activity which constitutes the exercise of a right of audience (within the meaning of that Act);]

"child" and "young person" have the same meaning as in the Children and Young Persons Act 1933;

"civil prisoner" has the meaning given to it by section 48(2)(c) above;

"guardian", in relation to a child or young person, has the same meaning as in the Children and Young Persons Act 1933;

"place of safety", in relation to a person who is not a child or young person, means any police station, prison or remand centre, or any hospital the managers of which are willing temporarily to receive him, and in relation to a child or young person has the same meaning as in the Children and Young Persons Act 1933;

["responsible clinician", in relation to a person liable to be detained in a hospital within the meaning of Part 2 of this Act, means the approved clinician with overall responsibility for the patient's case.]

(2)   Any reference in this Part of this Act to an offence punishable on summary conviction with imprisonment shall be construed without regard to any prohibition or restriction imposed by or under any enactment relating to the imprisonment of young offenders.

(3)   [...]

(4)   Any reference to a hospital order, a guardianship order or a restriction order in section 40(2), (4) or (5), section 41(3) to (5), or section 42 above or section 69(1) below shall be construed as including a reference to any order or direction under this Part of this Act having the same effect as the first-mentioned order; and the exceptions and modifications set out in Schedule 1 to this Act in respect of the provisions of this Act described in that Schedule accordingly include those which are consequential on the provisions of this subsection.

(5)   Section 34(2) above shall apply for the purposes of this Part of this Act as it applies for the purposes of Part II of this Act.

(6)   References in this Part of this Act to persons serving a sentence of imprisonment shall be construed in accordance with section 47(5) above.

(7)   Section 99 of the Children and Young Persons Act 1933 (which relates to the presumption and determination of age) shall apply for the purposes of this Part of this Act as it applies for the purposes of that Act.

Amendments

The amendments to this section were made by the Legal Services Act 2007 s.208, Sch.21 para.59 and the Mental Health Act 2007 ss.11(7), 55, Sch.11 Pt 1.

Definitions

1-750   approved clinician: s.145(1).
hospital: s.145(1) and see subs.(5) of this section.
the managers: s.145(1).
patient: s.145(1).
application for admission for treatment: ss.3, 145(1).
mental disorder: ss.1, 145(1).
hospital order: ss.37, 145(1).
guardianship order: ss.37, 145(1).
restriction order: ss.41, 145(1).

Subsection (1)

1-751   Under s.107(1) of the Children and Young Persons Act 1933, "child" means a person under the age of 14 years, "young person" means a person who has attained the age of 14 years and is under the age of 18 years, "guardian", in relation to a child or young person, includes any person who, in the opinion of the relevant court, has for the time being the care of the child or young person, and "place of safety" means a community home provided by a local authority or a controlled community home, any police station, or any hospital, surgery, or any other suitable place, the occupier of which is willing temporarily to receive a child or young person.

Responsible clinician   See the note on s.34(1).

Subsection (4)

Having the same effect   An interim hospital order made under s.38 does not have the same effect as **1-752**
a hospital order made under s.37: see the note on s.40(3).

Subsection (6)

In *R. v Fort* [2013] EWCA Crim 2332; [2014] M.H.L.R. 334 at paras 82 to 83, it was held that the   **1-753**
extension of the phrase "sentence of imprisonment" in this provision applies only to persons who are
actually "serving" a sentence and that it cannot extend to the phrase "deciding to impose a sentence of
imprisonment" in s.45A(1)(b) so as to include "deciding to impose a sentence of detention or custody
for life".

PART IV CONSENT TO TREATMENT

General Note

The extent to which the Mental Health Act 1959 gave authority to the responsible medical officer to   **1-754**
treat a detained patient without his consent was unclear. The opinion of the Department of Health and
Social Security was that where the purpose of detention was treatment, the Act gave implied authority
for treatment to be imposed. During the 1970s the correctness of this opinion was questioned by a
number of commentators: see paras 3.57 to 3.59 of the *Butler Committee*, Joe Jacob, "The right of the
mental patient to his psychosis", *Modern Law Review*, 1976, vol.39, pp.221–235, and Ch.11 of Phil Fennell's *Treatment Without Consent: Law Psychiatry and the Treatment of Mentally Disordered People
since 1895* (1996).

The purpose of this Part is to clarify the extent to which treatment for mental disorder can be imposed
on patients who are liable to be detained under the Act. It provides for three categories of treatment which
have different legal consequences. They are (1) the most serious treatments which require the patient's
consent and a second opinion (s.57); (2) treatments that can be given without consent subject to a second
opinion (s.58); and (3) treatments that can be given only with the consent of a capable patient or to an
incapable patient subject to a second opinion (s.58A). Treatments that do not come within these
categories can be imposed on a patient who is liable to be detained and who understands the nature and
purpose of the treatment, but expressly withholds consent (s.63). The safeguards provided for by ss.57,
58 and 58A can be overridden on a temporary basis if the treatment is required urgently (s.62).

Paragraph 24.7 of the *Code of Practice* states:

"Where reasonably practicable, treatment should be based on a strong evidence-base. Professionals
should ensure that any treatment is compliant with the current guidelines and standards about what
is appropriate treatment. Examples include, National Institute for Health and Care Excellence (NICE)/
Social Care Institute for Excellence (SCIE) guidelines, NICE quality standards and Department of
Health Care Programme Approach (CPA) guidance. In the case of medications that are used to treat
mental disorder, particular care is required when prescribing medications that exceed the maximum
dosage listed in the British National Formulary (BNF) or where multiple medications are used to treat
a patient."

The central importance of treatment in the scheme of the Act was explained by the Court of Appeal
in *R. (on the application of B) v Dr SS (Responsible Medical Officer)* [2006] EWCA Civ 28; [2006]
M.H.L.R. 131 at para.43:

"The MHA is primarily concerned with the compulsory detention of patients suffering from mental
disorders in order that they may receive treatment for those disorders. The compulsory detention is
justified because it is necessary in order to ensure that the patient receives the treatment. Ensuring
that the patient receives the treatment is justified because this is necessary for the health or safety of
the patient or for the protection of others."

The Explanatory Notes to the Mental Health Act 2007 at para.57, explain the frequent use of the
phrase "approved clinician in charge of treatment" rather than "responsible clinician" (RC) in this Part
and in Pt IVA:

"In the majority of cases the AC in charge of the treatment will be the patient's RC, but where, for example, the RC is not qualified to make decisions about a particular treatment (e.g. medication if the RC is not a doctor or a nurse prescriber) then another appropriately qualified professional will be in charge of that treatment, with the RC continuing to retain overall responsibility for the patient's case."

Approved Clinicians owe a duty of care to the patient whenever they propose or administer treatment under this Part (*R. (on the application of Wilkinson) v Responsible Medical Officer Broadmoor Hospital* [2001] EWCA Civ 1545; [2002] 1 W.L.R. 419 para.68).

A Court will not order a clinician to treat a patient contrary to her professional judgment (*AVS v A NHS Foundation Trust and A PCT* [2011] EWCA Civ 7, following *R. (on the application of Burke) v GMC* [2005] EWCA Civ 1003) and, on an application for judicial review, it is not the duty of the court to investigate requests for alternative forms of treatment or "second opinions" from patients unhappy or dissatisfied with their treatment (*YZ v NHS Trust* [2015] EWHC 2296 (Admin); [2015] M.H.L.R. 394 at para.35).

The provision of information about risk to patients

1-755   In *Montgomery v Lanarkshire Health Board* [2015] UKSC 11, the Supreme Court comprehensively reviewed the case law on a doctor's obligation to warn a patient of the risks of treatment. The substantive judgment was given by Lords Kerr and Reed who held that the correct position is that:

"87. ... An adult person of sound mind is entitled to decide which, if any, of the available forms of treatment to undergo, and her consent must be obtained before treatment interfering with her bodily integrity is undertaken. The doctor is therefore under a duty to take reasonable care to ensure that the patient is aware of any material risks involved in any recommended treatment, and of any reasonable alternative or variant treatments. The test of materiality is whether, in the circumstances of the particular case, a reasonable person in the patient's position would be likely to attach significance to the risk, or the doctor is or should reasonably be aware that the particular patient would be likely to attach significance to it.

88. The doctor is however entitled to withhold from the patient information as to a risk if he reasonably considers that its disclosure would be seriously detrimental to the patient's health. The doctor is also excused from conferring with the patient in circumstances of necessity, as for example where the patient requires treatment urgently but is unconscious or otherwise unable to make a decision. It is unnecessary for the purposes of this case to consider in detail the scope of those exceptions."

Their Lordships said that three further points should be made: first, assessing the significance of a risk is fact-sensitive and cannot be reduced to percentages. Second, in order to advise, the doctor must engage in dialogue with her patient. Third, the therapeutic exception (see para.88) is limited, and should not be abused (paras 89–91).

Mental Capacity Act 2005

1-756   With the exception of the provision of electro-convulsive therapy under s.58A to a patient who is incapable of consenting to that treatment, an advance decision refusing medical treatment for mental disorder made by the patient under s.24 of the 2005 Act is rendered ineffective if the patient comes within the scope of this Part (s.28 of the 2005 Act). If the patient is mentally incapacitated, the advance decision should be treated as an expression of the patient's wishes and feelings about the treatment in question which should be taken into account by the psychiatrist before a decision is made on whether to provide the patient with the treatment. Psychiatrists "should, for example, consider whether it is possible to use a different form of treatment not refused by the advance decision. If it is not, they should explain why to the patient" (*Code of Practice*, para.9.9).

Neither a donee of a lasting power of attorney nor a deputy appointed by the Court of Protection can consent to treatment coming within the scope of this Part on the patient's behalf (s.28 of the 2005 Act).

In *Cheshire and Wirral Partnership NHS Foundation Trust v Z* [2016] EWCOP 56, Hayden J. said, at para.21, that although s.28 of the 2005 Act "effectively prohibits the making of a declaration [in Court of Protection proceedings] concerning coercive treatment where it falls within Part IV of the Mental Health Act 1983", given that the application "is heard in the Court of Protection, sitting in the High Court, I would have had the scope to make the declarations under the Inherent Jurisdiction".

Human Rights Act 1998

The *Code of Practice* states: **1-757**

"24.42 Clinicians authorising or administering treatment without consent under the Act are performing a function of a public nature and must therefore comply with the Human Rights Act (HRA) 1998, which gives effect in the UK to certain rights and freedoms guaranteed under the European Convention on Human Rights (ECHR).

24.43 In particular, the following should be noted:

- compulsory administration of treatment which would otherwise require consent is invariably an infringement of article 8 of the ECHR (respect for family and private life). However, it may be justified where it is in accordance with law (in this case the procedures in the Act) and where it is proportionate to a legitimate aim (in this case, the reduction of the risk posed by a person's mental disorder and the improvement of their health)
- compulsory treatment is capable of being inhuman treatment (or in extreme cases even torture) contrary to article 3 of the ECHR, if its effect on the person concerned reaches a sufficient level of severity. But the European Court of Human Rights has said that a measure which is convincingly shown to be of medical necessity from the point of view of established principles of medicine cannot in principle be regarded as inhuman and degrading.

24.44 Scrupulous adherence to the requirements of the legislation and good clinical practice should ensure that there is no such incompatibility. If clinicians have concerns about a potential breach of a person's human rights they should seek senior clinical and, if necessary, legal advice."

In *M v Ukraine* [2013] M.H.L.R. 255, the European Court of Human Rights said at para.76:

"The international community has developed a set of relevant principles under which the validity of a patient's consent to psychiatric treatment can be ensured. In particular, under principle 11(2) of the UN Principles [for the Protection of Persons with Mental Illness] an agreement to psychiatric treatment implies that a patient has been provided with adequate and understandable information, in a form and language he or she understands on the diagnostic assessment; the purpose, method, likely duration and expected benefit of the proposed treatment; alternative modes of treatment, including those less intrusive; possible pain or discomfort, risks and side-effects of the proposed treatment. The [European Committee for the Prevention of Torture and Inhuman or Degrading Treatment or Punishment] has specified that consent to treatment can only be qualified as free and informed if it is based on full, accurate and comprehensible information about the patient's condition and the treatment proposed."

United Nations Convention on the Rights of Persons with Disabilities

The power to impose treatments for mental disorder on non-consenting mentally capable patients **1-758** conflicts with art.25(d) of this Convention (see the General Note to the Act under *International*) which requires States to:

"Require health professionals to provide care of the same quality to persons with disabilities as to others, including on the basis of free and informed consent by, inter alia, raising awareness of the human rights, dignity, autonomy and needs of persons with disabilities through training and the promulgation of ethical standards for public and private health care".

Code of Practice

Guidance on this Part is contained in Chs 24 and 25. **1-759**

[Patients to whom Part 4 applies

56.—(1)   Section 57 and, so far as relevant to that section, sections 59 to 62 **1-760** below apply to any patient.

(2)   Subject to that and to subsection (5) below, this Part of this Act applies to a patient only if he falls within subsection (3) or (4) below.

(3)   A patient falls within this subsection if he is liable to be detained under this Act but not if—

    (a)   he is so liable by virtue of an emergency application and the second medical recommendation referred to in section 4(4)(a) above has not been given and received;

    (b)   he is so liable by virtue of section 5(2) or (4) or 35 above or section 135 or 136 below or by virtue of a direction for his detention in a place of safety under section 37(4) or 45A(5) above; or

    (c)   he has been conditionally discharged under section 42(2) above or section 73 or 74 below and he is not recalled to hospital.

(4)   A patient falls within this subsection if—

    (a)   he is a community patient; and

    (b)   he is recalled to hospital under section 17E above.

(5)   Section 58A and, so far as relevant to that section, sections 59 to 62 below also apply to any patient who—

    (a)   does not fall within subsection (3) above;

    (b)   is not a community patient; and

    (c)   has not attained the age of 18 years.]

Amendment

This section was inserted by the Mental Health Act 2007 s.34(2).

Definitions

1-761   patient: s.145(1).
emergency application: s.4(1).
hospital: ss.64(1), 145(1).
community patient: ss.17A(7), 145(1).

General Note

1-762   This section identifies the categories of patients to whom this Part applies. Treatments provided under s.57 apply to all patients, irrespective of their legal status (subs.(1)). Subject to that, treatments provided under this Part apply to patients who are liable to be detained under the Act, with the exception of the categories set out in subs.(3). It also applies to patients who are subject to hospital orders made under s.5(2)(a) of the Criminal Procedure (Insanity) Act 1964 because such an order has the same meaning as a hospital order made under s.37 (see s.5(4) of the 1964 Act). With the exception of s.57, a community patient is not subject to this Part unless he has been recalled to hospital under s.17E (subs.(4)), in which case the provisions of s.62A will apply. The medical treatment of community patients is governed by Pt IVA. An informal child patient who is not subject to a community treatment order is subject to s.58A (subs.(5)).

There is an argument to support the contention that patients who are liable to be detained under s.3 and who are either sentenced, or are committed or remanded to custody, by a court for a period of less than six months continue to be subject to the provisions of this Part: see the General Note to s.22.

Patients who do not come within the scope of this Part can be treated for both mental and physical disorders under common law rules if they are mentally capable of consenting to the treatment, and under the Mental Capacity Act 2005 if they are mentally incapable of making a decision relating to the treatment in question and the treatment is in their best interests.

The use of restraint to administer treatment

1-763   The *Code of Practice* states:

"26.99 Physical restraint may, on occasion, need to be used to administer rapid tranquillisation by intramuscular injection to an unwilling patient, where the patient may lawfully be treated without consent. It must not be used unless there is such legal authority, whether under the Act (see provisions for treatment in chapter 24), the MCA or otherwise. Rapid tranquillisation must not be used to treat an informal patient who has the capacity to refuse treatment and who has done so.

26.100 The use of restraint to administer treatment in non-emergency circumstances should be avoided wherever possible, but may sometimes be necessary, especially if an emergency situation would be likely to occur if the treatment were not administered. The decision to use restraint should be discussed first with the clinical team and should be properly documented and justified in the patient's notes."

Subsection (1)

This subsection extends the protection provided by s.57 to informal patients. It was originally enacted **1-764** as a result on an opposition amendment to the 1982 Act which found favour with the Minister for Health who accepted the argument that "if a course of treatment is so drastic that a detained patient's consent alone should not justify it and that there should be further safeguards, it is difficult to see why the same provisions should not apply to an informal patient" (*Hansard*, HC Vol.29, col.81).

Subsection (3)

Liable to be detained   As this provision refers to a patient who is "liable to be detained" rather than **1-765** to a patient who is actually detained, the provisions of this Part are triggered when the patient has been made subject to a duly completed application made under Pt II or to an order of the court made under Pt III. It is the existence of the application or order, rather than the acceptance of the application or order by the detaining hospital, that results in the patient being "liable to be detained".

Patients who have been granted leave of absence from hospital under s.17 continue to be "liable to be detained" and are subject to the provisions of this Part. It is therefore important that during such leave of absence the patient's General Practitioner is informed of the content of any certificates given under this Part as she will be bound by them.

Patients who are subject to guardianship are not "liable to be detained" and do not come within the scope of this Part.

Paragraph (c)

A patient who has been conditionally discharged   The Reference Guide, at para.23.29, states that **1-766** a patient's conditional discharge constitutes a break in the continuity of the patient's detention with the result that three month period provided for in s.58(1)(b) applies when the patient is recalled to hospital.

Treatment requiring consent and a second opinion

57.—(1)   This section applies to the following forms of medical treatment for **1-767** mental disorder—

(a)   any surgical operation for destroying brain tissue or for destroying the functioning of brain tissue; and

(b)   such other forms of treatment as may be specified for the purposes of this section by regulations made by the Secretary of State.

(2)   Subject to section 62 below, a patient shall not be given any form of treatment to which this section applies unless he has consented to it and—

(a)   a registered medical practitioner appointed for the purposes of this Part of this Act by [the regulatory authority] (not being the [responsible clinician (if there is one) or the person in charge of the treatment in question]) and two other persons appointed for the purposes of this paragraph by [the regulatory authority] (not being registered medical practitioners) have certified in writing that the patient is capable of understanding the nature, purpose and likely effects of the treatment in question and has consented to it; and

(b) the registered medical practitioner referred to in paragraph (a) above has certified in writing that [it is appropriate for the treatment to be given.]

(3) Before giving a certificate under subsection (2)(b) above the registered medical practitioner concerned shall consult two other persons who have been professionally concerned with the patient's medical treatment [but, of those persons—

(a) one shall be a nurse and the other shall be neither a nurse nor a registered medical practitioner; and

(b) neither shall be the responsible clinician (if there is one) or the person in charge of the treatment in question.]

(4) Before making any regulations for the purpose of this section the Secretary of State shall consult such bodies as appear to him to be concerned.

Amendments

The amendments to this section were made by the Mental Health Act 2007 ss.6(2)(a), 12(2) and the Health and Social Care Act 2008 s.52, Sch.3 para.2.

Definitions

1-768
medical treatment: s.145(1), (4).
mental disorder: ss.1, 145(1).
patient: ss.56, 145(1).
the regulatory authority: s.145(1).
responsible clinician: s.64(1).

General Note

1-769
This section, which applies to all patients irrespective of their age or legal status, provides that certain of the most serious forms of medical treatment for mental disorder can only be given if the patient consents to the treatment and three independent people appointed by the Care Quality Commission (the Commission) or, in relation to Wales, Healthcare Inspectorate Wales, one being a doctor, have certified that the patient understands the treatment and has consented to it. If the patient is either not capable of consenting to the treatment or does not consent to it, the treatment cannot proceed. The independent doctor must also certify that it is appropriate for the treatment to be given. Before issuing the certificate the doctor must consult with two persons, other than the patient's doctor, who have been professionally concerned with the patient's treatment. The certificate of consent and the certificate relating to the need for treatment together make up Form T1 of the English Regulations and Form CO1 of the Welsh Regulations.

As treatments provided under this section require the patient's consent, they "cannot, therefore, be given to any young person or child who does not have the competence or capacity to consent, even if a person with parental responsibility consents" (*Code of Practice*, para.19.79).

Paragraph 13.51 of the *Code of Practice* on the Mental Capacity Act 2005 states:

"The combined effect of section 57 of the Mental Health Act and section 28 of the Mental Capacity Act is, effectively, that a person who lacks the capacity to consent to [a section 57 treatment] may never be given it. Healthcare staff cannot use the Mental Capacity Act as an alternative way of giving these kinds of treatment. Nor can an attorney [of a lasting power of attorney] or deputy [appointed by the Court of Protection] give permission for them on a person's behalf."

In *X v A, B and C and the Mental Health Act Commission* (1991) 9 B.M.L.R. 91, Morland J. held that the only legal relationship between the three persons appointed under subs.(2) (a) and the Commission's predecessor, the Mental Health Act Commission (MHAC), is that of appointees and appointor. It is the Commission on behalf of the Secretary of State who appoints the panel. It then becomes the exclusive function of the panel to carry out their responsibilities and the Commission have no further responsibility or duty in relation to a person who is aggrieved by the actions of the panel. When carrying out their functions under subs.(2)(a) the panel had to discharge duties which had quasi-judicial hallmarks and which were in the field of public administrative law. Consequently, no common law duty of care is owed by the panel in private law to the patient. His Lordship said at 96:

> "It may very well be although I reach no definitive conclusion about it, that a doctor giving an opinion, which was negligent, that electro-convulsive therapy should be given, that that opinion, being in the certificate given under section 58(3)(b) [now see s.58A] could be in breach of a common law duty in private law. In my judgment the reason for that is that the doctor, qua doctor, is giving a medical opinion about a patient, albeit not his. Similar considerations would apply to a doctor's certificate … given under section 57(2)(b)."

If a patient is given treatment under this section, the approved clinician in charge of the patient's treatment (AC) must provide the Commission with reports on the treatment and the patient's condition (s.61).

The provision of information about risk to patients

See the General Note to this Part.   **1-770**

Code of Practice

Guidance on this section is given in Ch.25. Paragraphs 25.9 and 25.10 state: **1-771**

> "A decision to administer treatments to which section 57 applies requires particularly careful consideration, given their significance and sensitivity. Hospitals proposing to offer such treatments are strongly encouraged to agree with the CQC the procedures which will be followed to implement the requirements of section 57.
>
> Before asking the CQC to put in hand the process of issuing a certificate, referring professionals should personally satisfy themselves that the patient is capable of giving valid consent and is willing to consent. The restrictions and procedures imposed by section 57 should be explained to the patient, and it should be made clear to the patient that their willingness to receive treatment does not necessarily mean that the treatment will be given."

Paragraph 19.79 of the Code deals with the application of this section to children and young people:

> "Treatment covered by section 57 of the Act (primarily neurosurgery for mental disorder) cannot be given to a child or young person who does not personally consent to it, whether they are detained or not. These treatments cannot, therefore, be given to any young person or child who does not have the competence or capacity to consent, even if a person with parental responsibility consents. If such treatment is proposed in respect of a child or young person who has the competence or capacity to consent (such cases are likely to be rare), the requirements set out under section 57 of the Act must be met before the treatment can be given and these are explained in chapter 25 (paragraphs 25.7 – 25.10). The child or young person is eligible for help from an IMHA and must be informed of this right."

Subsection (1)

Paragraph (a)   Only a handful of cases are referred to the Commission for neurosurgery for mental   **1-772** disorder (sometimes called "psychosurgery") each year. It is very rare for a detained patient to be referred.

As Deep Brain Stimulation (DBS) is a procedure that involves implanting electrodes on the brain rather than "destroying brain tissue", the procedure would not appear to come within the scope of this section. DBS is regulated in Scotland by the Mental Health (Medical treatment subject to safeguards) (Section 234) (Scotland) Regulations 2005 (SSI 2005/291). BDS is defined in reg.1(2) of those Regulations as "the focal modulation of the activity of specific brain regions by direct electrical stimulation delivered by electrodes which are stereotactically implanted in the brain and attached to a programmable control unit inserted in the chest which delivers electrical stimuli administered repeatedly, over an extended period".

Paragraph (b); Other forms of treatment   Regulation 27(1) of the English Regulations and reg.38(1) of the Welsh Regulations specify "the surgical implantation of hormones for the purposes of reducing male sex drive" as a form of treatment to which this section shall apply. The patient must be mentally disordered as well as having an abnormal sex drive for him to come within the scope of this section.

In *R. v Mental Health Act Commission Ex p. X* (1988) 9 B.M.L.R. 77, DC at 85, the court found that the term "hormone" included synthetically produced hormones as well as the naturally occurring substance, but did not include hormone analogues, such as Goserelin, which are separate substances well known at the time the regulations were made. It was therefore held that Goserelin, even though approximately 100 times more powerful than the naturally occurring substance, is not a hormone within the meaning of reg.16. Stuart-Smith L.J. said at 83: "If Parliament passes legislation on the control of leopards, it is not to be presumed that leopards include tigers on the basis that they are larger and fiercer". On the question whether a particular procedure comes within the scope of "surgical implant" the court held that "in the end it is ... a question of fact and degree". The court took the view that a wide bore disposable syringe used for implanting the Goserelin was more like a conventional injection and could not be described as "surgical". It would appear that an incision must be made if an implant is to be categorised as being "surgical". The effect of this judgment is that if the administration of Goserelin is used as a treatment for mental disorder, it is governed by s.58(1)(b).

There have only been four referrals (only one of which was proceeded with) of patients for hormone implantation and there have been no referrals since 1988. "This is probably because the most widely used sexual suppressant, cyproterone acetate (Androcur), is administered by mouth" (Phil Fennell, *Treatment Without Consent: Law Psychiatry and the Treatment of Mentally Disordered People since 1845* (1996) p.188).

Regulations   See subs.(4). The *Code of Practice* can also specify treatments to which this section will apply (s.118(2)).

Secretary of State   The functions of the Minister under this section, so far as exercisable in relation to Wales, are exercised by the Welsh Ministers (see the General Note to the Act).

Subsection (2)

1-773   **Registered medical practitioner**   See the note on s.58(3)(a).

Person in charge of the treatment   Who need not be an approved clinician: see s.64(1A).

Appointed ... by the Secretary of State   The Commission (or, in Wales, Health Inspectorate Wales) will appoint the doctor and the two other persons referred to in this paragraph (Health and Social Care Act 2008 s.52(1)(a)). Those appointed may include members or employees of the Commission (Health and Social Care Act 2008 s.52(2)). They must be allowed to interview the patient and inspect his records, and the doctor must be allowed to examine the patient: see s.119. The three appointed persons have a duty to act fairly (*R. v Mental Health Act Commission Ex p. X*, above). Having been appointed these people are not regulated by the Commission but are exercising their own independent judgment (*X v A, B and C and the Mental Health Act Commission* (1991) 9 B.M.L.R. 91). It is therefore the case that their decisions cannot be appealed against to the Commission. As the appointed persons are discharging a public law function, their decisions can be challenged by way of a judicial review. The appointed persons are "public authorities" for the purposes of s.6 of the Human Rights Act 1998 because they "exercise functions of a public nature" (s.6(3)(b)).

Consented to it   See *M v Ukraine* [2013] M.H.L.R. 255, which is noted under Human Rights Act 1998 in the General Note to this Part, "The provision of information about risk to patients" which is also noted in the General Note to this Part, and paras 19.24–19.37 of the *Code of Practice* which focus on assessing the capacity or competence of children and young persons to consent to treatment.

Paragraph 25.17 of the *Code of Practice* states:

"Where approved clinicians certify the treatment of a patient who consents, they should not rely on the certificate as the only record of their reasons for believing that the patient has consented to the treatment. A record of their discussion with the patient including any capacity assessment, should be made in the patient's notes as normal."

In *Re R (A Minor) (Wardship: Medical Treatment)* [1991] 4 All E.R. 177, 184, CA, Lord Donaldson MR said that "consent by itself creates no obligation to treat". Patients must consent themselves: consent cannot be provided by a donee of a lasting power of attorney or a deputy appointed by the Court of

Protection (Mental Capacity Act 2005 s.28). "Consent" is not defined in the Act, although the *Code of Practice* provides the following definition at para.24.34:

"Consent is the voluntary and continuing permission of a patient to be given a particular treatment, based on a sufficient knowledge of the purpose, nature, likely effects and risks of that treatment, including the likelihood of its success and any alternatives to it. Permission given under any unfair or undue pressure is not consent."

The notion of consent is problematic when detained patients are being treated and it is important that professionals do not confuse compliance with consent: see, for example, M. Larkin et al., "Making sense of 'consent' in a constrained environment", Int. J. of Law and Psychiatry, 32, (2009), 176–183. "An apparent consent will not be a true consent if it has been obtained by fraud, misrepresentation, duress or fundamental mistake"; per Stuart-Smith L.J. in *R. v Mental Health Act Commission Ex p. X*, above, at 85. Ultimately, whether there was a true consent is always a question of fact (*Freeman v Home Office (No.2)* [1984] 1 Q.B. 524). If consent is subsequently withdrawn, the treatment cannot proceed (s.60(1)). Subject to s.62, if the patient loses capacity before the completion of the treatment, the treatment cannot continue (s.60(1A), (1B)).

Both the patient's consent and the doctor's certificate may apply to a plan of treatment (s.59).

Paragraph (a)

Certified in writing   This certificate is not a substitute for a standard consent form. The certificate **1-774** must be in the form set out in Form T1: see s.64(2) and reg.27(1) of the English Regulations (Form CO1 and reg.40(1) of the Welsh Regulations). The appointed persons have to be satisfied as to the patient's capacity and to the fact of consent before a certificate can be issued. In forming a view as to whether the patient has consented to the treatment, the appointed persons would need to be satisfied that the patient had been provided with sufficient information to enable a valid consent to be given: see the note on "consented to it", above. It is the responsibility of the doctor proposing to treat the patient to ensure that sufficient information has been provided.

Capable of understanding   See the note on this phrase in s.58(3)(a).

Nature, purpose and likely effects of the treatment   See the note on this phrase in s.58(3)(a).

Paragraph (b)

Appropriate for the treatment to be given   See the note to s.58(3)(b).   **1-775**

Certified   The appointed doctor is required to reach an independent view of the desirability and propriety of the AC's proposal: *R. (on the application of Wilkinson) v The Responsible Medical Officer Broadmoor Hospital* [2001] EWCA Civ 1545; [2002] 1 W.L.R. 419, noted in s.58(3)(b) under "certified".

The Commission has the power to withdraw the authority to treat provided by the certificate by issuing a notice under s.61(3).

Appropriate for the treatment to be given   See s.64(3).

Subsection (3)

See the notes on s.58(4).   **1-776**

Treatment requiring consent or a second opinion

58.—(1)   This section applies to the following forms of medical treatment for   **1-777** mental disorder—

    (a)   such forms of treatment as may be specified for the purposes of this section by regulations made by the Secretary of State;

    (b)   the administration of medicine to a patient by any means (not being a form of treatment specified under paragraph (a) above or section 57 above [or section 58A(1)(b) below]) at any time during a period for which he is liable to be detained as a patient to whom this Part of this Act applies if three months or more have elapsed since the first occasion in that period when medicine was administered to him by any means for his mental disorder.

(2) The Secretary of State may by order vary the length of the period mentioned in subsection (1)(b) above.

(3) Subject to section 62 below, a patient shall not be given any form of treatment to which this section applies unless—

(a) he has consented to that treatment and either the [approved clinician in charge of it] or a registered medical practitioner appointed for the purposes of this Part of this Act by [the regulatory authority] has certified in writing that the patient is capable of understanding its nature, purpose and likely effects and has consented to it; or

(b) a registered medical practitioner appointed as aforesaid (not being the [responsible clinician or the approved clinician in charge of the treatment in question]) has certified in writing that the patient is not capable of understanding the nature, purpose and likely effects of that treatment or [being so capable] has not consented to it but that [it is appropriate for the treatment to be given.]

(4) Before giving a certificate under subsection (3)(b) above the registered medical practitioner concerned shall consult two other persons who have been professionally concerned with the patient's medical treatment, [but, of those persons—

(a) one shall be a nurse and the other shall be neither a nurse nor a registered medical practitioner; and

(b) neither shall be the responsible clinician or the approved clinician in charge of the treatment in question.]

(5) Before making any regulations for the purposes of this section the Secretary of State shall consult such bodies as appear to him to be concerned.

Amendments

The amendments to this section were made by the Mental Health Act 2007 ss.6(2)(b), 12(3), 28(2) and the Health and Social Care Act 2008 s.52, Sch.3 para.3.

Definitions

1-778   medical treatment: s.145(1), (4).
mental disorder: ss.1, 145(1).
patient: ss.56, 145(1).
the regulatory authority: s.145(1).
responsible clinician: s.64(1).
approved clinician: s.145(1).

General Note

1-779   This section provides that certain forms of treatment shall not be given to a patient unless the patient consents or an independent medical practitioner appointed by the Care Quality Commission (the Commission) or, in relation to Wales, Healthcare Inspectorate Wales, has certified that either the patient is incapable of giving consent or that the patient should receive the treatment even though he has not consented to it. The independent doctor is usually referred to as a SOAD (second opinion appointed doctor). If the patient consents to the treatment, either the approved clinician in charge of the patient's treatment (AC) or a SOAD must certify that the consent has been properly given. Treatments governed by this section may be given in emergencies under s.62 prior to the involvement of a SOAD.

If a child patient who is subject to this Part of the Act is either not consenting to, or is incapable of consenting to the proposed treatment, the provisions of this section must be satisfied before the treatment can be given. There is no provision which enables a person with parental responsibility over such a patient to consent to the treatment on his behalf.

A SOAD certificate provides an authority to provide treatment; it is not a direction to do so. In the *Wilkinson* case, below, Hale L.J. said, at para.71, that although this section is not phrased in terms of permission to treat, the only sensible construction is that it does confer permission to treat in the two circumstances set out in subs.(3).

If a patient is given treatment under this section, the patient's AC must provide the Commission with reports on the treatment and the patient's condition (s.61).

The SOAD system is presumably based on the assumption that where there is a significant disagreement between the SOAD and the patient's AC about the treatment that the patient should receive, the opinion of the SOAD is to be preferred because the patient's interests would be better served by that opinion. There is no evidence to suggest that this assumption is correct, or that patients derive any benefit from the SOAD system. On the other hand, it has been said by some psychiatrists that the knowledge that their treatment decisions will be subject to outside peer review acts as a beneficial constraint on decision making. Having reviewed research on the operation of this section, Peter Bartlett and Ralph Sandland's conclusion is that "the SOAD system has done little to protect patients from overenthusiastic treatment regimes or abuses of their legal rights" (*Mental Health Law: policy and practice*, 2007, p.332). An alternative procedure was suggested in the Preface to the 13th edition of this Manual.

Remote assessments by SOADs

The position that the CQC takes on this issue is outlined in para.22 of its evidence to the Joint Parliamentary Committee which considered the Mental Health Bill:

> "In respect of the use of remote technology for SOAD assessments, we believe this should be available in all circumstances where a second opinion is required under the Act, not just for cases of emergency ECT, where in fact SOADs feel an in-person assessment is the preferred option. This is supported by evidence we have obtained from our own survey of 75 patients who had received second opinions, where only a minority expressed a positive wish for an in-person meeting with a SOAD. At the height of the pandemic, CQC used remote technology to continue providing SOAD service. The SOAD service continues, in part, to operate using remote communication, including between the patient and appointed doctor for some cases. We are therefore keen to ensure that an option to use remote technology continues, to maintain the service and meet the expected increase in demand."

The evidence, which is dated September 9, 2022, can be accessed at: *https://committees.parliament.uk/writtenevidence/111375/pdf.*

Human Rights Act 1998 and procedural issues

This section, which enables mentally capacitated patients to be treated without their consent subject to limited safeguards, does not sit easily with a principle identified by the Committee for the Prevention of Torture and Inhuman or Degrading Treatment or Punishment. In para.41 of its eighth report (1998) the Committee, which, in effect, polices art.3 of the European Convention on Human Rights (ECHR) in respect of persons deprived of their liberty on behalf of the Council of Europe, states:

1-780

> "Patients should, as a matter of principle, be placed in a position to give their free and informed consent to treatment. The admission of a person to a psychiatric establishment on an involuntary basis should not be construed as authorising treatment without his consent. It follows that every competent patient, whether voluntary or involuntary, should be given the opportunity to refuse treatment or other medical intervention. Any derogation from this fundamental principle should be based upon law and only relate to clearly and strictly defined exceptional circumstances."

The question whether the procedures set out in this section provide patients with safeguards that are sufficient to avoid a breach of art.8 of the ECHR is raised by the decision of the European Court of Human Rights in *X v Finland* [2012] M.H.L.R. 318 which is considered in the note on s.63 under this heading.

Article 6 of the ECHR does not entitle a patient in every case to challenge a treatment plan before an independent and impartial tribunal before being subjected to it (*R. (on the application of Wilkinson) v The Responsible Medical Officer Broadmoor Hospital* [2001] EWCA Civ 1545; [2002] 1 W.L.R. 419 at para.34). In *R. (on the application of N) v Dr M* [2002] EWCA Civ 1789; [2003] M.H.L.R. 157, the Court of Appeal held that:

1.   Any alleged breach of a patient's art.6 rights based on the way in which the SOAD had conducted the certification process would fall away on the judge deciding the disputed facts for himself on an application for judicial review.

2.   There was no requirement under art.6 for the judge to hear oral evidence on the issue.

In *Wilkinson*, a patient with a heart condition was being forcibly treated under this section in a situation where there were disputes about whether he was mentally capable and whether the treatment was in his best interests. The court held that on an application for a judicial review of the decision to treat, it would be necessary for the court to reach its own view on the disputed issues, which required them to be determined by cross-examination of the psychiatrists who had been involved with the patient's treatment. Apart from determining the issue of capacity, the court would be required to consider whether the treatment (a) would threaten the patient's life and so be impermissible under art.2, (b) would be degrading and so be impermissible under art.3, and (c) would not be justifiable as both necessary and proportionate under art.8(2) given the extent to which it would invade the appellant's right to privacy. Simon Brown L.J. said at para.29: "The precise equivalence under section 58(3)(b) between incompetent patients and competent but non-consenting patients seems to me increasingly difficult to justify". Wilkinson is authority for the proposition that a court, albeit exercising a judicial review function, does so, not on a *Wednesbury* basis (see *Associated Provincial Picture House Ltd v Wednesbury Corporation* [1948] 1 K.B. 223), but by deciding the matter for itself on the merits after full consideration of the evidence whether oral, or in writing. The patient's subsequent complaint to the European Court of Human Rights that his treatment constituted a breach of arts 3, 6 and 8 of the ECHR was declared inadmissible (*Wilkinson v United Kingdom* [2006] M.H.L.R. 142).

1-781   *Wilkinson* was considered in *R. (on the application of N) v Dr M*, above, where the Court of Appeal held that:

1.   Contrary to what was said in *Wilkinson*, it should not often be necessary to adduce oral evidence with cross-examination where there are disputed issues of fact and opinion in cases where the need for forcible medical treatment of a patient is being challenged on human rights grounds. [In *R. (on the application of JB) v Dr A. Haddock* [2006] EWCA Civ 961; [2006] M.H.L.R. 306, the Court of Appeal did not see any conflict between Wilkinson and N. Auld L.J. said at para.65: "[T]he court in *Wilkinson*, could not have intended or contemplated that every case would require the hearing and testing of oral medical evidence, especially where, as here, none of the parties requested it". In *R. (on the application of Taylor) v Haydn-Smith* [2005] EWHC 1668 (Admin); [2005] M.H.L.R. 327, para.8, Collins J. said: "In my view it will only be in a rare case that [adducing oral evidence] will be appropriate. If the court has the relevant medical notes, the reasoned decisions by the doctors concerned, statements from the doctors and other professionals, and comments on any opposing views, it is difficult to see why oral evidence should be needed". Also see *M v South West Hospital and St George's Mental Health NHS Trust* [2008] EWCA Civ 1112 paras 22–24].

2.   For a judge to be satisfied that it is appropriate to give permission for treatment where the patient does not consent to it he had to be satisfied that the proposed treatment was both in the patient's best interests and was "medically necessary" as that phrase should be understood and applied for the purposes of art.3 of the ECHR.

3.   The standard of proof required is that the court should be satisfied that medical necessity has been "convincingly" shown (*Herczegfalvy v Austria* (1992) E.H.R.R. 437 at 484, para.82).

4.   The answer to the question whether the proposed treatment has been convincingly shown to be medically necessary will depend on a number of factors, including (a) how certain is it that the patient does suffer from a treatable mental disorder; (b) how serious a disorder is it; (c) how serious a risk is presented to others; (d) how likely is it that, if the patient does suffer from such a disorder, the proposed treatment will alleviate the condition; (e) how much alleviation is there likely to be; (f) how likely is it that the treatment will have adverse consequences for the patient; and (g) how severe may they be. The court rejected a submission that, in a case where there is a responsible body of opinion that a patient is not suffering from a treatable condition, that the treatment is not in the patient's best interests and is not medically necessary, then it cannot be convincingly shown that the treatment proposed is in the patient's best interests or medically necessary.

Where there is an issue as to the patient's consent or his capacity to consent under subs.(3) (b), the Court of Appeal in *R. (on the application of JB) v Dr A. Haddock*, above, identified the following three-stage process:

1. The first stage is that of the AC in seeking to initiate the treatment in question.
2. The second stage is for a SOAD to issue a certificate under subs.(3)(b) authorising the treatment on the basis of medical or therapeutic necessity. Auld L.J. said at para.34(ii): "[T]he SOAD's task is a medical one, to be undertaken on the *Bolam* principle, which is likely in almost all cases to involve consideration of the best interests of the patient, and may also take into account non-clinical factors".
3. At the third stage it is for the court to determine whether the *Herczegflavy* medical or therapeutic "necessity" for the treatment has been "convincingly" established by conducting a full merits review of the lawfulness of the SOAD's certificate.

The requirement on a court to be convinced of medical necessity in the light of the medical and other evidence is not capable of being expressed in terms of a standard of evidential proof. Auld L.J. said at para.42: "It is rather a value judgment as to the future—a forecast—to be made by a court in reliance on medical evidence according to a standard of persuasion. If it is to be expressed in forensic terms at all, it is doubtful whether it amounts to more than satisfaction of medical necessity on a balance of probabilities ...". His Lordship also said, at para.14, that courts:

"in determining whether forcible treatment of a patient has been 'convincingly shown' to be medically necessary, should, as the Court said in *R. (on the application of B) v Dr SS (RMO)* [2005] EWHC 86 (Admin), pay particular attention to the views of those charged with his care and well-being. And, as Simon Brown L.J. ... observed in [*Wilkinson*, above,] at para.31, courts should not be astute to overrule a treatment plan decided upon by the [AC] and certified by a SOAD following the required consultation with two others concerned with the patient's care; see also *Herczegfalvy*, at para.86".

In *R. (on the application of B) v Dr SS (Responsible Medical Officer)* [2006] EWCA Civ 28; [2006] M.H.L.R. 131, paras 66–68, the Court of Appeal said that:　　　　　　**1-782**

1. Where the real issue is whether the patient should be detained in a mental hospital at all, that issue is one that should be referred to a tribunal in the first instance, rather than be the subject of judicial review proceedings. In such circumstances the appropriate course may well be on the application for permission to grant an interim injunction and adjourn the application pending a hearing before the tribunal.
2. Where the challenge is not to the grounds for detention but to the treatment itself, careful consideration should be given to the procedure to ensure, in so far as is possible, that there are not protracted and expensive legal proceedings requiring oral evidence from medical witnesses where there is no prima facie case that anything untoward has occurred. It is, of course, essential that the requirements of art.6 are satisfied but this does not mean that permission must be given for judicial review proceedings where the papers do not disclose any arguable grounds for this.
3. Section 58 imposes preconditions to compulsory treatment which ought to ensure that this is not imposed unless there is a convincing therapeutic case for it. They will only do so, however, if the SOAD satisfies herself that the treatment in question should be imposed. This requires a truly independent assessment, not merely approval of the AC's decision on the basis that it is not manifestly unsound. If s.58 is properly complied with then issues requiring cross-examination of medical witnesses should not often arise.

In *R. (on the application of B) v Dr SS* [2005] EWHC 1936 (Admin); [2005] M.H.L.R. 347, Charles J. said, at para.231, that when there is no distinct and separate challenge to the certificate of the SOAD in judicial review proceedings, nonetheless (a) the SOAD should be joined to obtain a binding order in respect of his certificate and to give him the opportunity to make separate representations from the AC if he so wishes, and (b) if possible at an early directions hearing the issues of permission and the further participation of the SOAD should be addressed. In a postscript to his judgment in *R. (on the application of B) v Haddock* [2005] EWHC 921 (Admin); [2005] M.H.L.R. 317 at paras 38, 39, Collins J. said that it will be rare that it is necessary for a SOAD to be represented where she has granted a certificate in a case where the decision of the AC is under attack, although it will be necessary to treat the SOAD as a defendant. In this case it was confirmed that the *Herczegfalvy* test only applies to the administration of the proposed treatment; it does not apply to the determination whether the patient suffers from a mental disorder.

R. (on the application of N) v Dr M, above, was applied in *R. (on the application of PS) v G* [2003]　　**1-783**
EWHC 2335 (Admin); [2004] M.H.L.R. 1, where Silber J. held that where medical treatment is

administered to a patient against his will, art.3 will be contravened if:

(i) the treatment reaches the minimum level of severity of ill-treatment, taking into account all the circumstances, including the positive and adverse mental and physical consequences of the treatment, the nature and context of the treatment, the manner and method of its execution, its duration and, if relevant, the sex, age and health of the patient; and

(ii) the medical or therapeutic necessity for the treatment has not been convincingly shown to exist.

With regard to (i), the European Court of Human Rights has held that the minimum level of severity threshold would only be met if the treatment involved "actual physical injury or intense physical or mental suffering" (*Pretty v United Kingdom* (2002) 35 E.H.R.R. 1 at para.52).

His Lordship said, at para.123, that where the patient has capacity, his lack of consent, while an important factor in determining whether treatment engages art.3, cannot be decisive and that there is no basis for concluding that the patient's objections automatically and inevitably override all other issues except where the interests of other people would be affected if the medication was not administered.

With regard to a claim made under art.8 of the ECHR, his Lordship held that the phrase "in accordance with law" in that article means that the common law "best interests test" must be satisfied in that the treatment must be in accordance with responsible and competent professional opinion, a less invasive form of treatment which would be likely to achieve the same beneficial results for the patient is not available, and it is necessary that the treatment should be given to the patient with regard to (a) his resistance to treatment, (b) the degree to which treatment is likely to alleviate or prevent deterioration of his condition, (c) the risk that he presents to himself or to others, (d) the consequences of the treatment not being given and (e) any possible adverse affects of the treatment.

The decisions in *Wilkinson*, *N* and *PS* were considered by Silber J. in *R. (on the application of B) v Dr SS* [2005] EWHC 86 (Admin); [2005] M.H.L.R. 96, where the claimant asserted that subs.(3)(b) when considered with s.3 of the Human Rights Act authorises the compulsory treatment of a patient who has capacity to refuse to consent only where it is shown that (a) such treatment is necessary for the protection of the public from serious harm or (b) without such treatment serious harm is likely to result to his health, alternatively is incompatible with the requirements of art.3 and/or art.8 and/or art.14 of the ECHR. In particular, the claimant contended that the fact that the objection to the treatment by a patient with capacity is merely an important factor in determining whether a ECHR right is engaged is wrong in law. Although his Lordship found that the claim could not be pursued because of its academic nature, he held that:

1. The proposed treatment of anti-psychotic medication which was a therapeutic necessity would not amount to a breach of arts 3 or 8 merely because the patient had capacity to consent but did not consent. Treatment that was a therapeutic necessity could not be regarded as "inhuman or degrading" for the purposes of art.3. So far as art.8 was concerned, art.8(1) was engaged but treatment that was a therapeutic necessity could be justified under art.8(2) provided that it was in accordance with the law. Thus it had to satisfy both the "best interests" test at common law and the express requirements of s.58.

2. In deciding whether treatment was a therapeutic necessity, the fact that the patient did not consent to it was an important factor.

3. There was no need to "read down" s.58 and that the section was compatible with the ECHR.

His Lordship also rejected the claim that the present law amounts to unlawful discrimination in breach of art.14 against a patient with capacity for reasons which included the fact that the suggested comparators were not in an analogous position and there was an objective and reasonable justification for overriding the wishes of a patient where s.58 applied.

It became clear to his Lordship during the course of the hearing that where a SOAD's certificate has been obtained difficulties arise because the certificate only lasts for three months, but under the present arrangements, the challenge in the courts to the certificate is invariably not completed in time for the treatment to be administered within the three month period. Proposals on how to resolve this problem are set out in Appendix II to the judgment. They have been endorsed by the lead judge of the Administrative Court and the Head of the Administrative Court Office. Paragraph 12 of Appendix II states:

"The best way forward would be to ensure that when any claim is brought challenging the decision of the [AC] or the SOAD to authorise medical treatment to a patient who does not consent, there should be a speedy and automatic oral case management hearing two working days after the challenge application is brought. The Mental Health Act Commission has suggested that at that case management hearing 'one of the relevant factors to take into account when making directions at such a hearing is whether the SOAD has advised on the Form [T3] that a further second opinion be obtained, and if so, at what stage'. I agree with that suggestion. Unless an application for interim relief is made very quickly, it is unlikely that an interim order would be appropriate without at least a hearing at which other parties were represented. All parties should attend that hearing and the court could then consider a timetable for steps leading up to the hearing of the substantive claim within a timetable, which would be speedy and which would enable all parties to have sufficient time in which to present their cases. In many cases, it would be appropriate at the initial hearing to order a rolled-up hearing at which the court could consider the permission application and then proceed to deal with the substantive application."

These remarks should be read subject to the comments about procedure made by the Court of Appeal in *R. (on the application of B) v Dr SS*, above. **1-784**

The cases set out above were considered by Charles J. in *R. (on the application of B) v Dr SS* [2005] EWHC 1936 (Admin); [2005] M.H.L.R. 347. His Lordship held that:

1. The capacity of the patient is relevant to an assessment under art.3 of medical necessity, to assessments under s.58 and thus to whether what is proposed is "in accordance with the law" for the purposes of art.8(2). However, whether or not a patient has capacity does not carry significant weight. The correct approach is to take account of the wishes of the patient against a background of his understanding of and approach to the issues relating to the relevant treatment and to his appreciation of whether he is being forced to accept the treatment and the effects this could have.

2. Inhuman and degrading treatment under art.3 would not be demonstrated where it was convincingly shown to the court's satisfaction that the treatment was a therapeutic necessity. The phrase "convincingly shown" introduces a high standard of proof and that the language of the English criminal and civil standards of proof should not be imported into it.

3. Article 8 was engaged whether or not the patient had capacity. The issue was justification under art.8(2). Such justification did not require that it should be convincingly shown that the treatment was a therapeutic necessity. The conventional three-fold test fell to be applied: was the treatment: (i) in accordance with the law; (ii) for a legitimate aim; and (iii) necessary in a democratic society? Treatment would be in accordance with the law if it fell within the terms of s.58. His Lordship accepted a submission on behalf of the Secretary of State that the common law should not be considered as a separate and distinct consideration in determining whether the treatment being proposed was "in accordance with the law". His Lordship said at para.91:

   "[T]he s.58 MHA test is a distinct test set by Parliament for a particular situation and purpose and when it applies it supplants or suspends the common law. In my view when applying the statutory test the courts should remember this, whilst at the same time taking appropriate guidance from the approach at common law in applying the 'best interests test' and, I add, to the right to autonomy at common law."

This decision was upheld by the Court of Appeal ([2006] EWCA Civ 28; [2006] M.H.L.R. 131). The court held that:

1. On the findings of fact made by Charles J., the imposition of proposed anti-psychotic medication will be lawful under English law and will not infringe the ECHR.

2. The judge was correct to hold that: (i) capacity is not the crucial factor in determining whether treatment can be administered without consent; and (ii) when considering the severity of treatment the fact that it is imposed by compulsion is more significant than the question of whether the patient has or has not capacity to consent to the treatment.

3. It was wrong to claim that in order to avoid infringing the ECHR treatment can only be given to a competent patient against his will if the treatment is not only a "therapeutic necessity" but is also necessary for the protection of the public or to prevent the patient from suffering serious harm. The court endorsed the acceptance by Silber J. in the *PS* case of the submission that "the decision to administer anti-psychotic medication has to be considered in the context that the medication is likely to lead to the claimant being rehabilitated rather than remaining subject to long-term incarceration."

The court found that it was not necessary for it to decide whether a best interests test had to be satisfied in addition to provisions set out in s.58 in order to meet requirements of art.8(2). However, the court made a number of observations on this issue which are set out in the notes on subs.(3)(b) under the heading "Appropriate for the treatment to be given".

For the compatibility of the three-month stabilising period established by subs.(1)(b) with art.8 of the ECHR, see the notes to "three months or more" in that provision.

Covert administration of medication

1-785   Covert medication is the administration of medication in disguised form without the patient's knowledge or consent. This usually involves disguising the medication by administering it in food or drink. As a result, the patient is unknowingly taking the medication. In *A Local Authority v P* [2018] EWCOP 10, Baker J. said at para.55:

> "Covert medical treatment is a serious interference with an individual's right to respect for private life under Article 8 [of the ECHR]."

In para.5.8 of its *Sixth Biennial Report*, 1993–1995, the Mental Health Act Commission made the following comments about the covert administration of medication (the references are to the 1999 edition of the *Code of Practice*):

> "One of the problems associated with covert administration is that it is clearly impossible to attempt to negotiate consent to such treatment and covert administration is seemingly precluded by paragraph 16.11 in the *Code of Practice* and by section 58(3)(a) of the Act, unless it has been certified as acceptable by a Second Opinion Doctor under section 58(3)(b). In contrast, it has been argued that a doctor may be entitled to withhold information from the patient under paragraph 15.13 of the Code but must be prepared to justify that decision. However, for that to be valid, the treatment must be 'in accordance with practice accepted at the time by a responsible body of medical opinion skilled in the particular form of treatment in question' (*Code of Practice* para.15.19). It would seem appropriate therefore for this matter to be considered by the Royal College of Psychiatrists and the Royal College of Nursing. Meanwhile, professional judgment must be relied upon in making decisions on this important ethical issue."

That the MHAC gave such equivocal advice on this issue is to be regretted. The quotation reproduced by the MHAC is from the case of *Bolam v Friern Hospital Management Committee* [1957] 1 W.L.R. 582, which laid down the general approach to be adopted by the courts to questions of medical negligence. The argument that this common law test can override the clear statutory language of subs.(3)(a), where it is stated that "a patient shall not be given … treatment to which this section applies unless … he has consented to that treatment", is clearly erroneous and should not be followed. The MHAC's slightly modified final position on this issue was set out at paras 6.38 to 6.48 of its *Twelfth Biennial Report*, 2005– 2007. The legal position is that the covert administration of medication can only be given to a detained patient under the powers contained in either s.63 (i.e. during the three-month period provided for in subs.(1)(b)) or under subs.(3)(b). Before treatment is administered covertly, the RC should consider: (a) why it is not "practicable" to seek the patient's consent (*Code of Practice* para.24.41), and (b) whether, for the purposes of art.8(2) of the European Convention on Human Rights, the giving of covert medication is a proportionate response to the aim of improving the patient's health or reducing the risk posed by the patient (*Code of Practice* para.24.43). The fact that the RC has considered these issues should be recorded in the patient's notes. Although an application to the court is not necessary in every case "there will undoubtedly be cases in which an application will be required (or desirable) because of the particular circumstances that appertain, and there should be no reticence about involving the court in such cases" (*An NHS v Y* [2018] UKSC 46, per Lady Black at para.126). Although it would be lawful to administer medication provided under either s.63 or subs. (3)(b) forcibly (if that is clinically possible), the RC might consider that the alternative of administering the medication covertly would be less invasive of the patient's physical integrity. While it is the case that a certificate granted under subs.(3)(b) can authorise the covert administration of medication to a patient who is mentally capable of "understanding the nature, purpose and likely effects" of the treatment but is objecting to it, the patient will obviously be aware that the treatment is likely to be given to him at some time in the future.

It is suggested that the RC discusses the appropriateness of the covert administration of the medication with the SOAD, and that the SOAD be invited to agree to such action and to confirm this on Form T3 (subs.(3)(b) as supplemented by s.64(3)). If a mentally incapable patient is informal, the treatment can be given under the authority of the Mental Capacity Act 2005 if the treatment is assessed as being in the best interests of the patient. Some guidance on the covert administration of medication to mentally incapacitated patients in the context of a deprivation of liberty authorisation was given by District Judge Bellamy in *Re AG* [2016] EWCOP 37. The guidance included the following at para.36:

> "(i)   if a person lacks capacity and is unable to understand the risks to their health if they do not take their prescribed mediation and the person is refusing to take the medication then it should only be administered covertly in exceptional circumstances;

(ii)   before the medication is administered covertly there must be a best interest decision which includes the relevant health professionals and the person's family members;

(iii)   if it is agreed that the administration of covert medication is in their best interests then this must be recorded and placed in the person's medical records/care home records and there must be an agreed management plan including details of how it is to be reviewed; …"

The fact that medication is being administered covertly could be disclosed to the patient on an application or a reference to the tribunal being made: see the note to r.14(2) of the Tribunal Rules.

The CQC has published "Brief guide: Covert Medicines in Mental Health Services" (2022) which can be accessed on its website (*www.cqc.org.uk*). The Royal College of Psychiatry has published a "College Statement on Covert Administration of Medicines" which can be accessed at: *www.cambridge.org/core/journals/psychiatric-bulletin/article/college-statement-on-covert-administration-of-medicines/F0FAD544C59EF28D167D49A8F4BA921E*.

Placebo medication

In its *Eighth Biennial Report*, 1997–1999, at para.6.17, the MHAC said that "as an inert substance, a placebo does not fall within the definition of 'medicine' and, therefore, falls outside the provisions of section 58" (in its *Tenth Biennial Report* 2001–2003, para.10.52, the MHAC stated that this represented a "provisional" view). This approach fails to address the reality of the situation which is that a placebo is offered to the patient as a "medicine" which, hopefully, will lead to an improvement in his condition. The fact that any improvement in the patient's condition is triggered by a psychological rather than a physiological reaction does not disqualify the substance from being categorised as a "medicine". It is instructive to note that the *Shorter Oxford English Dictionary* states that a placebo was first described, in 1811, as a "medicine given more to please than to benefit the patient". A more recent definition is "a pill, medicine, etc. prescribed more for psychological reasons than for any physiological effect" (*Oxford English Reference Dictionary* (1996)). Given that in *B v Croydon Health Authority* [1995] 1 All E.R. 683, the Court of Appeal held that "medical treatment" included "a range of acts ancillary to the core treatment that the patient is receiving", and that ancillary treatment would include treatment which is "concurrent with the core treatment", it would seem that the administration of placebo medication is the administration of a medicine for the medical treatment of the patient's mental disorder for the purposes of subs.(1)(b). However, in most cases the practical reality is that placebo medication cannot be given to either mentally capable or mentally incapable patients who come within the scope of this Part as in both instances the patient must be given an explanation of the nature, purpose and effect of the medication in order that his capacity to consent to the treatment can be assessed.   **1-786**

The provision of information about risk to patients

See the General Note to this Part.   **1-787**

The Mental Capacity Act 2005

See the General Note to this Part.   **1-788**

The Code of Practice

Guidance on this section is given in Ch.25 at paras 25.11 to 25.18.   **1-789**

Subsection (1)

Paragraph (a)

Such forms of treatment   No treatments have been specified under this provision.   **1-790**

Regulations   See subs.(5). There is no power equivalent to that contained in s.118(2) for treatments to be specified for the purposes of this section by the *Code of Practice*.

Secretary of State   The functions of the Minister under this section, so far as exercisable in relation to Wales, are exercised by the Welsh Ministers (see the General Note to the Act).

Paragraph (b)   This paragraph enables a course of medication to be imposed on a patient coming   **1-791**

within the scope of this Part for up to three months without the patient's consent and without the need to obtain an independent medical opinion. The protection provided by this section does not come into play until three months have elapsed since the commencement of the treatment. Authorisation for imposing treatment on the patient during the initial three months is given by s.63. Medication that is specified in regulations made under para.(a), above, and medication that is a s.57 or s.58A treatment does not come within the scope of this paragraph.

The approach to be taken by a court when considering an application for the judicial review of decisions made by the patient's AC and a SOAD to administer medication under this section, notwithstanding the patient's refusal to consent to that treatment, is considered in the cases noted under *Human Rights Act 1998 and procedural issues*, above.

Medicine   Or any combination of medicines. Paragraph 25.18 of the *Code of Practice* states:

"Certificates under this section must clearly set out the specific forms of treatment to which they apply. All the relevant drugs should be listed, including medication to be given 'as required' (prn), either by name or by the classes described in the British National Formulary (BNF). If drugs are specified by class, the certificate should state clearly the number of drugs authorised in each class, and whether any drugs within the class are excluded. The maximum dosage and route of administration should be clearly indicated for each drug or category of drugs proposed. This can exceed the dosages listed in the BNF, but particular care is required in these cases."

Phil Fennell reports that the "most striking aspect of the medication cases [he studied] was the surprisingly high number of occasions where BNF recommended dose limits were exceeded (12 per cent of the medicines cases), and in a small number of cases the very large margin by which they were exceeded" (*Treatment Without Consent*, 1996, p.216). In November 2014, the Royal College of Psychiatrists issued a revised "Consensus statement on high-dose antipsychotic medication" which contains recommendations in relation to the decision to treat patients in excess of BNF recommended limits. The statement can be accessed at: *www.rcpsych.ac.uk/docs/default-source/improving-care/better-mh-policy/college-reports/college-report-cr190.pdf?sfvrsn=54f5d9a2_2*.

Only medicine that is prescribed as treatment for the patient's mental disorder is "medicine" for the purpose of this section. This can include medication which is aimed at relieving the symptoms of the patient's mental disorder or which is ancillary to the core treatment that the patient is receiving: see s.145(4) and *B v Croydon Health Authority* [1995] 1 All E.R 683 CA, which is considered in the note on s.63. Medicines do not come within the scope of this section merely because they have an effect on the patient's mental state.

Paragraph 25.13 of the *Code of Practice* states:

"Section 58 does not apply to medication administered as part of electro-convulsive therapy (ECT). That is covered by section 58A instead."

The fact that medication administered to a patient under this section might continue to have effect after the three month period has expired or after the patient has ceased to be detained is not legally relevant.

Three months or more   Month means calendar month (Interpretation Act 1978 Sch.1). The first day of treatment should be included in the calculation of this period. Although the patient's consent to be treated during this period is not required, consent should be sought "wherever practicable" (*Code of Practice*, para.24.41; also see the General Note to this Part). Given that most detentions last less than three months, this provision provides limited protection to patients. During the debates on the Mental Health (Amendment) Bill, the Minister of State said:

"The three-month period is considered appropriate because of the time that it allows for an optimum regime of medication to be identified—or, at least, for certain options to be ruled out before a certificate is needed. Different medications need to be tried before the most suitable one is identified" (*Hansard*, HL Vol.688, cols 494,495).

The three-month period must be continuous. The period is not broken on (1) the patient being granted leave of absence or being absent without leave; (2) the patient being transferred to another hospital whilst continuing to be detained; (3) the authority to detain the patient being renewed under s.20; (4) a change of medication; (5) the medication not being administered continuously; (6) the patient being made subject to a community treatment order or having his community treatment order revoked; and (7) the section under which the patient is detained being changed. As the medication must be given "at any time during a period for which [the patient] is liable to be detained", the three-month period will clearly be broken by the patient's discharge from detention. This situation could occur where the patient's detention is found to be unlawful, he is discharged from that detention, and is then immediately re-detained. The three-month period is also broken "if a Part 2 patient is discharged without becoming a CTO patient or if the patient is placed under guardianship, or upon the conditional discharge of a restricted patient" (*Code of Practice*, para.25.12). "A patient's move between detention and CTO does not change the date on which the three-month period expires" (*Code of Practice*, para.25.16).

In the Scottish case of *Petition of WM* [2002] M.H.L.R. 367, the Court of Session (Outer House) held that the three month period set out in Pt X of the Mental Health (Scotland) Act 1984 during which the consent of a mentally competent detained patient is not required for treatment of his mental disorder did not violate art.8 of the ECHR. Although there was a closely defined departure from the principle of personal autonomy, the court found that the requirement of proportionality was not breached. The approach taken in *WM* was followed with regard to the three month period established by subs.(1)(b) in the unreported case of *R. (on the application of AM) v Central and North West London Mental Health NHS Trust*, February 1, 2007 (see Radcliffes Le Brasseur, Mental Health Law Briefing No.116). The question whether these findings are compatible with the patient's rights under art.8 is raised by the decision of the European Court of Human Rights in *X v Finland* [2012] M.H.L.R. 318, which is considered in the note on s.63 under the heading "Human Rights Act 1998".

First occasion in that period   The three-month period starts from the first occasion when medicine for mental disorder is given to a patient who is detained under a section which is not excluded by s.56(3). For example, if a patient is initially detained under s.4, which is subsequently converted to a s.2, and is then detained under s.3 the three-month period will start from the first time that medicine was administered to the patient after the second medical recommendation referred to in s.4(4) was received. The period starts irrespective of whether the patient has consented to the treatment.

Subsection (3)

Concurrent use of Forms T2 and T3   If a mentally capable patient consents to some of the treatment that is being provided for him (for example, anti-depressant medication) but does not consent to the remainder of his treatment (for example, anti-psychotic medication), then both of the procedures set out in paras (a) and (b) should be followed. The position of the Mental Health Act Commission had been that if a patient consents to treatment A but does not consent to treatment B, a Form T3 issued under s.58(3)(b) should be completed and treatment A should be included on the form as part of the patient's plan of treatment as authorised by s.59: see *Policy Briefing for Commissioners*, Issue 3, Annex 2, p.4. This is to misinterpret the effect of s.59. If the patient consents to a treatment, s.58(3)(a) requires a statutory procedure involving the use of Form T2 to be followed: the treatment "shall not be given" unless the form is completed. If the patient does not consent to a treatment, s.58(3)(b) provides for a different procedure involving the use of Form T3 to be followed. Section 59 allows either Form to relate to a plan of treatment which would allow for variations in the treatment that the patient receives under the authority granted by the Form. Section 59 does not allow for the mandatory procedure set out in s.58(3)(a) to be disregarded on the ground that the treatment in question will be included in the patients plan of treatment under s.58(3)(b). The MHAC subsequently accepted the correctness of this opinion "where a patient genuinely consents to a part of a treatment plan but refuses to consent to the remainder" ("Guidance Note for Commissioners on consent to treatment and the Mental Health Act 1983", 2008, para.9.1). The CQC adopts the same stance: see the May 2012 revision of the Guidance Note.

It is submitted that where concurrent Forms T2 and T3 are in place: (1) the Forms should be annotated to refer to each other; and (2) with regard to patients who have either fluctuating mental capacity or who frequently change their minds about consenting to treatment, it would be permissible for Form T2 to be issued with respect to a particular medication and for Form T3 covering the same medication to be relied on at a time when the patient either lacks capacity or is objecting to the medication.

Paragraph (a)   This paragraph applies to a capacious patient who consents to the treatment.

Section 1(2) of the Mental Capacity Act 2005 states that a "person must be assumed to have capacity unless it is established that he lacks capacity". The CQC turns this principle on its head by stating that "where a person is in the situation of requiring specialist inpatient mental health care under the powers of the Act, the assumption of capacity should be backed up by an evidential record" ("Monitoring the Mental Health Act in 2011/12", pp.69,70). It is not clear what should comprise the "evidential record"; presumably the CQC means that a record of a formal capacity assessment of the patient should be made, a requirement that is not to be found in the Act. It is submitted that the assumption of capacity established by s.1(2) of the 2005 Act applies to this provision, and that a formal capacity assess-

1-792

1-793

ment is only required if the patient's diagnosis, presentation or history suggests that the assumption might be rebutted. The assumption of capacity makes redundant the CQC's claim that a capacity assessment should be undertaken before the first administration of every patient's treatment ("Monitoring the Mental Health Act in 2014/15", p.55). The *Code of Practice* states at para.25.17:

> "Where approved clinicians certify the treatment of a patient who consents, they should not rely on the certificate as the only record of their reasons for believing that the patient has consented to the treatment. A record of their discussion with the patient including any capacity assessment, should be made in the patient's notes as normal."

See the note on "consented to it" in s.57(2).

Approved clinician in charge   See the note on "Approved Clinician" in s.145(1).

Registered medical practitioner   A registered medical practitioner means "a fully registered person within the meaning of the Medical Act 1983 who holds a licence to practise under that Act" (Interpretation Act 1978 Sch.1).

A visit by a SOAD for the purposes of this paragraph should only be requested if ACs "are genuinely unable to determine for themselves whether the patient has the capacity to consent or whether the patient is in fact consenting" (*Code of Practice*, para.25.44).

Appointed ... by the secretary of state   The Commission (or, in Wales, Health Inspectorate Wales) makes the appointment (Health and Social Care Act 2008 s.52(1)(b)). Both the Commission and HIW require appointees to be GMC registered and to hold a current licence to practise. Those appointed may include members or employees of the Commission (ibid., s.52(2)). There is no requirement for the SOAD to be an AC. It is rare for a SOAD to issue a certificate under this paragraph. This could happen where, contrary to the prior opinion expressed by the patient's AC, the SOAD finds that the patient is both competent and consenting to the treatment. The SOAD has a right of access to the patient and his records: see s.119. Once appointed, the SOAD is not subject to regulation by the Commission but will exercise her own independent judgment (*X v A, B and C and the Mental Health Act Commission*, noted in the General Note to s.57).

As a person who is exercising "functions of a public nature", the SOAD is a "public authority" for the purposes of s.6 of the Human Rights Act 1998: see s.6(3)(b) and *R. (on the application of Wilkinson) v The Responsible Medical Officer Broadmoor Hospital* [2001] EWCA Civ 1545; [2002] 1 W.L.R. 419, where Hale L.J. said that the SOAD is "performing a statutory watchdog function on behalf of the public to protect detained persons who are in an especially vulnerable position" (para.71).

Certified   Using Form T2: see s.64(2) and reg.27(2) of the English Regulations (in Wales, Form CO2: see reg.40(2) of the Welsh Regulations). Neither the Act nor the English or Welsh Regulations provide for the renewal of the Form. Paragraph 25.18 of the *Code of Practice* states:

> "Certificates under this section must clearly set out the specific forms of treatment to which they apply. All the relevant drugs should be listed, including medication to be given 'as required' (prn), either by name or by the classes described in the British National Formulary (BNF). If drugs are specified by class, the certificate should state clearly the number of drugs authorised in each class, and whether any drugs within the class are excluded. The maximum dosage and route of administration should be clearly indicated for each drug or category of drugs proposed. This can exceed the dosages listed in the BNF, but particular care is required in these cases."

The statement in para.25.83 of the *Code of Practice* that Form T2 ceases to authorise treatment where there "is a permanent change in the approved clinician in charge of the patient's treatment" is, it is submitted, incorrect as para.(a) merely states that the completion of the Form gives authority for the treatment to be provided. There is nothing in either the Act or the regulations which supports the contention that the validity of Form T2 ends on a change of status of the signatory. It would be surprising if a permanent change of AC rendered the Form ineffective, while the long term absence of the AC did not have such an effect. The wording of this section supports the contention that the authority to treat provided by the Form will only end if the patient's consent is withdrawn, the patient becomes mentally incapable of consenting to the treatment, the patient ceases to be detained, or the treatment specified in the Form changes. It would be good practice for a fresh Form to be completed at the earliest opportunity where there is either a permanent change of AC or the AC is likely to be absent for a considerable time because the new or acting AC will need to review the patient's medication and completing the Form will provide evidence of the review. The approach taken here has been implicitly endorsed by the National MHA Policy Advisor to the CQC who has stated in an email dated March 13, 2019, which was posted on the MHLO website, that para.25.83 "appears to describe a legal position when it is in fact describing a good practice issue".

Capable of understanding   In *R. (on the application of B) v Dr SS (Responsible Medical Officer)* [2006] EWCA Civ 28 paras 33, 34, Lord Phillips C.J. said that it was arguable that the words "capable of understanding the nature, purpose and likely effects of" the treatment do not go far enough to define capacity and that whatever "the precise test of capacity to consent to treatment, we think that it is plain that a patient will lack that capacity if he is not able to appreciate the likely effects of having or not having the treatment". The judgment in this case was delivered before the implementation of the Mental Capacity Act 2005. Despite the differences in the wording of the two tests, it is suggested that in cases where there is doubt about the patient's capacity the test set out in ss.2 and 3 of that Act should be used to determine whether the patient is capable of understanding the treatment in question. Given the obiter remarks of Hale L.J. in *R. (on the application of Wilkinson) v Responsible Medical Officer Broadmoor Hospital* [2001] EWCA Civ 1545; [2002] 1 W.L.R. 419 at paras 65, 66, it is likely that the courts would endorse this approach which has been adopted by the *Code of Practice* at para.24.31.

In *R. (on the application of B) v Dr G* [2005] EWHC 1936 (Admin), Charles J. held that a patient who did not accept that he is mentally ill was mentally incapacitated on the ground that he could not "use and weigh" the information relating to his need for medication to treat his mental illness (see s.3(1)(c) of the 2005 Act). As s.1(2) of the 2005 Act states that a person must be assumed to have capacity unless it is established that he lacks capacity, a formal assessment of capacity would only be required if there is reason to believe that the presumption could be rebutted: see the note on the CQC's report on "Monitoring the Mental Health Act in 2011/12", above.

In *R. v Mental Health Act Commission Ex p. X* (1988) 9 B.M.L.R. 77, Stuart-Smith L.J. noted, obiter, at 85, that the words in this subsection "are 'capable of understanding' and not 'understands'. Thus the question is capacity and not actual understanding". In para.6.12 of its Fourth Biennial Report 1989–1991, the Mental Health Act Commission (MHAC) stated that the judgment in this case "appeared to suggest that consent rests not on actual understanding but simply on the patient's intellectual capacity to understand". The MHAC reported that it had "taken legal advice on this approach and advised all [Second Opinion Appointed Doctors] to continue with their approach of requiring both a capacity and adequate understanding of the treatment and its consequences". It is submitted that the MHAC's advice is correct as Stuart-Smith L.J.'s remarks do little more than distinguish the two elements of this provision, i.e. the patient's capacity and the patient's consent. In any event Stuart-Smith L.J.'s formulation, at 86, of the requirements of a valid consent— "No doubt consent has to be an informed consent in that [the patient] knows the nature and likely effect of the treatment"—is supportive of the MHAC's approach. It would also be difficult to establish whether a patient is capable of understanding particular information without, at the same time, also establishing that he actually does understand that information. However, in *R. (on the application of B) v Secretary of State for Health* [2005] EWHC 86 (Admin); [2005] M.H.L.R. 96 para.87, Silber J. said that Stuart-Smith L.J.'s comment on this phrase "might mean that a patient might be regarded as having capacity even if he does not actually understand the nature, purpose and likely effects of the treatment". This formulation is not compatible with the approach taken by the Court of Appeal in B, above. His Lordship endorsed the finding of Hale L.J. in *R. (on the application of Wilkinson) v The Responsible Medical Officer Broadmoor Hospital*, that the threshold for capacity is a low one and said at para.91:

"The present low threshold for capacity recognises correctly the great importance to be attached to principles of autonomy, but it also means that the case for non-consensual treatment of those with capacity is increased."

Nature, purpose and likely effects of the treatment   Prior to the passing of the Mental Capacity Act 2005, Thorpe J. held that this formulation is declaratory of the common law position relating to information that must be given to a patient before a valid consent can be obtained (*Re C (Refusal of Medical Treatment)* [1994] 1 All E.R. 819 at 824).

Consented to it   It is submitted that in this context, "likely" means "more likely than not": see the note on "likely to act" in s.25(1).

Paragraph (b)   This paragraph allows for the provision of medical treatments that come within the scope of this section to mentally incapacitated patients and to mentally capable non-consenting patients if a certificate by a SOAD is provided. If treatment is regulated by this section, it cannot be provided to   **1-794**

a mentally incapable detained patient under the authority of the Mental Capacity Act 2005: see s.28 of that Act. This means that if such a patient has made a valid and applicable advance decision (AD) under the 2005 Act refusing a treatment which comes within the scope of this section, the AD is not binding on the clinician. However, clinicians should try to abide by the patient's wishes as expressed in the AD if this is practicable (*Code of Practice*, para.9.9).

The decision-making process to be followed where treatment is provided under this provision was identified by the Court of Appeal in *R. (on the application of JB) v Dr A. Haddock*, which is noted under Human Rights Act 1998 and procedural issues, above.

This section does not place the patient's AC under an obligation to continue to provide a treatment to a patient which is specified in the statutory form after it has become clinically inappropriate to do so.

Certified   Form T3 should be used: see s.64(2) and reg.27(2) of the English Regulations (in Wales, Form CO3 and reg.40(2) of the Welsh Regulations). This section does not identify how close to the expiration of the three-month period the Form should be completed.

Although the *Code of Practice*, at para.25.48, states that the SOAD should "interview the patient in private if possible", neither interviewing the patient nor medically examining him is a legal requirement. Therefore, a SOAD can give a certificate if the patient is either unwilling or too disturbed to be interviewed.

In its "Guidance note for Commissioners on consent to treatment and the Mental Health Act 1983", the CQC states:

"8.2 The validity of a Form T3 is unaffected by changes in approved clinician or even detaining hospital. If a patient is transferred to another hospital under s.19 the Form T3 from their original hospital remains valid.

8.3 Whilst SOADs have the right to authorise time-limited authorisations Forms T3 are not time-limited, and the Code of Practice gives no guidance on when they should be reviewed. However, the Commission has taken the general view that Forms T3 should not normally be extant for more than two years. Commissioners who encounter Forms T3 that are more than two years old should pass the details of the form to the Commission Secretariat so that further investigation can take place.

8.4 If a patient gives genuine and consistent consent to the treatment authorised on a Form T3, the Approved Clinician should complete a Form T2 to replace that authority. Where consent fluctuates, it may be appropriate to continue treating under the authority of Form T3. However, the *Code of Practice* [(25.88)] states that any certificate issued on the basis that a patient is incapable of consent will cease to authorise treatment upon that patient regaining capacity. Similarly, where T3 states that the patient is capable but refusing consent, but subsequently the patient loses capacity, that certificate must no longer be deemed to authorise treatment and a further second opinion is required. The same approach should, of course, be applied where patients cease to consent and a Form T2 is extant."

In *R. (on the application of Wilkinson) v The Responsible Medical Officer Broadmoor Hospital* [2001] EWCA Civ 1545, the Court of Appeal said that the SOAD doctor is required to reach her own independent view of the desirability and propriety of the AC's proposal. Simon Brown L.J. said at paras 32, 33:

"The evidence before us, however, suggests that his approach to the [AC's] proposal is perhaps more akin to that of a review than to forming his own primary judgment on the question. Indeed, in the advice issued by the Mental Health Act Commission to Second Opinion Appointed Doctors in April 1999 it is stated:

'The treatment authorised … may not be in accord with the SOAD's personal practice but should be reasonable in the opinion of the SOAD, i.e. the SOAD is not offering an 'academic' second opinion or imposing a treatment plan on the RMO.'

Whilst, of course, it is proper for the SOAD to pay regard to the views of the [AC] who has, after all, the most intimate knowledge of the patient's case, that does not relieve him of the responsibility of forming his own independent judgment as to whether or not 'the treatment should be given'. And certainly, if the SOAD's certificate and evidence is to carry any real weight in cases where … the treatment plan is challenged, it will be necessary to demonstrate a less deferential approach than appears to be the norm."

Brooke and Hale L.JJ. expressed their agreement with these obiter comments.

1-795   The question whether fairness requires a SOAD to give reasons for a decision which sanctions the violation of the autonomy of a mentally competent adult patient was considered by the Court of Appeal in *R. (on the application of Wooder) v Feggetter* [2002] EWCA Civ 554; [2002] M.H.L.R. 178. It was held that:

(i)   a SOAD owes a duty to give in writing the reasons for her opinion when certifying under this section that a mentally competent detained patient should be given medication against his will;

(ii)   there is no requirement for a SOAD to dot every "i" and cross every "t" when giving her reasons. So long as she gives his reasons clearly on what she reasonably regards as the substantive points on which she formed her clinical judgment, this will suffice;

(iii)   the court will only grant a patient permission to challenge the reasons if it can be shown that there is a real prospect of establishing that a SOAD has not addressed any substantive point which she should have addressed, or that there is some material error underlying the reasons that she gave;

(iv)   the reasons need not be disclosed to the patient if either the SOAD or the AC considers that such disclosure would be likely to cause serious harm to the physical or mental health of the patient or any other person;

(v)   the SOAD should send a statement of her reasons to the AC or to the hospital together with any opinion she may have on the desirability of withholding them from the patient on "serious harm" grounds. The AC should then make them available to the patient to read, unless it is a case in which reliance can properly be placed on the "serious harm" exception from disclosure; and

(vi)   although the reasons should be prepared and disclosed to the patient as soon as practicable, it may not always be appropriate to delay treatment once the SOAD's certificate has been given.

These findings would also apply to a mentally competent child patient. Their Lordships left open the question whether fairness also requires the AC's report to the SOAD to be disclosed to the patient in order that the patient can address its contents when interviewed by the SOAD.

A consideration of the implications of this decision is set out in the following paragraphs of the *Code of Practice*:

"25.63 SOADs must provide written reasons in support of their decisions to approve specific treatments for patients. SOADs do not have to give an exhaustive explanation, but should provide their reasons for what they consider to be the substantive points on which they made their clinical judgement. These reasons can be recorded on the certificate itself when it is given, or can be provided to the clinician in charge of the treatment separately as soon as possible afterwards.

25.64 A certificate may be acted on even though the SOAD's reasons have yet to be received. If there is no pressing need for treatment to begin immediately, it is preferable to wait until the reasons are received, especially if the patient is likely to be unhappy with the decision.

25.65 When giving reasons, SOADs will need to indicate whether, in their view, disclosure of the reasons to the patient would be likely to cause serious harm to the patient's physical or mental health or to that of any other person. The responsible clinician should take into account this view when deciding whether or not to disclose the reasons to the patient. The expectation is that in the overwhelming majority of cases the patient should be able to see the SOAD's reasons.

25.66 It is the personal responsibility of the clinician in charge of the treatment to communicate the results of the SOAD visit to the patient. This need not wait until any separate statement of reasons has been received from the SOAD. But when a separate statement is received from the SOAD, the patient should be given the opportunity to see it as soon as possible, unless the clinician in charge of the treatment (or the SOAD) thinks that it would be likely to cause serious harm to the physical or mental health of the patient or any other person."

Although in *R. (on the application of Lee-Hirons) v Secretary of State for Justice* [2014] EWCA Civ 553, para.27, Sir Stanley Burnton indicated that the decision in *Wooder* is not authority for the requirement for the SOAD's reasons to be given in writing, it is suggested that this be done and the guidance given in para.25.63 of the Code followed.

Although the Commission has no power to attach a time limit to a Form T3, it can withdraw the power to treat provided by the Form T3 by issuing a notice under s.61(3).

Not capable of understanding   See the note on para.(a). If the patient regains capacity, see s.60(1C), (1D).

Not consented to it   The 1978 White Paper suggested that the following principle be adopted in cases where the patient's consent is not forthcoming: "where it is not possible to agree with the patient the form the treatment is to take and the consultant feels the imposition of treatment is essential he should, wherever there is a choice, select the method of treatment the patient finds least objectionable or which would represent the minimum interference with the patient" (Cmnd. 7320 para.6.18).

Appropriate for the treatment to be given   See s.64(3). When considering this matter (as it was prior to the amendment made by the 2007 Act), the SOAD "should have regard for the [RC's] greater experience than his of the patient", per Auld L.J. in the *Dr Haddock* case, below, at para.46. In *R. (on the application of B) v Dr SS (Responsible Medical Officer)* [2006] EWCA Civ 28 at para.62, the Court of Appeal said that the phrase "likelihood of its alleviating or preventing a deterioration of his condition", which was removed by the 2007 Act:

> "should not be equated with the test of whether treatment is in the best interests of a patient. That question will depend on wider considerations than the simple question of efficacy of the treatment, such as whether an alternative and less invasive treatment will achieve the same result. The distress that will be caused to the patient if the treatment has to be imposed by force will also be a relevant consideration. English common law and medical ethics both require that medical treatment shall not be imposed without the consent of the patient unless treatment is considered to be in the best interests of the patient. Thus, while the specified criteria are obviously critical to the decision of whether the treatment should be given, they are not the only considerations relevant to that question. The SOAD has to certify that the treatment should be given and we do not see how he can properly do that unless satisfied that the treatment is in the best interests of the patient."

In *R. (on the application of JB) v Dr A. Haddock* [2006] EWCA Civ 961; [2006] M.H.L.R. 306 at para.45, Auld L.J. said that considerations such as these "underline the composite nature of the question of medical necessity. It is one to which the answer will always be one of value judgment derived from other value judgments on often difficult and complex questions of diagnosis and prognosis on which there may be some difference of medical opinion".

It is submitted that the comments made in these two cases are equally applicable to the phrase substituted by the 2007 Act.

Subsection (4)

1-796   The identification and role of the "statutory consultees" is considered in the following paragraphs of the *Code of Practice*:

> "25.54 The Act does not specify who the statutory consultees should be, but they should be people whose knowledge of the patient and the patient's treatment can inform the SOAD when making decisions as to the patient's capacity to consent to or refuse treatment and the appropriateness of the proposed treatment, and will commonly be members of the wider multi-disciplinary team. People who may be particularly well placed to act as statutory consultees are those who have detailed and/or up-to-date knowledge of the patient. For part 4A certificates, it is permissible for one of the two consultees to be a medical doctor, but that person cannot be the responsible clinician; typically a general practitioner (GP) may be consulted.
>
> 25.55 The statutory consultees whom the SOAD proposes to consult should consider whether they are sufficiently concerned professionally with the patient's care to fulfil the function. If not, or if a consultee feels that someone else is better placed to fulfil the function, they should make this known to the clinician in charge of the treatment and to the SOAD in good time.
>
> 25.56 Statutory consultees may expect a private discussion with the SOAD and to be listened to with consideration. Issues that the consultees may be asked about include, but are not limited to:

> - the proposed treatment and the patient's ability to consent to it
> - their understanding of the past and present views and wishes of the patient
> - other treatment options and the way in which the decision on the treatment proposal was arrived at
> - the patient's progress and the views of the patient's carers, and
> - where relevant, the implications of imposing treatment on a patient who does not want it and the reasons why the patient is refusing treatment.

> 25.57 If the SOAD wishes to speak to the statutory consultees face-to-face, the hospital managers should ensure that the SOAD is able to do so.
>
> 25.58 SOADs should make a record of their consultation with statutory consultees, which will become part of the patient notes.
>
> 25.59 SOADs should, where appropriate, consult a wider range of people who are concerned with the patient's care than those required by the Act. That might include the patient's GP, nearest relative, family and carers, and any independent mental health advocate or other advocate representing the patient."

The Act does not place an obligation on any person to act as a consultee under this provision and the SOAD is not placed under an obligation to accept the nurse or "other person" put forward by the AC as a potential consultee.

If there is a significant delay in identifying an appropriate consultee, consideration could be given to treating the patient under the authority of s.62 until the completion of the consultation process.

Two other persons   In *R. (on the application of B) v Haddock* [2005] EWHC 921 (Admin); [2005] M.H.L.R. 317 para.8, Collins J. said that the SOAD "should, if he thinks it desirable to do so, consult with others than the two statutory consultees, including (with the patient's consent) the patient's nearest relative, family, carers or advocate".

Who have been professionally concerned with the patient's medical treatment   And will therefore have some direct knowledge of the patient. A particular involvement with the patient is therefore required; it would not be sufficient for a potential consultee merely to have general responsibilities on the ward where the patient is being treated.

The fact that consultation must take place with two persons who have been concerned with the patient's medical treatment, rather than with persons who are so concerned, means that a consultation can take place with a person who has no current involvement with the patient. Such a consultation can only take place if identifying the person concerned was a reasonable action for the authorities to take given the non-availability of a person with a current involvement in the patient's treatment (*R. (on the application of W) v Feggetter* [2000] M.H.L.R. 200)).

Nurse   Means a qualified nurse whose name appears on the register maintained by the Nursing and Midwifery Council (Nursing and Midwifery Order 2001 (SI 2002/253) art.5).

The other   The Mental Health Act Commission in its Fifth Biennial Report 1991–1993, at para.7.16, reports that identifying the "other person" is a "major source of difficulty for SOADs when undertaking second opinion visits". While recognising that the issue has not yet been tested in the courts, the MHAC "concluded that to require the statutory 'other' consultee to be invariably professionally qualified and included in a professional register would be unnecessarily restrictive". At the same time the MHAC expressed its "grave doubts about the validity of some certificates which, for example, refer to the 'ward clerk', 'Gymnasium technician' and 'Occupational Therapy Aid' ". The MHAC suggested that "the appointed doctor should endeavour to meet with somebody whose qualifications, experience and knowledge of the patient should enable them to make an effective contribution to the work of the multidisciplinary team". As Parliament has required the "other person" to be "professionally concerned" as opposed to being merely "concerned" with the patient's medical treatment, it is submitted that the other person must hold a recognised professional qualification which is directly relevant to the "medical treatment" of the patient as defined in s.145(1). Persons falling into this category could include psychologists, occupational therapists, pharmacists, psychotherapists, physiotherapists, art/music therapists and social workers. The MHAC subsequently revised its position on this issue and supported the approach advocated here: see para.9 of its Guidance Note, noted below.

In its Guidance Note "People with Nursing Qualifications and Consultation with the 'other' Professional in Second Opinions under the Mental Health Act" (2008), the MHAC stated that:

"it has decided to interpret the law as preventing someone who is registered as a nurse from being the 'other' consultee, whether or not s/he is acting as a nurse or even practicing in another profession (e.g. as a psychologist or social worker). We take this view on the basis that the Act requires the person not to 'be' a nurse, rather than specifying that the person's professional relationship with the patient must not involve a nursing role" (para.3).

Accordingly, the MHAC "asked SOADs to no longer accept professionals who are registered nurses as the 'other' consultee on their Second Opinion visits" (para.5). The CQC has adopted a similar stance (personal communication). SOADs, who must exercise their own independent judgment and do not act under the direction of the MHAC's successor, the Care Quality Commission (*X v A B C and the Mental Health Act Commission* (1991) 9 B.M.L.R. 91), should be cautious about accepting this advice for the following reasons:

1.   The "other" consultee must be "professionally concerned" with the patient's medical treatment. If, for example, the other consultee is a psychologist who is providing the patient with psychological therapies and she also happens to have a nursing qualification, that person is professionally concerned with the patient's medical treatment in her capacity as a psychologist.

On this interpretation, the phrase "the other shall be neither a nurse nor a registered medical practitioner" should be interpreted as meaning "the other shall be neither a nurse nor a registered medical practitioner who is treating the patient in her professional capacity as a nurse or a registered medical practitioner."

2. It is difficult to imagine that Parliament, when enacting this provision, understood that it was placing an obligation on SOADs to ask every "other" consultee whether he or she is also registered as a nurse.

An Independent Mental Health Advocate who is assisting the patient cannot be a consultee as she is representing the patient's interests and is not involved in the patient's treatment.

In the sample studied by Phil Fennell, by far the largest category of "other persons" consulted was that of social worker. He reports that "the duty to consult the other professional is ... seen as a tiresome formality" (*Treatment Without Consent*, 1996, p.208).

[Electro-convulsive therapy, etc.

1-797 **58A.**—(1) This section applies to the following forms of medical treatment for mental disorder—

 (a) electro-convulsive therapy; and

 (b) such other forms of treatment as may be specified for the purposes of this section by regulations made by the appropriate national authority.

 (2) Subject to section 62 below, a patient shall be not be given any form of treatment to which this section applies unless he falls within subsection (3), (4) or (5) below.

 (3) A patient falls within this subsection if—

 (a) he has attained the age of 18 years;

 (b) he has consented to the treatment in question; and

 (c) either the approved clinician in charge of it or a registered medical practitioner appointed as mentioned in section 58(3) above has certified in writing that the patient is capable of understanding the nature, purpose and likely effects of the treatment and has consented to it.

 (4) A patient falls within this subsection if—

 (a) he has not attained the age of 18 years; but

 (b) he has consented to the treatment in question; and

 (c) a registered medical practitioner appointed as aforesaid (not being the approved clinician in charge of the treatment) has certified in writing—

  (i) that the patient is capable of understanding the nature, purpose and likely effects of the treatment and has consented to it; and

  (ii) that it is appropriate for the treatment to be given.

 (5) A patient falls within this subsection if a registered medical practitioner appointed as aforesaid (not being the responsible clinician (if there is one) or the approved clinician in charge of the treatment in question) has certified in writing—

 (a) that the patient is not capable of understanding the nature, purpose and likely effects of the treatment; but

 (b) that it is appropriate for the treatment to be given; and

 (c) that giving him the treatment would not conflict with—

  (i) an advance decision which the registered medical practitioner concerned is satisfied is valid and applicable; or

  (ii) a decision made by a donee or deputy or by the Court of Protection.

 (6) Before giving a certificate under subsection (5) above the registered medical practitioner concerned shall consult two other persons who have been professionally concerned with the patient's medical treatment but, of those persons—

(a)   one shall be a nurse and the other shall be neither a nurse nor a registered medical practitioner; and

(b)   neither shall be the responsible clinician (if there is one) or the approved clinician in charge of the treatment in question.

(7)   This section shall not by itself confer sufficient authority for a patient who falls within section 56(5) above to be given a form of treatment to which this section applies if he is not capable of understanding the nature, purpose and likely effects of the treatment (and cannot therefore consent to it).

(8)   Before making any regulations for the purposes of this section, the appropriate national authority shall consult such bodies as appear to it to be concerned.

(9)   In this section—

(a)   a reference to an advance decision is to an advance decision (within the meaning of the Mental Capacity Act 2005) made by the patient;

(b)   "valid and applicable", in relation to such a decision, means valid and applicable to the treatment in question in accordance with section 25 of that Act;

(c)   a reference to a donee is to a donee of a lasting power of attorney (within the meaning of section 9 of that Act) created by the patient, where the donee is acting within the scope of his authority and in accordance with that Act; and

(d)   a reference to a deputy is to a deputy appointed for the patient by the Court of Protection under section 16 of that Act, where the deputy is acting within the scope of his authority and in accordance with that Act.

(10)   In this section, "the appropriate national authority" means—

(a)   in a case where the treatment in question would, if given, be given in England, the Secretary of State;

(b)   in a case where the treatment in question would, if given, be given in Wales, the Welsh Ministers.]

Amendment

This section was inserted by the Mental Health Act 2007 s.27.

Definitions

medical treatment: s.145(1), (4). **1-798**
mental disorder: ss.1, 145(1).
patient: ss.56, 124(1).
responsible clinician: s.64(1).
approved clinician: ss.64(1B), 145(1).

General Note

This section provides that, except in an emergency, electro-convulsive therapy (ECT) and any other **1-799**
treatment provided for in regulations made under this section may only be given to the patient if the patient either consents to the treatment, or a second opinion appointed doctor (SOAD) has certified that it is appropriate for the treatment to be given. It applies to adult detained patients who come within the scope of this Part, apart from those who are subject to community treatment orders (s.56(5)), and to all patients who are under the age of 18 (whether or not they are detained) (subss.(4), (7)). Consent and certification can be given for a plan of treatment involving more than one administration of ECT (s.59). If a mentally capable patient refuses to consent to the treatment, it cannot be given. The advice given to the patient by the AC should be recorded (*St George's Healthcare NHS Trust v S* [1998] 3 All E.R. 673 at 703). If the patient withdraws consent, the treatment must either not proceed or must be halted

(s.60(1)). A patient who loses capacity before the completion of the treatment is treated as if he had withdrawn consent and the remaining treatment has to be considered as a separate treatment (s.60(1A),(1B)). In both situations, the treatment can continue pending compliance with this section if its discontinuance would cause serious suffering to the patient (s.62(2)).

A certificate issued by a SOAD under Pt IVA will not provide authority for treatment under this section to be given to a community patient who has capacity or competence to consent but refuses consent when recalled to hospital or when the community treatment order is revoked (s.62A(4)).

If a mentally capable patient consents to the ECT, the consent must be certified by either the approved clinician in charge of the patient's treatment (AC) or a SOAD (subs.(3)). For child patients, both detained and informal (s.56(5)), the consent and the appropriateness of the treatment must be certified by a SOAD (subs.(4)). A new SOAD certificate is not required merely because a child reaches the age of 18. If the child is informal, there must also be authority to treat the child (subs.(7)).

Where the patient lacks the capacity to consent, a SOAD must certify that the patient is "not capable of understanding the nature, purpose and likely effects of the treatment" and that it is appropriate for the treatment to be given (subs.(5)(a),(b)). Before issuing the certificate the SOAD must consult with two persons who have been professionally concerned with the patient's medical treatment; one must be a nurse and the other shall be neither a nurse nor a doctor nor the patient's responsible clinician (RC) or the AC (subs.(6)). The SOAD cannot complete a certificate under subs.(5) if to do so would conflict with:

(i)   an advance decision of the patient not to receive the treatment in question, which the SOAD is satisfied is valid and applicable;

(ii)   a decision made by the donee of a lasting power of attorney or a deputy appointed by the Court of Protection if the donee or deputy has the authority to refuse the treatment on behalf of the patient; or

(iii)   an order of the Court of Protection.

[NB. Under the terms of the Mental Capacity Act 2005, a person under the age of 18 cannot make an advance decision or execute a lasting power of attorney: see ss.24(1) and 10(1)(a) of the 2005 Act.]

The SOAD's certificate provides authority for the ECT to be given; it does not require it to be given. "In all cases, SOADs should indicate on the certificate the maximum number of administrations of ECT which it approves" (Code of Practice, para.25.23). If a SOAD has certified that the patient lacks the capacity to consent to the ECT, the clinician who would administer the ECT should confirm at the time when the treatment is to be given that the patient's capacity status has not changed. If the patient is refusing the ECT and the clinician assesses the patient as being mentally capable of making that decision, the ECT should not be given.

This section is subject to the emergency provisions contained in s.62 (subs.(2)). Treatment under s.62, including the administration of medicine as part of ECT (see reg.27(4) of the English Regulations and reg.38(2) of the Welsh Regulations), can be given to a mentally incapacitated patient even though the patient has made a valid and applicable advance decision refusing ECT. However, the treatment could not continue under this section if the SOAD is satisfied that the patient has made such an advance decision (subs.(5)(c)(i)). Although the rationale for invoking s.62 in respect of incapacitated patients who require treatment urgently is clear, the fact that a capacious patient can be given treatment under s.62 conflicts with the underlying purpose of this section which is to respect the wishes of such patients. Baroness Murphy, a distinguished psychiatrist, said that she could not:

"envisage a clinical situation where section 62 should ever be given to a patient who has capacity. Such treatment exists to treat profoundly depressed people who have usually stopped eating and drinking and who are seriously at risk of dehydration and death before the treatment takes effect. As the British Psychological Society has pointed out, evidence from [the] Northwick Park studies shows that if a nurse can sit with a patient day in and day out over the course of a three or four-day weekend and get liquid into him one way or another through a drip and so forth, ECT can usually be avoided. But sometimes it is necessary. Sometimes the circumstances are not right and the patient may pull out the drip and refuse treatment. But I cannot understand how such a situation could arise with a patient who had full capacity. The nature of the illness is such that it would not happen" (*Hansard*, HL Vol.689, col.978)."

An informal adult incapacitated patient could be given ECT under the authority of the Mental Capacity Act 2005 if the treatment is deemed to be in the patient's best interests. Such treatment could not be provided if the patient had made a valid and applicable advance decision refusing ECT or if a donee or a deputy had refused such treatment on the patient's behalf. In 2012/13, 1 per cent of serious medical treatment decisions made under s.37 of the 2005 Act involved the administration of ECT ("The Sixth

Year of the Independent Mental Capacity Advocacy (IMCA) Service: 2012/2013", p.26). Paragraph 13.65 of the *Code of Practice* states:

"If ECT is to be given to an individual who lacks capacity and is under a DoLS authorisation or Court of Protection order, consideration should be given to seeking an independent second medical opinion before treatment which could, in principle, be given under the MCA (remembering that a DoLS authorisation only authorises the deprivation of liberty, not the treatment)."

Code of Practice

Guidance on this section is given in Ch.25 at paras 25.19 to 25.25. The application of this section to patients who are under the age of 18 is considered in the Code at paras 19.80 to 19.88. **1-800**

Subsection (1)

Regulations Regulation 27(3) of the English Regulations and reg.38(2) of the Welsh Regulations specify the administration of medicines as part of the ECT as being a form of treatment to which this section applies. Such medicines could include anaesthetics and muscle relaxants. **1-801**

Appropriate national authority See subs.(10).

Subsection (3)

Approved clinician in charge See s.64(1B). **1-802**

Capable of understanding; Nature, purpose and likely effects See the notes on these phrases in s.58(3)(a).

Certified in writing Using Form T4: see reg.24(3) of the English Regulations (in Wales, Form CO4: see reg.40(3) of the Welsh Regulations).

Consented to it See the note on this phrase in s.57(2). The problems associated with obtaining a patient's informed consent to ECT were considered by the MHAC in its *Eleventh Biennial Report*, 2003–2005, at paras 4.74, 4.75.

Subsection (4)(a)

Not attained the age of 18 years Such patients are entitled to an independent mental health advocate in the circumstances set out in s.130C(3)(b). **1-803**

Subsection (4)(c)

Certified in writing Using Form T5 (in Wales, Form CO5). A fresh certificate is not required just because a young person reaches the age of 18. **1-804**

Appropriate for the treatment to be given See s.64(3). This criterion does not apply to adult patients.

Subsection (5)

Certified in writing Using Form T6 (in Wales, Form CO6). **1-805**

Paragraph (c)

The legal responsibility for being satisfied that an advance decision made by the patient is both "valid and applicable" is that of the SOAD. This could cause difficulties for the SOAD if there is a dispute about either the validity or the applicability of the decision. For example, the AC might dispute the existence of an advance decision in a case where the spouse of the patient claims that the patient had made an oral advance decision refusing ECT some time ago. In this situation the SOAD could not automatically rely on the judgment of the AC; the SOAD would have to form an opinion as to which view is to be preferred **1-806** in order that she can be "satisfied" that a valid and applicable advance decision is in place. It would be difficult for the SOAD to reach such an opinion without interviewing the spouse, and possibly other relatives and the patient's GP. Such enquiries could prove to be very time consuming. In this example, such interviews would not be required if the SOAD concluded that the provision of ECT to the patient constituted a "life-sustaining treatment" for the purposes of s.25 of the Mental Capacity Act 2005, in which case the advance decision must be in writing, signed and witnessed, and must contain a statement that the decision is to take effect even if life is at risk. If, after investigation, the SOAD continued to have doubts about the validity or the applicability of an advance decision, an application would have to be made to the Court of Protection for the matter to be determined. In the meantime, the ECT could be provided if it is either life-sustaining or would prevent a serious deterioration of the patient's condition (s.26(5) of the 2005 Act).

The SOAD should also make enquiries to ascertain whether a donee or deputy has been appointed under the 2005 Act and, if so, whether the donee or deputy has the authority to make a decision to refuse ECT. The SOAD should also ascertain whether the Court of Protection has ordered that ECT should not be given to the patient. This information should be noted on the patient's medical record.

Subsection (6)

1-807   See the notes on s.58(4).

Subsection (7)

1-808   This subsection applies to mentally incapacitated patients who come within the scope of s.56(5) i.e. informal patients under 18 who cannot give consent. As this section does not "by itself confer sufficient authority" for providing treatment to such patients, authority to treat must be found elsewhere. The Reference Guide states at para.23.50 that, depending on the circumstances, that authority to treat might, for example, come from "a court order, or, in the case of a young person aged 16 or 17, the provisions of the MCA". It might also come from parental consent for younger children. Accordingly, s.28 of the 2005 Act, which gives preference to Pt IV in respect of treatments that come within its scope, does not apply to treatments provided under this section if the patient comes within the scope of this subsection: see s.28(1A) of the 2005 Act. The *Code of Practice*, at para.19.85, states that "careful consideration should be given as to whether to rely on parental consent" as such a decision is likely to be outside the "zone of parental responsibility". If parental consent is not relied upon, either an application under the Act or, if the Act is not applicable, an application to the court should be considered.

Plans of treatment

1-809   **59.**   Any consent or certificate under section 57 [, 58 or 58A] above may relate to a plan of treatment under which the patient is to be given (whether within a specified period or otherwise) one or more of the forms of treatment to which that section applies.

Amendment

The words in square brackets were substituted by the Mental Health Act 2007 s.28(3).

Definition

1-810   patient: s.145(1).

General Note

1-811   This section enables any consent or certificate obtained for the purposes of s.57, s.58 or s.58A to relate to a plan of treatment which would involve one or more of the treatments specified under the same section. Such a plan would allow for variations in treatment within the context of the treatment objectives and enable the approved clinician to respond rapidly to the patient's reaction to a particular drug or dosage. The plan could include a time scale for the administration of treatments. A patient may withdraw consent to a plan of treatment under s.60(2). "Treatment plans are usually described in terms of the drug categories recorded in the British National Formulary" (Mental Health Act Commission, *Fifth Biennial Report* 1991–1993, para.7.7).

Code of Practice

The Code states: **1-812**

"24.45 Treatment plans are essential for patients being treated for mental disorder under the Act. A patient's responsible clinician is responsible for ensuring that a treatment plan is in place for that patient.

24.46 A treatment plan should include a description of the immediate and long-term goals for the patient and should give a clear indication of the treatments proposed and the methods of treatment.

24.47 The treatment plan should form part of a coherent care plan under the CPA (or its equivalent), and be recorded in the patient's notes (see chapter 34).

24.48 Psychological therapies should be considered as a routine treatment option at all stages, including the initial formulation of a treatment plan and each subsequent review of that plan. Any programme of psychological intervention should form part of the agreed treatment plan and be recorded in the patient's notes as such.

24.49 Wherever possible, the whole treatment plan should be discussed with the patient. Patients should be encouraged and assisted to make use of advocacy support available to them, if they want it. This includes, but need not be restricted to, independent mental health advocacy services under the Act. Where patients cannot (or do not wish to) participate in discussion about their treatment plan, any views they have expressed previously should be taken into consideration (see chapter 9)."

Withdrawal of consent

60.—(1) Where the consent of a patient to any treatment has been given for the **1-813** purpose of section 57[, 58 or 58A] above, the patient may, subject to section 62 below, at any time before the completion of the treatment withdraw his consent, and those sections shall then apply as if the remainder of the treatment were a separate form of treatment.

[(1A) Subsection (1B) below applies where—
    (a) the consent of a patient to any treatment has been given for the purposes of section 57, 58 or 58A above; but
    (b) before the completion of the treatment, the patient ceases to be capable of understanding its nature, purpose and likely effects.

(1B) The patient shall, subject to section 62 below, be treated as having withdrawn his consent, and those sections shall then apply as if the remainder of the treatment were a separate form of treatment.

(1C) Subsection (1D) below applies where—
    (a) a certificate has been given under section 58 or 58A above that a patient is not capable of understanding the nature, purpose and likely effects of the treatment to which the certificate applies; but
    (b) before the completion of the treatment, the patient becomes capable of understanding its nature, purpose and likely effects.

(1D) The certificate shall, subject to section 62 below, cease to apply to the treatment and those sections shall then apply as if the remainder of the treatment were a separate form of treatment.]

(2) Without prejudice to the application of [subsections (1) to (1D)] above to any treatment given under the plan of treatment to which a patient has consented, a patient who has consented to such a plan may, subject to section 62 below, at any time withdraw his consent to further treatment, or to further treatment of any description, under the plan.

Amendment

The words in square brackets were substituted and inserted by the Mental Health Act 2007 ss.28(4), 29(2) and (3).

Definition

1-814   patient: ss.56, 145(1).

General Note

1-815   This section provides for a patient to withdraw his consent to treatment under ss.57, 58 or 58A or to a plan of treatment under s.59. On the withdrawal of consent, the remainder of the treatment must be considered as a separate treatment for the purposes of those sections. It is submitted that the three-month period referred to in s.58(1)(b) is not re-activated on a patient withdrawing consent to be treated by medication. A patient cannot therefore be treated for a fresh period of three months in the absence of consent before the independent medical opinion referred to in s.58(3)(b) is obtained.

Subsection (1)

1-816   **Withdraw his consent**   The withdrawal of consent can be made in writing, orally, or through the patient's behaviour, e.g. by physically resisting the administration of the treatment.

Subsections (1A) to (1D)

1-817   The effect of these subsections is:

1.   If a mentally capable patient who has consented to a s.57, s.58 or s.58A treatment loses his capacity to consent, the patient is to be treated as having withdrawn his consent to the treatment.
2.   If a s.58 or s.58A treatment is being given to a mentally incapable patient but, before the treatment has been completed, the patient becomes mentally capable of consenting to the treatment, the remainder of the treatment is to be treated as a separate form of treatment for the purposes of certification under those sections.

In both instances, the treatment that the patient is receiving can continue if the approved clinician considers that stopping it would cause serious suffering to the patient (s.62(2)).

Review of treatment

1-818   **61.**—(1)   Where a patient is given treatment in accordance with section 57(2)[,58(3)(b) or 58A(4) or (5)] above[, or by virtue of section 62A below in accordance with a Part 4A certificate (within the meaning of that section) [that falls within section 64C(4) below],] a report on the treatment and the patient's condition shall be given [by the approved clinician in charge of the treatment] to [the regulatory authority]—

(a)   on the next occasion on which the [responsible clinician] furnishes a report [under section 20(3)[, 20A(4) or 21B(2) above in respect] of the patient]; and

(b)   at any other time if so required by [the regulatory authority].

(2)   In relation to a patient who is subject to a restriction order [, limitation direction] or restriction direction subsection (1) above shall have effect as if paragraph (a) required the report to be made—

(a)   in the case of treatment in the period of six months beginning with the date of the order or direction, at the end of that period;

(b)   in the case of treatment at any subsequent time, on the next occasion on which the [responsible clinician] makes a report in respect of the patient under section 41(6) [, 45B(3)] or 49(3) above.

(3) [the regulatory authority] may at any time give notice […] directing that, subject to section 62 below, a certificate given in respect of a patient under section 57(2)[, 58(3)(b) or 58A(4) or (5)] above shall not apply to treatment given to him [whether in England or Wales] after a date specified in the notice and sections 57[, 58 and 58A] above shall then apply to any such treatment as if that certificate had not been given.

[(3A) The notice under subsection (3) above shall be given to the approved clinician in charge of the treatment.]

Amendments

The amendments to this section were made by the Mental Health (Patients in the Community) Act 1995 s.2(5), the Crime (Sentences) Act 1997 s.55, Sch.4 para.12(7), the Mental Health Act 2007 ss.12(4), 28(5), 34(3), the Health and Social Care Act 2008 s.52, Sch.3 para.4 and the Health and Social Care Act 2012 s.299(7).

Definitions

the regulatory authority: s.145(1).   **1-819**
limitation direction: s.145(1).
patient: ss.56, 145(1).
responsible clinician: s.64(1).
approved clinician: s.145(1).
restriction direction: s.145(1).
restriction order: s.145(1).

General Note

This section provides for the periodic review by the Care Quality Commission (the Commission) or,   **1-820**
in relation to Wales, the Welsh Ministers (in practice, Health Inspectorate Wales) of treatment which is being given under either s.57(2), s.58(3)(b), s.58A(4) or (5) or, following a recall from a community treatment order, under s.62A in accordance with a Pt IVA certificate. The trigger for the review is set out in paras (a) and (b) of subs.(1). A review is not required where a patient has consented to treatment being given to him under s.58(3)(a) or s.58A(3) (which does not apply to child patients) or where an approved clinician has provided a Pt IVA certificate with regard to a capacious, consenting patient.
With regard to treatment provided under s.62A, the Reference Guide states:

"24.49 [A] report must be given automatically to CQC under section 61 if treatment is given on the basis of a Part 4A certificate to a CTO patient who has been recalled to hospital, including one whose CTO is then revoked, in lieu of a SOAD certificate under section 58 or 58A (see paragraphs 24.32 to 24.43). This will only apply to treatment to which the patient either did not, or could not consent.
24.50 In such cases, a report must be submitted by the approved clinician in charge of the treatment at the same time it would have to be given if the treatment had, in fact, been given on the basis of section 58 or 58A SOAD certificate (see paragraphs 23.63 – 23.65). This means the approved clinician must make a report to CQC on the next occasion that the responsible clinician submits a report under section 20 to renew the patient's detention, under section 20A to extend the patient's CTO, or under section 21B to confirm the patient's detention or CTO after absence without leave for more than 28 days."

The CQC's "Section 61–Review of Treatment Form", previously Form MHAC 1, does not relate to s.57(2) treatments. A separate form, which can be obtained from the CQC's Mental Health Operations team, must be used for such treatments.

Code of Practice

The Code states: **1-821**

"25.76 Although the Act does not require the validity of certificates to be reviewed after any particular period, it is good practice for the clinician in charge of the treatment to review them (in consultation with the responsible clinician, if different) at regular intervals.

25.77 The clinician in charge of any treatment given in accordance with a SOAD certificate must provide a written report on that treatment and the relevant patient's condition at any time if requested to do so by the CQC under sections 61 or 64H of the Act. This is in addition to the reports they are automatically required to provide periodically under those sections. Copies of reports should be given to patients.

25.78 Under sections 61 and 64H, the CQC may also, at any time, direct that a certificate is no longer to approve either some or all of the treatments specified in it from a particular date.

25.79 However, where the CQC revokes approval in that way, treatment (or a course of treatment) which is already in progress may continue, pending a new certificate, if the clinician in charge of it considers that discontinuing it would cause the patient serious suffering (section 62 (2)).

25.80 This exception only applies pending compliance with the relevant requirement to have a certificate – in other words, while steps are taken to obtain a new certificate. It cannot be used to continue treatment under section 57 or section 58A against the wishes of a patient who has the capacity to refuse the treatment, because in those cases there is no prospect of obtaining a new certificate."

The legal status of the Code was considered by the House of Lords in *R. (on the application of Munjaz) v Mersey Care National Health Service Trust* [2005] UKHL 58; [2005] M.H.L.R 276 where it was held that the guidance it contains could be departed from if there were cogent reasons for doing so: see further the notes to s.118. Such reasons, which would have been present when a decision was made to administer medication to the patient covertly, would provide justification for not supplying the patient with a copy of a report under this section which disclosed that medication was being administered covertly.

Subsection (1)

1-822   **Report on the treatment and the patient's condition**   The approved clinician (AC) in charge of the patient's treatment should report on the treatment and the patient's response to it. There is no requirement under paragraph (a) for the AC to report on an *informal* patient who has been treated under s.57. However, the Commission can require such a report to be made under para.(b).

Approved clinician in charge of the treatment   See s.64(1A), (1B).

On the next occasion   And on each subsequent occasion when such a report is made.

Subsection (2)

1-823   This subsection specifies the timing of the treatment review in respect of patients who are subject to a restriction order, limitation direction or restriction direction.

Subsection (3)

1-824   This subsection provides that the Commission may at any time give notice to the AC that a certificate given under ss.57(2), 58(3)(b) or s.58A(4) or (5) shall cease to apply after the date it specifies. If the AC wished to continue with the treatment specified in the notice she would need to start afresh with the procedures laid down in ss.57, 58 or s.58A, unless the criteria for urgent treatment set out in s.62(2) were satisfied.

Urgent treatment

1-825   62.—(1)   Sections 57 and 58 above shall not apply to any treatment—

(a)   which is immediately necessary to save the patient's life; or

(b)   which (not being irreversible) is immediately necessary to prevent a serious deterioration of his condition; or

(c)   which (not being irreversible or hazardous) is immediately necessary to alleviate serious suffering by the patient; or

(d)   which (not being irreversible or hazardous) is immediately necessary and represents the minimum interference necessary to prevent the patient from behaving violently or being a danger to himself or to others.

[(1A) Section 58A above, in so far as it relates to electro-convulsive therapy by virtue of subsection (1)(a) of that section, shall not apply to any treatment which falls within paragraph (a) or (b) of subsection (1) above.

(1B) Section 58A above, in so far as it relates to a form of treatment specified by virtue of subsection (1)(b) of that section, shall not apply to any treatment which falls within such of paragraphs (a) to (d) of subsection (1) above as may be specified in regulations under that section.

(1C) For the purposes of subsection (1B) above, the regulations—
   (a) may make different provision for different cases (and may, in particular, make different provision for different forms of treatment);
   (b) may make provision which applies subject to specified exceptions; and
   (c) may include transitional, consequential, incidental or supplemental provision.]

(2) Sections 60 and 61(3) above shall not preclude the continuation of any treatment or of treatment under any plan pending compliance with section 57[, 58 or 58A] above if the [approved clinician in charge of the treatment] considers that the discontinuance of the treatment or of treatment under the plan would cause serious suffering to the patient.

(3) For the purposes of this section treatment is irreversible if it has unfavourable irreversible physical or psychological consequences and hazardous if it entails significant physical hazard.

Amendments

The amendments to this section were made by the Mental Health Act 2007 ss.12(5), 28(6) and (7).

Definitions

patient: ss.56, 145(1).   **1-826**
approved clinician: s.145(1).

General Note

This section states that the procedural safeguards provided for in ss.57 and 58 shall not apply to the   **1-827**
categories of urgent treatment set out in paras (a) to (d) of subs.(1). Treatments provided under this section cannot be approved retrospectively by the attendance of a second opinion appointed doctor and the issuing of a certificate. Where the treatment is ECT provided under s.58A, urgent treatment can only be given if either of the grounds set out in para.(a) or (b) are satisfied (subs.(1A)). Where the treatment is another form of s.58A treatment (to be determined by regulations made under s.58A), the Secretary of State (for England) or the Welsh Ministers (for Wales) may make regulations regarding which of the criteria in subs.(1) are to apply to that treatment (subss.(1B), (1C)). Existing treatments can continue if the "serious suffering" criterion set out in subs.(2) is satisfied.

This section, which is not applicable to any treatment that does not come within the remit of either ss.57, 58 or s.58A, for example patients who are detained under ss.135 or 136, does not place a treating clinician under a legal obligation to assess the patient's mental capacity to consent to the treatment.

The purpose of this section is to provide for treatment to be given as a response to an urgent situation. If it is proposed to continue with the treatment thereafter, the procedures set out under ss.57, 58 or s.58A should be observed. Paragraph 25.41 of the *Code of Practice* states:

"Urgent treatment under [this section] can continue only for as long as it remains immediately necessary. If it is no longer immediately necessary, the normal requirements for certificates apply. Although certificates are not required where treatment is immediately necessary, the other requirements of [Part 4] of the Act still apply. The treatment is not necessarily allowed just because no certificate is required."

The Mental Health Act Commission expressed its concern "about treatment given in emergency situations which fall outside the Consent to Treatment provisions of the Act. Some treatment is described as being given under the provisions of section 62 when in fact the patient is either not detained or is held under the short-term holding powers of the Act to which section 62 does not apply" (*Fifth Biennial Report* 1991–1993, para.7.12). If treatment is to be given in these circumstances, it must be justified under either the common law or the Mental Capacity Act 2005.

Although there is no statutory form to be completed when this section is invoked, the *Code of Practice*, at para.25.42 states:

"Hospital managers should monitor the use of these exceptions to the certificate requirements to ensure that they are not used inappropriately or excessively. They are advised to provide a form (or other method) by which the clinician in charge of the treatment in question can record details of:

- the proposed treatment
- why it is immediately necessity to give the treatment, and
- the length of time for which the treatment was given."

Subsection (1)

1-828 The test in this provision is not one of mere necessity; the treatment must be *immediately* necessary. The immediacy refers to the need for treatment and not to the consequences that would flow if the treatment was not provided. It follows that depot medication can be given under this provision even though the effect of the treatment is not immediate, i.e. the treatment is immediately required to ensure that the patient's medication level does not drop below the therapeutic dose.

As treatment under this section is provided under the authority of s.63 (see the note on "shall not apply", below), it is for the approved clinician (AC) who is for the time being in charge of the patient's treatment to determine whether the criteria set out in this subsection are satisfied. Such a determination can be made over the telephone. Under s.63, the AC can direct an appropriately qualified person who is not an approved clinician to provide the treatment.

Sections 57 and 58 As the treatments covered by s.57 are not emergency treatments, it is difficult to envisage the circumstances that would lead a doctor to consider invoking this section in respect of such treatments.

Shall not apply Which means that the treatment can be given to a detained patient without consent by virtue of the power given to the patient's AC by s.63. As s.63 does not apply to informal patients, the AC must find a justification under the Mental Capacity Act 2005 for proceeding without the patient's consent if she plans to give a s.57 treatment to a mentally incapable informal patient in any of the circumstances set out in paras (a) to (d).

Subsections (1A) to (1C)

1-829 These subsections enable emergency ECT to be provided if either of the criteria set out in paras (a) or (b) of subs.(1) is satisfied. As this section does not apply to treatments given under s.58A, treatment under this section can be given to a mentally incapacitated patient even though the patient has made an advance decision under the Mental Capacity Act 2005 refusing a s.58A treatment. There are no statutory limitations to the number of ECT treatments that can be given under this section. For an expression of doubt as to whether such treatment should be given to capacious patients, see the comments of Baroness Murphy noted in the General Note to s.58A. The administration of medicine as part of ECT may also be provided (reg.27(4) of the English Regulations and reg.38(2) of the Welsh Regulations); see further the General Note to s.58A.

Subsection (2)

1-830 This subsection provides that an existing course of treatment or a plan of treatment can continue notwithstanding that the patient has withdrawn his consent if the AC considers that discontinuing the treatment or plan of treatment would cause the patient *serious* suffering. It also applies to patients who lose capacity to consent before the completion of the treatment (s.60(1A)) and where the Commission has given a notice under s.61(3). The treatment must cease as soon as its cessation would no longer cause the patient serious suffering.

Approved clinician in charge of the treatment   See s.64(1A), (1B).

Subsection (3)

Paragraph 6.25 of the White Paper Cmnd. 7320 contains the following definitions of "irreversible"   **1-831**
and "hazardous" treatments: "irreversible treatments" are "treatments which necessitate the removal or
destruction of brain tissue or are designed to effect irreversible change in cerebral or bodily functions";
"hazardous treatments" are "treatments where the risk of adverse reaction or the severity of such reaction would be disproportionate to the degree of benefit the treatment is likely to confer or the prospect
of success".
ECT is not regarded as an irreversible treatment.

Unfavourable   At the Special Standing Committee the Under-Secretary of State cited the removal of
a brain tumour and the removal of a diseased thyroid as examples of treatments which are irreversible
and which can be reasonably expected to have favourable consequences. (Sitting of June 29, 1982.)

[Treatment on recall of community patient or revocation of order

62A.—(1)   This section applies where—   **1-832**
    (a)   a community patient is recalled to hospital under section 17E above;
       or
    (b)   a patient is liable to be detained under this Act following the revoca-
       tion of a community treatment order under section 17F above in
       respect of him.

(2)   For the purposes of section 58(1)(b) above, the patient is to be treated as if
he had remained liable to be detained since the making of the community treatment order.

(3)   But section 58 above does not apply to treatment given to the patient if—
    (a)   the certificate requirement is met for the purposes of section 64C or
       64E below; or
    (b)   as a result of section 64B(4) or 64E(4) below, the certificate require-
       ment would not apply (were the patient a community patient not
       recalled to hospital under section 17E above).

(4)   Section 58A above does not apply to treatment given to the patient if there
is authority to give the treatment, and the certificate requirement is met, for the
purposes of section 64C or 64E below.

(5)   In a case where this section applies [and the Part 4A certificate falls within
section 64C(4) below], the certificate requirement is met only in so far as—
    (a)   the Part 4A certificate expressly provides that it is appropriate for one
       or more specified forms of treatment to be given to the patient in that
       case (subject to such conditions as may be specified); or
    (b)   a notice having been given under subsection (5) of section 64H below,
       treatment is authorised by virtue of subsection (8) of that section.

(6)   Subsection (5) above shall not preclude the continuation of any treatment,
or of treatment under any plan, pending compliance with section 58 or 58A above
[or 64B or 64E below] if the approved clinician in charge of the treatment considers that the discontinuance of the treatment, or of the treatment under the plan,
would cause serious suffering to the patient.

[(6A)   In a case where this section applies and the certificate requirement is no
longer met for the purposes of section 64C(4A) below, the continuation of any treatment, or of treatment under any plan, pending compliance with section 58 or 58A
above or 64B or 64E below shall not be precluded if the approved clinician in

charge of the treatment considers that the discontinuance of the treatment, or of treatment under the plan, would cause serious suffering to the patient.]

(7) In a case where subsection (1)(b) above applies, subsection (3) above only applies pending compliance with section 58 above.

(8) In subsection (5) above—

"Part 4A certificate" has the meaning given in section 64H below; and
"specified", in relation to a Part 4A certificate, means specified in the certificate.]

Amendments

This section was inserted by the Mental Health Act 2007 s.34(4). The amendments to it were made by the Health and Social Care Act 2012 s.299(8)–(10).

Definitions

1-833
community patient: ss.17A(7), 145(1).
hospital: s.145(1).
patient: ss.56, 145(1).
community treatment order: ss.17A(7), 145(1).
approved clinician: s.145(1).

General Note

1-834
This complex section regulates the treatment of the mental disorders of community patients who have either been recalled to hospital under s.17E, or who have had their community treatment order (CTO) revoked under s.17F (subs.(1)). Subject to the exceptions set out in subs.(3), the treatment of such patients cannot proceed unless it is permitted by this Part of the Act. This means that if a certificate under Pt IV was in place before the CTO was made and the certificate covers the patient's current treatment needs and consent status, the certificate remains valid and a fresh certificate will not be required. Note, however, that the *Code of Practice*, at para.25.85, states, without explanation, that it is "not good practice" to rely on such certificates even though they are "technically valid".

In the case of administration of medicine, a certificate is not required if "the patient is still within the period before which a certificate is required i.e. either one month has elapsed from the time when the CTO was made or the three month period from when medication was first given to the patient, as provided for in s.58(1)(b) has not elapsed" (Explanatory Notes, para.127). The patient can be treated with medication for his mental disorder without formality during this period. For the purpose of calculating the three-month period, patients are to be treated as if they had remained liable to be detained since the making of the CTO (subs.(2)). In other words, the three-month period does not start afresh on the patient's recall.

Patients who come within the scope of this section will *not* be subject to Part IV if the Pt IVA certificate requirement set out in s.64C or 64E is met (subs.(3)(a)). Under subs.(5), the certificate requirement is met only in so far as:

(i) the certificate expressly provides that it is appropriate for the specified treatment to be given on recall, and giving the treatment would not be contrary to any condition attached to the certificate, or
(ii) although the regulatory body has given notice under s.64H(5) that the treatment must stop, the treatment can continue under s.64H(8) because its discontinuance would cause serious suffering to the patient.

By virtue of the amendment made to subs.(5) by the Health and Social Care Act 2012, a "new certificate under s.58 or 58A is not required if the treatment in question is already covered by an approved clinician's Part IVA certificate [Form CTO 12] provided that the patient continues to consent to the treatment (and still has the capacity to do so)" (Explanatory Notes to the 2012 Act, para.1531).

Unless the SOAD's Part IVA certificate specifies otherwise, it will authorise the treatment even if the patient has capacity to refuse it. However, the certificate will not provide authority for treatment under s.58A to be given to a patient who has capacity or competence to consent but refuses consent when recalled to hospital or when the CTO is revoked (subs.(4)).

Existing treatment which does not satisfy the certification requirement can be continued, pending compliance with s.58 or s.58A, if the approved clinician in charge of the patient's treatment considers that its discontinuance would cause serious suffering to the patient (subss.(6), (6A)). In addition, in cases of urgency the provisions of s.62 or 64G will apply.

If the patient's CTO is revoked, with the patient being once again detained in hospital for treatment, treatment can be given on the authority of a Pt IVA certificate only until a s.58 or s.58A certificate can be arranged (subs.(7)).

The medical treatment of a CTO patient who is admitted to hospital informally is governed by Pt IVA.

Subsection (6A)

Paragraph 1532 of the Explanatory Notes to the Health and Social Care Act 2012 states: **1-835**

"Section 62A ... provides that, even if the treatment has not been expressly approved by a SOAD's Part 4A certificate, it may be continued while a new SOAD certificate is sought, if the approved clinician in charge thinks stopping the treatment would cause the patient serious suffering. [Subsection (6A)] extends that to include cases where (either before or during recall) the patient withdraws consent to treatment to which an approved clinician's Part 4A certificate applies, or loses capacity to consent to it. As amended, section 62A [allows] an approved clinician to continue giving medication to a patient who has withdrawn consent if they consider that its discontinuance would cause serious suffering to the patient, but it does not allow electro-convulsive therapy to be given against such a patient's will (because it is not possible to obtain a SOAD certificate authorising electro-convulsive therapy for a detained patient who has capacity to consent, but is refusing to do so)."

Treatment not requiring consent

63.   The consent of a patient shall not be required for any medical treatment   **1-836**
given to him for the mental disorder from which he is suffering[, not being a form
of treatment to which section 57, 58 or 58A above applies,] if the treatment is given
by or under the direction of the [approved clinician in charge of the treatment].

Amendment

The words in square brackets were substituted by the Mental Health Act 2007 ss.12(6), 28(8).

Definitions

patient: ss.56, 145(1).   **1-837**
medical treatment: s.145(1), (4).
mental disorder: ss.1, 145(1).
approved clinician: s.145(1).

General Note

This section provides that the consent of a patient to whom this Part applies (see s.56) is not required   **1-838**
for treatment which does not fall within ss.57, 58 or s.58A if it is given by or under the direction of the "approved clinician in charge of the treatment". Paragraph 67 of the Explanatory Notes to the Mental Health Act 2007 explains why this phrase, rather than "responsible clinician", is used in this Part:

"In the majority of cases the AC in charge of the treatment will be the patient's RC, but where, for example, the RC is not qualified to make decisions about a particular treatment (e.g. medication if the RC is not a doctor or a nurse prescriber) then another appropriately qualified professional will be in charge of that treatment, with the RC continuing to retain overall responsibility for the patient's case."

A positive decision to impose non-consensual medical treatment pursuant to this section is a public law decision susceptible to judicial review: see *R. (on the application of B) v Haddock (Responsible Medical Officer)* [2006] EWCA Civ 961; [2006] M.H.L.R. 306.

In *Nottinghamshire Healthcare NHS Trust v RC* [2014] EWCOP 1317, Mostyn J. held that where the approved clinician makes a decision *not* to impose treatment under this section, and where the consequences of that decision may prove to be life-threatening, then the NHS trust in question would be well advised to apply to the High Court for declaratory relief. His Lordship said at para.21:

> "The hearing will necessarily involve a 'full merits review' of the initial decision. It would be truly bizarre if such a full merits review were held where a positive decision was made under s.63, but not where there was a negative one, especially where one considers that the negative decision may have far more momentous consequences (i.e. death) than the positive one."

The principles the court should apply where it conducts a full merits review on an application for declaratory relief in circumstances where a decision has been made not to impose potentially life-saving treatment under this section were identified at para.26:

> "Obviously the expressed wishes of the patient will be highly relevant. If there is an advance decision in place under ss.24 and 26 of the Mental Capacity Act then this will weigh most heavily in the scales. The Hippocratic duty to seek to save life, or the benign but paternalistic view that it is in someone's best interests to remain alive must all surely be subservient to the right to sovereignty over your own body. Beyond this, considerations such as whether the treatment would be futile will no doubt be relevant; for example, if the repair of a laceration would inevitably be followed by a new one or if the patient was suffering from another unrelated terminal disease."

In this case, his Lordship said that, notwithstanding the existence of power under this section, it would be an abuse of power "even to think about imposing a blood transfusion on [a patient who is a Jehovah's Witness] having regard to my findings that he presently has capacity to refuse blood products and, were such capacity to disappear for any reason, the advance decision [that he had made refusing a blood transfusion] would be operative. To impose a blood transfusion would be a denial of a most basic freedom" (para.42). His Lordship therefore declared that the decision of the patient's RC not to impose a blood transfusion on the patient was lawful. The approach adopted by Mostyn J. in RC was followed by Moor J. in A Midlands *NHS Trust v RD* [2021] EWCOP 35, where the following declarations were granted:

1. RD lacked capacity to make decisions about her nutritional intake and about her care and treatment in general; and,
2. it was in RD's best interests to receive the care in her care plan, specifically that it was lawful not to take any steps towards forcing nutrition against her wishes, notwithstanding that, by so doing, it might in the short-term prevent her death.

Also see *A Mental Health Trust v BG* [2022] EWCOP 26, where declarations were granted with respect to BG, who was detained under s.3, that BG lacked capacity to make decisions about her care and treatment, including nutrition and hydration, and that it was in BG's best interests that no further treatment be provided against her wishes (including any artificial nutrition and hydration, and any life-saving treatment).

As a decision to impose non-consensual treatment under this section is susceptible to judicial review, the common law duty of fairness requires the patient's AC to record her reasons for taking that decision: see the judgment of Hickinbottom L.J in *R. (on the application of Help Refugees Ltd) v Secretary of State for the Home Department* [2018] EWCA Civ 2098 at para.122.

The Minister for Health's response to the argument that detained patients should not be forced to receive treatment is contained in the following passage from his speech to the Special Standing Committee:

> "[That argument would] lead us to conclude that those who were forcibly detained and had lost their liberty against their will … should be kept in custody in places in which they received no treatment despite the fact that those who looked after them would have to gaze on them knowing perfectly well that some treatment could be given to alleviate their suffering and distress and enable them eventually to recover their liberty. Hospitals are places of treatment and we cannot have hospitals in which people are locked up and left to wander about without receiving treatment" (sitting of June 29, 1982).

The Government's response to the criticism that this provision might authorise a disturbingly wide range of interventions was given by Lord Elton who emphasised that it was not intended to apply to "borderline" or "experimental" treatments, but to "things which a person in hospital for treatment ought to undergo for his own good and for the good of the running of the hospital and for the good of other patients … perfectly routine, sensible treatment" (*Hansard* H.L. Vol.426, col.107).

This section "does not absolve the doctor of his ordinary duties of care towards his patient, judged on the usual *Bolam/Bolitho* principles" (*R. (on the application of Wilkinson) v The Responsible Medical Officer Broadmoor Hospital* [2001] EWCA Civ 1545; [2002] 1W.L.R. 419 per Hale L.J. at para.68). There is no statutory form for treatments given under the authority of this section.

Human Rights Act 1998

In *B v Croydon Health Authority*, below, counsel for the patient submitted that if the meaning of **1-839** "medical treatment for … mental disorder" was wide enough to include ancillary forms of treatment, this section would involve a breach of art.8 of the European Convention on Human Rights (ECHR). He referred to *Herczegfalvy v Austria* (1993) 15 E.H.R.R. 437 at 485 where the European Court of Human Rights (ECtHR) said that a measure constituting an interference with private life and therefore prima facie contrary to art.8(1) (like involuntary tube feeding) can only be justified under art.8(2) if, among the other requirements of that article, its terms are sufficiently precise to enable the individual "to foresee its consequences for him". In rejecting counsel's submission, Hoffmann L.J. said at 688: "In my judgment section 63 amply satisfies this test. There is no conceptual vagueness about the notion of treating the symptoms or consequences of a mental disorder, although naturally there will be borderline cases. But there is no question of exercise of arbitrary power".

In *X v Finland* [2012] M.H.L.R. 318, the ECtHR considered whether the procedure in the Finnish Mental Health Act which allows for the forcible administration of medication was compatible with the patient's rights under art.8. The Court said at para.220:

"The Court considers that forced administration of medication represents a serious interference with a person's physical integrity and must accordingly be based on a 'law' that guarantees proper safeguards against arbitrariness. In the present case such safeguards were missing. The decision to confine the applicant to involuntary treatment included an automatic authorisation to proceed to forced administration of medication when the applicant refused the treatment. The decision-making was solely in the hands of the treating doctors who could take even quite radical measures regardless of the applicant's will. Moreover, their decision-making was free from any kind of immediate judicial scrutiny: the applicant did not have any remedy available whereby she could require a court to rule on the lawfulness, including proportionality, of the forced administration of medication and to have it discontinued."

The Court concluded that "even if there could be said to be a general legal basis for the measures provided for in Finnish law, the absence of sufficient safeguards against forced medication by the treating doctors deprived the applicant of the minimum degree of protection to which she was entitled under the rule of law in a democratic society" (para.221). This finding, together with a similar finding in *LM v Slovenia, June 12, 2014 (App. No.32863/05)*, raises the question of whether treatment given under this section during the three-month period provided for in s.58(1)(b), treatment which is given at the sole discretion of the patient's approved clinician and which can involve the use of force on an unwilling patient, breaches art.8 on the ground that it contains no safeguards against arbitrariness. The contention that the availability of judicial review (see the *Wilkinson* line of cases noted under s.58) provides a sufficient and practical safeguard for the patient against involuntary treatment is open to doubt.

The approach that the domestic courts adopt when determining whether the forcible medical treatment of a patient breaches either art.3 or art.8 of the ECHR is considered in the note on s.58 under the heading *Human Rights Act 1998 and procedural issues*.

Mental Capacity Act 2005

See the General Note to this Part. **1-840**

Consent … shall not be required However, consent should be sought "wherever practicable" (*Code of Practice*, para.24.41; also see the General Note to this Part). Although treatments which do not come within ss.57, 58 or 58A may be given to a patient without his consent, "in practice it is impossible to undertake many of the therapies concerned without a patient's co-operation" (Cmnd. 8405, para.37).

Medical treatment … for the mental disorder The leading case on the meaning of this phrase is *B v Croydon Health Authority* [1995] 1 All E.R. 683, where the Court of Appeal held that:

(i) a range of acts ancillary to the core treatment that the patient is receiving fall within the term "medical treatment" as defined in s.145(1);

(ii) treatment is capable of being ancillary to the core treatment if it is nursing and care "concurrent with the core treatment or as a necessary prerequisite to such treatment or to prevent the patient from causing harm to himself or to alleviate the consequences of the disorder …" (per Hoffmann L.J. at 687);

(iii)   relieving the symptoms of the mental disorder is just as much a part of treatment as relieving its underlying cause (NB This finding is reflected in s.145(4) which was inserted by the 2007 Act.); and

(iv)   treatment for a physical disorder will not amount to a treatment for a mental disorder where the treatment for the physical disorder is entirely unconnected with the pre-existing mental disorder.

In *St George's Healthcare NHS Trust v S* [1998] 3 All E.R. 673 at 693, Judge L.J. said that the *Croydon* case is authority for the proposition that this section "may apply to the treatment of any condition which is integral to the mental disorder".

In the *Croydon* case, the Court of Appeal held that the force feeding of a patient who was suffering from borderline personality disorder was treatment which fell within the scope of this section because such treatment was aimed at treating a symptom of the disorder which was a refusal to eat in order to inflict self harm. The force feeding of a patient suffering from either anorexia nervosa or depression can also come within the scope of this section: see *Re KB* [1997] 2 F.L.R. 180 and *Re VS (Adult: Mental Disorder)* (1995) 3 Med.L.Rev. 292.

If a question comes before the court as to whether the proposed force feeding of a patient comes within the scope of this section, it will necessarily be a "matter on which the Court will be heavily reliant upon medical, and in particular, psychiatric evidence. The inter-relationship between the patient's mental disorder and the treatment which is proposed, is in my view one primarily of medical expertise rather than legal analysis" (*JK v A Local Health Board* [2019] EWHC 67 (Fam); [2020] M.H.L.R. 190, per Lieven J. at para.69).

In *A Healthcare; B NHS Trust v CC* [2020] EWHC 574 (Fam); [2020] M.H.L.R. 336, a case where dialysis was found to be treatment for a manifestation of the patient's mental disorder, Lieven J. said, at para.56(i):

"The physical condition CC is now in, by which dialysis is critical to keep him alive, is properly described as a manifestation of his mental disorder. There is a very real prospect that if he was not mentally ill he would self-care in a way that would have not led to the need for dialysis. Further, CC's refusal of dialysis is very obviously a manifestation of his mental disorder and dialysis treatment is therefore treatment within the scope of section 63 MHA 1983."

The following findings were made:

1.   A submission that for this section to apply, the *primary* purpose of the treatment must be to treat the mental disorder was rejected. Rather, it is sufficient "that a purpose of the proposed treatment is to alleviate a manifestation of the mental disorder" (para.37).

2.   In most if not all cases where this section is relied upon, the treatment will involve some use of medication, often sedation. It would make no sense of the statute for sedation to be dealt with under one statutory route (i.e. s.58) and other forms of treatment to be dealt with by a wholly different one. In any event, where the proposed treatment is very urgent and potentially life-saving the case will fall within s.62(1) and as such s.58 is excluded (paras 46,47).

3.   As this section "can be used as authority to provide medical treatment to CC, including by dialysis treatment and by the use of light physical restraint and chemical restraint (if required), it is unnecessary for the court to exercise its discretion and make a contingent declaration pursuant to section 15(1)(c) MCA 2005 that it is lawful to treat CC in accordance with the proposed dialysis treatment plan in the event that he lacks capacity to make a decision regarding dialysis treatment at the relevant time" (para.56(v)).

In *Norfolk and Suffolk NHS Foundation Trust v HJ* [2023] EWFC 92 one of the issues before the court was whether treatment for HJ's chronic constipation came within the scope of this section. David Lock KC, sitting as a Deputy High Court Judge, said at para.8:

"The fact that HJ's presenting mental health state can, to an extent, be improved or can deteriorate depending on her physical condition does not mean that her mental health condition is caused by her physical health problems. She may well present with fewer symptoms of her mental health condition when she is in good physical health and not in pain, but her gastrointestinal illness is not the cause of her Bipolar Affective Disorder. It follows that, as agreed between the parties, the administration of enemas falls outside the scope of section 63 MHA even applying the expanded scope of section 63 arising from cases such as *B v Croydon Health Authority* [1995] Fam 133."

In this case, the Trust accepted "that HJ's resistance to treatment for her chronic constipation is closely related to the mental disorders from which she suffers" (para.7).

In *R. v Collins and Ashworth Hospital Authority Ex p. Brady* [2000] M.H.L.R. 17, Kay J., held that as the patient's hunger strike was a manifestation or symptom of his personality disorder, the force feeding of the patient came within this section because it constituted a form of treatment for his disorder. His Lordship said at para.44:

> "On any view, and to a high degree of probability, s.63 was triggered because what arose was the need for medical treatment for the mental disorder from which the Applicant was and is suffering. The hunger strike is a manifestation or symptom of the personality disorder. The fact (if such it be) that a person without mental disorder could reach the same decision on a rational basis in similar circumstances does not avail the Applicant because he reached and persists in his decision because of his personality disorder."

The *Croydon* and *Brady* cases were distinguished in *A NHS Trust v Dr A* [2013] EWHC 2442 (COP), a case where the patient went on hunger strike in the delusional belief that this would force the UK Border agency to return his passport. Baker J. accepted the evidence of the patient's responsible clinician (RC) that she did not consider it appropriate to use this section to treat the patient as she did not consider that force feeding him in the circumstances of the case to be a medical treatment for his mental disorder, but rather for a physical disorder that arose from his decision to refuse food. In declining to make a declaration that artificial nutrition and hydration could be administered to the patient under this section, but declaring that such treatment could be provided under the authority of the inherent jurisdiction of the High Court, his Lordship said that although the patient's decision to refuse food was flawed in part because his mental disorder deprived him of the capacity to use and weigh information relevant to the decision and that this lead to the conclusion that the physical disorder is in part a consequence of his mental disorder, the disorder was "not obviously either a manifestation or a symptom of the mental disorder". His lordship held that the patient could not be force fed under the Mental Capacity Act (MCA), even though he did not have capacity, because this Act had primacy over the MCA when a person is detained in hospital under the hospital treatment regime: see Sch.1A of the MCA.

His Lordship said at para.80:

> "[I]t is generally undesirable to extend the meaning of medical treatment under the MHA too far so as to bring about deprivation of liberty in respect of sectioned or sectionable patients beyond what is properly within the ambit of the MHA. I recognise the need for identifying, where possible, a clear dividing line between what is and what is not treatment for a mental disorder within the meaning of the MHA; but I venture to suggest that in medicine, as in the law, it is not always possible to discern clear dividing lines. In case of uncertainty, where there is doubt as to whether the treatment falls within s.145 and s.63, the appropriate course is for an application to be made to the court to approve the treatment. That approach ensures that the treatment given under s.63 of the MHA will be confined to that which is properly within the definition of s.145 as amended. It would help to ensure that patients with mental disorders are, so far as possible, treated informally rather than under section. Finally, it ensures compliance with Art.8 [of the ECHR] and provides the patient with a more effective remedy than would otherwise be available, namely a forensic process to determine whether the treatment is in his best interests."

In *JK v A Local Health Board*, above, Lieven J. said that in the situation contemplated by Baker J. the court could make declaratory order under the inherent jurisdiction (para.66) and that "any decision under the inherent jurisdiction both as to whether proposed treatment falls within s.63, as being for a manifestation of the mental disorder; and as to whether it is 'treatment' within s.145 under the MHA, must also involve a full merits review" (para.68).

In *Nottinghamshire Healthcare NHS Trust v RC* [2014] EWHC 1317 (COP), Mostyn J. was required to determine whether a blood transfusion provided to a patient who had engaged in significant self-harm would amount to treatment of a symptom or manifestation of his underlying mental disorder. In holding that it was, his Lordship said at para.31:

> "It cannot be disputed that the act of self harming, the slashing open of the brachial artery, is a symptom or manifestation of the underlying personality disorder. Therefore to treat the wound in any way is to treat the manifestation or symptom of the underlying disorder. So, indisputably, to suture the wound would be squarely within s.63. As would be the administration of a course of antibiotics to prevent infection. A consequence of bleeding from the wound is that haemoglobin levels are lowered. While it is strictly true, as Dr Latham says, that 'low haemoglobin is not wholly a manifestation or symptom of personality disorder', it is my view that to treat the low haemoglobin by a blood

transfusion is just as much a treatment of a symptom or manifestation of the disorder as is to stitch up the wound or to administer antibiotics."

Although the proposed treatment came within the scope of this section, Mostyn J. held that the patient's RC was "completely correct" when she decided not to use this section to impose a blood transfusion on a mentally capable patient who was refusing the treatment for strongly held religious reasons: see further the General Note to this section.

Mostyn J.'s finding in *RC* is consistent with the finding in the *Croydon* case that treatment under this section can include the medical and surgical treatment for the physical consequences of self-poisoning or self-injury if the self-poisoning or self-injury can be categorised as either the consequence of or a symptom of the patient's mental disorder. The treatment could include measures taken to prevent a patient from interfering with a self-inflicted wound. In *Croydon*, Hoffmann L.J. said at 687, 688:

"It would seem strange to me if a hospital could, without the patient's consent, give him treatment directed to alleviating a psychopathic disorder showing itself in suicidal tendencies, but not without such consent be able to treat the consequences of the suicide attempt".

1-841   The *Croydon* case was applied by Wall J. in *Tameside and Glossop Acute Services Trust v CH* [1996] 1 F.L.R. 762, a case where a pregnant patient who was suffering from schizophrenia had been detained under s.3. She had the delusional belief that the doctors who were caring for her wished to harm her baby. The baby was not developing well and the obstetrician took the view that if the pregnancy was allowed to continue the baby might die in the womb. For that reason the obstetrician wished to induce labour and, if necessary, perform a caesarean section. The trust sought a declaration that it would be lawful to carry out such treatment without the patient's consent and to use any necessary force to restrain her in order to facilitate the treatment. Wall J. held, at 773, that there were "several strands in the evidence" which brought the proposed treatment within the scope of this section:

"First, there is the proposition that an ancillary reason for the induction and, if necessary, the birth by caesarean section is to prevent a deterioration in the [patient's] mental state. Secondly, there is the clear evidence of [the patient's psychiatrist] that in order for the treatment of her schizophrenia to be effective, it is necessary for her to give birth to a live baby. Thirdly, the overall structure of her treatment requires her to receive strong anti-psychotic medication. The administration of that treatment has been necessarily interrupted by her pregnancy and cannot be resumed until her child is born. It is not, therefore, I think stretching language unduly to say that achievement of a successful outcome of her pregnancy is a necessary part of the overall treatment of her mental disorder."

His Lordship granted the declaration sought, distinguishing *Re C (Adult: Refusal of Medical Treatment)* [1994] 1 All E.R. 819 where a schizophrenic patient was held to have the mental capacity to refuse treatment for gangrene which was considered to be life threatening, on the ground that "C's gangrene was not likely to affect his mental condition: the manner in which the delivery of the [patient's] child is treated is likely to have a direct effect on her mental state". As the patient's pregnancy was neither a symptom nor a consequence of her mental disorder, this finding appears to allow a doctor to claim that the treatment of a condition which has no apparent connection with the patient's mental disorder comes within the scope of this section if such treatment will either enhance, or prevent a deterioration of, the patient's mental condition. Treatment proposed in circumstances that are similar to those that were present in *Tameside* should not proceed in the absence of approval by the court: see *A NHS Trust v Dr A*, above.

One reason why a declaration was sought in the *Tameside* case was the fact that the obstetrician might have had to use force on the patient. Wall J. held that it was permissible, should the doctor deem it to be clinically necessary, to use restraint to the extent to which it may be reasonably required in order to achieve the delivery by the patient of a healthy baby. It is therefore lawful for doctors and nurses to use restraint, so far as reasonably required and clinically necessary, to administer treatment under this section. His Lordship agreed, at 774, with counsel's proposition that "in cases in which the question of restraint arose or was likely to arise, and the doctor was doubtful about the lawfulness of the application of restraint or the use of force, an application should be made to the court for a declaration that the treatment would be lawful". In *R. (on the application of Wilkinson) v The Responsible Medical Officer Broadmoor Hospital* [2001] EWCA Civ 1545; [2002] 1 W.L.R. 419, Hale L.J. said, at para.64, that where a mentally incapacitated patient is "actively opposed to a course of action, the benefits which it holds for him will have to be carefully weighed against the disadvantages of going against his wishes, especially if force is required to do this". It is submitted that these remarks, which were concerned with the application of the "best interests" test under common law, are equally applicable to the situation of a detained patient, irrespective of patient's mental capacity.

The decision in the *Croydon* case brings the monitoring of the blood of a patient who is being treated with Clozapine within the definition of treatment for mental disorder for the purposes of this section because such monitoring is clearly ancillary to the core treatment for his mental disorder. Treatments which are given to respond to the side effects of the patient's core treatment also come within the scope of this section, e.g. antiparkinsonian agents used to alleviate the motor side effects of anti-psychotic medication.

Deep-brain stimulation (i.e. the implantation of electrodes in the brain that are activated by the patient through an external stimulator) comes within the scope of this section if the procedure is used to treat the patient's mental disorder and it does not involve an operation for the destruction of brain tissue or function, in which case it will come within the scope of s.57. The CQC has recommended that "that the Mental Health regulations should extend the safeguards of section 57 to the use of [deep-brain stimulation] as a treatment for mental disorder (CQC, "*Monitoring the Mental Health Act in 2013/2014*", p.60). See also the note on s.57(1)(a).

The fact that a remedy can be bought in the High Street does not prevent it from being a medical treatment for the purposes of this section. Such treatments would include St John's Wort prescribed for mild to moderate depression and fish oils prescribed to enhance the efficacy of anti-psychotic drugs: see further, MHAC, *Twelfth Biennial Report* 2005–2005 paras 6.49–6.54.

If a patient's refusal to pay attention to his personal hygiene or to be treated for a physical condition is assessed as being a manifestation or symptom of his mental disorder, the patient can be washed and/or treated under the authority of the *Croydon* case as both nursing and specialist care come within the definition of "medical treatment" in s.145(1). If a non-detained patient is mentally incapable of making decisions about such matters, intervention must be justified under the Mental Capacity Act 2005.

Approved clinician   Who can direct an appropriately qualified person who is not an approved clinician to provide the treatment.

Supplementary provisions for Part IV

64.—(1)   In this Part of this Act ["the responsible clinician" means the approved clinician with overall responsibility for the case] of the patient in question and "hospital" includes a [registered establishment].   **1-842**

[(1A)   References in this Part of this Act to the approved clinician in charge of a patient's treatment shall, where the treatment in question is a form of treatment to which section 57 above applies, be construed as references to the person in charge of the treatment.]

[(1B)   References in this Part of this Act to the approved clinician in charge of a patient's treatment shall, where the treatment in question is a form of treatment to which section 58A above applies and the patient falls within section 56(5) above, be construed as references to the person in charge of the treatment.

(1C)   Regulations made by virtue of section 32(2)(d) above apply for the purposes of this Part as they apply for the purposes of Part 2 of this Act.]

(2)   Any certificate for the purposes of this Part of this Act shall be in such form as may be prescribed by regulations made by the Secretary of State.

[(3)   For the purposes of this Part of this Act, it is appropriate for treatment to be given to a patient if the treatment is appropriate in his case, taking into account the nature and degree of the mental disorder from which he is suffering and all other circumstances of his case.]

Amendments

The amendments to this section were made by the Care Standards Act 2000 s.116, Sch.4 para.9(2) and the Mental Health Act 2007 ss.6(3), 12(7), 28(9).

Definitions

1-843   approved clinician: s.145(1).
patient: s.145(1).
hospital: s.145(1).
registered establishment: ss.34(1), 145(1).

General Note

Subsection (1)

1-844 **Responsible clinician**   See the note on s.34(1).

Approved clinician in charge of a patient's treatment   This clinician will not be subject to the supervision of another clinician in respect of the provision of the treatment in question. The Reference Guide states at para.23.11:

"Where a patient has a responsible clinician in overall charge of their case, the responsible clinician need not be in charge of any particular form of treatment. There may be different clinicians in charge of different forms of treatment."

Any dispute between the RC and the AC concerning the medical treatment of the patient that cannot be resolved through discussion would have to be referred to the hospital management for resolution.

Subsection (2)

1-845 **Secretary of State**   Or, in relation to Wales, the Welsh Ministers (see the General Note to the Act and SI 1999/672 art.2, Sch.1).

Subsection (3)

1-846   Note the circularity of this definition.

[PART IVA TREATMENT OF COMMUNITY PATIENTS NOT RECALLED TO HOSPITAL]

General Note

1-847   This Part authorises the provision of "relevant treatment" (see s.64A) to either a mentally capable or mentally incapable community patient who has not been recalled to hospital under s.17E. It also applies to "patients on CTOs who are in hospital without having been recalled (e.g. if they have been admitted to hospital voluntarily)" (*Code of Practice*, para.24.14). A community patient is a patient in respect of whom a community treatment order is in force (s.17A(7)). Such patients can only be given treatment if they consent or, if they lack the capacity to consent, do not actively object. Treatment can also be given in emergencies to a mentally incapable patient who resists it. The medical treatment of community patients who have been recalled to hospital is governed by s.62A.
The requirements of this Part are of two types: authority and certification. Although there must always be authority to give the treatment, the certificate requirement does not always apply.
The *Code of Practice* states:

"24.17 Part 4A patients, who have the capacity to consent to or refuse a treatment, may not be given that treatment unless they consent. There are no exceptions to this rule, even in emergencies. The effect is that treatment can be given without their consent only if they are recalled to hospital.
24.18 For part 4A patients, aged 18 and over, who lack the capacity to consent to or to refuse a treatment, it may be given if someone who has lasting power of attorney (an attorney) or a Court of Protection appointed deputy consents on their behalf. Similarly it may be given in the case of those aged 16 and over if a deputy consents to the treatment on their behalf.
24.19 Part 4A patients who lack capacity to consent to or refuse a treatment may also be given it, without anyone's consent by or under the direction of the approved clinician in charge of the treatment, unless:

•   in the case of a patient aged 18 or over, the treatment would be contrary to a valid and applicable advance decision made by the patient (see chapter 9)

[372]

- in the case of a patient aged 18 or over, the treatment would be against the decision of someone with the authority under the MCA 2005 to refuse it on the patient's behalf (an attorney, a deputy or the Court of Protection), or
- in the case of a patient aged 16 or over, the treatment would be against the decision of a deputy who has authority to refuse it on the patient's behalf, or force needs to be used in order to administer the treatment and the patient objects to the treatment."

The authority to treat CTO patients was summarised by Lady Hale in *Welsh Ministers v PJ* [2018] UKSC 66; [2018] M.H.L.R. 411 at para.16(iv):

"There is only authority to treat a community patient in three circumstances, which reflect the circumstances in which it would be possible to treat him without a CTO, but with some extra procedural safeguards, the details of which need not concern us. The three circumstances are: first, where there is a valid consent, given either by a patient who has capacity to give it or, if he does not, by a donee of a lasting power of attorney or a deputy appointed by the Court of Protection who has power to give it, or by the Court of Protection (section 64C(2)); second, where the patient lacks capacity and it is possible to give him the treatment without using force (section 64D); or third, where emergency treatment is needed by a patient who lacks capacity (section 64G). Extra procedural safeguards are required for particular treatments, including long term medication and ECT. But there is nothing in the MHA to authorise the giving of medical treatment to a community patient who has the capacity to consent to it and does not give that consent."

There is no requirement for the treatment provided under this Part to be given in a clinical setting.

Code of Practice

Guidance on this Part is contained in Ch.24.   **1-848**

[Meaning of "relevant treatment"

64A.— In this Part of this Act "relevant treatment", in relation to a patient,   **1-849**
means medical treatment which—
    (a)   is for the mental disorder from which the patient is suffering; and
    (b)   is not a form of treatment to which section 57 above applies.]

Amendment

This section was inserted by the Mental Health Act 2007 s.35(1).

Definitions

medical treatment; s.145(1), (4).   **1-850**
mental disorder: ss.1, 145(1).
patient: s.145(1).

General Note

The meaning of the phrase "medical treatment ... for the mental disorder" was explained by the Court   **1-851**
of Appeal in *B v Croydon Health Authority* [1995] 1 All E.R. 683 which is considered in the note on
s.63.
Section 57 treatments are regulated by the requirements of that section which apply to "any patient"
receiving such treatment (s.56(1)).

[Adult community patients

64B.—(1) This section applies to the giving of relevant treatment to a com-   **1-852**
munity patient who—
    (a)   is not recalled to hospital under section 17E above; and

(b)   has attained the age of 16 years.

(2)   The treatment may not be given to the patient unless—

(a)   there is authority to give it to him; and

(b)   if it is section 58 type treatment or section 58A type treatment, the certificate requirement is met.

(3)   But the certificate requirement does not apply if—

(a)   giving the treatment to the patient is authorised in accordance with section 64G below; or

(b)   the treatment is immediately necessary and—

(i)   the patient has capacity to consent to it and does consent to it; or

(ii)   a donee or deputy or the Court of Protection consents to the treatment on the patient's behalf.

(4)   Nor does the certificate requirement apply in so far as the administration of medicine to the patient at any time during the period of one month beginning with the day on which the community treatment order is made is section 58 type treatment.

(5)   The reference in subsection (4) above to the administration of medicine does not include any form of treatment specified under section 58(1)(a) above.]

Amendment

This section was inserted by the Mental Health Act 2007 s.35(1).

Definition

1-853   community patient: ss.17A(7), 145(1).

General Note

1-854   This section and s.64C provide authority to treat a community patient who is over the age of 16 if

(a)   there is authority to give it to him because either the patient has capacity and consents to the treatment (even the emergency treatment of such patients requires their consent), or a donee or a deputy or the Court of Protection consents to it on his behalf, or it is authorised under s.64D (treatment for patients who lack capacity) or 64G (emergency treatment for patients who lack capacity) (subs.(2)(a) and s.64C(2)) and,

(b)   if it is a treatment coming within the scope of s.58 or 58A, the certificate requirement is met in that a SOAD (or the approved clinician in charge of the treatment if the patient is capacious and has consented to the treatment (s.64C(4A),(4B)) has certified that the treatment (or a plan of treatment (s.64H(1)) should be given to the patient (subs.(2)(b) and s.64C(4)).

The certificate requirement does *not* apply if the treatment:

(i)   is emergency treatment given to a mentally incapacitated patient which is authorised under s.64G (subs.(3)(a)), or

(ii)   is immediately necessary (see s.64C(5)–(7)) and either the patient has the capacity to consent to it and does consent to it or a donee or a deputy of a mentally incapacitated patient consents to the treatment on his behalf (subs.(3)(b)), or

(iii)   is medication coming within the scope of s.58(1)(b) and the medication is being given to the patient within a month of the CTO being made (subss.(4), (5)) or three months from when the medication was first given to the patient (whether in the community or in hospital), whichever is later. The three month period is relevant because s.58 only applies to medicines after three months have elapsed since they were first given.

The situations set out in paras (i) and (ii) allow for treatment to continue pending a SOAD visit after the one or three-month period mentioned in para.(iii) has elapsed, as long as the relevant criteria are satisfied.

If a certificate is withdrawn by the regulatory authority, the treatment can continue pending compliance with this section if the person in charge of the treatment considers that the discontinuance of the treatment would cause serious suffering to the patient (s.64H(5)–(9)).

Where treatment has been given on the basis of a Pt IVA certificate, the person in charge of the treatment must send the regulatory authority a report on the treatment and the patient's condition if required by that authority (s.64H(4)).

Subsection (1)

Relevant treatment   See s.64C(3).   **1-855**

Hospital   See s.64K(7).

Subsection (2)(a)

See s.64C(2).   **1-856**

Subsection (2)(b)

The meaning of a "section 58 type treatment or section 58A type treatment" is explained in s.64C(3).   **1-857**

Certificate requirement   See s.64C(4).

Subsection (3)(b)

Immediately necessary   See s.64C(5) to (9) and reg.28(2) of the English Regulations and reg.39(a)   **1-858**
of the Welsh Regulations.

Capacity to consent   See s.64K(2). The emergency treatment of patients who lack capacity or competence is governed by s.64G.

Donee; deputy   The decision must be within the scope of the authority of the donee or deputy: see s.64K(4), (5).

Subsection (4)

Period of one month   The certificate requirement also does not apply during the period of three   **1-859**
months from the date when the medication was first given to the patient: see the note on s.64C(4). The SOAD certificate is required from the later of the two periods.

[Section 64B: supplemental

64C.—(1)   This section has effect for the purposes of section 64B above.   **1-860**

(2)   There is authority to give treatment to a patient if—

(a)   he has capacity to consent to it and does consent to it;

(b)   a donee or deputy or the Court of Protection consents to it on his behalf; or

(c)   giving it to him is authorised in accordance with section 64D or 64G below.

(3)   Relevant treatment is section 58 type treatment or section 58A type treatment if, at the time when it is given to the patient, section 58 or 58A above (respectively) would have applied to it, had the patient remained liable to be detained at that time (rather than being a community patient).

(4)   The certificate requirement is met in respect of treatment to be given to a patient if—

(a)   a registered medical practitioner appointed for the purposes of Part 4 of this Act (not being the responsible clinician or the person in charge of the treatment) has certified in writing that it is appropriate for the treatment to be given or for the treatment to be given subject to such conditions as may be specified in the certificate; and

(b) if conditions are so specified, the conditions are satisfied.

[(4A) Where there is authority to give treatment by virtue of subsection (2)(a), the certificate requirement is also met in respect of the treatment if the approved clinician in charge of the treatment has certified in writing that the patient has capacity to consent to the treatment and has consented to it.

(4B) But, if the patient has not attained the age of 18, subsection (4A) does not apply to section 58A type treatment.]

(5) In a case where the treatment is section 58 type treatment, treatment is immediately necessary if—

(a) it is immediately necessary to save the patient's life; or

(b) it is immediately necessary to prevent a serious deterioration of the patient's condition and is not irreversible; or

(c) it is immediately necessary to alleviate serious suffering by the patient and is not irreversible or hazardous; or

(d) it is immediately necessary, represents the minimum interference necessary to prevent the patient from behaving violently or being a danger to himself or others and is not irreversible or hazardous.

(6) In a case where the treatment is section 58A type treatment by virtue of subsection (1)(a) of that section, treatment is immediately necessary if it falls within paragraph (a) or (b) of subsection (5) above.

(7) In a case where the treatment is section 58A type treatment by virtue of subsection (1)(b) of that section, treatment is immediately necessary if it falls within such of paragraphs (a) to (d) of subsection (5) above as may be specified in regulations under that section.

(8) For the purposes of subsection (7) above, the regulations—

(a) may make different provision for different cases (and may, in particular, make different provision for different forms of treatment);

(b) may make provision which applies subject to specified exceptions; and

(c) may include transitional, consequential, incidental or supplemental provision.

(9) Subsection (3) of section 62 above applies for the purposes of this section as it applies for the purposes of that section.]

Amendments

This section was inserted by the Mental Health Act 2007 s.35(1). Subss.(4A) and 4(B) were inserted by the Health and Social Care Act 2012 s.299(2).

Definitions

1-861   patient: s.145(1).
community patient: ss.17A(7), 145(1).
responsible clinician: ss.34(1), 64K(6).

General Note

Subsection (2)(a)

If the patient has fluctuating capacity, capacity should be regularly re-assessed. With the exception **1-862**
of s.58A treatments, a mentally capable patient may only be treated without consent on him being
recalled to hospital (s.62A).

Subsection (2)(b)

If a valid consent has been given by a donee or deputy or the Court of Protection (i.e. the consent is **1-863**
valid in that the donee or deputy have the authority to make such a decision (s.64K(4),(5))) the treatment may be given despite the objections of the incapacitated patient. Consent cannot be given if the
patient has capacity. The donee, deputy and the court have an obligation to act in the best interests of
the patient: see ss.4 and 16(3) of the Mental Capacity Act 2005.

Subsection (4)

Apart from capacious consenting patients (see subss.(4A) and (4B)), all community patients receiv- **1-864**
ing the type of treatment which falls under s.58 or 58A must have that treatment certified by a SOAD
in accordance with the provisions of this Part. For treatment specified in s.58(1)(b), i.e. medication, a
certificate is not required immediately, but must be in place after a certain period. This period is one
month from when a patient leaves hospital or three months from when the medication was first given
to the patient (whether that medication was given in the community or in hospital), whichever is later.
The SOAD must certify in writing that it is appropriate for the treatment to be given. The one month
period is specified in s.64B(4). The legal rationale for the alternative period of three months from when
the medication was first given is that during that period the provision of medication is not a "section 58
type treatment" (see subs.(3)) as that section would not have applied to it during that period.
A certificate for a s.58A type treatment is required immediately before the treatment is started.

Certified in writing   Although the *Code of Practice*, at para.25.48, states that the SOAD should
"interview the patient in private if possible", neither interviewing the patient nor medically examining
him is a legal requirement. Therefore, a SOAD can give a certificate if the patient is unwilling to be
interviewed. Before giving a certificate, the SOAD must undertake the consultation exercise provided
for in s.64H(3). Form CTO11 must be used: see reg.28(1) of the English Regulations (in Wales, Form
CO7: see reg.40(4) of the Welsh Regulations).
The SOAD's role when completing the Form is confined to considering whether it would be appropriate for the treatment to be given to the patient. In other words, the SOAD is not required to confirm the
patient's consent to the treatment as the two conditions set out in s.64B(2) are not dependent on each
other. This interpretation is supported by the following advice that the Mental Health Act Commission
(MHAC) received from the Department of Health which is reproduced in the Commission's *Thirteenth
Biennial Report* 2007–2009, at para.3.73:

""Appropriateness" does not include [legal] authority. The Act itself provides that treatment cannot
lawfully be given unless there is authority to do so, and sets out when such authority will exist. So
it is not necessary ... for SOADs to concern themselves with the question of whether there would
be authority to give the treatment. So, in effect, the SOAD is required to consider whether it would
be appropriate for the treatment to be given, assuming there were legal authority to give it."

Paragraph 25.32 of the *Code of Practice* states:

"When giving part 4A certificates, SOADs do not have to certify whether a patient has, or lacks,
capacity to consent to the treatments in question, nor whether a patient with capacity is consenting
or refusing. They may make it a condition of their approval that particular treatments are given only
in certain circumstances. For example, they might specify that a particular treatment is to be given
only with the patient's consent. Similarly, they might specify that a medication may be given up to
a certain dosage if the patient lacks capacity to consent, but that a higher dosage may be given with
the patient's consent."

The fact that a patient who is subject to a community treatment order does not consent to treatment that
is deemed to be appropriate for him suggests that long term s.17 leave would be the more appropriate
option.

Conditions   The Explanatory Notes to the Mental Health Act 2007 state at para.134:

"The SOAD may specify within the certificate that certain treatment can be given to the patient only if certain conditions are satisfied: so, for example, the SOAD could specify that a particular antipsychotic and dosage can only be given in the community if the patient retains capacity to consent to it. The SOAD can also specify whether and if so what treatments can be given to the patient on recall to hospital and the circumstances in which the treatment can be given. For example, the SOAD can specify, if appropriate, that an antipsychotic can be given to the patient on recall without the patient's consent."

If the certificate specifies conditions, the treatment may only be given in accordance with those conditions.

Subsection (4)(a)

1-865   **Appropriate for the treatment to be given**   See ss.64K(8) and 64(3).

Subsections (4A) and (4B)

1-866   These subsections provide that, if the patient consents to the treatment in question, the approved clinician in charge of the treatment will satisfy the certificate requirement by issuing their own Part IVA certificate stating that the patient consents to the treatment and has the capacity to do so. This certificate is sufficient to meet the certificate requirement so long as the patient continues to consent and has capacity to do so: see s.64FA. The subsections do not apply to electro-convulsive therapy for patients under 18. That is because, unless it is an emergency, treatments covered by section 58A may not be given to any patient under 18 (whether or not they are otherwise subject to the Act) without the approval of a SOAD.

For the position where the patient either loses capacity or withdraws his consent, see s.64FA.

Approved clinician in charge   See the note on "Approved Clinician" in s.145(1).

Certified in writing   Using Form CTO 12 (in Wales, Form CO8).

Subsection (5)

1-867   In this provision, the immediacy refers to the need for treatment and not to the consequences that would flow if the treatment was not provided.

Subsection (6)

1-868   Treatment under this provision can be given to a mentally incapacitated patient even though the patient has made an advance decision refusing ECT.

Subsection (9)

1-869   Section 62(3) defines "irreversible" and "hazardous".

[Adult community patients lacking capacity

1-870   **64D.**—(1)   A person is authorised to give relevant treatment to a patient as mentioned in section 64C(2)(c) above if the conditions in subsections (2) to (6) below are met.

(2)   The first condition is that, before giving the treatment, the person takes reasonable steps to establish whether the patient lacks capacity to consent to the treatment.

(3)   The second condition is that, when giving the treatment, he reasonably believes that the patient lacks capacity to consent to it.

(4)   The third condition is that—

(a)   he has no reason to believe that the patient objects to being given the treatment; or

(b) he does have reason to believe that the patient so objects, but it is not necessary to use force against the patient in order to give the treatment.

(5) The fourth condition is that—

    (a) he is the person in charge of the treatment and an approved clinician; or

    (b) the treatment is given under the direction of that clinician.

(6) The fifth condition is that giving the treatment does not conflict with—

    (a) an advance decision which he is satisfied is valid and applicable; or

    (b) a decision made by a donee or deputy or the Court of Protection.

(7) In this section—

    (a) reference to an advance decision is to an advance decision (within the meaning of the Mental Capacity Act 2005) made by the patient; and

    (b) "valid and applicable", in relation to such a decision, means valid and applicable to the treatment in question in accordance with section 25 of that Act.]

Amendment

This section was inserted by the Mental Health Act 2007 s.35(1).

Definitions

relevant treatment: s.64A.   **1-871**
patient: s.145(1).
approved clinician: s.145(1).

General Note

This section sets out the conditions that must be satisfied before relevant treatment (see s.64A) can   **1-872**
be provided to a community patient who lacks the capacity to consent to the treatment. It provides authority to give treatment to the patient for the purposes of ss.64B(2)(a): see 64C(2)(c). The treatment cannot be given if force would have to be used to ensure that an objecting patient received the treatment (subs.(4)), or if it conflicts with a valid and applicable advance decision made under the Mental Capacity Act 2005 (the 2005 Act) or a decision made by a donee, a deputy or the Court of Protection (subs.(6)). Note that s.64G allows for force to be used to provide treatment to a mentally incapacitated patient in an emergency.

Nothing in this section excludes a person's liabilities resulting from his or her negligence in undertaking anything authorised to be done under it (s.64I).

Subsection (2)

The capacity of the patient to consent to the treatment should be assessed using the test set out in   **1-873**
ss.2 and 3 of the 2005 Act (s.64K(2)).

In *R. (on the application of B) v Dr G* [2005] EWHC 1936 (Admin), Charles J. held that a patient who did not accept that he is mentally ill was mentally incapacitated on the ground that he could not "use and weigh" the information relating to his need for medication to treat his mental illness (see s.3(1)(c) of the 2005 Act).

Subsection (4)

The factors to be considered in determining whether a patient objects to the treatment are set out in   **1-874**
s.64J. If the patient does not object to the treatment, the use of force, which is not defined, is permitted under this section "in cases where, for example, the patient is suffering from tremor and physical force is needed as a practical measure to administer the treatment" (Explanatory Notes, para.130).

In unreported cases considered in the October 2018 issue of 39 Essex Chambers "Mental Capacity Report" at p.8, Keehan J., sitting in the Court of Protection, used the Mental Capacity Act 2005 to endorse the provision of forced covert medication in the community for two objecting CTO patients.

Section 64B(3)(b)(ii) provides for a CTO patient to receive treatment if the Court of Protection consents to the treatment on the patient's behalf.

Force The *Code of Practice* states that "force means the actual use of physical force on the patient" (para.24.20).

Subsection (5)(b)

1-875   The patient's GP can only prescribe medication for the patient's mental disorder if it is covered by the SOAD certificate or if a donee or deputy has consented to the medication on the patient's behalf.

Subsection (6)

1-876   Under the terms of the 2005 Act a person who is under the age of 18 cannot make an advance decision or execute a lasting power of attorney.

Advance decision   See subs.(7).

Donee or deputy   The decision must be within the scope of the authority of the donee or deputy: see s.64K(4), (5).

[Child community patients

1-877   **64E.**—(1)   This section applies to the giving of relevant treatment to a community patient who—
  (a)   is not recalled to hospital under section 17E above; and
  (b)   has not attained the age of 16 years.
  (2)   The treatment may not be given to the patient unless—
  (a)   there is authority to give it to him; and
  (b)   if it is section 58 type treatment or section 58A type treatment, the certificate requirement is met.
  (3)   But the certificate requirement does not apply if—
  (a)   giving the treatment to the patient is authorised in accordance with section 64G below; or
  (b)   in a case where the patient is competent to consent to the treatment and does consent to it, the treatment is immediately necessary.
  (4)   Nor does the certificate requirement apply in so far as the administration of medicine to the patient at any time during the period of one month beginning with the day on which the community treatment order is made is section 58 type treatment.
  (5)   The reference in subsection (4) above to the administration of medicine does not include any form of treatment specified under section 58(1)(a) above.
  (6)   For the purposes of subsection (2)(a) above, there is authority to give treatment to a patient if—
  (a)   he is competent to consent to it and he does consent to it; or
  (b)   giving it to him is authorised in accordance with section 64F or 64G below.
  (7)   Subsections [(3) to (4A) and (5) to (9)] of section 64C above have effect for the purposes of this section as they have effect for the purposes of section 64B above [; and for the purpose of this subsection, subsection (4A) of section 64C above has effect as if—
  (a)   the references to treatment were references only to section 58 type treatment,
  (b)   the reference to subsection (2)(a) of section 64C were a reference to subsection (6)(a) of this section, and

    (c)   the reference to capacity to consent were a reference to competence to consent.].

(8)   Regulations made by virtue of section 32(2)(d) above apply for the purposes of this section as they apply for the purposes of Part 2 of this Act.]

Amendments

This section was inserted by the Mental Health Act 2007 s.35(1). The amendments to subs.(7) were made by the Health and Social Care Act 2012 s.299(3).

Definitions

relevant treatment: s.64A. **1-878**
community patient: ss.17A(7), 145(1).
community treatment order: ss.17A(1), 145(1).
hospital: ss.64K(7), 145(1).

General Note

This section identifies when relevant treatment (see s.64A) can be provided to a community patient **1-879** who is under the age of 16 and who has not been recalled to hospital under s.17E. Such treatment cannot be provided to the patient unless

    (a)   he is competent to consent to it and does consent to it, or the giving of the treatment is authorised by s.64F (treatment for child patients lacking competence) or s.64G (emergency treatment for child patients lacking competence) (subss.(2)(a), (6)), and

    (b)   if it is a treatment coming within the scope of s.58 or s.58A, the certificate requirement is met in that a SOAD (or the approved clinician in charge of the treatment if the patient is mentally competent and has consented to the treatment (subs.(7)) has certified that the treatment (or plan of treatment (s.64H(1)) should be given (subs. (2)(b), (7) and s.64C(4)).

The certificate requirement does not apply if the treatment:

    (i)   is emergency treatment which is authorised under s.64G (subs.(3)(a)), or

    (ii)   is immediately necessary (subss.(3)(b), (7), s.64C(5), (6)), or

    (iii)   is medication coming within the scope of s.58(1)(b) and the medication is being given to the patient within a month of the CTO being made (subss.(4), (5)) or three months from when the medication was first given to the patient (whether in the community or in hospital), whichever is later.

A certificate for a s.58A type treatment is required immediately before the treatment is started.

If a certificate is withdrawn by the regulatory authority, the treatment can continue pending compliance with the this section if the person in charge of the treatment considers that the discontinuance of the treatment would cause serious suffering to the patient (s.64H(5)-(9)).

A parent (or another person with parental responsibility) cannot either consent to or refuse treatment for mental disorder on behalf of a child who is subject to a CTO: see para.19.114 of the *Code of Practice*.

Code of Practice

See paras 19.24 to 19.37 of the Code which are concerned with assessing the competence of children **1-880** to consent to treatment.

Subsection (2)

The meaning of "section 58 type treatment or section 58A type treatment" is explained in s.64C(3) **1-881** (subs.(7)).

Subsection (3)(b)

1-882   **Immediately necessary**   See reg.28(2) of the English Regulations and reg.39(a) of the Welsh Regulations.

[Child community patients lacking competence

1-883   **64F.**—(1)   A person is authorised to give relevant treatment to a patient as mentioned in section 64E(6)(b) above if the conditions in subsections (2) to (5) below are met.

(2)   The first condition is that, before giving the treatment, the person takes reasonable steps to establish whether the patient is competent to consent to the treatment.

(3)   The second condition is that, when giving the treatment, he reasonably believes that the patient is not competent to consent to it.

(4)   The third condition is that—

    (a)   he has no reason to believe that the patient objects to being given the treatment; or

    (b)   he does have reason to believe that the patient so objects, but it is not necessary to use force against the patient in order to give the treatment.

(5)   The fourth condition is that—

    (a)   he is the person in charge of the treatment and an approved clinician; or

    (b)   the treatment is given under the direction of that clinician.]

Amendment

This section was inserted by the Mental Health Act 2007 s.35(1).

Definition

1-884   relevant treatment: s.64A.
patient: s.145(1).
approved clinician: s.145(1).

General Note

1-885   This section sets out the conditions that must be satisfied before relevant treatment (see s.64A) can be provided to a community patient who is under the age of 16 and who lacks the competence to consent to the treatment. Children lack competence (the equivalent to "capacity" for adults) if they do not have sufficient understanding and intelligence to enable them fully to understand what is involved in a proposed treatment: see paras 19.34 to 19.37 of the *Code of Practice*. The treatment cannot be given if force would have to be used to ensure that an objecting patient received the treatment (subs.(4)); but force can be used in an emergency (s.64G). As is the case with capacious adults, treatment cannot be given to a child in the community who is competent to consent and does not consent to it.

A person with parental responsibility for a child patient may not consent on the child's behalf to treatment for mental disorder (or refuse it) while the child is a community patient: see para.19.114 of the *Code of Practice*.

Nothing in this section excludes a person's liabilities resulting from his or her negligence in undertaking anything authorised to be done under it (s.64I).

Code of Practice

1-886   See the note to s.64E under this heading.

Subsection (4)

The factors to be considered in determining whether a patient objects to the treatment are set out in s.64J.

1-887

[Withdrawal of consent

64FA.—(1).   Where the consent of a patient to any treatment has been given as mentioned in section 64C(2)(a) above for the purposes of section 64B or 64E above, the patient may at any time before the completion of the treatment withdraw his consent, and those sections shall then apply as if the remainder of the treatment were a separate form of treatment.

1-888

(2)   Subsection (3) below applies where—
  (a)   the consent of a patient to any treatment has been given as mentioned in section 64C(2)(a) above for the purposes of section 64B or 64E above; but
  (b)   before the completion of the treatment, the patient loses capacity or (as the case may be) competence to consent to the treatment.

(3)   The patient shall be treated as having withdrawn his consent and section 64B or (as the case may be) section 64E above shall then apply as if the remainder of the treatment were a separate form of treatment.

(4)   Without prejudice to the application of subsections (1) to (3) above to any treatment given under the plan of treatment to which a patient has consented, a patient who has consented to such a plan may at any time withdraw his consent to further treatment, or to further treatment of any description, under the plan.

(5)   This section shall not preclude the continuation of any treatment, or of treatment under any plan, pending compliance with section 58, 58A, 64B or 64E above if the approved clinician in charge of the treatment considers that the discontinuance of the treatment, or of treatment under the plan, would cause serious suffering to the patient.]

Amendment

This section was inserted by the Health and Social Care Act 2012 s.299(4).

Definitions

approved clinician: s.145(1).
patient: s.145(1).

1-889

General Note

The section provides that a community patient who has consented to treatment may at any time withdraw that consent. It also sets out what happens if a patient who has consented to treatment subsequently loses the capacity to do so. In both cases, the patient will be treated as having withdrawn consent to the treatment in question. A consequence of this is that any approved clinician's certificate relating to the treatment would no longer be valid, and a SOAD's certificate would be required instead. However, subs.(5) provides that treatment may continue whilst a new certificate is being sought, if the approved clinician considers that stopping the treatment would cause serious suffering to the patient. Subsection (5) does not allow treatment to continue against the wishes of a patient who still has capacity to consent, unless the patient is recalled to hospital. This is because a SOAD's certificate does not provide legal authority to give the treatment to a capacious, non-consenting patient.

1-890

[Emergency treatment for patients lacking capacity or competence

64G.—(1)   A person is also authorised to give relevant treatment to a patient as mentioned in section 64C(2)(c) or 64E(6)(b) above if the conditions in subsections (2) to (4) below are met.

1-891

(2) The first condition is that, when giving the treatment, the person reasonably believes that the patient lacks capacity to consent to it or, as the case may be, is not competent to consent to it.

(3) The second condition is that the treatment is immediately necessary.

(4) The third condition is that if it is necessary to use force against the patient in order to give the treatment—

    (a) the treatment needs to be given in order to prevent harm to the patient; and

    (b) the use of such force is a proportionate response to the likelihood of the patient's suffering harm, and to the seriousness of that harm.

(5) Subject to subsections (6) to (8) below, treatment is immediately necessary if—

    (a) it is immediately necessary to save the patient's life; or

    (b) it is immediately necessary to prevent a serious deterioration of the patient's condition and is not irreversible; or

    (c) it is immediately necessary to alleviate serious suffering by the patient and is not irreversible or hazardous; or

    (d) it is immediately necessary, represents the minimum interference necessary to prevent the patient from behaving violently or being a danger to himself or others and is not irreversible or hazardous.

(6) Where the treatment is section 58A type treatment by virtue of subsection (1)(a) of that section, treatment is immediately necessary if it falls within paragraph (a) or (b) of subsection (5) above.

(7) Where the treatment is section 58A type treatment by virtue of subsection (1)(b) of that section, treatment is immediately necessary if it falls within such of paragraphs (a) to (d) of subsection (5) above as may be specified in regulations under section 58A above.

(8) For the purposes of subsection (7) above, the regulations—

    (a) may make different provision for different cases (and may, in particular, make different provision for different forms of treatment);

    (b) may make provision which applies subject to specified exceptions; and

    (c) may include transitional, consequential, incidental or supplemental provision.

(9) Subsection (3) of section 62 above applies for the purposes of this section as it applies for the purposes of that section.]

Amendment

This section was inserted by the Mental Health Act 2007 s.35(1).

Definitions

1-892   relevant treatment: s.64A.
patient: s.145(1).

General Note

1-893   This section sets out the criteria that must be satisfied before relevant treatment (see s.64A) can be given in an emergency to adult community patients who lacks capacity or child community patients who lacks competence, and identifies in subs.(4) when force can be used in order to provide such treatment. The requirement to obtain a certificate from a SOAD does not apply to such treatment (s.64B(3)(a)). The person providing the treatment need not be acting under the direction of an approved clinician (*Code of Practice*, para.24.24).

Emergency treatment can be provided in those rare situations where it is in the best interests of the patient to be immediately treated with force in the community rather than be transported to hospital under the recall power contained in s.17E for the treatment to be provided there. Such treatment can be given even if it conflicts with an advance decision to refuse the treatment or a decision of a donee or a deputy. The provisions of subs.(5) are virtually identical to the criteria that must be satisfied before urgent treatment can be given under s.62.

The emergency circumstances in which s.58A type treatment can be given are more limited than the circumstances in which other treatments can be given in an emergency: see subss.(6) to (8).

Nothing in this section excludes a person's liabilities resulting from his or her negligence in undertaking anything authorised to be done under it (s.64I).

Code of Practice

This section is considered in the following paragraphs of the Code: **1-894**

"24.24 In an emergency, treatment can also be given to part 4A patients who lack capacity to consent to or refuse a treatment (and who have not been recalled to hospital) by anyone, whether or not they are acting under the direction of an approved clinician.

24.25 It is an emergency only if the treatment is immediately necessary to:

* save the patient's life
* prevent a serious deterioration of the patient's condition and the treatment does not have unfavourable physical or psychological consequences which cannot be reversed
* alleviate serious suffering by the patient and the treatment does not have unfavourable physical or psychological consequences which cannot be reversed and does not entail significant physical hazard, or
* prevent patients behaving violently or being a danger to themselves or others and the treatment represents the minimum interference necessary for that purpose, does not have unfavourable physical or psychological consequences which cannot be reversed and does not entail significant physical hazard.

If the treatment is ECT (or medication administered as part of ECT), only the first two categories above apply.

24.26 Where treatment is immediately necessary in these terms, it can be given even though it conflicts with an advance decision or the decision of someone who has the authority under the MCA to refuse it on the patient's behalf.

24.27 In addition, force may be used (whether or not the patient objects), provided that:

* the treatment is necessary to prevent harm to the patient, and
* the force used is proportionate to the likelihood of the patient suffering harm and to the seriousness of that harm.

24.28 These are the only circumstances in which force may be used to treat patients on CTOs who object, without recalling them to hospital. This exception is for situations where the patient's interests would be better served by being given urgently needed treatment by force outside hospital rather than being recalled to hospital. This might, for example, be where the situation is so urgent that recall is not realistic, or where taking patients to hospital would exacerbate their condition, damage their recovery or cause them unnecessary anxiety or suffering. Situations like this should be exceptional."

Subsection (1)

Treatment   Including the treatment specified in reg.28(3) of the English Regulations and reg.39(b)   **1-895**
of the Welsh Regulations.

Subsection (2)

Lacks capacity   See s.64K(2).   **1-896**

Subsection (3)

Immediately necessary   See subss.(5) to (8) and the note on this phrase in s.62(1).   **1-897**

Subsection (4)

1-898   Although physical force cannot be used to provide treatment in order to prevent harm to others, treatment which is aimed at preventing harm to the patient could also have that effect. For example, treatment which is aimed at preventing the patient being aggressive to others could have the effect of preventing harm to the patient through possible retaliation.

Subsection (9)

1-899   Section 62(3) defines "irreversible" and "hazardous".

[Certificates: supplementary provisions

1-900   **64H.**—(1)   A certificate under section 64B(2)(b) or 64E(2)(b) above (a "Part 4A certificate") may relate to a plan of treatment under which the patient is to be given (whether within a specified period or otherwise) one or more forms of section 58 type treatment or section 58A type treatment.

(2)   A Part 4A certificate shall be in such form as may be prescribed by regulations made by the appropriate national authority [; and the regulations may make different provision for the different descriptions of Part 4A certificate].

(3)   Before giving a Part 4A certificate [that falls within section 64C(4) above], the registered medical practitioner concerned shall consult two other persons who have been professionally concerned with the patient's medical treatment but, of those persons—

(a)   at least one shall be a person who is not a registered medical practitioner; and

(b)   neither shall be the patient's responsible clinician or the person in charge of the treatment in question.

(4)   Where a patient is given treatment in accordance with a Part 4A certificate [that falls within section 64C(4) above], a report on the treatment and the patient's condition shall be given by the person in charge of the treatment to the [regulatory authority] if required by that authority.

(5)   The [regulatory authority] may at any time give notice directing that a Part 4A certificate [that falls within section 64C(4) above] shall not apply to treatment given to a patient after a date specified in the notice, and the relevant section shall then apply to any such treatment as if that certificate had not been given.

(6)   The relevant section is—

(a)   if the patient is not recalled to hospital in accordance with section 17E above, section 64B or 64E above;

(b)   if the patient is so recalled or is liable to be detained under this Act following revocation of the community treatment order under section 17F above—

(i)   section 58 above, in the case of section 58 type treatment;

(ii)   section 58A above, in the case of section 58A type treatment; (subject to section 62A(2) above).

(7)   The notice under subsection (5) above shall be given to the person in charge of the treatment in question.

(8)   Subsection (5) above shall not preclude the continuation of any treatment or of treatment under any plan pending compliance with the relevant section if the person in charge of the treatment considers that the discontinuance of the treatment or of treatment under the plan would cause serious suffering to the patient.

(9)   In this section, "the appropriate national authority" means—

(a) in relation to community patients in respect of whom the responsible hospital is in England, the Secretary of State;

(b) in relation to community patients in respect of whom the responsible hospital is in Wales, the Welsh Ministers.]

Amendments

This section was inserted by the Mental Health Act 2007 s.35(1). The amendments to it were made by the Health and Social Care Act 2008 s.52, Sch.3 para.5 and the Health and Social Care Act 2012 s.299(5).

Definitions

patient: s.145(1).   **1-901**
the regulatory authority: s.145(1).
medical treatment: s.145(1),(4).
responsible clinician: ss.64K(6), 145(1).
hospital: ss.64K(7), 145(1).
community treatment order: ss.17A(3), 145(1).
responsible hospital: ss17A(7), 145(1).

General Note

Subsection (2)

Appropriate national authority   See subs.(9).   **1-902**

Subsection (3)

This provision requires that any SOAD certifying that treatment is appropriate in the case of a com-   **1-903**
munity patient must first have consulted with two persons who have been professionally concerned with the patient's treatment, at least one of whom shall not be a doctor, and neither of whom may be the responsible clinician or approved clinician in charge of the treatment in question. As such, there is no positive requirement to consult with a specific type of professional, in contrast to the arrangements for SOAD visits to detained patients under Part IV, where one of the statutory consultees must be a nurse. Paragraph 24.26 of the Reference Guide states:

"[T]he certificate would not authorise any treatment if, at the time it is proposed to give the treatment, the person who is now the patient's responsible clinician or the approved clinician in charge of the treatment in question happens to be one of the two people who were originally consulted by the SOAD before giving the certificate."

The *Code of Practice* guidance on the identification and role of the statutory consultees is reproduced in the notes to s.58(4).

Subsection (4)

For reviews of treatment by the CQC, see s.61 under the heading *Code of Practice*.   **1-904**

Subsections (4), (5)

The regulatory authority   Is the Care Quality Commission or, in relation to Wales, the Welsh   **1-905**
Ministers (in practice, Healthcare Inspectorate Wales) (s.145(1)).

Subsection (5)

Relevant section   See subs.(6).   **1-906**

[Liability for negligence

1-907   **64I.—** Nothing in section 64D, 64F or 64G above excludes a person's civil liability for loss or damage, or his criminal liability, resulting from his negligence in doing anything authorised to be done by that section.]

Amendment

This section was inserted by the Mental Health Act 2007 s.35(1).

[Factors to be considered in determining whether patient objects to treatment

1-908   **64J.—**(1) In assessing for the purposes of this Part whether he has reason to believe that a patient objects to treatment, a person shall consider all the circumstances so far as they are reasonably ascertainable, including the patient's behaviour, wishes, feelings, views, beliefs and values.

    (2) But circumstances from the past shall be considered only so far as it is still appropriate to consider them.]

Amendment

This section was inserted by the Mental Health Act 2007 s.35(1).

Definition

1-909   patient: s.145(1).

General Note

1-910   An objection is not rendered invalid because a view is taken that it is unreasonable. "The question is simply whether the patient objects – the reasonableness (or unreasonableness) of the objection is irrelevant" (*Code of Practice*, para.24.20). The Code offers the following guidance on identifying whether patient objects:

> "24.21 In deciding whether patients object to treatment, all the relevant evidence should be taken into account, so far as it reasonably can be. In many cases, patients will be perfectly able to state their objection, either verbally or by their dissenting behaviour. In other cases, especially where patients are unable to communicate (or only able to communicate to a limited extent), clinicians will need to consider the patient's behaviour, wishes, feelings, views, beliefs and values, both present and past, so far as they can be ascertained.
> 24.22 If there is reason to think that a patient would object, if able to do so, then the patient should be taken to be objecting. Occasionally, it may be that the patient's behaviour initially suggests an objection to being treated, but is in fact not directed at the treatment at all. In that case the patient would not be taken to be objecting."

[Interpretation of Part 4A

1-911   **64K.—**(1) This Part of this Act is to be construed as follows.

    (2) References to a patient who lacks capacity are to a patient who lacks capacity within the meaning of the Mental Capacity Act 2005.

    (3) References to a patient who has capacity are to be read accordingly.

    (4) References to a donee are to a donee of a lasting power of attorney (within the meaning of section 9 of the Mental Capacity Act 2005) created by the patient, where the donee is acting within the scope of his authority and in accordance with that Act.

(5) References to a deputy are to a deputy appointed for the patient by the Court of Protection under section 16 of the Mental Capacity Act 2005, where the deputy is acting within the scope of his authority and in accordance with that Act.

(6) Reference to the responsible clinician shall be construed as a reference to the responsible clinician within the meaning of Part 2 of this Act.

(7) References to a hospital include a registered establishment.

(8) Section 64(3) above applies for the purposes of this Part of this Act as it applies for the purposes of Part 4 of this Act.]

Amendment

This section was inserted by the Mental Health Act 2007 s.35(1).

Definition

patient: s.145(1).   **1-912**
hospital: s.145(2).
registered establishment: ss.34(1), 145(1).

General Note

Subsection (6)

Responsible clinician   See s.34(1) and the notes thereto.   **1-913**

PART V MENTAL HEALTH REVIEW TRIBUNALS

CONSTITUTION, ETC.

Mental Health Review [Tribunal for Wales]

65.—[(1)   There shall [be a Mental Health Review Tribunal for Wales.]   **1-914**

(1A)   The purpose of [that tribunal] is to deal with applications and references by and in respect of patients under the provisions of this Act.]

(2)   The provisions of Schedule 2 to this Act shall have effect with respect to the constitution of [the Mental Health Review Tribunal for Wales].

(3)   Subject to the provisions of Schedule 2 to this Act, and to rules made by the Lord Chancellor under this Act, the jurisdiction of [the Mental Health Review Tribunal for Wales] may be exercised by any three or more of its members, and references in this Act to [the Mental Health Review Tribunal for Wales] shall be construed accordingly.

[(4)   The Welsh Ministers may pay to the members of the Mental Health Review Tribunal for Wales such remuneration and allowances as they may determine, and defray the expenses of that tribunal to such amount as they may determine, and may provide for that tribunal such officers and servants, and such accommodation, as that tribunal may require.]

Amendments

The amendments to this section were made by the Mental Health Act 2007 s.38(2) and SI 2008/2883 art.9, Sch.3 para.45.

Definition

1-915   patient: s.145(1).

General Note

Wales—The Mental Health Review Tribunal for Wales

1-916   This section, together with Sch.2, provides for the establishment of a Mental Health Review Tribunal for Wales. This Tribunal, which has a President and covers the whole of Wales, has its office within the Welsh Parliament's administrative building in Cardiff. The equivalent tribunal in England, the First-tier Tribunal (Mental Health), was established under the Tribunals, Courts and Enforcement Act 2007 (the 2007 Act). The two tribunals have identical powers and duties to discharge patients and to make recommendations.

One curious difference between the two tribunals is that while the requirement for a practicing medical practitioner to have a licence to practice has been disapplied with respect to First-tier Tribunal medical members by SI 2008/2692, r.1(2), similar action has not been taken with respect to medical members of the Welsh tribunal. The position of the Welsh medical member is governed by Sch.2, para.1(b), which states that a medical member must be a registered medical practitioner, and Sch.1 to the Interpretation Act 1978 which defines a registered medical practitioner as "a fully registered person within the meaning of the Medical Act 1983 who holds a licence to practise under that Act".

The website of the Mental Health Review Tribunal for Wales is: *https:// mentalhealthreviewtribunal.gov.wales/*.

England—The First-tier Tribunal (Mental Health)

1-917   In the report of his Review of Tribunals, *Tribunals for Users—One System, One Service*, published in August 2001, Sir Andrew Leggatt recommended extensive reform to the tribunals system. He recommended that tribunals should be brought together in a single system, that they should become separate from their current sponsoring departments, and that such a system be administered instead by a single Tribunals Service. The Government agreed and its response is to be found in the 2007 Act. The Act creates two new, generic tribunals, the First-tier Tribunal and the Upper Tribunal, into which existing tribunal jurisdictions have been transferred: see SI 2008/2833 art.3, Sch.1. The Upper Tribunal is primarily an appellate tribunal from the First-tier Tribunal.

The 2007 Act also provides for the establishment of "chambers" within the two tribunals which enable tribunals to be grouped appropriately. A Health, Education and Social Care Chamber has been created which, inter alia, has functions relating to "applications and references by and in respect of patients under the provisions of the Mental Health Act 1983 or paragraph 5(2) of the Schedule to the Repatriation of Prisoners Act 1984" (SI 2008/2684 art.5(h)). The tribunal within the Health, Education and Social Care Chamber that deals with mental health cases is known as the First-tier Tribunal (Mental Health). Each Chamber is headed by a Chamber President and the tribunals judiciary is headed by a Senior President of Tribunals. The First-tier Tribunal (Mental Health) only has jurisdiction in England.

The 2007 Act also provides for the membership of the tribunals and the making of Tribunal Procedure Rules, which can be supplemented by means of practice directions. The First-tier Tribunal (Health, Education and Social Care Chamber) Rules 2008 (SI 2008/2699) (the Tribunal Rules) and related practice directions are reproduced in Part 3.

An account of various aspects of the operation of the First-tier Tribunal (Mental Health) can be found in the General Note to the Tribunal Rules.

Appeals (Also see the notes to r.46 of the Tribunal Rules in Part 3)

1-918   A decision, apart from an "excluded decision" but including an interlocutory decision (*LS v London Borough of Lambeth* [2010] UKUT 461 (AAC)), of the First-tier Tribunal (and the Mental Health Review Tribunal for Wales: see s.78A) may be appealed to the Administrative Appeals Chamber of the Upper Tribunal (s.11 of the 2007 Act and SI 2008/2684, arts 6, 7(a)(i) and (iv)), and a decision of the Upper Tribunal may be appealed to the Court of Appeal. However, the Court of Appeal cannot grant permission to appeal from a refusal of the Upper Tribunal to review its decision to refuse permission to appeal. The only remedy of the aggrieved party is by way of judicial review (*Samuda v Secretary of State for Work and Pensions* [2014] EWCA Civ 1; [2014] 3 All E.R. 201). Permission to appeal to the Court of Appeal should only be granted if the appeal raises an important point of principle or practice, or there is some other compelling reason for the Court of Appeal to consider the appeal (*RH v South London and Maudsley NHS Foundation Trust* [2010] EWCA Civ 1273; [2010] M.H.L.R. 341, para.36). An appeal to the Upper Tribunal can only succeed if "the making of the decision concerned involved the making of an error on a point of law" (s.12(1) of the 2007 Act).

The rights of appeal may only be exercised with permission of the First-tier Tribunal or the Upper Tribunal itself. If the Upper Tribunal exercises its discretion to set aside the decision of the First-tier Tribunal it must either remit the case to the tribunal with directions for its reconsideration, or remake the decision: see s.12(2) of the 2007 Act. The procedure of the Upper Tribunal, which is a superior court of record (2007 Act s.3(5)) and can therefore lay down authoritative precedents, is governed by the Tribunal Procedure (Upper Tribunal) Rules 2008 (SI 2008/2698). The Upper Tribunal has a similar power to that of the First-tier Tribunal to review its own decisions, and to take similar actions following a review (2007 Act s.10). The Upper Tribunal has published a leaflet on "Appealing to the Administrative Appeals Chamber of the Upper Tribunal from the First-tier Tribunal Mental Health Decisions", a form for applying for permission to appeal (Form UT3), and a guidance note to accompany the form. The Upper Tribunal also deals with most of the judicial review cases relating to the tribunal which previously would have been dealt with by the High Court. Applications to the Upper Tribunal for judicial review may be made by virtue of ss.15 to 18 of the 2007 Act where the application does not seek a declaration of incompatibility under the Human Rights Act 1998 and it is within the scope of *Practice Direction (Upper Tribunal: Judicial Review Jurisdiction)* [2009] 1 W.L.R. 327. In *R. (on the application of OK) v First-tier Tribunal* [2017] UKUT 22 (AAC) at para.3, UT Judge Jacobs said: "The existence of a right of appeal, is usually (although not necessarily) a bar to bringing judicial review proceedings: *R (Khan) v Secretary of State for the Home Department* [2015] 1 WLR 747". The Upper Tribunal is subject to the jurisdiction of the High Court by way of judicial review but only where there is an important point of principle or practice or some other compelling reason to review the case (*R. (on the application of Cart) v The Upper Tribunal* [2011] UKSC 28; [2011] 4 All E.R. 127).

The Upper Tribunal does not have any habeas corpus jurisdiction (*AS v First-tier Tribunal*, Upper Tribunal Case No.JR/3048/2012 para.3).

As it is exercising a jurisdiction of equivalent status, the Upper Tribunal is not bound by decisions of the High Court, but will follow them unless convinced they are wrong (*Secretary of State for Justice v RB* [2010] UKUT 454 (AAC); [2011] M.H.L.R. 37, para.47).

Rules of Precedence in the Upper Tribunal

The following guidelines were identified by the Upper Tribunal in *Dorset Healthcare NHS Foundation Trust v MH* [2009] UKUT 4 (AAC); [2009] M.H.L.R. 102, para.37:　　**1-919**

"(i)　　Judges of the Upper Tribunal in the Administrative Appeals Court (AAC) speak with equal authority. All their decisions may be cited to the Upper Tribunal, First-tier Tribunals and other tribunals from which appeals to the AAC come and the appropriate decision-making authorities. Where they decide questions of legal principle they must be followed by the appropriate decision-making authorities and the tribunals below in cases involving the application of that principle, unless they can be distinguished. It should be borne in mind that similarity in underlying facts does not automatically give rise to similarity in the principle to be applied and questions of fact should not be elevated into questions of legal principle.

(ii)　　If confronted with decisions which conflict, the appropriate decision-making authority and tribunals below must prefer the decision of a Three-Judge Panel of the AAC to that of a single judge.

(iii)　　In so far as the AAC is concerned, on questions of legal principle, a single judge shall follow a decision of a Three-Judge Panel of the AAC ... unless there are compelling reasons why he should not, as, for instance, a decision of a superior court affecting the legal principles involved. A single judge in the interests of comity and to avoid confusion on questions of legal principle normally follows the decisions of other single judges. It is recognised however that a slavish adherence to this could lead to the perpetuation of error and he is not bound to do so."

Habeas Corpus and Judicial Review

If a patient considers that his detention was unlawful he can attempt to secure his release by making　　**1-920** an application to the High Court for a writ of habeas corpus. The writ of habeas corpus, which requires the detaining body to show lawful justification for a detention, runs to the party having the applicant in his custody (the hospital managers) and not the doctor who made medical recommendation in support of an application under Pt II (*R. v South Western Hospital, Managers Ex p. M* [1994] 1 All E.R. 161). If the writ is issued, the applicant must be released. An alternative course of action would be to make an application for the judicial review of the decision to detain him. Most cases that would in the past have resulted in applications to the High Court for the judicial review of a tribunal decision will now be dealt with as appeals on points of law to the Upper Tribunal, which also has a judicial review jurisdiction (see above). The Upper Tribunal has no jurisdiction over the decisions of hospital managers taken under s.23.

The distinction between the habeas corpus and judicial review procedures was explained by Lord Donaldson M.R. in the following extract from his judgment in *R. v Secretary of State for the Home Department Ex p. Cheblak* [1991] 2 All E.R. 319 at 322, 323, a case where the applicant was seeking to challenge his arrest and the decision to deport him:

"Although, as I have said, the two forms of relief which Mr. Cheblak seeks are inter-related on the facts of his case, they are essentially different. A writ of habeas corpus will issue where someone is detained without any authority or the purported authority is beyond the powers of the person authorising the detention and so is unlawful. *The remedy of judicial review* is available where the decision or action sought to be impugned is within the powers of the person taking it but, due to procedural error, a misappreciation of the law, a failure to take account of relevant matters, a taking account of irrelevant matters or the fundamental unreasonableness of the decision or action, it should never have been taken. In such a case the decision or action is lawful, unless and until it is set aside by a court of competent jurisdiction. In the case of detention, if the warrant, or the underlying decision to deport, were set aside but the detention continued, a writ of habeas corpus would issue."

The distinction between the two forms of proceedings was applied to the Act in *Re S-C (Mental Patient: Habeas Corpus)* [1996] 1 All E.R. 532, CA, where the patient was challenging the lawfulness of his detention on the ground that the application for his detention under s.3 was not "duly completed" as required by s.6(1) because a condition precedent relating to the application was not present in that the patient's nearest relative had not been consulted as required by s.11(4). The Court held that as the patient's challenge was not directed to an administrative decision but to the jurisdiction of the hospital managers to detain him, an application for habeas corpus was the appropriate remedy rather than proceedings for judicial review. In *B v Barking Havering and Brentwood Community Healthcare NHS Trust* [1999] 1 F.L.R. 106, CA, Lord Woolf M.R. referred to a passage in the judgment of Sir Thomas Bingham M.R. in Re S-C where his Lordship said that on the facts of that case "an application for habeas corpus is *an* appropriate, and possibly even the appropriate course to pursue". Lord Woolf expressed his disagreement with the suggestion that "possibly" an application for habeas corpus was the only procedure that was appropriate. While accepting that in *Re S-C* habeas corpus was an appropriate procedure, his Lordship suggested that judicial review was equally appropriate and would even have advantages over habeas corpus. His Lordship would discourage applications for habeas corpus unless it was clear that no other form of relief would be required. Where applications were made for both judicial review and habeas corpus, the proceedings should be harmonised if at all possible. In the Northern Irish case of *Re SM's Application for a Writ of Habeas Corpus* [2020] NIQB 73, Keegan J. said at para.4:

"[H]abeas corpus has more than once been found by the European Court of Human Rights to be an inadequate remedy because it fails to provide the court with sufficiently intensive powers to review the factual basis or judgments upon which detention has been ordered. This flows from *X v United Kingdom* [1982] 4 EHRR 188 and *HL v United Kingdom* [2005] 40 EHRR 32."

In this case, an application for habeas corpus was refused where a patient remained detained in hospital under the Mental Health (Northern Ireland) Order 1986 despite a mental health tribunal finding that he ought to be conditionally discharged. The hospital was seeking declaratory relief in the High Court as to the lawfulness of the conditions to be imposed and whether they would breach the patient's rights under art.5 of the ECHR. The court found that that was an appropriate course of action, provided it took place within a reasonable time.

1-921   In *Re Doreen Trew* [2000] M.H.L.R. 53, the applicant submitted that the court considering the remedy of habeas corpus is not limited to considering whether the procedural requisites for detention are met, but can also take action where there is inadequate evidence to justify the detention. Owen J., in refusing the application, held that although there was authority to support the contention that habeas corpus is available when there is no evidence to justify the decision to detain (see *R. v Board of Control Ex p. Rutty* [1956] 2 Q.B. 109), this does not support an argument that when a case before a tribunal is strong, but no decision has been given because the tribunal adjourned the hearing, the court hearing the application can consider the evidence, sideline the tribunal, and find that the tribunal should discharge. His Lordship said that in these circumstances "it is evident that the tribunal should make the decision".

The court or Upper Tribunal considering an application for judicial review is exercising a public law jurisdiction and is not required to grant the application even if unlawfulness is established. In order to succeed in an application one of the established grounds must be made out, namely illegality, irrationally or procedural impropriety. The court will also consider whether there has been a breach of the applicant's rights under the European Convention on Human Rights (*R. v Secretary of State for the Home Department, Ex p. Daly* [2001] 2 A.C. 532, HL).

If, on an application for judicial review an order quashing the decision of the tribunal to discharge the patient is made, this has the effect of treating the decision to discharge as never having been made and restoring the patient to the status of a detained patient (*R. (on the application of Wirral Health Authority and Wirral Borough Council) v Mental Health Review Tribunal and DE* [2001] EWCA Civ 1901; [2002] M.H.L.R. 34). However, the remedies afforded on judicial review are as flexible as justice requires and the need for a fresh tribunal decision does not automatically require a quashing order. In *R. (on the application of the Secretary of State for the Home Department) v Mental Health Review Tribunal and BR* [2005] EWCA Civ 1616; [2006] M.H.L.R. 172, the patient appealed against the effect of a quashing order made following a successful appeal by the Secretary of State against a decision by a tribunal that the patient be unconditionally discharged from hospital. The issue before the tribunal was whether discharge should be absolute or conditional, not whether he was entitled to be discharged at all. The effect of the quashing order was to allow the patient to be detained again, which is what happened. On allowing the appeal, the Court of Appeal made orders quashing as much of the tribunal's decision as granted the patient an absolute discharge, and declaring that pending a rehearing the patient is entitled to be treated as having been conditionally discharged. Sedley L.J. said at para.16:

"Modern public law is quite capable enough to do this if necessary, and here it was called for by the requirements both of the common law and the European Convention on Human Rights that nobody is to be deprived of his liberty except according to law."

APPLICATIONS AND REFERENCES CONCERNING PART II PATIENTS

Applications to tribunals

66.—(1) Where—   **1-922**
- (a) a patient is admitted to a hospital in pursuance of an application for admission for assessment; or
- (b) a patient is admitted to a hospital in pursuance of an application for admission for treatment; or
- (c) a patient is received into guardianship in pursuance of a guardianship application; or
- [(ca) a community treatment order is made in respect of a patient; or
- (cb) a community treatment order is revoked under section 17F above in respect of a patient; or]
  [...]
- (e) a patient is transferred from guardianship to a hospital in pursuance of regulations made under section 19 above; or
- (f) a report is furnished under section 20 above in respect of a patient and the patient is not discharged [under section 23 above]; or
- [(fza) a report is furnished under section 20A above in respect of a patient and the patient is not discharged under section 23 above; or]
- [(fa) a report is furnished under subsection (2) of section 21B above in respect of a patient and subsection (5) of that section applies (or subsections (5) and (6)(b) of that section apply) in the case of the report; or
- [(faa) a report is furnished under subsection (2) of section 21B above in respect of a community patient and subsection (6A) of that section applies (or subsections (6A) and (6B)(b) of that section apply) in the case of the report; or]
  [...]

(g)   a report is furnished under section 25 above in respect of a patient who is detained in pursuance of an application for admission for treatment [or a community patient]; or
[...]

(h)   an order is made under section 29 above [on the ground specified in paragraph (c) or (d) of subsection (3) of that section] in respect of a patient who is or subsequently becomes liable to be detained or subject to guardianship under Part II of this Act [or who is a community patient],

an application may be made to [the appropriate tribunal] within the relevant period—

    (i)   by the patient (except in the cases mentioned in paragraphs (g) and (h) above) [...] and

    (ii)   in the cases mentioned in paragraphs (g) and (h) above, by his nearest relative.

(2)   In subsection (1) above "the relevant period" means—

    (a)   in the case mentioned in paragraph (a) of that subsection, 14 days beginning with the day on which the patient is admitted as so mentioned;

    (b)   in the case mentioned in paragraph (b) of that subsection, six months beginning with the day on which the patient is admitted as so mentioned;

    (c)   in the [case mentioned in paragraph (c)] of that subsection, six months beginning with the day on which the application is accepted;

    [(ca)   in the case mentioned in paragraph (ca) of that subsection, six months beginning with the day on which the community treatment order is made;

    (cb)   in the case mentioned in paragraph (cb) of that subsection, six months beginning with the day on which the community treatment order is revoked;]

    (d)   [in the case mentioned in paragraph (g)] of that subsection, 28 days beginning with the day on which the applicant is informed that the report has been furnished;

    (e)   in the case mentioned in paragraph (e) of that subsection, six months beginning with the day on which the patient is transferred;

    (f)   in the case mentioned in paragraph (f) [or (fa) of that subsection, the period or periods] for which authority for the patient's detention or guardianship is renewed by virtue of the report;

    [(fza)   in the cases mentioned in paragraphs (fza) and (faa) of that subsection, the period or periods for which the community treatment period is extended by virtue of the report;]
[...]

    (g)   in the case mentioned in paragraph (h) of that subsection, 12 months beginning with the date of the order, and in any subsequent period of 12 months during which the order continues in force.

[(2A)   Nothing in subsection (1)(b) above entitles a community patient to make an application by virtue of that provision even if he is admitted to a hospital on being recalled there under section 17E above.]

(3)   Section 32 above shall apply for the purposes of this section as it applies for the purposes of Pt II of this Act.

[(4)   In this Act "the appropriate tribunal" means the First-tier Tribunal or the Mental Health Review Tribunal for Wales.

(5)   For provision determining to which of those tribunals applications by or in respect of a patient under this Act shall be made, see section 77(3) and (4) below.]

Amendments

The amendments to this section were made by the Mental Health Act 2007 ss.1(4), 25, 36(3), 55, Sch.1 para.13, Sch.11 Pts 1 and 5 and SI 2008/2883 art.9, Sch.3 para.46.

Definitions

patient: s.145(1).   **1-923**
hospital: ss.79(6), 145(1).
application for admission for assessment: ss.2, 145(1).
application for admission for treatment: ss.3, 145(1).
guardianship application: s.7(1).
nearest relative: ss.26(3), 145(1).
community treatment order: ss.17A(7), 145(1).
community patient: ss.17A(7), 145(1).
community treatment period: ss.20A(2), 145(1).
the appropriate tribunal: subs.(4).

General Note

This section identifies the occasions on which a patient or his nearest relative may make an applica-   **1-924**
tion to a tribunal. By virtue of ss.132(1)(b) and 132A, hospital managers have a duty to inform patients of their right to make an application. If either the patient or the nearest relative changes his mind subsequent to making an application, the application must proceed unless it is formally withdrawn with the consent of the tribunal under r.17 the Tribunal Rules. An application lapses if the patient is no longer subject to the provisions of the Act. Application forms and other tribunal information can be accessed at: *www.gov.uk/courts-tribunals/first-tier-tribunal-mental-health*.

In *VS v St Andrew's Healthcare* [2018] UKUT 250 (AAC); [2018] M.H.L.R. 337 at para.2, UT Judge Jacobs identified the test of capacity required by a patient to bring proceedings before the tribunal:

"The patient must understand that they are being detained against their wishes and that the First-tier Tribunal is a body that will be able to decide whether they should be released."

In *SM v Livewell CIC* [2020] UKUT 191 (AAC); [2021] M.H.L.R. 131, para.77, the Upper Tribunal held that "the test of capacity formulated in *VS* is accurate and appropriate". The UT said that the test "is deliberately couched at a low level" (para.77e) and that in "summary the applicant must have sufficient understanding that she is detained and that the Tribunal has the power to release her from that detention" (para.87a). The UT emphasised that:

"i.   The test is less demanding than that required for the conduct of an application.
ii.   It is not necessary that the patient has a sophisticated understanding of the powers of the Tribunal: it is sufficient if she understands that the Tribunal can order her release" (para.87b).

The court made the following observations at para.86: (i) wherever possible the applicant and her representatives should be alerted that her capacity to make the application may be an issue and (ii) if the tribunal considers that the applicant's capacity has fluctuated and, while she did not have capacity at the time of the application, she does have capacity at the time of the hearing, the tribunal should consider inviting the applicant to make a fresh application, abridging any of the procedural obligations and proceeding to consider the substance of the application.

With regard to suggesting a referral to the Secretary of State, the court said at para.88:

"(a)   The Code says that hospital managers should raise this possibility with the Secretary of State if, among other reasons, the patient lacks capacity to do so herself.
(b)   However, the Code also says that anyone can make such a suggestion to the Secretary of State. The IMHA who will have seen the patient and had the opportunity to assess their

wishes would be well suited to make the suggestion to the Secretary of State, if the IMHA considered that the patient wished to leave but lacked capacity to make an application to the Tribunal.

(c)   A third possibility would be the Tribunal itself. In a case, such as the present, where the Tribunal had found (a) that the patient lacked capacity, but (b) wished to leave the hospital, it would have been very sensible for the Tribunal to have done so.

(d)   Indeed, in other cases (uncomplicated by the patient's pregnancy and imminent confinement in this case) a combination of these factors may well lead the Tribunal to consider whether, before striking out the application, it would be sensible to adjourn for a short period to see if the Secretary of State wished to make a reference so that the Tribunal could consider as expeditiously as possible whether the statutory conditions for detention were made out"

Although an application has to be made in writing, it can be signed by any person authorised by the patient to do so on his behalf: see r.32(1) of the Tribunal Rules. This could be a relative, a social worker, an advocate, or a nurse, provided that the patient has sufficient capacity to authorise that person to act for him.

Donees of lasting powers of attorneys and deputies appointed by the Court of Protection are able to exercise a patient's rights to apply to the tribunal for discharge from detention, guardianship or a community treatment order (CTO) if they have the relevant authority under the LPA or the order of the court appointing them and the patient concerned lacks the capacity to do so themselves. Such an application would be made "in respect of" the patient for the purposes of s.77(3): also see para.7.7 of the *Code of Practice* and the notes on r.32(1)(b) of the Tribunal Rules.

In *R. (on the application of OK) v First-tier Tribunal* [2017] UKUT 22 (AAC), an application to the tribunal had been made by a solicitor on behalf of the patient. The tribunal found that the patient, who was detained under s.3, lacked the mental capacity to authorise another person to act on his behalf. In striking out the application using the power under r.8 of the Tribunal Rules, UT Judge Jacobs said that the approach that had been advocated by the House of Lords *R. (on the application of H) v Secretary of State for Health* [2005] UKHL 60 with respect to a mentally incapacitated patient whose s.2 detention had been extended by s.29(4) was equally applicable to the case before him. This approach required the Secretary of State to use the power under s.67(1) to make a reference to the tribunal in order to avoid a violation of the patient's rights under art.5(4) of the European Convention on Human Rights: also note the following paragraphs of the *Code of Practice*:

"37.45 Hospital managers should consider asking the Secretary of State to make a reference in respect of any patients whose rights under article 5(4) of the ECHR might otherwise be at risk of being violated because they are unable (for whatever reason) to have their cases considered by the Tribunal speedily following their initial detention or at reasonable intervals afterwards.

37.46 In particular, they should normally seek such a reference in any case where:

- a patient's detention under section 2 has been extended under section 29 of the Act pending the outcome of an application to the county court for the displacement of their nearest relative
- the patient lacks the capacity to request a reference, or
- either the patient's case has never been considered by the Tribunal, or a significant period has passed since it was last considered."

It is therefore the case that if a reference is made under s.67(1), a Convention right is not violated in a situation where a patient either lacks the capacity to decide to apply to the tribunal or to authorise anyone to make an application on his behalf. The H case is considered in the note on Human Rights Act 1998 in s.29.

In *R. v South Thames Mental Health Review Tribunal Ex p. M* [1998] C.O.D. 38, Collins J. held that the right of a patient to make an application to a tribunal is founded on the patient's admission, which is something that happens in a moment of time, and not on his detention. Applying this ruling to the situation of a patient who is admitted and detained under s.2 and who is subsequently detained under s.3 during the currency of the s.2, his Lordship held that the following passage from para.5.3 of the *Code of Practice* (1993 edition) is correct:

"Changing a patient's status from section 2 to section 3 will not deprive him of a Mental Health Review Tribunal hearing if the change takes place after a valid application has been made to the Tribunal but before it has been heard. The patient's right to apply for a Tribunal under section 66(1)(b) in the first period of detention after his change of status are unaffected."

His Lordship said that in these circumstances the tribunal must consider the patient's case by using the s.3 criteria set out in s.72(1)(b).

Ex p.M was distinguished by Plender J. in *R. (on the application of MN) v Mental Health Review Tribunal* [2008] EWHC 3383 (Admin). In *GM v Dorset Healthcare NHS Trust* [2020] UKUT 152 (AAC) which is noted below, UT Judge Jacobs applied the approach that had been adopted in *MN* and said that "there is no universal rule that applies in all cases of a change of status and that the significance of a change of status depends upon the proper analysis of the relevant sections of the Act" (para.36).

Does an application to the tribunal by a s.3 patient lapse on the patient being made subject to CTO? This question was answered in *AA v Cheshire and Wirral Partnership NHS Foundation Trust* [2009] UKUT 195 (AAC); [2009] M.H.L.R. 308 where UT Judge Rowland held that a tribunal has the power—or, if the conditions of s.72(1)(c) are satisfied, a duty—to direct that a person subject to a CTO be discharged notwithstanding that that person made the application to the tribunal while liable to be detained under s.2 or 3. Therefore, an application to the tribunal made by or on behalf of a person detained under s.2 or 3 does not lapse if a CTO is made in respect of that person before the application is determined. The tribunal will consider the case using the CTO criteria. Judge Rowland said at para.61:

> "[P]arties need to co-operate sensibly with each other and the First-tier Tribunal if a patient is made the subject of a CTO while an application to the tribunal is pending. In particular, it will clearly be incumbent on any representative of the applicant to inform the tribunal as soon as possible whether or not the application is being withdrawn and it is also clearly incumbent on all parties to inform the tribunal whether or not a postponement of any hearing that has already been fixed will be required in the light of the change of circumstances."

In *KF v Birmingham and Solihull Mental Health NHS Foundation Trust* [2010] UKUT 185 (AAC); [2010] M.H.L.R. 176, a three judge panel of the Upper Tribunal (UT) was satisfied that AA was correctly decided. The issue of principle that was considered in this case was: what should happen where an appeal from a tribunal's substantive decision on a s.2 application is overtaken by the patient's detention under s.3. Having undertaken a comprehensive analysis, the tribunal concluded that:

> "… any movement from s.2 to s.3 or to community patient status does not affect the continuing validity of an extant and undetermined application or reference to the First-tier Tribunal. The application or reference still falls to be determined by the tribunal in accordance with the patient's status at the time of the actual hearing and subject to the relevant criteria under section 72(1)(a)-(c)" (para.59).

The use of the tribunal's case management powers to deal with the practical consequences of this finding was considered at para.60:

> "The effective use of the First-tier Tribunal's case management powers should enable outstanding proceedings to be consolidated, heard and determined together…. [T]he position may be more complicated where there is a change in the patient's status from s.3 to a CTO. Different clinicians and other mental health professionals may become involved in the patient's care and reports provided by the professionals who were involved in the patient's care whilst he or she was an in-patient may not address the criteria which the First-tier Tribunal will have to consider at the hearing in accordance with the patient's status at that time. This is an important factor which judges dealing with case management will need to keep firmly in mind when using case management powers, to ensure that cases are dealt with in a timely fashion and that, when appropriate and possible, hearing dates already fixed are retained for the hearing of the new application or reference. Appropriate and imaginative use of the case management powers should be encouraged to ensure that the relevant professionals are able to provide the required reports in time, notwithstanding the presence of a sometimes rapidly changing landscape in respect of the patient's status."

It is not always appropriate for the tribunal to refuse permission to appeal a s.2 application on the ground that the appeal was academic because the patient had in the meantime been detained under s.3. The UT said at para.30 (also see the note to r.17 of the Tribunal Rules):

> "In general, unless there is good reason why not, if the First-tier Tribunal is asked to review a tribunal decision on a s.2 application, and concludes that it involves an error of law, then the appropriate way forward is for the First-tier Tribunal to set aside the substantive decision and to re-list the case for hearing together with any existing s.3 application."

The UT rejected a submission that the discharge of the patient should inevitably result in the tribunal declining to continue with the proceedings as there "may well be circumstances in which it remains appropriate for there to be further scrutiny of the initial tribunal decision, notwithstanding the individual's subsequent discharge. There may be a danger that a future decision-maker may give inappropriate weight to a flawed decision. Moreover, there may be an urgent need for the legal principles at stake to be clarified" (para.41).

In *R. (on the application of SR) v Mental Health Review Tribunal* [2005] EWHC 2923 (Admin); [2006] M.H.L.R. 121 Stanley Burnton J. held that an application to a tribunal under s.3 did not survive if the patient was discharged and made subject to "after-care under supervision" under the repealed s.25A. The reasoning in this case was described as being "defective" by UT Judge Jacobs in *AD'A v Cornwall Partnership NHS Trust* [2020] UKUT 110 (AAC); [2021] M.H.L.R. 101. Consequentially the decision "should not be applied beyond its immediate context, which no longer obtains" (para.21). In *AD'A*, the patient made an application to the tribunal while she was detained under s.3. She was subsequently sent to a care home on s.17 leave and was received into guardianship under s.7. The tribunal decided that it did not have jurisdiction after the guardianship came into effect and struck out the proceedings. Judge Jacobs held that the tribunal had been wrong to strike out the patient's case for want of jurisdiction. The tribunal's jurisdiction arose from the s.3 application, and none of the subsequent changes (including a new right to apply to tribunal, different tribunal powers, and different parties) affected that jurisdiction. Judge Jacobs said at para.18:

> "The tribunal's powers are conferred on it in exercise of its jurisdiction. They are not themselves matters of jurisdiction. The jurisdiction remains the same: to decide whether to discharge the patient. The conditions that decide how the jurisdiction to discharge is to be exercised have changed, but the ultimate issue for the tribunal has not.
>
> The change in the parties could be effected by substitution of the local social services authority for the managers under rule 9(1)(b)."

AD'A was applied by Judge Jacobs in *DD v Sussex Partnership NHS Foundation Trust* [2022] UKUT 166 (AAC); [2022] M.H.L.R. 380, where it was held that the tribunal retained jurisdiction on an application made by the patient who was subject to hospital and restriction orders when the application was made, but who had been conditionally discharged before the hearing.

In *SM v Livewell CIC* [2020] UKUT 191 (AAC); [2021] M.H.L.R. 131, para.55, the Upper Tribunal said:

> "The decisions in *ex parte M* [[1998] C.O.D. 38] and *SR* were recently subjected to penetrating analysis by Judge Jacobs in *AD'A v Cornwall Partnership NHS Trust* … and we respectfully agree with his conclusion, including with his view that the reasoning of *ex parte M* is sound."

If the patient's case was referred to the tribunal when the patient was detained under s.3 (after a community treatment order had been revoked) but the patient has become subject to a new community treatment order by the time of the hearing, the tribunal retains jurisdiction and has to apply the community treatment order criteria (*PS v Camden and Islington NHS Foundation Trust* [2011] UKUT 143 (AAC)).

In *GM v Dorset Healthcare NHS Trust* [2020] UKUT 152 (AAC); [2021] M.H.L.R. 107, Judge Jacobs held that when a patient who was detained pursuant to s.3 is made subject to a hospital order without a restriction order, the tribunal has no jurisdiction on any application or reference that was lodged before the order was made. Judge Jacobs said that the rationale for his decision "is the obvious one that as the order has been made by a court, there has been judicial oversight of the initial detention" (para.8).

Cases where the First-tier Tribunal retains jurisdiction despite a change in the patient's status

In the *DD case*, above, at para.20. Judge Jacobs conveniently listed the cases cited above where the First-tier Tribunal retains jurisdiction despite a change in the patient's status after the date of their application but before it is heard and decided. The decisions are:

- Detention changed from s.2 to s.3: *KF v Birmingham and Solihull Mental Health Foundation Trust* [2010] UKUT 185 (AAC).
- Detention under s.3 changed to a community treatment order: *AA v Cheshire and Wirral Partnership NHS Foundation Trust* [2009] UKUT 195 (AAC).
- Detention under s.3 (after a community treatment order had been revoked) changed to a new community treatment order: *PS v Camden and Islington NHS Foundation Trust* [2011] UKUT 143 (AAC).

- Detention under s.3 changed to guardianship: *AD'A v Cornwall Partnership NHS Trust* [2020] UKUT 110 (AAC).
- Restrictions under ss.47/49 changed to restrictions under ss.37/41: *S v Elysium Healthcare and the Secretary of State for Justice* [2021] UKUT 186 (AAC).

His Lordship said at para.21:

"This outcome is not, though, inevitable. It will not apply if it is inconsistent with the structure of the Mental Health Act. That is what happened in *GM v Dorset Healthcare NHS Trust and the Secretary of State for Justice* [2020] UKUT 152 (AAC) [see above]. I decided that the First-tier Tribunal lost jurisdiction on an application that had been made when the patient was liable to be detained under section 3 but was later made the subject of a hospital order without a restriction before the hearing."

For patients who have been placed under hospital or guardianship orders by a court under s.37, subss.(1) and (2) of this section read as follows:

"(1) Where—
- [(ca) a community treatment order is made in respect of a patient; or
- (cb) a community treatment order is revoked under section 17F above in respect of a patient; or]
- (e) a patient is transferred from guardianship to a hospital in pursuance of regulations made under section 19 above; or
- (f) a report is furnished under section 20 above in respect of a patient and the patient is not discharged; or
- (fza) a report is furnished under section 20A above in respect of a patient and the patient is not discharged under section 23 above; or
- (fa) a report is furnished under subsection (2) of section 21B above in respect of a patient and subsection (5) of that section applies (or subsections (5) and (6)(b) of that section apply) in the case of the report; or
- (faa) a report is furnished under subsection (2) of section 21B above in respect of a community patient and subsection (6A) of that section applies (or subsections (6A) and (6B)(b) of that section apply) in the case of the report;

an application may be made to the appropriate tribunal within the relevant period by the patient.
(2)   In subsection (1) above 'the relevant period' means—
- (ca) in the case mentioned in paragraph (ca) of that subsection, six months beginning with the day on which the community treatment order is made;
- (cb) in the case mentioned in paragraph (cb) of that subsection, six months beginning with the day on which the community treatment order is revoked;
- (d) in the case mentioned in paragraph (gb) of that subsection, 28 days beginning with the day on which the applicant is informed that the report has been furnished;
- (e) in the case mentioned in paragraph (e) of that subsection, six months beginning with the day on which the patient is transferred;
- (f) in the case mentioned in paragraph (f) [or (fa) of that subsection, the period or periods] for which authority for the patient's detention or guardianship is renewed by virtue of the report; or
- (fza) in the cases mentioned in paragraphs (fza) and (faa) of that subsection, the period or periods for which the community treatment period is extended by virtue of the report" (Sch.1, Pt 1, paras 2,9)."

The effect of subss.(1)(f), (2)(f), as amended by Sch.1, is to enable a hospital order patient to make his first application to a tribunal during the *second* six months of his detention. The rationale for this is explained in the note to s.69(1). Thereafter the patient's entitlement to make applications corresponds to the entitlements accruing on renewal of the authority to detain Pt II patients.

Applications by or on behalf of hospital and guardianship order patients can also be made under s.69. Applications by restricted patients are governed by s.70.

Subsection (1)

1-925   **Paragraph (a); application for admission for assessment**   If the patient's status changes to a s.3 patient, see *R. v South Thames Mental Health Review Tribunal Ex p. M*, above. Patients admitted under s.4 are not excluded as an application under that section is "an application for admission for assessment" (s.4(1)) which is founded on one medical recommendation. An application which was made immediately after the patient's admission would automatically lapse if the second medical recommendation required by s.4(4) was not forthcoming.

Paragraph (b); application for admission for treatment   If the patient does not make an application within six months of his admission, including any period of detention under s.2 (s.68(5)(b)), the hospital managers will automatically refer the case to the tribunal (s.68(1)(b), (2)). A patient who is subject to a hospital order can make his first application to a tribunal during the *second* six months of his detention: see above and the note on *Applications to the First-tier Tribunal (Mental Health) or the Mental Health Review Tribunal for Wales* under s.37.

A conditionally discharged patient who has been made subject to an application under s.3 has a right to make an application under this paragraph (*R. v North West London Mental Health NHS Trust Ex p. Stewart* [1997] C.O.D. 42).

Paragraph (e)   A patient who does not exercise his right to apply to a tribunal within six months of the transfer (subs.(2)(e)) will have his case automatically referred to a tribunal by the hospital managers (s.68(1)(e), (2)).

Paragraph (g)   The tribunal has no jurisdiction to deal with the application if the responsible clinician's report under s.25 has been withdrawn before the application was sent to or received by the tribunal: see *DP v Hywel Dda Health Board* [2011] UKUT 381 (AAC); [2011] M.H.L.R. 394, a case where the report was withdrawn after the hospital had received legal advice that the relative who had ordered the patient's discharge under s.23 was not the patient's nearest relative. The Upper Tribunal left open the question whether it would have jurisdiction if the report had not been withdrawn.

In *MA v Secretary of State for Health* [2012] UKUT 474 (AAC), UT Judge Levenson held that the fact that the patient's nearest relative does not have a right to make an application under this provision in respect of a patient who has been detained for assessment and whose detention has been extended by virtue of the operation of s.29(4), does not violate art.6 of the European Convention on Human Rights.

Paragraph (h)   Applications under this paragraph can only be made by nearest relatives who have been displaced by the court on the grounds that they have unreasonably objected to an application being made or have used (or were likely to use) their powers of discharge without due regard to the welfare of the patient or the interests of the public.

Paragraph (i): the patient   If the patient is mentally incapacitated, see *R. (on the application of OK) v First-tier Tribunal*, above.

An application   In *AD'A v Cornwall Partnership NHS Trust* [2020] UKUT 110 (AAC); [2021] M.H.L.R. 101, Judge Jacobs said that "the legislation [in s.77(2)] limits the number of applications within a period, but not the number of hearings that take place within that period" (para.21).

The making of an application is the process for beginning the proceedings before the tribunal: see *R. (on the application of SR) v Mental Health Review Tribunal* [2005] EWHC 2923 (Admin); [2006] M.H.L.R. 121 para.20, where the court held that the statutory restriction contained in s.77(2) is not on more than one application being made to a tribunal in any specified period because more than one application can be made in any period, if it is of a different kind from that made in that period (para.26).

Nearest relative   Or, except in relation to para.(h), an acting nearest relative. Where an acting nearest relative has been appointed under s.29 that person exercises the right of the nearest relative to make applications to a tribunal under this section and under s.69 (s.29(1)). However, the supplanted nearest relative can make one application to a tribunal for the patient's discharge within the periods specified in subs.(2)(g) (s.29(6)).

The nearest relative could consider using his or her powers of discharge under s.23(2)(a) as an alternative to making an application to a tribunal.

If the patient is a ward of court the nearest relative cannot make an application to a tribunal without the leave of the High Court (s.33(2)).

Subsection (2)

14 days   The application must be received by the tribunal within the 14-day period: see r.32(1)(c) of   **1-926**
the Tribunal Rules. However, if the tribunal office is closed during the whole of the 14th day, the application will be validly received if it arrives at that office at any time during the first succeeding day
on which the office is open (i.e. the next business day). So if the final day for receiving the application
would otherwise be Christmas Day, the application can be validly received on December 27 (unless it
is a weekend, in which case it would be the following Monday) (*R. (on the application of Modaresi) v
Secretary of State for Health* [2011] EWCA Civ 1359; [2011] M.H.L.R. 311). At the Supreme Court
hearing of this case, which was concerned with the scope of the Secretary of State's power under s.67(1),
Lady Hale said that it would be helpful if the *Code of Practice* advised that the hospital should ensure
that tribunal applications which have been given to hospital staff are transmitted to the tribunal without
delay ([2013] UKSC 53, para.32).

Beginning with   Means "including" (*Zoan v Rouamba* [2000] 2 All E.R. 620, CA).

References to tribunals by Secretary of State concerning Part II patients

67.—(1)   The Secretary of State may, if he thinks fit, at any time refer to [the   **1-927**
appropriate tribunal] the case of any patient who is liable to be detained or subject
to guardianship [...] under Part II of this Act [or of any community patient].

(2)   For the purpose of furnishing information for the purposes of a reference
under subsection (1) above any registered medical practitioner [or approved clini-
cian] authorised by or on behalf of the patient may, at any reasonable time, visit the
patient and examine him in private and require the production of and inspect any
records relating to the detention or treatment of the patient in any hospital [or to any
after-care services provided for the patient under section 117 below].

(3)   Section 32 above shall apply for the purposes of this section as it applies
for the purposes of Part II of this Act.

Amendments

The amendments to this section were made by SI 2008/2883 art.9, Sch.3 para.47, the Mental Health
(Patients in the Community) Act 1995 s.2(1), Sch.1 para.8 and the Mental Health Act 2007 ss.13(2)(a),
32(4), 55, Sch.3 para.19, Sch.11 Pt 5.

Definitions

the appropriate tribunal: ss.66(4), 145(1).   **1-928**
community patient: ss.17A(7), 145(1).
approved clinician: s.145(1).
hospital: ss.79(6), 145(1).
patient: s.145(1).

General Note

This section enables the Secretary of State (or, in relation to Wales, the Welsh Ministers) to refer a   **1-929**
patient who is liable to be detained, or subject to guardianship or to a community treatment order to a
tribunal at any time. It also provides for either a registered medical practitioner or an approved clinician to visit and examine the patient, including a community patient, and to inspect relevant records relating to the patient, for the purposes of gathering information for the reference. A failure to allow such a
person to undertake this function could amount to an offence under s.129.

The Secretary of State for Justice has a similar power to refer the case of a restricted patient to a
tribunal under s.71(1).

The following information, which is taken from the website of Mental Health Law Online, was
circulated to Mental Health Lawyers Association members on 1/7/21, based on an email from Sarah
Johnston (Deputy Chamber President) on 30/6/21:

"SM v Livewell Southwest – New Process for References
Deputy Chamber President, Judge Johnston, described the system the Tribunal has put in place in cooperation with the Department of Health to ensure that a reference can be made on the day the Tribunal is sitting where the patient has been found to lack capacity to make the application.

If the Tribunal finds the patient did not have the capacity to apply to the Tribunal but the Tribunal decides it is the interests of justice to continue with a hearing after hearing submissions from the parties, the Department of Health has agreed to make an urgent reference on behalf of the Secretary of State for Health under Section 67 of the Mental Health Act 1983 so that the case can continue as listed that day.

In this situation, the Tribunal Judge will contact the Department of Health and if the reference is able to be made, the Hearing may be able to continue on the day."

Anyone may request a referral. Requests for referrals with respect to patients detained in England should be sent to:

Department of Health and Social Care
3rd Floor,
39 Victoria Street,
London SW1H 0EU
Tel: Matthew Lees, MHA Policy lead (020 7210 5774)
E-mail:mentalhealthact2007@dhsc.gov.uk; matthew.lees@dhsc.gov.uk

The address for patients detained in Wales is:

Head of Mental Health, Vulnerable Groups & Offenders Branch
Welsh Government
Cathays Park
Cardiff CF10 3NQ

The following guidance has been published by the Department of Health (April 22, 2013):

"Information required to support the request
Your letter will need to set out clearly why a Secretary of State's reference under s.67 is being sought. You will need to read the guidance and complete the tribunal *referral* form and *not* the application form on the Tribunals Service website *http://www.justice.gov.uk/forms/hmcts/ts-mh* when requesting a s.67 reference and attach it to your letter. Please do not sign or date the *referred* form. In addition to the information to be given in the form, please indicate in your letter the length of time the patient has been on the section of the Act.

The issues that the Secretary of State for Health will take into account when considering making a reference under section 67
The issues that the Secretary of State for Health will take into account include but are not limited to:
   the reason for the request;
   the length of time since the case was last considered by a Tribunal (if ever);
   the length of time it may be before an application may (or a reference must) be made under other sections of the Act; and
   whether any decision being sought falls within the remit of a Tribunal.
These are not, however, the only factors. Each case will be considered on its merits. The Secretary of State will not refer cases where the patient has already been discharged from their section.

If the Secretary of State makes a reference under s.67, he will ask the Tribunal Secretariat to make the necessary arrangements, and the person who made the request will be informed."

The *Code of Practice* states:

"37.45 Hospital managers should consider asking the Secretary of State to make a reference in respect of any patients whose rights under article 5(4) of the ECHR might otherwise be at risk of being violated because they are unable (for whatever reason) to have their cases considered by the Tribunal speedily following their initial detention or at reasonable intervals afterwards.
   37.46 In particular, they should normally seek such a reference in any case where:

[402]

- a patient's detention under section 2 has been extended under section 29 of the Act pending the outcome of an application to the county court for the displacement of their nearest relative
- the patient lacks the capacity to request a reference, or
- either the patient's case has never been considered by the Tribunal, or a significant period has passed since it was last considered."

For the need for the Secretary of State to make a reference with respect to a s.3 patient who lacks the mental capacity to make an application to the tribunal, see *R. (on the application of OK) v First-tier Tribunal* which is noted in the General Note to s.66. For the need for a reference to be made when a patient's s.2 detention has been extended by the operation of s.29(4), see the notes on s.29 under the heading Human Rights Act 1998.

In *R. (on the application of Modaresi) v Secretary of State for Health* [2013] UKSC 53; [2014] M.H.L.R. 51, the Supreme Court held that the Secretary of State's discretion to make a reference under this provision is underpinned by his duty to avoid a breach of art.5(4) of the European Convention on Human Rights. There is no breach of art.5(4) if a patient who, through no fault of her own, loses her opportunity to make an application to the tribunal under s.2 and is then detained under s.3 before the s.2 expires. In these circumstances, a request to the tribunal for an urgent hearing of the patient's s.3 application should be made. The disadvantage of the patient having to use up her s.3 application at an early stage was not such as to make it unlawful for the Secretary of State to decline to use his power under this section in the expectation that she would apply under s.3. Lord Carnwath, who gave the lead judgment of the court, said at para.22:

"The position might well have been different … if she had continued to be detained under s.2 [due to an application having being made to displace her nearest relative], and had not acquired a separate right under s.3. In circumstances where she had lost her right of immediate access to the tribunal wholly through the fault of the trust, itself an agent of the state for these purposes, it could well be said that the Secretary of State had a positive duty to remedy the position. It is however unnecessary to decide that point, which does not arise on the facts before us."

Guidance on suggesting a referral to the Secretary of State by either the hospital managers, an IMHA or the tribunal itself if the patient lacks the mentally capacity to make an application to the tribunal is provided by the Upper Tribunal in *SM v Livewell CIC* [2020] UKUT 191 (AAC), at para.88:

"a. The Code says that hospital managers should raise this possibility with the Secretary of State if, among other reasons, the patient lacks capacity to do so herself.
b. However, the Code also says that anyone can make such a suggestion to the Secretary of State. The IMHA who will have seen the patient and had the opportunity to assess their wishes would be well suited to make the suggestion to the Secretary of State, if the IMHA considered that the patient wished to leave but lacked capacity to make an application to the Tribunal.
c. A third possibility would be the Tribunal itself. In a case, such as the present, where the Tribunal had found (a) that the patient lacked capacity, but (b) wished to leave the hospital, it would have been very sensible for the Tribunal to have done so.
d. Indeed, in other cases (uncomplicated by the patient's pregnancy and imminent confinement in this case) a combination of these factors may well lead the Tribunal to consider whether, before striking out the application, it would be sensible to adjourn for a short period to see if the Secretary of State wished to make a reference so that the Tribunal could consider as expeditiously as possible whether the statutory conditions for detention were made out."

If the reference is made, there is no deadline within which the tribunal must hear the reference.

In a case known to the author, a tribunal judge contemplated setting aside a reference on the ground that the patient had the required mental capacity to make an application at the time when the request for the reference was made. The tribunal has no jurisdiction to set aside a reference.

Subsection (1)

Secretary of State In practice, the Secretary of State for Health. The functions of the Minister, so far as exercisable in relation to Wales, are exercised by the Welsh Ministers (see the General Note to the Act).

1-930

Subsection (2)

1-931 **Registered medical practitioner** Means "a fully registered person within the meaning of the Medical Act 1983 who holds a licence to practise under that Act" (Interpretation Act 1978, Sch.1).

[Duty of managers of hospitals to refer cases to tribunal

1-932 **68.**—(1) This section applies in respect of the following patients—

(a) a patient who is admitted to a hospital in pursuance of an application for admission for assessment;

(b) a patient who is admitted to a hospital in pursuance of an application for admission for treatment;

(c) a community patient;

(d) a patient whose community treatment order is revoked under section 17F above;

(e) a patient who is transferred from guardianship to a hospital in pursuance of regulations made under section 19 above.

(2) On expiry of the period of six months beginning with the applicable day, the managers of the hospital shall refer the patient's case to [the appropriate tribunal].

(3) But they shall not do so if during that period—

(a) any right has been exercised by or in respect of the patient by virtue of any of paragraphs (b), (ca), (cb), (e), (g) and (h) of section 66(1) above;

(b) a reference has been made in respect of the patient under section 67(1) above, not being a reference made while the patient is or was liable to be detained in pursuance of an application for admission for assessment; or

(c) a reference has been made in respect of the patient under subsection (7) below.

(4) A person who applies to a tribunal but subsequently withdraws his application shall be treated for these purposes as not having exercised his right to apply, and if he withdraws his application on a date after expiry of the period mentioned in subsection (2) above, the managers shall refer the patient's case as soon as possible after that date.

(5) In subsection (2) above, "the applicable day" means—

(a) in the case of a patient who is admitted to a hospital in pursuance of an application for admission for assessment, the day on which the patient was so admitted;

(b) in the case of a patient who is admitted to a hospital in pursuance of an application for admission for treatment—

(i) the day on which the patient was so admitted; or

(ii) if, when he was so admitted, he was already liable to be detained in pursuance of an application for admission for assessment, the day on which he was originally admitted in pursuance of the application for admission for assessment;

(c) in the case of a community patient or a patient whose community treatment order is revoked under section 17F above, the day mentioned in sub-paragraph (i) or (ii), as the case may be, of paragraph (b) above;

(d) in the case of a patient who is transferred from guardianship to a hospital, the day on which he was so transferred.

(6) The managers of the hospital shall also refer the patient's case to [the ap-

propriate tribunal] if a period of more than three years (or, if the patient has not attained the age of 18 years, one year) has elapsed since his case was last considered by such a tribunal, whether on his own application or otherwise.

(7)   If, in the case of a community patient, the community treatment order is revoked under section 17F above, the managers of the hospital shall also refer the patient's case to [the appropriate tribunal] as soon as possible after the order is revoked.

(8)   For the purposes of furnishing information for the purposes of a reference under this section, a registered medical practitioner or approved clinician authorised by or on behalf of the patient may at any reasonable time—

(a)   visit and examine the patient in private; and

(b)   require the production of and inspect any records relating to the detention or treatment of the patient in any hospital or any after-care services provided for him under section 117 below.

(9)   Reference in this section to the managers of the hospital—

(a)   in relation to a community patient, is to the managers of the responsible hospital;

(b)   in relation to any other patient, is to the managers of the hospital in which he is liable to be detained.]

Amendments

This section was inserted by the Mental Health Act 2007 s.37(3). The references to the appropriate tribunal in subss.(2), (6) and (7) were substituted by SI 2008/2883 art.9, Sch.3 para.48.

Definitions

application for admission for assessment: ss.2, 145(1).
application for admission for treatment: ss.3, 145(1).
the appropriate tribunal: ss.66(4), 145(1).
approved clinician: s.145(1).
community patient: ss.17A(7), 145(1).
community treatment order: ss.17A(7), 145(1).
hospital: ss.34(2), 79(6), 145(1).
the managers: s.145(1) and see subs.(9) of this section.
responsible hospital: ss.17A(7), 145(1).
patient: s.145(1).

1-933

General Note

This section requires the hospital managers to refer a patient to a tribunal in specified circumstances. The purpose of the referral system is to "ensure that patients who lack the ability or initiative to make an application to a Tribunal ... have the safeguard of an independent review of their case" (Cmnd.8405, para.24).

1-934

Part II patients

The key provisions for patients who are subject to Part II are:

1-935

1.   A requirement to make a referral to the tribunal six months from the day on which the patient was first detained, whether under s.2 for assessment (including s.2 patients whose detention has been extended by virtue of the operation of s.29(4)) or s.3 for treatment (including patients who are subsequently placed on a community treatment order (CTO)), or the day on which he was detained in hospital following a transfer from guardianship (subs.(2)). The day in question is defined as "the applicable day" (subs.(5)). A s.3 patient must be referred even though he has had a tribunal hearing while detained under s.2. In such cases, the applicable is the day on which the patient was admitted under s.2 (subs.(5)(b)(ii)). The applicable day for a patient

who was detained under either s.2 or 3 is not affected by the patient being subsequently placed on a CTO (subs.(5)(c)). Under s.68A, the six-month period can be reduced by order of the Secretary of State, in relation to hospitals in England, or the Welsh Ministers, in relation to hospitals in Wales.

2. The hospital managers also have a duty to make a referral if the tribunal has not considered the patient's case at a hearing in three years (or one year if the patient is under 18) (subs.(6)). The order making power under s.68A can be used to reduce the three-year and one-year periods.

3. The duty to make a referral in respect of a CTO patient rests with the hospital managers of the responsible hospital (subs.(9)(a)).

4. The hospital managers of the detaining hospital must refer the case of a community patient to the tribunal as soon as possible after the CTO is revoked (subs.(7)).

5. Either a registered medical practitioner or an approved clinician may visit and examine the patient, including a community patient, and inspect relevant records relating to the patient for the purposes of gathering information for the reference (subs.(8)). A failure to allow such a person to undertake this function could amount to an offence under s.129.

In *PS v Camden and Islington NHS Foundation Trust* [2011] UKUT 143 (AAC); [2011] M.H.L.R. 159, UT Judge Jacobs said that the difficulties encountered by the tribunal when faced with a referred CTO patient who does not wish to co-operate or even participate in the tribunal proceedings might be tackled in the following manner:

"One power that the tribunal could use is the power to stay proceedings under rule 5(3)(j) of the Tribunal Procedure (First-tier Tribunal) (Health, Education and Social Care Chamber) Rules 2008. However, it might be considered an abuse of that power if it were effectively used as a means of permanent disposal or as a means of avoiding deciding the case at all.

More appropriate, perhaps, would be for the tribunal to arrange block hearings of community treatment references on the limited information that it is able to obtain.... The tribunal can use its powers under rules 5 and 15 to give directions on evidence from the responsible clinician and others that is appropriate in all the circumstances, taking account of the overriding objective and, in particular, of the need to act proportionately under rule 2(2)(a)" (paras 25, 26).

For the need for hospital managers to request the Secretary of State to make a reference to the tribunal under s.67(1) in a situation where a s.2 patient has had his detention extended under s.29(4), see the note on Human Rights Act 1998 in s.29.

Any change in the patient's legal status, for example from a s.3 to a community patient, does not affect the continuing validity of an extant and undetermined reference to the First-tier Tribunal (*KF v Birmingham and Solihull Mental Health NHS Foundation Trust* [2010] UKUT 185 (AAC)).

The fact that a reference has been made under this section does not prevent the patient from making an application under s.66(1)(f) during the period of detention when the reference takes place. Although s.77(2) prohibits the making of more than one application during a specific period of detention, a reference is not an application.

Patients who are absent without leave at the point at which they should be referred to the tribunal must be referred on their return to hospital (s.21(3)).

Part III patients

1-936 For the application of this section to Part III patients who have been made subject to hospital orders without restrictions or to guardianship orders, see Sch.1 Pt 1, paras 2, 10 which provide that:

1. Only patients who are transferred from a guardianship order to a hospital order will be referred by the hospital managers after six months. Other patients will not have their cases referred at that time because, as their initial detention will have been considered by the sentencing court, they cannot apply to the tribunal themselves during that period.

2. The duty to make a referral at three years (or one year) applies to all unrestricted Part III patients, including hospital order patients who have been placed on a CTO. i.e. a referral cannot be made in respect of an unrestricted hospital order patient until after the three year (or one year period) period has been reached.

The start date for calculating when a reference should be made for a restricted patient whose restrictions have ended (a "notional hospital order" patient) is the date when the restrictions ceased to have effect: see ss.41(5). Otherwise the period starts from the date when the order was made or, for patients transferred from hospitals from outside England or Wales, the date of the patient's admission to hospital in England or Wales (or the date when they were treated as being subject to a CTO).

Under s.71(2), the Secretary of State for Justice must refer the case of a restricted patient whose case has not been considered by the tribunal for three years.

Human Rights Act 1998

In *MH v United Kingdom* (2014) 58 E.H.R.R. 35; [2014] M.H.L.R. 249 at para.87, the European Court of Human Rights held that the failure to provide the means for a mentally incapacitated patient to bring proceedings to challenge a detention under s.2 constituted a violation of art.5(4) of the European Convention on Human Rights. The Court said at para.82: **1-937**

"As the right set forth in Article 5(4) of the Convention is guaranteed to everyone, it is clear that special safeguards are called for in the case of detained mental patients who lack legal capacity to institute proceedings before judicial bodies. However, it is not for this Court to dictate what form those special safeguards should take, provided that they make the right guaranteed by Article 5(4) as nearly as possible as practical and effective for this particular category of detainees as it is for other detainees. While automatic judicial review might be one means of providing the requisite safeguard, it is not necessarily the only means."

The Government's response to this judgment can be found in the following information that was provided to the Council of Europe on February 18, 2015:

"Since the events giving rise to this case took place, the 1983 Act has been substantially amended by the Mental Health Act 2007. This has addressed the violation identified in the judgment by introducing provisions on independent mental health advocates (IMHA). An IMHA is there to offer patients advice as to how the 1983 Act applies to them and give them an idea about what rights they have. They can represent patients including by accompanying them to any meetings and consultations, speak on their behalf and contact a lawyer for them. For example, there is now a duty under section 130D of the 1983 Act for a specified person to take such steps as are practicable to ensure that a patient understands the help that is available to them from an IMHA and how to obtain that help. There is now a duty upon local authorities to make arrangements to enable an IMHA to be available to help any patient liable to be detained under the 1983 Act.

To further protect persons lacking capacity, the Government made amendments to the relevant statutory guidance which applies in England: the *"Code of Practice Mental Health Act 1983"*. The amendments make clear that if a patient lacks capacity to decide whether to seek help from an IMHA, an IMHA should be introduced to the patient so that the IMHA can explain what help they can offer. The revised Code was laid before Parliament on 15 January 2015 and will come into force on 1 April 2015.

In Wales, the Mental Health Act Code of Practice for Wales provides guidance on all aspects of the 1983 Act. It currently specifies that hospital managers should always consider a referral to the Tribunal for someone in the applicant's circumstances, lacking capacity, and where otherwise necessary."

The Government's response can be accessed at: *https://wcd.coe.int/ViewDoc.jsp?id=2293953&Site =CM*.

Subsection (2)

Beginning with   Means "including" (*Zoan v Rouamba* [2000] 2 All E.R. 620, CA). **1-938**

Managers of the hospital   See subs.(9).

Subsection (3)

The purpose of this provision is to prevent duplication of proceedings. **1-939**

Subsection (6)

The wording of this provision means that there could be no reference if the tribunal had never previously considered the case, such as a patient who has been made subject to a hospital order made by a court under s.37. However, the *Code of Practice* states that a reference should be made where "[t]hree **1-940** years have passed without their case being considered by the Tribunal (one year if they are under 18)" (para.37.39 and fig.20; also see the Reference Guide at para.6.51 and fig.32). Although the wording of the Act does not support the interpretation given in the Code, in order to provide the patient with the safeguard that Parliament presumably intended, it is suggested that the approach taken by the Code should be followed.

Attained the age of 18 years   At the date of the referral. This date is reached at the commencement of the patient's 18th birthday (Family Law Reform Act 1969 s.9(1)).

Considered   At a hearing.

Subsection (7)

1-941   In *PS v Camden and Islington NHS Foundation Trust* [2011] UKUT 143 (AAC); [2011] M.H.L.R. 159, the Upper Tribunal held that a decision of the First-tier tribunal to treat a reference made under this provision as having lapsed on the ground that the patient had been made the subject of a fresh CTO following the revocation of the previous CTO was unlawful. UT Judge Jacobs criticised the hospital managers for not making the reference until 12 days after the revocation.

[Power to reduce periods under section 68

1-942   **68A.**—(1)   The appropriate national authority may from time to time by order amend subsection (2) or (6) of section 68 above so as to substitute for a period mentioned there such shorter period as is specified in the order.

(2)   The order may include such transitional, consequential, incidental or supplemental provision as the appropriate national authority thinks fit.

(3)   The order may, in particular, make provision for a case where—

    (a)   a patient in respect of whom subsection (1) of section 68 above applies is, or is about to be, transferred from England to Wales or from Wales to England; and

    (b)   the period by reference to which subsection (2) or (6) of that section operates for the purposes of the patient's case is not the same in one territory as it is in the other.

(4)   A patient is transferred from one territory to the other if—

    (a)   he is transferred from a hospital, or from guardianship, in one territory to a hospital in the other in pursuance of regulations made under section 19 above;

    (b)   he is removed under subsection (3) of that section from a hospital or accommodation in one territory to a hospital or accommodation in the other;

    (c)   he is a community patient responsibility for whom is assigned from a hospital in one territory to a hospital in the other in pursuance of regulations made under section 19A above; [or]

    (d)   on the revocation of a community treatment order in respect of him under section 17F above he is detained in a hospital in the territory other than the one in which the responsible hospital was situated; [...]

    (e)   [...]

(5)   Provision made by virtue of subsection (3) above may require or authorise the managers of a hospital determined in accordance with the order to refer the patient's case to [the appropriate tribunal].

(6)   In so far as making provision by virtue of subsection (3) above, the order—

    (a)   may make different provision for different cases;

    (b)   may make provision which applies subject to specified exceptions.

(7)   Where the appropriate national authority for one territory makes an order

under subsection (1) above, the appropriate national authority for the other territory may by order make such provision in consequence of the order as it thinks fit.

(8)　An order made under subsection (7) above may, in particular, make provision for a case within subsection (3) above (and subsections (4) to (6) above shall apply accordingly).

(9)　In this section, "the appropriate national authority" means—
- (a)　in relation to a hospital in England, the Secretary of State;
- (b)　in relation to a hospital in Wales, the Welsh Ministers.]]

Amendments

This section was inserted by the Mental Health Act 2007 s.37(3). The amendments to it were made by SI 2008/2883 art.9, Sch.3 para.49 and the Health and Social Care Act 2012 s.42(2).

Definitions

patient: s.145(1).
hospital: ss.34(2), 79(6), 145(1).
community patient: ss.17A(7), 145(1).
community treatment order: ss.17A(7), 145(1).
responsible hospital: ss.17A(7), 145(1).
the managers: s.145(1).
the appropriate tribunal: ss.66(4), 145(1).

1-943

General Note

This section enables the Secretary of State and the Welsh Ministers to make an order reducing the referral periods specified in s.68. It also "enables the order to include any consequential provisions that may be required to ensure that patients who are transferred from England to Wales or vice versa between the period of referral in one territory and the other do not miss out on a referral to the tribunal by virtue of the transfer" (Explanatory Notes, para.154). There is no power to lengthen the periods. At the time of writing, no orders have been made under this provision.

1-944

Subsection (1)

Appropriate national authority　See subs.(9).

1-945

By order　See s.143(1).

APPLICATIONS AND REFERENCES CONCERNING PART III PATIENTS

Applications to tribunals concerning patients subject to hospital and guardianship orders

69.—(1)　Without prejudice to any provision of section 66(1) above as applied by section 40(4) above, an application to [the appropriate tribunal] may also be made—

1-946

- [(a)　in respect of a patient liable to be detained in pursuance of a hospital order or a community patient who was so liable immediately before he became a community patient, by the nearest relative of the patient in any period in which application may be made by the patient under any such provision as so applied;] and
- (b)　in respect of a patient placed under guardianship by a guardianship order—
  - (i)　by the patient, within the period of six months beginning with the date of the order;

[409]

(ii)   by the nearest relative of the patient, within the period of 12 months beginning with the date of the order and in any subsequent period of 12 months.

(2)   Where a person detained in a hospital—

(a)   is treated as subject to a hospital order [, hospital direction] or transfer direction by virtue of section 41(5) above, [or section 80B(2), 82(2) or 85(2) below.] [...]; or

(b)   is subject to a direction having the same effect as a hospital order by virtue of section

[...] 47(3) or 48(3) above,

then, without prejudice to any provision of Part II of this Act as applied by section 40 above, that person may make an application to [the appropriate tribunal] in the period of six months beginning with the date of the order or direction mentioned in paragraph (a) above or, as the case may be, the date of the direction mentioned in paragraph (b) above.

[(3)   The provisions of section 66 above as applied by section 40(4) above are subject to subsection (4) below.

(4)   If the initial detention period has not elapsed when the relevant application period begins, the right of a hospital order patient to make an application by virtue of paragraph (ca) or (cb) of section 66(1) above shall be exercisable only during whatever remains of the relevant application period after the initial detention period has elapsed.

(5)   In subsection (4) above—

(a)   "hospital order patient" means a patient who is subject to a hospital order, excluding a patient of a kind mentioned in paragraph (a) or (b) of subsection (2) above;

(b)   "the initial detention period", in relation to a hospital order patient, means the period of six months beginning with the date of the hospital order; and

(c)   "the relevant application period" means the relevant period mentioned in paragraph (ca) or (cb), as the case may be, of section 66(2) above.]

Amendments

The amendments to this section were made by the Mental Health Act 2007 ss.32(4), 39(2), 55, Sch.3 para.20, Sch.5 Pt 2 para.18, Sch.11 Pt 5, the Domestic Violence, Crime and Victims Act 2004 s.58(2), Sch.11 and SI 2008/2883 art.9, Sch.3 para.50.

Definitions

1-947

the appropriate tribunal: ss.66(4), 145(1).
patient: s.145(1).
hospital: ss.34(2), 79(6), 145(1).
hospital order: ss.37, 55(4), 145(1).
hospital direction: ss.45A(3)(a), 145(1).
guardianship order: s.55(4).
transfer direction: ss.47, 145(1).
nearest relative: ss.26(3), 145(1).
community patient: ss.17A(7), 145(1).

General Note

1-948

This section specifies when a tribunal application can be made by the nearest relative, or an acting nearest relative appointed by the county court under s.29, of a patient who has been placed under a hospital order made by a court under s.37 or has been subsequently placed on a community treatment order. The application can only be made within the same period that allows for the patient to make an application. The right of the nearest relative to make an application can be exercised even through the patient has made an application during the same period. This section also enables tribunal applications to be made in respect of guardianship order patients and provides an opportunity for certain other patients who have been transferred from prison to hospital after having committed offences to have their cases reviewed by a tribunal within six months of their transfer. Applications by restricted patients are governed by s.70.

Subsection (1)

Period in which an application may be made by the patient   See subss.(3) to (5).   **1-949**

Subsection (2)

This subsection affects: **1-950**

"certain categories of patient whose cases have not recently been looked at by a court but who are, simply by reason of the way [this Act is] put together, deemed to be detained as though subject to a fresh hospital order. [...] As a result of [Schedule 1, Part 1, paragraphs 2, 9], such patients, who may already have been in hospital for a substantial period, would have a six months' gap during which they were not entitled to apply to a Tribunal and had not just had their cases looked at by a court ... [This subsection removes] that gap. In addition, [it] seeks to meet the concern which has been expressed ... about the position of patients immediately after they have been transferred from prison. Again, the grounds for their detention in hospital will not previously have been considered by a court. The Government now accept that such people should have an immediate right to a Tribunal hearing"; per Lord Belstead, *Hansard* HL, Vol.427, col.868."

Applications to tribunals concerning restricted patients

70.   A patient who is a restricted patient within the meaning of section 79 below   **1-951**
and is detained in a hospital may apply to [the appropriate tribunal]—
    (a)   in the period between the expiration of six months and the expiration of 12 months beginning with the date of the relevant hospital order [, hospital direction] or transfer direction; and
    (b)   in any subsequent period of 12 months.

Amendments

The amendments to this section were made by SI 2008/2883 art.9, Sch.3 and by the Crime (Sentences) Act 1997 s.55, Sch.4 para.12(9).

Definitions

patient: s.145(1).   **1-952**
restricted patient: s.79(1).
hospital: ss.79(6), 145(1).
the appropriate tribunal: ss.66(4), 145(1).
the relevant hospital direction: s.79(2)–(5).
the relevant hospital order: s.79(2)–(5).
the relevant transfer direction: s.79(2)–(5).

General Note

This section provides for a tribunal application to be made by a restricted patient during the second   **1-953**
six months of the duration of the hospital order or transfer direction, and at yearly intervals thereafter. A nearest relative cannot make an application because a restricted patient has no nearest relative. Section 69(2)(b) provides patients who are made the subject of a restricted transfer direction with an additional right to make an application to the tribunal during the first six months starting with the date of the direction. Section 71(2) requires the Secretary of State to refer the case of any restricted patient whose case has not been considered by the tribunal within the last three years.

A tribunal considering an application made by a restricted patient under this section has no power to adjourn the proceedings so as to monitor the patient's progress in the hope that a projected course of treatment would eventually permit it to discharge the patient (*R. v Nottingham Mental Health Review Tribunal Ex p. Secretary of State for the Home Department The Times,* March 25, 1987).

An application made under this section ceases to have effect if the patient ceases to be a restricted patient and becomes an unrestricted patient. However, it is the practice of the tribunal to treat such an application as converted into one made under s.69(2)(a) so as to avoid the patient being placed under a disadvantage to which he would have otherwise have been placed of having to wait six months before he could make an application (*R. (on the application of MN) v Mental Health Review Tribunal*) [2008] EWHC 3383 (Admin); [2009] M.H.L.R. 98). *MN* was distinguished by the Upper Tribunal in *CS v Elysium Healthcare* [2021] UKUT 186 (AAC). The issue in *CS* was whether a tribunal application made when a patient was one type of restricted patient remains valid if, before it is determined, the patient becomes a different type of restricted patient. In this case, the patient was originally a restricted patient by virtue of a transfer direction together with a restriction direction (s.47/49) and, subsequently, a restricted patient by virtue of a hospital order together with a restriction order (s.37/41). The UT held that the MHRT for Wales had erred in law in finding that it lacked jurisdiction to determine the application made when the patient was subject to the s.47/49 transfer direction as the patient had remained a restricted patient throughout: see s.79.

A restricted patient whose restriction order has ceased to have effect is treated as if he had been admitted to hospital as an unrestricted patient on the date when the restriction order ceased to have effect: see s.41(5).

Beginning with

Including the date of the hospital order or transfer direction (*Zoan v Rouamba* [2001] 2 All E.R. 620 CA).

References by Secretary of State concerning restricted patients

1-954   **71.**—(1)   The Secretary of State may at any time refer the case of a restricted patient to [the appropriate tribunal].

(2)   The Secretary of State shall refer to [the appropriate tribunal] the case of any restricted patient detained in a hospital whose case has not been considered by such a tribunal, whether on his own application or otherwise, within the last three years.

(3)   The Secretary of State may by order vary the length of the period mentioned in subsection (2) above.

[(3A)   An order under subsection (3) above may include such transitional, consequential, incidental or supplemental provision as the Secretary of State thinks fit.]

(4)   Any reference under subsection (1) above in respect of a patient who has been conditionally discharged and not recalled to hospital shall be made to the tribunal for the area in which the patient resides.

(5), (6)   [*Repealed by the Domestic Violence, Crime and Victims Act 2004 s.58(2), Sch.11*].

Amendments

The amendments to this section were made by the Mental Health Act 2007 s.37(4) and SI 2008/ 2883 art.9, Sch.3 para.52.

Definitions

1-955   restricted patient: s.79(1).
the appropriate tribunal: ss.66(4), 145(1).
hospital: ss.34(2), 79(6), 145(1).
patient: s.145(1).

General Note

This section provides that the Secretary of State may, and in certain circumstances must refer the case **1-956** of a restricted patient, including a conditionally discharged patient, to a tribunal. Such a referral does not affect the patient's right to apply to the tribunal directly.

For the duty of the Secretary of State to refer to the tribunal a conditionally discharged patient who has been recalled to hospital, see s.75(1).

Subsection (1)

The nature of the Secretary of State's discretion under this provision was examined in *R. (on the ap-* **1-957** *plication of C) v The Secretary of State for the Home Department* [2001] EWHC Admin 501; [2001] M.H.L.R. 100, where Collins J. held that:

(i) the discretion of the Secretary of State to refer a case in a situation where the tribunal has reached a decision is not untrammelled, in that the Secretary of State must pay proper respect to the decision of the tribunal. He should not use his power merely because he disagreed with the decision reached by the tribunal; and

(ii) a reference can be made: (a) where the decision of the tribunal has been ruled unlawful or stayed by the court on judicial review; (b) where the tribunal has imposed a condition that has proved impossible to put into effect; and (c) where there has been a material change of circumstances. With regard to (c), to be consistent with the patient's rights under art.5 of the European Convention on Human Rights, a reference should only be made if the Secretary of State has formed the view that it is probable that the material in question would have affected the decision of the tribunal in that it would have decided either that a more onerous condition be imposed or that a conditional discharge would not have been ordered.

This case went to appeal and point (ii)(c) of Collins J.'s judgment must be read subject to the following finding of the Court of Appeal. If a change in the patient's circumstances is brought to the Secretary of State's attention after a tribunal has made a deferred conditional discharge but before discharge has been directed, he should utilise the procedure set out in *R. (on the application of IH) v The Secretary of State for the Home Department* [2002] EWCA Civ 646, by inviting the tribunal to reconsider its decision. He should not make a referral to a fresh tribunal under this provision (*R. (on the application of C) v Secretary of State for the Home Department* [2002] EWCA Civ 647; [2002] M.H.L.R. 105). The decision of the Court of Appeal in *IH* in so far as it relates to the ability of the tribunal to reconsider its decision was affirmed by the House of Lords in *R. v Secretary of State for the Home Department Ex p. IH* [2003] UKHL 59; [2004] 1 All E.R. 412, which is noted under s.73(7).

Secretary of State   Functions under this provision have not been transferred to Welsh Ministers (see the General Note to the Act and SI 1999/672 art.2, Sch.1).

Subsection (2)

This provision applies to a restricted patient who has received a deferred conditional discharge but **1-958** three years have elapsed without the conditions being met or the tribunal reconvening to consider the case.

Subsection (3)

At the time of writing, no order has been made under this provision. **1-959**

DISCHARGE OF PATIENTS

Powers of tribunals

72.—[(1)   Where application is made to [the appropriate tribunal] by or in **1-960** respect of a patient who is liable to be detained under this Act [or is a community patient], the tribunal may in any case direct that the patient be discharged, and—

(a)   the tribunal shall direct the discharge of a patient liable to be detained under section 2 above if [it is] not satisfied—

(i)   that he is then suffering from mental disorder or from mental

[413]

disorder of a nature or degree which warrants his detention in a hospital for assessment (or for assessment followed by medical treatment) for at least a limited period; or

   (ii) that his detention as aforesaid is justified in the interests of his own health or safety or with a view to the protection of other persons;

 (b) the tribunal shall direct the discharge of a patient liable to be detained otherwise than under section 2 above if [it is] not satisfied—

   (i) that he is then suffering from [mental disorder or from mental disorder] of a nature or degree which makes it appropriate for him to be liable to be detained in a hospital for medical treatment; or

   (ii) that it is necessary for the health or safety of the patient or for the protection of other persons that he should receive such treatment; or

   (iia) that appropriate medical treatment is available for him; or]

   (iii) in the case of an application by virtue of paragraph (g) of section 66(1) above, that the patient, if released, would be likely to act in a manner dangerous to other persons or to himself.

[(c) the tribunal shall direct the discharge of a community patient if [it is] not satisfied—

   (i) that he is then suffering from mental disorder or mental disorder of a nature or degree which makes it appropriate for him to receive medical treatment; or

   (ii) that it is necessary for his health or safety or for the protection of other persons that he should receive such treatment; or

   (iii) that it is necessary that the responsible clinician should be able to exercise the power under section 17E(1) above to recall the patient to hospital; or

   (iv) that appropriate medical treatment is available for him; or

   (v) in the case of an application by virtue of paragraph (g) of section 66(1) above, that the patient, if discharged, would be likely to act in a manner dangerous to other persons or to himself.]]

[(1A) In determining whether the criterion in subsection (1)(c)(iii) above is met, the tribunal shall, in particular, consider, having regard to the patient's history of mental disorder and any other relevant factors, what risk there would be of a deterioration of the patient's condition if he were to continue not to be detained in a hospital (as a result, for example, of his refusing or neglecting to receive the medical treatment he requires for his mental disorder).]

(2) [...]

(3) A tribunal may under subsection (1) above direct the discharge of a patient on a future date specified in the direction; and where a tribunal [does not] direct the discharge of a patient under that subsection the tribunal may—

   (a) with a view to facilitating his discharge on a future date, recommend that he be granted leave of absence or transferred to another hospital or into guardianship; and

   (b) further consider his case in the event of any such recommendation not being complied with.

[(3A) Subsection (1) above does not require a tribunal to direct the discharge of a patient just because [it thinks] it might be appropriate for the patient to be discharged (subject to the possibility of recall) under a community treatment order; and a tribunal—

[414]

(a)   may recommend that the responsible clinician consider whether to make a community treatment order; and

(b)   may (but need not) further consider the patient's case if the responsible clinician does not make an order.]

(4)   Where application is made to [the appropriate tribunal] by or in respect of a patient who is subject to guardianship under this Act, the tribunal may in any case direct that the patient be discharged, and shall so direct if [it is] satisfied—

(a)   that he is not then suffering from [mental disorder]; or

(b)   that it is not necessary in the interests of the welfare of the patient, or for the protection of other persons, that the patient should remain under such guardianship.

[(4A)   […]]

(5)   […]

(6)   Subsections (1) to [(4)] above apply in relation to references to [the appropriate tribunal] as they apply in relation to applications made to [the appropriate tribunal] by or in respect of a patient.

(7)   Subsection (1) above shall not apply in the case of a restricted patient except as provided in sections 73 and 74 below.

Amendments

The amendments to this section were made by the Mental Health Act 1983 (Remedial Order) Order 2001 (SI 2001/3712) art.3, the Mental Health Act 2007 ss.1(4), 2(8), 32(4), 55, Sch.1 para.14, Sch.3 para.21, Sch.11 Pts 1, 2 and 5 and SI 2008/2883 art.9, Sch.3 para.53.

Definitions

the appropriate tribunal: ss.66(4), 145(1).   **1-961**
patient: s.145(1).
appropriate medical treatment: ss.3(4), 145(1).
community patient: ss.17A(7), 145(1).
mental disorder: ss.1, 145(1).
hospital: ss.34(2), 79(6), 145(1).
medical treatment: s.145(1), (4).
responsible clinician: ss.34(1), 79(6).
community treatment order: ss.17A(7), 145(1).
restricted patient: s.79(1).

General Note

This section empowers tribunals to discharge patients from hospital, guardianship or community treat-   **1-962**
ment orders (CTOs) and directs tribunals to discharge such patients if specified criteria are satisfied. For detained and community patients, the discharge can take place at a specified future date (subs.(3)).

The powers of the tribunal are confined to the powers set out in this section which can be read compatibly with human rights jurisprudence. The tribunal therefore has no jurisdiction to consider European Convention on Human Rights (ECHR) issues: see *Secretary of State for Justice v MM; Welsh Ministers v PJ* [2017] EWCA Civ 194; [2017] M.H.L.R. 282 where the Court of Appeal said at para.59:

"Neither the Convention nor the Human Rights Act 1998 confer jurisdiction on a tribunal. There is nothing in the general role and function of a tribunal that permits it to exercise a function that it does not have by statute."

This finding was not challenged by Supreme Court when the case was appealed: see [2018] UKSC 66. The decision in *MM* and *PJ* was followed in *Djaba v West London Mental Health Trust* [2017] EWCA Civ 436; [2017] M.H.L.R. 345 where the Court of Appeal held that this section does not require a "proportionality assessment" to be conducted, pursuant to arts 5 and/or 8 of the ECHR and the 1998 Act, taking into account the conditions of the patient's detention. It is therefore the case that this section does not provide the tribunal with a power to regulate the conditions of the patient's detention or matters such as the availability of visiting rights for members of a patient's family. Arden L.J. said that a patient "must apply for judicial review to the Administrative Court if he considers that the conditions of his detention are disproportionate and do not comply with the Convention. That Court is able to carry out a sufficient review on the merits to meet the requirements of the Convention" (para.55). However, note that in *Welsh Ministers v PJ* [2018] UKSC 66; [2018] M.H.L.R. 411, Lady Hale said that while the "MHRT has no jurisdiction over the conditions of treatment and detention in hospital, ... these can be relevant to whether the statutory criteria for detention are made out, especially in borderline cases" (para.33).

The tribunal's powers under this section are confined to granting or refusing relief in respect of persons who are liable to be detained or liable to be recalled; it has no power to consider either the validity of the admission which gave rise to the liability to be detained (*R. v East London and The City Mental Health Trust Ex p. Brandenburg* [2003] UKHL 58; [2004] 1 All E.R. 400 para.9(3)) or issues relating to a patient's consent to medical treatment: see *SH v Cornwall Partnership NHS Trust* [2012] UKUT 290 (AAC); [2012] M.H.L.R. 383 where UT Judge Jacobs said at para.15:

"Judicial oversight *by the First-tier Tribunal* is limited to the issue whether the person should be subject to the Act. The treatment of patients under the Act is subject to judicial oversight *by the courts*, but not by the First-tier Tribunal."

When determining whether a compliant mentally incapacitated patient's detention is either warranted for the purposes of subs.(1)(a)(i) or is necessary for the purposes of subs.(1)(b) (ii), the tribunal must consider whether the patient should be detained under this Act, or whether the assessment or treatment in the proposed circumstances should be founded on the Mental Capacity Act 2005 (MCA) and any deprivation of liberty it involves should be authorised under the deprivation of liberty safeguards (DOLS). To do that, the tribunal has to consider whether the MCA and its DOLS alternative are applicable and available and, if so, whether and when they should be used. In making its decision, the tribunal has to consider which alternative best achieves the objective of ensuring the patient's assessment or treatment in the least restrictive way. As the tribunal has no power to compel a DOL authorisation, a decision to discharge the patient should usually be deferred to enable the relevant DOLS authorisation to be sought: see *AM v South London & Maudsley NHS Foundation Trust* [2013] UKUT 365 (AAC); [2014] M.H.L.R. 181, per Charles J. at paras 34, 74 and 75. *AM* is considered in Part 6 under the heading "The 1983 Act or the 2005 Act?" and the note on *The detention of compliant mentally incapable patients* in the General Note to Part II. It is suggested that adjourning the hearing, rather that deferring the decision, would be the appropriate option as the deferred discharge would have to take effect even if a DOL authorisation had not been obtained: also see *Perkins v Bath District Health Authority*, which is noted under subs.(3). There is no reason why the DOL safeguards cannot be applied in anticipation of the patient being discharged from detention: see Sch.A1, para.63 of the MCA and *DN v Northumberland Tyne and Wear NHS Foundation Trust* which is noted under subs.(1)(b).

The legality of a decision to make an application to detain a patient immediately after a decision of a tribunal to discharge him is considered in the General Note to s.3 under the heading "The re-sectioning of a patient subsequent to a discharge by the First-tier Tribunal (Mental Health), the Mental Health Review Tribunal for Wales or a Hospital Manager's Panel".

Human Rights Act 1998

1-963   In *Cumbria, Northumberland Tyne & Wear NHS Foundation Trust v EG* [2021] EWHC 2990 (Fam); [2022] M.H.L.R. 309, Lieven J. held that where the recall of a conditionally discharged restricted patient to hospital would breech his rights under art.5(1)(e) of the European Convention on Human Rights (ECHR), the interpretative power in s.3 of the Human Rights Act 1998 could be applied to construe the Mental Health Act so as to be compatible with the patient's Convention rights. This case is considered in the notes on subs.(1)(b)(i), below.

In *R. (on the application of H) v Mental Health Review Tribunal* [2002] EWHC 1522 (Admin); [2002] M.H.L.R. 362, a declaration of incompatibility was sought on the basis that this section does not authorise a tribunal to consider and to determine questions such as whether a hospital is a particularly suitable hospital in terms of the degree of security or in terms of geographical proximity to the family of a patient. With regard to the latter point, it was claimed that as this section does not empower a tribunal to consider or to determine the rights of a patient or the members of his family under art.8 it is incompatible with the ECHR. The application was rejected on the authority of *Re S (Care Plan)* [2002] UKHL 10; [2002] 2 All E.R. 192, where the House of Lords held that a lacuna in an Act, or a failure to provide an effective remedy for a violation of a Convention right, does not lead to the conclusion that the Act is incompatible with that Convention right or the provisions of the Convention in question.

The question whether the continued detention of an asymptomatic patient contravenes art.5 of the

ECHR was considered by the Court of Appeal in *R. (on the application of H) v Mental Health Review Tribunal, North and North East London Region* which is noted under "nature or degree" in subs.(1)(b)(i), below.

Article 5 protects against arbitrary detention; it does not incorporate any additional requirement of proportionality. There is therefore no need for the court to consider whether this section, which sets out a test to prevent arbitrary detention, is itself a proportional response to art.5(1)(e) (*R. (on the application of CS) v Mental Health Review Tribunal* [2004] EWHC 2958 (Admin); [2004] M.H.L.R. 355); also see *DL-H v Devon Partnership NHS Trust*, below, and the General Note, above. The detention itself can only be justified "where other, less severe, measures have been considered and found to be insufficient to safeguard the individual or public interest which might require that the person concerned be detained" (*X v Finland* [2012] M.H.L.R. 318, para.151).

The question whether a decision not to discharge a patient who had been granted a conditional discharge by a tribunal due to a failure to put in place appropriate after-care facilities in the community constitutes a violation of art.5 is considered in the notes on s.117 under this heading.

Subsection (1)

This provision requires a tribunal to discharge an unrestricted detained patient if it is not satisfied as to any one of the criteria set out in (a)(i), (ii) or (b)(i), (ii), (iii). A community patient must be discharged if the tribunal is not satisfied as to any one of the criteria set out in (c)(i), (ii), (iii), (iv) or (v). When determining whether criterion (c)(iii) is met, the tribunal must consider the matters set out in subs.(1A). A tribunal is not required to discharge a patient because it considers that it might be appropriate for the patient to be made subject to a community treatment order (CTO) (subs.3A).

1-964

This provision also provides the tribunal with discretion to discharge the patient even though it considers that the relevant criteria are satisfied: see the note on "May in any case direct that the patient be discharged", below.

In *MH v Mental Health Review Tribunal for Northern Ireland* [2014] NIQB 87, Horner J., sitting in the High Court of Justice in Northern Ireland, said that the tribunal should have expressly dealt with a claim by the patient that if he was discharged, he would remain in the hospital as a voluntary patient.

In *DL-H v Devon Partnership NHS Trust* [2010] UKUT 102 (AAC); [2010] M.H.L.R. 162, UT Judge Jacobs rejected a submission that the tribunal had to apply a test of proportionality to the patient's detention:

> "The tribunal must discharge the patient unless detention for treatment is necessary for the patient's health or safety or for the protection of others. The legislation authorises detention by reference to the twin requirements of treatment and protection, moderated by the word 'necessary'. That is a demanding test and provides ample protection for the patient without the need for any additional consideration of proportionality." (para.27)"

This issue was also addressed in the *CS* case which is noted under Human Rights Act 1998, above.

As essentially the same criteria have to be applied in relation to admission and discharge (*Reid v Secretary of State for Scotland* [1999] 1 All E.R. 481, per Lord Clyde at 503 and *R. v East London and City Mental Health NHS Trust Ex p. Brandenburg* [2001] EWCA Civ 239; [2001] M.H.L.R. 36, per Lord Phillips at paras 17, 18; also see *R. v Upper Tribunal* [2021] M.H.L.R. 323), reference should be made to the notes on the admission criteria under ss.2(2) and 3(2). As the patient may be on leave of absence under s.17 at the time of the tribunal hearing, reference should also be made to the notes on s.20(4) and to the notes on "appropriate for him to be liable to be detained in a hospital for medical treatment" in para.(b)(i), below. It is not fatal to a decision of a tribunal if it does not expressly consider whether the patient meets the admission criteria, so long as it considers the discharge criteria and provided that in the process it has effectively considered all the criteria that would be relevant to admission: see *R. (on the application of H) v Mental Health Review Tribunal, North and East London Region* [2000] M.H.L.R. 242 where Crane J. said at para.52:

> "Moreover, if the question is asked, namely would the admission criteria be fulfilled if this patient presented today, that question undoubtedly requires amplification in the case of a patient detained in hospital. If a doctor is considering admission criteria, he must ask himself whether there is a risk of failure to take medication in the future and of a consequent deterioration. So, similarly, if the patient is already in hospital, a similar question must be asked. If he is no longer in hospital, to what extent is there a risk of a failure to take medication and of consequent deterioration? It would plainly be too simplistic a question simply to ask, if he were as he is today, would he qualify for admission?"

A similar approach was adopted by Latham J. in *R. v London South West Region Mental Health Review*

Tribunal Ex p. Moyle [1999] M.H.L.R. 195, para.34, where his Lordship said that although the discharge criteria mirror the admission criteria:

"the patient applying for discharge is ex hypothesi in a different situation from the person who is in the community. As a patient, he or she is receiving care and medication in the controlled environment of the hospital and not ... free to exercise his or her own wishes. In a case like the present, the assessment of risk must involve a judgment as to the extent to which release into the community will give rise to the likelihood that he or she will not comply with medication, with the consequences described by the psychiatrist".

It is therefore submitted that the patient's RC should not be asked: "Would the patient's current mental state justify making an application?". Rather, she should be asked to identify the consequences for the patient and/or the public if the tribunal decided to discharge the patient.

The question of what after-care services will be available in the community is relevant to the issue of whether the criteria in this provision are met: see *R. (on the application of Ashworth Hospital Authority) v Mental Health Review Tribunal for the West Midlands and North West Regions*, noted under para.(b). However, it is not essential for the tribunal to have specific information about aftercare in every case: see *AM v West London MH NHS Trust & Secretary of State for Justice* [2012] UKUT 382 where UT Judge Jacobs said at para.29:

"On the tribunal's findings, Mr M had not yet progressed to the point where the issue of aftercare that was actually available would arise. Without some acceptance or insight, Mr M could not progress to the point where his management in the community could even be tested by unescorted leave, let alone where he could be conditionally discharged."

On refusing permission to appeal in this case, Richards L.J. said:

"[It] seems to me ... that it must, as a matter of principle, be open to a Tribunal to conclude in the circumstances of a particular case that information or better information of aftercare is incapable of affecting the decision, and that an adjournment to secure its provision could achieve nothing beyond additional expense and delay and would therefore be inappropriate" ([2013] EWCA Civ 1010, para.9).

Also see the obiter comments of UT Judge Wright in *AF v Nottinghamshire NHS Trust* [2015] UKUT 216 (AAC); [2015] M.H.L.R. 347 which are reproduced in the General Note to s.117 under the heading *Applications to the First-tier Tribunal (Mental Health) and to the Hospital Managers*.

This subsection only applies to restricted patients to the extent provided for in ss.73 and 74 (subs.(7)).

Application   Or a reference made by the Secretary of State (subs.(6)).

In respect of a patient who is liable to be detained under this Act or is a community patient   In *KF v Birmingham and Solihull Mental Health NHS Foundation Trust* [2010] UKUT 185 (AAC); [2010] M.H.L.R. 176, para.57, the Upper Tribunal said:

(i)   in the context of references, these words refer to the patient's status both at the date the reference is made and at the subsequent hearing of that reference;

(ii)   a patient may therefore fall within this provision by being liable to be detained under the Act when the reference is made and by being a community patient at the time of the hearing; and

(iii)   sub-paragraphs (a) to (c) of subs.(1) refer *only* to the patient's status as at the time of the hearing (not the date of the reference), and set out the legal tests to be applied depending on the patient's particular status at that time (see *AA v Cheshire and Wirral Partnership NHS Trust* [2009] UKUT 195 (AAC) at para.45).

May in any case direct that the patient be discharged   The tribunal has power to discharge the patient even though the legal grounds for compulsory detention or a CTO still subsist. The discharge could take place some time after the tribunal's decision (subs.(3)). This discretion should only be exercised in "exceptional circumstances" where the tribunal is "satisfied that the identified needs [of the patient] for treatment and protection can be properly catered for". It "will almost certainly only be appropriate where discharge would be consistent with the existence of the statutory criteria in [this subsection]" (*GA v Betsi Cadwaladr University LHB* [2013] 0280 (AAC); [2014] M.H.L.R. 27, per Judge Jacobs at paras 22 and 24).

In a case known to the author, the tribunal exercised its discretionary power to discharge a detained patient to enable him to join his parents in the USA and to receive treatment for his mental disorder there. Also see *Northamptonshire Healthcare NHS Foundation Trust v ML* [2014] EWCOP 2 where a discretionary discharge was ordered by the tribunal in a situation where the patient's reaction to an intensive behavioural intervention programme had resulted in him being placed in seclusion on multiple occasions.

Where the discharge of a patient who has been detained under s.2 has been barred by the RC issuing a report under s.25, a tribunal is not obliged to consider the dangerousness criterion in that section when exercising its discretion to discharge even if the patient's detention under s.2 has been extended by the operation of s.29(4). Whether it does so will depend on its assessment of the facts of an individual case (*R. (on the application of MH) v Secretary of State for Health* [2004] EWHC 56 (Admin); [2004] M.H.L.R. 155).

Paragraph (a)

The tribunal must discharge the patient from detention under s.2 if it is not satisfied as to either of the criteria set out in paras (i) and (ii).

1-965

Discharge   This term has to be read in a way which is compatible with art.5(1) of the European Convention on Human Rights. Consequently a person is discharged from detention if he is no longer deprived of his liberty (*R.(on the application of Secretary of State for the Home Department) v Mental Health Review Tribunal* [2002] EWHC 1128 (Admin); [2002] M.H.L.R. 241). The Court of Appeal proceeded on the assumption this proposition was correct ([2002] EWCA Civ 1868; [2003] M.H.L.R. 202). In *Secretary of State for Justice v KC* [2015] UKUT 376 (AAC); [2015] M.H.L.R. 369, Charles J. said that this and earlier cases need "to be considered having regard to [the decision of the Supreme Court in *P v Cheshire West and Chester Council* [2014] UKSC 19] and in particular its conclusion that a wide range of circumstances and settings can give rise to the result that on an objective assessment a person is deprived of his liberty" (para.87).

Satisfied   The burden of proof is placed on the detaining authority to satisfy the tribunal as to the matters set out in this provision. In *R. (on the application of N) v Mental Health Review Tribunal (Northern Region)* [2005] EWCA Civ 1605; [2006] 4 All E.R. 194, the Court of Appeal held that:

1.   The correct standard of proof to be applied by the tribunal under this section and s.73 is the civil standard of proof on the balance of probabilities (or preponderance of probability). Richards L.J. said at para.62:

> "Although there is a single *standard* of proof, it is flexible in its *application*. In particular, the more serious the allegation or the more serious the consequences if the allegation is proved, the stronger must be the evidence before a court will find the allegation proved on the balance of probabilities. Thus the flexibility of the standard lies not in any adjustment to the degree of probability required for an allegation to be proved (such that a more serious allegation has to be proved to a higher degree of probability), but in the strength or quality of the evidence that will in practice be required for an allegation to be proved on the balance of probabilities."

2.   In relation to this section and s.73, no more than cogent evidence that was accepted as correct will be required in order to satisfy the tribunal, on the balance of probabilities, that the conditions for continuing detention are met. Demanding an especially high evidential requirement would subvert the obvious purpose of the Act which sought both to protect the interests of the individual whose ability to act in his own best interests was impaired and at the same time enable a proportionate balance to be struck between individual and public interests.

3.   The findings in 1 and 2 are in full conformity with the requirements of the ECHR.

4.   The standard of proof has a potential part to play in the decision-making process even in relation to issues that are the subject of judgment and evaluation. Richards L.J said at para.103:

> "We ... think it likely that the tribunal's task will be made easier if, instead of dividing up the issues into matters that are susceptible to proof to a defined standard and those that are not, it approaches the entire range of issues by reference to the standard of proof on the balance of probabilities, whilst recognising that in practice the standard of proof will have a much more important part to play in the determination of disputed issues of fact that it will generally have in matters of judgment as to appropriateness and necessity."

The finding made by Richards L.J. at point 1 was endorsed by the House of Lords in *Re D* [2008] UKHL

33 para.27, where Lord Carswell said that it "effectively states in concise terms the proper state of the law on this topic". Lord Carswell stated that he would add one small qualification to the statement made by Richard's L.J. concerning the seriousness of the anticipated consequences. His view was that this should be considered as no more than a facet of the seriousness of the allegation. The following example was given, at para.28, to illustrate the point:

"[I]f it is alleged that a bank manager has committed a minor peculation, that could entail very serious consequences for his career, so making it less likely that he would risk doing such a thing."

Then suffering The term "then" refers to the time of the tribunal's review and the tribunal has no power to consider the validity of the admission which gave rise to the liability to detain. The tribunal will doubtless endeavour to assess a patient's condition in the round, and in considering issues of health, safety and public protection under this provision and under sub-para.(b)(ii) it cannot ignore the foreseeable future consequences of discharge, but the temporal reference of "then" is clear and the tribunal is not called upon to make an assessment which will remain accurate indefinitely or for any given period of time (*R. v East London and The City Mental Health Trust Ex p. Brandenburg* [2003] UKHL 58 para.9(3)).

Mental disorder There is no requirement for a diagnosis of the patient's mental disorder to have been made (*JP v South London and Maudsley NHS Foundation Trust* [2012] UKUT 486 (AAC), para.13). In this case, UT Judge Lane said that the "Tribunal would be entitled to accept a report prepared by a doctor [who had not seen the patient] from medical notes, though it would have to be examined with care to justify the Tribunal's conclusions" (para.16).

Nature or degree See the note on para.(b)(i), below.

Warrants See *AM v South London & Maudsley NHS Foundation Trust* [2013] UKUT 365 (AAC); [2014] M.H.L.R. 181 which is noted in the General Note to this section.

Detention Or the patient's liability to be detained during a period of leave of absence granted under s.17 (*R. v Barking Havering and Brentford Community Healthcare NHS Trust* [1999] 1 F.L.R. 106).

Protection of other persons See the note on para.(b)(ii), below.

Paragraph (b)

1-966 The tribunal must discharge the patient from detention under s.3 if they are not satisfied as to any one of the criteria set out in paras (i), (ii) and (iii). Where a tribunal is considering the matters specified in paras (i) or (ii) they must bear in mind the distinction between the two matters and "one must somehow be able to read from the reasons the issue to which the reasons are directed" (*R. v Mental Health Review Tribunal Ex p. Pickering* [1986] 1 All E.R. 99 at 104, per Forbes J.). In *MD v Mersey Care NHS Trust* [2013] UKUT 0127 (AAC); [2013] M.H.L.R. 164, UT Judge Jacobs said at para.8:

"The criteria in section 72(1)(b) may be separate, but they are also related in the sense that evidence may be relevant to more than one. Similarly, the conclusion in respect of one criterion may be relevant to another. As Latham J. recognised in *R v London South and South West Region Mental Health Review Tribunal, ex parte Moyle* [1999] MHLR 195, the legal tests may be different but the facts found in relation to one test may determine the application of another."

In *MD*, it was accepted that risk is relevant to both paras (i) and (ii), but it is not necessarily relevant to the issue of whether appropriate treatment is available for a patient under para. (iia): see the notes on s.3(2)(d).

In *R. (on the application of Ashworth Hospital Authority) v Mental Health Review Tribunal for West Midlands and North West Regions* [2001] EWHC Admin 901; [2002] M.H.L.R. 13, Stanley Burnton J. said at para.64:

"[S]atisfaction of the criteria for the discharge of a patient under [this provision] may depend on the availability of suitable after-care. If no such after-care is available, it may follow that it is appropriate for the patient to be liable to be detained, or that it is necessary for him to receive treatment in a hospital".

This case was appealed and the following observations of Stanley Burnton J. were endorsed by the Court of Appeal:

"If there is uncertainty as to the putting in place of the after-care arrangements on which satisfaction of the discharge criteria depends, the tribunal should adjourn ... to enable them to be put in place, indicating their views and giving appropriate directions" ([2002] EWCA Civ 923; [2002] M.H.L.R. 314).

In *DN v Northumberland Tyne and Wear NHS Foundation Trust* [2011] UKUT 327 (AAC); [2011] M.H.L.R. 249, UT Judge Jacobs held that there was no reason why the deprivation of liberty safeguards contained in the Mental Capacity Act 2005 cannot be applied in anticipation of the patient being discharged from detention and moving to a care home as long as he was not "within the scope of the Mental Health Act" on his discharge (see Sch.1A of the 2005 Act). This would enable suitable arrangements, in particular those relating to him accessing alcohol, to be in place on his arrival at the care home. Also see *Secretary of State for Justice v KC* [2015] UKUT 376 (AAC) noted under "Conditions" in s.73(4).

Discharge   See the note on para.(a).

Sub-paragraph (i)

Then suffering   See the note on para.(a).   **1-967**

Mental disorder   If the person has a learning disability, the disability must be associated with abnormally aggressive or seriously irresponsible conduct (s.1(2A), (2B)).

Nature or degree   The meaning of this phrase is considered in the note on s.3(2)(a). In *R. v The Mental Health Review Tribunal or the South Thames Region Ex p. Smith* (1999) 47 B.M.L.R. 104, the tribunal refused to discharge the patient who was suffering from paranoid schizophrenia, the symptoms of which were well controlled by medication. On refusing the patient's application to judicially review this decision, Popplewell J. said:

"[At the time of the tribunal hearing the patient] was in a stable condition and it is quite clear that the illness was not of a degree which of itself made it appropriate for him to be liable to be detained. The reason for that was because he had a chronic condition which was static. However, the nature of the condition was that it might cease to be static so that the interpretation that nature is in some way unchanging in one view may be right, but the effect of the condition is that because of its very nature it may not remain static. It seems to me that if the facts upon which the tribunal rely have shown that it may not be static, that goes to the nature of the condition. The degree in the instant case, in relation to his condition, was not relevant because it was static and stable."

His Lordship continued:

"If one had simply to look at the degree it would have been right for the discharge to take place, but the nature of the condition was such that it was clear that he should not be discharged. It may well be in a great number of cases that nature and degree involve much the same questions ... and it maybe that tribunals will be wise, if they have any doubts about it, to include them both [in their conclusions]."

Smith was followed by Latham J. in *R. v London and South West Region Mental Health Review Tribunal Ex p. Moyle* [1999] M.H.L.R. 195 where his Lordship, when considering the position of a patient with a history of relapsing, said:

"The correct analysis, in my judgment, is that the nature of the illness of a patient such as the applicant is that it is an illness which will relapse in the absence of medication. The question that then has to be asked is whether the nature of that illness is such as to make it appropriate for him to be liable to be detained in hospital for medical treatment. Whether it is appropriate or not will depend upon an assessment of the probability that he will relapse in the near future if he were free in the community."

Moyle is also considered in the note on "Appropriate for him to be liable to be detained in hospital for medical treatment", below.

A finding by a tribunal that the patient's "illness is of a nature to justify detention in hospital but not at present of a degree" constituted a misdirection of law because it erroneously treated "nature or degree" as conjunctive rather than disjunctive. Separate consideration of nature and degree is needed (*R. (on the application of the Home Secretary) v Mental Health Review Tribunal* [2003] EWHC 2864 (Admin); [2004] M.H.L.R. 91 para.57). In *R. (on the application of the Secretary of State for the Home Department) v Mental Health Review Tribunal and CH* [2005] EWHC 746 (Admin); [2005] M.H.L.R. 199, Stanley Burnton J. said, at para.33, that he had "some sympathy" with the difficulties faced by tribunals in addressing the statutory criteria and the distinction between "nature" and "degree", and that in many cases "the distinction is elusive, and it may not matter under which head the question is addressed".

The question whether the continued detention of an asymptomatic patient contravenes art.5 of the ECHR was considered by the Court of Appeal in *R. (on the application of H) v Mental Health Review Tribunal, North and North East London Region* [2001] EWCA Civ 415; [2001] M.H.L.R. 48, where Lord Phillips M.R. said at para.33:

"The circumstances of the present case, which are similar to those considered by Latham J. in [*Moyle*], are not uncommon. A patient is detained who is unquestionably suffering from schizophrenia. While in the controlled environment of the hospital he is taking medication, and as a result of the medication is in remission. So long as he continues to take the medication he will pose no danger to himself or to others. The nature of the illness is such, however, that if he ceases to take the medication he will relapse and pose a danger to himself or to others. The professionals may be uncertain whether, if he is discharged into the community, he will continue to take the medication. We do not believe that Article 5 requires that the patient must always be discharged in such circumstances. The appropriate response should depend upon the result of weighing the interests of the patient against those of the public having regard to the particular facts. Continued detention can be justified if, but only if, it is a proportionate response having regard to the risks that would be involved in discharge."

Appropriate for him to be liable to be detained in a hospital for medical treatment The term "appropriate" does not include the conditions of a patient's detention (*Djaba v West London Mental Health Trust* [2017] EWCA Civ 436; [2017] M.H.L.R. 345 para.51).

In *R. (on the application of the Secretary of State for the Home Department) v Mental Health Review Tribunal)* [2002] EWHC 1128 (Admin); [2002] M.H.L.R. 241 para.24, Elias J. cited the observations of Lord Phillips in *H*, above, and said:

"In determining whether it is appropriate to detain a patient in hospital, the interests of the patient have to be weighed against those of the public, and the tribunal has to determine whether the detention is proportional to the risks involved. If it is not satisfied that it is a proportional response to those risks to detain the patient, then he must be discharged."

A judgment on proportionality also has to be made with respect to the risk to the patient's health should he be discharged from detention even if there is no risk to the public. In *Smirek v Williams* [2000] M.H.L.R. 38, the Court of Appeal in a permission hearing held that it can be appropriate for a patient to be liable to be detained in a hospital if the evidence is that, without being detained in hospital, the patient will not take the medication that is required to prevent the deterioration of a chronic mental illness.

In *Cumbria, Northumberland Tyne & Wear NHS Foundation Trust v EG* [2021] EWHC 2990 (Fam); [2022] M.H.L.R. 309, EG was a conditionally discharged restricted patient. He has been receiving treatment at a care home on s.17(3) leave for 7 years. His treatment had no physical connection to the hospital where he had been detained, even though the treatment had been supervised from the hospital. The conditions of the discharge included that EG must live at the care home, which amounted to a deprivation of his liberty. In the absence of such arrangements, EG was assessed as posing a risk of harm to others. In 2018, the Supreme Court in *Secretary of State for Justice v MM* [2018] UKSC 60 held that a restricted patient cannot be discharged from hospital under this Act on conditions that amounted to a deprivation of liberty. The evidence showed that being in hospital, even as an out-patient, was positively counter-therapeutic for EG. A recall to hospital would therefore breech his art.5 ECHR rights. Due to the decision in *MM*, EG was subject to a "technical" recall, which did not involve his physical return to hospital, and his case was automatically referred to the First-tier tribunal. The tribunal considered that it had no choice under the existing case law, including the cases noted below, but to discharge EG because the criteria under s.72(1)(b)(i) were not met. This decision was reached even though it was accepted that discharge did not serve the interests of any party, including EG, or the public. On an appeal of the decision of the tribunal, Lieven J. said that where the recall of a conditionally discharged restricted patient to hospital would breech his rights under art.5(1)(e) of the ECHR, the interpretative power in s.3 of the Human Rights Act 1998 could be applied to construe the Mental Health Act so as to be compatible with the patient's Convention rights. On adopting this approach, her Ladyship held that it is possible to read the s.72(1)(b) that makes the phrase "liable to be detained" mean "liable in law to be detained for treatment, even where that treatment is being provided in the community, so long as it could lawfully be provided in hospital" (para.70). Her Ladyship concluded that it "is therefore possible to construe s.72 as to not require the Tribunal to discharge, even where the link to the hospital is tenuous (as here), where such a construction is necessary in order to avoid a breach of Article 5" (para.73).

The phrase "liable to be detained" includes patients who have been granted leave of absence from hospital under s.17 (*R. v Hallstrom Ex p. W* [1986] 2 All E.R. 306 at 312). In *R. (on the application of Epsom and St Helier NHS Trust) v Mental Health Review Tribunal* [2001] EWHC Admin 101; [2001] M.H.L.R. 8, the Trust challenged the decision of the tribunal to discharge the patient. The tribunal's decision was made on the ground that as the patient, who had been granted leave of absence under s.17 to reside in a nursing home, was not receiving in-patient treatment it was not "appropriate for her to be liable to be detained in hospital for medical treatment". Sullivan J. held that:

1. The decision of the Court of Appeal in *R. v Barking Havering and Brentwood Community Healthcare NHS Trust* [1999] 1 F.L.R. 106 is authority for the proposition that one has to look at the whole course of the patient's treatment. To do so, one has to look at the past, present and future (para.46).
2. It would be inconsistent with the scheme of the Act if the mere prospect, that at some unspecified future time in-patient treatment would or might be required, compelled a tribunal to reject a patient's application for discharge (para.51). His Lordship said at para.52:

> "The matter has to be looked at in the round, including the prospect of future in-patient treatment, but there will come a time when, even though it is certain that treatment will be required at some stage in the future, the timing of that treatment is so uncertain that it is no longer 'appropriate' for the patient to continue to be liable to detention. It is the tribunal's function to use its expertise to decide whether the certainty, or the possibility, of the need for in-patient treatment at some future date makes it 'appropriate' that the patient's liability to detention shall continue."

His Lordship's references to "in-patient treatment" should now be read as if they were references to "hospital treatment": see *R. (on the application of DR) v Mersey Care NHS Trust* [2002] EWHC 1810 (Admin); [2002] M.H.L.R. 386.

Subsequent to the decision in the *Epsom* case, the interpretation of this provision was considered in *R. (on the application of CS) v Mental Health Review Tribunal* [2004] EWHC 2958 (Admin); [2004] M.H.L.R. 355. Pitchford J. formulated the question for decision in that case as:

> "[W]as CS's mental illness of a nature and degree which made it appropriate for her to receive treatment, a significant and justified component of which was treatment in hospital?" (para.39)."

In *DB v Betsi Cadwaladr UHB* [2021] UKUT 53 (AAC); [2021] M.H.L.R. 335, the patient had been on leave under s.17 since October 2019. He had not set foot in the hospital since that date (i.e. for 11 months). His "virtual bed", as his solicitor put it, was at two different sites during his leave. Throughout that time, DB had been living in a care home with supervised leave in the community.

UT Judge Jacobs applied *CS* and held that:

1. It is not sufficient for the tribunal to find that that the administration of medication in a care home was a significant component of the patient's care plan; the tribunal must also find that a significant component of that plan was being provided in hospital (para.11).
2. Liability to detention under s.17 is not a fallback when other options, such as a CTO, are unsuitable or unavailable: if the statutory conditions for detention are not met, the tribunal must direct discharge (para.13).

In *CM v Derbyshire Healthcare NHS Foundation Trust* [2011] UKUT 129 (AAC); [2011] M.H.L.R. 153, UT Judge Levenson held that:

> "If the nature of a patient's illness is such that it will relapse in the absence of medication, then whether the nature is such as to make it appropriate for him to be liable to be detained in hospital for medical treatment depends on an assessment of the probability that he will relapse in the near future if he were free in the community and on whether the evidence is that without being detained in hospital he will not take the medication (*Smirek v Williams* (2000) 1 MHLR 38 - CA; *R v MHRT ex parte Moyle* [2000] Lloyd's LR 143 – High Court)" (para.12)."

This finding was challenged by UT Judge Ward in *LW v Cornwall Partnership NHS Trust* [2018] UKUT

408; [2019] M.H.L.R. 6 who said at para.24 that he did "not regard either *ex p Moyle* or *Smirek* as providing an authoritative basis for the views expressed at para 12 of *CM*". He said at para.27:

> "... I do accept that the time within which a relapse is thought likely to occur is a material consideration but am unable to discern a principle that such a relapse must be 'soon' or 'in the near future'. While clearly the case for detention may prove to be stronger if it is, that falls short of accepting Mr Pezzani's formulation that proximity in time 'determines' the decision about whether a detained patient is entitled to discharge."

It is submitted that the opinion expressed by Judge Ward is to be preferred as, unlike the judgment in *CM*, it was preceded by a detailed analysis of the case law.

The *Barking, Epsom, DR* and *CS* cases, which should be read subject to the decision in *Cumbria, Northumberland Tyne & Wear NHS Foundation Trust v EG*, above, are also considered in the note on s.20(4). In *SL v Ludlow Street Healthcare* [2015] UKUT 398 (AAC); [2015] M.H.L.R. 390 UT Judge Jacobs, having accepted the *Epsom, DR* and *CS* cases as "correctly stating the law" (para.34), made the following obiter comments at para.35 under the heading "Dangers to avoid":

> "There are two dangers that tribunals must bear in mind in applying the approach set out in the cases. First, the tribunal must not reason by analogy from the facts of those cases. It must apply the principles established by the cases, but their application can only be undertaken by reference to the facts and circumstances of the case before the tribunal. Even small differences may justify, or even require, a different analysis. Second, it is not sufficient merely to repeat the language of the principles. The tribunal must, of course, make sufficient findings of fact to support, and provide an explanation that justifies, its conclusion."

Sub-paragraph (ii)

1-968   **Necessary**   See *AM v South London & Maudsley NHS Foundation Trust* [2013] UKUT 365 (AAC); [2014] M.H.L.R. 181 which is noted in the General Note to this section. The standard "is one of necessity, not desirability" (*Reid v Secretary of State for Scotland* [1999] 1 All E.R. 481 per Lord Clyde at 504). The test of necessity is "demanding" (*DL-H v Devon Partnership NHS Trust* [2010] UKUT 102 (AAC); [2010] M.H.L.R. 162 per Judge Jacobs at para.27).

Protection of other persons   It is submitted that this phrase covers both protection from serious psychological harm as well as protection from physical harm: see the note on this phrase in s.2(2) and *Re Whitbread* which is noted under "Dangerous" in s.25(1).

The Court of Appeal in *R. v Vowles* [2015] EWCA Crim 45; [2016] M.H.L.R. 66 at para.35(iv) said:

> "The concept of burden of proof is not relevant in risk evaluation, even though the risk may be defined differently. This was determined by the courts in relation to the Parole Board: see *R (Sim) v Parole Board* [2004] QB 1288; *R (Brooks) v Parole Board* [2004] EWCA Civ 80. We agree with the submission that there is no difference in principle to the assessment of risk before the FTT."

In *AM v Partnerships in Care Ltd* [2015] UKUT 659; [2016] M.H.L.R. 214, the Upper Tribunal considered whether the tribunal is required to make findings of fact in order to support its conclusion that the patient who had allegedly committed rapes on fellow patients required assessment and appropriate treatment as to sexual violence. UT Judge Markus held that:

1.   Where an assessment of risk relies on past acts, those acts must be proved to the civil standard; a tribunal cannot find that a risk exists merely on the basis of unproven allegations.

2.   A decision on the likelihood of a future happening must be founded on a basis of present facts and the inferences fairly to be drawn therefrom (*Re (H)(Minors) (Sexual Abuse: Standard of Proof)* [1996] A.C. 563 at 590 applied).

3.   The conditions under this section of which a tribunal has to be satisfied involve mixed questions of fact and judgment or evaluation. But the judgment or evaluation of what is likely to occur must be based on fact. This does not mean that a tribunal could only be satisfied of the risk of sexual violence if it is satisfied that the rapes occurred. As Lord Nicholl observed in *Re H* at page 591E: "The range of facts which may properly be taken into account is infinite". In this case, relevant facts might involve aspects of the patient's sexual or other history, his behaviour towards others, things that he said, and his attitudes.

In *R. v Parole Board Ex p. Bradley* [1990] 3 All E.R. 828 at 836 DC, Stuart-Smith L.J., on examining this provision, said that "the precise level of risk is not (surely cannot be) spelt out". Bradley was referred to in *R. (on the application of N) v Mental Health Review Tribunal* [2001] EWHC Admin 1133; [2002] M.H.L.R. 70, where Gibbs J. made the following comments on risk assessment at paras 53–54:

"It is submitted that there was a requirement on the Tribunal itself to quantify the risk in the face of Dr Gravett's expressed inability at this stage, to do so. I accept ... that there may arise a stage at which a Tribunal must reasonably be required to quantify a risk. It depends on the context. If it was clear that all available evidence was there for it to consider but that the tribunal simply walked away from its responsibility and sat on the fence, then there would be justice in the criticism. I acknowledge also that even where the medical evidence before it does not enable it to quantify the risk there must come, or may come, a point in where continuous deferment of quantification is unreasonable ... Here the context is one in which Dr Gravett is, in my judgment, clearly expressing the view that there is a substantial and unacceptable, in unquantifiable, risk. There is a project for the treatment of the [patient], partially completed, one of the purposes of which is to define that risk more closely. There is, in my judgment, nothing wrong in principle in the psychiatrist, pending the outcome of that process, defining the possible range of risk widely. Nor, in my judgment, is there anything wrong in principle with the Tribunal accepting the psychiatrist's view. It is, in my judgment, unreasonable in that context to say that the Tribunal should attempt the impossible and reach some kind of assessment of risk which would be in danger of amounting to purely arbitrary speculation."

In *R. (on the application of Munday) v Secretary of State for the Home Department* [2009] EWHC 3638 (Admin), para.30, Burnett J. said:

"Although psychiatrists or other medical health professionals or social supervisors with their knowledge of a person might be in a position to express a view about risk, it is by its nature an exercise of evaluation which does not necessarily call for expert medical input."

The fact that a patient could pose a risk to the public for reasons unconnected with his mental illness is not relevant to the tribunal's decision (*R. (on the Application of Li) v Mental Health Review Tribunal* [2004] EWHC 51 (Admin)).

That he should receive such treatment   Compare with the criterion set out in para.(a)(ii).

Sub-paragraph (iia)

Appropriate medical treatment   An analysis of the appropriate medical treatment test and the ap-   **1-969**
proach that the tribunal should adopt when considering it is contained in the notes on s.3(2)(d).

Sub-paragraph (iii)

Paragraph (g) of section 66(1)   Which provides for an application to a tribunal to be made by a near-   **1-970**
est relative on the issue by the RC of a report under s.25, barring the nearest relative's discharge powers. Although the tribunal is under a duty to consider the "dangerousness" criterion where an application has been made by a nearest relative under s.66(1)(g), there is no such duty in the case of an application by the patient, although the tribunal is entitled to take it into account when deciding whether to exercise its discretionary power to discharge (*R. (on the application of W) v Mental Health Review Tribunal* [2004] EWHC 3266 (Admin); [2005] M.H.L.R. 134).

The test in para.(iii) is much narrower than that in para.(ii). It implies a likely serious psychological or physical injury to the patient or to some other person. A mere suspicion that the patient might be dangerous is not sufficient: see the notes on "likely to act" and "dangerous" in s.25(1). If they are not satisfied as to the criterion set out in this paragraph, the tribunal must discharge the patient, even if detention is still justified under paras (i) and (ii).

Section 66(1)(g) does not apply to patients who are detained under Pt III: applications made by or in respect of such patients are governed by s.69(1)(a) (*R. (on the application of Central and North West London Mental Health NHS Trust) v Mental Health Review Tribunal (Southern Region)* [2005] EWHC 337 (Admin); [2005] M.H.L.R. 183).

If released   As this phrase does not necessarily refer to immediate release, the tribunal could make an order for the deferred discharge of the patient (*R. (on the application of B) v Mental Health Review Tribunal* [2003] EWHC 815 (Admin); [2003] M.H.L.R. 218 para.8).

Sub-paragraph (iii)

Likely to act   It is submitted that in this context, "likely" means "more likely than not": see the note on "likely to act" in s.25(1).

Paragraph (c)

1-971   This paragraph states that if the tribunal is not satisfied as to any of the matters set out in (i) to (v) in relation to a community patient, the patient must be discharged. Sub-paragraphs (i) to (iv) replicate the criteria set out in s.17A(5)(a), (b), (d) and (e) and reference should be made to the notes thereto. The tribunal also has a general discretion to discharge the patient.

In *Welsh Ministers v PJ* [2018] UKSC 66; [2018] M.H.L.R. 411, the Supreme Court held at paras 30 to 34 that:

1. The tribunal has no power to revoke or vary the conditions attached to a CTO.
2. The patient's actual situation on the ground as described in the reports presented to the tribunal may well be relevant to whether the criteria for the CTO are made out.
3. If the tribunal identifies a state of affairs amounting to an unlawful deprivation of liberty, it is within its powers to explain to all concerned what the true legal effect of a CTO is.
4. If the reality is that the patient is being unlawfully detained, the remedy is either habeas corpus or judicial review.
5. A conscientious RC can be expected not to impose a condition on a CTO which deprives a patient of his liberty, and this is reinforced by the duties under s.132A to provide information to a patient and (usually) his nearest relative about the effect of a CTO.

The correct approach to the likelihood of relapse if a patient, once free of the CTO, does not take his or her medication and the possible consequences if such a relapse were to occur was considered by UT Judge Ward in *LW v Cornwall Partnership NHS Trust* [2018] UKUT 408; [2019] M.H.L.R. 6 where it was held that a defined degree of imminence of likely relapse is not required in order to justify a patient's discharge from a CTO. Judge Ward summarised his conclusions at para.49:

"(a)   in cases where there is a risk of a relapse which might necessitate recall, it will be a relevant consideration when it is thought likely such a relapse will occur;

(b)   that factor is not of itself determinative; other factors, including the risk to the patient and/or others if a relapse were to occur, may also be relevant;

(c)   the authorities do not establish as a matter of law that likely relapse must be 'soon', 'in the near future' or within the permitted duration of a CTO for discharge to be lawfully refused;

(d)   the case for discharge may be stronger if the anticipated timescale for relapse is protracted, but all relevant circumstances must be taken into account in deciding what is 'appropriate' for the purposes of s.72(1)(c); ...

(f)   I have reached these conclusions primarily from consideration of the statutory framework of CTOs and the legislative purposes behind them. I do not accept that there is a necessary and complete read-across from authorities relating to s.3. Even were I to be wrong in that, I consider that the cases cited do not provide authority for a requirement that relapse be likely soon or in the near future if the patient is to be refused discharge."

In *GA v Betsi Cadwaladr University LHB* [2013] 0280 (AAC); [2014] M.H.L.R. 27, UT Judge Jacobs held that the tribunal had no jurisdiction under this provision to deal with issues of consent to treatment when a patient was on a CTO. Judge Jacobs had previously analysed the legislation in *SH v Cornwall Partnership NHS Trust* [2012] M.H.L.R 383 where he reached the following conclusion at para.16:

"The result is that the tribunal has the right to order the release of the patient, but no more. It does not have power to order that the patient be recalled to hospital. Nor does it have any power to direct the responsible authority to take any steps in respect of the patient's treatment, including steps to allow it to give treatment without consent. Those would be surprising limitations on the tribunal's powers, if it had jurisdiction to deal with issues of consent. The tribunal can make recommendations about treatment (as under s.72(3A)(a)), but they are powers only. It has no right to impose that recommendation on the clinical staff."

Sub-paragraph (i)

Mental disorder   If the person has a learning disability, the disability must be associated with   **1-972**
abnormally aggressive or seriously irresponsible conduct (s.1(2A), (2B)).

Sub-paragraph (iii)

See subs.(1A).   **1-973**

Sub-paragraph (iv)

In *PM v Midlands Partnership NHS Foundation Trust* [2020] UKUT 69 (AAC); [2020] M.H.L.R.   **1-974**
320, the issue before UT Judge Church was "whether the lawfulness of administering medication to a
Part 4A patient is relevant to a tribunal's assessment of whether the medical treatment proposed by the
responsible authority was appropriate and available, or whether such a consideration, like consent, is
something that comes into play only at the later stage of deciding whether to give the treatment"
(para.9.4). In this case, a CTO patient was refusing her depot medication. At the time of the tribunal hearing, the certificate requirement under Part 4A did not have to be satisfied until two days after the hearing.
Although a SOAD referral had been made by the patient's RC, it was not known when a SOAD would
be available to assess the patient. Judge Church held that while the lack of SOAD approval may, but
will not always be relevant to the issue of "appropriateness" (para.9.10), it was not open to the tribunal
to find that the treatment was "available" to the patient (para.10). Judge Church said that the fact that
SOAD approval was not required on the day that the tribunal sat did not undermine his finding because
when determining whether the criteria set out in s.72(1)(c) were satisfied that determination must not
be based on a mere "snapshot". At para.10.14, he said that the following approach taken by Sullivan J.
in *R. (on the application of Epsom and St Helier NHS Trust) v Mental Health Review Tribunal* [2001]
EWHC Admin 101; [2001] M.H.L.R. 8 should be adopted:

"[O]ne has to look at the whole course of treatment. To do so, one has to look at the past, present
and future. It is not enough to say that a patient is not receiving treatment at a particular time"
(para.47).

Two points can be made about the decision in *PM*: First, Judge Church said at para.8.4:

"However, it is clear from the Tribunal's decision with reasons that the only medical treatment the
Tribunal relied upon in deciding to uphold Miss M's CTO was the administration of her prescribed
depot antipsychotic medication. Further, the Tribunal did not make findings as to the activities
involved in monitoring Miss M or as to the purpose of those activities which would have been sufficient to support a decision that the monitoring activities themselves amounted to medical treatment.
I therefore restrict my analysis in the rest of this decision to the proposed medical treatment that the
Tribunal did rely on: the administration of prescribed psychotropic medication."

It is unusual for a tribunal to find that medication is the only medical treatment that the patient is
receiving.
Second, what if SOAD approval for the medication was not required until, for example, two weeks
after the tribunal hearing? It is unclear from the judgment whether the medical treatment would be said
to be unavailable in such a situation if it was not known when the SOAD's assessment would take place.
It is suggested that the approach taken in this case should only be followed where the need for a
certificate is imminent and no SOAD visit has been arranged.

Sub-paragraph (v)

See the notes on para.(b)(iii), above.   **1-975**

Subsection (1A)

See the notes on s.17A(6).   **1-976**

Subsection (3)

This provision enables the tribunal to defer the patient's discharge to a future date. If the tribunal   **1-977**
decides not to exercise its power of deferment, it may make a recommendation that the patient be either

granted leave of absence, or transferred to another hospital or into guardianship and may reconsider the case if the recommendation is not complied with. As a patient who is subject to a deferred discharge continues to be "liable to be detained", the RC retains the power to grant leave of absence during the period of deferment.

The power to defer discharge applies to situations where the tribunal has exercised either its mandatory or its discretionary duty to discharge (*R. v Mental Health Review Tribunal for the North Thames Region Ex p. Pierce* (1996) 36 B.M.L.R. 137). A different conclusion was reached by Stephens J., sitting in the High Court in Northern Ireland, who, on considering an equivalent provision in art.77(2) of the Mental Health (Northern Ireland) Order 1986, held that the power to defer discharge is confined to a discretionary discharge (*X's Application (No.2)* [2009] NIQB 2).

If a detained patient is made subject to a CTO during a period of deferred discharge, the CTO will end on the discharge taking effect as the s.3 application upon which the CTO is based will no longer be in place. Placing the patient of a CTO in this situation would therefore be a pointless exercise. This was accepted as being the correct legal position in *MP v Mersey Care NHS Trust* [2011] UKUT 107 (AAC); [2011] M.H.L.R. 146, para.14.

Deferral cannot be used to test whether a patient is ready for discharge: see *CNWL NHS Foundation Trust v H-JH* [2012] UKUT 210 (AAC); [2012] M.H.L.R. 305, a case where a deferred discharge was held to be lawful where the reason for the deferral was to allow an opportunity for the patient's RC to reduce the patient's medication. The reason for this was not to make the patient ready for release, but because she had been complaining about the medication's side-effects. In this case, UT Judge Jacobs identified at para.22 the action that could be taken by a detaining authority if the condition of a CTO patient deteriorated after a deferred discharge had been made in respect of him:

"An authority's powers have to be considered at two stages: (i) before the discharge takes effect; and (ii) thereafter. As to (i), the community treatment order remains in force until the discharge takes effect. Until then, a patient remains liable to have her medication changed and to be recalled to hospital. As to (ii), it is possible to detain a patient immediately following discharge. ... It is permissible to re-admit a patient on the basis of 'information not known to the tribunal which puts a significantly different complexion on the case as compared with that which was before the tribunal' [see *R. v East London and The City Mental Health NHS Trust Ex p. Brandenburg* which is considered in the General Note to s.3]."

The discharge on a future date of a patient who is found by the tribunal not to be suffering from a mental disorder would be in danger of violating art.5(1)(e) of the ECHR if the delay between the decision to discharge and the date of discharge was excessive: see *Johnson v United Kingdom* (1999) 27 E.H.R.R. 296, noted in art.5(1)(e) under "persons of unsound mind". Also see the note on Human Rights Act 1998 in s.73.

Deferment can be used to enable preparations to be made to receive a patient back into the community, although there is no power for the tribunal to reconsider the deferment if circumstances show that what is required to provide after-care services to the patient cannot be put in place. In *R. (on the application of H) v Ashworth Hospital Authority* [2002] EWCA Civ 923; [2002] M.H.L.R. 362, Dyson L.J. said at para.68:

"If the tribunal had any doubt as to whether [after-care] services would be available, they should have adjourned to obtain any necessary information. I regard the alternative of a deferral [...] as less satisfactory ... [I]f the tribunal is in doubt as to whether suitable after-care arrangements will be available, it is difficult to see how they can specify a particular date for discharge. In cases of doubt, the safer course is to adjourn."

In *JMcG v Devon Partnership NHS Trust (MH)* [2017] UKUT 348 (AAC); [2017] M.H.L.R. 360, UT Judge Knowles said that the decision in *H* "reinforces the need for care on the part of tribunals when deciding if a deferred discharge is appropriate. It moreover accords with my view that deferred discharge is permissible in a limited number of situations which almost but not always centre on the arrangements for a patient's after-care. It will be a matter for the good sense of tribunals to discern whether there is both sufficient and certain information about after-care such that a particular date for discharge can be specified" (para.29).

The power to defer discharge may also be used in a case of an application made by a nearest relative under s.66(1)(g): see *R. (on the application of B) v Mental Health Review Tribunal* [2003] EWHC 815 (Admin); [2003] M.H.L.R. 218, where Stanley Burnton J. said at para.8:

"If a tribunal, on the evidence before it, comes to the conclusion that a patient, if released immediately, would be likely to act in a manner dangerous to other persons, or to himself or herself, but that if proper after-care arrangements are put in place that will not be the position, in my judgement, it is clear that the tribunal may make an order for a deferred discharge under section 72(3) deferring discharge to a date when it is reasonably assured that the appropriate aftercare arrangements will be in place."

In *Perkins v Bath District Health Authority; R. v Wessex Health Review Tribunal Ex p. Wiltshire CC* 4 B.M.L.R. 145, the tribunal directed the patient's discharge from s.2 but directed that the patient's discharge be deferred "to give an adequate opportunity to those responsible to consider whether an application for treatment might be appropriate". Although counsel for the tribunal was prepared to accept that a tribunal cannot defer discharge under this provision to enable the authorities to decide whether there is some other basis for lawful detention, the Court of Appeal was not required to resolve the point. It is likely that counsel's concession would be upheld if the point was required to be resolved. The tribunal could defer discharge if it was felt that the patient would be fit for discharge at the expiration of a further short period of treatment.

Direct the discharge of a patient under that subsection   i.e. under subs.(1) which is concerned with the powers of tribunals to discharge unrestricted patients. This subsection does not therefore apply to patients who are subject to restriction orders (*R. v Oxford Mental Health Authority Review Tribunal Ex p. Smith*, January 25, 1995 CA). A submission that art.5(4) of the ECHR requires that this subsection be construed to apply to restricted patients was rejected by Collins J. in *R. (on the application of the Secretary of State for the Home Department) v Mental Health Review Tribunal* [2001] A.C.D. 62.

The power to defer does not apply to patients who are subject to guardianship because applications under subs.(1) can only be made in respect of patients who are "liable to be detained".

Date specified in the direction   In *JMcG v Devon Partnership NHS Trust (MH)*, above, UT Judge Knowles held obiter that "a tribunal, when exercising its power pursuant to s.72(3) to direct discharge on a specified future date, cannot specify a future date for discharge after that on which the authority for the patient's discharge expires" (para.32). With regard to the alternative of granting an adjournment, Judge Knowles said:

"If the tribunal was considering an adjournment beyond the date of the order authorising detention, there was nothing to prevent it taking that course since this would not have the same legal effect as a discharge pursuant to section 72(3). Of course, during the period of any adjournment, the Responsible Clinician could have used his/her powers to discharge the patient from liability to be detained in which case the adjournment and indeed the application to the tribunal would have been rendered academic" (para.37).

The date specified in the direction cannot be changed by the tribunal subsequent to the communication to the patient of the decision to defer discharge: see *Secretary of State for the Home Department v Oxford Regional Mental Health Review Tribunal* [1987] 3 All E.R. 8, noted under s.73(7).

Recommend   There is no power under this provision to make a recommendation with a view to doing something other than "facilitating the discharge of the patient on a future date". For example, there is no power to make a recommendation for the transfer of the patient to another hospital more convenient for him or his family (*R. (on the application of H) v Mental Health Review Tribunal*, below) or to make a recommendation which is contingent upon an event occurring, such as the patient's mental disorder being stabilised. For judicial guidance on the making of extra-statutory recommendations, see the remarks of UT Judge Rowland in *C v Birmingham and Solihull Mental Health NHS Trust* [2012] UKUT 178 (AAC) which are reproduced in the General Note to s.73.

A failure to make a recommendation is not amenable to judicial review because it is not a final decision (*R. (on the application of LH) v Mental Health Review Tribunal* [2002] EWHC 170 (Admin); [2002] M.H.L.R. 130), although a failure to give reasons for not making a recommendation might be susceptible to judicial review in circumstances where the contentions and material before the tribunal justified its consideration of such a recommendation (*R. (on the application of H) v Mental Health Review Tribunal* [2002] EWHC 1522 (Admin); [2002] M.H.L.R. 362 para.24). The appropriate procedure now would be for an application to be made to the tribunal under r.49 of the Tribunal Rules for it to review its decision. This happened in *RB v Nottinghamshire Healthcare NHS Trust* [2011] UKUT 73 (AAC); [2011] M.H.L.R. 296 where UT Judge Jacobs made the following comments on the tribunal's power to make recommendations:

"The first question is whether to make a recommendation at all. The more obvious the recommendation, the more likely it is that the authority will consider it anyway. So recommendations are likely to be made in those cases where the authority has not considered the possibility or would be unlikely to do so. If the tribunal does make a recommendation, it has to take account of the tenuous nature of its control. This makes it essential to consider very carefully the timescale and the directions that the tribunal might give in order (i) to apply its moral pressure on the authority and (ii) to be fully informed by the time it has to decide whether to reconvene. It may, for example, be appropriate for the tribunal to direct that a progress report be provided shortly before a specified date so that it can decide if there is any practical purpose in reconvening. Finally, the tribunal has to decide whether to reconvene. In making that decision, it has to decide what practical value this would serve. It has no power to enforce the recommendation and is not reconvening for that purpose. It has the power to embarrass the authority into explaining its thinking or, possibly, into compliance. But it has to make a judgment on what it can practically achieve, if anything." (para.16)

In this case, Judge Jacobs said that the tribunal's power to make a recommendation must be exercised judicially, tempered by the reality that it has no power to coerce (para.12). The tribunal should have given reasons for its decision to make a recommendation (para.13) and for exercising its discretion not to reconvene (para.15). In *RN v Curo Care* (2011) UKUT 263 (AAC); [2011] M.H.L.R. 337, Judge Jacobs held that the tribunal should also give reasons if it is asked to make a recommendation and declines to do so; see also *H*, above.

Transferred to another hospital   The lack of a power to secure the transfer of a patient to another hospital does not breech art.5 of the ECHR (*MP v Nottinghamshire Healthcare NHS Trust* [2003] EWHC 1782 (Admin); [2003] M.H.L.R. 381).

In *R. (on the application of L) v West London Mental Health NHS Trust* [2012] EWHC 3200 (Admin); [2013] M.H.L.R. 297, para.178, Stadlen J. said that it should "be noted that the Tribunal's power to recommend a transfer may only be exercised with a view to facilitating the patient's discharge. Although that may coincide with a conclusion that the patient's continued detention in a high security hospital is not necessary for the protection of himself or others it may not necessarily be so".

Further consider his case   The tribunal will set a time limit at the expiration of which it will reconsider the case. It may then decide to reconvene the hearing. At such a hearing the tribunal has all the powers available that it enjoyed at the original hearing (*Mental Health Review Tribunal v Hempstock* (1998) 39 B.M.L.R. 123). *Hemstock* was applied in *R. (on the application of O) v Mental Health Review Tribunal* [2006] EWHC 2659 (Admin); [2006] M.H.L.R. 326, where Collins J. held that the phrase "his case" meant the patient's application to the tribunal. Accordingly, that application and the tribunal's powers in respect of it, including the power to agree to the patient's request for his application to be withdrawn, remain extant after the tribunal has made a recommendation under this provision.

Subsection (3A)

1-978   This subsection, which is only relevant in a case where the tribunal is not under a positive duty to discharge (*MP v Mersey Care NHS Trust* [2011] UKUT 107 (AAC); [2011] M.H.L.R. 146, para.45), states that a tribunal is not required to discharge a patient because they think it might be appropriate for the patient to be made subject to a CTO. If the tribunal has formed such a view, they can recommend to the RC that she considers applying for a CTO and can reconvene in the event of the recommendation not being followed. As a recommendation can only be made where the tribunal is not under a duty to discharge the patient and as the patient would satisfy the criteria for detention under subs.(1)(b), at the reconvened hearing, the exercise by the tribunal of its discretionary power to discharge in this situation is likely to be a rare occurrence.

If the patient's representative requests the tribunal to make a recommendation under this provision and that request is denied, the tribunal should explain its reasons. In order to make a recommendation, the tribunal does not have to be satisfied that the conditions for a CTO are satisfied (*RN v Curo Care* (2011) UKUT 263 (AAC); [2011] M.H.L.R. 337).

Subsection (4)

1-979   This subsection enables the tribunal to discharge a patient under guardianship and directs the tribunal to discharge the patient if either of the criteria set out in paras (a) or (b) is satisfied. The tribunal does not have the power either to defer the patient's discharge from guardianship or to make recommendations with a view to facilitating discharge at a later date.

The possible use of the powers of guardianship is relevant when considering the test in this subsection (*GW v Gloucestershire County Council* [2016] UKUT 499 (AAC); [2017] M.H.L.R. 80, per UT Judge Jacobs at para.10).

In *NL v Hampshire County Council* [2014] UKUT 475 (AAC); [2015] M.H.L.R. 338 Judge Jacobs said at para.20:

> "Given the importance of the welfare of those suffering from a mental disorder and of the need for protection of other persons, it is difficult to imagine a case in which the tribunal could properly exercise its discretion to discharge [a guardianship patient] without there being appropriate safeguards to ensure the necessary treatment and protection."

With regard to the availability of alternative placement options, in *KD v A Borough Council*, below, Charles J. said at para.64:

> "The FTT is an investigative tribunal. But this does not mean that it has to embark on an investigation of and so identify all available options and initiate the gathering of evidence about them. Rather, in my view the parties have the primary obligation of providing and advancing:
>
> (i)   evidence on the available options, including sufficient detail of their terms and availability,
>
> (ii)   evidence to support argument that an identified option is or would be the appropriate option (which may have to include evidence on other possibilities), and
>
> (iii)   argument on the application of the 'necessity test' set by [this subsection] to the identified and competing options."

A guardianship patient can be the subject of a deprivation of liberty authorisation made under Sch.A1 of the Mental Capacity Act 2005 (DOLS): see Sch.1A, Case D of the 2005 Act and *KD v A Borough Council* [2015] UKUT 251 (AAC); [2015] M.H.L.R. 343, para.39. This issue is considered in the note on *The use of guardianship to authorise the deprivation of a person's liberty* in s.8.

When Parliament responded to the declaration of incompatibility made by the Court of Appeal in *R. (on the application of H) v Mental Health Review Tribunal, North and East London Region* [2001] EWCA Civ 415; [2001] M.H.L.R. 48, by approving the Mental Health Act 1983 (Remedial Order) 2001 (SI 2001/3712), it did not act to amend this subsection by requiring the tribunal to be positively satisfied that the criteria justifying guardianship continue to exist before refusing to order a patient's discharge.

Note the failure in this provision to reproduce the "nature or degree" requirement which is found in s.7(2)(a).

Paragraph (a)

Mental disorder   If the person has a learning disability, the disability must be associated with abnormally aggressive or seriously irresponsible conduct (s.1(2A), (2B)). **1-980**

Paragraph (b)

Welfare   See the note on s.7(2). **1-981**

Power to discharge restricted patients

73.—[(1)   Where an application to [the appropriate tribunal] is made by a restricted patient who is subject to a restriction order, or where the case of such a patient is referred to [the appropriate tribunal], the tribunal shall direct the absolute discharge of the patient if— **1-982**

(a)   [the tribunal is] not satisfied as to the matters mentioned in paragraph (b)(i) [, (ii) or (iia)] of section 72(1) above; and

(b)   [the tribunal is] satisfied that it is not appropriate for the patient to remain liable to be recalled to hospital for further treatment.

(2)   Where in the case of any such patient as is mentioned in subsection (1) above—

(a)   paragraph (a) of that subsection applies; but

(b)   paragraph (b) of that subsection does not apply,

the tribunal shall direct the conditional discharge of the patient.]

(3)   Where a patient is absolutely discharged under this section he shall thereupon cease to be liable to be detained by virtue of the relevant hospital order, and the restriction order shall cease to have effect accordingly.

(4)   Where a patient is conditionally discharged under this section—

(a)   he may be recalled by the Secretary of State under subsection (3) of section 42 above as if he had been conditionally discharged under subsection (2) of that section; and

(b)   the patient shall comply with such conditions (if any) as may be imposed at the time of discharge by the Tribunal or at any subsequent time by the Secretary of State.

(5)   The Secretary of State may from time to time vary any condition imposed (whether by the Tribunal or by him) under subsection (4) above.

(6)   Where a restriction order in respect of a patient ceases to have effect after he has been conditionally discharged under this section the patient shall, unless previously recalled, be deemed to be absolutely discharged on the date when the order ceases to have effect and shall cease to be liable to be detained by virtue of the relevant hospital order.

(7)   A Tribunal may defer a direction for the conditional discharge of a patient until such arrangements as appear to the Tribunal to be necessary for that purpose have been made to [its satisfaction]; and where by virtue of any such deferment no direction has been given on an application or reference before the time when the patient's case comes before the Tribunal on a subsequent application or reference, the previous application or reference shall be treated as one on which no direction under this section can be given.

(8)   This section is without prejudice to section 42 above.

Amendments

The amendments to this section were made by the Mental Health Act 1983 (Remedial) Order 2001 (SI 2001/3712) art.4, the Mental Health Act 2007 s.4(9) and SI 2008/2883 art.9, Sch.3 para.54.

Definitions

1-983

the appropriate tribunal: ss.66(4), 145(1).
restricted patient: s.79(1).
restriction order: ss.41, 145(1).
hospital: ss.34(2), 79(6), 145(1).
relevant hospital order: s.79(2)–(5).

General Note

1-984

This section requires the tribunal to order either the absolute or conditional discharge of a restricted patient if the requirements of subss.(1) or (2) are satisfied. The tribunal also has the power to attach conditions to a conditional discharge (subs.(4)) and to defer the discharge (subs.(7)). The conditions of a conditional discharge can be varied by the Secretary of State (subs.(5)). The tribunal has no general discretion to order the discharge of a restricted patient where the statutory criteria are not met and has no power to adjourn the patient's application to give an opportunity for the patient's condition to improve or to see if an improvement already made is sustained (*R. v Nottingham Mental Health Review Tribunal Ex p. Secretary of State for the Home Department The Times,* October 12, 1988 CA). Neither has the tribunal the power to order the deferred discharge of a restricted patient (*JMcG v Devon Partnership NHS Trust (MH)* [2017] UKUT 348 (AAC), para.24).

As essentially the same criteria have to be applied in relation to admission and discharge (*Reid v Secretary of State for Scotland* [1999] 1 All E.R. 481, per Lord Clyde at 503 and *R. v East London and City Mental Health NHS Trust Ex p. Brandenburg* [2001] EWCA Civ 239; [2001] M.H.L.R. 36, per Lord

Phillips at paras 17, 18; also see *R. v Upper Tribunal* [2021] M.H.L.R. 323), reference should be made to the notes on the admission criteria under ss.2(2) and 3(2). The implications of this mirroring of the admission and discharge criteria are examined in the General Note to s.72.

The powers of the tribunal are confined to the powers set out in this section which can be read compatibly with human rights jurisprudence. The tribunal therefore has no jurisdiction to consider European Convention on Human Rights (ECHR) issues: see *Secretary of State for Justice v MM; Welsh Ministers v PJ* [2017] EWCA Civ 194; [2017] M.H.L.R. 282 where the Court of Appeal said at para.59:

> "Neither the Convention nor the Human Rights Act 1998 confer jurisdiction on a tribunal. There is nothing in the general role and function of a tribunal that permits it to exercise a function that it does not have by statute."

This finding was not challenged by Supreme Court when the case was appealed: see [2018] UKSC 66. The decision in *MM* and *PJ* was followed in *Djaba v West London Mental Health Trust* [2017] EWCA Civ 436; [2017] M.H.L.R. 345 where the Court of Appeal held that this section does not require a "proportionality assessment" to be conducted, pursuant to arts 5 and/or 8 of the ECHR and the 1998 Act, taking into account the conditions of the patient's detention. It follows that this section does not provide the tribunal with a power to regulate the conditions of the patient's detention or matters such as the availability of visiting rights for members of a patient's family. Arden L.J. said that a patient "must apply for judicial review to the Administrative Court if he considers that the conditions of his detention are disproportionate and do not comply with the Convention. That Court is able to carry out a sufficient review on the merits to meet the requirements of the Convention" (para.55). However, note that in *Welsh Ministers v PJ* [2018] UKSC 66; [2018] M.H.L.R. 411, at para.33, Lady Hale said that while the "MHRT has no jurisdiction over the conditions of treatment and detention in hospital, ... these can be relevant to whether the statutory criteria for detention are made out, especially in borderline cases".

A restricted patient who is no longer suffering from a mental disorder remains a "patient" for the purposes of this section until he is discharged absolutely (*R. v Merseyside Mental Health Review Tribunal Ex p. K* [1990] 1 All E.R. 694 CA). The relevant extract from the judgment of Butler-Sloss L.J. is reproduced in the note on "patient" in s.145(1); also see *Johnson v United Kingdom*, noted under subs.(2).

The relationship between the Secretary of State and the tribunal has been described as being one of "constructive tension"; per the Parliamentary Under-Secretary of State, Department for Constitutional Affairs (*Hansard*, HL Vol.688, col.740).

The legality of a decision to make an application to detain a patient immediately after a decision of a tribunal to discharge him is considered in the General Note to s.3.

Extra – statutory recommendations

Although the tribunal has no power under this section to make recommendations (*Grant v Mental Health Review Tribunal, The Times,* April 26, 1986; *R. v Oxford Mental Health Authority Review Tribunal Ex p. Smith*, January 25, 1995 CA), the following Written Answer was given by Mr Douglas Hogg MP, a Home Office Minister, to a question on what would happen if a tribunal which had considered the case of a restricted patient included in its decision a recommendation that the patient be granted leave of absence or be transferred to another hospital or be transferred to guardianship: **1-985**

> "Any such recommendation received in the Home Office [now the Ministry of Justice] is acknowledged, and any comments are offered which can usefully be made at that stage. Correspondence with the tribunal is copied to the patient's [responsible clinician] since it is for this officer to consider the recommendation in the first instance. If the [responsible clinician] submits a proposal based on a tribunal's recommendation, full account is taken of the tribunal's views. At any subsequent hearing of the case, the statement which the Home Office provides will explain the outcome of any recommendation which the tribunal had made" (*Hansard* HC Vol.121, cols 261, 262, October 28, 1987).

In *C v Birmingham and Solihull Mental Health NHS Trust* [2013] EWCA Civ 701; [2014] M.H.L.R. 23, the Court of Appeal held that the ministerial answer given by Mr Hogg did not give rise to a legitimate expectation that a patient had a right to have a request for an extra-statutory recommendation heard by the tribunal. A patient therefore has no right to challenge a decision of the tribunal to refuse to make such a recommendation. At the Upper Tribunal hearing of this case ([2012] UKUT 178 (AAC); [2012] M.H.L.R. 292), UT Judge Rowland said at para.35:

"In the absence of any formalisation, some inconsistency – even if more perceived than actual – in the approaches of the First-tier Tribunal to the making of extra-statutory recommendations seems inevitable. Courts and tribunals of all types and at all levels make comments or suggestions that are not necessary for their decisions. It is a matter of judgment when to do so and among the matters taken into consideration are likely to be whether the court or tribunal considers itself sufficiently well informed to make a useful comment or suggestion and whether doing so is likely to be seen as inappropriate interference with another body's decision making. I will not express any view as to the circumstances in which the First-tier Tribunal should or should not make extra-statutory recommendations in mental health cases, save that, if some panels are routinely spending a great deal of time considering issues not necessary for the exercise of their statutory functions for no better reason than that a party has asked them to do so, I would deprecate that practice."

A tribunal cannot use its power to adjourn an application to enable it to decide whether an extra-statutory recommendation should be made (*R. (on the application of the Secretary of State for the Home Department) v Mental Health Review Tribunal* [2000] M.H.L.R. 209).

If an extra-statutory recommendation is made, the question of risk has ultimately to be determined by the Secretary of State who is the statutory decision-maker, and not by the court or the tribunal. The court could not substitute its own decision, and would afford the decision-maker a margin of discretion, though it would scrutinise the decision and ensure that all relevant material has been taken into account. The recommendation is an important input, but it is not determinative. Article 8 of the ECHR did not alter the legal framework (*R. (on the application of P) v Mersey Care NHS Trust* [2003] EWHC 994 (Admin); [2004] M.H.L.R. 107). In *R. (on the application of RA) v Secretary of State for the Home Department* [2002] EWHC 1618 (Admin); [2003] M.H.L.R. 54, para.59, Crane J. said that the Secretary of State should (i) respond with reasonable promptness to recommendations made by the tribunal and (ii) follow them in the absence of sound reasons or new circumstances. Also see the note on this case in subs.(7).

The Tribunal's approach to issues arising under art.8 of the ECHR

1-986   See the notes on s.75 under this heading.

Human Rights Act 1998

1-987   In *MP v Nottinghamshire Healthcare NHS Trust* [2003] EWHC 1782 (Admin); [2003] M.H.L.R. 381, Silber J. held that art.5 of the ECHR does not require the tribunal to be able to secure the transfer of a restricted patient to less secure accommodation.

There have been a number of cases on whether the power to defer a patient's discharge under subs.(7) is compatible with art.5 of the ECHR: see the notes on subs.(7).

In *Johnson v United Kingdom* (1997) 27 E.H.R.R. 296, the Court held that the absence of a power to ensure that the deferred conditional discharge of a patient who is found not to be suffering from mental disorder is not unreasonably delayed, is a violation of art.5; also see *Kolanis v United Kingdom* (2006) 42 E.H.R.R. 12; [2005] M.H.L.R. 238. In *R. v Camden and Islington Health Authority Ex p. K* [2001] EWCA Civ 240; [2001] 3 W.L.R.553, the Court of Appeal said that the decision of the House of Lords in *Secretary of State for the Home Department v Oxford Regional Mental Health Review Tribunal* [1987] 3 All E.R. 8, to the effect that should it prove to be impossible to implement the conditions specified by a tribunal on a deferred conditional discharge, that tribunal could not consider whether to impose alternative conditions, may not be consistent with art.5 as interpreted by the Court in *Johnson*. The *Oxford* case was subsequently found to be incompatible with the ECHR and was overruled by the House of Lords in *R. (on the application of H) v Secretary of State for the Home Department* [2003] UKHL 59; [2004] 1 All E.R. 412 where it was held that it was not the case that, because the tribunal lacked the power to secure compliance with its conditions, it lacked the coercive power which is one of the essential attributes of a court for the purposes of art.5. Lord Bingham said at para.26:

"What Article 5(1)(e) and (4) require is that a person of unsound mind compulsorily detained in hospital should have access to a court with power to decide whether the detention is lawful and, if not, to order his release. This power the tribunal had. Nothing in Article 5 suggests that discharge subject to conditions is impermissible in principle, and nothing in the Convention jurisprudence suggests that the power to discharge conditionally (whether there are specific conditions or a mere liability to recall), properly used, should be viewed with disfavour."

The conditional discharge regime set out in this section is therefore not incompatible with art.5. This was implicitly confirmed by the European Court of Human Rights in *Kolanis v United Kingdom*, above.

The question whether a decision not to discharge a patient because of a failure to put in place appropriate after-care facilities in the community would constitute a violation of art.5 is considered in the General Note to s.117 under this heading.

Although it was accepted by Sullivan L.J. in *RH v South London and Maudsley NHS Foundation Trust* [2010] EWCA Civ 1273; [2010] M.H.L.R. 341, para.27, that conditions imposed on a conditional discharge are capable of amounting to an interference with a patient's rights under art.8, the granting of a discharge with a condition that the patient continues to accept medication will not contravene that article if one of the grounds in art.8(2) is satisfied (*L v Sweden*, noted Part 5 under art.8(2) under "protection of health"). Also see *RP v Dudley and Walsall Mental Health Partnership NHS Trust* [2016] UKUT 204 (AAC)which is noted under The Tribunal's approach to issues arising under art.8 of the ECHR in the General Note to s.75.

Subsection (1)

The effect of this subsection is that a tribunal must order the *absolute* discharge of a restricted patient if: **1-988**

(i)   they are not satisfied that he is then suffering from mental disorder of a nature or degree which makes it appropriate for him to be liable to be detained in a hospital for medical treatment; *or*

(ii)   they are not satisfied that it is necessary for the health and safety of the patient or for the protection of other persons that he should receive such treatment; *or*

(iii)   they are not satisfied that appropriate medical treatment is available for him; *and*

(iv)   they are satisfied that it is not appropriate for the patient to remain liable to be recalled to hospital for further treatment.

In *Secretary of State for Justice v RB* [2012] 1 W.L.R. 2043, Arden L.J. said that "the conditions referred to in section 73(1)(a) mirror the detention criteria in section 3" (para.25).

In *SLL v Priory Heath Care and Secretary of State for Justice* [2019] UKUT 323 (AAC); [2020] M.H.L.R. 178, UTJ Thomas Church said, at para.59:

"While I don't accept the narrow argument Mr Pezzani put forward about the Tribunal being required to decide the matters set out in all three limbs of section 72(1)(b) MHA, I am persuaded by the thrust of the Appellant's case that the Tribunal erred in law in failing to apply the proper test under section 73(1)(b) MHA. This required it to make findings on substantially similar matters, albeit on a forward-looking basis rather than on the basis of an assessment of the state of play at the time of the Decision, and it required the Tribunal to make a decision on the appropriateness of the Appellant remaining subject to the power of recall on the basis of those findings. It did not do so (or, if it did, it failed to explain how it did so). Simply stating that it was not satisfied that it was not appropriate for the Appellant to continue to be liable to be recalled to hospital for further treatment was not enough. Either way, this amounts to a material error of law."

An absolute discharge has the effect of extinguishing both the hospital order and the restriction order (subs.(3)). In *R. (on the application of L) v West London Mental Health NHS Trust* [2012] EWHC 3200 (Admin); [2013] M.H.L.R. 297 Stadlen J. said at para.266:

"Discharge directly from a high security hospital like Broadmoor is extremely rare. A staged discharge involving normally at least a period in a medium security hospital is much more usual. There are reasons unconnected with the severity or nature of a patient's mental disorder which make it likely that a patient who is transferred to a high security hospital will experience a longer passage of time before he is ultimately discharged than would be the case if he were not so transferred."

In *Secretary of State for the Home Department v KE (Nigeria)* [2017] EWCA Civ 1382, Hickinbottom L.J. said that "it is common for orders never to be absolutely discharged because, even if an offender is conditionally discharged into the community, the risk of a recurrence of the mental disorder or its symptoms – and thus of danger to the public – remains" (para.5).

There is no power in the tribunal to defer an absolute discharge (*R. (on the application of Secretary of State for Home Department) v Mental Health Review Tribunal* [2004] EWHC 1029 (Admin); [2004] M.H.L.R. 184).

If the High Court quashes an order of the tribunal granting a conditionally discharged patient an absolute discharge, the court can declare that pending a rehearing the patient is to be treated as if he had been conditionally discharged: see *R. (on the application of the Secretary of State for the Home Department) v Mental Health Review Tribunal and BR* [2005] EWCA Civ 1616, noted in the General Note to s.65 under the heading *Habeas Corpus and Judicial Review*.

Referred to such a tribunal   See the note on this term in s.75(1).

Satisfied   See the note on s.72(1)(a).

Matters mentioned in paragraph (b)(i), (ii) or (iia) of section 72(1)   Reference should be made to the notes thereto.

Recalled to hospital for further treatment   This paragraph is relevant only to the question of whether any discharge should be conditional or absolute. The tribunal would have to be satisfied at the time of the hearing that it would not be appropriate for the patient to remain liable to be recalled to hospital to receive treatment that might be required at some time in the future. In *R. (on the application of the Secretary of State) v Mental Health Tribunal* [2001] EWHC Admin 849; [2002] M.H.L.R. 260, the Administrative Court quashed the decision of the tribunal to grant the patient an absolute discharge on the ground that the tribunal ignored this provision when giving the reasons for its decision. Pill L.J. said at para.25: "The possible consequences for the safety of member of the public and the patient, when an order of absolute discharge is made are such that the question of liability to be recalled must be dealt with expressly". This case was cited in *R. (on the application of Secretary of State for Home Department) v Mental Health Review Tribunal*, above, para.21, where Moses J. said that even where the tribunal conclude that the patient is not mentally disordered, "it is incumbent upon the tribunal in cases of restricted patients to go on to consider whether it is satisfied that it is not appropriate for the patient to remain liable to be recalled to hospital for further treatment".

In *SLL v Priory Heath Care and Secretary of State for Justice*, above, UT Judge Church said:

"34. Given that the power of recall in respect of a conditionally discharged patient can only be exercised for the purpose of the patient receiving further treatment, and given that the patient may be recalled to hospital only (and nowhere else) it is difficult to see how the question of the appropriateness of a patient continuing to be subject to the power of recall could properly be determined without the tribunal making findings about:

a.   whether the patient now suffers from a mental disorder which may be expected to endure or has, now or in the past, suffered from a mental disorder which may be expected to recur;

b.   if the answer to the question posed in paragraph a. is 'yes', how likely it is that the patient might experience symptoms of such mental disorder in the future;

c.   what kind of treatment might be available in hospital to treat such mental disorder;

d.   what can reasonably be expected to change in consequence of the patient receiving such treatment in hospital (in other words, what purpose is to be served by the recall?); and

e.   (given the 'least restrictive' principal that informs the MHA regime) whether any alternative strategies are available which might manage the risks associated with future deteriorations in the patient's mental health effectively but which place less restriction on the patient's liberty than the patient continuing to be subject to the power of recall.

35. Such findings would, no doubt, be based on evidence of the patient's past experience (of the chronicity of his mental disorder, its symptoms, its response to treatment, the prognosis and the attendant risks), but the findings themselves must be forward-looking in nature."

Subsection (2)

1-989   The effect of this subsection is that a tribunal must direct the *conditional* discharge of a restricted patient if:

(i)   they are not satisfied that he is then suffering from mental disorder of a nature or degree which makes it appropriate for him to be liable to be detained in a hospital for medical treatment; *or*

(ii)   they are not satisfied that it is necessary for the health and safety of the patient or for the protection of other persons that he should receive such treatment *or*

(iii)   they are not satisfied that appropriate medical treatment is available to him.

For the conditions that can be attached to the discharge, see below. The discharge can be deferred under subs.(7).

This section does not attach, or empower the attachment of, any sanction for failure to comply with a condition. The Secretary of State has a general power of recall under subs. (4)(a), but there is nothing to make recall an automatic sanction for non-compliance with a specific condition (*R. (on the application of SH) v Mental Health Review Tribunal* [2007] EWHC 884 (Admin), [2007] M.H.L.R. 234, para.26).

In *R. (on the application of H) v Secretary of State for the Home Department* [2003] UKHL 59; [2004] 1 All E.R. 412, Lord Bingham said at para.26:

"[T]he conditional discharge regime, properly used, is of great benefit to patients and the public, and conducive to the Convention object of restricting the curtailment of personal liberty to the maximum, because it enables tribunals to ensure that restricted patients compulsorily detained in hospital represent the hard core of those who suffer from mental illness, are a risk to themselves or others and cannot be effectively treated and supervised otherwise than in hospital. If there is any possibility of treating and supervising a patient in the community, the imposition of conditions permits that possibility to be explored and, it may be, tried."

In *R. (on the application of H) v Secretary of State for the Home Department* [2002] EWCA Civ 646; [2002] M.H.L.R. 87, para.98, the Court of Appeal summarised the position where a tribunal is considering ordering a conditional discharge:

1. The tribunal can, at the outset, adjourn the hearing to investigate the possibility of imposing conditions. [In *DC v Nottinghamshire Healthcare NHS Trust* [2012] UKUT 92 (AAC); [2012] M.H.L.R. 238, para.19, UT Judge Jacobs said that this must mean that the tribunal can adjourn at any time before it is under a duty to direct a discharge.]

2. The tribunal can make a provisional decision to make a conditional discharge on specified conditions, including submitting to psychiatric supervision, but defer directing a conditional discharge while the authorities responsible for after-care under s.117 make the necessary arrangements to enable the patient to meet those conditions.

3. The tribunal should meet after an appropriate interval to monitor progress in making these arrangements if they have not been put in place.

4. Once the arrangements have been made, the tribunal can direct a conditional discharge without holding a further hearing.

5. If problems arise with making arrangements to meet the conditions, the tribunal has a number of options, depending on the circumstances.

   (a) It can defer for a further period, perhaps with suggestions as to how any problems can be overcome.

   (b) It can amend or vary the proposed conditions to seek to overcome the difficulties that have been encountered.

   (c) It can order a conditional discharge without specific conditions, thereby making the patient subject to recall.

   (d) It can decide that the patient must remain detained in hospital for treatment.

6. It will not normally be appropriate for a tribunal to direct a conditional discharge on conditions with which the patient will be unable to comply because it has not proved possible to make the necessary arrangements.

The court identified a "categorical difference" between the case of a patient who had been found by the tribunal not to be mentally disordered and who did not therefore satisfy the criteria identified in *Winterwerp v Netherlands* (1979) 2 E.H.R.R. 387, and the case of a patient who did satisfy the *Winterwerp* criteria and the tribunal considered that he could be satisfactorily treated and supervised in the community. [The *Winterwerp* case determined that detention on the ground of mental disorder is only lawful under art.5 of the ECHR if (1) there is objective medical evidence that the patient suffers from mental disorder; (2) the mental disorder is of a kind or degree warranting compulsory confinement; and (3) the mental disorder persists.] In the former case, if the conditions of discharge were not met the alternative was not continued detention but discharge, either absolutely or subject only to a condition of recall. In this situation the conditional discharge must not be deferred beyond a reasonable limited period if a violation of art.5(4) is to be avoided. In the latter case, if the tribunal's conditions proved impossible to meet the alternative was continued detention.

The implications of the decision in *H* were explained by Mance L.J. in *W v Doncaster MBC* [2004] EWCA Civ 378; [2004] M.H.L.R. 201 at paras 72, 73:

"The central question is whether the *Winterwerp* criteria for detention are satisfied. If a person is no longer suffering from any mental illness, these criteria are clearly not met. If someone is still suffering from mental illness, they may or may not be met. It may still be possible to release the person in question into the community, either unconditionally or in the expectation that he or she will receive treatment there under appropriate conditions. In the latter case, there are two alterative possibilities. Upon true analysis, the provision of the expected treatment either may or may not be regarded by the tribunal as an essential pre-requisite of discharge from detention: contrast paragraphs 91 and 96 of the Master of the Rolls judgment in [the Court of Appeal], quoted with approval in the House of Lords at … paragraphs 24 and 28.

If such treatment is an essential pre-requisite of discharge (as it was in *H*), but it proves impossible to provide, then continuing detention is lawful, although the impossibility of providing the treatment envisaged by the tribunal means that the matter will have to return to the tribunal for reconsideration: [2003] UKHL 59, paragraph 27. If such treatment is not an essential pre-requisite to discharge, then, although discharge may be delayed for a period while efforts are made to arrange the expected treatment, discharge cannot be unreasonably delayed, even if it proves impossible to arrange it: see *Johnson v United Kingdom* (1997) 27 E.H.R.R. 296)."

The decision of the Court of Appeal in *H*, above, that a Health Authority was not under an absolute obligation to procure compliance with the tribunal's conditions was affirmed by the House of Lords ([2003] UKHL 59; [2004] 1 All E.R. 413) where it was held that the obligation is for the authority to use its best endeavours to secure compliance. The tribunal has "no power to require any psychiatrist to act in a way which conflicted with the conscientious professional judgment of that psychiatrist" (per Lord Bingham at para.29; also see *R. v Camden and Islington Health Authority Ex p. K* [2001] EWCA Civ 240 CA, noted in the General Note to s.117). The House of Lords found it unnecessary to determine whether in this context psychiatrists were or could be a hybrid public authority within the meaning of s.6 of the Human Rights Act 1998. If such a finding were made it would have the effect of requiring a psychiatrist to supervise a patient who had been conditionally discharged by a tribunal even though the psychiatrist was professionally opposed to conditions attached to the discharge. It is unlikely that the courts would countenance such an outcome.

In *Kolanis v United Kingdom* (1987) 27 E.H.R.R. 296, the ECtHR confirmed that where a tribunal finds that a patient may be conditionally discharged,

"new issues of lawfulness may arise where the detention nonetheless continues due, for example, to difficulties in fulfilling the conditions. It follows that such patients are entitled under Art.5(4) to have the lawfulness of that continued detention determined by a court with requisite promptness" (para.80).

However, where the treatment considered to be necessary as a condition of discharge was not available, there could be no question of interpreting art.5(1)(e) as requiring discharge without the stipulated conditions for the protection of the applicant and the public being fulfilled, or as imposing an absolute obligation on the authorities to ensure that those conditions were fulfilled (para.71).

A conditionally discharged patient can apply to a tribunal for his absolute discharge under s.75.

Paragraph (b) of that subsection does not apply   In *R. v Mental Health Review Tribunal Ex p. Cooper*, unreported, February 14, 1990, Rose J. held that the tribunal could direct a conditional discharge, rather than an absolute discharge, solely for therapeutic reasons and that it was not the case that the maintenance of liability to recall under para.(b) of subs.(1) of this section can only be proper if the applicant poses some danger to others.

Conditional discharge   For the nature of the conditions that can be imposed, see subs.(4). A conditional discharge can be deferred under subs.(7).

Subsection (4)

Paragraph (a)

1-990   *May be recalled*   And have his case referred to a tribunal under s.75(1)(a). Only the Secretary of State can recall the patient to hospital: see the note on s.42(3). Guidance for the clinical and social supervisors on the recall of conditionally discharged patients can be accessed at: *www.gov.uk/government/ publications/recall-of-conditionally-discharged-restricted-patients.*

1-991   **Paragraph (b)**

1-991   *Conditions*   In *R. (on the application of SC) v Mental Health Review Tribunal* [2005] EWHC 17 (Admin), Munby J examined the purpose behind the power to impose a conditional discharge. Having reviewed the relevant cases, his Lordship noted at para.36:

"These cases show that the purpose of conditional discharge is not necessarily to impose a requirement for ongoing treatment for a classified mental disorder. It may be no more, to use the words of the Tribunal in the present case, than to ensure monitoring 'in case the clinical picture unexpectedly changes in the future'."

An after-care body is not placed under an absolute obligation to satisfy the conditions imposed by the tribunal: see the note on subs.(2).

In *Secretary of State for Justice v MP* [2013] UKUT 025 (AAC), UT Judge Jacobs said at para.20:

"It is permissible to direct a conditional discharge without imposing any further conditions, as envisaged by section 73(4)(b). A tribunal is under a duty to explain its decision, including a decision not to impose further conditions. In some cases, the circumstances alone may be sufficient to show why the tribunal did not impose conditions. This is not such a case. The tribunal found that Mr P had a drug-induced psychosis and that he had continued to use drugs. Indeed, he said that he would do if he were discharged. The tribunal found that that involved a risk of self-neglect. In those circumstances, the tribunal was under a duty to explain why it did not impose conditions."

This section does not empower the attachment of any sanction for failure to comply with a condition, but provides for a general power of recall which, except in an emergency situation, cannot be exercised without up to date medical evidence being obtained by the Secretary of State: see the notes to s.42(3). A patient does not commit an offence by breeching a condition of his discharge.

In *Secretary of State for Justice v MM* [2018] UKSC 60; [2018] M.H.L.R. 392, the issue to be resolved by the Supreme Court was whether the conditions imposed on a conditional discharge can, if the patient consents, be so restrictive as to amount to a deprivation of liberty within the meaning of art.5 of the European Convention on Human Rights. Lady Hale, who gave the main judgment, held that the word "discharge" in this subsection, when referring to the conditional discharge of restricted patients, must mean actual discharge from the hospital in which the patient is currently detained, as he remains liable to be detained (para.20). Although her Ladyship said that there is nothing in this Act which expressly prohibits a condition which amounts to a detention or deprivation of liberty in another setting, there were compelling reasons not to construe this subsection in this way. The most compelling reason is that such a power would be contrary to the whole scheme of this Act, which provides in detail for only two forms of detention (in a place of safety for up to 36 hours, or in a hospital), each with associated specific powers to convey a patient there, to detain him and to retake him if he absents himself from such detention without leave. There is no equivalent express power to convey a conditionally discharged restricted patient to the place where he is required to live or to detain him there, nor is he liable to be taken into custody and returned anywhere unless and until he is recalled to hospital by the Secretary of State (paras 33–36). The fact that a conditionally discharged restricted patient can apply far less frequently than a hospital patient to the tribunal for his release indicates that Parliament did not consider that such patients might be subject to conditions which required the same degree of protection as those deprived of their liberty (para.37). Accordingly, Lady Hale held that this Act does not permit the tribunal to impose conditions amounting to detention or a deprivation of liberty upon a conditionally discharged restricted patient (para.38). A similar conclusion had been reached in *Secretary of State for Justice v RB* [2011] EWCA Civ 1608; [2012] M.H.L.R. 131, where the Court of Appeal said, at para.66, that the tribunal may be able to express some helpful non-statutory recommendations for the Secretary of State to exercise his powers of transfer in an appropriate case.

In *MM*, Lady Hale said:

"Whether the Court of Protection could authorise a future deprivation, once the First-tier Tribunal has granted a conditional discharge, and whether the First-tier Tribunal could defer its decision for this purpose, are not issues which it would be appropriate for this court to decide at this stage in these proceedings" (para.27).

These issues were addressed in *MC v Sygnet Behavioural Health Ltd* [2020] UKUT 230 (AAC); [2021] M.H.L.R. 157 where UT Judge Jacobs held that the First-tier tribunal has the power to coordinate its decision to discharge a mentally incapacitated patient on a conditional discharge with the provision of authority under the Mental Capacity Act 2005 to deprive him of his liberty. Judge Jacobs said that if an advance authorisation had been obtained (either by a DoLs authorisation or by an order of the court) the "tribunal may be able to proceed to a conditional discharge without more ado. If it has not, there are two possibilities that have been discussed in the cases. It may be that there are other and better approaches, but if there are I cannot think of them. I certainly do not intend to limit the First-tier Tribunal to these approaches if there is a more appropriate option" (para.29). The two approaches are:

The different hats approach
If appropriate, the same judge could sit in the Court of Protection and in the First-tier Tribunal to

ensure that all decisions could be made that would allow the patient to be conditionally discharged on appropriate conditions and with the benefit of a deprivation of liberty authorisation" (para.30).

"The ducks in a row approach
If it not possible or appropriate for some reason to follow the same hat approach, it would be a proper use of the tribunal's powers to adjourn, to make a provisional decision or to defer discharge in order to allow the necessary authorisation to be arranged" (para.32).

The choice between the two approaches "may come to little more than a matter of preference for the tribunal. It may, though, depend on how sure the tribunal is that the mental capacity decision will be put in place and how confident it is of the terms of any such decision (the terms of the care package, for example)" (para.32). Judge Jacobs further held that his finding did not involve "a violation of the Convention right under Article 14 of the European Convention on Human Rights, read together with Article 5 or Article 8" (para.33).

The Secretary of State's policy on the discharge of restricted patients on conditions that involve a deprivation of liberty is set out in "Guidance: Discharge conditions that amount to deprivation of liberty" which is reproduced in Part 4. A decision of the tribunal to direct a deferred conditional discharge with a care plan that amounts to a deprivation of liberty is considered at para.4.1 of the guidance.

In *Re AB (Inherent Jurisdiction: Deprivation of Liberty)* [2018] EWHC 3103 (Fam), Mrs Justice Gwynneth Knowles used the inherent jurisdiction of the High Court as a means of providing lawful authorisation for conditions of discharge amounting to a deprivation of liberty for a capacitous patient. The Secretary of State considers that the court did not adopt the correct approach in this case: see para.3 of the Guidance document, noted above. A contrary opinion to that given by Mrs Justice Gwynneth Knowles was expressed by Cobb J. in *Wakefield MDC & Wakefield CCG v DN* [2019] EWHC 2306 (Fam) and by Lieven J. in *Cumbria, Northumberland Tyne & Wear NHS Foundation Trust v EG* [2021] EWHC 2990 (Fam): see the General Note to the Act under *"Inherent Jurisdiction"*.

In *Secretary of State for Justice v SB* [2013] UKUT 320 (AAC); [2014] M.H.L.R. 46, para.29, UT Judge Levenson held that the cumulative effect of the conditions of discharge imposed by the tribunal, which were imposed largely to protect the public, "would amount to detention and to an unlawful deprivation of liberty such that it could hardly be characterised as a discharge at all". The meaning of a deprivation of liberty is considered in Part 6.

In *Re T (A child: murdered parent)* [2011] EWHC 1185 (Fam); [2011] M.H.L.R. 133, it was held that the family court (i) does not have the power to vary or discharge the conditions imposed by the tribunal, (ii) is not constrained by the conditions imposed by the tribunal, and (iii) can make orders under its jurisdiction that have the effect of supplementing the protection provided to victims by the tribunal's conditions. Judge Bellamy, sitting as a Judge of the High Court, said at para.76:

"The problem of conflict between an order of this court and conditions imposed by the Tribunal does not arise [in this case]. The question of the approach to be taken where there may be such a conflict is, therefore, academic. That said, it seems to me that in any case in which the court is seriously considering making an order which, if complied with, would cause a patient to be in breach of conditions imposed by a Tribunal, the appropriate course would be for the court to invite the Secretary of State to set out his position to the court and, in particular, to indicate whether and if so to what extent he is prepared to vary the conditions imposed by the Tribunal in order to enable the court's order to take effect without risk of the patient being in breach of the conditions."

1-992   When imposing conditions the tribunal may have regard not only to considerations relating to treatment itself, but also to the question of risk, both to the patient and to the public. The proportionate response to the risk posed by the patient may be achieved by the imposition of suitable conditions on a conditional discharge rather than by continuing the patient's detention (*R. (on the application of the Secretary of State for the Home Department) v Mental Health Review Tribunal* [2002] EWHC 1128 (Admin); [2002] M.H.L.R. 241,at paras 26 and 27). A tribunal has a duty to impose such conditions of discharge of a restricted patient as it considers necessary, even if was in no position to enforce those conditions and it was apparent that it would be difficult to put in place arrangements to enable the conditions to be satisfied (*R. v Mental Health Review Tribunal, Ex p. Hall* [2000] 1 W.L.R. 1323 CA). However, only reasonable conditions can be imposed and a condition that the tribunal positively knows will be impossible or highly unlikely to be put into effect is not reasonable. If necessary, the tribunal should use its power of adjournment to ascertain whether conditions which appear attractive are achievable (*R. (on the application of H) v Secretary of State for the Home Department* [2002] EWCA Civ 646; [2002] M.H.L.R.87). The tribunal should give reasons for its decision to impose conditions. It would be helpful in a situation where the patient continues to suffer from an underlying mental illness which can only be managed in the community provided the conditions imposed are implemented if the tribunal says so when it orders the patient's conditional discharge (*W v Doncaster MBC* [2004] EWCA Civ 378; [2004] M.H.L.R. 201).

In *R. (on the application of SH) v Mental Health Review Tribunal* [2007] EWHC 884 (Admin); [2007] M.H.L.R. 234 paras 18–20, Holman J. said that a condition: (a) could not lawfully be capricious; (b) must be relevant and for a proper purpose within the scope of the Act; and (c) is subject to the principle of legality as described by Lord Hoffmann in *R. v Secretary of State for the Home Department, Ex p. Simms* [2000] 2 A.C. 115, i.e. the courts presume that even the most general words were intended to be subject to the basic rights of the individual.

The tribunal cannot lawfully impose a condition which effectively makes the conditional discharge subject to the agreement of some other body, such as the Ministry of Justice, as such a requirement is not a condition of discharge, but a pre-condition to discharge (*R. (on the application of Secretary of State for the Home Department) v Mental Health Review Tribunal* [2007] EWHC 2224 (Admin); [2008] M.H.L.R. 212).

Although a condition may require that the patient attends for treatment, treatment cannot be forced upon him in the absence of his consent because conditionally discharged patients are not subject to the consent to treatment provisions contained in Pt IV (s.56(3)(c)). In *R. (on the application of SH) v Mental Health Review Tribunal*, above, Holman J. held that:

(i)   a condition that the patient "shall comply" with medication prescribed by his responsible [clinician] was lawfully imposed as it did not interfere with the patient's absolute right to choose whether to accept treatment, nor did it interfere with his rights under art.8(1) the ECHR;

(ii)   the condition must be read as respecting and being subject to the patient's own final choice, which must be his real or true choice; and

(iii)   a tribunal should not impose such a condition unless it has a proper basis for anticipating that the patient does and will consent to the treatment in question.

His Lordship said, at para.42, that it would be preferable for a tribunal, when imposing a similar condition to add words such as the following: "subject always to his right to give or withhold consent to treatment on any given occasion".

In an unreported decision of the First-tier Tribunal, a condition attached to a conditional discharge was removed on a review on the grounds that the condition had not been explicitly discussed with the patient or the clinical team during the tribunal proceedings and there had been no opportunity for the patient to make representations in relation to the condition.

With regard to a patient who lacks the mental capacity to make a decision about medical treatment, the Mental Capacity Act 2005 (MCA) may permit treatment which is in his best interests, but will only permit coercion in order to impose treatment in very limited circumstances (MCA ss.5 and 6).

The usual conditions relate to supervision, residence and medical treatment; see further, the notes on s.42(2) under the heading "Subject to conditions". In his *"Review of Homicides by Patients with Severe Mental Illness"* (March 2006), Professor Tony Maden made the following recommendation at p.63: "In patients subject to a restriction order there should always be consideration of setting conditions relating to abstinence from drugs or alcohol and the standard procedure should be immediate recall if that condition is breached".

After a conditional discharge the patient's progress in the community will be monitored by the Ministry of Justice in the same way as that of a patient conditionally discharged by the Secretary of State, and the Secretary of State may vary conditions imposed by the tribunal (subs.(5)).

If any   The tribunal is not obliged to impose conditions on a conditionally discharged patient. In practice, it is unlikely that a patient will be conditionally discharged without conditions being imposed either by the tribunal or the Secretary of State. The Secretary of State can impose conditions even though the tribunal has not.

Secretary of state   Functions under this provision have not been transferred to Welsh Ministers (see the General Note to the Act and SI 1999/672 art.2, Sch.1).

Subsection (7)

A tribunal may defer   A deferred discharge is a mechanism that postpones the coming into effect of a direction ordering the patient's conditional discharge until the tribunal is satisfied that suitable arrangements have been put in place to enable the conditions to be met. There is no power in the tribunal to defer an absolute discharge (*R. (on the application of the Secretary of State for the Home Department) v Mental Health Review Tribunal* [2004] EWHC 1029 (Admin)). The deferment cannot be to a fixed

1-993

date (*Secretary of State for the Home Department v Oxford Regional Mental Health Review Tribunal* [1987] 3 All E.R. 8, at 13).

UT Judge Jacobs examined the operation of this provision in *DC v Nottinghamshire Healthcare NHS Trust* [2012] UKUT 92 (AAC); [2012] M.H.L.R. 238, at paras 25 and 26:

"The language of section 73(7) is important. The tribunal does not defer the patient's conditional discharge. It defers the direction for the discharge. That is what section 73(7) says and it is significant. That presupposes that there is a direction to discharge ready to take effect. Until there is, there is nothing to defer. That means that the conditions for discharge must be identified and included in the direction. The deferral allows time for the necessary arrangements to be made. That means the arrangements necessary for the conditional discharge. And it is impossible to make those arrangements without knowing what the conditions for the discharge are. Section 73(7), by its terms, operates until the tribunal is satisfied that the arrangements are in place. Once it is, there is nothing left for the tribunal to do except to lift the deferral.

In summary, the tribunal cannot exercise the power in section 73(7) unless it finds that the patient should not be detained but should be subject to recall and it formulates a direction, including conditions for discharge, that can take effect if the necessary arrangements can be made. Until then, it is free to adjourn."

Judge Jacobs considered when this provision may not be used at para.28:

"The tribunal may not bypass the detention and discharge conditions and use section 73(7) as (i) a device for gathering information that it needs. Nor may it bypass difficulties in formulating conditions for discharge and use section 73(7) to gather the information it needs to decide (ii) whether a conditional discharge would be possible or (iii) what conditions might be appropriate. The proper approach in all three circumstances is to adjourn for the information to be obtained. It is only permissible to use section 73 when (a) it is able to find, on the balance of probabilities, that the patient should not be detained but should be subject to recall, and (b) it has drafted the conditions for the discharge."

It is unlawful for a tribunal to make a "wait and see" decision to defer discharge for the purpose of seeing whether any change in the patient's circumstances might arise and thus provide material which will point to the correct decision in the application: see *R. (on the application of the Secretary of State for the Home Department) v Mental Health Review Tribunal* [2002] EWHC 2043 (Admin); [2002] M.H.L.R. 381, where the tribunal used its power under this provision to await the results of a therapeutic assessment of the patient. It is also unlawful for a tribunal to defer a discharge until arrangements are made to secure the patient's admission to another hospital (*Secretary of State for the Home Department v Mental Health Review Tribunal for the Mersey Regional Health Authority* [1986] 3 All E.R. 233).

In *R. (on the application of H) v Secretary of State for the Home Department* [2002] EWCA Civ 646; [2002] M.H.L.R. 87, the Court of Appeal considered the problem that can develop where a tribunal determines that a restricted patient is entitled to release on condition that he receives psychiatric supervision, but no psychiatrist can be found who is prepared to provide that supervision. In *Secretary of State for the Home Department v Oxford Regional Mental Health Review Tribunal* [1987] 3 All E.R. 8, the House of Lords had held that in this situation a tribunal cannot subsequently reconvene to reconsider its original decision that the patient be discharged. The Court of Appeal held that:

1. The decision of the House of Lords could lead to the patient finding himself "in limbo" should it prove impossible to make the necessary arrangements for him to comply with the proposed condition.

2. The period spent "in limbo" may last too long to be compatible with art.5(4) of the ECHR and may result in the patient being detained in violation of art.5(1) of the Convention: see *Johnson v United Kingdom* (1997) 27 E.H.R.R. 296.

3. Tribunals should no longer proceed on the basis that they cannot reconsider a decision to direct a conditional discharge on specified conditions where, after deferral and before directing discharge, there is a material change of circumstances. Such a change may be demonstrated by fresh material placed before or obtained by a tribunal. Such material may, for instance, show that the patient's condition has relapsed. It may show that the patient's condition has improved. It may demonstrate that it is not possible to put in place arrangements necessary to enable the conditions that the tribunal proposed to impose on the patient to be satisfied. The original decision should be treated as a provisional decision, and the tribunal should monitor progress towards implementing it so as to ensure that the patient is not left "in limbo" for an unreasonable length of time.

4. Accordingly, where a tribunal decides (i) that a restricted patient is suffering from mental

disorder for which psychiatric treatment is necessary for the health or safety of the patient or for the protection of other persons and (ii) that detention in hospital is not necessary if, but only if, psychiatric treatment is provided in the community, the tribunal can properly make a provisional decision to direct a conditional discharge, but defer giving that direction to enable arrangements to be made for providing psychiatric treatment in the community. The Health Authority subject to the s.117 duty will then be bound to use its best endeavours to put in place the necessary aftercare. If it fails to use its best endeavours it will be subject to judicial review. If, despite its best endeavours, the Health Authority is unable to provide the necessary services, the tribunal must think again (see the note on this case under subs.(2)). If, as is likely in those circumstances, it concludes that it is necessary for the patient to remain detained in hospital in order to receive the treatment, it should record that decision.

The decision of the Court of Appeal was affirmed by the House of Lords in *R. (on the application of H) v Secretary of State for the Home Department* [2003] UKHL 59; [2004] 1 All E.R. 412 where their Lordships overruled *Secretary of State for the Home Department v Oxford Regional Mental Health Review Tribunal*.

If a change in the patient's circumstances or the availability of additional material relating to the patient is brought to the Secretary of State's attention after deferral but before discharge has been directed, he should utilise the procedure set out in *H* by inviting the tribunal to reconsider its decision. He should not make a referral to a fresh tribunal using his power under s.71(1) (*R. (on the application of C) v Secretary of State for the Home Department* [2002] EWCA Civ 647; [2002] M.H.L.R. 105). If the tribunal departs from its original reasoning, it must identify a material change in circumstances which may be demonstrated by fresh material placed before or obtained by the tribunal (*LC v DHIC (CHL)* [2010] UKUT 319 (AAC); [2010] M.H.L.R.337).

When a deferred conditional discharge has been granted by a tribunal, leave of absence, with the consent of the Secretary of State (see s.41(3)(c)), is the normal method designed by the Act to facilitate the patient's discharge from hospital by, for example, providing for overnight stays in a hostel. The Secretary of State should only use his power under s.42(2) to grant such a patient a conditional discharge if there is some development that the tribunal is unable to deal with: see *R. (on the application of RA) v Secretary of State for the Home Department* [2002] EWHC 1618 (Admin); [2003] M.H.L.R. 54 where Crane J. held that an extra-statutory recommendation made by a tribunal has legal force where it is linked to the satisfaction of conditions imposed by a tribunal as part of a deferred conditional discharge: see further the General Note, above.

A deferment should not result in the patient's discharge being unreasonably delayed: see the decision of the European Court of Human Rights (ECtHR) in *Johnson v United Kingdom* (1997) 27 E.H.R.R. 296. Subsequent to this decision the Department of Health wrote to health and social services authorities asking the authorities "to give priority to ensuring that all cases of deferred conditional discharge are implemented within six months of the [tribunal's] decision".

It is desirable for there to be, as far as practicable, a continuation of the membership of a tribunal which is to monitor and continue to consider a deferred conditional discharge: see *R. (on the application of A) v Secretary of State for the Home Department and the Mental Health Review Tribunal* [2003] EWHC 270 (Admin); [2005] M.H.L.R. 144, where Stanley Burnton J. said at para.16:

> "Where a relatively short time has passed between the original decision and its reconsideration, the advantages and the fairness involved in requiring the original constitution to reconsider the matter must be greater than when a considerable time has passed."

Have been made to their satisfaction   The wording of this provision clearly implies that the tribunal is required to formally indicate whether the arrangements that have been put in place to enable the patient to be discharged are satisfactory.

The previous application or reference   The patient cannot be discharged on the basis of the earlier deferred direction: the matter must be considered afresh.

Subsection (8)

Section 42   Which, inter alia, empowers the Secretary of State to discharge the patient from hospital either absolutely or subject to conditions.   **1-994**

Restricted patients subject to restriction directions

74.—(1)   Where an application to [the appropriate tribunal] is made by a   **1-995**
restricted patient who is subject to [a limitation direction or] a restriction direc-

[443]

tion, or where the case of such a patient is referred to [the appropriate tribunal], the Tribunal—

(a) shall notify the Secretary of State whether, in [its] opinion, the patient would, if subject to a restriction order, be entitled to be absolutely or conditionally discharged under section 73 above; and

(b) if [the tribunal notifies] him that the patient would be entitled to be conditionally discharged, may recommend that in the event of his not being discharged under this section he should continue to be detained in hospital.

(2) If in the case of a patient not falling within subsection (4) below—

(a) the Tribunal [notifies] the Secretary of State that the patient would be entitled to be absolutely or conditionally discharged; and

(b) within the period of 90 days beginning with the date of that notification the Secretary of State gives notice to the Tribunal that the patient may be so discharged,

the Tribunal shall direct the absolute or, as the case may be, the conditional discharge of the patient.

(3) Where a patient continues to be liable to be detained in a hospital at the end of the period referred to in subsection (2)(b) above because the Secretary of State has not given the notice there mentioned, the managers of the hospital shall, unless [the tribunal has] made a recommendation under subsection (1)(b) above, transfer the patient to a prison or other institution in which he might have been detained if he had not been removed to hospital, there to be dealt with as if he had not been so removed.

(4) If, in the case of a patient who is subject to a transfer direction under section 48 above, the Tribunal [notifies] the Secretary of State that the patient would be entitled to be absolutely or conditionally discharged, the Secretary of State shall, unless [the tribunal has] made a recommendation under subsection (1)(b) above, by warrant direct that the patient be remitted to a prison or other institution in which he might have been detained if he had not been removed to hospital, there to be dealt with as if he had not been so removed.

(5) Where a patient is transferred or remitted under subsection (3) or (4) above [the relevant hospital direction and the limitation direction or, as the case may be,] the relevant transfer direction and the restriction direction shall cease to have effect on his arrival in the prison or other institution.

[(5A) Where [the tribunal has] made a recommendation under subsection (1)(b) above in the case of a patient who is subject to a restriction direction or a limitation direction—

(a) the fact that the restriction direction or limitation direction remains in force does not prevent the making of any application or reference to the Parole Board by or in respect of him or the exercise by him of any power to require the Secretary of State to refer his case to the Parole Board, and

(b) if the Parole Board make a direction or recommendation by virtue of which the patient would become entitled to be released (whether unconditionally or on licence) from any prison or other institution in which he might have been detained if he had not been removed to hospital, the restriction direction or limitation direction shall cease to have effect at the time when he would become entitled to be so released.]

(6) Subsections (3) to (8) of section 73 above shall have effect in relation to this section as they have effect in relation to that section, taking references to the relevant hospital order and the restriction order as references to [the hospital direction and the limitation direction or, as the case may be, to] the transfer direction and the restriction direction.

(7) This section is without prejudice to subsections 50 to 53 above in their application to patients who are not discharged under this section.

Amendments

The amendments to this section were made by the Crime (Sentences) Act 1997 s.55, Sch.4 para.12, the Criminal Justice Act 2003 s.295 and SI 2008/2883 art.9, Sch.3 para.55.

Definitions

the appropriate tribunal: ss.66(4), 145(1).
restricted patient: s.79(1).
restriction direction: ss.49, 145(1).
restriction order: ss.41, 145(1).
hospital: ss.34(2), 79(6), 145(1).
hospital direction: s.145(1).
limitation direction: s.145(1).
the managers: s.145(1).
relevant hospital direction: s.79(2)-(5).
relevant hospital order: s.79(2)-(5).
relevant transfer direction: s.79(2)-(5).
transfer direction: ss.47, 145(1).

1-996

General Note

This section, which should be read with s.50, provides for the procedure to be adopted on an application to a tribunal by a patient who has been transferred from prison to hospital under either s.47 or 48, subject to a restriction direction made under s.49, or has been made the subject of hospital and limitation directions under s.45A. It also applies to references to tribunals made in respect of such patients by the Secretary of State. A patient who has been transferred subject to a restriction direction ceases to be subject to restrictions on reaching his release date had he remained in prison (s.50(2)(3)).

1-997

The reason for the distinction between the regimes for discharge set out in s.73 and in this section was explained by Irwin J. in *R. (on the application of LV) v Secretary of State for Justice* [2014] EWHC 1495 (Admin) at para.48:

"In making a hospital order and a restriction order the judge in the crown court is conducting the definitive sentencing exercise in the case. Whereas, the prisoner who is transferred to hospital and made subject of a restriction direction may very likely be suffering from a mental disorder which arose after his sentence began. The statutory provisions preserve the capacity of such a prisoner to apply to the Parole Board irrespective of – indeed as if there had never been – a transfer direction and a restriction direction. The considerations which arise for the Parole Board are different and additional to those which arise for the Tribunal, either in respect of a patient subject to a hospital order and a restriction order, or in respect of a patient subject to a transfer direction and a restriction direction."

The Reference Guide describes the effect of this section:

"6.89 As with other restricted patients, the Tribunal has no general discretion to discharge patients subject to hospital and limitation directions or restricted transfer directions.

6.90 In addition, because these patients are liable to resume serving their sentence of imprisonment, or its equivalent, if they no longer require treatment in hospital, special arrangements apply where the Tribunal believes that the criteria for discharge from detention are met.

6.91 The criteria for the discharge of patients subject to these directions are the same as those for patients subject to restricted hospital orders – see paragraphs 6.81 and 6.82.

6.92 Where the Tribunal decides that such a patient would be entitled to be discharged absolutely or conditionally if the patient were subject to a restriction order ... it must inform the Secretary of State for Justice.

6.93 If the patient would be entitled to conditional discharge, the Tribunal may recommend that the patient continue to be detained in hospital, rather than going to prison or other custodial institution, if the patient is not, in fact, discharged.

6.94 In the case of patients who are remand prisoners or other unsentenced prisoners subject to restricted transfer directions under section 48, the Secretary of State has no discretion. If the Tribunal has decided that such a patient would be entitled to be conditionally discharged and has made a recommendation for the patient's continued detention in hospital, the patient remains detained and subject to the restriction direction or limitation direction. Otherwise, the Secretary of State must issue a warrant directing the person's return to prison, or any other place of detention in which the patient could have been detained but for being in hospital.

6.95 In the case of a sentenced prisoner subject to hospital and limitation directions or a restricted transfer direction under section 47, the Secretary of State has the discretion to agree to the patient's discharge.

6.96 In these cases, the Secretary of State has 90 days from being informed of the Tribunal's findings in which to give notice that the patient may be discharged. If the Secretary of State does not do so, the patient must be returned to prison, or its equivalent, unless the Tribunal has recommended that the patient remain in hospital if not conditionally discharged.

6.97 Where sentenced prisoners subject to hospital and limitation directions or transfer directions remain in hospital only as a result of a recommendation by the Tribunal, they have the right to apply to the Parole Board for release once they have served the minimum period set by the court (the 'tariff' period) in the same way as other prisoners. If that point has already been reached when the Tribunal recommendation is first acted on, the Secretary of State will refer their case automatically to the Parole Board."

In *R. (on the application of Abu-Rideh) v Mental Health Review Tribunal* [2004] EWHC 1999 (Admin); [2004] M.H.L.R. 308 at paras 19–22, Gage J. adopted the following summary, drafted by counsel, of the effect of this section in the case of a patient subject to a direction made under s.48 and a restriction direction made under s.49 who appears before a tribunal:

1. The tribunal must, if not satisfied *either* that the patient is suffering from a mental disorder of a nature or degree which makes it appropriate for him to be liable to be detained in a hospital for medical treatment *or* that it is necessary for the health and safety of the patient or the protection of others that he continue to receive medical treatment in hospital, make a recommendation for discharge under s.74(1)(a).
2. If the tribunal is satisfied that it is not appropriate for the patient to remain liable to be recalled to hospital, they must recommend the patient's absolute discharge; if they are not so satisfied, they must recommend the patient's conditional discharge (s.73(1)(b) and 73(2)).
3. If the tribunal recommends the patient's conditional discharge then it may also make a recommendation under s.74(1)(b) that, in the event of his not being discharged under s.74, the patient should continue to be detained in hospital. If the Secretary of State accepts the recommendation the patient remains in hospital notwithstanding he no longer satisfies the criteria for detention under the Act (or under art.5(1)(e) [of the European Convention on Human Rights]).
4. By virtue of s.74(4) a patient subject to a transfer direction under s.48 *cannot* be discharged by the Secretary of State under s.74 either absolutely or conditionally. His discharge powers under s.74(2) only apply to serving prisoners transferred under s.47. The patient will automatically be remitted back to the place of his former detention if the recommendation is for absolute discharge *or* if a recommendation for conditional discharge has been made without a recommendation under s.74(1)(b). If a recommendation has been made under s.74(1)(b) the patient is not automatically remitted back to their place of detention and he will remain detained until remitted back to prison by the Secretary of State under s.53, discharged by the Secretary of State under s.42(2) or the justification for his underlying detention expires.

In *AC v Partnerships in Care Ltd and Secretary of State for Justice* [2012] UKUT 450 (AAC); [2013] M.H.L.R., UT Judge Jacobs said at para.16:

"The tribunal in this case decided that 'conditional discharge would envisage the discharge being subject only to such conditions as the tribunal could properly impose under s.73(4).' That is precisely correct. The tribunal's jurisdiction is limited to issues of discharge. It has no power to impose conditions as to release, which is the exclusive preserve of the Parole Board. The tribunal was right to refuse to take account of the conditions that might be imposed by the Parole Board."

The policy of the Secretary of State on receiving a notification under paras (a) and (b) of subs.(1) is set out in the note on s.50(1)(b).

Subsection (1)

Patient   See the note on "any such patient" in s.73(2).   **1-998**

Secretary of State   Functions under this provision have not been transferred to Welsh Ministers (see the General Note to the Act and SI 1999/672 art.2, Sch.1).

Discharge   In the context of para.(a) this term means only discharge from hospital; it does not exclude consideration of discharge back to prison (*R. (on the application of Abu-Rideh) v Mental Health Review Tribunal*, above).

Subsection (2)

In *R. v Vowles* [2015] EWCA Crim 45; [2016] M.H.R.L. 66 Lord Thomas CJ, who gave the judg-   **1-999**
ment of the Court, said that this "sub-section imposed on the Secretary of State an obligation to notify the FTT within 90 days of his decision in relation to [the patient's] discharge. It was the policy of the Secretary of State set out in Chapter 10 of the MHCS Casework Manual never to agree to a conditional discharge in such cases. The case therefore had to be referred to the Parole Board".

Beginning with   Including the date of the notification (*Zoan v Rouamba* [2000] 2 All E.R. 620 CA).

Conditional discharge   A patient who has been conditionally discharged under this provision is not subject to the consent to treatment provisions contained in Pt IV (s.56(3)(c)).

Subsection (5)

Relevant hospital direction … relevant transfer direction   See s.79(2).   **1-1000**

Subsection (5A)

This subsection, which was inserted as a response to the decision of the European Court of Human   **1-1001**
Rights in *Benjamin and Wilson v United Kingdom* (2003) 36 E.H.R.R. 1, relates to transferred prison-ers detained in hospital beyond their release date whose detention in hospital has been found by the tribunal to be no longer justified by their mental disorder, but who the tribunal has recommended should remain in hospital, rather than return to prison, in the event that the Secretary of State does not agree to discharge them from hospital. It provides that the fact that restrictions under the Act remain in force does not prevent an application or reference to the Parole Board for release. It further provides that if the Parole Board directs or recommends release, the restrictions cease to have effect at the time he is entitled to release. The effect of this is that the transferred prisoner is assured access to the Parole Board, and the possibility of release on licence, once he has reached his release date and the tribunal find he is no longer appropriately detained in hospital for medical treatment.

Subsection (6)

Relevant hospital order   See s.79(2).   **1-1002**

Applications and references concerning conditionally discharged restricted patients

75.—(1)   Where a restricted patient has been conditionally discharged under   **1-1003**
section 42(2), 73 or 74 above and is subsequently recalled to hospital—

   (a)   the Secretary of State shall, within one month of the day on which the patient returns or is returned to hospital, refer his case to [the appropri-ate tribunal]; and

   (b)   section 70 above shall apply to the patient as if the relevant hospital order [, hospital direction] or transfer direction had been made on that day.

[447]

(2)   Where a restricted patient has been conditionally discharged as aforesaid but has not been recalled to hospital he may apply to [the appropriate tribunal]—

    (a)   in the period between the expiration of 12 months and the expiration of two years beginning with the date on which he was conditionally discharged; and

    (b)   in any subsequent period of two years.

(3)   Sections 73 and 74 above shall not apply to an application under subsection (2) above but on any such application the Tribunal may—

    (a)   vary any condition to which the patient is subject in connection with his discharge or impose any condition which might have been imposed in connection therewith; or

    (b)   direct that the restriction order [, limitation direction] or restriction direction to which he is subject shall cease to have effect;

and if the tribunal [gives] a direction under paragraph (b) above the patient shall cease to be liable to be detained by virtue of the relevant hospital order [, hospital direction] or transfer direction.

Amendments

The amendments to this section were made by the Crime (Sentences) Act 1997 s.55, Sch.4 para.12(13), the Mental Health Act 2007 s.41 and SI 2008/2883 art.9, Sch.3 para.56.

Definitions

1-1004   restricted patient: s.79(1).
hospital: ss.34(2), 79(6), 145(1).
the appropriate tribunal: ss.66(4), 145(1).
limitation direction: s.145(1).
hospital direction: s.145(1).
the relevant hospital direction: s.79(2)-(5).
the relevant hospital order: s.79(2)-(5).
the relevant transfer direction: s.79(2)-(5).
restriction order: ss.41, 145(1).
restriction direction: ss.49, 145(1).
restricted patient: s.79(1).

General Note

1-1005   This section directs the Secretary of State to refer the case of a conditionally discharged restricted patient who has been recalled to hospital to a tribunal (subs.(1)). It also provides for a tribunal application to be made by a conditionally discharged restricted patient who has not been recalled to hospital (subs.(2)). On hearing such an application the tribunal has the power to vary the conditions of the discharge, to impose new conditions, or to direct that the restriction order, restriction direction or hospital direction shall cease to have effect (subs.(3)).

A restricted patient who is no longer suffering from a mental disorder remains a "patient" for the purposes of this section until discharged absolutely (*R. v Merseyside Mental Health Review Tribunal Ex p. K* [1990] 1 All E.R. 694 CA).

Human Rights Act 1998

1-1006   In *Secretary of State for Justice v Rayner* [2008] EWCA Civ 176; [2008] M.H.L.R. 115, the Court of Appeal held that this section was capable of satisfying the requirement of art.5(4) of the European Convention on Human Rights (ECHR) for the lawfulness of the patient's detention to be decided "speedily" if the Secretary of State referred the patient's case to the tribunal with reasonable dispatch, having regard to all the material circumstances. Keene L.J., who gave the only judgment of substance, said, at para.25, that one would normally expect a reference to be made within days, not weeks, of the return of the patient to hospital, and normally within a few days. The court also considered whether subs.(1)(b) of this section, which has the effect of enabling a recalled patient to make an application to a tribunal only after six months has elapsed since his return to hospital, violates the entitlement in art.5(4) for the patient to "take proceedings" to challenge the lawfulness of the detention. In concluding that it did not, his Lordship said at para.46:

"I conclude that while s.75 ..., if it stood alone, might now not be regarded as sufficient to achieve the protection of Art.5(4) rights required by the ECHR and the Strasbourg jurisprudence, the combination of that statutory mechanism, the right of the patient to enforce the Secretary of State's statutory duty (as interpreted in the light of the Convention) by way of judicial review, and the right of the patient to challenge the lawfulness of his detention directly in the courts on its substantive merits by judicial review and/or habeas corpus does suffice to comply with Art.5(4). The patient has direct access as of right to the courts and can obtain swift redress if he is being unlawfully detained. I would only add that, as a matter of procedure, if judicial review has to be resorted to by a patient, he or she would normally find it quicker and more effective to apply for an order enforcing the Secretary of State's statutory duty rather than embark on a direct challenge in the courts to the lawfulness of the detention."

In *R. (on the application of SC) v Mental Health Review Tribunal and the Secretary of State for Health* [2005] EWHC 17 (Admin); [2005] M.H.L.R. 31, Munby J. held that subs.(3)is not incompatible with arts 6 and 8 of the ECHR as the relevant law is both sufficiently foreseeable and adequate to protect the patient from all risk of arbitrariness.

The Tribunal's approach to issues arising under art.8 of the ECHR

In *RP v Dudley and Walsall Mental Health Partnership NHS Trust* [2016] UKUT 204 (AAC); [2016] **1-1007** M.H.L.R. 270, UT Judge Jacobs said that:

1. The terms of s.6 of the Human Rights Act 1998 does not mean that the tribunal is expected to deal with art.8 issues separately in every case. Any consideration of art.8 can be subsumed in the tribunal's discussion of the statutory criteria (para.11).
2. Decisions on art.8 depend on their facts. They are not unique in that, but there is always a danger in reasoning by comparison with the facts of other cases when so much depends on the circumstances of the individual case. The correct approach is to reason by reference to the terms of art.8 and the principles established by the case law, not by comparison of facts (para.13).
3. Accepting that art.8 is engaged by virtue of the conditions imposed on a conditional discharge, the issue is whether the interference is authorised under art.8(2). That breaks down into two questions. First: was the interference in accordance with law? That will depend on the whether the statutory conditions under the Mental Health Act were satisfied. Second: was the interference necessary in a democratic society in the interests of public safety, for the protection of health, or for the protection of the rights and freedoms of others? Again, those questions reflect the statutory criteria (para.16).
4. In the vast majority of cases, the Tribunal can deal adequately with art.8 by focusing on the statutory criteria, but with art.8 providing an additional protection in an individual case. It is possible, for example, that the conditions imposed on a conditional discharge might represent an unjustified interference with private or family live. The tribunal is entitled to expect a representative to draw attention to any specific art.8 issues that arise. This does not absolve the tribunal of all responsibility under s.6 of the Human Rights Act 1998; tribunals cannot ignore obvious issues that arise before them. Their responsibility is greater when a patient is not represented by solicitors or counsel (para.17).
5. There is a difference between violations of art.8 that are bound to arise from the tribunal's decision and those that only arise from the way its decision may be implemented. The former are the tribunal's responsibility; the latter are not. Most conditions that are imposed on conditional discharges are capable of being operated oppressively, but in practice they are not. It is understood when the conditions are imposed that they will be applied reasonably and according to the circumstances at the time. Intervention may be light-handed or heavy-handed as required. The application of art.8 will be calibrated to the needs of the patient and the public. The tribunal is likely to be concerned to ensure that the conditions are reasonable in principle (para.18).

Subsection (1)

1-1008   **Within one month**   Disregarding the day of the patient's return to hospital (*Stewart v Chapman* [1951] 2 K.B. 792). The referral should normally be made within a few days of the patient's return to hospital (*Secretary of State for Justice v Rayner*, above). If the patient is already in the hospital as an informal patient when he is recalled, the one-month period runs from the date of the recall (*R. (on the application of Rayner) v Secretary of State for the Home Department* [2007] EWHC 1028 (Admin); [2007] 1 W.L.R. 2239, para.7).

Refer his case to the Appropriate Tribunal   The tribunal will exercise its powers under s.73. In *R. v Mental Health Review Tribunal for Merseyside Ex p. Kelly* [1998] 39 B.M.L.R. 114, Keene J. said that he could:

> "see that in general terms the events leading up to a recall of a patient may not be relevant to the issues arising under s.72(1)(b)(i) and (ii) [see s.73(1)(a)] ... However, it is also true that such events prior to a patient's recall may be relevant. Diagnosis of and opinions as to such matters as are referred to in the relevant statutory paragraphs are not arrived at by ignoring events which have happened. The behaviour of the patient may well be material to such diagnosis and opinions. It will depend at least partly on how the expert witness or witnesses have arrived at their conclusions."

In this case, his Lordship declared that the decision of the tribunal was ultra vires in that it was contrary to the rules of natural justice because of a refusal by the tribunal to allow the cross-examination of the patient's responsible clinician on statements that he had made in his report to the tribunal concerning allegations that had been made about the patient's conduct prior to his recall to hospital.

Although the tribunal may consider events leading up to the recall, there is no jurisdiction to examine "the underlying circumstances of the mechanics of the recall and particularly the extent to which there had been discussion between [the patient's responsible clinician and the Mental Health Casework Section]" (*R. (on the application of Munday) v Secretary of State for the Home Department* [2009] EWHC 3638 (Admin), para.23, per Burnett J.).

Paragraph (b)

1-1009   The effect of this provision is that a recalled patient may not make an application to a tribunal until six months after his return to hospital.

Subsection (2)

1-1010   **Conditionally discharged**   A patient is conditionally discharged for the purposes of calculating time under this provision, not on the date when the tribunal decided that he be discharged subject to conditions being met, but on the date when he actually leaves hospital once those conditions had been met: see *R. v Canons Park Mental Health Review Tribunal Ex p. Martins* (1995) 26 B.M.L.R. 134 where Ognall J. followed Mann J.'s finding in *Secretary of State for the Home Department v Mental Health Review Tribunal for the Mersey Regional Health Authority* [1986] 3 All E.R. 233 at 237 that:

> "The word 'discharge' as employed in sections 72 to 75 of the Act of 1983 means, and in my judgment can only mean, release from hospital. The release may be absolute or it may be conditional."

Not been recalled to hospital   A conditionally discharged restricted patient who has been brought back to hospital under either s.2 or s.3 has not been "recalled to hospital" as such a recall can only be made by the Secretary of State under s.42(3).

May apply   To the tribunal for the area in which he resides (s.77(4)).

Beginning with   Including the date of his conditional discharge (*Zoan v Rouamba* [2000] 2 All E.R. 620 CA) which is day when he leaves hospital: see the note on "Conditionally discharged" above.

Subsection (3)

1-1011   Under this provision a tribunal is not "concerned so much with finding facts which are capable of exact demonstration but rather with a process of judgment, evaluation and assessment which involves the appreciation and evaluation of inherently imprecise and often differing or conflicting psychiatric evidence" (*R. (on the application of DJ v Mental Health Review Tribunal* [2005] EWHC 587 (Admin); [2005] M.H.L.R. 56, para.102, per Munby J.).These observations were followed by the Court of Appeal in *R. (on the application of N) v Mental Health Review Tribunal (Northern Region)* [2005] EWCA Civ 1605; [2006] 4 All E.R. 194, at para.98.

In *R. (on the application of SC) v Mental Health Review Tribunal and the Secretary of State for Health* [2005] EWHC 17 (Admin); [2005] M.H.L.R. 31 paras 56, 57, Munby J. said that a patient who makes an application under subs.(2) will have been convicted of an offence grave enough to merit a possible sentence of imprisonment, found to have been suffering from a mental disorder meriting detention in hospital for treatment, and to have presented a risk of re-offending such that a restriction order was necessary for the protection of the public from serious harm; and found by a tribunal to be someone who, although not requiring detention for treatment for the time being, nonetheless required to remain liable to recall. Accordingly, when exercising its powers under this provision, the tribunal:

"will need to consider such matters as the nature, gravity and circumstances of the patient's offence, the nature and gravity of his mental disorder, past present and future, the risk and likelihood of the patient re-offending, the degree of harm to which the public may be exposed if he re-offends, the risk and likelihood of a recurrence or exacerbation of any mental disorder, and the risk and likelihood of his needing to be recalled in the future for further treatment in hospital. The tribunal will also need to consider the nature of any conditions previously imposed, whether by the tribunal or by the Secretary of State, under ss.42(2), 73(4)(b) or 73(5), the reasons why they were imposed and the extent to which it is desirable to continue, vary or add to them."

His Lordship said, at para.60, that the effect of this provision:

"is not to *preclude* the tribunal from considering the kind of factors which fall for consideration under s.73. Rather ... the effect is that the tribunal, when exercising its discretion under s.75(3), is not constrained by the mandatory terms of s.73 which bind the approach of the tribunal when considering the exercise of its powers under s.73."

His Lordship further stated, at para.59, that:

"in effect, one of the key questions that the tribunal will wish to ask is whether it is—as s.73(1)(b) puts it—'satisfied that it is not appropriate for the patient to remain liable to be recalled to hospital for further treatment.' If the tribunal is not so satisfied, then it is difficult to see that it could be appropriate for it to make an order under s.75(3)(b)."

In *RH v South London and Maudsley NHS Foundation Trust* [2010] EWCA Civ 1273; [2010] M.H.L.R. 341, para.29, the Court of Appeal held that Munby J.'s formulation of the question to be asked by the tribunal under this provision, which is set out at para.59 of his judgment and which places the burden of proof on the patient, does not violate the ECHR.

SC was applied by UT Judge Ward in *DA v Central and North West London NHS Foundation Trust* [2021] UKUT 101 (AAC); [2022] M.H.L.R. 72 where it was held on an application under this section that there is nothing intrinsically irrational in removing the conditions of a conditional discharge while maintaining the liability to recall the patient. Judge Ward said at para.23:

"What makes a conditional discharge 'conditional' is the liability to recall. I therefore do not consider that irrationality necessarily arises by retaining a liability to recall while jettisoning conditions previously in force. What matters, rather, are the reasons in the circumstances of the case for retaining liability to recall (on the one hand) and dispensing with the conditions (on the other)."

GENERAL

Visiting and examination of patients

76.—(1)   For the purpose of advising whether an application to [the appropriate tribunal] should be made by or in respect of a patient who is liable to be detained or subject to guardianship […] under Part II of this Act [or a community patient,] or of furnishing information as to the condition of a patient for the purposes of such an application, any registered medical practitioner [or approved clinician] authorised by or on behalf of the patient or other person who is entitled to make or has made the application—   **1-1012**

(a) may at any reasonable time visit the patient and examine him in private, and

(b) may require the production of and inspect any records relating to the detention or treatment of the patient in any hospital [or to any after-care services provided for the patient under section 117 below].

(2) Section 32 above shall apply for the purposes of this section as it applies for the purposes of Part II of this Act.

Amendments

The amendments to this section were made by the Mental Health Act 2007 ss.13(2)(b), 32(4), 55, Sch.3 para.22, Sch.11 Pt 5 and SI 2008/2883 art.9, Sch.3 para.57.

Definitions

1-1013   the appropriate tribunal: ss.66(4), 145(1).
community patient: s.17A(7).
approved clinician: s.145(1).
patient: s.145(1).
hospital: ss.34(2), 79(6), 145(1).

General Note

1-1014   This section, which is applied to patients who have been placed under hospital, restriction or guardianship orders by a court under s.37 or 41 of the Act (Sch.1 Pt 1 para.1; Pt 2 para.1), provides for a medical practitioner or approved clinician to be authorised by or on behalf of the patient, or anyone else entitled to make an application to a tribunal, to advise on whether an application should be made, or to provide information on the patient's condition for the purposes of an application. The authorised person may visit and examine the patient, and inspect relevant records.

Where the patient's nearest relative is the applicant to the tribunal, para.12.9 of the *Code of Practice* states:

"Where nearest relatives have a right to apply to the Tribunal, they too may authorise independent doctors or approved clinicians [under this section]. The patient's consent is not required for authorised doctors or approved clinicians to see their records, and they should be given prompt access to the records they wish to see."

A failure to allow authorised persons to carry out their functions under this section could amount to an obstruction under s.129.

Subsection (1)

1-1015   **Furnishing information**   In *W v Egdell* [1990] 1 All E.R. 835, the Court of Appeal held that where a medical practitioner is called on to examine a patient with a view to providing an independent psychiatric report to support the patient's application to a tribunal, he owes a duty not only to his patient but also a duty to the public. His duty to the public would enable him to place before the proper authorities the results of his examination if, in his opinion, the public interest so required. This would be so whether or not the patient instructed him not to do so. Bingham L.J. said at 852, 853:

"There is one consideration [in this case] which in my judgment ... weighs the balance of public interest decisively in favour of disclosure. It may be shortly put. Where a man has committed multiple killings under the disability of serious mental illness, decisions which may lead directly or indirectly to his release from hospital should not be made unless a responsible authority is properly able to make an informed judgment that the risk of repetition is so small as to be acceptable. A consultant psychiatrist who becomes aware, even in the course of a confidential relationship, of information which leads him, in the exercise of what the court considers a sound professional judgment, to fear that such decisions may be made on the basis of inadequate information and with a real risk of consequent danger to the public is entitled to take such steps as are reasonable in all the circumstances to communicate the grounds of his concern to the responsible authorities."

Registered medical practitioner   Means "a fully registered person within the meaning of the Medical Act 1983 who holds a licence to practise under that Act" (Interpretation Act 1978 Sch.1).

General provisions concerning tribunal applications

77.—(1)   No application shall be made to [the appropriate tribunal by or in   **1-1016** respect of a patient under this Act] except in such cases and at such times as are expressly provided by this Act.

(2)   Where under this Act any person is authorised to make an application to [the appropriate tribunal] within a specified period, not more than one such application shall be made by that person within that period but for that purpose there shall be disregarded any application which is withdrawn in accordance with [Tribunal Procedure Rules or] rules made under section 78 below.

(3)   Subject to subsection (4) below an application to [a tribunal] authorised to be made by or in respect of a patient under this Act shall be made by notice in writing addressed

[(a)   in the case of a patient who is liable to be detained in a hospital, [to the First-tier Tribunal where that hospital is in England and to the Mental Health Review Tribunal for Wales where that hospital is in Wales];

(b)   in the case of a community patient, [to the First-tier Tribunal where the responsible hospital is in England and to the Mental Health Review Tribunal for Wales where that hospital is in Wales];

(c)   in the case of a patient subject to guardianship, [to the First-tier Tribunal where the patient resides in England and to the Mental Health Review Tribunal for Wales where the patient resides in Wales].]

(4)   Any application under section 75(2) above shall be made [to the First-tier Tribunal where the patient resides in England and to the Mental Health Review Tribunal for Wales where the patient resides in Wales].

Amendments

The amendments to this section were made by the Mental Health Act 2007 s.32(4), Sch.3 para.23, SI 2008/2883 art.9, Sch.3 para.58 and SI 2009/1307 art.5, Sch.1 para.161.

Definitions

patient: s.145(1).   **1-1017**
community patient: s.17A(7).
the appropriate tribunal: ss.66(4), 145(1).
hospital: ss.34(2), 79(6), 145(1).
responsible hospital: ss.17A(7), 145(1).

General Note

This section provides, in subss.(1) and (2), that there is no right to apply to a tribunal apart from those   **1-1018** situations expressly provided for in the Act, that where the Act gives rise to a right to make an application within a specified period only one such application may be made within that period, and that where the tribunal authorises the withdrawal of an application the applicant can re-apply during the relevant period. Where a patient is transferred between England and Wales, a tribunal application made in one country counts as an application to a tribunal in the other.

Subsections (3) and (4) determine whether an application should be made to the First-tier Tribunal (Mental Health) or the Mental Health Review Tribunal for Wales.

Subsection (2)

1-1019   See the note on "an application" in s.66(1).

Withdrawn in accordance with the rules   References cannot be withdrawn.

Subsection (4)

1-1020   **Application under section 75(2)**   By a restricted patient who has been conditionally discharged from hospital.

Resides   See the note on this term in s.7(5).

Procedure of [Mental Health Review Tribunal for Wales]

1-1021   **78.**—(1)   The Lord Chancellor may make rules with respect to the making of applications to [the Mental Health Review Tribunal for Wales] and with respect to the proceedings of [that tribunal] and matters incidental to or consequential on such proceedings.

(2)   Rules made under this section may in particular make provision—

   (a)   for enabling [the tribunal], or the [President] of [the tribunal], to postpone the consideration of any application by or in respect of a patient, or of any such application of any specified class, until the expiration of such period (not exceeding 12 months) as may be specified in the rules from the date on which an application by or in respect of the same patient was last considered and determined [under this Act by the tribunal or the First-tier Tribunal];

   [(b)   for the transfer of proceedings to or from the Mental Health Review Tribunal for Wales in any case where, after the making of the application, the patient is moved into or out of Wales;]

   (c)   for restricting the persons qualified to serve as members of [the tribunal] for the consideration of any application, or of an application of any specified class;

   (d)   for enabling [the tribunal] to dispose of an application without a formal hearing where such a hearing is not requested by the applicant or it appears to the tribunal that such a hearing would be detrimental to the health of the patient;

   (e)   for enabling [the tribunal] to exclude members of the public, or any specified class of members of the public, from any proceedings of the tribunal, or to prohibit the publication of reports of any such proceedings or the names of any persons concerned in such proceedings;

   (f)   for regulating the circumstances in which, and the persons by whom, applicants and patients in respect of whom applications are made to [the tribunal] may, if not desiring to conduct their own case, be represented for the purposes of those applications;

   (g)   for regulating the methods by which information relevant to an application may be obtained by or furnished to the tribunal, and in particular for authorising the members of [the tribunal], or any one or more of them, to visit and interview in private any patient by or in respect of whom an application has been made;

   (h)   for making available to any applicant, and to any patient in respect of whom an application is made to [the tribunal], copies of any documents obtained by or furnished to the tribunal in connection with the application, and a statement of the substance of any oral information so obtained or furnished except where the Tribunal considers it undesirable in the interests of the patient or for other special reasons;

(i) for requiring [the tribunal], if so requested in accordance with the rules, to furnish such statements of the reasons for any decision given by the tribunal as may be prescribed by the rules, subject to any provision made by the rules for withholding such a statement from a patient or any other person in cases where the tribunal considers that furnishing it would be undesirable in the interests of the patient or for other special reasons;

(j) for conferring on the [tribunal] such ancillary powers as the Lord Chancellor thinks necessary for the purposes of the exercise of [its] functions under this Act;

(k) for enabling any functions of [the tribunal] which relate to matters preliminary or incidental to an application to be performed by the [President] of the tribunal.

(3) Subsections (1) and (2) above apply in relation to references to [the Mental Health Review Tribunal for Wales] as they apply in relation to applications to [that tribunal] by or in respect of patients.

(4) Rules under this section may make provision as to the procedure to be adopted in cases concerning restricted patients and, in particular—

(a) for restricting the persons qualified to serve as [chairman] of [the tribunal] for the consideration of an application or reference relating to a restricted patient;

[(b) for the transfer of proceedings to or from the tribunal in any case where, after the making of a reference or application in accordance with section 71(4) or 77(4) above, the patient begins or ceases to reside in Wales.]

(5) Rules under this section may be so framed as to apply to all applications or references or to applications or references of any specified class and may make different provision in relation to different cases.

(6) Any functions conferred on the [President] of [the Mental Health Review Tribunal for Wales] by rules under this section may […], be exercised by another member of that tribunal appointed by him for the purpose.

(7) [The Mental Health Review Tribunal for Wales] may pay allowances in respect of travelling expenses, subsistence and loss of earnings to any person attending the Tribunal as an applicant or witness, to the patient who is the subject of the proceedings if he attends otherwise than as the applicant or a witness and to any person (other than [an authorised person (within the meaning of Part 3)]) who attends as the representative of an applicant.

(8) […]

(9) [Part I of the Arbitration Act 1996] shall not apply to any proceedings before [the Mental Health Review Tribunal for Wales] except so far as any provisions of that Act may be applied, with or without modifications, by rules made under this section.

Amendments

The amendments to this section were made by the Arbitration Act 1996 s.107(1), Sch.3 para.40, the Mental Health Act 2007 ss.38, 55, Sch.11 Pt.6, SI 2008/2883 art.9, Sch.3 para.59 and the Legal Services Act 2007 s.208, Sch.21 para.60.

Definitions

1-1022   patient: s.145(1).
restricted patient: s.79(1).

General Note

1-1023   The Mental Health Review Tribunal for Wales Rules 2008 (SI 2008/2705 (L.17)) govern the practice and procedure to be followed in proceedings before the Mental Health Review Tribunal for Wales.

Subsection (1)

1-1024 **The lord chancellor**   The functions of the Lord Chancellor under this section have been transferred to the Welsh Ministers (Welsh Ministers (Transfer of Functions) Order 2018 (SI 2018/644) art.20).

Subsection (2)

1-1025 **Paragraph (a); president of a tribunal**   See Sch.2 para.2.

Paragraph (b); area of the tribunal   See s.65(1).

Subsection (4)

1-1026 **Qualified to serve as chairman of the tribunal**   Provision for restricting those who can act as chairman in cases relating to restricted patients is made in r.11(2) of the Welsh Rules. There is no equivalent provision in the Tribunal Rules.

Subsection (7)

1-1027 **Loss of earnings**   This would not cover the payment of a fee for representing the client or acting as an expert witness.

Attending   Expenses cannot be paid for preparatory work.

Authorised person   Is defined in s.55(1).

[Appeal from the Mental Health Review Tribunal for Wales to the Upper Tribunal

1-1028   **78A.**—(1)   A party to any proceedings before the Mental Health Review Tribunal for Wales may appeal to the Upper Tribunal on any point of law arising from a decision made by the Mental Health Review Tribunal for Wales in those proceedings.

(2)   An appeal may be brought under subsection (1) above only if, on an application made by the party concerned, the Mental Health Review Tribunal for Wales or the Upper Tribunal has given its permission for the appeal to be brought.

(3)   Section 12 of the Tribunals, Courts and Enforcement Act 2007 (proceedings on appeal to the Upper Tribunal) applies in relation to appeals to the Upper Tribunal under this section as it applies in relation to appeals to it under section 11 of that Act, but as if references to the First-tier Tribunal were references to the Mental Health Review Tribunal for Wales.]

Amendment

This section was inserted by SI 2008/2883 art.9, Sch.3 para.60.

General Note

As the Mental Health Review Tribunal for Wales is not administered through the Courts and Tribunal **1-1029**
Service, this section ensures that the onward appeal right to the Upper Tribunal which is enjoyed by the
First-tier Tribunal (Mental Health) is also available in Wales.

Interpretation of Part V

79.—(1)   In this Part of this Act "restricted patient" means a patient who is **1-1030**
subject to a restriction order [, limitation direction] or restriction direction and this
Part of this Act shall, subject to the provisions of this section, have effect in relation to any person who
  [(a)   is treated by virtue of any enactment as subject to a hospital order and
      a restriction order; or]
  (b)   [...]
  [(c)   is treated as subject to a hospital order and a restriction order, or to a
      hospital direction and a limitation direction, or to a transfer direction
      and a restriction direction, by virtue of any provision of Part 6 of this
      Act (except section 80D(3), 82A(2) or 85A(2) below),]
as it has effect in relation to a restricted patient.

(2)   Subject to the following provisions of this section, in this Part of this Act
"the relevant hospital order" [, "the relevant hospital direction"] and "the relevant
transfer direction," in relation to a restricted patient, mean the hospital order [, the
hospital direction] or transfer direction by virtue of which he is liable to be detained
in a hospital.

(3)   In the case of a person within paragraph (a) of subsection (1) above, references in this Part of this Act to the relevant hospital order or restriction order shall
be construed as references to the direction referred to in that paragraph.

(4)   In the case of a person within paragraph (b) of subsection (1) above, references in this Part of this Act to the relevant hospital order or restriction order shall
be construed as references to the order under the provisions mentioned in that
paragraph.

(5)   In the case of a person within paragraph (c) of subsection (1) above, references in this Part of this Act to the relevant hospital order, [the relevant hospital
direction,] the relevant transfer direction, the restriction order [, the limitation direc-
tion] or the restriction direction or to a transfer direction under section 48 above
shall be construed as references to the hospital order, [hospital direction,] transfer
direction, restriction order, [limitation direction,] restriction direction or transfer
direction under that section to which that person is treated as subject by virtue of
the provisions mentioned in that paragraph.

[(5A)   Section 75 above shall, subject to the modifications in subsection (5C)
below, have effect in relation to a qualifying patient as it has effect in relation to a
restricted patient who is conditionally discharged under section 42(2), 73 or 74
above.

(5B)   A patient is a qualifying patient if he is treated by virtue of section 80D(3),
82A(2) or 85A(2) below as if he had been conditionally discharged and were subject
to a hospital order and a restriction order, or to a hospital direction and a limitation direction, or to a transfer direction and a restriction direction.

(5C)   The modifications mentioned in subsection (5A) above are—

    (a)   references to the relevant hospital order, hospital direction or transfer direction, or to the restriction order, limitation direction or restriction direction to which the patient is subject, shall be construed as references to the hospital order, hospital direction or transfer direction, or restriction order, limitation direction or restriction direction, to which the patient is treated as subject by virtue of section 80D(3), 82A(2) or 85A(2) below; and

    (b)   the reference to the date on which the patient was conditionally discharged shall be construed as a reference to the date on which he was treated as conditionally discharged by virtue of a provision mentioned in paragraph (a) above.]

(6)   In this Part of this Act, unless the context otherwise requires, "hospital" means a hospital [, and "the responsible clinician" means the responsible clinician,] within the meaning of Part II of this Act.

(7)   [*Repealed by SI 2008/2883 art.9, Sch.3 para.61*]

Amendments

The amendments to this section were made by the Domestic Violence, Crime and Victims Act 2004 s.58, Sch.10 para.21(a), Sch.11 of that Act, SI 2005/2078 Sch.1 para.2(3), the Crime (Sentences) Act 1997 s.55, Sch.4 para.12(14)(15) and the Mental Health Act 2007 ss.13(3), 38(4), 39(2), Sch.5 Pt 2 para.19.

Definitions

1-1031   patient: s.145(1).
restriction order: ss.41, 145(1).
restriction direction: ss.49, 145(1).
hospital order: ss.37, 145(1).
transfer direction: ss.47, 145(1).
hospital direction: s.145(1).
limitation direction: s.145(1).

General Note

Subsection (6)

1-1032   **Hospital**   See s.34(2).

PART VI REMOVAL AND RETURN OF PATIENTS WITHIN UNITED KINGDOM, ETC

General Note

1-1033   This Part deals with the transfer between the United Kingdom jurisdictions and the Channel Islands or the Isle of Man of patients who are subject to certain compulsory powers. It ensures that the patients remain in legal custody whilst in transit and that they are liable to equivalent compulsory powers on their arrival in the receiving jurisdiction. It also provides, in s.86, powers for moving mentally disordered patients who are neither British citizens nor Commonwealth citizens with the right of abode in the United Kingdom from hospitals in England and Wales to countries abroad.

The procedure to be followed on the removal of a patient to England under this Part is set out in regs 15 and 16 of the English Regulations and reg.29 of the Welsh Regulations.

Corresponding legislative provisions

1-1034   Corresponding legislative provisions relating to transfers from Scotland and Northern Ireland can be found in figures 88 and 90 of Ch.34 of the Reference Guide.

The Parliament of the Isle of Man, the Tynwald, has produced a helpful table which sets out equivalent provisions from the mental health legislation of the Isle of Man, England and Wales, Scotland, Northern Ireland and Jersey: see Schs 1, 2 and 3 to the Mental Health (Transfer of Patients) (Equivalent Provisions of Relevant Territories) Regulations 2009 (Statutory Document 117/09). The table can be accessed at: *https://www.tynwald.org.im/spfile?file=/links/tls/SD/2009/2009-SD-0117.pdf.*

Scotland   The Mental Welfare Commission for Scotland has published "Cross border transfers, cross   **1-1035**
border absconding and cross border visits under mental health law – a factsheet for practitioners" which
can be accessed at at the Commission's website (*http://www.mwcscot.org.uk*).

Contact details (taken from Ch.34 of the Reference Guide)

Scotland   **1-1036**
Directorate for Population Health Improvement Mental Health, St Andrews House, Regents Road,
Edinburgh, EH1 3DG
Telephone: 0131 244 5668
Email: andy.lawson2@scotland.gsi.gov.uk
For cases concerned with criminal proceedings email: restrictedpatients@scotland.gsi.gov.uk

Northern Ireland
Mental Health Unit, Department of Health, Social Services and Public
Safety, D1.4 Castle Buildings, Stormont Estate, Belfast BT4 3SQ
Telephone: 028 9052 2562
Fax: 028 9052 2500
Email: mentalhealthunit@dhsspsni.gov.uk
States of Jersey
Community Mental Health Service, 20 La Chasse, St Helier, Jersey,
Channel Islands, JE24UE
Tel: 01534 445841
Fax: 01534 445140
Email: health@gov.je

Bailiwick of Guernsey
Corporate Headquarters, Rue Mignot, St Andrews, Guernsey, Channel
Islands, GY6 8TW
Tel: 01481 725241
Fax: 01481 235341
Email: healthandwellbeing@gov.gg

Isle of Man
Department of Health and Social Care, Mental Health Service, Cronk Coar,
Noble's Hospital, Braddan, Isle of Man, IM4 4RF
Telephone: 01624 656015
Fax: 01624 642805
Email: mentalhealthcustomerservices.dh@gov.im

[Removal to and from Scotland

Removal of patients to Scotland

80.—(1)   If it appears to the Secretary of State, in the case of a patient who is   **1-1037**
for the time being liable to be detained [...] under this Act (otherwise than by virtue
of section 35, 36 or 38 above), that it is in the interests of the patient to remove him
to Scotland, and that arrangements have been made for admitting him to a hospital
[...] there [or, where he is not to be admitted to a hospital, for his detention in
hospital to be authorised by virtue of the Mental Health (Care and Treatment)
(Scotland) Act 2003 or the Criminal Procedure (Scotland) Act 1995], the Secretary
of State may authorise his removal to Scotland and may give any necessary directions for his conveyance to his destination.

(2)—(6)   [*Repealed in relation to England and Wales by SI 2005/2078 art.16,
Sch.3*]

(7)　In this section "hospital" has the same meaning as in the [Mental Health (Care and Treatment) (Scotland) Act 2003].

[(8)　Reference in this section to a patient's detention in hospital being authorised by virtue of the Mental Health (Care and Treatment) (Scotland) Act 2003 or the Criminal Procedure (Scotland) Act 1995 shall be read as including references to a patient in respect of whom a certificate under one of the provisions listed in section 290(7)(a) of the Act of 2003 is in operation.]

Amendments

The amendments to this section were made by SI 2003/2078 Sch.1 para.2(4) and the Mental Health Act 2007 s.55, Sch.11 Pt 7. The cross-heading immediately above this section was substituted by s.39(2), Sch.5 Pt 1 para.2.

Definitions

1-1038　　patient: s.145(1).
hospital: subs.(7).
restriction order: ss.41, 145(1).
restriction direction: ss.49, 145(1).

General Note

1-1039　　This section enables the Secretary of State (or, for certain categories of patient, the Welsh Ministers) to transfer a patient who is detained (otherwise than under s.35, 36 or 38) in England or Wales to Scotland without a break in the powers of detention. The Secretary of State (or the Welsh Ministers) must be satisfied that such a move is in the interests of the patient.

Transfer to Scotland requires the approval of Scottish Ministers in accordance with the Mental Health (Cross Border transfers: patients subject to detention requirements or otherwise in hospital) (Scotland) Regulations 2005 (SSI 2005/467) which regulate both the removal of patients from Scotland as well as the reception of patients in Scotland. In terms of the reception of patients into Scotland, reg.24 sets out that the consent of Scottish Ministers is required for any patients coming into Scotland and lists the information that needs to be made available to Scottish Ministers to allow them to consider a request for transfer; this includes details of the relevant measures to which the patient is currently subject. Scottish Ministers are then required, under reg.24(5) to consider the request and give notice to the relevant hospital managers whether their consent has been given. Regulation 30(5) provides that, following reception into Scotland, the order to which a patient is now subject will be treated as if that measure was made or given on the date when the order the patient was subject to immediately preceding transfer was made or given. Given this, difficulties have arisen where a patient is received into a Scottish hospital with only a few days left to run on their order. In such cases, there is often insufficient time for the Scottish responsible medical officer to adequately discharge her responsibilities in relation to the appropriate assessment and possible re-detention of a patient. In view of this "it will now be our practice in considering requests for the consent of Scottish Ministers to the transfer of patients into Scotland to request that, where an application is made under the 2005 Regulations for a patient to transfer into Scotland, there must be a minimum of 10 days and, where possible, at least 14 days left before the expiry of their existing detention order" (Letter from the Mental Health Division of the Primary and Community Directorate, January 29, 2010). The Department of Health or the Welsh Ministers (or the Ministry of Justice for restricted patients) will seek approval directly from the Scottish Executive. When the transfer is completed, the application, order or direction on the basis of which the patient was detained in England, ceases to have effect and cannot be revived. For the patient to return to England a further transfer would be necessary, in accordance with Scottish legislation, which will require the agreement of the Scottish Ministers.

Once the transfer of a detained patient has been agreed in principle between the sending and receiving hospitals, the sending hospital should write to:

Department of Health and Social Care 3rd Floor,
39 Victoria Street,
London, SW1H 0EU

The Department of Health and Social Care has devised a pro-forma (Gateway ref. 14651) for completion by responsible hospitals in England to request transfer of non-restricted patients to a hospital outside England and Wales. The pro-forma should be completed by or on behalf of the managers of the responsible hospital in England. The Department's e-mail address for this purpose is: mentalhealthact2007@dhsc.gov.uk.

For patients who are detained in Wales, the information should be sent to:

The National Assembly for Wales
Cathays Park
Cardiff, CF10 3NQ
Tel: 029 20825111

Full details of the proposed transfer of a restricted patient should be sent to:

Mental Health Casework Section
14th Floor, Southern House Wellesley Road
Croydon, CR0 1XG
Tel: 020 3334 3555

For the effect of a transfer under this section on the existing application, see s.91.

Subsection (1)

Secretary of state   The functions of the Secretary of State, so far as exercisable in relation to Wales, **1-1040** are exercised by the Welsh Ministers (see the General Note to the Act and SI 1999/672 art.2, Sch.1, as varied by SI 2000/253 art.4, Sch.3) except in relation to a patient who is subject to one or more of the following, namely:

(a)   a restriction order;
(b)   a hospital direction;
(c)   a limitation direction; or
(d)   a restriction direction,

made under ss.41, 45A or, as the case may be, 49.

Conveyance to his destination   General provisions relating to the custody, conveyance and detention of patients are contained in s.137. The Reference Guide, at para.35.13, states:

"The Scottish Ministers may also give directions about the patient's conveyance once in Scotland under Scottish regulations (or authorise the patient's intended responsible medical officer in Scotland to do so)".

[Transfer of responsibility for community patients to Scotland

80ZA.—(1)   If it appears to the appropriate national authority, in the case of a **1-1041** community patient, that the conditions mentioned in subsection (2) below are met, the authority may authorise the transfer of responsibility for him to Scotland.

(2)   The conditions are—

(a)   a transfer under this section is in the patient's interests; and
(b)   arrangements have been made for dealing with him under enactments in force in Scotland corresponding or similar to those relating to community patients in this Act.

(3)   The appropriate national authority may not act under subsection (1) above while the patient is recalled to hospital under section 17E above.

(4)   In this section, "the appropriate national authority" means—

(a)   in relation to a community patient in respect of whom the responsible hospital is in England, the Secretary of State;
(b)   in relation to a community patient in respect of whom the responsible hospital is in Wales, the Welsh Ministers.]

Amendment

This section was inserted by the Mental Health Act 2007 s.39(2), Sch.5 Pt 1 para.3(1).

Definitions

1-1042   community patient: ss.17A(7), 145(1).
patient: s.145(1).
hospital: ss.34(2), 92(1), 145(1).
responsible hospital: ss.17A(7), 145(1).

General Note

1-1043   This section enables a community patient who has not been recalled to hospital to be transferred to Scotland as long as the transfer is in the patient's best interests and arrangements have been made for dealing with him or her under the corresponding legislation in Scotland. In practice, this means "a CTO under the Mental Health (Care and Treatment) (Scotland) Act 2003 (or a compulsion order under the Criminal Procedure (Scotland) Act 1995), which does not authorise the patient's detention in hospital" (Reference Guide, para.35.22). The Mental Health (England and Wales Cross-border transfer: patients subject to requirements other than detention) (Scotland) Regulations 2008 (SSI 2008/356) enable the cross-border transfer of Scottish patients on community-based orders to England and Wales and allow patients on community treatment orders in England and Wales to transfer to Scotland. The arrangements for the transfer will be made by either the Secretary of State or the Welsh Ministers depending on the location of the responsible hospital.

A transfer of responsibility for a patient on a CTO does not give anyone any power to convey the patient to Scotland against the patient's will (Reference Guide, para.35.26).

The Department of Health and Social Care has devised a pro-forma (Gateway ref. 14651) for completion by responsible hospitals in England to request transfer of community patients to Scotland. The pro-forma should be completed by or on behalf of the managers of the responsible hospital in England. The Department's e-mail address for this purpose is: mentalhealthact2007@dhsc.gov.uk.

There is no power to transfer a guardianship patient to guardianship in Scotland. For the effect of a transfer under this section on the existing order, see s.91.

[

[Transfer of responsibility for conditionally discharged patients to Scotland]

1-1044   **80A.**—(1)   If it appears to the Secretary of State, in the case of a patient who—

(a)   is subject to a restriction order under section 41 above; and

(b)   has been conditionally discharged under section 42 or 73 above, that a transfer under this section would be in the interests of the patient, the Secretary of State may, with the consent of the Minister exercising corresponding functions in Scotland, transfer responsibility for the patient to that Minister.]

(2)—(3)   [Repealed in relation to England and Wales by SI 2005/2078, art.16, Sch.3]

Amendments

This section was inserted by the Crime (Sentences) Act 1997 s.48, Sch.3 para.1. The heading was substituted by the Mental Health Act 2007 s.39(2), Sch.5 Pt 1 para.4.

Definitions

1-1045   patient: s.145(1).
restriction order: ss.41, 145(1).

General Note

1-1046   This section makes provision for the transfer of responsibility for conditionally discharged restricted patients from England and Wales to Scotland. It enables the Secretary of State to authorise such a transfer where it appears to be in the interests of the patient, and where the relevant Scottish Minister has consented to the transfer.

For the effect of a transfer under this section on the existing order, see s.91.

Corresponding legislative provisions

See the General Note to this Part under this heading.   **1-1047**

Secretary of State   Functions under this provision have not been transferred to Welsh Ministers (see the General Note to the Act and SI 1999/672 art.2, Sch.1).

[Removal of detained patients from Scotland

80B.—(1)   This section applies to a patient if—   **1-1048**

(a)   he is removed to England and Wales under regulations made under section 290(1)(a) of the Mental Health (Care and Treatment) (Scotland) Act 2003 ("the 2003 Act");

(b)   immediately before his removal, his detention in hospital was authorised by virtue of that Act or the Criminal Procedure (Scotland) Act 1995; and

(c)   on his removal, he is admitted to a hospital in England or Wales.

(2)   He shall be treated as if, on the date of his admission to the hospital, he had been so admitted in pursuance of an application made, or an order or direction made or given, on that date under the enactment in force in England and Wales which most closely corresponds to the enactment by virtue of which his detention in hospital was authorised immediately before his removal.

(3)   If, immediately before his removal, he was subject to a measure under any enactment in force in Scotland restricting his discharge, he shall be treated as if he were subject to an order or direction under the enactment in force in England and Wales which most closely corresponds to that enactment.

(4)   If, immediately before his removal, the patient was liable to be detained under the 2003 Act by virtue of a transfer for treatment direction, given while he was serving a sentence of imprisonment (within the meaning of section 136(9) of that Act) imposed by a court in Scotland, he shall be treated as if the sentence had been imposed by a court in England and Wales.

(5)   If, immediately before his removal, the patient was subject to a hospital direction or transfer for treatment direction, the restriction direction to which he is subject by virtue of subsection (3) above shall expire on the date on which that hospital direction or transfer for treatment direction (as the case may be) would have expired if he had not been so removed.

(6)   If, immediately before his removal, the patient was liable to be detained under the 2003 Act by virtue of a hospital direction, he shall be treated as if any sentence of imprisonment passed at the time when that hospital direction was made had been imposed by a court in England and Wales.

(7)   Any directions given by the Scottish Ministers under regulations made under section 290 of the 2003 Act as to the removal of a patient to which this section applies shall have effect as if they were given under this Act.

(8)   Subsection (8) of section 80 above applies to a reference in this section as it applies to one in that section.

(9)   In this section—

"hospital direction" means a direction made under section 59A of the Criminal Procedure (Scotland) Act 1995; and "transfer for treatment direction" has the meaning given by section 136 of the 2003 Act.]

Amendment

This section was inserted by the Mental Health Act 2007 s.39(2), Sch.5 Pt 1 para.4(1).

Definitions

1-1049   patient: s.145(1).
hospital: ss.34(2), 92(1), 145(1).

General Note

1-1050   This section applies to a detained patient who is transferred from Scotland to England or Wales. The date of his hospital admission will be the date of his arrival at the hospital in England or Wales under the provision in force which most closely corresponds to the legislation that the patient was detained under in Scotland. For example, if a patient who is detained in Scotland under the equivalent of s.3 is transferred to England on August 1, he will be treated as if he had been admitted to the hospital in England on August 1 under s.3. Such a patient is therefore given the same powers to apply to a tribunal as those enjoyed by a s.3 patient (s.69(2)). These powers are also enjoyed by the patient's nearest relative (s.69(1), as applied by s.55(4)).

Paragraph 34.28 of the Reference Guide states:

"In practice, the Scottish Executive will generally ask the Department of Health (or the Ministry of Justice for restricted patients) to confirm that arrangements have been made. The Secretary of State for Justice will not, in practice, agree to the transfer of a restricted patient to England unless satisfied that the proposed arrangements will enable the patient's safe management in England."

The Mental Health (Care and Treatment) (Scotland) Act 2003 provides for the transfer of patients subject to a detention requirement or otherwise in hospital from Scotland and for patients subject to corresponding measures in England and Wales to be received in Scotland. The Mental Health (Cross-border transfer: patients subject to detention requirement or otherwise in hospital) (Scotland) Regulations 2005 (SSI 2005/467) make provision for those transfers to take place. Provisions consequential on the 2003 Act for England and Wales are made in the Mental Health (Care and Treatment) (Scotland) Act 2003 (Consequential Provisions) Order (SI 2005/2078) which is reproduced in Part 2.

Form M1 should be completed on the patient's admission to the English or Welsh hospital: see reg.15(2) of the English Regulations (in Wales, Form TC7: see reg.29 of the Welsh Regulations).

Requesting a transfer warrant

1-1051   The Reference Guide states:

"35.9 Requests for the transfer of restricted patients should be made to the Ministry of Justice. The Act only provides for the transfer of patients between hospitals in different jurisdictions but not the transfer between a prison in one jurisdiction and a hospital in another. If such a transfer is being contemplated, it will need to be undertaken in two stages. Either the patient will be transferred from prison to hospital and from there to a hospital in the other jurisdiction or from prison to another prison and then prison to hospital. Although this might appear complicated, it can be agreed in principle with the patient only having to move once.

35.10 For patients detained under section 2 of the Act, the Scottish authorities require there to be at least 10 days and preferably 14 days remaining on the section 2 when the transfer takes place. This means that the pro-forma for such a transfer should be completed as soon as it is known that the patient is to be transferred to Scotland and the hospital in England has been advised that there is a bed available for the patient at the receiving hospital in Scotland. The completed pro-forma should be faxed or emailed to the Department of Health by day 11 (day 14 at the very latest) and the hospital in England would need to transfer the patient by day 18 (preferably by day 14). A warrant issued for a patient detained under section 2 would not be valid beyond day 18 of the patient's detention."

Subsection (3)

Most closely corresponds   See the table set out at figure 88 of Ch.34 of the Reference Guide and the   **1-1052**
General Note to this Part under the heading Corresponding legislative provisions.

[Removal of patients subject to compulsion in the community from Scotland

80C.—(1)   This section applies to a patient if—   **1-1053**

    (a)   he is subject to an enactment in force in Scotland by virtue of which regulations under section 289(1) of the Mental Health (Care and Treatment) (Scotland) Act 2003 apply to him; and

    (b)   he is removed to England and Wales under those regulations.

(2)   He shall be treated as if on the date of his arrival at the place where he is to reside in England or Wales—

    (a)   he had been admitted to a hospital in England or Wales in pursuance of an application or order made on that date under the corresponding enactment; and

    (b)   a community treatment order had then been made discharging him from the hospital.

(3)   For these purposes—

    (a)   if the enactment to which the patient was subject in Scotland was an enactment contained in the Mental Health (Care and Treatment) (Scotland) Act 2003, the corresponding enactment is section 3 of this Act;

    (b)   if the enactment to which he was subject in Scotland was an enactment contained in the Criminal Procedure (Scotland) Act 1995, the corresponding enactment is section 37 of this Act.

(4)   "The responsible hospital", in the case of a patient in respect of whom a community treatment order is in force by virtue of subsection (2) above, means the hospital to which he is treated as having been admitted by virtue of that subsection, subject to section 19A above.

(5)   As soon as practicable after the patient's arrival at the place where he is to reside in England or Wales, the responsible clinician shall specify the conditions to which he is to be subject for the purposes of section 17B(1) above, and the conditions shall be deemed to be specified in the community treatment order.

(6)   But the responsible clinician may only specify conditions under subsection (5) above which an approved mental health professional agrees should be specified.]

Amendment

This section was inserted by the Mental Health Act 2007 s.39(2), Sch.5 Pt 1 para.4(1).

Definitions

patient: s.145(1).   **1-1054**
community treatment order: ss.17A(7), 145(1).
hospital: ss.34(2), 92(1), 145(1).
responsible clinician: ss.34(1), 145(1).
approved mental health professional: s.145(1).

General Note

This section applies to a patient who is subject to compulsion in the community in Scotland who is   **1-1055**
transferred to England or Wales. On arrival at the place where he is required to reside in England or

Wales, the patient will be treated as if he had been admitted to a hospital in England or Wales on that date under s.3 or s.37 and a community treatment order (CTO) had been made discharging him from that hospital. As soon as practicable after the patient's arrival, the hospital managers should complete Form M1: see reg.15(2) of the English Regulations (in Wales, Form TC7: see reg.29 of the Welsh Regulations) and the patient's responsible clinician should complete Form CTO 9: see subs.(5) and reg.16(2)(4) of the English Regulations.

The Mental Health (England and Wales Cross-border transfer: patients subject to requirements other than detention) (Scotland) Regulations 2008 (SSI 2008/356) allow for patients who are subject to community based orders to be transferred from Scotland.

[Transfer of conditionally discharged patients from Scotland

1-1056   **80D.**—(1)   This section applies to a patient who is subject to—

(a)   a restriction order under section 59 of the Criminal Procedure (Scotland) Act 1995; and

(b)   a conditional discharge under section 193(7) of the Mental Health (Care and Treatment) (Scotland) Act 2003 ("the 2003 Act").

(2)   A transfer of the patient to England and Wales under regulations made under section 290 of the 2003 Act shall have effect only if the Secretary of State has consented to the transfer.

(3)   If a transfer under those regulations has effect, the patient shall be treated as if—

(a)   on the date of the transfer he had been conditionally discharged under section 42 or 73 above; and

(b)   he were subject to a hospital order under section 37 above and a restriction order under section 41 above.

(4)   If the restriction order to which the patient was subject immediately before the transfer was of limited duration, the restriction order to which he is subject by virtue of subsection (3) above shall expire on the date on which the first-mentioned order would have expired if the transfer had not been made.]

Amendment

This section was inserted by the Mental Health Act 2007 s.39(2), Sch.5 Pt 1 para.4(1).

Definitions

1-1057   patient: s.145(1).
hospital order: ss.37, 145(1).
restriction order: ss.41, 145(1).

General Note

1-1058   This section makes provision for the transfer of a conditionally discharged patient from Scotland to England or Wales. On his arrival in England or Wales the patient will be treated as if he was a restricted patient who had been granted a conditional discharge under either ss.42 or 73. The transfer can only take place if the Secretary of State (subs.(2)) and the Scottish Ministers (Mental Health (Cross-border transfer: patients subject to detention requirement or otherwise in hospital) (Scotland) Regulations 2005 (SSI 2005/467)) have consented to it.

REMOVAL TO AND FROM NORTHERN IRELAND

Removal of patients to Northern Ireland

1-1059   **81.**—(1)   If it appears to the Secretary of State, in the case of a patient who is for the time being liable to be detained or subject to guardianship under this Act (otherwise than by virtue of section 35, 36 or 38 above), that it is in the interests of the patient to remove him to Northern Ireland, and that arrangements have been made for admitting him to a hospital or, as the case may be, for receiving him into guardianship there, the Secretary of State may authorise his removal to Northern Ireland and may give any necessary directions for his conveyance to his destination.

(2)   Subject to the provisions of subsections (4) and (5) below, where a patient liable to be detained under this Act by virtue of an application, order or direction under any enactment in force in England and Wales is removed under this section and admitted to a hospital in Northern Ireland, he shall be treated as if on the date of his admission he had been so admitted in pursuance of an application made, or [a restriction order or a restriction direction] made or given, on that date under the corresponding enactment in force in Northern Ireland, and, [where he is subject to a hospital order and a restriction order or a transfer direction and a restriction direction under any enactment in this Act, as if he were subject to a hospital order and a restriction order or a transfer direction and a restriction direction under the corresponding enactment] in force in Northern Ireland.]

(3)   Where a patient subject to guardianship under this Act by virtue of an application, order or direction under any enactment in force in England and Wales is removed under this section and received into guardianship in Northern Ireland, he shall be treated as if on the date on which he arrives at the place where he is to reside he had been so received in pursuance of an application, order or direction under the corresponding enactment in force in Northern Ireland, and as if the application had been accepted or, as the case may be, the order or direction had been made or given on that date.

(4)   Where a person removed under this section was immediately before his removal liable to be detained by virtue of an application for admission for assessment under this Act, he shall, on his admission to a hospital in Northern Ireland, be treated as if he had been admitted to the hospital in pursuance of an application [for assessment under Article 4 of the Mental Health (Northern Ireland) Order 1986] made on the date of his admission.

(5)   Where a person removed under this section was immediately before his removal liable to be detained by virtue of an application for admission for treatment under this Act, he shall, on his admission to a hospital in Northern Ireland, be treated as if [he were detained for treatment under Part II of the Mental Health (Northern Ireland) Order 1986 by virtue of a report under Article 12(1) of that Order made on the date of his admission.]

(6)   Where a person removed under this section was immediately before his removal liable to be detained under this Act by virtue of a transfer direction given while he was serving a sentence of imprisonment (within the meaning of section 47(5) above) imposed by a court in England and Wales, he shall be treated as if the sentence had been imposed by a court in Northern Ireland.

(7)   Where a person removed under this section was immediately before his removal subject to a [...] restriction direction of limited duration, [the [...] restriction direction] to which he is subject by virtue of subsection (2) above shall expire on the date on which [the first mentioned [..] restriction direction would have expired if he had not been so removed.

(8)   In this section "hospital" has the same meaning as in the Mental Health [(Northern Ireland) Order 1986].

Amendments

The amendments to this section were made by the Mental Health (Northern Ireland Consequential Amendments) Order 1986 (SI 1986/596) art.2 and the Mental Health Act 2007 ss.39(2), 55, Sch.5 Pt 1 para.5, Sch.11 Pt 8.

Definitions

1-1060
patient: s.145(1).
hospital order: ss.37, 145(1).
restriction order: ss.41, 145(1).
restriction direction: ss.49, 145(1).
application for admission for assessment: ss.2, 145(1).
application for admission for treatment: ss.3, 145(1).
transfer direction: ss.47, 92(5), 145(1).

General Note

1-1061   This section enables the Secretary of State (or, for certain categories of patient in relation to Wales, the Welsh Ministers) to transfer a patient who is detained (otherwise than under ss.35, 36 or 38) or subject to guardianship in England or Wales to Northern Ireland without a break in the powers of detention or guardianship. The Secretary of State (or the Welsh Ministers) must be satisfied that such a move is in the interests of the patient and that suitable arrangements have been made for admitting him to hospital or receiving him into guardianship in Northern Ireland. On arrival in Northern Ireland the patient will become subject to the equivalent Northern Irish legislation, and the application or direction made in England or Wales will cease to have effect.

Once the transfer of a detained patient has been agreed in principle between the sending and receiving hospitals, the sending hospital should contact either the Department of Health and Social Care or the National Assembly for Wales. Details of the proposed transfer of a restricted patient should be sent to the Ministry of Justice. The Department of Health and Social Care has devised a pro-forma to be used by hospitals in England for non-restricted patients: see the General Note to s.80.

For the effect of a transfer under this section on the existing application, see s.91.

Transitional provision

1-1062   The repeal of the reference to restriction orders made in subs.(7) shall have no effect in respect of:

(a)   a restriction order for a specified period made before October 1, 2007, or

(b)   an order made outside England and Wales which is treated under the 1983 Act as if it were a restriction order for a specified period (Mental Health Act 2007 s.40(7) and SI 2007/2798 art.2(d)).

Subsection (1)

1-1063 **Secretary of state**   See the note on s.80(1).

Guardianship   Paragraph 36.23 of the Reference Guide states:

"In practice, a request for a transfer warrant should be made by, or on behalf of, the patient's responsible local authority in England to the Department of Health using the same pro-forma as for detained patients. The request should explain why the transfer would be in the patient's interests, the arrangements that have been agreed for the patient to be received into guardianship in Northern Ireland, and whether, and if so why, the patient needs to be kept in custody while being taken there."

Arrangements   For the transmission of information about these arrangements, see the General Note to s.80.

Subsection (6)

1-1064 **Transfer direction**   See s.92(5).

Subsection (8)

Hospital   Is defined in art.2(1) and (2A) of the 1986 Order.   **1-1065**

[Removal of community patients to Northern Ireland

81ZA.—(1)   Section 81 above shall apply in the case of a community patient   **1-1066**
as it applies in the case of a patient who is for the time being liable to be detained
under this Act, as if the community patient were so liable.

(2)   Any reference in that section to the application, order or direction by virtue
of which a patient is liable to be detained under this Act shall be construed, for these
purposes, as a reference to the application, order or direction under this Act in
respect of the patient.]

Amendment

This section was inserted by the Mental Health Act 2007 s.39(2), Sch.5 Pt 1 para.6.

Definitions

community patient: ss.17A(7), 145(1).   **1-1067**
patient: s.145(1).

General Note

The Reference Guide states: **1-1068**

"36.19 At the time of publication, there is no equivalent of a CTO under Northern Ireland legislation, so responsibility for patients on a CTO may not be transferred to a hospital in Northern Ireland.
    36.20 If it is in their interests, patients on a CTO may instead be transferred to detention in
Northern Ireland under a transfer warrant [issued under s.81], as if (in effect) they had never become
a patient on a CTO.
    36.21 In practice, a request for the transfer of a patient on a CTO should be made to the Depart-
ment of Health by, or on behalf of, the managers of the patient's responsible hospital."

[Transfer of responsibility for patients to Northern Ireland

81A.—(1)   If it appears to the Secretary of State, in the case of a patient who—   **1-1069**
    [(a) is subject to a hospital order under section 37 above and a restriction
           order under section 41 above or to a transfer direction under section
           47 above and a restriction direction under section 49 above;] and
    (b) has been conditionally discharged under section 42 or 73 above, that
           a transfer under this section would be in the interests of the patient, the
           Secretary of State may, with the consent of the Minister exercising cor-
           responding functions in Northern Ireland, transfer responsibility for the
           patient to that Minister.

(2)   Where responsibility for such a patient is transferred under this section, the
patient shall be treated—
    (a) as if on the date of the transfer he had been conditionally discharged
           under the corresponding enactment in force in Northern Ireland; and
    (b) as if he were subject to [a hospital order and a restriction order, or to
           a transfer direction and a restriction direction,] under the correspond-
           ing enactment in force in Northern Ireland.

(3)   Where a patient responsibility for whom is transferred under this section
was immediately before the transfer subject to a […] or restriction direction of
limited duration, the [. .] or restriction direction to which he is subject by virtue of

subsection (2) above shall expire on the date on which the first-mentioned [...] direction would have expired if the transfer had not been made.]

Amendments

This section was inserted the Crime (Sentences) Act 1997 s.48, Sch.3 para.2. The amendments to it were made by the Mental Health Act 2007 ss.39(2), 55, Sch.5 Pt 1 para.7, Sch.11 Pt 8.

Definitions

1-1070   patient: s.145(1).
hospital order: ss.37, 145(1).
transfer direction: ss.47, 145(1).
restriction order: ss.41, 145(1).
restriction direction: ss.49, 145(1).

General Note

1-1071   This section makes provision for the transfer of responsibility for conditionally discharged restricted patients from England and Wales to Northern Ireland. It is an equivalent provision to s.80A and reference should be made to the notes on that section.

Corresponding legislative provisions

1-1072   See the General Note to this Part under this heading.

Transitional provision

1-1073   The repeal of the reference to restriction orders in subs.(3) shall have no effect in respect of:

(a)   a restriction order for a specified period made before October 1, 2007, or
(b)   an order made outside England and Wales which is treated under the 1983 Act as if it were a restriction order for a specified period (Mental Health Act 2007 s.40(7) and SI 2007/2798 art.2(d)).

Subsection (1)

1-1074   **Secretary of state**   Functions under this provision have not been transferred to Welsh Ministers (see the General Note to the Act and SI 1999/672, art.2, Sch.1).

Removal to England and Wales of patients from Northern Ireland

1-1075   **82.**—(1)   If it appears to the responsible authority, in the case of a patient who is for the time being liable to be detained or subject to guardianship under the Mental Health [(Northern Ireland) Order 1986 (otherwise than by virtue of Article 42, 43 or 45 of that Order)], that it is in the interests of the patient to remove him to England and Wales, and that arrangements have been made for admitting him to a hospital or, as the case may be, for receiving him into guardianship there, the responsible authority may authorise his removal to England and Wales and may give any necessary directions for his conveyance to his destination.

(2)   Subject to the provisions of [subsections (4) and (4A)] below, where a patient who is liable to be detained under the [Mental Health (Northern Ireland) Order 1986] by virtue of an application, order or direction under any enactment in force in Northern Ireland is removed under this section and admitted to a hospital in England and Wales, he shall be treated as if on the date of his admission he had been so admitted in pursuance of an application made, or an order or direction made or given, on that date under the corresponding enactment in force in England and Wales and, [where he is subject to a hospital order and a restriction order or a

transfer direction and a restriction direction under any enactment in that Order, as if he were subject to a hospital order and a restriction order or a transfer direction and a restriction direction under the corresponding enactment] in force in England and Wales].

(3) Where a patient subject to guardianship under the [Mental Health (Northern Ireland) Order 1986] by virtue of an application, order or direction under any enactment in force in Northern Ireland is removed under this section and received into guardianship in England and Wales, he shall be treated as if on the date on which he arrives at the place where he is to reside he had been so received in pursuance of an application, order or direction under the corresponding enactment in force in England and Wales and as if the application had been accepted or, as the case may be, the order or direction had been made or given on that date.

[(4) Where a person removed under this section was immediately before his removal liable to be detained for treatment by virtue of a report under Article 12(1) or 13 of the Mental Health (Northern Ireland) Order 1986, he shall be treated, on his admission to a hospital in England and Wales, as if he had been admitted to the hospital in pursuance of an application for admission for treatment made on the date of his admission.

(4A) Where a person removed under this section was immediately before his removal liable to be detained by virtue of an application for assessment under Article 4 of the Mental Health (Northern Ireland) Order 1986, he shall be treated, on his admission to a hospital in England and Wales, as if he had been admitted to the hospital in pursuance of an application for admission for assessment made on the date of his admission.]

(5) Where a patient removed under this section was immediately before his removal liable to be detained under the [Mental Health (Northern Ireland) Order 1986] by virtue of a transfer direction given while he was serving a sentence of imprisonment (within the meaning of [Article 53(5) of that Order)] imposed by a court in Northern Ireland, he shall be treated as if the sentence had been imposed by a court in England and Wales.

(6) Where a person removed under this section was immediately before his removal subject to [a restriction order or restriction direction] of limited duration, the restriction order or restriction direction to which he is subject by virtue of subsection (2) above shall expire on the date on which the [first-mentioned restriction order or restriction direction] would have expired if he had not been so removed.

(7) In this section "the responsibility authority" means the Department of Health and Social Services for Northern Ireland or, in relation to a patient who is subject to [a restriction order or restriction direction], the [Department of Justice in Northern Ireland].

Amendments

The amendments to this section were made by the Mental Health (Northern Ireland Consequential Amendments) Order 1986 (SI 1986/596) art.2, the Mental Health Act 2007 s.39(2), Sch.5 Pt 1 para.8 and SI 2010/976, Sch.14 para.28.

Definitions

1-1076   patient: s.145(1).
hospital: ss.34(2), 92(1), 145(1).
application for admission for assessment: ss.2, 145(1).
application for admission for treatment: ss.3, 145(1).
hospital order: ss.37, 145(1).
transfer direction: ss.47, 145(1).
restriction order: ss.41, 145(1).
restriction direction: ss.49, 145(1).

General Note

1-1077   This section provides that a patient who is detained or subject to guardianship in Northern Ireland may be transferred to England or Wales without a break in the powers of detention or guardianship. On arrival in England or Wales the patient will become subject to detention or guardianship under the Act. Paragraph 34.33 of the Reference Guide states:

> "In practice, the Northern Ireland authorities will generally ask the Department of Health (or the Ministry of Justice for restricted patients) to confirm that arrangements have been made for the patient to be admitted to hospital or received into guardianship in England or Wales. The Secretary of State for Justice will not, in practice, agree to the transfer of a restricted patient to England unless satisfied that the proposed arrangements will enable the patient's safe management in England."

Applications to the First-tier Tribunal (Mental Health) or the Mental Health Review Tribunal for Wales

1-1078   A patient who has been transferred under this section has a right to apply to a tribunal within six months of his transfer (ss.66(1), 69(2)(a)). The patient's nearest relative has similar rights to make an application (s.69(1), as applied by s.55(4)).

Subsection (1)

1-1079   **Appears**   In the Northern Ireland case *Re JR49 (Application for Judicial Review)* [2011] NIQB 41; [2011] M.H.L.R. 351, para.39, Treacy J. said that the term "appears" in this context "means 'is deemed or judged to' after all appropriate investigations and assessments have been completed". His Lordship said that the "level of the investigation and assessment required will depend on the gravity of the decision involved. As we know a decision to transfer a patient to England against his family's wishes and his own ascertainable wishes is a very grave decision indeed which demands the best informed and most anxious scrutiny".

Interests of the patient   Means making a choice "which brings more benefits to the patient than any other choice that could be made, i.e. the choice of the best option" (see *Re JR49*, above, para.34).

Subsection (2)

1-1080   **Date of his admission**   Which must be recorded on Form M1: see reg.15 of the English Regulations (in Wales, Form TC7: see reg.29 of the Welsh Regulations).

Corresponding enactment   See the table set out at figure 89 of Ch.34 of the Reference Guide and the General Note to this Part under the heading Corresponding legislative provisions.

Subsection (3)

1-1081   **Date on which he arrives**   Which should be recorded on Form M1: see the note on "date of his admission" in subs.(2).

Subsection (6)

1-1082   **Restriction direction**   See s.92(4)(b).

[Transfer of responsibility for [conditionally discharged] patients to England and Wales from Northern Ireland

82A.—(1)   If it appears to [the Department of Justice in Northern Ireland], in **1-1083** the case of a patient who—

    (a)   is subject to a restriction order or restriction direction under Article 47(1) or 55(1) of the Mental Health (Northern Ireland) Order 1986; and

    (b)   has been conditionally discharged under Article 48(2) or 78(2) of that Order,

        that a transfer under this section would be in the interests of the patient, [the Department of Justice in Northern Ireland] may, with the consent of the Secretary of State, transfer responsibility for the patient to the Secretary of State.

(2)   Where responsibility for such a patient is transferred under this section, the patient shall be treated—

    (a)   as if on the date of the transfer he had been conditionally discharged under section 42 or 73 above; and

    [(b)   as if he were subject to a hospital order under section 37 above and a restriction order under section 41 above or to a transfer direction under section 47 above and a restriction direction under section 49 above.]

(3)   Where a patient responsibility for whom is transferred under this section was immediately before the transfer subject to a restriction order or restriction direction of limited duration, the restriction order or restriction direction to which he is subject by virtue of subsection (2) above shall expire on the date on which the first-mentioned order or direction would have expired if the transfer had not been made.

    (4)   [...]

Amendments

This section was inserted by the Crime (Sentences) Act 1997 s.48, Sch.3 para.3. The amendments to it were made by SI 2010/976, Sch.14 para.28 and the Mental Health Act 2007 s.39(2), Sch.5 Pt 1 para.9.

Definitions

patient: s.145(1).   **1-1084**
hospital order: ss.37, 145(1).
restriction order: ss.41, 145(1).
restriction direction: ss.41, 145(1).
transfer direction: ss.47, 145(1).

General Note

This section enables the Secretary of State to authorise the transfer of a conditionally discharged **1-1085** restricted patient from Northern Ireland to England and Wales. The expiry date of the original order or direction is not effected by the transfer.

Subsection (1)

Secretary of state   Functions under this provision have not been transferred to Welsh Ministers (see **1-1086** the General Note to the Act and SI 1999/672 art.2, Sch.1).

REMOVAL TO AND FROM CHANNEL ISLANDS AND ISLE OF MAN

Removal of patients to Channel Islands or Isle of Man

1-1087   **83.**   If it appears to the Secretary of State, in the case of a patient who is for the time being liable to be detained or subject to guardianship under this Act (otherwise than by virtue of section 35, 36 or 38 above), that it is in the interests of the patient to remove him to any of the Channel Islands or to the Isle of Man, and that arrangements have been made for admitting him to a hospital or, as the case may be, for receiving him into guardianship there, the Secretary of State may authorise his removal to the island in question and may give any necessary directions for his conveyance to his destination.

Definitions

1-1088   patient: s.145(1).
hospital: ss.34(2), 92(1), 145(1).

General Note

1-1089   This section provides for patients who are detained or subject to guardianship in England or Wales to be transferred to the Channel Islands or the Isle of Man by the Secretary of State (or, for certain categories of patient in relation to Wales, the Welsh Ministers) without a break in the powers of detention or guardianship. It does not apply to patients who travel to the Channel Islands or the Isle of Man and who are not detained in hospital or received into guardianship on arrival there. Transfers may require the approval of the relevant island authorities in accordance with the local legislation. The Department of Health and Social Care (or the Ministry of Justice) will seek this as necessary. The Department of Health and Social Care has devised a pro-forma to be used by hospitals in England for non-restricted patients: see the General Note to s.80.

For the effect of a transfer under this section on the existing application, see s.91.

If a patient is granted escorted leave of absence under s.17 to travel to the Isle of Man or any of the Channel Islands, the escort would have no jurisdiction on arrival there.

Secretary of state

See the note on s.80(1).

Guardianship

The Reference Guide states at para.37.24:

"In practice, a request for a transfer warrant should be made by, or on behalf of, the patient's responsible local authority in England to the Department of Health. The request should explain why the transfer would be in the patient's interests, the arrangements that have been agreed for the patient to be received into guardianship in the island in question, and whether, and if so why, the patient needs to be kept in custody while being taken there. The transfer may also have to be agreed with the relevant island authorities in accordance with local legislation."

Arrangements

For the transmission of information about these arrangements, see the General Note to s.80.

Conveyance

General provisions relating to the custody, conveyance and detention of patients are contained in s.137.

[Removal or transfer of community patients to Channel Islands or Isle of Man

83ZA.—(1) Section 83 above shall apply in the case of a community patient **1-1090** as it applies in the case of a patient who is for the time being liable to be detained under this Act, as if the community patient were so liable.

(2)   But if there are in force in any of the Channel Islands or the Isle of Man enactments ("relevant enactments") corresponding or similar to those relating to community patients in this Act—

(a)   subsection (1) above shall not apply as regards that island; and

(b)   subsections (3) to (6) below shall apply instead.

(3)   If it appears to the appropriate national authority, in the case of a community patient, that the conditions mentioned in subsection (4) below are met, the authority may authorise the transfer of responsibility for him to the island in question.

(4)   The conditions are—

(a)   a transfer under subsection (3) above is in the patient's interests; and

(b)   arrangements have been made for dealing with him under the relevant enactments.

(5)   But the authority may not act under subsection (3) above while the patient is recalled to hospital under section 17E above.

(6)   In this section, "the appropriate national authority" means—

(a)   in relation to a community patient in respect of whom the responsible hospital is in England, the Secretary of State;

(b)   in relation to a community patient in respect of whom the responsible hospital is in Wales, the Welsh Ministers.]

Amendment

This section was inserted by the Mental Health Act 2007 s.39(2), Sch.5 Pt 1 para.10.

Definition

community patient: ss.17A(7), 145(1).   **1-1091**
hospital: ss.34(2), 92(1), 145(1).
patient: s.145(1).
responsible hospital: ss.17A(1), 145(1).

General Note

This section and s.85ZA provide for community patients to be transferred from England and Wales   **1-1092** to the Channel Islands and the Isle of Man and vice versa. The Reference Guide states:

"37.21 If there is no equivalent of a CTO in the island in question, patients on a CTO may instead be transferred to detention in the island under a transfer warrant [made under s.83], as if (in effect) they had never become a patient on a CTO.

37.22 In practice, a request for the transfer of a patient on a CTO should be made to the Department of Health by, or on behalf of, the managers of the patient's responsible hospital. At the time of publication the Isle of Man legislation contains provision for 'After-care under supervision' (section 28 et seq). The Jersey Mental Health Act 1969 [now see the Mental Health (Jersey) Law 2016] contains no provision equivalent to the CTO. The Mental Health Law 2010 of the Bailiwick of Guernsey does contain provision for CTOs (section 26 et seq)."

[Transfer of responsibility for conditionally discharged patients to Channel Islands or Isle of Man

1-1093   **83A.**   If it appears to the Secretary of State, in the case of a patient who—

    (a) is subject to a restriction order or restriction direction under section 41 or 49 above; and

    (b) has been conditionally discharged under section 42 or 73 above, that a transfer under this section would be in the interests of the patient, the Secretary of State may, with the consent of the authority exercising corresponding functions in any of the Channel Islands or in the Isle of Man, transfer responsibility for the patient to that authority.]

Amendments

This section was inserted by the Crime (Sentences) Act 1997 s.48, Sch.3 para.4. The heading was substituted by the Mental Health Act 2007 s.39(2), Sch.5 Pt 1 para.10.

Definitions

1-1094   patient: s.145(1).
restriction order: ss.41, 145(1).
restriction direction: ss.49, 145(1).

General Note

1-1095   This section provides a procedure for the Secretary of State to authorise the transfer of a conditionally discharged restricted patient from England and Wales to the Channel Island or the Isle of Man.
For the effect of a transfer under this section on the existing order or direction, see s.91.

Corresponding legislative provisions

1-1096   See the General Note to this Part under this heading.

Secretary of state   Functions under this provision have not been transferred to Welsh Ministers (see the General Note to the Act and SI 1999/672, art.2, Sch.1).

Removal to England and Wales of offenders found insane in Channel Islands and Isle of Man

1-1097   **84.**—(1)   The Secretary of State may by warrant direct that any offender found by a court in any of the Channel Islands or in the Isle of Man to be insane or to have been insane at the time of the alleged offence, and ordered to be detained during Her Majesty's pleasure, be removed to a hospital in England and Wales.

    (2)   A patient removed under subsection (1) above shall, on his reception into the hospital in England and Wales, be treated as if he [were subject to a hospital order together with a restriction order […]

    (3)   The Secretary of State may by warrant direct that any patient removed under this section from any of the Channel Islands or from the Isle of Man be returned to the island from which he was so removed, there to be dealt with according to law in all respects as if he had not been removed under this section.

Amendments

The amendments to this section were made by the Domestic Violence, Crime and Victims Act 2004 s.58(1), Sch.10 para.22 and the Mental Health Act 2007 s.55, Sch.11 Pt 8.

Definitions

hospital: ss.34(2), 92(1), 145(1). **1-1098**
patient: s.145(1).
hospital order: ss.37, 145(1).
restriction order: ss.41, 145(1).

General Note

This section enables the Secretary of State to transfer to a hospital in England or Wales an offender **1-1099**
who has been found to be insane by a court in the Channel Islands or Isle of Man. On arrival at the
hospital, the patient will be treated as if he were subject to a hospital order with restrictions (subs.(2)).
   Form M1 should be completed on the patient's admission to the English or Welsh hospital: see
reg.15(2) of the English Regulations (in Wales, Form TC7: see reg.29 of the Welsh Regulations).
   For procedure and tribunal rights, see the General Note to s.82.

Transitional provision

The repeal of the reference to restriction orders made for a specified period in subs.(2) shall have no **1-1100**
effect in respect of—

(a)   a restriction order for a specified period made before October 1, 2007, or
(b)   an order made outside England and Wales which is treated under the 1983 Act as if it were a
      restriction order for a specified period (Mental Health Act 2007 s.40(7) and SI 2007/2798
      art.2(d)).

Subsection (1)

Secretary of State   Functions under this provision have not been transferred to Welsh Ministers (see **1-1101**
the General Note to the Act and SI 1999/672 art.2, Sch.1).

Patients removed from Channel Islands or Isle of Man

   85.—(1)   This section applies to any patient who is removed to England and **1-1102**
Wales from any of the Channel Islands or the Isle of Man under a provision corresponding to section 83 above and who immediately before his removal was liable to be detained or subject to guardianship in the island in question under a provision corresponding to an enactment contained in this Act (other than section 35, 36
or 38 above).

   (2)   Where the patient is admitted to a hospital in England and Wales he shall
be treated as if on the date of his admission he had been so admitted in pursuance
of an application made, or an order or direction made or given, on that date under
the corresponding enactment contained in this Act and, where he is subject to an
order or direction restricting his discharge, as if he were subject [to a hospital order
and a restriction order or to a hospital direction and a limitation direction or to a
transfer direction and a restriction direction].

   (3)   Where a patient is received into guardianship in England and Wales, he shall
be treated as if on the date on which he arrives at the place where he is to reside he
had been so received in pursuance of an application, order or direction under the
corresponding enactment contained in this Act and as if the application had been
accepted or, as the case may be, the order or direction had been made or given on
that date.

   (4)   Where the patient was immediately before his removal liable to be detained
by virtue of a transfer direction given while he was serving a sentence of imprisonment imposed by a court in the island in question, he shall be treated as if the
sentence had been imposed by a court in England and Wales.

(5)   Where the patient was immediately before his removal subject to an order or direction restricting his discharge, being an order or direction of limited duration, the restriction order or restriction direction to which he is subject by virtue of subsection (2) above shall expire on the date on which the first-mentioned order or direction would have expired if he had not been removed.

(6)   While being conveyed to the hospital referred to in subsection (2) or, as the case may be, the place referred to in subsection (3) above, the patient shall be deemed to be in legal custody, and section 138 below shall apply to him as if he were in legal custody by virtue of section 137 below.

(7)   In the case of a patient removed from the Isle of Man the reference in subsection (4) above to a person serving a sentence of imprisonment includes a reference to a person detained as mentioned in section 60(6)(a) of the Mental Health Act 1974 (an Act of Tynwald).

Amendment

In subs.(2) the words in square brackets were substituted by the Mental Health Act 2007 s.39(2), Sch.5 Pt 1 para.11.

Definitions

1-1103   patient: s.145(1).
hospital: ss.34(2), 92(1), 145(1).
hospital order: ss.37, 145(1).
hospital direction: ss.45A(3), 145(1).
limitation direction: ss.45A(3), 145(1).
restriction order: ss.41, 145(1).
restriction direction: ss.49, 145(1).
transfer direction: ss.47, 92(5), 145(1).

General Note

1-1104   This section provides for a patient who is detained or subject to guardianship in the Channel Islands or the Isle of Man to be transferred to England or Wales without a break in the powers of detention or guardianship.

The Reference Guide states:

"34.38 Patients transferred from the Isle of Man or the Channel Islands are treated on their arrival in England or Wales as if subject to the application, order or direction which corresponds to the provisions to which they were subject in the island in question. Advice should be sought from the island authorities or from the Department of Health or the Ministry of Justice, as applicable, if there is doubt about what the relevant corresponding provision is. Patients subject to the equivalent of remand to hospital under sections 35 or 36, or an interim hospital order under section 38, cannot be transferred.

34.39 For patients transferred from the Isle of Man who become subject to the equivalent of hospital directions or restriction directions in England, detention under sections 53 and 54 of the Mental Health Act 1998, is treated, where relevant, as if it were a sentence of imprisonment which has been given by a court in England or Wales."

For the procedure to be followed when a patient is transferred to England or Wales, see reg.15 of the English Regulations and reg.29 of the Welsh Regulations. On the patient's arrival in England or Wales, Form M1 should be completed.

Corresponding legislative provisions

1-1105   See the General Note to this Part under this heading.

Applications to the First-tier Tribunal (Mental Health) or the Mental Health Review Tribunal for Wales

A patient who has been transferred under this section has a right of appeal to a tribunal within six months of his transfer (ss.66(1), 69(2)(a)). The patient's nearest relative has similar rights to make an application (s.69(1), as applied by s.55(4)). **1-1106**

[Responsibility for community patients transferred from Channel Islands or Isle of Man

85ZA.—(1) This section shall have effect if there are in force in any of the **1-1107** Channel Islands or the Isle of Man enactments ("relevant enactments") corresponding or similar to those relating to community patients in this Act.

(2) If responsibility for a patient is transferred to England and Wales under a provision corresponding to section 83ZA(3) above, he shall be treated as if on the date of his arrival at the place where he is to reside in England or Wales—

    (a)   he had been admitted to the hospital in pursuance of an application made, or an order or direction made or given, on that date under the enactment in force in England and Wales which most closely corresponds to the relevant enactments;
            and

    (b)   a community treatment order had then been made discharging him from the hospital.

(3) "The responsible hospital", in his case, means the hospital to which he is treated as having been admitted by virtue of subsection (2) above, subject to section 19A above.

(4) As soon as practicable after the patient's arrival at the place where he is to reside in England or Wales, the responsible clinician shall specify the conditions to which he is to be subject for the purposes of section 17B(1) above, and the conditions shall be deemed to be specified in the community treatment order.

(5) But the responsible clinician may only specify conditions under subsection (4) above which an approved mental health professional agrees should be specified.]

Amendment

This section was inserted by the Mental Health Act 2007 s.39(2), Sch.5 Pt 1 para.12.

Definitions

community patient: ss.17A(1), 145(1). **1-1108**
patient: s.145(1).
hospital: ss.34(2), 92(1), 145(1).
community treatment order: ss.17A(7), 145(1).
responsible clinician: ss.34(1), 145(1).
approved mental health professional: s.145(1).

General Note

See the General Notes to ss.83ZA and 85. **1-1109**

Subsection (4)

Shall specify the conditions   On form CTO 9: see reg.16(4) of the English Regulations. **1-1110**

[Responsibility for conditionally discharged patients transferred from Channel Islands or Isle of Man

1-1111   **85A.**—(1)   This section applies to any patient responsibility for whom is transferred to the Secretary of State by the authority exercising corresponding functions in any of the Channel Islands or the Isle of Man under a provision corresponding to section 83A above.

(2)   The patient shall be treated—

(a)   as if on the date of the transfer he had been conditionally discharged under section 42 or 73 above; and

[(b)   as if he were subject to a hospital order under section 37 above and a restriction order under section 41 above, or to a hospital direction and a limitation direction under section 45A above, or to a transfer direction under section 47 above and a restriction direction under section 49 above.]

(3)   Where the patient was immediately before the transfer subject to an order or direction restricting his discharge, being an order or direction of limited duration, the restriction order[, limitation direction] or restriction direction to which he is subject by virtue of subsection (2) above shall expire on the date on which the first-mentioned order or direction would have expired if the transfer had not been made.]

Amendments

This section was inserted by the Crime (Sentences) Act 1997 s.48, Sch.3 para.4. The amendments to it were made by the Mental Health Act 2007 s.39(2), Sch.5 Pt 1 paras 12, 13.

Definitions

1-1112   patient: s.145(1).
hospital order: ss.37, 145(1).
hospital direction: ss.45A(3), 145(1).
limitation direction: ss.45A(3), 145(1).
restriction order: ss.41, 145(1).
restriction direction: ss.49, 145(1).

General Note

1-1113   This section states that a patient who has been transferred from the Channel Islands or the Isle of Man under a provision that corresponds to s.83A, shall be treated as if on the date of the transfer he was a conditionally discharged restricted patient. Also see the General Note to s.85.

Corresponding legislative provisions

1-1114   See the General Note to this Part under this heading.

Subsection (1)

1-1115   **Secretary of state**   Functions under this provision have not been transferred to Welsh Ministers (see the General Note to the Act and SI 1999/672 art.2, Sch.1).

REMOVAL OF ALIENS

Removal of alien patients

1-1116   **86.**—(1)   This section applies to any patient who is neither a British citizen nor a Commonwealth citizen having the right of abode in the United Kingdom by virtue of section 2(1)(b) of the Immigration Act 1971, being a patient who is receiving treatment for [mental disorder] as an in-patient in a hospital in England and Wales or a hospital within the meaning of the Mental Health Act [(Northern Ireland) Order 1986] and is detained pursuant to—

(a) an application for admission for treatment or [a report under Article 12(1) or 13 of that Order];

(b) a hospital order under section 37 above or [Article 44 of that Order]; or

(c) an order or direction under this Act (other than under section 35, 36 or 38 above) or [under that Order (other than under Article 42, 43 or 45 of that Order] having the same effect as such a hospital order.

(2) If it appears to the Secretary of State that proper arrangements have been made for the removal of a patient to whom this section applies to a country or territory outside the United Kingdom, the Isle of Man and the Channel Islands and for his care or treatment there and that it is in the interests of the patient to remove him, the Secretary of State may, subject to subsection (3) below—

(a) by warrant authorise the removal of the patient from the place where he is receiving treatment as mentioned in subsection (1) above, and

(b) give such directions as the Secretary of State thinks fit for the conveyance of the patient to his destination in that country or territory and for his detention in any place or on board any ship or aircraft until his arrival at any specified port or place in any such country or territory.

(3) The Secretary of State shall not exercise his powers under subsection (2) above in the case of any patient except with the approval of [the appropriate tribunal] or, as the case may be, of the Mental Health Review Tribunal for Northern Ireland.

[(4) In relation to a patient receiving treatment in a hospital within the meaning of the Mental Health (Northern Ireland) Order 1986, the reference in subsection (1) above to mental disorder shall be construed in accordance with that Order [and any reference in subsection (2) or (3) to the Secretary of State shall be construed as a reference to the Department of Justice in Northern Ireland].]

Amendments

The amendments to this section were made by the Mental Health (Northern Ireland Consequential Amendments) Order 1986 (SI 1986/596) art.2, the Mental Health Act 2007 s.1(4), Sch.1 para.15, SI 2010/976 Sch.14 para.28 and SI 2008/2883 art.9, Sch.3 para.62.

Definitions

patient: s.145(1). **1-1117**
mental disorder: s.145(1), and see subs.(4) of this section.
hospital: ss.34(2), 92(2), 145(1).
application for admission for treatment: ss.3, 145(1).
hospital order: ss.37, 145(1).
the appropriate tribunal: ss.66(4), 145(1).

General Note

This section empowers the Secretary of State (or, for certain purposes, the Welsh Ministers) to **1-1118** authorise the removal to any country abroad of certain detained in-patients (see subs.(1)) who do not have a right of abode in this country and who are receiving in-patient treatment for mental disorder (subs.(2)). It does not apply to detained patients who have been granted leave of absence under s.17. Before they exercise their powers the Secretary of State or the Welsh Ministers must have obtained the approval of the appropriate tribunal (subs.(3)).

The main purpose of this section is to "enable patients who are either irrationally opposed to their removal, or are unable to express a view, to be compulsorily removed to another country when this is judged to be in their best interests. It is also used to enable patients to be kept under escort on their journey home if this is necessary" (Cmnd. 7320, para.8.26).

"Guidance: The Repatriation and Removal of Restricted Patients to and from England and Wales", Mental Health Casework Section, November 2021, states:

"5.2 Repatriation under section 86 of the MHA 1983

If the Responsible Clinician feels that repatriation would be in the best interests of the patient but the patient does not wish to return to their home country, they can consider compulsory repatriation under section 86. This section can only be used where a patient is detained for in-patient treatment (use of section 86 is not appropriate where the patient is likely to be discharged within 6 months).

Under the provisions of section 86, the consent of the patient is not required for repatriation where the patient is either opposed to their removal or unable to express a view. Repatriation under section 86 must however be approved by the First-tier Tribunal (Health, Education and Social Care) in England or the Mental Health Review Tribunal in Wales. It remains for the respective Tribunals to determine what they deem as appropriate in respect to the arrangements that should be made for the arrival of the patient in their State of nationality. However, MHCS understand it will be broadly similar to what is considered by the MHCS in the above section.

Repatriation is ... effected after the use of conditional discharge by the Secretary of State under section 42 of the Act.

5.3 Arrangements for Repatriation

Those patients who are being considered for repatriation under the MHA 1983 will ordinarily be subject to immigration control and therefore liable for deportation under the Immigration Act 1971. As a consequence the Home Office will normally make the arrangements for the patient's removal from the United Kingdom and MHCS will not issue the discharge warrant until such time as the removal is imminent."

If the patient is not a restricted patient, the patient will be granted leave of absence under s.17 to travel to the port of embarkation. The Secretary of State will use his power under s.42 to conditionally discharge a restricted patient, subject to the condition that he is taken directly to the port of embarkation. In *MJ (Angola) v Secretary of State for the Home Department* [2010] EWCA Civ 557, the Court of Appeal held that it was lawful for the Secretary of State to (a) use s.42 for this purpose and (b) make a decision to deport a person who is a restricted patient.

In *R. (on the application of X) v Secretary of State for the Home Department* [2001] 1 W.L.R. 740; [2000] M.H.L.R. 67, the Court of Appeal held that where a person detained under the Act had no basis for remaining in the UK under the Immigration Act 1971, the Secretary of State was entitled to remove him under the provisions of that Act, and was not obliged to do so only in accordance with his power of removal under this section. Schiemann L.J. said at para.28:

"There appears to us no reason why the two regimes should not run in parallel in the case of a person who is both an immigrant and mentally ill. Clearly if the [Secretary of State] proposes to use his Immigration Act powers in relation to a mentally ill person that illness will be a factor which he must take into account."

In *MJ (Angola) v Secretary of State for the Home Department*, above, para.28, the Court of Appeal said that when exercising powers under the 1971 Act, the Secretary of State "must have regard to the patient's mental illness and any barriers to securing proper care and treatment in the country of destination".

There is nothing to prevent a patient who has been removed under this section from applying for readmission to the UK. If the patient was subject to a hospital order with restrictions when he was removed, both the hospital order and the restriction order will remain in force (s.91(2)). Otherwise the application, order or direction will cease to have effect when the patient leaves the UK (s.91(1)).

Proposals for the removal of Pt II patients detained in English hospitals should be made to the Secretary of State for Health and Social Care (Mental Health Legislation, 3rd Floor North, 39 Victoria St, Westminster, London, SW1H 0EU). Proposals for the removal of Pt III patients should be made to the Secretary of State for Justice (Mental Health Casework Section, 14th Floor, Southern House, Wellesley Road, Croydon CR0 1XG).

Functions under this section, so far as exercisable in relation to Wales, are transferred to the Welsh Ministers except in relation to a patient who is subject to a restriction order made under s.41, a hospital direction made under s.45A(3)(a), a limitation direction made under s.45A(3)(b), or a restriction direction made under s.49 (SI 2008/1786 art.2).

The Reference Guide states at para.38.8:

"Before deciding whether to seek the agreement of the Tribunal, the Department of Health or the Ministry of Justice will need to have details of the reasons for the proposed transfer and the arrangements that have or could be made for the patient's transport (in the UK and abroad) and for the patient's subsequent care and treatment. In practice, the Departments will expect the managers of the hospital in which the patient is detained to provide this information and (if the case is referred to the Tribunal) to provide any further information which the Tribunal requires."

As an alternative to the use of this section, the voluntary repatriation of restricted patients can be considered. "Guidance: The Repatriation and Removal of Restricted Patients to and from England and Wales", above, at para.5.1 states:

"Voluntary repatriation under the MHA 1983 is an arrangement whereby the Secretary of State conditionally discharges the patient, subject to the condition that the patient is taken directly to a port of embarkation and from there to their home country. This process is appropriate for a foreign national offender, who is nearing discharge and who can be considered for deportation by the Home Office. This process is not appropriate if the patient is likely to remain detained for a considerable period due to their treatment needs and the risk they continue to pose to the public.

The process is largely in the hands of the responsible clinician (RC), and allows the RC the opportunity to contact and liaise with psychiatric services abroad to ensure that suitable care would be available for the patient on his or her return home. In order for a patient to be repatriated in this way, the RC needs to be satisfied that:

a. The patient is willing to return;
b. The authorities in his home country are prepared to accept them;
c. There are acceptable arrangements for continued treatment, including detention if appropriate; and
d. There are suitable transport arrangements.

If all of these provisions were met, a request for repatriation should be made to the MHCS through the submission of the application form in Annex C. Once satisfied that the conditions are met, MHCS can issue a conditional discharge under section 42 of the MHA 1983 on behalf of the Secretary of State. The patient can then be conveyed, in accordance with the conditions of the discharge, to their State of nationality."

A similar approach, which would not involve either the Mental Health Casework Section or the Secretary of State, can be adopted for the voluntary repatriation of consenting non-restricted patients.

Guidance

See "Guidance: The Repatriation and Removal of Restricted Patients to and from England and **1-1119** Wales", noted above. The guidance covers the following topics: Principles of Repatriation, Statutory Mechanisms for Repatriation, Repatriation under the Repatriation of Prisoners Act 1984, Repatriation under the Mental Health Act 1983, Repatriation of British Nationals Detained in Hospitals Abroad, and Repatriation and Victims. Annex A to the guidance contain a "List of Countries with an International Transfer Arrangement with the UK". The guidance can be accessed at: *www.gov.uk/government/ publications/repatriation-of-foreign-national-restricted-patients*.

UK Borders Act 2007

Section 32 of the UK Borders Act 2007 makes provision for the deportation of certain categories of **1-1120** foreign criminals where this is conducive to the public good. Section 33 of that Act provides that if the criminal is made the subject of a hospital order, a guardianship order, a hospital direction or a transfer direction, there is not an automatic assumption that deportation is conducive to the public good.

Travel Restriction Orders

Section 33 of the Criminal Justice and Police Act 2001 gives power in some circumstances to the **1-1121** Crown Court to make travel restriction orders in relation to offenders convicted of drug trafficking offences. Such orders prohibit the offender from leaving the UK for a specified period after release from custody. Section 37 of that Act provides that a travel restriction order made in relation to any person shall not prevent that person being removed from the UK under a prescribed removal power. The Schedule to the Travel Restrictions Order (Prescribed Removal Powers) Order 2002 (SI 2002/313) designates subs.2(a) and (b) of this section as a prescribed removal power for the purposes of s.37.

Human Rights Act 1998

1-1122   The removal of a patient under this section could involve a breach of art.3 of the European Convention on Human Rights (ECHR) if there is a real risk of the patient being the subject of inhuman or degrading treatment in the country to which he is sent.

In *D v United Kingdom* (1997) 24 E.H.R.R. 423 para.54, the European Court of Human Rights (ECtHR) said:

"[T]he court emphasises that aliens who have served their prison sentences and are subject to expulsion cannot in principle claim any entitlement to remain in the territory of a Contracting State in order to continue to benefit from the medical, social or other forms of assistance provided by the expelling State during their stay in prison".

The same principle would apply to persons who are detained under this Act: also see the notes to art.3 in Part 5.

Article 8 of the ECHR is engaged in deportation cases. In *Maslov v Austria* (2008) E.H.R.R. 20, para.75, the ECtHR held that "for a settled migrant who has lawfully spent all or the major part of his or her childhood and youth in the host country very serious reasons are required to justify expulsion. This is all the more so where the person concerned committed the offences underlying the expulsion measure as a juvenile".

Subsection (1)

1-1123   **United kingdom**   Means Great Britain and Northern Ireland (Interpretation Act 1978 s.5, Sch.1).

Subsection (2)

1-1124   The Act is silent as to the identity of those who are entitled to make requests for removal to the Secretary of State.

By warrant authorise   Paragraph 38.9 of the Reference Guide states:

"If the Secretary of State obtains the Tribunal's approval and decides to authorise the patient's transfer, the Secretary of State will issue a warrant which directs that the patient is taken directly to the point of embarkation and which may also include any appropriate directions to allow the patient to be conveyed, while remaining in legal custody, out of the UK. This includes being kept in custody while en route to another country, eg on a plane or ship. But the Secretary of State cannot authorise the patient being kept in custody or detained once the patient has arrived in another country – so any escort arrangements for the rest of the journey would have to be made under the law of that country, if that is allowed."

Conveyance ... and for his detention   General provisions relating to the custody, conveyance and detention of patients are contained in s.137.

Subsection (3)

1-1125   **The approval of the appropriate tribunal**   The Secretary of State will exercise his power under r.32(8) of the Tribunal Procedure (First-tier Tribunal) (Health, Education and Social Care Chamber) Rules 2008 (SI 2008/2699).

RETURN OF PATIENTS ABSENT WITHOUT LEAVE

General Note

Scotland

Authority for the retaking of patients who have absconded from hospitals or other places in Scotland **1-1126** is contained in art.8 of the Mental Health (Care and Treatment) (Scotland) Act 2003 (Consequential Provisions) Order 2005 (SI 2005/2078) which is reproduced in Part 2.

Patients absent from hospitals in Northern Ireland

87.—(1)   Any person who—   **1-1127**

(a)   under [Article 29 or 132 of the Mental Health (Northern Ireland) Order 1986] (which provide, respectively, for the retaking of patients absent without leave and for the retaking of patients escaping from custody); or

(b)   under the said [Article 29 as applied by Article 31 of the said Order] (which makes special provision as to persons sentenced to imprisonment),

may be taken into custody in Northern Ireland, may be taken into custody in, and returned to Northern Ireland from, England and Wales by an [approved mental health professional], by any constable or by any person authorised by or by virtue of the [said Order] to take him into custody.

(2)   This section does not apply to any person who is subject to guardianship.

Amendments

The amendments to this section were made by the Mental Health (Northern Ireland Consequential Amendments) Order 1986 (SI 1986/596) art.2 and the Mental Health Act 2007 s.21, Sch.2 para.7.

Definitions

patient: s.145(1).   **1-1128**
absent without leave: ss.18(6), 145(1).
approved mental health professional: s.145(1), (1AC).

General Note

This section permits a patient from Northern Ireland who has either escaped from custody or who is **1-1129** absent without leave from a hospital, to be taken into custody in England or Wales and returned to Northern Ireland. It does not apply to patients subject to guardianship.

Subsection (1)

Returned   For the powers of a constable or approved mental health professional on taking the patient **1-1130** into custody and returning him to Northern Ireland, see s.137. The period during which the patient may be returned may not be the same as it is for patients subject to similar forms of detention in England. Advice should be sought from the Northern Ireland authorities on this point.

Patients absent from hospitals in England and Wales

88.—(1)   Subject to the provisions of this section, any person who, under sec- **1-1131** tion 18 above or section 138 below or under the said section 18 as applied by section 22 above, may be taken into custody in England and Wales may be taken into custody in, and returned to England and Wales from, [Northern Ireland].

[(2)   For the purposes of the enactments referred to in subsection (1) above in their application by virtue of this section, the expression "constable" includes an officer or constable of the Police Service of Northern Ireland.]

(3) For the purposes of the said enactments in their application by virtue of this section [...], any reference to an [approved mental health professional] shall be construed as including a reference—

    (a) [...];

    (b) [...] to any [approved social worker within the meaning of the Mental Health (Northern Ireland) Order 1986.]

(4) This section does not apply to any person who is subject to guardianship.

Amendments

The amendments to this section were made by the Mental Health Act 2007 ss.21, 39(2), 55, Sch.2 para.7, Sch.5 Pt 1 para.14, Sch.11 Pt 7 and the Mental Health (Northern Ireland Consequential Amendments) Order 1986 (SI 1986/596) art.2.

Definition

1-1132   approved mental health professional: s.145(1).

General Note

1-1133   This section permits patients from England or Wales who are absent without leave from hospital or who have escaped from custody, to be taken into custody in, and returned to England and Wales from Northern Ireland. It does not apply to patients who are subject to guardianship. The patient must be taken into custody within the time limits specified in ss.18 and 22.

For patients who have absconded to Scotland, see the General Note to s.18.

Patients absent from hospitals in the Channel Islands or Isle of Man

1-1134   **89.**—(1) Any person who under any provision corresponding to section 18 above or 138 below may be taken into custody in any of the Channel Islands or the Isle of Man may be taken into custody in, and returned to the island in question from, England and Wales by an [approved mental health professional] or a constable.

(2) This section does not apply to any person who is subject to guardianship.

Amendment

The words in square brackets in subs.(1) were substituted by the Mental Health Act 2007 s.21, Sch.2 para.7.

Definition

1-1135   approved mental health professional: s.145(1).

General Note

1-1136   The purpose of this section is to ensure that a detained patient who absconds to England or Wales from the Channel Islands or the Isle of Man can be apprehended and returned to the island in question. It does not apply to patients who are subject to guardianship.

The Explanatory Notes state at para.167:

"The Channel Islands and the Isle of Man have powers of their own, which they can use to return patients from England and Wales."

Returned

For the powers of a constable or approved mental health professional, see s.137. The period during which the patient may be returned may not be the same as it is for patients subject to similar forms of detention in England. Advice should be sought from the relevant authority on this point.

GENERAL

Regulations for purposes of Part VI

90.   Section 32 above shall have effect as if references in that section to Part II **1-1137** of this Act included references to this Part of this Act[, so far as this Part of this Act applies to patients removed to England and Wales or for whom responsibility is transferred to England and Wales.]

Amendment

In this section the words in square brackets were substituted by the Mental Health Act 2007, s.39(2), Sch.5 Pt 1 para.15.

Definition

patient: s.145(1).   **1-1138**

General provisions as to patients removed from England and Wales

91.—(1)   Subject to subsection (2) below, where a patient liable to be detained **1-1139** or subject to guardianship by virtue of an application, order or direction under Part II or III of this Act (other than section 35, 36 or 38 above) is removed from England and Wales in pursuance of arrangements under this Part of this Act, the application, order or direction shall cease to have effect when he is duly received into a hospital or other institution, or placed under guardianship [or, where he is not received into a hospital but his detention in hospital is authorised by virtue of the Mental Health (Care and Treatment) (Scotland) Act 2003 or the Criminal Procedure (Scotland) Act 1995], in pursuance of those arrangements.

(2)   Where the Secretary of State exercises his powers under section 86(2) above in respect of a patient who is detained pursuant to a hospital order under section 37 above and in respect of whom a restriction order is in force, those orders shall continue in force so as to apply to the patient if he returns to England and Wales […].

[(2A)   Where responsibility for a community patient is transferred to a jurisdiction outside England and Wales (or such a patient is removed outside England and Wales) in pursuance of arrangements under this Part of this Act, the application, order or direction mentioned in subsection (1) above in force in respect of him shall cease to have effect on the date on which responsibility is so transferred (or he is so removed) in pursuance of those arrangements.]

[(3)   Reference in this section to a patient's detention in hospital being authorised by virtue of the Mental Health (Care and Treatment) (Scotland) Act 2003 or the Criminal Procedure (Scotland) Act 1995 shall be read as including references to a patient in respect of whom a certificate under one of the provisions listed in section 290(7)(a) of the Act of 2003 is in operation.]

[487]

MENTAL HEALTH ACT 1983

Amendments

The amendments to this section were made by SI 2005/2078 Sch.1 para.2(7) and the Mental Health Act 2007 ss.39(2), 55, Sch.5 Pt 1 para.16, Sch.11 Pt 8.

Definitions

1-1140   patient: s.145(1).
hospital: ss.34(2), 92(2), 145(1).
hospital order: ss.37, 145(1).
restriction order: ss.41, 145(1).
community patient: ss.17A(7), 145(1).

General Note

1-1141   This section provides that, with one exception, when a patient is removed from England or Wales under a provision in this Part, any application, order or direction made in respect of him (other than s.35, 36 or 38) will cease to have effect on arrival at his destination (subs.(1)) or, in the case of a community patient, the date on which responsibility for the patient is transferred (subs.(2A)). The exception is that if a patient who is subject to a hospital order with restrictions is removed, both the hospital order and the restriction order will remain in force (subs.(2)).

Transitional provision

1-1142   The repeal of the reference to restriction orders made for a specified period in subs.(2) shall have no effect in respect of—

    (a)   a restriction order for a specified period made before October 1, 2007, or
    (b)   an order made outside England and Wales which is treated under the 1983 Act as if it were a restriction order for a specified period (Mental Health Act 2007 s.40(7) and SI 2007/2798 art.2(d)).

Interpretation of Part VI

1-1143   **92.**—(1)   References in this Part of this Act to a hospital, being a hospital in England and Wales, shall be construed as references to a hospital within the meaning of Part II of this Act.

[(1A)   References in this Part of this Act to the responsible clinician shall be construed as references to the responsible clinician within the meaning of Part 2 of this Act.]

(2)   Where a patient is treated by virtue of this Part of this Act as if he had been removed to a hospital in England and Wales in pursuance of a direction under Part III of this Act, that direction shall be deemed to have been given on the date of his reception into the hospital.

(3)   [...]

[(4)   Sections 80 to 85A above shall have effect as if—

    (a)   any hospital direction under section 45A above were a transfer direction under section 47 above; and
    (b)   any limitation direction under section 45A above were a restriction direction under section 49 above.

(5)   Sections 80(5), 81(6) and 85(4) above shall have effect as if any reference to a transfer direction given while a patient was serving a sentence of imprisonment imposed by a court included a reference to a hospital direction given by a court after imposing a sentence of imprisonment on a patient.]

Amendments

The amendments to this section were made by the Mental Health Act 2007 ss.39(2), 55, Sch.5 Pt 1 para.17, Sch.11 Pt 1 and the Crime (Sentences) Act 1997 s.55, Sch.4 para.16.

Definitions

responsible clinician: ss.34(1), 145(1).   **1-1144**
patient: s.145(1).
mental disorder: ss.1, 145(1).
hospital direction: s.145(1).
transfer direction: s.145(1).
limitation direction: s.145(1).
restriction direction: s.145(1).

Subsection (1)

Hospital   See s.34(2).   **1-1145**

Part VII

[*Repealed by the Mental Capacity Act 2005 s.67(2), Sch.7.*]   **1-1146**

Part VIII Miscellaneous Functions of Local Authorities and the Secretary of State

[Approved mental health professionals

Approval by local social services authority

114.—(1)   A local social services authority may approve a person to act as an   **1-1147**
approved mental health professional for the purposes of this Act.

(2)   But a local social services authority may not approve a registered medical practitioner to act as an approved mental health professional.

(3)   Before approving a person under subsection (1) above, a local social services authority shall be satisfied that he has appropriate competence in dealing with persons who are suffering from mental disorder.

(4)   The appropriate national authority may by regulations make provision in connection with the giving of approvals under subsection (1) above.

(5)   The provision which may be made by regulations under subsection (4) above includes, in particular, provision as to—

(a)   the period for which approvals under subsection (1) above have effect;

(b)   the courses to be undertaken by persons before such approvals are to be given and during the period for which such approvals have effect;

(c)   the conditions subject to which such approvals are to be given; and

(d)   the factors to be taken into account in determining whether persons have appropriate competence as mentioned in subsection (3) above.

(6)   Provision made by virtue of subsection (5)(b) above may relate to courses approved or provided by such person as may be specified in the regulations (as well as to courses approved under section [114ZA or] 114A below).

(7)   An approval by virtue of subsection (6) above may be in respect of a course in general or in respect of a course in relation to a particular person.

(8)   The power to make regulations under subsection (4) above includes power to make different provision for different cases or areas.

(9)   In this section "the appropriate national authority" means—
  (a)   in relation to persons who are or wish to become approved to act as approved mental health professionals by a local social services authority whose area is in England, the Secretary of State;
  (b)   in relation to persons who are or wish to become approved to act as approved mental health professionals by a local social services authority whose area is in Wales, the Welsh Ministers.

(10)   In this Act "approved mental health professional" means—
  (a)   in relation to acting on behalf of a local social services authority whose area is in England, a person approved under subsection (1) above by any local social services authority whose area is in England, and
  (b)   in relation to acting on behalf of a local social services authority whose area is in Wales, a person approved under that subsection by any local social services authority whose area is in Wales.

Amendments

This section was substituted by the Mental Health Act 2007 s.18. The amendment to subs.(6) was made by the Health and Social Care Act 2012 s.217(3).

Definitions

1-1148   local social services authority: s.145(1).
          mental disorders. ss.1, 145(1).
          approved mental health professional: s.145(1C) and see subs.(10) of this section.

General Note

1-1149   This section provides for the approval of approved mental health professionals (AMHPs) by local social services authorities. AMHPs do not have to be employed by the local authority that approves them. AMHPs perform key functions under the Act: see the note on "For the purposes of this Act" in subs.(1). AMHPs can be drawn from social workers; first level nurses, whose field of practice is mental health or learning disability nursing; occupational therapists; and chartered psychologists: see the Mental Health (Approved Mental Health Professionals) (Approval) (England) Regulations (SI 2008/1206), which are reproduced in Pt 2. The equivalent regulations for Wales are SI 2008/2436 (W.209). As at October 2019, a survey conducted by Skills for Care found that 94% of AMHPs are social workers (*www.skillsforcare.org.uk/adult-social-care-workforce-data/Workforce-intelligence/documents/AMHPs-Briefing.pdf*). A registered medical practitioner is specifically prohibited from being approved to act as an AMHP (subs.(2)). Although all of the professionals involved in an assessment of the patient for detention may be employed by the NHS, "the skills and training required of AMHPs aim to ensure that they provide an independent social perspective" (Explanatory Notes to the Mental Health Act 2007, para.64).
    An AMHP acts in a personal capacity when performing functions under the Act (see the notes on subs.(10) and on "that professional" in s.13(1A)). Even though an AMHP acts as an independent statutory decision maker, as an AMHP acts on behalf of the local authority that authority will be vicariously liable for any lack of care or bad faith on behalf of the AMHP (*TTM v London Borough of Hackney* [2010] EWHC 1349 (Admin); [2010] M.H.L.R. 214, para.35). In *TTM*, Collins J. said that he could see no reason in principle why an AMHP should not owe a duty of care to the patient, thus giving rise to a possible action for negligent behaviour (para.36). Both the finding on vicarious liability and the conclusion reached on the duty of care owed by an AMHP were implicitly affirmed on appeal: see [2011] EWCA Civ 4; [2011] 3 All E.R. 529 at paras 59 and 97.
    The *Code of Practice*, at para.14.35, states that local authorities should ensure that sufficient AMHPs are available to carry out their functions under the Act and that arrangements must be in place to provide a 24-hour service that can respond to patient's needs. The Association of Directors of Adult Social Services issued an advice note to its members in July 2008 on "Local Social Services Authorities (LS-SAs) and the Approved Mental Health Professional Role". In order to meet its obligations under this section, the Association recommends that LSSAs "enter into a contractual arrangement with the individual AMHP to cover remuneration, training requirements, disciplinary procedures, access to legal advice and legal indemnity whilst carrying out duties on behalf of the LSSA" (para.5.1).

The approval of an AMHP is made by the LSSA (subs.(1)) and the AMHP acts on behalf of the authority (s.145(1AC)). A person may be approved as an AMHP by only one LSSA at any time. Approval will only be granted if the authority is satisfied that the applicant has appropriate competence in dealing with mentally disordered people (subs.(3)) and complies with any regulations issued by the Secretary of State if the authority is located in England, or the Welsh Ministers if the authority is located in Wales (subss.(4)–(8)).

Although an AMHP can only be approved by one LSSA, she can perform AMHP functions in the area of another LSSA (or LSSAs) if that authority has authorised the AMHP to perform such functions on its behalf. Confirmation of the authorisation can be given informally, e.g. by e-mail. On such an authorisation being made, the AMHP must notify the approving LSSA (SI 2008/1206, reg.5(b)). The Reference Guide states at para.30.5:

"Being approved by a local authority to be an AMHP is not the same as being permitted by a local authority to act on its behalf. It is for each local authority to establish its own arrangements for determining which AMHPs may act as such on its behalf and when they may do so. A local authority may arrange for AMHPs to act on its behalf even though they are approved by a different local authority."

Schedule 1 to SI 2008/2561 requires LSSAs to treat as an AMHP a person who had been approved as an ASW by an LSSA in Wales immediately before November 3, 2008.

AMHPs approved in England but acting in Wales (and vice versa) [section 114(10)]

Under this heading, paras.30.29 to 30.31 of the Reference Guide state: **1-1150**

"AMHPs approved by an English local authority may only act on behalf of local authorities which are also in England. In order to act on behalf of local authorities in Wales, they would need also to be approved as an AMHP by a local authority in Wales, in accordance with the corresponding regulations made by the Welsh Ministers.

There is nothing to prevent an AMHP acting in Wales on behalf of an English local authority where necessary.

For example, an AMHP acting on behalf of an English local authority can make applications for admission to hospitals in Wales, or apply for a warrant under section 135 of the Act to a magistrates' court in Wales. Similarly, an AMHP acting on behalf of a Welsh local authority can make applications to hospitals in England or to English magistrates' courts."

In cross-border situations, the AMHP acting on behalf of the English LSSA should use the statutory forms that are applicable in Wales, and vice versa.

Partnership arrangements

LASSAs are prevented from entering into agreements under s.75 of the National Health Service Act **1-1151** 2006 for NHS Trusts to exercise functions under this section on their behalf: see NHS Bodies and Local Authorities Partnership Arrangements Regulations 2000 (SI 2000/617) reg.6(a)(iv). SI 2000/617 has effect as if made under s.75, by virtue of the National Health Service (Consequential Provisions) Act 2006 s.4, Sch.2 Pt 1 para.1.

Human Rights Act 1998

An AMHP who is performing functions under the Act is exercising "functions of a public nature" **1-1152** and is therefore a "public authority" for the purposes of the 1998 Act: see s.6(3)(b) of that Act and *R. (on the application of Wilkinson) v Responsible Medical Officer Broadmoor Hospital* [2001] EWCA Civ 1545; [2002] 1 W.L.R. 419, at para.61. The effect of this is that it is unlawful for an AMHP to act in a way which is incompatible with a patient's rights under the European Convention on Human Rights (s.6(1) of the 1998 Act).

Subsection (1)

Approve An AMHP should be provided with documentary evidence of her approval as some sec- **1-1153** tions of the Act require the production of such a document. There is no statutory form that can be used for this purpose. The document, which should be authenticated by a senior officer of the approving authority, could read as follows: "[Name] has been approved under s.114 of the Mental Health Act 1983 to perform the functions of an Approved Mental Health Professional under that Act". It would be advisable to reproduce s.115, which provides AMHPs with a power of entry and inspection, on the document.

For the purposes of this act   AMHPs perform functions under the following sections of the Act: ss.4, 6, 8, 10, 11, 13, 14, 17A, 17B, 17F, 20A, 18, 21B, 29, 30, 40, 47, 87, 88, 89, 115, 130B, 145, 135, 136 and 138.

Subsection (2)

1-1154   Doctors cannot be appointed as AMHPs, even if they also have a qualification listed in the approval regulations.

Subsection (3)

1-1155   **Appropriate competence**   See the competencies set out in Sch.2 to SI 2008/1206. The approving LSSA should have a mechanism in place to enable it to be satisfied that AMHPs continue to possess "appropriate competence" after approval.

Subsection (4)
Appropriate national authority
1-1156   See subs.(9).

Regulations   See SIs 2008/1206 and SI 2008/2436 (W.209), noted above.

Subsection (10)

1-1157   This provision enables an AMHP acting on behalf of an English local authority to perform AMHP functions in Wales, and an AMHP acting on behalf of a Welsh local authority to perform AMHP functions in England: see the General Note, above, under the heading *AMHPs approved in England but acting in Wales (and vice versa) [section 114(10)]*.

Acting on behalf of a local social services authority   Concern was expressed in Parliament during the passage of the 2007 Act that if an AMHP is said to be acting on behalf of a LSSA, the authority could in some way direct the decisions of the AMHP. The Government denied that this was the case. Baroness Royall, speaking for the Government, said:

"An AMHP is required to make an independent decision about whether to make an application. I can assure your Lordships that nothing changes this. Paragraph 5(2) of Schedule 2 [which amends s.13 of the Act] makes it clear that AMHPs must make an application only if they are personally satisfied that it is necessary and proper to do so. The decision cannot be overturned by the local social services authority for which they are acting. The AMHP acts independently and will continue to do so in their decision making.
    The [Act] makes it clear [in s.145(1AC)] that an AMHP carries out their functions on behalf of the LSSA. This underlines the independence of the AMHP from the trust that may employ the doctors who also examine a patient's case for admission. It also ensures that the responsibility for providing that an AMHP service is in place clearly lies with the LSSA, whether or not it chooses to enter into arrangements with another body, such as a trust, to provide the service" (*Hansard*, HL Vol.688, cols 681,682).

As AMHPs act on behalf of the appointing LSSA, that authority should provide legal advice on AMHP responsibilities to AMHPs, including those who are not employees of the authority. It might not always be easy to determine when an AMHP is performing the functions of an AMHP and, therefore, acting on behalf of the LSSA, and when the AMHP is performing her normal professional role and being accountable to her employer, which might not be the LSSA.

Approval of courses: England

1-1158   **[114ZA.**—(1)   [Social Work England] may approve courses for persons who are, or wish to become, approved to act as approved mental health professionals by a local social services authority whose area is in England.

(2)   [Social Work England] must publish a list of—

(a) the courses which are approved under this section, and

(b) the courses which have been, but are no longer, approved under this section and the periods for which they were so approved.

(3) The functions of an approved mental health professional are not to be considered to be relevant social work for the purposes of Part 4 of the Care Standards Act 2000.

(4) [...]]

[(5) Social Work England may charge fees for approving courses under subsection (1).

(6) In this section "Social Work England" means the body corporate established by section 36(1) of the Children and Social Work Act 2017.]

Amendment

This section was inserted by the Health and Social Care Act 2012 s.217(2). The amendments to it were made by SI 2018/893, reg.39.

Definitions

approved mental health professional: s.145(1), (1AC). **1-1159**
local social services authority: s.145(1).

General Note

This section enables the Social Work England to approve courses for the training of English AMHPs, **1-1160**
regardless of the trainees' profession.

[

[Approval of courses: Wales]

114A.—[(1) The [Social Care Wales] may, in accordance with rules made by **1-1161**
it, approve courses for persons who are, or wish to become, approved to act as approved mental health professionals by a local social services authority whose area is in Wales.]

[(2) For that purpose—

(a) subsections (2), (3), (4)(a) and (7) of section 114 of the Regulation and Inspection of Social Care (Wales) Act 2016 apply as they apply to approvals given, rules made and courses approved under that section, and

(b) sections 73 to 75 and section 115 of that Act apply accordingly.]

(3) [...]

(4) The functions of an approved mental health professional shall not be considered to be relevant social work [for the purposes of Parts 3 to 8 of the Regulation and Inspection of Social Care (Wales) Act 2016].

(5) The [...] [Social Care Wales] may also carry out, or assist other persons in carrying out, research into matters relevant to training for approved mental health professionals.]

Amendments

This section was inserted by the Mental Health Act 2007 s.19. The amendments to it were made by the Health and Social Care Act 2012 s.217(4)–(8) and the Regulation and Inspection of Social Care (Wales) Act 2016 Sch.3 Pt 2 para.38.

[493]

Definitions

1-1162   approved mental health professional: s.145(1), (1AC).
local social services authority: s.145(1)‚

General Note

1-1163   This section enables Social Care Wales to approve courses for the training of Welsh AMHPs, regardless of the trainees' profession.

Powers of entry and inspection

1-1164   [**115.**—(1) An approved mental health professional may at all reasonable times enter and inspect any premises (other than a hospital) in which a mentally disordered patient is living, if he has reasonable cause to believe that the patient is not under proper care.

(2) The power under subsection (1) above shall be exercisable only after the professional has produced, if asked to do so, some duly authenticated document showing that he is an approved mental health professional.]

Amendment

This section was substituted by the Mental Health Act 2007 s.21, Sch.2 para.8.

Definitions

1-1165   approved mental health professional: s.145(1), (1AC).
hospital: s.145(1).
mentally disordered patient: s.1(2).
patient: s.145(1).

General Note

1-1166   This section provides approved mental health professionals (AMHPs) with a power to enter and inspect premises where a mentally disordered patient is believed to be living. It does not provide the AMHP with authority to remove the patient. The power, which is not limited to premises within the area of the AMHP's approving authority, does not apply to NHS hospitals.

Section 42(1) of the Care Act 2014 requires a local authority to undertake an adult safeguarding enquiry where it:

"has reasonable cause to suspect that an adult in its area (whether or not ordinarily resident there)—

(a)   has needs for care and support (whether or not the authority is meeting any of those needs),

(b)   is experiencing, or is at risk of, abuse or neglect, and

(c)   as a result of those needs is unable to protect himself or herself against the abuse or neglect or the risk of it".

A visiting headquarters, as defined by art.3 of the Visiting Forces and International Headquarters (Application of Law) Order 1999 (SI 1999/1736), is exempted from the operation of this section (art.12, Sch.5).

Wales

1-1167   Section 127 of the Social Services and Well-being (Wales) Act 2014 enables applications to be made to magistrates' courts for adult protection and support orders. The purpose of such orders is to enable an authorised officer to speak in private to a person suspected of being an adult at risk to establish whether he or she can make decisions freely, to assess whether the person is an adult at risk and to establish whether any action should be taken, and if so, what action.

Subsection (1)

All reasonable times   The reasonableness of the time will presumably depend upon the urgency of   **1-1168**
the situation.

Enter and inspect   This section does not empower the AMHP to force entry on to the premises, or
to override the owner's refusal to give permission to enter. The Court of Appeal has held that a wife who
is the co-owner of a house may give permission for a person to enter the house, and that person shall
not be a trespasser, notwithstanding that the husband purports to refuse permission: see *Slade v Guscott*,
July 28, 1981, (unreported; transcript available on Lexis). There is also authority for the proposition that
a co-occupier of premises can allow entry to another person: see *R. v Thornley* (1981) 72 Cr. App. R
302 where Dunn L.J. said: "It was accepted in this Court that the judge was right to direct the jury that
when the police officers entered the house they were not trespassers because they had been invited to
enter by the appellant's wife who was co-occupier". Permission to enter premises may also be given by
a landlord in a situation where the tenant does not enjoy an exclusive right of occupation: see *R. v Rosso*
[2003] EWCA Crim 3242, noted in the General Note to s.135.
  If entry is refused, the AMHP could point out to the person concerned that a refusal to allow the
inspection to take place would constitute an offence under s.129. If this information fails to impress the
obstructor and entry is still denied, the AMHP should consider whether the facts of the case would justify
making an application to a magistrate under s.135 for a warrant authorising a policeman to enter the
premises by force. The police also have powers to enter premises without a warrant under s.17(1)(e) of
the Police and Criminal Evidence Act 1984 and under the common law: see the General Note to s.135.
  Whether the common law doctrine of necessity would provide a defence if force is used to gain entry
to private property to apprehend a dangerous mentally disordered person in cases where there is an imminent threat of serious harm either to that person or to others and action is required before the arrival
of the police is doubted by Brenda Hale: see *Mental Health Law* (6th edn, p.130).

Premises   Which could include a care home or a private dwelling.

Mentally disordered patient   The use of this phrase rather than the term "patient" (see s.145(1)), suggests that this section can only be invoked in respect of persons who have been diagnosed as being
mentally disordered.

Subsection (2)

Produced, if asked to do so   The right of entry is not dependent upon someone being available to   **1-1169**
whom the document can be produced (*Grove v Eastern Gas Board* [1952] 1 K.B. 77).

Duly authenticated document   See the note on "approve" in s.114(1).

VISITING PATIENTS

Welfare of certain hospital patients
  116.—(1)   Where a patient to whom this section applies is admitted to a hospital   **1-1170**
[, independent hospital or care home] in England and Wales (whether for treatment for mental disorder or for any other reason) then, without prejudice to their
duties in relation to the patient apart from the provisions of this section, the authority shall arrange for visits to be made to him on behalf of the authority, and shall
take such other steps in relation to the patient while in the hospital [, independent
hospital or care home] as would be expected to be taken by his parents.
  (2)   This section applies to—
      [(a)   a child or young person—
          (i)   who is in the care of a local authority by virtue of a care order
              within the meaning of the Children Act 1989, or

      (ii)   in respect of whom the rights and powers of a parent are vested in a local authority by virtue of section 16 of the Social Work (Scotland) Act 1968;]

   (b)   a person who is subject to the guardianship of a local social services authority under the provisions of this Act [...]; or

   (c)   a person the functions of whose nearest relative under this Act [...] are for the time being transferred to a local social services authority.

Amendments

The amendments to this section were made by the Care Standards Act 2000 s.116, Sch.4 para.9(5), the Courts and Legal Services Act 1990 s.116, Sch.16 para.42 and SI 2005/2078 art.16, Sch.3.

Definitions

1-1171   patient: s.145(1).
hospital: s.145(1).
care home; s.145(1).
independent hospital: s.145(1).
mental disorder: ss.1, 145(1).
local social services authority: s.145(1).
nearest relative: ss.26(3), 145(1).

General Note

1-1172   This section obliges local authorities to arrange for visits to be made to certain categories of patients who have been admitted to NHS hospitals, independent hospitals and care homes. It also requires local authorities to take other steps in relation to such patients as would be expected to be taken by patients' parents. There is no requirement that the patients concerned need to be receiving treatment for mental disorder.

Section 131A places a qualified duty on hospital managers to place mentally disordered children who are admitted to hospital, whether informally or under compulsion, in a child friendly environment.

Where a child is provided with accommodation by any Local Health Board, Special Health Authority, NHS Trust, NHS Foundation Trust or local education authority for a period of three months, s.85 of the Children Act 1989 requires that body to notify the appropriate officer of the responsible local authority who shall take steps to ensure that the child's welfare is safeguarded. Similar responsibilities are placed on the proprietors of care homes and independent hospitals by s.86 of the 1989 Act. Following a notification under s.85 or 86, the local authority must arrange for the child to be visited (Children Act 1989 s.86A). Such visits must be carried out in accordance with the Visits to Children in Long-term Residential Care Regulations 2011 (SI 2011/1010).

Paragraph 19.123 of the *Code of Practice* states:

"Local authorities are under a duty in the Children Act 1989 to:

- promote contact between children and young people who are children in need, or looked after children, and their families, if they live away from home, and to help them get back together (paragraphs 10 and 15 of Schedule 2 to the Children Act 1989), and
- arrange for people (independent visitors) to visit, advise and befriend children and young people looked after by the authority wherever they are, if they have not been regularly visited by their parents (paragraph 17 of Schedule 2 to the Children Act 1989)."

The Secretary of State and, in relation to Wales, the Welsh Ministers (see the General Note to the Act and SI 1999/672 art.2, Sch.1) have the power to conduct, or assist other persons in conducting, research into this section so far as it relates to children looked after by local authorities (Children Act 1989 s.83).

Subsection (1)

Such other steps   Which could include seeking a discussion with the hospital doctors about the   **1-1173**
patient's condition, ensuring that the patient's domestic arrangements are catered for during the stay in
hospital, and providing a child patient with toys and reading matter.

Subsection (2)

Paragraph (a) child   This section does not apply to children who are wards of court.   **1-1174**

Paragraph (c) for the time being transferred to a local social services authority   By virtue of s.29.

AFTER-CARE

After-care
117.—(1)   This section applies to persons who are detained under section 3   **1-1175**
above, or admitted to a hospital in pursuance of a hospital order made under section 37 above, or transferred to a hospital in pursuance of [a hospital direction made
under section 45A above or] a transfer direction made under section 47 or 48 above,
and then cease to be detained and [(whether or not immediately after so ceasing)]
leave hospital.

(2)   It shall be the duty of the [[integrated care board] or] [...] [Local Health
Board] and of the local social services authority to provide [or arrange for the provision of], in co-operation with relevant voluntary agencies, after-care services for any
person to whom this section applies until such time as the [[integrated care board]
or] [...] [Local Health Board] and the local social services authority are satisfied
that the person concerned is no longer in need of such services [; but they shall not
be so satisfied in the case of a [community patient while he remains such a patient.]]

[(2A)   ...]

[(2B)   Section 32 above shall apply for the purposes of this section as it applies for the purposes of Part II of this Act.]

[(2C)   References in this Act to after-care services provided for a patient under
this section include references to services provided for the patient—

(a)   in respect of which direct payments are made under
   (i)   sections 31 to 33 of the Care Act 2014 (as applied by Schedule 4
      to that Act),
   (ii)   sections 50, 51 and 53 of the Social Services and Well-being
      (Wales) Act 2014 (as applied by Schedule A1 to that Act), or
   (iii)   regulations under] section 12A(4) of the National Health Service
      Act 2006, and
(b)   which would be provided under this section apart from [those sections (as so supplied) or] the regulations.]

[(2D)   Subsection (2), in its application to the [integrated care board], has effect [as if the words "provide or" were omitted].

(2E)   The Secretary of State may by regulations provide that the duty imposed
on the [integrated care board] by subsection (2) is, in the circumstances or to the
extent prescribed by the regulations, to be imposed instead on another [integrated
care board] or [NHS England].

(2F)   Where regulations under subsection (2E) provide that the duty imposed
by subsection (2) is to be imposed on [NHS England], subsection (2D) has effect
as if the reference to the [integrated care board] were a reference to [NHS England].

[497]

(2G)   Section 272(7) and (8) of the National Health Service Act 2006 applies to the power to make regulations under subsection (2E) as it applies to a power to make regulations under that Act.]

(3)   In this [section "the [[integrated care board]] or] [...] [Local Health Board]" means the [[integrated care board] or] [...] [Local Health Board], and "the local social services authority" means the local social services authority[—

(a)   if, immediately before being detained, the person concerned was ordinarily resident in England, for the area in England in which he was ordinarily resident;

(b)   if, immediately before being detained, the person concerned was ordinarily resident in Wales, for the area in Wales in which he was ordinarily resident; or

(c)   in any other case], for the area] in which the person concerned is resident or to which he is sent on discharge by the hospital in which he was detained.

[(4)   Where there is a dispute about where a person was ordinarily resident for the purposes of subsection (3) above—

(a)   if the dispute is between local social services authorities in England, section 40 of the Care Act 2014 applies to the dispute as it applies to a dispute about where a person was ordinarily resident for the purposes of Part 1 of that Act;

(b)   if the dispute is between local social services authorities in Wales, section 195 of the Social Services and Well-being (Wales) Act 2014 applies to the dispute as it applies to a dispute about where a person was ordinarily resident for the purposes of that Act;

(c)   if the dispute is between a local social services authority in England and a local social services authority in Wales, it is to be determined by the Secretary of State or the Welsh Ministers.

(5)   The Secretary of State and the Welsh Ministers shall make and publish arrangements for determining which of them is to determine a dispute under subsection (4)(c); and the arrangements may, in particular, provide for the dispute to be determined by whichever of them they agree is to do so.]

[(6)   In this section, "after-care services", in relation to a person, means services which have both of the following purposes—

(a)   meeting a need arising from or related to the person's mental disorder; and

(b)   reducing the risk of a deterioration of the person's mental condition (and, accordingly, reducing the risk of the person requiring admission to a hospital again for treatment for mental disorder).]

Amendments

The amendments to this section were made by the Health Authorities Act 1995 s.2(1), Sch.1 para.107(8), the Mental Health (Patients in the Community) Act 1995 s.2(1), Sch.1 para.15, Crime (Sentences) Act 1997 s.55, Sch.4 para.12(17), Sch.11 Pt 5, the National Health Service Reform and Health Care Professions Act 2002 s.2(5), Sch.1 para.47, SI 2007/961 art.3, Sch. para.13(9), the Mental Health Act 2007 s.32(4), Sch.3 para.24 and the Health Act 2009 s.13, Sch.1 para.3, the Health and Social Care Act 2012 s.40, the Care Act 2014 s.75 and the Health and Care Act 2022 Sch.1 para.1, Sch.4 para.16.

Definitions

hospital: s.145(1).
hospital order: ss.37, 145(1).
hospital direction: s.145(1).
Local Health Board: s.145(1), and see subs.(3) of this section.
transfer direction: ss.47, 145(1).
local social services authority: s.145(1), and see subs.(3) of this section.

Transitional Provisions

This section applies to patients who on September 30, 1983 were detained for treatment under s.26 of the Mental Health Act 1959 and to patients were subject to the equivalent of a hospital order or a transfer direction made under Part 5 of that Act on that date (Sch.5, para.6).

The Explanatory Notes to the Care Act 2014 state:

"Subsection (12) [of section 75] provides that the changes to the commissioning responsibility made by subsections (3) and (4) will not apply where a person is already in receipt of section 117 services when these changes come into force. The current authority will remain responsible for commissioning those services for as long as the person concerned continues to need them."

For the case law that applied before the commencement of subss.(3) and (4) on April 1, 2015, reference should be made to the notes on this section in the 17th edition of this Manual.

General Note

This section, which applies to patients of all ages who come within its scope, imposes an enforceable joint duty on the relevant health and social services authorities to provide or to arrange to provide after-care services for certain categories of mentally disordered patients who have ceased to be detained and leave hospital (or prison, having spent part of their sentence detained in hospital). It originated as an opposition amendment to the Mental Health (Amendment) Bill 1981. The then Government initially opposed it in the mistaken belief that it merely duplicated the general duties to provide services under the National Health Service Act 1977. Unlike the duties under that Act, the duty under this section applies to individual patients that come within its scope: see further, Tim Spencer-Lane, *Care Act Manual* (2019), para.1-709A.

Health Service Circular HSC 2000/003: Local Authority Circular LAC 2000(3) states:

"Social services and health authorities should establish jointly agreed local policies on providing Section 117 Mental Health Act after-care. Policies should set out clearly the criteria for deciding which services fall under Section 117 Mental Health Act and which authorities should finance them".

The fact that the duty under this section is a joint one does not mean that the costs incurred in providing services under this section should be shared between the authorities irrespective of the nature of the service being provided. The allocation of costs will depend on the specific aftercare service being provided. The duty is joint in the sense that the authorities must collaborate and plan together when providing, or arranging to provide, services under subs. (6) that come within the scope of their health or social care responsibilities. Paragraph 7.23 of "Care and Support Statutory Guidance", Department of Health, states:

"Section 117 of the MHA places a duty on the NHS and local authorities to provide aftercare and this will usually involve a joint assessment (often under the Care Programme Approach) including an assessment of the person's care and support needs, a care and support or support plan and subsequent review (which may reach a decision that a person is no longer in need of aftercare)."

Paragraph 45 of Annex A to the guidance states that as the legislative requirement for a care and support plan under the Care Act 2014 does not apply to this section, the care plan should instead be drawn up under guidance on the Care Programme Approach. N.B. The Care programme Approach has been replaced by the Community Mental Health Framework.

The duty to provide after-care services is a freestanding one i.e. the services are provided under this section alone. It is not a "gateway" provision which places a duty on the "responsible after-care bodies" to prove services under other legislation such as the Children Act 1989 and the National Health

Service Act 2006 (*R. v Manchester City Council Ex p. Stennett* [2002] UKHL 34). When discharging their duties under this section, integrated care boards and local authorities may provide the person with direct payments (subs.(2C)). A local authority may authorise a third party to exercise on its behalf a function under this section (Care Act 2014 s.79). Functions under this section are NHS functions for the purposes of the NHS Bodies and Local Authorities Partnership Arrangements Regulations 2000 (SI 2000/617): see *Partnership arrangements*, below.

Section 54 and Sch.3 to the Nationality, Immigration and Asylum Act 2002 have the effect of preventing local authorities from providing support under the provisions listed in the Schedule to certain categories of refugees and asylum seekers. As this section does not appear in the list of provisions set out in Sch.3, the duty under this section applies to patients irrespective of their country of origin.

The nature of the obligation placed on authorities by this section was considered in *R. v Ealing District Health Authority Ex p. Fox* [1993] 3 All E.R. 170 where Otton J. held that (1) a "proper interpretation of this section to be that it is a continuing duty in respect of any patient who may be discharged and falls within s.117, although the duty to any particular patient is only triggered at the moment of discharge"; and (2) a Health Authority "acts unlawfully in failing to seek to make practical arrangements for after-care prior to [a] patient's discharge from hospital where such arrangements are required by a [tribunal] in order to enable the patient to be conditionally discharged from hospital".

In *R. v Mental Health Review Tribunal Ex p. Hall* [1999] 3 All E.R. 132, Scott Baker J. said, at 143:

"In my judgment *Ex p. Fox* supports the following propositions which I accept to be the law: (i) an authority's duty to provide after-care services includes a duty to set up the arrangements that will be required on discharge. It is not a duty that arises for the first time at the moment of discharge; (ii) an authority with a duty to provide after-care arrangements acts unlawfully by failing to seek to make arrangements for the fulfilling of conditions imposed by a [tribunal] under section 73(2); (iii) if such an authority is unable to make the necessary arrangements it must try to obtain them from another authority; (iv) if arrangements still cannot be made an impasse should not be allowed to continue; the case must be referred back to a [tribunal] through the Secretary of State."

Fox and *Hall* were considered by Stanley Burnton J. in *R. (on the application of W) v Doncaster MBC* [2003] EWHC 192 (Admin); [2004] M.H.L.R. 189. His Lordship held that:

1. Neither *Fox* nor *Hall* is authority for the proposition that in a contested case the after-care bodies are placed under a duty to put in place after-care arrangements before the decision of a tribunal because the duty under this section only arises if (i) the patient has been in hospital under one of the provisions specified in subs.(1); (ii) the patient ceases to be detained; and (iii) the patient leaves hospital. His Lordship said at para.34:

    "It would be wasteful of the limited resources of (in this case) a local social services authority for it to have to plan and make arrangements for the after-care of all patients whose applications come before [tribunals]. Most applications are contested, and a relatively small proportion of contested applications succeed".

    His Lordship noted that in *R. v Mental Health Review Tribunal Ex p. Hall* [1994] 4 All E.R. 883, 890, Kennedy L.J. said that the terms of para.27.7 of the 1999 edition of the *Code of Practice* suggest that a care plan "at least in embryo" should be available before a tribunal hearing takes place.

2. In the case of a restricted patient the bodies are normally bound before actual discharge to endeavour to put in place the arrangements required by the tribunal as conditions of a conditional discharge, or which the tribunal requires before a deferred discharge takes effect, or which the tribunal provisionally decides should be put in place.

3. With both restricted and non-restricted patients where the discharge is not contested, the bodies should if practicable plan after-care before a tribunal hearing in order for it to be able to comply with its duty under this section on the patient's discharge.

1-1179   With regard to the first proposition set out by Scott Baker J. in *Hall*, his Lordship said, at para.39, that it is "confined to cases in which the tribunal has decided on the discharge of the patient, and the arrangements ... were those specified by the tribunal". In *W v Doncaster MBC* [2004] EWCA Civ 378; [2004] M.H.L.R. 201. Scott Baker L.J. said, at para.49, that Stanley Burnton J. was correct in his analysis and that the observations that had been made by Otton J. in *Fox* and by himself in *Hall* to the effect that there is a duty under this section to set up after-care arrangements prior to the patient's discharge should not be followed. His Lordship said at para.51:

"Although the section 117 duty does not bite on local authorities or health authorities until after the tribunal decision, they do not at that point start entirely from scratch. Most such authorities will be faced fairly frequently with circumstances in which they are expected to exercise their section 117 duty to help to rehabilitate mental patients within the community. It is reasonable to suppose therefore that they have procedures in place for coping with situations of this kind. Also, they certainly have the *power*, in appropriate cases, to start making plans before the tribunal sits. Kennedy L.J. in *Hall* referred to them as plans in embryo. Once the tribunal has made its decision it will be a case of tailoring their procedures to meet the needs of the particular case."

The nature of the duty imposed by this section in a case where the tribunal has ordered the conditional discharge of a restricted patient was considered in *R. v Camden and Islington Health Authority Ex p. K* [2001] EWCA Civ 240; [2001] M.H.L.R. 24, where the Court of Appeal confirmed that this section does not impose on Health Authorities an absolute obligation to satisfy any conditions that a tribunal may specify as prerequisites to the discharge of a patient. Lord Phillips M.R. said at para.29:

"[Section 117] imposes on Health Authorities a duty to provide after care facilities for the benefit of patients who are discharged from mental hospitals. The nature and extent of those facilities must, to a degree, fall within the discretion of the Health Authority which must have regard to other demands on its budget".

In *K*, Lord Phillips endorsed a concession that had been made by the Health Authority that a failure to use reasonable endeavours to fulfil conditions imposed by a tribunal, in the absence of strong reasons, would be likely to be an unlawful exercise of discretion: also see *R. (on the application of Worcestershire CC) v Secretary of State for Health and Social Care* [2023] UKSC 31, para.9. If, despite the exercise of all reasonable endeavours, it proves impossible for the after-care bodies to fulfil the tribunal's conditions, the continued detention of the patient would not violate art.5 of the European Convention on Human Rights (ECHR): also see the note on *Human Rights Act 1998*, below. In *R. v Secretary of State for the Home Department Ex p. IH* [2003] UKHL 59; [2004] 1 All E.R. 412, para.29, the House of Lords confirmed that the "best endeavours" principle (which is the same as the "reasonable endeavours" principle (*W v Doncaster MBC*, above, para.50)) applies whether under this section or in response to the conditions attached to a patient's discharge by the tribunal.

In *R. (on the application of B) v Camden LBC* [2005] EWHC 1366 (Admin); [2005] M.H.L.R. 258, **1-1180** B, a patient who had been made subject to a deferred conditional discharge, claimed that the defendants, in breach of their duties under this section and, in respect of the local authority, s.47 of the National Health Service and Community Care Act 1990, had caused his discharge to be delayed so as to give rise to a claim for damages for violating his rights under arts 5 and 8 of the ECHR. Section 47 of the 1990 Act, which continues to apply to this section, requires local authorities to provide services under this section to people who are assessed as having a need for such services. The issue between the parties as to the effect of this section was whether the duty imposed by subs.(2) arose before B's discharge. Stanley Burnton J. held that:

1. As the duty under subs.(2) is only owed to a person who ceases to be detained and leaves hospital, the duty could not have arisen until after the decision of the tribunal that the preconditions for B's discharge had been satisfied. However, there is a power to make preparatory after-care plans prior to the patient leaving hospital: see the obiter remarks of Scott Baker L.J. in the *Doncaster* case, above.

2. The practical effect of the concession endorsed by Lord Phillips in *K*, above, is that a s.117 authority is under a duty to use reasonable endeavours to fulfil the conditions attached by the tribunal to the conditional discharge before the discharge has taken place.

3. It is unrealistic and wrong to require s.117 authorities to act to provide residential accommodation without exploring funding issues. Resources are limited, and any authority is entitled to consider, without dragging its feet, whether a suggested placement would involve an efficient use of its resources, and therefore whether there is a possibility of that placement being funded by central government or by another authority.

4. A s.117 authority is not placed under a duty to monitor the condition of a detained patient with a view to deciding whether there is occasion to exercise their discretion to arrange for the provision of after-care services in case he is discharged. Where a patient is represented before the tribunal, the patient's solicitor should inform the s.117 authorities of the decision; and the hospital should do so too. His Lordship said, at para.72, that consideration should be given to sending the written tribunal decision to the s.117 authorities in any case where a deferred conditional discharge is ordered.

On the s.47 point, his Lordship held that:

1. The words "any person [who] may be in need of ... services [under this section]" in s.47(1)

refer to a person who may be in need at that time, or who may be about to be in need. A detained patient who is the subject of a deferred conditional discharge decision of a tribunal, which envisages his conditional discharge once s.117 after-care services are in place, is a person who "may be in need of such services", since if such services are available to him he will be discharged and immediately need them.

2.   However, the duty under s.47 does not arise until it "appears" to the local authority that a person may be in need, and it cannot appear to it that he may be in need unless it knows of his possible need. It follows that s.47 does not impose an obligation on a local authority to monitor a patient detained in hospital in case he should at some later time be in need. The decision of the local authority under s.47(1)(b) whether his needs call for the provision of services falls to be made by reference to the result of the assessment it has carried out. It follows that s.47 cannot require the local authority to monitor the situation of a patient to consider providing for his changed needs.

Stanley Burnton J.'s findings on the s.47 point was applied by Sales J. in *R. (on the application of NM) v The London Borough of Islington* [2012] EWHC 414 (Admin) where the question before the court was whether a prisoner who was awaiting discharge was a person who "may be in need" of community care services. Sales J. held that this phrase covered both cases of present need and a narrow penumbra of cases of reasonably predictable future need.

In *B*, Stanley Burnton J. said obiter, following the comments made by Scott Baker L.J. in *W v Doncaster MBC*, above, that even if the after-care bodies had been in breach of their duties to B under this section or s.47 of the 1990 Act and that breach had prolonged his detention, they would not have been liable for damages under ss.6 and 8 of the Human Rights Act 1998 for breaches of B's rights under arts 5 or 8 of the ECHR as it was only the detaining authority that could potentially be liable for such breaches. Permission to appeal this case was refused by Wall L.J. at an oral hearing held on February 21, 2006 ([2006] EWCA Civ 256).

If there is uncertainty as to the putting in place of the after-care arrangements in respect of a patient, a tribunal should adjourn to enable them to be put in place, indicating their views and giving appropriate directions (*R. (on the application of H) v Ashworth Hospital Authority* [2002] EWCA Civ 923; [2002] M.H.L.R. 314, per Dyson L.J. at para.68).

Wales

1-1181   The duty on health and social care bodies in Wales to provide services under this section was not amended by the Social Services and Well-being (Wales) Act 2014. For an account of the current legal position in Wales, see the "Rhydian: Social Welfare Law in Wales" section of Luke Clement's website: *www.lukeclements.co.uk/rhydian-social-welfare-law*.

National Health Service and Community Care Act 1990

1-1182   By virtue of para.51 of the Schedule to the Care Act 2014 and the Children and Families Act 2014 (Consequential Amendments) Order 2015 (SI 2015/914), the duty to assess under s.47 of the 1990 Act continues to apply in England for the purposes of the provision of services under this section. This means that the eligibility criteria for services provided under the Care Act 2014 do not apply to assessments for services provided under this section.

Human Rights Act 1998

1-1183   It does not automatically follow that a finding by an expert authority that the mental disorder which justified a patient's compulsory confinement no longer persists compels his immediate and unconditional release into the community (*Johnson v United Kingdom* (1999) 27 E.H.R.R. 296). It is therefore the case that if a patient who is deemed to pose a risk to the public is found no longer to be mentally disordered, discharge from detention can be delayed for a limited period until such time as appropriate after-care facilities are put in place. In *Johnson*, the Court said that the authority "should be able to retain some measure of supervision over the progress of the person once he is released into the community and to that end make his discharge subject to conditions" (para.63).

Whether a decision not to discharge a patient who had been granted a conditional discharge by a tribunal due to a failure to put in place appropriate after-care facilities in the community would constitute a violation of art.5 of the European Convention on Human Rights (ECHR) was considered by the House of Lords in *R. (on the application of H) v Secretary of State for the Home Department* [2003] UKHL 59: see the notes to s.73(7).

The question whether the ECHR places a general duty on states to provide community based services to respond to the needs of mentally disordered patients was considered by the Court of Appeal in *R. (on the application of H) v The Secretary of State for the Home Department* [2002] EWCA Civ 646; [2002] M.H.L.R. 87, where Lord Phillips M.R. said at para.87:

"We are not aware of any Strasbourg jurisprudence that indicates that a Member State owes a duty under the Convention to put in place facilities for the treatment in the community of those suffering from mental disorder so as to render it unnecessary to detain them in hospital."

In *Clunis v United Kingdom* [2001] M.H.L.R. 162, ECtHR, the applicant maintained that the failure of the authorities to implement their duties under this section amounted to a breach of the Government's positive obligations under art.8 of the ECHR, having regard to the harm which he had suffered. In declaring the complaint inadmissible, the Court said at paras 82, 83:

"[T]he Court considers that in the instant case there is no direct link between the measures which, in the applicant's view, should have been taken by Camden and the prejudice caused to his psychiatric well-being attendant on the realisation of the gravity of his act, his conviction and subsequent placement in a hospital placement without limit of time. The Court acknowledges that the assumption of responsibilities by the authorities of a Contracting State for the health of an individual may in certain defined contexts engage their liability under the Convention with respect to that individual as well as respect to third parties.

However, in the Court's opinion it cannot be said that Camden's failure to discharge its statutory duty under section 117 ... led inevitably to the fatal stabbing of Jonathan Zito. It is a matter of speculation as to whether the applicant would have consented to become an in-patient on a voluntary basis or followed a prescribed course of medication or co-operated in any other way with the authorities. In these circumstances, and without prejudice to the question as to whether Article 8 is applicable in the circumstances of this case, the Court finds that the applicant's complaint does not disclose an appearance of a violation of that Article."

In *W v Doncaster MBC* [2004] EWCA Civ 378 para.67, Scott Baker L.J. said that the ECHR places no greater obligation upon a s.117 after-care authority than domestic legislation.

The degree of judicial scrutiny required when assessing the lawfulness of s.117 after-care plans

In *R. (on the application of AK) v Islington LBC* [2021] EWHC 301 (Admin), para.26(iii), Judge **1-1184** Lickley QC, sitting as a deputy High Court judge, said that the court had to ensure that it did not take over the role of decision-maker. There was a need for objective and evidence-based analysis which should not involve "nit-picking" or making unrealistic expectations in criticising aspects of the after-care plan.

Charging for services provided under section 117

In *R. v Manchester City Council Ex p. Stennett* [2002] UKHL 34; [2002] M.H.L.R. 377, the House **1-1185** of Lords held that as this section imposes a freestanding duty to provide after-care services, and, as there is no express power to charge for services provided under it, such services must be provided free of charge.

At the first instance hearing ([1999] M.H.L.R. 149), Sullivan J. held that if a charged for service is being provided to the patient prior to the patient's admission under one of the provisions set out in subs.(1), that service would have to be provided free of charge on the patient's discharge from hospital if the provision of the service was a component of the patient's after-care plan. This finding is unaffected by the decision of the House of Lords.

The decision of the House of Lords, which is now subject to the additional cost provisions of the Care and Support and After-care (Choice of Accommodation) Regulations 2014 (SI 2014/2670) noted under s.117A, leads to the following consequences:

Case 1. A 50-year-old man with pre-senile dementia is admitted informally to hospital as a compliant mentally incompetent patient. He is assessed as requiring residential care on his discharge from hospital. He will almost certainly require such accommodation for the rest of his life. He could be charged for the accommodation by virtue of s.14 of the Care Act 2014.

Case 2. A 50-year-old man with pre-senile dementia and with identical needs to the man in Case 1 is admitted to hospital under s.3 because he happened not to be compliant when the crisis in his mental health occurred. He is assessed as requiring residential care on his discharge from hospital. He will almost certainly require such accommodation for the rest of his life. He will be provided with the accommodation without charge because he comes within the scope of s.117.

In *Stennett*, counsel for the local authority described this scenario as the anomaly of the compliant and non-compliant patients in adjacent beds. Lord Steyn rejected this view as being "too simplistic". His Lordship said that there:

"may well be a reasonable view that generally patients compulsorily admitted under ss.3 and 37 pose greater risks upon discharge to themselves and others than compliant patients. Moreover, Parliament necessarily legislates for the generality of cases" (para.13).

Nicolette Priaulx comments that the anomaly is far from "simplistic" in that it highlights "the manifest unfairness which can arise from differential treatment in circumstances where the 'need' of the patients are objectively no different at all" ("Charging for After-care services under Section 117 of the Mental Health Act 1983—The Final Word?", *Journal of Mental Health Law* (2002), 8, 313–322, at 317; see also Phil Fennell, All E.R. Rev. 2002, paras 18.57, 18.58). In *R. v Bournewood Community and Mental Health NHS Trust Ex p. L* [1998] 3 All E.R. 298 at 309, Lord Steyn described mentally incapable compliant patients as being "diagnostically indistinguishable from compulsory patients". The decision in *Stennett* has resulted in the charging for residential care provided to the mentally disordered operating in an arbitrary manner with free care being provided for those whose clinical and financial needs may not be as great as those who are charged for such care.

For many patients who are provided with after-care services under this section, the administration of medication for their mental disorder will be a key component of their after-care plan. "Psychiatric treatment" was identified as an after-care service by Lord Steyn in *Stennett* (at para.7). By virtue of the principle established in *Stennett*, medication provided as an after-care service is provided under this section and the National Health Service (Charges for Drugs and Appliances) Regulations 2015 (SI 2015/570) do not apply. The medication should therefore be provided free of charge. It is submitted that the operation of this principle to all patients who are subject to this section is not undermined by the fact that regs 6(5)(b), 8(4)(b) and 9(6)(b) of SI 2015/570 provide for a particular group of patient who are subject to this section, namely patients who are subject to community treatment orders, to be provided with medicines for the treatment of their mental disorder free of charge. The website of the NHS Business Services Authority states:

"To claim free prescriptions under Section 117 of the Mental Health Act, you must speak to the person who's overseeing your care package [i.e. the care co-ordinator]. It's their responsibility to arrange for the appropriate medication to be given at a prearranged place."

The three Local Government Ombudsmen, pursuant to their power under s.23(12A) of the Local Government Act 1974, produced a "Special Report" providing "advice and guidance on the funding of aftercare under s.117 of the Mental Health Act 1983" (2003). The report considers the extent to which authorities are liable for financial restitution to those who have been charged for s.117 services.

If a local authority refunds charges that were wrongly made for residential care provided under this section, the refund will be taken into account as capital by the Department of Work and Pensions in determining a claimant's entitlement to income support after the date of the repayment (Decision of the Social Security Commissioner (CIS/3760/2006), October 2007).

Damages for breach of the duty imposed by this section

1-1186   In *Henderson v Dorset Healthcare University NHS Foundation Trust* [2020] UKSC 43; [2022] M.H.L.R. 228, Ms Henderson brought proceedings against the Trust for negligence and breach of duty of care on the ground that, if she had been properly treated for her mental disorder, she would not have killed her mother and would not have been convicted of the offence of manslaughter. At the time of the killing, Ms Henderson, who was subject to a CTO and who "knew what she was doing and that it was legally and morally wrong" (per Lord Hamblen at para.142), was under the care of the local community mental health team. The Supreme Court rejected Ms Henderson's claim for damages on the grounds that the damages claimed by her were the consequence of: (i) the sentence imposed on her by the criminal court, and/or (ii) her criminal act of manslaughter. The damages were therefore irrecoverable by reason of the doctrine of illegality (or, to use the Latin maxim, "*ex turpi causa non oritur actio*") which prevents a claimant from being compensated for losses suffered in consequence of their own criminal act, irrespective of their degree of personal responsibility for their actions.

In *R. (on the application of W) v Doncaster MBC* [2003] EWHC 192 (Admin); [2004] M.H.L.R. 189, Stanley Burnton J. held that although a breach of the duty imposed by this section does not of itself give rise to a cause of action for damages for breach of statutory duty (*Clunis v Camden and Islington Health*

Authority [1998] 3 All. E.R. 180 followed), an authority whose breach of its duty causes the detention (or prolongs the detention) of a patient who would otherwise be discharged will normally cause an infringement of his rights under art.5(1) of the ECHR.

Restitution

The decision in *Clunis*, above, does not prevent a private law claim being pursued against a local **1-1187** authority for the restitution of sums spent on the care of a patient who is subject to this section (*Richards v Worcestershire CC* [2017] EWCA Civ 1998; [2017] M.H.L.R. 388).

Personal injury awards

A local authority may not have regard to the patient's ability to fund the cost of after-care services **1-1188** from damages awarded to him in his claim for personal injuries when determining whether or not to provide or arrange for the provision of after-care services under this section: see *Tinsley v Manchester City Council* [2017] EWCA Civ 1704; [2017] M.H.L.R. 381 where Longmore L.J. said at para.34:

"One understands that local authorities are concerned about the potential implications of the Administrative Court's decision especially since Schedule 4 to the Care Act 2014 applies sections 31 and 32 of that Act to the provision of after-care services, so that direct payments can be made instead, to those who have capacity to ask for them and to an authorised person on their behalf if they do not. That concern may, however, be over-stated. Few claimants who have been awarded the costs of private care will voluntarily seek local authority care while the funds for private care still exist. If they ask for direct payments, the provisions of the Care Act will have to be considered. Any argument about such provisions is for another day."

Personal Health Budgets

Regulation 32A of the NHS Commissioning Board and Clinical Commissioning Groups **1-1189** (Responsibilities and Standing Rules) Regulations 2012 (SI 2012/2996) extends the right to request a personal health budget (PHB) to a person in receipt of "that part of a package of care which is arranged and funded by a relevant body for a person to whom section 117(1) of the 1983 Act applies". A PHB is a sum of money the person can use to meet their identified needs under this section.

Direct payments

See subs.(2C). **1-1190**

"Top-up payments"

See s.117A. **1-1191**

NHS Continuing Healthcare

The *National Framework for NHS Continuing Healthcare and NHS-funded Nursing Care* (July 2022 **1-1192** (revised)) states:

"337. Responsibility for the provision of section 117 services lies jointly with local authorities and the ICB. Where an individual is eligible for services under section 117 these must be provided under section 117 and not under NHS Continuing Healthcare. It is important for ICBs to be clear in each case whether the individual's needs (or in some cases which elements of the individual's needs) are being funded under section 117, NHS Continuing Healthcare or any other powers.
338. There are no powers to charge for services provided under section 117, regardless of whether they are provided by the NHS or local authorities. Accordingly, the question of whether services should be free NHS services (rather than potentially charged-for social services) does not arise. It is not, therefore, necessary to assess eligibility for NHS Continuing Healthcare if all the services in question are in fact to be provided as after-care services under section 117.
339. However, a person in receipt of after-care services under section 117 may for example have ongoing needs that do not arise from, or are not related to, their mental disorder and that may, therefore, not fall within the scope of section 117. Also a person may be receiving services under section 117 and then develop separate physical health needs (e.g. through a stroke) which may then trig-

ger the need to consider NHS Continuing Healthcare, but only in relation to these separate needs, bearing in mind that NHS Continuing Healthcare must not be used to meet section 117 needs. Where an individual in receipt of section 117 services develops physical care needs resulting in a rapidly deteriorating condition which may be entering a terminal phase, consideration should be given to the use of the Fast Track Pathway Tool."

Independent Mental Health Advocates and Care Act Advocates

1-1193   Paragraph 7.23 of "Care and Support Statutory Guidance", Department of Health, states:

"Under the Mental Health Act 1983 (MHA) certain people, known as 'qualifying patients', are entitled to the help and support from an Independent Mental Health Advocate (IMHA). Section 117 of the MHA places a duty on the NHS and local authorities to provide aftercare and this will usually involve a joint assessment (often under the Care Programme Approach) including an assessment of the person's care and support needs, a care and support or support plan and subsequent review (which may reach a decision that a person is no longer in need of aftercare). Those people who do not retain a right to an IMHA, whose care and support needs are being assessed, planned or reviewed should be considered for an advocate under the Care Act, if they have substantial difficulty in being involved and if there is no appropriate person to support their involvement (see paragraph 7.32)."

Independent Mental Capacity Advocates

1-1194   Section 39 of the Mental Capacity Act 2005 applies if a local authority intends to arrange for a patient to be provided with long-stay residential accommodation under this section, or for the accommodation to be changed, if:

(i)   there is no-one apart from a professional or paid carer for the authority to consult in determining whether the placement would be in the patient's best interests; and

(ii)   the patient lacks the mental capacity to make a decision about the arrangements.

In this situation, the authority is required to instruct an independent mental capacity advocate (IMCA) to represent the patient and any information given, or submissions made, by the IMCA must be taken into account when a decision is made about the placement. Such consultation need not take place if the patient is likely to stay in the accommodation for less than eight weeks or if the need for the accommodation is urgent. However, the consultation must take place after the placement has been effected if the authority subsequently believes that the accommodation will be provided for the patient for at least eight weeks. Section 39 does not apply if the accommodation is provided as a result of an obligation imposed on the patient under this Act: see further, paras 1-380 to 1-387 of the *Mental Capacity Act Manual* (8th edn, 2018).

Partnership arrangements

1-1195   This section is prescribed as a NHS function which may be the subject of a partnership arrangement with local authorities under s.75 of the National Health Service Act 2006 (NHS Bodies and Local Authority Partnership Arrangements Regulations 2000 (SI 2000/617) reg.5). Section 75 enables NHS bodies and local authorities to pool resources, delegate functions and transfer resources from one body to another so that there can be a single provider of services. By virtue of reg.6 of SI 2000/617, this section is a health-related function of a local authority that may be the subject of a partnership arrangement. SI 2000/617 has effect as if made under s.75, by virtue of the National Health Service (Consequential Provisions) Act 2006 s.4, Sch.2 Pt 1 para.1.

Applications to the First-tier Tribunal (Mental Health) and to the Hospital Managers

1-1196   Paragraph 33.12 of the *Code of Practice* states:

"Where a Tribunal or hospital managers' hearing has been arranged for a patient who might be entitled to after-care under section 117 of the Act, the hospital managers should ensure that the relevant CCG and local authority have been informed. The CCG and local authority should consider putting practical preparations in hand for after-care in every case, but should in particular consider doing so where there is a strong possibility that the patient will be discharged if appropriate after-care can be arranged. Where the Tribunal has provisionally decided to give a restricted patient a conditional discharge, the CCG and local authority should do their best to put after-care in place which would allow that discharge to take place."

It is not essential for the tribunal to have specific information about aftercare in every case, in particular a case where the patient has not progressed to the point where the issue of after-care that was actually available would arise: see *AM v West London MH NHS Trust & Secretary of State for Justice* [2012] UKUT 382; [2012] M.H.L.R. 399. On refusing permission to appeal in this case, Richards L.J. said:

"[It] seems to me ... that it must, as a matter of principle, be open to a Tribunal to conclude in the circumstances of a particular case that information or better information of aftercare is incapable of affecting the decision, and that an adjournment to secure its provision could achieve nothing beyond additional expense and delay and would therefore be inappropriate" ([2013] EWCA Civ 1010; [2014] M.H.L.R. 174, para.9).

In *AF v Nottinghamshire NHS Trust* [2015] UKUT 216 (AAC); [2015] M.H.L.R. 347 para.50, UT Judge Wright observed obiter that the law does not

"require the social circumstances report to include details about s.117 after-care in every case. I say this because it is arguable that the terms of para.14(i) in the Practice Direction only require that the report includes details of the care pathway and s.117 after-care to be made available, so far as is known, and that may therefore absolve the report from including such information if it is not known, for example where no s.117 after-care '*is to be made available*' because the views of all those treating the patient is that he is not close to being able to be discharged".

Also see the judgment of Stanley Burnton J. in *R. (on the application of W) v Doncaster MBC* which is noted in the General Note, above.

Code of Practice

Guidance on this section is contained in Ch.33 of the Code. For the application of this section to children, see paragraph 19.111 of the Code which states: **1-1197**

"Prior to their discharge from hospital all children and young people should have an assessment of their needs, on which a care plan for their after-care is based. Guidance on the duty to provide after-care under section 117 of the Act, is set out in chapter 33. Such guidance is applicable to individuals of all ages, but in relation to children and young people additional factors will need to be considered. This may include ensuring that the after-care integrates with any existing provision made for looked after children and those with special educational needs or disabilities, as well as safeguarding vulnerable children. Whether or not section 117 of the Act applies, a child or young person who has been admitted to hospital for assessment and/or treatment of their mental disorder may be 'a child in need' for the purpose of section 17 of the Children Act 1989. See also paragraph 19.118 below in relation to children and young people with special educational needs."

With regard to the provision of information to patients, the Code states at para.4.30:

"When a detained patient or a community patient is discharged, or the authority for their detention or the CTO expires, this fact should be made clear to them. The patient should be given an explanation of what happens next, including any section 117 after-care or other services which are to be provided."

Subsection (1)

This section applies to patients of all ages who come within the scope of this provision. For qualifying patients who have been granted leave of absence under s.17, see the note on "cease to be detained and leave hospital", below.   **1-1198**

Detained under section 3   It is submitted that the duty under this section would not be engaged if, subsequent to the patient being admitted, the application for detention was found to be fundamentally defective: see the General Note to s.15.

Hospital order made under section 37   This section also applies to hospital order patients who have been made subject to restriction orders under s.41.

Transfer direction made under section 47 or 48   This section also applies to transfer direction patients who have been made subject of restriction directions under s.49.

The NHS has published "Transfer and remission of adult prisoners under the MHA: Good practice guidance" (2021) which can be accessed at: *https://www.england.nhs.uk/publication/guidance-for-the-transfer-and-remission-of-adult-prisoners-and-immigration-removal-centre-detainees-under-the-mental-health-act-1983*. Also see para.5.5 of guidance on the restricted patient system published by the Ministry of Justice and HM Prison and Probation Service. The guidance can be accessed at: *www.gov.uk/government/publications/mentally-disordered-offenders-the-restricted-patient-system*.

Paragraphs 17.6 and 17.7 of "Care and Support Statutory Guidance", Department of Health, state:

"Where prisoners have previously been detained under sections 47 and 48 of the Mental Health Act 1983 and transferred back to prison, their entitlement to section 117 aftercare should be dealt with in the same way as it would be in the community, apart from any provisions which are disapplied in custodial settings, such as direct payments and choice of accommodation, which are set out in more detail below. Section 117(3), as amended by the Care Act 2014, will apply in determining which local authority is responsible for commissioning or providing the section 117 after-care.

If the person was ordinarily resident in the area of a local authority immediately before being detained in hospital, that local authority will be responsible for the after-care while the person is in prison and upon their release from prison (see Chapter 19 for further detail on determination). However, if the person was not ordinarily resident in any area immediately before detention, the local authority responsible will be where the person is resident or where they have been discharged (i.e. the local authority responsible for the prison to which the person has been discharged). The local authority will be jointly responsible for after-care with NHS England while the person is in prison."

With regard to children returning to custody from hospital, see para.6.1 of *Procedure for the referral for assessment, and transfer to and from hospital (under Part III of the Mental Health Act 1983) of a child held in custody in England*, NHS, 2021, which is noted in the General Note to s.47 under the heading *Transfers of children*.

Cease to be detained and leave hospital   The duty to provide after-care services under this section extends to patients who, having been detained under s.3, are granted leave of absence under s.17 and have ceased to be detained and have left the hospital. In *R. v Richmond LBC Ex p. W* [1999] M.H.L.R. 155, Sullivan J. said at para.99:

"In my view, this section is dealing with a practical problem: what after-care is to be provided for a patient who has suffered from mental illness requiring inpatient treatment when he actually leaves hospital? A person on leave under section 17 is in just as much, if not more, need of care after he leaves hospital as a person who leaves hospital subject to guardianship or supervision. For the purposes of section 17, he has ceased to be detained, and left hospital. It would be remarkable if, in such circumstances there was no duty to provide him with after-care under section 117, even though it would almost certainly have been a condition of his being given leave that he should reside in particular accommodation."

The *Richmond* case was distinguished by the Court of Appeal in *R. (on the application of CXF) v Central Bedfordshire Council* [2018] EWCA Civ 2852; [2019] M.H.L.R. 16 where Leggatt L.J., who gave the only reasoned judgment, said at para.36 that he agreed with the following passage of the first instance judgment of Dinah Rose QC (sitting as a Deputy High Court Judge):

"As a matter of ordinary language, the phrase 'left hospital' is commonly used to refer to discharge from the care of a hospital, rather than simply leaving the premises for any period of time or any reason. If one person asks another 'have you left hospital yet?' they are not asking whether they have gone outside for a shopping trip. I note that, by contrast, s.17(4) refers to a patient on leave as 'absent from a hospital'. In short, a person may be 'absent from a hospital' (e.g. to go on a short trip outside the grounds), without having 'left hospital'."

His Lordship said that "it is a perfectly ordinary and natural use of language to say that a patient who is allowed to leave the hospital in which he is detained to go on a short trip in the custody of hospital staff is not a person who has 'left hospital'" (para.37) and that he could not accept that "it is inappropriate to describe a patient who is permitted to leave the hospital premises to go on a short escorted trip and then return as a person who is still 'detained' in the hospital" (para.32). It was therefore an "inescapable conclusion is that the claimant does not 'cease to be detained' or 'leave hospital' within the meaning of s.117(1) when he is escorted on day trips and is therefore not a person to whom s.117 applies" (para.44). However, his Lordship could "readily accept that there will be cases in which a patient granted leave of absence from hospital under s.17 does 'cease to be detained' and 'leave hospital' within the meaning of s.117(1) so as to become eligible to receive after-care services during the period of their absence". These would include "a person who is living in the community on leave of absence – either full-time or for part of the week" (para.39) which was the situation which Sullivan J. was addressing in the *Richmond* case where the person was "living in residential accommodation in the community" (para.41).

Whether or not immediately after so ceasing   This section applies to a patient who has been detained under one of the sections mentioned in this subsection and who subsequently acquires informal status prior to leaving hospital. It also applies to a patient who having been discharged from the s.3, is re-detained under another provision of the Act (e.g. under s.5(2)) prior to his discharge from hospital.

Subsection (2)

Duty   The nature of this joint duty is considered in the General Note to this section. The duty will last   **1-1199**
until the after-care bodies are satisfied that the patient no longer needs any after-care service for his mental disorder and have formally recorded their decision. The patient is not legally obliged to accept the after-care services that are offered. An unwillingness to receive after-care services should not be equated with an absence of a need for such services. A patient's continued refusal to receive after-care services should be confirmed by professional inquiry at appropriate intervals.

Integrated Care Board   For the identity of the relevant ICB, see subs.(3).

Or arrange for the provision of   ICBs and local authorities can commission as well as provide after-care services. They can commission services from each other as well as from external providers.

Local Social Services Authority   For the identity of the relevant social services authority, see subs.(3). There is no requirement for the authority's duty to be carried out by approved mental health profession-als (*Nottingham City Council v Unison* [2004] EWHC 893, para.24).

After-care services   See subs.(6).

Any person   If the person is a child, the local authority should ensure that it complies with its responsibilities under Pt III of the Children Act 1989.

Satisfied   The after-care bodies must be satisfied that the patient is no longer in need of any after-care service. This joint decision, which should be recorded and explained, should be communicated to relevant people and agencies. The after-care bodies cannot be so satisfied if the patient is a community patient (subs.(2)). A person who is diagnosed as no longer suffering from a mental disorder is clearly a person who no longer needs services under this section. A decision that a patient no longer qualifies for services under this section can only be made if the after-care bodies have monitored the patient's progress in the community since discharge. It "is for the authority responsible for providing particular services to take the lead in deciding whether those services are no longer required. The patient, his/her carer and other agencies should always be consulted" (Local Authority Circular LAC (2000) 3, para.4).
   Given the nature of after-care services, many patients will require after-care services for substantial periods. A patient should not be discharged from care under this section solely on the ground that: (1) he has been discharged from the care of a responsible clinician or specialist mental health services; (2) an arbitrary period has elapsed since the care was first provided; (3) the provision of care is successful in that he is well settled in the community or in residential care and the continuation of after-care is needed to prevent a relapse or further deterioration in his condition; (4) he is no longer subject to a com-munity treatment order or s.17 leave; (5) he returns to hospital as an informal patient or under s.2 and subsequently leaves the hospital; (6) the diagnostic category of the patient's mental disorder changes; or (7) the patient has been made the subject of a deprivation of liberty authorisation under the Mental Capacity Act 2005. Also see the *Code of Practice* at paras 33.21 and 33.23. With regard to (3), responsibility under this section could end if the needs that were being addressed after the patient became settled in a care home related to the patient's age and mental frailty rather than to the patient's mental disorder: see further "A report by the Health Service Ombudsman and the Local Government Ombuds-man about the provision of section 117 aftercare", HC 642, Oct 2012 which is noted under subs.(6).
   R. (on the Mwanza) v Greenwich LBC [2010] EWHC 1462 (Admin); [2010] M.H.L.R. 226 is author-ity for the proposition that if a patient's condition is relatively stable, there are no concerns arising from his non-engagement with after-care authorities, and a follow up letter has been sent to his GP, he may be discharged from this section: see para.87.

If a person is assessed as no longer coming within the scope of this section, he should be formally discharged from receiving s.117 services. In the absence of a discharge, it might be difficult to establish when the obligation to charge for services arose. Paragraph 33.22 of the *Code of Practice* states that after-care services "may be reinstated if it becomes obvious that they have been withdrawn prematurely, eg where a patient's mental condition begins to deteriorate immediately after services are withdrawn". Apart from this situation, if a patient has been discharged from this section, he will only be eligible to receive s.117 services again if he is re-detained under a qualifying section.

A patient's expressed wish to be "discharged" from this section has no legal effect if he continues to have a need for after-care services: see the report of the Local Government Ombudsman on an investigation into complaint no. 04/B/01280 against York City Council.

Subsection (2C)

1-1200   This provision brings within the scope of this section relevant services provided under the direct payments scheme. Also see reg.11 of the Care and Support (Direct Payments) Regulations (SI 2014/2871). The *Code of Practice* considers direct payments in the following paragraphs [By virtue of the Health and Care Act 2022, for references to CCGs and the NHS Commissioning Board substitute ICBs and NHS England respectively]:

"33.17 A local authority may make direct payments to pay for after-care services under section 117 of the Act. An adult who is eligible for after-care can request the local authority to make direct payments to them, if they have capacity to do this. If the adult lacks capacity to do so, the local authority can make direct payments to an authorised person or suitable person if certain conditions are met. A key condition is that the local authority must consider that making the direct payments to the 'authorised person' is an appropriate way to discharge their section 117 duty, and that they must be satisfied the 'authorised person' will act in the adult's best interests in arranging for the after-care.

33.18 If a local authority is providing or arranging accommodation as part of a patient's after-care, the patient and/or friends or relatives identified in regulations may make top-up payments to enable the patient to live in their preferred accommodation if certain conditions are met.

33.19 A CCG or the NHS Commissioning Board may also make direct payments in respect of after-care to the patient or, where the patient is a child or a person who lacks capacity, to a representative who consents to the making of direct payments in respect of the patient. A payment can only be made if valid consent has been given. In determining whether a direct payment should be made, a CCG or the NHS Commissioning Board is required to have regard to whether it is appropriate for a person with that person's condition, the impact of that condition on the person's life and whether a direct payment represents value for money. A payment can also, in certain circumstances, be made to a nominee."

Sections 31 to 33 of the Care Act 2014   As they apply to this section, these provisions are subject to Sch.4 to the 2014 Act which makes a number of modifications to the application of certain provisions of that Act to enable direct payments to be made in respect of services provided under this section.

Regulations made under section 12A   See the National Health Service (Direct Payments) Regulations 2013 (SI 2013/1617).

Subsection (2D)

1-1201   This provision makes clear that the duty of an integrated care board (or NHS England) is to commission, rather than provide after-care services.

Subsection (2E)

1-1202   See regs 5 to 8 of the National Health Service (Integrated Care Boards: Responsibilities) Regulations 2022 (SI 2022/635) which are noted under subs.(3) and reproduced in Part 2.

NHS England   Paragraph 33.8 of the *Code of Practice* states:

"The NHS Commissioning Board (NHS England) is responsible for a patient's aftercare if the aftercare services required are of the type that [NHS England] would be responsible for commissioning rather than [an ICB]. In these circumstances local authorities and [ICBs] should liaise with [NHS England] to ensure these services are commissioned promptly."

Subsection (3)

This provision is concerned with identifying the bodies that have a duty to provide services under **1-1203** this section. Its purpose is "to avoid anomalies which can currently arise where one local authority is responsible for commissioning section 117 services whilst another commissions any other services a person may need. They apply consistent after-care ordinary residence rules in England and Wales, in particular, in relation to which health body and local authority are responsible for commissioning after-care services" (Care Act 2014, Explanatory Notes, para.448). A transitional provision contained in s.75(12) of the 2014 Act is noted above.

The phrase "immediately before being detained" in paras (a) and (b) includes a detention under s.2 which precedes and leads to a subsequent detention under s.3 (*R. (on the application of (Worcestershire County Council v Essex County Council* [2014] EWHC 3557 (Admin); [2015] M.H.L.R. 93, para.14). It is submitted that the same approach should be taken to an interim hospital order made under s.38 which is immediately followed by a hospital order made under s.37, i.e. where there is a continuous period of detention under this Act, the patient's ordinary residence is to be determined at the point when the patient was first detained.

Registering a hospital patient to vote has no impact on identifying the responsible after-care bodies under this section because under s.7(2) of the Representation of the People Act 1983, a patient is regarded as being resident in the hospital only for the purposes of entitlement to be registered to vote.

Integrated Care Board   "Who Pays? Determining which NHS commissioner is responsible for commissioning healthcare services and making payment to providers" (June 2022) "sets out the framework for establishing which NHS commissioner will be responsible for commissioning and paying for an individual's NHS care" (para.1.1).

Regulations have been made which bring commissioning responsibility in line with the position on payment responsibility as set out "Who Pays?": see in regs.5 to 8 of the National Health Service (Integrated Care Boards: Responsibilities) Regulations 2022 (SI 2022/635) which are reproduced in Part 2, and para.18.2 of "Who Pays", below.

The general rules for determining responsibility between ICBs is set out in para.10.2 of "Who Pays?" which states:

"Where an individual is registered on the list of NHS patients of a GP practice, the ICB with core responsibility for the individual will be the ICB with which that GP practice is associated.

Where an individual is not registered with a GP practice, the ICB with core responsibility for the individual will be the ICB in whose geographic area the individual is 'usually resident'. (See Appendix 2 for more details on determining usual residence.)

Any one GP practice may have some individuals registered with it who are usually resident in one ICB and others who are usually resident in another. In that situation, the responsible ICB for all of the individuals registered with that practice will be the ICB with which that practice is associated.

Where an individual is registered with a GP practice which is associated with ICB A, but has then been accepted as a temporary resident by a GP practice which is associated with ICB B, the individual becomes the core responsibility of ICB B for that period of temporary residence."

A number of specific exceptions to these general rules include "Detention under the Mental Health Act and section 117 aftercare":

"*Background*
18.1 In the 2020 version of Who Pays? we sought to address confusion – and remove some perverse incentives – around NHS responsibilities for commissioning and payment where, under the Mental Health Act, patients (whether adults or children) are detained in hospital and where, following discharge, they then receive aftercare ('section 117 aftercare'). We established a separate rule on CCG responsibility for paying for detention and aftercare services, so that – in summary – the CCG which was responsible for the patient at the point of initial detention under the Act retained responsibility for paying for the detention, subsequent aftercare and any further detentions / aftercare until the patient was ultimately discharged from aftercare. This was different from the position set out in legislation, at that point, on CCG responsibilities for commissioning detention and aftercare services.
18.2 From 1 July 2022 onwards, the position is much simpler – because the new ICB Responsibilities Regulations now align the legislative position on responsibility for commissioning detention and

aftercare services with the rule on responsibility for paying providers which was introduced in the 2020 version of Who Pays? The new arrangements are described below.

What is the exception in relation to commissioning responsibility and who does it apply to?

18.3 For individuals who are detained under the Mental Health Act for the first time on or after 1 July 2022 (including where they are detained for the first time following discharge from s117 aftercare provided after a previous detention), the position on commissioning responsibility will be as follows – and the same rule will also apply to payment responsibility.

- NHS England will be responsible for payment for any period where the patient is treated by a prescribed specialised service.
- In respect of ICB-commissioned detention and aftercare services, the ICB responsible for commissioning and payment will be determined on the basis of the general rules at paragraph 10.2 above, applied at the point of the patient's initial detention in hospital under the Act (whether for assessment or treatment). This ICB will be known as the 'originating ICB'.
- This originating ICB will then retain responsibility for commissioning and payment throughout the initial detention (including any period of informal admission following detention, during which the patient is no longer detained but remains in hospital voluntarily), for the whole period for which any s117 aftercare is provided and for any subsequent repeat detentions or voluntary admissions from aftercare, until such point as the patient is finally discharged from s117 aftercare – regardless of where the patient is treated or placed, where they live or which GP practice they are registered with.

18.4 To clarify further:

- detention for assessment under s2 of the Mental Health Act does not trigger a right to s117 aftercare – but it does constitute detention for the purposes of the rule at paragraph 18.3; so if a patient is detained under s2 for assessment and then, while they are in hospital, this becomes an s3 detention for treatment, the 'point of initial detention' will be the date of the s2 detention;
- removal by the police to a place of safety under s136 of the Act does not constitute detention for the purposes of the rule at paragraph 18.3 (other rules set out in Who Pays? will apply as relevant, including those on emergency services in paragraph 17);
- the arrangements set out in paragraph 18.3 do not apply where an individual is deprived of their liberty under the Mental Capacity Act but is not detained pursuant to the Mental Health Act; in that instance, the general rule at paragraph 10.2 applies; and
- s117 aftercare services are services which are intended to meet a need that arises from or relates to an individual's mental health condition and which reduce the risk of deterioration in the individual's mental health which could otherwise lead to re-admission to hospital; an individual receiving s117 aftercare may therefore also be eligible for FNC or continuing care (see paragraph 41 of the NHS-funded Nursing Care Practice Guidance and paragraph 339 of the National Framework respectively); in such cases, payment responsibility for the FNC / continuing care will be determined separately under the rules in paragraphs 11.14-18 and paragraph 14 as applicable.

18.5 In this guidance we do not seek to describe how mental health services should be commissioned or how ICBs should work together to ensure that patients receive care that is appropriate to their needs, for example where a patient receiving s117 aftercare that is organised and paid for by ICB A but is actually delivered by a provider located in the area of ICB B where the patient is now resident. Materials are available to support commissioners and providers, such as the DHSC's Mental Health Act Code of Practice which sets out to 'encourage commissioners of services, health and care providers and professionals to deliver a holistic, whole person approach to care that is reflective of clinical best practice and quality'.

18.6 We are aware that there may be occasions where it is clinically necessary for someone to be admitted to an acute mental health bed before it has been possible to identify the responsible commissioner. Where this happens, the provider must make every effort, without delay, to establish which commissioner is responsible for funding the patient's care – and the relevant commissioners must engage with, and support, the provider in doing this. This will help to avoid disputes and ensure that the provider is paid in a timely manner.

Transitional arrangements for payment

18.7 Where a patient is detained in hospital for the first time on or after 1 July 2022, responsibility for commissioning and payment will be determined on the basis of the arrangements set out in paragraphs 18.3-4 above.

18.8 For patients already detained in hospital or receiving aftercare before 1 July 2022, NHS England continues to mandate (using its 14Z50 powers, as described in paragraph 4.5 above) the following transitional requirements (first set out in 2020 Who Pays?) in relation to payment responsibility for detention and aftercare. These transitional arrangements continue to operate by reference to the date when the 2020 version of Who Pays? came into effect – that is, 1 September 2020.

- Where, at 1 September 2020, a patient had been discharged from detention and was already receiving s117 aftercare, funded in part or whole by a CCG, that CCG (and its successor ICB where applicable) will remain responsible for funding the aftercare – and any subsequent further detentions or voluntary admissions – until such point as the patient is discharged from s117 aftercare.
- Where, at 1 September 2020, a patient was detained in hospital funded by a CCG, that CCG (and its successor ICB where applicable) will be responsible for funding the full period of detention and any necessary NHS aftercare on discharge – and any subsequent further detentions or voluntary admissions – until such point as the patient is discharged from s117 aftercare.
- Where, at 1 September 2020, a patient was detained in hospital funded by NHS England, the CCG/ICB which will be responsible for funding any further detention in a CCG/ICB-funded hospital setting and any necessary NHS aftercare (including any subsequent further detentions or voluntary admissions, until such point as the patient is discharged from s117 aftercare) will be determined as set out in paragraph 18.3 above – that is, on the basis of the general rules at paragraph 10.2 above, applied at the point of the patient's initial detention in hospital under the Act."

The guidance sets out how responsibility for payment is to be determined in specific scenarios at para.18.10 et seq.

Cross border issues within the UK are dealt with at para.19. Paragraph 19.2 states:

"Specific arrangements have been agreed between NHS England and the Welsh Government relating to responsibilities for commissioning and payment for patients living in defined areas along the England / Wales border. These arrangements apply to Flintshire, Wrexham, Powys, Monmouthshire and Denbighshire in Wales and the areas in England covered by NHS West Cheshire CCG, NHS Shropshire CCG, NHS Gloucestershire CCG, NHS Herefordshire CCG, NHS South Cheshire CCG, NHS Wirral CCG and NHS Telford and Wrekin. They are set out in 'England / Wales Cross Border Healthcare Services: Statement of values and principles'. Commissioners should refer to this for detailed guidance on issues relating to the defined border areas."

Attribution of responsibility to individual Health Boards in Scotland or Local Health Boards in Wales is a matter for the separate guidance published by the Scottish and Welsh Governments: see "Responsible Body Guidance for the NHS in Wales", and "Establishing the Responsible Commissioner: Guidance and Directions for Health Boards" (March 2013).

The functions of an ICB exercisable under this section may, subject to such restrictions and conditions as the ICB considers appropriate, be exercised jointly with a Local Health Board. These functions can be exercised by a joint committee of the ICB and the Local Health Board (SI 2013/261 regs 13, 14, Sch. para.18).

Local Social Services Authority In *R. (on the application of Worcestershire CC) v Secretary of State* **1-1204** *for Health and Social Care* [2023] UKSC 31, a patient was detained in the area of Local Authority A under s.3 and that authority accepted responsibility for providing her with services under s.117 on her discharge. The patient was then placed by Local Authority A in a residential placement in the area of Local Authority B and the period of detention came to an end. Local Authority A did not at any point take a decision under subs.(2) that the patient was no longer in need of after-care services. The patient was subsequently detained under s.3 in the area of Local Authority B. She was eventually discharged from the s.3 and the hospital and she again received services provided under s.117. The question before the court was which of Local Authority A or Local Authority B was responsible for providing the patient with s.117 services after her discharge from her second period of detention. The Supreme Court held that Local Authority A's duty to provide after-care services ended upon the patient's second detention under a qualifying section (paras 44 and 53). The Court said that this interpretation "is grounded in the language and purpose of section 117" (para.45) in that:

(i)   upon a person's second detention, he/she is no longer a person who has "ceased to be detained" (see subs.(1)) but is a person who is detained and is in hospital;

(ii)   it is implicit in the concept of "after-care" that the duty does not apply to people who are currently detained and receiving treatment in hospital; and

(iii)   the purpose of after-care, to reduce the risk of readmission, makes no sense in the context of a person who has already been readmitted to hospital (paras 45–53).

Upon the patient's second discharge a new duty to provide after-care services arose. Which local authority owed that duty depended upon where the patient was "ordinarily resident" immediately before the second detention. The Court held that although the patient lacked the mental capacity to decide where to live, the decision to live in a residential placement in Local Authority B was still made voluntarily as it was the result of a choice made by those with the power to make decisions on her behalf. Further, her residence in the residential placement was also adopted for settled purposes. As the term "ordinarily resident" in this provision should be given its usual meaning, it followed that immediately before the second detention the patient was ordinarily resident in the area of Local Authority B (paras 58 and 71)).

It should be noted that there will be cases in which a patient who has been granted short-term leave of absence from hospital under s.17 does not "cease to be detained" and "leave hospital" within the meaning of s.117(1) and is therefore not eligible for aftercare under this section: see *R. (on the application of CXF) v Central Bedfordshire Council NHS North Norfolk Clinical Commissioning Group*, which is noted under "Cease to be detained and leave hospital" in subs.(1).

The identity of the local authority which arranged for an AMHP to make an application under s.3 in respect of the person has no bearing on the question of which local authority has responsibility to provide services under this section.

Responsibility for assessing a person who is receiving services under this section for a possible readmission under the Act is that of the LSSA for the area where the person currently is, not that of the LSSA with responsibilities under this section if different: see s.13(1).

Ordinarily resident   Originally, the relevant authorities were those for where the person was "resident" before being detained or to where the person was sent on discharge, but by virtue of the amendments made to this section by the Care Act 2014, with effect from April 1, 2015, the authorities are those for where the person was "ordinarily resident" in England or Wales before being detained, and in other cases those for the place where the person was sent on discharge from hospital.

A person's place of ordinary residence is the place where they are in fact ordinarily resident as determined by the common law test rather than the place where they were deemed to be ordinarily resident for the purposes other local authority services provided under the Care Act 2014. Unlike the 1948 Act, this section does not contain a deeming provision. The leading case on the general approach to be taken to the words "ordinarily resident" is *R. v London Borough of Barnet, ex p. Shah* [1983] 2 A.C. 309. *Shah* and subsequent case law is considered in the note on "ordinarily resides" in s.26(4). In *R. (on the application of Worcestershire CC) v Secretary of State for Health and Social Care*, above, the court held that the analysis provided by the Supreme Court in *R. (on the application of Cornwall CC) v Secretary of State for Health* [2015] UKSC 46, which is noted under s.26(4), does not apply to the determination of a person's ordinary residence under this section (para.70).

The significance of s.39(4) of the Care Act 2014 is "in confirming that, unlike the rules in the adult social care legislation and the [Children Act] 1989, the ordinary residence rules in the 2014 Act and section 117 of the 1983 Act are not congruent with each other, so that a specific provision is needed to align them where they interact" (*R. (on the application of Worcestershire CC) v Secretary of State for Health and Social Care*, above, para.86).

For identifying the relevant local authority where prisoners who have previously been detained in hospital under ss.47 and 48 are transferred back to prison, see paras 17.6 and 17.7 of the "Care and Support Statutory Guidance" which are reproduced in the note on "Transfer direction made under section 47 or 48" in subs.(1).

In *R. (on the application of Hertfordshire County Council) v London Borough of Hammersmith and Fulham)* [2011] EWCA Civ 77; [2011] M.H.L.R. 76, it was held that during a period of detention under the Act the person is not "resident" for the purposes of this provision in the hospital in which he is detained. It is submitted that this finding also applies to the "ordinary residence" of the person.

Subsection (4) applies if there is a dispute between local authorities about where the person was ordinarily resident immediately before being detained.

Paragraph (c)

Although it is not possible for a patient to be a "resident" in a hospital during a period of detention **1-1205** (*R. (on the application of Hertfordshire CC) v London Borough of Hammersmith and Fulham*, above), it is possible for a detained patient who has subsequently attained informal status at the hospital to attain resident status. In *R. (on the application of Sunderland City Council) v South Tyneside Council* [2012] EWCA Civ 1232; [2013] 1 All E.R. 394, a case on this section prior to the introduction on an ordinary residence test in paras (a) and (b) by the Care Act 2014, the Court of Appeal held that:

1. The test of residence is not the same as the test of ordinary residence for the purposes of the National Assistance Act 1948 (following the decision in the *Hertfordshire CC* case, above).
2. If, during the course of a period of informal admission in hospital the patient ceased to have any other place of residence available to her on her discharge she was either a resident of the hospital or not resident anywhere.
3. Not being resident anywhere constitutes an ultimate default position, which should not be held to apply except in extreme and clear circumstances.

Subsection (4)

Paragraph (a)   Section 40 of the Care Act 2014 provides that where a dispute about where an adult **1-1206** is ordinarily resident cannot be resolved by local authorities in England, the local authorities involved may request a determination of ordinary residence to be made by the Secretary of State or a person appointed by the Secretary of State. The Care and Support (Disputes Between Local Authorities) Regulations 2014 (SI 2014/2829) set out the procedure to be followed. Section 41 the 2014 Act allows for expenditure borne by a local authority in the provision of services under this section, for a person ordinarily resident in the area of another local authority, to be recoverable from that other authority.

Paragraph (b)   Section 195 of the Social Services and Well-being (Wales) Act 2014, which came into **1-1207** force in April 2016, states that disputes of the nature described in para.(a) that occur between local authorities in Wales are to be determined by the Welsh Ministers or person appointed by the Welsh Ministers.

Paragraph (c)   A dispute that arises under this paragraph will be determined under the arrangements **1-1208** provided for in subs.(5).

Subsection (5)

Disputes between a local authority in England and a local authority in Wales about where a person **1-1209** was ordinarily resident are determined by the Secretary of State for Health or the Welsh Ministers under the following arrangements which were made under this provision and were published by the Department of Health and the Welsh Government in March 2015:

"1.   In these arrangements—

"dispute" means a dispute between at least one local authority in England and at least one local authority in Wales about where a person was ordinarily resident for the purposes of section 117(3) of the 1983 Act;
"the 1983 Act" means the Mental Health Act 1983;
"the lead authority" is the local authority in whose area the person to whom the dispute relates was living immediately before being detained under the 1983 Act.

2.   The Secretary of State will determine the dispute if the lead authority is in England.
3.   The Welsh Ministers will determine the dispute if the lead authority is in Wales.
4.   If there is a dispute as to where the person was living immediately before being detained under the 1983 Act, the Secretary of State and the Welsh Ministers will agree between themselves who will determine the dispute.
5.   The Secretary of State and Welsh Ministers (each referred to in this paragraph as a 'responsible Minister') agree that each will –
   a.   notify the other responsible Minister immediately on being made aware of the dispute;
   b.   agree in accordance with these arrangements which responsible Minister will determine the dispute, as soon as it is known where the person to whom the dispute relates was living immediately before being detained under the 1983 Act;

c. consult the other responsible Minister and take their views into account, prior to determining the dispute; and

d. notify the other responsible Minister of the outcome of the determination, prior to notifying the local authorities which are parties to the dispute.

6. These arrangements have effect from 1 April 2015.

Where the dispute is to be referred to the Secretary of State, local authorities should contact:

Department of Health Quality and Safety Team
Social Care Policy Division
Area 313B Richmond House
79 Whitehall
London
SW1A 2NS

Where the dispute is to be referred to the Welsh Ministers, local authorities should contact:

Mental Health & Vulnerable Groups Division
Health and Social Services Directorate General
Welsh Government
Cathays Park
Cardiff
CF10 3NQ
MentalHealthandVulnerableGroups@Wales.GSI.Gov.UK."

There is no process for determining ordinary residence disputes between English and Northern Irish authorities.

Subsection (6)

1-1210   The definition of after-care services contained in this provision is based on the judgment of Hickinbottom J. in *R. (on the application of Mwanza) v London Borough of Greenwich* [2010] EWHC 1462 (Admin); [2010] M.H.L.R. 226; see especially paras 63 and 67. With regard to after-care planning for children and young people, see para.19.111 of the Code of Practice which is reproduced under *Code of Practice*, above.

An individual who is receiving aftercare under this section is receiving care which is "intrinsically linked to medical treatment he has been receiving for his mental disorder" (*DM v Doncaster Metropolitan Borough Council* [2011] EWHC 3652 (Admin), para.64).

As an after-care service is a service which is aimed at "reducing the risk of the person requiring admission to a hospital again for treatment for mental disorder" (para.(b)), the treatment of a patient who is re-admitted to hospital when subject to this section is not an after-care service.

Although the definition gives a considerable discretion to the after-care bodies as to the nature and extent of the services that can be provided, the bodies "must have regard to other demands" on their budgets (*R. v Camden and Islington Health Authority, Ex p. K* [2001] EWCA Civ 240; [2001] M.H.L.R. 24, para.29).

Speaking for the Government during a debate on the definition, Earl Howe said:

"I reassure the House that the definition we are now considering is the result of extensive consultation. In consequence, we have added a positive objective to prevent deterioration as well as preventing readmission to hospital, and have further changed the clause to remove the definite article when referring to 'the mental disorder', for which the noble Lord made the case in Committee. This is intended to remove any doubt about our intention that the scope of aftercare covers more than just one form of mental disorder, and is not necessarily limited to the specific disorder or disorders for which a person was previously detained under the Act and which gave rise to the right to aftercare" (*Hansard*, HL Vol.748, col.600).

The duty under this section therefore extends to meeting needs arising from a mental disorder other than the one that the patient was suffering from when he was discharged from hospital. For example, if some time after discharge the patient is diagnosed as suffering from dementia, meeting relevant needs that arise from the dementia will come within the scope of this section.

Paragraph 33.4 of the *Code of Practice* states:

"CCGs and local authorities should interpret the definition of after-care services broadly. For example,

[516]

after-care can encompass healthcare, social care and employment services, supported accommodation and services to meet the person's wider social, cultural and spiritual needs, if these services meet a need that arises directly from or is related to the particular patient's mental disorder, and help to reduce the risk of a deterioration in the patient's mental condition."

However, taking a patient on escorted day trips from the hospital where he is detained cannot constitute "after-care services" within the meaning of this section (*R. (on the application of CXF) v Central Bedfordshire Council* [2018] EWCA Civ 2852; [2019] M.H.L.R. 16, para.42).

In *R. (on the application of Afework) v The Mayor and Burgesses of the London Borough of Camden* [2013] EWHC 1637 (Admin); [2014] M.H.L.R. 32, para.14, Mostyn J. said:

"After-care services ... would normally include (1) social work; (2) support in helping the ex-patient with problems of (a) employment, (b) accommodation or (c) family relationships; (3) the provision of domiciliary services; and (4) the use of day centre and residential facilities."

And in *R. v Manchester City Council Ex p. Stennett* [2002] UKHL 34, Lord Steyn said that "psychiatric treatment" (para.7) and "caring residential care" (para.15) would qualify as after-care services. It is submitted that these observations, which were made before the definition was enacted, have continuing relevance. For the provision of medication for the treatment of mental disorder for patients who come within the scope of this section, see the note on "*Charging for services provided under section 117*", above.

With regard to the provision of ordinary accommodation, in *Afework* Mostyn J. said, at para.16, that "basic or pure or ordinary accommodation" does not come within the concept of after-care services. His Lordship held "that as a matter of law s117(2) is only engaged vis-à-vis accommodation if:

i)   The need for accommodation is a direct result of the reason that the ex-patient was detained in the first place ('the original condition');
ii)   The requirement is for enhanced specialised accommodation to meet needs directly arising from the original condition; and
iii)   The ex-patient is being placed in the accommodation on an involuntary (in the sense of being incapacitated) basis arising as a result of the original condition" (para.19).

A local authority has power to provide accommodation to people who suffer from mental ill health under s.18 of the Care Act 2014.

The fact that a person was receiving a service, such as residential care, for his mental health needs prior to the admission to hospital does not mean that that service cannot be an "after-care" service for the purposes of this section. The residential care would have been provided under the Care Act 2014 prior to the admission (apart from self-funders), and under this section on discharge as long as the person still required the accommodation to meet his mental health needs. The person could therefore not be charged for the accommodation on returning to it from hospital even if he was charged for it prior to the admission. This interpretation is supported by the finding of Sullivan J. in the *Stennett* case which is noted under "*Charging for local authority services under section 117*", above.

The search for necessary after-care services should not be confined to those services and facilities provided directly by the health and social services authorities.

A need arising from or related to the person's mental disorder   Determining whether a need is "related to" the person's mental disorder will not always be easy. It is submitted that there must be a clear connection (not necessarily a casual connection) between the person's need and his mental disorder for the need is to come within the definition. A need which is related to the person's general well-being or to a physical disorder that is not related to the person's mental disorder would not be sufficient.

In *Afework*, above, Mostyn J. held that the patient's claim that his need for specialist accommodation came within the scope of this section failed because the need arose from a brain injury which he incurred after his discharge from hospital. This finding is consistent with the definition unless it could be argued that the circumstances that gave rise to the brain injury were directly related to the person's mental disorder.

If a person's need for residential care arises from his physical disability which requires full-time support for his daily living needs, the fact that he continues to suffer from the symptoms of mental disorder does not bring the residential care within the scope of this section: see "*A report by the Health Service Ombudsman and the Local Government Ombudsman about the provision of section 117 aftercare*", HC 642, Oct 2012.

Reducing the risk of a deterioration of the person's mental condition   The nature of the person's mental condition might have changed since his discharge from hospital. Speaking for the Government, Earl Howe said:

> "I reassure the House that the definition we are now considering is the result of extensive consultation. In consequence, we have added a positive objective to prevent deterioration as well as preventing readmission to hospital, and have further changed the clause to remove the definite article when referring to 'the mental disorder', for which the noble Lord made the case in Committee. This is intended to remove any doubt about our intention that the scope of aftercare covers more than just one form of mental disorder, and is not necessarily limited to the specific disorder or disorders for which a person was previously detained under the Act and which gave rise to the right to aftercare" (*Hansard*, HL, Vol.748. col.600)

Admission to a hospital   As either a detained or an informal patient.

[After-care: preference for particular accommodation

1-1211   **117A.**—(1)   The Secretary of State may by regulations provide that where—

    (a)   the local social services authority under section 117 is, in discharging its duty under subsection (2) of that section, providing or arranging for the provision of accommodation for the person concerned;

    (b)   the person concerned expresses a preference for particular accommodation; and.

    (c)   any prescribed conditions are met,

the local social services authority must provide or arrange for the provision of the person's preferred accommodation.

    (2)   Regulations under this section may provide for the person concerned, or a person of a prescribed description, to pay for some or all of the additional cost in prescribed cases.

    (3)   In subsection (2), "additional cost" means the cost of providing or arranging for the provision of the person's preferred accommodation less the amount that the local social services authority would expect to be the usual cost of providing or arranging for the provision of accommodation of that kind.

    (4)   The power to make regulations under this section—

    (a)   is exercisable only in relation to local social services authorities in England;

    (b)   includes power to make different provision for different cases or areas.]

Amendment

This section was inserted by the Care Act 2014 s.75(6).

Definition

1-1212   local social services authority: s.145(1).

General Note

1-1213   This section, which does not apply to local authorities in Wales, empowers the Secretary of State to make regulations to place a duty on a local authority to enable a person who qualifies for specialist accommodation under s.117 to live in accommodation of their choice, provided that conditions specified in the regulations are met. Ordinary accommodation does not come within the scope of s.117: see the *Afework* case noted under s.117(6). If the cost of the preferred accommodation is more expensive than the local authority would normally expect to pay, this will involve the person themselves or another person entering into a written agreement with the authority to pay some or all of the additional cost of the preferred accommodation. These additional payments are sometimes called "top-up payments".

Regulations

Regulations 4 and 5 of the Care and Support and After-care (Choice of Accommodation) Regula- **1-1214**
tions 2014 (SI 2014/2670), which were made under subss.(1), (2) and (4) of this section, state:

"**Application to after-care**

4.— Where—

(a) a local authority is, in discharging its duty under section 117(2) of the 1983 Act, providing or arranging for the provision of accommodation in England for a person;

(b) the person expresses a preference for particular accommodation (identifiable by reference to its address or provider); and

(c) the conditions in paragraph (2) are met,

the local authority must provide or arrange for the provision of the preferred accommodation in accordance with these Regulations.

(2) The following conditions must be met for the provision of preferred accommodation under
paragraph (1)—

(a) the person must be aged 18 or over;

(b) the accommodation which the local authority is providing or arranging must be of a
specified type;

(c) the preferred accommodation must be of the same type that the local authority has
decided to provide or arrange;

(d) the preferred accommodation must be suitable to meet the person's needs;

(e) the preferred accommodation must be available;

(f) where the preferred accommodation is not provided by the local authority, the provider
of the accommodation must agree to provide the accommodation to the person on the
local authority's terms; and

(g) where the cost to the local authority of providing or arranging for the provision of the
preferred accommodation is greater than the amount that the local authority would expect
to be the usual cost of providing or arranging for the provision of accommodation of that
kind, the additional cost conditions in paragraph (3) must also be met.

(3) The additional cost conditions referred to in paragraph (2)(g) are that—

(a) the local authority is satisfied that the person for whom the accommodation is to be
provided or another person ('the payer'), is willing and able to pay the additional cost
of the preferred accommodation for the period during which the local authority expects
to meet needs by providing or arranging for the provision of that accommodation; and

(b) the payer enters into a written agreement with the authority in which the payer agrees
to pay the additional cost.

(4) In a case to which paragraph (3) applies, the local authority must comply with the requirements of regulation 5(2), (3)(a) and (c) to (f), and (4).

(5) For the purposes of this regulation the additional cost that is to be met by the payer may be
less than the full amount of the additional cost referred to in section 117A(3) of the 1983 Act, if the
local authority agrees that a lesser amount should be paid.

(6) The specified types of accommodation are those referred to in regulation 2(2) but for the
purposes of this regulation any reference to 'an adult' in regulations 7 and 8 should be read as a reference to 'a person'.

The additional cost condition

5.—(1) The additional cost condition is met if—

(a) the local authority is satisfied that—

(i) a person other than the adult, or

(ii) in a case to which paragraph (5) applies, the adult, ('the payer') is able and
willing to pay the additional cost of the preferred accommodation for the period
during which the local authority expects to meet the adult's needs by providing or arranging for the provision of that accommodation; and

(b) the payer enters a written agreement with the local authority in which the payer agrees
to pay the additional cost.

(2) The local authority must provide the payer with access to sufficient information and advice
to enable the payer to understand the terms of the proposed written agreement before entering into

it.

(3) The written agreement must include—

    (a) the additional cost;

    (b) the amount specified in the adult's personal budget in relation to the provision of accommodation;

    (c) the frequency of payments;

    (d) details of the person to whom the payments are to be made;

    (e) provision for review of the agreement;

    (f) provisions about the matters specified in paragraph (4).

(4) The specified matters are—

    (a) the consequences of ceasing to make payments;

    (b) the effect of increases in charges made by the provider of the preferred accommodation;

    (c) the effect of changes in the payer's financial circumstances.

(5) The local authority may not agree with the adult for whom the accommodation is to be provided for that adult to pay the additional cost unless—

    (a) paragraph 2 of Schedule 2 to the Care and Support (Charging and Assessment of Resources) Regulations 2014 (the 12 week property disregard) applies to that adult; or

    (b) the adult and the local authority agree to enter into a deferred payment agreement in accordance with the Care and Support (Deferred Payment) Regulations 2014 in respect of the additional cost.

(6) For the purposes of this regulation the additional cost that is to be met by the payer may be less than the full amount of the additional cost referred to in section 30(3) of the Act, if the local authority agrees that a lesser amount should be paid."

Guidance

1-1215 Guidance on the regulations is contained in the following paragraphs of the Department of Health's *"Care and Support Statutory Guidance"*:

"Choice of accommodation and mental health after-care

44. Regulations made under section 117A of the Mental Health Act 1983 enable persons who qualify for after-care under section 117 to express a preference for particular accommodation if accommodation of the types specified in the regulations is to be provided as part of that after-care. Local authorities are required to provide or arrange the provision of the preferred accommodation if the conditions in the regulations are met.

45. The regulations give people who receive mental health after-care broadly the same rights to choice of accommodation as someone who receives care and support under the Care Act 2014. But some differences arise because after-care is provided free of charge and, as the legislative requirement for a care and support plan under the Care Act 2014 does not apply to section 117 after-care, the care plan should instead be drawn up under guidance on the Care Programme Approach (CPA). Care planning under the CPA should, if accommodation is an issue, include identifying the type of accommodation which is suitable for the person's needs and affording them the right to choice of accommodation set out in the regulations made under section 117A. The person should be fully involved in the care planning process.

46. An adult has the right to choose accommodation provided that:

- the preferred accommodation is of the same type that the local authority has decided to provide or arrange
- it is suitable for the person's needs
- it is available (see guidance in paras. 13-16) for mental health after-care purposes ('assessed needs' means needs identified in the CPA care plan)
- where the accommodation is not provided by the local authority, the provider of the accommodation agrees to provide the accommodation to the person on the local authority's terms (see guidance in para. 18)

47. The principles in paras. 5, 6, 7 and 40 apply equally where a local authority is providing, or arranging the provision of, accommodation in discharge of its after-care duty. The guidance in paras. 17 and 18 applies when the preferred choice cannot be met.

48. Where the cost of the person's preferred accommodation is more than the local authority would provide in a personal budget or local mental health after-care limit to meet the person's needs, then the local authority *must* arrange for them to be placed there, provided that either the person or a third party is willing and able to meet the additional cost.

49. The guidance in paras. 20 to 38 applies where the adult has chosen more expensive accommodation. For the purposes of section 117 after-care, however, references to a third party should be read as including the adult receiving the after-care (because an adult can also meet the additional cost when a local authority is providing, or arranging for the provision of accommodation in discharge of the after-care duty).

50. In securing the funds needed to meet the additional cost, one of the following will apply:

- a local authority may agree with the person and the provider, and in cases where a third party is paying the 'top-up', agree with that third party, that payment for the additional cost can be made directly to the provider with the local authority paying the remainder
- the person or the third party pays the 'top-up' amount to the local authority. The local authority then pays the full amount to the provider."

[After-care: exception for provision of nursing care

117B.—(1)   Section 117 does not authorise or require a local social services   **1-1216** authority […] in or in connection with the provision of services under that section, to provide or arrange for the provision of nursing care by a registered nurse.

(2)   In this section "nursing care by a registered nurse" means a service provided by a registered nurse involving—

(a)   the provision of care, or

(b)   the planning, supervision or delegation of the provision of care,

other than a service which, having regard to its nature and the circumstances in which it is provided, does not need to be provided by a registered nurse.]

Amendment

This section was inserted by SI 2015/914, reg.2, Sch. para.28. The amendment to it was made by SI 2016/413 reg.36.

Definition

local social services authority: s.145(1).   **1-1217**

General Note

This section ensures continuation of the current prohibition on the provision of registered nursing   **1-1218** care as defined in subs.(2) by a local social services authority under s.117.

FUNCTIONS OF THE SECRETARY OF STATE

Code of practice

118.—(1)   The Secretary of State shall prepare, and from time to time revise, a   **1-1219** code of practice—

(a)   for the guidance of registered medical practitioners[, approved clinicians], managers and staff of hospitals[, independent hospitals and care homes] and [approved mental health professionals] in relation to the admission of patients to hospitals [and registered establishments] under this Act [and to guardianship and [community patients] under this Act]; and

(b) for the guidance of registered medical practitioners and members of other professions in relation to the medical treatment of patients suffering from mental disorder.

[(1A) The Code which must be prepared, and from time to time revised, in relation to Wales shall also be for the guidance of independent mental health advocates appointed under arrangements made under section 130E below.]

(2) The code shall, in particular, specify forms of medical treatment in addition to any specified by regulations made for the purposes of section 57 above which in the opinion of the Secretary of State give rise to special concern and which should accordingly not be given by a registered medical practitioner unless the patient has consented to the treatment (or to a plan of treatment including that treatment) and a certificate in writing as to the matters mentioned in subsection (2)(a) and (b) of that section has been given by another registered medical practitioner, being a practitioner [appointed for the purposes of this section by the regulatory authority].

[(2A) The code shall include a statement of the principles which the Secretary of State thinks should inform decisions under this Act.

(2B) In preparing the statement of principles the Secretary of State shall, in particular, ensure that each of the following matters is addressed—
    (a) respect for patients' past and present wishes and feelings,
    (b) respect for diversity generally including, in particular, diversity of religion, culture and sexual orientation (within the meaning of section 35 of the Equality Act 2006),
    (c) minimising restrictions on liberty,
    (d) involvement of patients in planning, developing and delivering care and treatment appropriate to them,
    (e) avoidance of unlawful discrimination,
    (f) effectiveness of treatment,
    (g) views of carers and other interested parties,
    (h) patient wellbeing and safety, and
    (i) public safety.

(2C) The Secretary of State shall also have regard to the desirability of ensuring—
    (a) the efficient use of resources, and
    (b) the equitable distribution of services.

(2D) In performing functions under this Act persons mentioned in subsection (1)(a) or (b) [and subsection (1A)] shall have regard to the code.]

(3) Before preparing the code or making any alteration in it the Secretary of State shall consult such bodies as appear to him to be concerned.

(4) The Secretary of State shall lay copies of the code and of any alteration in the code before Parliament; and if either House of Parliament passes a resolution requiring the code or any alteration in it to be withdrawn the Secretary of State shall withdraw the code or alteration and, where he withdraws the code, shall prepare a code in substitution for the one which is withdrawn.

(5) No resolution shall be passed by either House of Parliament under subsection (4) above in respect of a code or alteration after the expiration of the period of 40 days beginning with the day on which a copy of the code or alteration was laid before that House; but for the purposes of this subsection no account shall be taken

of any time during which Parliament is dissolved or prorogued or during which both Houses are adjourned for more than four days.

(6)   The Secretary of State shall publish the code as for the time being in force.

[(7)   The Care Quality Commission may at any time make proposals to the Secretary of State as to the content of the code of practice which the Secretary of State must prepare, and from time to time revise, under this section in relation to England.]

Amendments

The amendments to this section were made by the Mental Health (Patients in the Community) Act 1995 s.2(1), Sch.1 para.16, the Care Standards Act 2000 s.116, Sch.4 para.9(6) and the Mental Health Act 2007 ss.8, 14(2), 21, 32(4), Sch.2 para.9, Sch.3 para.25, the Mental Health (Wales) Measure 2010 s.39 and the Health and Social Care Act 2008 s.52, Sch.3 para.6.

Definitions

approved clinician: s.145(1).   **1-1220**
the managers: s.145(1).
hospital: s.145(1).
registered establishment: ss.34(1), 145(1).
care home: s.145(1).
independent hospital: s.145(1).
approved mental health professional: s.145(1), (1AC).
patient: s.145(1).
community patient: ss.17A(7), 145(1).
medical treatment: s.145(1), (4).
mental disorder: ss.1, 145(1).
the regulatory body: s.145(1).

General Note

This section imposes a duty on the Secretary of State (and, in relation to Wales, the Welsh Ministers) **1-1221** to prepare, publish and from time to time revise, a *Code of Practice* for the guidance of those concerned with the admission, treatment, guardianship and supervised community treatment of mentally disordered patients. The Code can specify forms of treatment which give rise to special concern and which should not be given without the patient's consent and an independent second medical opinion (subs.(2)). The Code states that the Act and Code "support one another and should be read together" (Introduction, XVIII). The Welsh *Code of Practice* must provide guidance to independent mental health advocates appointed under s.130E (subs.(1A)).

Those who are mentioned in subss.(1) and (1A) must "have regard" to the Code (subs. (2D)). Those mentioned do not include integrated care boards, members of the First-tier Tribunal (Mental Health) and members of the Mental Health Review Tribunal for Wales. With regard to the position of integrated care boards, in *R. (on the application of AK) v Islington L.B.C.* [2021] EWHC 301 (Admin), Judge Lickley QC, sitting as a deputy High Court judge, said:

"[W]here two bodies [a local authority and an ICB] are responsible for the welfare of an individual, and in particular in a case of a vulnerable child, and are working together for the purposes of s.117 MHA 83 responsibilities imposed on the relevant local authority in the form of statutory guidance must be the applicable standard. It would make no logical sense to either dilute or reduce the status of the Code or to reduce the overall obligation to apply the guidance in such cases" (para.15).

A failure to have regard to the Code could be used in legal or disciplinary proceedings as prima facie evidence of either bad practice or unlawful behaviour, although the effect of non-compliance will largely depend upon the nature of the provision in the Code that has not been followed.

The following statement is made at para.XXV of the Introduction to the Code:

"Where the principles and guidance of the Code are not implemented, the CQC may use its regulatory powers to facilitate change and improvement in local services as a failure to apply the Act and its Code may show a breach of one of the registration requirements in the Health and Social Care Act 2008, (Regulated Activities) Regulations 2014, or Care Quality Commission (Registration) Regulations (2009)."

The legal status of the Code was considered by the House of Lords in *R. (on the application of Munjaz) v Mersey Care National Health Service Trust* [2005] UKHL 58; [2005] M.H.L.R 276, where it was contended that the policy of Ashworth Hospital relating to the seclusion of patients was unlawful because it provided for less frequent medical reviews, particularly after the first week of seclusion, than that laid down in the Code. Ashworth had also adopted a definition of seclusion that differed from that set out in the 1999 edition of the Code. It was held that:

1. The Code does not have the binding effect which a statutory provision or a statutory instrument would have. It is what it purports to be, guidance and not instruction.
2. The guidance in the Code should be given great weight. Although it is not instruction, the Code is much more than mere advice which an addressee is free to follow or not as it chooses. In other words, it is more than something to which those to whom it is addressed must "have regard to".
3. The Code contains guidance which should be considered with great care, and should be followed unless there are cogent reasons for not doing so. The reason need not be confined to the facts of an individual case; it can relate to a matter of policy. The requirement that cogent reasons must be shown for any departure sets a high standard which is not easily satisfied. With regard to subsection (2) of this section, Lord Bingham said, at para.69, that "any departure would call for even stronger reasons".
4. In reviewing any departures from the Code, the court should scrutinise the reasons given for departure with the intensity which the importance and sensitivity of the subject matters requires.
5. There were cogent reasons for Ashworth's decision not to follow the guidance in the Code, even though there were many eminent professional experts who took a different view. The reasons were:
    (a) The Code was directed at the generality of mental hospitals and did not address the special problems of high security hospitals;
    (b) The Code did not recognise the special position of patients whom it was necessary to seclude for longer than a very few days.
    (c) The statutory scheme, while providing for the Secretary of State to give guidance, deliberately left the power and responsibility of final decision to those who bear the legal and practicable responsibility for detaining, treating, nursing and caring for patients.
6. For the purpose of determining whether Ashworth's policy on seclusion was compatible with the European Convention on Human Rights (ECHR), the Code is irrelevant: if the policy is incompatible, consistency with the Code will not save it; if it is compatible, it requires no support from the Code. The policy on seclusion was compatible with the ECHR because it did not expose patients to a significant risk of treatment prohibited by art.3, did not amount to a separate deprivation of liberty which engages art.5, and any possible breach of art.8(1) was proportionate, in accordance with the law and had a purpose that fell within art.8(2). Lord Bingham said at para.34:

    "The procedure adopted by the Trust does not permit arbitrary or random decision-making. The rules are accessible, foreseeable and predictable. It cannot be said, in my opinion, that they are not in accordance with or prescribed by law."

The patient unsuccessfully claimed before the European Court of Human Rights that art.8 of the ECHR required that the Code should be interpreted as having the force of law which had universal application. The Court, in agreeing with the judgment of the House of Lords that Ashworth was justified in its decision to depart from the Code's guidance, found that there had been no violation of art.8 (*Munjaz v United Kingdom* [2012] M.H.L.R. 351).

It is suggested that the following circumstances could provide cogent reasons for not following the guidance contained in the Code:

1. A determination by the High Court that a particular aspect of the Code is not legally accurate (see, for example, *AR v Bronglais Hospital and Pembrokeshire and Derwen NHS Trust* [2001] EWHC Admin 792; [2001] M.H.L.R. 175, which is noted under s.12(2)).
2. A requirement of the Code has been made redundant by subsequent caselaw or legislation.
3. A statement in the Code being obviously legally incorrect e.g. the 2008 edition of the *Code of Practice for Wales* stating, at para.23.9, that, contrary to the provisions of s.25, the nearest rela-

tive of a guardianship patient has to give 72 hours notice of their intention to discharge the patient.

4. Legal advice being obtained which casts a significant doubt on the legal correctness of an aspect of the guidance.

5. Following the guidance would involve breaching the patient's rights under the ECHR.

6. A judgment is made that a particular aspect of the guidance should not be followed for safety or another cogent reason relating to the care or treatment of patients (see, for example, para.2.20.59 of the *Committee of Inquiry into the Personality Disorder Unit, Ashworth Special Hospital* (1999) where para.26.3 of the 1999 edition of the Code was described as being "untenable" in the context of a high security hospital).

Reasons for departing from the guidance in the Code "must be spelled out clearly, logically and consistently" (*Munjaz*, above, per Lord Hope at para.69).

The question in the *Munjaz* case was what weight a hospital authority should give to the Code when deciding how to exercise a function under the Act. In *R. (on the application of CXF) v Central Bedfordshire Council* [2018] EWCA Civ 2852; [2019] M.H.L.R. 16, at para.23, Leggatt L.J. said that there "is nothing in the judgment of the House of Lords [in *Munjaz*] which suggests that the Code can legitimately be treated as guidance on what the language of the Act itself means". His Lordship said that the position of the Code is analogous "to that of statutory regulations or other delegated legislation made under an Act of Parliament. Such regulations can only be used as an aid to the interpretation of the Act under which they are made if they were contemporaneously prepared, so that the draft regulations formed part of the background against which Parliament was legislating" (para.24).

In *An NHS Trust v Y* [2018] UKSC 46 at para.97, Lady Black held that a Code of Practice cannot create legal obligations.

In *R. v Secretary of State for Health Ex p. Pfizer Ltd* (1999) 2 C.C.L. Rep. 270, Collins J. held that Government guidance which is expressed in unqualified and mandatory language and which appeared to override the clinical judgment which a doctor was entitled to exercise in an individual case, was unlawful.

The Code can be accessed at: *www.mhlo.uk/k*. A separate Code of Practice for Wales was published in 2016. It can also be accessed at *www.mhlo.uk/k*.

Residual deprivation of liberty

In the *Munjaz* case, above, Lord Bingham said: **1-1222**

"In any event, the Ashworth policy, properly applied as one must assume, does not permit a [detained] patient to be deprived of any residual liberty to which he is properly entitled: seclusion must be for as short a period and in conditions as benign as will afford reasonable protection to others who have a right to be protected" (para.30).

Lord Bingham's judgment proceeded on the basis that if a person is detained by a state body in circumstances that satisfy the requirements of art.5 of the ECHR, he nonetheless retains a measure of "residual liberty" and that if that residual liberty was taken away the person would suffer a deprivation of liberty that would have to be justified. In *Norfolk and Suffolk NHS Foundation Trust v HJ* [2023] EWFC 92, David Lock KC, sitting as a Deputy High Court Judge, said, at para.27, that Lord Bingham's reasoning "was consistent with the ECtHR case of *Bollan v United Kingdom*, App No. 42117/98. In that case the ECtHR considered the case of a prisoner who complained that she was unlawfully deprived of her liberty by being secluded in her cell for two hours. The ECtHR (albeit in an admissibility decision) said 'The court does not exclude that measures adopted within a prison may disclose interferences with the right to liberty in exceptional circumstances'. However, the ECtHR also said in that case that 'modifications of the conditions of lawful detention ... fall outside the scope of Article 5 § 1 of the Convention'. Hence, it was a question of fact and degree as to whether a change in detention conditions which further curtailed a detained person's liberty amounted to a further deprivation of liberty. The question of justification or otherwise of that further deprivation of liberty would only arise if the line was crossed so that a further deprivation of liberty was established."

Mr Lock identified, at para.32, the following principles from the cases that had been cited to him that apply to an "assessment as to whether medical treatment provided to someone in lawful detention amounts to a further deprivation of their liberty:

(a) the starting point should be that it will only be in exceptional cases ... where something that happens to a person who has already been lawfully deprived of their liberty will amount to a further deprivation of that person's residual liberty;

(b) Article 5 will only arise in an exceptional case because the usual position is that '*Article 5(1)(e) is not in principle concerned with suitable treatment or conditions'* [*Ashingdane v United Kingdom* (1985) 7 EHRR 528]; and

(c)   the acid test for the engagement of article 5 in any case involving an alleged deprivation of residual liberty is whether there is an unacceptable element of arbitrariness in the actions which are taken by a state body and which are said to deprive a person of their residual liberty...."

The reasons why the ECtHR in the *Munjaz* case held that a secluded detained patient had not been the subject of a further deprivation of liberty are summarised in the note of "detention" under art.5(1)(e) in Part 5.

Reference Guide to the Act

1-1223   The following statement is set out in the Introduction to the Code:

"XVII The Reference Guide to the Mental Health Act 1983 is intended as a source of reference for people who want to understand the main provisions of the Mental Health Act 1983 and regulations under the Act, as amended at 1 April 2015, including by the Mental Health Act 2007, Health and Social Care Acts 2008 and 2012 and Care Act 2014.

XVIII Guidance on the way the Act should be applied in practice is given in this Code. The two documents support one another and should be read together, as well as with other material available to assist people to understand their duties, rights and responsibilities under the Act.

XIX The Reference Guide is not a definitive statement of the law. It is not a substitute for consulting the Act itself or for taking legal advice."

Although the Introduction states that the two documents should be "read together", the Reference Guide does not have the same legal status as the Code because it was not published under this section and was therefore not laid before Parliament.

The Reference Guide can be accessed at: *https://assets.publishing.service.gov.uk/government/uploads/ system/uploads/attachment_data/file/417412/Reference_Guide.pdf*.

Subsection (1)

1-1224   **Paragraph (a):**   Admission of patients to hospitals. This term is not limited to the actual admission process; it covers what happens to the patient after he has been detained (*R. v Mersey Care National Health Service Trust Ex p. Munjaz*, above, para.19).

Paragraph (b)   This provision is not limited to the hospital care of patients; it also covers patients cared for in the community. In *C v A local Authority* [2011] EWHC 1539 (Admin) the Code was held to apply in a residential special school which used seclusion.

The term "medical treatment", as defined in s.145(1), is wide enough to cover nursing and caring for a patient in seclusion, even though seclusion cannot properly form part of a treatment programme (*Munjaz*, above, para.19).

Subsection (2)

1-1225   **Specify forms of medical treatment**   The Code has not added to the forms of treatment covered by s.57.

Subsections (2A) to (2C)

1-1226   During the Parliamentary passage of the 2007 Act, the Minister of State said that "the question of how the Government should express principles to inform practitioners making decisions under the Act as amended by the Bill has dominated our discussions and caused a great deal of interest" (*Hansard*, HL Vol.690, col.118). A considerable amount of Parliamentary time was spent debating whether the principles should be contained in the Act or, as the Government preferred, in the Code of Practice. A compromise was eventually reached by the Government proposing an amendment which is given legislative effect in these provisions. The purpose of the amendment was described by the Minister of State:

"Our amendment places in statute a new requirement that the Secretary of State and Welsh Ministers include a statement of principles in the respective codes of practice for England and Wales, which should inform decision-making under the 1983 Act. The amendment legally obliges the Secretary of State and the Welsh Ministers to address certain fundamental issues in preparing this statement of principles" (*Hansard*, HL Vol.690, col.119).

Subsection (2A)

The five overarching principles are set out in Ch.1 of the Code. They are: 1-1227

"Least restrictive option and maximising independence
Where it is possible to treat a patient safely and lawfully without detaining them under the Act, the patient should not be detained. Wherever possible a patient's independence should be encouraged and supported with a focus on promoting recovery wherever possible.

Empowerment and involvement
Patients should be fully involved in decisions about care, support and treatment. The views of families, carers and others, if appropriate, should be fully considered when taking decisions. Where decisions are taken which are contradictory to views expressed, professionals should explain the reasons for this.

Respect and dignity
Patients, their families and carers should be treated with respect and dignity and listened to by professionals.

Purpose and effectiveness
Decisions about care and treatment should be appropriate to the patient, with clear therapeutic aims, promote recovery and should be performed to current national guidelines and/or current, available best practice guidelines.

Efficiency and equity
Providers, commissioners and other relevant organisations should work together to ensure that the quality of commissioning and provision of mental healthcare services are of high quality and are given equal priority to physical health and social care services. All relevant services should work together to facilitate timely, safe and supportive discharge from detention."

Guidance on these principles can be found in paras 1.2 to 1.24 of the Code. In *Secretary of State for Justice v MM* [2018] UKSC 60; [2018] M.H.L.R. 392 at para.24, Lady Hale said that it is "difficult to extract the principle of the 'least restrictive alternative' from the case law under article 5 [of the ECHR]".
Paragraph 1.23 of the Code states that all "five sets of principles are of equal importance, and should inform any decision made under the Act. The weight given to each principle in reaching a particular decision will need to be balanced in different ways according to the circumstances and nature of each particular decision".
Whether the requirement for the principles to "inform decisions" differs from the general duty of practitioners to "have regard" to the Code (subs.(2D)) is not clear.

Subsection (2C)

In her response to concern that had been expressed about this provision, the Minister of State said: 1-1228

"I can also reassure hon. Members that there is nothing sinister about the wording of proposed subsection (2C). [It] was drafted to include the fundamental matters considered most important in England and Wales. The Welsh national service framework for mental health has four underpinning principles: the so-called four Es of equality, equity, efficiency and effectiveness. When drafting the clause, we wanted to ensure that the Welsh principles were incorporated, given that the legislation covers England and Wales" (Public Bill Committee, col.208).

Subsection (2D)

The purpose of this provision is to give legislative effect to the decision of the House of Lords in *R.*   1-1229
(on the application of Munjaz) v Mersey Care NHS Trust (*Hansard*, HL Vol.690, col.118: also see the Explanatory Notes to the 2007 Act, para.45). The *Munjaz* case is considered above.

Practitioners approved for Part IV and section 118

119.—(1)   [The regulatory authority] may make such provision as [it] may with   1-1230
the approval of the Treasury determine for the payment of remuneration, allow-

ances, pensions or gratuities to or in respect of registered medical practitioners appointed [by the authority] for the purposes of Part IV of this Act and section 118 above and to or in respect of other persons appointed for the purposes of section 57(2)(a) above.

(2)   A registered medical practitioner or other person appointed [...] for the purposes of the provisions mentioned in subsection (1) above may, for the purpose of exercising his functions under those provisions [or under Part 4A of this Act], at any reasonable time—

    (a)   visit and interview and, in the case of a registered medical practitioner, examine in private any patient detained [in a hospital or registered establishment or any community patient in a hospital or [regulated establishment (other than a hospital)] or (if access is granted) other place]; and

    (b)   require the production of and inspect any records relating to the treatment of the patient [there].

  [(3)   In this section, "regulated establishment" means—

    (a)   an establishment in respect of which a person is registered under Part 2 of the Care Standards Act 2000; [...]

    (b)   premises used for the carrying on of a regulated activity, within the meaning of Part 1 of the Health and Social Care Act 2008, in respect of which a person is registered under Chapter 2 of that Part [; or

    (c)   premises at which—

        (i)   a care home service,

        (ii)   a secure accommodation service, or

        (iii)   a residential family centre service, within the meaning of the Regulation and Inspection of Social Care (Wales) Act 2016 (anaw 2) is provided by a person registered under Part 1 of that Act].]

Amendments

The amendments to this section were made by the Mental Health Act 2007 s.35(2), the Health and Social Care Act 2008 ss.52, 166, Sch.3 para.7, Sch.15 Pt.1, SI 2010/813 art.5(4) and SI 2018/195 reg.4.

Definitions

1-1231
    the regulatory authority: s.145(1).
    patient: s.145(1).
    residential establishment: ss.34(1), 145(1).
    community patient: ss.17A(7), 145(1).
    hospital: s.145(1).

General Note

1-1232
    This section provides for the payment of medical practitioners appointed by the Care Quality Commission or, in relation to Wales, the Welsh Ministers to carry out certain functions under the Act, and for them to have access to detained and community patients and their records.

Subsection (2)

1-1233
    Anyone who obstructs a person in the exercise of his functions under this section commits an offence under s.129.

Examine   Given the decision of the Divisional Court in *Devon Partnership NHS Trust v Secretary of State for Health and Social Care* [2021] EWHC 101 (Admin) (noted under s.11(5)), it is likely that a court would find that the physical presence of the examining doctor is required and that examining the patient cannot be undertaken by the use of remote technology.

[General protection of relevant patients

120.—(1)   The regulatory authority must keep under review and, where appropriate, investigate the exercise of the powers and the discharge of the duties conferred or imposed by this Act so far as relating to the detention of patients or their reception into guardianship or to relevant patients.

(2)   Relevant patients are—
 (a)   patients liable to be detained under this Act,
 (b)   community patients, and
 (c)   patients subject to guardianship.

(3)   The regulatory authority must make arrangements for persons authorised by it to visit and interview relevant patients in private—
 (a)   in the case of relevant patients detained under this Act, in the place where they are detained, and
 (b)   in the case of other relevant patients, in hospitals and regulated establishments and, if access is granted, other places.

(4)   The regulatory authority must also make arrangements for persons authorised by it to investigate any complaint as to the exercise of the powers or the discharge of the duties conferred or imposed by this Act in respect of a patient who is or has been detained under this Act or who is or has been a relevant patient.

(5)   The arrangements made under subsection (4)—
 (a)   may exclude matters from investigation in specified circumstances, and
 (b)   do not require any person exercising functions under the arrangements to undertake or continue with any investigation where the person does not consider it appropriate to do so.

(6)   Where any such complaint as is mentioned in subsection (4) is made by a Member of Parliament or a member of the National Assembly for Wales, the results of the investigation must be reported to the Member of Parliament or member of the Assembly.

(7)   For the purposes of a review or investigation under subsection (1) or the exercise of functions under arrangements made under this section, a person authorised by the regulatory authority may at any reasonable time—
 (a)   visit and interview in private any patient in a hospital or regulated establishment,
 (b)   if the authorised person is a registered medical practitioner or approved clinician, examine the patient in private there, and
 (c)   require the production of and inspect any records relating to the detention or treatment of any person who is or has been detained under this Act or who is or has been a community patient or a patient subject to guardianship.

(8)   The regulatory authority may make provision for the payment of remuneration, allowances, pensions or gratuities to or in respect of persons exercising functions in relation to any review or investigation for which it is responsible under subsection (1) or functions under arrangements made by it under this section.

(9)   In this section "regulated establishment" means—
 (a)   an establishment in respect of which a person is registered under Part 2 of the Care Standards Act 2000, […]
 (b)   premises used for the carrying on of a regulated activity (within the

1-1234

meaning of Part 1 of the Health and Social Care Act 2008) in respect of which a person is registered under Chapter 2 of that Part [, or

(c) premises at which—

(i) a care home service,

(ii) a secure accommodation service, or

(iii) [a residential family centre service, within the meaning of the Regulation and Inspection of Social Care (Wales) Act 2016 is provided by a person registered under Part 1 of that Act.]

Amendment

This section was substituted by the Health and Social Care Act 2008 s.52, Sch.3 para.8. The amendments to subs.(9) were made by SI 2018/195 reg.5.

Definitions

1-1235   the regulatory authority: s.145(1).
patients: s.145(1)
relevant patients: subs.(2).
community patient: ss.17A(1), 145(1).
hospital: s.145(1).
regulated establishment: subs.(9).
approved clinician: s.145(1).

General Note

1-1236   This section places a duty on the regulatory authority (i.e. the Care Quality Commission (CQC) or, in relation to Wales, the Welsh Ministers (s.145(1)) to review and, where appropriate, investigate the exercise of powers and the discharge of duties in relation to detention, supervised community treatment and guardianship under the Act. For the purposes of such reviews and investigations, the regulatory body can authorise persons to visit and examine patients in hospitals, and to inspect relevant records (subs.(7)). There is no right to enter private premises. For the duty to provide the regulatory body with relevant information, see s.120C. Reports of reviews and investigations may be published (s.120A). Under subs.(3), the regulatory body must make arrangements for authorised persons to visit and interview "relevant patients" as defined in subs.(2). The regulatory body must also make arrangements for authorised persons to investigate complaints concerning the exercise of powers under the Act in respect of detained or relevant patients. Such an investigation need not be either instigated or continued if this is considered not to be appropriate (subss. (4),(5)). It is an offence under s.129 to obstruct a person carrying out functions under this section.

Although the CQC does not have the power to investigate the deaths of detained patients, reg.17 of the Care Quality Commission (Registration) Regulations 2009 (SI 2009/3112) requires the registered person to notify the CQC without delay of the death of a service user who is liable to be detained under the Act (for Wales, see SI 2011/734 (W.112) reg.30). While not included in the regulations, the CQC also asks providers to provide information about the deaths of patients subject to community treatment orders (CQC, "*Monitoring the Mental Health Act in 2014/15*", p.24). Regulation 17 also requires the notification of the unauthorised absence (and return) of a service user who is liable to be detained in an English NHS establishment providing secure psychiatric services. A person who is "liable to be detained" includes a community patient who has been recalled to hospital in accordance with s.17E, but does not include a patient who has been conditionally discharged and not recalled to hospital (para.(3)(a)). Notification forms for both purposes may be downloaded from the Commission's website (*www.cqc.org.uk*).

One curious aspect of the duty imposed by this section is that the regulatory authority, as the sole provider of the second opinion appointed doctor service which operates in Pts IV and IVA, is required to review its own service provision.

The Optional Protocol to the United Nations Convention Against Torture, which the UK ratified in December 2003, requires states to establish a "national preventative mechanism" (NPM) to carry out a system of regular visits to places of detention in order to prevent torture and other cruel, inhuman or degrading treatment or punishment. The Government has designated a number of bodies to form the United Kingdom NPM, including the CQC and the Healthcare Inspectorate of Wales (*Hansard*, March

31, 2009, col.55WS). The website of the UK's NPM is: *www.nationalpreventivemechanism.org.uk/*. The UK's NPM has published *"Guidance: Isolation in detention"* (2017).

Subsection (1)

Regulatory authority   The functions of the Welsh Ministers under this section are exercised by the   **1-1237**
Health Inspectorate Wales (HIW).

Persons authorised by the CQC may include members or employees of the Commission (Health and Social Care Act 2008 s.52(2)). When performing its functions, the Commission must have regard to:

"the need to protect and promote the rights of people who use health and social care services (including, in particular, the rights of children, of persons detained under the Mental Health Act 1983, of persons who are deprived of their liberty in accordance with the Mental Capacity Act 2005, and of other vulnerable adults)" (2008 Act, s.4(1)(d)).

The contact details of the Commission and HIW for issues relating to the Mental Health Act are:

CQC Mental Health Act
Citygate
Gallowgate
Newcastle
NE1 4PA
tel no: 03000 616161

Healthcare Inspectorate Wales
Rhydycar Business Park,
Merthyr Tydfil
CF48 1UZ
tel no: 0300 062 8163

Subsection (4)

A complaint under this provision can be made by anyone, including patients, carers, staff or a member   **1-1238**
of the public.

Exercise of the powers or the discharge of the duties   In *R. v Mental Health Act Commission Ex p. Smith* (1998) 43 B.M.L.R. 174, complaints were made to the CQC's predecessor, the Mental Health Act Commission (MHAC), regarding a hospital patient who had committed suicide during a period when he was subject to detention under s.3 of the Act. There were four essential complaints:

(i)   it was said that the patient's original detention was neither appropriate nor legal;
(ii)   it was said that he was inappropriately detained in a secure unit for a period;
(iii)   it was alleged that the patient was given drugs in such quantities that it was unlikely that he could have given consent, and the level of dosage was inappropriate; and
(iv)   it was said that the patient was inadequately cared for during his detention, and his condition was not adequately assessed for the purposes of determining whether there was any risk of self harm.

The MHAC had always been prepared to accept jurisdiction to entertain complaint (i), was persuaded that it had jurisdiction to accept complaint (iii), but only to a limited extent, but considered that it did not have jurisdiction to entertain complaints (ii) and (iv). On a judicial review of the MHAC's decision, Latham J. held that it is too restrictive to construe this provision as referring only to the express powers and duties set down in the Act. Rights and duties which flow necessarily and by necessary implication from the patient's detention also come within its scope. It followed that any complaints arising out of the exercise of the power to detain, manage and control, and the duty to treat detained patients could be investigated by the MHAC. Accordingly, the MHAC had jurisdiction to consider complaints (ii) and (iv), and had an unrestricted jurisdiction to consider complaint (iii).

Subsection (7)

1-1239   It is submitted that the exercise of the power granted by para.(c) is not limited to authorised persons who are either registered medical practitioners or approved clinicians.

[Investigation reports

1-1240   **120A.**—(1)   The regulatory authority may publish a report of a review or investigation carried out by it under section 120(1).

(2)   The Secretary of State may by regulations make provision as to the procedure to be followed in respect of the making of representations to the Care Quality Commission before the publication of a report by the Commission under subsection (1).

(3)   The Secretary of State must consult the Care Quality Commission before making any such regulations.

(4)   The Welsh Ministers may by regulations make provision as to the procedure to be followed in respect of the making of representations to them before the publication of a report by them under subsection (1).]

Amendment

This section was inserted by the Health and Social Care Act 2008 s.52, Sch.3 para.9.

Definition

1-1241   the regulatory authority: s.145(1).

General Note

1-1242   Under s.84 of the Health and Social Care Act 2008, the Care Quality Commission must make copies of any reports published under the Act available for inspection at its offices by any person at any reasonable time and any person who requests a copy of the report is entitled to have one on payment of such reasonable fee (if any) as the Commission considers appropriate.

Subsection (2)

1-1243   No regulations have been made under this provision.

[Action statements

1-1244   **120B.**—(1)   The regulatory authority may direct a person mentioned in subsection (2) to publish a statement as to the action the person proposes to take as a result of a review or investigation under section 120(1).

(2)   The persons are—
(a)   the managers of a hospital within the meaning of Part 2 of this Act;
(b)   a local social services authority;
(c)   persons of any other description prescribed in regulations.

(3)   Regulations may make further provision about the content and publication of statements under this section.

(4)   "Regulations" means regulations made—
(a)   by the Secretary of State, in relation to England;
(b)   by the Welsh Ministers, in relation to Wales.]

Amendment

This section was inserted by the Health and Social Care Act 2008 s.52, Sch.3 para.9.

Definitions

the regulatory authority: s.145(1).
the managers: s.145(1).
hospital: s.145(1).
local social services authority: s.145(1).

General Note

This section enables the regulatory authority to require hospital managers, social services depart- **1-1246** ments and people to be prescribed in regulations to publish a statement of the action they propose to take in response to any recommendations following a review or investigation undertaken under s.120(1). Paragraph 223 of the Explanatory Notes on the Health and Social Care Act 2008 states:

"[It] is not only hospital managers and social services authorities and their staff who exercise relevant functions under the Mental Health Act and contribute to its operation. There may, therefore, be circumstances in which reviews or investigations make recommendations that are addressed (in whole or in part) to other people. In these cases, it would make sense for the people concerned to be asked directly to publish a report of the action they propose to take as a result. This might include, for example, other NHS bodies that are responsible for providing or commissioning services for patients subject to the Mental Health Act."

[Provision of information

120C.—(1) This section applies to the following persons— **1-1247**
  (a) the managers of a hospital within the meaning of Part 2 of this Act;
  (b) a local social services authority;
  (c) persons of any other description prescribed in regulations.

(2) A person to whom this section applies must provide the regulatory authority with such information as the authority may reasonably request for or in connection with the exercise of its functions under section 120.

(3) A person to whom this section applies must provide a person authorised under section 120 with such information as the person so authorised may reasonably request for or in connection with the exercise of functions under arrangements made under that section.

(4) This section is in addition to the requirements of section 120(7)(c).

(5) "Information" includes documents and records.

(6) "Regulations" means regulations made—
  (a) by the Secretary of State, in relation to England;
  (b) by the Welsh Ministers, in relation to Wales.]

Amendment

This section was inserted by the Health and Social Care Act 2008 s.52, Sch.3 para.9.

Definitions

the managers: s.145(1).
hospital: s.145(1).
local social services authority: s.145(1).
the regulatory authority: s.145(1).
information: subs.(5).

General Note

1-1249   This section obliges hospital managers, local social services authorities and prescribed people to provide the regulatory authority with information, including records and documents, that the authority may require in relation to its functions under s.120.

Paragraph 224 of the Explanatory Notes on the Health and Social Care Act 2008 states that examples "of the kind of information which might be requested are:

- statistical information on people subject to the formal powers under the Mental Health Act, including data relating to particular groups of patients such as children, adolescents, women, and black and ethnic minority patients;
- information on the use of particular powers, such as the granting of leave of absence;
- the number of deaths and other serious incidents;
- information on the use of seclusion in respect of patients."

[Annual reports

1-1250   **120D.**—(1)   The regulatory authority must publish an annual report on its activities in the exercise of its functions under this Act.

(2)   The report must be published as soon as possible after the end of each financial year.

(3)   The Care Quality Commission must send a copy of its annual report to the Secretary of State who must lay the copy before Parliament.

(4)   The Welsh Ministers must lay a copy of their annual report before the National Assembly for Wales.

(5)   In this section "financial year" means—

　　(a)   the period beginning with the date on which section 52 of the Health and Social Care Act 2008 comes into force and ending with the next 31 March following that date, and

　　(b)   each successive period of 12 months ending with 31 March.]

Amendment

This section was inserted by the Health and Social Care Act 2008 s.52, Sch.3 para.9.

Definitions

1-1251   the regulatory authority: s.145(1).
financial year: subs.(5).

General Note

1-1252   Both the Care Quality Commission and the Health Inspectorate Wales have taken a relaxed attitude to the meaning of the phrase "as soon as possible" in subs.(2): see p.69 of the December 2014 issue of "Keeping up to date", MHA and MCA Law Ltd.

Mental Health Act Commission

1-1253   **121.**   [*Repealed by the Health and Social Care Act 2008 s.166, Sch.15 Pt 1.*]

Provision of pocket money for in-patients in hospital

1-1254   **122.**—(1)   The [Welsh Ministers may (in relation to Wales)] pay to persons who are receiving treatment as in-patients (whether liable to be detained or not) in [...] hospitals wholly or mainly used for the treatment of persons suffering from mental disorder, such amounts as [the Welsh Ministers think fit] in respect of [those persons] occasional personal expenses where it appears to [the Welsh Ministers] that [those persons] would otherwise be without resources to meet those expenses.

(2)   For the purposes of the [...] the National Health Service (Wales) Act 2006], the making of payments under this section to persons for whom hospital services are provided under [that Act] shall be treated as included among those services.

Amendments

The amendments to this section were made by the Health Act 1999 s.65, Sch.5, the National Health Service (Consequential Provisions) Act 2006 s.2, Sch.1 para.67 and the Health and Social Care Act 2012 s.41.

Definitions

patient: s.145(1).   **1-1255**
hospital: s.145(1).
mental disorder: ss.1, 145(1).

General Note

By virtue of s.41 of the Health and Social Care Act 2012, this section only applies to Wales. The ef-   **1-1256**
fect of s.41 is explained at paras 452 to 454 of the Explanatory Memorandum to the 2012 Act:

"This section abolishes the power of the Secretary of State in section 122 of the 1983 Act to make payments to in-patients in mental health hospitals in respect of their occasional personal expenses, where they cannot meet those expenses themselves. In England, this power was previously delegated to PCTs by means of regulations. It is primarily used to provide small personal allowances for patients who have been transferred from prison to hospital under section 47 of the 1983 Act and who are therefore not eligible for social security benefits.
      CCGs [now ICBs] and the NHS Commissioning Board [now NHS England] would still be able to arrange for such payments to be made to NHS patients under the NHS Act. And the Secretary of State would be able to make regulations requiring such payments to be made, using the power to make 'standing rules' introduced in section 20.
      The section also removes this power entirely in Scotland (where it has no practical significance). This change does not affect the powers of the Scottish Ministers to make pocket-money payments under Scottish mental health legislation. This section does not affect the position in Wales, where the Secretary of State's powers are exercisable by the Welsh Ministers. Indeed, it amends section 122 to confer the power directly on the Welsh Ministers."

In *R. (on the application of Mitocariu) v Central and North West London NHS Foundation Trust* [2018] EWHC 126 (Admin); [2018] M.H.L.R 89 David Casement QC(sitting as a Deputy High Court Judge) was required to consider the powers or duties of NHS Foundation Trusts in circumstances where the patient receiving mental health care is or appears to be unable, for whatever reason, to fund occasional expenses. The Judge's conclusions are set out at para.40 of his judgment:

"The power exists under the [National Health Service Act 2006] to make what have been described as 'pocket money payments' to in-patients but that power only arises and can only be exercised for and in connection with functions identified under section 43 of the 2006 Act. The discretion of a foundation trust to make payments is limited to that which is commensurate with the therapeutic treatment being provided. There is no entitlement to payment neither is there a duty to make payment. The power that is held by the foundation trust is one which must take into account all the circumstances of the individual case including financial needs and the nature of the therapeutic treatment being provided."

The Judge also said that "a standardised approach involving making regular payments irrespective of and unrelated to the therapeutic needs of the patient would be outside of the powers granted to a foundation trust" (para.34).

Transfers to and from special hospitals

123.   [*Repealed by the Health and Social Care Act 2012 s.42(1).*]   **1-1257**

General Note

1-1258 The repeal of this section does not affect the validity of the detention of anyone who had been transferred under it prior to its repeal, nor prevent the recapture of anyone who escaped from custody while being transferred under it: see s.42(5) of the 2012 Act.

Default powers of Secretary of State

1-1259 **124.** *[Repealed by the National Health Service and Community Care Act 1990 s.66(2), Sch.10.]*

Inquiries

1-1260 **125.** *[Repealed by the Inquiries Act 2005 s.49, Sch.3.]*

PART IX OFFENCES

General Note

1-1261 Part I of the Sexual Offences Act 2003 creates a number of offences "against persons with a mental disorder impeding choice". They are:

- Sexual activity with a person with a mental disorder impeding choice (s.30).
- Causing or inciting a person, with a mental disorder impeding choice, to engage in sexual activity (s.31).
- Engaging in sexual activity in the presence of a person with a mental disorder impeding choice (s.32).
- Causing a person, with a mental disorder impeding choice, to watch a sexual act
- (s.33).
- Inducement, threat or deception to procure sexual activity with a person with a mental disorder (s.34).
- Causing a person with a mental disorder to engage in or agree to engage in sexual activity by inducement, threat or deception (s.35).
- Engaging in sexual activity in the presence, procured for inducement, threat or deception, of a person with a mental disorder (s.36).
- Causing a person with a mental disorder to watch a sexual act by inducement, threat or deception (s.37).

The 2003 Act also introduces a number of specific offences which relate to care workers. They elevate the position of trust and responsibility enjoyed by a care worker from a simple aggravating feature of an offence to an offence in its own right. The definition of care worker in s.42 is extremely broad and includes informal carers who provide services to the mentally disordered. The offences are:

- Care workers: sexual activity with a person with a mental disorder (s.38).
- Care workers: causing or inciting sexual activity (s.39).
- Care workers: sexual activity in the presence of a person with a mental disorder
- (s.40).
- Care workers: causing a person with a mental disorder to watch a sexual act (s.41).

"Guidance on Part I of the Sexual Offences Act 2003", which considers the offences set out above, is attached to Home Office Circular 21/2004.

Forgery, false statements, etc

1-1262 **126.**—(1) Any person who without lawful authority or excuse has in his custody or under his control any document to which this subsection applies, which is, and which he knows or believes to be, false within the meaning of Part I of the Forgery and Counterfeiting Act 1981, shall be guilty of an offence.

(2) Any person who without lawful authority or excuse makes or has in his custody or under his control, any document so closely resembling a document to which subsection (1) above applies as to be calculated to deceive shall be guilty of an offence.

(3)   The documents to which subsection (1) above applies are any documents purporting to be—
- (a)   an application under Part II of this Act;
- (b)   a medical [or other] recommendation or report under this Act; and
- (c)   any other document required or authorised to be made for any of the purposes of this Act.

(4)   Any person who—
- (a)   wilfully makes a false entry or statement in any application, recommendation, report, record or other document required or authorised to be made for any of the purposes of this Act; or
- (b)   with intent to deceive, makes use of any such entry or statement which he knows to be false,

shall be guilty of an offence.

(5)   Any person guilty of an offence under this section shall be liable—
- (a)   on summary conviction, to imprisonment for a term not exceeding six months or to a fine not exceeding the statutory maximum, or to both;
- (b)   on conviction on indictment, to imprisonment for a term not exceeding two years or to a fine of any amount, or to both.

Amendment

In subs.(3)(b) the words in square brackets were inserted by the Mental Health (Patients in the Community) Act 1995 s.2(1), Sch.1 para.17.

General Note

Under this section, it is an offence either to forge or make false statements in applications, recommendations or other documents made under the Act. Proceedings can be instituted by a local social services authority (s.130).   **1-1263**

Subsection (1)

Any person   Or corporation (Interpretation Act s.5, Sch.1).   **1-1264**

False   This term is defined for the purposes of the Forgery and Counterfeiting Act 1981 in s.9 of that Act. An entry or statement may be false on account of what it omits, even though the statement or entry itself is literally true (*R. v Lord Kylsant* [1932] 1 K.B. 442).

Subsection (2)

To deceive   "To deceive is … to induce a man to believe a thing to be true which is false, and which   **1-1265** the person practising the deceit knows or believes to be false", per Buckley J. in *Re London and Globe Finance Corporation Ltd* [1903] 1 Ch. 728 at 732. In *Weltham v DPP* [1961] A.C. 103 Lord Radcliffe extended the scope of Buckley J.'s obiter remarks to include the inducing of a man to believe a thing to be false which is true.

Ill-treatment of patients

127.—(1)   It shall be an offence for any person who is an officer on the staff   **1-1266** of or otherwise employed in, or who is one of the managers of, a hospital [, independent hospital or care home]—
- (a)   to ill-treat or wilfully to neglect a patient for the time being receiving treatment for mental disorder as an in-patient in that hospital or home; or
- (b)   to ill-treat or wilfully to neglect, on the premises of which the hospital or home forms part, a patient for the time being receiving such treatment there as an out-patient.

(2)　It shall be an offence for any individual to ill-treat or wilfully to neglect a mentally disordered patient who is for the time being subject to his guardianship under this Act or otherwise in his custody or care (whether by virtue of any legal or moral obligation or otherwise).

[...]

(3)　Any person guilty of an offence under this section shall be liable—

    (a)　on summary conviction, to imprisonment for a term not exceeding six months or to a fine not exceeding the statutory maximum, or to both;

    (b)　on conviction on indictment, to imprisonment for a term not exceeding [five years] or to a fine of any amount, or to both.

(4)　No proceedings shall be instituted for an offence under this section except by or with the consent of the Director of Public Prosecutions.

Amendment

The amendments to this section were made by the Care Standards Act 2000 s.116, Sch.4 para.9(8) and the Mental Health Act 2007 ss.42, 55, Sch.11 Pt 5.

Definitions

1-1267   the managers: s.145(1).
hospital: s.145(1).
independent hospital: s.145(1).
care home: ss.34(1), 145(1).
patient: s.145(1).
mental disorder: ss.1, 145(1).
mentally disordered: s.1(2).

General Note

1-1268   This section, which fortifies the common law duty of care owed by those who have custody of or treat or look after patients (*R. v Mersey Care National Health Service Trust Ex p. Munjaz* [2005] UKHL 58; [2006] 4 All E.R. 736 para.4), creates two separate offences. Under subs.(1) it is an offence for an employee or a manager of a hospital or care home to ill-treat or wilfully to neglect an in-patient or out-patient of that hospital or home. Under subs.(2) it is an offence for a guardian or some other person who has the custody or care of a mentally disordered person who is living in the community to ill-treat or wilfully to neglect that person. It is an essential pre-requisite for each offence that the victim is a mentally disordered person within the meaning of s.1 at the time when the offence is committed. An offence under this section is a "specified violent offence" for the purposes of s.306 of the Sentencing Act 2020.

In *R. v Newington* (1990) 91 Cr. App. R. 247, the Court of Appeal said that "ill-treatment" could not be equated with "wilfully to neglect". The court therefore advised the Crown Prosecution Service that, when proceedings were brought under this section, charges of "ill-treatment" and of "wilfully to neglect" should be put in separate counts in the indictment.

Proceedings under this section can either be instituted by the Director of Public Prosecutions, or by a local social services authority with the Director's consent (s.130 and subs.(4)). As s.139 does not apply to proceedings brought under this section (s.139(3)), prosecutions may be commenced without proof of bad faith or lack of reasonable care.

Under s.44 of the Mental Capacity Act 2005, it is an offence for either a lay or professional carer, a donee of a lasting power of attorney (or of an enduring power of attorney) or a deputy appointed by the Court of Protection to ill-treat or wilfully neglect a person who lacks, or is believed to lack, mental capacity.

Criminal Justice and Courts Act 2015

1-1269   Section 20 of the 2015 Act makes it an offence for an individual who has the care of another individual by virtue of being a care worker to ill-treat or wilfully neglect that individual. Paragraph 60 of Ministry of Justice Circular No.2015/01 states:

"Prior to the introduction of [this offence], prosecutions for a statutory offence of ill-treatment or wilful neglect can only occur in respect of persons receiving treatment for mental disorder, persons who lack mental capacity or, in certain circumstances, children."

A care worker is defined as an individual who is paid specifically to provide health care for adults or, with certain exceptions, children, or to provide adult social care. "Care worker" also includes an individual who is paid specifically to supervise or manage individuals providing such care, and a director or equivalent of an organisation providing such care. The Explanatory Notes to the Act state that the "intention is to ensure that the individual offence can apply to any individual perpetrator, not just those on the 'front line' of care provision. However, it will only apply where the individual supervisor, director, etc has themselves directly committed ill-treatment or wilful neglect. They will not commit the individual offence by virtue of the acts or omissions of others they supervise or manage".

Section 21 of the 2015 Act creates a separate offence relating to care providers. A care provider commits an offence if:

- an individual employed or otherwise engaged by the care provider ill-treats or wilfully neglects someone to whom they are providing health care or adult social care and to whom the care provider owes a relevant duty of care; and
- the way in which the care provider manages or organises its activities amounts to a gross breach of that duty of care; and
- if that breach had not occurred, the ill-treatment or wilful neglect would not have happened, or would have been less likely to happen.

Subsection (1)

Officer on the staff of the hospital "Officer" is not defined. The term could include a person who is **1-1270** neither a nurse nor a doctor.

Care home Registration of such a home by the regulatory authority is not the test of whether an establishment is a care home. The fact of being a care home triggers the obligation to register, not the reverse: see *R. v Davies and Poolton* [2000] Crim.L.R. 297, where the Court of Appeal held that it was not a requirement of an offence under this section that the accused should be aware that the establishment where she worked was a mental nursing home (now an independent hospital or a care home) and that the victim of ill-treatment or wilful neglect was receiving treatment for mental disorder. The relevant mens rea is found in the element of ill-treatment or wilful neglect that is the gist of the offence.

Ill-treat It is not necessary to establish a course of conduct as a single act, such as slapping the patient's face on one occasion, could constitute ill-treatment under this section (*R. v Holmes* [1979] Crim.L.R. 52, Bodmin Crown Court).

In *R. v Newington*, above, the Court of Appeal held that for there to be a conviction of ill-treatment under this section (the case in question was brought under subs.(2)), the Crown would have to prove: (1) deliberate conduct by the accused which could properly be described as ill-treatment irrespective of whether it damaged or threatened to damage the victim's health; (2) a guilty mind involving either an appreciation by the accused that she was inexcusably ill-treating a patient, or that she was reckless as to whether she was inexcusably acting in that way; and (3) that the victim was a mentally disordered person within the meaning of s.1. The court disapproved of a direction given by the trial judge "that violence would inevitably amount to ill-treatment" on the ground that violence necessarily used for the reasonable control of a patient would not amount to ill-treatment. As the court found that for the offence to have been committed there is no need for the prosecution to show that the treatment caused actual injury to the victim, it is clear that "ill-treatment" encompasses a wide range of conduct. M. J. Gunn has stated that the decision in *R. v Newington* suggests that an offence of ill-treatment "might deal with matters such as inadequate feeding, heating, etc., or the use of harsh words and gratuitous bullying as well as what would be ordinarily understood to be ill-treatment" (Journal of Forensic Psychiatry (1990) 1(3), at p.361; also see Gunn's commentary on this case at [1990] Crim. L.R. 595-597).

Wilfully The leading case on this term is *R. v Sheppard* [1981] A.C. 394 HL, a case brought under s.1(1) of the Children and Young Persons Act 1933 where it was held that the primary meaning of "wilful" is "deliberate", but it may also include recklessness. Lord Keith said at 418:

"It is used here to describe the mental element, which, in addition to the fact of neglect, must be proved ... The primary meaning of 'wilful' is 'deliberate'. So a parent who knows that his child needs medical care and deliberately, that is by conscious decision, refrains from calling a doctor, is guilty under the subsection. As a matter of general principle, recklessness is to be equiparated with deliberation. A parent who fails to provide medical care which his child needs because he does not care whether it is needed or not is reckless of his child's welfare. He too is guilty of an offence. But a parent who has genuinely failed to appreciate that his child needs medical care, through personal inadequacy or stupidity or both, is not guilty."

A direction of the kind suggested by Lord Keith's reasoning, suitably tailored to the facts of the case, should be given by the trail judge hearing a case under this section: see *R. v Morrell* [2002] EWCA Crim 2547, where Poole J. said at para.45:

"We do recognise the force of Crown counsel's argument that in the [appellant's] case, that of an experienced professional, unlike the feckless parent being considered by Lord Keith, questions of inadequacy or stupidity scarcely arose. Nonetheless there is or can be room for genuine mistake, even in an experienced practitioner, and we are quite satisfied that a suitably tailored direction should have been given".

In *R. v Salisu* [2009] EWCA Crim 2702; [2010] M.H.L.R. 58, a case involving appeals against convictions under this section, Hughes L.J. said that in *R. v G* [2003] UKHL 50; [2003] 4 All E.R. 765, the House of Lords had "made clear that recklessness involves subjective fault and actual foresight of risk" (para.11).

In *De Maroussem v Commissioner of Income Tax* [2004] UKPC 43 at para.41, the Privy Council held that the meaning to be attributed to the expression "wilful neglect" may vary according to the context but generally the expression should be taken to mean that there has been an intentional or purposive omission to do something that the person in question knows he or she has a duty to do.

Neglect   In the context of a verdict of neglect made at a Coroner's inquest, Sir Thomas Bingham MR said that neglect

"means a gross failure to provide adequate nourishment or liquid, or provide or procure basic medical attention or shelter or warmth for someone in a dependent position (because of youth, age, illness or incarceration) who cannot provide it for himself. Failure to provide medical attention for a dependent person whose physical condition is such as to show that he obviously needs it may amount to neglect. So it may be if it is the dependent person's mental condition which obviously calls for medical attention (as it would, for example, if a mental nurse observed that a patient had a propensity to swallow razor blades and failed to report this propensity to a doctor, in a case where the patient had no intention to cause himself injury but did thereafter swallow razor blades with fatal results). In both cases the crucial consideration will be what the dependent person's condition, whether physical or mental, appeared to be" (*R. v Humberside and Scunthorpe Coroner Ex p. Jamieson* [1994] 3 All E.R. 972 at 990, 991).

Patient   There is no requirement under this subsection for the victim to have been detained. The ill-treatment or wilful neglect of an in-patient need not have taken place on the hospital premises.

Subsection (2)

1-1271   **Mentally disordered patient**   Is a person who is either suffering or appearing to be suffering from mental disorder (*R. v Newington*, above). There is no need for the victim to be receiving treatment for mental disorder, to have had a history of in-patient treatment in a hospital, or to have been a detained patient or a detained patient on leave of absence from a hospital. At the time of the offence the victim could, for example, be living in his own home, with relatives or friends, or in a care home.

Otherwise in his custody or care   The custodians or carers could include social workers, care workers, teachers, relatives or friends. It is submitted that the use of the term "moral obligation" extends the scope of this section to include a family member, friend or volunteer who is caring for the mentally disordered person.

Assisting patients to absent themselves without leave, etc

1-1272   **128.**—(1)   Where any person induces or knowingly assists another person who is liable to be detained in a hospital within the meaning of Part II of this Act or is subject to guardianship under this Act [or is a community patient] to absent himself without leave he shall be guilty of an offence.

(2)   Where any person induces or knowingly assists another person who is in legal custody by virtue of section 137 below to escape from such custody he shall be guilty of an offence.

(3)   Where any person knowingly harbours a patient who is absent without leave or is otherwise at large and liable to be retaken under this Act or gives him any assistance with intent to prevent, hinder or interfere with his being taken into custody or returned to the hospital or other place where he ought to be he shall be guilty of an offence.

(4)   Any person guilty of an offence under this section shall be liable—
  (a)   on summary conviction, to imprisonment for a term not exceeding six months or to a fine not exceeding the statutory maximum, or to both;
  (b)   on conviction on indictment, to imprisonment for a term not exceeding two years or to a fine of any amount, or to both.

Amendment

In subs.(1) the words in square brackets were inserted by the Mental Health Act 2007 s.32(4), Sch.3 para.28.

Definitions

absent without leave: ss.18(6), 145(1).   **1-1273**
patient: s.145(1).
community patient: ss.17A(7), 145(1).
hospital: ss.34(2), 145(1).

General Note

Under this section, which applies to patients who are detained under both Parts 2 and 3 of the Act,   **1-1274**
to patients under guardianship, and to community patients, it is an offence to induce or to help a patient escape from custody or to absent himself from hospital or place where he is required to be without leave, or to harbour or prevent the recapture or return of such patients. The patient does not commit an offence by absenting himself without leave. Proceedings under this section can be instituted by local social services authorities (s.130).

Subsection (1)

Knowingly   The use of this term emphasises the requirement of mens rea (*R. v Dunne* (1998) 162 J.P.   **1-1275**
399 CA).

Subsection (3)

Other place where he ought to be   Such as a specified place of residence under guardianship or a   **1-1276**
community treatment order.

Obstruction

129.—(1)   Any person who without reasonable cause—   **1-1277**
  (a)   refuses to allow the inspection of any premises; or
  (b)   refuses to allow the visiting, interviewing or examination of any person by a person authorised in that behalf by or under this Act [or to give access to any person to a person so authorised]; or
  (c)   refuses to produce for the inspection of any person so authorised any document or record the production of which is duly required by him; or
  [(ca) fails to comply with a request under section 120C; or]

(d)   otherwise obstructs any such person in the exercise of his functions, shall be guilty of an offence.

(2)   Without prejudice to the generality of subsection (1) above, any person who insists on being present when required to withdraw by a person authorised by or under this Act to interview or examine a person in private shall be guilty of an offence.

(3)   Any person guilty of an offence under this section shall be liable on summary conviction to imprisonment for a term not exceeding three months or to a fine not exceeding level 4 on the standard scale or to both.

Amendments

The amendments to this section were made by the Mental Health (Patients in the Community) Act 1995 s.2(1), Sch.1 para.19 and the Health and Social Care Act 2008 s.52, Sch.3 para.10.

General Note

1-1278   This section specifies when a person commits the offence of obstruction under the Act. Proceedings can be instituted by a local social services authority (s.130).

A person who is suspected of committing an offence under this section could be arrested. This would enable the police to use reasonable force to prevent a continuation of the offence.

The Committee of Inquiry into Complaints about Ashworth Hospital stated that they were "inclined to the view that the right of silence is abrogated by [this section] which makes it an offence for anyone, without reasonable excuse, to obstruct an authorised investigation" (Cm. 2028, Vol.1, Ch. XIII, p.126). This opinion runs counter to the decision of the Divisional Court in *Rice v Connolly*, below.

Subsection (1)

1-1279   **Any person**   Or corporation (Interpretation Act 1978 s.5, Sch.1).

Obstructs   Cases on the offence of obstructing a policeman in the execution of his duty suggest that an offence under this section: (1) need not involve physical violence (*Hinchcliffe v Sheldon* [1955] 1 W.L.R. 1207); (2) is not committed on a mere refusal to answer questions or otherwise assist with enquiries (*Rice v Connolly* [1966] 2 Q.B. 414) or on advising a person not to answer questions (*Green v DPP* [1991] Crim. L.R. 782 DC); (3) will be committed if a person exercising powers under the Act approaches a person who she is entitled to approach and that person runs away (*Sekfali v DPP* [2006] EWHC 894 (Admin)); and (4) might be committed if a verbal warning of an impending inspection was given (*Green v Moore* [1982] 2 W.L.R. 671). There is also authority to support the contention that an offence is committed if the defendant's conduct makes it more difficult for an authorised person to carry out his duties: see the dictum of Lord Goddard C.J. in *Hinchcliffe v Sheldon*, above, at 1210 which was followed by the Divisional Court in *Lewis v Cox* [1984] 3 W.L.R. 875. In *Barge v British Gas Corporation* (1982) 81 L.G.R. 53, a case heard under the Trade Descriptions Act 1968, it was held that a refusal to co-operate will be an offence only in relation to a valid requirement which the enforcement officer is entitled to make.

During the Parliamentary passage of the 2007 Act, a Government Minister said that behaviour intended to stop a professional from making an independent decision that they are required to make under the Act could constitute the offence of obstruction (*Hansard*, HL Vol.688, col.749).

Subsection (2)

1-1280   **In private**   Although an approved mental health professional (AMHP) is required to interview a patient "in a suitable manner" before making an application under Pt II (s.13(2)), there is no express provision authorising the interview to be in private. A person who disrupts an AMHP's interview with a patient would be guilty of an offence under subs.(1)(d).

Prosecutions by local authorities

1-1281   **130.**   A local social services authority may institute proceedings for any offence under this Part of this Act, but without prejudice to any provision of this Part of this Act requiring the consent of the Director of Public Prosecutions for the institution of such proceedings.

Definition

local social services authority: s.145(1).   **1-1282**

General Note

This section empowers a local social services authority to institute proceedings for an offence al-   **1-1283**
leged to have been committed under this Part.

Local authority staff who are charged with the duty of investigating offences under this Part must have regard to relevant provisions of the Codes of Practice issued under the Police and Criminal Evidence Act 1984 (s.67(9)). In particular, the following caution must be administered to a suspect before any questions about the offence are put to him or her: "You do not have to say anything. But it may harm your defence if you do not mention when questioned something which you later rely on in court. Anything you do say may be given in evidence" (*Code of Practice C* (2019 revision), para.10.5).

Consent of the director of public prosecutions

Is required by s.127.

PART X MISCELLANEOUS AND SUPPLEMENTARY

MISCELLANEOUS PROVISIONS

[Independent mental health advocates]

130A.—(1)   [A local social services authority whose area is in England] shall   **1-1284**
make such arrangements as it considers reasonable to enable persons ("independent mental health advocates") to be available to help qualifying patients [for whom the authority is responsible for the purposes of this section].

(2)   The appropriate national authority may by regulations make provision as to the appointment of persons as independent mental health advocates.

(3)   The regulations may, in particular, provide—

   (a)   that a person may act as an independent mental health advocate only in such circumstances, or only subject to such conditions, as may be specified in the regulations;

   (b)   for the appointment of a person as an independent mental health advocate to be subject to approval in accordance with the regulations.

(4)   In making arrangements under this section, [a local social services authority] shall have regard to the principle that any help available to a patient under the arrangements should, so far as practicable, be provided by a person who is independent of any person who is professionally concerned with the patient's medical treatment.

(5)   For the purposes of subsection (4) above, a person is not to be regarded as professionally concerned with a patient's medical treatment merely because he is representing him in accordance with arrangements—

   (a)   under section 35 of the Mental Capacity Act 2005; or

   (b)   of a description specified in regulations under this section.

(6)   Arrangements under this section may include provision for payments to be made to, or in relation to, persons carrying out functions in accordance with the arrangements.

(7)   Regulations under this section—

(a) may make different provision for different cases;

(b) may make provision which applies subject to specified exceptions;

(c) may include transitional, consequential, incidental or supplemental provision.

Amendments

This section was inserted by the Mental Health Act 2007 s.30(2). The amendments to it were made by the Health and Social Care Act 2012 s.43.

Wales

This section has been amended in respect of Wales by the Mental Health (Wales) Measure 2010 s.53(1), Sch.1.

Definitions

1-1285 medical treatment: s.145(1), (4).
patient: s.145(1).
qualifying patient: s.130C(1)–(4).

Coronavirus Pandemic

1-1286 The NHS Guidance considers access to Independent Mental Health Advocates during the pandemic at p.44.

General Note

1-1287 This section places a duty on local authorities in England to make arrangements for independent mental health advocates (IMHAs) to be available to help "qualifying patients" who are defined in s.130C(2), (3) and (4). The mechanism for identifying which local authority is responsible for a qualifying patient is contained in s.130C(4A), (4B). In making arrangements under this section local authorities must have regard to the principle that any help provided under the arrangements to a qualifying patient should, as far as practicable, be provided by a person who is independent of anyone who is professionally concerned with the patient's treatment (subs.(4)). The IMHA must help the patient to obtain information about and to understand the matters set out in s.130B(1) and (2). The powers available to the IMHA are identified in s.130B(3), (4) and (7). A "responsible person", as defined in s.130D(2), has a duty to provide a qualifying patient with oral and written information about the IMHA service (s.130D(1), (4)). A qualifying patient can decline the services of an IMHA (s.130B(6)). Much of the detail of the IMHA scheme is set out in the Mental Health Act 1983 (Independent Mental Health Advocates) (England) Regulations 2008 (SI 2008/3166) which are made under subs.(2) and reproduced in Part 2 (for Wales, see SI 2008/2437 (W.210)).

Paragraph 4.11 of the Reference Guide states:

"The help which independent mental health advocacy services must provide also includes helping patients to exercise their rights, which can include representing them and speaking on their behalf. Independent mental health advocacy services are not designed to take the place of advice from, or representation by, qualified legal professionals."

Also see para.6.13 of the *Code of Practice* which states:

"The Act enables IMHAs to help patients to exercise their rights, which can include representing them and speaking on their behalf, eg by accompanying them to review meetings or hospital managers' hearings. IMHAs support patients in a range of other ways to ensure they can participate in the decisions that are made about their care and treatment, including by helping them to make applications to the Tribunal."

Although, as Fennell states, there is no specific provision in the Tribunal Rules which entitles IMHAs to attend tribunal hearings, the tribunal is unlikely to refuse permission given that r.2(2)(c) of the Rules requires the tribunal to ensure ", so far as practicable, that the parties are able to fully participate in the proceedings" (Phil Fennell, *Mental Health: Law and Practice* (2011) para.5.22). The IMHA can act as the patient's representative at hearings if this is the patient's wish. See further r.11(1) (for representing the patient) and (5) (for attending the hearing) of the Tribunal Rules and the General Note to the Rules under the heading "Independent Mental Advocacy Advocates". Also see para.2.2 of the Law Society Practice Note which is reproduced at Appendix D.

A concern about a perceived low take up rate by patients of the services of IMHAs has led Mental Health Reviewers of the CQC to advise that hospitals should either routinely provide the IMHA service with a list of all current detained patients or operate an "opt-out" system in that unless a patient states that he does not wish to be provided with the services of an IMHA, all detained patients should be referred to the service. Neither option is lawful as hospitals do not possess the statutory power to provide such lists or to make such referrals. In any event, the operation of such a system would involve a breach of patient confidentiality. For this reason, it is submitted that the following guidance set out at para.6.16 of the *Code of Practice* should not be followed: "If a patient lacks capacity to decide whether or not to obtain help from an IMHA, the hospital manager should ask an IMHA to attend the patient so that the IMHA can explain what they can offer to the patient directly": also see the extracts from the Code of Practice, below. The Health Committee of the House of Commons recommended that the IMHA service becomes an opt-out rather than an opt-in service (*Post-legislative scrutiny of the Mental Health Act 2007* (July 2013) para.45).

Hospital managers cannot withhold correspondence between patients and their IMHAs (s.134(3)(eb), (3A)).

Patients who lack the capacity to instruct an IMHA

A patient who lacks the capacity to decline the assistance of an IMHA (see s.130B(6)) is a qualify- **1-1288** ing patient for the purposes of s.130C. Paragraph 5.3 of "Independent Mental Health Advocacy-Guidance for Commissioners", NIMH for England, December 2008, which is headed "Instructed and non-instructed advocacy", offers the following guidance on patients who lack the capacity to instruct an advocate:

"Wherever possible IMHAs will take instruction from the person they are supporting. An IMHA may support a person to obtain information, explore options and carry out actions, but throughout this process the IMHA will be directed by the person and act only on their behalf. IMHAs may also provide non-instructed advocacy when helping patients who are unable to express their wishes clearly, or at all, because they lack the mental capacity to instruct or have difficulties communicating. When providing non-instructed advocacy, the IMHA will represent the patient's wishes (as far as those wishes are known) and ensure the patient's rights are respected. Where a patient qualifies for both an IMHA and an Independent Mental Capacity Advocate (IMCA), the IMCA will represent the patient in line with the IMCA's statutory role. An example is a qualifying patient who lacks capacity and it is being considered for cancer treatment: in this case, the IMCA would represent the patient in the decision making process for this treatment."

Code of Practice

Guidance on IMHAs is contained in Ch.6. Paragraph 6.3 of the Code states that "IMHAs should be **1-1289** independent of any person who has been professionally involved in the patient's medical treatment". Professionals "should remember that the normal rules on patient confidentiality apply to conversations with IMHAs, even when the conversation is at the patient's request. IMHAs have a right of access to patients' records in certain cases [see s.130B(4)], but otherwise professionals should be careful not to share confidential information with IMHAs, unless the patient has consented to the disclosure or the disclosure is justified on the normal grounds" (Code, para.6.29). With regard to patients seeking help from an IMHA, the Code states:

"6.21 A qualifying patient may request the support of an IMHA at any time after they become a qualifying patient. Patients have the right to access the independent mental health advocacy service itself, rather than the services of a particular IMHA, though where possible it would normally be good practice for the same IMHA to remain involved while the person remains subject to the Act.

6.22 IMHAs must also comply with any reasonable request to visit and interview a qualifying patient, if the request is made by the patient's nearest relative, an approved mental health professional (AMHP) or the patient's responsible clinician (if they have one).

6.23 AMHPs and responsible clinicians should consider requesting an IMHA to visit a qualifying patient if they think that the patient might benefit from an IMHA's visit but is unable, or unlikely, for whatever reason to request an IMHA's help themselves. If a patient lacks capacity to decide whether to seek help from an IMHA, an IMHA should be introduced to the patient.

6.24 Before requesting an IMHA to visit a patient, they should, wherever practicable, first discuss the idea with the patient, and give the patient the opportunity to decide for themselves whether to request an IMHA's help. AMHPs and responsible clinicians should not request an IMHA to visit where they know, or strongly suspect, that the patient does not want an IMHA's help, or the help of the particular IMHA in question.

6.25 Patients may refuse to be interviewed and do not have to accept help from an IMHA if they do not want it. Equally, a patient may choose to end the support they are receiving from an IMHA at any time."

Subsection (1)

1-1290 **Local social services authority**   See s.130(4A), (4B).

Subsection (2)

1-1291 **Appropriate national authority**   See s.130C(5), (6).

Subsection (4)

1-1292 **Professionally concerned**   See subs.(5).

Subsection (5)

1-1293 **Section 35 of the Mental Capacity Act 2005**   Which provides for the appointment of independent mental capacity act advocates.

Specified in regulations   See reg.7 of the Mental Health Act 1983 (Independent Mental Health Advocates) (England) Regulations 2008 (SI 2008/3166).
[

Arrangements under section 130A

1-1294   **130B.**—(1)   The help available to a qualifying patient under arrangements under section 130A above shall include help in obtaining information about and understanding—

(a)   the provisions of this Act by virtue of which he is a qualifying patient;

(b)   any conditions or restrictions to which he is subject by virtue of this Act;

(c)   what (if any) medical treatment is given to him or is proposed or discussed in his case;

(d)   why it is given, proposed or discussed;

(e)   the authority under which it is, or would be, given; and

(f)   the requirements of this Act which apply, or would apply, in connection with the giving of the treatment to him.

(2)   The help available under the arrangements to a qualifying patient shall also include—

(a)   help in obtaining information about and understanding any rights which may be exercised under this Act by or in relation to him; and

(b)   help (by way of representation or otherwise) in exercising those rights.

(3)   For the purpose of providing help to a patient in accordance with the arrangements, an independent mental health advocate may—

(a)   visit and interview the patient in private;

(b)   visit and interview any person who is professionally concerned with his medical treatment;

(c)   require the production of and inspect any records relating to his detention or treatment in any hospital or registered establishment or to any after-care services provided for him under section 117 above;

    (d)   require the production of and inspect any records of, or held by, a local social services authority which relate to him.

(4)   But an independent mental health advocate is not entitled to the production of, or to inspect, records in reliance on subsection (3)(c) or (d) above unless—

    (a)   in a case where the patient has capacity or is competent to consent, he does consent; or

    (b)   in any other case, the production or inspection would not conflict with a decision made by a donee or deputy or the Court of Protection and the person holding the records, having regard to such matters as may be prescribed in regulations under section 130A above, considers that—

        (i)   the records may be relevant to the help to be provided by the advocate; and

        (ii)   the production or inspection is appropriate.

(5)   For the purpose of providing help to a patient in accordance with the arrangements, an independent mental health advocate shall comply with any reasonable request made to him by any of the following for him to visit and interview the patient—

    (a)   the person (if any) appearing to the advocate to be the patient's nearest relative;

    (b)   the responsible clinician for the purposes of this Act;

    (c)   an approved mental health professional.

(6)   But nothing in this Act prevents the patient from declining to be provided with help under the arrangements.

(7)   In subsection (4) above—

    (a)   the reference to a patient who has capacity is to be read in accordance with the Mental Capacity Act 2005;

    (b)   the reference to a donee is to a donee of a lasting power of attorney (within the meaning of section 9 of that Act) created by the patient, where the donee is acting within the scope of his authority and in accordance with that Act;

    (c)   the reference to a deputy is to a deputy appointed for the patient by the Court of Protection under section 16 of that Act, where the deputy is acting within the scope of his authority and in accordance with that Act.]

Amendment

This section was inserted by the Mental Capacity Act 2007 s.30(2).

Definitions

medical treatment: s.145(1), (4).   **1-1295**
hospital: s.145(1).
registered establishment: s.145(1).
local social services authority: s.145(1).
nearest relative: s.145(1).
responsible clinician. ss.34(1), 145(1).
approved mental health professional: s.145(1), (1C).

General Note

1-1296   This section identifies the help that an IMHA who is acting under s.130A should provide to the patient (subss.(1), (2)) and the powers of the IMHA (subss.(3), (4), (7)). It also requires the IMHA to comply with the reasonable requests of specified persons to visit and interview the patient (subs.(5)) and provides the patient with the power to decline the assistance of an IMHA (subs.(6)).

Subsections (1),(2)

1-1297   Note that the IMHA is not entitled to adopt either a befriending or campaigning role.

Subsection (2)(b)

1-1298   Help under this provision could include providing assistance to the patient in bringing legal proceedings relating to his detention. The IMHA has no independent right to take such action.

Subsection (3)

1-1299   The normal rules of confidentiality apply to conversations between professionals and IMHAs: see para.6.29 of the *Code of Practice*.

Paragraph (d)

1-1300   Anyone who refuses, without reasonable cause, to produce records that an IMHA has a right to inspect may be guilty of the offence of obstruction under s.129.

Subsection (4)

1-1301   An IMHA's access to patients' records is considered in the following paragraphs of the *Code of Practice*:

> "6.30 Where the patient consents, IMHAs have a right to see any clinical or other records relating to the patient's detention or treatment in any hospital, or relating to any after-care services provided to the patient. An IMHA has a similar right to see any records relating to the patient held by a local authority.
> 6.31 Where the patient does not have the capacity (or in the case of a child, the competence) to consent to an IMHA having access to their records, the holder of the records must allow the IMHA access if they think that it is appropriate and that the records in question are relevant to the help to be provided by the IMHA.
> 6.32 When an IMHA seeks access to the records of a patient who does not have the capacity or the competence to consent, the person who holds the records should ask the IMHA to explain what information they think is relevant to the help they are providing to the patient and why they think it is appropriate for them to be able to see that information.
> 6.33 The Act does not define any further what it means by access being appropriate, so the record holder needs to consider all the facts of the case. But the starting point should always be what is in the patient's best interests and not (for example) what would be most convenient for the organisation which holds the records.
> 6.34 In deciding whether it is appropriate to allow the IMHA access, the holder of the records needs to consider whether disclosure of the confidential patient information contained in the records is justified.
> 6.35 The key consideration will therefore be whether the disclosure is in the patient's best interests. That decision should be taken in accordance with the Mental Capacity Act 2005 (MCA) (or, for children under 16, the common law).
> 6.36 Record holders should start from a general presumption that it is likely to be in the patient's interests to be represented by an IMHA who is knowledgeable about their case. But each decision must still be taken on its merits, and the record holder must, in particular, take into account what they know about the patient's wishes and feelings, including any written statements made in advance. (For further information on taking decisions in the best interests of people who lack capacity to make the decision themselves, please see the Code of Practice to the MCA.)
> 6.37 Records must not be disclosed if that would conflict with a decision made on the patient's behalf by the patient's attorney or deputy, or by the Court of Protection.

6.38 If the record holder thinks that disclosing the confidential patient information in the records to the IMHA would be in the patient's best interests, it is likely to be appropriate to allow the IMHA access to those records in all but the most exceptional cases."

Paragraph (b)

Capacity; donee; deputy   See subs.(7).   **1-1302**

Person holding the record   It is for this person, and not the IMHA, to determine whether to record is "relevant" and its production or inspection is "appropriate".

Subsection (7)

Capacity   Is to be determined by using the tests set out in ss.2 and 3 of the 2005 Act.   **1-1303**

[

Section 130A: supplemental

130C.—(1)   This section applies for the purposes of section 130A above.   **1-1304**

(2)   A patient is a qualifying patient if he is—
    (a)   liable to be detained under this Act (otherwise than by virtue of section 4 or 5(2) or (4) above or section 135 or 136 below);
    (b)   subject to guardianship under this Act; or
    (c)   a community patient.

(3)   A patient is also a qualifying patient if—
    (a)   not being a qualifying patient falling within subsection (2) above, he discusses with a registered medical practitioner or approved clinician the possibility of being given a form of treatment to which section 57 above applies; or
    (b)   not having attained the age of 18 years and not being a qualifying patient falling within subsection (2) above, he discusses with a registered medical practitioner or approved clinician the possibility of being given a form of treatment to which section 58A above applies.

(4)   Where a patient who is a qualifying patient falling within subsection (3) above is informed that the treatment concerned is proposed in his case, he remains a qualifying patient falling within that subsection until—
    (a)   the proposal is withdrawn; or
    (b)   the treatment is completed or discontinued.

[(4A)   A local social services authority is responsible for a qualifying patient if—
    (a)   in the case of a qualifying patient falling within subsection (2)(a) above, the hospital or registered establishment in which he is liable to be detained is situated in that authority's area;
    (b)   in the case of a qualifying patient falling within subsection (2)(b) above, that authority is the responsible local social services authority within the meaning of section 34(3) above;
    (c)   in the case of a qualifying patient falling within subsection (2)(c), the responsible hospital is situated in that authority's area;
    (d)   in the case of a qualifying patient falling within subsection (3)—
        (i)   in a case where the patient has capacity or is competent to do so, he nominates that authority as responsible for him for the purposes of section 130A above, or
        (ii)   in any other case, a donee or deputy or the Court of Protection,

or a person engaged in caring for the patient or interested in his welfare, nominates that authority on his behalf as responsible for him for the purposes of that section.

(4B)   In subsection (4A)(d) above—

    (a)   the reference to a patient who has capacity is to be read in accordance with the Mental Capacity Act 2005;

    (b)   the reference to a donee is to a donee of a lasting power of attorney (within the meaning of section 9 of that Act) created by the patient, where the donee is acting within the scope of his authority and in accordance with that Act;

    (c)   the reference to a deputy is to a deputy appointed for the patient by the Court of Protection under section 16 of that Act, where the deputy is acting within the scope of his authority and in accordance with that Act.]

(5)   References to the appropriate national authority are—

    (a)   in relation to a qualifying patient in England, to the Secretary of State;

    (b)   in relation to a qualifying patient in Wales, to the Welsh Ministers.

(6)   For the purposes of subsection (5) above—

    (a)   a qualifying patient falling within subsection (2)(a) above is to be regarded as being in the territory in which the hospital or registered establishment in which he is liable to be detained is situated;

    (b)   a qualifying patient falling within subsection (2)(b) above is to be regarded as being in the territory in which the area of the responsible local social services authority within the meaning of section 34(3) above is situated;

    (c)   a qualifying patient falling within subsection (2)(c) above is to be regarded as being in the territory in which the responsible hospital is situated;

    (d)   a qualifying patient falling within subsection (3) above is to be regarded as being in the territory determined in accordance with arrangements made for the purposes of this paragraph, and published, by the Secretary of State and the Welsh Ministers.]

Amendments

This section was inserted by the Mental Health Act 2007 s.30(2). The amendments to it were made by the Health and Social Care Act 2012 s.43.

Wales

This section has been amended in respect of Wales by the Mental Health (Wales) Measure 2010 s.53(1), Schs 1, 2.

Definitions

1-1305   community patient: ss.17A(7), 145(1).
approved clinician: s.145(1).
hospital: s.145(1).
registered establishment: ss.34(1), 145(1).
responsible hospital: ss.17A(7), 145(1).
local social services authority: s.145(1).

General Note

This section defines a "qualifying patient" (subss.(2) to (4)) and "the appropriate national author- **1-1306**
ity" (subss.(5), (6)) for the purposes of s.130A, and identifies which local authority is responsible for a
qualifying patient (subss.(4A), (4B)).

Subsection (2)(a)

A patient who is on s.17 leave is "liable to be detained" and is therefore included. The exclusions **1-1307**
reflect the fact that the IMHA service is not intended to be an emergency response service.

Subsections (3), (4)

The Reference Guide states, at para.4.5, that informal patients who qualify because they are being **1-1308**
considered for one of the treatments specified in subss.(3), "remain eligible until the treatment is finished,
or stopped, or it is decided that they will not be given the treatment for the time being".

Subsection (4A)

An advocacy service that has not been commissioned by a local authority is not an IMHA service **1-1309**
for the purposes of the Act.
Paragraph 6.6 of the *Code of Practice* states:

"To ensure that IMHA services reflect the diversity of the local population and that they are as
independent as possible, they are commissioned by local authorities, as follows:

- for detained patients, by the local authority for the area in which the hospital in which they
  are detained is located
- for community treatment order (CTO) patients, by the local authority for the area in which
  their responsible hospital is located
- for people subject to guardianship, by the local authority which is acting as the guardian
  or, if the patient has a private guardian, by the local authority for the area in which the
  private guardian lives."

The CQC's "Monitoring the Mental Health Act in 2016/2017" states at p.24:

"Some national services and independent hospitals find it difficult to persuade their local authority
to meet its responsibilities for commissioning IMHA services, despite the Health and Social Care Act
2012 clarifying the legal responsibilities involved [by inserting this provision into s.130C]. In other
cases, it seems that local authority provision of advocacy services has not met the needs of the hospital
and so the hospital has taken up the commissioning role to remedy this. These arrangements do raise
the question of the practical independence of the advocacy service."

Paragraph (a)

A conditionally discharged patient is liable to be detained in the hospital that discharged him **1-1310**
(*Secretary of State for Justice v MM* [2018] UKSC 60; [2018] M.H.L.R. 392, para.20).
[

Duty to give information about independent mental health advocates

130D.—(1)   The responsible person in relation to a qualifying patient (within **1-1311**
the meaning given by section 130C above) shall take such steps as are practicable
to ensure that the patient understands—

    (a)   that help is available to him from an independent mental health
          advocate; and

    (b)   how he can obtain that help.

  (2)   In subsection (1) above, "the responsible person" means—

    (a)   in relation to a qualifying patient falling within section 130C(2)(a) above (other than one also falling within paragraph (b) below), the managers of the hospital or registered establishment in which he is liable to be detained;

(b)   in relation to a qualifying patient falling within section 130C(2)(a) above and conditionally discharged by virtue of section 42(2), 73 or 74 above, the responsible clinician;

(c)   in relation to a qualifying patient falling within section 130C(2)(b) above, the responsible local social services authority within the meaning of section 34(3) above;

(d)   in relation to a qualifying patient falling within section 130C(2)(c) above, the managers of the responsible hospital;

(e)   in relation to a qualifying patient falling within section 130C(3) above, the registered medical practitioner or approved clinician with whom the patient first discusses the possibility of being given the treatment concerned.

(3)   The steps to be taken under subsection (1) above shall be taken—

(a)   where the responsible person falls within subsection (2)(a) above, as soon as practicable after the patient becomes liable to be detained;

(b)   where the responsible person falls within subsection (2)(b) above, as soon as practicable after the conditional discharge;

(c)   where the responsible person falls within subsection (2)(c) above, as soon as practicable after the patient becomes subject to guardianship;

(d)   where the responsible person falls within subsection (2)(d) above, as soon as practicable after the patient becomes a community patient;

(e)   where the responsible person falls within subsection (2)(e) above, while the discussion with the patient is taking place or as soon as practicable thereafter.

(4)   The steps to be taken under subsection (1) above shall include giving the requisite information both orally and in writing.

(5)   The responsible person in relation to a qualifying patient falling within section 130C(2) above (other than a patient liable to be detained by virtue of Part 3 of this Act) shall, except where the patient otherwise requests, take such steps as are practicable to furnish the person (if any) appearing to the responsible person to be the patient's nearest relative with a copy of any information given to the patient in writing under subsection (1) above.

(6)   The steps to be taken under subsection (5) above shall be taken when the information concerned is given to the patient or within a reasonable time thereafter.]

Amendment

This section was inserted by the Mental Health Act 2007 s.30(2).

Definitions

the managers: s.145(1).   **1-1312**
hospital: s.145(1).
registered establishment: s.145(1).
responsible hospital: ss.17A(7), 145(1).
local social services authority: s.145(1).
responsible clinician: ss.34(1), 145(1).
approved clinician: s.145(1).
community patient: ss.17A(7), 145(1).
nearest relative: s.145(1).

General Note

This section places a duty on the "responsible person", as defined in subs.(2), to take practicable steps   **1-1313**
to ensure that a qualifying patient understands the help that an IMHA can provide and how to obtain
such help (subs.(1)). The information, which has to be given both orally and in writing (subs.(4)), must
be given to the patient as soon as practicable after the patient becomes a qualifying patient (subs.(3)).
The nearest relative of a patient who comes within s.130C(2) (Part III patients do not have nearest relatives) must be given a written copy of the information that the patient receives unless the patient objects
(subss. (5), (6)).

[Independent mental health advocates: Wales

130E.—(1)   The Welsh Ministers shall make such arrangements as they   **1-1314**
consider reasonable to enable persons ("independent mental health advocates") to
be available to help—
    (a)   Welsh qualifying compulsory patients; and
    (b)   Welsh qualifying informal patients.
(2)   The Welsh Ministers may by regulations make provision as to the appointment of persons as independent mental health advocates.
(3)   The regulations may, in particular, provide—
    (a)   that a person may act as an independent mental health advocate only
        in such circumstances, or only subject to such conditions, as may be
        specified in the regulations;
    (b)   for the appointment of a person as an independent mental health
        advocate to be subject to approval in accordance with the regulations.
(4)   In making arrangements under this section, the Welsh Ministers shall have
regard to the principle that any help available to a patient under the arrangements
should, so far as practicable, be provided by a person who is independent of any
person who—
    (a)   is professionally concerned with the patient's medical treatment; or
    (b)   falls within a description specified in regulations made by the Welsh
        Ministers.
(5)   For the purposes of subsection (4) above, a person is not to be regarded as
professionally concerned with a patient's medical treatment merely because he is
representing him in accordance with arrangements–
    (a)   under section 35 of the Mental Capacity Act 2005; or
    (b)   of a description specified in regulations under this section.
(6)   Arrangements under this section may include provision for payments to be
made to, or in relation to, persons carrying out functions in accordance with the
arrangements.
(7)   Regulations under this section and sections 130F to 130H—
    (a)   may make different provision for different cases;

    (b)   may make provision which applies subject to specified exceptions;

    (c)   may include transitional, consequential, incidental or supplemental provision.]

Amendment

This section was inserted by the Mental Health (Wales) Measure 2010 s.31.

General Note

1-1315   This section places a duty on the Welsh Ministers to make arrangements for help to be provided by IMHAs. Such help must be made available to two client groups: Welsh qualifying compulsory patients, as defined in s.130I, and Welsh qualifying informal patents, as defined in s.130J. The nature of the help to be provided is set out in s.130F, for compulsory patients, and s.130G, for informal patients.

The Mental Health (Independent Mental Health Advocates) (Wales) Regulations 2011 (SI 2011/2501 (W.273)) have been made under this section.

[Arrangements under section 130E for Welsh qualifying compulsory patients

1-1316   **130F.**—(1)   The help available to a Welsh qualifying compulsory patient under arrangements under section 130E shall include help in obtaining information about and understanding—

    (a)   the provisions of this Act by virtue of which he is a qualifying compulsory patient;

    (b)   any conditions or restrictions to which he is subject by virtue of this Act;

    (c)   what (if any) medical treatment is given to him or is proposed or discussed in his case;

    (d)   why it is given, proposed or discussed;

    (e)   the authority under which it is, or would be, given; and

    (f)   the requirements of this Act which apply, or would apply, in connection with the giving of the treatment to him.

(2)   The help available under the arrangements to a Welsh qualifying compulsory patient shall also include—

    (a)   help in obtaining information about and understanding any rights which may be exercised under this Act by or in relation to him;

    (b)   help (by way of representation or otherwise)—

        (i)   in exercising the rights referred to in paragraph (a);

        (ii)   for patients who wish to become involved, or more involved, in decisions made about their care or treatment, or care or treatment generally;

        (iii)   for patients who wish to complain about their care or treatment;

    (c)   the provision of information about other services which are or may be available to the patient;

    (d)   other help specified in regulations made by the Welsh Ministers.]

Amendment

This section was inserted by the Mental Health (Wales) Measure 2010 s.32.

Definition

1-1317   medical treatment: s.145(1), (4).

General Note

This section sets out the nature of the help which must be made available for Welsh qualifying **1-1318** compulsory patients under arrangements made under s.130E.

[Arrangements under section 130E for Welsh qualifying informal patients

130G.—(1)   The help available to a Welsh qualifying informal patient under ar- **1-1319** rangements under section 130E shall include help in obtaining information about and understanding—

    (a)   what (if any) medical treatment is given to him or is proposed or discussed in his case;

    (b)   why it is given, proposed or discussed;

    (c)   the authority under which it is, or would be, given.

(2)   The help available under the arrangements to a Welsh qualifying informal patient shall also include—

    (a)   help (by way of representation or otherwise)—

        (i)   for patients who wish to become involved, or more involved, in decisions made about their care or treatment, or care or treatment generally;

        (ii)   for patients who wish to complain about their care or treatment;

    (b)   the provision of information about other services which are or may be available to the patient;

    (c)   other help specified in regulations made by the Welsh Ministers.]

Amendment

This section was inserted by the Mental Health (Wales) Measure 2010 s.33.

Definition

medical treatment: s.145(1), (4). **1-1320**

General Note

This section sets out the nature of the help which must be made available for Welsh qualifying **1-1321** informal patients under arrangements made under s.130E.

[Independent mental health advocates for Wales: supplementary powers and duties

130H.—(1)   For the purpose of providing help to a patient in accordance with **1-1322** arrangements made under section 130E, an independent mental health advocate may—

    (a)   visit and interview the patient in private;

    (b)   visit and interview–

        (i)   any person who is professionally concerned with his medical treatment;

        (ii)   any other person who falls within a description specified in regulations made by the Welsh Ministers;

    (c)   require the production of and inspect any records relating to his detention, treatment or assessment in any hospital or registered establishment or to any after-care services provided for him under section 117 above;

(d)   require the production of and inspect any records of, or held by, a local social services authority which relate to him.

(2)   But an independent mental health advocate is not entitled to the production of, or to inspect, records in reliance on subsection (1)(c) or (d) above unless—

    (a)   in a case where the patient has capacity or is competent to consent, he does consent; or

    (b)   in any other case, the production or inspection would not conflict with a decision made by a donee or deputy or the Court of Protection and the person holding the records, having regard to such matters as may be prescribed in regulations under section 130E above, considers that—

        (i)   the records may be relevant to the help to be provided by the advocate;

        (ii)   the production or inspection is appropriate.

(3)   For the purpose of providing help to a Welsh qualifying compulsory patient in accordance with the arrangements, an independent mental health advocate shall comply with any reasonable request made to him by any of the following for him to visit and interview the patient—

    (a)   the patient;

    (b)   the person (if any) appearing to the advocate to be the patient's nearest relative;

    (c)   the responsible clinician for the purposes of this Act;

    (d)   an approved mental health professional;

    (e)   a registered social worker who is professionally concerned with the patient's care, treatment or assessment;

    (f)   where the patient is liable to be detained in a hospital or registered establishment, the managers of the hospital or establishment or a person duly authorised on their behalf;

    (g)   the patient's donee or deputy.

(4)   For the purpose of providing help to a Welsh qualifying informal patient in accordance with the arrangements, an independent mental health advocate shall comply with any reasonable request made to him by any of the following for him to visit and interview the patient—

    (a)   the patient;

    (b)   the managers of the hospital or establishment in which the patient is an inpatient or a person duly authorised on their behalf;

    (c)   any person appearing to the advocate to whom the request is made to be the patient's carer;

    (d)   the patient's donee or deputy;

    (e)   a registered social worker who is professionally concerned with the patient's care, treatment or assessment.

(5)   But nothing in this Act prevents the patient from declining to be provided with help under the arrangements.

(6)   In subsection (2) above the reference to a patient who has capacity is to be read in accordance with the Mental Capacity Act 2005.

(7)   In subsection (4) above—

    (a)   "carer", in relation to a Welsh qualifying informal patient, means an individual who provides or intends to provide a substantial amount of care on a regular basis for the patient, but does not include any individual who provides, or intends to provide care by virtue of a contract of employment or other contract with any person or as a volunteer for a body (whether or not incorporated);

(b) "registered social worker" means a person included in the [social worker part

[…]of the register kept under section 80(1) of the Regulation and Inspection of Social Care (Wales) Act 2016.]

(8) In subsections (2) to (4) above—

(a) the reference to a donee is to a donee of a lasting power of attorney (within the meaning of section 9 of the Mental Capacity Act 2005) created by the patient, where the donee, in making the decision referred to in subsection (2) or the request referred to in subsection (3) or (4), is acting within the scope of his authority and in accordance with that Act;

(b) the reference to a deputy is to a deputy appointed for the patient by the Court of Protection under section 16 of that Act, where the deputy, in making the decision referred to in subsection (2) or the request referred to in subsection (3) or (4), is acting within the scope of his authority and in accordance with that Act.]

Amendment

This section was inserted by the Mental Health (Wales) Measure 2010 s.34. The amendments to subs.(7)(b) were made by the Regulation and Inspection of Social Care (Wales) Act 2016 Sch.3 Pt 2 para.39, SI 2016/1030 regs 119, 144 and SI 2019/761 r.15.

Definitions

local social services authority: s.145(1).   **1-1323**
hospital: s.145(1).
registered establishment: s.145(1).
patient: s.145(1).
nearest relative: s.145(1).
approved mental health professional: s.145(1), (1AC).
medical treatment: s.145(1), (4).

General Note

The Explanatory Notes to the Mental Health (Wales) Measure 2010 state at paras 59 to 63:   **1-1324**

"[This] section … applies in respect of both Welsh qualifying compulsory patients and Welsh qualifying informal patients. IMHAs may meet such patients in private, and visit and interview anyone professionally concerned with the patient's medical treatment. Regulations may be made by the Welsh Ministers to specify other persons who the IMHA may visit and interview.

Where a patient has the capacity, or is competent, to consent to records being made available to an IMHA (and does consent), the IMHA may require the production of any hospital or local authority records relating to the patient. If a patient lacks the capacity or is not competent to consent to records being made available to an IMHA, the record holder can still allow access to such records. The record holder can only do this if it is appropriate and relevant to the help the advocate will provide to the patient, and such access does not conflict with a valid decision of a donee of deputy (within the meaning of the Mental Capacity Act 2005).

An IMHA must meet with a Welsh qualifying compulsory patient on the reasonable request of the patient themselves, the patient's nearest relative, the responsible clinician, an approved mental health professional (AMHP), a social worker professionally concerned with the patient, hospital managers or a person duly authorised on their behalf, or the patient's donee or deputy.

An IMHA must meet with a Welsh qualifying informal patient on the reasonable request of the patient themselves, the hospital managers or a person duly authorised on their behalf, the patient's carer, the patient's donee or deputy, or a social worker professionally concerned with the care, treatment or assessment of the patient.

A patient is not obliged to accept the help provided or offered by an IMHA."

The Mental Health (Independent Mental Health Advocates) (Wales) Regulations 2011 (SI 2011/2501 (W.273)) have been made under this section.

[Welsh qualifying compulsory patients

1-1325 **130I.**—(1) This section applies for the purposes of section 130E above.

(2) A patient is a Welsh qualifying compulsory patient if he is—

(a) liable to be detained under this Act (other than under section 135 or 136 below) and the hospital or registered establishment in which he is liable to be detained is situated in Wales;

(b) subject to guardianship under this Act and the area of the responsible local social services authority within the meaning of section 34(3) above is situated in Wales; or

(c) a community patient and the responsible hospital is situated in Wales.

(3) A patient is also a Welsh qualifying compulsory patient if the patient is to be regarded as being in Wales for the purposes of this subsection and—

(a) not being a qualifying patient falling within subsection (2) above, he discusses with a registered medical practitioner or approved clinician the possibility of being given a form of treatment to which section 57 above applies; or

(b) not having attained the age of 18 years and not being a qualifying patient falling within subsection (2) above, he discusses with a registered medical practitioner or approved clinician the possibility of being given a form of treatment to which section 58A above applies.

(4) For the purposes of subsection (3), a patient is to be regarded as being in Wales if that has been determined in accordance with arrangements made for the purposes of that subsection and section 130C(3), and published, by the Secretary of State and the Welsh Ministers.

(5) Where a patient who is a Welsh qualifying compulsory patient falling within subsection (3) above is informed that the treatment concerned is proposed in his case, he remains a qualifying patient falling within that subsection until—

(a) the proposal is withdrawn; or

(b) the treatment is completed or discontinued.]

Amendment

This section was inserted by the Mental Health (Wales) Measure 2010 s.35.

Definitions

1-1326 approved clinician: s.145(1).
community patient: ss.17A(7), 145(1).
hospital: s.145(1).
patient: s.145(1).
registered establishment: ss.34(1), 145(1).
the responsible hospital: ss.17A(7), 145(1).

General Note

This section determines which patients are considered to be Welsh qualifying compulsory patients. **1-1327**

[Welsh qualifying informal patients

130J.—(1)   This section applies for the purposes of section 130E above.   **1-1328**
(2)   A patient is a Welsh qualifying informal patient if—
  (a)   the patient is an in-patient at a hospital or registered establishment situated in Wales;
  (b)   the patient is receiving treatment for, or assessment in relation to, mental disorder at the hospital or registered establishment; and
  (c)   no application, order, direction or report renders the patient liable to be detained under this Act.]

Amendment

This section was inserted by the Mental Health (Wales) Measure 2010 s.36.

Definitions

hospital: s.145(1).   **1-1329**
patient: s.145(1).
registered establishment: ss.34(1), 145(1).
mental disorder: ss.1, 145(1).

General Note

This section determines which patients are considered to be Welsh qualifying informal patients.   **1-1330**

[Duty to give information about independent mental health advocates to Welsh qualifying compulsory patients

130K.—(1)   The responsible person in relation to a Welsh qualifying   **1-1331**
compulsory patient (within the meaning given by section 130I above) shall take such steps as are practicable to ensure that the patient understands—
  (a)   that help is available to him from an independent mental health advocate; and
  (b)   how he can obtain that help.
(2)   In subsection (1) above, the "responsible person" means—
  (a)   in relation to a Welsh qualifying compulsory patient falling within section 130I(2)(a) above (other than one also falling within paragraph (b) below), the managers of the hospital or registered establishment in which he is liable to be detained; or
  (b)   in relation to a Welsh qualifying compulsory patient falling within section 130I(2)(a) above and conditionally discharged by virtue of section 42(2), 73 or 74 above, the responsible clinician;
  (c)   in relation to a Welsh qualifying compulsory patient falling within section 130I(2)(b) above, the responsible local social services authority within the meaning of section 34(3) above;
  (d)   in relation to a Welsh qualifying compulsory patient falling within section 130I(2)(c) above, the managers of the responsible hospital;
  (e)   in relation to a Welsh qualifying compulsory patient falling within section 130I(3) above, the registered medical practitioner or approved

clinician with whom the patient first discusses the possibility of being given the treatment concerned.

(3)   The steps to be taken under subsection (1) above shall be taken—

(a)   where the responsible person falls within subsection (2)(a) above, as soon as practicable after the patient becomes liable to be detained;

(b)   where the responsible person falls within subsection (2)(b) above, as soon as practicable after the conditional discharge;

(c)   where the responsible person falls within subsection (2)(c) above, as soon as practicable after the patient becomes subject to guardianship;

(d)   where the responsible person falls within subsection (2)(d) above, as soon as practicable after the patient becomes a community patient;

(e)   where the responsible person falls within subsection (2)(e) above, while the discussion with the patient is taking place or as soon as practicable thereafter.

(4)   The steps to be taken under subsection (1) above shall include giving the requisite information both orally and in writing.

(5)   The responsible person in relation to a Welsh qualifying compulsory patient falling within section 130I(2) above (other than a patient liable to be detained by virtue of Part 3 of this Act) shall, except where the patient otherwise requests, take such steps as are practicable to furnish any person falling within subsection (6) with a copy of any information given to the patient in writing under subsection (1) above.

(6)   A person falls within this subsection if—

(a)   the person appears to the responsible person to be the patient's nearest relative;

(b)   the person is a donee of a lasting power of attorney (within the meaning of section 9 of the Mental Capacity Act 2005) created by the patient and the scope of the donee's authority includes matters related to the care and treatment of the patient;

(c)   the person is a deputy appointed for the patient by the Court of Protection under section 16 of that Act and the scope of the deputy's authority includes matters related to the care and treatment of the patient.

(7)   The steps to be taken under subsection (5) above shall be taken when the information concerned is given to the patient or within a reasonable time thereafter.]

Amendment

This section was inserted by the Mental Health (Wales) Measure 2010 s.37.

Definitions

1-1332   approved clinician: s.145(1).
community patient: ss.17A(7), 145(1).
hospital: s.145(1).
patient: s.145(1).
nearest relative: s.145(1).
the managers: s.145(1).
registered establishment: ss.34(1), 145(1).
the responsible hospital: ss.17A(7), 145(1).

General Note

1-1333 The person(s) responsible for ensuring the patient understands that help from an IMHA is available is known as the "responsible person". Subsection (2) defines who the responsible person is in relation to the different groups of Welsh qualifying compulsory patients. The responsible person must provide written information regarding the IMHA service to the nearest relative, donee or deputy (if any) of a qualifying compulsory patient.

[Duty to give information about independent mental health advocates to Welsh qualifying informal patients

130L.—(1)   The responsible person in relation to a Welsh qualifying informal patient (within the meaning given by section 130J above) shall take such steps as are practicable to ensure that the patient understands—

    (a)   that help is available to him from an independent mental health advocate; and

    (b)   how he can obtain that help.

(2)   In subsection (1) above, the "responsible person" means the managers of the hospital or registered establishment to which the patient is admitted as an inpatient.

(3)   The steps to be taken under subsection (1) above shall be taken as soon as practicable after the patient becomes an in-patient.

(4)   The steps to be taken under subsection (1) above shall include giving the requisite information both orally and in writing.

(5)   The responsible person in relation to a Welsh qualifying informal patient shall, except where the patient otherwise requests, take such steps as are practicable to furnish any person falling within subsection (6) with a copy of any information given to the patient in writing under subsection (1) above.

(6)   A person falls within this subsection if—

    (a)   the person appears to the responsible person to be a carer of the patient;

    (b)   the person is a donee of a lasting power of attorney (within the meaning of section 9 of the Mental Capacity Act 2005) created by the patient and the scope of the donee's authority includes matters related to the care and treatment of the patient;

    (c)   the person is a deputy appointed for the patient by the Court of Protection under section 16 of that Act and the scope of the deputy's authority includes matters related to the care and treatment of the patient.

(7)   In subsection (6), "carer", in relation to a Welsh qualifying informal patient, means an individual who provides or intends to provide a substantial amount of care on a regular basis for the patient, but does not include any individual who provides, or intends to provide care by virtue of a contract of employment or other contract with any person or as a volunteer for a body (whether or not incorporated);

(8)   The steps to be taken under subsection (5) above shall be taken when the information concerned is given to the patient or within a reasonable time thereafter.]

Amendment

This section was inserted by the Mental Health (Wales) Measure 2010 s.38.

Definitions

1-1335

hospital: s.145(1).
the managers: s.145(1).
patient: s.145(1).
registered establishment: ss.34(1), 145(1).

General Note

1-1336   This section provides for "information-giving" arrangements in respect of Welsh qualifying informal patients. It is similar to those provided for Welsh qualifying compulsory patients in s.130K.

Informal admission of patients

1-1337   **131.**—(1) Nothing in this Act shall be construed as preventing a patient who requires treatment for mental disorder from being admitted to any hospital or [registered establishment] in pursuance of arrangements made in that behalf and without any application, order or direction rendering him liable to be detained under this Act, or from remaining in any hospital or [registered establishment] in pursuance of such arrangements after he has ceased to be so liable to be detained.

[(2) Subsections (3) and (4) below apply in the case of a patient aged 16 or 17 years who has capacity to consent to the making of such arrangements as are mentioned in subsection (1) above.

(3) If the patient consents to the making of the arrangements, they may be made, carried out and determined on the basis of that consent even though there are one or more persons who have parental responsibility for him.

(4) If the patient does not consent to the making of the arrangements, they may not be made, carried out or determined on the basis of the consent of a person who has parental responsibility for him.

(5) In this section—

(a) the reference to a patient who has capacity is to be read in accordance with the Mental Capacity Act 2005; and

(b) "parental responsibility" has the same meaning as in the Children Act 1989.]

Amendments

The amendments to this section were made by the Care Standards Act 2000 s.116, Sch.4 para.9(2), the Children Act 1989 s.108(5), Sch.13 para.48(5) and the Mental Health Act 2007 s.43.

Definitions

1-1338

patient: s.145(1).
mental disorder: ss.1, 145(1).
hospital: s.145(1).
registered establishment: ss.34(1), 145(1).

General Note

1-1339   This section, which applies to mentally capable patients who consent to their admission and to patients lacking such capacity who do not object to their admission (*R. v Bournewood NHS Trust, Ex p. L* [1998] 3 All E.R. 289), provides that a patient can either enter hospital for treatment for mental disorder on an informal basis, or remain in hospital on an informal basis once the authority for the original detention has come to an end. It also provides that in the case of patients aged 16 or 17 years who have the capacity to consent to their informal admission to hospital for treatment for their mental disorder, they may consent (or may not consent) to the admission and their decision cannot be overridden by a person with parental responsibility for them. If such a child does not consent to the admission, he could be admitted for compulsory treatment under Pt II if the relevant criteria are satisfied.

The informal admission to hospital of any compliant mentally incapacitated patient can be provided under the Mental Capacity Act 2005 (MCA) if he is not being deprived of his liberty in the hospital. The *Code of Practice* is therefore incorrect when it states that a "person with a learning disability or autism cannot be informally admitted if they do not have capacity to consent to or refuse that admission and treatment" (para.20.30). An assessment should be undertaken if it is thought that a patient is being deprived of his liberty as a failure either to detain the patient under this Act or to authorise the deprivation under Sch.A1 of the 2005 Act on a finding that the patient was being deprived of his liberty would violate the patient's rights under art.5 of the European Convention on Human Rights (*HL v United Kingdom* (2005) 40 E.H.R.R. 32; [2004] M.H.L.R. 236). If the patient is not compliant to either being admitted to hospital or to being treated there for his mental disorder, this Act has to be invoked: see the discussion on *The detention of compliant mentally incapable patients* in the General Note to Part II. The nature of a deprivation of liberty is considered in Part 6.

The question of whether a person has the mental capacity to consent to admission as an informal patient "will be likely to include consideration of the person's capacity to agree (a) to the relevant admission to hospital for the relevant purpose, (b) to stay in hospital whilst its purpose is carried out and (c) to the circumstances relating to a possible deprivation of liberty that will prevail during that admission" (*AM v South London & Maudsley NHS Foundation Trust* [2013] UKUT 365 (AAC); [2014] M.H.L.R. 181, per Charles J. at para.40). In *A Primary Care Trust v LDV* [2013] EWHC 272 (Fam), a case decided under the MCA 2005, Baker J., without "seeking to set any sort of precedent", said that "the clinicians and the court should ask whether [the patient] has the capacity to understand, retain and weigh the following information:

(1)   that she is in hospital to receive care and treatment for a mental disorder;
(2)   that the care and treatment will include varying levels of supervision (including supervision in the community), use of physical restraint and the prescription and administration of medication to control her mood;
(3)   that staff at the hospital will be entitled to carry out property and personal searches;
(4)   that she must seek permission of the nursing staff to leave the hospital, and, until the staff at the hospital decide otherwise, will only be allowed to leave under supervision;
(5)   that if she left the hospital without permission and without supervision, the staff would take steps to find and return her, including contacting the police (para. 39).

This list requires the patient to possess a high level of capacity. Indeed, some members of the hospital staff might find it difficult to satisfy this capacity test without the assistance of written prompts. Assessors should bear in mind the following note of caution expressed by Peter Jackson J. at para.26 of *Heart of England NHS Foundation Trust v JB* [2014] EWCOP 342:

"What is required here is a broad, general understanding of the kind that is expected from the population at large. JB is not required to understand every last piece of information about her situation and her options: even her doctors would not make that claim. It must also be remembered that common strategies for dealing with unpalatable dilemmas – for example indecision, avoidance or vacillation – are not to be confused with incapacity. We should not ask more of people whose capacity is questioned than of those whose capacity is undoubted."

It is suggested that a more appropriate list than the one suggested by Baker J. might be: can the patient understand, retain and weigh the information that he is being admitted to hospital informally and that this means that, subject to s.5, he can leave whenever he wants, that treatment for his mental disorder might involve the administration of medication, that during his stay in hospital he will be subject to hospital rules, and that the rules might involve placing restrictions on him.

Although informal admission should be the preferred mode of admission, there is nothing in the Act which expressly prevents an application being made in respect of a mentally capable patient who is willing to enter hospital as an informal patient. While it is true that s.5 can be invoked to prevent an informal patient from leaving hospital, circumstances can arise which justify the use of compulsion on "willing" patients. Compulsion should be used where its absence would place the patient's safety and/or the safety of others at significant risk. Paragraph 14.16 of the *Code of Practice* states:

"Compulsory admission should, in particular, be considered where a patient's current mental state, together with reliable evidence of past experience, indicates a strong likelihood that they will have a change of mind about informal admission, either before or after they are admitted, with a resulting risk to their health or safety or to the safety of other people."

Paragraph 14.16 (as it appeared in the previous edition of the Code) was endorsed by Charles J. in *AM v South London & Maudsley NHS Foundation Trust*, above, at para.20.

In *R. v Kirklees Metropolitan Borough Council Ex p. C* [1992] 2 F.L.R. 117, Kennedy J., on an application for the judicial review of a decision by the local authority to consent to the admission of an adolescent girl to a psychiatric hospital, held that an admission to a psychiatric hospital can be lawful even though it does not take place within the framework of the Act, which did not cover all eventualities. His Lordship found that there is no reason to conclude that the right to arrange an informal admission is limited to the terms of this section. If that were the case it would produce the surprising result that no one, adult or child, who had not been diagnosed as being mentally disordered, could ever be admitted to a psychiatric hospital for assessment. This section did not apply to the patient because there was no evidence that she required "treatment for mental disorder" (see subs.(1)). The local authority was entitled to consent on the patient's behalf because a care order had been made in respect of her and at the material time she was not "Gillick competent". On affirming this decision at [1993] 2 F.L.R. 187, the Court of Appeal confirmed that although the informal admission of a patient for assessment is not covered by this section, there is nothing to prohibit such an admission taking place under common law. The effect of this decision is merely to fill a gap in the statutory scheme, a gap which was described by Lloyd L.J., at 190, as being "odd".

J. Bindman and his colleagues found that a third of patients who had been admitted informally to a psychiatric hospital felt highly coerced at admission, and the majority were uncertain that they were free to leave the hospital ("Perceived coercion at admission to psychiatric hospital and engagement with follow up", Soc. Psychiatry Psychiatric Epidemiol (2005) 40: 160–166). Informal patients should therefore "have their legal position and rights explained to them" (*Code of Practice*, para.4.49). Paragraph 4.51 of the Code states:

"Informal patients must be allowed to leave if they wish, unless they are to be detained under the Act. Both the patient and, where appropriate, their carer and advocate should be made aware of this right with information being provided in a format and language the patient understands. Local policies and arrangements about movement around the hospital and its grounds must be clearly explained to the patients concerned. Failure to do so could lead to a patient mistakenly believing that they are not allowed to leave hospital, which could result in an unlawful deprivation of their liberty and a breach of their human rights."

Human Rights Act 1998

1-1340   In *M v Ukraine* [2013] M.H.L.R. 255, the Court said at paras 71 and 77:

"[I]f in-patient psychiatric treatment is voluntary this presupposes that the patient has the guaranteed right to stop any further treatment and to leave the hospital whenever he or she wishes to do so. This freedom of action is subject to mental health practitioners' authority to refuse to discharge the patient, provided that the relevant compulsory admission procedures are immediately applied, following which the person shall be treated as an involuntary patient. …

[T]he Court takes the view that a person's consent to admission to a mental health facility for in-patient treatment can be regarded as valid for the purpose of the Convention only where there is sufficient and reliable evidence suggesting that the person's mental ability to consent and comprehend the consequences thereof has been objectively established in the course of a fair and proper procedure and that all the necessary information concerning placement and intended treatment has been adequately provided to him."

Article 5 of the European Convention on Human Rights (ECHR), which as aimed at preventing unjustified deprivations of liberty, applies to children. In *Nielsen v Denmark* (1989) 11 E.H.R.R. 175, the European Court of Human Rights (ECtHR) found that no deprivation of liberty had occurred when the mother of a 12 year-old boy consented to his admission to a psychiatric hospital against his wishes and that of his father. Among the factors that were cited in support of this decision, the court emphasised at para.72:

(i)   the fact that the mother was the sole holder of parental responsibility in respect of the child. The court said that the "care and upbringing of children normally and necessarily require that the parents or an only parent decide where the child must reside and also impose, or authorise others to impose, various restrictions on the child's liberty". However, it accepted that "the rights of the holder of parental authority cannot be unlimited and that it is incumbent on the State to provide safeguards against abuse";

(ii)   that the "restrictions to which the [child] was subject were no more than the normal requirements for the care of a child of 12 years of age receiving treatment in hospital"; and

(iii)   its view that the child "was still of an age at which it would be normal for a decision to be made by the parent against the wishes of the child".

The court concluded by stating that it "must be possible for a child like the applicant to be admitted to hospital at the request of the holder of parental rights, a case which is clearly not covered by paragraph 1 of Article 5". This statement was made because the child, not having been diagnosed as being mentally ill, was not detained as a person of unsound mind so as to bring the case within art.5(1)(e).

Schedule 3 of the Mental Capacity Act 2005

Schedule 3 makes provision as to the private international law of England and Wales in relation to those who are over the age of 16 who, as a result of impairment or insufficiency of their personal faculties (which is not a test of lack of mental capacity), cannot protect their interests. In particular, it gives effect in England and Wales to the Convention on the International Protection of Adults (Cm.5881) which was signed at The Hague on January 13, 2000 and entered into force on January 1, 2009. It does so on a very wide basis in that the Schedule provides for the mutual recognition of "protective measures", which can include detention in a psychiatric institution, imposed by a foreign court regardless of whether that court is located in a Convention country. This means that Sch.3 comes into play whenever a cross-border "incapacity" issue arises. The aims of the Convention are set out in art.1. They are to: **1-1341**

- provide for the protection in international situations of adults who, by reason of impairment or insufficiency in their personal faculties, are not in a position to defend their interests
- establish rules on jurisdiction, applicable law, international recognition and enforcement of protective measures which are to be respected by all Contracting States, and co-operation between Contracting States.
- The basis of the jurisdiction is habitual residence, not best interests: (*Re MN* [2010] EWHC 1926 (Fam), para.38). The habitual residence of the person therefore determines which State authorities have jurisdiction over his person and property.

A detailed analysis of the jurisdiction of the Court of Protection to recognise and enforce foreign protective measures under Sch.3 was provided by Baker J. in *Health Service Executive of Ireland v PA* [2015] EWCOP 38. (also see his Lordships judgment in *HSE v PD* [2015] EWCOP 48). The case law on Sch.3 was analysed by Hayden J. in *The Health Service Executive of Ireland v Ellern Mede Moorgate* [2020] EWCOP 12. A "Comparison of protections under MHA and under Schedule 3" is set out in an Appendix to the judgment in this case. In *PA*, Baker J. held that:

"[W]hen considering applications to recognise and enforce compulsory psychiatric placements under Schedule 3, the limited review [undertaken by the Court] should encompass the Court being satisfied that (1) the *Winterwerp* criteria are met and (2) that the individual's right to challenge the detention under Article 5(4) is effective (i.e. that they have a right to take proceedings to challenge the detention and the right to regular reviews thereafter)" (para.96).

Schedule 3 is examined in *International Protection of Adults*, edited by Richard Frimston, Alexander Ruck Keene, Claire van Overdijk, and Adrian Ward, 2015.

Code of Practice

Guidance on the informal admission of children and young people in contained in Ch.19. With regard to the provision of information for informal hospital patients, the Code states: **1-1342**

"4.49 Although the Act does not impose any duties to give information to informal patients, these patients should have their legal position and rights explained to them.

4.50 Informal patients should be provided with relevant information (eg about how to make a complaint and consent requirements for treatment).

4.51 Informal patients must be allowed to leave if they wish, unless they are to be detained under the Act. Both the patient and, where appropriate, their carer and advocate should be made aware of this right with information being provided in a format and language the patient understands. Local policies and arrangements about movement around the hospital and its grounds must be clearly explained to the patients concerned. Failure to do so could lead to a patient mistakenly believing that they are not allowed to leave hospital, which could result in an unlawful deprivation of their liberty and a breach of their human rights."

Children aged 16 or 17 (see paras 19.53–19.64 of the Code of Practice)

1-1343   Subsections (2) to (5) provide that patients aged 16 or 17 who have the capacity to consent to their admission to a hospital for treatment for mental disorder can consent or not consent to such arrangements on their own behalf. If the patient consents to the making of the arrangements, he can be informally admitted to hospital, and the consent cannot be over-ridden by a person with parental responsibility for him. If the patient does not consent to the making of the arrangements, he cannot be informally admitted on the basis of consent from a person with parental responsibility.

The capacity of the patient to consent to the arrangements should be assessed according to the test set out in ss.2 and 3 of the MCA bearing in mind that under s.1(2) of that Act the patient is assumed to have capacity. The assessment of a patient's capacity to consent to an informal admission is considered above. If the young person lacks the capacity to consent to the admission, para.19.57 of the *Code of Practice* states:

> "Where a young person aged 16 or 17 lacks capacity it may be possible for them to be admitted informally, in accordance with the MCA, unless the admission and treatment amounts to a deprivation of liberty. In cases where the MCA cannot authorise informal admission, but the admission is thought to be necessary, consideration should be given to as whether the criteria for admission under the Act are met. If the Act is not applicable, legal advice should be sought on the need to seek authorisation from the court before further action is taken."

Where the patient is assessed as lacking the mental capacity to consent to his admission, it may be possible for a person with parental responsibility to consent to the admission on the young person's behalf. However, it is not possible for a person with parental responsibility to consent to any subsequent deprivation of the young person's liberty: see *Re D (A Child)* [2019] UKSC 42; [2020] M.H.L.R. 135 where the Supreme Court held that it is not within the scope of parental responsibility for parents to consent to a placement which deprived their 16 or 17 year old child of his or her liberty. Lady Hale identified the "crux of the matter" as being summed up in the question "Do the restrictions fall within normal parental control for a child of this age or do they not?" (para.39). It is not possible for the deprivation of liberty of a young person to be authorised under the deprivation of liberty procedure set out in Sch.A1 of the MCA: see para.13 of Sch.A1.

Children under the age of 16 (see paras 19.65–19.70 of the Code of Practice)

1-1344   Where a child who is assessed as having Gillick capacity (or competence) to decide about their admission to hospital for assessment and/or treatment of their mental disorder consents to this, they may be admitted to hospital as an informal patient. If a child who has *Gillick* capacity objects to being admitted for treatment, any confinement must be authorised either by this Act or the High Court. Where the child does not have *Gillick* capacity, a person with parental responsibility can consent to the admission and to any subsequent deprivation of liberty on the child's behalf if they are acting in the best interests of the child: see *Re RN (Deprivation of Liberty and Parental Consent)* [2022] EWHC 2576 (Fam), para.34. The "Court will only become involved if there is a dispute between the parents and the local authority or other State body, such as the NHS, or between the parents themselves, as to what is in the child's best interests", per HHJ Burrows (sitting as a High Court Judge) in *Lancashire CC v PX* [2022] EWHC 2379 (Fam), at para.56. It is not possible for a deprivation of liberty of a child to be authorised under the deprivation of liberty procedure set out in Sch.A1 of the MCA: see para.13 of Sch.A1.

Gillick capacity

1-1345   For a child to have *"Gillick* capacity", he or she has to be of sufficient understanding and intelligence to understand fully the decision being proposed to be taken (*Gillick v West Norfolk and Wisbech Area Health Authority* [1985] 3 All E.R. 402). In *Re S (Child as parent: Adoption: Consent)* [2017] EWHC 2729 (Fam), Cobb J. said that when assessing *Gillick* capacity he regarded it "as appropriate, and indeed helpful, to read across to, and borrow from, the relevant concepts and language of the Mental Capacity Act 2005" (para 15). His Lordship considered it helpful to test Gillick capacity in the following way:

> "[T]he child should be of sufficient intelligence and maturity to:
>
> (i)   Understand the nature and implications of the decision and the process of implementing that decision;
>
> (ii)   Understand the implications of not pursuing the decision;

(iii)   Retain the information long enough for the decision-making process to take place;

(iv)   Weigh up the information and arrive at a decision;

(v)   Communicate that decision" (para.18).

The nature of *Gillick* capacity (or competence) is identified in the Code at paras 19.34 to 19.37.

Hospitals as "secure accommodation"

If the main objective is to detain the child because of the child's behavioural disturbance rather than   **1-1346**
to hospitalise the child to provide medical treatment for the child's mental disorder, it might be appropriate to invoke s.25 of the Children Act 1989 (the equivalent provision in Wales is s.119 of the Social
Services and Well-being (Wales) Act 2014) which sets out the criteria that must be satisfied before a child
can be placed in secure accommodation. Secure accommodation is "accommodation designed for, or
having as its primary purpose, the restriction of liberty … [H]owever, premises which are not designed
as secure accommodation may become secure accommodation because of the use to which they are put
in the particular circumstances of the individual case", per Baker L.J. in *Re B*, below, at para.59. Under
reg.3(1) of the Children (Secure Accommodation) Regulations 1991 (SI 1991/1505), accommodation
in a children's home "shall not be used as secure accommodation unless in the case of accommodation
in England, it has been approved by the Secretary of State for that use".

The criteria under s.25 are that one or other of two circumstances are established:

(i)   A history of absconding, a likelihood of future absconding and, if he did abscond, he is likely
to suffer significant harm; or

(ii)   He is likely to injure himself or other persons if kept in any other description of
accommodation.

The child's welfare is a relevant but not paramount consideration and the requirements in s.1 of the
Children Act 1989 are not applicable (*Re M (A Minor) (Secure Accommodation Order)* [1995] 3 All E.R.
407).

The approach of the court is that such orders will "only very rarely be appropriate" and "must always
remain a measure of last resort" (*Re SS (Secure Accommodation Order)* [2014] EWHC 4436 (Fam), cited
in *Re X (Secure Accommodation: Lack of Provision)* [2023] EWHC 129 (Fam) at para.4.

Regulation 5 of SI 1991/1505 provides that s.25 does not apply to a child who is detained under any
provision of the Mental Health Act, although it will apply if the child is granted leave of absence under
s.17 (*Hereford and Worcester County Council v S* [1993] 2 F.L.R. 360). Section 25 will also apply if
the child is either admitted informally under this section or is admitted under the common law powers
identified in *R. v Kirklees Metropolitan Borough Council Ex p. C* [1992] 2 F.L.R. 117, if the unit of the
hospital where the child is being accommodated is "secure accommodation".

The s.25 scheme was extensively analysed by the Court of Appeal in *Re B (Secure Accommodation
Order)* [2019] EWCA Civ 2025. Baker L.J. said at para.101:

"Where the local authority cannot apply under s.25 because one or more of the relevant criteria are
not satisfied, it may be able to apply for leave to apply for an order depriving the child of liberty under
the inherent jurisdiction if there is reasonable cause to believe that the child is likely to suffer
significant harm if the order is not granted: s.100(4) Children Act."

In *Re T (A Child)* [2021] UKSC 35, the Supreme Court confirmed that the use of the inherent jurisdiction to authorise the deprivation of liberty in a placement in England which was not a registered
children's home or approved for use as secure accommodation, is permissible, but expressed grave
concern about its use to fill a gap in the child care system caused by inadequate resources. The Court
confirmed that the use of the inherent jurisdiction in such a case did not contravene art.5 of the ECHR.
Also see *Tameside MBC v AM* [2021] EWHC 2472 (Fam) and *A Mother v Derby City Council* [2021]
EWCA Civ 1867.

To assist individual local authorities in searching for a secure placement, the Secure Welfare
Coordination Unit was established by the Department for Education in May 2016.

Transfers of children

Procedure for the referral for assessment, and transfer to and from hospital (under Part II of the   **1-1347**
Mental Health Act 1983) of a child held in secure accommodation under welfare grounds in England
(NHS, 2021) provides guidance on the procedure for transferring to and from hospital under Part II of
the Act a looked after child who is in secure accommodation on welfare grounds. The procedure cov-

ers the duties of secure children's homes (SCHs) in identifying and transferring children, and the action that must be taken by other agencies involved. The procedure applies to SCHs in England. The guidance can be accessed at: *https://www.england.nhs.uk/wp-content/uploads/2021/11/B0721_i_Children-and-young-persons-Mental-Health-Act-transfers-guidance-part-II-welfare-protocol.pdf.*

The power of the High Court to make declarations regarding the detention of child patients

1-1348   In *Re C (Detention: Medical Treatment)* [2017] 2 F.L.R. 180, above, a 16-year-old child needed treatment for anorexia nervosa in a private psychiatric unit in circumstances where the unit would not accept patients who were detained under this Act and where there were sound reasons for not instituting care proceedings. Wall J. held that:

(i)   the High Court has the power under the inherent jurisdiction to order the detention of a child in a specified institution for the purpose of medical treatment being administered to the child without her agreement (see *Re W (A Minor) (Medical Treatment)* [1992] 4 All E.R. 627);

(ii)   the court has power to authorise the use of reasonable force (if necessary) to detain the child in the institution and to ensure that any necessary treatment is received (see *Norfolk and Norwich Healthcare (NHS) Trust v W* [1996] 2 F.L.R. 613);

(iii)   as the clinic was not "secure accommodation" for the purposes of s.25 of the Children Act 1989 and the attendant regulations (see above), the inherent jurisdiction was not ousted. An application under s.25 for a secure accommodation order would have had to have been made if the clinic did constitute secure accommodation;

(iv)   although s.25 did not apply, the court should pay careful attention to the scheme laid down by Parliament under that section, and an order should not be made under the inherent jurisdiction unless the s.25 criteria are, by analogy to the facts of the case, met. The rights given to a child who is the subject of a s.25 application should be made available, and equivalent safeguards to those provided for in s.25 should be built into the order; and

(v)   although consideration should always be given to alternative avenues (for example, under s.31 of the Children Act or the Mental Health Act) a refusal to exercise the inherent jurisdiction on the basis that an alternative avenue was available could lead to the child falling between several statutory stools, and not receiving the treatment that he or she needs. A primary purpose of the inherent jurisdiction is to fill lacunae in the statutory schemes; if the court is satisfied that in the particular circumstances of the case no statutory scheme is available, it should not hesitate to use its powers under the inherent jurisdiction.

In *Re X (A Child) (Jurisdiction: Secure Accommodation)* [2016] EWHC 2271 (Fam); [2017] Fam 80, para.32, Munby P. said:

"It is in my judgment quite clear that a judge exercising the inherent jurisdiction of the court ... with respect to children ... has power to direct that the child ... in question shall be placed at and remain in a specified institution such as, for example, a hospital, residential unit, care home or secure unit. It is equally clear that the court's powers extend to authorising that person's detention in such a place and the use of reasonable force (if necessary) to detain him and ensure that he remains there."

Further guidance on the use of the inherent jurisdiction has been provided in the cases noted by Munby P. in *Re A-F (Children)* [2018] EWHC 138 (Fam) at para.27.
[

Accommodation, etc. for children

1-1349   **131A.**—(1)   This section applies in respect of any patient who has not attained the age of 18 years and who—

(a)   is liable to be detained in a hospital under this Act; or

(b)   is admitted to, or remains in, a hospital in pursuance of such arrangements as are mentioned in section 131(1) above.

(2)   The managers of the hospital shall ensure that the patient's environment in the hospital is suitable having regard to his age (subject to his needs).

(3)   For the purpose of deciding how to fulfil the duty under subsection (2) above, the managers shall consult a person who appears to them to have knowledge

or experience of cases involving patients who have not attained the age of 18 years which makes him suitable to be consulted.

(4)   In this section, "hospital" includes a registered establishment.]

Amendment

This section was inserted by the Mental Health Act 2007 s.31(3).

Definitions

patient: s.145(1).   **1-1350**
hospital: s.145(1) and see subs.(4) of this section.
the managers: s.145(1).
registered establishment: ss.34(1), 145(1).

General Note

This section places a duty on hospital managers to ensure that the hospital environment of a detained   **1-1351**
or informal mentally disordered patient who is under the age of 18 is "suitable having regard to his age (subject to his needs)" (subss.(1), (2)). The duty extends to children and young people who are detained in hospital as a place of safety under ss.135 or 136. Prior to making a decision about how to fulfil this duty, the managers must consult with a suitable person as defined in subs.(3). This person is likely to be a child and adolescent mental health services professional.

The Minister of State said:

"We have used the word 'environment' because what matters to a child or young person goes well beyond mere physical segregation from older people. … By using the word 'environment' we can ensure not only that children and young people have separate facilities, but that they are appropriate physical facilities, with staff who have the right training to understand and address their specific needs as children, and a hospital routine that will allow their personal, social and educational development to continue as normally as possible" (*Hansard*, HC, Vol.461, col.1144).

Paragraph 91 of "Post-legislative assessment of the Mental Health Act 2007", Cm 8408, states that "admission to an adult ward may be the most appropriate option [for young people] because of (a) overriding need when a young person needs immediate admission for their safety or that of others, and (b) atypical need when, even if a CAMHS (Child and Adolescent Mental Health Service) bed was available, an adult ward is the most appropriate clinical placement": see further, paras 19.94 et seq of the *Code of Practice*.

A registered person must notify the Care Quality Commission where a person under the age of 18 has been admitted to an adult psychiatric unit for more than 48 hours (Care Quality Commission (Registration) Regulations 2009 (SI 2009/3112) reg.18(2)(h)). A form that must be used for this purpose may be downloaded from the Commission's website (*www.cqc.org.uk*). In 2021/22, "these notifications showed there was a 32% rise in the number of under 18s admitted to adult psychiatric wards (260 admissions in 2021/22 compared with 197 in 2020/21). The main reason given for admitting the child to an adult ward (70%, 182 admissions) was because there was no alternative mental health inpatient or outreach service available for children and young people. In over half of the notifications received, providers recorded that the child needed to be admitted immediately for their safety (58%, 152 admissions). Only 13% of providers recorded that admission to the adult ward was clinically preferred and 4% that it was socially the preferred option" ("Monitoring the Mental Health Act in 2021/22", CQC, 2022)

Under ss.85 and 86 of the Children Act 1989 where a child is to be accommodated by a Local Health Board or NHS trust for a consecutive period of at least three months, or where a child is to be accommodated in a care home or independent hospital for a similar period, the accommodating authority or the person carrying on the home must notify the local authority for the area where the child is ordinarily resident. The local authority is then placed under a duty to determine whether the child's welfare is being adequately safeguarded and to consider whether it should exercise any of its functions under the 1989 Act in respect of the child.

See s.140 for the duty of health bodies to notify local authorities of the arrangements that are in force for the provision of accommodation or facilities designed to be specially suitable for mentally disorder child patients.

Article 37(c) of the United Nations Convention on the Rights of the Child states that "every child deprived of liberty shall be separated from adults unless it is considered in the child's best interest not to do so". The United Kingdom entered the following reservation to this aspect of the Convention:

> "Where at any time there is a lack of suitable accommodation or adequate facilities for a particular individual in any institution in which young offenders are detained, or where the mixing of adults and children is deemed to be mutually beneficial, the United Kingdom reserves the right not to apply Article 37(c) in so far as those provisions require children who are to be detained to be accommodated separately from adults."

Code of Practice

1-1352 This section is considered in Ch.36 at paras 19.90 to 19.104.

Duty of managers of hospitals to give information to detained patients
1-1353 **132.**—(1) The managers of a hospital or [registered establishment] in which a patient is detained under this Act shall take such steps as are practicable to ensure that the patient understands—

    (a)   under which of the provisions of this Act he is for the time being detained and the effect of that provision; and

    (b)   what rights of applying to a [tribunal] are available to him in respect of his detention under that provision;

and those steps shall be taken as soon as practicable after the commencement of the patient's detention under the provision in question.

(2) The managers of a hospital or [registered establishment] in which a patient is detained as aforesaid shall also take such steps as are practicable to ensure that the patient understands the effect, so far as relevant in his case, of sections 23, 25, 56 to 64, 66(1)(g), 118 and 120 above and section 134 below; and those steps shall be taken as soon as practicable after the commencement of the patient's detention in the hospital or [establishment].

(3) The steps to be taken under subsections (1) and (2) above shall include giving the requisite information both orally and in writing.

(4) The managers of a hospital or [registered establishment] in which a patient is detained as aforesaid shall, except where the patient otherwise requests, take such steps as are practicable to furnish the person (if any) appearing to them to be his nearest relative with a copy of any information given to him in writing under subsections (1) and (2) above; and those steps shall be taken when the information is given to the patient or within a reasonable time thereafter.

Amendments

The amendments to this section were made by the Care Standards Act 2000 s.116, Sch.4 para.9(2), the Mental Health Act 2007 s.32 (4), Sch.3 para.29 and SI 2008/2883 art.9, Sch.3 para.63.

Definitions

1-1354 the managers: s.145(1).
patient: s.145(1).
hospital: s.145(1).
registered establishment: ss.34(1), 145(1).
nearest relative: ss.26(3), 145(1).

General Note

1-1355 This section requires the managers of NHS and independent hospitals to inform detained patients of their legal position and rights. It applies to patients who are detained under the "holding powers" contained in s.5 and to patients who are detained in hospital under either s.135 or s.136. It does not apply to a community patient who has been recalled to hospital unless the patient's community treatment order is revoked and the patient becomes a detained patient (see s.17G), and there is no requirement to give information to patients who are detained under the Act in places other than a hospital, e.g. a patient who is detained in a police station under s.136. Unless the patient requests otherwise, the information must also be given to the patient's nearest relative or acting nearest relative. Section 132A places a similar duty on hospital managers with respect to community patients. There is also a duty placed on hospital managers to inform patients when their detention is renewed (s.20(3); also see reg.26(1)(b) of the English Regulations and reg.8 of the Welsh Regulations). It would clearly be good practice for a detained patient to be informed when he attains informal status.

As a result of the decision in *R. (on the application of Wooder) v Feggetter and Mental Health Act Commission* [2002] EWCA Civ 554, noted under s.58(3)(b), a patient should be informed of the reasons for the imposition of treatment given without consent under s.58.

Regulation 26 of the English Regulations and regs 8, 22, 39 and 32 of the Welsh Regulations state that the nearest relative of the patient must be informed of various statutory events concerning the patient unless the patient objects to the information being provided or providing the information would not be practicable.

Human Rights Act 1998

In accordance with art.5(2) of the European Convention on Human Rights, the managers should inform the patient of the reason why he is being detained under the Act (*Van de Leer v Netherlands* (1990) 12 E.H.R.R. 567).   **1-1356**

Code of Practice

Guidance on this section and on providing information to patients, nearest relatives, carers and others is given in Ch.4. Guidance on providing information to those who are detained and are under 18 is contained in paras 19.75 to 19.77 of the Code. In addition to the obligations set out in this section, the Code states: **1-1357**

> "4.15 Patients should also be told the essential legal and factual grounds for their detention or CTO. For the patient to be able to adequately and effectively challenge the grounds for their detention or their CTO, should they wish, they should be given the full facts rather than simply the broad reasons. This should be done promptly and clearly. They should be told they may seek legal advice, and assisted to do so if required.
>
> 4.16 In addition, a copy of the detention or CTO documentation should be made available to the patient as soon as practicable and as a priority, unless the hospital managers are of the opinion (based on the advice of the authors of the documents) that the information disclosed would adversely affect the health or wellbeing of the patient or others. It may be necessary to remove any personal information about third parties.
>
> 4.17 Where the section of the Act under which the patient is being detained changes, they must be provided with the above information to reflect the new situation. The same applies where a detained patient becomes subject to a CTO."

Paragraph 4.28 of the Code states:

> "Those with responsibility for patient care should ensure that patients are reminded from time to time of their rights and the effects of the Act. It may be necessary to give the same information on a number of different occasions or in different formats and to check regularly that the patient has fully understood it. Information given to a patient who is unwell may need to be repeated when their condition has improved. It is helpful to ensure that patients are aware that an IMHA can help them to understand the information."

Information about how to make a complaint to the service commissioner, the CQC or Parliamentary and Health Ombudsmen should also be readily available (Code, para.4.63).

Leaflets

Model leaflets on patients' rights that have been designed to assist hospitals and local social services authorities to meet their legal obligations under this section have been produced by the Department of   **1-1358**

Health. They can be accessed on the website of Mental Health Law online at: *www.mhlo.uk/v*. Foreign-language information leaflets can be accessed at: *www.mhlo.uk/g*.

Information about firms of solicitors who could represent patients at tribunal and managers' hearings

1-1359 This issue is best addressed by looking separately at the position of patients who lack the mental capacity to instruct a solicitor and patients who possess such capacity:

Mentally Incapacitated Patients

Hospital staff should not approach a solicitor with a request to represent a mentally incapacitated patient. Apart from a situation where either a court appointed deputy or the donee of a lasting power of attorney instructs a solicitor to represent a mentally incapacitated patient, solicitors are prevented by their professional Code of Conduct from acting for a client who lacks capacity: see para.4.2 of Appendix D. Although the First-tier Tribunal has the power under r.11 of the Tribunal Rules to appoint a solicitor to represent such patients, hospital managers do not have an equivalent power. An independent mental health advocate can represent the patient at both the tribunal and managers' hearings (s.130B(2)(b)).

Mentally Capable Patients

Hospital staff should not recommend a particular firm of solicitors to a patient because, as well as the clear conflict of interest issues that arise, solicitors will have a legitimate cause for complaint if they are not recommended. If the patient does not have a solicitor and wishes to be represented, staff should provide the patient with a list of local solicitors who are accredited by the Law Society to represent patients at tribunal hearings. Independent mental health advocates can assist patients with their choice of an appropriate solicitor.

Subsection (1)

1-1360 **Such steps as are practicable**   The steps must include giving the requisite information both orally and in writing (subs.(3)). It is clearly not practicable for staff to attempt to provide the information orally to a patient who is either too ill to understand the information, refuses to listen to staff, or becomes significantly distressed when the attempt is made. If the patient initially fails to understand the information or is too distressed to receive it, staff should make further attempts to provide the information if it is considered that the patient's mental state has improved to the extent that such an attempt would be likely to succeed. In appropriate cases, the managers should use an interpreter.

In *LM v Slovenia*, June 12, 2014, (App.No.32863/05), the European Court of Human Rights held that a delay of four days between the patient's detention and the giving of reasons breached art.5(2) of the European Convention on Human Rights.

For the time being detained   This provision requires the patient to be provided with the relevant information when the section under which he is detained changes.

Rights of applying to a tribunal   If the patient (or his nearest relative) has missed an opportunity to apply to a tribunal because of a failure to provide the information set out in this provision, the patient (or his representative) should request that the Secretary of State refers the case to the tribunal under either s.67 or s.71.

Subsection (2)

1-1361 Sections 23, 25 and 66(1)(a) are concerned with the powers of the responsible clinician, the hospital managers and the nearest relative to discharge the patient, ss.56 to 64 contain the consent to treatment provisions, s.118 provides for the publishing of the *Code of Practice*, s.120 is concerned with the Care Quality Commission and the Welsh Ministers' functions relating to the general protection of patients who are subject to the Act and s.134 deals with the withholding of detained patient's correspondence.

Subsection (4)

1-1362 Paragraph 4.32 of the Code states:

"When a patient detained under the Act or subject to a CTO is given information, they should be told that the written information will also be supplied to their nearest relative, so that they can discuss their views about sharing this information and following this discussion, raise any concerns or object to the sharing of some or all of this information. There should be discussion with the patient at the earliest possible time as to what information they are happy to share and what they would like to be kept private."

With regard to the patient's rights under the European Convention on Human Rights (ECHR), the Code states at para.4.36:

"In addition, occasionally there will be cases where [the duties to provide information to nearest relatives] do not apply because disclosing information about the patient to the nearest relative cannot be considered practicable, on the grounds that it would have a detrimental impact on the patient that is disproportionate to any advantage to be gained from informing the nearest relative. This would therefore be a breach of the patient's right to privacy under article 8 of the ECHR. The risk of this is greatest where the nearest relative is someone whom the patient would not have chosen themselves. Before disclosing information to nearest relatives without a patient's consent, the person concerned must consider whether the disclosure would be likely to:

- put the patient at risk of physical harm or financial or other exploitation
- cause the patient emotional distress or lead to a deterioration in their mental health, or
- have any other detrimental effect on their health or wellbeing and, if so, whether the advantages to the patient and the public interest of the disclosure outweigh the disadvantages to the patient, in the light of all the circumstances of the case.""

If the patient is mentally incapable of requesting that the information be not copied to his nearest relative, the information should be sent unless the patient, when mentally capable, had indicated that the nearest relative should not be contacted by the hospital. This opinion is subject to the note on "such steps as are practicable", below.

Patient otherwise requests   It is submitted that the patient should be informed of the provisions of this subsection at the same time as he is given the information required by subss.(1) and (2). A nearest relative will usually be informed about an admission under s.2 (s.11(3)) and consulted about an admission under s.3 (s.11(4)).

Such steps as are practicable   If the hospital managers consider that it might not be practicable to copy the information to the nearest relative of a patient on the ground that knowledge that the nearest relative had been contacted might cause the patient's rights under art.8 of the ECHR to be violated, the managers should adopt the approach identified in *TW v Enfield Borough Council* [2014] EWCA Civ 362; [2014] M.H.L.R. 415 in order to reach a decision: see the notes to "not reasonably practicable" in s.11(4).

[Duty of managers of hospitals to give information to community patients

132A.—(1)   The managers of the responsible hospital shall take such steps as **1-1363** are practicable to ensure that a community patient understands—

(a)   the effect of the provisions of this Act applying to community patients; and

(b)   what rights of applying to a [tribunal] are available to him in that capacity; and those steps shall be taken as soon as practicable after the patient becomes a community patient.

(2)   The steps to be taken under subsection (1) above shall include giving the requisite information both orally and in writing.

(3)   The managers of the responsible hospital shall, except where the community patient otherwise requests, take such steps as are practicable to furnish the person (if any) appearing to them to be his nearest relative with a copy of any information given to him in writing under subsection (1) above; and those steps shall be taken when the information is given to the patient or within a reasonable time thereafter.]

Amendments

This section was inserted by the Mental Health Act 2007 s.32(4), Sch.3 para.30. The reference to the tribunal in subs.(1)(b) was substituted by SI 2008/2883 art.9, Sch.3 para.64.

Definitions

1-1364   the managers: s.145(1).
responsible hospital: ss.17A(7), 135(1).
community patient: ss.17A(7), 145(1).
nearest relative: s.145(1).

General Note

1-1365   This section places a duty on the managers of the responsible hospital to inform a community patient, both orally and in writing, of the legal effect of being a community patient and of his rights to make an application to a tribunal. The information provided should include information about the conditions which the patient is required to keep and the circumstances in which the RC may recall the patient to hospital: see para 4.13 of the *Code of Practice*. Unless the patient otherwise requests, the written information must also be sent to the patient's nearest relative. This section mirrors the duty contained in s.132 and reference should be made to the notes on that section. There is also a duty placed on hospital managers to inform a patient when his CTO renewed (s.20A(5); also see reg.26(1)(g) of the English Regulations and reg.22(2) of the Welsh Regulations).

Code of Practice

1-1366   Reference should be made to the note to s.132 under this heading.

Duty of managers of hospitals to inform nearest relatives of discharge

1-1367   **133.**—(1)   Where a patient liable to be detained under this Act in a hospital or [registered establishment] is to be discharged otherwise than by virtue of an order for discharge made by his nearest relative, the managers of the hospital or [registered establishment] shall, subject to subsection (2) below, take such steps as are practicable to inform the person (if any) appearing to them to be the nearest relative of the patient; and that information shall, if practicable, be given at least seven days before the date of discharge.

[(1A)   The reference in subsection (1) above to a patient who is to be discharged includes a patient who is to be discharged from hospital under section 17A above.

(1B)   Subsection (1) above shall also apply in a case where a community patient is discharged under section 23 or 72 above (otherwise than by virtue of an order for discharge made by his nearest relative), but with the reference in that subsection to the managers of the hospital or registered establishment being read as a reference to the managers of the responsible hospital.]

(2)   Subsection (1) above shall not apply if the patient or his nearest relative has requested that information about the patient's discharge should not be given under this section.

Amendments

The amendments to this section were made by the Care Standards Act 2000 s.116, Sch.4 para.9(2) and the Mental Health Act 2007 s.32(4), Sch.3 para.31.

Definitions

patient: s.145(1).   **1-1368**
hospital: s.145(1).
registered establishment: ss.34(1), 145(1).
nearest relative: ss.26(3), 145(1).
the managers: s.145(1).
community patient: ss.17A(7), 145(1).
responsible hospital: ss.17A(7), 145(1).

General Note

This section places a duty on the managers of NHS and independent hospitals to inform the nearest **1-1369**
relative of a detained patient that the patient is about to be discharged from detention (including being
discharged subject to a community treatment order) or discharged from a community treatment order
(other than a discharge ordered by the patient's nearest relative). The information should be given at least
seven days before the date of discharge if this is practicable. The duty does not arise if either the patient
or his nearest relative has requested that this information should not be given.

Restricted patients, patients remanded to hospital under s.35 or s.36 and patients subject to interim
hospital orders under s.38 do not have nearest relatives for the purposes of the Act.

Subsection (1)

Such steps as are practicable   See the note on s.132(4).   **1-1370**

Correspondence of patients

134.—(1)   A postal packet addressed to any person by a patient detained in a **1-1371**
hospital under this Act and delivered by the patient for dispatch may be withheld
from [the postal operator concerned]—

>   (a)   if that person has requested that communications addressed to him by
>   the patient should be withheld; or
>   (b)   subject to subsection (3) below, if the hospital is [one at which high
>   security psychiatric services are provided] and the managers of the
>   hospital consider that the postal packet is likely—
>   (i)   to cause distress to the person to whom it is addressed or to any
>   other person (not being a person on the staff of the hospital); or
>   (ii)   to cause danger to any person;

and any request for the purposes of paragraph (a) above shall be made by a notice
in writing given to the managers of the hospital, [or] the [approved clinician with
overall responsibility for the patient's case] […].

(2)   Subject to subsection (3) below, a postal packet addressed to a patient
detained [under this Act in a hospital at which high security psychiatric services are
provided] may be withheld from the patient if, in the opinion of the managers of
the hospital, it is necessary to do so in the interests of the safety of the patient or
for the protection of other persons.

(3)   Subsections (1)(b) and (2) above do not apply to any postal packet addressed by a patient to, or sent to a patient by or on behalf of—

>   (a)   any Minister of the Crown [or the Scottish Ministers] or Member of
>   either House of Parliament [or a Member of the Scottish Parliament]
>   [or of the Northern Ireland Assembly];
>   [(aa)   any of the Welsh Ministers, the Counsel General of the [Welsh Govern-
>   ment] or a member of the National Assembly for Wales;]

[(b)   any judge or officer of the Court of Protection, any of the Court of Protection Visitors or any person asked by that Court for a report under section 49 of the Mental Capacity Act 2005 concerning the patient;]

(c)   the Parliamentary Commissioner for Administration, [the Scottish Public Services Ombudsman] [the Public Services Ombudsman for Wales] the Health Service Commissioner for England, [...] or a Local Commissioner within the meaning of Part III of the Local Government Act 1974;

[(ca)   the Care Quality Commission;]

(d)   [the First-tier Tribunal or the Mental Health Review Tribunal for Wales];

(e)   [NHS England] [, an integrated care board,] [...] [[[Local Health Board] [or Special Health Authority] [...], a local social services authority, a Community Health Council [...]] [a] [local probation board established under section 4 of the Criminal Justice and Court Services Act 2000] [or a provider of probation services];

[(ea)   a provider of a patient advocacy and liaison service for the assistance of patients at the hospital and their families and carers;

(eb)   a provider of independent advocacy services for the patient;]

(f)   the managers of the hospital in which the patient is detained;

(g)   any legally qualified person instructed by the patient to act as his legal adviser; or

(h)   the European Commission of Human Rights or the European Court of Human Rights

[and for the purposes of paragraph (d) above the reference to the First-tier Tribunal is a reference to that tribunal so far as it is acting for the purposes of any proceedings under this Act or paragraph 5(2) of the Schedule to the Repatriation of Prisoners Act 1984.]

[(3A)   In subs.(3) above—

(a)   "a patient advocacy and liaison service" means a service of a description prescribed by regulations made by the Secretary of State, and

[(b)   "independent advocacy services" means services provided under—

(i)   arrangements under section 130A [or section 130E] above;

(ii)   arrangements under [section 223A of the Local Government and Public Involvement in Health Act 2007] or section 187 of the National Health Service (Wales) Act 2006; or

(iii)   arrangements of a description prescribed as mentioned in paragraph (a) above.]

(4)   The managers of a hospital may inspect and open any postal packet for the purposes of determining—

(a)   whether it is one to which subsection (1) or (2) applies, and

(b)   in the case of a postal packet to which subsection (1) or (2) above applies, whether or not it should be withheld under that subsection;

and the power to withhold a postal packet under either of those subsections includes power to withhold anything contained in it.

(5)   Where a postal packet or anything contained in it is withheld under subsection (1) or (2) above the managers of the hospital shall record that fact in writing.

(6)   Where a postal packet or anything contained in it is withheld under subsection (1)(b) or (2) above the managers of the hospital shall within seven days give

notice of that fact to the patient and, in the case of a packet withheld under subsection (2) above, to the person (if known) by whom the postal packet was sent; and any such notice shall be given in writing and shall contain a statement of the effect of [section 134A(1) to (4)].

(7)   The functions of the managers of a hospital under this section shall be discharged on their behalf by a person on the staff of the hospital appointed by them for that purpose and different persons may be appointed to discharge different functions.

(8)   The Secretary of State may make regulations with respect to the exercise of the powers conferred by this section.

(9)   In this section [and section 134A] "hospital" has the same meaning as in Part II of this Act, [and "postal operator" and] "postal packet" [have] the same meaning as in [Part 3 of the Postal Services Act 2011].

Amendments

The amendments to this section were made by the Scotland Act 1998 (Consequential Modifications) (No.2) Order 1999 (SI 1999/1820) art.4, Sch.2 para.71, the Northern Ireland Act 1998 s.99, Sch.13 para.5(2), the Government of Wales Act 1998 s.125, Sch.12 para.22, the Health Act 1999 s.65, Sch.4 para.68, the Mental Capacity Act 2005 s.67(1), Sch.6 para.29(2), the Mental Health Act 2007 ss.14(4), 30(3), SI 2007/1388 art.3, Sch.1 para.18, the Public Services Ombudsman (Wales) Act 2005 s.39, Sch.6 para.21, Sch.7, the Health and Social Care Act 2008 s.52, Sch.3 para.11, the Health Authorities Act 1995 s.2(1), Sch.1 para.107(10), the Health Act 1999 (Supplementary, Consequential, etc., Provisions) Order 2000 (SI 2000/90) Sch.1 para.16(7), the Criminal Justice and Court Services Act 2000 s.74, Sch.7 para.74, the NHS Reform and Health Care Professions Act 2002 s.19(6), the National Health Service Reform and Health Care Professions Act 2002 (Supplementary, Consequential, etc. Provisions) Regulations 2002 (SI 2002/2469) reg.4, Sch.1, SI 2007/961 art.3, Sch. para.13(10), SI 2008/912 art.3, Sch.1 Pt 1 para.7, the Local Government and Public Involvement in Health Act 2007 s.241, Sch.18 Pt 18, the Health and Social Care Act 2001 s.67, Sch.5 para.6, SI 2008/2883 art.9, Sch.3 para.65, the Postal Services Act 2011 s.91, Sch.12 para.115, the Mental Health (Wales) Measure 2010 s.53(1), Sch.1, the Health and Social Care Act 2012 s.44, Sch.5 para.29, the Wales Act 2014 s.4(4)(a) and the Health and Care Act 2022 Sch.1 para.1, Sch.4 para.17.

Definitions

patient: s.145(1).   **1-1372**
hospital: ss.34(2), 145(1).
approved clinician: s.145(1).
high security psychiatric services: s.145(1).
special managers: s.145(1).
the managers: s.145(1).
local social services authority: s.145(1).
Local Health Board: s.145(1).
Special Health Authority: s.145(1).

General Note

This section provides authority for the inspection and withholding of a detained patient's outgoing   **1-1373**
and incoming mail. It does not apply to patients on community treatment orders. There is no authority for the hospital managers to censor correspondence, i.e. to strike out certain passages in a letter. However, there is power to withhold something contained in a postal packet (subs.(4)). A patient whose mail is withheld under subs.(1)(b) or (2) can have the decision reviewed by the Care Quality Commission (CQC) or, in relation to Wales, the Welsh Ministers (s.134A). For the procedure to be adopted when mail is opened and inspected, see reg.29 of the English Regulations and reg.41 of the Welsh Regulations.

If either a detained or an informal patient is sent articles of potential danger, such as weapons, explosives or matches, through the mail, s.3(1) of the Criminal Law Act 1967 and the common law provide authority for hospital staff to take reasonable measures to prevent the patient from receiving or keeping the article in his possession (see further, "*A review of the Mental Health Act 1959*" D.H.S.S. (1976), para.10.28, and Appendix A).

This section does not confer on a hospital a power to require the return of a patient's mail once it has reached its destination. In *Broadmoor Hospital Authority v R* [2000] 2 All E.R. 727, the Court of Appeal refused the hospital's application for an injunction requiring the return of a draft manuscript of a book which had been sent by a patient to his agent. The hospital considered that the contents of the book, if published, would be prejudicial to the interests of the sender and would cause distress to the family of his victim. The court held that it could, if appropriate, grant an injunction to restrain an activity outside the hospital if it could be shown that it was having a sufficiently significant impact on the security of the hospital or the treatment of a patient: see further the General Note to the Act under the heading "Injunctions to support an authority's performance of its duties under the Act".

Further provisions relating to items brought to hospital premises for patients, patients' access to computer equipment and mobile phones, patients' post and patients' telephone calls for patients at high security hospitals can be found in the High Security Psychiatric Services (Arrangements for Safety and Security) Directions 2013 which are reproduced at Appendix C. In *R. v Franey Ex p. Warren* [1998] EWHC 5, Turner J., in refusing leave to bring judicial review proceedings, held that the decision of the Chief Executive of Broadmoor Hospital to remove, inter alia, personal computers from patients' rooms was a lawful decision which did not prevent patients from communicating with the authorities or the courts. Arrangements had been made for patients to have access to their computers in the hospital's day areas.

A person commits an offence under s.84 of the Postal Services Act 2000 if, without reasonable excuse, he intentionally delays or opens a postal packet in the course of its transmission by post. Under the Investigatory Powers Act 2016 any deliberate interception of communications in the United Kingdom which is without lawful authority, for example under this section, is also an offence.

The Malicious Communications Act 1988 makes provision for the prosecution of persons who send or deliver letters or other articles with the intent to cause distress or anxiety.

Human Rights Act 1998

1-1374   A restriction on a patient's freedom to communicate with others constitutes an interference with the patient's right to respect for his private life under art.8(1) of the European Convention on Human Rights (ECHR). Such an interference will contravene art.8 unless it is "in accordance with the law", pursues one or more of the legitimate aims referred to in art.8(2) and is "necessary in a democratic society" in order to achieve them. It is likely that the power contained in this section does not contravene art.8, given the interpretation that the Court has given to art.8(2) in *Herczegfalvy v Austria* (1993) 15 E.H.R.R. 437, at paras 85 to 92; also see the note on art.10(2) of the ECHR in Part 5.

Code of Practice

1-1375   Paragraph 4.27 of the Code states:

"Detained patients must be told that their letters for posting may be withheld if the person to whom it is addressed asks the hospital managers to do so. Patients in high security psychiatric hospitals must be told about the other circumstances in which their correspondence may be withheld, the procedures that will be followed and of their right to ask the CQC to review the decisions taken."

Subsection (1)

1-1376   This subsection authorises a person appointed by the hospital managers (subss.(4), (7)) to withhold a detained patient's outgoing mail if the addressee has requested that the communications addressed to him or her by the patient should be withheld. The outgoing mail of patients detained in a high security psychiatric hospital can also be withheld if it is felt that the communication is likely to cause distress or danger to any person. This provision could be used to withhold, for example, threatening letters, letters to victims of crime, or letters containing dangerous objects. There is no provision equivalent to that which was contained in s.36 of the Mental Health Act 1959 which authorised the withholding of outgoing mail which would "be likely to prejudice the interests of the patient".

Postal packet   Is defined in subs.(9).

Withheld   Paragraph 5.14 of the Reference Guide states:

"In practice, because a patient can ask the CQC to review the decision within six months of receiving the notice, anything addressed to a patient which is withheld should be retained for at least six months, unless it is necessary to give it to the police or other similar body. After that – assuming the CQC is not in the process of reviewing the decision – it may be returned to the sender, if that can be done safely."

Paragraph (a)   The review procedure set out in s.121(7)(8) does not apply to outgoing mail which is withheld under this paragraph.

Contrary to what is stated in the *Code of Practice* at para.37.37, there is no obligation placed on the hospital managers to inform the patient that mail has been withheld under this paragraph. Such an obligation exists if the mail is withheld under para.(b): see subs.(6).

Paragraph (b): managers of the hospital   Who shall comply with their obligation under subs.(6). This function shall be discharged by a member of the hospital staff (subs. (7)).

Likely   It is submitted that in this context, "likely" means "more likely than not": see the note on "likely to act" in s.25(1).

Distress   The level of distress that has to be experienced is not identified.

Approved clinician   It is submitted that the request remains valid if, subsequent to it being made, the identity of the approved clinician changes.

Subsection (2)

This subsection authorises the withholding of the incoming mail of a patient detained in a high   **1-1377**
security hospital if it is considered that such action is necessary in the interests of the safety of the patient or for the protection of other persons. Either the patient or the sender can have the decision reviewed by the CQC or, in relation to Wales, the Welsh Ministers (s.134A). There is no power to withhold incoming mail on the ground that it would cause distress to the patient.

Paragraph 1.127 of the Mental Health Act Commission's *Thirteenth Biennial Report* 2007–2009, states:

"Legal advice received by the MHAC in 1997 suggested that the first ground under s.134(2) for withholding mail addressed to High Security Hospital patients ('necessary in the interests of the safety of the patient') should not be deemed to extend to include the patient's health or welfare. However, the second ground ('protection of others') might apply individually in these cases to the authors of the letters, or indeed to classes of persons, such as women or children, provided that the actual risk posed by the patient should he receive such material is clearly expressed. Such a risk could, in our view, be related to the patient's pathology and the treatment he is receiving for it, but a decision must be taken on the facts of any individual case."

Although there is no power to withhold the incoming mail of a patient who is detained in a hospital which is not a high security hospital, para.1.135 of the MHAC's *Thirteenth Biennial Report* states:

"Some medium secure hospital policies stipulate that, whilst it is unlawful to withhold incoming mail from a patient, or to open mail addressed to a patient without that patient's permission, if a staff member has concerns about the possible contents of a particular package or letter, it is acceptable for the patient to be advised that he or she may only open it in a controlled environment (i.e. the nurses' office) in the presence of staff. Once open, the contents may be treated like any other item of patient property and confiscated if necessary. The MHAC accepts the need for such arrangements as a last resort, but they should be carefully monitored and reviewed to ensure that they are and continue to be a justified interference with the patient's rights to privacy, and must never [be] used as a blanket measure irrespective of individual risk assessment."

The managers   Who shall comply with their obligation under subs.(6). This function shall be discharged by a member of the hospital staff (subs.(7)).

Subsection (3)

1-1378   This subsection excludes the provisions of subss.(1)(b) and (2) in respect of certain bodies and individuals. Any person or body listed in this subsection can request that communications addressed to him or her by the patient be withheld (subs.(1)(a)).

Although the Criminal Cases Review Commission is not a body that is listed in this provision, it is suggested that, given the function of the Commission, letters addressed to it should not be opened unless the Commission has requested otherwise.

The Mental Health Act Commission held the view that:

> "patient telephone calls to the same organisations [listed in this subsection] should attract a similar degree of privacy and that whilst any supervision of phone calls should not generally include listening into the contents of the calls (in certain circumstances this may be necessary) such listening in should never take place when the patient's phone call is with one of the specific organisations referred to above" (MHAC, *Sixth Biennial Report* 1993–1995, para.9.8).

Any policy that restricts a patient's access to a telephone must be consistent with the patient's rights under art.8 of the ECHR (*Valle v Finland* [2000] M.H.L.R. 255).

Patient advocacy and liaison service   See the note of "Regulations" in subs.(3A).

Subsection (3A)

1-1379   **Regulations**   For the purposes of subs.(3)(ea), above, "patient advocacy and liaison service" is defined in reg.31(1) of the English Regulations.

For the purposes of para.(b)(iii), the prescribed arrangements are arrangements in respect of independent mental capacity advocates: see reg.31(2) of the English Regulations and reg.42 of the Welsh Regulations.

Subsection (4)

1-1380   **The managers**   See subs.(7).

Open   It will not usually be necessary to open the mail of patients who are not detained in high security hospitals, as the requirements of subs.(1)(a) can be met by looking at the addresses on patients' outgoing mail. However, it would be permissible for such mail to be opened if staff had a reasonable suspicion that a postal packet contained letters which the patient wanted the addressee to forward to people who had requested that mail be withheld. In high security psychiatric hospitals it will be necessary to open both outgoing and incoming mail if there is a reasonable suspicion that either subs.(1) or (2) applies. If, as a result of the inspection, nothing is withheld from the patient, the procedure set out in reg.29(1) of the English Regulations should be followed.

Although the issue has not been tested in the courts, it is likely that the inspection of the contents of a postal packet can include viewing the contents of a computer disc.

Subsection (5)

1-1381   **Record**   See reg.29(2) of the English Regulations and reg.41(a) of the Welsh Regulations.

Withheld   The obligation to record does not apply to the opening of mail under subs.(4).

Subsection (6)

1-1382   **Notice**   See reg.29(3) of the English Regulations.

Subsection (7)

1-1383   **Shall be discharged**   The hospital managers must appoint a member of staff to discharge their functions under this section. This person will need to consult with the patient's responsible clinician before a decision is made to withhold post.

Subsection (8)

Secretary of state   The functions of the Minister, so far as exercisable in relation to Wales, are **1-1384**
exercised by the Welsh Ministers (see the General Note to the Act and SI 1999/672, art.2, Sch.1).

Subsection (9)

Postal operator   By virtue of s.125(1) of the Postal Services Act 2000, the definition of this phrase **1-1385**
is to be found in s.27(3) to (5) of the Postal Services Act 2011 which reads as follows:

> "(3)   'postal operator' means a person who provides—
>   (a)   the service of conveying postal packets from one place to another by post, or
>   (b)   any of the incidental services of receiving, collecting, sorting and delivering postal
>   packets.
> (4)   A person is not to be regarded as a postal operator merely as a result of receiving postal
> packets in the course of acting as an agent for, or otherwise on behalf of, another.
> (5)   The Secretary of State may make regulations prescribing circumstances in which subsec-
> tion (4) is not to apply."

Postal packet   Means "a letter, parcel, packet or other article transmitted by post": Postal Services Act
2000 s.125(1).

[Review of decisions to withhold correspondence

134A.—(1)   The regulatory authority must review any decision to withhold a **1-1386**
postal packet (or anything contained in it) under subsection (1)(b) or (2) of section
134 if an application for a review of the decision is made—
  (a)   in a case under subsection (1)(b) of that section, by the patient; or
  (b)   in a case under subsection (2) of that section, either by the patient or
        by the person by whom the postal packet was sent.

(2)   An application under subsection (1) must be made within 6 months of
receipt by the applicant of the notice referred to in section 134(6).

(3)   On an application under subsection (1), the regulatory authority may direct
that the postal packet (or anything contained in it) is not to be withheld.

(4)   The managers of the hospital concerned must comply with any such
direction.

(5)   The Secretary of State may by regulations make provision in connection
with the making to and determination by the Care Quality Commission of applications under subsection (1), including provision for the production to the Commission of any postal packet which is the subject of such an application.

(6)   The Welsh Ministers may by regulations make provision in connection with
the making to them of applications under subsection (1), including provision for the
production to them of any postal packet which is the subject of such an application.]

Amendment

This section was inserted by the Health and Social Care Act 2008 s.52, Sch.3 para.12.

Definitions

the regulatory authority: s.145(1).   **1-1387**
postal packet: s.134(9).
patient: s.145(1).
the managers: s.145(1).
hospital: ss.34(2), 145(1) (by virtue of s.134(9)).

General Note

1-1388   This section provides that the Care Quality Commission or, in relation to Wales, the Welsh Ministers must review any decision made under s.134(1)(b) or (2) to withhold a postal packet or anything contained within it if an application is made by a person specified in subs.(1)(a) or (b) within the timescale set out in subs.(2). Subsection (3) provides that such a review could result in the regulatory authority directing that the postal packet is not withheld.

Although the CQC upholds very few appeals without qualification, it reports that a "larger number of appeals result in a compromise, for instance where elements of the postal packet are released or alternative arrangements are made that are acceptable to the sender or the intended recipient of postal packages. In 2013/14, four cases were resolved in that way" (CQC, "*Monitoring the Mental Health Act in 2013/2014*", p.26).

Warrant to search for and remove patients

1-1389   **135.**—(1)   If it appears to a justice of the peace, on information on oath laid by an [approved mental health professional], that there is reasonable cause to suspect that a person believed to be suffering from mental disorder—

(a)   has been, or is being, ill-treated, neglected or kept otherwise than under proper control, in any place within the jurisdiction of the justice, or

(b)   being unable to care for himself, is living alone in any such place,

the justice may issue a warrant authorising any constable [...] to enter, if need be by force, any premises specified in the warrant in which that person is believed to be, and, if thought fit, to remove him to a place of safety with a view to the making of an application in respect of him under Part II of this Act, or of other arrangements for his treatment or care.

[(1A)   If the premises specified in the warrant are a place of safety, the constable executing the warrant may, instead of removing the person to another place of safety, keep the person at those premises for the purpose mentioned in subsection (1).]

(2)   If it appears to a justice of the peace, on information on oath laid by any constable or other person who is authorised by or under this Act or under [article 8 of the Mental Health (Care and Treatment) (Scotland) Act 2003 (Consequential Provisions) Order 2005] to take a patient to any place, or to take into custody or retake a patient who is liable under this Act or under the said [article 8] to be so taken or retaken—

(a)   that there is reasonable cause to believe that the patient is to be found on premises within the jurisdiction of the justice; and

(b)   that admission to the premises has been refused or that a refusal of such admission is apprehended,

the justice may issue a warrant authorising any constable [...] to enter the premises, if need be by force, and remove the patient.

(3)   A patient who is removed to a place of safety in the execution of a warrant issued [under subsection (1)][, or kept at the premises specified in the warrant under subsection (1A),] may be detained there for a period not exceeding [the permitted period of detention].

[(3ZA)   In subsection (3), "the permitted period of detention" means—

(a)   the period of 24 hours beginning with—

(i)   in a case where the person is removed to a place of safety, the time when the person arrives at that place;

(ii)   in a case where the person is kept at the premises specified in the warrant, the time when the constable first entered the premises to execute the warrant; or

(b) where an authorisation is given in relation to the person under section 136B, that period of 24 hours and such further period as is specified in the authorisation.]

[(3A) A constable, an approved mental health professional or a person authorised by either of them for the purposes of this subsection may, before the end of [the permitted period of detention] mentioned in subsection (3) above, take a person detained in a place of safety under that subsection to one or more other places of safety.

(3B) A person taken to a place of safety under subsection (3A) above may be detained there for a period ending no later than the end of [the permitted period of detention] mentioned in subsection (3) above.]

(4) In the execution of a warrant issued under subsection (1) above, [a constable] shall be accompanied by an [approved mental health professional] and by a registered medical practitioner, and in the execution of a warrant issued under subsection (2) above [a constable] may be accompanied—

(a) by a registered medical practitioner;

(b) by any person authorised by or under this Act or under [article 8 of the Mental Health (Care and Treatment) (Scotland) Act 2003 (Consequential Provisions) Order 2005] to take or retake the patient.

(5) It shall not be necessary in any information or warrant under subsection (1) above to name the patient concerned.

(6) In this section "place of safety" means residential accommodation provided by a local social services authority under [Part 1 of the Care Act 2014 or] [Part 4 of the Social Services and Well-being (Wales) Act 2014] […], a hospital as defined by this Act, a police station, [an independent hospital or care home] for mentally disordered persons or any other suitable place […].

[(7) For the purpose of subsection (6)—

(a) a house, flat or room where a person is living may not be regarded as a suitable place unless—

(i) if the person believed to be suffering from a mental disorder is the sole occupier of the place, that person agrees to the use of the place as a place of safety;

(ii) if the person believed to be suffering from a mental disorder is an occupier of the place but not the sole occupier, both that person and one of the other occupiers agree to the use of the place as a place of safety;

(iii) if the person believed to be suffering from a mental disorder is not an occupier of the place, both that person and the occupier (or, if more than one, one of the occupiers) agree to the use of the place as a place of safety;

(b) a place other than one mentioned in paragraph (a) may not be regarded as a suitable place unless a person who appears to the constable exercising powers under this section to be responsible for the management of the place agrees to its use as a place of safety.]

[(8) This section is subject to section 136A which makes provision about the removal and taking of persons to a police station under this section.]

Amendments

The amendments to this section were made by SI 2005/2078 Sch.1 para.2(9), the Police and Criminal Evidence Act 1984 s.119, Sch.6 para.26, Sch.7, the National Health Service and Community Care Act 1990 s.66(2), Sch.10, the Care Standards Act 2000 s.116, Sch.4 para.9(9), the Mental Health Act 2007 ss.21, 44(2), Sch.2 para.10, SI 2015/914 Sch. para.29, SI 2016/413 reg.37 and the Policing and Crime Act 2017 ss.80(2), (3) and 81 (2), (3), (4).

Definitions

1-1390
    approved mental health professional: s.145(1), (1AC).
    mental disorder: ss.1, 145(1).
    patient: s.145(1).
    local social services authority: s.145(1).
    hospital: ss.34(2), 145(1).
    independent hospital: s.145(1).
    care home: s.145(1).

General Note

1-1391
    This section provides in subs.(1) and (1A) for a magistrate to issue a warrant authorising a constable to enter premises, using force if necessary, for the purpose of either removing a mentally disordered person who is not liable to be detained to a place of safety (subs.(1)) or, if the premises specified in the warrant are a place of safety, keep the person in the premises (subs.(1A)) for the permitted period of detention which is usually 24 hours but can be extended for a further 12 hours under s.136B (subss.(3),(3ZA)). The person can be transferred to another place of safety during the permitted period of detention (subss.(3) (A), (3)(B)) and reasonable force may be used in the transfer if this proves to be necessary (s.137). A warrant issued under subs.(2) is used where the person concerned is either liable to be detained or is required to reside at a particular place under the terms of guardianship, a community treatment order (CTO) or under the Scottish legislation.

    The existence of the warrant, which provides a means by which an entry which would otherwise be a trespass becomes a lawful act, does not mean that it must be executed; the decision to do so is that of the constable. The warrant is executed once entry to the premises has been effected by the constable, either by force, or by invitation if the occupier is aware of the warrant. However, if the occupier of the premises allows entry without knowledge of the existence of the warrant and without the constable producing the warrant, it is submitted that the warrant has not been executed as long as the occupier's consent to the entry is not withdrawn. Any police officer can execute the warrant: see the note on "constable" in s.136(1).

    By virtue of Sch.1 to the Magistrates Courts Fees Order 2008 (SI 2008/1052) (as amended) a fee of £20 shall be charged for the issuing of a warrant under this section. Local authorities can use the fee account system to ensure that payment for the warrant does not become a delaying factor: see *www.justice.gov.uk/courts/fees/payment-by-account.*

    For the power of a constable to search the person to whom a warrant that has been issued under subs.(1) or (2) relates, see s.136C. If a person escapes while being taken to or detained in a place of safety, he can only be retaken within the period specified in s.138(3).

    In *Ward v Commissioner of Police for the Metropolis* [2005] UKHL 32; [2005] 3 All E.R. 1013, the House of Lords held that when issuing a warrant under subs.(1) a magistrate has no power to impose a condition that the constable executing it should be accompanied by a *named* approved mental health professional (AMHP) and/or medical practitioner. The reasoning adopted by the House of Lords would also apply to warrants issued under subs.(2).

    Sections 5 and 6 of the Mental Capacity Act 2005 do not confer on police officers authority to remove mentally incapacitated persons to hospital or other places of safety for the purposes set out in this section (*R. (on the application of Sessay) v South London and Maudsley NHS Foundation Trust)* [2011] EWHC 2617 (QB); [2012] M.H.L.R. 94).

    The consent to treatment provisions contained in Part IV do not apply to a patient who is detained under this section (s.56(3)(b)). If the person is mentally capable of making a decision about treatment, the common law enables him to refuse to be treated for either a physical or mental disorder. However, if the person is assessed as being mentally incapable of making a decision about treatment, the treatment can be provided under the Mental Capacity Act 2005 if it is deemed to be in his best interests.

Restraint can be used in the provision of the treatment if its use is both necessary and proportionate to prevent harm to the person (2005 Act s.6).

Where an adult who has been removed under this section is admitted to accommodation provided under ss.18 or 19 of the Care Act 2014 or to any hospital, and it appears to the local social services authority that there is a danger of loss or damage to moveable property in the local authority's area because the adult is unable (whether permanently or temporarily) to protect or deal with the property and no other suitable arrangements have been or are being made, s.47 of the 2014 Act places the authority under a duty to take reasonable steps to prevent or mitigate the loss or damage. The authority has the power to enter the person's home in order to carry out this duty if certain criteria are satisfied, and to recover its reasonable expenses. The equivalent duty in Wales is contained in s.58 of the Social Services and Well-being (Wales) Act 2014.

The Government's "Mental Health Crisis Care Concordat" (2014) is a national agreement between services and agencies involved in the care and support of people in crisis, including people who are detained under this section. It sets out how organisations will work together better to make sure that people get the help they need when they are having a mental health crisis. The Concordat can be accessed at: *www.crisiscareconcordat.org.uk*. The Welsh Government published a Concordat for Wales in 2015. It can be accessed at: *http://democratiaeth.sirgar.llyw.cymru/documents/s28668/Concordat.pdf ?LLL=1*.

Treatment in an A and E department: when does the clock start ticking?

See the General Note to s.136 under this heading. **1-1393**

Police and Criminal Evidence Act 1984 (PACE)

Section 15(1) of PACE states: **1-1394**

"This section and section 16 … have effect in relation to the issue to constables under any enactment, including an enactment contained in an Act passed after this Act, of warrants to enter and search premises, and an entry on or search of premises under a warrant is unlawful unless it complies with this section and section 16 …"

Although it would appear from the heading of this section that a warrant issued to a constable under either subs.(1) or (2) comes within the scope of ss.15 and 16 of PACE, the wording of s.15(4), which states that the "constable shall answer on oath any question that the justice of the peace … hearing the application asks him", suggests that the two sections only relate to warrants issued on the application of a constable. However, in *Ward v Commissioner of Police for the Metropolis*, above, Lady Hale said, at para.27, that she was "inclined to the view" that ss.15 and 16 do apply to warrants issued under this section. It is submitted that the view expressed by Lady Hale should be followed and that the following requirements of PACE be satisfied:

1. The application for the warrant shall be made without notice and the information laid before the magistrate must be in writing (s.15(3)).
2. The warrant shall authorise an entry on one occasion only unless it specifies that it authorises multiple entries (either unlimited or limited to a specified maximum) (s.15(5), (5A)).
3. The warrant shall specify the name of the person who applies for it, the date on which it is issued, and the fact that it was issued under the Mental Health Act (s.15(6)).
4. The warrant shall identify, so far as is practicable, the person to be sought (s.15(6)).
5. Apart from a warrant that authorises multiple entries where as many copies as are reasonably required may be made, two copies shall be made of the warrant and the copies shall be clearly certified as copies (s.15(7), (8)). One copy is retained by the police and the other is handed to the occupier of the premises. It is suggested that a third copy be taken for retention by the person in charge of the place of safety to which the patient is removed.
6. Entry and search under the warrant must be within three months from the date of its issue (s.16(3)).
7. Entry and search under the warrant must be at a reasonable hour unless it appears to the constable executing it that the purpose of the search may be frustrated on an entry at a reasonable hour (s.16(4)).
8. If the occupier of the premises is present at the time when the constable seeks to execute the warrant, the constable shall (a) identify himself; (b) produce the warrant to him; and (c) supply him with a copy of it. If the occupier of the premises is not present but some other person

who appears to the constable to be in charge of the premises is present, the above procedure will be followed in respect of that other person. If there is no person present who appears to the constable to be in charge of the premises, he shall leave a copy of the warrant in a prominent place on the premises (s.16(5), (6), (7)).

9.   A search under the warrant may only be a search to the extent required for the purpose for which the warrant was issued (s.16(8)).

10.   The constable executing the warrant shall make an endorsement on it stating whether the person sought was found (s.16(9)).

11.   A warrant which has been executed, or which has not been executed within the time authorised for its execution, shall be returned to the designated officer for the local justice area in which the justice was acting who shall retain it for a period of 12 months. During this period the occupier of the premises to which the warrant relates shall be allowed to inspect the warrant (s.16(10), (10A), (11), (12)).

The powers of the Police under PACE

1-1395   Under s.117 of PACE, the constable may use reasonable force, if necessary, when executing the warrant, which can include restricting the movement of those in occupation of the premises while the premises are being searched (*DPP v Meaden* [2003] EWHC 3005 (Admin), para.32). *Meaden* was applied by the Court of Appeal in *Connor v Chief Constable of Merseyside Police* [2006] EWCA Civ 1549, where it was held, at paras 67 and 69, that the power of the police when executing a warrant extended to taking reasonable and necessary steps to detain the occupants of the premises who might otherwise put lives in danger or themselves be put in danger. "Guidance on Responding to People with Mental Ill Health or Learning Disabilities", National Police Improvement Agency (2010), para.6.8.7, states that a warrant permits "a degree of control of others within the premises to ensure the safety of everyone present".

Code of Practice C on the "Detention, Treatment and Questioning of Persons by Police Officers", which is issued under PACE, applies to a person who has been removed to a police station as a place of safety under this section (para.1.10). The implications of this requirement are set out in the General Note to s.136.

In *D'Souza v Director of Public Prosecutions* [1992] 4 All E.R. 545, the House of Lords held that the power to obtain a warrant under subs.(2) of this section is not the exclusive method of gaining access to premises in order to retake a detained patient who has absconded from hospital and that an alternative is provided for in s.17(1)(d) of PACE. Section 17(1)(d) states that a policeman "may enter and search any premises for the purpose ... of recapturing a person who is unlawfully at large and whom he is pursuing". The leading speech in the House of Lords was given by Lord Lowry who held, at 556, that the

"verb in the clause 'whom he is pursuing' is in the *present continuous* tense and therefore, give or take a few seconds or minutes—this is a question of degree—the pursuit must be almost contemporaneous with the entry into the premises. There must, I consider, be an act of pursuit, that is a chase, however short in time or distance. It is not enough for the police to form an intention to arrest, which they put into practice by resorting to the premises where they believe that the person whom they seek may be found."

His Lordship further held, at 553, 554, that if a person who is lawfully detained in hospital under s.6(2) goes absent without leave, he is by virtue of s.18(1) liable to be taken into custody and returned to the hospital, and is therefore "unlawfully at large" for the purposes of s.17(1)(d).

Section 17(1)(e) of PACE provides the police with the power to enter and search any premises without a warrant if such action is required to save "life or limb" or to prevent "serious damage to property". In *Baker v Crown Prosecution Service* [2009] EWHC 299 (Admin), the Divisional Court held that:

1.   The power enables the police to enter premises where permission has not been given if there is a reasonable belief that the requirements of s.17(1)(e) are satisfied. The requirements will not be satisfied if the police merely have a concern for the welfare of someone within the premises (*Syed v Director of Public Prosecutions* [2010] EWHC 81 (Admin)). [In *Nassinde v Chester Magistrates Court* [2020] EWHC 3329 (Admin) at para.10, Macur L.J. said that the "threshold is high".]

2.   The words "saving life or limb" (a) refer to a degree of apprehended *serious* bodily injury and (b) are wide enough to cover saving a person from seriously harming himself or herself, as well as seriously harming third parties.

3.   The power to search in s.17 is only a power to search to the extent that is reasonably required for the purpose for which the power of entry is exercised; it is not a general power to search.

Although s.17(1)(e) does not provide the police with authority to remove any person from the premises, the police could arrest the person for any offence that might have been committed.

PACE has not removed the common law power of the police to enter private premises without a warrant to prevent a breach of the peace occurring if they reasonably believe that an imminent breach of the peace, usually an assault, is likely to occur on the premises (*McLeod v Commissioner of Police of the Metropolis* [1994] 4 All E.R. 553 CA). The nature of a breach of the peace is considered in Appendix A.

Human Rights Act 1998

1-1396

Use of this section involves an interference with the mentally disordered person's home and private life that must be justified under art.8(2) of the European Convention on Human Rights. Entry to the person's home must be a proportionate measure in all the circumstances and the reasons adduced to justify the search must be relevant and sufficient (*McLeod v United Kingdom* (1999) 27 E.H.R.R. 493). In *Camenzind v Switzerland* (1999) 28 E.H.R.R. 458 at para.45, the European Court of Human Rights held that the State's governing legislation and practice must afford adequate and effective safeguards against abuse if the test of proportionality is to be satisfied. Although it has been argued that the failure to give formal notification to the mentally disordered person of an impending application for a warrant under this section might breach art.8, it is likely that a court would find that the adjudication of the application by a magistrate provides the safeguard required.

Code of Practice

1-1397

Chapter 16, which considers this section, should be read with caution because its contents do not reflect the significant amendments that have been made to this section by the Policing and Crime Act 2017.

Guidance

1-1398

Joint Department of Health and Home Office guidance to support the implementation of changes to the police powers and places of safety provisions contained in this section made by the Policing and Crime Act 2017 can be accessed at: *www.gov.uk/government/uploads/system/uploads/attachment_data/file/656025/Guidance_on_Police_Powers.PDF*.

Right Care Right Person

See the General Note to s.136 under this heading.

Subsection (1)

1-1399

This subsection enables an AMHP, when acting on behalf of a local social services authority, to make an application to a magistrate for a warrant authorising a constable to enter premises where a mentally disordered person is believed to be living for the purpose of removing that person to a place of safety if an initial assessment indicates that removal is required (subs.(1)). However, if the premises specified in the warrant are a place of safety, the constable executing the warrant may, instead of removing the person to another place of safety, keep the person at those premises (subs.(1A)). There is no requirement for an intended place of safety to be identified before the warrant is executed. The constable must be accompanied by a doctor and an AMHP when executing the warrant (subs.(4)). The power to enter the premises includes a power to search those premises in order to find the person believed to be suffering from mental disorder (*Ward v Commissioner of Police for the Metropolis*, above, para.23).

It is not a precondition for the making of an application that admission to the premises has been refused. An application could be made where consent to entry is likely to be given in circumstances where the person is thought likely to be either violent or to immediately abscond once entry has been effected. In other words, the warrant is being sought not to gain entry but to provide authority to the police to effectively manage the risks which will have been identified in the application. In the absence of a warrant, the legal powers of the police in such a situation would be limited to using their powers under either s.3 of the Criminal Law Act 1967 or to prevent a breach of the peace (see Appendix A). A constable has the power to search the person to whom a warrant that has been issued under this subsection relates in the circumstances specified in s.136C.

Once entry to the premises has been effected, an assessment of the person for detention under the Act can be undertaken. The Home Office Impact Assessment on the Policing and Crime Bill states: "If deemed safe and appropriate by the AMHP, a mental health assessment should be able to take place in a person's home once entry has been gained through a s.135 warrant. This ratifies existing practice in many areas (where a person consents), can be a much more practicable option for professionals as well as desirable for the individual being assessed, and can ultimately reduce unnecessary pressure on health-based places of safety" (para.27.7). It is submitted that if either the assessing doctor concludes on her initial examination that the person is not mentally disordered or if a decision is taken that no further action need to be taken with respect to the person, the power for the professionals to remain in the premises lapses.

Paragraph 16.8 of the *Code of Practice* states:

"The AMHP and the doctor may convene a mental health assessment in the person's home if it is safe and appropriate to do so and the person consents to this. In taking this decision, consideration should be given as to who else is present, particularly if a person might be distressed by the assessment taking place in these circumstances."

During the debates on the Mental Health Bill, a Government Minister said: "Under [this] provision, the ill-treatment, neglect, lack of proper control or inability to care for onself need not be linked to the existence of the mental disorder from which the person is suffering" (*Hansard*, HL Vol.688, col.663).

A warrant can be issued though the name of the mentally disordered person is not known (subs.(5)). The relevant premises must be specified in the warrant.

Justice of the peace   The *Code of Practice* states:

"16.11 Magistrates have to be satisfied that it is appropriate to issue a warrant. They are likely to ask applicants why they are applying for a warrant, whether reasonable attempts to enter without a warrant have been made and, if not, why not. Although it is not necessary for permission to enter to have been refused in order for a section 135(1) warrant to be granted, applicants should provide documented reasons for seeking a warrant if they have not already tried to gain access.

16.12 Magistrates should ensure that section 135 warrants can be granted in a timely way, taking into account that situations can be very urgent and that it should be possible to grant a warrant outside of normal business hours."

Information   There is no requirement for the person who is the subject of the application to be informed of the fact that it is being made: see the note on Human Rights Act 1998, above.

Approved mental health professional   Only an AMHP acting on behalf of a local authority can apply for a warrant to be issued under this subsection. If the person has a care co-ordinator who is not an AMHP, he or she can accompany the AMHP applicant and provide evidence to the magistrate.

Believed to be suffering from mental disorder   But has not yet reliably been shown to be so (*Ward v Commissioner of Police for the Metropolis*, above, para.13).

Kept otherwise than under proper control   This phrase encompasses not only the situation where a person is being subjected to a degree of improper control, but also the situation where a person is suffering from the absence of control.

Unable to care for himself   Paragraph (b) is aimed at a mentally disordered person who is living alone and is unable to look after himself appropriately. As "care" is a broad term which encompasses matters that relate to a person's daily needs, a warrant could be applied for where the main cause of concern is the apparent failure of the person to take essential prescribed medication. It is suggested that the AMHP would have to satisfy the magistrate that a failure to take the medication would have serious consequences for the well-being of the person who lacked the mental capacity to make a decision about taking the medication.

Living alone   The suggestion by the Royal College of Psychiatrists that this section should also provide for a situation where two mentally disordered people were living together and were unable to care for themselves was not adopted (Cmnd. 7320, para.2.21).

Premises   This term is not defined. Although it is generally taken to mean a house or building, together with its land and outbuildings, the courts have adopted wider definitions in different contexts. In *Maunsell v Olins* [1975] 1 All E.R. 16 at 19, HL, Viscount Dilhorne said:

"'Premises' is an ordinary word of the English language which takes colour and content from the context in which it is used. ... It has, in my opinion, no recognised and established primary meaning."

In s.23(c) of the Police and Criminal Evidence Act 1984, the definition of "premises" in that Act includes "any tent or moveable structure". In the context of this section, it is submitted that the term includes any place where the person is living, which can include a caravan or a tent.

Access to premises can be effected lawfully if a co-owner or, possibly, a co-occupier of the premises gives permission for the mental health professionals to enter: see the note on "enter and inspect" in s.115. If permission is granted to enter premises, such as a hotel, where members of the public can reside, a warrant under this section is not required to enter a room in the premises that the mentally disordered person is occupying if that person has no right of exclusive occupation of the room (*R. v Rosso* [2003] EWCA Crim 3242; [2003] M.H.L.R. 404). In *Rosso*, the Court of Appeal, at para.19, determined whether the person had an exclusive right to occupy a room by asking the following questions:

1.   Does the occupant have a right to exclude others from the room?
2.   Does the occupant have the right to deny anybody access to the room?

As the answer to both questions was "no", no such right existed.

A lodger who rents a room in a house where he shares facilities with his landlord does not have the right to deny his landlord access to the room. As the lodger does not have an exclusive right to occupy the room, the landlord has the right to grant mental health professionals access.

In *Ward v Commissioner of Police for the Metropolis*, above, the person concerned had locked herself in her car which was apparently located on her premises. The policeman executing the warrant gained access to the car and the person was taken to the place of safety by ambulance.

If thought fit, to remove him   This section does not specify whose decision this is. It is suggested that the constable's role is to gain entry to the premises and to ensure the safety of the doctor and the AMHP, whose joint role is to assess whether the person should be removed to a place of safety for further assessment there. However, the person need not be removed in the circumstances specified in subs.(1A).

In *Ward v Commissioner of Police for the Metropolis*, above, Lady Hale said that "professionals should be able to help the police officer to decide whether or not it is 'fit' to take the person concerned to a place of safety" (para.12). Although para.16.16 of the Code of Practice states that the "police should not normally be needed to transport the person or to escort them for a section 135 warrant", this provision allocates responsibility for transporting the patient to the police. In *Ward*, Lady Hale said that it may be "that the police officer can authorise others, such as the ambulance service or an [AMHP], to transport the person to the place of safety rather than doing it himself" (para.23).

For general provisions relating to the conveyance of patients from one place to another, see s.137.

Other arrangements   Such as an informal admission to hospital, or the provision of community care services at the person's home.

Subsection (1A)

This subsection enables the constable who executes the warrant not to remove the person to a place   **1-1400** of safety if the premises specified in the warrant are a place of safety. A place of safety is defined in subss.(6) and (7).

Subsection (2)

This subsection provides for the issue of a warrant to a constable to enter premises, using force if   **1-1401** necessary, for the purposes of taking or retaking a patient who is already liable to be detained into custody. It also applies to a patient under guardianship, a CTO or the Scottish legislation who has absconded from a place where he is required to reside or has absconded while being taken to that place. The warrant authorises the removal of the patient to the place where he is required to be. The warrant can only be issued if admission to the premises has been refused or that refusal can be anticipated. The constable may be accompanied by a doctor or any other person, such as an AMHP, who is authorised to take or retake the patient when executing the warrant (subs.(4)).

A constable has the power to search the person to whom a warrant that has been issued under this subsection relates in the circumstances specified in s.136C.

Also note the power of the police under s.17(1)(d) of the Police and Criminal Evidence Act 1984 which is considered in the General Note to this section under *The powers of the Police under PACE*.

Person Authorised   The persons authorised to retake patients under s.18 (and who can therefore be applicants under this provision) are, in addition to a constable, any officer on the staff of the hospital, any AMHP or any person authorised by the hospital managers, or, in the case of a patient subject to guardianship, any officer on the staff of a local social services authority, or any person authorised by the guardian or a local social services authority. For community patients, see s.18(2A). Mental Health Act administrators, care co-ordinators and nurses have made applications under this provision.

Also note the power of the police under s.17(1)(d) of the Police and Criminal Evidence Act 1984 which is considered in the General Note to this section.

Subsection (3)

1-1402 **Place of safety** Is defined in subss.(6) and (7). For restrictions on the use of police stations as places of safety under this section, see s.136A. If entry to the preferred place of safety is refused, it is lawful to take the person to another place of safety. The patient can be transferred from one place of safety to another during the permitted period of detention (subss.(3A), (3B)):

The permitted period of detention Which only applies to warrants issues under subs.(1). The permitted period of detention is a maximum of 24 hours. The Care Quality Commission reported in "Monitoring the Mental Health Act in 2021/22" that this time limit is regularly breached because of delays in accessing an inpatient bed. If, exceptionally, a police station is used as the place of safety, the period can extended for a maximum of 12 hours: see subs.(3ZA). If the place of safety is a hospital, this period cannot be continued under s.5(2) or (4) as it is Parliament's intention that the assessment be completed within the permitted period: see *R. v Wilson Ex p. Williamson* [1996] C.O.D. 42, noted in the General Note to s.2.

Subsections (3A), (3B)

1-1403 These provisions, which respond to concern that was expressed during debates on the 2007 Act about mentally disordered people being detained in a police cell (see for e.g. *Hansard*, HL Vol. 689, col.1467), enable a person who has been detained in a place of safety under this section to be transferred to another one before the permitted period of detention expires. Such a transfer does not have the effect of increasing the permitted period. Guidance on transfers between places of safety is reproduced in the notes on s.136(3), (4).

Subsection (4)

1-1404 **Approved Mental Health Professional** Who need not be the AMHP who made the application to the magistrate.

1-1405 **Subsection (6)** For guidance on "Places that can be used as a place of safety" see the Guidance document, noted above. Paragraphs 3.1 and 3.2 of the document state:

"The legislation continues to provide for a range of locations to be used as a place of safety, which allows for local flexibility to respond to different situations. A person in mental health crisis should be taken to or kept at a place of safety that best meets their needs. The expectation remains that, with limited exceptions, the person's needs will most appropriately be met by taking them to a 'health-based' place of safety – a dedicated section 136 suite where they can be looked after by properly trained and qualified mental health and other medical professionals. There will however, there will be situations in which it is appropriate to use other suitable places, or where other suitable places can supplement the use of health-based places of safety.

The use of other suitable places should not reduce the number or use of health-based places of safety. However local commissioners may wish to consider increasing local place of safety capacity by entering into formal arrangements with third parties (such as charities, voluntary sector or private providers) to establish additional, bespoke places of safety; or by undertaking contingency planning with local partners to identify potential temporary places should all other facilities be unavailable for some reason; or both."

For the use of police stations as places of safety, see s.136A. Where a hospital is used as a place of safety, the provisions of s.132 apply.

Other suitable place This phrase is qualified by subs.(7). The deletion of the phrase "the occupier of which is willing temporarily to receive the patient" in this provision by s.81(2) of the Policing and Crime

Act 2017 is aimed at removing barriers to using community-run places of safety or other alternatives which could not be said to have a single "occupier".

The suitable place could be either the home of a relative or friend of the person or a community based health or social care facility.

Subsection (7)   This provision restricts the use of a house, flat or room as a place of safety to speci-   **1-1406**
fied circumstances.

Although the term "house" is usually interpreted as meaning a building for people to live in, it is submitted that it should be given an expansive interpretation so as to include a houseboat or a caravan if that is the person's home. The Guidance states that para.(a) "would not normally apply if the person is located in a private room in a care or residential home where a person lives" (para.2.5).

The effect of para.(a) is summarised in the following table taken from para.3.9 of the Guidance document:

"Scenario	Agreement required
If the person believed to be suffering from a mental disorder is the sole occupier of the place.	That person agrees to the use of the place as a place of safety;
If the person believed to be suffering from a mental disorder is an occupier of the place but not the sole occupier.	Both that person and one of the other occupiers agree to the use of the place as a place of safety.
If the person believed to be suffering from a mental disorder is not an occupier of the place.	Both that person and the occupier (or, if more than one, one of the occupiers) agree to the use of the place as a place of safety."

The person believed to be suffering from a mental disorder must be mentally capable of giving his agreement. Paragraph 3.10 of the Guidance states:

"When seeking agreement to use a private dwelling or other premises as a place of safety, the police officer should ensure that the relevant persons understand the purpose for which the place will be used, and the support arrangements that will be put in place to safeguard the person (and any others present) pending an assessment. It should be made clear that there is no legal obligation on them to accede to such a request. The request for and giving of this agreement should be recorded."

Paragraph (b) is concerned with the identification of "any other suitable place" in subs. (6), i.e. a place other than the specific places listed in that provision. It states that a place other than one mentioned in para.(a) cannot be regarded as being a "suitable place" unless the person who is responsible for the management of that place agrees to it being used as a place of safety. The agreement of a senior manager who is at the place at the relevant time would be sufficient.

[Removal etc of mentally disordered persons without a warrant]

136.—[(1)   If a person appears to a constable to be suffering from mental   **1-1407**
disorder and to be in immediate need of care or control, the constable may, if he
thinks it necessary to do so in the interests of that person or for the protection of
other persons—

(a)   remove the person to a place of safety within the meaning of section
135, or

(b)   if the person is already at a place of safety within the meaning of that
section, keep the person at that place or remove the person to another
place of safety.

(1A)   The power of a constable under subsection (1) may be exercised where
the mentally disordered person is at any place, other than—

(a)   any house, flat or room where that person, or any other person, is living, or

(b)   any yard, garden, garage or outhouse that is used in connection with
the house, flat or room, other than one that is also used in connection
with one or more other houses, flats or rooms.

(1B)   For the purpose of exercising the power under subsection (1), a constable
may enter any place where the power may be exercised, if need be by force.]

[(1C)   Before deciding to remove a person to, or to keep a person at, a place of safety under subsection (1), the constable must, if it is practicable to do so, consult—

    (a)   a registered medical practitioner,

    (b)   a registered nurse,

    (c)   an approved mental health professional, or

    (d)   a person of a description specified in regulations made by the Secretary of State.]

(2)   A person [removed to, or kept at] a place of safety under this section may be detained there for a period not exceeding [the permitted period of detention] for the purpose of enabling him to be examined by a registered medical practitioner and to be interviewed by an [approved mental health professional] and of making any necessary arrangements for his treatment or care.

[(2A)   In subsection (2), "the permitted period of detention" means—

    (a)   the period of 24 hours beginning with—

        (i)   in a case where the person is removed to a place of safety, the time when the person arrives at that place;

        (ii)   in a case where the person is kept at a place of safety, the time when the constable decides to keep the person at that place; or

    (b)   where an authorisation is given in relation to the person under section 136B, that period of 24 hours and such further period as is specified in the authorisation.]

[(3)   A constable, an approved mental health professional or a person authorised by either of them for the purposes of this subsection may, before the end of [the permitted period of detention] mentioned in subsection (2) above, take a person detained in a place of safety under that subsection to one or more other places of safety.

(4)   A person taken to a place of a safety under subsection (3) above may be detained there for a purpose mentioned in subsection (2) above for a period ending no later than the end of [the permitted period of detention] mentioned in that subsection.]

[(5)   This section is subject to section 136A which makes provision about the removal and taking of persons to a police station, and the keeping of persons at a police station, under this section.]

Amendments

The amendments to this section were made by the Mental Health Act 2007 ss.21, 44(3), Sch.2 para.10 and the Crime and Policing Act 2017 ss.80 (4)–(7), 81(5), 82(3).

Definitions

1-1408   mental disorder: ss.1, 145(1).
    approved mental health professional: s.145(1), (1AC).

General Note

1-1409   This section, which is usually invoked "where a person's abnormal behaviour is causing nuisance or offence" (Cmnd. 7320, para.2.2.2), empowers a constable to either remove a person to a place of safety or, if the person is already at a place of safety, keep the person at that place or remove the person to another place of safety (subs.(1)) for the permitted period of detention which is usually 24 hours but can be extended for a further 12 hours under s.136B (subss.(2),(2A)). The power can only be exercised if the constable considers that the person is suffering from mental disorder and is in immediate need of care or control. The power may be exercised at any place other than a private dwelling (subs. (1A)). The constable may use force to enter a place where the power needs to be exercised (subs.(1B)), and may use restraint on the person being detained (*Collins v Wilcock* [1984] 1 W.L.R. 1172). Before exercising the power the constable must, where it is practicable, consult with a person specified in subs.(1C). In accordance with art.5(2) of the European Convention on Human Rights, the constable should inform the person of the reason why he is being detained under this section (*Van de Leer v Netherlands* (1990) 12 E.H.R.R. 567). For restrictions on the use of police stations as places of safety under this section, see s.136A. As many people who are detained under this section could be charged with a criminal offence, it provides a key pathway into mental health care.

When initiating his power to detain under this section, the constable has a power to search the person (see s.32 of PACE, noted below). On arrival at the place of safety (or on transfer to a second place of safety), a power of search is granted to the constable by s.136C(3).

It is for the constable to determine whether he is detaining a person under this section; he cannot make a determination which is conditional on a subsequent confirmation by a superior officer. The person can be detained for the purpose of being examined by a doctor and interviewed by an approved mental health professional (AMHP) in order that suitable arrangements can be made for his treatment or care (subs.(2)). It is therefore the case that the detention can continue after the assessment has been completed until such time, within the permitted period, that the necessary arrangements have been put in place. The need for the constable to remain at the place of safety during the period of detention is considered in the note on subs.(2). The authority to detain under this section ends immediately if the doctor's assessment leads her to conclude that the person is not mentally disordered. The further detention of the patient in these circumstances would be unlawful: see the note on "Human Rights Act 1998", below. The detained person can be transferred to another place of safety as long as the permitted period has not expired (subss.(3), (4)). There is nothing to prevent a patient who is already liable to be detained under the Act, for example a patient on s.17 leave, from being detained under this section. If, subsequent to the person's arrival at the place of safety, it is discovered that the person is currently a patient who is liable to be detained under the Act, the power under this section falls away and the appropriate absence without leave procedure should be activated.

The powers contained in this section:

"inevitably require that the person concerned can be kept safe in the sense that harm to himself or others is prevented until he can be seen by a doctor and, if necessary, given some form of sedation … A police officer in exercising his powers under s.136 is entitled to use reasonable force. If someone is violent, he can be restrained" (*R. on the application of Anderson) v HM Coroner for Inner North Greater London* [2004] EWHC 2729 (Admin); [2004] M.H.L.R. 324 paras 8, 9, per Collins J.).

Sections 5 and 6 of the Mental Capacity Act 2005 do not confer on the police authority to remove mentally incapacitated persons to hospital or other places of safety for the purposes set out in this section (*R. (on the application of Sessay) v South London and Maudsley NHS Foundation Trust)* [2011] EWHC 2617 (QB); [2012] M.H.L.R. 94). Sessay is authority for the proposition that the staff of a hospital's accident and emergency or out-patient department can hold a patient for a brief period while awaiting the arrival of the police to exercise their power under this section if such action is necessary to prevent the patient from causing harm to himself or to another: also see Appendix A.

A person who is detained under this section is not subject to the consent to treatment provisions contained in Pt IV (s.56(3)(b)). If the person is mentally capable of making a decision about treatment, the common law enables him to refuse to be treated for either a physical or mental disorder. However, if the person is assessed as being mentally incapable of making a decision about treatment, the treatment can be provided under the Mental Capacity Act if it is deemed to be in his best interests. It is submitted that there is a common law power to sedate both mentally capable and mentally incapable persons in an emergency if the sedation is used to restrain that person from causing harm to others: see *R. (on the application of Munjaz) v Mersey Care NHS Trust* [2003] EWCA Civ 1036 which is considered in Appendix A. If the police have concerns about the physical health of the person who has been detained under this section, he could be taken directly to the local A and E department for assessment: see below.

As an alternative to invoking this section with respect to a person under the age of 18, the police could consider using their power under s.46 of the Children Act 1989 which provides that where a constable has reasonable cause to believe that a child would otherwise be likely to suffer significant harm, he may "remove the child to suitable accommodation and keep him there" (ibid., subs.(1)(a)).

The power to arrest under this section was specifically preserved by s.26 and Sch.2 of the Police and Criminal Evidence Act 1984 (PACE) (the references below are to sections of PACE). Apart from providing the arresting policeman with a power to search the person concerned at a place other than a police station (see s.32 and para.16.68 of the *Code of Practice*), this means that a person who has been removed to a place of safety under this section is given the following rights: to be told that they have been arrested and the grounds for the arrest as soon as practicable (s.28), to have another person of his choice informed of his removal (s.56) and to consult a solicitor privately at any time (s.58). Although s.58 relates to a patient who is being "held in custody in a police station or *other premises*", the wording of the section suggests that it is not intended to apply where a patient is detained under this section in a place other than a police station. Section 58 states that where a patient makes a request to consult privately with a solicitor, the time when the request was made "shall be recorded in the custody record" (s.58(2)). Under para.2.1 of *Code of Practice* C (2019 revision), a custody record is only opened in respect of "each person brought to a police station under arrest or arrested at the station having gone there voluntarily". As the mandatory requirement in s.58(2) cannot be satisfied in respect of a patient who is detained in a place other than a police station, it would appear that s.58 does not apply in such circumstances. Paragraph 16.69 of the *Code of Practice* states that hospital managers should facilitate "access to legal advice ... whenever it is requested". Although a person who has been detained under this section has technically been arrested, there is no requirement for a caution to be administered and this should not be done.

There is no statutory form that can be used to record an admission of a person to a hospital which is acting as a place of safety under this section. If such an admission takes place, the hospital should not record it on Form H3 (in Wales, Form HO14) as no application has been made in respect of that person: see reg.4(4) of the English Regulations and reg.4(3) of the Welsh Regulations.

If a person is removed to a hospital under this section, the managers of the hospital are obliged to give that person information under s.132.

A person who escapes while being taken to or detained in a place of safety can only be retaken within the period specified in s.138(3).

The fact that a person has been detained by the police under this section could be disclosed to a potential employer in an enhanced criminal record certificate issued under s.113B(4) of the Police Act 1997 if the relevant criteria are satisfied. Paragraph 37 of "Statutory Disclosure Guidance" (Home Office, 2015) states that the "fact of detention under sections 135(1) or 136 of the Mental Health Act 1983 is unlikely, in itself, to be sufficient to justify disclosure".

The Government's "Mental Health Crisis Care Concordat" (2014) is a national agreement between services and agencies involved in the care and support of people in crisis, including people who are detained under this section. It sets out how organisations will work together better to make sure that people get the help they need when they are having a mental health crisis. The Concordat can be accessed at: *www.crisiscareconcordat.org.uk*. The Welsh Government published a Concordat for Wales in 2015. It can be accessed at: *http://democratiaeth.sirgar.llyw.cymru/documents/s28668/Concordat.pdf ?LLL=1*.

Detention for mental health assessments at police stations

1-1410   If it is considered that an arrested person needs an urgent mental health assessment, he could be assessed at the police station by mental health professionals. The assessment could result in an application being made to a hospital to detain him. If the application cannot be actioned due to a failure to identify a hospital which is willing to admit the patient, it is arguable that it would not be possible to continue the patient's detention at the police station after the expiration of the 24-hour period allowed for by PACE by detaining him under s.136 on the ground that the patient's continued detention would constitute an illegitimate extension of the PACE detention period. The website of the College of Policing states:

"Where the obligation to release someone from PACE detention creates a situation where the health and safety of the detainee is at risk due to their mental health, detention under s 136 may be considered and may be lawfully relied upon in a police station. Any decision to remove someone to a place of safety should be taken as if that person had just been encountered. Under PACE persons should not be solely held in police custody pending a mental health assessment or pending the identification of a bed for that person's admission. Detention under PACE must be justified against the evidential and investigative criteria in s 34 and s 37 PACE and reconsidered by the review officers in s 40 or s 41" (*https://www.college.police.uk/app/mental-health/mental-health-detention#the-decision-to-use-section-136-mha-1983*).

In the absence of a significant change in the patient's presentation, the use of s.136 immediately after the patient has been released from police custody after having been the subject of a full mental health assessment is of doubtful legality as the patient has already been the subject of an assessment under this Act.

A person detained under s.136 can be taken directly to a police station acting as the place of safety if the requirements set out in the Mental Health Act 1983 (Places of Safety) Regulations 2017 (which are reproduced in Part 2) are satisfied. PACE Code of Practice C, which is concerned with the "Detention, Treatment and Questioning of Persons by Police Officers", applies to persons who have been removed to a police station under both this s.136 and s.135 (para.1.10). Paragraph 3.16 of Code C states:

> "It is imperative that a person detained under the Mental Health Act 1983, section 135 or 136, be assessed as soon as possible within the permitted period of detention specified in that Act. A police station may only be used as a place of safety in accordance with The Mental Health Act 1983 (Places of Safety) Regulations 2017. If that assessment is to take place at the police station, an approved mental health professional and a registered medical practitioner shall be called to the station as soon as possible to carry it out. ...The appropriate adult has no role in the assessment process and their presence is not required. Once the detainee has been assessed and suitable arrangements made for their treatment or care, they can no longer be detained under section 135 or 136. A detainee must be immediately discharged from detention if a registered medical practitioner, having examined them, concludes they are not mentally disordered within the meaning of the Act."

As an alternative to conducting the relevant assessments at the police station, the person could be transferred to a health-based place of safety: see subs.(3) and (4).

The attendance of an "appropriate adult" at the police station is necessary if a person who, having been detained under s.136, has also been arrested for a criminal offence. This happened in *Francis v Director of Public Prosecutions* (1997) 36 B.M.L.R. 180, where the Divisional Court held that detention under this section does not give rise to any legal bar to any subsequent use of the breath specimen procedure under s.7 of the Road Traffic Act 1988. The court held that the fact of detention under s.136, while giving rise to obligations on the police, was not determinative of the issue of whether the procedure could be used, and that the propriety or fairness of using the procedure in such circumstances fell to be decided on the facts. *"Guidance on Responding to People with Mental Ill Health or Learning Disabilities"*, National Police Improvement Agency (2010), para.6.4.4.1, states that "there is nothing in law . . . to prevent police officers from using s.136 and the power of arrest for a criminal offence in the same case at the same time". If a person who has been detained under s.136 has also been arrested for a criminal offence, the appropriate adult should not be the AMHP who has been involved with that person's mental health assessment.

Treatment in an A and E department: when does the clock start ticking?

It is the opinion of the author that a person who is detained under this section can be treated for the **1-1411** physical consequences of his mental disorder, for example suturing a wound caused by a suicide attempt, if the person either consents or, if he is mentally incapable of giving his consent, the treatment is in his best interests. The time taken to undertake this procedure would therefore be counted in calculating the 24 hour "permitted period of detention" specified in subs.(2). But what if, as a result of a medical emergency, a person who has been detained under this section requires immediate treatment for an unrelated physical injury or disorder in a hospital's Accident and Emergency department before being transferred to the intended place of safety. Does the "permitted period of detention" start when the person is admitted to the department, or does it start when he arrives at the intended place of safety? Section 135(6) defines a place of safety as including a hospital. Does this mean that an A and E department automatically becomes a place of safety for the purposes of this section if the police take the person there for emergency treatment? If it does, in order to comply with subs.(2), arrangements must be put in place for the examination and interview of the person to take place at the department. Take the example of a patient who having been detained under this section is being transported to a health based place of safety by the police. During the conveyance the patient has a heart attack and the police are advised to take the patient to an A and E department. On arrival at the department the patient is given treatment to respond to the heart attack which lasts for some time. Is it the case that the patient is detained under this section while he is being treated for his heart attack, or has the patient's heart attack superseded the section 136 detention? In the latter case, the "permitted period of detention" does not commence at the patient's arrival at the department. Put another way, is the department being used as a place of safety even though the functions of a place of safety under this section are not being undertaken? The answer to this question is not clear, and there has been conflicting official advice on the issue.

The statutory guidance contained in the *Code of Practice* for Wales (2017) states at para.16.46:

> "If, in exceptional circumstances, a police officer needs to take a person to an emergency department after detaining that person under section 136, for the emergency medical assessment or treatment of their physical health this should not be treated as an admission to a place of safety. Detention under section 136 will begin when the person is taken to the appropriate place of safety for the assessment of their mental health."

A contrary opinion was expressed by the non-statutory Joint Department of Health and Home Office guidance (2018) ("the Guidance") to support the implementation of changes made to this section by the Policing and Crime Act 2017 which states at para.4.4:

"If a person subject to section 135 or 136 is taken first to an Emergency Department of a hospital for treatment of an illness or injury (before being removed to another place of safety) the detention period begins at the point when the person arrived at the Emergency Department (because a hospital is a place of safety)."

This opinion can be contrasted with the previous stance taken by the Department of Health and the Home Office in the "*Review of the Operation of Sections 135 and 136 of the Mental Health Act 1983*" (2014) where the following footnote appears at p.59:

"For example, if the person is first taken to an emergency department and has to wait there for some hours, it is unclear whether this should be 'counted' as being within the 72 hours maximum length of detention."

The *Code of Practice* for England does not directly address this issue.

Given that the circumstances contemplated by para.16.46 of the Welsh Code will be rarely encountered, what approach should be taken by practitioners where no interview and examination for the purpose of this section has been undertaken at the A and E department?

Factors in favour of the approach advocated by the Guidance are:

1. As the liberty of the individual is at issue, it could be argued that a restrictive interpretation should be adopted and time should begin to run from the time when the person arrives at the A and E department.
2. While the agreement of the manager of a place specified in s.135(7)(b) is required before the place can be considered to be a place of safety, no such agreement is required with regard to a hospital being used as a place of safety: see s.135(6).

Factors in favour of the approach advocated by the *Code of Practice* for Wales are:

1. It might be considered perverse to count time spent in an A and E department which is not performing the functions of a place of safety. On this argument, time spent in an A and E department should only be counted if the department is being used as a place of safety for the purposes of this section, i.e. for the purposes set out in subs.(2).
2. Only a doctor who is involved in the person's mental health assessment can authorise an extension under s.136B.
3. If a hospital's A and E department is being used as a place of safety, the hospital must comply with its obligations under s.132 of the Act which include identifying the detained person's nearest relative. It is unlikely that A and E staff will possess the expertise necessary to comply with these obligations.
4. The fact that that some people who have been taken to an A and E department as a place of safety under this section have spent the whole of the "permitted period of detention" being treated for their physical health raises an issue about the legality of their detention.

There is case law which is supportive of not counting time spent in an A and E department where no mental health assessment has been undertaken. In *Webley v St George's Hospital NHS Trust*, which is considered in the General Note to s.6 under the heading *Treatment in an A and E department en route to the hospital named in the application*, a patient who was subject to an application under s.2 had been detained in an A and E department for physical treatment for two hours prior to his intended admission to the hospital named in the application (the A and E department was located at a different hospital). No point was taken in the case as to the authority for detaining the patient at the department pending his arrival at the hospital named in the application. It is submitted that the authority is to be found in s.137 and that s.137 would also provide authority for detaining a person in an A and E department prior to his arrival at the intended place of safety.

As an element of uncertainty about the correct legal position does not constitute a "cogent reason" for departing from the *Code of Practice* (see the General Note to s.118), the approach that should be adopted practitioners in Wales is clear: they should follow the guidance contained in the *Code of Practice* for Wales as long as the interview and examination procedures required by this section are not commenced in the A and E department. In the absence of guidance on this issue being provided either by the courts or the *Code of Practice* for England, practitioners in England should obtain legal advice as to which approach to adopt. In the author's opinion, the approach advocated by the *Code of Practice* for Wales is to be preferred. Those providing advice should bear in mind that it is clearly unsatisfactory for different approaches to this important issue being followed in the two countries.

In an email dated December 8, 2017, a Welsh Government civil servant wrote to practitioners in Wales in the following terms: "It is our intention that paragraph 16.46 of the *Code of Practice* for Wales 2016 will be reviewed and revisited at the earliest opportunity. Until the Code is revisited, paragraph 4.4 of the recently published England and Wales guidance should be regarded as the Welsh Government position". No explanation was provided to justify this change of opinion. It should be noted that a statutory Code of Practice cannot be amended by a civil servant's email as the statutory procedure set out in s.118 has not been followed.

Human Rights Act 1998

In *Winterwerp v Netherlands* (1979) 2 E.H.R.R. 387 at para.39, the European Court of Human Rights **1-1412** (ECtHR) held that "except in emergency cases", an individual "should not be deprived of his liberty unless he has been reliably shown to be of 'unsound mind'". The court has subsequently said that it cannot "be inferred from the Winterwerp judgment that [a medical report on the patient] must in all conceivable cases be obtained before rather than after the confinement of a person on the ground of unsoundness of mind" (*X v United Kingdom* (1981) 4 E.H.R.R. 188, para.41; also see *Varbanov v Bulgaria* [2000] M.H.L.R. 263, para.47). As the power under this section applies to a person who appears to be in immediate need of care or control and lasts for a relatively brief period, it is clearly an emergency measure which complies with art.5(1)(e) of the European Convention on Human Rights (ECHR). The continued detention of a person under this section subsequent to a finding by the assessing doctor that the person was not mentally disordered would contravene the ECHR as there would be no ground under art.5(1)(e) to detain him: see further the notes on subs.(2).

Although it could be argued that using a police station as a place of safety contravenes art.5(1)(e) of the ECHR because it does not provide a therapeutic environment for the medical assessment (*Aerts v Belgium* (2000) 29 E.H.R.R. 50), the ECtHR has held that a person can be placed temporarily in an establishment not specifically designed for the detention of mental health patients before being transferred to the appropriate institution, provided that the waiting period is not excessively long (*Morsink v the Netherlands* [2005] M.H.L.R. 161, paras 67–69). However, art.3 of the ECHR could be breeched if the relevant threshold is reached. This occurred in *MS v United Kingdom* (2012) 55 E.H.R.R. 23 where a severely mentally ill person was detained under this section in a police cell for more than 72 hours (which was the maximum period of detention under this section prior to its amendment by the Policing and Crime Act 2017) in a situation where "no psychiatric treatment could be provided for him" (para.41). During his time in police custody, MS, who "was in direct need of appropriate psychiatric treatment" (para.44), banged his head against the cell wall, beat his chest, stripped naked, drank from the toilet bowl, ranted incoherently and appeared to smear himself with food or faeces. The ECtHR held that, even though there was no intention to humiliate or debase MS, the conditions which he had to endure "were an affront to human dignity and reached the thresholds of degrading treatment for the purposes of art.3" (para.45). It is submitted that there would be no breech of art.3 in a case of this nature if the detainee is transferred to a psychiatric facility without undue delay.

The death of a person who has been detained under this section following a disproportionate use of restraint or a failure to prevent the suicide of a person who was known to be a suicide risk could engage art.2 of the ECHR: see the notes on art.2 in Part 5.

Code of Practice

Chapter 16, which considers this section, should be read with caution because its contents do not **1-1413** reflect the significant amendments that have been made to this section by the Policing and Crime Act 2017.

Guidance

Joint Department of Health and Home Office guidance to support the implementation of changes to **1-1414** the police powers and places of safety provisions contained in this section made by the Policing and Crime Act 2017 can be accessed at: *www.gov.uk/government/uploads/system/uploads/attachment_data/ file/656025/Guidance_on_Police_Powers.PDF*.

The Royal College of Psychiatrists has published "*Standards on the use of Section 136 of the Mental Health Act 1983 (England and Wales)*" CR159 (2011) which considers all aspects of the process of detaining and assessing a person under this section. This has been supplemented by "Guidance for commissioners: service provisions for Section 136 of the Mental Health Act 1983", Position Statement PS2/2013, April 2013.

Right Care Right Person

1-1415   This document (RCRP) sets out a collective national commitment from the Home Office, Department of Health & Social Care, the National Police Chiefs' Council, Association of Police and Crime Commissioners, and NHS England to work to end the inappropriate and avoidable involvement of police in responding to incidents involving people with mental health needs. It states that where it is appropriate for the police to be involved in responding, this will continue to happen, but the police should only be involved for as long as is necessary, and in conjunction with health and/or social care services. RCRP provides a framework for assisting police with decision-making about when they should be involved in responding to reported incidents involving people with mental health needs. Information about RCRP, which has already been implemented in several local areas, can be accessed at: *https://www.gov.uk/government/publications/national-partnership-agreement-right-care-right-person/national-partnership-agreement-right-care-right-person-rcrp.*

Subsection (1)

1-1416   If there is serious concern about the immediate safety of a person who is on private premises which are not a place of safety (see s.135(7)) and the police are refused access to the premises, the police might be able to use their power under s.17(1)(e) of PACE to gain access. Section 17(1)(e) is considered in the General Note to s.135 under *The powers of the Police under PACE.*

A person   Children of any age may be detained under this section. As an alternative to invoking this section, any person under 18 years of age may be taken into police protection under s.46 the Children Act 1989.

Constable   Means the office of constable, and not the rank of constable (Police Act 1996 s.29, Sch.4). Therefore, any police officer can exercise this power.

Appears … to be suffering from mental disorder   No medical evidence is needed. All that is required is that the constable has a reasonable belief that the person is mentally disordered within the meaning of s.1.

Remove   Subs.(1B) enables a police officer to enter any place where this section can be invoked (if necessary by force) to remove a person. A person who is being conveyed to a place of safety is deemed to be in legal custody (s.137) and, as the person has been arrested, reasonable force may be used to facilitate the removal. The constable owes a duty of care to the person being conveyed: see *Webley v St George's Hospital NHS Trust* [2014] EWHC 299 (QB) which is noted under *Treatment in an A and E department en route to the hospital named in the application* in s.6.

This section does not specify who, other than the constable, might have the power to convey the person to the place of safety. The Butler Committee, at para.9.2, had "no doubt" that the constable's power "extends to persons acting under his direction, such as the ambulance staff who are taking the disordered person to hospital". And in *Ward v Commissioner of Police for the Metropolis* [2005] UKHL 32; [2005] 3 All E.R. 1013, a case decided under s.135, Lady Hale said that it may be "that the police officer can authorise others, such as the ambulance service or an [AMHP], to transport the person to the place of safety rather than doing it himself" (para.23). In this situation, those conveying the person would have the powers of a constable during the conveyance (s.137(2)). Paragraph 16.41 of the *Code of Practice* states:

> "People taken to a health-based place of safety should be transported there by an ambulance or other health transport arranged by the police who should, in the case of section 136, also escort them in order to facilitate hand-over to healthcare staff."

The Mental Health Crisis Care Concordat (2014) states at p.31:

> "The NHS ambulance services in England are planning to introduce a single national protocol for the transportation of section 136 patients, which will provide agreed response times and a standard specification for use by [integrated care boards]."

In the absence of an explicit power to detain the person in the community, the constable can only hold the person for a brief period measured in minutes while awaiting the arrival of an ambulance or other health transport.

Subsection (1A)

This provision identifies the places where this section cannot be invoked. Apart from those places, **1-1417** this section can be invoked anywhere, including railway lines, cars, cinemas, hospital wards, schools, police stations, accident and emergency departments, and offices, as long as the person is in need of immediate care or control. Paragraph 2.5 of the Guidance (see above) states:

"The places in which section 136(1) does not apply should be clear in the majority of cases – for example if the person is located in a living room or garden of a self-contained private dwelling. However, in other scenarios it may be less clear-cut. Section 136(1)(a) would not normally apply if the person is located in a private room in a care or residential home where a person lives."

Although a caravan does not come within the description of a "house, flat or room", it is suggested that this section should not be invoked if a person is living in a caravan and the caravan is treated by the person as their home.

The use of the phrase "is living" in para.(a) rather than the phrase "is staying" implies that the person must normally reside at that place and is not there on a temporary basis. In the absence of exceptional circumstances, hotel guests are staying at a hotel rather than living there.

In *McMillan v CPS* [2008] EWHC 1457 (Admin), a police constable was held to have acted lawfully when he physically escorted a woman from a private garden to a public footpath and then arrested her for the criminal offence of being drunk and disorderly in a public place. The court noted, at para.12, that at the Magistrates' Court the Justices had "rejected any suggestion that [Ms McMillan] was being moved from a private place to a public place simply so as to justify an arrest outside the garden for an offence which had a public place requirement". It follows that although a police constable has the right to escort a person from a garden to a public place if, for example, that is necessary either to diffuse an emotionally fraught situation or to lawfully remove a trespasser (see *Winzar v Chief Constable of Kent, The Times,* March 28, 1983), it would not be lawful to remove the person solely for the purpose of bringing him or her within the scope of this section.

Subsection (1C)

This provision requires a constable to consult with a health professional before deciding to remove **1-1418** the person to, or keep the person at, a place of safety if the constable considers that undertaking such consultation is practicable. Triage schemes have an important role to play in enabling a constable to meet this requirement. The constable's judgment on practicability will be influenced by the fact that he will have assessed the person as being in immediate need of care or control (subs.(1)). It submitted that detaining the person while the consultation takes place would be unlawful if the detention lasted for more than a brief period measured in minutes. The decision to remove the person is that of the constable, not the consultee.

Paragraph 2.11 of the Guidance (see above) states:

"The police officer should seek to ascertain, and the healthcare professional being consulted should offer, where possible, information or advice regarding:

- an opinion on whether this appears to be a mental health issue based on professional observation and, if possible, questioning of the person;
- whether other physical health issues may be of concern or contributing to behaviour (e.g. substance misuse, signs of physical injury or illness);
- whether the person is known to local health service providers;
- if so, whether it is possible to access medical records or any care plan to determine medical history and suggested strategies for appropriately managing a mental health crisis;
- whether in the circumstances, the proposed use of section 136 powers is appropriate;
- where it is determined that use of section 136 powers is appropriate – identification of a suitable health based place of safety, and facilitation of access to it;
- where it is determined that use of section 136 powers is not appropriate – identification and implementation of alternative arrangements (such as escorting the person home, to their own doctor, to hospital, or to a community place of calm/respite)".

Practicable Among the factors that the police officer will take into account when making a judgement on practicability are:

"• whether there are established local arrangements for undertaking such consultation

- (for example, street triage schemes ...);
- the time it is likely to take to carry out the consultation;
- whether the person appearing to suffer from a mental disorder is likely to remain cooperative and present during the time taken to undertake a consultation; and
- whether it is safe to undertake a consultation or whether the behaviour of the person requires immediate action in the interests of safety" (Guidance, para.2.13).

With regard to the first bullet point, the Guidance states that where local arrangements are not in place, "it is less likely to be practicable to consult" (para.2.14).

Paragraph (d)

1-1419 An occupational therapist and a paramedic are specified for the purposes of this provision by reg.8 of the Mental Health Act 1983 (Places of Safety) Regulations 2017 (SI 2017/1036).

Subsection (2)

1-1420 The identification of those who have the power to detain a person under this provision is set out in the following extract from the Butler Committee at para.9.2:

"The powers of detention given by section 136(2) are not conferred expressly on the police, but are given to any person who is a party to the detention of the disordered person once he has been brought to a place of safety".

It follows that the power to detain the person continues even though the police have left the place of safety.

Bearing in mind that the only power given to the police under this section is to remove the person to a place of safety, the police officer is only legally obliged to remain there if his presence is required to ensure the safety of the patient and staff: see para.16.34 of the *Code of Practice* which states:

"[Local] policies should cover arrangements for police officers to remain in attendance when a person arrives at a health-based place of safety. Healthcare staff, including ambulance staff, should take responsibility for the person as soon as possible, including preventing the person from absconding before the assessment can be carried out. The police officer should not be expected to remain until the assessment is completed; the officer should be able to leave when the situation is agreed to be safe for the patient and healthcare staff."

The Care Quality Commission is incorrect when it states that the police officer is obliged "to wait with the person during the assessment" (*Monitoring the use of the Mental Health Act in 2009/10*, p.33). "Guidance on Responding to People with Mental Ill Health or Learning Disabilities", National Police Improvement Agency (2010) states that in general, "the police should only need to stay where, in their professional judgement, there is a medium to high risk of violence or breach of the peace" (para.6.4.7.3).

The authority to detain under this section ends immediately if the doctor's assessment leads her to conclude that the person is not mentally disordered. This is the case even if the person has not been seen by an AMHP (*Code of Practice*, para.16.50). The further detention of the patient in these circumstances would be unlawful: see the note on *Human Rights Act 1998*, above. Following an inquest into the death of James Emmerson, the Assistant Coroner of the Bedfordshire and Luton Coroner Service issued a Regulation 28 report on "action to prevent other deaths", dated January 5, 2020. Under the heading "Confusion generated by the Department of Health Guide 'Mental Health Act 1983 Code of Practice'", the report states that the interpretation of para.16.50 of the Code as meaning that assessment by an AMPH was not a "required formality" after a finding by the examining doctor that the detained person was not mentally disordered was "deeply flawed". The Assistant Coroner considered that an arrangement that precluded the detained person not being seen by an AMHP in all cases "contravened both the spirit and the letter of the Mental Health Act 1983". It is submitted that the opinion of the Assistant Coroner is not correct. A precondition of the use of this section is that the person "appears ... to be suffering from mental disorder". If the examining doctor finds that this precondition is not satisfied, the legal justification for the use of this section to detain the person falls away. It follows that there is no power to further detain the person in order for him to be seen by an AMHP. Further detention of the person would contravene art.5(1)(e) of the ECHR: see *Winterwerp v Netherlands*, noted under *Human Rights Act 1998*, above.

In its *Second Biennial Report*, 1985–87, at para.11.1(e), the MHAC reported that it had:

"found that doubt exists when the person brought to the hospital [under this section] has been examined by the doctor but no [AMHP] is available to conduct the interview. The legal consequences of failure to provide an [AMHP] interview are open to debate. Has the person to remain in detention even though the doctor does not consider that compulsory admission is necessary, until the [AMHP] is available? Good practice would suggest that if the delay is going to be considerable (say more than four hours) then the requirements of the section shall be deemed to have been fulfilled so that detention may end. The case where the doctor decides that compulsory admission is appropriate is more controversial, since Parliament clearly intended that the [AMHP's] opinion would be of great importance both in providing a safeguard for the rights of the individual and in deciding what arrangements are most appropriate to provide the care which the person needs."

It is submitted that, in the absence of a finding that the person is not mentally disordered, the wording of this subsection clearly envisages the person being both examined by a doctor and interviewed by an AMHP and that in both of the situations identified by the MHAC the patient will remain subject to detention under this section until the interview by the AMHP takes place and any necessary arrangements for the patient's treatment or care have been put in place. In the passage quoted, the MHAC appeared to assume that the sole purpose of being removed to a place of safety is to assess the patient for possible compulsory admission under the Act. Such an outcome is, in fact, only one of a number of options that would be considered on an assessment. The MHAC adopted a more orthodox approach to this section in its *Ninth Biennial Report 1999–2001* at paras 4.7–4.9.

The IPCC's report on the "Investigation into West Yorkshire Police contact with Martin Middleton" (2004) states that where a police station is used as the place of safety this section "does not give a custody sergeant the discretion to release someone or refuse to authorise the detention of a person who has been detained under s.136 before an assessment has been carried out". After the assessment has been carried out, the discretion should not be exercised by the custody sergeant until the "necessary arrangements" have been put in place.

Contrary to an opinion that is sometimes heard, it is not unlawful for a person who has drunk alcohol to be assessed in a place of safety under this section. In other words, there is no need for the assessment to be delayed until the person blows zero on the Intoximeter. To delay intervention until complete sobriety is achieved could put a person who is an alcoholic at physical risk. Paragraph 16.44 of the *Code of Practice* states that "intoxication (whether through drugs or alcohol) should not be used as a basis for exclusion from places of safety, except in circumstances set out in the local policy, where there may be too high a risk to the safety of the individual or staff. Health-based places of safety should not be conducting tests to determine intoxication as a reason for exclusion".

Place of safety   Is defined in s.135(6), (7) (subs.(1)). The choice of place of safety is that of the police irrespective of whether that place has been designated as a place of safety in local protocols. If hospitals are acting as places of safety, although the person is often taken to an area of the hospital called a "Section 136 suite", any part of the hospital can be used. For the use of police stations as places of safety, see s.136A. A constable has the power to search the person at the place of safety in the circumstances specified in s.136C.

If the police have concerns about the physical health of the person, he could be taken directly to the local A and E department: see *Treatment in an A and E department: when does the clock start ticking*, above.

If a person who is severely mentally disordered is detained in a police station as the place of safety, he should be transferred to hospital under subs.(3) and (4) at the earliest opportunity: see *MS v United Kingdom*, noted under *Human Rights Act 1998*, above. People detained in police custody under this section are kept in the same style of cell as those arrested for crimes.

Detained   "Detention" is "a matter of fact … not a legal concept" (*Upadrasta v Commissioner of the City of London Police* [2023] EWHC 1853 (KB), para.87).

The permitted period of detention   The permitted period of detention is a maximum of 24 hours. The Care Quality Commission reported in "Monitoring the Mental Health Act in 2021/22" that this time limit is regularly breached because of delays in accessing an inpatient bed. The period can extended for a further period not exceeding 12 hours: see subs.(2A) and s.136B. The permitted period cannot be extended by invoking either the common law or the Mental Capacity Act 2005 (*R. (on the application of Sessay) v South London and Maudsley NHS Foundation Trust* [2011] EWHC 2617 (QB); [2012] M.H.L.R. 94). What is the situation if a capacious patient is assessed as being at risk of committing suicide? Lady Hale has said:

"But what can be done when a patient who does have capacity is about to do harm to himself? It is probably always lawful to prevent someone committing suicide ... Following the Human Rights Act, there is a positive duty, stemming from the right to life protected by art.2 of the ECHR, to take reasonable steps to protect the life of a detained or informal patient where there is a real and immediate risk to life about which the authorities knew or also have known at the time ...

Obviously, there are limits to what can be done to control a patient who is not liable to be detained under the Act, and anything done would have to be proportionate to the likelihood and severity of the possible arm. If there is any doubt, it is safer to section the patient under the MHA" (Brenda Hale, *Mental Health Law*, 2017, para.6-024).

The power to detain under this section will lapse as soon as the person has been examined and interviewed and it is considered that no further arrangements need be made for his treatment or care. If it is determined that such arrangements have to be made, the person can continue to be detained, subject to the permitted period, while the arrangements are put in place (*Code of Practice*, para.16.27). If the assessment by the AMHP and the doctor has resulted in an application being made under Part 2 to detain the person, the patient can continue to be detained under this provision, within the permitted period of detention, pending arrangements for transporting the patient to the admitting hospital being put in place. If a decision is taken to admit the person to hospital under s.2, the admission should be actioned without undue delay: see *Sessay*, above, at para.56.

As the permitted period starts from the time when the person arrives at the place which is being used as a place of safety, a record of the time of arrival there should be made. If the place of safety is a hospital, this period cannot be continued under s.5(2) or (4) as it is Parliament's intention that the assessment be completed within that period; see *R. v Wilson Ex p. Williamson* [1996] C.O.D. 42, noted in the General Note to s.2 and the *Code of Practice* at para.16.76.

Examined   Given the decision of the Divisional Court in *Devon Partnership NHS Trust v Secretary of State for Health and Social Care* [2021] EWHC 101 (Admin) (noted under s.11(5)), it is likely that a court would find that the physical presence of the examining doctor is required and that examining the patient cannot be undertaken by the use of remote technology.

Registered medical practitioner   Wherever possible, the examining doctor should be approved by the Secretary of State or the Welsh Ministers under s.12, or by another person by virtue of s.12ZA or 12ZB (*Code of Practice*, para.16.46). A registered medical practitioner means "a fully registered person within the meaning of the Medical Act 1983 who holds a licence to practise under that Act" (Interpretation Act 1978 Sch.1).

Approved mental health professional   There is no power to detain the person in order for him to be interviewed by an AMHP if the examining doctor has concluded that the person is not mentally disordered: see above. However, the person could agree to be interviewed.

Although this section is silent on the issue, to be consistent with the duty placed on local authorities under s.13(1) it is submitted that the responsibility for providing an AMHP to undertake the interview rests with the local authority for the area where the place of safety is located. This conclusion is reinforced by the following extract from para.16.28 of the *Code of Practice*:

"Local authorities should also have arrangements in place so that the nearest AMHP can attend, although consideration should always be given to whether an AMHP from the person's home authority, with the benefit of local knowledge and understanding of any relevant history, could reasonably travel to assess the person. These arrangements should also ensure that, when a place of safety serves an area that includes more than one local authority, the relevant AMHP services work together to ensure continuity of care and timely attendance."

The CQC found that 61 per cent of health bases places of safety reported that "AMHPs refused to start assessments until a bed was available" (*A safer place to be*, October 2014, p.38). Such refusals are certainly inappropriate and possibly unlawful as the purpose of an assessment under this section is not confined to assessing whether the person should be detained under the Act.

Necessary arrangements   These could include detention under the Act, informal admission to hospital, or making arrangements for the person to be assessed for the possible provision of community care services.

If it is established that the patient is absent without leave from the detaining hospital, he can be immediately returned to that hospital under the authority of s.18. If the patient is either on leave of absence under s.17 or is subject to a community treatment order, the patient's responsible clinician should be contacted to establish whether the patient is going to be recalled to hospital.

Subsections (3),(4)

These provisions, which respond to concern that was expressed during debates on the 2007 Act about mentally disordered people being detained in a police cell (see, for e.g., *Hansard*, HL Vol. 689, col.1467), enable a person who has been detained in a place of safety under this section to be transferred to another one before the permitted period of detention has expired. A transfer under this provision is not required if the person is transferred between separate units of a place of safety. **1-1421**

Before a transfer takes place, the agreement of a person in control of the new place of safety to accept the patient must be obtained. On arrival at the new place of safety, the person in control should be informed, preferably in writing, of the time when the original detention under this section started.

A constable has the power to search a person who has been transferred from one the place of safety to another in the circumstances specified in s.136C.

The transfer of a person between places of safety is considered in the following paragraphs of the *Code of Practice*:

"16.53 A person removed to a place of safety under section 135(1) or section 136 may be moved to a different place of safety within the [permitted period of detention]. Transfers should take place only when it is in the person's best interests. The maximum period of detention begins from the time of the person's arrival at the first place of safety to which they are taken and cannot be extended if the person is transferred to another place of safety.

16.54 The person may be taken to the second or subsequent place of safety by transport arranged by a police officer, the AMHP or a person authorised by either a police officer or the AMHP.

16.55 A person may be transferred before their assessment has begun, while it is in progress, or after it is completed and they are waiting for any necessary arrangements for their care or treatment to be put in place. If it is unavoidable, or it is in the person's interests, an assessment begun by one AMHP or doctor may be taken over and completed by another, either in the same location or at another place to which the person is transferred.

16.56 Although it may be helpful for local policies to outline circumstances in which a person is usually to be transferred between places of safety, the decision in each case should reflect the individual circumstances, including the person's needs and the level of risk. For example, where the purpose of the transfer would be to move a person from a police station to a more appropriate health-based place of safety, the benefit of that move needs to be weighed against any delay it might cause in the person's assessment and any distress that the journey might cause them. Any delays resulting from transferring the person cannot result in an overall period of detention which exceeds 72 hours.

16.57 Unless it is an emergency, a person should not be transferred without the agreement of an AMHP, a doctor or another healthcare professional who is competent to assess whether the transfer would put the person's health or safety (or that of other people) at risk. Someone with the authority to effect a transfer should proceed by agreement wherever possible. It is for those professionals to decide whether they first need to see the person personally.

16.58 A person should never be moved from one place of safety to another unless it has been confirmed that the new place of safety is willing and able to accept them."

[Use of police stations as places of safety

136A.—(1)   A child may not, in the exercise of a power to which this section applies, be removed to, kept at or taken to a place of safety that is a police station. **1-1422**

(2)   The Secretary of State may by regulations—
   (a)   provide that an adult may be removed to, kept at or taken to a place of safety that is a police station, in the exercise of a power to which this section applies, only in circumstances specified in the regulations;
   (b)   make provision about how adults removed to, kept at or taken to a police station, in the exercise of a power to which this section applies, are to be treated while at the police station, including provision for review of their detention.

(3)   Regulations under this section—
   (a)   may make different provision for different cases;

(b) may make provision that applies subject to specified exceptions;

(c) may include incidental, supplementary or consequential provision or transitional, transitory or saving provision.

(4) The powers to which this section applies are—

(a) the power to remove a person to a place of safety under a warrant issued under section 135(1);

(b) the power to take a person to a place of safety under section 135(3A);

(c) the power to remove a person to, or to keep a person at, a place of safety under section 136(1);

(d) the power to take a person to a place of safety under section 136(3).

(5) In this section—

(a) "child" means a person aged under 18;

(b) "adult" means a person aged 18 or over.]

Amendment

This section was inserted by the Policing and Crime Act 2017 s.81(6).

General Note

1-1423 This section prevents the use of a police station as a place of safety in any circumstances where the detainee is under 18 years of age. It also confers on the Secretary of State the power to make regulations to restrict the circumstances in which police stations may be used as a place of safety for adults (aged 18 years or over) and to make provision for the treatment of such adults whilst so detained, including provision for the review of their detention.

The Mental Health Act 1983 (Places of Safety) Regulations 2017 (SI 2017/1036), which are reproduced in Part 2, have been made under this section. The criteria for using police stations as a place of safety in the regulations are very restrictive. It is therefore likely that police stations will be rarely used for this purpose.

[Extension of detention

1-1424 **136B.**—(1) The registered medical practitioner who is responsible for the examination of a person detained under section 135 or 136 may, at any time before the expiry of the period of 24 hours mentioned in section 135(3ZA) or (as the case may be) 136(2A), authorise the detention of the person for a further period not exceeding 12 hours (beginning immediately at the end of the period of 24 hours).

(2) An authorisation under subsection (1) may be given only if the registered medical practitioner considers that the extension is necessary because the condition of the person detained is such that it would not be practicable for the assessment of the person for the purpose of section 135 or (as the case may be) section 136 to be carried out before the end of the period of 24 hours (or, if the assessment began within that period, for it to be completed before the end).

(3) If the person is detained at a police station, and the assessment would be carried out or completed at the station, the registered medical practitioner may give an authorisation under subsection (1) only if an officer of the rank of superintendent or above approves it.]

Amendment

This section was inserted by the Policing and Crime Act 2017 s.82(4).

General Note

1-1425 This section makes provision for the registered medical practitioner who is responsible for the examination of a person detained under s.135 or 136 to authorise the extension of the permitted period of detention (24 hours) by a maximum of 12 hours where the condition of the person makes it necessary to do so. The further period of detention, which may be less than the maximum of 12 hours, must be specified in the authorisation (s.136(2A) (b)). Where both the place of safety at which the person is being held and the intended place of assessment is a police station, authorisation to extend the permitted period of detention will also require the approval of a police officer of the rank of superintendent or above. There is nothing to prevent this approval being given verbally.

If the person is being treated for a physical disorder in A&E as well as being assessed under s.136, the authorisation must be made by the doctor who is assessing the person's mental disorder.

Subsection (1)

The registered medical practitioner   Who need not be approved under s.12, s.12ZA or 12ZB. A   **1-1426** registered medical practitioner means "a fully registered person within the meaning of the Medical Act 1983 who holds a licence to practise under that Act" (Interpretation Act 1978, Sch.1).

Authorise   There is no statutory form.

Subsection (2)

Condition of the person   Paragraph 4.6 of the Guidance (see the note on *Guidance* in s.136) states: **1-1427**

"These are that, because of the person's condition (physical or mental), it is not practicable to complete a Mental Health Act assessment within the 24 hour period. This might arise, for example, if the person is too mentally distressed, or is particularly intoxicated with alcohol or drugs and cannot co-operate with the assessment process. A delay in attendance by an Approved Mental Health Professional or medical practitioner is not a valid reason for extending detention."

It is submitted that if communication with the person is not possible in the absence of an interpreter, an extension under this provision is permitted to enable an interpreter to be present at the assessment.

[Protective searches

136C.—(1)   Where a warrant is issued under section 135(1) or (2), a constable   **1-1428** may search the person to whom the warrant relates if the constable has reasonable grounds for believing that the person—
  (a)   may present a danger to himself or herself or to others, and
  (b)   is concealing on his or her person an item that could be used to cause physical injury to himself or herself or to others.
  (2)   The power to search conferred by subsection (1) may be exercised—
  (a)   in a case where a warrant is issued under section 135(1), at any time during the period beginning with the time when a constable enters the premises specified in the warrant and ending when the person ceases to be detained under section 135;
  (b)   in a case where a warrant is issued under section 135(2), at any time while the person is being removed under the authority of the warrant.
  (3)   Where a person is detained under section 136(2) or (4), a constable may search the person, at any time while the person is so detained, if the constable has reasonable grounds for believing that the person—
  (a)   may present a danger to himself or herself or to others, and
  (b)   is concealing on his or her person an item that could be used to cause physical injury to himself or herself or to others.
  (4)   The power to search conferred by subsection (1) or (3) is only a power to search to the extent that is reasonably required for the purpose of discovering the item that the constable believes the person to be concealing.
  (5)   The power to search conferred by subsection (1) or (3)—
  (a)   does not authorise a constable to require a person to remove any of his or her clothing other than an outer coat, jacket or gloves, but

(b)   does authorise a search of a person's mouth.

(6)   A constable searching a person in the exercise of the power to search conferred by subsection (1) or (3) may seize and retain anything found, if he or she has reasonable grounds for believing that the person searched might use it to cause physical injury to himself or herself or to others.

(7)   The power to search a person conferred by subsection (1) or (3) does not affect any other power to search the person.]

Amendment

This section was inserted by the Policing and Crime Act 2017 s.83.

General Note

1-1429   The purpose of the search power contained in this section is to enable police officers to maintain the safety of all concerned during the exercise of their functions under s.135 or 136. The power is limited to circumstances where the police have reasonable grounds to believe that the person who is the subject of the s.135 warrant or who has been detained under s.136 is concealing a dangerous item and presents a danger to themselves or others. This section also requires that the search is only to the extent that is reasonably required to discover the item, and is limited to a search of the person's outer clothing and mouth. These safeguards are comparable to those found in s.32 of PACE.

With regard to warrants issued under s.135, the authority to search the person to whom the warrant relates lasts until either the end of the period of detention under s.135(1) or until the person who has been detained under s.135(2) has been returned to the place where he is required to be. Where a person is detained under s.136, he can be immediately searched under the authority of s.32 of PACE, which in noted in the General Note to s.136, and can also be searched under this section once he has arrived at the place of safety. Anything found on the person can be retained if the criteria set out in subs.(6) are satisfied.

Subsection (1)

1-1430   **Person**   Of any age.

Subsection (3)

1-1431   The term "item" includes any article or substance capable of being used as either a weapon or to cause self-harm.

Provisions as to custody, conveyance and detention

1-1432   **137.**—(1)   Any person required or authorised by or by virtue of this Act to be conveyed to any place or to be kept in custody or detained in a place of safety or at any place to which he is taken under section 42(6) above shall, while being so conveyed, detained or kept, as the case may be, be deemed to be in legal custody.

(2)   A constable or any other person required or authorised by or by virtue of this Act to take any person into custody, or to convey or detain any person shall, for the purposes of taking him into custody or conveying or detaining him, have all the powers, authorities, protection and privileges which a constable has within the area for which he acts as constable.

(3)   In this section convey includes any other expression denoting removal from one place to another.

General Note

1-1433   This section specifies the circumstances whereby a person is deemed to be in legal custody for the purposes of the Act. It also provides that a person who is required or authorised to detain or convey a person who is in legal custody shall have the powers of a constable when so acting. That person owes a duty of care to the patient: see *Webley v St George's Hospital NHS Trust* [2014] EWHC 299 (QB) which is noted under *Treatment in an A and E department en route to the hospital named in the application* in s.6(1). A person who escapes from legal custody can be retaken under s.138.

In *E v DPP* [2002] EWHC 433 (Admin) DC at para.20, Forbes J. said that "for a person to be in custody, his liberty must be subject to such constraint or restriction that he can be said to be confined by another in the sense that the person's immediate freedom of movement is under the direct control of another. Whether that is so in any particular case will depend on the facts of that case". This passage was cited in *Korcala v Polish Judicial Authority* [2017] EWHC 167 (Admin) DC, where Nicol J. said, at para.26, that he could "see no distinction of any significance in the terms 'detention' and 'custody' in s.137 (or any other relevant part of the Mental Health Act 1983)".

The powers contained in this section do not include the power to use force to enter premises to remove a person simply because he or she was believed to be suffering from a mental disorder or was a person liable to be taken into custody under the Act (*R. v Rosso* [2003] EWCA Crim 3242; [2003] M.H.L.R. 404 para.17). Section 135 should be used in such circumstances.

Subsection (2)

In *R. v Broadmoor Special Hospital Authority and The Secretary of State for the Department of* **1-1434**
Health Ex p. SH and D, February 5, 1998, Potts J. held that this subsection was concerned with the limited function of detention for the purpose of conveyance to hospital, not with detention once there. This finding was referred to without comment when this case reached the Court of Appeal: see [1998] C.O.D. 199.

Powers ... which a constable has   Which include the powers to arrest a person who is wilfully obstructing him in the execution of his duties, to use reasonable force in effecting an arrest, to prevent a person from escaping, to secure the conveyance of the person, and to require other persons to assist him in the execution of his duties.

Retaking of patients escaping from custody

138.—(1)   If any person who is in legal custody by virtue of section 137 above   **1-1435**
escapes, he may, subject to the provisions of this section, be retaken—

    (a)   in any case, by the person who had his custody immediately before the escape, or by any constable or [approved mental health professional];

    (b)   if at the time of the escape he was liable to be detained in a hospital within the meaning of Part II of this Act, or subject to guardianship under this Act, [or a community patient who was recalled to hospital under section 17E above,] by any other person who could take him into custody under section 18 above if he had absented himself without leave.

(2)   A person to whom paragraph (b) of subsection (1) above applies shall not be retaken under this section after the expiration of the period within which he could be retaken under section 18 above if he had absented himself without leave on the day of the escape unless he is subject to a restriction order under Part III of this Act or an order or direction having the same effect as such an order; and subsection (4) of the said section 18 shall apply with the necessary modifications accordingly.

(3)   A person who escapes while being taken to or detained in a place of safety under section 135 or 136 above shall not be retaken under this section [—

    (a)   in a case where the person escapes while being removed to a place of safety in the execution of a warrant under section 135(1) or under section 136(1), after the end of the period of 24 hours beginning with the escape;

    (b)   in a case where the person escapes after the beginning of the period that is the permitted period of detention in relation to the person under section 135(3ZA) or 136(2A), after the end of that period (taking into account any authorisation under section 136B(1) that was given before the person escaped).]

[607]

(4) This section, so far as it relates to the escape of a person liable to be detained in a hospital within the meaning of Part II of this Act, shall apply in relation to a person who escapes—

(a) while being taken to or from such a hospital in pursuance of regulations under section 19 above, or of any order, direction or authorisation under Part III or VI of this Act (other than under section 35, 36, 38, 53, 83 or 85) [...]; or

(b) while being taken to or detained in a place of safety in pursuance of an order under Part III of this Act (other than under section 35, 36 or 38 above) pending his admission to such a hospital,

as if he were liable to be detained in that hospital and, if he had not previously been received in that hospital, as if he had been so received.

(5) In computing for the purposes of the power to give directions under section 37(4) above and for the purposes of sections 37(5) and 40(1) above the period of 28 days mentioned in those sections, no account shall be taken of any time during which the patient is at large and liable to be retaken by virtue of this section.

(6) Section 21 above shall, with any necessary modifications, apply in relation to a patient who is at large and liable to be retaken by virtue of this section as it applies in relation to a patient who is absent without leave and references in that section to section 18 above shall be construed accordingly.

Amendments

The amendments to this section were made by the Mental Health Act 2007 ss.21, 32(4), Sch.2 para.10, Sch.3 para.32, the Health and Social Care Act 2012 s.42(3) and the Policing and Crime Act 2017 s.82(5).

Definitions

1-1436   approved mental health professional: s.145(1), (1AC).
absent without leave: ss.18(6), 145(1).
restriction order: ss.41, 145(1).
patient: s.145(1).
community patient: ss.17A(7), 145(1).
hospital: s.145(1).

General Note

1-1437   This section provides for the retaking of persons who have escaped from legal custody. The retaking can only take place within the relevant time scales. Section 18 identifies the action that can be taken when a detained patient, a community patient or a patient subject to guardianship absents himself without leave.

A patient who has been made subject to an application under Pt II and who escapes whilst on the way to hospital can only be retaken if he can be apprehended within the relevant period set out in either para.(a) or para.(b) of s.6(1).

Although the power to retake the person can be exercised anywhere, this section does not provide authority for force to be used to enter premises where the patient is believed to be. An application to a magistrate under s.135(2) should be made if such action is deemed to be necessary.

A person who assists another person who is in legal custody to escape commits an offence under s.128(2).

The power of the police to arrest under this section was specifically preserved by s.26 and Sch.2 of the Police and Criminal Evidence Act 1984 (PACE). This means that the arresting policeman has a power under s.32 of PACE to search the patient at a place other than a police station. Section 72 of the Criminal Justice Act 1967 also provides for a power of arrest under this provision, but only if a warrant of arrest has been issued by a magistrate.

Subsections (1), (4)

Hospital within the meaning of part II   See s.34(2).   **1-1438**

Subsection (6)   The effect of this subsection is that if the patient is retaken within the last week of   **1-1439**
the period during which he can be retaken, the authority to detain will end a week after the day he is
retaken.

Protection for acts done in pursuance of this Act

139.—(1)   No person shall be liable, whether on the ground of want of jurisdic-   **1-1440**
tion or on any other ground, to any civil or criminal proceedings to which he would
have been liable apart from this section in respect of any act purporting to be done
in pursuance of this Act or any regulations or rules made under this Act, […] unless the act was done in bad faith or without reasonable care.

(2)   No civil proceedings shall be brought against any person in any court in
respect of any such act without the leave of the High Court; and no criminal
proceedings shall be brought against any person in any court in respect of any such
act except by or with the consent of the Director of Public Prosecutions.

(3)   This section does not apply to proceedings for an offence under this Act,
being proceedings which, under any other provision of this Act, can be instituted
only by or with the consent of the Director of Public Prosecutions.

(4)   This section does not apply to proceedings against the Secretary of State
or against [[NHS England] [, an integrated care board,]] a […] [Local Health Board]
[or Special Health Authority] […] [or against a National Health Service trust
established under [the National Health Service Act 2006 or the National Health
Service (Wales) Act 2006]] [or NHS foundation trust] [or against the Department
of Justice in Northern Ireland] [or against a person who has functions under this Act
by virtue of section 12ZA in so far as the proceedings relate to the exercise of those
functions].

(5)   In relation to Northern Ireland the reference in this section to the Director
of Public Prosecutions shall be construed as a reference to the Director of Public
Prosecutions for Northern Ireland.

Amendments

The amendments to this section were made by the Mental Capacity Act 2005 s.67(2), Sch.7, the
National Health Service and Community Care Act 1990 s.66(1), Sch.9 para.24(7), the Health Authorities Act 1995 s.2(1), Sch.1 para.107(11), the National Health Service Reform and Health Care Profes-
sions Act 2002 (Supplementary, Consequential, etc. Provisions) Regulations 2002 (SI 2002/2469) reg.4,
Sch.1, the Health and Social Care (Community Health and Standards) Act 2003 s.34, Sch.4 para.56, SI
2007/961 art.3, Sch. para.13(11), the National Health Service (Consequential Provisions) Act 2006 s.2,
Sch.1 para.6, SI 2010/976 para.28, the Health and Social Care Act 2012 s.38(3), Sch.5 para.30 and the
Health and Care Act 2022 Sch.1 para.1, Sch.4 para.18.

Definitions

Local Health Board: s.145(1).   **1-1441**
Special Health Authority: s.145(1).

General Note

This section, which has its origins in s.330 of the Lunacy Act 1890, provides that: (1) apart from   **1-1442**
proceedings against the Secretary of State or a body mentioned in subs.(4) and proceedings under s.127,
no civil or criminal proceedings can be brought against any person in any court in respect of an act
purporting to be done under the Act without the leave of the High Court or the Director of Public

Prosecutions; and (2) for such proceedings to succeed the court must be satisfied that the person proceeded against acted in bad faith or without reasonable care.

During the passage of the 1982 Act, the Government resisted an amendment to exclude the provisions of this section for informal patients on the ground that this would remove the protection given to someone who purports to do something under the Act when he believes that the patient is a detained patient. The Minister for Health gave the following illustration in support of this argument:

> "An ambulance man ... has a patient in his charge whom he believes is a detained patient because he is told so. Therefore, he is told that he should prevent the patient escaping. If the patient attempts to go off and he takes steps to stop him escaping, he might be liable to an action thereafter, but he would be protected if we retain [this section] with its present wording" (*Hansard* HC, Vol.29, col.173).

This interpretation is consistent with the use of the term "purporting" in this provision. Although there is Crown Court authority for the contention that this section does not cover acts done in respect of informal patients (*R. v Runighian* [1977] Crim. L.R. 361), Cox J. in *Lebrooy v Hammersmith and Fulham LBC* [2006] EWHC 1976 (QB); [2006] M.H.L.R. 253 at para.15, rejected a submission that this section "only applies to those who have been detained under [the] Act". It is submitted that the Government's approach is correct, and that although this section does not apply to every act done in respect of informal patients, it does apply to an informal patient if the individual undertaking the act genuinely believes on reasonable grounds at the relevant time that he or she is acting under a provision of the Act.

This section's scope does not extend to claims made under s.7 of the Human Rights Act 1998: see the decision of the Court of Appeal in *TTM v London Borough of Hackney* which is noted under *Human Rights Act 1998*, below. Neither does it not affect the right of a patient to apply to the High Court for his discharge by means of a writ of habeas corpus (*R. v Governor of Pentonville Prison Ex p. Azam* [1974] A.C. 18 at 31). *Azam* was cited in *R. v Hallstrom Ex p. W* [1985] 3 All E.R. 775 where the Court of Appeal held that leave under this section is also not required for applications for judicial review.

In *Winch v Jones* [1985] 3 All E.R. 97, the Court of Appeal held that the test to be applied by the court when considering to grant leave under this section was whether, on the materials immediately available to the court, the applicant's complaint appeared to deserve the fuller investigation which will be possible if the intended applicant is allowed to proceed. Sir John Donaldson M.R. said, at 102, that this section:

> "is intended to strike a balance between the legitimate interests of the applicant to be allowed, at his own risk as to costs, to seek the adjudication of the courts on any claim which is not frivolous, vexatious or an abuse of the process and the equally legitimate interests of the respondent to such an application not to be subjected to the undoubted exceptional risk of being harassed by baseless claims by those who have been treated under the Mental Health Acts".

In *Seal v Chief Constable of South Wales Police* [2007] UKHL 31; [2007] 4 All E.R. 177, para.20, Lord Bingham said that the judgment in *Winch v Jones* set the threshold for obtaining leave "at a very unexacting level ... an applicant with an arguable case will be granted leave". Lord Brown said, at para.70, that "the test is now simply whether the case deserves further investigation by the court". Both remarks were made obiter. In *Johnston v Chief Constable of Merseyside Police* [2009] EWHC 2969 (QB); [2009] M.H.L.R. 343, Coulson J. considered whether the test identified by Sir John Donaldson in *Which v Jones* should be modified to take account of CPR Part 24 which introduced a new emphasis on allowing claims to go to trial only where they have a real prospect of success. His Lordship concluded, at para.15, "that a court faced with an application for permission under section 139(2) of the Act must strive to apply the test set out by Sir John Donaldson MR in *Winch v Jones* ..., with the proviso that the court should also consider whether, in all the circumstances, the proposed claim has a real prospect of success". *Winch v Jones* and *Johnston v Chief Constable of Merseyside Police* were cited in *DD v Durham County Council* [2013] EWCA Civ 96; [2013] M.H.L.R. 85, para.23, as authority for the proposition that the threshold under this section is "a low one". The same conclusion was reached by Yip J. in *Appiah v Leeds City Council* [2022] EWHC 2546 (KB) at para.19.

A successful application under subs.(2) of this section does not inhibit a judge on an application to strike out reaching a conclusion following fuller investigation that a statement of claim should be struck out as disclosing no reasonable cause of action (*X v A, B and C and the Mental Health Act Commission* (1991) 9 B.M.L.R. 91).

Article 12 of the Mental Health (Care and Treatment) (Scotland) Act 2003 (Consequential Provisions) Order 2005 (SI 2005/2078), which is reproduced in Pt 2, extends the protection afforded by this section to acts done in pursuance of that Order.

Human Rights Act 1998

On rejecting a claim that subs.(2) violates art.6(1) of the European Convention on Human Rights **1-1443** (ECHR), the European Court on Human Rights (ECtHR) confirmed in *Seal v United Kingdom* ((2011) 54 E.H.R.R. 6) that the "right of access to court is not absolute and may be subject to limitations" (para.75) and accepted the Government's argument that subs.(2) "is aimed at providing an additional layer of protection for those exercising sensitive powers under the 1983 Act and does not assume that all those who are, or have been, subject to compulsory powers contained in the Mental Health Act 1983 are vexatious litigants" (para.77). A claim that subs.(2) would violate art.6 if it is read together with art.14 was rejected in *TW v London Borough of Enfield* [2013] EWHC 1180 (QB); [2013] M.H.L.R. 214 at para.39. The ECtHR in *Salontaji-Drobnjak v Serbia (App.No.36500/05) Oct 13, 2009*, para.133, said that limitations on a mentally disordered patient's right of access to a court must be proportionate.

This section should be "read down" under s.3 of the 1998 Act so as to permit a patient's claim under s.7 of that Act for judicial review and damages for unlawful detention to proceed without leave (*TTM v London Borough of Hackney* [2011] EWCA Civ 4; [2011] 3 All E.R. 529, para.66).

The power to control the activities of detained patients

In *Pountney v Griffiths* [1976] A.C. 314, the House of Lords quashed the conviction of a nurse who **1-1444** had been charged with assaulting a patient when ushering the patient to his ward after a visit from the patient's family on the ground that leave to prosecute had not been obtained under subs.(2) of this section. Their Lordships approved the finding of Lord Widgery C.J. in the Court of Appeal that "when a male nurse is on duty and exercising his functions of controlling the patients in the hospital, acts done in pursuance of such control are acts within the scope of [s.139] and are thus protected by the section". Although the Act provides for the detention and treatment of patients, it nowhere explicitly refers to the control of patients. The House of Lords held that:

(i) subs.(2) extends to any act, provided that it had been carried out in purported pursuance of the Act, and that its scope is not limited to acts done or purported to be done in pursuance of functions specifically provided for in the terms of the Act; and

(ii) treating patients necessarily involves the exercise of discipline and control, and that suitable arrangements for visits to patients by family and friends was an obvious part of the patient's treatment.

In *R. (on the application of E.) v Ashworth Hospital Authority* [2001] EWHC Admin 1089; [2002] M.H.L.R. 150, Richards J., in holding that the power to control what patients wear is a necessary incident of the power to detain, said that to be lawful the implied power must be exercised:

(i) for the purpose of detention and/or treatment rather than for some ulterior purpose;

(ii) in accordance with *Wednesbury* principles of reasonableness; and

(iii) compatibly with the ECHR and in particular with art.8.

Pountney v Griffiths was cited by Auld L.J. in *R. v Broadmoor Special Hospital and the Secretary of State for the Department of Health Ex p. S, H, and D* [1998] C.O.D. 199, where the Court of Appeal held that the exercise of discipline and control in respect of a detained patient includes, where necessary, a power to search patients with or without cause and despite individual medical objections. To be lawful, a hospital's search policy must:

(i) be proportionate to the level of risk posed by the patient population to the maintenance of a safe and therapeutic environment; and

(ii) take account of a patient's right to respect for private life under art.8 of the ECHR.

The application of art.8 to the searching of patients is considered in the notes on that article in Pt 5 under the heading "Private life". A strip and intimate body search could also engage art.3: see *Wainwright v United Kingdom* (2007) 44 E.H.R.R. 40, paras 42, 43, noted in the General Note to art.3. The *Code of Practice* guidance on personal and other searches is contained in Ch.8.

In the *Broadmoor* case, Auld L.J. said that both the 1959 and 1983 Acts:

"leave unspoken many of the necessary incidents of control flowing from a power of detention for treatment, including: the power to restrain patients, to keep them in seclusion …, to deprive them of their personal possessions for their own safety and to regulate the frequency and manner of visits to them …".

Observations to a similar effect were made by Lord Woolf M.R. in *Broadmoor Hospital Authority v R.* [2000] 2 All E.R. 727 at para.26. In *R. v Mersey Care National Health Service Trust Ex p. Munjaz* [2005] UKHL 58; [2006] 4 All E.R. 736, Lord Bingham said at para.34:

"[T]he power to seclude a patient within a hospital is implied from the power to detain as a 'necessary ingredient flowing from a power of detention for treatment'".

It is submitted that the cases cited above provide authority for a hospital to enforce the rules that it has put in place to regulate the activities of detained patients as long as such rules are a necessary and proportionate response to the risks that have been identified. A legal basis for the use of restraint can also be found in the provisions considered in Appendix A.

In *Munjaz v United Kingdom* [2012] M.H.L.R. 351, the European Court of Human Rights held that in certain circumstances the seclusion of a detained patient could amount to a further deprivation of his liberty under art.5: see the note in "detention" under art.5(1)(e) in Part 5. The *Code of Practice* guidance on seclusion and on long-term segregation is contained in Ch.26. Seclusion is defined at para.26.103:

"Seclusion refers to the supervised confinement and isolation of a patient, away from other patients, in an area from which the patient is prevented from leaving, where it is of immediate necessity for the purpose of the containment of severe behavioural disturbance which is likely to cause harm to others."

Long-term segregation is described at para.26.150:

"Long-term segregation refers to a situation where, in order to reduce a sustained risk of harm posed by the patient to others, which is a constant feature of their presentation, a multi-disciplinary review and a representative from the responsible commissioning authority determines that a patient should not be allowed to mix freely with other patients on the ward or unit on a long-term basis. In such cases, it should have been determined that the risk of harm to others would not be ameliorated by a short period of seclusion combined with any other form of treatment. The clinical judgement is that, if the patient were allowed to mix freely in the general ward environment, other patients or staff would continue to be exposed to a high likelihood of serious injury or harm over a prolonged period of time. Where consideration is being given to long-term segregation, wherever appropriate, the views of the person's family and carers should be elicited and taken into account. The multi-disciplinary review should include an IMHA in cases where a patient has one."

The power to control includes the power to restrain patients as long as its use is necessary and proportionate. To avoid breaches of the ECHR the restraint must satisfy the test of "medical necessity": see *Herczegfalvy v Austria* (1992) 15 E.H.R.R. 437 and the General Note to art.3 in Part 5. A legal basis for the use of restraint can also be found in the provisions considered in Appendix A.

Information about the Government's *Positive and Safe* programme and relevant NICE guidance are noted in the General Note to the Mental Health Units (Use of Force) Act 2018.

Isolating detained patients

1-1445   In the context of the coronavirus pandemic, the DHSC has provided the following guidance:

"In most cases, when a patient is already detained under the Mental Health Act 1983 (MHA), the powers provided by this legislation will be available and can lawfully be relied upon, so long as the patient's refusal to self-isolate is connected to their mental disorder, or the measures are necessary to support the overall purpose of the MHA, ie detaining the patient in a safe and secure environment, where they can be treated for their mental disorder. Crucially, the decision about whether these MHA powers should actually be used to isolate a patient should still be made on a case-by-case basis, considering the individual circumstances of the patient" ("Legal guidance for services supporting people of all ages during the coronavirus pandemic: Mental health, learning disability and autism, specialised commissioning", NHSE and NHSI, v.4, January 25, 2021).

Subsection (1)

1-1446   This "subsection does not create any cause of action and only relates to pre-existing possible liability. It creates a hurdle for a plaintiff to surmount"; per Morland J. in *X v A, B and C and the Mental Health Act Commission* (1991) 9 B.M.L.R. 91 at 96.

Person   Or corporation (Interpretation Act 1978 s.5, Sch.1).

Shall be liable   The question whether the protection of this section can be claimed by a health body in a situation where that body is vicariously liable for any shortcomings of a doctor employee in the performance of duties vested in him or her personally by the Act is undecided: see the conflicting opinions of Brooke and Hale L.JJ. in *R. (on the application of Wilkinson) v The Responsible Medical Officer Broadmoor Hospital* [2001] EWCA Civ 1545; [2002] 1 W.L.R. 419, at paras 42 and 58.

Civil or criminal proceedings   The proceedings need not necessarily involve a patient.

In *Dunnage v Randall* [2015] EWCA Civ 673; [2015] M.H.L.R. 117 the Court of Appeal held that there was no principle that requires the law to excuse from liability in negligence a defendant who fails to meet the normal standard of care partly because of a medical problem. Vos L.J. said at para.131:

> "In my judgment, only defendants whose attack or medical incapacity has the effect of entirely eliminating any fault or responsibility for the injury can be excused. It is only defendants in that category that have not actually broken their undoubted duty of care. The actions of a defendant, who is merely impaired by medical problems, whether physical or mental, cannot escape liability if he causes injury by failing to exercise reasonable care."

There is no presumption of anonymity in High Court proceedings relating to the use of compulsory powers under the Act. In each case the court is required to weigh up the rights of the patient under art.8 of the ECHR with the right to freedom of expression under art.10 (*R. (on the application of C) v Secretary of State for Justice* [2016] UKSC 2).

Act purporting to be done in pursuance of this act   In *TW v London Borough of Enfield* [2013] EWHC 1180) (QB); [2013] M.H.L.R. 214, para.41, Bean J. said that it is clear from *TTM v Hackney LBC* [2011] EWCA Civ 4; [2011] M.H.L.R. 171 that in order to be compliant with the ECHR this provision is to be read as though the following words were added to this phrase "or is otherwise unlawful, for example because of a contravention of s.11(4)". Although nearly all such acts will relate to detained patients, this section also applies to patients who are subject to guardianship and community treatment orders.

Whether the protection afforded by this section applies to omissions, such as a failure to detain a person under the Act, is undecided. In *R. (on the application of W) v Doncaster M.B.C.* [2003] EWHC 192 (Admin); [2004] M.H.L.R. 189, Stanley Burnton J. said that he would have been "reluctant to accept [a] submission that s.139(1) does not apply to an omission or failure to act, and is confined to positive acts. I do not think that Parliament intended there to be any such illogical and unmeritorious distinction in the application of that section" (para.55).

In the unreported case of *Ashingdane v Secretary of State for Social Services*, February 18, 1980, the Court of Appeal held that the immunity conferred by this section is confined to an act done by a person to whom authority to do an act of that type is expressly or impliedly conferred by the Act or by regulations made under it. Applying this test, the Court held that the decision of a nurses' union not to allow patients who were subject to restriction orders to be transferred to a particular hospital was a policy decision which fell outside their express or implied authority and was not, therefore, covered by this section.

This section was engaged in a case where it was alleged that the defendants had made maliciously false, defamatory allegations in medical notes made by them in conection with the management and care of the claimant when he had suffered from mental illness: see *Lebrooy v Hammersmith and Fulham LBC* [2006] EWHC 1976 (QB); [2006] M.H.L.R. 253.

Acted in bad faith or without reasonable care   In *Richardson v London County Council* [1957] 1 W.L.R. 751 it was held that: (1) whether a person has acted in bad faith or without reasonable care is a question of fact with the burden of proof lying with the applicant; and (2) this section offers protection even though the person proceeded against acted either without jurisdiction or misconstrued the Act, as long as the misconstruction was one which the Act was reasonably capable of bearing.

In *R. (on the application of Wilkinson) v The Responsible Medical Officer Broadmoor Hospital* [2001] EWCA Civ 1545; [2002] 1 W.L.R. 419, at para.57, Hale L.J., citing *Richardson*, said that it may well be that the immunity provided by this section does not relieve against "a negligent mistake of law as to the extent of the legal authority conferred by the Act".

If bad faith were established, there could be a private law claim based on misfeasance in public office (*TTM v London Borough of Hackney* [2010] EWHC 1349 (Admin), para.36).

Subsection (2)

1-1447   Failure to obtain the necessary leave or consent required by this provision before the proceedings are begun renders the proceedings a nullity (*Seal v Chief Constable of South Wales Police* [2007] UKHL 31; [2007] 4 All E.R. 177).

Civil proceedings   This phrase does not include proceedings for judicial review. Acts purportedly done in pursuance of the Act can therefore be reviewed even if bad faith or lack of reasonable care are not alleged (*R. v Hallstrom, Ex p. W* [1986] 2 All E.R. 306).

Leave   The leave of a High Court judge is required even if the case would normally be heard in the county court. An appeal lies to the Court of Appeal against a judge's decision but either the leave of the judge or of the Court of Appeal is required before the appeal can be made (*Moore v Commissioner of Metropolitan Police* [1968] 1 Q.B. 26). A Master or District Judge may not make orders or grant interim remedies in applications under this section (CPR Practice Direction 2B, Allocation of Cases to Levels of Judiciary, para.3(1)(g)).

Although a Master is not empowered to grant leave under this provision, in *Upadrasta v Commissioner of the City of London Police* [2023] EWHC 1853 (KB) an order by a Master granting leave was declared to be valid in accordance with the operation of the common law doctrine of de facto authority.

The onus is on the applicant to satisfy the court or the D.P.P. that the proceedings should be commenced (*Carter v Commissioner of Police for the Metropolis* [1975] 1 W.L.R. 507 CA). The "overriding objective" set out in Pt 1 of the Civil Procedure Rules 1998 has no application to an application for leave under this section (*C v South London and Maudsley Hospital National Health Service Trust* [2001] M.H.L.R. 269).

Subsection (3)

1-1448   **Consent of the director of public prosecutions**   Is required for proceedings under s.127.

Subsection (4)

1-1449   **Does not apply**   The acts of a local social services authority performed in pursuance of the Act are protected by this section.

An approved mental health professional (AMHP) who is employed by a health body is acting on behalf of a local social services authority when performing the functions of an AMHP and is therefore protected by this section: see s.145(1AC).

Secretary of State   Or the Welsh Ministers (see the General Note to this Act and SI 2000/253, Sch.3).

Notification of hospitals having arrangements for reception of urgent cases

1-1450   **140.**   It shall be the duty of [every [integrated care board] and of] every [Local Health Board] to give notice to every local social services authority for an area wholly or partly comprised within the [area of the [[integrated care board] or] [Local Health Board]] specifying the hospital or hospitals administered by [or otherwise available] [to the [[integrated care board] or] [Local Health Board]] in which arrangements are from time to time in force [—

    (a)   for the reception of patients in cases of special urgency;

    (b)   for the provision of accommodation or facilities designed so as to be specially suitable for patients who have not attained the age of 18 years.]

Amendments

The amendments to this section were made by the National Health Service and Community Care Act 1990 s.66(1), Sch.9 para.24(8), the Health Authorities Act 1995 s.2(1), Sch.1 para.107(12), the National Heath Service Reform and Health Care Professions Act 2002 s.2(5), Sch.2 para.48, the Mental Health

Act 2007 s.31(4), SI 2007/961 art.3, Sch. para.13(12), the Health and Social Care Act 2012 s.45 and the Health and Care Act 2022 Sch.4 para.19.

Definitions

Local Health Board: s.145(1).   **1-1451**
local social services authority: s.145(1).
hospital: s.145(1).
patient: s.145(1).

General Note

This section, which is based on a similar provision in s.132 of the Mental Health Act 1959, requires   **1-1452**
relevant health bodies to notify local social services authorities within their area of the arrangements
that are in force for the reception of mentally disordered patients to hospital in cases of special urgency
and the provision of accommodation or facilities designed to be specially suitable for child patients who
are mentally disordered. The patients may be either detained or informal. Paragraph 14.77 of the *Code
of Practice* states:

> "If the doctors reach the opinion that the patient needs to be admitted to hospital, it is their responsibil-
> ity to take the necessary steps to secure a suitable hospital bed; it is not the responsibility of the
> applicant. In some cases, it could be agreed locally between the local authority and the relevant NHS
> bodies and communicated to the AMHP that this will be done by any AMHP involved in the
> assessment."

Paragraph 14.78 of the *Code of Practice* states:

> "Clinical commissioning groups (CCGs) [now integrated care boards] are responsible for commis-
> sioning mental health services to meet the needs of their areas. Under section 140 of the Act, CCGs
> have a duty to notify local authorities in their areas of arrangements which are in force for the recep-
> tion of patients in cases of special urgency or the provision of appropriate accommodation or facili-
> ties specifically designed for patients under the age of 18. The arrangements should include details
> of which providers in their area can receive patients in cases of special urgency and provide accom-
> modation or facilities designed to be specifically suitable for patients under the age of 18. CCGs
> should provide a list of hospitals and their specialisms to local authorities which will help inform
> AMHPs as to where these hospitals are. This should in turn help inform AMHPs as to where beds
> are available in these circumstances if they are needed."

Although this section does not oblige the specified hospitals to admit patients in an emergency or to
maintain the capacity to facilitate such admissions, a refusal to admit should only be made with good
reason. If a hospital bed cannot be found for a patient who requires admission, it is the responsibility
of the local health and social services authorities to provide the patient with appropriate treatment and/or
care until a bed is found: see the note on *Delay in finding a hospital bed for a patient who has been assessed under the Act* in s.6.

As independent hospitals can be "otherwise available" to commissioners, ICBs and LHBs could enter
into contacts with independent hospitals to provide hospital places to patients when bed capacity in NHS
hospitals is exhausted.

The Mental Health Act Commission suggested that if a patient cannot be admitted to hospital in an
emergency for want of a bed the approved mental health professional should complete an application,
making it out to the hospital which has been the subject of a notification under this provision, and convey
the patient to that hospital. For a comment on this suggestion, see the note on "to hospital" in s.6(1).

For the duty to provide suitable accommodation and facilities for children, see s.131A. Also note the
duty placed by s.39 on integrated care boards and Local Health Boards to provide the courts with
information as to the availability of hospital places.

Members of Parliament suffering from mental illness

141.—   [*Repealed by the Mental Health (Discrimination) Act 2013 s.1(1)*]   **1-1453**

General Note

1-1454   Section 1(2) of the Mental Health (Discrimination) Act 2013 abolished any rule of the common law which disqualifies a person from membership of the House of Commons on grounds of mental illness.

Pay, pensions, etc. of mentally disordered persons

1-1455   **142.**—(1)   Where a periodic payment falls to be made to any person by way of pay or pension or otherwise in connection with the service or employment of that or any other person, and the payment falls to be made directly out of moneys provided by Parliament or the Consolidated Fund [or the Scottish Consolidated Fund], or other moneys administered by or under the control or supervision of a government department, the authority by whom the sum in question is payable, if satisfied after considering medical evidence that the person to whom it is payable (referred to in this section as "the patient") is incapable by reason of mental disorder of managing and administering his property and affairs, may, instead of paying the sum to the patient, apply it in accordance with subsection (2) below.

(2)   The authority may pay the sum or such part of it as they think fit to the institution or person having the care of the patient, to be applied for his benefit and may pay the remainder (if any) or such part of the remainder as they think fit—

   (a)   to or for the benefit of persons who appear to the authority to be members of the patient's family or other persons for whom the patient might be expected to provide if he were not mentally disordered, or

   (b)   in reimbursement, with or without interest, of money applied by any person either in payment of the patient's debts (whether legally enforceable or not) or for the maintenance or other benefit of the patient or such persons as are mentioned in paragraph (a) above.

(3)   In this section "government department" does not include a Northern Ireland department.

Amendment

The words in square brackets in subsection (1) were inserted by the Scotland Act 1998 (Consequential Modifications) (No.2) Order 1999 (SI 1999/1820) art.4, Sch.2 para.71.

Definition

mental disorder: ss.1, 145(1).

Repeal

1-1456   Although this section has been repealed by the Mental Capacity Act 2005 s.67(2), Sch.7 it is reproduced because of the terms of s.67(1), Sch.6 para.29(5) and (6) of that Act which state:

"(5)   Sub-paragraph (6) applies where, before the [repeal of s.142 on October 1, 2007], an authority has, in respect of a person referred to in that section as 'the patient', made payments under that section—

   (a)   to an institution or person having the care of the patient, or

   (b)   in accordance with subsection (2)(a) or (b) of that section.

(6)   The authority may, in respect of the patient, continue to make payments under that section to that institution or person, or in accordance with subsection (2)(a) or (b) of that section, despite the [repeal of s.142]".

General Note

1-1457   Under this section provision is made in the case of any pay, pension or similar payment payable by Parliament or the Government, for direct payment to the institution or person having the care of the patient. Any sums which remain can be paid to members of the patient's family, or to other persons for whom the patient might be expected to provide were he not mentally disordered, or to reimburse people who have paid his debts or helped to maintain him or his family. This section applies to any person who "is incapable by reason of mental disorder of managing and administering his property and affairs" and is not limited to either detained or hospital patients.

[Regulations as to approvals in relation to England and Wales

142A.— The Secretary of State jointly with the Welsh Ministers may by **1-1458** regulations make provision as to the circumstances in which—

    (a) a practitioner approved for the purposes of section 12 above, or

    (b) a person approved to act as an approved clinician for the purposes of this Act, approved in relation to England is to be treated, by virtue of his approval, as approved in relation to Wales too, and vice versa.]

Amendment

This section was inserted by the Mental Health Act 2007 s.17.

Definition

approved clinician: s.145(1).   **1-1459**

General Note

This section gives the Secretary of State, jointly with Welsh Ministers, the power to set out in regula- **1-1460** tions the circumstances in which approval in England under s.12, and approval as an approved clini- cian should be considered to mean approval in Wales, and vice versa.

The Mental Health (Mutual Recognition) Regulations 2008 (SI 2008/1204), which are reproduced in Pt 2, have been made under this section.

[Delegation of powers of managers of NHS foundation trusts

142B.—(1) The constitution of an NHS foundation trust may not provide for **1-1461** a function under this Act to be delegated otherwise than in accordance with provi- sions made by or under this Act.

(2) Paragraph 15(3) of Schedule 7 to the National Health Service Act 2006 (which provides that the powers of a public benefit corporation may be delegated to a committee of directors or to an executive director) shall have effect subject to this section.]

Amendment

This section was inserted by the Mental Health Act 2007 s.45(3).

General Note

Schedule 7 of the National Health Service Act 2006 sets out mandatory requirements for the contents **1-1462** of the constitution of a NHS foundation trust. The effect of this section is that the constitution may not permit the trust's functions under this Act to be delegated to executive directors or committees of direc- tors unless that is permitted by this Act.

General provisions as to regulations, orders and rules

1-1463   **143.**—(1)   Any power of the Secretary of State or the Lord Chancellor to make regulations, orders or rules under this Act shall be exercisable by statutory instrument.

(2)   Any Order in Council under this Act [or any order made [by the Secretary of State] under section 54A [or 68A(7)][...] above] and any statutory instrument containing regulations [made by the Secretary of State, or rules made,] under this Act shall be subject to annulment in pursuance of a resolution of either House of Parliament.

(3)   No order shall be made [by the Secretary of State] under section [45A(10)] [68A(1)]) or 71(3) above unless a draft of it has been approved by a resolution of each House of Parliament.

[(3A)   Subsections (3B) to [(3DB)] apply where power to make regulations or an order under this Act is conferred on the Welsh Ministers (other than by or by virtue of the Government of Wales Act 2006).

(3B)   Any power of the Welsh Ministers to make regulations or an order shall be exercisable by statutory instrument.

(3C)   Any statutory instrument containing regulations, or an order under section 68A(7) above, made by the Welsh Ministers shall be subject to annulment in pursuance of a resolution of the National Assembly for Wales.

(3D)   No order shall be made under section 68A(1) above by the Welsh Ministers unless a draft of it has been approved by a resolution of the National Assembly for Wales.

[(3DA)   Subsection (3C) does not apply to regulations to which subsection (3DB) applies.

(3DB)   A statutory instrument which contains (alone or with other provisions) the first regulations to be made under any of the following provisions—

   (a)   section 130E(2),
   (b)   section 130E(4)(b),
   (c)   section 130E(5)(b),
   (d)   section 130F(2)(d),
   (e)   section 130G(2)(c), or
   (f)   section 130H(1)(b)(ii),

must not be made unless a draft of the instrument containing the regulations has been laid before, and approved by resolution of, the National Assembly for Wales.

(3E)   In this section—

   (a)   references to the Secretary of State include the Secretary of State and the Welsh Ministers acting jointly; and
   (b)   references to the Welsh Ministers include the Welsh Ministers and the Secretary of State acting jointly.]

[(4)   This section does not apply to rules which are, by virtue of section 108 of this Act, to be made in accordance with Part 1 of Schedule 1 to the Constitutional Reform Act 2005.]

Amendments

The amendments to this section were made by the Criminal Justice Act 1991 s.27(3), the Mental Health Act 2007 ss.37(5), 47(2), (3), 55, Sch.11 Pt 6, the Crime (Sentences) Act 1997 s.55, Sch.4 para.12(18), the Mental Health (Wales) Measure 2010 s.40 and the Constitutional Reform Act 2005 s.12, Sch.1 para.16.

General Note

Subsection (1)

Secretary of State   Or, in relation to Wales, the Welsh Ministers (see the General Note to the Act and SI 1999/672 art.2, Sch.1).   **1-1464**

The lord chancellor   Who cannot transfer his functions under this provision to another person (Constitutional Reform Act 2005 s.19, Sch.7).

Power to amend local Acts

144.   Her Majesty may by Order in Council repeal or amend any local enact-   **1-1465**
ment so far as appears to Her Majesty to be necessary in consequence of this Act.

Interpretation
145.—(1)   In this Act, unless the context otherwise requires—   **1-1466**

"absent without leave" has the meaning given to it by section 18 above and related expressions [(including expressions relating to a patient's liability to be returned to a hospital or other place)] shall be construed accordingly;

"application for admission for assessment" has the meaning given in section 2 above;

"application for admission for treatment" has the meaning given in section 3 above;

["the appropriate tribunal" has the meaning given by section 66(4) above;]

["approved clinician" means a person approved by the Secretary of State [or another person by virtue of section 12ZA or 12ZB above] (in relation to England) or by the Welsh Ministers (in relation to Wales) to act as an approved clinician for the purposes of this Act;]

["approved mental health professional" has the meaning given by section 114, above;]

["care home"—

(a)   has the same meaning as in the Care Standards Act 2000 in respect of a care home in England; and

(b)   means a place in Wales at which a care home service within the meaning of Part 1 of the Regulation and Inspection of Social Care (Wales) Act 2016 is provided wholly or mainly to persons aged 18 or over;]

["community patient" has the meaning given in section 17A above;]

["community treatment order" and "the community treatment order" have the meanings given in section 17A above;]

["the community treatment period" has the meaning given in section 20A above;]

[...]

["high security psychiatric services" has the same meaning as in [section 4 of the National Health Service Act 2006 or section 4 of the National Health

Service (Wales) Act 2006]]
"hospital" means—
- (a) any health service hospital within the meaning of [National Health Service Act 2006 or the National Health Service (Wales) Act 2006]; and
- (b) any accommodation provided by a local authority and used as a hospital or on behalf of the Secretary of State under [the National Health Service Act 2006, or of the Welsh Ministers under the National Health Service (Wales) Act 2006] [; and
- (c) any hospital as defined by section 206 of the National Health Service (Wales) Act 2006 which is vested in a Local Health Board;]

and "hospital within the meaning of Part II of this Act" has the meaning given in section 34 above;

["hospital direction" has the meaning given in section 45A(3)(a) above;]

"hospital order" and "guardianship order" have the meanings respectively given in section 37 above;

["independent hospital"—
- (a) in relation to England, means a hospital as defined by section 275 of the National Health Service Act 2006 that is not a health service hospital as defined by that section, and
- (b) in relation to Wales, has the same meaning as in the Care Standards Act 2000;]

"interim hospital order" has the meaning given in section 38 above;

["limitation direction" has the meaning given in section 45A(3)(b) above;]

["Local Health Board" means a Local Health Board established under section 11 of the National Health Services (Wales) Act 2006;]

["local social services authority" means—
- (a) an authority in England which is a local authority for the purposes of Part 1 of the Care Act 2014, or
- (b) an authority in Wales which is a local authority for the purposes of the Social Services and Well-being (Wales) Act 2014;]

"the managers" means—
- (a) in relation to a hospital vested in the Secretary of State for the purposes of his functions under [the National Health Service Act 2006, or in the Welsh Ministers for the purposes of their functions under the National Health Service (Wales) Act 2006], and in relation to any accommodation provided by a local authority and used as a hospital by or on behalf of the Secretary of State under [the National Health Service Act 2006, or of the Welsh Ministers under the National Health Service (Wales) Act 2006,] [the Secretary of State where the Secretary is responsible for the administration of the hospital or] the [...] [...] [[Local Health Board] or Special Health Authority] responsible for the administration of the hospital;
- (b) [...];
- [(bb) in relation to a hospital vested in [...] a National Health Service trust, [...] the trust;]
- [(bc) in relation to a hospital vested in an NHS foundation trust, the trust;]
- [(bd) in relation to a hospital vested in a Local Health Board, the Board;]

    [(c)   in relation to a registered establishment—
          (i)   if the establishment is in England, the person or persons registered as a service provider under Chapter 2 of Part 1 of the Health and Social Care Act 2008 in respect of the regulated activity (within the meaning of that Part) relating to the assessment or medical treatment of mental disorder that is carried out in the establishment, and
         (ii)   if the establishment is in Wales, the person or persons registered in respect of the establishment under Part 2 of the Care Standards Act 2000;] and in this definition "hospital" means a hospital within the meaning of Part II of this Act;

"medical treatment" includes nursing, [psychological intervention and specialist mental health habilitation, rehabilitation and care (but see also subsection (4) below);]

["mental disorder" has the meaning given in section 1 above (subject to [section 86(4));]

[...];

"nearest relative," in relation to a patient, has the meaning given in Part II of this Act;

"patient"
    [...] means a person suffering or appearing to be suffering from mental disorder;

[...]

["registered establishment" has the meaning given in section 34 above;]

["the regulatory authority" means—
      (a)   in relation to England, the Care Quality Commission;
      (b)   in relation to Wales, the Welsh Ministers;]

[...]

["the responsible hospital" has the meaning given in section 17A above;]

"restriction direction" has the meaning given to it by section 49 above;

"restriction order" has the meaning given to it by section 41 above;

["Special Health Authority" means a Special Health Authority established under [section 28 of the National Health Service Act 2006, or section 22 of the National Health Service (Wales) Act 2006];]

[...]
[...]
[...]
[...]

"transfer direction" has the meaning given to it by section 47 above.

[(1AA)   Where high security psychiatric services and other services are provided at a hospital, the part of the hospital at which high security psychiatric services are provided and the other part shall be treated as separate hospitals for the purposes of this Act.]

[(1AB)   References in this Act to appropriate medical treatment shall be construed in accordance with section 3(4) above.]

[(1AC)   References in this Act to an approved mental health professional shall be construed as references to an approved mental health professional acting on behalf of a local social services authority, unless the context otherwise requires.]

[(1A)   ...]

(2)   [...]

(3)   In relation to a person who is liable to be detained or subject to guardianship [or a community patient] by virtue of an order or direction under Part III of this Act (other than under section 35, 36, or 38), any reference in this Act to any enactment contained in Part II of this Act or in section 66 or 67 above shall be construed as a reference to that enactment as it applies to that person by virtue of Part III of this Act.

[(4)   Any reference in this Act to medical treatment, in relation to mental disorder, shall be construed as a reference to medical treatment the purpose of which is to alleviate, or prevent a worsening of, the disorder or one or more of its symptoms or manifestations.]

Amendments

The amendments to this section were made by the National Health Service and Community Care Act 1990 s.66(1), Sch.9 para.24(9), the Health Authorities Act 1995 s.2(1), Sch.1 para.107(14), the Mental Health (Patients in the Community) Act 1995 s.1(2), Sch.1 para.20, the Health Act 1999 s.65, Sch.4 para.69, the Crime (Sentences) Act 1997 s.55, Sch.4 para.12(19), the Health Act 1999 (Supplementary, Consequential, etc. Provisions) Order 2000 (SI 2000/90) Sch.1 para.16(9), the Care Standards Act 2000 ss.116, 117(2) Sch.4 para.9(10), Sch.6, the National Health Service and Health Care Professions Act 2002 s.2(5), Sch.2 para.49, the National Health Service Reform and Health Care Professions Act 2002 (Supplementary, Consequential, etc. Provisions) Regulations 2002 (SI 2002/2469) reg.4, Sch.1, the Mental Health Act 2007 ss.1(4), 4, 7(2)(3), 14(5), 21, 32(4), 46, Sch.1 para.17, Sch.2 para.11(2)(3), Sch.3 para.34, SI 2007/961 art.3, Sch. para.13(13), SI 2008/2883 art.9, Sch.3 para.66, the Health and Social Care Act 2008 s.52, Sch.3 para.13 and SI 2010/813, art.5(5), the Mental Health Act 2007 s.55, Sch.11 Pt 5, the Statute Law (Repeals) Act 1993 s.1(1), Sch.1 Pt XIV, Group 2, the Mental Health (Amendment) Act 1994 s.1, the Mental Capacity Act 2005 s.67(2), Sch.7, the Health and Social Care (Community Health and Standards) Act 2003 s.34, Sch.4 para.57, the Health Act 1999 s.65, Sch.4 para.69, Sch.5, the National Health Service (Consequential Provisions) Act 2006 s.2, Sch.1 para.70, the Health and Social Care Act 2012 s.39(4), Sch.5 para.31, the Mental Health (Discrimination) Act 2013 s.1(1), Sch., para.1(1), the Care Act 2014 s.75(13) and SI 2018/195 reg.6.

General Note

Subsection (1)

1-1467   **Approved Clinician**   The Secretary of State's "Mental Health Act 1983–Instructions with respect to the exercise of an approval function in relation to approved clinicians 2015", which establish the criteria for approval as an Approved Clinician (AC), can be accessed at: *www.gov.uk/government/uploads/ system/uploads/attachment_data/file/489216/2015_AC_Instructions.pdf*. Approval is for the whole of England. Unlike s.12, no explicit test for approval of an AC is given in the Act. Doctors who are approved as ACs are automatically approved as doctors who are approved under s.12(2) (s.12(2A)). For Wales, see the Mental Health Act 1983 Approved Clinician (Wales) Directions 2008. See s.142A for the mutual recognition of approval as an AC in England and Wales.

With regard to medical treatment, an AC, who will not necessarily be the patient's responsible clinician, can only carry out treatment which she is qualified to give. An independent prescriber who is not a doctor but who is an AC could therefore be the AC in charge of medicines she can prescribe.

The Mental Health (Approval Functions) Act 2012 was passed to retrospectively validate the approval of clinicians where the approval function had been unlawfully delegated: see the note on the 2012 Act in the General Note to s.12.

High security psychiatric services   These comprise:

"hospital accommodation and services for persons who are—(a) liable to be detained under the

Mental Health Act 1983, and (b) in the opinion of the Secretary of State require treatment under conditions of high security on account of their dangerous, violent or criminal propensities" (National Health Service Act 2006 s.4(1)).

The National Health Service Commissioning Board [now NHS England] has been directed to perform certain functions with respect to high security psychiatric services: see the High Security Psychiatric Services (National Health Service Commissioning Board) Directions 2013.

Hospital   The definition of hospital in s.275(1) of the 2006 Act is very broad:

"'hospital' means—
- (a) any institution for the reception and treatment of persons suffering from illness,
- (b) any maternity home, and
- (c) any institution for the reception and treatment of persons during convalescence or persons requiring medical rehabilitation,

and includes clinics, dispensaries and out-patient departments maintained in connection with any such home or institution, and 'hospital accommodation' must be construed accordingly".

In *Re Couchman's Will Trusts* [1952] Ch. 391, Danckwerts J. considered a similar definition in s.79(1) of the National Health Service Act 1946 and held that:

1. "Reception" means taking people into a building and keeping them there. An institution that confines itself to treating patients as out-patients does not qualify.
2. The phrase "maintained in connection with" means maintained in connection with a particular hospital. It does not cover a clinic which was "maintained for the purpose of dealing with people who needed subsequent treatment, and it would have dealt with persons coming from any hospital—a hospital, perhaps in another country—or with persons who were not connected with any hospital".

The definition, which is not confined to mental hospitals (*IM (Nigeria) v Secretary of State for the Home Department* [2013] EWCA Civ 1561, para.19), does not include an independent hospital, which is brought within the scope of the Act by s.34(1), (2) and s.55(5).

By virtue of s.8(1) of the Health and Social Care Act 2008 and reg.3 and Sch.1, para.5 to SI 2014/2936, a hospital which provides for the assessment or medical treatment (other than surgical procedures) of patients detained under the Act (with the exception of s.135 or 136) must be registered for that activity by the Care Quality Commission. Such registration "is not required to provide assessment or treatment of mental disorder to patients who are detained by another authority, but admitted to the treating hospital under the powers to grant leave of absence from the place of detention under MHA 1983, section 17. This will be the case even if the detaining authority authorises that the patient remains in the custody of the treating hospital" ("Use of the Mental Health Act 1983 in general hospitals without a psychiatric unit" CQC, April 2010).

The holding powers contained in s.5(2) and (4) can be invoked in any hospital in England or Wales. It is clearly impracticable for a hospital to seek registration with the CQC on the ground that such powers might be invoked at some point in the future. Although the CQC has encouraged general hospitals to register to assess and treat detained patients, it is understood that the CQC turns a "blind eye" to occasions when the holding powers are used in a general hospital that is not so registered.

Prison healthcare centres are excluded from the definition as such facilities are provided under prison legislation. Responsibility for prison health care was fully transferred from HM Prison Service to the NHS in April 2006. The Government has stated that "prisoners should have access to the same range and quality of services appropriate to their needs as are available to the general population through the NHS" (*Changing the Outlook*, DH and MHPS, 2001, p.5). This policy was considered in *Roberts v Secretary of State for Justice* [2009] EWHC 2321 (Admin), where Michael Supperstone QC, sitting as a deputy judge of the High Court, said at para.20:

"In my view, if there is any restriction on the access that prisoners have to health services so that prisoners are not provided with access to the same range and quality of healthcare services as the general public receives, it is in the public interest that such restriction be published and made generally known."

In *Riviere v France* (App.No.33834/03) the European Court of Human Rights observed that Recommendation No. R (98) 7 of the Committee of Ministers of the Council of Europe concerning the ethical and organisational aspects of health care in prison provides that prisoners suffering from serious mental disturbance should be kept and cared for in a hospital facility that was adequately equipped and possessed appropriately trained staff.

The managers   General guidance on the functions of the hospital managers is given in Ch.37 of the *Code of Practice*. Managers are accountable for the lawfulness of each patient's detention under the Act (ss.6(2), 40(1)(b)). In *South Staffordshire and Shropshire Healthcare NHS Foundation Trust v The Hospital Managers of St George's Hospital* [2016] EWHC 1196 (Admin); [2016] M.H.L.R. 273, paras 26, 27, Cranston J. held that a panel of the hospital managers exercising powers under s.23 to discharge a patient was sufficiently separate from and independent of the Trust that appointed it to enable the Trust in "quite exceptional circumstances" to bring a judicial review challenge to its decision.

The *Code of Practice* states:

"37.3 Hospital managers have the authority to detain patients under the Act. They have the primary responsibility for seeing that the requirements of the Act are followed. In particular, they must ensure that patients are detained only as the Act allows, that their treatment and care accord fully with its provisions, and that they are fully informed of, and are supported in exercising, their statutory rights.

37.4 As managers of what the Act terms 'responsible hospitals', hospital managers have equivalent responsibilities towards CTO patients, even if those patients are not actually being treated at one of their hospitals."

When a detained patient is transferred to the detention of different hospital managers, any outstanding responsibilities of the original hospital managers, such as the duty to hold a review, are transferred to the new hospital managers.

The managers of an independent hospital act as a "public authority" within s.6 of the Human Rights Act 1998 when making decisions relating to the staffing and/or facilities to be provided to a detained patient (*R. (on the application of A) v Partnerships in Care* [2002] EWHC 529 (Admin); [2002] 1 W.L.R. 2610).

"Hospitals vested in the Secretary of State" include hospitals vested in the Welsh Ministers for the purposes of their functions under the National Health Service (Wales) Act 2006 (see the General Note to the Act and SI 2000/253, Sch.3).

1-1468   **Medical treatment**   In *Secretary of State for Justice v RB* [2011] EWCA Civ 1608; [2012] M.H.L.R. 131, paras 25, 26, the Court of Appeal said that the policy of the Act is treatment, not containment.

The definition of medical treatment, which should be considered along with subs.(4), is inclusive, not exhaustive. It includes interventions that are not ordinarily considered to be "medical". The definition does not deal with the willingness of any person to accept treatment (*R. (on the application of SP) v Secretary of State for Justice* [2010] EWCA Civ 1590; [2011] M.H.L.R. 65, para.4). Medical treatment for the purposes of the Act includes the specific treatments mentioned in Pt IV.

Cases on the definition prior to its amendment by the 2007 Act confirmed that the mere fact of being cared for or nursed is sufficient to constitute medical treatment (the amendment requires the care to be of a specialist nature): see, for example *R. v Mersey Mental Health Review Tribunal Ex p. D, DC The Times,* April 13, 1987, where the continued detention of the patient was upheld even though there was nothing other than nursing care that could be provided for him. Ward round reviews may be part of a patient's medical treatment (*KL v Somerset Partnership NHS Foundation Trust* [2011] UKUT 233 (AAC); [2011] M.H.L.R. 194, para.9). In *R. (on the application of Epsom and St Helier NHS Trust) v Mental Health Review Tribunal* [2001] EWHC Admin 101; [2001] M.H.L.R. 8, Sullivan J. said at para.47:

"[O]ne has to look at the whole course of treatment. To do so, one has to look at the past, present and future. It is not enough to say that a patient is not receiving treatment at a particular time."

In *Re Ian Brady*, December 11, 2013, at para.207, the First-tier Tribunal (Mental Health) "observed that this sub-section does not seek to provide a comprehensive definition. It sets out various actions which may be taken when seeking to assist a patient. There may be a degree of overlap of the nature of that assistance encompassed by the items mentioned but they must also connote some different action. Thus, in the opinion of the Tribunal whilst 'specialist care' may include 'nursing' it must also encompass other actions. Conversely, 'nursing' does not necessarily encompass 'specialist care'. This indicates the width of meaning of the term 'treatment'".

As the definition of mental disorder in s.1(2) includes "paraphilias like fetishism or paedophilia" (Explanatory Notes, para.24), medication which acts as a sexual suppressant could be medical treatment for the purposes of this provision.

In *R. (on the application of Munjaz) v Mersey Care National Health Service Trust* [2005] UKHL 58;

[2005] M.H.L.R. 276, para.19, Lord Bingham said that the definition of "medical treatment" in this subsection is "wide enough to cover the nursing and caring of a patient in seclusion, even though seclusion cannot properly form part of a treatment programme".

Enquiries made to a third party about either the patient's diagnosis or treatment are enquiries made with a view to treatment and do not themselves constitute treatment: see *R. (on the application of O'Reilly) v Blenheim Healthcare Ltd* [2005] EWHC 241 (Admin), para.14 where Stanley Burnton J. said that it "does not follow from [the judgment in *B v Croydon Health Authority* [1995] 1 All E.R. 683] that acts carried out for the purposes of treatment, or with a view to deciding on treatment, are themselves treatment".

Practical examples of psychological interventions include "cognitive therapy, behaviour therapy and counselling" (Explanatory Notes, para.39).

A decision to transfer a patient to another hospital can, in certain circumstances, be regarded as part of the patient's medical treatment: see *R. (on the application of F) v Oxfordshire Mental Healthcare NHS Trust* [2001] EWHC 535 (Admin); [2002] M.H.L.R. 140 where Sullivan J. said at para.68:

> "Treatment includes rehabilitation, and I can envisage cases where transfer to a particular institution because of the particular form of therapy available there would be a necessary step in the patient's rehabilitation."

In *WH v Llanarth Court Hospital* [2015] UKUT 695 (AAC); [2016] M.H.L.R. 245, UT Judge Knowles Q.C. held that visits by the patient to a hospital to which he might be transferred was "rehabilitative planning" that came within the scope of this definition (para.53). Also see *C v Birmingham and Solihull Mental Health NHS Trust* [2013] EWCA Civ 701, para.15, where Laws L.J. accepted a submission that "leave of absence and transfer are, or may be, functions of a patient's treatment, sometimes an important part".

An illustration of the distinction between habilitation and rehabilitation was given by Mr Terry Davis MP at the Special Standing Committee on the Mental Health (Amendment) Bill 1982:

> "'Habilitation' would cover those cases in which someone, probably a child, was so severely mentally impaired that he had never learnt certain social skills such as being able to eat or communicate in some way. The remedying of that impairment cannot be called 'rehabilitation' because that person never had those skills, so one has to use the word 'habilitation' in its technical sense" (Sitting of June 22, 1982).

Patient A person can become a patient who is subject to this Act regardless of their nationality.

In *R. v Davies* [2000] Crim. L.R. 297, the Court of Appeal considered a similar definition of patient found in s.22 of the Registered Homes Act 1984. The court said:

> "It is obvious that a person may be receiving treatment for mental disorder, without actually suffering from it, if he or she *appears* to be suffering from it. Much medical diagnosis and treatment is based on probability, not certainty or therefore, in some cases, actuality."

In *R. v Merseyside Mental Health Review Tribunal Ex p. K* [1990] 1 All E.R. 694 CA, the appellant, a restricted patient, sought judicial review of the tribunal's decision on the ground that once it had found as a fact that he was not suffering from mental disorder he was no longer a "patient" as defined in this section and he was therefore entitled to an absolute discharge. The Court of Appeal affirmed the tribunal's decision to grant the patient a conditional discharge and held that a restricted patient remains a "patient" until he is discharged absolutely. Butler-Sloss L.J. said at 699:

> "At the time the offender is detained under a hospital order he is a patient within the interpretation of section 145. By section 41(3)(a) a restricted patient continues to be liable to be detained until discharged under section 73 and, in my judgment, remains a patient until he is discharged absolutely, if at all, by the tribunal. Any other interpretation of the word 'patient' makes nonsense of the framework of the 1983 Act and the hoped-for progression to discharge of the treatable patient, treatable being a prerequisite of his original admission."

Regulatory authority The regulatory functions of the Welsh Ministers under the Act are performed by Healthcare Inspectorate Wales.

Subsection (1AA)

1-1469   If a hospital contains a unit where high security services are provided, that unit is treated as a separate hospital for the purposes of the Act.

Subsection (1AC)

1-1470   The fact that the AMHP acts on behalf of the local authority does not provide the authority with a power to direct the AMHP to make a particular decision while performing a function under the Act: see the note on s.114(10).

In *DD v Durham County Council* [2012] EWHC 1053 (QB); [2012] M.H.L.R. 245, para.21, Eady J. said:

> "It seems clear from this [provision] that the legislative purpose is to ensure that there will be a local social services authority available to stand in the shoes of any AMHP against whom a claim is made. The section is neutral as to whether there has to exist any employment or other contractual relationship between the relevant authority and the AMHP in question."

Subsection (3)

1-1471   I gratefully adopt Phil Fennell's interpretation of this obscurely drafted provision:

> "For certain purposes, such as the renewal of detention, and entitlement to [tribunals hearings], parties liable to be detained under Part III are treated as if liable to be detained under section 3. What section 145(3) does is to ensure that this happens subject to the modifications specified in sections 40(4), 41(3) and (5), 55(4) and Schedule 1, Part 1... . The modifications relate to the powers to remand and to sentence to interim hospital orders. People who are on remand remain under the jurisdiction of the courts. They are liable to be detained, but they remain under the jurisdiction of the courts rather than the mental health system. The reason that they are expressly mentioned in section 145(3) is that they have no rights to seek discharge from a [tribunal]" ("Double Detention under the Mental Health Act 1984—A Case of Extra Parliamentary Legislation?" [1991] J.S.W.F.L. 200).

Subsection (4)

1-1472   This provision was tabled as an amendment to the Mental Health Bill by a backbencher. It received cross party support and was accepted by the Government because of the concerns that had been expressed about the absence of any reference to therapeutic benefit in the appropriate treatment test: see the notes on s.3(2)(d). The test set out here is one of an intention to bring about therapeutic benefit, rather than the likelihood of achieving such benefit. In *MD v Nottinghamshire Health Care NHS Trust* [2010] UKUT 59 (AAC); [2010] M.H.L.R. 93, para.34, UT Judge Jacobs said:

> "Section 145(4) provides that it is sufficient if the treatment is for the purpose of preventing a worsening of the symptoms or manifestations. That envisages that the treatment required may not reduce risk. It is also sufficient if it will alleviate but one of the symptoms or manifestations, regardless of the impact on the risk posed by the patient."

The *Code of Practice* states:

> "23.4 Purpose is not the same as likelihood. Medical treatment must be for the purpose of alleviating or preventing a worsening of mental disorder even if it cannot be shown, in advance, that a particular effect is likely to be achieved.
>
> 23.5 Symptoms and manifestations include the way a disorder is experienced by the individual concerned and the way in which the disorder manifests itself in the person's thoughts, emotions, communication, behaviour and actions. It should be remembered that not every thought or emotion or every aspect of the behaviour, of a patient suffering from mental disorder will be a manifestation of that disorder."

Baroness Royall, speaking for the Government, explained the distinction between symptoms and manifestations:

> "[S]ymptoms and manifestations are intended to cover all the ways that the disorder affects the

patient's functioning, in terms of how the patient thinks, feels or believes. While there is almost certainly some overlap between the two, broadly speaking we think that 'symptoms' covers the consequences of which patients themselves complain while 'manifestations' more obviously covers the evidence of the disorder as seen by other people. In the end, the important point is not the distinction between the two words but the certainty that between them they cover the whole gamut of what can be addressed by medical treatment" (*Hansard*, HL Vol.693, col.835).

Application to Scotland

146. Sections 42(6), 80, […], 116, […], […], […], 137, 139(1), […], 142, 143 (so far as applicable to any Order in Council extending to Scotland) and 144 above shall extend to Scotland together with any amendment or repeal by this Act or any provision of Schedule 5 to this Act relating to any enactment which so extends; but, except as aforesaid and except so far as it relates to the interpretation or commencement of the said provisions, this Act shall not extend to Scotland. **1-1473**

Amendments

The words omitted were repealed by the Mental Capacity Act 2005 s.67(2), Sch.7, the Mental Health Act 2007 s.55, Sch.11 Pts 5 and 7, the Health and Social Care Act 2013 s.41 and the Mental Health (Discrimination) Act s.1(1), Sch., para.1(2).

Definition

patient: s.145(1). **1-1474**

General Note

This section provides for a limited application to the Act to Scotland. **1-1475**

Application to Northern Ireland

147. Sections 81, 82, 86, 87, 88 (and so far as applied by that section sections 18, 22, and 138), […], section 128 (except so far as it relates to patients subject to guardianship), 137, 139, […], 142, 143 (so far as applicable to any Order in Council extending to Northern Ireland) and 144 above shall extend to Northern Ireland together with any amendment or repeal by this Act of or any provision of Schedule 5 to this Act relating to any enactment which so extends; but except as aforesaid and except so far as it relates to the interpretation or commencement of the said provisions, this Act shall not extend to Northern Ireland. **1-1476**

Amendments

The amendments to this section were made by the Mental Capacity Act 2005 s.67(2), Sch.7 and the Mental Health (Discrimination) Act 2013 s.1(1), Sch., para.1(3).

Definition

patient: s.145(1). **1-1477**

General Note

This section provides for a limited application of the Act to Northern Ireland. **1-1478**

Consequential and transitional provisions and repeals

148.—(1) Schedule 4 (consequential amendments) and Schedule 5 (transitional and saving provisions) to this Act shall have effect but without prejudice to the **1-1479**

operation of sections 15 to 17 of the Interpretation Act 1978 (which relate to the effect of repeals).

(2)   Where any amendment in Schedule 4 to this Act affects an enactment amended by the Mental Health (Amendment) Act 1982 the amendment in Schedule 4 shall come into force immediately after the provision of the Act of 1982 amending that enactment.

(3)   The enactments specified in Schedule 6 to this Act are hereby repealed to the extent mentioned in the third column of that Schedule.

Short title, commencement and application to Scilly Isles

1-1480   **149.**—(1)   This Act may be cited as the Mental Health Act 1983.

(2)   Subject to subsection (3) below and Schedule 5 to this Act, this Act shall come into force on September 30, 1983.

(3)   [Repealed by the Statute Law (Repeals) Act 2004, Sch.1, Pt 17, Group 8.]

(4)   Section 130(4) of the National Health Service Act 1977 (which provides for the extension of that Act to the Isles of Scilly) shall have effect as if the references to that Act included references to this Act.

General Note

Subsection (4)

1-1481   The Isles of Scilly (Mental Health) Order 1985 (SI 1985/149) extends the Act to the Isles of Scilly from March 12, 1985, with the modification that the expression "local social services authority" in the Act shall, in relation to the Isles, mean the Council of the Isles of Scilly.

SCHEDULES

SCHEDULE 1

APPLICATION OF CERTAIN PROVISIONS TO PATIENTS SUBJECT TO HOSPITAL AND GUARDIANSHIP ORDERS

Sections 40(4), 41(3) and (5), and 55(4)

PART I

PATIENTS NOT SUBJECT TO SPECIAL RESTRICTIONS

1-1482   **1.**   Sections 9, 10, 17 [to 17C, 17E, 17F, 20A], [21 to 21B], [...], [26] to 28, 31, 32, 34, 67 and 76 shall apply in relation to the patient without modification.

2.   Sections [...], [17D, 17G, 18 to 20, 20B], 22, 23[, 66 and 68] shall apply in relation to the patient with the modifications specified in [paragraphs 2A] [to 10] below.

2A   In section 17D(2)(a) for the reference to section 6(2) above there shall be substituted a reference to section 40(1)(b) below.

2B   In section 17G—

    (a)   in subsection (2) for the reference to section 6(2) above there shall be substituted a reference to section 40(1)(b) below;

    (b)   in subsection (4) for paragraphs (a) and (b) there shall be substituted the words "the order or direction under Part 3 of this Act in respect of him were an order or direction for his admission or removal to that other hospital"; and

    (c)   in subsection (5) for the words from "the patient" to the end there shall be substituted the words "the date of the relevant order or direction under Part 3 of this Act were the date on which the community treatment order is revoked".]

3.   [...]

4.   In section 18 subsection (5) shall be omitted.

5.   In section 19(2) for the words from "as follows" to the end of the subsection there shall be substituted the words "as if the order or direction under Part III of this Act by virtue of which he was liable to be detained or subject to guardianship before being transferred were an order or direction for his admission or removal to the hospital to which he is transferred, or placing him under the guardianship of the authority or person into whose guardianship he is transferred, as the case may be".

5A In section 19A(2), paragraph (b) shall be omitted.]

6. In section 20—

    (a) in subsection (1) for the words from "day on which he was" to "as the case may be" there shall be substituted the words "date of the relevant order or direction under Part III of this Act;" [...]

6A In section 20B(1), for the reference to the application for admission for treatment there shall be substituted a reference to the order or direction under Part 3 of this Act by virtue of which the patient is liable to be detained.]

7. In section 22 for references to an application for admission or a guardianship application there shall be substituted references to the order or direction under Part III of this Act by virtue of which the patient is liable to be detained or subject to guardianship.

8. In section 23(2)—

    (a) in paragraph (a) the words "for assessment or" shall be omitted; and

    (b) in paragraphs (a) [to (c)] the references to the nearest relative shall be omitted.

[...]

9. In section 66—

    (a) in subsection (1), paragraphs (a), (b), (c), (g) and (h), the words in parenthesis in paragraph (i) and paragraph (ii) shall be omitted; and

    (b) in subsection (2), paragraphs (a), (b), (c) and (g) [, and in paragraph (d), "(g)", shall be omitted.]

10. In section 68—

    (a) in subsection (1) paragraph (a) shall be omitted; and

    (b) subsections (2) to (5) shall apply if the patient falls within paragraph (e) of subsection (1), but not otherwise.]

Amendments

The amendments to this Part were made by the Mental Health (Patients in the Community) Act 1995 s.2(1), Sch.1, the Mental Health Act 2007 ss.32(4), 36(4), 37(6), 55, Sch.3 para.36, Sch.11 Pts 1 and 5 and the Health and Social Care Act 2012 s.39.

Part II

Patients Subject to Special Restrictions

1. Sections [...] 32 and 76 shall apply in relation to the patient without modification. **1-1483**

2. Sections [17, 18, 19], 22, 23 and 34 shall apply in relation to the patient with the modifications specified in paragraphs 3 to 8 below.

3. In section 17—

    (a) in subsection (1) after the word "may" there shall be inserted the words "with the consent of the Secretary of State";

    [(aa) subsections (2A) and (2B) shall be omitted;]

    (b) in subsection (4) after the words ["the responsible clinician"] and after the words ["that clinician"] there shall be inserted the words "or the Secretary of State"; and

    (c) in subsection (5) after the word "recalled" there shall be inserted the words ["by the responsible clinician"], and for the words from "he has ceased" to the end of the subsection there shall be substituted the words "the expiration of the period of [twelve] months beginning with the first day of his absence on leave".

4. In section 18 there shall be omitted—

    (a) in subsection (1) the words "subject to the provisions of this section"; and

    (b) subsections (3), (4) and (5).

5. In section 19—

    (a) in subsection (1) after the word "may" in paragraph (a) there shall be inserted the words "with the consent of the Secretary of State", and the words from "or into" to the end of the subsection shall be omitted; [...]

    (b) in subsection (2) for the words from "as follows" to the end of the subsection there shall be substituted the words "as if the order or direction under Part III of this Act by virtue of which he was liable to be detained before being transferred were an order or direction for his admission or removal to the hospital to which he is transferred" [and

(c) in subsection (3) after the words "may at any time" there shall be inserted the words ", with the consent of the Secretary of State",]

6. In section 22, subsections (1) and (5) shall not apply.]

7. In section 23—
   (a) in subsection (1) references to guardianship shall be omitted and after the word "made" there shall be inserted the words "with the consent of the Secretary of State and"
   (b) in subsection (2)—
       (i) in paragraph (a) the words "for assessment or" and "or by the nearest relative of the patient" shall be omitted; and
       (ii) paragraph (b) shall be omitted.

8. In section 34, in subsection (1) the definition of "the nominated medical attendant" and subsection (3) shall be omitted.

Amendments

The amendments to this Part were made by the Mental Health Act 2007 ss.11(8), 33(4), 33(3), Sch.3 para.37, the Crime (Sentences) Act 1997 ss.49(3), 56(2), Sch.6 and the Health and Social Care Act 2012 s.39.

SCHEDULE 2

MENTAL HEALTH REVIEW [TRIBUNAL FOR WALES]

Section 65(2)

1-1484

1. [The Mental Health Review Tribunal for Wales] shall consist of—
   (a) a number of persons (referred to in this Schedule as "the legal members") appointed by the Lord Chancellor and having such legal experience as the Lord Chancellor considers suitable;
   (b) a number of persons (referred to in this Schedule as "the medical members") being registered medical practitioners appointed by the Lord Chancellor [...]; and
   (c) a number of persons appointed by the Lord Chancellor [...] and having such experience in administration, such knowledge of social services or such other qualifications or experience as the Lord Chancellor considers suitable.

1A. As part of the selection process for an appointment under paragraph 1(b) or (c) the Judicial Appointments Commission shall consult the Secretary of State.]

2. [Subject to paragraph 2A below,] the members of [the Mental Health Review Tribunal for Wales] shall hold and vacate office under the terms of the instrument under which they are appointed, but may resign office by notice in writing to the Lord Chancellor; and any such member who ceases to hold office shall be eligible for re-appointment.

2A. A member of [the Mental Health Review Tribunal for Wales] shall vacate office on the day on which he attains the age of [75].]

3.[(1) [...]

(2) The Lord Chancellor shall appoint one of the legal members of the Mental Health Review Tribunal for Wales to be the President of that tribunal.]

4. Subject to rules made by the Lord Chancellor under section 78(2)(c) above, the members who are to constitute [the Mental Health Review Tribunal for Wales] for the purposes of any proceedings or class or group of proceedings under this Act shall be appointed by the [President] of the tribunal or [...], by another member of the tribunal appointed for the purpose by the [President]; and of the members so appointed—
   (a) one or more shall be appointed from the legal members;
   (b) one or more shall be appointed from the medical members; and
   (c) one or more shall be appointed from the members who are neither legal nor medical members.

5.—[(1) A member of the First-tier Tribunal who is eligible to decide any matter in a case under this Act may, at the request of the President of the Mental Health Review Tribunal for Wales and with the approval of the Senior President of Tribunals, act as a member of the Mental Health Review Tribunal for Wales.

[(1A) A member of a tribunal listed in section 59 of the Wales Act 2017 (the Welsh tribunals) who is not a member of the Tribunal but who is eligible to decide any matter in a case under this Act may, at the request of the President of the Mental Health Review Tribunal for Wales and with the approval of the President of Welsh Tribunals, act as a member of the Mental Health Review Tribunal for Wales.]

(2)   Every person while acting under this paragraph may perform any of the functions of a member of the Mental Health Review Tribunal for Wales.

(3)   Until section 38(7) of the Mental Health Act 2007 comes into force, the reference in sub-paragraph (1) [or (1A)] to the President of the Mental Health Review Tribunal for Wales is to be read as a reference to the chairman of the tribunal.]

6.   Subject to any rules made by the Lord Chancellor under section 78(4)(a) above, where the [President] of the tribunal is included among the persons appointed under para.4 above, he shall be [chairman] of the tribunal; and in any other case the [chairman] of the tribunal shall be such one of the members so appointed (being one of the legal members) as the [President] may nominate.

Amendments

The amendments to this Schedule were made by the Judicial Pensions and Retirement Act 1993 s.26, Sch.6 para.40, the Constitutional Reform Act 2005 ss.15, 146, Sch.4 para.158(3), Sch.18 Pt.2; the Mental Health Act 2007 s.38(7)(b); SI 2008/2833 art.9, Sch.3 para.67, SI 2009/1307 art.5, Sch.1 para.162, SI 2017/1038 arts 3 and 4 (for transitional provisions), the Wales Act 2017 s.62(3) and the Public Service Pensions and Judicial Offices Act 2022 Sch.1(1) para.18.

General Note

The President and members of the MHRT for Wales are subject to the selection process set out in ss.86 to 93 of the Constitutional Reform Act 2005 (s.85, Sch.14 Pt 3).   **1-1485**

Paragraph 1

The Lord Chancellor   Who, in the exercise of his functions under this provision in relation to Wales,   **1-1486**
is required to consult with the Welsh Ministers with regard to -appointments made under paragraphs (b) and (c) (see the General Note to the Act and SI 1999/672 art.5, Sch.2). The Lord Chancellor cannot transfer his functions under this paragraph, or under paras 2 or 3, to another person (Constitutional Reform Act 2005 s.19, Sch.7).

Paragraph 1(b)

A "registered medical practitioner" means "a fully registered person within the meaning of the Medi-   **1-1487**
cal Act 1983 who holds a licence to practise under that Act" (Interpretation Act 1978 Sch. 1)

Paragraph 5

This allows members of the First-tier Tribunal who may hear mental health cases to sit in the Mental   **1-1488**
Health Review Tribunal for Wales. There is no reciprocal arrangement.

SCHEDULE 3

Section 113

[Repealed by the Mental Capacity Act 2005 s.67(2), Sch.7.]   **1-1489**

SCHEDULE 4

Consequential Amendments

Section 148

[*Not reproduced.*]   **1-1490**

SCHEDULE 5

Transitional and Saving Provisions

Section 148

1.   Where any period of time specified in an enactment repealed by this Act is current at the com-   **1-1491**
mencement of this Act, this Act shall have effect as if the corresponding provision of this Act had been in force when that period began to run.

2. Nothing in this Act shall affect the interpretation of any provision of the Mental Health Act 1959 which is not repealed by this Act and accordingly sections 1 and 145(1) of this Act shall apply to any such provision as if it were contained in this Act.

3. Where, apart from this paragraph, anything done under or for the purposes of any enactment which is repealed by this Act would cease to have effect by virtue of that repeal it shall have effect as if it had been done under or for the purposes of the corresponding provisions of this Act.

4. [...]

5. [...]

6. This Act shall apply in relation to any authority for the detention or guardianship of a person who was liable to be detained or subject to guardianship under the Mental Health Act 1959 immediately before September 30, 1983 as if the provisions of this Act which derive from provisions amended by section 1 or 2 of the Mental Health (Amendment) Act 1982 and the amendments in Sch.3 to that Act which are consequential on those sections were included in this Act in the form the provisions from which they derive would take if those amendments were disregarded but this provision shall not apply to any renewal of that authority on or after that date.

7. [...]

8. [...]

9.—(1) [...]

(2) Section 20(2) of this Act shall have effect in relation to any authority renewed before October 1, 1983 with the substitution for the words "six months" of the words "one year" and for the words "one year" in both places they occur of the words "two years".

(3) [...]

10. [...]

11. [...]

12. [...]

13. [...]

14. [...]

15. The provisions of this Act which derive from sections 24 to 27 of the Mental Health (Amendment) Act 1982 shall have effect in relation to a transfer direction given before September 30, 1983 as well as in relation to one given later, but where, apart from this paragraph, a transfer direction given before September 30, 1983 would by virtue of the words in section 50(3) of this Act which are derived from section 24(3) of the Mental Health (Amendment) Act 1982 have ceased to have effect before that date it shall cease to have effect on that date.

16. The words in section 42(1) of this Act which derive from the amendment of section 66(1) of the Mental Health Act 1959 by section 28(1) of the Mental Health (Amendment) Act 1982 and the provisions of this Act which derive from section 28(3) of and Sch.1 to that Act have in relation to a restriction order or, as the case may be, a restriction direction made or given before September 30, 1983 as well as in relation to one made or given later, but—

(a) any reference to a tribunal under section 66(6) of the said Act of 1959 in respect of a patient shall be treated for the purposes of subsections (1) and (2) of section 77 of this Act in their application to sections 70 and 75(2) of this Act as an application made by him; and

(b) sections 71(5) and 75(1)(a) of this Act do not apply where the period in question has expired before September 30, 1983.

17. Section 91(2) of this Act shall not apply in relation to a patient removed from England and Wales before September 30, 1983.

18. [...]

19. [...]

20. The repeal by the Mental Health (Amendment) Act 1982 of section 77 of the Mental Health Act 1959 does not affect subsection (4) of that section in its application to a transfer direction given before September 30, 1983, but after the coming into force of this Act that subsection shall effect for that purpose as if for the references to subsection (6) of section 60, Part IV of that Act and the provisions of that Act there were substituted respectively references to section 37(8), Part III and the provisions of this Act.

21. Any direction to which section 71(4) of the Mental Health Act 1959 applied immediately before the commencement of this Act shall have the same effect as a hospital order together with a restriction order, made without limitation of time.]

22. [...]

23. For any reference in any enactment, instrument, deed or other document to a receiver under Part

VIII of the Mental Health Act 1959 there shall be substituted a reference to a receiver under Part VII of this Act.

24. Nothing in this Act shall affect the operation of the proviso to section 107(5) of the Mental Health Act 1959 in relation to a charge created before the commencement of this Act under that section.

25. Nothing in this Act shall affect the operation of subsection (6) of section 112 of the Mental Health Act 1959 in relation to a charge created before the commencement of this Act by virtue of subsection (5) of that section.

26. [...]

27. Nothing in this Act shall affect the operation of section 116 of the Mental Health Act 1959 in relation to orders made, directions or authorities given or other instruments issued before the commencement of this Act.

28. References to applications, recommendations, reports and other documents in section 126 of this Act shall include those to which sections 125 of the Mental Health Act 1959 applied immediately before the commencement of this Act and references in section 139 of this Act to the acts to which that section applies shall include those to which section 141 of the said Act of 1959 applied at that time.

29. The repeal by the Mental Health Act 1959 of the Mental Treatment Act 1930 shall not affect any amendment effected by section 20 of that Act in any enactment not repealed by the said Act of 1959.

30. The repeal by the Mental Health Act 1959 of the provisions of the Lunacy Act 1890 and of the Mental Deficiency Act 1913 relating to the superannuation of officers or employees shall not affect any arrangements for the payment of allowances or other benefits made in accordance with those provisions and in force on November 1, 1960.

31.—(1) Any patient who immediately before the commencement of this Act was liable to be detained in a hospital or subject to guardianship by virtue of para.9 of Sch.6 to the Mental Health Act 1959 shall unless previously discharged continue to be so liable for the remainder of the period of his treatment current on November 1, 1960.

(2) The patient may before the expiration of the period of treatment referred to in sub-paragraph (1) above apply to a Mental Health Review Tribunal.

32. Any patient who immediately before the commencement of this Act was liable to be detained or subject to guardianship by virtue of an authority which had been renewed under para.11 of Sch.6 to the Mental Health Act 1959 shall unless previously discharged continue to be so liable during the period for which that authority was so renewed.

33.—(1) This paragraph applies to patients who at the commencement of this Act are liable to be detained or subject to guardianship by virtue of para.31 or 32 above.

(2) Authority for the detention or guardianship of the patient may on the expiration of the relevant period, unless the patient has previously been discharged, be renewed for a further period of two years.

(3) Sections 20(3) to (10) and 66(1)(f) of this Act shall apply in relation to the renewal of authority for the detention or guardianship of a patient under this paragraph as they apply in relation to the renewal of authority for the detention or guardianship of the patient under section 20(2).

(4) In this paragraph "the relevant period" means—

    (a) in relation to a patient liable to be detained or subject to guardianship by virtue of the said paragraph 31, the period of his treatment referred to in that paragraph;

    (b) in relation to a patient detained by virtue of the said paragraph 32, the period for which authority for the detention or guardianship of the patient has been renewed under paragraph 11 of Schedule 6 to the 1959 Act;

    (c) in relation to a patient the authority for whose detention or guardianship has previously been renewed under this paragraph, the latest period for which it has been so renewed.

34.—(1) Any patient who is liable to be detained in a hospital or subject to guardianship by virtue of para.31 above shall (subject to the exceptions and modifications specified in the following provisions of this paragraph) be treated as if he has been admitted to the hospital in pursuance of an application for admission for treatment under Part II of this Act or had been received into guardianship in pursuance of a guardianship application under the said Part II and had been so admitted or received as a patient suffering from the form or forms of mental disorder recorded under para.7 of Sch.6 to the Mental Health Act 1959 or, if a different form or forms have been specified in a report under section 38 of the Act as applied by that paragraph, the form or forms so specified.

(2) Section 20 of this Act shall not apply in relation to the patient, but the provisions of para.33 above shall apply instead.

(3) Any patient to whom para.9(3) of Sch.6 to the Mental Health Act 1959 applied at the commencement of this Act who fell within paragraph (b) of that paragraph shall cease to be liable to be detained on attaining the age of 25 years unless, during the period of two months ending on the date when he attains that age, the responsible medical officers records his opinion under the following provisions of this Schedule that the patient is unfit for discharge.

(4)   If the patient was immediately before November 1, 1960 liable to be detained by virtue of section 6, 8(1) or 9 of the Mental Deficiency Act 1913, the power of discharging him under section 23 of this Act shall not be exercisable by his nearest relative, but his nearest relative may make one application in respect of him to [the appropriate tribunal] in any period of 12 months.

35.—(1)   The responsible medical officer may record for the purposes of para.34(3) above his opinion that a patient detained in a hospital is unfit for discharge if it appears to the responsible medical officer—

(a)   that if that patient were released from the hospital he would be likely to act in a manner dangerous to other persons or to himself, or would be likely to resort to criminal activities; or

(b)   that that patient is incapable of caring for himself and that there is no suitable hospital or other establishment into which he can be admitted and where he would be likely to remain voluntarily;

and where the responsible medical officer records his opinion as aforesaid he shall also record the grounds for his opinion.

(2)   Where the responsible medical officer records his opinion under this paragraph in respect of a patient, the managers of the hospital or other persons in charge of the establishment where he is for the time being detained or liable to be detained shall cause the patient to be informed, and the patient may, at any time before the expiration of the period of 28 days beginning with the date on which he is so informed, apply to a Mental Health Review Tribunal.

(3)   On any application under sub-paragraph (2) above the tribunal shall, if satisfied that none of the conditions set out in paragraphs (a) and (b) of sub-paragraph (1) above are fulfilled, direct that the patient be discharged, and subsection (1) of section 72 of this Act shall have effect in relation to the application as if paragraph (b) of that subsection were omitted.

36.   Any person who immediately before the commencement of this Act was deemed to have been named as the guardian of any patient under para.14 of Sch.6 to the Mental Health Act 1959 shall be deemed for the purposes of this Act to have been named as the guardian of the patient in an application for his reception into guardianship under Part II of this Act accepted on that person's behalf by the relevant local authority.

37.—(1)   This paragraph applies to patients who immediately before the commencement of this Act were transferred patients within the meaning of para.15 of Sch.6 to the Mental Health Act 1959.

(2)   A transferred patient who immediately before the commencement of this Act was by virtue of sub-paragraph (2) of that paragraph treated for the purposes of that Act as if he were liable to be detained in a hospital in pursuance of a direction under section 71 of that Act shall be treated as if he were so liable in pursuance of a [hospital order together with a restriction order, made without limitation of time].

(3)   A transferred patient who immediately before the commencement of this Act was by virtue of sub-paragraph (3) of that paragraph treated for the purposes of the Act as if he were liable to be detained in a hospital by virtue of a transfer direction under section 72 of that Act and as if a direction restricting his discharge had been given under section 74 of that Act shall be treated as if he were liable by virtue of a transfer direction under section 47 of this Act and as if a restriction direction had been given under section 49 of this Act.

(4)   Section 84 of this Act shall apply to a transferred patient who was treated by virtue of sub-paragraph (5) of that paragraph immediately before the commencement of this Act as if he had been removed to a hospital under section 89 of that Act as if he had been so removed under the said section 84.

(5)   Any person to whom sub-paragraph (6) of that paragraph applied immediately before the commencement of this Act shall be treated for the purposes of this Act as if he were liable to be detained in a hospital in pursuance of a transfer direction given under section 48 of this Act and as if a restriction direction had been given under section 49 of this Act […].

38.   Any patient who immediately before the commencement of this Act was treated by virtue of sub-paragraph (1) of para.16 of Sch.6 to the Mental Health Act 1959 as if he had been conditionally discharged under section 66 of that Act shall be treated as if he had been conditionally discharged under section 42 of this Act and any such direction as is mentioned in paragraph (b) of that sub-paragraph shall be treated as if it had been given under the said section 42.

39.   […]

40.   A person who immediately before the commencement of this Act was detained by virtue of para.19 of Sch.6 to the Mental Health Act 1959 may continue to be detained until the expiration of the period of his treatment current on November 1, 1960 or until he becomes liable to be detained or subject to guardianship under this Act, whichever occurs first, and may be so detained in any place in which he might have been detained under that paragraph.

[634]

41. Any opinion recorded by the responsible medical officer under the foregoing provisions of this Schedule shall be recorded in which form as may be prescribed by regulations made by the Secretary of State.

42.—(1) In the foregoing provisions of this Schedule—

(a) references to the period of treatment of a patient that was current on November 1, 1960 are to the period for which he would have been liable to be detained or subject to guardianship by virtue of any enactment repealed or excluded by the Mental Health Act 1959, or any enactment repealed or replaced by any such enactment as aforesaid, being a period which began but did not expire before that date; and

(b) "the responsible medical officer" means—

(i) in relation to a patient subject to guardianship, the medical officer authorised by the local social services authority to act (either generally or in any particular case or for any particular purpose) as the responsible medical officer;

(ii) in relation to any other class of patient, the registered medical practitioner in charge of the treatment of the patient.

(2) Subsection (2) of section 34 of this Act shall apply for the purposes of the foregoing provisions of this Schedule as it applies for the purposes of Part II of this Act.

(3) The sentence or other period of detention of a person who was liable to be detained or subject to guardianship immediately before November 1, 1960 by virtue of an order under section 9 of the Mental Deficiency Act 1913 shall be treated for the purposes of the foregoing provisions of this Schedule as expiring at the end of the period for which that person would have been liable to be detained in a prison or other institution if the order had not been made.

(4) For the purposes of the foregoing provisions of this Schedule, an order sending a person to an institution or placing a person under guardianship made before March 9, 1956 on a petition presented under the Mental Deficiency Act 1913 shall be deemed to be valid if it was so deemed immediately before the commencement of this Act by virtue of section 148(2) of the Mental Health Act 1959.

43. [...]

44. [...]

45. [...]

46. [...]

Amendments

The amendments to this Schedule were made by the Health Authorities Act 1995 s.5(1), Sch.3, the Statute Law (Repeals) Act 2004 Sch.1 Pt 17, the Mental Capacity Act 2005 s.67(2), Sch.7, the Mental Health Act 2007 s.55, Sch.11 Pt 1, the Domestic Violence, Crime and Victims Act 2004 s.58(1), Sch.10 para.23 and SI 2008/2833 art.9, Sch.3 para.68.

Definitions

local social services authority: s.145(1). **1-1492**
approved mental health professional: s.145(1).
application for admission for treatment: ss.3, 145(1).
patient: s.145(1).
nearest relative: ss.26(3), 145(1).
hospital order: ss.37, 145(1).
transfer direction: ss.47, 145(1).
restriction order: ss.41, 145(1).
restriction direction: ss.49, 145(1).
mental disorder: ss.2, 145(1).
hospital: s.145(1).
the managers: s.145(1).
appropriate tribunal: ss.66(4), 135(1).

General Note

This Schedule makes provision to cover the transition from the Mental Health Act 1959, as amended **1-1493** by the Mental Health (Amendment) Act 1982, to this Act. It therefore affects patients detained on or before the commencement date of this Act (September 30, 1983) and anything which was in the process of being done at that date.

Paragraph 1

1-1494 This paragraph states the general rule that any period of time specified in legislation which was in force on September 30, 1983 will be replaced by the corresponding provision in this Act, calculated from the time when the original order or application was made. This rule is subject to the important exceptions set out in para.9.

Paragraph 6

1-1495 This paragraph ensures that the changes in the definitions of mental disorder will not affect the authority to detain somebody who was detained prior to September 30, 1983. This paragraph does not apply to the renewal of authority.

Paragraph 9

1-1496 When an authority to detain a patient admitted for treatment or to subject a patient to guardianship is renewed before October 1, 1983 the duration of the authority applicable under the 1959 Act (of one or two years) will continue to apply. However, where the authority has been renewed for two years and less than 16 months has passed since the renewal by September 30, 1983, that period of detention will expire after 18 months rather than two years. If that detention is subsequently renewed the period of one year will apply.

Paragraphs 31 to 42

1-1497 Inter alia, provide authority for the continued detention or guardianship of patents whose detention or guardianship commenced before the Mental Health Act 1959 came into force.

SCHEDULE 6

REPEALS

Section 134

1-1498 [*Not reproduced.*]

MENTAL HEALTH UNITS (USE OF FORCE) ACT 2018

(2018 c.27)

An Act to make provision about the oversight and management of the appropriate use of force in relation to people in mental health units; to make provision about the use of body cameras by police officers in the course of duties in relation to people in mental health units; and for connected purposes.

[1st November 2018]

CONTENTS

SECTION

General Note

The purpose of this Act, which started life as a private members bill sponsored by Steve Reed MP, **1-1499** is to increase the oversight and management of the use of force in mental health units. The Act provides for relevant health organisations that operate mental health units to appoint a responsible person (s.2) who can delegate his functions (s.10). The responsible person has a duty to publish a policy on the use of force by staff in the mental health unit, and information for patients about the use of force (ss.3, 4). The responsible person must also provide training for staff relating to the use of force (s.5), keep a record of any use of force by staff who work in the unit (s.6), and have regard to relevant guidance whenever a patient dies or suffers a serious injury in a mental health unit (s.9). The Act requires the Secretary of State to ensure that statistics about the use of force in mental health units are published annually (s.7), to publish an annual report following a review of relevant reports relating to the use of force in mental health units (s.8), and to publish guidance about the functions of the responsible person and health bodies under the Act (s.11). The Act also requires police officers to wear and operate body cameras when attending a mental health unit where this is reasonably practicable (s.12).

Introducing the Mental Health Units (Use of Force) Act Bill, Steve Reed MP described the events leading up to the death of his constituent Olaseni (also known as Seni) Lewis, who had been a patient at the Bethlem Royal Hospital in Croydon in 2010. Mr Reed stated that following an incident in which Mr Lewis had attempted to leave the hospital's mental health unit, he was restrained face down by police officers, suffered a heart attack and died four days later. Consequently, Mr Reed described the Bill as "Seni's Law". Mr Reed claimed Seni Lewis's case was not an isolated incident, stating that prone restraint "was used over 9,000 times in the last year alone", and that "46 mental health patients [have] died following restraint between 2000 and 2014".

The Act will generate a great deal of paperwork. It is to be hoped that this activity will result in positive outcomes for patients.

Statutory Guidance on the Act (referred to throughout the Act as "the guidance")

1-1500   See s.11. The *guidance* is "not intended to override" the guidance in the *Code of Practice* "but sits alongside it" (p.13).

Code of Practice on the Mental Health Act 1983

1-1501   Guidance on restrictive interventions for people receiving treatment for a mental disorder is contained in Ch.26 of the Code. The Code states that restrictive interventions should be used for no longer than necessary to prevent harm to the patient or others, be a proportionate response to that harm, and be the least restrictive option (para.26.37). The Code further states that patients "should not be deliberately restrained in a way that impacts on their airway, breathing or circulation" and that that prone restraint must not be used "unless there are cogent reasons for doing so" (para.26.70).

Care Quality Commission

1-1502   The Act does not provide the CQC with any new powers.

Positive and Safe programme

1-1503   In April 2014, the Department of Health launched the *Positive and Safe* programme, which aims to reduce use of restrictive interventions across all health and adult social care. As part of the programme, the Department published new guidelines on ending the deliberate use of face-down restraint for people receiving care. *Positive and Proactive care: Reducing the need for restrictive interventions* provides non-statutory guidance for adult health and social care staff to develop a culture where restrictive interventions are only ever used as a last resort, and only then for the shortest possible time. The guidance is intended to inform the Care Quality Commission's (CQC) programme of regular monitoring and inspection against CQC standards. The guidance can be accessed at: *https://assets.publishing.service.gov.uk/government/uploads/system/uploads/attachment_data/file/300293/JRA_DoH_Guidance_on_RP_web_accessible.pdf*.

NICE guidance

1-1504   The NICE guidelines on *Violence and aggression: short-term management in mental health, health and community settings* (May 2015) recommends ways to reduce the use of restrictive interventions, such as through staff training and de-escalation techniques. The guidelines state that a restrictive intervention should only be used if de-escalation techniques and other preventative strategies have failed and there is a risk of harm to the service user or other people if no action is taken. They also state that sufficient numbers of trained staff, including a doctor trained in resuscitation, should be immediately available (pp.30, 31). The guidelines can be accessed at: *www.nice.org.uk/guidance/ng10*.

The NICE quality standard on *Violent and aggressive behaviours in people with mental health problems* (June 2017), which can be accessed at *www.nice.org.uk/guidance/qs154*, recommends that people who use mental health services who have been violent or aggressive should be supported to identify successful de-escalation techniques and make advance statements about the use of restrictive interventions. The standard states that if a restrictive intervention is used, the patient's physical health should be monitored during and after physical restraint.

The Police Use of Restraint in Mental Health & Learning Disability Settings

A multi-agency "Memorandum of Understanding" on this topic, which is intended "to outline when and how the responsibilities of the police service fit in to the established roles and responsibilities of care providers" (p.4), can be accessed via the website of the College of Policing at: *www.college.police.uk/ Pages/Home.aspx.* **1-1505**

The Restraint Reduction Network

The website of this organisation (*http://restraintreductionnetwork.org*) states that the "Network has an ambitious vision to reduce reliance on restrictive practices and make a real difference in the lives of people". **1-1506**

Wales

Although the Act extents to England and Wales (s.17(1)), it only applies in relation to mental health units in England (s.1(3)). **1-1507**

Human Rights Act 1998

A "Memorandum from the Department of Health and Social Care to the Joint Committee on Human Rights" states that the "Department considers that the Bill engages, or potentially engages, Articles 2, 3 and 8 of the ECHR, and Article 1 of the First Protocol. The Department does not consider that the provisions of the Bill infringe these rights" (para.6). **1-1508**

Commencement

Regulation 2 of SI 2021/1372 brought into force on 31 March 2022 ss.1 to 6, 9 to 11, 13 and 15. Section 11(3) was brought into force on 28 October 2019 by SI 2019/1373 and s.12 was brought into force on August 18, 2022 by SI 2022/909. **1-1509**

KEY DEFINITIONS

Key definitions

1.—(1)   This section applies for the purposes of this Act. **1-1510**

(2)   "Mental disorder" has the same meaning as in the Mental Health Act 1983.

(3)   "Mental health unit" means—

(a)   a health service hospital, or part of a health service hospital, in England, the purpose of which is to provide treatment to in-patients for mental disorder, or

(b)   an independent hospital, or part of an independent hospital, in England—

(i)   the purpose of which is to provide treatment to in-patients for mental disorder, and

(ii)   where at least some of that treatment is provided, or is intended to be provided, for the purposes of the NHS.

(4)   In subsection (3)(b)(ii) the reference to treatment provided for the purposes of the NHS is to be read as a service provided for those purposes in accordance with the National Health Service Act 2006.

(5)   "Patient" means a person who is in a mental health unit for the purpose of treatment for mental disorder or assessment.

(6)   References to "use of force" are to—

(a)   the use of physical, mechanical or chemical restraint on a patient, or

(b)   the isolation of a patient.

(7)   In subsection (6)—

"physical restraint" means the use of physical contact which is intended to prevent, restrict or subdue movement of any part of the patient's body;

"mechanical restraint" means the use of a device which—

(a) is intended to prevent, restrict or subdue movement of any part of the patient's body, and

(b) is for the primary purpose of behavioural control;

"chemical restraint" means the use of medication which is intended to prevent, restrict or subdue movement of any part of the patient's body;

"isolation" means any seclusion or segregation that is imposed on a patient.

Definitions

1-1511   health service hospital: s.13.
independent hospital: s.13.
the NHS: s.13

General Note

1-1512   This section defines some important terms used in the Act.

Subsection (2)

1-1513   Mental disorder is defined in s.1(2) of the 1983 Act as "any disorder or disability of the mind".

Subsection (3)

1-1514   **Mental Health Unit**   The *guidance* states at p.16:

"The following services are considered to be outside of the definition of a mental health unit (this is not an exhaustive list) and therefore not covered by the requirements of the Act:

• accident and emergency departments of emergency departments
• section 135 and 136 suites that are outside of a mental health unit
• outpatient departments or clinics
• mental health transport vehicles."

Subsection (5)

1-1515   **Patient**   Both detained and informal patients (of any age) come within the scope of the Act.

Subsection (7)(b)

1-1516   **Seclusion Or Segregation**   The definitions of these terms are set out in Annex A of the Mental Health Act 1983: Code of Practice which applies to patients detained in mental health units:

"Seclusion refers to the supervised confinement and isolation of a patient, away from other patients, in an area from which the patient is prevented from leaving, where it is of immediate necessity for the purpose of the containment of severe behavioural disturbance which is likely to cause harm to others."

"Long term segregation refers to a situation where, in order to reduce a sustained risk of harm posed by the patient to others, which is a constant feature of their presentation, a patient is not allowed to mix freely with other patients on the ward/unit on a long term basis. In such cases, it should have been determined that the risk to others is not subject to amelioration by a short period of seclusion combined with any other form of treatment; the clinical judgement is that if the patient were allowed to mix freely in the general ward environment, other patients or staff would almost continuously be open to potentially serious injury or harm."

Mental health units to have a responsible person

2.—(1) A relevant health organisation that operates a mental health unit must **1-1517** appoint a responsible person for that unit for the purposes of this Act.

(2) The responsible person must—

(a) be employed by the relevant health organisation, and

(b) be of an appropriate level of seniority.

(3) Where a relevant health organisation operates more than one mental health unit that organisation must appoint a single responsible person in relation to all of the mental health units operated by that organisation.

Definitions

mental health unit: s.1(3).   **1-1518**
responsible person: s.13.

General Note

This section requires a relevant health organisation that operates a mental health unit to appoint a **1-1519** responsible person for that unit. "Relevant health organisation" is defined in s.13. The responsible person, who has key responsibilities under the Act, must be employed by the organisation and be of an appropriate level of seniority (subs.(2)). Subsection (3) provides that if a relevant health organisation runs more than one mental health unit, the same responsible person must be appointed in relation to all of the mental health units.

Guidance

See pp.16–18.   **1-1520**

Policy on use of force

3.—(1) The responsible person for each mental health unit must publish a **1-1521** policy regarding the use of force by staff who work in that unit.

(2) Where a responsible person is appointed in relation to all of the mental health units operated by a relevant health organisation, the responsible person must publish a single policy under subsection (1) in relation to those units.

(3) Before publishing a policy under subsection (1), the responsible person must consult any persons that the responsible person considers appropriate.

(4) The responsible person must keep under review any policy published under this section.

(5) The responsible person may from time to time revise any policy published under this section and, if this is done, must publish the policy as revised.

(6) If the responsible person considers that any revisions would amount to a substantial change in the policy, the responsible person must consult any persons that the responsible person considers appropriate before publishing the revised policy.

(7) A policy published under this section must set out what steps will be taken to reduce the use of force in the mental health unit by staff who work in that unit.

Definitions

1-1522   responsible person: s.13.
mental health unit: s.1(3).
staff: s.13.
relevant health organisation: s.13.

General Note

1-1523   This section imposes a duty on the responsible person for each mental health unit to publish (subs.(1)) and keep under review (subs.4)) a policy on the use of force on patients by staff who work in the unit. The policy must set out what steps will be taken to reduce the use of force by staff who work in the unit (subs.(7)). The effect of subs.(2) is that there is to be a single policy across all the mental health units operated by a relevant health organisation. A consultation process must precede the publication of the policy (subs.3) which can be revised (subs.(5)). Subsection (6) requires the responsible person to consult any persons that they consider appropriate when considering any revisions to the policy that would amount to a substantial change.

In the Public Bill Committee in the House of Commons, the Member in Charge of the Bill said:

"A written policy will effectively govern the use of force within the units, and there is a real opportunity for NHS trusts to work with service users and their families to formalise and replicate the best of what many are already doing to reduce the use of force. The use of force varies enormously across NHS trusts. Some already have robust policies in place to minimise the use of force but others do not. The amendment will put an end to the regional disparity between trusts. Based on currently available figures, the variation can be as wide as between 5% and 50% of patients being subject to the use of force while attending mental health units for treatment."

Guidance

1-1524   See pp.18–24.

Information about use of force

1-1525   **4.**—(1)   The responsible person for each mental health unit must publish information for patients about the rights of patients in relation to the use of force by staff who work in that unit.

(2)   Before publishing the information under subsection (1), the responsible person must consult any persons that the responsible person considers appropriate.

(3)   The responsible person must provide any information published under this section—

    (a)   to each patient, and

    (b)   to any other person who is in the unit and to whom the responsible person considers it appropriate to provide the information in connection with the patient,

unless the patient (where paragraph (a) applies) or the other person (where paragraph (b) applies) refuses the information.

(4)   The information must be provided to the patient—

    (a)   if the patient is in the mental health unit at the time when this section comes into force, as soon as reasonably practicable after that time;

    (b)   in any other case, as soon as reasonably practicable after the patient is admitted to the mental health unit.

(5)   The responsible person must take whatever steps are reasonably practicable to ensure that the patient is aware of the information and understands it.

(6)   The responsible person must keep under review any information published under this section.

(7) The responsible person may from time to time revise any information published under this section and, if this is done, must publish the information as revised.

(8) If the responsible person considers that any revisions would amount to a substantial change in the information, the responsible person must consult any persons that the responsible person considers appropriate before publishing the revised information.

Definitions

responsible person: s.13. **1-1526**
mental health unit: s.1(3).
patient: s.1(5).
use of force: s.1(6), (7).
staff: s.13.

General Note

This section imposes a duty on the responsible person to publish information for patients about the **1-1527** rights of patients in relation to the use of force by staff who work in the unit (subs. (1)). Before publishing the information, the responsible person is required to consult any persons they consider appropriate (subs.(2)).

Subsection (3) requires the responsible person to provide the information to each patient, and to any person who is in the unit and to whom the responsible person considers it appropriate to provide the information in connection with the patient, such as a family member. However, the duty to provide the information does not apply if the recipient refuses the information (subs.(3)(b)).

Subsection (4) requires the information to be provided to the patient as soon as reasonably practicable after the patient is admitted to the unit, or if the patient is already in the mental health unit when this provision comes into force, as soon as reasonably practicable after that time. Subsection (5) requires the responsible person to take reasonably practicable steps to make sure the patient is aware of the information and understands it.

Subsections (6) and (7) require the responsible person to keep the information under review and to publish any revisions to the information. If the revisions would amount to a substantial change, the responsible person must also consult any person they consider appropriate before publishing the revised information (subs.(8)).

In the Public Bill Committee in the House of Commons, the Member in Charge of the Bill said:

"It is important that any patient entering a mental health unit is aware of what may or may not be done to them regarding the use of force, so that if people in the unit seek to do things to them that go beyond their rights, they are able to call it out and stop it. This applies not just to the individual concerned, but to their carers, family members or close relatives who might be there with them, who are often unfamiliar with mental health units and have equally high levels of concern. It is important that they, too, are aware of what their loved one's rights are."

Guidance

See pp.24–29. **1-1528**

Subsection (5)

This provision does not require the patient to possess the level of mental capacity set out in ss.2 and **1-1529** 3 of the Mental Capacity Act 2005.

Training in appropriate use of force

5.—(1) The responsible person for each mental health unit must provide train- **1-1530** ing for staff that relates to the use of force by staff who work in that unit.

(2)   The training provided under subsection (1) must include training on the following topics—

(a)   how to involve patients in the planning, development and delivery of care and treatment in the mental health unit,

(b)   showing respect for patients' past and present wishes and feelings

(c)   showing respect for diversity generally,

(d)   avoiding unlawful discrimination, harassment and victimisation,

(e)   the use of techniques for avoiding or reducing the use of force,

(f)   the risks associated with the use of force,

(g)   the impact of trauma (whether historic or otherwise) on a patient's mental and physical health,

(h)   the impact of any use of force on a patient's mental and physical health,

(i)   the impact of any use of force on a patient's development,

(j)   how to ensure the safety of patients and the public, and

(k)   the principal legal or ethical issues associated with the use of force.

(3)   Subject to subsection (4), training must be provided—

(a)   in the case of a person who is a member of staff when this section comes into force, as soon as reasonably practicable after this section comes into force, or

(b)   in the case of a person who becomes a member of staff after this section comes into force, as soon as reasonably practicable after they become a member of staff.

(4)   Subsection (3) does not apply if the responsible person considers that any training provided to the person before this section came into force or before the person became a member of staff—

(a)   was given sufficiently recently, and

(b)   is of an equivalent standard to the training provided under this section.

(5)   Refresher training must be provided at regular intervals whilst a person is a member of staff.

(6)   In subsection (5) "refresher training" means training that updates or supplements the training provided under subsection (1).

Definitions

1-1531   responsible person: s.13.
mental health unit: s.1(3).
use of force: s.1(6), (7).
patient: s.1(5).

General Note

1-1532   This section requires the responsible person to provide training for staff who work in the mental health unit about the use of force by staff (subs.(1)). The training must cover the specific topics set out in subs.(2). Subsection (3) requires training to be provided as soon as reasonably practicable after a person becomes a member of staff, and for people who are already a member of staff when this section comes into force as soon as is reasonably practicable after that time. However, subs.(3) does not apply if the responsible person considers that a member of staff was provided with training of an equivalent standard sufficiently recently.

Subsection (5) requires refresher training, as defined in subs.(6), to be carried out at regular intervals for staff at the unit.

The Code of Practice on the Mental Health Act requires that all hospitals have a policy on training for staff who may be exposed to violence or aggression in their work or who may need to be involved in the application of a restrictive intervention (para.26.175). It also states that staff should only use restrictive interventions for which they have received training (para.26.65).

Guidance

See pp.29–45.   **1-1533**

Subsection (1)

Staff   See the definition of "staff" in s.13. In the Public Bill Committee in the House of Commons,   **1-1534** the Member in Charge of the Bill said:

> "Only people working in a professional capacity would be able to use force on patients; any volunteers would not be able to do so."

REPORTING

Recording of use of force

6.—(1)   The responsible person for each mental health unit must keep a record   **1-1535** of any use of force by staff who work in that unit in accordance with this section.

(2)   Subsection (1) does not apply in cases where the use of force is negligible.

(3)   Whether the use of force is "negligible" for the purposes of subsection (1) is to be determined in accordance with guidance published by the Secretary of State.

(4)   Section 11(3) to (6) apply to guidance published under this section as they apply to guidance published under section 11.

(5)   The record must include the following information—

  (a)   the reason for the use of force;

  (b)   the place, date and duration of the use of force;

  (c)   the type or types of force used on the patient;

  (d)   whether the type or types of force used on the patient formed part of the patient's care plan;

  (e)   name of the patient on whom force was used;

  (f)   a description of how force was used;

  (g)   the patient's consistent identifier;

  (h)   the name and job title of any member of staff who used force on the patient;

  (i)   the reason any person who was not a member of staff in the mental health unit was involved in the use of force on the patient;

  (j)   the patient's mental disorder (if known);

  (k)   the relevant characteristics of the patient (if known);

  (l)   whether the patient has a learning disability or autistic spectrum disorders;

  (m)   a description of the outcome of the use of force;

  (n)   whether the patient died or suffered any serious injury as a result of the use of force;

  (o)   any efforts made to avoid the need to use force on the patient;

  (p)   whether a notification regarding the use of force was sent to the person or persons (if any) to be notified under the patient's care plan.

(6)   The responsible person must keep the record for 3 years from the date on which it was made.

(7)   In subsection (5)(g) the "patient's consistent identifier" means the consistent identifier specified under section 251A of the Health and Social Care Act 2012.

(8)   This section does not permit the responsible person to do anything which, but for this section, would be inconsistent with—

    (a)   any provision of the data protection legislation, or

    (b)   a common law duty of care or confidence.

(9)   In subsection (8) "the data protection legislation" has the same meaning as in the Data Protection Act 2018 (see section 3 of that Act).

(10)   In subsection (5)(k) the "relevant characteristics" in relation to a patient mean—

    (a)   the patient's age;

    (b)   whether the patient has a disability, and if so, the nature of that disability;

    (c)   the patient's status regarding marriage or civil partnership;

    (d)   whether the patient is pregnant;

    (e)   the patient's race;

    (f)   the patient's religion or belief;

    (g)   the patient's sex;

    (h)   the patient's sexual orientation.

(11)   Expressions used in subsection (10) and Chapter 2 of Part 1 of the Equality Act 2010 have the same meaning in that subsection as in that Chapter.

Definitions

1-1536   responsible person: s.13.
mental health unit: s.1(3).
use of force: s.1(6), (7).
patient: s.1(5).
Mental disorder: s.1(2).

General Note

1-1537   As a means of effecting greater scrutiny, this section imposes a duty on the responsible person to keep a record of any use of force on a patient by staff who work in that unit (subs.(1)). The duty to keep a record does not apply if the use of force is "negligible" as defined in the guidance (subss.(2),(3)). By virtue of subs.(4), the Secretary of State must consult such persons as he or she considers appropriate before publishing the guidance or any substantial changes to it, and must keep the guidance under review (see s.11(3)–(6)).

The precise information to be recorded is set out in subs.(5) as elaborated in subss.(7), (10) and (11).

The responsible person must keep the record for three years from the date it was made (subs.(6)). Subsection (8) provides that nothing in this section permits the responsible person to do anything that is inconsistent with data protection legislation, as defined in subs.(9), or the common law duty of care or confidence. This has the effect of preserving the patient's legal rights in relation to their information.

Subsection (3)

1-1538   **Negligible**   Paragraph 7 of a letter dated September 7, 2018, from Lord O'Shaughnessy, Parliamentary Under Secretary of State for Health, to Lord Blencathra, Chairman of Parliament's Delegated Powers and Regulatory Reform Committee states:

> "The Government considered carefully whether the meaning of a 'negligible' use of force could be set out in regulations, or indeed on the face of the Bill. However, the range of techniques that may be used for physical interventions alone is many and varied – from the most serious such as prone restraint, to something as simple as guiding a patient by the elbow down a corridor, or through the right doorway. Further, what is 'negligible' will generally be a matter of degree rather than kind. It was concluded that the meaning would be more effectively illustrated through example case studies in guidance. This would also allow for more rapid revision to take account of changes in practice."

Paragraph 8 of the letter states that the "decision to require 'negligible' to be determined in accordance with the guidance (rather than requiring responsible persons simply to 'have regard to' the guidance) was taken to ensure consistency of approach to recording uses of force across the sector".

The *guidance* defines "negligible use of force" at p.46:

"Negligible does not mean irrelevant to a person's experience of care or treatment. We expect that negligible use of force will only apply in a very small set of circumstances. Whenever a member of staff makes a patient do something against their will, the use of force must always be recorded. If a member of staffs' contact with a patient goes beyond the minimum necessary in order to carry out therapeutic or caring activities, then it is not a negligible use of force and must be recorded.

The use of force can only be considered negligible where it involves light or gentle and proportionate pressure."

Guidance

See pp.45–53.   **1-1539**

Statistics prepared by mental health units

7.—(1)   The Secretary of State must ensure that at the end of each year statistics   **1-1540**
are published regarding the use of force by staff who work in mental health units.

(2)   The statistics must provide an analysis of the use of force in mental health units by reference to the relevant information recorded by responsible persons under section 6.

(3)   In subsection (2) "relevant information" means the information falling within section 6(5)(b), (c), (k), (l) and (n).

Definitions

use of force: s.1(6), (7).   **1-1541**
mental health unit: s.1(3).
staff: s.13.

General Note

In the Public Bill Committee in the House of Commons, the Member in Charge of the Bill said: **1-1542**

"[This section] places a duty on the Secretary of State to ensure that statistics on the use of force against mental health patients are published annually. That will allow us to identify trends in the way, and against whom, force is being used, and whether its use is reducing as intended, or whether some groups, such as BAME patients or women patients, are experiencing disproportionate use of force, as appears to be the evidence from the existing inadequate statistics."

Annual report by the Secretary of State

8.—(1)   As soon as reasonably practicable after the end of each calendar year,   **1-1543**
the Secretary of State—

(a)   must conduct a review of any reports made under paragraph 7 of Schedule 5 to the Coroners and Justice Act 2009 that were published during that year relating to the death of a patient as a result of the use of force in a mental health unit by staff who work in that unit, and

(b)   may conduct a review of any other findings made during that year relating to the death of a patient as a result of the use of force in a mental health unit by staff who work in that unit.

(2)   Having conducted a review under subsection (1), the Secretary of State must publish a report that includes the Secretary of State's conclusions arising from that review.

(3)   The Secretary of State may delegate the conduct of a review under subsection (1) and the publication of a report under subsection (2).

(4)   For the purposes of subsection (1)(b) "other findings" include, in relation to the death of a patient as a result of the use of force in a mental health unit, any finding or determination that is made—

    (a)   by the Care Quality Commission as the result of any review or investigation conducted by the Commission, or

    (b)   by a relevant health organisation as the result of any investigation into a serious incident.

Definitions

1-1544   use of force: s.1(6), (7).
staff: s.13.
mental health unit: s.1(3).
patient: s.1(5).
use of force: s.1(6), (7).
relevant health organisation: s.13.

General Note

1-1545   Subsection (1) requires the Secretary of State to conduct a review of any reports made by a coroner during each calendar year under para.7 of Sch.5 to the Coroners and Justice Act 2009 which relate to the death of a patient as a result of the use of force by staff in a mental health unit. The Secretary of State may also review any "other findings" (see subs.(4)) made during that year relating to the death of a patient as a result of a use of force by staff in a mental health unit. The review is to be conducted as soon as reasonably practicable after the end of each calendar year. Once the review has been conducted, subs.(2) requires the Secretary of State to publish a report that includes any conclusions as a result of the review. Subsection (3) provides that the Secretary of State is able to delegate the responsibility to conduct the review and the publication of the report following the review.

Subsection (1)

1-1546   In the Public Bill Committee in the House of Commons, the Member in Charge of the Bill said:

"The purpose of the amendment and the clause is to ensure that all findings from coroners' reports over a year are collated by the Secretary of State and published in an annual report, with the Secretary of State's conclusions on how the state is learning from any incidents that occurred during that year.

    That is an important step towards transparency and a culture in which lessons are learned quickly and effectively. A striking element of the findings in coroners' reports over the years is how frequently the same recommendations are made again and again. If there was learning in the system and those lessons were being applied, that repetition would be far less likely to occur.

    The proposal is to ensure that when those findings are made, they do not vanish into the ether; they must to properly understood and incorporated into the future development of best practice, to keep mental health patients safe. Amendment 70 would make the necessary provisions for the Secretary of State to carry out the publication of the reports."

INVESTIGATION OF DEATHS

Investigation of deaths or serious injuries

1-1547   **9.**   When a patient dies or suffers a serious injury in a mental health unit, the responsible person for the mental health unit must have regard to any guidance relating to the investigation of deaths or serious injuries that is published by—

    (a)   the Care Quality Commission (see Part 1 of the Health and Social Care Act 2008);

    (b)   [*Repealed by Health and Care Act 2022 Sch.5 para.102*];

(c) the National Health Service Commissioning Board (see section 1H of the National Health Service Act 2006);

(d) *[Repealed by Health and Care Act 2022 s.36(3)]*;

(e) a person prescribed by regulations made by the Secretary of State.

Definitions

patient: s.1(5).   **1-1548**
mental health unit: s.1(3).
responsible person: s.13.

General Note

This section places the NHS serious incident framework on a statutory footing. If a patient dies or **1-1549** suffers from a serious injury in a mental health unit the responsible person must have regard to any guidance relating to the investigations of deaths or serious injuries that is published by any of the bodies specified in paras (a) to (d). Paragraph (e) enables the Secretary of State to prescribe further persons whose guidance a responsible person must have regard to under this section.

At the Report Stage of the Bill, the Minister said:

"[Section 9] requires that when a patient dies or suffers a serious injury in a mental health unit, the responsible person must have regard to the relevant guidance relating to investigations of deaths or serious injuries, published by a list of organisations that are responsible for regulation: for example, NHS Improvement and the Care Quality Commission. That means that in the current NHS Improvement guidance, the NHS serious incident framework, which was last revised in 2015, will be put on a statutory footing. The framework outlines the process for conducting investigations of deaths and other serious incidents in the NHS for the purpose of learning to prevent recurrence. It requires the treating clinician to report an unexpected death when natural causes are not suspected. All deaths of detained patients must be reported to the coroner, the CQC and the provider's commissioner as serious incidents. That will ensure that all deaths in custody are automatically reported.

If the death occurred in a mental health in-patient or hospital setting, NHS providers are responsible for ensuring that there is an appropriate investigation into the death of a patient detained under the Mental Health Act, or where the Mental Capacity Act 2005 applies. The death of a voluntary in-patient will also be investigated by the coroner, and under the NHS serious incident framework, if it was violent or unnatural. These are not inquiries into how a person died, as that is a matter for coroners, and they are not conducted to hold any individual or organisation to account. Other processes exist for that purpose, including criminal or civil proceedings, disciplinary procedures, employment law, and systems of service and professional regulation. That is an important point, because overlapping interests will need to be managed. I hope that I can give the hon. Gentleman some comfort, and reassure him that we are tackling the real problem that the Bill is intended to tackle." (Hansard, 15 June 2018.)

Guidance

See pp.54–56.   **1-1550**

DELEGATION

Delegation of responsible person's functions

10.—(1) The responsible person for each mental health unit may delegate any **1-1551** functions exercisable by the responsible person under this Act to a relevant person only in accordance with this section.

(2) The responsible person may only delegate a function to a relevant person if the relevant person is of an appropriate level of seniority.

(3) The delegation of a function does not affect the responsibility of the responsible person for the exercise of the responsible person's functions under this Act.

(4)   The delegation of a function does not prevent the responsible person from exercising the function.

(5)   In this section "relevant person" means a person employed by the relevant health organisation that operates the mental health unit.

Definitions

1-1552   responsible person: s.13.
mental health unit: s.1(3).
relevant health organisation: s.13.

General Note

1-1553   This section provides that the responsible person for each mental health unit may delegate their functions under the Act to a "relevant person" in accordance with subs.(2), (3) and (4). "Relevant person" is defined in subs.(5).

Guidance

1-1554   See pp.56–57.

GUIDANCE

Guidance about functions under this Act

1-1555   **11.**—(1)   The Secretary of State must publish guidance about the exercise of functions by responsible persons and relevant health organisations under this Act.

(2)   In exercising functions under this Act, responsible persons and relevant health organisations must have regard to guidance published under this section.

(3)   Before publishing guidance under this section, the Secretary of State must consult such persons as the Secretary of State considers appropriate.

(4)   The Secretary of State must keep under review any guidance published under this section.

(5)   The Secretary of State may from time to time revise the guidance published under this section and, if this is done, must publish the guidance as revised.

(6)   If the Secretary of State considers that any revisions would amount to a substantial change in the guidance, the Secretary of State must consult such persons as the Secretary of State considers appropriate before publishing any revised guidance.

Definitions

1-1556   responsible person: s.13.
relevant health organisation: s.13.

General Note

1-1557   Subsection (1) requires the Secretary of State to publish guidance about the exercise of functions by the responsible persons and relevant health organisations. Before publishing guidance, the Secretary of State must consult anyone that he or she thinks is appropriate (subs.(3)). When a responsible person or relevant health organisation exercises functions under the Act they must have regard to the guidance (subs.(2)). The Secretary of State must keep the guidance under review (subs.(4)). If revisions made to the guidance amount to a substantial change, the Secretary of State must consult with anyone he or she thinks is appropriate before publishing the revised guidance (subss.(5)–(6)).

The guidance was published in December, 2021. It can be accessed at: *www.gov.uk/government/ publications/mental-health-units-use-of-force-act-2018.*

Subsection (2)

Have regard to   This phrase means that the guidance must be considered; but it can be disregarded   **1-1558** where the circumstances suggest that other considerations outweigh the guidance.

Subsection (3)

Consult   "In practice this will mean consulting with experts in the field of restrictive interventions and   **1-1559** those with lived experience, which the Government considers is appropriate for this type of guidance" (Letter from Lord O'Shaughnessy, Parliamentary Under Secretary of State for Health, to Lord Blencathra, Chairman of Parliament's Delegated Powers and Regulatory Reform Committee, September 7, 2018, para.9).

VIDEO RECORDING

Police body cameras

12.—(1)   If a police officer is going to a mental health unit on duty that involves   **1-1560** assisting staff who work in that unit, the officer must take a body camera if reasonably practicable.

(2)   While in a mental health unit on duty that involves assisting staff who work in that unit, a police officer who has a body camera there must wear it and keep it operating at all times when reasonably practicable.

(3)   Subsection (2) does not apply if there are special circumstances at the time that justify not wearing the camera or keeping it operating.

(4)   A failure by a police officer to comply with the requirements of subsection (1) or (2) does not of itself make the officer liable to criminal or civil proceedings.

(5)   But if those requirements appear to the court or tribunal to be relevant to any question arising in criminal or civil proceedings, they must be taken into account in determining that question.

(6)   In this section—

"body camera" means a device that operates so as to make a continuous audio and video recording while being worn;
"police officer" means—
(a)   a member of a police force maintained under section 2 of the Police Act 1996,
(b)   a member of the metropolitan police force,
(c)   a member of the City of London police force,
(d)   a special constable appointed under section 27 of the Police Act 1996, or
(e)   a member or special constable of the British Transport Police Force.

Definitions

mental health unit: s.1(3).   **1-1561**
staff: s.13.

General Note

1-1562   Subsection (1) imposes a duty on police officers to take a body camera if it is reasonably practicable to do so whenever they attend a mental health unit on duty that involves helping staff who work in that unit. "Police officer" is defined in subs.(6). If the police officer has a body camera they must wear it and keep it operating at all times when reasonably practicable (subs.(2)), unless, as set out in subs.(3), there are special circumstances that justify not wearing or not operating the camera. Any failure to comply with the requirements of subs.(1) or (2) does not of itself make the police officer liable to criminal or civil proceedings (subs.(4)).

Subsection (5) provides that if the requirements of subs.(1) or (2) are relevant to any question that arises in criminal or civil proceedings, those requirements must be taken into account to determine that question.

Interpretation

Interpretation

1-1563   **13.**   In this Act—

"health service hospital" has the same meaning as in section 275(1) of the National Health Service Act 2006;

"independent hospital" has the same meaning as in section 145(1) of the Mental Health Act 1983;

"the NHS" has the same meaning as in section 64(4) of the Health and Social Care Act 2012;

"responsible person" means a person appointed under section 2(1);

"relevant health organisation" means—

    (a)   an NHS trust;

    (b)   an NHS foundation trust;

    (c)   any person who provides health care services for the purposes of the NHS within the meaning of Part 3 of the Health and Social Care Act 2012;

"staff" means any person who works for a relevant health organisation that operates a mental health unit (whether as an employee or a contractor) who—

    (a)   may be authorised to use force on a patient in the unit,

    (b)   may authorise the use of force on a particular patient in the unit, or

    (c)   has the function of providing general authority for the use of force in the unit.

Final provisions

Transitional provision

1-1564   **14.**   The Secretary of State may by regulations make such transitional, transitory or saving provision in connection with the coming into force of any provision of this Act.

Financial provisions

1-1565   **15.**   There is to be paid out of money provided by Parliament—

    (a)   any expenditure incurred under or by virtue of this Act, and

    (b)   any increase attributable to this Act in the sums payable under any other Act out of money so provided.

Regulations

16.—(1)   Regulations under this Act are to be made by statutory instrument.   **1-1566**

(2)   Regulations under this Act are subject to annulment in pursuance of a resolution of either House of Parliament (other than regulations made under section 17(3)).

Commencement, extent and short title

17.—(1)   This Act extends to England and Wales only.   **1-1567**

(2)   This section and section 16 come into force on the day on which this Act is passed.

(3)   The other provisions of this Act come into force on such day as the Secretary of State may appoint by regulations.

(4)   Regulations under this section may appoint different days for different purposes or areas.

(5)   This Act may be cited as the Mental Health Units (Use of Force) Act 2018.

PART 2: DELEGATED LEGISLATION

DELEGATED LEGISLATION

The Mental Health (Care and Treatment) (Scotland) Act 2003 (Consequential Provisions) Order 2005

(SI 2005/2078)

Dated July 21, 2005 and made by the Secretary of State for Constitutional Affairs under the Scotland Act 1998 (c.46) sections 104, 112(1) and 113

General Note

This Order makes provision consequential on the Mental Health (Care and Treatment) (Scotland) Act **2-001**
2003. Only those articles that extend to England and Wales are reproduced.

Article 8 provides that any person who may be taken into custody in Scotland under the 2003 Act or regulations made under that Act may be taken into custody in any other part of the UK and returned to Scotland. Article 10 makes it an offence in England and Wales and in Northern Ireland to do anything in relation to a person subject to the 2003 Act that would be an offence under s.316 of the 2003 Act if done in Scotland. Section 316 makes it an offence to induce or assist patients to abscond. Article 11 provides that where patients are being conveyed to any place in England, Wales or Northern Ireland by virtue of the 2003 Act or this Order they will be in legal custody while being conveyed through those territories and that persons taking patients into custody or conveying or detaining them by virtue of the 2003 Act or this Order will have all the powers and privileges of a constable. Article 12 extends the protection afforded by s.139 of the 1983 Act to acts done in pursuance of this Order.

The Mental Welfare Commission for Scotland has produced a factsheet on "Cross border transfers, cross border absconding and cross border visits under mental health law" (June, 2021). It can be accessed at: *https://www.mwcscot.org.uk/sites/default/files/2021-07/Cross-border-guidance_AdviceNote_2021.pdf.*

Citation, commencement, interpretation and extent

1.—(1)   This Order may be cited as the Mental Health (Care and Treatment)   **2-002**
(Scotland) Act 2003 (Consequential Provisions) Order 2005 and, subject to paragraph (2), shall come into force on 5th October 2005.

(2)   The entry in Schedule 3 to this Order in respect of the Mental Health (Scotland) Act 1984 shall come into force immediately after the coming into force of the entry in Schedule 5 to the 2003 Act in respect of the Mental Health (Scotland) Act 1984.

(3)   In this Order, unless the context otherwise requires—

"the 1995 Act" means the Criminal Procedure (Scotland) Act 1995;
"the 2003 Act" means the Mental Health (Care and Treatment) (Scotland) Act 2003;
"hospital", except as provided in articles 2(7) and 4(8), has the meaning given in section 329(1) of the 2003 Act;
"hospital direction" means a direction made under section 59A of the 1995 Act;
"patient" has the meaning given in section 329(1) of the 2003 Act;
"restriction order" means an order made under section 59 of the 1995 Act; and
"transfer for treatment direction" has the meaning given by section 136 of the 2003 Act.

(4)   A reference in this Order to "a patient whose detention in hospital was authorised by virtue of the 2003 Act or the 1995 Act" shall be read as including

references to a patient in respect of whom a certificate under one of the provisions listed in section 290(7)(a) of the 2003 Act is in operation.

(5) [...]

(6) Articles 4, 5, 6, 7 and 9 extend to Northern Ireland only.

(7) Articles 8, 10, 11 and 12(2) extend to England and Wales and Northern Ireland only.

(8) Articles 12(1), 13 and 14 extend to Scotland only.

(9) Subject to paragraph (10), the modifications in Schedules 1 and 2 and the repeals in Schedule 3 have the same extent as the provisions being modified or repealed.

(10) Those modifications and repeals do not extend to Scotland other than the modifications in paragraphs 1(4)(b), 5 and 6 of Schedule 1 and paragraph 20 of Schedule 2 and the repeal in Schedule 3 of the Mental Health (Scotland) Act 1984.

Amendment

Paragraph (5) was repealed by the Mental Health Act 2007 s.55, Sch.11 Pt 7.

[Patients absent from hospitals or other places in Scotland]

2-003   **8.**—(1) Subject to the provisions of this article, any person who may be taken into custody in Scotland under—

(a) sections 301 to 303 of the 2003 Act; or

(b) regulations made under section [289, 290, 309, 309A] or 310 of that Act, may be taken into custody in, and returned to Scotland from, any other part of the United Kingdom.

(2) For the purposes of the enactments referred to in paragraph (1), in their application by virtue of this article to England and Wales or Northern Ireland–

(a) "constable" includes a constable in England or Wales or a constable of the Police Service of Northern Ireland, as the case may be; and

(b) "mental health officer" includes—

(i) in England and Wales, any approved [mental health professional] within the meaning of the Mental Health Act 1983; and

(ii) in Northern Ireland, any approved social worker within the meaning of the Mental Health (Northern Ireland) Order 1986.

Amendments

The amendments to this article were made by the Mental Health Act 2007 s.39(2), Sch.5 Pt 2 para.21(3) and SI 2008/2828 art.20.

Assisting patients to absent themselves without leave etc.

2-004   **10.**—(1) Any person who in England and Wales or Northern Ireland does anything in relation to a person whose detention in hospital is authorised by the 2003 Act which, if done in Scotland, would make him guilty of an offence under section 316 of the 2003 Act shall be guilty of an offence.

(2) Where a person is charged with an offence under paragraph (1) as it applies to section 316(1)(b) of the 2003 Act, it shall be a defence for such person to prove that the doing of that with which the person is charged—

(a) did not obstruct the discharge by any person of a function conferred or imposed on that person by virtue of the 2003 Act or this Order; and

(b) was intended to protect the interests of the patient.

(3) Any person guilty of an offence under this article shall be liable—

(a) on summary conviction, to imprisonment for a term not exceeding 3 months or to a fine not exceeding level 5 on the standard scale;

(b) on conviction on indictment, to imprisonment for a term not exceeding 2 years or to a fine, or both.

Provisions as to custody, removal and detention

11.—(1) Any person required or authorised by or by virtue of the 2003 Act or **2-005** by virtue of this Order to be moved to any place or to be kept in custody or detained in a place of safety shall, while being so moved, kept or detained, as the case may be, be deemed to be in legal custody.

(2) A constable or any other person required or authorised by or by virtue of that Act or by virtue of this Order to take any person into custody, or to move or detain any person shall, for the purposes of taking him into custody or moving or detaining him, have all the powers, authorities, protection and privileges which a constable has—

(a) in the case of a constable, within the area for which he acts as constable; and

(b) in the case of any other person, in the area where he has taken any person into custody or is moving or detaining him.

Protection for acts done under this Order

12.—(1) No person shall be liable, whether on ground of want of jurisdiction **2-006** or on any other ground, to any civil or criminal proceedings to which he would have been liable apart from this paragraph in respect of any act purporting to be done in pursuance of this Order, unless the act was done in bad faith or without reasonable care.

(2) Section 139 of the Mental Health Act 1983 (which relates to protection for acts done in pursuance of that Act) shall apply in respect of any act purporting to be done in pursuance of articles [4 to 11] of this Order.

Amendment

The amendment to para.(2) was made by the Mental Health Act 2007 s.39(2), Sch.5 Pt 2 para.21(4).

THE MENTAL HEALTH (MUTUAL RECOGNITION) REGULATIONS 2008

(SI 2008/1204)

Dated April 28, 2008 and made by the Secretary of State and the Welsh Ministers acting jointly under the Mental Health Act 1983, section 142A

General Note

These regulations set out the circumstances in which a practitioner approved in England for the **2-007** purposes of s.12 of the Act or a person approved in relation to England to act as an approved clinician for the purposes of the Act may be treated as approved in relation to Wales by virtue of that approval, and vice versa. They apply where a patient is liable to be detained, subject to a community treatment order or subject to guardianship under the Act. This flexibility is particularly helpful in areas near the border between England and Wales, where services are accessed for patients across that border.

Citation, commencement and interpretation

2-008   **1.**—(1)   These Regulations may be cited as the Mental Health (Mutual Recognition) Regulations 2008 and shall come into force on 3rd November 2008.

(2)   In these Regulations, "the Act" means the Mental Health Act 1983.

Approval under section 12(2) of the Act

2-009   **2.**—(1)   Any person who is approved in relation to England for the purposes of section 12(2) of the Act, or treated as approved by virtue of section 12(2A) of the Act, shall in all circumstances relevant to the purposes of section 12(2) be treated as approved in relation to Wales.

(2)   Any person who is approved in relation to Wales for the purposes of section 12(2) of the Act, or treated as approved by virtue of section 12(2A) of the Act, shall in all circumstances relevant to the purposes of section 12(2) be treated as approved in relation to England.

Person approved to act as an approved clinician

2-010   **3.**—(1)   The circumstances in which a person who is approved to act as an approved clinician in relation to England shall be treated, by virtue of his approval, as approved in relation to Wales too are where—

(a)   the approved clinician is acting in respect of a patient who is liable to be detained in accordance with the provisions of the Act or is subject to a community treatment order,

(b)   the patient is in Wales, and

(c)   the patient's relevant hospital is in England.

(2)   The circumstances in which a person who is approved to act as an approved clinician in relation to Wales shall be treated, by virtue of his approval, as approved in relation to England too are where—

(a)   the approved clinician is acting in respect of a patient who is liable to be detained in accordance with the provisions of the Act or is subject to a community treatment order,

(b)   the patient is in England, and

(c)   the patient's relevant hospital is in Wales.

(3)   In this regulation, "relevant hospital"—

(a)   in respect of a patient liable to be detained, means the hospital in which the patient is liable to be detained in accordance with the provisions of the Act;

(b)   in respect of a patient subject to a community treatment order, has the same meaning as "the responsible hospital".

Guardianship

2-011   **4.**—(1)   In relation to a patient subject to guardianship, the circumstances in which a responsible local social services authority in England may treat a person who is approved to act as an approved clinician in relation to Wales as approved in relation to England in order to authorise that person to be the patient's responsible clinician are where—

(a)   the patient is in Wales, or

(b)   the patient receives medical treatment for mental disorder in Wales.

(2)   In relation to a patient subject to guardianship, the circumstances in which a responsible local social services authority in Wales may treat a person who is approved to act as an approved clinician in relation to England as approved in rela-

tion to Wales in order to authorise that person to be the patient's responsible clinician are where—

    (a)   the patient is in England, or

    (b)   the patient receives medical treatment for mental disorder in England.

(3)   In relation to a patient subject to guardianship, the circumstances in which a person approved to act as an approved clinician in England shall be treated as approved to act as an approved clinician in relation to Wales are where—

    (a)   that approved clinician has been authorised to act as the patient's responsible clinician by the patient's responsible local social services authority in England, and

    (b)   that approved clinician is acting in respect of a patient who is in Wales.

(4)   In relation to a patient subject to guardianship, the circumstances in which a person approved to act as an approved clinician in Wales shall be treated as approved to act as an approved clinician in relation to England are where—

    (a)   that approved clinician has been authorised to act as the patient's responsible clinician by the patient's responsible local social services authority in Wales, and

    (b)   that approved clinician is acting in respect of a patient who is in England.

(5)   In this regulation, "responsible local social services authority" has the same meaning as in section 34(3) of the Act.

The Mental Health (Conflicts of Interest) (England) Regulations 2008

(SI 2008/1205)

Dated April 28, 2008 and made by the Secretary of State under the Mental Health Act 1983, section 12A

General Note

These regulations, which are considered in Ch.39 of the Code of Practice, only apply to applications made under Part 2 of the Act. They set out the circumstances in which there is a potential conflict of interest such that an approved mental health professional (AMHP) cannot make an application mentioned in s.11(1) of the Act, or a registered medical practitioner cannot make a medical recommendation for the purposes of such an application. A registered medical practitioner means "a fully registered person within the meaning of the Medical Act 1983 who holds a licence to practise under that Act" (Interpretation Act 1978 Sch.1).   **2-012**

An AMHP considering making such an application, or a registered medical practitioner considering giving a medical recommendation for the purposes of such an application, will have a potential conflict of interest if the reasons set out in the regulations apply. These may be financial reasons (reg.4), business reasons (reg.5), professional reasons (reg.6) or because of a personal relationship existing between the assessor and another assessor, or between the assessor and the patient or, where the application is to be made by the patient's nearest relative, the nearest relative (reg.7).

There is provision for an AMHP or a registered medical practitioner to make an application or a medical recommendation despite a potential conflict of interest for professional reasons in specified circumstances in cases of urgent necessity where there would otherwise be a delay with a serious risk to the health or safety of the patient or to others (reg.6).

Other potential conflicts

Under this heading, the Code of Practice states: **2-013**

"39.15 There may be circumstances not covered by these regulations where the assessor feels, nonetheless, that there is (or could be seen to be) a potential conflict of interest. Assessors should work on the principle that in any situation where they believe that the objectivity or independence of their decision is (or could be seen to be) undermined then they should not become involved or should withdraw.

39.16 These regulations do not cover potential conflicts of interest relating to a community treatment order (CTO). The responsible clinician responsible for making the decision as to whether to place a patient on a CTO, or any decision to revoke a CTO, should not have any financial interest in the outcome of the decision. Responsible clinicians should not be considered to have a financial interest in a hospital on the sole basis that they work there. Similarly, the responsible clinician should not be a relative of the patient.

39.17 These regulations do not cover potential conflicts of interest relating to renewal of detention or guardianship. The persons involved in making the decision as to whether to renew the detention (the responsible clinician and other professionals consulted by the responsible clinician) or the guardianship (the appropriate practitioner) should not have any financial interest in the outcome of the decision."

As these regulations do not cover the situation set out in para.39.15, it is not appropriate for the guidance to use mandatory terms in that paragraph. It is submitted that the final phrase of the paragraph should read: "they should consider not becoming involved or should consider withdrawing".

The guidance contained in para.39.17, which relates to renewals made under s.20 should not be followed in so far as it applies to the responsible clinician of a detained patient or to the appropriate practitioner of a patient who is subject to the guardianship because they are the only professionals who can trigger a renewal.

Wales

2-014   The Welsh Ministers have made separate Regulations in relation to Wales: see the Mental Health (Conflicts of Interest) (Wales) Regulations 2008 (SI 2008/2440) (W.213).

Citation, commencement and application

2-015   **1.**—(1)   These Regulations may be cited as the Mental Health (Conflicts of Interest) (England) Regulations 2008 and shall come into force on 3rd November 2008.

(2)   These Regulations apply to England only.

Interpretation

2-016   **2.**   In these Regulations—

"the Act" means the Mental Health Act 1983;
"AMHP" means an approved mental health professional;
"application" means an application mentioned in section 11(1) of the Act;
"assessor" means—
    (a)   an AMHP, or
    (b)   a registered medical practitioner.

General

2-017   **3.**   Regulations 4 to 7 set out the circumstances in which there would be a potential conflict of interest within the meaning of section 12A(1) of the Act such that an AMHP shall not make an application or a registered medical practitioner shall not give a medical recommendation.

Potential conflict for financial reasons

2-018   **4.**—(1)   A assessor shall have a potential conflict of interest for financial reasons if the assessor has a financial interest in the outcome of a decision whether or not to make an application or give a medical recommendation.

(2)   Where an application for the admission of the patient to a hospital which

is a registered establishment is being considered, a registered medical practitioner who is on the staff of that hospital shall have a potential conflict of interest for financial reasons where the other medical recommendation is given by a registered medical practitioner who is also on the staff of that hospital.

General Note

Paragraph 39.6 of the Code of Practice states: **2-019**

"An assessor will have a conflict of interest for financial reasons if the assessor stands to make a financial benefit (or loss) for their decision. There will not be a potential conflict of interest for financial reasons where an assessor is paid a fee for making an application or giving a medical recommendation if it is paid regardless of the outcome of the assessment."

Paragraph (2)

Paragraph 39.4 of the Code of Practice states: **2-020**

"The current regulations require that where the patient is to be admitted to an independent hospital and the doctor providing one of the medical recommendations is on the staff of that independent hospital, the other medical recommendation must be given by a doctor who is not on the staff of that independent hospital. That is, there will be a potential conflict if both doctors giving recommendations are on the staff of the independent hospital. It is also good practice for doctors on the staff of an NHS trust or NHS foundation trust to ensure that one of the recommendations is given by a doctor not on the staff of that trust."

The "good practice" point made in the final sentence is not a legal requirement.
Regulation 4(3) of the Welsh Regulations prevents either recommending doctor from being on the staff of the admitting independent hospital.

Potential conflict of interest for business reasons

5.—(1)   When considering making an application or considering giving a medi-   **2-021**
cal recommendation in respect of a patient, an assessor shall have a potential conflict of interest for business reasons if both the assessor and the patient or another assessor are closely involved in the same business venture, including being a partner, director, other office-holder or major shareholder of that venture.

(2)   Where the patient's nearest relative is making an application, a registered medical practitioner who is considering giving a medical recommendation in respect of that patient shall have a potential conflict of interest for business reasons if that registered medical practitioner and the nearest relative are both closely involved in the same business venture, including being a partner, director, other office-holder or major shareholder of that venture.

General Note

The Code of Practice states: **2-022**

"39.7 An assessor will have a potential conflict of interest if both that assessor and one of the other assessors, the patient or the nearest relative (if the nearest relative is the applicant) are closely involved in the same business venture. Being 'closely involved' is not defined in the regulations. Examples could include being a partner in a partnership, being a director or other office-holder of a company, or being a major shareholder in it. This will apply even if the business venture is not associated with the provision of services for the care and treatment of persons with a mental disorder.
39.8 Business ventures include any form of commercial enterprise from which the person concerned stands to profit. Such people include: directors and major investors in a company (of any size) which provides goods or services for profit; partners in a general practitioner (GP) practice; partners in a business established as a limited liability partnership. Involvement in a business venture

does not include involvement in societies and similar organisations which are essentially non-commercial, and from which the people concerned do not stand to profit."

Potential conflict of interest for professional reasons

2-023   **6.**—(1)   When considering making an application or considering giving a medical recommendation in respect of a patient, an assessor shall have a potential conflict of interest for professional reasons if the assessor—

    (a)   directs the work of, or employs, the patient or one of the other assessors making that consideration;

    (b)   except where paragraph (3) applies, is a member of a team organised to work together for clinical purposes on a routine basis and—

        (i)   the patient is a member of the same team, or

        (ii)   the other two assessors are members of the same team.

(2)   Where the patient's nearest relative is making an application, a registered medical practitioner who is considering giving a medical recommendation in respect of that patient shall have a potential conflict of interest for professional reasons if that registered medical practitioner—

    (a)   directs the work of, or employs, the nearest relative, or

    (b)   works under the direction of, or is employed by, the patient's nearest relative.

(3)   Paragraph (1)(b) shall not prevent a registered medical practitioner giving a medical recommendation or an AMHP making an application if, in their opinion, it is of urgent necessity for an application to be made and a delay would involve serious risk to the health or safety of the patient or others.

General Note

2-024   The Code of Practice states:

"39.9 Regulations set out that a conflict of interest for professional reasons will occur where:

-     the assessor is in a line management or employment relationship with one of the other assessors or the patient or the nearest relative (where the nearest relative is the applicant)
-     the assessor is a member of the same team as the patient, or
-     where there are three assessors, all of them are members of the same team.

39.10 A line management relationship will exist whether an assessor manages, or is managed by, one of the other assessors, the patient or the nearest relative (where the nearest relative is the applicant). Similarly an employment relationship will exist whether the assessor employs, or is employed by, one of the other assessors, the patient or the nearest relative (where the nearest relative is the applicant).

39.11 For the purposes of the regulations a team is defined as a group of professionals who work together for clinical purposes on a routine basis. That might include a community mental health team, a crisis resolution or home treatment team, or staff on an in-patient unit (but not necessarily the staff of an entire hospital)."

Although para.39.4 of the Code states that it is "good practice for doctors on the staff of an NHS trust or NHS foundation trust to ensure that one of the recommendations is given by a doctor not on the staff of that trust", the Act allows for two doctors on the staff of the same Trust to provide medical recommendations as long as one doctor does not have management responsibility for the other.

Paragraph (1)

2-025   Sub-paragraphs (a) and (b) provide alternative reasons for identifying a potential conflict of interest.

Paragraph (3)

Urgent necessity   The Code of Practice states: **2-026**

"39.12 If there is a case of urgent necessity all three assessors may be from the same team. However, this should happen only in a genuine emergency, where the patient's need for urgent assessment outweighs the desirability of waiting for another assessor who has no potential conflict of interest. Any decisions made to proceed despite a potential conflict of interest should be recorded, with reasons, in case notes.

39.13 In a case of urgent necessity it is preferable to proceed with three assessors, despite a potential conflict of interest, rather than make the application under section 4 of the Act with only two assessors (one doctor and one AMHP) (see paragraphs 15.6 – 15.8).

39.14 There are no other circumstances in which potential conflict of interest can be set aside because of urgent necessity."

In their opinion   This criterion is to be judged by adopting a subjective test.

Potential conflict of interest on the basis of a personal relationship

7.—(1)   A assessor who is considering making an application or considering   **2-027**
giving a medical recommendation in respect of a patient, shall have a potential
conflict of interest on the basis of a personal relationship if that assessor is—

(a)   related to a relevant person in the first degree;

(b)   related to a relevant person in the second degree;

(c)   related to a relevant person as a half-sister or half-brother;

(d)   the spouse, ex-spouse, civil partner or ex-civil partner of a relevant
person, or

(e)   living with a relevant person as if they were a spouse or a civil partner.

(2)   For the purposes of this regulation—

(a)   "relevant person" means another assessor, the patient, or, if the nearest relative is making the application, the nearest relative;

(b)   "related in the first degree" means as a parent, sister, brother, son or
daughter and includes step relationships;

(c)   "related in the second degree" means as an uncle, aunt, grandparent,
grandchild, first cousin, nephew, niece, parent-in-law, grandparent-in-
law, grandchild-in-law, sister-in-law, brother-in-law, son-in-law,
daughter-in-law and includes step relationships;

(d)   references to step relationships and in-laws in sub-paragraph (b) and
(c) are to be read in accordance with section 246 of the Civil Partnership Act 2004.

THE MENTAL HEALTH (APPROVED MENTAL HEALTH PROFESSIONALS) (APPROVAL) (ENGLAND) REGULATIONS 2008

(SI 2008/1206)

Dated April 28, 2008 and made by the Secretary of State under the Mental Health
Act 1983, section 114

General Note

These regulations set out a number of matters in connection with the giving by local social services   **2-028**
authorities (LSSAs) in England of approvals to persons to act as approved mental health professionals
(AMHPs) for the purposes of the Act.

Before a person can be approved (or re-approved) in England to act as an AMHP by a LSSA, the person must have appropriate competence. In deciding whether it is satisfied that the person has appropriate competence, the LSSA must take into account that the person has at least one of the professional requirements set out in Sch.1 and the matters set out in Sch.2 (reg.3).

Before a person can be approved to act as an AMHP if he or she has not been approved before, that person must have completed a course within the last five years that was approved by Social Work England or Social Care Wales. The period for which an AMHP is approved (or re-approved) is five years (reg.4). Approval (or re-approval) is subject to specified conditions (reg.5).

The approval shall be suspended for any period that the AMHP is suspended from the register or list relevant to the AMHP's professional requirements (reg.6).

The approval or re-approval of an AMHP will end when the period of approval expires or before that in specified circumstances. When the approval ends, the LSSA must inform the AMHP and any other LSSA for which it knows that AMHP has agreed to act. If one LSSA approves a person to act as an AMHP who is already approved by another, it must inform that other LSSA (reg.7).

Each LSSA is required to keep records with specified details of AMHPs for whom it is the approving LSSA (reg.8).

Wales

2-029   The Welsh Ministers have made separate regulations relating to the approval of persons to act as AMHPs in relation to Wales: see the Mental Health (Approval of Persons to be Approved Mental Health Professionals) (Wales) Regulations 2008 (SI 2008/2436) (W.209). The Schedule to Mental Health Act 2007 (Commencement No.8 and Transitional Provisions) Order 2008 (SI 2008/2561) requires LSSAs to treat as AMHPs a person who has been approved as an approved social worker by an LSSA in Wales immediately before November 3, 2008.

Transitional Provisions

2-030   See paras 4 and 5 of the Schedule to the Mental Health Act 2007 (Commencement No.7 and Transitional Provisions) Order 2008 (SI 2008/1900) and para.84(5) of Sch.1, Pt 2 to the Health and Social Care Act 2012 (Consequential Provision—Social Workers) Order 2012 (SI 2012/1479).

Citation, commencement and application

2-031   **1.**—(1)   These Regulations may be cited as the Mental Health (Approved Mental Health Professionals) (Approval) (England) Regulations 2008 and shall come into force on 3rd November 2008.

(2)   These Regulations apply to England only.

Interpretation

2-032   **2.**   In these Regulations—

"the Act" means the Mental Health Act 1983;

"AMHP" means an approved mental health professional;

"approve" and "approval" include "re-approve" and "re-approval";

"approving LSSA" means the local social services authority in England that has approved the person to act as an AMHP;

[…];

"LSSA" means a local social services authority in England;

"professional requirements" means the requirements set out in Schedule 1;

["Social Care Wales" has the meaning given by section 67 of the Regulation and Inspection of Social Care (Wales) Act 2016.]

Amendments

The definition of "General Social Care Council" was repealed by SI 2012/1479 Sch.1 Pt 2 para.84. The definition of "Social Care Wales" was inserted by SI 2017/52 Sch.1 para.17(2)(b).

Granting approval

3.—(1)   An LSSA may only approve a person to act as an AMHP if it is satis-   **2-033**
fied that the person has appropriate competence in dealing with persons who are suffering from mental disorder.

(2)   In determining whether it is satisfied a person has appropriate competence,
the LSSA must take into account the following factors—
     (a)   that the person fulfils at least one of the professional requirements, and
     (b)   the matters set out in Schedule 2.

(3)   Before an LSSA may approve a person to act as an AMHP who has not been
approved, or been treated as approved, before in England and Wales, the person
must have completed within the last five years a course approved by [[Social Work
England] under section 114ZA of the Mental Health Act 1983 or by] [Social Care
Wales].

[(4)   In this regulation "Social Work England" means the body corporate
established by section 36(1) of the Children and Social Work Act 2017.]

Amendments

The amendments to para.(3) were made by SI 2012/1479 Sch.1 Pt 2 para.84 and SI 2017/52 Sch.1
para.17(3) and by SI 2018/893, reg.43(2)(a). Paragraph (4) was inserted by SI 2018/893, reg.43(2)(b).

Period of approval

4.   An LSSA may approve a person to act as an AMHP for a period of five years.   **2-034**

Conditions

5.   When any approval is granted under these Regulations, it shall be subject to   **2-035**
the following conditions—
     (a)   in each year that the AMHP is approved, the AMHP shall complete at
         least 18 hours of training agreed with the approving LSSA as being
         relevant to their role as an AMHP;
     (b)   the AMHP shall undertake to notify the approving LSSA in writing as
         soon as reasonably practicable if they agree to act as an AMHP on
         behalf of another LSSA, and when such agreement ends;
     (c)   the AMHP shall undertake to cease to act as an AMHP and to notify
         the approving LSSA immediately if they are suspended from any of the
         registers or listings referred to in the professional competencies, or if
         any such suspension ends, and
     (d)   the AMHP shall undertake to cease to act as an AMHP and to notify
         the approving LSSA immediately if they no longer meet at least one
         of the professional requirements.

Suspension of approval

6.—(1)   If at any time after being approved, the registration or listing required   **2-036**
by the professional requirements of a person approved to act as an AMHP is
suspended, the approving LSSA shall suspend that AMHP's approval for as long
as the AMHP's registration or listing is suspended.

(2)   Where an AMHP's approval is suspended, that person may not act as an
AMHP unless and until the suspension of approval is ended by the approving LSSA
in accordance with subsection (3).

(3)   Where the approving LSSA is notified that the suspension of the AMHP's registration or listing has ended, the approving LSSA shall, unless it is not satisfied the AMHP has appropriate competence in dealing with persons suffering from mental disorder, end the suspension of approval.

(4)   Where the suspension of approval has ended, the approval shall continue to run for any unexpired period of approval, unless the approving LSSA ends it earlier in accordance with regulation 7.

End of approval

2-037   **7.**—(1)   Except where paragraph (2) applies, a person shall cease to be approved to act as an AMHP at the end of the day on which their period of approval expires.

(2)   Except where regulation 6 applies, the approving LSSA shall end the approval of a person it has approved to act as an AMHP before their period of approval expires—

    (a)   in accordance with a request in writing to do so from that AMHP;

    (b)   if it is no longer satisfied that the AMHP has appropriate competence taking into account the matters set out in Schedule 2;

    (c)   immediately upon becoming aware that the AMHP—

        (i)   is no longer a person who meets at least one of the professional requirements;

        (ii)   is in breach of any of the conditions set out in regulation 5, or

        (iii)   has been approved to act as an AMHP by another LSSA.

(3)   When an approval ends, the approving LSSA shall notify the AMHP immediately that the approval has ended and give reasons for ending the approval.

(4)   When an approval ends, the approving LSSA shall notify that fact to any other LSSA for whom it knows the AMHP has agreed to act as an AMHP.

(5)   If an LSSA approves a person as an AMHP knowing that that AMHP is already approved by another LSSA, it shall notify the previous approving LSSA.

General Note

Paragraph (2)(b),(c)(i)(ii)

2-038   The AMHP has no right of appeal against the decision of the local authority.

Records

2-039   **8.**—(1)   The approving LSSA shall keep a record of each AMHP it approves which shall include—

    (a)   the name of the AMHP;

    (b)   the AMHP's profession;

    (c)   the AMHP's date of approval;

    (d)   details of any period of suspension under regulation 6;

    (e)   details of the completion of training to comply with regulation 5(a);

    (f)   details of any previous approvals as an AMHP within the previous five years;

    (g)   the names of other LSSAs for whom the AMHP has agreed to act as an AMHP, and

    (h)   the date of and reason for the end of approval, if applicable.

(2)   The record referred to in paragraph (1) shall be retained by the approving LSSA for a period of five years commencing with the day on which the AMHP's approval ended.

SCHEDULE 1

PROFESSIONAL REQUIREMENTS

Regulation 2

2-040

The professional requirements are as follows—
- (a)   [...];
- (b)   a first level nurse, registered in Sub-Part 1 of the Nurses' Part of the Register maintained under article 5 of the Nursing and Midwifery Order 2001, with the inclusion of an entry indicating their field of practice is mental health or learning disabilities nursing;
- (c)   an occupational therapist registered in Part 6 [...] of the Register maintained under article 5 of the [Health and Social Work Professions Order 2001]; [...]
- (d)   a chartered psychologist who is listed in the British Psychological Society's Register of Chartered Psychologists and who holds a relevant practising certificate issued by that Society. [; or
- (e)   a social worker registered in the register of social workers in England maintained under section 39(1) of the Children and Social Work Act 2017].

Amendments

The amendments to this Schedule were made by SI 2012/1479 Sch.1 Pt 1 para.54, Sch.1 Pt 2 para.84 and SI 2019/1094, Sch.3 para.20.

SCHEDULE 2

MATTERS TO BE TAKEN INTO ACCOUNT TO DETERMINE COMPETENCE

Regulation 3(2)

Key Competence Area 1: Application of Values to the AMHP Role

2-041

1.   Whether the applicant has—
- (a)   the ability to identify, challenge and, where possible, redress discrimination and inequality in all its forms in relation to AMHP practice;
- (b)   an understanding of and respect for individuals' qualities, abilities and diverse backgrounds, and is able to identify and counter any decision which may be based on unlawful discrimination;
- (c)   the ability to promote the rights, dignity and self determination of patients consistent with their own needs and wishes, to enable them to contribute to the decisions made affecting their quality of life and liberty, and
- (d)   a sensitivity to individuals' needs for personal respect, confidentiality, choice, dignity and privacy while exercising the AMHP role.

Key Competence Area 2: Application of Knowledge: The Legal and Policy Framework

2.(1)   Whether the applicant has—
- (a)   appropriate knowledge of and ability to apply in practice—
  - (i)   mental health legislation, related codes of practice and national and local policy guidance, and
  - (ii)   relevant parts of other legislation, codes of practice, national and local policy guidance, in particular the Children Act 1989, the Children Act 2004, the Human Rights Act 1998 and the Mental Capacity Act 2005;
- (b)   a knowledge and understanding of the particular needs of children and young people and their families, and an ability to apply AMHP practice in the context of those particular needs;
- (c)   an understanding of, and sensitivity to, race and culture in the application of knowledge of mental health legislation;
- (d)   an explicit awareness of the legal position and accountability of AMHPs in relation to the Act, any employing organisation and the authority on whose behalf they are acting;

(e)   the ability to—
      (i)   evaluate critically local and national policy to inform AMHP practice, and
      (ii)   base AMHP practice on a critical evaluation of a range of research relevant to evidence-based practice, including that on the impact on persons who experience discrimination because of mental health.

(2)   In paragraph (1), "relevant" means relevant to the decisions that an AMHP is likely to take when acting as an AMHP.

Key Competence Area 3: Application of Knowledge: Mental Disorder

3.   Whether the applicant has a critical understanding of, and is able to apply in practice—
    (a)   a range of models of mental disorder, including the contribution of social, physical and development factors;
    (b)   the social perspective on mental disorder and mental health needs, in working with patients, their relatives, carers and other professionals;
    (c)   the implications of mental disorder for patients, their relatives and carers, and
    (d)   the implications of a range of treatments and interventions for patients, their relatives and carers.

Key Competence Area 4: Application of Skills: Working in Partnership

4.   Whether the applicant has the ability to—
    (a)   articulate, and demonstrate in practice, the social perspective on mental disorder and mental health needs;
    (b)   communicate appropriately with and establish effective relationships with patients, relatives, and carers in undertaking the AMHP role;
    (c)   articulate the role of the AMHP in the course of contributing to effective inter-agency and inter-professional working;
    (d)   use networks and community groups to influence collaborative working with a range of individuals, agencies and advocates;
    (e)   consider the feasibility of and contribute effectively to planning and implementing options for care such as alternatives to compulsory admission, discharge and aftercare;
    (f)   recognise, assess and manage risk effectively in the context of the AMHP role;
    (g)   effectively manage difficult situations of anxiety, risk and conflict, and an understanding of how this affects the AMHP and other people concerned with the patient's care;
    (h)   discharge the AMHP role in such a way as to empower the patient as much as practicable;
    (i)   plan, negotiate and manage compulsory admission to hospital or arrangements for supervised community treatment;
    (j)   manage and co-ordinate effectively the relevant legal and practical processes including the involvement of other professionals as well as patients, relatives and carers, and
    (k)   balance and manage the competing requirements of confidentiality and effective information sharing to the benefit of the patient and other persons concerned with the patient's care.

Key Competence Area 5: Application of Skills: Making and Communicating Informed Decisions

5.   Whether the applicant has the ability to—
    (a)   assert a social perspective and to make properly informed independent decisions;
    (b)   obtain, analyse and share appropriate information having due regard to confidentiality in order to manage the decision-making process including decisions about supervised community treatment;
    (c)   compile and complete statutory documentation, including an application for admission;
    (d)   provide reasoned and clear verbal and written reports to promote effective, accountable and independent AMHP decision making;
    (e)   present a case at a legal hearing;
    (f)   exercise the appropriate use of independence, authority and autonomy and use it to inform their future practice as an AMHP, together with consultation and supervision;
    (g)   evaluate the outcomes of interventions with patients, carers and others, including the identification of where a need has not been met;
    (h)   make and communicate decisions that are sensitive to the needs of the individual patient, and

    (i)   keep appropriate records with an awareness of legal requirements with respect to record keeping and the use and transfer of information.

The Mental Health (Hospital, Guardianship and Treatment) (England) Regulations 2008

(SI 2008/1184)

Dated April 28, 2008 and made by the Secretary of State under the Mental Health Act 1983, sections 9, 17F(2), 19(1) and (4), 31(1), (2) and 3, 57(1)(b), 58A(1)(b), 64(2), 64H(2), 134(3A)(a) and 134(8)

General Note

These regulations are the principal regulations dealing with the exercise of powers in respect of persons who are liable to be detained, or subject to a community treatment order or guardianship under the Act. They provide for certain applications, recommendations and records under the Act to be in the form set in the Forms in Sch.1.
    The amendments made to these regulations by SI 2020/1072, which add electronic communication to the permitted methods of service, do not apply in Wales.

2-042

Wales

The Welsh Ministers have made separate regulations in relation to Wales (the "Welsh Regulations"): see the Mental Health (Hospital, Guardianship, Community Treatment and Consent to Treatment) (Wales) Regulations 2008 (SI 2008/2439) (W.212).

2-043

The use of electronic forms

See the notes on Sch.1 under this heading.

2-044

Code of Practice

The receipt and scrutiny of documents is considered in Ch.35.

2-045

PART 1

GENERAL

Citation and commencement
1.—(1)   These Regulations may be cited as the Mental Health (Hospital, Guardianship and Treatment) (England) Regulations 2008 and shall come into force on 3rd November 2008.
    (2)   These Regulations apply to England only.

2-046

Interpretation
2.—(1)   In these Regulations—

    "the Act" means the Mental Health Act 1983;
    "bank holiday" includes New Year's Day, Good Friday, Easter Monday, Christmas Day and Boxing Day;
    "business day" means any day except Saturday, Sunday or a bank holiday;
    "the Commission" means the [Care Quality Commission] referred to in section 121;

2-047

"document" means any application, recommendation, record, report, order, notice or other document;

"electronic communication" has the same meaning as in section 15(1) of the Electronic Communications Act 2000;

"guardianship patient" means a person who is subject to guardianship under the Act;

"private guardian", in relation to a patient, means a person, other than a local social services authority, who acts as guardian under the Act;

"responsible registered establishment" is a registered establishment which is a responsible hospital;

"served", in relation to a document, includes addressed, delivered, given, forwarded, furnished or sent.

(2)　Unless otherwise stated, any reference in these Regulations to—
   (a)　a numbered section is to the section of the Act bearing that number;
   (b)　an alphanumeric form is a reference to the form in Schedule 1 bearing that designation.

Amendment

The amendment to the definition of "the Commission" was made by SI 2009/462 art.12, Sch.5 para.25(a).

Documents

2-048　**3.**—(1)　Except in a case to which paragraph (2), (3), (4) or (5) applies, or in a case to which regulation 6(3) (recall notices in respect of community patients) applies, any document required or authorised to be served upon any authority, body or person by or under Part 2 of the Act (compulsory admission to hospital, guardianship or community treatment orders) or these Regulations may be served by [...]—
   (a)　[delivering it to] the authority, body or person upon whom it is to be served;
   [(b)　sending it by means of electronic communication to the authority, body or person upon whom it is to be served, if that authority, body or person agrees];
   (c)　[...] sending it by pre-paid post addressed to—
      (i)　the authority or body at their registered or principal office; or
      (ii)　the person upon whom it is to be served at that person's usual or last known residence, or
   (d)　[...] delivering it using an internal mail system operated by the authority, body or person upon whom it is to be served, if that authority, body or person agrees.

[(1A)　In paragraphs (1)(a) and (b) references to the authority, body or person upon whom a document is to be served include any person authorised by that authority, body or person to receive it.

(1B)　Paragraph (1)(b) does not apply where the person to whom the document is to be served is—
   (a)　a patient liable to be detained in hospital under Part 2 of the Act,
   (b)　a community patient, or
   (c)　a guardianship patient.]

[(2)　Any application for the admission of a patient to a hospital under Part 2 of the Act shall be served by—

     (a)   delivering the application to an officer of the managers of the hospital to which it is proposed that the patient shall be admitted who is authorised by them to receive it, or

     (b)   sending the application by means of electronic communication to the managers of the hospital to which it is proposed that the patient shall be admitted, whether or not those managers agree.]

(3)   Where a patient is liable to be detained in a hospital under Part 2 of the Act—

     (a)   any order by the nearest relative of the patient under section 23 for the patient's discharge, and

     (b)   the notice of such order given under section 25(1), shall be served either by—

         (i)   delivery of the order or notice at that hospital to an officer of the managers authorised by the managers to receive it, [...]

        (ii)   sending it by pre-paid post to those managers at that hospital, [...]

       (iii)   delivering it using an internal mail system operated by the managers upon whom it is to be served, if those managers agree[, or

       (iv)   sending it by means of electronic communication to the managers at that hospital, if those managers agree.]

(4)   Where a patient is a community patient—

     (a)   any order by the nearest relative of the patient under section 23 for the patient's discharge, and

     (b)   the notice of such order given under section 25(1A), shall be served by—

         (i)   delivery of the order or notice at the patient's responsible hospital to an officer of the managers authorised by the managers to receive it,

        (ii)   sending it by pre-paid post to those managers at that hospital, [...]

       (iii)   delivering it using an internal mail system operated by the managers upon whom it is to be served, if those managers agree, [or,

       (iv)   sending it by means of electronic communication to the managers at the hospital, if those managers agree.]

(5)   Any report made under subsection (2) of section 5 (detention of patient already in hospital for 72 hours) shall be served by—

     (a)   delivery of the report to an officer of the managers of the hospital authorised by those managers to receive it, [...]

     (b)   delivering it using an internal mail system operated by the managers upon whom it is to be served, if those managers agree [, or

     (c)   sending it by means of electronic communication to the managers of the hospital, if those managers agree.]

(6)   Where a document referred to in this regulation is sent by pre-paid—

     (a)   first class post, service is deemed to have taken place on the second business day following the day of posting;

     (b)   second class post, service is deemed to have taken place on the fourth business day following posting,

unless the contrary is shown.

(7)   Where a document under this regulation is delivered using an internal mail system, service is considered to have taken place immediately it is delivered into the internal mail system.

[(7A)

    (a)   Subject to sub-paragraph (b), where a document under this regulation is served by means of electronic communication, service is considered to have taken place immediately after it is sent to the recipient.

    (b)   Where an order or notice referred to in paragraphs (3) or (4) is sent by means of electronic communication, service is considered to have taken place at the beginning of the next business day after the day on which the order or notice was sent.]

[(8)

    (a)   Subject to sections 6(3) and 8(3) (proof of applications), any document—

        (i)   required or authorised by or under Part 2 of the Act or these Regulations, and

       (ii)   purporting to be signed by a person required or authorised by or under that Part or these Regulations to do so,

    shall be received in evidence and be deemed to be such a document without further proof.

    (b)   For the purposes of sub-paragraph (a)—

        (i)   "signed" includes using an electronic signature;

       (ii)   "electronic signature" has the same meaning as in section 7(2) of the Electronic Communications Act 2000.]

(9)   Where under Part 2 of the Act or these Regulations the managers of a hospital are required to make any record or report, that function may be performed by an officer authorised by those managers in that behalf.

[(9A)   Where under these Regulations a document may be served on hospital managers by means of electronic communication, that document may also be served on an officer of the managers of the hospital authorised by those managers to receive it.]

(10)   Where under these Regulations the decision to accept service by a particular method requires the agreement of the managers of a hospital, that agreement may be given by an officer authorised by those managers in that behalf.

Amendments

The amendments to this rule were made by SI 2020/1072, reg.2.

Definitions

2-049   document: reg.2(1).
served: reg.2(1).
the Act: reg.2(1).

General Note

2-050   The regulation sets out rules on how documents required under the Act are to be served.

Paragraph (1)

2-051   **Prepaid post**   See para.(6). If a notice of recall to hospital is sent to the patient's last known residence, he becomes absent without leave if there is a failure to respond to the notice.

Internal mail system   See para.(7).

Paragraph (1B)

This paragraph creates an exception to the general rule that documents may be served electronically. It provides that documents may not be served by means of electronic communication alone on patients liable to be detained in hospital, or patients subject to guardianship or community treatment orders.

2-052

Paragraph (2)

This paragraph allows for detention applications to be sent to hospital managers electronically, whether or not the managers agree.

2-053

Served The application documents cannot be served by post.

Officer In *R. (on the application of PD) v West Midlands and North West Mental Health Review Tribunal* [2004] EWCA Civ 311; [2004] M.H.L.R. 174, the Court of Appeal held that the meaning of "officer" will depend upon the context in which it is used, and that in the context of a tribunal hearing an "officer" means a person holding office and taking part in the management of the authority that is detaining the patient. It is submitted that in the context of these regulations, which are largely concerned with process issues rather than decision making, the meaning of "officer" should be extended to embrace an "employee". Paragraph 35.7 of the Code of Practice states:

> "Hospital managers should formally delegate their duties to receive and scrutinise admission documents to a limited number of officers, who may include clinical staff on wards. Someone with the authority to receive admission documents should be available at all times at which patients may be admitted to the hospital. A manager of appropriate seniority should take overall responsibility on behalf of the hospital managers for the proper receipt and scrutiny of documents."

Paragraph (3)(b)(i)

Any challenge as to whether a nearest relative's notice of discharge under s.25(1) was properly served must be made to the High Court on an application for judicial review. As a creature of statute, the First-tier Tribunal (Mental Health) has no jurisdiction in the matter.

2-054

Served Also see r.25(2). In *Re GK (Patient: Habeas Corpus)* [1999] M.H.L.R. 128, the nearest relative of a patient who had been admitted to hospital under s.3 handed a letter to the ward receptionist requesting the patient's discharge. This took place on May 27. The nearest relative was told that the letter would be handed to the appropriate person, namely the Mental Health Act administrator. The letter was received by the administrator on June 3. On that day, as no barring report under s.25 had been issued, the nearest relative arrived on the ward, seeking the discharge of the patient. A barring report was then made. In rejecting an application for habeas corpus, the court held that the purpose of this provision was to ensure that an order for discharge came to the notice of the proper authorised person without delay. That being the case, the handing of the letter to the ward receptionist did not satisfy that requirement and was not good delivery. The notice was served when the letter was received by the administrator on June 3.

In *K v Hospital Managers of the Kingswood Centre* [2014] EWCA Civ 1332; [2015] M.H.L.R. 75, the letter requesting discharge was faxed to the hospital by the patient's solicitor and then put into the in-tray of the authorised person who worked part-time and did not return to her desk for four days (including the weekend). The Court of Appeal, on finding that the legislative scheme had been correctly applied in *Re GK*, held that the method of delivery used by the solicitor was not prescribed by this regulation. The court agreed with the following submission made on behalf of the hospital:

> "A hospital can be expected to put in place systems to deal with methods of delivery that are prescribed. That is not the circumstance here. It is submitted that they should not be expected to provide for a non-prescribed method of delivery. Delivery to a general fax number is not a prescribed form of service, the deeming provisions do not apply to it and the default prescribed method of delivery then governs service so that it is not until the authorised officer has the order delivered to her that time begins to run" (para.15).

It was therefore the case that the 72 hour notice period did not start to run from the time when the discharge order was received at the hospital's fax machine; it started to run from the time when it was received by the officer authorised by the hospital managers. The court said that non-prescribed methods of service "might include e-mail and social networking, both of which, like attempted fax service, are regularly excluded from commercial methods of service because in the context of the purpose to be served, the risk of non-delivery is too great" (para.19).

Authorised by the managers to receive it Under the appropriate scheme of delegation.

Paragraph (7A)

2-055 This paragraph provides that documents sent electronically are considered served immediately after they have been sent. This is the case except for discharge orders or notices sent by nearest relatives, which are considered served at the beginning of the next business day after the day on which they are sent.

Paragraph (8)

2-056 **Electronic signature** *"Guidance on the electronic communication of statutory forms under the Mental Health Act"*, DHSC, 2021, para.4 states:

"Electronic signatures on forms have the same meaning as in section 7(2) of the Electronic Communications Act 2000. This states that an electronic signature is 'so much of anything in electronic form as is incorporated into or otherwise logically associated with any electronic communication or electronic data; and purports to be used by the individual creating it to sign'. As such, electronic signatures on electronically submitted statutory forms may be a typed name or initials, a scan or photo of a wet ink signature, or an electronically drawn signature, among other options meeting the definition specified above."

Purporting to be signed The term "purporting" refers to the identity of the signatory rather than the nature of the signature.

Without further proof The officer checking the document may take certain statements at face value. For example, there is no need to check that the doctor who states that she is a registered medical practitioner is so registered, or that the mental health professional who states that she is an approved mental health practitioner has been approved under s.114.

Paragraphs (9), (10)

2-057 **Officer authorised** See the note on "officer" in para.2, above.

PART 2

PROCEDURES AND RECORDS RELATING TO HOSPITAL ADMISSIONS, GUARDIANSHIP AND COMMUNITY TREATMENT ORDERS

Procedure for and record of hospital admissions
2-058 **4.**—(1) Subject to paragraph (2), for the purposes of admission to hospital under Part 2 of the Act—
    (a) any application for admission for assessment under section 2 shall be in the form set out—
        (i) where made by the nearest relative, in Form A1,
        (ii) where made by an approved mental health professional, in Form A2;
    (b) any medical recommendation for the purposes of section 2 shall be in the form set out—
        (i) in the case of joint recommendations, in Form A3,
        (ii) in any other case, in Form A4;

    (c)   any application for admission for treatment under section 3 shall be in the form set out—

        (i)   where made by the nearest relative, in Form A5,

       (ii)   where made by an approved mental health professional, in Form A6;

    (d)   any medical recommendation for the purposes of section 3 shall be in the form set out—

        (i)   in the case of joint recommendations, in Form A7,

       (ii)   in any other case, in Form A8;

    (e)   any emergency application under section 4 shall be in the form set out—

        (i)   where made by the nearest relative, in Form A9,

       (ii)   where made by an approved mental health professional, in Form A10;

    (f)   any medical recommendation for the purposes of section 4 shall be in the form set out in Form A11;

    (g)   any report made under subsection (2) of section 5 (detention of in-patient already in hospital for a maximum 72 hours) by—

        (i)   the registered medical practitioner or approved clinician in charge of the treatment of the patient, or

       (ii)   any person nominated by the registered medical practitioner or approved clinician to act for them,

    shall be in the form set out in Part 1 of Form H1 and the hospital managers shall record receipt of that report in Part 2 of that Form;

    (h)   any record made under subsection (4) of section 5 (power to detain an in-patient for a maximum of 6 hours) by a nurse of the class for the time being prescribed for the purposes of that subsection shall be in the form set out in Form H2.

  (2)   For the purposes of any medical recommendation under sections 2, 3, 4 and 7 (admission for assessment, admission for treatment, admission for assessment in cases of emergency and application for guardianship respectively) in the case of—

    (a)   a single recommendation made in respect of a patient whom a doctor has examined in Wales, the medical recommendation shall be in the form required by Regulations made by the Welsh Ministers to similar effect for Wales;

    (b)   joint recommendations made in respect of a patient whom both doctors have examined in Wales, the medical recommendation shall be in the form required by Regulations made by the Welsh Ministers to similar effect for Wales;

    (c)   joint recommendations made in respect of a patient whom one doctor has examined in Wales and one doctor has examined in England, the medical recommendation shall either be in the form required by these Regulations or in the form required by Regulations made by the Welsh Ministers to similar effect for Wales.

  (3)   For the purposes of section 15 (rectification of applications and recommendations), the managers of the hospital to which a patient has been admitted in pursuance of an application for assessment or for treatment may authorise an officer on their behalf—

    (a)   to consent under subsection (1) of that section to the amendment of the application or any medical recommendation given for the purposes of the application;

    (b)   to consider the sufficiency of a medical recommendation and, if the recommendation is considered insufficient, to give written notice as required by subsection (2) of that section.

(4)   Where a patient has been admitted to a hospital pursuant to an application under section 2, 3 or 4 (admission for assessment, admission for treatment and admission for assessment in cases of emergency respectively), a record of admission shall be made by the managers of that hospital in the form set out in Part 1 of Form H3 and shall be attached to the application.

(5)   Where a patient has been admitted to a hospital pursuant to an application under section 4 (admission for assessment in cases of emergency), a record of receipt of a second medical recommendation in support of the application for admission of the patient shall be made by the managers in the form set out in Part 2 of Form H3 and shall be attached to the application.

Definition

2-059   the Act: reg.2(1).

General Note

Paragraph (1)

Shall be in the form set out

2-060   See the General Note to Sch.1.

Paragraph (2)

2-061   This paragraph sets out when the equivalent Welsh forms are to be used for medical recommendations for patients who have been examined by doctors in Wales. If patients who are admitted to hospitals in Wales are medically examined in England, the medical recommendation forms set out in these Regulations must be used: see reg.(4)(4) of the Welsh Regulations. The application to the Welsh hospital will be made using a Welsh application form: see reg.(4)(1) of the Welsh Regulations and para.8.64 of the Reference Guide.

Paragraph (3)

2-062   **An officer**   See the note on reg.3(2). This officer is unlikely to be the person who records the patient's admission for the purposes of reg.4(4). The scrutiny of documents for the purposes of possible rectification "should happen at the same time as the documents are received or as soon as possible afterwards (and certainly no later than the next working day)" (Code of Practice, para.35.11). Also see the notes to s.6(3).

Paragraph (4)

2-063   The patient is "admitted" at the time when he arrives at the hospital and either the application for detention is handed to an authorised person or it is sent to the hospital managers electronically (reg.3(2)). The time and date of the admission should by recorded on Form H3, which is an administrative record and does not provide authority for the detention: see below.

Form H3   If an application has been "duly completed" for the purposes of s.6(1), a failure to comply with the requirement to complete this form would not invalidate the detention of a patient made pursuant to an application because the application is "sufficient authority" to detain the patient (s.6(2)). The form should be completed retrospectively on the omission being discovered.

Procedure for and acceptance of guardianship applications

5.—(1) For the purposes of section 7 (application for guardianship)— **2-064**
    (a) an application for guardianship shall be in the form set out—
        (i) where made by the nearest relative, in Part 1 of Form G1,
        (ii) where made by an approved mental health professional, in Part 1 of Form G2;
    (b) where a person other than a local social services authority is named as guardian, the statement of willingness of that person to act as guardian shall be in the form set out in Part 2 of Form G1 or, as the case may be, G2;
    (c) any medical recommendation shall be in the form set out—
        (i) in the case of joint recommendations, in Form G3,
        (ii) in any other case, in Form G4.

(2) Where an application for guardianship is accepted by the responsible local social services authority, it shall record its acceptance of the application in the form set out in Form G5 (which shall be attached to the application).

Procedure for and records relating to community treatment orders

6.—(1) For the purposes of section 17A (community treatment orders)— **2-065**
    (a) an order made by the responsible clinician shall be in the form set out in Parts 1 and 3 of Form CTO1;
    (b) the agreement of the approved mental health professional shall be in the form set out in Part 2 of Form CTO1;
    (c) as soon as reasonably practicable, the responsible clinician shall furnish the managers of the responsible hospital with that order.

(2) For the purposes of section 17B (conditions in community treatment orders)—
    (a) the conditions to which the patient is subject whilst the order remains in force shall be in the form set out in Form CTO1;
    (b) a variation of any of those conditions by the responsible clinician shall be in the form set out in Form CTO2;
    (c) as soon as reasonably practicable, the responsible clinician shall furnish the managers of the responsible hospital with Form CTO2.

(3) For the purposes of section 17E (power to recall a community patient to hospital)—
    (a) a responsible clinician's notice recalling a patient to hospital shall be in the form set out in Form CTO3;
    (b) as soon as reasonably practicable, the responsible clinician shall furnish the managers of the hospital to which the patient is recalled with a copy of the notice recalling the patient to hospital;
    (c) where the patient is recalled to a hospital which is not the responsible hospital, the responsible clinician shall notify the managers of the hospital to which the patient is recalled in writing of the name and address of the responsible hospital;
    (d) the managers of the hospital to which the patient is recalled shall record the time and date of the patient's detention pursuant to that notice in the form set out in Form CTO4.

(4)   Where the patient's responsible hospital is in Wales, the patient's recall shall be effected in accordance with Regulations made by the Welsh Ministers to similar effect for Wales.

(5)   A responsible clinician's notice recalling a patient to hospital for the purposes of section 17E (power to recall a community patient to hospital) in Form CTO3 shall be served by—

    (a)   delivering it by hand to the patient,

    (b)   delivering it by hand to the patient's usual or last known address, or

    (c)   sending it by pre-paid first class post addressed to the patient at the patient's usual or last known address.

(6)   Notice of recall in Form CTO3 is considered served—

    (a)   in the case of sub-paragraph 5(a), immediately on delivery of the notice to the patient;

    (b)   in the case of sub-paragraph 5(b), on the day (which does not have to be a business day) after it is delivered;

    (c)   in the case of sub-paragraph 5(c), on the second business day after it was posted.

(7)   As soon as practicable following the patient's recall, the managers of the responsible hospital shall take such steps as are reasonably practicable to—

    (a)   cause the patient to be informed, both orally and in writing, of the provisions of the Act under which the patient is for the time being detained and the effect of those provisions, and

    (b)   ensure that the patient understands the effect, so far as is relevant to the patient's case, of sections 56 to 64 (consent to treatment).

(8)   For the purposes of section 17F (powers in respect of recalled patients)—

    (a)   an order referred to in subsection (4) (responsible clinician's order revoking a community treatment order) shall be in the form set out in Parts 1 and 3 of Form CTO5;

    (b)   a statement of an approved mental health professional referred to in that subsection (signifying agreement with the responsible clinician's opinion and that it is appropriate to revoke the order) shall be in the form set out in Part 2 of Form CTO5;

    (c)   as soon as practicable, the responsible clinician shall furnish the managers of the hospital to which the patient is recalled with that Form;

    (d)   where the patient is recalled to a hospital which is not the responsible hospital, the managers of that hospital shall (as soon as reasonably practicable) furnish the managers of the hospital which was the patient's responsible hospital prior to the revocation of the patient's community treatment order, with a copy of Form CTO5.

Definition

2-066   the Act: reg.2(1).
       served: reg.2(1).

General Note

Paragraph (4)

Where a community patient's responsible hospital is in Wales, the patient's recall to hospital is be   **2-067**
effected in accordance with the Welsh Regulations and the appropriate Welsh form (Form CP5) should
be used (even if the patient is to be recalled to a hospital in England).

Paragraph (7)

This is similar to the duty that hospital managers have under s.132 of the Act in respect of detained   **2-068**
patients as patients recalled from a community treatment order do not count as detained patients for the
purposes of s.132.

Transfer from hospital to hospital or guardianship

7.—(1)   This regulation shall apply in respect of any patient ("a hospital   **2-069**
patient") to whom section 19(1)(a) applies and who is not a patient transferred
under—

   (a)   section 19(3) (transfer between hospitals under the same managers), or
   (b)   section 123(1) and (2) (transfers between and from special hospitals).
   (2)   A hospital patient may be transferred to another hospital where—
   (a)   an authority for transfer is given by the managers of the hospital in
         which the patient is liable to be detained in the form set out in Part 1
         of Form H4, and
   (b)   those managers are satisfied that arrangements have been made for the
         admission of the patient to the hospital to which the patient is being
         transferred within a period of 28 days beginning with the date of the
         authority for transfer.
   (3)   Upon completion of the transfer of the patient, the managers of the hospital
to which the patient is transferred shall record the patient's admission in the form
set out in Part 2 of Form H4.
   (4)   A hospital patient may be transferred into the guardianship of a local social
services authority, or a person approved by a local social services authority, where—
   (a)   an authority for transfer is given by the managers of the hospital in
         which the patient is detained in the form set out in Part 1 of Form G6;
   (b)   the transfer has been agreed by the local social services authority,
         which will be the responsible local social services authority if the
         proposed transfer takes effect;
   (c)   that local social services authority has specified the date on which the
         transfer shall take place;
   (d)   the managers of the transferring hospital have recorded the agree-
         ment of the local social services authority referred to in paragraph (b)
         and the date for transfer referred to in paragraph (c), in the form set out
         in Part 1 of that Form;
   (e)   in the case of a person other than a local social services authority be-
         ing named as guardian, the agreement of that person to act as guard-
         ian is recorded in the form set out in Part 2 of that Form.
   (5)   A hospital patient who is detained in a registered establishment—
   (a)   may be transferred from that registered establishment to another
         registered establishment where both are under the same management,
         and paragraph (2) shall not apply, and

(b) where such a patient is maintained under a contract with [an integrated care board], a Local Health Board, [...], National Health Service trust, National Health Service foundation trust, a Special Health Authority [, NHS England] or the Welsh Ministers, any authority for transfer required under paragraph (2)(a) or, as the case may be, (4)(a), and the record (where relevant) required under paragraph (4)(d), may be made or given by an officer of that [body] authorised by that [body], board or trust in that behalf, or by those Ministers, instead of by the managers.

(6) The functions of the managers referred to in this regulation may be performed by an officer authorised by them in that behalf.

Amendments

The amendments to this regulation were made by SI 2013/235 art.11, Sch.2 para.117, SI 2022/634 reg.34(2), Sch.1 and the Health and Care Act 2022 Sch.1 para.1(3).

General Note

2-070   See reg.10 for transfers between Wales and England.

Paragraph (2)

2-071   The conveyance of a patient who is transferred to another hospital is governed by reg.11.

Transferred to another hospital   There must be a physical transfer of the patient within the 28 day period allowed for in para.(b).

Paragraph (4)(c)

2-072   **Date on which the transfer takes place**   The patient could be granted leave of absence under s.17 to take up residence in the place where he will be required to reside before that date.

Paragraph 5(d)

2-073   The effect of this provision is explained in the Reference Guide:

"10.13 If an NHS patient is detained in an independent hospital, an authorisation to transfer the patient to a hospital under different managers, but not the same managers, may also be given by an officer of the relevant NHS body who has been authorised by that body to do so.

10.14 In other words, the relevant NHS body can authorise the patient's transfer without the agreement of the managers of the independent hospital. For restricted patients, the agreement of the Secretary of State for Justice is still required."

Paragraph (6)

2-074   **Officer**   See the note on reg.3(2).

Transfer from guardianship to guardianship or hospital

2-075   **8.**—(1) A guardianship patient may be transferred into the guardianship of another local social services authority or person where—

(a) an authority for transfer is given by the guardian in the form set out in Part 1 of Form G7;

    (b)   that transfer has been agreed by the receiving local social services authority, which will be the responsible local social services authority if the proposed transfer takes effect;

    (c)   that local social services authority has specified the date on which the transfer shall take place;

    (d)   the guardian has recorded the agreement of the receiving local social services authority mentioned in paragraph (b) and the date for transfer mentioned in paragraph (c) in Part 1 of that Form;

    (e)   a person other than a local social services authority is named in the authority for transfer as proposed guardian, the statement of willingness of that person to act as guardian is recorded in the form set out in Part 2 of that Form.

(2)   An authority for transfer to hospital of a guardianship patient may be given by the responsible local social services authority in the form set out in Part 1 of Form G8 where—

    (a)   an application for admission for treatment has been made by an approved mental health professional in the form set out in Form A6;

    (b)   that application is founded on medical recommendations given by two registered medical practitioners in accordance with section 12 in the form set out—

        (i)   in the case of joint recommendations, in Form A7;

        (ii)   in any other case, in Form A8;

    (c)   the responsible local social services authority is satisfied that arrangements have been made for the admission of the patient to that hospital within the period of 14 days beginning with the date on which the patient was last examined by a registered medical practitioner for the purposes of paragraph (b).

(3)   Where paragraph (2)(a) applies, for the purposes of the application referred to in that paragraph, sections 11(4) (consultation with nearest relative) and 13 (duty of approved mental health professional) shall apply as if the proposed transfer were an application for admission for treatment.

(4)   On the transfer of a guardianship patient referred to in paragraph (2), a record of admission shall be made by the managers of the hospital to which the patient is transferred in the form set out in Part 2 of Form G8 and shall be attached to the application referred to in paragraph (2)(a).

(5)   Where the conditions of paragraph (2) are satisfied, the transfer of the patient must be effected within 14 days of the date on which the patient was last examined, failing which the patient will remain subject to guardianship.

(6)   The functions of the managers referred to in this regulation may be performed by an officer authorised by them in that behalf.

Definition

guardianship patient: reg.2(1).   **2-076**

General Note

A patient who has been transferred from guardianship to hospital has a right to apply to a tribunal within six months of the day of the transfer (s.66(1)(e), (2)(e)). If the patient does not exercise this right, the hospital managers must automatically refer the case to the tribunal (s.68(1)).   **2-077**

Paragraph (1)(e)

2-078   Person other than a local social services authority. Who, after the transfer has been completed, must appoint a doctor to act as the nominated medical attendant of the patient and send relevant details to the local social services authority (reg.22).

Paragraph (2)

2-079   The provisions of s.15 of the Act concerning the rectification of applications and medical recommendations do not apply to documents given in support of a transfer. The application and recommendations should therefore be scrutinised carefully to ensure that they comply with legislative requirements before the authority for transfer is signed. Minor errors can be corrected without affecting the validity of the transfer.

The patient must be admitted to the hospital within 14 days beginning with the date of the latter of the two medical examinations on which the medical recommendations are based (reg.11(1)(b)).

Paragraph (6)

2-080   **Officer**   See the note on reg.3(2).

Transfer of community patients recalled to hospital

2-081   **9.**—(1)   The managers of a hospital in which a community patient is detained, having been recalled to hospital, may authorise the transfer of that patient to another hospital.

(2)   Where the hospital to which the patient has been recalled and the hospital to which the patient is being transferred are not under the same management, a transfer may only take place if the requirements of paragraphs (3) to (5) are satisfied.

(3)   Those requirements are that the managers of the hospital to which the patient was recalled—

   (a)   authorise the transfer of the patient in the form set out in Part 1 of Form CTO6, and

   (b)   are satisfied that arrangements have been made for the admission of the patient to the hospital to which the patient is being transferred.

(4)   The managers of the hospital from which the patient is being transferred shall furnish the managers of the hospital to which the patient is being transferred with a copy of Form CTO4 (record of patient's detention in hospital after recall) before, or at the time of, the patient's transfer.

(5)   On the transfer of the patient, the managers of the hospital to which the patient is transferred shall record the patient's admission in the form set out in Part 2 of Form CTO6.

(6)   Where—

   (a)   a patient has been recalled to a registered establishment, and

   (b)   that patient is maintained under a contract with [an integrated care board,] Local Health Board, [...], National Health Service trust, National Health Service foundation trust, a Special Health Authority [, NHS England] or the Welsh Ministers,

any authority for transfer required under paragraph (3)(a) may be given by an officer of that [body] authorised by that [body] in that behalf, or by those Ministers, instead of the managers.

(7)   The functions of the managers referred to in this regulation may be performed by an officer authorised by them in that behalf.

Amendments

The amendments to this regulation were made by SI 2013/235 art.11, Sch.2 para.117, SI 2022/634 reg.34(3), Sch.1 and the Health and Care Act 2022 Sch.1 para.1(3).

General Note

This regulation allows community patients who have been recalled to one hospital to be transferred **2-082** to another, provided this is done within the 72-hour maximum period allowed for a patient to be detained following recall: see s.17F(6). The requirements are similar to those for the transfer of detained patients between hospitals under reg.7. In particular, no statutory form is required when managers authorise the transfer of a patient between hospitals which are both under their own management. The conveyance of a patient who is transferred under this provision is governed by reg.12. Assignment of responsibility for community patients between one hospital and another is dealt with in reg.17. For the responsibility to inform the patient's nearest relative of the assignment, see reg.26(1)(h) (reg.32(b) of the Welsh Regulations).

If a recalled patient is to be transferred from a hospital in Wales to one in England, the transfer must be authorised and recorded in accordance with the Welsh Regulations. Transfers from England to Wales are to be made in accordance with these regulations.

Paragraph (7)

Officer   See the note on reg.3(2).   **2-083**

Transfers from England to Wales and from Wales to England

10.—(1)   Where a patient who is liable to be detained or is subject to guardian- **2-084** ship under the Act is transferred from a hospital or guardianship in England to a hospital or guardianship in Wales, that transfer shall be subject to the conditions in these Regulations.

(2)   Where a patient who is liable to be detained or is subject to guardianship under the Act is transferred from a hospital or guardianship in Wales to a hospital or guardianship in England, that transfer and the duty to record the admission of a patient so transferred shall be subject to such conditions as may be prescribed in Regulations made by the Welsh Ministers to similar effect for Wales.

(3)   Where paragraph (2) applies and any Regulations made by the Welsh Ministers to similar effect for Wales provide for authority to convey a patient in Wales, those Regulations shall provide authority to convey the patient whilst in England.

General Note

This regulation deals with transfers of detained and guardianship patients between England and **2-085** Wales. Its main effect is that, if a patient is to be transferred from Wales to England, the procedure in the Welsh Regulations is to be followed.

Conveyance to hospital on transfer from hospital or guardianship

11.—(1)   Where the conditions of regulation 7(2) or 8(2) are satisfied, the **2-086** authority for transfer given in accordance with those regulations shall be suf- ficient authority for the following persons to take the patient and convey the patient to the hospital to which the patient is being transferred within the periods speci- fied—

    (a)   in a case to which regulation 7(2) applies—

        (i)   an officer of the managers of either hospital, or

> (ii) any person authorised by the managers of the hospital to which the patient is being transferred,

within the period of 28 days beginning with the date of the authority for transfer;

> (b) in a case to which regulation 8(2) applies—
>> (i) an officer of, or
>> (ii) any person authorised by,

the responsible local social services authority, within the period of 14 days beginning with the date on which the patient was last examined by a medical practitioner for the purposes of regulation 8(2)(b).

> (2) Paragraph (1) shall apply to a patient who—
>> (a) is liable to be detained under the Act and is removed to another hospital in circumstances to which section 19(3) applies, as if the authority given by the managers for that transfer were an authority for transfer given in accordance with regulation 7(2);
>> (b) is liable to be detained in a hospital at which high security psychiatric services are provided and who, pursuant to a direction given by the Secretary of State under section 123(1) or (2) (transfers to and from special hospitals), is removed or transferred to another hospital, as if that direction were an authority for transfer given in accordance with regulation 7(2).

> (3) In a case to which regulation 7(5)(a) applies, an officer of or any other person authorised by the managers of the registered establishment may take and convey the patient to the registered establishment to which the patient is being transferred.

General Note

2-087   Paragraph 10.19 of the Reference Guide states:

> "In all cases [of patients being conveyed to hospital], patients are deemed to be in legal custody while being conveyed, which means that the person conveying them can take steps to stop them absconding, and retake them if they do ....If they abscond while being transferred, they are also treated as if they were absent without leave (AWOL) from both hospitals—which affects who may take them into custody and allows them to be returned to either hospital ... ."

Conveyance from hospital to hospital following recall of community patients

2-088   **12.** Where the conditions of regulation 9(1) or (3) are satisfied, the authority for transfer given in accordance with that regulation shall be sufficient authority for the following persons to take the patient and convey him to the hospital to which he is being transferred—

> (a) an officer of the managers of either hospital, or
> (b) any person authorised by the managers of the hospital to which the patient is being transferred,

within the period of 72 hours beginning with the time of the patient's detention pursuant to the patient's recall under section 17E (power to recall to hospital).

Renewal of authority for detention or guardianship and extension of community treatment period

2-089   **13.**—(1) Any report for the purposes of section 20(3) (medical recommendation for renewal of authority to detain) shall be in the form set out in Parts 1 and 3 of Form H5.

(2)   The statement for the purposes of section 20(5A) (agreement with medical recommendation for renewal of authority to detain) shall be in the form set out in Part 2 of Form H5.

(3)   The receipt of Form H5 shall be recorded by the managers of the hospital in which the patient is liable to be detained in the form set out in Part 4 of that Form.

(4)   Any report for the purposes of section 20(8) (medical recommendation for renewal of guardianship) shall be in the form set out in Part 1 of Form G9.

(5)   The responsible social services authority shall record receipt of Form G9 in the form set out in Part 2 of that Form.

(6)   For the purposes of section 20A (community treatment period)—

- (a)   a report for the purposes of subsection (4) of that section (responsible clinician's report extending the community treatment period) shall be in the form set out in Parts 1 and 3 of Form CTO7;
- (b)   a statement for the purposes of subsection (8) of that section (approved mental health professional's statement that it is appropriate to extend the order) shall be in the form set out in Part 2 of Form CTO7.

(7)   The managers of the responsible hospital shall record the receipt of Form CTO7 in the form set out in Part 4 of that Form.

Detention, guardianship or community treatment after absence without leave for more than 28 days

14.—(1)   In relation to a patient who is liable to be detained—   **2-090**

- (a)   any report for the purposes of section 21B(2) (authority for detention or guardianship of patients who are taken into custody or return after more than 28 days) shall be in the form set out in Part 1 of Form H6, and
- (b)   the receipt of that report shall be recorded by the managers of the hospital in which the patient is liable to be detained in the form set out in Part 2 of that Form.

(2)   In relation to a patient who is subject to guardianship—

- (a)   any report for the purposes of section 21B(2) shall be in the form set out in Part 1 of Form G10, and
- (b)   the receipt of that report shall be recorded by the responsible local social services authority in the form set out in Part 2 of that Form.

(3)   In relation to a community patient—

- (a)   any report for the purposes of section 21B(2) shall be in the form set out in Part 1 of Form CTO8, and
- (b)   the receipt of that report shall be recorded by the managers of the responsible hospital in the form set out in Part 2 of that Form.

Removal to England

15.—(1)   This regulation shall apply to a patient who is removed from Scotland,   **2-091**
Northern Ireland, any of the Channel Islands or the Isle of Man to England ("a removed patient") under—

- (a)   section 82, 84 or 85 (as the case may be), or
- (b)   regulations made under section 290 of the Mental Health (Care and Treatment) (Scotland) Act 2003 (removal and return of patients within United Kingdom).

(2)   Where a removed patient is liable to be detained in a hospital, the managers of the hospital shall record the date on which the patient is admitted to the hospital in the form set out in Form M1.

(3)   The managers of the hospital shall take such steps as are reasonably practicable to inform the person (if any) appearing to them to be the patient's nearest relative as soon as practicable of the patient's admission to hospital.

(4)   Where a removed patient is received into guardianship—

    (a)   the guardian shall record the date on which the patient arrives at the place at which the patient is to reside on the patient's reception into guardianship under the Act in the form set out in Form M 1;

    (b)   the guardian shall take such steps as are reasonably practicable to inform the person (if any) appearing to them to be the patient's nearest relative as soon as practicable that the patient has been received into guardianship under the Act;

    (c)   a private guardian shall notify the responsible local social services authority of the—

        (i)   date mentioned in sub-paragraph (a), and

        (ii)   particulars mentioned in regulation 22(1)(b) and (e).

Definition

2-092   private guardian: reg.2(1).

General Note

2-093   This regulation deals with the statutory forms to be used to record the arrival in England of detained and guardianship patients from Scotland, Northern Ireland, and any of the Channel Islands or the Isle of Man.

Paragraphs (3),(4)(b)

2-094   **Such steps as are reasonably practicable**   Paragraph 4.36 of the *Code of Practice* states:

"In addition, occasionally there will be cases where these duties do not apply because disclosing information about the patient to the nearest relative cannot be considered practicable, on the grounds that it would have a detrimental impact on the patient that is disproportionate to any advantage to be gained from informing the nearest relative. This would therefore be a breach of the patient's right to privacy under article 8 of the European Convention on Human Rights (ECHR). The risk of this is greatest where the nearest relative is someone whom the patient would not have chosen themselves. Before disclosing information to nearest relatives without a patient's consent, the person concerned must consider whether the disclosure would be likely to:

- put the patient at risk of physical harm or financial or other exploitation
- cause the patient emotional distress or lead to a deterioration in their mental health, or
- have any other detrimental effect on their health or wellbeing and, if so, whether the advantages to the patient and the public interest of the disclosure outweigh the disadvantages to the patient, in the light of all the circumstances of the case."

Removal to England of patients subject to compulsion in the community

2-095   **16.**—(1)   This regulation shall apply to a patient who is removed from Scotland, any of the Channel Islands or the Isle of Man to England under—

    (a)   section 289(1) of the Mental Health (Care and Treatment) (Scotland) Act 2003 (crossborder transfer: patients subject to requirement other than detention) in the case of Scotland; or

(b) section 85ZA (responsibility for community patients transferred from any of the Channel Islands or the Isle of Man) in the case of any of the Channel Islands or the Isle of Man.

(2) The managers of the responsible hospital shall record the date on which the patient arrived at the place where the patient is to reside in the form set out in Form M1.

(3) The managers of the hospital shall take such steps as are reasonably practicable to inform the person (if any) appearing to them to be the patient's nearest relative as soon as practicable that the patient is a community patient.

(4) The conditions specified by the responsible clinician under section 80C(5) (removal of patients subject to compulsion in the community from Scotland) or section 85ZA(4), shall be recorded by that responsible clinician in Part 1 of Form CTO9.

(5) The approved mental health professional's agreement to the conditions referred to in paragraph (4) shall be recorded by that approved mental health professional in Part 2 of Form CTO9.

General Note

This regulation deals with the reception of patients in England or Wales as community patients on their transfer from Scotland, any of the Channel Islands or the Isle of Man.   2-096

Paragraph (3)

See the note on reg.15(3), (4)(b) above.   2-097

Assignment of responsibility for community patients

17.—(1) This regulation applies to a community patient whether or not the patient has been recalled to hospital in accordance with section 17E (power to recall to hospital).   2-098

(2) Responsibility for a patient referred to in paragraph (1) may be assigned by the managers of the responsible hospital to any other hospital whether or not that other hospital is under the same management as the responsible hospital.

(3) Responsibility for a patient shall not be assigned to a hospital which is not under the same management as the responsible hospital unless—

(a) an authority for the assignment is given by the managers of the assigning responsible hospital in the form set out in […] Form CTO10;

(b) that [assignment] has been agreed by the managers of the hospital which will be the responsible hospital if the proposed [assignment] takes effect;

(c) the managers of the hospital referred to in (b) have specified the date on which the [assignment] shall take place;

(d) the managers of the assigning responsible hospital record—
(i) the agreement of the managers of the new responsible hospital to the assignment, and
(ii) the date on which the assignment is to take place,

in the form set out in that Form.

(4) The managers of the receiving hospital must notify the patient in writing of—

(a)   the assignment, either before it takes place or as soon as reasonably practicable thereafter; and

(b)   their name and address (irrespective of whether or not there are any changes in the managers).

(5)   Where responsibility for a patient is assigned from a responsible registered establishment to another hospital which is not under the same management and the patient is maintained under a contract with [an integrated care board,] Local Health Board, [...], National Health Service trust, National Health Service foundation trust, a Special Health Authority [, NHS England] or the Welsh Ministers, any authority for [assignment] required under paragraph (3)(a), and the record required under paragraph (3)(b), may be given by an officer of that [body] authorised by it in that behalf, or by those Ministers, instead of by the managers.

(6)   Any hospital to which a patient has been assigned may, in accordance with the provisions of this regulation, assign the patient to another hospital.

(7)   The functions of the managers referred to in this regulation may be performed by an officer authorised by them in that behalf.

Amendments

The amendments to this regulation were made by SI 2008/2560 reg.2(2), SI 2013/235 art.11, Sch.2 para.117, SI 2022/634 reg.34(4), Sch.1 and the Health and Care Act 2022 Sch.1 para.1(3).

General Note

2-099   This regulation sets out the procedure to be followed to authorise the reassignment of responsibility for a community patient from one hospital to another. No statutory form is required when managers authorise the transfer of responsibility for the patient between hospitals which are both under their management.

If responsibility is to be assigned from a hospital in Wales to one in England, the assignment must be made in accordance with the Welsh Regulations. This regulation should be followed for assignments from England to Wales.

Paragraph (5)

2-100   Paragraph 26.133 of the Reference Guide states:

"If an independent hospital is the responsible hospital for an NHS patient, an officer authorised by the relevant NHS body may also authorise the patient's transfer to another hospital under different management. The relevant NHS body is the one which has contracted with the independent hospital to act as the responsible hospital."

Paragraph (7)

2-101   **Officer**   See the note on reg.3(2).

Discharge of patients

2-102   **18.**   For the purposes of section 23 (discharge of patients) a responsible clinician's order for the discharge of—

(a)   a patient liable to be detained under the Act, or a community patient, shall be sent to the managers of the hospital in which the patient is liable to be detained or the responsible hospital (as applicable) as soon as practicable after it is made;

(b)   a guardianship patient, shall be sent to the guardian as soon as practicable after it is made.

Definition

guardianship patient: reg.2(1).   **2-103**

General Note

This regulation deals with the discharge of a patient under s.23 of the Act by the responsible clinician.   **2-104**
There is no statutory form to be used for this purpose in England; a letter to the appropriate body would
suffice. In Wales, if an RC discharges a patient from detention Form HO17 must be used. This Form
must also be used in Wales if the hospital managers order discharge: see reg.7 of the Welsh Regulations.

Delegation of hospital managers' functions under the Act

19. The functions of the managers of a hospital in respect of the following—   **2-105**
   (a) notifying local social services authorities under section 14 (social
        reports) of patients detained on the basis of applications by their near-
        est relatives;
   (b) authorising persons under section 17(3) (leave of absence from
        hospital) to keep in custody patients who are on leave of absence who
        are subject to a condition that they remain in custody;
   (c) authorising persons under sections 18(1) and (2A) (return and readmis-
        sion of patients absent without leave) to take and return detained and
        community patients respectively who are absent without leave,
may be performed by any person authorised by them in that behalf.

General Note

For the avoidance of doubt, this regulation expressly allows hospital managers to authorise a person   **2-106**
to exercise on their behalf the functions set out in paras (a), (b) and (c).

Delegation of managers' functions under the Domestic Violence, Crime and Victims Act 2004

20. The functions of the managers of a hospital under sections 35 to 44B of the   **2-107**
Domestic Violence, Crime and Victims Act 2004 (provision of information to
victims of patients under the Act etc.) may be performed by any person authorised
by them in that behalf.

General Note

The Explanatory Memorandum to these regulations states: **2-108**

"The Committee's attention is drawn to section 45(4) of the Domestic Violence, Crime and Victims
Act 2004 which provides that a function conferred on the managers of a hospital under sections 35
to 44B of that Act is to be treated as a function of those managers under Part 3 of the 1983 Act for
the purposes of section 32(3) of the 1983 Act (regulations as to delegation of managers' functions,
etc). Section 32(3) of the 1983 Act, in turn, allows for the delegation of the functions of hospital
managers under the 1983 Act."

Delegation by local social services authorities

21.—(1) Except as provided by paragraph (2), a local social services author-   **2-109**
ity may delegate its functions under Parts 2 and 3 of the Act and these Regulations
in the same way and to the same persons as its functions referred to in the Local
Government Act 1972 may be delegated in accordance with section 101 of that Act.

(2)   The function of the local social services authority under section 23 (discharge of patients) may not be delegated otherwise than in accordance with that section.

General Note

2-110   This regulation confirms that local social services authorities to whom s.101 of the Local Government Act 1972 applies (those authorities who do not operate executive arrangements) may delegate their functions under Pts II and III of the Act (apart from decisions made under s.23), and under these regulations, in any way and to any person to whom they could delegate them under that section. Authorities which operate executive arrangements have separate and extensive powers of delegation under the Local Government Act 2000.

Part 3

Functions of Guardians and Nearest Relatives

Duties of private guardians

2-111   **22.**—(1)   It shall be the duty of a private guardian—
- (a)   to appoint a registered medical practitioner to act as the nominated medical attendant of the patient;
- (b)   to notify the responsible local social services authority of the name and address of the nominated medical attendant;
- (c)   in exercising the powers and duties of a private guardian conferred or imposed by the Act and these Regulations, to comply with such directions as that authority may give;
- (d)   to furnish that authority with all such reports or other information with regard to the patient as the authority may from time to time require;
- (e)   to notify that authority—
  - (i)   on the reception of the patient into guardianship, of the private guardian's address and the address of the patient,
  - (ii)   except in a case to which paragraph (f) applies, of any permanent change of either address, before or not later than 7 days after the change takes place;
- (f)   on any permanent change of the private guardian's address, where the new address is in the area of a different local social services authority, to notify that authority—
  - (i)   of that address and that of the patient,
  - (ii)   of the particulars mentioned in paragraph (b),
  and to notify the authority which was formerly responsible of the permanent change in the private guardian's address;
- (g)   in the event of the death of the patient, or the termination of the guardianship by discharge, transfer or otherwise, to notify the responsible local social services authority as soon as reasonably practicable.

(2)   Any notice, reports or other information under this regulation may be given or furnished in any other way (in addition to the methods of serving documents provided for by regulation 3(1)) to which the relevant local social services authority agrees, including orally […].

Amendment

The amendment to para.(2) was made by SI 2020/1072, reg.3.

Definition

private guardian: reg.2(1).   **2-112**

General Note

Paragraph (1)(a)

The nominated medical attendant is responsible for examining the patient for the purposes of renew-   **2-113**
ing guardianship (ss.20(6), 34(1)). This doctor could be the patient's general practitioner.

Visits to patients subject to guardianship

23. The responsible local social services authority shall arrange for every   **2-114**
patient received into guardianship under the Act to be visited at such intervals as
the authority may decide, but—
   (a) in any case at intervals of not more than 3 months, and
   (b) at least one such visit in any year shall be made by an approved clini-
        cian or a practitioner approved by the Secretary of State for the
        purposes of section 12 (general provisions as to medical
        recommendations).

General Note

Paragraph (b)

The approved clinician need not be a medical practitioner.   **2-115**

Performance of functions of nearest relative

24.—(1) Subject to the conditions of paragraph (7), any person other than— **2-116**
   (a) the patient;
   (b) a person mentioned in section 26(5) (persons deemed not to be the
        nearest relative), or
   (c) a person in respect of whom the court has made an order on the
        grounds set out in section 29(3)(b) to (e) (which sets out the grounds
        on which an application to the court for the appointment of a person
        to exercise the functions of a nearest relative may be made) for so long
        as an order under that section is in effect,
may be authorised in accordance with paragraph (2) to act on behalf of the nearest
relative in respect of the matters mentioned in paragraph (3).

(2) [The] authorisation mentioned in paragraph (1) must be given in writing by
the nearest relative.

(3) The matters referred to in paragraph (1) are the performance in respect of
the patient of the functions conferred upon the nearest relative under—
   (a) Part 2 of the Act (as modified by Schedule 1 to the Act as the case may
        be), and
   (b) section 66 (applications to tribunals).

(4) An authorisation given under paragraph (1) shall take effect upon its receipt
by the person authorised.

(5)   Subject to the conditions of paragraph (7), the nearest relative of a patient may give notice in writing revoking that authorisation.

(6)   Any revocation of such authorisation shall take effect upon the receipt of the notice by the person authorised.

(7)   The conditions mentioned in paragraphs (1) and (5) are that the nearest relative shall immediately notify—

    (a)   the patient;

    (b)   in the case of a patient liable to be detained in a hospital, the managers of that hospital;

    (c)   in the case of a patient subject to guardianship, the responsible local social services authority and the private guardian, if any;

    (d)   in the case of a community patient, the managers of the responsible hospital, of the authorisation or, as the case may be, its revocation.

(8)   […].

Amendments

The amendments to this regulation were made by SI 2020/1072, reg.4.

Definitions

2-117   private guardian: reg.2(1).
electronic communication: reg.2(1).

General Note

2-118   This regulation enables the patient's nearest relative to delegate the functions specified in para.(3) to another person at any time. The delegate can exercise all of the functions of nearest relative with the exception that, by virtue of the legal principle delegatus non potest delegare, he or she does not have the power to further delegate such functions to another. By virtue of Sch.1 to the Interpretation Act 1978, which defines a person as including a corporation, a local authority may be authorised to act as the delegate under this provision (see s.116(2)(c)). Although the authority could not further delegate the functions of nearest relative, there is nothing to prevent the functions of nearest relative being exercised by a named officer under the authority's scheme of delegation. In order to avoid the appearance of a conflict of interest, that officer should not be an Approved Mental Health Professional (AMHP). A delegation cannot be made to the persons identified in para.(1)(a),(b) or (c).

The patient, who cannot prevent the nearest relative from making a delegation, does not need to be subject to the Act's provisions at the time when the delegation is made. If this is the case, the only formality that is required is for the nearest relative to give written notice of the authorisation to the delegate and for the patient to be notified of the authorisation.

A letter will suffice; there is no statutory form that needs to be completed. The letter, which should be signed and dated, could be written along the following lines:

"I [insert name] of [insert address] being the nearest relative of [insert patient's name and address] for the purposes of the Mental Health Act 1983, hereby delegate my powers of nearest relative to [insert name] of [insert address]. I confirm that [insert name] has consented to act as the nearest relative of [insert patient's name]"

Notification to one of the bodies mentioned in para.(7) is required if the patient is subject to the Act's provisions at the time of the authorisation. However, it would be sensible for the relevant body to be notified before it becomes necessary to utilise the provisions of the Act. That body should check whether the author of the letter is in fact the patient's nearest relative and whether the delegate has agreed to the delegation. If a delegation is made, the nearest relative may revoke it at any time by notifying the authorised person in writing (para.(5)).

If an AMHP suspects that the nearest relative might not have possessed the required mental capacity at the time when the delegation was made, the AMHP should attempt to assess the nearest relative's capacity. If the assessment, together with the result of enquiries made by the AMHP, suggests that the nearest relative was likely to have been mentally incapacitated at the relevant time, an application should be made to the Court of Protection to determine the issue.

A delegation made under this provision would end on the delegate withdrawing his or her agreement to perform the functions of nearest relative, on the death of the nearest relative or on the nearest relative ceasing to have that status by virtue of the operation of either s.26 or s.29 of the Act.

An acting nearest relative appointed by the court under s.29 cannot exercise the power contained in this provision but must apply to the county court under s.30 for the s.29 order to be varied if he or she no longer wishes to perform the functions of acting nearest relative.

Paragraph (1)

Any person   The person authorised need not be a relative of the patient. Although there is no require-   **2-119**
ment for the person concerned to have consented to the delegation, it must be assumed that such consent is a pre-condition of delegation.

Discharge by nearest relative

25.—(1)   Any report given by the responsible clinician for the purposes of sec-   **2-120**
tion 25 (restrictions on discharge by nearest relative)—

(a)   shall be in the form set out in Part 1 of Form M2, and

(b)   the receipt of that report by—

    (i)   the managers of the hospital in which the patient is liable to be detained, or

    (ii)   the managers of the responsible hospital in the case of a community patient, shall be in the form set out in Part 2 of that Form.

[(2)   In addition to the methods of serving documents provided for by regulation 3(1), reports under this regulation may be furnished by transmission by facsimile, if the managers of the hospital agree.]

Amendment

Paragraph (2) was substituted by SI 2020/1072, reg.5.

General Note

Paragraph 32.25 of the *Code of Practice* contains an illustrative letter of discharge which is   **2-121**
reproduced in the notes on s.25(1).

PART 4

PROVISION OF INFORMATION

26.—(1)   Unless the patient requests otherwise, where —   **2-122**

(a)   a patient is to be or has been transferred from hospital to hospital pursuant to section 19 or section 123 (regulations as to transfer of patients and transfer to and from special hospitals respectively), the managers of the hospital to which the patient is to be or has been transferred shall take such steps as are reasonably practicable to cause the person (if any) appearing to them to be the patient's nearest relative to be informed of that transfer before it takes place or as soon as practicable thereafter;

(b)   a patient's detention is renewed pursuant to a report furnished under section 20 (duration of authority), the managers of the responsible hospital shall take such steps as are reasonably practicable to cause the person (if any) appearing to them to be the patient's nearest relative to be informed of that renewal as soon as practicable following their decision not to discharge the patient;

(c) by virtue of section 21B(7) (patients who are taken into custody or return after more than 28 days) a patient's detention is renewed pursuant to a report furnished under section 21B(2), the managers of the responsible hospital in which the patient is liable to be detained shall take such steps as are reasonably practicable to cause the person (if any) appearing to them to be the patient's nearest relative to be informed of that renewal as soon as practicable following their decision not to discharge the patient;

(d) by virtue of section 21B(5) and (6) (patients who are taken into custody or return after more than 28 days), a patient's detention is renewed retrospectively pursuant to a report furnished under section 21B(2), the managers of the hospital in which the patient is liable to be detained shall take such steps as are reasonably practicable to cause the patient and the person (if any) appearing to them to be the patient's nearest relative to be informed of that renewal as soon as practicable following their receipt of that report;

(e) a patient's period of community treatment is extended pursuant to a report furnished under section 20A (community treatment period), the managers of the responsible hospital shall take such steps as are reasonably practicable to cause the person (if any) appearing to them to be the patient's nearest relative to be informed of that extension as soon as practicable following their decision not to discharge the patient;

(f) by virtue of section 21B(7A) (patients who are taken into custody or return after more than 28 days) a patient's period of community treatment is extended pursuant to a report furnished under section 21B(2), the managers of the responsible hospital shall take such steps as are reasonably practicable to cause the person (if any) appearing to them to be the patient's nearest relative to be informed of that extension as soon as practicable following their decision not to discharge the patient;

(g) by virtue of section 21B(6A) and (6B) (patients who are taken into custody or return after more than 28 days) a patient's period of community treatment is extended retrospectively pursuant to a report furnished under section 21B(2), the managers of the responsible hospital shall take such steps as are reasonably practicable to cause the patient and the person (if any) appearing to them to be the patient's nearest relative to be informed of that extension as soon as practicable following their receipt of that report;

(h) a patient is to be or has been assigned to another hospital which assumes responsibility for that patient as a community patient, the managers of the hospital to which the patient is to be or has been assigned shall take such steps as are reasonably practicable to cause the person (if any) appearing to them to be the patient's nearest relative to be informed of that assignment before or as soon as practicable following it taking place;

(i) a patient is to be or has been transferred from hospital to guardianship pursuant to section 19 (regulations as to transfer of patients), the

[696]

responsible local social services authority shall take such steps as are reasonably practicable to cause the person appearing to it to be the patient's nearest relative to be informed of that transfer before it takes place or as soon as practicable thereafter;

(j) a patient is to be or has been transferred from the guardianship of one person to the guardianship of another person pursuant to section 19 (regulations as to transfer of patients), the new responsible local social services authority shall take such steps as are reasonably practicable to cause the person (if any) appearing to it to be the patient's nearest relative to be informed of that transfer before it takes place or as soon as practicable thereafter;

(k) a patient's guardianship becomes vested in the local social services authority or the functions of a guardian are, during the guardian's incapacity, transferred to the authority or a person approved by it under section 10 (transfer of guardianship in case of death, incapacity, etc of guardian), the responsible local social services authority shall take such steps as are reasonably practicable to cause the person (if any) appearing to it to be the patient's nearest relative to be informed of that vesting, or as the case may be, transfer before it takes place or as soon as practicable thereafter;

(l) a patient's guardianship is renewed pursuant to a report furnished under section 20 (duration of authority), the responsible local social services authority shall take such steps as are reasonably practicable to cause the person (if any) appearing to it to be the patient's nearest relative to be informed of that renewal as soon as practicable following the decision of the responsible local social services authority [not] to discharge the patient;

(m) by virtue of section 21B(7) (patients who are taken into custody or return after more than 28 days) a patient's guardianship is renewed pursuant to a report furnished under section 21B(7), the responsible local social services authority shall take such steps as are reasonably practicable to cause the person (if any) appearing to it to be the patient's nearest relative to be informed of that renewal as soon as practicable following the decision of the responsible local social services authority not to discharge the patient;

(n) by virtue of section 21B(5) and (6) (patients who are taken into custody or return after more than 28 days) a patient's guardianship is renewed retrospectively pursuant to a report furnished under section 21B(2), the responsible local social services authority shall take such steps as are reasonably practicable to cause the patient and person (if any) appearing to it to be the patient's nearest relative to be informed of that renewal as soon as practicable following the receipt by the responsible local social services authority of that report.

(2) Where paragraph (1)(m) or (n) applies, the responsible local social services authority shall, as soon as practicable inform the private guardian (if any) of its receipt of a report furnished under section 21B (patients who are taken into custody or return after more than 28 days).

(3) Upon a patient becoming subject to guardianship under the Act, the responsible local social services authority shall take such steps as are reasonably practicable to cause to be informed both the patient and the person (if any) appear-

ing to the authority to be the patient's nearest relative of the rights referred to in paragraph (4).

(4) Those rights are—

    (a) the patient's rights under section 66 (applications to tribunals),

    (b) the nearest relative's right, as the case may be, to—

        (i) discharge the patient under section 23 (discharge of patients), or

        (ii) make an application under section 69 (application to tribunals concerning patients subject to hospital and guardianship orders where the patient is, or is treated as being, subject to guardianship under section 37).

(5) Where information referred to in paragraph (1)(d), (g) or (n), or in paragraph (3) is to be given to the patient, it shall be given both orally and in writing.

(6) Where information referred to in paragraph (1) [or (3)] is to be given to the person appearing to be the patient's nearest relative, it shall be given in writing.

(7) Where information referred to in paragraph (2) is to be given to the private guardian, it shall be given in writing.

(8) [...]

(9) The functions of the managers referred to in this regulation may be performed by an officer authorised by them in that behalf.

Amendments

The amendments to this regulation were made by SI 2008/2560 reg.2(3) and SI 2020/1072, reg.6.

General Note

2-123   This regulation sets out when hospital managers and local authorities are required to give information about various statutory events relating to the patient's detention, supervised community treatment or guardianship to the patient's nearest relative (and sometimes patients themselves and, where applicable, private guardians). This requirement is in addition to the duties placed on hospital managers by ss.132, 132A and 133 of the Act to give information to patients and their nearest relatives. The information must not be given to the nearest relative if this is the patient's wish (para.(1)) or it is not "reasonably practicable" to provide the information: see the note on reg.15(3), (4)(b), above.

PART 5

CONSENT TO TREATMENT

Consent to treatment

2-124   27.—(1) For the purposes of section 57 (treatment requiring consent and a second opinion)—

    (a) the form of treatment to which that section shall apply, in addition to the treatment mentioned in subsection (1)(a) of that section (any surgical operation for destroying brain tissue or for destroying the functioning of brain tissue), shall be the surgical implantation of hormones for the purpose of reducing male sexual drive, and

    (b) the certificates required for the purposes of subsection (2)(a) and (b) of that section shall be in the form set out in Form T1.

(2)   For the purposes of section 58 (treatment requiring consent or a second opinion) the certificates required for the purposes of subsection (3)(a) and (b) of that section shall be in the form set out in Forms T2 and T3 respectively.

(3)   For the purposes of section 58A (electro-convulsive therapy, etc.)—

    (a)   the form of treatment to which that section shall apply, in addition to the administration of electro-convulsive therapy mentioned in subsection (1)(a) of that section, shall be the administration of medicine as part of that therapy; and

    (b)   the certificates required for the purposes of subsections (3), (4) and (5) of that section shall be in the form set out in Forms T4, T5 and T6 respectively.

(4)   Section 58A does not apply to treatment by way of the administration of medicine as part of electro-convulsive therapy where that treatment falls within section 62(1)(a) or (b) (treatment immediately necessary to save the patient's life or to prevent a serious deterioration in the patient's condition).

General Note

Paragraph (1)(a)

The oral administration of hormones for the purpose of reducing the male sex drive does not come within the scope of s.57.   **2-125**

Paragraph (4)

This provides that administration of medicine as part of ECT (like ECT itself: see para.(3)(a)) does not require a certificate from a SOAD if it is immediately necessary to save the patient's life or to prevent a serious deterioration of his condition.   **2-126**

Part 6

Treatment of Community Patients not Recalled to Hospital

28.—(1)   For the purposes of Part 4A of the Act (treatment of community patients not recalled to hospital), the certificates required for the purposes of sections 64B(2)(b) and 64E(2)(b) (which set out when treatment under Part 4A of the Act may be given to adult and child community patients respectively) shall be in the form set out in Form CTO11 [except where paragraph (1A) applies].   **2-127**

[(1A)   Where there is authority to give treatment to a patient by virtue of section 64C(2)(a) or section 64E(6)(a), the certificate required for the purposes of sections 64B(2)(b) and 64E(2)(b) shall be in the form set out in Form CTO12.]

(2)   Treatment of a patient to whom section 64B(3)(b) or section 64E(3)(b) applies (adult and child patients for whom treatment is immediately necessary), may include treatment by way of administration of medicine as part of electro-convulsive therapy but only where that treatment falls within section 64C(5)(a) or (b) (treatment immediately necessary to save the patient's life or to prevent a serious deterioration in the patient's condition).

(3)   Treatment of a patient to whom section 64G (emergency treatment for patients lacking capacity or competence) applies may include treatment by way of the administration of medicine as part of electro-convulsive therapy but only where that treatment falls within section 64G(5)(a) or (b) (treatment immediately neces-

sary to save the patient's life or to prevent a serious deterioration in the patient's condition).

Amendments

The amendments to this rule were made by SI 2012/1118 reg.2(2).

General Note

2-128   This regulation makes similar provision to reg.27(2) to (4) in respect of patients who are subject to community treatment orders and who have not been recalled to hospital.

PART 7

CORRESPONDENCE OF PATIENTS

Inspection and opening of postal packets

2-129   **29.**—(1)   Where under section 134(4) (inspection and opening of postal packets addressed to or by patients in hospital) any postal packet is inspected and opened, but neither the packet nor anything contained in it is withheld under section 134(1) or (2) the person appointed who inspected and opened it, shall record in writing—

(a)   that the packet had been so inspected and opened,

(b)   that nothing in the packet has been withheld, and

(c)   the name of the person appointed and the name of the hospital, and shall, before resealing the packet, place the record in that packet.

(2)   Where under section 134(1) or (2) any postal packet or anything contained in it is withheld by the person appointed—

(a)   that person shall record in a register kept for the purpose—

(i)   that the packet or anything contained in it has been withheld,

(ii)   the date on which it was so withheld,

(iii)   the grounds on which it was so withheld,

(iv)   a description of the contents of the packet withheld or of any item withheld, and

(v)   the name of the person appointed; and

(b)   if anything contained in the packet is withheld, the person appointed shall record in writing—

(i)   that the packet has been inspected and opened,

(ii)   that an item or items contained in the packet have been withheld,

(iii)   a description of any such item,

(iv)   the name of the person appointed and the name of the hospital, and

(v)   in any case to which section 134(1)(b) or (2) applies, the further particulars required for the purposes of section 134(6),

and shall, before resealing the packet, place the record in that packet.

(3)   In a case to which section 134(1)(b) or (2) applies—

(a)   the notice required for the purposes of section 134(6) shall include—

(i)   a statement of the grounds on which the packet in question or anything contained in it was withheld, and

(ii)   the name of the person appointed who so decided to withhold that packet or anything contained in it and the name of the hospital; and

(b)   where anything contained in a packet is withheld the record required by paragraph (2)(b) shall, if the provisions of section 134(6) are otherwise satisfied, be sufficient notice to the person to whom the packet is addressed for the purposes of section 134(6).

(4)   For the purposes of this regulation "the person appointed" means a person appointed under section 134(7) to perform the functions of the managers of the hospital under that section.

Review of decisions to withhold postal packets

30.—(1)   Every application for review by the Commission under [section **2-130** 134A(1) (review of decisions to withhold correspondence)] shall be—

(a)   made in such manner as the Commission may accept as sufficient in the circumstances of any particular case or class of case and may be made otherwise than in writing, and

(b)   made, delivered or sent to an office of the Commission.

(2)   Any person making such an application shall furnish to the Commission the notice of the withholding of the postal packet or anything contained in it, given under section 134(6), or a copy of that notice.

(3)   For the purpose of determining any such application the Commission may direct the production of such documents, information and evidence as it may reasonably require.

Amendment

In para.(1), the words in square brackets were substituted by SI 2009/462 art.12, Sch.5 para.25(b).

Definition

the Commission: reg.2(1).   **2-131**

Patient advocacy and liaison services and independent mental capacity advocate services

31.—(1)   In section 134 (correspondence of patients), for the purposes of **2-132** subsection (3)(ea) "patient advocacy and liaison service" means a service affording assistance in the form of advice and liaison for patients, their families and carers provided by—

(a)   an NHS trust,

(b)   an NHS foundation trust,

[(c)   [an integrated care board], or

(d)   [NHS England].]

(2)   For the purposes of section 134(3A)(b)(iii), the prescribed arrangements are arrangements in respect of independent mental capacity advocates made under section 35 to 41 of the Mental Capacity Act 2005 (independent advocacy service).

Amendment

The amendments to this regulation were made by SI 2013/235 art.11, Sch.2 para.117, SI 2022/634 Sch.1 and the Health and Care Act 2022 Sch.1 para.1(3).

PART 8

REVOCATIONS

Revocations

2-133   **32.**   The Regulations specified in column 1 of Schedule 2 are hereby revoked to the extent mentioned in column 3 of that Schedule.

SCHEDULE 1

Regulations 4–9, 13–17, 25, 27 and 28

Amendments

The amendments to Forms A7, A9, H2, CTO8 and CTO 11 were made by SI 2008/2560 reg.2(4). Form CTO 12 was inserted by SI 2012/1118, reg.2(3). The remaining amendments to the Forms were made by SI 2020/1072, reg.7.

General Note

2-134   Health bodies and local authorities can produce their own forms as long as the wording set out in this Schedule is reproduced. A handwritten form would suffice in an emergency if printed forms were not available. An alternative course of action would be to remove the appropriate pages from this Manual. Copies of the forms can be downloaded from the Mental Health Law Online website at: *www.mhlo.uk/f*. Welsh forms can also be accessed from the MHLO website.

The use of a form which failed to produce the exact wording set out in these regulations would not necessarily invalidate the application or recommendation because minor departures would be regarded by the courts as being de minimis, i.e. too trivial to be of any consequence. In *R. (on the application of SP) v Secretary of State for Justice* [2010] EWCA Civ 1590; [2011] M.H.L.R. 65, the Court of Appeal confirmed the validity of a transfer direction made under s.47 of the Act where one of the reporting doctors had used an obsolete form. It is likely that a court would find a patient's detention to be unlawful if the statutory criteria set out in the form failed to reproduce the correct wording in some material respect.

A doctor who completes a medical recommendation on a form prescribed by the English or Welsh Regulations is acting in a clinical capacity, often in circumstances of considerable stress and urgency. The doctor is not "obliged to do any more than complete the form according to his or her professional judgment in the prescribed manner". It would be "wholly inappropriate" to treat that part of the form which requires the doctor to state the reasons why detention is required in the same way as a reasoned determination following a tribunal hearing (*R. (on the application of H) v Oxfordshire Mental Healthcare NHS Trust* [2002] EWHC Admin 465; [2002] M.H.L.R. 282, paras 70, 71, per Sullivan J.). In *Re RS's Application for Judicial Review* [2015] NICA 30, the Court of Appeal in Northern Ireland said that the decision in *H.* is authority for the proposition that the "statutory prescribed forms envisage the provision of summary reasons" (para.36).

The use of electronic forms

2-135   The Forms in this Schedule have been amended by the Mental Health (Hospital, Guardianship and Treatment) (England) (Amendment) Regulations 2020 (SI 2020/1072), which apply to England only. Paragraph 1 of "*Guidance on the electronic communication of statutory forms under the Mental Health Act*", published by the Department of Health and Social Care (*www.gov.uk/government/publications/ electronic-communication-of-statutory-forms-under-the-mental-health-act/guidance-on-the-electronic- communication-of-statutory-forms-under-the-mental-health-act*) states:

"The amended 2008 regulations enable statutory forms and other documents under Part 2 of the MHA to be served electronically, but only where the receiving body, authority or person agrees to accept electronic service of these forms.

There are a couple of exceptions to this:

- where an approved mental health professional (AMHP), or a nearest relative wishes to serve an application for detention. In this case, electronic communication to the hospital managers or their officers is always permitted (no agreement needed). Hospital managers are not entitled to reject a validly made application solely on the grounds of it being completed and communicated electronically (see section 2 for further guidance)
- where the recipient is a patient. In all such cases, statutory forms and other notifications for the information of the patient must continue to be served in hard copy. For example, the community treatment order recall form must continue to be served in hard copy and the patient should continue to be notified in hard copy if someone is authorised by a nearest relative to act on their behalf under regulation 24 of the 2008 regulations. Electronic communication can, however, be used as an additional means of providing the patient with the information, if that is their preference (see section 3 for further guidance)

Note that all electronic forms, apart from the discharge order form, should be considered 'served' once they have been successfully sent."

Paragraph 4 of the guidance states:

"Electronic forms should be considered equivalent in status to paper forms. Neither is more valid than the other. This means that, for example, where forms authorising an individual's detention are in an electronic format and they need to be transferred from one hospital to another, there should be no question over the validity of these forms by the receiving hospital simply because they're electronic.
...
Hospital managers in each local or regional trust should lead the creation of a multi-agency protocol that all providers agree to abide by. The protocol should cover:

- establishment of a default secure email address(es) for sending statutory forms and all other relevant correspondence to, either directly or in copy
- arrangements to monitor and action emails to this inbox in an appropriate and timely manner
- how the storage of complete records will be safely and securely maintained as outlined earlier in this section, whether electronically or in hard copy."

Transitional and saving provisions are set out in reg.8 of SI 2020/1072:

"(1)   Nothing in these Regulations affects the validity of any form set out in Schedule 1 which is served on an authority, body or person before the date on which these Regulations come into force.

(2)   Paragraph (3) applies to any document required by the 2008 Regulations to be served in a form set out in Schedule 1 and which is served on any authority, body or person between the date on which these Regulations come into force and 1st February 2021.

(3)   Where a document to which this paragraph applies is served other than by means of electronic communication, a requirement to serve that document in a form set out in Schedule 1 is met if—

    (a)   the document is served in a form set out in that Schedule as amended by these Regulations, or

    (b)   the document is served in a form set out in that Schedule as it applied immediately before the date on which these Regulations come into force."

Electronic signatures

The use of electronic signatures is permitted by reg.3(8)(b). Guidance on electronic signatures is reproduced in the note on that provision.

2-136

Using English or Welsh forms

2-137   For the use of the appropriate forms in cross-border cases, see the note on r.4(2) and the General Note to s.13 of the Act under the heading *Use of statutory documentation in England and Wales*.

Faxed forms

2-138   Although only reg.25(2)(a) provides specific authority for a form to be served by fax, it is submitted that a faxed reproduction of a completed form can be acted upon if (a) the recipient confers with the signatory by telephone to confirm that that the form was completed by the signatory; and (b) the original is delivered to the recipient at the earliest opportunity. The Mental Health Act Commission endorsed the use of faxed forms (MHAC, *Sixth Biennial Report*, 1993–1995, para.3.13).

Scanned documents

2-139   Provided that the scanning process and procedures are compliant with the British Standards Institution's Code of Practice for *"Evidential Weight and Legal Admissibility of Electronically Stored Information"*, the paper versions of Forms used under the Act can be destroyed under confidential conditions. Information about the Code of Practice can be accessed at *www.bsigroup.com*.

Lost forms

2-140   If the forms that were used to provide authority for the patient's detention or guardianship are lost, the authority for the detention or guardianship no longer exists and a fresh assessment under the Act must be undertaken if it is considered that the patient has a continuing need for either detention or guardianship. However, if copies of the original forms were made there would be no need for a fresh assessment if the signatories endorsed the relevant copy as a true copy of the original form.

Retention of statutory forms

2-141   The retention of health records is governed by the "Records Management Code of Practice for Health and Social Care" which was published by the Information Governance Alliance in 2016. The Code can be accessed at: *https://transform.england.nhs.uk/information-governance/guidance/records-management-code*.

FORMS FOR USE IN CONNECTION WITH COMPULSORY ADMISSION TO HOSPITAL, GUARDIANSHIP AND TREATMENT

FORM A1

Regulation 4(1)(a)(i)

2-142   **Mental Health Act 1983 section 2—application by nearest relative for admission for assessment**

To the managers of [name and address of hospital]

I [[PRINT your full name, address and, if sending by means of electronic communication, email address]] apply for the admission of [PRINT full name and address of patient] for assessment in accordance with Part 2 of the Mental Health Act 1983.

Complete (a) or (b) as applicable and delete the other.

(a)   To the best of my knowledge and belief I am the patient's nearest relative within the meaning of the Act

I am the patient's [state your relationship with the patient].

(b)   I have been authorised to exercise the functions under the Act of the patient's nearest relative by a county court/the patient's nearest relative *[delete the phrase which does not apply]*, and a copy of the authority is attached to this application.

I last saw the patient on [date], which was within the period of 14 days ending on the day this application is completed.

This application is founded on two medical recommendations in the prescribed form.

If neither of the medical practitioners had previous acquaintance with the patient before making their recommendations, please explain why you could not get a recommendation from a medical practitioner who did have previous acquaintance with the patient:—

....

....

....

If you need to continue on a separate sheet please indicate here [ ] and attach that sheet to this form]

Signed ....

Date ....

FORM A2

Regulation 4(1)(a)(ii)

Mental Health Act 1983 section 2—application by an approved mental health professional for admission for assessment   **2-143**

To the Managers of [name and address of hospital]

I [[PRINT your full name, address and, if sending by means of electronic communication, email address]] apply for the admission of [PRINT full name and address of patient] for assessment in accordance with Part 2 of the Mental Health Act 1983.

I am acting on behalf of [PRINT name of local social services authority] and am approved to act as an approved mental health professional for the purposes of the Act by *[delete as appropriate]*

that authority

[name of local social services authority that approved you, if different]

Complete the following if you know who the nearest relative is.

Complete (a) or (b) as applicable and delete the other.

(a)   To the best of my knowledge and belief [PRINT full name and address] is the patient's nearest relative within the meaning of the Act.

(b)   I understand that [PRINT full name and address] has been authorised by a county court/the patient's nearest relative* to exercise the functions under the Act of the patient's nearest relative. *[*Delete the phrase which does not apply]*

I have/have not yet* informed that person that this application is to be made and of the nearest relative's power to order the discharge of the patient. *[*Delete the phrase which does not apply]*

Complete the following if you do not know who the nearest relative is.

Delete (a) or (b).

(a)   I have been unable to ascertain who is the patient's nearest relative within the meaning of the Act.

(b)   To the best of my knowledge and belief this patient has no nearest relative within the meaning of the Act.

The remainder of the form must be completed in all cases.

I last saw the patient on [date], which was within the period of 14 days ending on the day this application is completed.

I have interviewed the patient and I am satisfied that detention in a hospital is in all the circumstances of the case the most appropriate way of providing the care and medical treatment of which the patient stands in need.

This application is founded on two medical recommendations in the prescribed form.

If neither of the medical practitioners had previous acquaintance with the patient before making their recommendations, please explain why you could not get a recommendation from a medical practitioner who did have previous acquaintance with the patient—

....

....

....

[If you need to continue on a separate sheet please indicate here [ ] and attach that sheet to this form]

Signed ....

Date ....

FORM A3

Regulation 4(1)(b)(i)

Mental Health Act 1983 section 2—joint medical recommendation for admission for assessment   **2-144**

We, registered medical practitioners, recommend that [PRINT full name and address of patient] be admitted to a hospital for assessment in accordance with Part 2 of the Mental Health Act 1983.

I [[PRINT full name, address and, if sending by means of electronic communication, email address of first practitioner]] last examined this patient on [date].

*I had previous acquaintance with the patient before I conducted that examination.

*I am approved under section 12 of the Act as having special experience in the diagnosis or treatment of mental disorder.

[*Delete if not applicable]

I [[PRINT full name, address and, if sending by means of electronic communication, email address of second practitioner]] last examined this patient on [date].

*I had previous acquaintance with the patient before I conducted that examination.

*I am approved under section 12 of the Act as having special experience in the diagnosis or treatment of mental disorder.

*[*Delete if not applicable]*

In our opinion

(a)   this patient is suffering from mental disorder of a nature or degree which warrants the detention of the patient in hospital for assessment (or for assessment followed by medical treatment) for at least a limited period,

AND

(b)   ought to be so detained

        (i)   in the interests of the patient's own health

        (ii)   in the interests of the patient's own safety

        (iii)   with a view to the protection of other persons

[*Delete the indents not applicable]

Our reasons for these opinions are:

[Your reasons should cover both (a) and (b) above. As part of them: describe the patient's symptoms and behaviour and explain how those symptoms and behaviour lead you to your opinion; explain why the patient ought to be admitted to hospital and why informal admission is not appropriate.]

....

....

....

[If you need to continue on a separate sheet please indicate here [ ] and attach that sheet to this form]

Signed ....

Date ....

Signed ....

Date ....

NOTE: AT LEAST ONE OF THE PRACTITIONERS SIGNING THIS FORM MUST BE APPROVED UNDER SECTION 12 OF THE ACT.

FORM A4

Regulation 4(1)(b)(ii)

2-145   **Mental Health Act 1983 section 2—medical recommendation for admission for assessment**

I [[PRINT full name, address and, if sending by means of electronic communication, email address of medical practitioner]], a registered medical practitioner, recommend that [PRINT full name and address of patient] be admitted to a hospital for assessment in accordance with Part 2 of the Mental Health Act 1983.

I last examined this patient on [date].

*I had previous acquaintance with the patient before I conducted that examination.

*I am approved under section 12 of the Act as having special experience in the diagnosis or treatment of mental disorder.

*[*Delete if not applicable]*

In my opinion,

(a)   this patient is suffering from mental disorder of a nature or degree which warrants the detention of the patient in hospital for assessment (or for assessment followed by medical treatment) for at least a limited period,

AND

(b)   ought to be so detained

        (i)   in the interests of the patient's own health

        (ii)   in the interests of the patient's own safety

        (iii)   with a view to the protection of other persons

*[*Delete the indents not applicable]*

My reasons for these opinions are:

[Your reasons should cover both (a) and (b) above. As part of them: describe the patient's symptoms and behaviour and explain how those symptoms and behaviour lead you to your opinion; explain why the patient ought to be admitted to hospital and why informal admission is not appropriate.]

....

....

....

[If you need to continue on a separate sheet please indicate here [ ] and attach that sheet to this form]

Signed ....

Date ....

Form A5

Regulation 4(1)(c)(i)

Mental Health Act 1983 section 3—application by nearest relative for admission for treatment **2-146**

To the Managers of [name and address of hospital]

I [[PRINT your full name, address and, if sending by means of electronic communication, email address]] apply for the admission of [PRINT full name and address of patient] for treatment in accordance with Part 2 of the Mental Health Act 1983.

Complete either (a) or (b) as applicable and delete the other

(a)   To the best of my knowledge and belief I am the patient's nearest relative within the meaning of the Act.

I am the patient's [state relationship with the patient].

(b)   I have been authorised to exercise the functions under the Act of the patient's nearest relative by a county court/the patient's nearest relative *[delete the phrase which does not apply]*, and a copy of the authority is attached to this application.

I last saw the patient on [date], which was within the period of 14 days ending on the day this application is completed.

This application is founded on two medical recommendations in the prescribed form.

If neither of the medical practitioners had previous acquaintance with the patient before making the recommendations, please explain why you could not get a recommendation from a medical practitioner who did have previous acquaintance with the patient—

....

....

....

....

....

[If you need to continue on a separate sheet please indicate here [ ] and attach that sheet to this form]

Signed ....

Date ....

Form A6

Regulation 4(1)(c)(ii)

Mental Health Act 1983 section 3—application by an approved mental health professional for admission for treatment **2-147**

To the managers of [name and address of hospital]

I [[PRINT your full name, address and, if sending by means of electronic communication, email address]] apply for the admission of [PRINT full name and address of patient] for treatment in accordance with Part 2 of the Mental Health Act 1983.

I am acting on behalf of [name of local social services authority] and am approved to act as an approved mental health professional for the purposes of the Act by *[delete as appropriate]*

that authority

[name of local social services authority that approved you, if different]

Complete the following where consultation with the nearest relative has taken place.

Complete (a) or (b) and delete the other.

(a)   I have consulted [PRINT full name and address] who to the best of my knowledge and belief is the patient's nearest relative within the meaning of the Act.

(b)   I have consulted [PRINT full name and address] who I understand has been authorised by a county court/the patient's nearest relative* to exercise the functions under the Act of the patient's nearest relative.

[*Delete the phrase which does not apply]

That person has not notified me or the local social services authority on whose behalf I am acting that he or she objects to this application being made

Complete the following where the nearest relative has not been consulted.

Delete whichever two of (a), (b) and (c) do not apply.

(a)   I have been unable to ascertain who is this patient's nearest relative within the meaning of the Act.

(b)   To the best of my knowledge and belief this patient has no nearest relative within the meaning the Act.

(c)   I understand that [PRINT full name and address] is

(i)   this patient's nearest relative within the meaning of the Act,

(ii)   authorised to exercise the functions of this patient's nearest relative under the Act,

[Delete either (i) or (ii)]

but in my opinion it is not reasonably practicable/would involve unreasonable delay *[delete as ap-*

[707]

propriate] to consult that person before making this application, because—

....

....

[If you need to continue on a separate sheet please indicate here [ ] and attach that sheet to this form]
The remainder of this form must be completed in all cases.
I saw the patient on [date], which was within the period of 14 days ending on the day this application is completed.

I have interviewed the patient and I am satisfied that detention in a hospital is in all the circumstances of the case the most appropriate way of providing the care and medical treatment of which the patient stands in need.

This application is founded on two medical recommendations in the prescribed form.

If neither of the medical practitioners had previous acquaintance with the patient before making their recommendations, please explain why you could not get a recommendation from a medical practitioner who did have previous acquaintance with the patient—

....

....

[If you need to continue on a separate sheet please indicate here [ ] and attach that sheet to this form]

Signed ....

Date ....

FORM A7

Regulation 4(1)(d)(i)

2-148 **Mental Health Act 1983 section 3—joint medical recommendation for admission for treatment**

We, registered medical practitioners, recommend that [PRINT full name and address of patient] be admitted to a hospital for treatment in accordance with Part 2 of the Mental Health Act 1983.

I [[PRINT full name, address and, if sending by means of electronic communication, email address of first practitioner]] last examined this patient on [date].

*I had previous acquaintance with the patient before I conducted that examination.

*I am approved under section 12 of the Act as having special experience in the diagnosis or treatment of mental disorder.

*[*Delete if not applicable]*

I [[PRINT full name, address and, if sending by means of electronic communication, email address of second practitioner]] [last examined this patient on [date].]

*I had previous acquaintance with the patient before I conducted that examination.

*I am approved under section 12 of the Act as having special experience in the diagnosis or treatment of mental disorder.

*[*Delete if not applicable]*

In our opinion,

(a)   this patient is suffering from mental disorder of a nature or degree which makes it appropriate for the patient to receive medical treatment in a hospital,

AND

(b)   it is necessary

    (i)   for the patient's own health

    (ii)   for the patient's own safety

    (iii)   for the protection of other persons

[delete the indents not applicable]

that this patient should receive treatment in hospital, AND

(c)   such treatment cannot be provided unless the patient is detained under section 3 of the Act,

because—[Your reasons should cover (a), (b) and (c) above. As part of them: describe the patient's symptoms and behaviour and explain how those symptoms and behaviour lead you to your opinion; say whether other methods of treatment or care (eg out-patient treatment or social services) are available and, if so, why they are not appropriate; indicate why informal admission is not appropriate.]

....

....

[If you need to continue on a separate sheet please indicate here [ ] and attach that sheet to this form]

....

We are also of the opinion that, taking into account the nature and degree of the mental disorder from which the patient is suffering and all the other circumstances of the case, appropriate medical treat-

ment is available to the patient at the following hospital (or one of the following hospitals):—
[Enter name of hospital(s). If appropriate treatment is available only in a particular part of the hospital, say which part.]

....

....

....

Signed ....
Date ....
Signed ....
Date ....

NOTE: AT LEAST ONE OF THE PRACTITIONERS SIGNING THIS FORM MUST BE AP-PROVED UNDER SECTION 12 OF THE ACT.

FORM A8

Regulation 4(1)(d)(ii)

Mental Health Act 1983 section 3—medical recommendation for admission for treatment   **2-149**
I [[PRINT full name, address and, if sending by means of electronic communication, email address of practitioner]], a registered medical practitioner, recommend that [PRINT full name and address of patient] be admitted to a hospital for treatment in accordance with Part 2 of the Mental Health Act 1983.
I last examined this patient on [date].
*I had previous acquaintance with the patient before I conducted that examination.
*I am approved under section 12 of the Act as having special experience in the diagnosis or treatment of mental disorder.
*[*Delete if not applicable]*
In my opinion,
(a)   this patient is suffering from mental disorder of a nature or degree which makes it appropriate for the patient to receive medical treatment in a hospital,
AND
(b)   it is necessary
     (i)   for the patient's own health
     (ii)   for the patient's own safety
     (iii)   for the protection of other persons
[delete the indents not applicable]
that this patient should receive treatment in hospital,
    AND
(c)   such treatment cannot be provided unless the patient is detained under section 3 of the Act,
because — [Your reasons should cover (a), (b) and (c) above. As part of them: describe the patient's symptoms and behaviour and explain how those symptoms and behaviour lead you to your opinion; say whether other methods of treatment or care (eg out-patient treatment or social services) are available and, if so, why they are not appropriate; indicate why informal admission is not appropriate.]

....

....

....

[If you need to continue on a separate sheet please indicate here [ ] and attach that sheet to this form]
I am also of the opinion that, taking into account the nature and degree of the mental disorder from which the patient is suffering and all the other circumstances of the case, appropriate medical treatment is available to the patient at the following hospital (or one of the following hospitals):—

....

....

[Enter name of hospital(s). If appropriate treatment is available only in a particular part of the hospital, say which part.]

Signed ....
Date ....

FORM A9

Regulation 4(1)(e)(i)

Mental Health Act 1983 section 4—emergency application by nearest relative for admission for   **2-150**
assessment
THIS FORM IS TO BE USED ONLY FOR AN EMERGENCY APPLICATION To the managers of [name and address of hospital]
I [[PRINT your full name, address and, if sending by means of electronic communication, email address]] apply for the admission of [PRINT full name and address of patient] for assessment in accord-

ance with Part 2 of the Mental Health Act 1983.

Complete (a) or (b) as applicable and delete the other.

(a)   To the best of my knowledge and belief I am the patient's nearest relative within the meaning of the Act.

I am the patient's [state your relationship with the patient].

(b)   I have been authorised to exercise the functions under the Act of the patient's nearest relative by a county court/the patient's nearest relative *[delete the phrase which does not apply]*, and a copy of the authority is attached to this application.

I last saw the patient on [date] [at time]], which was within the last 24 hours.

In my opinion it is of urgent necessity for the patient to be admitted and detained under section 2 of the Act and compliance with the provisions of Part 2 of the Act relating to applications under that section would involve undesirable delay.

This application is founded on a medical recommendation in the prescribed form.

If the medical practitioner did not have previous acquaintance with the patient before making the recommendation, please explain why you could not get a recommendation from a medical practitioner who did have previous acquaintance with the patient—

....

....

....

[If you need to continue on a separate sheet please indicate here [ ] and attach that sheet to this form]

Signed ....

Date ....

Time ....

FORM A10

Regulation 4(1)(e)(ii)

2-151   **Mental Health Act 1983 section 4—emergency application by an approved mental health professional for admission for assessment**

THIS FORM IS TO BE USED ONLY FOR AN EMERGENCY APPLICATION To the managers of [name and address of hospital]

I [[PRINT your full name, address and, if sending by means of electronic communication, email address]] apply for the admission of [PRINT full name and address of patient] for assessment in accordance with Part 2 of the Mental Health Act 1983.

I am acting on behalf of [name of local social services authority] and am approved to act as an approved mental health professional for the purposes of the Act by *[delete as appropriate]* that authority

[name of local social services authority that approved you, if different].

I last saw the patient on [date] at [time], which was within the last 24 hours.

I have interviewed the patient and I am satisfied that detention in a hospital is in all the circumstances of the case the most appropriate way of providing the care and medical treatment of which the patient stands in need.

In my opinion it is of urgent necessity for the patient to be admitted and detained under section 2 of the Act and compliance with the provisions of Part 2 of the Act relating to applications under that section would involve undesirable delay.

This application is founded on a medical recommendation in the prescribed form.

If the medical practitioner did not have previous acquaintance with the patient before making the recommendation, please explain why you could not get a recommendation from a medical practitioner who did have previous acquaintance with the patient—

....

....

....

[If you need to continue on a separate sheet please indicate here [ ] and attach that sheet to this form]

Signed ....

Date ....

Time ....

FORM A11

Regulation 4(1)(f)

2-152   **Mental Health Act 1983 section 4—medical recommendation for emergency admission for assessment**

THIS FORM IS TO BE USED ONLY FOR AN EMERGENCY APPLICATION

I [[PRINT name, address and, if sending by means of electronic communication, email address of medical practitioner]], a registered medical practitioner, recommend that [PRINT full name and address of patient] be admitted to a hospital for assessment in accordance with Part 2 of the Mental Health Act 1983.

I last examined this patient on [date] at [time].

*I had previous acquaintance with the patient before I conducted that examination.

*I am approved under section 12 of the Act as having special experience in the diagnosis or treatment of mental disorder.

*[*Delete if not applicable]*

I am of the opinion,

(a)   this patient is suffering from mental disorder of a nature or degree which warrants the detention of the patient in hospital for assessment (or for assessment followed by medical treatment) for at least a limited period,

AND

(b)   this patient ought to be so detained
- (i)   in the interests of the patient's own health
- (ii)   in the interests of the patient's own safety
- (iii)   with a view to the protection of other persons,
  [delete the indents not applicable]

AND

(c)   it is of urgent necessity for the patient to be admitted and detained under section 2 of the Act.

My reasons for these opinions are: [Your reasons should cover (a), (b) and (c) above. As part of them: describe the patient's symptoms and behaviour and explain how those symptoms and behaviour lead you to your opinion; and explain why the patient ought to be admitted to hospital urgently and why informal admission is not appropriate.]

....

....

....

[If you need to continue on a separate sheet please indicate here [ ] and attach that sheet to this form]

Compliance with the provisions of Part 2 of the Act relating to applications under section 2 would involve undesirable delay, because— [Say approximately how long you think it would take to obtain a second medical recommendation and what risk such a delay would pose to the patient or to other people.]

....

....

[If you need to continue on a separate sheet please indicate here [ ] and attach that sheet to this

Signed ....

Date ....

Time ....

Form H1

Regulation 4(1)(g)

Mental Health Act 1983 section 5(2)—report on hospital in-patient   **2-153**

Part 1

(To be completed by a medical practitioner or an approved clinician qualified to do so under section 5(2) of the Act)

To the managers of [name and address of hospital]

I am [PRINT full name]

and I am *[Delete (a) or (b) as appropriate]*

(a)   the registered medical practitioner/the approved clinician (who is not a registered medical practitioner) *[delete the phrase which does not apply]*

(b)   a registered medical practitioner/an approved clinician (who is not a registered medical practitioner)* who is the nominee of the registered medical practitioner or approved clinician (who is not a registered medical practitioner) *[*delete the phrase which does not apply]*

in charge of the treatment of [PRINT full name of patient], who is an in-patient in this hospital and not at present liable to be detained under the Mental Health Act 1983.

It appears to me that an application ought to be made under Part 2 of the Act for this patient's admission to hospital for the following reasons—

....

....

....

[The full reasons why informal treatment is no longer appropriate must be given. If you need to continue on a separate sheet please indicate here [ ] and attach that sheet to this form.]

I am furnishing this report by: *[Delete the phrase which does not apply]* consigning it to the hospital managers' internal mail system today at [time]

[today sending it to the hospital managers, or a person authorised by them to receive it, by means of electronic communication]

delivering it (or having it delivered) by hand to a person authorised by the hospital managers to receive it.

Signed ....
Date ....

Part 2

(To be completed on behalf of the hospital managers)

This report was *[Delete the phrase which does not apply]*

furnished to the hospital managers through their internal mail system

[furnished to the hospital managers, or a person authorised by them to receive it, by means of electronic communication]

delivered to me in person as someone authorised by the hospital managers to receive this report at [time] on [date]

Signed ....
on behalf of the hospital managers
PRINT NAME ....
Date ....

FORM H2

Regulation 4(1)(h)

2-154 **Mental Health Act 1983 section 5(4)—record of hospital in-patient**

To the managers of [name and address of hospital]

[PRINT full name of the patient]

It appears to me that—

(a) this patient, who is receiving treatment for mental disorder as an in-patient of this hospital, is suffering from mental disorder to such a degree that it is necessary for the patient's health or safety or for the protection of others for this patient to be immediately restrained from leaving the hospital;

AND

(b) it is not practicable to secure the immediate attendance of a registered medical practitioner or an approved clinician [(who is not a registered medical practitioner)] for the purpose of furnishing a report under section 5(2) of the Mental Health Act 1983.

I am [PRINT full name], a nurse registered—

[Delete whichever do not apply]

(a) in Sub-Part 1 of the register, whose entry includes an entry to indicate the nurse's field of practice is mental health nursing;

(b) in Sub-Part 2 of the register, whose entry includes an entry to indicate the nurse's field of practice is mental health nursing;

(c) in Sub-Part 1 of the register, whose entry includes an entry to indicate the nurse's field of practice is learning disabilities nursing;

(d) in Sub-Part 2 of the register, whose entry includes an entry to indicate the nurse's field of practice is [learning disabilities nursing].

Signed ....
Date ....
Time ....

FORM H3

Regulation 4(4) and (5)

2-155 **Mental Health Act 1983 sections 2, 3 and 4—record of detention in hospital**

(To be attached to the application for admission)

Part 1

[Name and address of hospital]

[PRINT full name of patient]

Complete (a) if the patient is not already an in-patient in the hospital.

Complete (b) if the patient is already an in-patient.

Delete the one which does not apply.

(a)   The above named patient was admitted to this hospital on [date of admission to hospital] at [time] in pursuance of an application for admission under section [state section] of the Mental Health Act 1983.

(b)   An application for the admission of the above named patient (who had already been admitted to this hospital) under section [state section] of the Mental Health Act 1983 was received by me on behalf of the hospital managers on [date] at [time] and the patient was accordingly treated as admitted for the purposes of the Act from that time.

Signed ....
on behalf of the hospital managers

PRINT NAME ....

Date ....

Part 2

(To be completed only if the patient was admitted in pursuance of an emergency application under section 4 of the Act)

On [date] at [time] I received, on behalf of the hospital managers, the second medical recommendation in support of the application for the admission of the above named patient.

Signed ....
on behalf of the hospital managers
PRINT NAME ....
Date ....

NOTE: IF THE PATIENT IS BEING DETAINED AS A RESULT OF A TRANSFER FROM GUARDIANSHIP, THE PATIENT'S ADMISSION SHOULD BE RECORDED IN PART 2 OF THE FORM G8 WHICH AUTHORISED THE TRANSFER.

Form H4

Regulation 7(2)(a) and 7(3)

Mental Health Act 1983 section 19—authority for transfer from one hospital to another under different managers   **2-156**

Part 1

(To be completed on behalf of the managers of the hospital where the patient is detained)

Authority is given for the transfer of [PRINT full name of patient] from [name and address of hospital in which the patient is liable to be detained] to [name and address of hospital to which patient is to be transferred] in accordance with the Mental Health (Hospital, Guardianship and Treatment) (England) Regulations 2008 within 28 days beginning with the date of this authority.

Signed ....
on behalf of the managers of the first named hospital
PRINT NAME ....
Date ....

Part 2

Record of Admission

(This is not part of the authority for transfer but is to be completed at the hospital to which the patient is transferred)

This patient was transferred to [name of hospital] in pursuance of this authority for transfer and admitted to that hospital on [date of admission to receiving hospital] at [time].

Signed ....
on behalf of the managers of the receiving hospital
PRINT NAME ....
Date ....

Form H5

Regulation 13(1), (2) and (3)

Mental Health Act 1983 section 20—renewal of authority for detention   **2-157**

Part 1

(To be completed by the responsible clinician)

To the managers of [name and address of hospital in which the patient is liable to be detained] I examined [PRINT full name of patient] on [date of examination].

The patient is liable to be detained for a period ending on [date authority for detention is due to expire].

I have consulted [PRINT full name and profession of person consulted] who has been professionally concerned with the patient's treatment.

In my opinion,

(a)   this patient is suffering from mental disorder of a nature or degree which makes it appropriate for the patient to receive medical treatment in a hospital,

AND

[713]

(b)   it is necessary
      (i)   for the patient's own health
      (ii)   for the patient's own safety
      (iii) for the protection of other persons
[delete the indents not applicable]
that this patient should receive treatment in hospital,

    because— [Your reasons should cover both (a) and (b) above. As part of them: describe the patient's symptoms and behaviour and explain how those symptoms and behaviour lead you to your opinion; say whether other methods of treatment or care (eg out-patient treatment or social services) are available and, if so, why they are not appropriate.]

    ....
    ....
    ....

    [If you need to continue on a separate sheet please indicate here [ ] and attach that sheet to this form]
    Such treatment cannot be provided unless the patient continues to be detained under the Act, for the following reasons — [Reasons should indicate why informal admission is not appropriate.]

    ....
    ....
    ....

    [If you need to continue on a separate sheet please indicate here [ ] and attach that sheet to this form.]
    I am also of the opinion that, taking into account the nature and degree of the mental disorder from which the patient is suffering and all the other circumstances of the case, appropriate medical treatment is available to the patient.

Signed ....
PRINT NAME ....
Profession ....
Date ....

Part 2
(To be completed by a professional who has been professionally concerned with the patient's medical treatment and who is of a different profession from the responsible clinician)

I agree with the responsible clinician that: this patient is suffering from mental disorder of a nature or degree which makes it appropriate for the patient to receive medical treatment in a hospital; it is necessary for the patient's own health or safety or for the protection of other persons that the patient should receive treatment and it cannot be provided unless the patient continues to be detained under the Act; and that, taking into account the nature and degree of the mental disorder from which the patient is suffering and all other circumstances of the case, appropriate medical treatment is available to the patient.

Signed ....
PRINT NAME ....
Profession ....
Date ....

Part 3
(To be completed by the responsible clinician)

I am furnishing this report by: *[Delete the phrase which does not apply]*
    today consigning it to the hospital managers' internal mail system.
    [today sending it to the hospital managers, or a person authorised by them to receive it, by means of electronic communication.]
    sending or delivering it without using the hospital managers' internal mail system.

Signed ....
PRINT NAME ....
Date ....

Part 4
(To be completed on behalf of the hospital managers)

This report was *[Delete the phrase which does not apply]*
    furnished to the hospital managers through their internal mail system.
    [furnished to the hospital managers, or a person authorised by them to receive it, by means of electronic communication.]
    received by me on behalf of the hospital managers on [date].

Signed ....
on behalf of the hospital managers
PRINT NAME ....
Date ....

FORM H6

Regulation 14(1)(a) and (b)

Mental Health Act 1983 section 21B—authority for detention after absence without leave for more than 28 days

2-158

Part 1

(To be completed by the responsible clinician)

To the managers of [name and address of hospital in which the patient is liable to be detained] I examined [PRINT full name of patient] on [date of examination] who:

(a)   was absent without leave from hospital or the place where the patient ought to have been beginning on [date absence without leave began];

(b)   was/is* liable to be detained for a period ending on [date authority for detention would have expired, apart from any extension under section 21, or date on which it will expire]; *[*delete the phrase which does not apply]* and

(c)   returned to the hospital or place on [date].

I have consulted [PRINT full name of approved mental health professional] who is an approved mental health professional.

I have also consulted [PRINT full name and profession of person consulted] who has been professionally concerned with the patient's treatment.

In my opinion,

(a)   this patient is suffering from mental disorder of a nature or degree which makes it appropriate for the patient to receive medical treatment in a hospital,

AND

(b)   it is necessary

      (i)   for the patient's own health

      (ii)   for the patient's own safety

      (iii) for the protection of other persons [delete the indents not applicable]

that this patient should receive treatment in hospital,

because— [Your reasons should cover both (a) and (b) above. As part of them: describe the patient's symptoms and behaviour and explain how those symptoms and behaviour lead you to your opinion; say whether other methods of treatment or care (eg out-patient treatment or social services) are available and, if so, why they are not appropriate.]

....

....

....

[If you need to continue on a separate sheet please indicate here [ ] and attach that sheet to this form]

Such treatment cannot be provided unless the patient continues to be detained under the Act, for the following reasons— [Reasons should indicate why informal admission is not appropriate.]

....

....

[If you need to continue on a separate sheet please indicate here [ ] and attach that sheet to this form]

I am also of the opinion that, taking into account the nature and degree of the mental disorder from which the patient is suffering and all other circumstances of the case, appropriate medical treatment is available to the patient.

The authority for the detention of the patient is/is not* due to expire within a period of two months beginning with the date on which this report is to be furnished to the hospital managers. *[*Delete the phrase which does not apply]*

Complete the following only if the authority for detention is due to expire within that period of two months.

This report shall/shall not* have effect as a report duly furnished under section 20(3) for the renewal of the authority for the detention of the patient. *[*Delete the phrase which does not apply]*

Complete the following in all cases.

I am furnishing this report by: *[Delete the phrase which does not apply]*

today consigning it to the hospital managers' internal mail system.

[today sending it to the hospital managers, or a person authorised by them to receive it, by means of electronic communication.]

sending or delivering it without using the hospital managers' internal mail system.

Signed ....

PRINT NAME ....

Date ....

Part 2

[715]

(To be completed on behalf of the hospital managers)
This report was *[Delete the phrase which does not apply]*
    furnished to the hospital managers through their internal mail system
    [furnished to the hospital managers, or a person authorised by them to receive it, by means of electronic communication]
    received by me on behalf of the hospital managers on [date]

Signed ....
on behalf of the hospital managers
PRINT NAME ....
Date ....

Form G1

Regulation 5(1)(a)(i) and (1)(b)

Mental Health Act 1983 section 7—guardianship application by nearest relative
Part 1
(To be completed by the nearest relative)

2-159   To the [name of local social services authority]

I [[PRINT your full name, address and, if sending by means of electronic communication, email address]] apply for the reception of [PRINT full name and address of patient] into the guardianship of [PRINT full name and address of proposed guardian] in accordance with Part 2 of the Mental Health Act 1983.

Complete (a) or (b) as applicable and delete the other.
(a)   To the best of my knowledge and belief I am the patient's nearest relative within the meaning of the Act. I am the patient's [state your relationship with the patient].
(b)   I have been authorised to exercise the functions under the Act of the patient's nearest relative by a county court/the patient's nearest relative *[delete the phrase which does not apply]*, and a copy of the authority is attached to this application.

*The patient's date of birth is [date]
OR
*I believe the patient is aged 16 years or over.
*[*Delete the phrase which does not apply.]*

I last saw the patient on [date], which was within the period of 14 days ending on the day this application is completed.

This application is founded on two medical recommendations in the prescribed form.

If neither of the medical practitioners had previous acquaintance with the patient before making their recommendations, please explain why you could not get a recommendation from a medical practitioner who did have previous acquaintance with the patient—

....
....

[If you need to continue on a separate sheet please indicate here [ ] and attach that sheet to this form]

Signed ....
Date ....

Part 2*
[*Complete only if proposed guardian is not a local social services authority]
(To be completed by the proposed guardian)

My full name and address is as entered in Part 1 of this form and I am willing to act as the guardian of the above named patient in accordance with Part 2 of the Mental Health Act 1983.

Signed ....
Date ....

Form G2

Regulation 5(1)(a)(ii) and 5(1)(b)

Mental Health Act 1983 section 7—guardianship application by an approved mental health professional

Part 1
(To be completed by the approved mental health professional)

2-160   To the [name of local social services authority]

I [[PRINT your full name, address and, if sending by means of electronic communication, email address]] apply for the reception of [PRINT full name and address of patient] into the guardianship of [PRINT full name and address of proposed guardian] in accordance with Part 2 of the Mental Health Act 1983.

I am acting on behalf of [name of local social services authority] and am approved to act as an ap-

proved mental health professional for the purposes of the Act by *[delete as appropriate]*
that authority
[name of local social services authority that approved you, if different.]
Complete the following where consultation with the nearest relative has taken place.
Complete (a) or (b) as applicable and delete the other.
(a)   I have consulted [PRINT full name and address] who to the best of my knowledge and belief is the patient's nearest relative within the meaning of the Act;
(b)   I have consulted [PRINT full name and address] who I understand has been authorised by a county court/ the patient's nearest relative to exercise the functions under the Act of the patient's nearest relative. *[Delete the phrase which does not apply]*
That person has not notified me or the local social services authority on whose behalf I am acting that he or she objects to this application being made.
Complete the following where the nearest relative has not been consulted. Delete whichever two of (a), (b) and (c) do not apply.
(a)   I have been unable to ascertain who is this patient's nearest relative within the meaning of the Act,
OR
(b)   to the best of my knowledge and belief this patient has no nearest relative within the meaning of the Act,
OR
(c)   [PRINT full name and address] is
          (i)   this patient's nearest relative within the meaning of the Act,
          (ii)   authorised to exercise the functions of this patient's nearest relative under the Act,
[Delete either (i) or (ii)]

          but in my opinion it is not reasonably practicable/would involve unreasonable delay *[delete as appropriate]* to consult that person before making this application, because—

....
....
[If you need to continue on a separate sheet please indicate here [ ] and attach that sheet to this form]
The remainder of Part 1 of this form must be completed in all cases.
I last saw the patient on [date], which was within the period of 14 days ending on the day this application is completed.
*The patient's date of birth is [date]
OR
*I believe the patient is aged 16 years or over.
*[*Delete the phrase which does not apply.]*
This application is founded on two medical recommendations in the prescribed form.
If neither of the medical practitioners had previous acquaintance with the patient before making their recommendations, please explain why you could not get a recommendation from a medical practitioner who did have previous acquaintance with the patient—

....
....
[If you need to continue on a separate sheet please indicate here [ ] and attach that sheet to this form]
Signed ....
Date ....

Part 2*
[*Complete only if proposed guardian is not a local social services authority]
(To be completed by the proposed guardian)
My full name and address is as entered in Part 1 of this form and I am willing to act as the guardian of the above named patient in accordance with Part 2 of the Mental Health Act 1983.
Signed ....
Date ....

FORM G3
Regulation 5(1)(c)(i)

Mental Health Act 1983 section 7—joint medical recommendation for reception into guardianship
We, registered medical practitioners, recommend that [PRINT full name and address of patient] be   **2-161**
received into guardianship in accordance with Part 2 of the Mental Health Act 1983.
I [[PRINT full name, address and, if sending by means of electronic communication, email address of first practitioner]] last examined this patient on [date], and
[*delete if not applicable]*

* I had previous acquaintance with the patient before I conducted that examination.

* I am approved under section 12 of the Act as having special experience in the diagnosis or treatment of mental disorder.

I [[PRINT full name, address and, if sending by means of electronic communication, email address of second practitioner]] last examined this patient on [date], and

[*delete if not applicable]

* I had previous acquaintance with the patient before I conducted that examination.

* I am approved under section 12 of the Act as having special experience in the diagnosis or treatment of mental disorder.

In our opinion,

(a)   this patient is suffering from mental disorder of a nature or degree which warrants the patient's reception into guardianship under the Act,

AND

(b)   it is necessary
    (i)   in the interests of the welfare of the patient
    (ii)   for the protection of other persons
[delete (i) or (ii) unless both apply]
that the patient should be so received.

Our reasons for these opinions are:

[Your reasons should cover both (a) and (b) above. As part of them: describe the patient's symptoms and behaviour and explain how those symptoms and behaviour lead you to your opinion; and explain why the patient cannot appropriately be cared for without powers of guardianship.]

....
....
....

[If you need to continue on a separate sheet please indicate here [ ] and attach that sheet to this form]

Signed ....
Date ....
Signed ....
Date ....

NOTE: AT LEAST ONE OF THE PRACTITIONERS SIGNING THIS FORM MUST BE APPROVED UNDER SECTION 12 OF THE ACT.

Form G4

Regulation 5(1)(c)(ii)

Mental Health Act 1983 section 7—medical recommendation for reception into guardianship

2-162   I [PRINT full name, address and, if sending by means of electronic communication, email address of practitioner]], a registered medical practitioner recommend that [PRINT full name and address of patient] be received into guardianship in accordance with Part 2 of the Mental Health Act 1983.

I last examined this patient on [date].

*I had previous acquaintance with the patient before I conducted that examination.

*I am approved under section 12 of the Act as having special experience in the diagnosis or treatment of mental disorder. *[*Delete if not applicable]*

In my opinion,

(a)   this patient is suffering from mental disorder of a nature or degree which warrants the patient's reception into guardianship under the Act,

AND

(b)   it is necessary
    (i)   in the interests of the welfare of the patient
    (ii)   for the protection of other persons
[delete (i) or (ii) unless both apply]
that the patient should be so received. My reasons for these opinions are:

[Your reasons should cover both (a) and (b) above. As part of them: describe the patient's symptoms and behaviour and explain how those symptoms and behaviour lead you to your opinion; and explain why the patient cannot appropriately be cared for without powers of guardianship.]

....
....
....

[If you need to continue on a separate sheet please indicate here [ ] and attach that sheet to this form]

Signed ....
Date ....

FORM G5

Regulation 5(2)

Mental Health Act 1983 section 7—record of acceptance of guardianship application
(To be attached to the guardianship application)
[PRINT full name and address of patient]   **2-163**
This application was accepted by/on behalf* of the local social services authority on [date].
[*Delete the phrase that does not apply]

Signed ....
on behalf of the responsible local social services authority
PRINT NAME ....
Date ....

FORM G6

Regulation 7(4)(a), (d) and (e)

Mental Health Act 1983 section 19—authority for transfer from hospital to guardianship
Part 1
(To be completed on behalf of the managers of the hospital where the patient is detained)
Authority is given for the transfer of [PRINT full name of patient] who is at present liable to be   **2-164**
detained in [name and address of hospital] to the guardianship of [PRINT full name and address of
proposed guardian] in accordance with the Mental Health (Hospital, Guardianship and Treatment)
(England) Regulations 2008.
This transfer was agreed by the [name of local social services authority] on [date of confirmation].
The transfer is to take place on [date].

Signed ....
on behalf of the hospital managers
PRINT NAME ....

Date ....

Part 2*
[*Complete only if proposed guardian is not a local social services authority]
(To be completed by the proposed private guardian)
My full name and address is as entered in Part 1 of this form and I am willing to act as the guardian
of the above named patient in accordance with Part 2 of the Mental Health Act 1983.

Signed ....
Date ....
*IF THE GUARDIAN IS TO BE A PRIVATE GUARDIAN, THE TRANSFER MAY NOT TAKE PLACE
UNTIL BOTH PARTS OF THIS FORM ARE COMPLETED*

FORM G7

Regulation 8(1)(a), (d) and (e)

**Mental Health Act 1983 section 19— authority for transfer of a patient from the guardianship
of one guardian to another**
Part 1
(To be completed by the present guardian)
Authority is given for the transfer of [PRINT full name and address of patient] from the guardian-   **2-165**
ship of [PRINT full name and address of the present guardian] to the guardianship of [PRINT full name
and address of the proposed guardian] in accordance with the Mental Health (Hospital, Guardianship
and Treatment) (England) Regulations 2008.
This transfer was agreed by the [name of local social services authority] on [date of confirmation].
The transfer is to take place on [date].

Signed ....
the guardian/on behalf of the local social services authority which is the guardian
[Delete whichever does not apply]
PRINT NAME ....
Date ....

PART 2*
[*Complete only if proposed guardian is not a local social services authority]
(To be completed by the proposed private guardian)
My full name and address is as entered in Part 1 of this form and I am willing to act as the guardian
of the above named patient in accordance with Part 2 of the Mental Health Act 1983.

Signed ....
Date ....

IF THE NEW GUARDIAN IS TO BE A PRIVATE GUARDIAN, THE TRANSFER MAY NOT TAKE PLACE UNTIL BOTH PARTS OF THIS FORM ARE COMPLETED

FORM G8

Regulation 8(2) and (4)

Mental Health Act 1983 section 19— authority for transfer from guardianship to hospital

Part 1

(To be completed on behalf of the local social services authority)

2-166   Authority is given for the transfer of [PRINT full name and address of patient] who is at present under the guardianship of [name and address of guardian] to [name and address of hospital] in accordance with the Mental Health (Hospital, Guardianship and Treatment) (England) Regulations 2008.

Signed ....

on behalf of the local social services authority

PRINT NAME ....

Date ....

Part 2

RECORD OF ADMISSION

(This is not part of the authority for transfer but is to be completed at the hospital to which the patient is transferred)

This patient was admitted to the above named hospital in pursuance of this authority for transfer on [date of admission to receiving hospital] at [time].

Signed ....

on behalf of the managers of the receiving hospital

PRINT NAME ....

Date ....

FORM G9

Regulation 13(4) and (5)

Mental Health Act 1983 section 20 — renewal of authority for guardianship

Part 1

2-167   *(To be completed by the responsible clinician or nominated medical attendant)*

To   [name of guardian]

[name of responsible local social services authority if it is not the guardian]

I examined [PRINT full name and address of patient] on [date].

The patient is subject to guardianship for a period ending on [date authority for guardianship is due to expire].

In my opinion,

(a)   this patient is suffering from mental disorder of a nature or degree which warrants the patient's reception into guardianship under the Act,

AND

(b)   it is necessary

(i)   in the interests of the welfare of the patient

(ii)   for the protection of other persons

[delete (i) or (ii) unless both apply]

that the patient should remain under guardianship under the Act.

My reasons for these opinions are:

[Your reasons should cover both (a) and (b) above. As part of them: describe the patient's symptoms and behaviour and explain how those symptoms and behaviour lead you to your opinion; and explain why the patient cannot appropriately be cared for without powers of guardianship.]

....

....

....

[If you need to continue on a separate sheet please indicate here [ ] and attach that sheet to this form]

Signed ....

*Responsible clinician

*Nominated medical attendant

*[*Delete whichever does not apply]*

PRINT NAME ....

Date ....

Part 2

(To be completed on behalf of the responsible local social services authority)

This report was received by me on behalf of the local social services authority on [date].

Signed ....

on behalf of the local social services authority

PRINT NAME ....

Date ....

FORM G10

Regulation 14(2)(a) and (b)

Mental Health Act 1983 section 21B — authority for guardianship after absence without leave for more than 28 days

Part 1

(To be completed by the responsible clinician or nominated medical attendant) **2-168**

To   [name of guardian]

[name of responsible local social services authority if it is not the guardian]

I examined [PRINT full name and address of patient] on [date of examination] who:

(a)   was absent without leave from the place where the patient is required to reside beginning on [date absence without leave began];

(b)   was/is* subject to guardianship for a period ending on [date authority for guardianship would have expired, apart from any extension under section 21, or date on which it will expire]; *[*delete phrase which does not apply]* and

(c)   returned to that place on [date].

In my opinion,

(a)   this patient is suffering from mental disorder of a nature or degree which warrants the patient's reception into guardianship under the Act,

AND

(b)   it is necessary

(i)   in the interests of the welfare of the patient

(ii)   for the protection of other persons

[delete (i) or (ii) unless both apply]

that the patient should remain under guardianship under the Act.

My reasons for these opinions are:

[Your reasons should cover both (a) and (b) above. As part of them: describe the patient's symptoms and behaviour and explain how those symptoms and behaviour lead you to your opinion; and explain why the patient cannot appropriately be cared for without powers of guardianship.]

....

....

....

[If you need to continue on a separate sheet please indicate here [ ] and attach that sheet to this form]

The authority for the guardianship of the patient is/is not* due to expire within a period of two months beginning with the date on which this report is to be furnished. *[*Delete the phrase which does not apply]*

Complete the following only if the authority for guardianship is due to expire within that period of two months.

This report shall/shall not* have effect as a report duly furnished under section 20(6) for the renewal of the authority for the guardianship of the patient. *[*Delete the phrase which does not apply]*

Signed ....

*Responsible clinician

*Nominated medical attendant

*[*Delete whichever does not apply]*

PRINT NAME ....

Date ....

Part 2

(To be completed on behalf of the responsible local social services authority)

This report was received by me on behalf of the local social services authority on [date].

Signed ....

on behalf of the local social services authority

PRINT NAME ....

Date ....

Regulation 15(2), (4)(a) and 16(2)

Mental Health Act 1983 Part 6—date of reception of a patient in England

2-169   [PRINT full name of patient]

*was admitted to [name and address of hospital] at [time] on [date]

*was received into the guardianship of [name and address of guardian] on [date]

*became a community patient as if discharged from [name and address of responsible hospital], on [date].

[*Complete as appropriate and delete the others]

Signed ....
on behalf of the hospital managers/
on behalf of the local social services authority/
the private guardian
[Delete whichever do not apply]
PRINT NAME ....
Date ....

Regulation 25(1)(a) and (b)

Mental Health Act 1983 section 25—report barring discharge by nearest relative

Part 1

(To be completed by the responsible clinician)

2-170   To the managers of [name and address of hospital]

[Name of nearest relative] gave notice at [time] on [date] of an intention to discharge [PRINT full name of patient].

I am of the opinion that the patient, if discharged, would be likely to act in a manner dangerous to other persons or to himself or herself.

The reasons for my opinion are—

....
....
....

[If you need to continue on a separate sheet please indicate here [ ] and attach that sheet to this form]

I am furnishing this report by: *[Delete the phrase which does not apply]*

consigning it to the hospital managers' internal mail system today at [time].

[today sending it to the hospital managers, or a person authorised by them to receive it, by means of electronic communication.]

sending or delivering it without using the hospital managers' internal mail system.

Signed ....
Responsible clinician
PRINT NAME ....
[Email address (if applicable)..........]
Date ....
Time ....

Part 2

(To be completed on behalf of the hospital managers)

This report was: *[Delete the phrase which does not apply]*

furnished to the hospital managers through their internal mail system.

[furnished to the hospital managers, or a person authorised by them to receive it, by means of electronic communication.]

received by me on behalf of the hospital managers at [time] on [date].

Signed ....
on behalf of the hospital managers
PRINT NAME ....
Date ....

Regulation 27(1)(b)

Mental Health Act 1983 section 57—certificate of consent to treatment and second opinion

(Both parts of this certificate must be completed)

[722]

Part 1

I [[PRINT full name, address and, if sending by means of electronic communication, email address]], a registered medical practitioner appointed for the purposes of Part 4 of the Act (a SOAD), and we [PRINT full name, address and profession], being two persons appointed for the purposes of section 57(2)(a) of the Act, certify that [PRINT full name and address of patient]

2-171

(a)   is capable of understanding the nature, purpose and likely effects of: [Give description of treatment or plan of treatment. Indicate clearly if the certificate is only to apply to any or all of the treatment for a specific period.]

....
....
....

[If you need to continue on a separate sheet please indicate here [ ] and attach that sheet to this form] AND

(b)   has consented to that treatment.

Signed ....
Date ....
Signed ....
Date ....
Signed ....
Date ....

Part 2
(To be completed by SOAD only)

I, the above named registered medical practitioner appointed for the purposes of Part 4 of the Act have consulted [PRINT full name of nurse] a nurse and [PRINT full name and profession] who have been professionally concerned with the medical treatment of the patient named above and certify that it is appropriate for the treatment to be given.

My reasons are as below/I will provide a statement of my reasons separately. *[Delete as appropriate]* [When giving reasons please indicate if, in your opinion, disclosure of the reasons to the patient would be likely to cause serious harm to the physical or mental health of the patient or to that of any other person.]

....
....
....

If you need to continue on a separate sheet please indicate here [ ] and attach that sheet to this form.]

Signed ....
Date ....

Form T2

Regulation 27(2)

Mental Health Act 1983 section 58(3)(a)—certificate of consent to treatment

I [[PRINT full name, address and, if sending by means of electronic communication, email address]], the approved clinician in charge of the treatment described below/a registered medical practitioner appointed for the purposes of Part 4 of the Act (a SOAD) *[delete the phrase which does not apply]* certify that [PRINT full name and address of patient]

2-172

(a)   is capable of understanding the nature, purpose and likely effects of: [Give description of treatment or plan of treatment. Indicate clearly if the certificate is only to apply to any or all of the treatment for a specific period.]

....
....
....

[If you need to continue on a separate sheet please indicate here [ ] and attach that sheet to this form.] AND

(b)   has consented to that treatment.

Signed ....
Date ....

Form T3

Regulation 27(2)

Mental Health Act 1983 section 58(3)(b)—certificate of second opinion

I [[PRINT full name, address and, if sending by means of electronic communication, email address]], a registered medical practitioner appointed for the purposes of Part 4 of the Act (a SOAD), have consulted [PRINT full name of nurse], a nurse and [PRINT full name and profession] who have been

2-173

professionally concerned with the medical treatment of [PRINT full name and address of patient].

I certify that the patient— *[Delete the phrase which does not apply]*

(a)   is not capable of understanding the nature, purpose and likely effects of

(b)   has not consented to

the following treatment: [Give description of treatment or plan of treatment. Indicate clearly if the certificate is only to apply to any or all of the treatment for a specific period.]

....

....

....

[If you need to continue on a separate sheet please indicate here [ ] and attach that sheet to this form] but that it is appropriate for the treatment to be given.

My reasons are as below/I will provide a statement of my reasons separately. *[Delete as appropriate]* [When giving reasons please indicate if, in your opinion, disclosure of the reasons to the patient would be likely to cause serious harm to the physical or mental health of the patient, or to that of any other person.]

....

....

....

[If you need to continue on a separate sheet please indicate here [ ] and attach that sheet to this form.]

Signed ....

Date ....

FORM T4

Regulation 27(3)(b)

Mental Health Act 1983 section 58A(3)—certificate of consent to treatment (patients at least 18 years old)

THIS FORM IS NOT TO BE USED FOR PATIENTS UNDER 18 YEARS OF AGE

2-174   I [[PRINT full name, address and, if sending by means of electronic communication, email address]], the approved clinician in charge of the treatment described below/a registered medical practitioner appointed for the purposes of Part 4 of the Act (a SOAD) *[delete as appropriate]* certify that [PRINT full name and address of patient] who has attained the age of 18 years,

(a)   is capable of understanding the nature, purpose and likely effects of: [Give description of treatment or plan of treatment. Indicate clearly if the certificate is only to apply to any or all of the treatment for a specific period.]

....

....

[If you need to continue on a separate sheet please indicate here [ ] and attach that sheet to this form] AND

(b)   has consented to that treatment.

Signed ....

Date ....

FORM T5

Regulation 27(3)(b)

Mental Health Act 1983 section 58A(4)—certificate of consent to treatment and second opinion (patients under 18)

THIS FORM IS ONLY TO BE USED FOR PATIENTS UNDER 18 YEARS OF AGE

2-175   I [[PRINT full name, address and, if sending by means of electronic communication, email address]], a registered medical practitioner appointed for the purposes of Part 4 of the Act (a SOAD) certify that [PRINT full name and address of patient] who has not yet attained the age of 18 years,

(a)   is capable of understanding the nature, purpose and likely effects of: [Give description of treatment or plan of treatment. Indicate clearly if the certificate is only to apply to any or all of the treatment for a specific period./a:author-amendment]

....

....

[If you need to continue on a separate sheet please indicate here [ ] and attach that sheet to this form] AND

(b)   has consented to that treatment.

In my opinion it is appropriate for that treatment to be given.

My reasons are as below/I will provide a statement of my reasons separately. *[Delete as appropri-*

ate] [When giving reasons please indicate if, in your opinion, disclosure of the reasons to the patient would be likely to cause serious harm to the physical or mental health of the patient, or to that of any other person.]

....

....

....

[If you need to continue on a separate sheet please indicate here [ ] and attach that sheet to this form.]

Signed ....

Date ....

Form T6

Regulation 27(3)(b)

Mental Health Act 1983 section 58A(5)—certificate of second opinion (patients who are not capable of understanding the nature, purpose and likely effects of the treatment)

I [[PRINT full name, address and, if sending by means of electronic communication, email address]], a registered medical practitioner appointed for the purposes of Part 4 of the Act (a SOAD), have consulted [PRINT full name of nurse] a nurse and [PRINT full name and profession] who have been professionally concerned with the medical treatment of [PRINT full name and address of patient].

2-176

I certify that the patient is not capable of understanding the nature, purpose and likely effects of: [Give description of treatment or plan of treatment. Indicate clearly if the certificate is only to apply to any or all of the treatment for a specific period.]

....

....

....

[If you need to continue on a separate sheet please indicate here [ ] and attach that sheet to this form] but that it is appropriate for the treatment to be given.

My reasons are as below/I will provide a statement of my reasons separately. *Delete as appropriate* [When giving reasons please indicate if, in your opinion, disclosure of the reasons to the patient would be likely to cause serious harm to the physical or mental health of the patient or to that of any other person.]

....

....

....

[If you need to continue on a separate sheet please indicate here [ ] and attach that sheet to this form.]

I further certify that giving the treatment described above to the patient would not conflict with—

(i) any decision of an attorney appointed under a Lasting Power of Attorney or deputy (appointed by the Court of Protection) of the patient as provided for by the Mental Capacity Act 2005

(ii) any decision of the Court of Protection, or

(iii) any advance decision to refuse treatment that is valid and applicable under the Mental Capacity Act 2005.

Signed ....

Date ....

Form CTO1

Regulation 6(1)(a), (b) and 6(2)(a)

Mental Health Act 1983 section 17A—community treatment order

2-177

(Parts 1 and 3 of this form are to be completed by the responsible clinician and Part 2 by an approved mental health professional)

Part 1

I [[PRINT full name, address and, if sending by means of electronic communication, email address of the responsible clinician]] am the responsible clinician for [PRINT full name and address of patient]. In my opinion,

(a) this patient is suffering from mental disorder of a nature or degree which makes it appropriate for the patient to receive medical treatment,

(b) it is necessary for

(i) the patient's health

(ii) the patient's safety

(iii) the protection of other persons

[delete any phrase which is not applicable]

that the patient should receive such treatment;

[725]

(c)   such treatment can be provided without the patient continuing to be detained in a hospital provided the patient is liable to being recalled to hospital for medical treatment;

(d)   it is necessary that the responsible clinician should be able to exercise the power under section 17E(1) to recall the patient to hospital;

(e)   taking into account the nature and degree of the mental disorder from which the patient is suffering and all other circumstances of the case, appropriate medical treatment is available to the patient.

My opinion is founded on the following grounds—

....

....

....

[If you need to continue on a separate sheet please indicate here [ ] and attach that sheet to this form]

I confirm that in determining whether the criterion at (d) above is met, I have considered what risk there would be of deterioration of the patient's condition if the patient were not detained in hospital, with regard to the patient's history of mental disorder and any other relevant factors.

Conditions to which the patient is to be subject by virtue of this community treatment order

The patient is to make himself or herself available for examination under section 20A, as requested.

If it is proposed to give a certificate under Part 4A of the Act in the patient's case, the patient is to make himself or herself available for examination to enable the certificate to be given, as requested.

The patient is also to be subject to the following conditions (if any) under section 17B(2) of the Act:

....

....

....

[If you need to continue on a separate sheet please indicate here [ ] and attach that sheet to this form]

I confirm that I consider the above conditions to be made under section 17B(2) of the Act are necessary or appropriate for one or more of the following purposes:

•   to ensure that the patient receives medical treatment

•   to prevent risk of harm to the patient's health or safety

•   to protect other persons.

Signed ....
Date ....

Part 2

I [PRINT full name and address] am acting on behalf of [name of local social services authority] and am approved to act as an approved mental health professional for the purposes of the Act by *[delete as appropriate]*

that authority

[name of local social services authority that approved you, if different].

I agree that:

(i)   the above patient meets the criteria for a community treatment order to be made

(ii)   it is appropriate to make a community treatment order, and

(iii)   the conditions made above under section 17B(2) are necessary or appropriate for one or more of the purposes specified.

Signed ....
Approved mental health professional
Date ....

Part 3

I exercise my power under section 17A of the Mental Health Act 1983 to make a community treatment order in respect of the patient named in Part 1 of this Form.

This community treatment order is to be effective from [date] at [time].

Signed...............
Responsible clinician
Date...............

THIS COMMUNITY TREATMENT ORDER IS NOT VALID UNLESS ALL THREE PARTS ARE COMPLETED AND SIGNED

IT MUST BE FURNISHED AS SOON AS PRACTICABLE TO THE MANAGERS OF THE HOSPITAL IN WHICH THE PATIENT WAS LIABLE TO BE DETAINED BEFORE THE ORDER WAS MADE

FORM CTO2

Regulation 6(2)(b)

2-178   **Mental Health Act 1983 section 17B—variation of conditions of a community treatment order**

I [[PRINT full name, address and, if sending by means of electronic communication, email address of the responsible clinician]] am the responsible clinician for [PRINT full name and address of the community patient].

I am varying the conditions attaching to the community treatment order for the above named patient. The conditions made under section 17B(2), as varied, are: [List the conditions as varied in full (including any which are not being varied) or state that there are no longer to be any such conditions.]

....
....
....

[If you need to continue on a separate sheet please indicate here [ ] and attach that sheet to this form] The variation is to take effect from [date].

I confirm that I consider the above conditions to be necessary or appropriate for one or more of the following purposes:

• to ensure that the patient receives medical treatment
• to prevent risk of harm to the patient's health or safety
• to protect other persons.

Signed ....
Responsible clinician
Date ....

THIS FORM MUST BE FURNISHED AS SOON AS PRACTICABLE TO THE MANAGERS OF THE RESPONSIBLE HOSPITAL

Form CTO3

Regulation 6(3)(a)

Mental Health Act 1983 section 17E—community treatment order: notice of recall to hospital   **2-179**
(To be completed by the responsible clinician)
I notify you, [PRINT name of community patient], that you are recalled to [PRINT full name and address of the hospital] under section 17E of the Mental Health Act 1983.
Complete either (a) or (b) below and delete the one which does not apply.
(a)   In my opinion,
    (i)   you require treatment in hospital for mental disorder, AND
    (ii)   there would be a risk of harm to your health or safety or to other persons if you were not recalled to hospital for that purpose.
This opinion is founded on the following grounds—

....
....
....

[If you need to continue on a separate sheet please indicate here [ ] and attach that sheet to this form]
(b)   You have failed to comply with the condition imposed under section 17B of the Mental Health Act 1983 that you make yourself available for examination for the purpose of: *[delete as appropriate]*
    (i)   consideration of extension of the community treatment period under section 20A
    (ii)   enabling a Part 4A certificate to be given.

Signed ....
Responsible clinician
PRINT NAME ....
Date ....
Time ....

A COPY OF THIS NOTICE IS TO BE FORWARDED TO THE MANAGERS OF THE HOSPITAL TO WHICH THE PATIENT IS RECALLED AS SOON AS POSSIBLE AFTER IT IS SERVED ON THE PATIENT. IF THAT HOSPITAL IS NOT THE RESPONSIBLE HOSPITAL, YOU SHOULD INFORM THE HOSPITAL MANAGERS THE NAME AND ADDRESS OF THE RESPONSIBLE HOSPITAL.

This notice is sufficient authority for the managers of the named hospital to detain the patient there in accordance with the provisions of section 17E of the Mental Health Act 1983.

Form CTO4

Regulation 6(3)(d)

Mental Health Act 1983 section 17E — community treatment order: record of patient's detention in hospital after recall   **2-180**
[PRINT full name and address of patient] ('the patient') is currently a community patient.
In pursuance of a notice recalling the patient to hospital under section 17E of the Act, the patient was detained in [full name and address of hospital] on [enter date and time at which the patient's detention

in the hospital as a result of the recall notice began].

Signed ....
on behalf of the hospital managers
PRINT NAME ....
Date ....
Time ....

Form CTO5

Regulation 6(8)(a) and (b)

2-181   Mental Health Act 1983 section 17F(4)—revocation of community treatment order
(Parts 1 and 3 of this form are to be completed by the responsible clinician and Part 2 by an approved mental health professional)

Part 1

I [[PRINT full name, address and, if sending by means of electronic communication, email address of the responsible clinician]] am the responsible clinician for [PRINT full name and address of community patient] who is detained in [name and address of hospital] having been recalled to hospital under section 17E(1) of the Act.

In my opinion,

(a)   this patient is suffering from mental disorder of a nature or degree which makes it appropriate for the patient to receive medical treatment in a hospital,
AND
(b)   it is necessary for
  (i)   the patient's own health
  (ii)   the patient's own safety
  (iii)   the protection of other persons
[delete the indents not applicable]
that this patient should receive treatment in hospital,
AND
(c)   such treatment cannot be provided unless the patient is detained for medical treatment under the Act,
because— [Your reasons should cover (a), (b) and (c) above. As part of them: describe the patient's symptoms and behaviour and explain how those symptoms and behaviour lead you to your opinion; say whether other methods of treatment or care (eg out-patient treatment or social services) are available and, if so, why they are not appropriate; indicate why informal admission is not appropriate.]

....
....
....

[If you need to continue on a separate sheet please indicate here [ ] and attach that sheet to this form]

I am also of the opinion that taking into account the nature and degree of the mental disorder from which the patient is suffering and all other circumstances of the case, appropriate medical treatment is available to the patient at the hospital named above.

Signed ....
Responsible clinician
Date ....

Part 2

I [[PRINT full name, address and, if sending by means of electronic communication, email address]] am acting on behalf of [name of local social services authority] and am approved to act as an approved mental health professional for the purposes of the Act by *[delete as appropriate]*
that authority
[name of local social services authority that approved you, if different].
I agree that:
(i)   the patient meets the criteria for detention in hospital set out above and
(ii)   it is appropriate to revoke the community treatment order.

Signed ....
Approved mental health professional
Date ....

Part 3

I exercise my power under section 17F(4) to revoke the community treatment order in respect of the patient named in Part 1 who has been detained in hospital since [time] on [date], having been recalled under section 17E(1).

Signed ....
Responsible clinician

Date ....

THIS REVOCATION ORDER IS NOT VALID UNLESS ALL THREE PARTS ARE COMPLETED AND SIGNED

IT MUST BE SENT AS SOON AS PRACTICABLE TO THE MANAGERS OF THE HOSPITAL IN WHICH THE PATIENT IS DETAINED

Form CTO6

Regulation 9(3)(a) and (5)

Mental Health Act 1983 section 17F(2)—authority for transfer of recalled community patient to a hospital under different managers   **2-182**

(To be completed on behalf of the managers of the hospital in which the patient is detained by virtue of recall)

Part 1

This form authorises the transfer of [PRINT full name of patient] from [name and address of hospital in which the patient is detained] to [name and address of hospital to which patient is to be transferred] in accordance with the Mental Health (Hospital, Guardianship and Treatment) (England) Regulations 2008.

I attach a copy of Form CTO4 recording the patient's detention in hospital after recall.

*The hospital in which the patient is currently detained is the patient's responsible hospital.

*The hospital to which the patient is to be transferred is the patient's responsible hospital.

*The patient's responsible hospital is [name and address of responsible hospital].

[Delete the phrases which do not apply]*

Signed ....
on behalf of managers of the first named hospital
PRINT NAME ....
Date ....

Part 2 Record of Admission

(This is not part of the authority for transfer but is to be completed at the hospital to which the patient is transferred)

This patient was admitted to [name of hospital] in pursuance of this authority for transfer on [date of admission to receiving hospital] at [time].

Signed ....
on behalf of managers of the receiving hospital
PRINT NAME ....
Date ....

Form CTO7

Regulation 13(6)(a) and (b), and 13(7)

Mental Health Act 1983 section 20A — community treatment order: report extending the community treatment period   **2-183**

Parts 1 and 3 of this form are to be completed by the responsible clinician and Part 2 by an approved mental health professional. Part 4 is to be completed by or on behalf of the managers of the responsible hospital.

Part 1

To the managers of [name and address of the responsible hospital]

I am [[PRINT full name, address and, if sending by means of electronic communication, email address of the responsible clinician]] the responsible clinician for [PRINT full name and address of patient].

The patient is currently subject to a community treatment order made on [enter date]. I examined the patient on [date].

In my opinion,

(a) this patient is suffering from mental disorder of a nature or degree which makes it appropriate for the patient to receive medical treatment;

(b) it is necessary for
   (i)   the patient's health
   (ii) the patient's safety
   (iii) the protection of other persons
[delete any indent which is not applicable]
   that the patient should receive such treatment;

[729]

(c)   such treatment can be provided without the patient continuing to be detained in a hospital provided the patient is liable to being recalled to hospital for medical treatment;

(d)   it is necessary that the responsible clinician should continue to be able to exercise the power under section 17E(1) to recall the patient to hospital;

(e)   taking into account the nature and degree of the mental disorder from which the patient is suffering and all other circumstances of the case, appropriate medical treatment is available to the patient.

My opinion is founded on the following grounds—

....

....

[If you need to continue on a separate sheet please indicate here [ ] and attach that sheet to this form]

I confirm that in determining whether the criterion at (d) above is met, I have considered what risk there would be of deterioration of the patient's condition if the patient were to continue not to be detained in hospital, with regard to the patient's history of mental disorder and any other relevant factors.

Signed ....
Responsible clinician
Date ....

Part 2

I [[PRINT full name, address and, if sending by means of electronic communication, email address]] am acting on behalf of [name of local social services authority] and am approved to act as an approved mental health professional for the purposes of the Act by *[delete as appropriate]*

that authority

[name of local social services authority that approved you, if different]. I agree that:

(i)   the patient meets the criteria for the extension of the community treatment period and

(ii)   it is appropriate to extend the community treatment period.

Signed ....
Approved mental health professional
Date ....

Part 3

Before furnishing this report, I consulted [PRINT full name and profession of person consulted] who has been professionally concerned with the patient's treatment.

I am furnishing this report by: *[Delete the phrase which does not apply]*

today consigning it to the hospital managers' internal mail system.

[today sending it to the hospital managers, or a person authorised by them to receive it, by means of electronic communication.]

sending or delivering it without using the hospital managers' internal mail system.

Signed ....
Responsible clinician
Date ....

THIS REPORT IS NOT VALID UNLESS PARTS 1, 2 & 3 ARE COMPLETED AND SIGNED

Part 4

This report was *[Delete the phrase which does not apply]*

furnished to the hospital managers through their internal mail system.

[furnished to the hospital managers, or a person authorised by them to receive it, by means of electronic communication.]

received by me on behalf of the hospital managers on [date].

Signed ....
on behalf of the managers of the responsible hospital
PRINT NAME ....
Date ....

FORM CTO8

Regulation 14(3)(a) and (b)

Mental Health Act 1983 section 21B—authority for extension of community treatment period after absence without leave for more than 28 days

Part 1

(To be completed by the responsible clinician)

2-184   To the managers of [enter name and address of responsible hospital]

I am [[PRINT full name, address and, if sending by means of electronic communication, email address of the responsible clinician]] the responsible clinician for [PRINT full name and address of patient]. I examined the patient on [date of examination] who:

(a)   was recalled to hospital on [date] under section 17E of the Mental Health Act 1983;

(b)   was absent without leave from hospital beginning on [date absence without leave began];

(c)   was/is *[delete as appropriate]* subject to a community treatment order for a period ending on [date community treatment order would have expired, apart from any extension under section 21, or date on which it will expire]; and

(d)   returned to the hospital on [date].

I have consulted [PRINT full name of approved mental health professional] who is an approved mental health professional.

I have also consulted [PRINT full name and profession of person consulted] who has been professionally concerned with the patient's treatment.

In my opinion,

(a)   this patient is suffering from mental disorder of a nature or degree which makes it appropriate for the patient to receive medical treatment;

(b)   it is necessary for

    (i)   the patient's health

    (ii)   the patient's safety

    (iii) the protection of other persons

[delete any indent which is not applicable]

that the patient should receive such treatment;

(c)   such treatment can be provided without the patient continuing to be detained in a hospital provided the patient is liable to being recalled to hospital for medical treatment;

(d)   it is necessary that the responsible clinician should continue to be able to exercise the power under section 17E(1) to recall the patient to hospital;

(e)   taking into account the nature and degree of the mental disorder from which the patient is suffering and all other circumstances of the case, appropriate medical treatment is available to the patient.

I confirm that in determining whether the criterion at (d) above is met, I have considered what risk there would be of deterioration of the patient's condition if the patient were to continue not to be detained in hospital, with regard to the patient's history of mental disorder and any other relevant factors.

My opinion is founded on the following grounds—

....

....

[If you need to continue on a separate sheet please indicate here [ ] and attach that sheet to this form]

The community treatment order is/is not* due to expire within a period of two months beginning with the date on which this report is to be furnished to the managers of the responsible hospital. *[*Delete the phrase which does not apply]*

[Complete the following only if the community treatment order is due to expire within that period of two months]

This report shall/shall not* have effect as a report duly furnished under section 20A(4) for the extension of the community treatment period for this patient. *[*Delete the phrase which does not apply]*

Complete the following in all cases.

I am furnishing this report by: *[Delete the phrase which does not apply]*

today consigning it to the hospital managers' internal mail system.

[today sending it to the hospital managers, or a person authorised by them to receive it, by means of electronic communication.]

sending or delivering it without using the hospital managers' internal mail system.

Signed..............
Date..............

Part 2
(To be completed on behalf of the managers of the responsible hospital)
This report was [Delete the phrase which does not apply]

furnished to the hospital managers through their internal mail system. received by me on behalf of the hospital managers on [date].

[furnished to the hospital managers, or a person authorised by them to receive it, by means of electronic communication.]

Signed ....
on behalf of the hospital managers
PRINT NAME ....
Date ....

FORM CTO9

Regulation 16(4) and (5)

Mental Health Act 1983 Part 6—community patients transferred to England

Part 1

(To be completed by the responsible clinician)

2-185   I [[PRINT full name, address and, if sending by means of electronic communication, email address of the responsible clinician]] am the responsible clinician for [PRINT full name and address of patient] who is treated as if subject to a community treatment order having been transferred to England.

The patient is to be subject to the following conditions by virtue of that community treatment order:

The patient is to make himself or herself available for examination under section 20A, as requested.

If it is proposed to give a certificate under Part 4A of the Act in the patient's case, the patient is to make himself or herself available for examination to enable the certificate to be given, as requested.

The patient is also to be subject to the following conditions (if any) under section 17B(2) of the Act:

....

....

[If you need to continue on a separate sheet please indicate here [ ] and attach that sheet to this form]

I confirm that I consider the above conditions to be made under section 17B(2) of the Act are necessary or appropriate for one or more of the following purposes:

- to ensure that the patient receives medical treatment
- to prevent risk of harm to the patient's health or safety
- to protect other persons.

Signed ....

Responsible clinician

Date ....

Part 2

(To be completed by the approved mental health professional)

I [[PRINT full name, address and, if sending by means of electronic communication, email address]] am acting on behalf of [name of local social services authority] and am approved to act as an approved mental health professional for the purposes of the Act by *[Delete as appropriate]*

that authority

[name of local social services authority that approved you, if different].

I agree that the conditions made above under section 17B(2) are necessary or appropriate for one or more of the purposes specified.

Signed ....

Approved mental health professional

Date ....

THE PATIENT IS NOT SUBJECT TO THE CONDITIONS SET OUT IN THIS FORM UNLESS BOTH PARTS OF THE FORM ARE COMPLETED.

FORM CTO10

Regulation 17(3)(a) and (d)(i) and (ii)

Mental Health Act 1983 section 19A—authority for assignment of responsibility for community patient to hospital under different managers

(To be completed on behalf of the responsible hospital)

2-186   This form gives authority for the assignment of responsibility for [PRINT full name and address of patient] from [name and address of responsible hospital] to [name and address of hospital to which responsibility is to be assigned in accordance with the Mental Health (Hospital, Guardianship and Treatment) (England) Regulations 2008.

This assignment was agreed by the managers of the hospital to which the responsibility is to be assigned on [date of confirmation]

The assignment is to take place on [date].

Signed ....

on behalf of managers of first named hospital

PRINT NAME ....

Date ....

FORM CTO11

Regulation 28(1)

Mental Health Act 1983 section 64C(4) — certificate of appropriateness of treatment to be given to community patient (Part 4A certificate)

[...]

2-187   I [[PRINT full name, address and, if sending by means of electronic communication, email address]] am a registered medical practitioner appointed for the purposes of Part 4 of the Act (a SOAD).

I have consulted [PRINT full name and profession] and [full name and profession] who have been professionally concerned with the medical treatment of [PRINT full name and address of patient] who is subject to a community treatment order.

I certify that it is appropriate for the following treatment to be given to this patient while the patient is not recalled to hospital, subject to any conditions specified below. The treatment is: [Give description of treatment or plan of treatment.]

....
....
....

I specify the following conditions (if any) to apply: [Conditions may include time-limits on the approval of any or all of the treatment.]

....
....
....

I certify that it is appropriate for the following treatment (if any) to be given to this patient following any recall to hospital under section 17E of the Act, subject to any conditions specified below. The treatment is: [Give description of treatment or plan of treatment].

....
....
....

I specify the following conditions (if any) to apply to the treatment which may be given to the patient following any recall to hospital under section 17E: [Conditions may include time-limits on the approval of any or all of the treatment.]

....
....
....

My reasons are as below/I will provide a statement of my reasons separately. *[Delete as appropriate]* [When giving reasons please indicate if, in your opinion, disclosure of the reasons to the patient would be likely to cause serious harm to the physical or mental health of the patient, or to that of any other person.]

....
....
....

[If you need to continue on a separate sheet for any of the above please indicate here [ ] and attach that sheet to this form.]

Signed ....
Date ....

Form CTO12

Regulation 28(1A)

Mental Health Act 1983 section 64C(4A)–certificate that community patient has capacity to consent (or if under 16 is competent to consent) to treatment and has done so (Part 4A consent certificate)

(To be completed on behalf of the responsible hospital)

I [[PRINT full name, address and, if sending by means of electronic communication, email address]] am the approved clinician in charge of the treatment of [PRINT full name and address of patient] who is subject to a community treatmen order.

2-188

I certify that this patient has the capacity/is competent to consent [delete the one that is not appropriate] and has consented to the following treatment. The treatment is: [Give description of treatment or plan of treatment.]

Signed ....
Date ....

Amendment

This Form was inserted by SI 2012/1118 reg.2(3).

SCHEDULE 2

Revocations

Regulations 32

[Not reproduced]

2-189

The Mental Health Act 1983 (Independent Mental Health Advocates) (England) Regulations 2008

(SI 2008/3166)

Dated December 9, 2008, and made by the Secretary of State under the Mental Health Act 1983, section 130A, and the National Health Service Act 2006, sections 7, 8, 14, 19, 75, 272(7) and (8) and 233(4).

General Note

2-190 Section 130A of the Act provides that local authorities shall make arrangements to enable Independent Mental Health Advocates (IMHAs) to be available to help qualifying patients. These regulations contain provisions about the arrangements for the appointment of IMHAs and as to who can be appointed to act as an IMHA.

Citation, commencement and extent

2-191 **1.**—(1) These Regulations may be cited as the Mental Health Act 1983 (Independent Mental Health Advocates) (England) Regulations 2008.

(2) These Regulations shall come into force on 1st April 2009.

(3) These Regulations apply in relation to England only.

Interpretation

2-192 **2.** In these Regulations—

"the Act" means the Mental Health Act 1983;

["commissioning body" means a local social services authority whose area is in England;]

"IMHA" means an independent mental health advocate;

"provider of advocacy services" means a person (including a voluntary organisation) that employs or engages individuals who may be made available to act as an IMHA but does not include a commissioning body;

["section 130A functions" means the functions under section 130A of the Act of a local social services authority whose area is in England.]

Amendments

The amendments to this regulation were made by SI 2013/261 reg.16(2).

[Circumstances in which a person may be appointed to be an Independent Mental Health Advocate

2-193 **3.**—(1) A commissioning body, in exercising section 130A functions, may enter into arrangements to appoint an individual to act as an IMHA only if the commissioning body is satisfied that the conditions set out in regulation 6 are satisfied.

(2) A commissioning body, in exercising section 130A functions, may enter into arrangements with a provider of advocacy services only if such arrangements include a term that the provider is satisfied that the conditions set out in regulation 6 are satisfied in respect of an individual made available by the provider to act as an IMHA.

(3) A commissioning body may only enter into the arrangements described in paragraphs (1) or (2) above where it has had due regard to the diverse circumstances

(including but not limited to the ethnic, cultural and demographic needs) of qualifying patients.]

Amendment

This regulation was substituted by SI 2013/261 reg.16(3).

4.   [*Repealed by SI 2013/261 reg.16(4)*]   **2-194**

5.   [*Repealed by SI 2013/261 reg.16(5)*]   **2-195**

Independent Mental Health Advocates: conditions

6.—(1)   A person may not act as an IMHA unless the conditions specified in   **2-196**
paragraph (2) are satisfied.

(2)   Those conditions are that the person referred to in paragraph (1)—

    (a)   has appropriate experience or training or an appropriate combination of experience and training;

    (b)   is a person of integrity and good character;

    (c)   is able to act independently of any person who is professionally concerned with the qualifying patient's medical treatment; and

    (d)   is able to act independently of any person who requests that person to visit or interview the qualifying patient.

(3)   For the purposes of the condition referred to in paragraph (2)(a) regard must be had to standards in guidance that may be issued from time to time by the Secretary of State.

(4)   The standards referred to in paragraph (3) may include any qualification that the Secretary of State may determine as appropriate.

[(5)   For the purposes of the condition referred to in paragraph (2)(b) there must be obtained, in respect of that person, an enhanced criminal record certificate issued pursuant to section 113B of the Police Act 1997 which includes—

    (a)   where the qualifying patient has not attained the age of 18, suitability information relating to children (within the meaning of section 113BA of the Police Act 1997);

    (b)   where the qualifying patient has attained the age of 18, suitability information relating to vulnerable adults (within the meaning of section 113BB of that Act).]

Amendment

Paragraph (5) was substituted by SI 2009/2376 reg.3.

General Note

Details of the IMHA scheme for England can be found in "Independent Mental Health Advocacy-   **2-197**
Guidance for Commissioners", NIMH in England, December 2008, which can be accessed at: *http://
data.parliament.uk/DepositedPapers/Files/DEP2009-0095/DEP2009-0095.pdf.*

Persons not professionally concerned with a patient's medical treatment

7.   For the purposes of section 130A(5) of the Act a person is not to be regarded   **2-198**
as professionally concerned with a qualifying patient's medical treatment if that person—

    (a)   is representing the patient in accordance with—

        (i)   arrangements made for the purposes of section 130A functions;

(ii)   arrangements made other than for the purposes of that section;

(b)   has in the past represented the qualifying patient in accordance with arrangements referred to in sub-paragraph (a) and in doing so was not otherwise professionally concerned in that patient's treatment.

The Mental Health Act 1983 (Places of Safety) Regulations 2017

(SI 2017/1036)

Made on October 24, 2017 by The Secretary of State in exercise of the powers conferred by sections 136(1C)(d) and 136A(2) and (3) of the Mental Health Act 1983

General Note

2-199   The Explanatory Note to these Regulations reads as follows:

"These Regulations specify the circumstances in which a police station can be used as a place of safety for an adult, for the purposes of powers in sections 135 and 136 of the Mental Health Act 1983 (that is, powers to remove or take an adult to, or to keep an adult at, a place of safety), as amended by the Policing and Crime Act 2017. Where a police station is used, the Regulations also describe the safeguards and steps to be taken to protect the person detained.

Regulation 2 provides that a police station can only be used as a place of safety for an adult where the person exercising, or authorising the exercise of, the power under section 135 or section 136 is satisfied that: (a) the behaviour of the adult presents an imminent risk of serious injury or death to that adult or to others; (b) as a result, no other place of safety in the police area in which the adult is located can reasonably be expected to detain them; and (c) the adult will have access to a healthcare professional, so far as is reasonably practicable, throughout the period in which they are detained at the police station.

Regulation 2 further provides that, where the person considering using a police station as a place of safety is a police officer, they must, if reasonably practicable, consult with a registered medical practitioner, a registered nurse, an approved mental health professional, an occupational therapist or a paramedic, before making the decision.

The decision to use a police station as a place of safety must be authorised by an officer of the rank of inspector or above.

Regulations 4 to 7 set out how adults detained at a police station must be treated during the period that they are detained.

They require the custody officer to ensure that the welfare of the adult is checked at least every thirty minutes by a healthcare professional, and any appropriate action is taken for their treatment and care, and that so far as reasonably practicable a healthcare professional is present and available to the adult at all times. In any case where it is no longer possible for those requirements to be met, the adult must be taken to another place of safety. (However, there is no requirement to transfer the adult to another place of safety where arrangements have been made for a mental health assessment to be carried out at the police station, the transfer would delay such an assessment taking place, and the delay would be likely to cause the adult distress.)

They also require the custody offer to review the adult's behaviour at least once an hour, so that the custody officer can consider (if reasonably practicable, with the advice of a healthcare professional) whether it is still the case that the adult's behaviour presents an imminent risk that no other place of safety in the police area can manage. If the custody officer determines that those circumstances no longer exist, the adult must be transferred to another place of safety that is not a police station. (Again, there is no requirement to transfer the adult where arrangements have been made for a mental health assessment to be carried out at the police station, the transfer would delay the assessment taking place, and the delay would be likely to cause the adult distress.) The frequency of the reviews may be reduced to no less than once every three hours if the adult is sleeping, and a healthcare professional has not identified any risk sufficient to warrant waking them more frequently.

The Regulations do not apply where a person's removal began, or the warrant for their removal was issued, before the coming into force of these Regulations.

The Mental Health Act 1983 requires that, before making a decision to remove a person to, or to keep a person at, a place of safety under section 136(1) the constable must, if it is reasonably practicable to do so, consult a registered medical practitioner, a registered nurse, an approved mental health professional, or a person of a specified description. These Regulations specify an occupational therapist and a paramedic for the purposes of that provision.

A full regulatory impact assessment has not been produced for this instrument as no impact on the private or voluntary sector is foreseen."

Guidance

Joint Department of Health and Home Office guidance on these Regulations can be accessed at: **2-200** *www.gov.uk/government/uploads/system/uploads/attachment_data/file/656025/Guidance_on_Police_ Powers.PDF.*

Citation, commencement and interpretation

1.—(1)   These Regulations may be cited as the Mental Health Act 1983 (Places   **2-201** of Safety) Regulations 2017 and come into force on 11th December 2017.

(2)   In these Regulations—

"the Act" means the Mental Health Act 1983;

"custody officer" means a person who is appointed as, or who is performing the functions of, a custody officer within the meaning given in section 36 of the Police and Criminal Evidence Act 1984;

"healthcare professional" means a person who is a member of a profession mentioned in section 60(2) of the Health Act 1999.

Circumstances in which a police station may be used as a place of safety

2.—(1)   An adult ("A") may only be removed to, kept at, or taken to, a place   **2-202** of safety that is a police station in the exercise of a power to which section 136A of the Act applies where—

(a)   the decision-maker is satisfied that—

(i)   the behaviour of A poses an imminent risk of serious injury or death to A, or to another person,

(ii)   because of that risk, no place of safety other than a police station in the relevant police area can reasonably be expected to detain A, and

(iii)   the requirement in sub-paragraph (b) of regulation 4(1) will be met, and

(b)   where the decision-maker is not an officer of the rank of inspector or above, an officer of that rank or above authorises that A may be removed to, kept at, or taken to a place of safety that is a police station.

(2)   Before determining that the circumstances in paragraphs (i) to (iii) of paragraph (1)(a) exist, a decision-maker who is a constable must, if it is reasonably practicable to do so, consult—

(a)   a registered medical practitioner,

(b)   a registered nurse,

(c)   an approved mental health professional, or

(d)   a person of a description specified in regulation 8(1).

(3)   In this regulation—

"decision-maker" means—

(a)   in relation to the exercise of a power under section 135(1) or 136(1) of the Act, the constable exercising that power,

(b)   in relation to the exercise of a power under section 135(3A) or 136(3) of the Act, the constable or approved mental health professional who—

(i)   exercises that power, or

(ii)   authorises a person to exercise that power,

"relevant police area" means the police area in which A is located when a power to which section 136A of the Act applies begins to be exercised in relation to A.

General Note

2-203   Under para.(1)(a)(iii), before the police decision-maker can agree to a police station being used as a place of safety, he or she must be satisfied under reg.4 that a healthcare professional will be present and available to the detained person throughout the period of detention.

Even though the behaviour of the detained person might satisfy the criteria set out in this regulation, para.4.19 of the Guidance (see above) states that nothing in these regulations "overrides provisions in PACE Code C on the custody officer sending for an ambulance or referring the person to a hospital for emergency treatment if deemed necessary".

If the detained person ceases to meet the criteria, he should be taken to a place of safety other than a police station (reg.5).

Requirements when a police station is used as a place of safety

2-204   **3.**   Regulations 4 to 7 apply when an adult is detained at a police station under section 135 or section 136 of the Act.

2-205   **4.**—(1)   A custody officer at the police station must ensure that—

(a)   the welfare of the detained adult ("D") is checked by a healthcare professional at least once every thirty minutes, and any appropriate action is taken for the treatment and care of D, and

(b)   so far as is reasonably practicable, a healthcare professional is present and available to D throughout the period in which D is detained at the police station.

(2)   Subject to regulation 7, in any case where either or both of the requirements in paragraph (1)(a) and (b) is not met, the custody officer must arrange for D to be taken to another place of safety.

General Note

2-206   Subject to the exception set out in para.7, if the custody officer is not able to satisfy the requirements of para.(1)(a) and/or (b), the detained adult *must* be taken to another place of safety.

2-207   **5.**—(1)   A custody officer at the police station must, subject to paragraph (2) and regulations 6 and 7—

(a)   review the behaviour of D at least once an hour and determine whether the circumstances in regulation 2(1)(a)(i) and (ii) exist, and

(b)   where those circumstances are determined not to exist, arrange for D to be taken to a place of safety other than a police station.

(2)   Before making a determination under paragraph (1)(a), the custody officer must, where reasonably practicable, consult the healthcare professional that carried out the most recent check by virtue of regulation 4(1)(a).

General Note

2-208   The requirement under para.(1)(b) to take the detained person to another place of safety is subject to the exception contained in para.7.

2-209   **6.**   The frequency of the reviews referred to in regulation 5(1)(a) may be reduced, to no less than once every three hours, where—

(a)   D is sleeping, and

(b) a healthcare professional who has checked D's welfare by virtue of regulation 4(1)(a) has not, in the most recent check, identified any risk that would require D to be woken more frequently.

7. The requirements to take D to a place of safety in regulation 4(2) and regulation 5(1)(b) do not apply where—   **2-210**
    (a) arrangements have been made which would enable an assessment of D for the purpose of section 135 or (as the case may be) section 136 of the Act to be commenced sooner at the police station than at another place of safety, and
    (b) to postpone the assessment would be likely to cause distress to D.

Persons to be consulted

8.—(1) The following persons are specified for the purposes of section 136(1C)(d) of the Act—   **2-211**
    (a) an occupational therapist,
    (b) a paramedic.
(2) For the purposes of paragraph (1)—
    (a) an occupational therapist is a person registered in the register established and maintained by the Health and Care Professions Council under article 5 of the [Health Professions Order 2001], in the part relating to occupational therapists, and
    (b) a paramedic is a person registered in that register, in the part relating to paramedics.

Amendment

The words in square brackets in para.(2)(a) were substituted by SI 2019/1094, Sch.2 para.37.   **2-212**

NATIONAL HEALTH SERVICE (INTEGRATED CARE BOARDS: RESPONSIBILITIES) REGULATIONS 2022

(SI 2022/635)

Dated June 9, 2022, and made by the Secretary of State for Health and Social Care in exercise of the powers conferred by sections 3(2)(b), 3A(2)(b) and 272(8) of, and paragraph 9(2)(b) of Schedule 1 to, the National Health Service Act 2006[1] and section 117(2E) of the Mental Health Act 1983.

General Note

These Regulations, which came into force on July 1, 2022 (reg.1), are reproduced only in so far as they relate to responsibilities to provide after-care services under s.117 of the Mental Health Act.   **2-213**
An Explanatory Memorandum to these Regulations, prepared by the Department of Health and Social Care, is reproduced below. **It needs to be read in the light of the decision of the Supreme Court in** *R. (on the application of Worcestershire CC) v Secretary of State for Health and Social Care* **[2023] UKSC 31 which is considered in the notes on s.117(3) of the 1983 Act.**

"Mental health services during the course of a patient's detention

7.4   Where an application to detain a patient under the MHA 1983 is made on or after the date this instrument comes into force, the ICB responsible for commissioning mental health services for the patient during the course of their detention will be the ICB that had core responsibility at the time the relevant application resulting in the patient's detention was made. This is irrespective of where the patient is detained, including in the area of another ICB. A relevant application is an application made after a person is discharged from a previous period of after-care services relating to detention under the MHA 1983 or, where there is no previous detention, the first application for detention made. The new policy seeks to introduce continuity in commissioning responsibility. As long as a person discharged from hospital has not been discharged from after-care services arranged under section 117(2) of the MHA 1983, the ICB that had core responsibility at the time the relevant application to detain is made continues to have responsibility for commissioning mental health services for periods of further detention, regardless of whether the patient becomes (under NHS England's rules under section 14Z31) the core responsibility of a different ICB in that time.

7.5   Under the position with CCGs, a CCG had additional responsibility for every person who was liable to be detained under the MHA 1983 in a hospital or registered establishment in the CCG's area. This instrument therefore represents a change in policy on commissioning responsibility for mental health services and will bring commissioning responsibility in line with the position on payment responsibility as set out in NHS England's "Who Pays?" document since 2020. The policy aim is to support continuity of clinical care for patients whilst preventing any perverse incentives for ICBs to place a patient in a hospital or registered establishment in a different ICB area to avoid commissioning responsibility.

7.6   This instrument also provides continuity of treatment for patients who are in detention on the coming into force of this instrument, are detained on or after the coming into force of this instrument pursuant to an application made before it came into force and for patients in receipt of after-care services on the coming into force this instrument (but in all cases, not discharged from after-care services). The policy intention is that in those scenarios, the ICB that had core responsibility for the patient on the date these regulations come into force continues to have responsibility for commissioning mental health services, even for periods of further detention, provided that the patient has not been discharged from after-care services, regardless of whether the patient becomes (under NHS England's rules under section 14Z31) the core responsibility of a different ICB.

7.7   *After-care services: imposition of ICB responsibility* In relation to after-care services under section 117(2) of the MHA 1983, this instrument sets out that the ICB that had the responsibility to arrange the mental health services during the patient's detention that preceded the after-care services to be provided, will continue to have responsibility to commission the after-care services. This is to ensure continuity in clinical care for patients and also align the commissioning responsibility with the payment responsibility under NHS England's "Who Pays?" document.

7.8   This instrument also applies to a scenario where the patient is in receipt of after-care services relating to a period of detention from which they were discharged prior to this instrument coming into force. The policy intention is that the ICB that had core responsibility for that patient on the date this instrument comes into force will be responsible for arranging that patient's after-care services.

7.9   Where a patient was in NHS England-commissioned detention that began before this instrument came into force and is discharged into ICB-commissioned after-care services on or after the coming into force of this instrument, then the ICB that had core responsibility on the date of the patient's discharge into ICB-commissioned aftercare services will be responsible for commissioning the provision of such services. On the other hand, where the NHS England-commissioned detention began on or after this instrument came into force, the ICB that had core responsibility for the patient on the first day of the patient's detention, will be responsible for commissioning the after-care services.

7.10   *After-care services: imposition of NHS England responsibility* An ICB does not have to arrange the provision of after-care services under section 117(2) of the MHA 1983 where the person is receiving after-care services under section 117(2) which, if they had been provided under the 2006 Act, would be a service that NHS England had a duty to arrange. This reflects the position with CCGs under the Standing Rules Regulations."

Additional persons for whom an ICB has responsibility: persons detained under the Mental Health Act 1983 pursuant to an application made on or after the coming into force of these Regulations

2-214   **5.**—(1)   For the purposes of sections 3 and 3A of the NHS Act 2006 (duties and powers of ICBs to commission certain health services), in addition to the group of people for whom it has core responsibility (see section 14Z31 of that Act), an ICB has responsibility to arrange for the provision of mental health services during the course of the person's detention under the Mental Health Act 1983 for each person—

   (a) who is detained under the Mental Health Act 1983 in a hospital or registered establishment pursuant to a relevant application made on or after the coming into force of these Regulations;

   (b) who is a qualifying patient within the meaning of section 130C of the Mental Health Act 1983; and

   (c) for whom the ICB had core responsibility when the relevant application resulting in the person's detention was made.

(2)   In this regulation, an application for detention, made in respect of a person, is an application for the person's admission to a hospital or registered establishment made in accordance with Part 2 of the Mental Health Act 1983.

(3)   In this regulation—

   "exclusion period", in relation to a person who is detained under the Mental Health Act 1983, means a period—

      (a) beginning with the person's detention under the Mental Health Act 1983; and

      (b) ending with the person's next discharge from after-care services;

   "relevant application" means an application for detention made outside of the exclusion period.

General Note

The Explanatory Note to the Regulations states: **2-215**

"Regulation 5 prescribes that an ICB is responsible for a person who is detained under the Mental Health Act 1983 in a hospital or registered establishment, is a qualifying patient within the meaning of section 130C of the Mental Health Act 1983, and for whom the ICB had core responsibility when the relevant application resulting in the person's detention was made. A relevant application is an application made after a person is discharged from a previous period of after-care services relating to detention under the Mental Health Act 1983 or, where there is no previous detention, the first application for detention made in relation to the person. Any application for detention made while the person is in detention or has been discharged into after-care services but not discharged from those services, is not relevant for the purposes of determining responsibility under this provision."

Additional persons for whom an ICB has responsibility: other persons detained, or in detention, under the Mental Health Act 1983

6.—(1)   For the purposes of sections 3 and 3A of the NHS Act 2006 (duties and   **2-216** powers of ICBs to commission certain health services), in addition to the group of people for whom it has core responsibility (see section 14Z31 of that Act), an ICB has responsibility to arrange for the provision of mental health services during the course of the person's detention under the Mental Health Act 1983 for each person—

   (a) to whom paragraph (2), (3) or (4) applies;

   (b) who is a qualifying patient within the meaning of section 130C of the Mental Health Act 1983; and

   (c) for whom the ICB has core responsibility on the coming into force of these Regulations.

(2)   This paragraph applies to a person who—

   (a) was in detention under the Mental Health Act 1983 on the coming into force of these Regulations; and

    (b)   either—
        (i)   has not been discharged from that detention; or
        (ii) where the person has been discharged from that detention, has not been discharged from after-care services subsequent to that detention prior to being further detained under the Mental Health Act 1983.

(3) This paragraph applies to a person who—

    (a)   is detained under the Mental Health Act 1983 on or after the coming into force of these Regulations in pursuance of an application for detention made before these Regulations came into force; and

    (b)   either—
        (i)   has not been discharged from that detention; or
        (ii) where the person has been discharged from that detention, has not been discharged from after-care services subsequent to that detention prior to being further detained under the Mental Health Act 1983.

(5) This paragraph applies to a person who—

    (a)   was being provided with after-care services on the coming into force of these Regulations in relation to a period of detention under the Mental Health Act 1983 occurring before these Regulations came into force;

    (b)   has not been discharged from those after-care services;

    (c)   is detained under that Act after the coming into force of these Regulations ("detention 2") (regardless of when the application for detention relating to detention 2 was made); and

    (d)   either—
        (i)   has not been discharged from detention 2; or
        (ii) where the person has been discharged from detention 2, has not been discharged from after-care services subsequent to detention 2 prior to being further detained under the Mental Health Act 1983.

(6) In this regulation—

    (a)   an application for detention, made in relation to a person, is an application for the person's admission to a hospital or registered establishment made in accordance with Part 2 of the Mental Health Act 1983;

    (b)   references to a person's detention are to a person's detention in a hospital or registered establishment.

General Note

2-217   The Explanatory Note to the Regulations states:

"Regulation 6 prescribes that an ICB is responsible for a person who is a qualifying patient within the meaning of section 130C of the Mental Health Act 1983, for whom the ICB has responsibility on the coming into force of these Regulations and in relation to whom paragraph (2), (3) or (4) of that regulation applies. Paragraph (2) applies to a person who was in detention under the Mental Health Act 1983 when these Regulations came into force and who either has not been discharged from that detention or has not been discharged from after-care services subsequent to that detention. Paragraph (3) applies to a person who is detained on or after the coming into force of these Regulations pursuant to an application made before these Regulations came into force and who either has not been discharged from that detention or has not been discharged from after-care services subsequent to that detention. Paragraph (4) applies to a person who was being provided with mental health after-care services on the coming into force of these Regulations in relation to a period of detention occurring before the coming into force of these Regulations, is not discharged from those after-care services, is subsequently re-detained after the coming into force of these Regulations and who either has not been discharged from that period of detention or has not been discharged from after-care services subsequent to that detention."

After-care services: imposition of ICB responsibility

7.—(1)   The duty imposed by section 117(2) of the Mental Health Act 1983 on   **2-218**
an ICB to arrange for the provision of after-care services for a person to whom that
section applies is to be imposed instead on another ICB ("ICB A") in the
circumstances described in paragraph (2), (3), (4) or (5).

(2)   The circumstances described in this paragraph are—
    (a)   ICB A had responsibility to arrange for the provision of mental health
        services to the person during the detention to which the after-care
        services relate; and
    (b)   the person is usually resident in England.

(3)   The circumstances described in this paragraph are—
    (a)   the after-care services relate to a period of detention from which the
        person was discharged before these Regulations came into force;
    (b)   ICB A has core responsibility for the person on the coming into force
        of these Regulations; and
    (c)   the person is usually resident in England.

(4)   The circumstances described in this paragraph are—
    (a)   the after-care services relate to a period of detention the provision of
        which was arranged by NHS England;
    (b)   the period of detention began before these Regulations came into force;
    (c)   the person is discharged from that period of detention on, or after, the
        coming into force of these Regulations;
    (d)   ICB A had core responsibility for the person on the date of their
        discharge from that period of detention;
    (e)   regulation 8 does not apply to the after-care services; and
    (f)   the person is usually resident in England.

(5)   The circumstances described in this paragraph are—
    (a)   the after-care services relate to a period of detention the provision of
        which was arranged by NHS England;
    (b)   the period of detention began on, or after, the coming into force of
        these Regulations;
    (c)   ICB A had core responsibility for the person on the first day of the
        person's detention;
    (d)   regulation 8 does not apply to the after-care services; and
    (e)   the person is usually resident in England.

General Note

The Explanatory Note to the Regulations states: **2-219**

"Regulation 7 imposes the duty to provide mental health after-care services on another ICB in one
of four specified circumstances, as follows—

•   the ICB has responsibility to arrange for the provision of mental health services to the
    person during the detention to which the after-care services relate and the person is usu-
    ally resident in England (paragraph (2));
•   the after-care services relate to a period of detention from which the person was discharged
    before these Regulations came into force, the ICB has core responsibility for the person
    when these Regulations came into force and the person is usually resident in England
    (paragraph (3));

- the after-care services relate to a period of detention the provision of which was arranged by NHS England, the period of detention began before these Regulations came into force, the person is discharged from that period of detention on, or after, the coming into force of these Regulations, the ICB had core responsibility for the person on the date of their discharge from detention, regulation 8 does not apply to the after-care services and the person is usually resident in England (paragraph (4)); or
- the after-care services relate to a period of detention the provision of which was arranged by NHS England, the period of detention began on, or after, the coming into force of these Regulations, the ICB had core responsibility for the person on the first day of the person's detention, regulation 8 does not apply to the after-care services and the person is usually resident in England (paragraph (5))."

After-care services: imposition of NHS England responsibility

2-220   **8.**—(1)   The duty imposed by section 117(2) of the Mental Health Act 1983 on an ICB to arrange for the provision of after-care services for a person to whom that section applies is to be imposed instead on NHS England in the circumstances described in paragraph (2).

(2)   The circumstances described in this paragraph are that the person is receiving after-care services under section 117 of the Mental Health Act 1983 which, if it were being provided under the NHS Act 2006, would be a service the provision of which NHS England had a duty to arrange (see sections 3B and 4 of the NHS Act 2006).

General Note

2-221   The Explanatory Note to the Regulations states:

"Regulation 8 imposes the duty to arrange the provision of mental health after-care services for a person on NHS England where the person is receiving after-care services under section 117 of the Mental Health Act 1983 which, if it were being provided under the NHS Act 2006, would be a service the provision of which NHS England had a duty to arrange."

PART 3: PRACTICE AND PROCEDURE

CIVIL PROCEDURE RULES 1998

Civil Procedure Rules 1998

(SI 1998/3132)

PART 8

ALTERNATIVE PROCEDURE FOR CLAIMS

Practice Direction 49E – Alternative Procedure for Claims

...   3-001

Applications under Mental Health Act 1983

19.1 In this paragraph—   3-002
(1) a section referred to by a number refers to the section so numbered in the Mental Health Act 1983 and "Part II" means Part II of that Act;
(2) "hospital manager" means the manager of a hospital as defined in section 145(1) of the Act; and
(3) "place of residence" means, in relation to a patient who is receiving treatment as an in-patient in a hospital or other institution, that hospital or institution.

19.2 The claim form must be filed—
(1) in the County Court hearing centre serving the patient's place of residence is situated; or
(2) in the case of an application under section 30, in the court or County Court hearing centre that made the order under section 29 which the application seeks to discharge or vary.

19.3 Where an application is made under section 29 for an order that the functions of the nearest relative of the patient are to be exercisable by some other person—
(1) the nearest relative must be made a respondent, unless—
    (a) the application is made on the grounds that the patient has no nearest relative or that it is not reasonably practicable to ascertain whether he has a nearest relative; or
    (b) the court orders otherwise; and
(2) the court may order that any other person shall be made a respondent.

19.4 Subject to paragraph 19.5, the court may accept as evidence of the facts relied upon in support of the application, any report made—
(1) by a medical practitioner; or
(2) by any of the following acting in the course of their official duties –
    (a) a probation officer;

(b) an officer of a local authority;

(c) an officer of a voluntary body exercising statutory functions on behalf of a local authority; or

(d) an officer of a hospital manager.

19.5 The respondent must be informed of the substance of any part of the report dealing with his fitness or conduct that the court considers to be material to the determination of the claim.

19.6 An application under Part II shall be heard in private unless the court orders otherwise.

19.7 The judge may, for the purpose of determining the application, interview the patient. The interview may take place in the presence of, or separately from, the parties. The interview may be conducted elsewhere than at the court. Alternatively, the judge may direct the district judge to interview the patient and report to the judge in writing.

General Note

3-003 This provision is concerned with applications to the County Court under ss.29 and 30 of the Act. The court, on hearing an application under s.29, has the power to make an interim order: see below and the General Note to s.29.

In order to achieve judicial continuity, in *Northamptonshire Healthcare NHS Foundation Trust v ML* [2014] EWCOP 2, Hayden J. reserved to himself any application to displace the nearest relative of the patient by constituting himself as a judge of the County Court.

Paragraph 19.3

3-004 With regard to the power of the court to order that the nearest relative not be made a respondent, para.5.21 of the *Code of Practice* states:

"If the patient has any concerns that any information given to the court on their views on the suitability of the nearest relative may have implications for their own safety, an application can be made to the court seeking its permission not to make the current nearest relative a party to the proceedings. The reasons for the patient's concerns should be set out clearly in the application."

Neither the wording of this paragraph nor the judgment of the Court of Appeal in *Lewis v Gibson* [2007] EWCA Civ 587; [2005] M.H.L.R. 309, preclude an application for an interim displacement being made without notice being given to the nearest relative: see *R. (on the application of Holloway) v Oxfordshire County Council* [2007] EWHC 776 (Admin) which is considered in the General Note to s.29. In *Lewis v Gibson*, the Court of Appeal endorsed the Official Solicitor's proposal for the implementation of this paragraph, as it appeared in CCR, Ord.49 r.12, in such a way as to ensure compliance with the patient's rights under the European Convention on Human Rights. Thorpe L.J. said at para.40:

"Although [this paragraph] does not require it, I support the Official Solicitor's conclusion that the patient must be served with the proceedings and notified of the right to be joined. Second the County Court Judge must at the earliest stage enquire whether the patient has been so served and ensure that appropriate steps are taken to secure the patient's Article 6 and 8 rights. Third he should extend his enquiry into the patient's capacity in order to ensure that a person willing to act as litigation friend has been identified and served. These precautions must be taken even in cases where urgent relief is sought. I accept the Official Solicitor's submission that it is difficult to conceive of circumstances in which a patient could lawfully be deprived of any opportunity to participate in proceedings. Any justification would have to address the patient's Article 6 and 8 rights."

Paragraph 19.5

3-005 To comply with the requirement of this paragraph, it is sufficient if a report is handed to the respondent's legal adviser in circumstances where the legal adviser can give advice and take instructions:

see *(B(A) v B(L) (Mental Health: Patient)* [1980] 1 W.L.R. 116) which is considered in the note on s.29(3)(c). *B(A)* was considered by Hale L.J. in *R. (on the application of S) v Plymouth City Council* [2002] EWCA Civ 388, paras 36 to 38, where her Ladyship held that:

(i)   this paragraph, as it appeared in CCR Ord.49, r.12, imposes a minimum obligation;

(ii)   the court has to comply with the rules of natural justice, which normally require that anything relevant to the court's decision be seen by both parties to the dispute;

(iii) the right to see all the documents in a case may be outweighed by other considerations, but there must be a clear and proper public objective and the limitation must be proportionate to that objective;

(iv)   in general, one would expect disclosure of all the information put before the court in proceedings under s.29 for the purposes of establishing that the nearest relative has "exercised without due regard to the welfare of the patient or the interests of the public his power to discharge the patient from guardianship, or is likely to do so", unless there was a demonstrable risk of harm to the patient or others in so doing; and

(v)   in principle, the approach of a court in a s.29 application should be no less open than that of a Mental Health Review Tribunal.

Paragraph 19.6

The publication of information relating to proceedings before any court sitting in private shall be a contempt of a court where the proceedings are brought under the Act authorising an application or reference to be made to the First-tier Tribunal, the Mental Health Review Tribunal for Wales or to a county court (Administration of Justice Act 1960 s.12(1)(b)).   **3-006**

Paragraph 19.7

In using this power, the judge will act in accordance with s.6(1) of the Human Rights Act 1998 and will not act in a way which is incompatible with the patient's rights under art.5 of the ECHR *(R. (on the application of MH) v Secretary of State for Health* [2004] EWHC 56 (Admin); [2004] M.H.L.R. 155 at para.45).   **3-007**

TRIBUNAL PROCEDURE RULES 2008

Tribunal Procedure (First-tier Tribunal) (Health, Education and Social Care Chamber) Rules 2008   3-008

(SI 2008/2699)

Made 9 October 2008.
Laid before Parliament 15 October 2008.
Coming into force 3 November 2008.

CONTENTS

PART 1 INTRODUCTION

After consulting in accordance with paragraph 28(1) of Schedule 5 to the Tribunals, Courts and Enforcement Act 2007, the Tribunal Procedure Committee has made the following Rules in exercise of the power conferred by sections 9(3), 22 and 29(3) and (4) of, and Schedule 5 to, that Act.

The Lord Chancellor has allowed the Rules in accordance with paragraph 28(3) of Schedule 5 to the Tribunals, Courts and Enforcement Act 2007.

Coronavirus Pandemic

3-009   A number of Practice Directions and guidance notes were made during to the pandemic. They, together with other relevant documents, can all be accessed at the website of Mental Health Law Online (*www.mhlo.uk/bh*).

General Note

3-010   An account of the genesis of the First-tier Tribunal (Mental Health) and of rights of appeal from decisions of the tribunal to the Upper Tribunal can be found in the General Note to s.65 of the Act.

These Rules are concerned with the conduct of proceedings before the First-tier Tribunal in mental health cases. A failure to comply with the Rules does not render the tribunal proceedings void (r.7).

Tribunal jurisdiction

As it is a creature of statute, a tribunal has no inherent jurisdiction; its jurisdiction is confined to that conferred on it by statute. The function of a tribunal is limited to reviewing the justification for the patient's continued detention, guardianship or supervised community treatment by considering evidence relating to the relevant statutory grounds for discharge. It has no power to consider the validity of the original decision to bring the patient within the scope of the Act (*R. v East London and The City Mental Health Trust Ex p. Brandenburg* [2003] UKHL 58; [2004] 1 All E.R. 400 at para.9(3); also see *Secretary of State for Justice v MP* [2013] UKUT 25 (AAC) at para.11). Neither has it jurisdiction to determine whether a patient had been detained under the appropriate section of the Act nor to investigate the circumstances that led to the powers of the Act being invoked. However, such circumstances would need to be taken account of when the tribunal considers the patient's condition at the time of the hearing. **3-011**

Although the tribunal will receive a significant amount of evidence on the medical and other treatment that the patient is receiving, the tribunal's task is confined to considering such evidence only in so far as it relates to the statutory grounds (*SH v Cornwall Partnership NHS Trust* [2012] UKUT 290 (AAC); [2012] M.H.L.R. 383 and *GA v Betsi Cadwaladr University LHB* [2013] 280 (AAC); [2014] M.H.L.R. 27). In *Secretary of State for Justice v MM; Welsh Ministers v PJ* [2017] EWCA Civ 194; [2017] M.H.L.R. 202, the Court of Appeal said at para.32:

"A First-tier Tribunal [FtT] and the Mental Health Review Tribunal for Wales [MHRTW] are inferior tribunals. Unlike the Upper Tribunal [UT], they are not a superior court of record (see s.3(5) Tribunals Courts Enforcement Act 2007 [TCEA]) nor do they possess the powers, rights, privileges and authority of the High Court granted to the UT by s.25(1)(a) TCEA. The FtT and the MHRTW cannot make binding declarations or exercise the judicial review jurisdiction of the High Court or the UT. Neither the FtT/MHRTW nor the UT is able to exercise the jurisdiction of the Court of Protection, although this should not be taken to suggest that a judge authorised in a tribunal jurisdiction cannot also sit in the Court of Protection and vice versa so that in an appropriate circumstance the judge might exercise both jurisdictions concurrently or separately on the facts of a particular case."

The court also said that neither the European Convention on Human Rights nor the Human Rights Act 1998 confer jurisdiction on a tribunal (para.59).

In *Djaba v West London Mental Health Trust* [2017] EWCA Civ 436, Arden L.J. said at para.58:

"[The established position is that] where the question whether the detention complies with the European Convention on Human Rights ('the Convention') is not expressly within the powers of the tribunals but can be heard in other proceedings, section 3 of the Human Rights Act 1998 does not require the powers of the tribunals to be interpreted by reference to the Convention to give them the powers to consider Convention-compliance as well. The same principle applies here too. In this case, the appellant must apply for judicial review to the Administrative Court if he considers that the conditions of his detention are disproportionate and do not comply with the Convention. That Court is able to carry out a sufficient review on the merits to meet the requirements of the Convention."

In refusing permission to appeal this case on March 15, 2018, the Court said:

"It cannot be ruled out that the conditions of a patient's detention in hospital might be relevant to whether or not the statutory criteria for detention are met and therefore whether continued detention is compatible with the patient's Article 5 rights. But there is no doubt, on the factual findings in this case, that the statutory conditions for detention are met and therefore that the patient's Article 5 rights have not been violated."

In *R. (on the application of B) v Dr SS* [2005] EWCA Civ 28; [2006] M.H.L.R. 131, Phillips L.C.J. said at para.65:

"Whilst the jurisdiction of MHRTs extends to the propriety of detention for treatment it does not extend to issues relating to the propriety of treatment pursuant to section 58. There is, however, an obvious overlap between the question of whether a patient is suffering from mental illness which justifies admission for treatment and the question of whether treatment should be administered under section 58. In each case an issue can arise as to whether the proposed treatment is likely to alleviate or prevent a deterioration of the patient's condition. Equally, there may be a seminal question as to whether the patient is suffering from a relevant mental illness at all."

Human Rights Act 1998

3-012   As a "public authority" for the purposes of the 1998 Act, the tribunal is required to act in a way which is compatible with the rights contained in the European Convention on Human Rights (ECHR) and these Rules must be read and given effect in a way which is compatible with such rights: see ss.3 and 6 of the 1998 Act. Articles 5(4) and 6(1) of the ECHR are particularly relevant to the operation of the tribunal: see Pt 5. In *MD v Nottinghamshire Health Care NHS Trust* [2010] UKUT 59 (AAC); [2010] M.H.L.R. 93, para.47, UT Judge Jacobs said:

> "[T]he tribunal, like all judicial bodies, is under a duty to comply with the Convention right to a hearing. As part of that duty, it must ensure an equality of arms as that is understood in the Strasbourg jurisprudence. It is relevant that the tribunal is not merely a body that hears evidence, finds facts and decides on arguments. It is, as I have said, a body with its own expertise. Its use of that expertise is an important contribution to ensuring an equality of arms. The psychiatrist on the panel makes an examination of the patient and the panel uses its collective knowledge, experience and expertise to assess the evidence. Both those tasks are performed independently. They reduce the need, which may exist in the court system, for the parties to have their own expert evidence. Patients are, of course, entitled to produce evidence on their own behalf. My point is simply that greater access to experts is not a necessary, or the only, way to ensure the equality of arms that the law requires."

Article 5 of the ECHR does not enable a patient who has failed before a tribunal and who had a favourable medical opinion which had not been accepted by the tribunal, to be bound to be granted leave to bring judicial review proceedings to challenge the tribunal's decision (*R. (on the application of MacDonald) v Mental Health Review Tribunal* [2001] EWHC Admin 1032, at para.18).

Mental Capacity Act 2005

3-013   In *SM v Livewell CIC* [2020] UKUT 191 (AAC); [2021] M.H.L.R. 131, para.47, the Upper Tribunal said:

> "Existing caselaw establishes that in relation to questions of capacity, the FtT in its mental health jurisdiction should apply the principles and approach set out in the Mental Capacity Act 2005 ('MCA 2005') and the Code of Practice".

The Tribunal's approach to issues arising under art.8 of the ECHR

3-014   See the note under this heading in the General Note to s.75.

Tribunal procedure and the rules of natural justice

3-015   As it is a creature of statute, a tribunal is obliged to follow the procedure laid down in these Rules and where the Rules are silent on a point of procedure the tribunal must follow the rules of natural justice, i.e. it should act in a fair and unbiased way and should provide an opportunity for each party to adequately state his case (*Secretary of State for the Home Department v Oxford Regional Mental Health Review Tribunal* [1987] 3 All E.R. 8 HL). The forming and expression of a provisional opinion by a member of the tribunal does not give rise to unfairness: see the General Note to r.34 and *Re Application for Judicial Review* [2008] NIQB 75, at para.24.

In *MB v BEH MH NHS Trust* [2011] UKUT 328 (AAC): [2011] M.H.L.R. 246, the presiding judge at the tribunal hearing had "clearly indicated that the application for discharge had no prospect of success" (para.15; see also para.8 where the judge was reported as having invited the patient to withdraw his application). On those facts, UT Judge Levenson held that there had been a breach of natural justice, agreeing with counsel for the appellant that the presiding judge had:

> "... 'expressed himself in such a way as to give rise to reasonable apprehension that he had formed a preconceived concluded opinion ... [the appellant] was effectively told that he should give up. It was an indication by the tribunal that he had no possibility of success'."

Order of evidence

In *Re F* [2021] MHLO 6 (FTT), the tribunal, without first consulting the patient's representative, **3-016** directed that the patient give evidence first in a video hearing, and rejected a submission that the responsible authority should be heard first. The representative stated that the judge had referred to a policy which required this order of evidence in such hearings (the panel judge accepted it was possible she used the term 'policy'). On review, the Senior Tribunal Judge decided that there was a clear error of law: if the justification for the direction on the order of evidence included reference to a policy, whether that was intended to convey a tribunal wide policy or a policy specific to this judge it would constitute an unlawful fetter of the tribunals' discretionary powers. There is no policy that patients must give evidence first in video hearings as the order of evidence is a case specific decision (see r.5).

The role of the tribunal

In *AMA v Greater Manchester West Mental Health NHS Foundation Trust* [2015] UKUT 36 (AAC); **3-017** [2015] M.H.L.R. 133, Charles J. said at para.35:

"(i)   The main purpose of Article 5 [of the European Convention on Human Rights] is to provide that no one should be deprived of their liberty in an arbitrary manner.

(ii)   The reviewing body, and so the [First-tier Tribunal], must consider whether the reasons that initially justified detention continue and review the substantive and procedural conditions that are essential for the deprivation of liberty to be lawful.

(iii)   Article 5(4) applies to those reviews and is directed to ensuring that there is a fair procedure for reviewing the lawfulness of a detention.

(iv)   To my mind the most important principles to take into account in the decision making process of the [First-tier Tribunal] are: (a) the underlying purpose and importance of the review and so the need to fairly and thoroughly assess the reasons for the detention, (b) the vulnerability of the person who is its subject and what is at stake for that person (i.e. a continuation of a detention for an identified purpose), (c) the need for flexibility and appropriate speed, (d) whether, without representation (but with all other available assistance and the prospect of further reviews), the patient will practically and effectively be able to conduct their case, and if not whether nonetheless (e) the tribunal is likely to be properly and sufficiently informed of the competing factors relating to the case before it and so able to carry out an effective review. (As to this the tribunal should when deciding the case review this prediction).

(v)   The presumption of capacity and the requirement for it to be assessed by reference to the relevant decision, issue or activity must be remembered but care needs to be taken not to embark on unnecessary assessments and to maintain flexibility to achieve the underlying purpose, namely a practical and effective review of a deprivation of liberty in an appropriate timescale."

Findings of fact

For the approach to be taken by the tribunal where disputed allegations underpin the responsible **3-018** authority's submissions, see *AM v Partnerships in Care Ltd* [2015] UKUT 659 which is noted under s.72(1)(b)(ii).

Concessions

In *NL v Hampshire County Council* [2014] UKUT 475 (AAC); [2015] M.H.L.R. 338, UT Judge **3-019** Jacobs said at para.24:

"[T]ribunals are not required to accept concessions unless they are satisfied that they are correct. That applies to matters of fact and law. Tribunals are entitled to require the parties to satisfy them by evidence and argument that concessions are sound and, if they fail to do so, tribunals are not obliged to accept them."

Bias of tribunal members

In *Equilibrium Health Care v AK* [2013] UKUT 543 (AAC; [2015] M.H.L.R. 338); [2014] M.H.L.R. **3-020** 268, para.11, UT Judge Jacobs said:

"Bias comes in different forms. Two are relevant in this case: actual bias and the real possibility of bias. The test for actual bias is whether the tribunal member is partial in the sense of favouring one side or being hostile to another. The test for the real possibility of bias is 'whether the fair-minded and informed observer, having considered the facts, would conclude that there was a real possibility that the tribunal was biased': Lord Hope in *Porter v Magill* [2002] 2 AC 357 at [103]."

The attributes of a fair-minded and informed observer were examined by the House of Lords in *Helow v Secretary of State for the Home Department* [2009] 2 All E.R. 1031 at paras 2 and 3.

The principles of "apparent bias" which can be drawn from the case law were identified by UT Judge Ramshaw in *JG v Kent and Medway NHS and Social Care Partnership Trust* [2019] UKUT 187 (AAC); [2020] M.H.L.R. 95 at para.13. In this case, at the commencement of a hearing of the First-tier Tribunal the judge spoke to the patient and his representative explaining that his colleagues had suggested that he inform them that he had accessed a Court of Appeal judgment in respect of the patient in a connected matter. Although Judge Ramshaw rejected submissions made on behalf of the patient that by acting as he did the First-tier Tribunal judge showed bias, he said that although the judge had acted "very unwisely" and that what he did "was clearly procedurally irregular" he considered that the irregularity "was remedied (albeit only just) by informing the appellant and his representative at the outset of the hearing" (para.48).

The question whether the tribunal was biased because the consultant psychiatrist who sat as a member of the tribunal was an employee of the detaining NHS Trust was addressed in *R. (on the application of PD) v West Midlands and North West Mental Health Review Tribunal* [2004] EWCA Civ 311; [2004] M.H.L.R 174, which is considered in the General Note to r.34. PD was applied in *R. (on the application of M) v Mental Health Review Tribunal* [2005] EWHC 2791 (Admin); [2006] M.H.L.R. 46, where Bennett J. confirmed that cases involving a consideration of bias are fact-sensitive and that an examination of case precedent was of limited value (also see *PD* at para.8). His Lordship found that the fair-minded and informed observer, having taken account of the facts of the case, would not say that there was a real possibility of bias on the part of a judge when sitting as a legal member of the tribunal in November 2004 on the ground that he had imposed a hospital order and a restriction order on the patient in September 2003.

Every application for the recusal of a tribunal member on the ground of bias must be decided on the facts and circumstances of the individual case. If in any case there is real ground for doubt, that doubt should be resolved in favour of recusal (*Locabail (UK) Ltd v Bayfield Properties Ltd* [2000] 1 All E.R. 65 at para.25). In the *Equilibrium Health Care* case, Judge Jacobs said that "decisions on recusal are best challenged, if at all, after the proceedings are concluded" (para.34).

Tribunal hearings

3-021   Under para.4 of the Practice Statement "Composition of Tribunals in relation to matters that fall to be decided by the Health, Education and Social Care Chamber on or after 18 January 2010", issued by the Senior President of Tribunals on December 16, 2009, a "decision that disposes of proceedings or determines a preliminary issue made at, or following, a hearing [in respect of a mental health case] must be made by:

    (a)   One judge; and
    (b)   One other member who is a registered medical practitioner; and
    (c)   One other member who has substantial experience of health, or social care matters".

There may be exceptional cases in which fairness requires that every member of the tribunal is of the same sex: see the judgment of UT Judge Wikeley in *CB v SSWP (ESA)* [2020] UKUT 15 (AAC) at paras 21 to 24.

In *W v Egdell* [1989] 1 All E.R. 1089 at 1095, Scott J. described the nature of a hearing before a tribunal as inquisitional, not adversarial. Tribunal procedure was said by Stanley Burnton J. to be "to a significant extent inquisitional" in *R. (on the application of Ashworth Hospital Authority) v Mental Health Review Tribunal for the West Midlands and North West Regions* [2001] EWHC Admin 901; [2002] M.H.L.R. 13, para.16. In the opinion of Collins J., "it is not particularly helpful to label the proceedings one way or the other" (*R. (on the application of X) v Mental Health Review Tribunal* [2003] EWHC 1272 (Admin); [2003] M.H.L.R. 299, para.24).

There is nothing to prevent the chairman of a tribunal from presiding over more than one hearing involving the same patient (*R. v Oxford Regional Mental Health Review Tribunal Ex p. Mackman, The Times*, June 2, 1986). This ruling would undoubtedly apply to other members of the tribunal.

Rule 39 establishes when a tribunal hearing may proceed in the absence of a party or the patient.

Panel membership

In *Re A* [2020] MHLO 14 (FTT) an interlocutory decision was made to set aside a decision to refuse **3-022**
the patient's request for an all-female panel. The main factor in the decision was the overriding objective set out in r.2, in particular para.(2)(c) ensuring, so far as practicable, that the parties are able to
participate fully. The patient's mental state meant that she could only attend the hearing or pre-hearing
medical examination if the panel were all female. The judge referred to obiter guidance on single-sex
panels that had been given in a social entitlement case (*CB v SSWP* [2020] UKUT 15 (AAC)), where
UT Judge Wikeley said:

> "[I]t is not helpful for those involved in the judicial process to characterise a request for an all-
> female panel in terms of it being an attempt by the claimant to 'choose their own tribunal'. Rather,
> the question is whether such a solution is fair and just and ensures 'so far as is practicable, that the
> parties are able to participate fully in the proceedings' (rule 2(2)(c)), bearing in mind also the other
> considerations in rule 2" (para.24).

Accommodation for hearings

The responsibility for identifying the location of a hearing is that of Her Majesty's Courts and **3-023**
Tribunal Service (MHCTS). If a responsible authority wishes to invite the tribunal to hold a hearing in
the hospital where the patient is (or has been) detained, the hospital must comply with guidance on
"Minimum requirements for tribunal hearings to be held in hospitals" which was issued by HMCTS in
June 2022. The guidance can be accessed on the Mental Health Law Online website at: *www.mhlo.uk/
de*.
The *Code of Practice* states under the heading "Accommodation for hearings":

> "12.36 The managers of a hospital in which a Tribunal hearing is to be held should provide suitable
> accommodation for that purpose. The hearing room should be private, quiet, clean and adequately
> sized and furnished. It should not contain confidential information about other patients. If the room
> is used for other purposes, care should be taken to ensure that any equipment (such as a video camera
> or a two way mirror) would not have a disturbing effect on the patient.
> 12.37 The patient should have access to a separate room in which to hold any private discus-
> sions that are necessary – eg with their representative – as should the Tribunal members, so that they
> can discuss their decision.
> 12.38 Where a patient is being treated in the community, the hospital managers should consider
> whether a hospital venue is appropriate. They may wish to discuss alternatives with the Tribunal
> office."

Victims

(Also see Ch.40 of the *Code of Practice*.) **3-024**
A victim is not a party to the proceedings (r.1(3)).
In *R. (on the application of Maher) v First-tier Tribunal (Mental Health)* [2023] EWHC 34 (Admin),
Stacey J. considered the relationship between the presumption of privacy in cases involving the mental
health of a patient and the open justice principle as it applied to a decision not to provide a victim of
the reasons for the decision of the tribunal to conditionally discharge the patient. This case is considered
in the General Note to r.14.
The Government has published "Make a victim representation to the Mental Health Tribunal" which
can be accessed at: *https://www.gov.uk/mental-health-tribunal-victim-representations*. Also see "Victims
of violent or sexual offences: Mental Health Tribunal" which can be accessed at: *https://www.gov.uk/
guidance/victims-of-violent-or-sexual-offences-mental-health-tribunal*.
The Ministry of Justice has published "Duties to victims under the Domestic Violence, Crime and
Victims Act 2004: Guidance for clinicians" which can be accessed at: *https://
assets.publishing.service.gov.uk/government/uploads/system/uploads/attachment_data/file/614535/
guidance-dvcv-act.pdf*.
A *Code of Practice for Victims of Crime*, published by the Ministry of Justice, can be accessed at:
*https://www.gov.uk/government/publications/the-code-of-practice-for-victims-of-crime/code-of-
practice-for-victims-of-crime-in-england-and-wales-victims-code*.

Independent Mental Health Advocates

The Courts and Tribunals Service has published a guidance note on the "*Role of the Independent* **3-025**
Mental Health Advocate (IMHA) in First-tier Tribunal (Mental Health) hearings" (2011) which can be

accessed at the Mental Health Law Online website at: *mhlo.uk/bg*. Paragraph 3.2 of the guidance note states:

"The role that the IMHA plays in a tribunal hearing should ... be informed by the statutory provisions and the Code of Practice, but the role should also take account of the requirements of The Tribunal Procedure (First-tier Tribunal) (Health, Education and Social Care Chamber) Rules 2008. The overriding objective in Rule 2 refers to '(c) ensuring, so far as practicable, that the parties are able to participate fully in the proceedings' and the tribunal must, of course, give effect to the overriding objective in exercising its powers. In general, therefore, the tribunal should enable and support the IMHA in the discharge of his or her legitimate functions before the tribunal."

Information for patients

3-026   The *Code of Practice* states:

"4.22 Hospital managers should ensure that patients are offered assistance to request a hospital managers' hearing or make an application to the Tribunal, and that the applications are transmitted to the Tribunal without delay. They should also be told:

- how to contact a suitably qualified legal representative (and should be given assistance to do so if required)
- that free legal aid may be available, and
- how to contact any other organisation which may be able to help them make an application to the Tribunal.

4.23 It is particularly important that patients are well-informed and supported to make an application to the Tribunal if they are on a CTO, do not otherwise have regular contact with their nearest relative or people who could help them make an application, or lack capacity. If a patient lacks capacity to decide whether to seek a review of detention or a CTO, an IMHA should be introduced to the patient so that the IMHA can explain what help they can offer.

4.24 Patients whose CTOs are revoked, and conditionally discharged patients recalled to hospital, should be told that their cases will be referred automatically to the Tribunal."

Interpretation services

3-027   See para.12.40 of the *Code of Practice* which states:

"It is important that patients and their representatives are able to understand and participate in the Tribunal hearing. This includes providing information in formats that they understand and, if required, providing interpretation services free of charge, including sign language. Hospital managers and local authorities should inform the Tribunal well in advance if they think any such services might be necessary."

Legal Aid

3-028   Paragraph 6.21 of the Reference Guide states:

"Legal Aid is available through the Legal Aid Agency to fund legal advice and representation for patients before the First-tier Tribunal, without requiring any assessment of the patients' means. Legal Aid for appeals to the Upper Tribunal is means-tested and subject to a merits test."

Code of Practice

3-029   Guidance on the role of the tribunal is given in Ch.12.

Wales

3-030   Separate rules, which are not reproduced in this Manual, have been made to govern the practice and procedure to be followed in proceedings before the Mental Health Review Tribunal for Wales: see the Mental Health Review Tribunal for Wales Rules 2008 (SI 2008/2705 (L.17) (the "Welsh Rules")).

PART 1

INTRODUCTION

Citation, commencement, application and interpretation

1.—(1)   These Rules may be cited as the Tribunal Procedure (First-tier Tribunal)   **3-031**
(Health, Education and Social Care Chamber) Rules 2008 and come into force on
3rd November 2008.

[(2)   These Rules apply to proceedings before the Health, Education and Social
Care Chamber of the First-tier Tribunal.]

(3)   In these Rules—

"the 2007 Act" means the Tribunals, Courts and Enforcement Act 2007;
"applicant" means a person who—
- (a)   starts Tribunal proceedings, whether by making an application, an appeal, a claim or a reference;
- (b)   makes an application to the Tribunal for leave to start such proceedings; or
- (c)   is substituted as an applicant under rule 9(1) (substitution and addition of parties);

"childcare provider" means a person who is a childminder or provides day care
as defined in [section 19 of the Children and Families (Wales) Measure
2010], or a person who provides childcare as defined in section 18 of the
Childcare Act 2006;
"disability discrimination in schools case" means proceedings concerning disability discrimination in the education of a child [or young person] or related
matters;
"dispose of proceedings" includes, unless indicated otherwise, disposing of a
part of the proceedings;
"document" means anything in which information is recorded in any form, and
an obligation under these Rules or any practice direction or direction to
provide or allow access to a document or a copy of a document for any
purpose means, unless the Tribunal directs otherwise, an obligation to
provide or allow access to such document or copy in a legible form or in a
form which can be readily made into a legible form;
[...]
["health service case" means a case under the National Health Service Act
2006, the National Health Service (Wales) Act 2006, regulations made under
either of those Acts, or regulations having effect as if made under either of
those Acts by reason of section 4 of and Schedule 2 to the National Health
Service (Consequential Provisions) Act 2006;]
"hearing" means an oral hearing and includes a hearing conducted in whole
or in part by video link, telephone or other means of instantaneous two-
way electronic communication;
"legal representative" means [a person who, for the purposes of the Legal
Services Act 2007, is an authorised person in relation to an activity which
constitutes the exercise of a right of audience or the conduct of litigation
within the meaning of that Act];
"mental health case" means proceedings brought under the Mental Health Act
1983 or paragraph 5(2) of the Schedule to the Repatriation of Prisoners Act
1984;

"nearest relative" has the meaning set out in section 26 of the Mental Health Act 1983;

"party" means—

    (a)   in a mental health case, the patient, the responsible authority, the Secretary of State (if the patient is a restricted patient or in a reference under rule 32(8) (seeking approval under section 86 of the Mental Health Act 1983)), and any other person who starts a mental health case by making an application;

    (b)   in any other case, a person who is an applicant or respondent in proceedings before the Tribunal or, if the proceedings have been concluded, a person who was an applicant or respondent when the Tribunal finally disposed of all issues in the proceedings;

"patient" means the person who is the subject of a mental health case;

"practice direction" means a direction given under section 23 of the 2007 Act;

"respondent" means—

    [(a)   in an appeal against an order made by a justice of the peace, the person who applied to the justice of the peace for the order;]

    (b)   in an appeal against any other decision, the person who made the decision;

    [(c)   in proceedings on a claim brought under paragraph 3 of Schedule 17 to the Equality Act 2010 (disabled pupils: enforcement)—

        (i)   the local authority or the governing body, where the school concerned is a maintained school;

        (ii)   the proprietor, where the school concerned is an independent school;]

    (d)   [...]

    [(da)   in an application for, or for a review of, a stop order under the National Health Service (Optical Charges and Payments) Regulations 1997—

        (i)   the supplier, where the Secretary of State is the applicant;

        (ii)   the Secretary of State, where the supplier is the applicant;

    (db)   in any other [health service case] —

        (i)   the practitioner, performer or person against whom the application is made, where [NHS England] [or Local Health Board] is, or is deemed to be, the applicant;

        (ii)   [NHS England] [or Local Health Board] that served the notice, obtained the order or confirmation of the order, where any other person is the applicant; [...]

    [(dc)   in an application under section 127(5) of the Education and Skills Act 2008, the Secretary of State; or]

    (e)   a person substituted or added as a respondent under rule 9 (substitution and addition of parties);]

"responsible authority" means—

    (a)   in relation to a patient detained under the Mental Health Act 1983 in a hospital within the meaning of Part 2 of that Act, the managers (as defined in section 145 of that Act);

    (b)   in relation to a patient subject to guardianship, the responsible

> local social services authority (as defined in sectic
> Mental Health Act 1983);
>
> (c) in relation to a community patient, the ma
> responsible hospital (as defined in section 14⁵
> Health Act 1983);
>
> (d) [...]
>
> "restricted patient" has the meaning set out in section 79(1) of the Mental
> Health Act 1983;
>
> ["special educational needs case" means proceedings concerning—
>
> (a) an EHC needs assessment within the meaning of section 36(2)
> of the Children and Families Act 2014, [...]
>
> [(aa) a detained person's EHC needs assessment within the mean-
> ing of section 70(5) of the Children and Families Act 2014, or]
>
> (b) an EHC plan within the meaning of section 37(2) of that Act,
> of a child or young person who has or may have special educational needs;]
>
> "Suspension Regulations" means regulations which provide for a right of ap-
> peal against a decision to suspend, or not to lift the suspension of, a person's
> registration as a childcare provider;
>
> "Tribunal" means the First-tier Tribunal;
>
> "working day" means any day except a Saturday or Sunday, Christmas Day,
> Good Friday or a bank holiday under section 1 of the Banking and Financial
> Dealings Act 1971.
>
> ["young person" means, in relation to a special educational needs case or a dis-
> ability discrimination in schools case, a person over compulsory school age
> but under 25].

Amendments

The amendments to this rule were made by SI 2010/15 r.15, SI 2010/2653 r.3, SI 2011/651 r.3(2),
SI 2013/477 r.11, SI 2014/2128 r.20, SI 2015/1510 r.9, S1 2017/1169 r.5 and the Health and Care Act
2022 Sch.1 para.1(3).

General Note

Paragraph (3)

Party The identity of the responsible authority in para.(a) can change if the patient is subject to a   **3-032**
transfer under s.19 of the Act after the decision under challenge has been made. An independent mental
health advocate for the patient is not a party to the proceedings.

Respondent The tribunal can give a direction adding a person to the proceedings as a respondent
(r.9(2)).

Overriding objective and parties' obligation to co-operate with the Tribunal

   2.—(1) The overriding objective of these Rules is to enable the Tribunal to deal   **3-033**
with cases fairly and justly.

   (2) Dealing with a case fairly and justly includes—

     (a) dealing with the case in ways which are proportionate to the impor-
tance of the case, the complexity of the issues, the anticipated costs and
the resources of the parties;

     (b) avoiding unnecessary formality and seeking flexibility in the proceed-
ings;

     (c) ensuring, so far as practicable, that the parties are able to participate
fully in the proceedings;

(d) using any special expertise of the Tribunal effectively; and

(e) avoiding delay, so far as compatible with proper consideration of the issues.

(3) The Tribunal must seek to give effect to the overriding objective when it—

(a) exercises any power under these Rules; or

(b) interprets any rule or practice direction.

(4) Parties must—

(a) help the Tribunal to further the overriding objective; and

(b) co-operate with the Tribunal generally.

Definitions

3-034 Tribunal: r.1(3).
party: r.1(3).
practice direction: r.1(3).

General Note

3-035 This rule establishes that the tribunal's overriding objective when performing functions under these Rules is to deal with cases fairly and justly. It also requires parties to help the tribunal to further this objective and to co-operate with the tribunal. It cannot be taken into account when interpreting the Act (para.3).

The objective of dealing with cases fairly and justly:

"includes the avoidance of unnecessary applications and unnecessary delay. That requires parties to cooperate and liaise with each other concerning procedural matters, with a view to agreeing a procedural course promptly where they are able to do so, before making any application to the tribunal. This is particularly to be expected where parties have legal representation. Parties should endeavour to agree disclosure issues without the need for the tribunal to make a ruling. However, even where a direction from the tribunal may be required (for example, where a responsible authority holding medical records requires an order for the disclosure of medical records to overcome issues of confidentiality or arising from the Data Protection Act, or where there are genuine issues as to how most appropriately to proceed), it will assist the tribunal to further the overriding objective if the parties can identify any directions they are able to agree, subject to the approval of the tribunal. Where they are unable to agree every aspect, this liaison will at least have the advantage of crystallising their positions, and more clearly identifying the issue(s) upon which the tribunal will have to rule. We stress that, in the context of an urgent application in the mental health jurisdiction, this liaison between the parties must not lead to any unavoidable delay" (*Dorset Healthcare NHS Foundation Trust v MH* [2009] UKUT 4 (AAC); [2009] M.H.L.R. 102 at para.13)."

According to UT Judge Jacobs, the objective also "includes ensuring full participation, so far as practicable. Rule 14(2) requires the tribunal to have regard to the interests of justice. Justice and fairness generally require openness. Sometimes, they are not compatible and a compromise is possible": see *RM v St Andrew's Healthcare* at para.31. *RM* is noted under r.14(2).

For the application of the overriding objective to a decision to agree to the patient's request for the establishment of an all-female panel, see the General Note to these Rules under the heading, "Panel membership".

Paragraph (2)

3-036 **includes** The list is not exclusive.

Paragraph (4)

3-037 This paragraph was not included in the Welsh Rules because it was felt that placing an obligation on the patient to co-operate with the tribunal was undesirable. The Law Commission has recommended that the Welsh Rules should contain this obligation (*Devolved Tribunals in Wales Report*, Law Com No.403, para..6.121).

In *MD v Nottinghamshire Health Care NHS Trust* [2010] UKUT 59 (AAC); [2010] M.H.L.R. 93, para.46, Judge Jacobs said that the duties placed on the parties under this paragraph "must include making their experts available to comply with any directions that are given by the tribunal".

Paragraph (b) requires the patient's representative to assist the tribunal by identifying issues specific to art.8 of the European Convention on Human Rights that arise in a particular case (*RP v Dudley and Walsall Mental Health Partnership NHS Trust* [2016] UKUT 204 (AAC); [2016] M.H.L.R. 270, para.11).

Alternative dispute resolution and arbitration

3.—(1) The Tribunal should seek, where appropriate—   **3-038**

    (a) to bring to the attention of the parties the availability of any appropriate alternative procedure for the resolution of the dispute; and

    (b) if the parties wish and provided that it is compatible with the overriding objective, to facilitate the use of the procedure.

(2) Part 1 of the Arbitration Act 1996 does not apply to proceedings before the Tribunal.

Definitions

    Tribunal: r.1(3).   **3-039**
    party: r.1(3).

General Note

    Although this rule is not applicable to mental health cases, the tribunal could draw the attention of a   **3-040**
patient to the availability of relevant complaint procedures.

PART 2

GENERAL POWERS AND PROVISIONS

Delegation to staff

4.—(1) Staff appointed under section 40(1) of the 2007 Act (tribunal staff and   **3-041**
services) [or section 2(1) of the Courts Act 2003 (court officers, staff and services)] may, [if authorised by] the Senior President of Tribunals [under paragraph 3(3) of Schedule 5 to the 2007 Act], carry out functions of a judicial nature permitted or required to be done by the Tribunal.

(2) […]

(3) Within 14 days after the date on which the Tribunal sends notice of a decision made by a member of staff under paragraph (1) to a party, that party may apply in writing to the Tribunal for that decision to be considered afresh by a judge.

Amendments

    The amendments to this rule were made by SI 2020/651 r.2(2)(a).

Definitions

    the 2007 Act: r.1(3).   **3-042**
    Tribunal: r.1(3).
    party: r.1(3).

General Note

    This rule enables judicial functions, such as case management, to be undertaken by tribunal staff if   **3-043**
this is authorised by the Senior President of Tribunals.

[761]

A Practice Statement on "Delegation of functions to registrars, tribunal case workers and authorised tribunal staff on or after 8 July 2016" was issued by the Senior President of Tribunals. It is reproduced below.

Case management powers

3-044 **5.**—(1) Subject to the provisions of the 2007 Act and any other enactment, the Tribunal may regulate its own procedure.

(2) The Tribunal may give a direction in relation to the conduct or disposal of proceedings at any time, including a direction amending, suspending or setting aside an earlier direction.

(3) In particular, and without restricting the general powers in paragraphs (1) and (2), the Tribunal may—

    (a)   extend or shorten the time for complying with any rule, practice direction or direction, unless such extension or shortening would conflict with a provision of another enactment containing a time limit;

    (b)   consolidate or hear together two or more sets of proceedings or parts of proceedings raising common issues, or treat a case as a lead case;

    (c)   permit or require a party to amend a document;

    (d)   permit or require a party or another person to provide documents, information or submissions to the Tribunal or a party;

    (e)   deal with an issue in the proceedings as a preliminary issue;

    (f)   hold a hearing to consider any matter, including a case management issue;

    (g)   decide the form of any hearing;

    (h)   adjourn or postpone a hearing;

    (i)   require a party to produce a bundle for a hearing;

    (j)   stay proceedings;

    (k)   transfer proceedings to another court or tribunal if that other court or tribunal has jurisdiction in relation to the proceedings and—

        (i)   because of a change of circumstances since the proceedings were started, the Tribunal no longer has jurisdiction in relation to the proceedings; or

        (ii)   the Tribunal considers that the other court or tribunal is a more appropriate forum for the determination of the case; or

    (l)   suspend the effect of its own decision pending the determination by the Tribunal or the Upper Tribunal of an application for permission to appeal against, and any appeal or review of, that decision.

Definitions

3-045 the 2007 Act: r.1(3).
Tribunal: r.1(3).
practice direction: r.1(3).
party: r.1(3).
document: r.1(3).
hearing: r.1(3).

General Note

3-046 This rule, which states that a direction under this rule can be given on the application of one or more of the parties or by the tribunal on its own initiative, should be read with r.6. It enables the tribunal to give case management directions so as to facilitate: (1) the speedy determination of the case in compliance with the art.5(4) of the European Convention on Human Rights (ECHR); and (2) the overriding objective of dealing with cases fairly and justly under r.2. It is supplemented by r.15. The tribunal and the Upper Tribunal are reluctant to grant permission to appeal against case management decisions: see the notes to r.46. As an alternative to an appeal, a party could apply to the tribunal under r.6(5) to either amend, suspend or set aside the direction.

Under paras 9 and 10 of the Practice Statement "Composition of Tribunals in relation to matters that fall to be decided by the Health, Education and Social Care Chamber on or after 18 January 2010", issued by the Senior President of Tribunals on December 16, 2009, where the tribunal:

"has given a decision that disposes of proceedings ('the substantive decision'), any matter decided under, or in accordance with, Rule 5(3)(l) or Part 5 of [these] Rules or section 9 of the Tribunals, Courts and Enforcement Act 2007 must be decided by one judge, unless the Chamber President considers it appropriate that it is decided either by:—

(a) the same members of the Tribunal as gave the substantive decision; or
(b) a Tribunal ... comprised of different members of the Tribunal to that which gave the substantive decision.

Any other decision, including striking out a case under Rule 8 ... (except at, or following, a hearing) or giving directions under Rule 5 ... (whether or not at a hearing) must be made by:—

(a) One judge."

A Case Management Request Form (CMR 1) is available as a means of ensuring that applicants provide the necessary information under the Rules when applying for directions and other interlocutory matters.

In *B v Mental Health Review Tribunal and the Secretary of State for the Home Department* [2002] EWHC Admin 1553; [2003] M.H.L.R. 19, Scott Baker J. said at para.49:

"At each stage the tribunal should have had in mind the delay that has occurred until then and given directions against that background. The longer the delay that has occurred the more aggressive the directions will need to be to ensure early disposal of the case. There comes a time when the convenience of expert witnesses must cede to the need for the tribunal to conclude a substantive hearing".

A tribunal does not have the power to make a direction after it has determined an application. It is therefore not possible for a tribunal to incorporate a direction into the reasons that it gives for a decision not to discharge the patient, unless the case has not been fully determined because the tribunal has reserved to itself the possibility of reconvening by virtue of s.72(3)(b) or s.72(3A)(b).

The tribunal cannot use its power under this provision either to circumvent its obligations under the Act or to direct a party to do something which it is prevented from doing by legislation (*DC v Nottinghamshire Healthcare NHS Trust* [2012] UKUT 92 (AAC); [2012] M.H.L.R. 238). Neither can it require a party to undertake a task which it is not otherwise legally obliged to perform under the Act, e.g. to direct the after-care bodies to provide the tribunal with a fully developed after-care plan prior to the hearing: see *W v Doncaster MBC* [2004] EWCA Civ. 378; [2004] M.H.L.R. 201 which is noted under s.117.

It is advisable for a without notice direction to include a reference to the right to make an application under r.(6)(5) if there is an objection to the direction (*Dorset Healthcare NHS Foundation Trust v MH* [2009] UKUT 4 (AAC); [2009] M.H.L.R. 102 at para.35).

Paragraph (3)(a)

The following provisions of the Act contain time limits which relate to tribunal applications or references which cannot be altered by the tribunal under this provision: ss.66(1),(2), 68(2), 69(1),(2),(4), 70, 71(2), and 75(1). **3-047**

Paragraph (3)(d)

This provision enables tribunals to direct those who are late in producing reports to do so forthwith. **3-048** It also enables the tribunal to direct a party or other person to produce a document that the party or person had no intention of submitting to the tribunal. A failure to comply with such a requirement could result in the tribunal using its power under r.16.

Where a nearest relative makes an application under s.66(1)(g) of the Act and applies for the disclosure of the patient's medical records, the tribunal must undertake a balancing exercise between the various interests involved. In *R. (on the application of S) v Plymouth City Council* [2002] EWCA Civ 388; [2002] M.H.L.R. 118, at para.48. Hale L.J. said that the interests that need to be considered include the confidentiality of the information sought; the proper administration of justice; the rights of both the patient and the nearest relative to respect for their family life and adequate involvement in decision-making processes about it; the patient's right to respect for his private life; and the protection of the patient's health and welfare and/or the protection of other people. In *TR v Ludlow Street Healthcare Ltd* [2011] UKUT (AAC); [2011] M.H.L.R. 190, UT Judge Jacobs considered *S* and said that "the consent of the patient, and the patient's capacity to give consent, are not decisive and have to be balanced along with other factors" (para.14).

A patient's victim could be invited to make written submissions to the tribunal under this provision.

Paragraph (3)(h)

3-049 In *Mental Health Tribunals: Law, Policy and Practice* (2013), Philip Fennel et al state that these Rules "do not define postponement or adjournment, but an adjournment is generally understood to be a decision made at the tribunal hearing, whereas a postponement decision is made before the hearing commences" (p.217).

Adjourn Any party may make an application to adjourn a hearing at any time. When exercising the power to adjourn, the tribunal should bear in mind the overriding objective in r.2 and the requirement in art.5(4) of the ECHR for a speedy decision: also see the remarks of Scott Baker J. in the *B* case, noted above.

The power to adjourn "must be exercised judicially and in accordance with the overriding objective in rule 2. As a procedural power, it cannot be exercised to override the provisions of the substantive legislation. In particular, a tribunal cannot adjourn if it is obliged to give a decision under section 73 of the 1983 Act" (*DC v Nottinghamshire Healthcare NHS Trust* [2012] UKUT 92 (AAC); [2012] M.H.L.R. 238, per Judge Jacobs at para.23). In *RC v NHS Islington* [2013] UKUT 0167 (AAC), para.11, UT Judge Bano ruled that the power to adjourn had to be exercised judicially on the facts of each case and that a fixed rule of policy by a tribunal in relation to the grant of postponements or adjournments would constitute an unlawful fetter of its discretionary powers. In this case, the UT held that the tribunal's policy of only allowing an adjournment to a fixed date was unlawful.

A decision not to adjourn a hearing can be appealed, but entertaining such interlocutory appeals is not to be encouraged because it is usually better to wait until the substantive appeal has been decided to determine whether the interlocutory decision had any material bearing on the lawfulness of the substantive decision arrived at by the First-tier Tribunal on the appeal: see *AF v Nottinghamshire NHS Trust* [2015] UKUT 216 (AAC); [2015] M.H.L.R. 347, para.39, and the cases noted in the General Note to r.46.

In *B v Mental Health Review Tribunal* [2002] EWHC Admin 1553; [2003] M.H.L.R. 19, Scott Baker J. held that:

1. It is not good practice to adjourn a hearing without any indication of when it will be resumed. If for some reason it is impossible to identify a specific date at the moment of adjournment, it is perfectly in order to say that the adjourned hearing will take place no later than a certain date.
2. What is required is not only a return date when the case could be heard but also some clear directions to ensure that all the expert evidence was available for the adjourned hearing. To provide for expert evidence to be obtained sequentially is a recipe for delay.
3. There is no reason why experts should not meet at an early stage to try and identify, and if possible narrow, any differences of opinion.
4. An adjournment should not be granted without giving the patient's representatives an opportunity to be heard.
5. Brief reasons should be given for a decision to adjourn.

B was applied in *R. (on the application of X) v Mental Health Review Tribunal* [2003] EWHC 1272 (Admin); [2003] M.H.L.R. 299, where Collins J. held that:

1. Although the tribunal will normally rely upon the material that is put before it by the parties, the tribunal has power of its own motion to adjourn for the purposes of obtaining information, even though the parties have decided not to put that information before it.
2. The tribunal should not adjourn a case unless it regards it as necessary for the purpose of doing justice and of reaching the right result in a given case, and in deciding whether it is necessary, it will have to balance the need which it perceives for the extra information against any delay that that will occasion to the determination of the application before it.

A tribunal should give serious consideration to an adjournment if the tribunal considers that the absence of a doctor from a hearing "is likely to affect materially the weight they feel able to give to the opinions expressed in their written reports, and if that is likely to be critical to their ultimate decision", or if it has concerns about the availability of the after-care services that will be available for the patient (*R. (on the application of H) v Ashworth Hospital Authority* [2000] EWCA Civ 923; [2002] M.H.L.R. 314 at paras 68, 85).

In *AM v West London MH NHS Trust & Secretary of State for Justice* [2012] UKUT 382; [2012] M.H.L.R. 399, the patient had not progressed to the point where the issue of aftercare that was actually available would arise. Judge Jacobs said at para.16:

> "The tribunal's decision, including its approach to adjournments for further information, should be informed by its knowledge, expertise and assessment of the possibilities. In that context, I do not accept that it is essential for the tribunal to have specific information about aftercare in every case. It is an individual judgment to be made in the circumstances of the particular case."

On refusing permission to appeal in this case, Richards L.J. said:

> "[It] seems to me ... that it must, as a matter of principle, be open to a Tribunal to conclude in the circumstances of a particular case that information or better information of aftercare is incapable of affecting the decision, and that an adjournment to secure its provision could achieve nothing beyond additional expense and delay and would therefore be inappropriate" ([2013] EWCA Civ 1010; [2014] M.H.L.R. 174, para.9).

An application for an adjournment should be granted if the reason for the application is to gain further information with a view to persuading the tribunal to recommend a transfer under s.72(3), which was not possible without further information about the patient's previous placement and treatment which was not contained in the reports before the tribunal (*LB v BMH*, Upper Tribunal, UT Judge Levenson, March 14, 2017).

The power to adjourn can only be exercised in relation to a function which the Act either permits or requires the tribunal to do. In the case of a restricted patient, the tribunal cannot therefore adjourn for the sole purpose of assisting its determination of whether to exercise its non-statutory discretion to recommend the patient's transfer to another hospital; it can only adjourn for the purpose of assisting it in determining whether the patient should be discharged or not and, if a discharge is being considered, what conditions should be attached to it (*R. (on the application of the Secretary of State for the Home Department v Mental Health Review Tribunal* [2000] M.H.L.R. 209).

As the tribunal has no power to consider the validity of the admission which gave rise to the patient's liability to be detained (*R. v East London and The City Mental Health Trust Ex p. Brandenburg* [2003] UKHL 58), the tribunal has no power to adjourn an application to enable the parties to consider an alleged defect in the admission papers. Any concerns that the patient's legal representative might have about the contents of the statutory documentation should be raised with the hospital prior to the hearing.

It is unlawful to adjourn the proceedings so as to monitor the patient's progress in the hope that a projected course of treatment would eventually permit the tribunal to discharge the patient (*R. v Nottinghamshire Mental Health Review Tribunal Ex p. Secretary of State for the Home Department The Times,* October 12, 1988 CA). It is submitted that any adjournment that purports to exercise a general supervisory function over the patient's progress would be unlawful.

In *R. v Mental Health Review Tribunal Ex p. Cleveland* (1989) CO/819/88, unreported, Popplewell J. upheld the decision of a tribunal not to adjourn the proceedings to enable the applicant to submit further evidence on the ground that even if the evidence sought had been available it would not have effected the tribunal's decision.

The patient's Responsible Clinician can discharge the patient from liability to be detained during the adjournment period (*JMcG v Devon Partnership NHS Trust (MH)* [2017] UKUT 348 (AAC), para.37).

Hearing   This term embraces the proceedings before the tribunal until it reaches its formal decision (*R. (on the application of X) v Mental Health Review Tribunal*, above at para.20).

Paragraph (3)(k)

The provision enables a case to be transferred to the Mental Health Review Tribunal for Wales if a patient is transferred to a Welsh hospital. Rule 23(2) of the Welsh Rules provides the MHRT for Wales with an equivalent power.   **3-050**

Coronavirus temporary rule (decisions without a hearing)

3-051   **5A.—**   [Revoked by SI 2020/416 r.1(2)]

Procedure for applying for and giving directions

3-052   **6.—**(1)   The Tribunal may give a direction on the application of one or more of the parties or on its own initiative.

(2)   An application for a direction may be made—

    (a)   by sending or delivering a written application to the Tribunal; or

    (b)   orally during the course of a hearing.

(3)   An application for a direction must include the reason for making that application.

(4)   Unless the Tribunal considers that there is good reason not to do so, the Tribunal must send written notice of any direction to every party and to any other person affected by the direction.

(5)   If a party, or any other person given notice of the direction under paragraph (4), wishes to challenge a direction which the Tribunal has given, they may do so by applying for another direction which amends, suspends or sets aside the first direction.

Definitions

3-053   Tribunal: r.1(3).
party: r.1(3).
hearing: r.1(3).

General Note

3-054   This rule enables the tribunal to make a direction on the application of a party or on its own initiative and provides a mechanism to enable a party to challenge a direction made by the tribunal.

Failure to comply with rules etc

3-055   **7.—**(1)   An irregularity resulting from a failure to comply with any requirement in these Rules, a practice direction or a direction, does not of itself render void the proceedings or any step taken in the proceedings.

(2)   If a party has failed to comply with a requirement in these Rules, a practice direction or a direction, the Tribunal may take such action as it considers just, which may include—

    (a)   waiving the requirement;

    (b)   requiring the failure to be remedied;

    (c)   exercising its power under rule 8 (striking out a party's case);

    (d)   exercising its power under paragraph (3); or

    (e)   except in mental health cases, restricting a party's participation in the proceedings.

(3)   The Tribunal may refer to the Upper Tribunal, and ask the Upper Tribunal to exercise its power under section 25 of the 2007 Act in relation to, any failure by a person to comply with a requirement imposed by the Tribunal—

    (a)   to attend at any place for the purpose of giving evidence;

    (b)   otherwise to make themselves available to give evidence;

    (c)   to swear an oath in connection with the giving of evidence;

    (d)   to give evidence as a witness;

    (e)   to produce a document; or

    (f)   to facilitate the inspection of a document or any other thing (including any premises).

Definitions

practice direction: r.1(3).   **3-056**
party: r.1(3).
Tribunal: r.1(3).
mental health case: r.1(3).
document: r.1(3).

General Note

This rule identifies the options open to the tribunal should a party fail to comply with these Rules, a   **3-057**
practice direction or a direction. The tribunal also has the option of using its power under r.16 to summons witnesses and to order the production of documents. Also see "Enforcement Procedure, Directions and Summonses", below.

Paragraph (3)

Section 25 of the 2007 Act vests the Upper Tribunal with the powers of the High Court to require   **3-058**
the attendance and examination of witnesses and the production and inspection of documents, together
with such other matters as are incidental to its functions.

Striking out a party's case
8.—(1)   With the exception of paragraph (3), this rule does not apply to mental   **3-059**
health cases.
    (2)   [*Not reproduced*].
    (3)   The Tribunal must strike out the whole or a part of the proceedings if the
Tribunal—
        (a)   does not have jurisdiction in relation to the proceedings or that part of
them; and
        (b)   does not exercise its power under rule 5(3)(k)(i) (transfer to another
court or tribunal) in relation to the proceedings or that part of them.
    (4)   [*Not reproduced*]
    (5)   The Tribunal may not strike out the whole or a part of the proceedings under
paragraph (3) or (4)(b) or (c) without first giving the applicant an opportunity to
make representations in relation to the proposed striking out.
    (6)–(9)   [*Not reproduced*]

Definitions

mental health case: r.1(3).   **3-060**
Tribunal: r.1(3)

General Note

A decision made under this rule must be made by a judge: see the General Note to r.5. The decision   **3-061**
carries the right of appeal to the Upper Tribunal (*R. (on the application of OK) v First-tier Tribunal*
[2017] UKUT 22 (AAC), para.3). Also see the notes on r.35(4).
Notwithstanding the terms of para.(1), in the *OK* case, above, UT Judge Jacobs said at para.16:

"Rule 8 is strangely constructed. It begins by providing that only paragraph (3) applies to mental
health cases, but paragraph (5) then makes provision for cases within that paragraph. The most
sensible interpretation is that paragraph (5) also applies to mental health cases, in so far as it relates
to paragraph (3). Otherwise, the reference to paragraph (3) in paragraph (5) would be redundant."

In *VS v St Andrew's Healthcare* [2018] UKUT 250 (AAC), [2018] M.H.L.R. 337, Judge Jacobs said that "provided that the proceedings were conducted fairly, the Upper Tribunal is unlikely to regard the use of withdrawal rather than strike out as a material error of law" (para.33).

Paragraph (3)

3-062   This paragraph allows mental health cases to be struck out without a hearing where the tribunal has no jurisdiction. The author has been informed by an NHS Trust that this paragraph was invoked to strike out a case on the ground that the tribunal considered that the documentation relating to the "sectioning" of the patient revealed an error which rendered the patient's detention unlawful. It is submitted that such action would be ultra vires as the tribunal has no jurisdiction to consider the legal validity of the statutory documentation. In this case, the patient lost her opportunity to have her application considered by the tribunal, yet remained a detained patient because the Trust did not agree with the opinion expressed by the tribunal.

Substitution and addition of parties

3-063   **9.**—(1)   The Tribunal may give a direction substituting a party if—

(a)   the wrong person has been named as a party; or

(b)   the substitution has become necessary because of a change in circumstances since the start of proceedings.

(2)   The Tribunal may give a direction adding a person to the proceedings as a respondent.

(3)   If the Tribunal gives a direction under paragraph (1) or (2) it may give such consequential directions as it considers appropriate.

Definitions

3-064   Tribunal: r.1(3).
party: r.1(3).
respondent: r.1(3).

General Note

Paragraph (1)

3-065   Where the responsible hospital for a patient made subject to a community treatment order is not the same as the hospital where the patient was formerly detained, this provision can be used to substitute the managers of the responsible hospital as a party in place of the managers of the other hospital.

Orders for costs

3-066   **10.**—(1)   Subject to paragraph (2), the Tribunal may make an order in respect of costs only—

(a)   under section 29(4) of the 2007 Act (wasted costs) [and costs incurred in applying for such costs]; or

(b)   if the Tribunal considers that a party or its representative has acted unreasonably in bringing, defending or conducting the proceedings.

(2)   The Tribunal may not make an order under paragraph (1)(b) in mental health cases.

(3)   The Tribunal may make an order in respect of costs on an application or on its own initiative.

(4)   A person making an application for an order under this rule must—

(a)   send or deliver a written application to the Tribunal and to the person against whom it is proposed that the order be made; and

(b)   send or deliver a schedule of the costs claimed with the application.

(5)   An application for an order under paragraph (1) may be made at any time

during the proceedings but may not be made later than 14 days after the date on which the Tribunal [sends—

    (a)   a decision notice recording the decision which finally disposes of all issues in the proceedings; or

    (b)   notice under rule 17(6) that a withdrawal which ends the proceedings has taken effect].

(6)   The Tribunal may not make an order under paragraph (1) against a person (the "paying person") without first—

    (a)   giving that person an opportunity to make representations; and

    (b)   if the paying person is an individual, considering that person's financial means.

(7)   The amount of costs to be paid under an order under paragraph (1) may be ascertained by—

    (a)   summary assessment by the Tribunal;

    (b)   agreement of a specified sum by the paying person and the person entitled to receive the costs ("the receiving person"); or

    (c)   assessment of the whole or a specified part of the costs [, including the costs of the assessment,] incurred by the receiving person, if not agreed.

(8)   Following an order for assessment under paragraph (7)(c), the paying person or the receiving person may apply to a county court for a detailed assessment of costs in accordance with the Civil Procedure Rules 1998 on the standard basis or, if specified in the order, on the indemnity basis.

[(9)   Upon making an order for the assessment of costs, the Tribunal may order an amount to be paid on account before the costs or expenses are assessed.]

Amendments

The amendments to this rule were made by SI 2013/477 rr.12,13,14 and 15.

Definitions

Tribunal: r.1(3).   **3-067**
party: r.1(3).
mental health case: r.1(3).

General Note

In *RB v Nottinghamshire Healthcare NHS Trust* [2011] UKUT 135 (AAC); [2011] M.H.L.R. 299,   **3-068**
UT Judge Jacobs reviewed the powers to make a costs order and concluded that "(i) the Upper Tribunal has power only to award costs where the First-tier Tribunal could do so; (ii) in a mental health case, that tribunal has power only to make a wasted costs order; (iii) a wasted costs order may only be made against a legal or other representative. There is no statutory authority to make an order for costs against the First-tier Tribunal" (para.6).

Paragraph (1)(b)

This paragraph does not apply to mental health cases (para.(2)).   **3-069**

Representatives

   11.—(1)   A party may appoint a representative (whether a legal representative   **3-070**
or not) to represent that party in the proceedings.

   [(1A)   Where a child or young person is a party to proceedings, that child or young person may appoint a representative under paragraph (1).]

(2)   If a party appoints a representative, that party (or the representative if the representative is a legal representative) must send or deliver to the Tribunal and to each other party written notice of the representative's name and address.

(3)   Anything permitted or required to be done by a party under these Rules, a practice direction or a direction may be done by the representative of that party, except—

(a)   signing a witness statement; or

(b)   signing an application notice under rule 20 (the application notice) if the representative is not a legal representative.

(4)   A person who receives due notice of the appointment of a representative—

(a)   must provide to the representative any document which is required to be provided to the represented party, and need not provide that document to the represented party; and

(b)   may assume that the representative is and remains authorised as such until they receive written notification that this is not so from the representative or the represented party.

(5)   At a hearing a party may be accompanied by another person whose name and address has not been notified under paragraph (2) but who, subject to paragraph (8) and with the permission of the Tribunal, may act as a representative or otherwise assist in presenting the party's case at the hearing.

(6)   Paragraphs (2) to (4) do not apply to a person who accompanies a party under paragraph (5).

(7)   In a mental health case, if the patient has not appointed a representative, the Tribunal may appoint a legal representative for the patient where—

(a)   the patient has stated that they do not wish to conduct their own case or that they wish to be represented; or

(b)   the patient lacks the capacity to appoint a representative but the Tribunal believes that it is in the patient's best interests for the patient to be represented.

(8)   In a mental health case a party may not appoint as a representative, or be represented or assisted at a hearing by—

(a)   a person liable to be detained or subject to guardianship [...], or who is a community patient, under the Mental Health Act 1983; or

(b)   a person receiving treatment for mental disorder at the same hospital as the patient.

Amendments

The amendments to this rule were made by SI 2013/477 r.16 and SI 2014/2128 r.21.

Definitions

3-071   party: r.1(3).
legal representative: r.1(3).
Tribunal: r.1(3).
practice direction: r.1(3).
document: r.1(3).
patient: r.1(3).

General Note

3-072   This rule enables a party, including a child or young person (para.(1A)), to appoint a representative to represent that party in the proceedings. The representative need not be legally qualified (para.(1)). A representative is entitled to question witnesses and to make submissions to the tribunal (*R. (on the application of Mersey Care NHS Trust) v Mental Health Review Tribunal* [2003] EWHC 1182 (Admin); [2003] M.H.L.R. 354). Subject to para.(8), a patient is entitled to have anyone, including an independent mental health advocate, to act as a representative. In *AMA v Greater Manchester West Mental Health NHS Foundation Trust* [2015] UKUT 36 (AAC); [2015] M.H.L.R. 133 at para.50, Charles J. said that unless an order of the Court of Protection appointing a welfare deputy expressly so provides it does not appoint the deputy to act as the patient's representative in proceedings under this Act.

Apart from the exceptions noted in para.(3), the representative can act on behalf of the party. Written notice of the appointment must be given to the tribunal and to other parties (para.(2)). Documents which are provided to the representative need not be provided to the represented party (para.(4)(a)). Provision is made in para.(5) for a party to be represented or otherwise assisted by a person who has not given prior notice to the tribunal. Paragraph (7), which enables the tribunal to appoint a legal representative for the patient, applies where the patient has said that he either does not wish to conduct the case or does not wish to be represented, or the patient lacks the capacity to appoint a representative. Paragraph (8) disqualifies certain persons from acting as a representative. Neither these Rules nor the Act provide for a litigation friend to represent a mentally incapacitated patient before the tribunal.

Although the patient's responsible clinician (RC) is usually seen as the appropriate person to represent the responsible authority at a hearing, there is nothing to prevent another member of staff, such as a nurse or a Mental Health Act administrator, from performing this role. Paragraphs 12.31 and 12.32 of the *Code of Practice* state:

"12.31 Responsible clinicians can attend the hearing solely as a witness or as the nominated representative of the responsible authority. As a representative of the responsible authority, the responsible clinician has the ability to call and cross examine witnesses and to make submissions to the Tribunal. This may not always be desirable where it is envisaged that the responsible clinician will have to continue working closely with a patient.

12.32 Responsible authorities should therefore consider whether they want to send an additional person to represent their interests, allowing the responsible clinician to appear solely as a witness. Responsible clinicians should be clear in what capacity they are attending the Tribunal, as they may well be asked this by the panel."

Being identified as the responsible authority's representative does not require the representative to perform all of the tasks usually associated with the role. A major advantage of being identified as the representative is that it provides the person concerned with the opportunity of question witnesses should the need arise. A representative can also make final submissions at the end of the hearing. It is submitted that a representative who is a member of the clinical team which is treating the patient cannot be excluded from the hearing at the request of the patient while the patient gives evidence: see *R. (on the application of Mersey Care NHS Trust) v Mental Health Review Tribunal*, above. If the tribunal did decide to interview the patient in the absence of the representative, the requirements of art.6 of the European Convention on Human Rights and the rules of natural justice would require that any salient facts that were divulged by the patient during the interview be communicated to the representative. A note of caution about the responsible authority being represented by the patient's RC has been expressed by C. Jones et al in "Mental health tribunals in England and Wales: a representative's guide", *Advances in Psychiatric Treatment* 2013; 19, 40–47.

The Law Society has published a Practice Note on *"Representation before mental health tribunals"*, December 2019, which is reproduced at Appendix D. Also see paras 24 to 28 of "Enforcement Procedure, Direction and Summonses" which is reproduced below.

The role of the legal representative

This was considered by Charles J. in the "Overview" section of his judgment in *YA v Central and North West London NHS Trust* [2015] UKUT 37 (AAC); [2015] M.H.L.R. 144. **3-073**

A. Patients with the capacity to provide instructions on all relevant matters relating to the conduct of the proceedings His Lordship said:

"(11) The position of a solicitor acting for a patient with capacity to instruct him to conduct the proceedings whether appointed by the patient or the tribunal is effectively the same as that under any other retainer for the purposes of proceedings, including the consideration of the capacity of the client to give and terminate instructions for that purpose. Generally, in such a case the appointment by the tribunal would have been under Rule 11(7)(a) and so based on the wish or request of the patient and so the patient effectively has the right to terminate the appointment even if formally the tribunal has to end it. Exceptionally, after an appointment under Rule 11(7)(b) it may be found as a result of change or an initial error that the patient has capacity to instruct the solicitor to conduct the proceedings and in such a case the patient would also effectively have a right of termination because the original basis for the appointment would have gone even if formally the tribunal has to end it.

(12)   Such a retainer would be to advise on and conduct the tribunal proceedings pursuant to the patient's instructions and subject to the solicitor's professional obligations and duties."

B.   Patients who do not have the capacity to provide instructions on all relevant matters relating to the conduct of the proceedings   His Lordship said:

"(15)   The main problems are likely to arise when (a) the legal representative's views on what is in the patient's best interests and those of the patient diverge in respect of issues where factors that the patient does not have capacity to give instructions on are relevant, (b) the patient wants the legal representative to advance an unarguable point and/or (c) the patient maintains that he does not want to be represented. In all of those situations it is to be noted that as approved by the Court of Appeal and found by the ECtHR in *RP* [2012] ECHR 1796, [2013] 2 FCR 77:

—   withdrawal of representation or the advancement of unreasoned or hopeless argument may well not promote (a) the patient's best interests, or (b) an effective and practical review of a deprivation of liberty, and thus the underlying purposes of Article 5 and its procedural safeguards,

—   representation of a patient by another against the patient's wishes as to any representation, or parts of it, is not contrary to Article 6 or in my view Article 5(4), although the departure from the views and wishes of the patient should only be when this is necessary, and

—   the failure to provide assistance to a litigant who lacks capacity may itself result in a breach of procedural safeguards.

(16)   The points that:

—   the grounds for the detention and its continuation should be tested and reviewed as effectively as is practicable, and

—   in many cases this can be done effectively by reference to the relevant statutory provisions and existing reports (and evidence from their authors and others)

—   strongly support the view that the appointment of the legal representative should continue and that the legal representative should act as follows:

(i)   so far as is practicable do what a competent legal representative would do for a patient who has capacity to instruct him to represent him in the proceedings and thus for example (a) read the available material and seek such other relevant material as is likely to be or should be available, (b) discuss the proceedings with the patient and in so doing take all practicable steps to explain to the patient the issues, the nature of the proceedings, the possible results and what the legal representative proposes to do,

(ii)   seek to ascertain the views, wishes, feelings, beliefs and values of the patient,

(iii)   identify where and the extent to which there is disagreement between the patient and the legal representative,

(iv)   form a view on whether the patient has capacity to give instructions on all the relevant factors to the decisions that found the disagreement(s),

(v)   if the legal representative considers that the patient has capacity on all those factors and so to instruct the representative on the areas of disagreement the legal-representative must follow those instructions or seek a discharge of his appointment,

(vi)   if the legal representative considers that the patient does not have or may not have capacity on all those issues, and the disagreements or other problems do not cause him to seek a discharge of his appointment, the legal representative should inform the patient and the tribunal that he intends to act as the patient's appointed representative in the following way:

—   he will provide the tribunal with an account of the patient's views, wishes, feelings, beliefs and values (including the fact but not the detail of any wish that the legal representative should act in a different way to the way in which he proposes to act, or should be discharged),

—   he will invite the tribunal to hear evidence from the patient and/or to allow the patient to address the tribunal (issues on competence to give evidence are in my view unlikely to arise but if they did they should be addressed before the tribunal),

— he will draw the tribunal's attention to such matters and advance such arguments as he properly can in support of the patient's expressed views, wishes, feelings, beliefs and values, and

— he will not advance any other arguments.

(17) In such circumstances, the tribunal should not in my view delve into the areas of disagreement or why the legal representative is of the view he cannot properly draw matters to the attention of the tribunal or advance argument. These may be apparent from the account of the patient's wishes or what they say directly to the tribunal but in my view the decisions on what the legal representative can and cannot argue are matters for the legal representative and not the tribunal who are charged with deciding whether the legal representative it has appointed should continue to act and not with how he should do so.

(18) Where there is no conflict between the wishes of the patient and his views the legal representative should still consider whether or not the patient has capacity to instruct him on all relevant factors and act on the patient's instructions if he concludes that the patient has that capacity. But if the legal representative concludes that the patient does not or may not have such capacity generally he should advance all arguable points to test the bases for the detention in hospital. In those circumstances it may or may not be appropriate to invite the tribunal to hear directly from the patient.

(19) Having determined the capacity test set by Rule 11(7)(b) the most important guiding principles to be applied under the best interests test (and so in deciding whether to exercise the power) are:

— the underlying purpose and importance of the review and so the need to fairly and thoroughly assess the reasons for the detention,

— the vulnerability of the person who is its subject and what is at stake for that person (i.e. a continuation of a detention for an identified purpose),

— the need for flexibility and appropriate speed,

— whether, without representation (but with all other available assistance and the prospect of further reviews), the patient will practically and effectively be able to conduct their case, and if not whether nonetheless

— the tribunal is likely to be properly and sufficiently informed of the competing factors relating to the case before it and so be able to carry out an effective review. (As to this the tribunal should when deciding the case review this prediction).

(20) To those I add (a) the nature and degree of the objections and of the distress caused to a patient if his or her wishes are not followed, (b) the likely impact of that distress on his or her well being generally and (c) the prospects that if a legal representative is appointed or not discharged that legal representative will seek a discharge of the appointment."

The role of the legal representative is also considered in the Law Society's Practice Note "Representation before mental health tribunals", and by UT Judge Rowland in *AA v Cheshire and Wirral Partnership NHS Foundation Trust* [2009] UKUT 195 (AAC); [2009] M.H.L.R. 308. In *YA*, Charles J. said at para.71:

"The Law Society submits (as it asserts in its Practice Note) that paragraph 20 of the decision in *AA* is incorrect in suggesting that even when the patient has full capacity and despite their instructions a solicitor may be under a duty to draw the tribunal's attention to particular matters that appear to be in the patient's best interests. I agree that that is incorrect and is inconsistent with the judge's correct comment at paragraph 15 that:

'A patient may be capable of giving valid instructions and, where valid instructions are given, a solicitor must act in accordance with them.'"

In *PI v West London Mental Health NHS Trust* [2017] UKUT (AAC), the issue before the Upper Tribunal was how the tribunal should react when, during the course of a tribunal hearing, it appeared that the patient no longer had capacity to appoint or instruct his solicitor. UT Judge Knowles cited Charles J.'s statement at para.105 of *YA* that the issue of a patient's capacity to appoint a representative, to give instructions and to participate in proceedings before the tribunal should be kept under review by all of those involved, not least the tribunal itself, and held that the tribunal erred in law by failing to give adequate reasons for its decision not to review the patient's capacity to give instructions to his legal representative during the hearing. Judge Knowles said at para.41:

"[T]he application for review of the patient's capacity required a considered response from the tribunal. I … accept the submission made on behalf of the patient that a short pause in the proceedings was desirable in order to:

(a)   establish whether the patient lacked capacity which may have meant him being seen on the ward;

(b)   ascertain the patient's wishes about the continuation of the hearing; and

(c)   ascertain whether the patient's legal representative remained instructed."

If a review established "a lack of capacity or indeed fluctuating capacity, the tribunal might well have made an appointment pursuant to Rule 11(7)(b) so that the patient could have continuation of representation dedicated to his best interests. That appointment could have been made on the basis that the appointment of the legal representative by the patient had been terminated by the loss of capacity thereby satisfying the terms of rule 11(7)" (para.46).

Human Rights Act 1998

3-074   See the notes on art.5(4) of the ECHR in Part 5.

An IMHA's relationship with the patient's legal representative

3-075   Paragraphs 5.1.1 to 5.1.3 of the guidance note on the "Role of the Independent Mental Health Advocate (IMHA) in First-tier Tribunal (Mental Health) hearings", noted in the General Note to these Rules, state:

"It is to be hoped that there will have been a discussion before the start of the hearing as to the role to be played by the IMHA. It would be appropriate for the tribunal judge to make a few opening remarks emphasising that the legal representative has the formal representational role, that the IMHA is there to assist the patient, the legal representative and the tribunal to understand each other–and that, if they need any time to consult in private, they should just ask.

If an IMHA infringes the proper role of the legal representative (for example starts to give unprompted evidence or asks questions or addresses the tribunal), the judge should politely ask them to stop, and clarify with the IMHA what it is they want to do, and why. The judge should then ask the legal representative whether they are content for this to happen. If the IMHA is seeking to open up something that the legal representative has not pursued, it may be appropriate for the IMHA and the legal representative to have a private discussion so that the IMHA does not unwittingly introduce an argument that may weaken the patient's case, or pursue irrelevant issues.

It should be recognised, of course, that tribunals are not purely adversarial and that the tribunal's inquisitorial role might be engaged by the introduction by the IMHA of fresh issues. However, it is also important to recognise that the overall conduct of the patient's case is in the hands of the legal representative, not the IMHA, and that the tribunal needs to be sensitive to the legal representative's wishes. For example, it is likely to be inappropriate for an IMHA to send a written statement from a patient to the tribunal in advance of the hearing, without prior discussion with the legal representative."

Paragraph (3)

3-076   This power includes the power to give a notice of withdrawal under r.17 (*AMA*, above, para.48).

Paragraph (7)

3-077   This provision enables the tribunal to appoint a legal representative for the patient where the patient has not appointed a representative. The role of the legal representative is considered above. For "sensible pragmatic reasons the appointment … is regularly made by a member of the tribunal staff pursuant to Rule 4" (*AMA v Greater Manchester West Mental Health NHS Foundation Trust* above, para.28). The tribunal has no power to grant funding for the representative (*R. (on the application of Brady) v The Lord Chancellor* [2017] EWHC 410 (Admin); [2017] M.H.L.R 274).

It is submitted that the tribunal cannot avoid using its power under this provision by utilising its case management powers to direct that the responsible authority appoints a legal representative for the patient on the ground that a direction cannot be used to require a party to undertake a task which it is not otherwise legally obliged to perform under the Act. In any event, such a direction would lead to the responsible authority being faced with a clear conflict of interest.

The Official Solicitor will not agree to act as the patient's legal representative: see *AA* at para.11.

Paragraph (b)

In *YA v Central and North West London NHS Trust* [2015] UKUT 37 (AAC); [2015] M.H.L.R. 144   **3-078**
Charles J. identified the factors that the tribunal should take into account in determining whether to exercise the power under this paragraph to appoint or to discharge the appointment of a legal representative when the patient is objecting to the appointment. The power only arises if the patient lacks capacity to make the appointment. His Lordship said:

"118. Having determined that the patient lacks capacity to appoint a representative the best interests test has to be applied.

119. In my view, the most important guiding principles on the application of that test are set out in paragraph 45 above, namely:

(i)   the underlying purpose and importance of the review and so the need to fairly and thoroughly assess the reasons for the detention,

(ii)   the vulnerability of the person who is its subject and what is at stake for that person (i.e. a continuation of a detention for an identified purpose),

(iii) the need for flexibility and appropriate speed,

(iv) whether, without representation (but with all other available assistance and the prospect of further reviews), the patient will practically and effectively be able to conduct their case, and if not whether nonetheless

(v)   the tribunal is likely to be properly and sufficiently informed of the competing factors relating to the case before it and so be able to carry out an effective review. (As to this the tribunal should when deciding the case review this prediction).

120. To those I add (a) the nature and degree of the objections and of the distress caused to a patient if his or her wishes are not followed, (b) the likely impact of that distress on his or her well being generally and (c) the prospects that if a legal representative is appointed or not discharged that legal representative will seek a discharge of the appointment."

In *SB v South London and Maudsley NHS Foundation Trust* [2020] UKUT 33 (AAC); [2020] M.H.L.R. 124, the patient wished to change the legal representative appointed for him by the tribunal under this paragraph. UT Judge Wikeley held that:

1.   The failure of standard court form MH6b to inform a detained mental health patient that he had 14 days to apply for a review of a direction appointing legal representatives for him meant that the appointment had involved a material error of law.

2.   Given that this rule makes no specific provision for the process by which appointments of legal representatives under para.(b) are to be reviewed and/or revoked, this could only be done by way of a case management decision under rule 5.

3.   By basing its decision not to review the appointment of the legal representative solely on the appointed solicitors' objection, the tribunal had abandoned its decision-making responsibility. By doing so, the tribunal had not reviewed the patient's capacity when faced with new evidence of instruction. In particular, the tribunal's approach seemingly ignored the principle that the test of capacity to instruct a legal representative is a lower test than the capacity required to conduct proceedings.

Best interests   In *YA*, above, Charles J. said at para.10 of his "Overview":

"[I]t is clear from the best interests test in Rule 11(7)(b) and the general requirement to act in the best interests of a person who lacks relevant capacity that the legal representative is not only appointed in the patient's best interests but must act in them (having regard to the relevant issues of fact and law that are relevant in the proceedings)."

Lacks the capacity   In *VS v St Andrew's Healthcare* [2018] UKUT 250 (AAC); [2018] M.H.L.R. 337, at para.16, UT Judge Jacobs said that he considered that "the capacity required to bring proceedings is less demanding than the capacity required to conduct them" (the test of capacity to bring proceedings is set out in the General Note to s.66). In this case, Judge Jacobs ruled that "a solicitor appointed under rule 11(7)(b) can make a request to withdraw an application to the tribunal if the representative feels that it would be in the best interests of the patient to do so where the patient has fluctuating capacity or does not understand or recall an application to the tribunal being submitted" (paras 23, 24).

The tribunal should not require the patient's responsible clinician (RC) to provide it with an assessment of the patient's mental capacity to instruct a solicitor as this would involve the RC in a conflict of interest in that the tribunal would be asking the RC to give an opinion on the capacity of an individual who is on the opposite side of the dispute. For the same reason, the patient's legal advocate should not follow the Law Society's advice that where the advocate is unable to form on opinion on the patient's mental capacity to provide instructions, the opinion of the patient's RC should be sought: see Appendix D, para.4.1. Conducting such an assessment might also be beyond the RC's area of competence. It is suggested that if, during her examination of the patient, the medical member of the tribunal suspects that the patient lacks the required capacity, she should inform her colleagues of her assessment. Guided by this assessment, the tribunal should then decide, applying the best interest test, whether to appoint a solicitor to represent the patient. The principles and approach set out in the Mental Capacity Act 2005 (see in particular ss.1 to 3) and its associated statutory guidance in the Code of Practice: Mental Capacity Act 2005 (see in particular Ch.4) should be applied (*YA*, above, para.30).

In *YA*, Charles J. said at para.58 that the "factors that the patient will have to be able to sufficiently understand, retain, use and weigh will be likely to include the following:

(i)   the detention, and so the reasons for it, can be challenged in proceedings before the tribunal who, on that challenge, will consider whether the detention in justified by the provisions of the MHA,

(ii)   in doing that, the tribunal will investigate and invite and consider questions and argument on the issues, the medical and other evidence and the legal issues,

(iii)   the tribunal can discharge the section and so bring the detention to an end,

(iv)   representation would be free,

(v)   discussion can take place with the patient and the representative before and so without the pressure of a hearing,

(vi)   having regard to that discussion a representative would be able to question witnesses and argue the case on the facts and the law, and thereby assist in ensuring that the tribunal took all relevant factual and legal issues into account,

(vii)   he or she may not be able to do this so well because of their personal involvement and the nature and complication of some of the issues (e.g. when they are finely balanced or depend on the likelihood of the patient's compliance with assessment or treatment or relate to what is the least restrictive available way of best achieving the proposed assessment or treatment),

(viii) having regard to the issues of fact and law his or her ability to conduct the proceedings without help, and so

(ix)   the impact of these factors on the choice to be made".

If it appears during the course of the hearing that the patient might no longer have capacity, see *PI v West London Mental Health NHS Trust*, above.

Calculating time

3-079   **12.**—(1)   An act required by these Rules, a practice direction or a direction to be done on or by a particular day must be done by 5pm on that day.

(2)   If the time specified by these Rules, a practice direction or a direction for doing any act ends on a day other than a working day, the act is done in time if it is done on the next working day.

(3)–(4)   [*These paragraphs do not apply to mental health cases*]

Definitions

3-080   practice direction: r.1(3).
working day: r.1(3).
Tribunal: r.1(3).

Sending and delivery of documents

3-081   **13.**—(1)   Any document to be provided to the Tribunal under these Rules, a practice direction or a direction must be—

(a) sent by pre-paid post or delivered by hand to the address specified for the proceedings;
(b) sent by fax to the number specified for the proceedings; or
(c) sent or delivered by such other method as the Tribunal may permit or direct.

[(1A) If the Tribunal permits or directs documents to be provided to it by email, the requirement for a signature on applications or references under rules 20(2), 22(4)(a) or 32(1)(b) may be satisfied by a typed instead of a handwritten signature.]

(2) Subject to paragraph (3), if a party provides a fax number, email address or other details for the electronic transmission of documents to them, that party must accept delivery of documents by that method.

(3) If a party informs the Tribunal and all other parties that a particular form of communication, other than pre-paid post or delivery by hand, should not be used to provide documents to that party, that form of communication must not be so used.

(4) If the Tribunal or a party sends a document to a party or the Tribunal by email or any other electronic means of communication, the recipient may request that the sender provide a hard copy of the document to the recipient. The recipient must make such a request as soon as reasonably practicable after receiving the document electronically.

(5) The Tribunal and each party may assume that the address provided by a party or its representative is and remains the address to which documents should be sent or delivered until receiving written notification to the contrary.

Amendment

Paragraph (1A) was inserted by SI 2011/651 reg.4(3).

Definitions

document: r.1(3).   **3-082**
Tribunal: r.1(3).
practice direction: r.1(3).
party: r.1(4).

Use of documents and information

14.—(1) The Tribunal may make an order prohibiting the disclosure or publica-   **3-083**
tion of—
(a) specified documents or information relating to the proceedings; or
(b) any matter likely to lead members of the public to identify any person whom the Tribunal considers should not be identified.

(2) The Tribunal may give a direction prohibiting the disclosure of a document or information to a person if—
(a) the Tribunal is satisfied that such disclosure would be likely to cause that person or some other person serious harm; and
(b) the Tribunal is satisfied, having regard to the interests of justice, that it is proportionate to give such a direction.

(3) If a party ("the first party") considers that the Tribunal should give a direction under paragraph (2) prohibiting the disclosure of a document or information to another party ("the second party"), the first party must—
(a) exclude the relevant document or information from any documents that will be provided to the second party; and
(b) provide to the Tribunal the excluded document or information, and the

reason for its exclusion, so that the Tribunal may decide whether the document or information should be disclosed to the second party or should be the subject of a direction under paragraph (2).

(4)   The Tribunal must conduct proceedings as appropriate in order to give effect to a direction given under paragraph (2).

(5)   If the Tribunal gives a direction under paragraph (2) which prevents disclosure to a party who has appointed a representative, the Tribunal may give a direction that the documents or information be disclosed to that representative if the Tribunal is satisfied that—

  (a)   disclosure to the representative would be in the interests of the party; and

  (b)   the representative will act in accordance with paragraph (6).

(6)   Documents or information disclosed to a representative in accordance with a direction under paragraph (5) must not be disclosed either directly or indirectly to any other person without the Tribunal's consent.

(7)   Unless the Tribunal gives a direction to the contrary, information about mental health cases and the names of any persons concerned in such cases must not be made public.

Definitions

3-084   Tribunal: r.1(3).
document: r.1(3).
party: r.1(3).
mental health case: r.1(3).

General Note

3-085   This rule enables the tribunal to make an order prohibiting the disclosure or publication of material relating to the proceedings to a person (para.(1)). Such an order can only be made if the tribunal is satisfied that the disclosure would be likely to cause serious harm to that person or another, and that it is proportionate, having regard to the interests of justice, to make such an order (para.(2)). Reasons for requesting the tribunal to exclude a document or information must be provided (para.(3)). An excluded document or information can be disclosed to the patient's representative (not necessarily a legal representative) as long as the representative does not disclose it further without the tribunal's consent (paras (5), (6)). Unless the tribunal directs otherwise, information about mental health cases must not be made public (para.(7)).

Although the tribunal is not explicitly required to give reasons for its decision on non-disclosure, a brief statement of reasons which avoids identifying the nature of the material under consideration should be given because the time limit for appealing the decision on a point of law is determined by the date when the person was sent "written reasons for the decision" (r.46(2)(a)).

The tribunal can decide to exclude the patient while the issue of non-disclosure is discussed (r.38(4)(b)) and can direct that a person be excluded from the hearing in order to give effect to a direction made under para.(2) (r.38(4)(c)).

In *R. (on the application of Maher) v First-tier Tribunal (Mental Health)* [2023] EWHC 34 (Admin), Stacey J. considered the relationship between the presumption of privacy in cases involving the mental health of a patient and the open justice principle. On holding that the Deputy Chamber President (DCP) had acted unlawfully when she decided not to provide a victim (who was the claimant) with the reasons for the tribunal's decision to order the conditional discharge of the patient, her Ladyship said:

"... Judge Johnston did not direct herself that departing from the open justice principle can only be justified in exceptional circumstances when they are strictly necessary to secure the proper administration of justice, but jumped straight to the presumption contained in the FTT Rules. As a consequence she did not engage with the purpose of the open justice principle which is to both assist in justice being done through transparency and also to enable the public to have confidence in the system [para.114].
...

The reasons for and against rebutting the presumption of privacy in mental health cases needed to be weighed against the open justice principle as a proportionality exercise for the FTT to undertake when considering whether to exercise its discretion. Without having set out the rationale for the open justice principle the exercise becomes unbalanced [para.116]".

Furthermore, the DCP had fallen into error by:

(i)   Focussing on the motives of the applicant in seeking to know the reasons, or the gist of the reasons, for the FTT's decision as those considerations should not have been given weight in the overall balance (para.118).

(ii)   Not directing herself that the extent of the derogation should be no more than is strictly necessary to achieve the desired purpose, and did not consider providing the victim with a gist or summary of the reasons (para.119).

(iii)   Not adequately explaining the reasons why a redacted version of the conditional discharge decision could not meet the privacy rights of the patient or why redacted reasons were not possible (para.120).

(iv)   Not engaging sufficiently with the reasons that the victim had put forward (para.121).

Stacey J. also accepted the claimant's arguments under the European Convention on Human Rights that the refusal to provide the gist of the reasons for the conditional discharge decision, when the Parole Board would have provided a gist of its reasons in similar circumstances, was unlawful discrimination under art.14 in relation to the claimant's art.8 rights.

In *Dorset Healthcare NHS Foundation Trust v MH* [2009] UKUT 4 (AAC); [2009] M.H.L.R. 102, the Upper Tribunal, after stating that the "starting point is that full disclosure of all relevant material should generally be given" (para.20), provided the following obiter guidance to assist parties who seek the disclosure of the patient's medical records (note that the published transcript has two paragraphs numbered 29):

"23. However, rule 14 does not provide the only procedure by which disclosure of documents can be withheld. The medical records of many patients contain documents from third parties which, irrespective of any harm to the patient that may ensure from their disclosure, may be sensitive. For example, a relative of a patient may provide details of his/her own medical condition which may be relevant to that person's ability to look after the patient if the patient were returned home: or simply set out reasons why, if the patient were returned home, relatives or potential carers would be unable to cope. Sometimes such documents are submitted to the responsible authority holding the medical records with an express requirement that they be kept confidential from the patient (and sometimes also from even the patient's solicitors). In any event, that authority often considers, rightly, that it owes a duty of confidence to the relevant third-parties and is unwilling to disclose documents to the patient (and occasionally even to the patient's solicitors) without an order. If the documents are relevant to the issues in an application made by the patient (as they usually will be), leaving aside the various common law and statutory obligations that fall on the responsible authority holding the medical records, there is an obvious potential tension between the Article 6 rights of the patient and the Article 8 rights of the third parties, and it is important that all of these rights are properly considered and maintained (see *R (B) v Crown Court at Stafford* [2007] 1 WLR 1524, especially at [23]). What is the correct approach in these circumstances?

24. As we have already observed, in dealing with such a situation the parties should first do all they can to agree the approach to be adopted and avoid applying to the tribunal unless it is essential. Disclosure does not and should not present a problem in the vast majority of cases.

25. Given the general rule in favour of full disclosure the burden will be on the responsible authority to demonstrate that it is appropriate to withhold disclosure of any particular documents.

26. Where there are third-party documents which the responsible authority considers may be confidential to the third-party, then, where this is practical, the authority may seek the relevant third parties' consent to disclosure. However, this may not be practical because of the delay that would be involved in identifying and locating the third parties.

27. In most cases where there are confidential third-party documents, it should be possible for the responsible authority to disclose all such documents to the patient's solicitors subject to an undertaking from the solicitors not to disclose to the patient third-party documents specifically identified by the authority. The solicitors can then take a view as to whether the third-party rights override the rights of the patient, or vice versa. Where they consider the documents ought to be disclosed to the patient, then they must make an application to the tribunal for disclosure.

28. In other circumstances, the responsible authority may take the view that the documents are so sensitive that they should not be disclosed even to the solicitors or they are unable to rely on an undertaking that the representative will not disclose to the patient documents received. However, an

undertaking from a solicitor (who owes a duty to the tribunal) will only not be acceptable in quite exceptional circumstances.

29. Where a responsible authority seeks to avoid disclosure of documents even to the patient's representative, then it should submit a skeleton argument setting out the reasons for resisting disclosure and should identify the documents in question. The skeleton argument, but not the documents, should be served on the patient's solicitors who will be given an opportunity to respond in writing.

29. In circumstances in which the responsible authority has served all of the documents on the solicitors subject to an undertaking, and the solicitor then wishes to disclose the documents (or some of them) to the patient, the procedure will be reversed; and the patient's solicitor should submit a skeleton argument setting out why it is considered appropriate to disclose the documents to the patient and the authority will be given the opportunity to respond in writing.

30. Where the exchange of skeleton arguments does not resolve the issue, then an application to the tribunal will be necessary. Where a patient's solicitor is seeking permission to disclose documents to a patient, then the application should be made by that solicitor: if a responsible authority is seeking to deny disclosure to even the patient's solicitor then the application should be made by the authority.

31. In most cases, any application should be capable of being determined by the tribunal on the day of the substantive hearing. However, there may be circumstances where the issue is more complicated, when it would be appropriate for the matter to be considered and determined by a single judge in advance of the substantive hearing. Depending on the circumstances and complexity this could be either on written submissions or by holding an oral hearing.

32. We can also envisage circumstances in which the tribunal will need to obtain information as to the third-party's views on the issue of disclosure. Where this occurs, the tribunal should notify the responsible authority which should then obtain this information and submit it to the tribunal, thus avoiding where possible any direct involvement by the third-party in the tribunal's procedures.

33. All of these steps can be taken under the general case management powers of the tribunal, particularly under rule 5(3)(d). The steps are all consistent with the specific provisions set out in rule 14, to which we have already made reference: and the parties should adopt a similar procedure in circumstances in which rule 14 might apply. Again in most instances those applications should be dealt with on the day of the substantive hearing and only exceptionally should it be necessary for a single judge to determine the issue on written submissions or by a separate hearing prior to the substantive hearing.

34. This guidance is intended to assist all parties who seek disclosure of medical records, and face requests for disclosure of medical records; and hopefully there will be few cases where the procedures suggested above will not suffice. However, this is only guidance and is not prescriptive for all cases. In cases where there are idiosyncratic features or complexities, it is always open to either party to make an application to the tribunal for specific directions or for a tribunal of its own motion to give appropriate directions."

The Data Protection Act 1998 provides patients with a right of access to their medical records. The patient's representative should obtain the written authority of the patient to apply for such access. In *NR's Application* [2015] NIQB 35, the following declaration was made by the High Court of Northern Ireland:

"The legal advisors of patients detained under the Mental Health (Northern Ireland) Order 1986 have a right, pursuant to Articles 5 and 6 of the European Convention on Human Rights to view their client's medical notes and records, in a practice and manner which safeguards the confidential and sensitive information therein, in advance of a Mental Health Review Tribunal Hearing as soon as reasonably practicable after reasonable notice has been given to the detaining trust accompanied by a properly executed written form of authority signed and dated by the detained patient."

The following guidance, which can be accessed at *http://www.mhlo.uk/bk*, is provided by the Courts and Tribunal Service in *Reports for Mental Health Tribunals* (2012) at pp.5, 6:

"If the Responsible Authority, or the source or author of the information, statement, report or document considers that the tribunal should give a direction prohibiting the disclosure of the material to the patient, they must:

a. separate and exclude the relevant information, statement, report or document from any other material submitted;

b. separately provide to the tribunal copies of the excluded information, statement, report or document, ensuring that the excluded material is clearly marked:

'NOT TO BE DISCLOSED TO THE PATIENT WITHOUT THE EXPRESS PERMIS-
SION OF THE TRIBUNAL'

c.   provide the tribunal with full written reasons for the proposed exclusion, so that the tribunal
      may decide for itself whether the grounds for exclusion have been made out and whether
      the information, statement, report or document should be disclosed to the patient, or whether
      it should be excluded."

Human Rights Act 1998

A decision by the tribunal not to disclose a document or information to the patient under para.(1)   **3-086**
would constitute an interference with the patient's right to respect for his private and family life under
art.8(1) of the European Convention on Human Rights (ECHR). Article 8(2) provides a justification for
such an interference on the ground of either protecting the patient's "health or morals" or the prevention of "disorder or crime". An interference on the general ground of protecting the "welfare of the
patient" is not allowed for.

In *Winterwerp v Netherlands (App.No.6301/73)*, the European Commission of Human Rights said
that the patient's lawyer had the right to examine the patient's file, but that it was not necessary for the
patient to be informed of all the evidence or that he be allowed access to all of the information in his
medical file. This approach was confirmed by the European Court of Human Rights in *Nikolova v
Bulgaria* (2001) E.H.R.R. 3 at para.58, where it was said that "[e]quality of arms is not ensured if counsel
is denied access to those documents in the investigation file which are essential in order effectively to
challenge the lawfulness of his client's detention".

In *Roberts v Nottinghamshire Healthcare NHS Trust* [2008] EWHC 1934 (QB); [2008] M.H.L.R.
294, at para.25, Cranston J. said that although a party has a right to a fair trial under art.6 "that does not
mean that he or she has an absolute or unqualified right to see every document": also see *Re B
(Disclosure to Parties)* [2001] 2 F.L.R. 2017 at para.56.

Although there has been no reported case which has considered the compatibility of this rule with
art.5(4) of the ECHR, in *McGrady's application for Judicial Review* [2003] NIQB 15, Kerr J. considered
a similar provision in r.12(2) of the Mental Health Review Tribunal Rules (Northern Ireland) 1986 (SI
1986/193). His Lordship said at paras 20 to 22:

"Where ... disclosure may cause harm to the applicant or to the informant, the tribunal must balance the right of the applicant under Art.5(4) with the interests that may be adversely affected if the
material is disclosed. In this context the tribunal will want to consider carefully whether the convention rights of the informant would be infringed if the material that that person has provided in
confidence is revealed to the applicant.

It appears to me that the tribunal will also take into account that the applicant's legal representatives have seen the material in question. While they may not disclose that material to the applicant,
they may nevertheless take his instructions on the themes with which the material is concerned. There
is no reason that the applicant should not be at liberty to present material to the tribunal on the matters raised in the addendum even if he remains unaware of its contents.

If the tribunal concludes that the addendum's contents should not be disclosed to the applicant it
should approach the assessment with care. It must keep in mind that details of the information have
not been revealed to the applicant. Its duty is to ensure that the proceedings are conducted fairly. This
duty arises under pre-incorporation law as well as under the convention. But the applicant is not
denied fairness simply because the material is withheld from him. As I have said, a balance must be
struck between, on the one hand, the requirement that an applicant applying for discharge should
generally have the opportunity to see and comment on all material adverse to him and, on the other,
that the safety of the informant should not be imperilled. Unfairness would arise if the tribunal failed
to acknowledge that the applicant has not been able to see and answer specifically the details of the
allegations made against him. Provided they are conscious of this and cater for it in their approach
to the assessment of the addendum, the proceedings will not be unfair to the applicant."

*Disclosure of the Victim's Evidence to the Patient in cases covered by the Domestic Violence, Crime and
Victims Act 2004*

See the note to r.15 under this heading.   **3-087**

Paragraph (2)

3-088   The tests in paras (a) and (b) which provide the tribunal with a power to order non-disclosure are "independent tests that are not to be merged" (*M v ABM University Health Board*), below, para.35).

The criterion of "serious harm" is not the exclusive rationale for non-disclosure, as issues of third party confidentiality may arise: see *Dorset Healthcare NHS Foundation Trust v MH*, above, and Kris Gledhill, "*The First Flight of the Fledgling: the Upper Tribunal's Substantive Debut*", J.M.H.L., Spring 2009, at 89–91.

In *RM v St Andrew's Healthcare* [2010] UKUT 119 (AAC); [2010] M.H.L.R. 176 UT Judge Jacobs said at para.31:

> "The Convention right under Article 6 guarantees a fair hearing. [*Secretary of State for the Home Department v AF (No.3)* [2009] UKHL 28; [2009] 3 All E.R. 643] shows how highly a fair hearing is rated in the balance with non-disclosure. ... The overriding objective in r.2 requires that the rules of procedure be applied so that cases are dealt with fairly and justly. This includes ensuring full participation, so far as is practicable. Rule 14(2) requires the tribunal to have regard to the interests of justice. Justice and fairness generally require openness. Sometimes, they are not compatible and a compromise is possible. It may, for example, be possible and necessary to conduct proceedings while concealing that the true prognosis is worse than the patient realises. In this case, I have set out the full implications of the tribunal's order. They involve more than a compromise between justice and openness. They involve the sacrifice of the patient's right to challenge his detention effectively."

In *RM*, which was a case where "a patient's best interests medically [clashed] with his best interests legally" (per Judge Jacobs at para.1), the non-disclosure order made by the First-tier tribunal referred to documents relating to the fact that the patient was being covertly medicated. Prior to being covertly medicated, the patient had been refusing medication and, as a consequence, had become very ill to the point where he was said to be at risk of sudden, unexpected death (para.3). However, Judge Jacobs found that disclosure "will, on the evidence, have some immediate adverse consequences for the claimant's condition" and that those "short-term consequences, while involving risk, do not justify the legal consequences that would follow from non-disclosure" (para.33). The question that had to be answered by the Upper Tribunal was: can the patient effectively challenge his detention without knowing that he was being covertly medicated? (para.26). The non-disclosure order was set aside on the ground that it would "exclude [the patient] completely from knowing the real process that was being followed and allow him to participate only in a pretence of a process" and "would severely hamper his legal team in participating effectively in that process" (para.32).

RM was distinguished in *M v ABM University Health Board* [2018] UKUT 120 (AAC); [2018] M.H.L.R 310 where the Mental Health Review Tribunal for Wales had made a direction under the equivalent Welsh Rule (r.17 of SI 2008/2705) for the non-disclosure of any information relating to the administration of covert medication to the patient. Unlike the position in *RM*, the patient in M lacked the mental capacity to appoint a representative. On allowing the patient's appeal against the tribunal's decision to make the direction, UT Judge Mitchell held that in deciding whether information about a patient's covert medication should be disclosed to a patient where (a) the patient lacks capacity to appoint a representative, and (b) disclosure would be likely to cause serious harm, a tribunal has an ongoing obligation to consider the extent to which the patient, despite his impaired mental capacity, is capable of participating in the proceedings (see r.2(2)(c)). A tribunal will then be in a position to decide whether, having regard to the interests of justice, it is proportionate to withhold covert medication information from the patient. When making this decision, the tribunal must bear in mind the difficulties that non-disclosure would cause for the patient's representative. Judge Mitchell said at para.98:

> "[I]t is necessary, in a case like Mr M's, to seek submissions from the parties as to the patient's ability to participate in the proceedings. A Tribunal may also decide it is necessary for this purpose to require the detaining authority to supply it with any formal mental capacity assessments that have been carried out."

The judge emphasised that the "fact that a patient lacks the mental capacity to appoint a legal representative does not mean the patient has no relevant wishes and feelings about his detention nor that any wishes and feelings fall out of account" and that a patient who lacked the "mental capacity to appoint a representative, might nevertheless have capacity to give instructions on some relevant issues" (para.95).

With regard to the decision in *RM*, Judge Mitchell said at para.94:

"In a case involving a patient who has capacity to appoint a legal representative, I can well understand why the failure to disclose information about covert medication may be considered so great a rupture in the fairness of proceedings that it could not be proportionate to withhold the information."

In *AF (No.3)* above, para.105, Baroness Hale said obiter:

"These days, a ... Tribunal would be unlikely to uphold a non-disclosure claim on the general ground that disclosure would be damaging to the doctor patient relationship. They would want to know precisely what it was in this doctor's evidence that might cause serious harm to this patient or to some other person and to weigh that damage against the interests of fairness. It will be an individualised balancing act carried out after discussion with the patient's own advocate and in the light of the opinions of the patient's own independent medical adviser."

In *RM*, Judge Jacobs said that a tribunal should draft non-disclosure orders in terms of information rather that documents. Although the terms of such an order would depend upon the facts of the individual case, the following was offered, at para.36, as "a useful starting point":

"'The Tribunal prohibits disclosure to the patient of:

(a)   information relating to ...;
(b)   any document containing or referring to that information, in particular—
    (i)   the reports of ...;
    (ii)   any other report prepared in connection with these proceedings; and
    (iii)   this order.'"

Paragraph (a) deals with the key issue of the information that must not be disclosed. It needs to be precise, clear and exhaustive. Paragraph (b) deals with the means by which disclosure might be made, directly or indirectly. It is supportive of paragraph (a) and need not be exhaustive.

The tribunal also needs to consider the patient's access to medical records. The order did not prohibit disclosure of the patient's medical records that, no doubt, contain details of his medication. A patient is entitled to access to medical records under section 7 of the Data Protection Act 1998. This is subject to the Data Protection (Subject Access Modification) (Health) Order 2000 (SI No 413). Article 5(1) contains an exemption from section 7 'to the extent to which the application of that section would be likely to cause serious harm to the physical or mental health or condition of the data subject or any other person.' That condition is effectively the same as rule 14(2)(a). The decision whether the exemption applies is made by the data controller.

Document   The natural limit of this provision is on documents that are relevant to the proceedings (*RM v St Andrew's Healthcare*, above, para.15).

Paragraph (a)

Would be likely to cause ... serious harm   In *M v ABM University Health Board*, above, Judge   **3-089**
Mitchell said at para.87:

"[S]ome types of 'serious harm' are more severe than others. To take a dramatic example, a likelihood of certain death is a more significant form of serious harm than a likelihood of a drastic but temporary deterioration in a patient's mental health. The nature of the likely serious harm must be relevant once the Tribunal goes on to decide whether, having regard to the interests of justice, nondisclosure would be proportionate."

A similar phrase is found in the Data Protection (Subject Access Modification) (Health) Order 2000 (SI 2000/413) para.5. In *Roberts v Nottinghamshire Healthcare NHS Trust* [2008] EWHC 1934 (QB); [2008] M.H.L.R. 294 at para.9, Cranston J. interpreted the phrase contained in the 2000 Order as follows:

"The question is whether there may very well be a risk of harm to health even if the risk falls short of being more probable that not. Harm to health could arise in various ways. In the context of mental health, it could be self harm or harm to others. The issue demands a factual enquiry: taking all matters into account such as the personality of the applicant, his past history, the care regime to which he is subject and so on, might there very well be a risk of harm to health on release of the data?"

His Lordship applied the judgment of Munby J. in *R (on the application of Lord) v Secretary of State for the Home Department* [2004] Prison Law Reports 65, where it was said that the term "likely ... connotes a degree of probability where there would be a significant and weighty chance of prejudice to the identified public interest. The degree of risk must be such that there 'may very well' be prejudice to those interests, even if the risk falls short of being more probable than not".

Paragraph (b)

3-090   **Proportionate**   It is submitted that in this context proportionality means that infringing the patient's right to the full disclosure of information about his treatment is a proportionate means of achieving the legitimate aim of protecting the patient and/or others from serious harm.

Paragraph (5)

3-091   With regard to the disclosure of a document to a representative in a different context, in *R (on the application of Mohamed) v Secretary of State for Defence* [2012] EWHC 3454 (Admin), Moses L.J. said at para.28:

> "The free and unencumbered ability to give and receive instructions is an important facet of open and fair trials. That ability is hampered if in some respects the lawyer is unable to disclose all the relevant evidence and material and, in that respect, the client is deprived of the opportunity to give informed instructions. But the degree to which that is of importance will vary from case to case. No lawyers should consent to such a [confidentiality] ring unless they are satisfied they can do so without harming their client's case. But provided the legal advisers are satisfied they can safely continue to act under a restriction, the inability to communicate fully with the client will not in such circumstances undermine the fundamental principles on which a fair application for judicial review depends."

Paragraphs 5.1.5 of the guidance note on the "Role of the Independent Mental Health Advocate (IMHA) in First-tier Tribunal (Mental Health) hearings" (see the General Note to these Rules) states that if an IMHA is appointed as the patient's representative, this "is likely to create considerable difficulty since, if the IMHA receives a document which is not to be disclosed to the patient, they will have had to undertake under Rule 14(5) not to disclose it or its contents to the patient. The IMHA might well consider that this undertaking conflicts with their general duty to the patient and, if so, the tribunal will be unable to disclose information to the IMHA because they will not be satisfied that the representative will act in accordance with Rule 14(6). This situation should be avoided to protect the patient's rights to effective legal representation".

Paragraph (7)

3-092   This paragraph should be considered in the context of the requirement under r.38(1) that all hearings must be held in private unless the tribunal considers that it is in the interests of justice for the hearing to be held in public.
   In *Pickering v Liverpool Daily Post and Echo Newspapers Plc* [1991] 1 All E.R. 622 HL, it was held that this rule, as it appeared in r.21(5) of the Mental Health Review Tribunal Rules 1983, did not prohibit the press from publishing the fact that the patient was applying to the tribunal for discharge, the date, time or place of the hearing, and the decision of the tribunal; also see *R. (on the application of Maher) v First-tier Tribunal (Mental Health)*, above .

Evidence and submissions
3-093   **15.**—(1)   Without restriction on the general powers in rule 5(1) and (2) (case management powers), the Tribunal may give directions as to—
   (a)   issues on which it requires evidence or submissions;
   (b)   the nature of the evidence or submissions it requires;
   (c)   whether the parties are permitted or required to provide expert evidence, and if so whether the parties must jointly appoint a single expert to provide such evidence;
   (d)   any limit on the number of witnesses whose evidence a party may put forward, whether in relation to a particular issue or generally;
   (e)   the manner in which any evidence or submissions are to be provided, which may include a direction for them to be given—

(i) orally at a hearing; or

(ii) by written submissions or witness statement; and

(f) the time at which any evidence or submissions are to be provided.

(2) The Tribunal may—

(a) admit evidence whether or not—

(i) the evidence would be admissible in a civil trial in England and Wales; or

(ii) the evidence was available to a previous decision maker; or

(b) exclude evidence that would otherwise be admissible where—

(i) the evidence was not provided within the time allowed by a direction or a practice direction;

(ii) the evidence was otherwise provided in a manner that did not comply with a direction or a practice direction; or

(iii) it would otherwise be unfair to admit the evidence.

(3) The Tribunal may consent to a witness giving, or require any witness to give, evidence on oath, and may administer an oath for that purpose.

(4)–(5) [*These paragraphs do not apply to mental health cases*]

Definitions

Tribunal: r.1(3).   **3-094**
party: r.1(3).
practice direction: r.1(3).

General Note

The Responsible Authority's duty to arrange for the attendance of its witnesses is considered at paras   **3-095**
20 to 23 of "*Enforcement Procedure, Directions and Summonses*" which is reproduced below.

The evaluation of expert evidence was considered by UT Judge Jacobs in *DL-H v West London Mental Health Trust* [2017] UKUT 387 (AAC); [2017] M.H.L.R. 372, who said that no "tribunal is obliged to accept expert evidence, even if all the evidence agrees, but it must have good reasons for not doing so" (para.18). It followed from this that there is no prohibition in principle on a tribunal substituting its diagnosis of the patient's mental disorder for that of the experts, including members of the clinical team, whose evidence was before the tribunal. The tribunal must have reasons for doing so and it must allow the patient's representative a chance to deal with its view before making a decision (paras 19, 20). Judge Jacobs also said that the "borderline between religious beliefs and mental disorder can be a fine one and one that is difficult to draw. It is right that evidence from both sides of the divide should be admissible to help the tribunal make a soundly-reasoned decision". It was also confirmed that there is no rule of evidence that "only the evidence of religious experts is admissible on matters of religion" (para.10).

The evidence of the patient's responsible clinician (RC) is likely to be of "particular centrality" in any hearing before the tribunal (*R. (on the application of Nottingham Healthcare NHS Trust) v Mental Health Review Tribunal* [2008] EWHC 2445 (Admin); [2008] M.H.L.R. 326 para.19). However, in *AC v Partnerships in Care Ltd and Secretary of State for Justice* [2012] UKUT 450 (AAC), Judge Jacobs said at para.11:

"[I]t does not always follow that greater knowledge means greater insight. The tribunal should have explained what it was in the RC's experience that made her view preferable."

The significance of the RC's evidence, and the way in which a tribunal should approach it, was touched upon in a different context by Dyson L.J in *R. (on the application of K) v West London Mental Health NHS Trust* [2006] EWCA Civ 118; [2006] M.H.L.R. 89 at para.70:

"The weight to be given to opinion of [RCs] must be a matter for the decision-maker having regard to all relevant circumstances. It is not appropriate to attempt an exhaustive definition of what these might be. But they will include how long the [RC] has been in charge of the treatment of the patient, the strength of conviction with which the [RC's] clinical judgment has been expressed, the weight of other clinical opinion and the reasons given by other medical practitioners for their disagreement with the opinion expressed by the [RC]."

The medical evidence that is given on behalf of the responsible authority need not come from the patient's RC. However, the medical evidence must be up to date (*R. v Mental Health Review Tribunal, London and North East Ex p. Manns* [1999] M.H.L.R. 101 at para.28). In *JP v South London and Maudsley NHS Foundation Trust* [2012] UKUT 486 (AAC), UT Judge Lane said that the "Tribunal would be entitled to accept a report prepared by a doctor [who had not seen the patient] from medical notes, though it would have to be examined with care to justify the Tribunal's conclusions" (para.16). If the tribunal concludes that it should hear evidence from the RC and the RC is not available, it could consider using its power to adjourn the hearing under r.5(3)(h).

The evidence should not be confined to justifying the patient's detention. It should also deal with the suitability of the regime that the patient is subject to as such information would be required if the patient's solicitor was minded to attempt to persuade the tribunal to recommend a transfer under s.72(3) (*LB v BMH*, Upper Tribunal, UT Judge Levenson, March 14, 2017).

Oral evidence given by the authors of clinical reports can only address the position as it is at the time of the hearing (*BB v South London & Maudsley NHS Trust* [2009] UKUT 157 (AAC); [2009] M.H.L.R. 302, para.10).

Human Rights Act 1998

3-096   The criteria for "lawful detention" under art.5(1)(e) of the European Convention on Human Rights entail that the review of lawfulness guaranteed by art.5(4) in relation to the continuing detention of a mental health patient should be made by reference to the patient's contemporaneous state of health, including his or her dangerousness, as evidenced by up-to-date medical assessments, and not by reference to past events at the origin of the initial decision to detain (*Rivera v Switzerland, February 18, 2014, (App.No.8300/06)*, para.60).

Evidence given by an Independent Mental Health Advocate

3-097   Paragraphs 6.1 and 6.2 of the guidance note on the "Role of the Independent Mental Health Advocate (IMHA) in First-tier Tribunal (Mental Health) hearings" (see the General Note to these Rules) state:

"It will not usually be appropriate for the IMHA to give evidence to the tribunal, as this is not their general role. However, there are occasions when the IMHA knows all about an issue that has arisen in the past in respect of the patient and will ask (or just begin) to give evidence to the tribunal.
      It is suggested that, if these circumstances arise without warning, the judge should stop the IMHA, and remind him or her that neither of the parties (patient or Responsible Authority) may wish them to give evidence, and if the panel is to seek evidence on its own initiative, it must have cogent reasons for doing so. Moreover, the giving of evidence may well result in the IMHA being cross-examined by the patient's legal representative and by any person representing the Responsible Authority, and being questioned by the panel. Should the IMHA still wish to give evidence, or remain undecided, the legal representative may then wish to have a private consultation with the IMHA in order to ensure that the representative understands the nature of any evidence the IMHA wishes to give, and to enable the representative to decide how they wish to proceed–for example, whether they wish to call the IMHA to give evidence, or whether there may be a better way to place the relevant information before the panel. The tribunal may regulate its own procedure [Rule 5(1)] and may give directions as to the admission and exclusion of evidence [Rule 15]."

Inference to be drawn from the fact that an independent psychiatrist who had visited a patient did not submit a report to the tribunal

3-098   In *MM v Nottinghamshire Healthcare NHS Trust* [2013] UKUT 107 (AAC), Judge Jacobs said at para.10:

"The First-tier Tribunal always has medical evidence from the clinical team. The medical member of the panel will have interviewed the patient. And the patient may have produced medical evidence in support of the application. I cannot imagine any realistic circumstances in which a tribunal, having such evidence, could properly rely on the failure by a patient to produce a report as a basis for drawing inferences that would affect the outcome. The tribunal's duty, and the only proper course, would be to decide on the evidence available rather than speculate on possible explanations of why the report was not produced."

Should a panel recuse themselves on account of having adjudicated on the admissibility of evidence at a preliminary hearing?

In *MM*, above, Judge Jacobs said at paras 12 to 14:   **3-099**

"I begin with the proposition that it is a judicial skill that judges should be able to disregard things that they have heard. ...
    This ability is recognised by the rules of procedure that apply in the First-tier Tribunal. Rule 15 of the Tribunal Procedure (First-tier Tribunal) (Health, Education and Social Care) Chamber 2008 allows tribunals to rule on the admissibility of evidence and on issues that may be presented. That will almost certainly involve the panel knowing at least something of that evidence or those issues. And the circumstances in which the panel has to make its ruling means that it may well have to be made by the same panel that hears the substantive case.
    My reasoning so far relates only to the judge. The other panel members come from different professional backgrounds and may be less experienced in putting matters out of their minds. Even if that is so, there is always a judge present and it is one of the duties of that judge to ensure that the other members of the panel disregard evidence that is not properly before them."

Paragraph (2)

This paragraph was considered in *LN v Surrey NHS Primary Care Trust* [2011] UKUT 76 (AAC)   **3-100**
where UT Judge Rowland said, at paras 22, 23, that the issue for the tribunal "is not whether evidence is admissible, i.e. whether it *can* be admitted, but is whether it *should* be admitted. Relevance is the key consideration. Irrelevant evidence should not be admitted".
    With regard to the use of hearsay evidence, Munby J. said in *R. (on the application of AN) v Mental Health Review Tribunal* [2005] EWHC 587 (Admin); [2005] M.H.L.R. 56 at para.129:

"If the tribunal is relying on hearsay evidence it must take into account the fact that it is hearsay and must have regard to the particular dangers involved in relying upon second, third or fourth hand hearsay. The tribunal must be appropriately cautious of relying upon assertions as to past events which are not securely recorded in contemporaneous notes, particularly if the only evidence is hearsay. The tribunal must be alert to the well-known problem that constant repetition in 'official' reports or statements may, in the 'official' mind, turn into established fact something which rigorous forensic investigation shows is in truth nothing more than 'institutional folklore' with no secure foundation in either recorded or provable fact. The tribunal must guard against too quickly jumping to conclusions adverse to the patient in relation to past events where the only direct evidence is that of the patient himself, particularly where there is no clear account in contemporaneous notes of what is alleged to have happened. In relation to past incidents which are centrally important to the decision it has to take the tribunal must bear in mind the need for proof to the civil standard of proof; it must bear in mind the potential difficulties of relying upon second or third hand hearsay; and, if the incident is really fundamental to its decision, it must bear in mind fairness may require the patient to be given the opportunity to cross-examine the relevant witness(es) if their evidence is to be relied on at all."

On appeal, the Court of Appeal said that it saw "no reason to disagree" with this guidance ([2005] EWCA Civ 1605; [2006] 4 All E.R. 194 at para.77).

Summoning of witnesses and orders to answer questions or produce documents

16.—(1)   On the application of a party or on its own initiative, the Tribunal   **3-101**
may—
    (a)   by summons require any person to attend as a witness at a hearing at the time and place specified in the summons; or
    (b)   order any person to answer any questions or produce any documents in that person's possession or control which relate to any issue in the proceedings.
    (2)   A summons under paragraph (1)(a) must—

(a) give the person required to attend 14 days' notice of the hearing, or such shorter period as the Tribunal may direct; and

(b) where the person is not a party, make provision for the person's necessary expenses of attendance to be paid, and state who is to pay them.

(3) No person may be compelled to give any evidence or produce any document that the person could not be compelled to give or produce on a trial of an action in a court of law.

(4) A summons or order under this rule must—

(a) state that the person on whom the requirement is imposed may apply to the Tribunal to vary or set aside the summons or order, if they have not had an opportunity to object to it; and

(b) state the consequences of failure to comply with the summons or order.

Definitions

3-102 party: r.1(3).
Tribunal: r.1(3).
hearing: r.1(3).

General Note

3-103 The issuing of summonses is considered in "Enforcement Procedure, Directions and Summonses" which is reproduced below.

The Senior President of Tribunals has issued a Practice Direction on "Child, Vulnerable Adult and Sensitive Witnesses" which is also reproduced below.

The tribunal can refer a person's failure to comply with a requirement imposed by it to the Upper Tribunal (r.7(3)). Provision is made in r.7 of the Tribunal Procedure (Upper Tribunal) Rules 2008 (SI 2008/2698) and s.25 of the Tribunals, Courts and Enforcement Act 2007 regarding the Upper Tribunal's options on such a reference being made.

Paragraph (1)

3-104 Although the summonsed person can be required to attend the hearing, he or she cannot be compelled to give evidence or to produce a document if para.(3) applies.

In *CB v Suffolk CC* [2010] UKUT 413 (AAC), a case involving a witness's failure to respond to a witness summons, the Upper Tribunal said that while it would not wish to suggest that every last avenue must always be explored to avoid issuing a witness summons, tribunals "should always consider alternatives to personal attendance available to them under relevant Tribunal Procedure Rules, including the power under r.16(1)(b) to order a person to answer any questions or produce any documents in that person's possession or control which relate to any issue in the proceedings". In this case, a fine of £500, with imprisonment in default, was imposed for failure to comply. In a letter to Mental Health Act administrators dated April 17, 2015, the Deputy Chamber President said that the tribunal "will keep records of witnesses who have failed to comply so that, if relevant, we can consider the witness's previous record of non-compliance when considering making a referral" (para.29).

Withdrawal

3-105 **17.**—(1) Subject to paragraphs (2) and (3), a party may give notice of the withdrawal of its case, or any part of it—

(a) [...] by sending or delivering to the Tribunal a written notice of withdrawal; or

(b) orally at a hearing.

(2) Notice of withdrawal will not take effect unless the Tribunal consents to the withdrawal except—

(a) in proceedings concerning the suitability of a person to work with children or vulnerable adults; [...]

(b) in proceedings started by a reference under section 67 or 71(1) of the Mental Health Act 1983[; or

(c)   where a local authority notifies the Tribunal before the expiry of the time limit for submitting a response that it will not oppose the appeal in a special educational needs case].

(3)   A party which started a mental health case by making a reference to the Tribunal under section 68, 71(2) or 75(1) of the Mental Health Act 1983 may not withdraw its case.

(4)   A party which has withdrawn its case may apply to the Tribunal for the case to be reinstated.

(5)   An application under paragraph (4) must be made in writing and be received by the Tribunal within 28 days after—

    (a)   the date on which the Tribunal received the notice under paragraph (1)(a); or

    (b)   the date of the hearing at which the case was withdrawn orally under paragraph (1)(b).

(6)   The Tribunal must notify each party in writing [that a withdrawal has taken effect under this rule].

[(7)   Where a local authority has notified the Tribunal before the expiry of the time limit for submitting a response that it will not oppose the appeal in a special educational needs case, the notice under paragraph (6) must state the date on which the Tribunal was so notified.]

Amendments

The amendments to this rule were made by SI 2013/477 r.17 and SI 2014/2128 r.22.

Definitions

party: r.1(3).
Tribunal: r.1(3).
hearing: r.1(3).

3-106

General Note

This rule, which enables an applicant to apply to the tribunal in writing to withdraw a case, does not apply to mandatory references (para.(3)). A discretionary reference may be withdrawn (para.(2)(b)). A withdrawal cannot take effect without the consent of the tribunal, apart from a discretionary reference by the Secretary of State made under s.67 or 71(1)) (para.(2)). If an application is withdrawn, the applicant can make a further application to the tribunal during the relevant period (s.77(2)). Provision is made for the reinstatement of a withdrawn case in paras (4) and (5).

3-107

The patient's solicitor appointed under r.11(7)(b) can make an application to withdraw on behalf of a mentally incapacitated patient (*VS v St Andrew's Healthcare* [2018] UKUT 250 (AAC), paras 23, 24, per UT Judge Jacobs speaking obiter).

The approach that the tribunal should adopt when considering an application to withdraw was identified by Charles J. in *AMA v Greater Manchester West Mental Health NHS Foundation Trust* [2015] UKUT 36 (AAC); [2015] M.H.L.R. 133 at para.37:

"(i)   the FtT must always ask for and consider who made the application to withdraw, how it was made, and perhaps most importantly the reasons for it and thus the continuation of a detention,

(ii)   the FtT must always make its own mind up on whether it should agree to it or conduct a review of the detention and give reasons for its decision, and

(iii)   if it is in doubt it should refuse consent and as a consequence carry out the review itself.

In effect the decision to give consent has to be based on a conclusion of the tribunal that continued detention under the MHA is justified for the reasons founding the application to withdraw (or other reasons)."

In the light of the judgment in *AMA* and para.12.24 of the *Code of Practice*, which states that the

"Tribunal is not bound to agree [to a withdrawal], especially if the withdrawal is merely tactical or is sought within 48 hours of the hearing", Judge Mark Hinchliffe, Deputy Chamber President, wrote to the Chairman of the Mental Health Lawyers Association as follows:

"I have decided that a withdrawal should not be agreed by staff with delegated powers if the withdrawal request was received less than 48 hours (not counting weekends etc) before the tribunal hearing, or if the withdrawal appears to be merely tactical—such as where the case is part-heard, or if there are two cases that ought to be heard together and an attempt is made to withdraw one of them, or if an application for a postponement or adjournment has been made and refused and the withdrawal appears to be an attempt to get round the refusal. Such withdrawals will be referred either to a Registrar, Salaried Judge, or Panel—who will apply the principles set out in *AMA*.

It follows, that for requests received less than 48 hours before the scheduled start of the hearing (not counting non-working days):

(1) the tribunal should always be provided with full reasons why the patient wants to withdraw the application (and thus agrees to the continuation of detention or a MHA order); and

(2) the tribunal must always make its own mind up on whether it should agree or, instead, proceed; and

(3) the tribunal will bear in mind that the need for, and right to, a periodic review of a patient's detention is an important safeguard and is necessary for Article 5 ECHR purposes. It should not be abandoned lightly, especially if the hearing may achieve some good; and

(4) if in doubt, the tribunal should (as Charles J suggests) refuse consent and, as a consequence, carry on with the hearing.

If the request is received after 4.30pm on the working day before the hearing, it will not be considered in advance, the panel will convene, and the decision whether or not to consent will be made by the panel, again applying the *AMA* principles" (accessed on the MHLO website at: *www.mhlo.uk/bd*.

In *MB v BEH MH NHS Trust* (2011) UKUT 328 (AAC); [2011] M.H.L.R. 246, UT Judge Levenson held that:

1. A decision of the tribunal to consent to a withdrawal is a judicial act which is appealable.

2. It is a breech of the rules of natural justice and fair procedure for a presiding judge to invite a patient to withdraw his application in such a way as to give rise to reasonable apprehension that he had formed a preconceived concluded opinion that the patient had no possibility of succeeding in his application.

With regard to point 2, it is permissible for the tribunal to express a preliminary view: see the General Note to r.34.

Withdrawals are considered in the Law Society's Practice Note on "Representation before Mental Health Tribunals" (see Appendix D) at para.6.9.

Paragraph (1)

3-108   **Before a hearing to consider the disposal of the proceedings**   An application to withdraw the case can be made after a recommendation has been made by the tribunal but before it reconvened to consider the case when the recommendation was not followed (*R. (on the application of O) v Mental Health Review Tribunal* [2006] EWHC 2659 (Admin); [2006] M.H.L.R. 326).

Paragraph (2)

3-109   **Unless the tribunal consents**   The tribunal should not consent "if it takes the view that [the application for withdrawal] is merely a tactical ploy and is not in the interests of the patient" (*R. (on the application of O) v Mental Health Review Tribunal*, above at para.41, Collins J.). An example of a tactical ploy was encountered by the author in a case where the tribunal agreed to a withdrawal where the application was made at the close of the hearing when it was clear that the tribunal was not going to order the patient's discharge.

O was considered by the Upper Tribunal in *KF v Birmingham and Solihull Mental Health NHS Foundation Trust* [2010] UKUT 185 (AAC); [2010] M.H.L.R. 176 at paras 37–38:

"In our view a First-tier Tribunal would certainly be justified in refusing consent to a withdrawal where it is no more than such a tactical ploy. However, that should not be taken as meaning that a

[790]

tribunal should *only* refuse its agreement in such a scenario. There is plainly no automatic right to withdraw, and we agree with both counsel that the case for accepting a withdrawal will depend very much on the particular circumstances of the case (or cases). The 1983 rules did not contain either the overriding objective or the extensive case management powers to which we have already made reference and the First-tier Tribunal should always have regard to those provisions when considering whether or not it is appropriate to consent to a withdrawal.

[Counsel] submitted that a patient's desire to make an application whenever legitimately possible within the terms of the Act can hardly amount to a 'tactical ploy'. In most cases we doubt whether it is helpful to use the terminology of 'tactical ploy'. The question is whether a patient who has both an outstanding s.2 application and a subsequent s.3 application in hand near the start of a six month period may be justified in seeking to withdraw the latter application in order to preserve the possibility of making such an application later in that period of treatment. There may be a number of relevant factors, for example the initial s.3 application may have been taken without the benefit of legal advice, and an individual's mental health may well change considerably over time. The danger of an unduly broad approach to the notion of a 'tactical ploy' is that a patient might be denied what would otherwise be a legitimate opportunity to question their continued detention."

In *VS v St Andrew's Healthcare* [2018] UKUT 250 (AAC), UT Judge Jacobs said at para.29:

"[The tribunal] has to take account of the interests of the patient, but that cannot alone be decisive. If it were, the tribunal proceedings would become a filter to test the strength of a patient's case for discharge, with withdrawal allowing the patient to abort the proceedings and preserve their position in the statutory timetable for applications. Tribunals are rightly alert to that possibility. It would abuse the process of the tribunal and affect the efficient operation of the tribunal."

Paragraph (4)   The approach that a tribunal should take when considering an application to reinstate   **3-110**
was identified by U.T. Judge Jacobs in *JS v South London and Maudsley NHS Foundation Trust and the Secretary of State for Justice* [2019] UKUT 172 (AAC); [2020] M.H.L.R. 88:

"16. As there is no right to reinstatement, the tribunal has a discretion whether or not to reinstate the party's 'case'. It must, like all discretions, be exercised judicially and that involves complying with the overriding objective of the tribunal's rules of procedure, which is 'to enable the Tribunal to deal with cases fairly and justly' (rule 2(1)). Mr Lewis argued that the patient had a legitimate expectation that his detention would be considered by a tribunal and that the default position should be to allow reinstatement 'unless there are strong reasons not to do so.' I do not accept that. What the patient is entitled to is to have an application for reinstatement considered properly in accordance with the overriding objective. I have already explained why it is not proper to disregard the fact that a tribunal has agreed to the patient withdrawing an application.

17. Considered methodically, the factors that the tribunal should take into account neatly divide into three. First, the tribunal should consider whether there is anything to undermine either the patient's application to withdraw or the tribunal's consent. Just to give some examples, the application may have been based on a misunderstanding of the facts or the law. Or there may be an issue whether the patient had capacity or gave informed consent. Or the tribunal's reasons for consenting may have been defective. Second, there may have been a change of circumstances that makes it appropriate to agree to reinstatement. Third, the tribunal will have to consider any other factors that may be relevant under the overriding objective. These will include: (a) the reasons given in support of the application, whatever they may be; (b) any prejudice to the patient in refusing consent; (c) any detriment to the other parties if consent is given; (d) any -prejudice to other patients if consent is given; and (d) any impact that reinstatement might have on the operation of the tribunal's mental health jurisdiction system as a whole."

Part 3

Proceedings before the Tribunal other than in mental health cases
[*Not reproduced*]

Part 4

Proceedings before the Tribunal in mental health cases

Chapter 1

Before the hearing

Application of Part 4

3-111   **31.**   This Part applies only to mental health cases.

Definition

3-112   mental health case: r.1(3).

Procedure in mental health cases

3-113   **32.**—(1)   An application or reference must be—
      (a)   made in writing;
      (b)   signed (in the case of an application, by the applicant or any person authorised by the applicant to do so); and
      (c)   sent or delivered to the Tribunal so that it is received within the time specified in the Mental Health Act 1983 or the Repatriation of Prisoners Act 1984.
    (2)   An application must, if possible, include—
      (a)   [name, address and date of birth] of the patient;
      (b)   if the application is made by the patient's nearest relative, the name, address and relationship to the patient of the patient's nearest relative;
      (c)   the provision under which the patient is detained, liable to be detained, subject to guardianship, [or] a community patient [...];
      (d)   whether the person making the application has appointed a representative or intends to do so, and the name and address of any representative appointed;
      (e)   the name and address of the responsible authority in relation to the patient.
    [(2A)   A reference must, if possible, include—
      (a)   the name and address of the person or body making the reference;
      (b)   the name, address and date of birth of the patient;
      (c)   the name and address of any representative of the patient;
      (d)   the provision under which the patient is detained, liable to be detained, subject to guardianship or a community patient (as the case may be);
      (e)   whether the person or body making the reference has appointed a representative or intends to do so, and the name and address of any representative appointed;
      (f)   if the reference is made by the Secretary of State, the name and address of the responsible authority in relation to the patient, or, in the

case of a conditionally discharged patient, the name and address of the responsible clinician and any social supervisor in relation to the patient.]

(3) Subject to rule 14(2) (withholding evidence likely to cause harm), when the Tribunal receives a document from any party it must send a copy of that document to each other party.

[(4) If the patient is a conditionally discharged patient—

    (a) upon being notified by the Tribunal of an application, the Secretary of State must immediately provide to the Tribunal the names and addresses of the responsible clinician and any social supervisor in relation to the patient; and

    (b) upon being notified by the Tribunal of an application or reference, the responsible clinician and any social supervisor named by the Secretary of State under this rule must send or deliver the documents specified in the relevant practice direction to the Tribunal so that they are received by the Tribunal as soon as practicable and in any event within 3 weeks after the notification.

(5) In proceedings under section 66(1)(a) of the Mental Health Act 1983 (application in respect of an admission for assessment), on the earlier of receipt of the copy of the application or a request from the Tribunal, the responsible authority must immediately send or deliver to the Tribunal a copy of—

    (a) the application for admission; and

    (b) the written medical recommendations on which that application was founded; and must as soon as practicable send or deliver to the Tribunal the documents specified in the relevant practice direction.

(6) If neither paragraph (4) nor (5) applies, the responsible authority must send or deliver the documents specified in the relevant practice direction to the Tribunal so that they are received by the Tribunal as soon as practicable and in any event within 3 weeks after the responsible authority made the reference or received a copy of the application or reference.

(7) If the patient is a restricted patient, a person or body providing a document to the Tribunal in accordance with paragraph (4)(b) or (6) must also send or deliver a copy of the document to the Secretary of State.

(7A) The Secretary of State must send the information specified in paragraph (7B) and any observations the Secretary of State wishes to make to the Tribunal as soon as practicable and in any event—

    (a) in proceedings under section 75(1) of the Mental Health Act 1983 (reference concerning a conditionally discharged restricted patient who has been recalled to hospital), within 2 weeks after the Secretary of State received the documents sent or delivered in accordance with paragraph (7);

    (b) otherwise, within 3 weeks after the Secretary of State received the documents sent or delivered in accordance with paragraph (7).

(7B) The information specified in this paragraph is—

    (a) a summary of the offence or alleged offence that resulted in the patient being detained in hospital subject to a restriction order or, in the case of a patient subject to a restriction or limitation direction, that resulted in the patient being remanded in custody, kept in custody or sentenced to imprisonment;

    (b) a record of any other criminal convictions or findings recorded against the patient;

(c)   full details of the history of the patient's liability to detention under the Mental Health Act 1983 since the restrictions were imposed;

(d)   any further information in the Secretary of State's possession that the Secretary of State considers relevant to the proceedings.]

(8)   If the Secretary of State wishes to seek the approval of the Tribunal under section 86(3) of the Mental Health Act 1983 [(removal of alien patients)], the Secretary of State must refer the patient's case to the Tribunal and the provisions of these Rules applicable to references under that Act apply to the proceedings.

[(9)   The responsible authority must make records relating to the detention or treatment of the patient and any after-care services available to the Tribunal on request and the Tribunal or an appropriate member of the Tribunal may, before or at the hearing, examine and take notes and copies of such records for use in connection with the proceedings.]

Amendments

The amendments to this rule were made by SI 2012/500 r.3 and SI 2014/514 r.17.

Definitions

3-114
applicant: r.1(3).
Tribunal: r.1(3).
patient: r.1(3).
nearest relative: r.1(3).
party: r.1(3).
responsible authority: r.1(3).
practice direction: r.1(3).

General Note

3-115   This Rule deals with applications and references to tribunals in mental health cases (paras (1), (2) and (2A)) and the submission of information to the tribunal by the responsible authority and the Secretary of State (paras (4)–(9)). Subject to r.14(2), a copy of every document received by the tribunal must be sent to each other party (para.(3)). An application may be withdrawn under r.17. Documents that are sent to the patient become the patient's property and he may disseminate them as he wishes.

With s.2 cases, the information set out in para.(5) must be sent to the tribunal prior to the hearing date. In other cases, the responsible authority must ensure that the tribunal receives the information required by the practice direction on mental health cases within three weeks of the authority making the reference or receiving a copy of the application or reference (para.(6)). If the patient is a restricted patient, the authority must also send the statement to the Secretary of State (para.(7)), and the Secretary of State must send the information specified in para.(7B) to the tribunal within the time limits set out in para.(7A). If the patient is a conditionally discharged patient, the patient's responsible clinician and any social supervisor named by the Secretary of State must send a statement containing the information required by the practice direction so that it is received by the tribunal within three weeks of them being notified by the tribunal of the application or reference (para.(4)).

The tribunal can remedy any defects in a report that it has received by exercising its power under r.7(2)(b).

Where the tribunal receives the information required by paras (4), (5) or (6) it must give notice of the proceedings to the persons and/or bodies specified in r.33.

There is provision for the time limits in this rule to be extended (r.5(3)(a)). See rr.12 and 13 for the calculation of time and methods of service.

The references in this Rule to "the relevant practice direction" are to "Practice Direction—First-Tier Tribunal, Health Education and Social Care Chamber, Statements and Reports in Mental Health Cases", which was issued on October 28, 2013, and is reproduced below. The Responsible Authority's duty to provide the tribunal with written evidence is considered in "Enforcement Procedure, Directions and Summonses" which is also reproduced below. The Tribunal Service has published *Reports for Mental Health Tribunals* (2012) which provides guidance, based on a previous edition of the Practice

Direction, for those who have to prepare reports for the tribunal. It can be accessed on the Mental Health Law Online website at: *www.mhlo.uk/bk.*

The authors of reports and their attendance at Tribunal hearings

In *AF v Nottinghamshire NHS Trust* [2015] UKUT 216 (AAC); [2015] M.H.L.R. 347 UT Judge **3-116** Wright observed obiter that:

1. The law does not require that the social circumstances report must "be prepared by a social worker or CPN and not a nurse, or that that report writer must be a different person to the person who prepares the nursing report. The important issue is not the professional title of the report writer but the relevance and quality of the information provided in the report and thus the report writer's position of knowledge in respect of that information" (para.45).
2. Neither does the law dictate "that the report writer, and that person alone, must attend the First-tier Tribunal hearing to speak to their report". It was therefore "not unlawful for a different person to attend before [the] tribunal" (para.49).

Also see the note on this case in the General Note to s.117 under the heading *Applications to the First-tier Tribunal (Mental Health) and to the Hospital Managers.*

Paper reviews

The CQC's "*Monitoring the Mental Health Act in 2013/2014*" reports, at p.41, that in 2012–13, "the **3-117** Tribunal introduced a system of 'paper reviews' for automatic referrals of CTO cases. This means that the Tribunal will not meet with the patient, but will carry out a review of the patient's records and reports. Since it was introduced, the Tribunal has reviewed 884 cases in this way. Patients are given the opportunity to object to having their case determined through a paper review, and will have a full hearing if they do so. In 2018/19, paper reviews took place in 583 CTO cases considered by the Tribunal" (CQC, "*Monitoring the Mental Health Act in 2018/19*", p.34, fig.13).

Paragraph (1)(b)

An application can only be made if the applicant either has the mental capacity to make it or to **3-118** authorise a person to sign the application on his behalf. In *VS v St Andrew's Healthcare* [2018] UKUT 250 (AAC); [2018] M.H.L.R. 337 at para.2, UT Judge Jacobs identified the test of capacity required by a patient to make an application:

"The patient must understand that they are being detained against their wishes and that the First-tier Tribunal is a body that will be able to decide whether they should be released."

If the patient does not satisfy this test, see *R. (on the application of OK) v First-tier Tribunal* [2017] UKUT 22 (AAC). VS and OK are noted in the General Note to s.66.

For the making of an urgent reference where tribunal finds the patient did not have the capacity to apply to the tribunal, but the tribunal decides it is the interests of justice to continue with a hearing, see the General Note to s.67.

Under the Mental Capacity Act 2005, a mentally capable person (the donor) can execute a legal document called a lasting power of attorney (LPA) which empowers another person (the donee) to act in his or her stead, either generally or for specific purposes. An act done by a donee can be treated as an act done by the donor. A LPA which confers on the donee (or donees) power to make decisions about the donor's personal welfare matters could cover the making of an application to a tribunal: see para.7.7 of the *Code of Practice* which states:

"Attorneys and deputies are able to exercise a patient's rights under the Act on their behalf, if they have the relevant authority under the LPA or the order of the court appointing them and the patient concerned lacks the capacity to do so themselves. In particular, personal welfare attorneys and deputies may be able to exercise the patient's various rights to apply to the Tribunal for discharge from detention, guardianship or a CTO."

A personal welfare LPA can only take effect after the donor has lost the mental capacity to make the decision in question. A donee could therefore make an application to a tribunal on the patient's behalf if:

(i) the welfare LPA either gives a general power to the donee or the power to make such an application has been specified by the donor; and

(ii)   the patient does not possess the mental capacity to make the application.

A deputy appointed by the Court of Protection under the 2005 Act to make personal welfare decisions on behalf of the patient can also make an application to the tribunal on the patient's behalf if such a power has been conferred on the deputy by the court and the patient does not have the mental capacity to make the application.

Paragraph (2)

3-119   There are no statutory forms. Application and referral forms produced by HM Courts and Tribunals Service can be accessed at the Mental Health Law Online website at: *www.mhlo.uk/y.*

Paragraph (3)

3-120   A failure to comply with this provision could give rise to a right to challenge the tribunal's decision under r.45. A failure to give notice to the Secretary of State in the case of a restricted patient would inevitably lead to the tribunal setting aside its decision under that rule as there would have been a breach of the most fundamental rule of natural justice in that the Secretary of State, as a vitally interested party whose role was to safeguard the public interest, was denied a hearing (*Secretary of State for the Home Department v Oxford Regional Mental Health Review Tribunal* [1987] 3 All E.R. 8, HL and *R. (on the application of the Secretary of State for the Home Department) v Mental Health Review Tribunal* [2004] EWHC 650 (Admin)).

Although this paragraph and the practice direction are mandatory, they are qualified by r.7: see *AM v West London MH NHS Trust & Secretary of State for Justice* [2012] UKUT 382 where UT Judge Jacobs said at para.12:

"The generalities of the rules, the practice direction and the code of practice give way to the practicalities and realities of the individual patient and the evidence. To take an obvious example, the patient's representative may tell the tribunal that detention is not disputed, but the tribunal is being invited to make a non-statutory recommendation. In those circumstances, it does not matter whether or not the practice direction has been complied with. Rule 7 provides the powers that a tribunal may need once the transition has taken place from case management to decision-making. In the example I have just given, it allows the tribunal to waive any failure to comply with the practice direction."

Paragraph (8)

3-121   **Section 86(3)**   Which states that the Secretary of State or the Welsh Ministers must not exercise their power to remove a patient from the UK under that section without the approval of the tribunal.

Paragraph (9)

3-122   HH Judge Sycamore, the Chamber President, issued the following guidance on this paragraph on March 11, 2014 (the guidance can be accessed at: *www.judiciary.gov.uk/wp-content/uploads/2014/08/hesc-rules-amendments-6-4.pdf*):

"As in all other types of legal proceedings, it is for the parties to draw the panel's -attention to any salient records or notes where there is sufficient time to do so. Therefore, if there are any aspects of the records or notes that any party considers the tribunal should consider, then they should prepare an extract and submit it to the tribunal, in advance.

It follows that, in all those cases where there is no pre-hearing examination or where the pre-hearing examination only arises because a patient fails to attend their hearing, tribunal doctors are not expected to routinely inspect the patient's records.

However, with a Section 2 pre-hearing examination or an examination properly requested or directed well in advance, the tribunal doctor should also inspect the patient's records – as has previously been the case. This Rule provides the authority for the tribunal doctor (or the panel as a whole) to have access to records upon request.

Finally, where a pre-hearing interview is not required, panels may consider giving patients an opportunity of speaking first and, again, at the end of the hearing. Many patients have things they want to say at the outset and, of course, much time will be saved by not having to feedback the tribunal doctor's preliminary opinion in such cases."

Notice of proceedings to interested persons

33. When the Tribunal receives the information required by rule 32(4), (5) or **3-123** (6) (procedure in mental health cases) the Tribunal must give notice of the proceedings—
- (a) where the patient is subject to the guardianship of a private guardian, to the guardian;
- (b) where there is an extant order of the Court of Protection, to that court;
- (c) subject to a patient with capacity to do so requesting otherwise, where any person other than the applicant is named by the authority as exercising the functions of the nearest relative, to that person;
- (d) [...] and
- (e) to any other person who, in the opinion of the Tribunal, should have an opportunity of being heard.

Amendment

The amendment to this rule was made by SI 2013/477 r.19.

Definitions

Tribunal: r.1(3). **3-124**
mental health case: r.1(3).
patient: r.1(3).
nearest relative: r.1(3).

General Note

A person who is notified under this rule may either attend and take part in the proceedings to such **3-125** extent as the tribunal considers proper, or provide written submissions to the tribunal (r.36).
The Government has published "Make a victim representation to the Mental Health Tribunal" which can be accessed at: *https://www.gov.uk/mental-health-tribunal-victim-representations.*

Paragraph (c)

The responsible authority should inform the tribunal of a capacious patient's objection to his near- **3-126** est relative being given notice of the proceedings.

Paragraph (e)

Any other person Including the victim of the patient. Victims need to be advised that any written **3-127** representations that are made under r.36(2)(b) will be disclosed to the patient unless r.14(2) applies.

[Medical examination of the patient

34.—(1) Where paragraph (2) applies, an appropriate member of the Tribunal **3-128** must, so far as practicable, examine the patient in order to form an opinion of the patient's mental condition, and may do so in private.
- (2) This paragraph applies—
  - (a) in proceedings under section 66(1)(a) of the Mental Health Act 1983(d) (application in respect of an admission for assessment), unless the Tribunal is satisfied that the patient does not want such an examination;
  - (b) in any other case, if the patient or the patient's representative has informed the Tribunal in writing, not less than 14 days before the hearing, that—

(i)   the patient; or

(ii) if the patient lacks the capacity to make such a decision, the patient's representative, wishes there to be such an examination; or

(c)   if the Tribunal has directed that there be such an examination.]

Amendment

This rule was substituted by SI 2014/514 r.18.

Definitions

3-129
hearing: r.1(3).
mental health case: r.1(3).
Tribunal: r.1(3).
patient: r.1(3).

General Note

3-130
Under this rule, the medical member of the tribunal will conduct a pre-hearing examination of the patient in all s.2 cases unless the patient does not want such an examination. In any other case, the tribunal doctor will not conduct such an examination unless:

- the tribunal is informed in writing by or on behalf of the patient, not less than 14 days before the hearing, that a pre-hearing examination is wanted, or
- the tribunal has directed that there must be such an examination. This will either be a direction by a salaried judge or Registrar in advance of the hearing, or a direction made by the panel because the patient has failed to attend the hearing.

The tribunal may not proceed with a hearing in the absence of the patient unless the requirements of this rule have been satisfied. However, the tribunal can proceed if the medical examination of the patient is either impractical or unnecessary: see r.39(2)(b) and the guidance reproduced below.

All requests for pre-hearing medical examinations must be made on either Form T129 (for patients) or Form CMR1 (for lawyers).

Under para.5 of the Practice Statement "Composition of Tribunals in relation to matters that fall to be decided by the Health, Education and Social Care Chamber on or after 18 January 2010", issued by the Senior President of Tribunals on December 16, 2009, the "appropriate member" is the member of the tribunal who is a registered medical practitioner. The medical member must be a fully registered person within the meaning of the Medical Act 1983 whether or not he or she holds a licence to practise under that Act (SI 2008/2692 r.1(2), as amended by SI 2009/1592 art.3). The position is different in Wales where the medical member of the Mental Health Review Tribunal for Wales has to have a licence to practise: see the General Note to s.65 under *Wales – The mental Health Review Tribunal for Wales*.

Although the tribunal will doubtless be guided by the medical member, it is the tribunal as a whole which determines issues relating to the patient's mental condition in the light of their own experience and examination of the patient (*R. v Trent Mental Health Review Tribunal Ex p. Ryan* [1992] C.O.D. 15 DC). In *MD v Nottinghamshire Health Care NHS Trust* [2010] UKUT 59 (AAC); [2010] M.H.L.R. 93, para.47, UT Judge Jacobs said that the presence of a psychiatrist on the tribunal panel reduces the need for parties to have their own expert evidence: see further the note on "Human Rights Act 1998" in the General Note to these Rules.

The question whether the tribunal was biased because the consultant psychiatrist who sat as a member of the tribunal was a consultant who was employed by the detaining NHS Trust was considered in *R. (on the application of PD) v West Midlands and North West Mental Health Review Tribunal* [2004] EWCA Civ 311; [2004] M.H.L.R 174, where it was alleged that the involvement of the psychiatrist in the decision was incompatible with art.6 of the European Convention on Human Rights (ECHR) and with natural justice and, in particular, the common law test of bias. The Court of Appeal held that the test of apparent bias under the ECHR and under public law is the same and that the court had to consider the case by applying the following test which had been established by the House of Lords in *Lawal v Northern Spirit Ltd* [2003] UKHL 35: would a fair minded and informed observer who is neither complacent nor unduly sensitive or suspicious conclude that there was a real possibility that the tribunal was biased when it made the decision under challenge. Applying this test to the facts of the case, the question was whether the reasonable and informed member of the public might suspect that someone in the position of the psychiatrist would be so concerned at the potential reaction of the managers of the trust if the patient were to be discharged, and the implications of such reaction for his own position, that this might consciously or unconsciously affect his decision. The court answered this question by rejecting the contention that an appearance of bias arises simply from the fact that the psychiatrist was employed by the detaining trust. The court said that an appearance of bias could have arisen if the psychiatrist had been employed at the hospital where the patient was detained. Also see the General Note to these Rules under the heading *Bias of tribunal members*.

In *DN v Switzerland* (2003) 37 E.H.R.R. 21; [2001] M.H.L.R. 117 the European Court of Human Rights held that the fact that a psychiatrist member of a court who, in his role as judge rapporteur, had previously prepared an expert opinion on the patient and had communicated his opinion on whether the patient's application should succeed to the court, constituted a violation of art.5(4) of the ECHR. The court said that the psychiatrist's position in the proceedings gave rise to legitimate fears in the applicant that "he had a preconceived opinion as to her request for release from detention and that he was not, therefore, approaching her case with due impartiality" (para.54). DN was applied in *R. (on the application of S) v Mental Health Review Tribunal* [2002] EWHC (Admin) 2522; [2003] M.H.L.R. 118, where Stanley Burnton J. held that:

1. This rule does not expressly require the medical member to form an opinion of the patient's mental condition: it requires him to take the steps necessary to form an opinion.
2. The medical member must not form a concluded opinion on the patient's mental condition until the conclusion of the hearing, since otherwise the outcome of the hearing would be prejudiced.
3. The forming and expression of a provisional opinion by the medical member does not give rise to unfairness.
4. As a matter of domestic law, there can be no objection to the expression of a provisional opinion by a medical member to his tribunal colleagues prior to the hearing, provided the other members are aware that is only a provisional opinion and treat it as such, and provided that they understand that they are free to disagree with it if the evidence and submissions before them lead them to a different conclusion.
5. The phrase "due impartiality" used by the court in *DN* requires a member of a tribunal not to have a preconceived concluded opinion on the merits of the patient's case. The court did not suggest that a provisional view formed before the commencement of the hearing is objectionable. If an otherwise impartial and independent member of a tribunal has a preconceived concluded opinion, or if he expresses himself in such a way as to give rise to reasonable apprehension that he has a preconceived concluded opinion, he lacks the necessary impartiality, but not otherwise.
6. It follows that this rule [as it appeared in the MHRT Rules 1983] is not inconsistent with the requirements of art.5(4) as interpreted in *DN*.

S was applied in *R. (on the application of RD) v Mental Health Review Tribunal* [2007] EWHC 781 (Admin) where Munby J. held that the power to express preliminary views was not confined to the medical member and that such views could relate to all aspects of the case.

Paragraph (1)

An appropriate member of the tribunal   See the General Note, above. The member will be protected by s.139 of the Act when acting under this rule.   **3-131**

Must, so far as practicable   This covers the situation where the patient refuses to see the medical member, is too disturbed to be examined, or is absent without leave.

An opinion of the patient's mental condition   The opinion must be provisional: see above. The tribunal is entitled to rely on the evidence of the medical member regarding the nature of the patient's mental disorder even if it conflicts with the evidence of the patient's responsible clinician (RC) and the patient's independent psychiatrist. However, any evidence or information which has only been made available to the member must be shown at least to the patient's representative so that he or she can have the opportunity to present countervailing arguments (*R. v Mental Health Review Tribunal Ex p. Clatworthy* [1985] 3 All E.R. 699 DC). In *R. (on the application of H) v Ashworth Hospital Authority* [2002] EWCA Civ 923; [2002] M.H.L.R. 314 at para.84 Dyson L.J. said:

"It seems to me both fair and sensible that, if the medical member of the tribunal has formed any views on the basis of his or her interview with the patient, the substance of those views should be communicated to the patient and/or those who are representing him. I cannot think of any good reason why this should not be a requirement, although I would not wish to rule out the possibility of exceptional cases where such a course may not be practicable."

This passage was cited by Stanley Burnton J. in *R. (on the application of S) v Mental Health Review Tribunal*, above, where his Lordship said, at para.34, that the following guidance taken from para.7 of "The Members' Handbook of the Mental Health Review Tribunals in England and Wales" must be followed:

> "[The medical member] must appreciate that he performs a dual role at the tribunal as a fact finder and as a decision-maker and it is therefore essential that his opinion of the patient's mental condition, if it differs significantly from that of the [RC], should have been disclosed to the patient and the representative at the outset of the hearing. Thus, a situation will be avoided where the members of the tribunal are acting on the basis of evidence known only to themselves which would, of course, be a breach both of fundamental principle, and likely to invalidate the decision."

Further guidance on this issue was provided in *R. (on the application of KW) v Avon and Wiltshire Mental Health Partnership NHS Trust and Bristol City Council* [2003] EWHC 919 (Admin); [2003] M.H.L.R. 315 (Admin) at para.25, where it was held that if the medical member makes a finding relevant to the existence of the patient's mental disorder, or forms a provisional opinion as to the existence or otherwise of a mental disorder, that view should be shared with the patient's RC in the course of the hearing.

CHAPTER 2

Hearings

[Restrictions on disposal of proceedings without a hearing]

3-132   **35.**—[(1)   Subject to the following paragraphs, the Tribunal must hold a hearing before making a decision which disposes of proceedings.]

(2)   This rule does not apply to a decision under Part 5.

[(3)   The Tribunal may make a decision on a reference under section 68 of the Mental Health Act 1983 (duty of managers of hospitals to refer cases to tribunal) without a hearing if the patient is a community patient aged 18 or over and either—

    (a)   the patient has stated in writing that the patient does not wish to attend or be represented at a hearing of the reference and the Tribunal is satisfied that the patient has the capacity to decide whether or not to make that decision; or

    (b)   the patient's representative has stated in writing that the patient does not wish to attend or be represented at a hearing of the reference.

(4)   The Tribunal may dispose of proceedings without a hearing under rule 8(3) (striking out a party's case).]

Amendments

The amendments to this rule were made by SI 2012/500 r.3.

Definitions

3-133   Tribunal: r.1(3).
dispose of proceedings: r.1(3).
hearing: r.1(3).

General Note

3-134   This rule states that, apart from the exceptions provided for in paragraphs (3) and (4), a tribunal must not make a decision which disposes of proceedings without holding a hearing.

In *PC v Cornwall Partnership NHS Trust* [2023] UKUT 64 (AAC), UT Jacobs said at para.14:

> "The general principle in all chambers of both the First-tier Tribunal and the Upper Tribunal is that a party has a right to a hearing and is entitled to attend that hearing. The rules (rule 1(3) in the rules for the Health, Education and Social Care Chamber) provide that this 'means an oral hearing'. They

also confer power on a tribunal to proceed without a hearing and to proceed with a hearing in the absence of a party. For mental health cases, those powers are more restricted. So rule 35(1) provides the default rule that the tribunal must hold a hearing in a mental health case; rule 35(3) then allows a patient to opt out of a hearing of their reference. Rule 39 contains additional restrictions in paragraph (2). The reason for the restrictions in rules 35(3) and 29(2) is to be found in the special importance of safeguards when a patient's liability to be detained is in issue. A tribunal must always operate within its rules of procedure and that is particularly important when liberty is at stake."

Paragraph (3)

This paragraph allows the tribunal to dispose of a reference under s.68 in respect of a community patient without a hearing in specified circumstances. **3-135**

Stated in writing The Courts and Tribunal Service has produced an explanatory leaflet (T128) which includes a form which enables the patient to indicate a preference with regard to attendance and representation.

The patient has the capacity to decide An assessment of capacity must be made by the patient's responsible clinician: see para.18(a) of the Practice Direction on Statements and Reports in Mental Health Cases, which is reproduced below.

Entitlement to attend a hearing

36.—(1) Subject to rule 38(4) (exclusion of a person from a hearing), each party to proceedings is entitled to attend a hearing. **3-136**

(2) Any person notified of the proceedings under rule 33 (notice of proceedings to interested persons) may—

(a) attend and take part in a hearing to such extent as the Tribunal considers proper; or

(b) provide written submissions to the Tribunal.

Definitions

party: r.1(3). **3-137**
hearing: r.1(3).
Tribunal: r.1(3).

General Note

Subject to the power of the tribunal in r.38(4) to exclude a person from a hearing, this rule states that a party is entitled to attend a tribunal hearing, and that an interested party may either attend and take part in a hearing to such extent as the tribunal considers proper or provide written submissions to the tribunal. A hearing can take place in the absence of a party if r.39 applies. **3-138**

Observers

The Courts and Tribunal Service has published "Guidance for the observation of tribunal hearings in the First-tier Tribunal Health Education and Social Care Chamber (Mental Health Jurisdiction)" which can be accessed on the MHLO website at: *http://www.mhlo.uk/be*. **3-139**

Paragraph (1)

Party Note r.11(5). **3-140**

Time and place of hearings

37.—(1) [In] proceedings under section 66(1)(a) of the Mental Health Act 1983 the hearing of the case must start within [10] days after the date on which the Tribunal received the application notice. **3-141**

[(1A) ...]

(2)   In proceedings under section 75(1) of that Act, the hearing of the case must start at least 5 weeks but no more than 8 weeks after the date on which the Tribunal received the reference.

(3)   The Tribunal must give reasonable notice of the time and place of the hearing (including any adjourned or postponed hearing), and any changes to the time and place of the hearing, to—

    (a)   each party entitled to attend a hearing; and

    (b)   any person who has been notified of the proceedings under rule 33 (notice of proceedings to interested persons).

(4)   The period of notice under paragraph (3) must be at least [21 days], except that—

    (a)   in proceedings under section 66(1)(a) of the Mental Health Act 1983 the period must be at least 3 working days; and

    (b)   the Tribunal may give shorter notice—

        (i)   with the parties' consent; or

        (ii)   in urgent or exceptional circumstances.

Amendment

The amendments to this rule were made by SI 2014/514 r.19, SI 2020/416, r.2(5), and SI 2022/1030 r.3.

Definitions

3-142

Tribunal: r.1(3).
party: r.1(3).
hearing: r.1(3).
working day: r.1(3).

General Note

3-143

This rule is concerned with the timing of tribunal hearings. In particular, it establishes the period within which the tribunal is required to list proceedings made under s.66(1)(a) (for patients who are detained under s.2) and for references made by the Secretary of State under s.75(1).

In *R. (on the application of C) v Mental Health Review Tribunal London South and South West Region* [2001] EWCA Civ 1110; [2001] M.H.L.R. 110, the Court of Appeal held that:

1.   A uniform policy that tribunal hearings requested by patients who had been detained under s.3 of the Act would be fixed eight weeks after the date of the application did not comply with art.5(4) of the European Convention on Human Rights (ECHR), which requires the lawfulness of the patient's detention to be decided speedily. Each application had to be heard as soon as reasonably practicable.

2.   However urgent the patient's demand for a hearing, such time could properly be allowed for preparation as was reasonably necessary to ensure that the tribunal was in a position adequately and fairly to adjudicate on the issues before it.

3.   There was nothing inconsistent with art.5(4) in having a target date of eight weeks maximum for the listing of hearings. In cases requiring eight weeks' preparation, that period would not conflict with the requirement that a decision on the application had to be reached speedily.

Lord Phillips M.R. said at para.60:

"It seems to me that the [appropriate] stage at which to fix a [hearing] date would be after receipt of the statement required by rule 6 [now see r.32], when the scope of the remaining activities that would need to take place before the hearing would be clear".

C was applied by Stanley Burnton J. in *R. (on the application of KB) v The Mental Health Review Tribunal and the Secretary of State for Health* [2002] EWHC 639 (Admin); [2003] M.H.L.R. 1 at para.31, where his Lordship said:

"What is a speedy decision in any case will depend on a number of factors, including the nature and importance of the subject matter of the case, the complexity of the issues, the preparation required before the hearing, and the evidence to be considered. Factors extraneous to the particular case may also be relevant, such as a sudden increase in similar applications, or the intervention of a holiday period. However, in my judgment the fact that a patient's case is perceived to be unmeritorious does not deprive him of his right to a speedy hearing; and similarly, if there is unjustified delay before the hearing, the fact that his case is belatedly held to be unmeritorious does not excuse the infringement of that right."

Having considered the causes of the delays involved in the cases before him, his Lordship said that:

1. In the ordinary way it should be practicable for tribunal hearings in s.3 cases to take place within eight weeks of the application.
2. Central government should ensure that tribunals are provided with the resources and administrative systems that would enable them to satisfy this expectation.
3. In any sensibly managed judicial system there are bound to be adjournments and cancelled hearings for a number of reasons: the illness of a judge or the unavailability of a necessary witness, the over-running of an earlier hearing, or the need to accommodate an urgent case. The postponement of a hearing for such reasons does not necessarily involve any infringement of a ECHR right. The correct approach to adopt in a case where there has been a delay in arranging a tribunal hearing is to consider whether the delay in question is, on the face of it, inconsistent with the requirement for a speedy hearing. If it is, the onus is on the state to excuse the delay. It may do so by establishing, for example, that the delay has been caused by a sudden and unpredictable increase in the workload of the tribunal, and it has taken effective and sufficient measures to remedy the problem. But if the state fails to satisfy that onus, the claimant will have established a breach of his right under art.5(4).

His Lordship said at para.48 that this approach is consistent with the judgment of the European Court of Human Rights in *Koendjbiharie v The Netherlands* (1990) 13 EHRR 820, where the Court said at para.29:

"On the face of it, a lapse of time of more than four months appears incompatible with the notion of speediness."

Whether the claimants in this case were entitled to awards of damages, and if so their amounts, was determined at [2003] EWHC Admin 193; [2003] M.H.L.R. 28. Stanley Burton L.J. said at para.73:

"Thus, even in the case of mentally ill claimants, not every feeling of frustration and distress will justify an award of damages. The frustration and distress must be significant: 'of such intensity that it would in itself justify an award of compensation for non-pecuniary damage' [*Silver v UK* (1983) 6 EHRR 62]. In my judgment, an important touchstone of that intensity in cases such as the present will be that the hospital staff considered it to be sufficiently relevant to the mental state of the patient to warrant its mention in the clinical notes."

Listing dates

The "Stakeholder bulletin Mental Health Tribunal administration Autumn 2017" states that if a party **3-144** is "unable to accommodate a hearing date that has been set then we would ask that you complete a CMR1 form requesting a change of hearing date which will be referred to a Judicial Officer for a decision. A hearing date cannot be changed by our administrative telephone team".

Paragraph (1)

This paragraph relates to patients who are detained under s.2 of the Act. **3-145**

Paragraph (4)

Where notice is unavoidably given late, the tribunal has the power to waive the irregularity under **3-146** r.7.

Public and private hearings

38.—(1) All hearings must be held in private unless the Tribunal considers that **3-147** it is in the interests of justice for the hearing to be held in public.

[803]

(2)   If a hearing is held in public, the Tribunal may give a direction that part of the hearing is to be held in private.

(3)   Where a hearing, or part of it, is to be held in private, the Tribunal may determine who is permitted to attend the hearing or part of it.

(4)   The Tribunal may give a direction excluding from any hearing, or part of it—

(a)   any person whose conduct the Tribunal considers is disrupting or is likely to disrupt the hearing;

(b)   any person whose presence the Tribunal considers is likely to prevent another person from giving evidence or making submissions freely;

(c)   any person who the Tribunal considers should be excluded in order to give effect to a direction under rule 14(2) (withholding information likely to cause harm); or

(d)   any person where the purpose of the hearing would be defeated by the attendance of that person.

(5)   The Tribunal may give a direction excluding a witness from a hearing until that witness gives evidence.

Definitions

3-148   hearing: r.1(3).
Tribunal: r.1(3).

General Note

3-149   Tribunal hearings are to be held in private unless the tribunal considers that the interests of justice require a public hearing (para.(1)). The hearing can be part public and part private (para.(2)). The overwhelming majority of hearings are held in private. The tribunal has the power to give directions excluding various categories of persons from both public and private hearings (paras (4), (5)).

The hearing must be conducted in accordance with r.2(2)(c) which requires the tribunal to deal with a case fairly and justly by "ensuring, so far as practicable, that the parties are able to participate fully in the proceedings".

For the relationship between the presumption of privacy in cases involving the mental health of a patient and the open justice principle see *R. (on the application of Maher) v First-tier Tribunal (Mental Health)* [2023] EWHC 34 (Admin) which is considered in the General Note to r.14. Also see the General Note to these Rules under *Tribunal procedure and the rules of natural justice and Order of evidence*.

In *AR v West London NHS Trust and the Secretary of State for Justice* [2020] UKUT 273 (AAC); [2021] M.H.L.R. 168, UT Judge Jacobs held that:

"1.   A patient does not need to have capacity to litigate in order to apply for a public hearing. When considering an application to have a public hearing, the tribunal has to decide whether the patient has the ability to conduct proceedings in general (para.13). If the patient does not have capacity to conduct proceedings, it would be necessary to appoint a legal representative for him under r.11(7)(b) (para.14).

2.   The quality of the patient's decision is only relevant in two ways. First, it may be evidence that the patient's decision-making is affected by 'an impairment of, or a disturbance in the functioning of, the mind or brain' for the purposes of s.2(1) of the Mental Capacity Act 2005. Second, it may be a factor to be taken into account, once the issue of competence has been decided, when applying r.38 as part of its assessment of whether a public hearing is in the interests of justice (para.22)."

Judge Jacobs identifies the following "more obvious salient features of a public hearing" at para.20:

"•   The tribunal's powers of disposal are the same, regardless of whether or not the hearing is held in public. Those powers will vary according to the nature of the case. Having the hearing in public will not affect the decision that the tribunal makes within the scope of its jurisdiction under the Mental Health Act 1983. It does not acquire power at a public hearing to deal with any issue that is outside its jurisdiction.

- The tribunal's procedural powers are also the same regardless of the form of the hearing. They include the power to exclude people from all or part of the hearing. The nature of the hearing will not affect the way that the hearing is conducted, the evidence that is relevant, what the patient is allowed to say, or the outcome of the case.
- Members of the public, including the press, are allowed to observe and may wish to do so, although they may not. They not allowed to take any part in the proceedings.
- A public hearing is no guarantee of publicity, even if members of the public do observe. The tribunal's power to limit disclosure remain the same as for a private hearing.
- A hearing may adversely affect the patient's health, for example as a result of receiving adverse publicity or realising that no one is interested in the case.
- Although the patient may want publicity, this may have a detrimental effect on others, such as his family or any victim."

In *AH v West London Mental Health Trust* [2010] UKUT 264 (AAC); [2010] M.H.L.R. 326, at para.44, the Upper Tribunal considered that the relevant factors in deciding whether it is in the interests of justice to direct a hearing in public are:

- Is it consistent with the subjective and informed wishes of the applicant (assuming he is competent to make an informed choice)?
- Will it have an adverse effect on his mental health in the short or long term, taking account of the views of those treating him and any other expert views?
- Are there any other special factors for or against a public hearing?
- Can practical arrangements be made for an open hearing without disproportionate burden on the authority?

The Upper Tribunal said, at para.25, that although the underlying assumption in this rule is that the interests of justice will normally require a hearing in private, having regard to the reasons for the exception to the right to a public hearing under art.6 of the European Convention of Human Rights (ECHR) the principal consideration remains the protection of the interests of the patient.

At a further hearing ([2011] UKUT 74 (AAC); [2011] M.H.L.R. 85), the Upper Tribunal directed that the tribunal must accede to the patient's request by holding a public hearing of his application. The UT said at para.22:

"It seems to us that once the threshold tests [set out in the four bullet points] above for establishing a right to a public hearing have been satisfied, art.6 of the ECHR (re-enforced by art.13 of the Convention on the Rights of Persons with Disabilities) requires that a patient should have the same or substantially equivalent right of access to a public hearing as a non-disabled person who has been deprived of his or her liberty, if this art.6 right to a public hearing is to be given proper effect. Such a right can only be denied a patient if enabling that right imposes a truly disproportionate burden on the state. The European Court of Human Rights has emphasised the need for special consideration to be given to the rights of particularly vulnerable groups such as the mentally disabled (see eg *Kiss v Hungary* [2010] M.H.L.R. 245, para 42)."

The UT made the following comments on the conduct of public hearings at para.23:

"How the right to a public hearing can practically and proportionately be achieved will depend on the facts of each individual case, including the facilities available in the hospital in question. On the evidence provided to us by the Broadmoor Hospital Clinical Director, it seems likely that if similar cases arise in the future, it should be possible for arrangements to be made between the hospital and the Tribunals Service for a hearing at the hospital with a video-link to suitable premises off-site where any interested members of the press or public can view the proceedings."

In *R. (on the application of Mersey Care NHS Trust) v Mental Health Review Tribunal* [2004] EWHC 1749 (Admin); [2005] 2 All E.R. 820, Beatson J. held that:

1. This rule, as it appeared in r.21 of the Mental Health Review Tribunal Rules 1983, creates a presumption that hearings before tribunals are private: now see para.(1) of this rule. Such a presumption can be justified under art.6 of the ECHR where it is considered necessary in the interests of morals, public order or national security or where required by the interests of juveniles or the protection of the private life of the parties (*B and P v United Kingdom* (2002) 34 E.H.R.R. 19 at para.39). In *AH v West London Mental Health Trust*, above, para.20, the Upper Tribunal said mental health cases can be added to this list.
2. The High Court has jurisdiction to commit for the contempt of an order of a tribunal: see

Pickering v Liverpool Daily Post and Echo Newspapers Plc [1991] 1 All E.R. 622, where the House of Lords held that a tribunal is, by virtue of s.19 of the Contempt of Court Act 1981 and s.12 of the Administration of Justice Act 1960, a "court" whose proceedings are subject to the law of contempt.

3. Although the general rule in s.12 of the 1960 Act is that the publication of information relating to proceedings before any court sitting in private shall not of itself be a contempt of court, proceedings in mental health tribunals are one of the exceptions so that publication of such information is itself a contempt: s.12(1)(b) of the 1960 Act.

4. Where a tribunal holds a public hearing, the control over publicity is by means of the "strict liability" rule in s.2 of the Contempt of Court Act 1981. The fact that the protection afforded by the strict liability rule would be only for a limited period coupled with the difficulty of determining in advance what kind of public comment about proceedings will create "a substantial risk that the course of justice ... will be seriously impeded or prejudiced" (s.2(2)) of the 1981 Act) mean that the tribunal's powers if the hearing is in public are significantly more limited than they are if it is in private.

5. Any restrictions on the right to "impart information and ideas" gained by attendance at a public hearing held by a mental health tribunal would prima facie require justification under art.10(2) of the ECHR.

It would be a contempt of court under the 1981 Act for sound recording equipment, including a mobile phone which is capable of recording sound, to be used at a tribunal hearing without permission.

Remote access to public hearings

3-150   With effect from June 28, 2022, a new framework governing remote access by non-participants to proceedings that are to be held in public was introduced by the Police, Crime, Sentencing and Courts Act 2022 which introduces new ss.85A and 85B into the Courts Act 2003 and the Remote Observation and Recording (Courts and Tribunals) Regulations 2022. The power can be exercised in "proceedings of any type" that are (a) in public, or (b) not open to the general public but "specific categories of person, or specific individuals, who are not taking part in the proceedings are entitled to be present by virtue of provision made by or under any enactment or of being authorised by the court" (reg.2).

This framework, which applies to all courts and tribunals, is explained in the Practice Guidance issued by the Lord Chief Justice and the Senior President of Tribunals on June 28, 2022. The guidance can be accessed at: *http://www.judiciary.uk/guidance-and-resources/practice-guidance-on-remote-observation-of-hearings-new-powers*. It applies whether the court is sitting in person, but enabling remote observation, or if the court is, itself, sitting remotely. In broad terms, its effect is to:

- provide judges with the power to make directions to enable members of the public to observe proceedings remotely (by video or audio);
- set down a series of considerations for judges to apply when deciding whether to make such a direction; and
- make it (by the Courts Act 2003 s.85B) a criminal offence to make an unauthorised recording during any such remote observation.

Observers

3-151   See the note under this heading in r.36.

Paragraph (3)

3-152   The tribunal can authorise a member of the clinical team to be present to hear the evidence of the patient contrary to the wishes of the patient (*R. (on the application of B) v South Region Mental Health Review Tribunal* [2008] EWHC 2356 (Admin); [2008] M.H.L.R. 312).

The guidance note on the "Role of the Independent Mental Health Advocate (IMHA) in First-tier Tribunal (Mental Health) hearings" (see the General Note to these Rules) states at para.4.1.1 that it "is not suggested that an IMHA needs to apply to the tribunal in advance for permission to attend a hearing".

Paragraph 4(b)

3-153   A representative has a right to question witnesses (*R. (on the application of Mersey Care NHS Trust v Mental Health Review Tribunal* [2003] EWHC 1182 (Admin): [2003] M.H.L.R. 354). It is therefore submitted that the responsible authority's representative, including a representative who is a member of the clinical team that is treating the patient, cannot be excluded under this provision. If the tribunal did decide to interview the patient in the absence of the representative, the requirements of art.6 of the ECHR and the rules of natural justice would require that any salient facts that were divulged by the patient during the interview be communicated to the representative.

Hearings in a party's absence

39.—(1)   Subject to paragraph (2), if a party fails to attend a hearing the   **3-154** Tribunal may proceed with the hearing if the Tribunal—

    (a)   is satisfied that the party has been notified of the hearing or that reasonable steps have been taken to notify the party of the hearing; and

    (b)   considers that it is in the interests of justice to proceed with the hearing.

[(2)   The Tribunal may not proceed with a hearing that the patient has failed to attend unless the Tribunal is satisfied that—

    (a)   the patient—

        (i)   has decided not to attend the hearing; or

        (ii)   is unable to attend the hearing for reasons of ill health; and

    (b)   an examination under rule 34 (medical examination of the patient)—

        (i)   has been carried out; or

        (ii)   is impractical or unnecessary.]

Amendment

Paragraph (2) was substituted by SI 2014/514 r.20.

Definitions

party: r.1(3).   **3-155**
hearing: r.1(3).
Tribunal: r.1(3).
patient: r.1(3).

General Note

This rule establishes when a tribunal hearing may proceed in the absence of a party or the patient.   **3-156**
The scope of this rule was explained by UT Judge Jacobs in *PC v Cornwall Partnership NHS Trust* [2023] UKUT 64 (AAC):

"5. Rule 39 is in two parts. The first part in paragraph (1) is positive. It sets out conditions that allow a tribunal to proceed in the patient's absence. The second part in paragraph (2) is negative. It set out circumstances in which a tribunal must not proceed. The rule uses the same word – 'may' – in both paragraphs, but it has a different meaning in each. In paragraph (1), it authorises the tribunal to proceed without requiring it to do so. In paragraph (2) with the addition of 'not', it is a prohibition. To put it another way, paragraph (2) contains condition precedents that must be satisfied before the power in paragraph (1) arises. I come back later to the importance of keeping the paragraphs separate.
6. Paragraph (2) contains two conditions. Both must be satisfied before the power to proceed arises. Paragraph (2)(a) deals with non-attendance. A tribunal may not proceed unless it is satisfied as a matter of fact that either the patient had decided not to attend or was unable to attend for reasons of ill health. If the tribunal is not so satisfied, it must not proceed, regardless of whether the conditions in paragraph (1) are satisfied. Paragraph (2)(b) deals with medical examinations."

In this case, Judge Jacobs held that "the tribunal did not make a finding to show that either paragraph (2)(a)(i) or (ii) was satisfied and it was not self-evident from what it did say that one or other of them must be satisfied. In those circumstances, paragraph (2) was not satisfied, regardless of any finding that might be made under paragraph (2)(b). Proceeding in the patient's absence was an error of law." (para.9)
If a patient fails to attend a hearing and the patient's legal representative leaves during the course of the hearing but after the tribunal had decided to refuse the representative's application to adjourn, it is incumbent on the tribunal to make a fresh assessment as to whether it was in the interests of justice to proceed with the hearing taking this development into account (*DA v Kent and Medway NHS and Social Care Trust* [2019] UKUT 348 (AAC); [2020] M.H.L.R. 178).

In *GL v Elysium Healthcare Hospital* [2020] UKUT 308 (AAC); [2021] M.H.L.R. 217, UT Judge Marcus set aside a decision of the First-tier Tribunal not to adjourn the hearing on the ground that the tribunal had decided to continue with a remote hearing despite the patient's legal representative requesting an adjournment due to the patient having legitimate concerns that the hearing could be overheard by a fellow patient. The tribunal had erred in failing to investigate and make any finding of fact relating to the patient's concerns.

Paragraph (2)

3-157   A tribunal should address how the criteria under this paragraph for proceeding with the hearing were satisfied in the written reasons for its decision provided under r.41(2): see the *DA v Kent and Medway NHS and Social Care Trust*, above.

Power to pay allowances

3-158   **40.**   The Tribunal may pay allowances in respect of travelling expenses, subsistence and loss of earnings to—

(a)   any person who attends a hearing as an applicant or a witness;

(b)   a patient who attends a hearing otherwise than as the applicant or a witness; and

(c)   any person (other than a legal representative) who attends as the representative of an applicant.

Definitions

3-159   Tribunal: r.1(3).
hearing: r.1(3).
applicant: r.1(3).
legal representative: r.1(3).

CHAPTER 3

Decisions

Decisions

3-160   **41.**—(1)   The Tribunal may give a decision orally at a hearing.

(2)   Subject to rule 14(2) (withholding information likely to cause harm), the Tribunal must provide to each party as soon as reasonably practicable after making [a decision (except a decision under Part 5) which finally disposes of all issues in the proceedings or of a preliminary issue dealt with following a direction under rule 5(3)(e)]—

(a)   a decision notice stating the Tribunal's decision;

(b)   written reasons for the decision; and

(c)   notification of any right of appeal against the decision and the time within which, and the manner in which, such right of appeal may be exercised.

(3)   The documents and information referred to in paragraph (2) must—

(a)   in proceedings under section 66(1)(a) of the Mental Health Act 1983, be provided at the hearing or sent within 3 working days after the hearing; and

(b)   in other cases, be provided at the hearing or sent within 7 days after the hearing.

(4)   The Tribunal may provide written reasons for any decision to which paragraph (2) does not apply.

Amendment

The amendment to para.2 was made by SI 2013/477 r.20.

Definitions

Tribunal: r.1(3).   **3-161**
hearing: r.1(3).
respondent: r.1(4).

General Note

Although the tribunal may give its decision orally at the hearing (para.(1)), it is required to provide   **3-162**
its written decision, the reasons for it, and information about any rights of appeal, to each party (para.(2))
within the time limits set out in para.(3).

A First-tier Tribunal consisting of more than one member is allowed to reach a decision by a majority by virtue of art.8 of the First-tier Tribunal and Upper Tribunal (Composition of Tribunal) Order 2008
(SI 2008/2835). There is no obligation placed upon the tribunal to state that a decision was given by a
majority. If the tribunal chooses to state that a decision was given by a majority, the statement of reasons
should provide "at least a brief statement of reasons for the dissent of the minority member" (*Secretary
of State for Work and Pensions v SS* [2010] UKUT 384 (AAC), para.10).

A tribunal has its statutory duty to perform and could not avoid that by accepting a submission that
it is bound to follow another tribunal's decision, even though there had been no change of circumstances.
There could be no res judicata (the legal principle that a matter which has been settled by a court cannot be reopened or challenged as to the matter decided) (*R. v South-West Thames Mental Health Review
Tribunal Ex p. Demetri (No.1)* [1997] C.O.D. 44 CA). However, there is nothing to prevent a previous
tribunal decision being placed before the tribunal hearing the patient's case. The weight to be given to
the decision will be a matter for that tribunal (*RH v South London and Maudsley NHS Foundation Trust*
[2010] EWCA Civ 1273; [2010] M.H.L.R. 341, para.35).

If a decision of a tribunal which appears to have been made without jurisdiction has not been quashed
by proceedings which were properly commenced within time, the decision must be treated as being a
valid decision (*Bath and North East Somerset Council v AJC* [1999] M.H.L.R. 184).

Paragraph (1)

In a decision on r.29(1) of the Tribunal Procedure (First-tier Tribunal) (Immigration and Asylum   **3-163**
Chamber) Rules 2014, which has identical wording to this paragraph, UT Judge Ockelton held that if
the tribunal gives a decision orally at a hearing, there is no power to revise or revoke the decision later.
It was also held that if "the written decision, when issued, is inconsistent with the oral decision, both
decisions, being decisions of the Tribunal, stand until set aside by a court of competent jurisdiction; but
neither party is entitled to enforce either decision until the matter has been sorted out on appeal" (*PAA
v Secretary of State for the Home Department* [2019] UKUT 13 (1AC)).

Paragraph (2)   **3-164**

Finally disposes   See r.42.   **3-164**

Written reasons for the decision   Excluding reasons which would be likely to cause serious harm to
the patient or another (r.14(2)). The reasons must contain numbered paragraphs (Practice Statement on
Form of Decisions and Neutral Citation, issued by the Senior President on October 31, 2008).

In *R. (on the application of Nash) v Chelsea College of Art and Design* [2001] EWHC 538, para.34
(i) Stanley Burnton J. said that "where there is a statutory duty to give reasons as part of the notification of the decision, so that (as Law J put it in *Northamptonshire County Council ex p D*) 'the adequacy
of the reasons is itself made a condition of the legality of the decision', only in exceptional circumstances
if at all will the Court accept subsequent evidence of the reasons".

The importance of the requirement for a decision-maker to give reasons was emphasised by Sedley
J. in *R. v Solihull Metropolitan Borough Council Housing Benefits Review Board Ex p. Simpson* (1993)

26 H.L.R. 370 at 377:

"A statutory duty imposed on a named decision maker to give reasons ... is not simply a bureaucratic chore or an opportunity for lawyers to find fault. It is, and is increasingly recognised as being, a fundamental aspect of good public administration (underpinned increasingly by law) because it focuses the decision maker's mind on exactly what it is that has to be decided, within what legal framework, and according to what relevant evidence and material. Experience shows that it will sometimes produce an opposite conclusion to that which was initially in the decision-makers mind before the rigour of formulating acceptable reasons was applied."

In *MS v North East London Foundation Trust* [2013] UKUT 092 (AAC) at para.15, UT Judge Jacobs said that the written reasons should:

- state what facts the tribunal found;
- explain how and why the tribunal made them;
- show how the tribunal applied the law to those facts.

Judge Jacobs returned to the issue of the adequacy of reasons in *DL-H v West London Mental Health Trust* [2017] UKUT 387 (AAC); [2017] M.H.L.R. 372 where he said at para.4:

"A tribunal's reasons have to be adequate, but adequacy is tested in a context and that context includes the whole of the evidence before the tribunal. Tribunals exercising different jurisdictions take different approaches to setting out the evidence. Some set it out extensively; others merely refer to it as required. And within jurisdictions, judges differ in their approaches. But whatever the approach of the particular jurisdiction or the individual judge, the Upper Tribunal is entitled to have regard to the whole of the evidence when considering whether the First-tier Tribunal's decision involved the making of an error of law."

Accordingly, it was open to the hospital on appeal to refer "to evidence that was before the tribunal but not mentioned in its reasons".

In *SLL*, below, UT Judge Church drew attention to the need to make the following finding relating to the least restrictive principle:

"(given the least restrictive [principle] that informs the MHA regime) whether any alternative strategies are available which might manage the risks associated with future deteriorations in the patient's mental health effectively but which place less restriction on the patient's liberty than the patient continuing to be subject to the power of recall" (para.34e).

The following aide memoire of matters which "may assist in the production of adequate and intelligible reasons" (para.11) was provided by UT Judge Knowles in *HK v Llanarth Court Hospital* [2014] UKUT 410 (AAC); [2015] M.H.L.R. 88:

"12. First, it would be helpful if tribunals were to set out their reasons by reference to the relevant criteria for detention. As Upper Tribunal Judge Jacobs observed in para.9 of *JL v Managers of Llanarth Court and SOS for Justice* [2011] UKUT 62 (AAC), it might be better if tribunals were to set out their reasons under the headings provided by the legal questions they have to determine. I agree. Using headings within the statement of reasons makes it easier to show that the tribunal has dealt with each of the legal criteria it has to address. I note that the First-tier Tribunal (Mental Health) in England has made template decisions using appropriate headings available to tribunal judges to assist them in reason writing.

13. Second, the tribunal's reasons should address how the tribunal dealt with any disputes as to either the law or the evidence. If this is not done, the unsuccessful party might believe that the tribunal has ignored important issues. In particular, failing to address explicitly any applications made by one or other of the parties may render a set of reasons inadequate. Such an omission certainly makes it more difficult for a party to know why they have been unsuccessful and additionally raises doubt as to whether the tribunal has dealt fairly with that party's case. However, it is not necessary for a set of reasons to resolve evidential matters which are irrelevant to the legal issues that the tribunal has to determine; a prudent tribunal though may wish to explain briefly why it has not resolved a factual dispute.

14. Third, the reasons themselves must be clear and unambiguous. It is not for a party to deduce the reasons for a decision.

15. Fourth, rehearsing what each witness told the tribunal is, without more liable to render a set of reasons erroneous in law. What is required is to explain (i) what facts the tribunal found as a result of that evidence and (ii) what conclusions on those facts the tribunal reached.

16. Fifth, it is not necessary for the tribunal's reasons to mention all of the evidence in a case. It is entitled to be selective in its references to evidence in its reasons though it should, as I have indicated in paragraph 13 above, identify and resolve evidence and applications which are in dispute."

In *A Mental Health Trust v M* (Case No.HM/0744/2017), Judge Jacobs accepted a submission of the Trust that given "the plethora of High Court and Upper Tribunal decisions that deal with the adequacy of reasons given by a tribunal ... no further judicial guidance is required".

The following notes of caution need to be made when considering the adequacy of reasons given to justify the decision of a tribunal:

(1)   the decision of a tribunal "is not required to be an elaborate formalistic product of refined legal draftsmanship" (*Meek v Birmingham City Council* [1987] I.R.L.R. 250, para.8, per Sir Thomas Bingham M.R.). In *SL v Ludlow Street Healthcare* [2015] UKUT 398 (AAC), para.41, Judge Jacobs said that the "test the Upper Tribunal applies is adequacy, not perfection";

(2)   tribunal reasons "are not intended to include a comprehensive and detailed analysis of the case, either in terms of fact or in law ... their purpose remains what it has always been, which is to tell the parties in broad terms why they lose or, as the case may be, win. I think it would be a thousand pities if these reasons began to be subjected to a detailed analysis and appeals were to be brought based upon any such analysis. This, to my mind, is to misuse the purpose for which the reasons are given" (*UCATT v Brain* [1981] I.R.L.R. 225, 227 per Donaldson L.J.);

(3)   "it is probable that in understanding and applying the law in their specialised field the tribunal will have got it right ... Their decisions should be respected unless it is quite clear that they have misdirected themselves in law" (*Secretary of State for the Home Department v AH (Sudan)* [2007] UKHL 49; [2008] 4 All E.R. 190, para.30, per Lady Hale: see also *R. (on the application of W) v Mental health Review Tribunal* [2004] EWHC 3266 (Admin); [2005] M.H.L.R. 134 at para.18); and

(4)   there is a danger of "elevating into general principles what are statements by judges made by reference to the facts and circumstances of particular cases but taken out of context" (*H v East Sussex County Council* [2009] EWCA Civ 249, para.15, per Waller L.J.).

The duty to give reasons under this provision (as it appeared in r.23 of the MHRT Rules 1983) was considered by the Court of Appeal in *R. (on the application of H) v Ashworth Hospital Authority* [2002] EWCA Civ 923; [2002] M.H.L.R. 314. The leading judgment was given by Dyson L.J. who adopted the approach taken by the Court of Appeal in *English v Emery Reimbold & Strick Ltd* [2002] EWCA Civ 605; [2002] 3 All E.R. 385 where Lord Phillips M.R. summarised the present state of the law regarding appeals from lower to higher courts. Lord Phillips said that, putting the matter at its simplest, "justice will not be done if it is not apparent to the parties why one has won and the other lost" (para.16). A judge should:

"provide an explanation as to why he has accepted the evidence of one expert and rejected that of another. It may be that the evidence of one or the other accorded more satisfactorily with facts found by the Judge. It may be that the explanation of one was more inherently credible than that of the other. It may simply be that one was better qualified, or manifestly more objective, than the other. Whatever the explanation may be, it should be apparent from the judgment" (para.20).

Dyson L.J. rejected a submission that inadequate reasons may be treated as adequate on the ground that inadequate resources were made available to the tribunal (para.76); also see *SLL v Priory Health Care and Secretary of State for Justice* [2019] UKUT 323 (AAC); [2020] M.H.L.R. 178 where the Upper Tribunal said: "The circumstances of the judge might explain why inadequate reasons were produced and they might make us more sympathetic to the writer of them, but they can't render inadequate reasons adequate" (para.101). Dyson L.J. said that "it is at least arguable" that the "informed audience point" (see *R. v Mental Health Review Tribunal Ex p. Booth*, noted below) "has less force in relation to a tribunal decision than to a decision by a lower court in the civil justice system". This is because, in the light of *R. v East London and City Mental Health NHS Trust Ex p. Brandenburg* [2003] UKHL 58; [2004] 1 All E.R. 400, it is essential that an approved mental health professional who is contemplating re-sectioning a patient subsequent to a tribunal discharge should know the facts and circumstances which a tribunal took into account when deciding to discharge a patient, and the reasons for its decision.

In *H*, the Court of Appeal found the tribunal's reasons to be inadequate for two principal reasons:

1.   The tribunal had failed to indicate the reasoning process by which they decided to accept the minority medical evidence and reject the majority medical evidence. Dyson L.J. said, at para.80, that the following passage from the judgment of Henry L.J. in *Flannery v Halifax Estate Agencies Ltd* [2001] 1 W.L.R. 377 at 381–382, is "as apt in relation to the decisions of tribunals as it is to lower courts generally":

[811]

"Where there is a straightforward factual dispute whose resolution depends simply on which witness is telling the truth about events which he claims to recall, it is likely to be enough for the judge (having no doubt, summarised the evidence) to indicate simply that he believes X rather than Y; indeed there may be nothing else to say. But where the dispute involves something in the nature of an intellectual exchange, with reasons and analysis advanced on either side, the judge must enter into issues canvassed before him and explain why he prefers one case over another. This is likely to apply particularly in litigation where as here there is disputed expert evidence; but it is not necessarily limited to such cases."

2. The tribunal failed to give any reasons for not adjourning in order to see whether suitable after-care would be made available for the patient, or whether an order for deferred discharge would be appropriate. In this case, the question of what aftercare arrangements would be available in the community was relevant to the issue of whether the statutory criteria were met.

With regard to point 1, if the tribunal has accepted the evidence of the patient as to the risk or lack of risk of him accepting medication if discharged into the community, and implicitly rejected the views of his responsible clinician and nurse, it is particularly important for the tribunal to explain the basis of its decision and the reasons for its preferring one witness to another (*R. (on the application of the Secretary of State for the Home Department) v Mental Health Review Tribunal and CH* [2005] EWHC 746 (Admin); [2005] M.H.L.R. 199 at para.35).

The fact that the responsible clinician had more experience of the patient than did another doctor is not of itself a reason for preferring her evidence. It does not always follow that greater knowledge means greater insight. The tribunal should explain what it was in the responsible clinician's experience that made her view preferable (*AC v Partnerships in Care Ltd and Secretary of State for Justice* [2012] UKUT 450 (AAC); [2013] M.H.L.R. 52).

The reasons "must be read as a whole, in a common sense way, not as a legal treatise"; per Sullivan J. in *R. (on the application of Epsom & St Helier NHS Trust v The Mental Health Review Tribunal* [2001] M.H.L.R. 8 at para.49. They must be "adequate and intelligible ... and must grapple with the important issues raised" (*R. v Mental Health Review Tribunal Ex p. Pickering* [1986] 1 All E.R. 99 at 102 per Forbes J.). It is therefore not sufficient for the tribunal's reasons merely to (1) recite the evidence or submissions (*J v Devon County Council* [2001] EWHC 958 (Admin)); or (2) recite the statutory criteria for discharge (*Bone v Mental Health Review Tribunal* [1985] 3 All E.R. 330).

In *RH v South London and Maudsley NHS Foundation Trust* [2010] UKUT 32 (AAC) [2010] M.H.L.R. 118, para.17, UT Judge Rowland said that where the tribunal merely disagreed with the conclusion to be drawn from the professional assessments when it came to considering whether a restriction order should cease to have effect, it was difficult to "give reasons beyond those required to show that the tribunal has directed itself correctly as to the law and to show to what matters the tribunal has had regard".

On a reconsideration of a decision that had been deferred under s.73(7) of the Act, it is impermissible for the tribunal in its reasons for not discharging the patient to take into account matters, such as risk factors, to which it had not referred in its original decision even though they must have been relevant then (*LC v DHIC* [2010] UKUT 319 (AAC); [2010] M.H.L.R. 337).

In *R. v Mental Health Review Tribunal Ex p. Booth* [1998] C.O.D. 203, Laws J. said:

"It has to be remembered ... that the quality of reasons required of a Mental Health Review Tribunal has to be looked at in light of the fact that the decision is addressed to an informed audience. Those who receive it and who are concerned with it will be familiar with the essential documents in the case ... They will be familiar with what has been said at the tribunal by way of oral evidence and what the issues there were which had been argued. Given that necessary familiarity, if there was a case in which it could still be said that the parties simply were not told why the tribunal arrived at the decision it did, then no doubt there would be a sound basis for a legal challenge."

This passage must be read subject to the caveat expressed by Dyson L.J. in *R. (on the Application of H) v Ashworth Hospital Authority*, above.

If the tribunal provides reasons that are considered to be inadequate, the review procedure should be invoked: see rr.47(1) and 49.

3-165   **Paragraph (3)(b)**

3-165   *7 Days*   Not 7 working days.

Paragraph (4) It is submitted that the overriding objective (r.2) requires the tribunal to provide reasons for all disputed decisions. **3-166**

Provisional decisions

42. For the purposes of this Part and Parts 1, 2 and 5, a decision with recommendations under section 72(3)(a) or (3A)(a) of the Mental Health Act 1983 or a deferred direction for conditional discharge under section 73(7) of that Act is a decision which disposes of the proceedings. **3-167**

Definition

dispose of proceedings: r.1(3). **3-168**

PART 5

Interpretation

43. In this Part— **3-169**

"appeal" means the exercise of a right of appeal on a point of law under section 11 of the 2007 Act; and

"review" means the review of a decision by the Tribunal under section 9 of the 2007 Act.

Definition

Tribunal: r.1(3). **3-170**

Clerical mistakes and accidental slips or omissions

44. The Tribunal may at any time correct any clerical mistake or other accidental slip or omission in a decision, direction or any document produced by it, by— **3-171**

    (a) sending notification of the amended decision or direction, or a copy of the amended document, to all parties; and

    (b) making any necessary amendment to any information published in relation to the decision, direction or document.

Definitions

Tribunal: r.1(3). **3-172**
document: r.1(3).
party: r.1(3).

Setting aside a decision which disposes of proceedings

45.—(1) The Tribunal may set aside a decision which disposes of proceedings, or part of such a decision, and re-make the decision or the relevant part of it, if— **3-173**

    (a) the Tribunal considers that it is in the interests of justice to do so; and

    (b) one or more of the conditions in paragraph (2) are satisfied.

(2) The conditions are—

[813]

(a) a document relating to the proceedings was not sent to, or was not received at an appropriate time by, a party or a party's representative;

(b) a document relating to the proceedings was not sent to the Tribunal at an appropriate time;

(c) a party, or a party's representative, was not present at a hearing related to the proceedings; or

(d) there has been some other procedural irregularity in the proceedings.

(3) A party applying for a decision, or part of a decision, to be set aside under paragraph (1) must make a written application to the Tribunal so that it is received no later than 28 days after the date on which the Tribunal sent notice of the decision to the party.

Definitions

3-174 Tribunal: r.1(3).
dispose of proceedings: r.1(3).
document: r.1(3).
party: r.1(3).
hearing: r.1(3).

General Note

3-175 This rule, which deals with procedural failings, not jurisdiction (*SK v Secretary of State for Work and Pensions* [2016] UKUT 529 (AAC)), enables the tribunal to set aside a decision, or part of a decision, which disposes of proceedings (see r.42) and to remake the decision or the relevant part of it on the ground of procedural irregularity if such action is in the interests of justice. An application form for this purpose (Form P9), together with a guidance note has been published by the Courts and Tribunal Service.

A decision by the tribunal to set aside a decision cannot be appealed to the Upper Tribunal (Tribunals, Courts and Enforcement Act 2007 s.11(1), (5)(d)(iii)).

A procedure for challenging a direction is contained in r.6(5).

Paragraph (3)

3-176 **28 Days** See rr.12 and 13 for the calculation of time and methods of service. There is provision for this time limit to be extended (r.5(3)(a)).

Application for permission to appeal

3-177 **46.**—(1) A person seeking permission to appeal must make a written application to the Tribunal for permission to appeal.

(2) An application under paragraph (1) must be sent or delivered to the Tribunal so that it is received no later than 28 days after the latest of the dates that the Tribunal sends to the person making the application—

[(za)] the relevant decision notice;]

(a) written reasons for the decision[, if the decision disposes of—

  (i) all issues in the proceedings; or

  (ii) subject to paragraph (2A), a preliminary issue dealt with following a direction under rule 5(3)(e);]

(b) notification of amended reasons for, or correction of, the decision following a review; or

(c) notification that an application for the decision to be set aside has been unsuccessful.

[(2A) The Tribunal may direct that the 28 days within which a party may send or deliver to the Tribunal an application for permission to appeal against a decision that disposes of a preliminary issue shall run from the date of the decision that disposes of all issues in the proceedings.]

[814]

(3) The date in paragraph (2)(c) applies only if the application for the decision to be set aside was made within the time stipulated in rule 45 (setting aside a decision which disposes of proceedings) or any extension of that time granted by the Tribunal.

(4) If the person seeking permission to appeal sends or delivers the application to the Tribunal later than the time required by paragraph (2) or by any extension of time under rule 5(3)(a) (power to extend time)—

    (a) the application must include a request for an extension of time and the reason why the application was not provided in time; and

    (b) unless the Tribunal extends time for the application under rule 5(3)(a) (power to extend time) the Tribunal must not admit the application.

(5) An application under paragraph (1) must—

    (a) identify the decision of the Tribunal to which it relates;

    (b) identify the alleged error or errors of law in the decision; and

    (c) state the result the party making the application is seeking.

Amendments

The amendments to this rule were made by SI 2013/477 r.21.

Definitions

appeal: r.43.   **3-178**
Tribunal: r.1(3).
review: r.43.
dispose of proceedings: r.43.
party: r.1(3).

General Note

For a consideration of appeals generally, see the General Note to s.65. Under s.11 of the Tribunals,   **3-179**
Courts and Enforcement Act 2007, an appeal lies to the Upper Tribunal "on any point of law arising from a decision made by the First-tier Tribunal". The Upper Tribunal can set aside the decision if it involves "an error on a point of law" (ibid., s.12(1); for Wales, see s.78A). In *TR v Ludlow Street Healthcare Ltd* [2011] UKUT 152 (AAC); [2011] M.H.L.R. 190, para.7, UT Judge Jacobs said that on "basic principle, I may give permission to appeal if there is a realistic prospect that the decision was erroneous in law or if there is some other good reason to do so (Lord Woolf MR in *Smith v Cosworth Casting Processes Ltd* [1997] 1 WLR 1538)". Lord Woolf's guidance in the *Smith* case "is capable of general application and is applied by the Upper Tribunal" (*Christie v Information Commissioner* [2022] UKUT 315 (AAC), per UT Judge Jacobs at para.21).

In *JLG v Managers of Llanarth Court* [2011] UKUT 62 (AAC); [2011] M.H.L.R. 74, para.3, Judge Jacobs provided guidance on the nature of an error of law:

> "The essence of the legal requirement for a tribunal's decision is that: (i) the tribunal asked itself the correct legal questions; (ii) it made findings of fact that were rationally based in the evidence; and (iii) it answered the legal questions appropriately given its findings of fact. Additionally, the tribunal must: (iv) give the parties a fair hearing; and (v) provide adequate reasons. In simple terms, the issue is whether the tribunal did its job properly."

Judge Jacobs further stated that when identifying whether an error of law exists, tribunals "are assumed to know the essentials of what their work involves". They therefore do not need to "spell out" fundamental matters such as the burden and standard of proof. The task of the Upper Tribunal is to examine whether "there is anything to indicate that [the tribunal] have exceptionally failed to apply the basic tools of their craft" (paras 5 and 6). See also the notes on r.41(2).

In *CNWL NHS Foundation Trust v H-JH* [2012] UKUT 210 (AAC); [2012] M.H.L.R. 305, para.12, Judge Jacobs described the Upper Tribunal's appellate role as follows:

> "In deciding whether the First-tier Tribunal made an error of law, the Upper Tribunal has no power

to undertake its own assessment of the evidence or to make its own findings of fact in substitution for those of the First-tier Tribunal. It must respect the fact-finding role, provided that the First-tier Tribunal carried out that task rationally and explained why it made its findings. To do otherwise would subvert the statutory limit of its jurisdiction."

The scope of this rule is not confined to appeals against the tribunal's decision which disposes of proceedings; an appeal lies against an interlocutory decision (*LS v London Borough of Lambeth* [2010] UKUT 461 (AAC)) In *RM v St Andrew's Healthcare* [2010] UKUT 119 (AAC), Judge Jacobs considered the approach that should be taken with regard to appeals against case management decisions. He said that although appellate courts are supportive of such decisions and "discourage appeals against them" as they "often have to be made with little time for analysis or reflection" (para.7), this "does not mean that [they] are immune from scrutiny" (para.8) and on "the spectrum of case management decisions, the non-disclosure order is more susceptible to scrutiny than most" (para.9). It was suggested in *Dorset Healthcare NHS Foundation Trust v MH* [2009] UKUT 4 (AAC) at para.19, that where case-management decisions are being challenged, the First-tier Tribunal can treat an application for permission to appeal as an application for a new direction if it is satisfied that the challenged direction is not appropriate.

There is nothing unfair in an initial application for permission to appeal being made to the judge who made the decision being challenged: see *AA v Cheshire and Wirral Partnership NHS Foundation Trust* [2009] UKUT 195 (AAC); [2009] M.H.L.R. 308, where Judge Rowland said at para.27:

"The advantage to a superior court or tribunal of having this kind of procedure is that it gives the judge whose decision is being challenged, who will have the relevant issues in mind, an opportunity to comment on the grounds of appeal and indicate whether he or she thinks there is anything in them."

Encouragement to respondents, especially public authority respondents, to take part in proceedings before the Upper Tribunal was given by Judge Rowland in *RH v South London and Maudsley NHS Foundation Trust* [2010] UKUT 32 (AAC); [2010] M.H.L.R. 118 at para.29 et seq. Public authorities will doubtless remain reluctant to take part in such proceedings when the decision under challenge is that of the tribunal, not the authority.

An application form for permission to appeal (Form P10), together with a guidance note has been published by the Courts and Tribunal Service. On receiving the application, the tribunal must first consider whether to review the decision in accordance with r.49 (r.47(1)). If permission to appeal is refused, reasons must be given (r.47(4)).

The principles that should be applied by an appellate tribunal

3-180   In *CICA v Hutton and the First-tier Tribunal* [2016] EWCA Civ 1305 at para.57, Gross L.J. summarised the principles that should be applied by an appellate tribunal reviewing the decision of a specialist tribunal:

"i)   First, this Court should exercise restraint and proceed with caution before interfering with decisions of specialist tribunals. Not only do such tribunals have the expertise which the 'ordinary' courts may not have but when a specialised statutory scheme has been entrusted by Parliament to tribunals, the Court should not venture too readily into their field.

ii)   Secondly, if a tribunal decision is clearly based on an error of law, then it must be corrected. This Court should not, however, subject such decisions to inappropriate textual analysis so as to discern an error of law when, on a fair reading of the decision as a whole, none existed. It is probable, as Baroness Hale said [in *AH (Sudan) v Home Secretary* [2007] UKHL 49 at para.40], that in understanding and applying the law within their area of expertise, specialist tribunals will have got it right. Moreover, the mere fact that an appellate tribunal or a court would have reached a different conclusion, does not constitute a ground for review or for allowing an appeal.

iii)   Thirdly, it is of the first importance to identify the tribunal of fact, to keep in mind that it and only it will have heard the evidence and to respect its decisions. When determining whether a question was one of 'fact' or 'law', this Court should have regard to context, as I would respectfully express it ('pragmatism', 'expediency' or 'policy', per [*R (Jones) v First-tier Tribunal* [2013] UKSC 19], so as to ensure both that decisions of tribunals of fact are given proper weight and to provide scope for specialist appellate tribunals to shape the development of law and practice in their field.

iv)   Fourthly, it is important to note that these authorities not only address the relationship between the courts and specialist appellate tribunals *but also* between specialist first-tier tribunals and appellate tribunals."

Paragraph (2)

28 Days   See rr.2 and 13 for the calculation of time and methods of service. There is provision for this time limit to be extended (r.5(3)(a)).   **3-181**

Tribunal's consideration of application for permission to appeal

47.—(1)   On receiving an application for permission to appeal the Tribunal must first consider, taking into account the overriding objective in rule 2, whether to review the decision in accordance with rule 49 (review of a decision).   **3-182**

(2)   If the Tribunal decides not to review the decision, or reviews the decision and decides to take no action in relation to the decision, or part of it, the Tribunal must consider whether to give permission to appeal in relation to the decision or that part of it.

(3)   The Tribunal must send a record of its decision to the parties as soon as practicable.

(4)   If the Tribunal refuses permission to appeal it must send with the record of its decision—

(a)   a statement of its reasons for such refusal; and

(b)   notification of the right to make an application to the Upper Tribunal for permission to appeal and the time within which, and the method by which, such application must be made.

(5)   The Tribunal may give permission to appeal on limited grounds, but must comply with paragraph (4) in relation to any grounds on which it has refused permission.

Definitions

appeal: r.43.   **3-183**
Tribunal: r.1(3).
party: r.1(3).

General Note

In *KF v Birmingham and Solihull Mental Health NHS Foundation Trust* [2010] UKUT 185 (AAC); [2010] M.H.L.R 201, para.19, the Upper Tribunal accepted the following analysis of the relevant legislative provisions that had been prepared by counsel: **3-184**

"On receipt of an application for permission to appeal, the First-tier Tribunal has a *discretion* as to whether to undertake a review (r.47(1)). If there is no review, the First-tier Tribunal has a *duty* to consider whether to give permission to appeal but a *discretion* as to whether or not to grant permission (r.47(2)). If permission is refused and the application is renewed before the Upper Tribunal, the Upper Tribunal also has a *discretion* as to whether to give permission (Tribunal Procedure (Upper Tribunal) Rules 2008, SI 2008/2698, r.21(2)). If permission is granted and the Upper Tribunal finds an error of law, it has a *discretion* as to whether to set aside the First-tier Tribunal decision (s.12(2)(a) of the 2007 Act), but if that tribunal decision is set aside, then the Upper Tribunal has a *duty* either to re-make the decision or to remit it to the First-tier Tribunal for a re-hearing (s.12(2)(b) of the 2007 Act)."

The UT said, at para.41, that there may be circumstances in which it is appropriate to grant either a review or permission to appeal notwithstanding the fact that the patient has been discharged:

"In many cases where the patient has since been released, there will be no individual or wider public interest in continuing proceedings, even where the decision of the First-tier Tribunal under challenge may well be suspect. To that extent we would agree that there may well be a presumption in practice against granting either a review or permission to appeal or against setting aside on appeal in such cases. However, we do not accept that it will *never* be appropriate to exercise such a procedural discretion in the patient's favour where he or she has already been released. We recognise that these are cases involving fundamental issues about the liberty of the subject. There may well be circumstances in which it remains appropriate for there to be further scrutiny of the initial tribunal decision, notwithstanding the individual's subsequent discharge. There may be a danger that a future decision-maker may give inappropriate weight to a flawed decision. Moreover, there may be an urgent need for the legal principles at stake to be clarified."

Application for review in special educational needs cases

3-185   **48.** [*Applies to special educational needs cases*]

Review of a decision
3-186   **49.**—(1)   The Tribunal may only undertake a review of a decision—
(a)   pursuant to rule 47(1) (review on an application for permission to appeal) if it is satisfied that there was an error of law in the decision; or
(b)   pursuant to rule 48 (application for review in special educational needs cases).

(2)   The Tribunal must notify the parties in writing of the outcome of any review, and of any right of appeal in relation to the outcome.

(3)   If the Tribunal takes any action in relation to a decision following a review without first giving every party an opportunity to make representations, the notice under paragraph (2) must state that any party that did not have an opportunity to make representations may apply for such action to be set aside and for the decision to be reviewed again.

Definitions

3-187   Tribunal: r.1(3).
review: r.43.
appeal: r.43.
party: r.1(3).

General Note

3-188   This power is intended to capture decisions that are clearly wrong in that there is an error of law in the decision, so avoiding the need for an appeal. As the propensity to fall into error is not confined to the English, it is unfortunate that this useful power has no equivalent in the Welsh Rules. The tribunal has the power to review a decision on its own initiative under s.9(2)(a) of the Tribunals, Courts and Enforcement Act 2007. The powers of the tribunal on undertaking a review are set out in s.9(4) to (6) of that Act:

"(4)   Where the First-tier Tribunal has under subsection (1) reviewed a decision, the First-tier Tribunal may in the light of the review do any of the following—
(a)   correct accidental errors in the decision or in a record of the decision;
(b)   amend reasons given for the decision;
(c)   set the decision aside.
(5)   Where under subsection (4)(c) the First-tier Tribunal sets a decision aside, the First-tier Tribunal must either—
(a)   re-decide the matter concerned, or
(b)   refer that matter to the Upper Tribunal.
(6)   Where a matter is referred to the Upper Tribunal under subsection (5)(b), the Upper Tribunal must re-decide the matter."

A decision by the tribunal either to review, or not to review a decision cannot be appealed to the Upper

Tribunal as it is an "excluded decision" (s.11(1),(5)(d)(i) of the 2007 Act). Although such a decision is not appealable, an application for the judicial review of the decision may be made to the Upper Tribunal by virtue of ss.15 to 18 of the 2007 Act where it does not seek a declaration of incompatibility under the Human Rights Act 1998 and it is within the scope of *Practice Direction (Upper Tribunal: Judicial Review Jurisdiction)* [2009] 1 W.L.R. 327 made by the Lord Chief Justice under s.18(6) of the 2007 Act. The Practice Direction specifies, with immaterial exceptions, "[a]ny decision of the First-tier Tribunal made under Tribunal Procedure Rules or section 9 of the 2007 Act where there is no right of appeal ...": see *RB*, below at para.11.

In *R (RB) v First-tier Tribunal (Review)* [2010] UKUT 160 (AAC); [2010] M.H.L.R. 192 the Upper Tribunal held that:

1. This Rule cannot be used to usurp the Upper Tribunal's function of determining appeals on contentious points of law. If the power is to be exercised to set aside the original decision because of a perceived error of law, this should only be done in clear cases (para.24). It should be possible to give brief reasons for the decision; it will be seldom be necessary to set out the facts or the background legislation or to cite at length from authorities (para.32).
2. Even if there is a clear error of law, the tribunal may decide not to review a decision but instead to give permission to appeal if it would be helpful to have an authoritative decision of the Upper Tribunal on the point (para.27).
3. Paragraph (3) of this Rule enables the First-tier Tribunal to take a robust approach when it first receives an application for permission to appeal because it enables it to take a decision without calling for representations by the other side, on the basis that if the other side objects there can be an application to set aside. However, in many cases it will be preferable to invite representations before concluding that an original decision should be set aside (para.26).
4. There may be occasions when it is desirable for a case to be reconsidered by the First-tier Tribunal so that further findings may be made even if it is likely to go to the Upper Tribunal eventually (para.28).
5. Where the First-tier Tribunal is to re-decide a case, the composition of the tribunal must be the same as was required for the original decision, although the particular judge and members may be different (para.29). [In *AA v Cheshire and Wirral Partnership NHS Foundation Trust* [2009] UKUT 195 (AAC); [2009] M.H.L.R. 308, the UT said that there is nothing unfair in a review being undertaken by the judge who made the decision being challenged].
6. The substantial element of judgment or discretion is no doubt a reason for review decisions not being appealable and it is also a reason for expecting that the Upper Tribunal will seldom interfere with review decisions when judicial review proceedings are brought (para.30).

RB was applied by UT Judge Wikeley in *R. (on the application of MP) v First-tier Tribunal* [2012] UKUT 231 (AAC) who said, at para.19, that there will need to be a "compelling case" to give permission to apply for the judicial review of a review decision.

When deciding whether to set aside a decision, it is relevant to consider whether such action could be of practical benefit to any of the parties. This is unlikely to be this case where a further hearing was due to take place which would consider the up-to-date position and would proceed on the basis that the previous decision would be erroneous in law (*BB v South London and Maudsley NHS Trust* [2009] UKUT 157 (AAC); [2009] M.H.L.R. 302).

In general, unless there is good reason why not, if the tribunal is asked to review a tribunal decision on a s.2 application where the patient has been subsequently detained under s.3, and concludes that it involves an error of law, then the appropriate way forward is for the tribunal to set aside the substantive decision and to re-list the case for hearing together with any existing s.3 application. The patient has the right to apply to withdraw that application under r.17. This approach has a number of practical ramifications. Some of the issues that may arise are as follows: (i) time limits; (ii) case management and consolidation; (iii) withdrawal; and (iv) provision of reports (*KF v Birmingham and Solihull Mental Health NHS Foundation Trust* [2010] UKUT 185 (AAC); [2010] M.H.L.R. 201 para.30).

A review decision cannot be used to criticise a decision that is under appeal (*RM v St Andrew's Healthcare* [2010] UKUT 119 (AAC); [2010] M.H.L.R. 176, para.5).

Power to treat an application as a different type of application

50. The Tribunal may treat an application for a decision to be corrected, set **3-189** aside or reviewed, or for permission to appeal against a decision, as an application for any other one of those things.

Definitions

3-190   Tribunal: r.1(3).
review: r.43.
appeal: r.43.

SCHEDULE

Rules 20(1)(a) and 21(1)(a)

3-191   [*The Schedule does not apply to mental health cases*]

PRACTICE DIRECTION

PRACTICE DIRECTION FIRST-TIER TRIBUNAL HEALTH EDUCATION AND SOCIAL CARE CHAMBER STATEMENTS AND REPORTS IN MENTAL HEALTH CASES

General Note

3-192   An equivalent Practice Direction relating to the Mental Health Review Tribunal for Wales was published in October 2019. It can be accessed at: *https://mentalhealthreviewtribunal.gov.wales/sites/ mentalhealthreview/files/2019-12/MHRT%20Practice%20Direction%20Oct%202019.pdf*.

3-193   1.   This Practice Direction is made by the Senior President of Tribunals with the agreement of the Lord Chancellor in the exercise of powers conferred by Section 23 of the Tribunals, Courts and Enforcement Act 2007. It applies to a "mental health case" as defined in Rule 1(3) the Tribunal Procedure (First-tier Tribunal) (Health, Education and Social Care Chamber) Rules 2008. Rule 32 requires that certain statements and reports must be sent or delivered to the tribunal (and, in restricted cases, to the Secretary of State) by the Responsible Authority, the Responsible Clinician and any Social Supervisor (as the case may be). This Practice Direction specifies the contents of such documents. It replaces the previous Practice Directions on mental health cases dated 30 October 2008 and 6 April 2012, with effect from 28 October 2013.

2.   In this Practice Direction "the Act" refers to the Mental Health Act 1983 (as amended by the Mental Health Act 2007).

3.   This Practice Direction contains five separate parts for the following categories of patient:
A.   IN-PATIENTS (NON-RESTRICTED AND RESTRICTED)
B.   COMMUNITY PATIENTS
C.   GUARDIANSHIP PATIENTS
D.   CONDITIONALLY DISCHARGED PATIENTS
E.   PATIENTS UNDER THE AGE OF 18.

4.   Responsible Authorities and authors of reports should refer to the relevant part of this Practice Direction, depending on the status of the patient under the Act.
SIR JEREMY SULLIVAN
SENIOR PRESIDENT OF TRIBUNALS
28 OCTOBER 2013

A. In-Patients (Non-Restricted and Restricted)

5. For the purposes of this Practice Direction, a patient is an in-patient if they are   **3-194**
detained in hospital to be assessed or treated for a mental disorder, whether admitted through civil or criminal justice processes, including a restricted patient (i.e. subject to special restrictions under the Act), and including a patient transferred to hospital from custody. A patient is to be regarded as an in-patient detained in a hospital even if they have been permitted leave of absence, or have gone absent without leave.

6. In the case of a restricted patient detained in hospital, the tribunal may make a provisional decision to order a Conditional Discharge. However, before it finally decides to grant a Conditional Discharge, the tribunal may defer its decision so that satisfactory arrangements can be made. The patient will remain an in-patient unless and until the tribunal finally grants a Conditional Discharge, so this part of the Practice Direction applies.

7. If the patient is an in-patient, the Responsible Authority must send or deliver to the tribunal the following documents containing the specified information in accordance with the relevant paragraphs below:
- *Statement of Information about the Patient.*
- *Responsible Clinician's Report, including any relevant forensic history.*
- *Nursing Report, with the patient's current nursing plan attached.*
- *Social Circumstances Report including details of any Care Pathway Approach (CPA) and/or Section 117 aftercare plan in full or in embryo and, where appropriate, the additional information required for patients under the age of 18, and any input from a Multi Agency Public Protection Arrangements (MAPPA) agency or meeting.*

8. In all in-patient cases, except where a patient is detained under Section 2 of the Act, the Responsible Authority must send to the tribunal the required documents containing the specified information, so that they are received by the tribunal as soon as practicable and in any event within 3 weeks after the Authority made or received the application or reference. If the patient is a restricted patient, the Authority must also, at the same time, send copies of the documents to the Secretary of State (Ministry of Justice).

9. Where a patient is detained under Section 2 of the Act, the Responsible Authority must prepare the required documents as soon as practicable after receipt of a copy of the application or a request from the tribunal. If specified information has to be omitted because it is not available, then this should be mentioned in the statement or report. These documents must be made available to the tribunal panel and the patient's representative at least one hour before the hearing is due to start.

10. The authors of reports should have personally met and be familiar with the patient. If an existing report becomes out-of-date, or if the status or the circumstances of the patient change after the reports have been written but before the tribunal hearing takes place (e.g. if a patient is discharged, or is recalled), the author of the report should then send to the tribunal an addendum addressing the up-to-date situation and, where necessary, the new applicable statutory criteria.

Statement of Information about the Patient – In-Patients

3-195 **11.** The statement provided to the tribunal must be up-to-date, specifically prepared for the tribunal, signed and dated, and must include:
a) the patient's full name, date of birth, and usual place of residence;
b) the full official name of the Responsible Authority;
c) the patient's first language/dialect and, if it is not English, whether an interpreter is required and, if so, in which language/dialect;
d) if the patient is deaf, whether the patient will require the services of British Sign Language Interpreters and/or a Relay Interpreter;
e) a chronological table listing:
   • the dates of any previous admissions to, discharge from, or recall to hospital, stating whether the admissions were compulsory or voluntary;
   • the date when the current period of detention in hospital originally commenced, stating the nature of the application, order or direction that is the authority for the detention of the patient;
   • the dates of any subsequent renewal of, or change in, the authority for the patient's detention, and any changes in the patient's status under the Act;
   • dates and details of any hospital transfers since the patient's original detention;
   • the date of admission or transfer to the hospital where the patient now is;
   • the dates and outcomes of any tribunal hearings over the last three years;
f) the name of the patient's Responsible Clinician and the date when the patient came under the care of that clinician;
g) the name and contact details of the patient's Care Co-ordinator, Community Psychiatric Nurse, Social Worker/AMHP or Social Supervisor;
h) where the patient is detained in an independent hospital, details of any NHS body that funds, or will fund, the placement;
i) the name and address of the local social services authority which, were the patient to leave hospital, would have a duty to provide Section 117 after-care services;
j) the name and address of the NHS body which, were the patient to leave hospital, would have a duty to provide Section 117 after-care services;
k) the name and address of any legal representative acting for the patient;
l) except in the case of a restricted patient, the name and address of the patient's Nearest Relative or of the person exercising that function, whether the patient has made any request that their Nearest Relative should not be consulted or should not be kept informed about the patient's care or treatment and, if so, the details of any such request, whether the Responsible Authority believes that the patient has capacity to make such a request and the reasons for that belief;
m) the name and address of any other person who plays a significant part in the care of the patient but who is not professionally involved;
n) details of any legal proceedings or other arrangements relating to the patient's mental capacity, or their ability to make decisions or handle their own affairs.

General Note

Guidance on drafting a Responsible Authority statement of information about the patient is provided **3-196** by C. Curran, P. Fennell and S. Burrows in "Responsible Authority Statements for Mental Health Tribunals in England under the 2013 Practice Direction" *Legal Action*, September 2014, pp.17–22.

Responsible Clinician's Report – In-Patients

12. The report must be up-to-date, specifically prepared for the tribunal and have **3-197** numbered paragraphs and pages. It should be signed and dated. The report should be written or counter-signed by the patient's Responsible Clinician. The sources of information for the events and incidents described must be made clear. This report should not be an addendum to (or reproduce extensive details from) previous reports, or recite medical records, but must briefly describe the patient's recent relevant medical history and current mental health presentation, and must include:

a) whether there are any factors that may affect the patient's understanding or ability to cope with a hearing and whether there are any adjustments that the tribunal may consider in order to deal with the case fairly and justly;

b) details of any index offence(s) and other relevant forensic history;

c) a chronology listing the patient's previous involvement with mental health services including any admissions to, discharge from and recall to hospital;

d) reasons for any previous admission or recall to hospital;

e) the circumstances leading up to the patient's current admission to hospital;

f) whether the patient is now suffering from a mental disorder and, if so, whether a diagnosis has been made, what the diagnosis is, and why;

g) whether the patient has a learning disability and, if so, whether that disability is associated with abnormally aggressive or seriously irresponsible conduct;

h) depending upon the statutory criteria, whether any mental disorder present is of a nature or degree to warrant, or make appropriate, liability to be detained in a hospital for assessment and/or medical treatment;

i) details of any appropriate and available medical treatment prescribed, provided, offered or planned for the patient's mental disorder;

j) the strengths or positive factors relating to the patient;

k) a summary of the patient's current progress, behaviour, capacity and insight;

l) the patient's understanding of, compliance with, and likely future willingness to accept any prescribed medication or comply with any appropriate medical treatment for mental disorder that is or might be made available;

m) in the case of an eligible compliant patient who lacks capacity to agree or object to their detention or treatment, whether or not deprivation of liberty under the Mental Capacity Act 2005 (as amended) would be appropriate and less restrictive;

n) details of any incidents where the patient has harmed themselves or others, or threatened harm, or damaged property, or threatened damage;

o) whether (in Section 2 cases) detention in hospital, or (in all other cases) the provision of medical treatment in hospital, is justified or necessary in the interests of the patient's health or safety, or for the protection of others;

p) whether the patient, if discharged from hospital, would be likely to act in a manner dangerous to themselves or others;

q) whether, and if so how, any risks could be managed effectively in the community, including the use of any lawful conditions or recall powers;

r) any recommendations to the tribunal, with reasons.

Nursing Report – In-Patients

3-198 **13.** The report must be up-to-date, specifically prepared for the tribunal and have numbered paragraphs and pages. It should be signed and dated. The sources of information for the events and incidents described must be made clear. This report should not recite the details of medical records, or be an addendum to (or reproduce extensive details from) previous reports, although the patient's current nursing plan should be attached. In relation to the patient's current in-patient episode, the report must briefly describe the patient's current mental health presentation, and must include:

a) whether there are any factors that might affect the patient's understanding or ability to cope with a hearing, and whether there are any adjustments that the tribunal may consider in order to deal with the case fairly and justly;

b) the nature of nursing care and medication currently being made available;

c) the level of observation to which the patient is currently subject;

d) whether the patient has contact with relatives, friends or other patients, the nature of the interaction, and what community support the patient has;

e) strengths or positive factors relating to the patient;

f) a summary of the patient's current progress, engagement with nursing staff, behaviour, cooperation, activities, self-care and insight;

g) any occasions on which the patient has been absent without leave whilst liable to be detained, or occasions when the patient has failed to return as and when required, after having been granted leave;

h) the patient's understanding of, compliance with, and likely future willingness to accept any prescribed medication or treatment for mental disorder that is or might be made available;

i) details of any incidents in hospital where the patient has harmed themselves or others, or threatened harm, or damaged property, or threatened damage;

j) any occasions on which the patient has been secluded or restrained, including the reasons why such seclusion or restraint was necessary;

k) whether (in Section 2 cases) detention in hospital, or (in all other cases) the provision of medical treatment in hospital, is justified or necessary in the interests of the patient's health or safety, or for the protection of others;

l) whether the patient, if discharged from hospital, would be likely to act in a manner dangerous to themselves or others;

m) whether, and if so how, any risks could be managed effectively in the community, including the use of any lawful conditions or recall powers;

n) any recommendations to the tribunal, with reasons.

General Note

3-199 Guidance on drafting an in-patient nursing report is provided by C. Curran, B. Leason and A. Deery in "Inpatient Nursing Reports and Current Nursing Plans for Mental Health Tribunals in England under the 2013 Practice Direction" *Legal Action*, November 2014, pp.30–36.

Social Circumstances Report – In-Patients

3-200 **14.** The report must be up-to-date, specifically prepared for the tribunal and have numbered paragraphs and pages. It should be signed and dated. The sources of information for the events and incidents described must be made clear. This report should not be an addendum to (or reproduce extensive details from) previous reports, but must briefly describe the patient's recent relevant history and current presentation, and must include:

a) whether there are any factors that might affect the patient's understanding or ability to cope with a hearing, and whether there are any adjustments that the tribunal may consider in order to deal with the case fairly and justly;

b) details of any index offence(s) and other relevant forensic history;

c) a chronology listing the patient's previous involvement with mental health services including any admissions to, discharge from and recall to hospital;

d) the patient's home and family circumstances;

e) the housing or accommodation available to the patient if discharged;

f) the patient's financial position (including benefit entitlements);

g) any available opportunities for employment;

h) the patient's previous response to community support or Section 117 after-care;

i) so far as is known, details of the care pathway and Section 117 after-care to be made available to the patient, together with details of the proposed care plan;

j) the likely adequacy and effectiveness of the proposed care plan;

k) whether there are any issues as to funding the proposed care plan and, if so, the date by which those issues will be resolved;

l) the strengths or positive factors relating to the patient;

m) a summary of the patient's current progress, behaviour, compliance and insight;

n) details of any incidents where the patient has harmed themselves or others, or threatened harm, or damaged property, or threatened damage;

o) the patient's views, wishes, beliefs, opinions, hopes and concerns;

p) except in restricted cases, the views of the patient's Nearest Relative unless (having consulted the patient) it would inappropriate or impractical to consult the Nearest Relative, in which case give reasons for this view and describe any attempts to rectify matters;

q) the views of any other person who takes a lead role in the care and support of the patient but who is not professionally involved;

r) whether the patient is known to any MAPPA meeting or agency and, if so, in which area, for what reason, and at what level – together with the name of the Chair of any MAPPA meeting concerned with the patient, and the name of the representative of the lead agency;

s) in the event that a MAPPA meeting or agency wishes to put forward evidence of its views in relation to the level and management of risk, a summary of those views (or an Executive Summary may be attached to the report); and where relevant, a copy of the Police National Computer record of previous convictions should be attached;

t) in the case of an eligible compliant patient who lacks capacity to agree or object to their detention or treatment, whether or not deprivation of liberty under the Mental Capacity Act 2005 (as amended) would be appropriate and less restrictive;

u) whether (in Section 2 cases) detention in hospital, or (in all other cases) the provision of medical treatment in hospital, is justified or necessary in the interests of the patient's health or safety, or for the protection of others;

v) whether the patient, if discharged from hospital, would be likely to act in a manner dangerous to themselves or others;

w) whether, and if so how, any risks could be managed effectively in the community, including the use of any lawful conditions or recall powers;

x) any recommendations to the tribunal, with reasons.

B. Community Patients

3-201 **15.** The Responsible Authority must send to the tribunal the following documents, containing the specified information, so that the documents are received by the tribunal as soon as practicable and in any event within 3 weeks after the Authority made or received the application or reference:

- *Statement of Information about the Patient.*
- *Responsible Clinician's Report, including any relevant forensic history.*
- *Social Circumstances Report including details of any Section 117 after-care plan and, where appropriate, the additional information required for patients under the age of 18, and any input from a Multi Agency Public Protection Arrangements (MAPPA) agency or meeting.*

16. The authors of reports should have personally met and be familiar with the patient. If an existing report becomes out-of-date, or if the status or the circumstances of the patient change after the reports have been written but before the tribunal hearing takes place (e.g. if a patient is recalled, or again discharged into the community), the author of the report should then send to the tribunal an addendum addressing the up-to-date situation and, where necessary, the new applicable statutory criteria.

Statement of Information about the Patient – Community Patients

3-202 **17.** The statement provided to the tribunal should be up-to-date, signed and dated, specifically prepared for the tribunal, and must include:

a) the patient's full name, date of birth, and current place of residence;

b) the full official name of the Responsible Authority;

c) the patient's first language/dialect and, if it is not English, whether an interpreter is required and, if so, in which language/dialect;

d) if the patient is deaf, whether the patient will require the services of British Sign Language Interpreters and/or a Relay Interpreter;

e) a chronological table listing:

- the dates of any previous admissions to, discharge from, or recall to hospital, stating whether the admissions were compulsory or voluntary, and including any previous instances of discharge on to a Community Treatment Order (CTO);
- the date of the underlying order or direction for detention in hospital prior to the patient's discharge onto the current CTO;
- the date of the current CTO;
- the dates of any subsequent renewal of, or change in, the authority for the patient's CTO, and any changes in the patient's status under the Act;
- the dates and outcomes of any tribunal hearings over the last three years;

f) the name of the patient's Responsible Clinician and the date when the patient came under the care of that clinician;

g) the name and contact details of the patient's Care Co-ordinator, Community Psychiatric Nurse, and/or Social Worker/AMHP;

h) the name and address of the local social services authority which has the duty to provide Section 117 after-care services;

i) the name and address of the NHS body which has the duty to provide Section 117 after-care services;

j) the name and address of any legal representative acting for the patient;

k) the name and address of the patient's Nearest Relative or of the person exercising that function, whether the patient has made any request that their Nearest Relative should not be consulted or should not be kept informed about the patient's care or treatment and, if so, the details of any such request, whether the Responsible Authority believes that the patient has capacity to make such a request and the reasons for that belief;

l) the name and address of any other person who plays a significant part in the care of the patient but who is not professionally involved;

m) details of any legal proceedings or other arrangements relating to the patient's mental capacity, or their ability to make decisions or handle their own affairs.

Responsible Clinician's Report – Community Patients

18.   The report must be up-to-date, specifically prepared for the tribunal and have **3-203** numbered paragraphs and pages. It should be signed and dated. This report should be written or counter-signed by the patient's Responsible Clinician. The sources of information for the events and incidents described must be made clear. The report should not be an addendum to (or reproduce extensive details from) previous reports, or recite medical records, but must briefly describe the patient's recent relevant medical history and current mental health presentation, and must include:

a) where the patient is aged 18 or over and the case is a reference to the tribunal, whether the patient has capacity to decide whether or not to attend or be represented at a tribunal hearing;

b) whether, if there is a hearing, there are any factors that may affect the patient's understanding or ability to cope with it, and whether there are any adjustments that the tribunal may consider in order to deal with the case fairly and justly;

c) details of any index offence(s) and other relevant forensic history;

d) a chronology listing the patient's previous involvement with mental health services including any admissions to, discharge from and recall to hospital;

e) reasons for any previous admission or recall to hospital;

f) the circumstances leading up to the patient's most recent admission to hospital;

g) the circumstances leading up to the patient's discharge onto a CTO;

h) any conditions to which the patient is subject under Section 17B, and details of the patient's compliance;

i) whether the patient is now suffering from a mental disorder and, if so, what the diagnosis is and why;

j) whether the patient has a learning disability and, if so, whether that disability is associated with abnormally aggressive or seriously irresponsible conduct;

k) whether the patient has a mental disorder of a nature or degree such as to make it appropriate for the patient to receive medical treatment;

l) details of any appropriate and available medical treatment prescribed, provided, offered or planned for the patient's mental disorder;

m) the strengths or positive factors relating to the patient;

n) a summary of the patient's current progress, behaviour, capacity and insight;

o) the patient's understanding of, compliance with, and likely future willingness to accept any prescribed medication or comply with any appropriate medical treatment for mental disorder that is or might be made available;

p) details of any incidents where the patient has harmed themselves or others, or threatened harm, or damaged property, or threatened damage;

s) whether it is necessary for the patient's health or safety, or for the protection of others, that the patient should receive medical treatment and, if so, why;

t) whether the patient, if discharged from the CTO, would be likely to act in a manner dangerous to themselves or others;

u) whether, and if so how, any risks could be managed effectively in the community;

v) whether it continues to be necessary that the Responsible Clinician should be able to exercise the power of recall and, if so, why;

w) any recommendations to the tribunal, with reasons.

Social Circumstances Report – Community Patients

3-204 **19.** The report must be up-to-date, specifically prepared for the tribunal and have numbered paragraphs and pages. It should be signed and dated. The sources of information for the events and incidents described must be made clear. This report should not be an addendum to (or reproduce extensive details from) previous reports, but must briefly describe the patient's recent relevant history and current presentation, and must include:

a) whether there are any factors that might affect the patient's understanding or ability to cope with a hearing, and whether there are any adjustments that the tribunal may consider in order to deal with the case fairly and justly;

b) details of any index offence(s), and other relevant forensic history;

c) a chronology listing the patient's previous involvement with mental health services including any admissions to, discharge from and recall to hospital;

d) the patient's home and family circumstances;

e) the housing or accommodation currently available to the patient;

f) the patient's financial position (including benefit entitlements);

g) any employment or available opportunities for employment;

h) any conditions to which the patient is subject under Section 17B, and details of the patient's compliance;

i) the patient's previous response to community support or Section 117 aftercare;

j) details of the community support or Section 117 after-care that is being, or could be made available to the patient, together with details of the current care plan;

k) whether there are any issues as to funding the current or future care plan and, if so, the date by which those issues will be resolved;

l) the current adequacy and effectiveness of the care plan;

m) the strengths or positive factors relating to the patient;

n) a summary of the patient's current progress, behaviour, compliance and insight;

o) details of any incidents where the patient has harmed themselves or others, or threatened harm, or damaged property, or threatened damage;

p)   the patient's views, wishes, beliefs, opinions, hopes and concerns;

q)   the views of the patient's Nearest Relative unless (having consulted the patient) it would inappropriate or impractical to consult the Nearest Relative, in which case give reasons for this view and describe any attempts to rectify matters;

r)   the views of any other person who takes a lead role in the care and support of the patient but who is not professionally involved;

s)   whether the patient is known to any Multi Agency Public Protection Arrangements (MAPPA) meeting or agency and, if so, in which area, for what reason, and at what level – together with the name of the Chair of any MAPPA meeting concerned with the patient, and the name of the representative of the lead agency;

t)   in the event that a MAPPA meeting or agency wishes to put forward evidence of its views in relation to the level and management of risk, a summary of those views (or an Executive Summary may be attached to the report); and where relevant, a copy of the Police National Computer record of previous convictions should be attached;

u)   whether it is necessary for the patient's health or safety, or for the protection of others, that the patient should receive medical treatment and, if so, why;

v)   whether the patient, if discharged from the CTO, would be likely to act in a manner dangerous to themselves or others;

w)   whether, and if so how, any risks could be managed effectively in the community;

x)   whether it continues to be necessary that the Responsible Clinician should be able to exercise the power of recall and, if so, why;

y)   any recommendations to the tribunal, with reasons.

C.   Guardianship Patients

20.   If the patient has been received into guardianship the Responsible Authority   **3-205**
must send to the tribunal the following documents, containing the specified information, so that they are received by the tribunal as soon as practicable and in any event within 3 weeks after the Authority made or received a copy of the application or reference:

- *Statement of Information about the Patient.*
- *Responsible Clinician's Report, including any relevant forensic history.*
- *Social Circumstances Report including details of any Care Pathway Approach (CPA) and, where appropriate, the additional information required for patients under the age of 18, and any input from a Multi Agency Public Protection Arrangements (MAPPA) agency or meeting.*

21.   The authors of reports should have personally met and be familiar with the patient. If an existing report becomes out-of-date, or if the status or the -circumstances of the patient change after the reports have been written but before the tribunal hearing takes place, the author of the report should then send to the tribunal an addendum addressing the up-to-date situation and, where necessary, the new applicable statutory criteria.

Statement of Information about the Patient – Guardianship Patients

3-206   **22.**   The statement provided to the tribunal should be up-to-date, signed and dated, specifically prepared for the tribunal, and must include:
  a)   the patient's full name, date of birth, and current place of residence;
  b)   the full official name of the Responsible Authority;
  c)   the patient's first language/dialect and, if it is not English, whether an interpreter is required and, if so, in which language/dialect;
  d)   if the patient is deaf, whether the patient will require the services of British Sign Language Interpreters and/or a Relay Interpreter;
  e)   a chronological table listing:
    • the dates of any previous admissions to, discharge from or recall to hospital, stating whether the admissions were compulsory or voluntary;
    • the dates of any previous instances of reception into guardianship;
    • the date of reception into current guardianship, stating the nature of the application, order or direction that constitutes the original authority for the guardianship of the patient;
    • the dates and outcomes of any tribunal hearings over the last three years;
  f)   the name and address of any private guardian;
  g)   the name of the patient's Responsible Clinician and the date when the patient came under the care of that clinician;
  h)   the name and contact details of the patient's Care Co-ordinator, Community Psychiatric Nurse, and/or Social Worker/AMHP;
  i)   the name and address of any legal representative acting for the patient;
  j)   the name and address of the patient's Nearest Relative or of the person exercising that function, whether the patient has made any request that their Nearest Relative should not be consulted or should not be kept informed about the patient's care or treatment and, if so, the details of any such request, whether the Responsible Authority believes that the patient has capacity to make such a request and the reasons for that belief;
  k)   the name and address of any other person who plays a significant part in the care of the patient but who is not professionally involved;
  l)   details of any legal proceedings or other arrangements relating to the patient's mental capacity, or their ability to make decisions or handle their own affairs.

Responsible Clinician's Report – Guardianship patients

3-207   **23.**   The report must be up-to-date, specifically prepared for the tribunal and have numbered paragraphs and pages. It should be signed and dated. The report should be written or counter-signed by the patient's Responsible Clinician. The sources of information for the events and incidents described must be made clear. This report should not be an addendum to (or reproduce extensive details from) previous reports, or recite medical records, but must briefly describe the patient's recent relevant medical history and current mental health presentation, and must include:
  a)   whether there are any factors that may affect the patient's understanding or ability to cope with a hearing, and whether there are any adjustments that the tribunal may consider in order to deal with the case fairly and justly;
  b)   details of any index offence(s), and other relevant forensic history;

[830]

c) a chronology listing the patient's previous involvement with mental health services including any admissions to, discharge from and recall to hospital, and any previous instances of reception into guardianship;

d) the circumstances leading up to the patient's reception into guardianship;

e) any requirements to which the patient is subject under Section 8(1), and details of the patient's compliance,

f) whether the patient is now suffering from a mental disorder and, if so, what the diagnosis is and why;

g) whether the patient has a learning disability and, if so, whether that disability is associated with abnormally aggressive or seriously irresponsible conduct;

h) details of any appropriate and available medical treatment prescribed, provided offered or planned for the patient's mental disorder;

i) the strengths or positive factors relating to the patient;

j) a summary of the patient's current progress, behaviour, capacity and insight;

k) the patient's understanding of, compliance with, and likely future willingness to accept any prescribed medication or comply with any appropriate medical treatment for mental disorder that is, or might be, made available;

l) details of any incidents where the patient has harmed themselves or others, or threatened harm, or damaged property, or threatened damage;

m) whether, and if so how, any risks could be managed effectively in the community;

n) whether it is necessary for the welfare of the patient, or for the protection of others, that the patient should remain under guardianship and, if so, why;

o) any recommendations to the tribunal, with reasons.

Social Circumstances Report – Guardianship Patients

24. The report must be up-to-date, specifically prepared for the tribunal and have **3-208** numbered paragraphs and pages. It should be signed and dated. The sources of information for the events and incidents described should be made clear. This report should not be an addendum to (or reproduce extensive details from) previous reports, but must briefly describe the patient's recent relevant history and current presentation, and must include:

a) whether there are any factors that might affect the patient's understanding or ability to cope with a hearing, and whether there are any adjustments that the tribunal may consider in order to deal with the case fairly and justly;

b) details of any index offence(s), and other relevant forensic history;

c) a chronology listing the patient's previous involvement with mental health services including any admissions to, discharge from and recall to hospital, and any previous instances of reception into guardianship;

d) the patient's home and family circumstances;

e) the housing or accommodation currently available to the patient;

f) the patient's financial position (including benefit entitlements);

g) any employment or available opportunities for employment;

h) any requirements to which the patient is subject under Section 8(1), and details of the patient's compliance,

i) the patient's previous response to community support;

j) details of the community support that is being, or could be, made available to the patient, together with details of the current care plan;

k) the current adequacy and effectiveness of the care plan;

l)   whether there are any issues as to funding the current or future care plan and, if so, the date by which those issues will be resolved;

m)   the strengths or positive factors relating to the patient;

n)   a summary of the patient's current progress, behaviour, compliance and insight;

o)   details of any incidents where the patient has harmed themselves or others, or threatened harm, or damaged property, or threatened damage;

p)   the patient's views, wishes, beliefs, opinions, hopes and concerns;

q)   the views of the guardian;

r)   the views of the patient's Nearest Relative unless (having consulted the patient) it would inappropriate or impractical to consult the Nearest Relative, in which case give reasons for this view and describe any attempts to rectify matters;

s)   the views of any other person who takes a lead role in the care and support of the patient but who is not professionally involved;

t)   whether the patient is known to any MAPPA meeting or agency and, if so, in which area, for what reason, and at what level – together with the name of the Chair of any MAPPA meeting concerned with the patient, and the name of the representative of the lead agency;

u)   in the event that a MAPPA meeting or agency wishes to put forward evidence of its views in relation to the level and management of risk, a summary of those views (or an Executive Summary may be attached to the report); and where relevant, a copy of the Police National Computer record of previous convictions should be attached;

v)   whether, and if so how, any risks could be managed effectively in the community;

w)   whether it is necessary for the welfare of the patient, or for the protection of others, that the patient should remain under guardianship and, if so, why;

x)   any recommendations to the tribunal, with reasons.

D. Conditionally Discharged Patients

3-209 **25.** A conditionally discharged patient is a restricted patient who has been discharged from hospital into the community, subject to a condition that the patient will remain liable to be recalled to hospital for further treatment, should it become necessary. Other conditions may, in addition, be imposed by the tribunal, or by the Secretary of State (Ministry of Justice).

26. This part only applies to restricted patients who have actually been granted a Conditional Discharge and who are living in the community. In the case of a restricted patient detained in hospital, the tribunal may make a provisional decision to order a Conditional Discharge. Before it finally grants a Conditional Discharge, the tribunal may defer its decision so that satisfactory arrangements can be put in place. Unless and until the tribunal finally grants a Conditional Discharge, the patient remains an in-patient, and so the in-patient part of this Practice Direction (and not this part) applies.

27. Upon being notified by the tribunal of an application or reference, the Responsible Clinician must send or deliver the Responsible Clinician's Report, and any Social Supervisor must send or deliver the Social Circumstances Report. If there is no Social Supervisor, the Responsible Clinician's report should also provide the required social circumstances information.

28. The required reports, which must contain the specified information, are:
- *Responsible Clinician's Report, including any relevant forensic history.*
- *Social Circumstances Report from the patient's Social Supervisor, including details of any Section 117 aftercare plan and, where appropriate, the additional information required for patients under the age of 18, and any input from a Multi Agency Public Protection Arrangements (MAPPA) agency or meeting.*

29. The reports must be sent or delivered to the tribunal so that they are received by the tribunal as soon as practicable and in any event within 3 weeks after the Responsible Clinician or Social Supervisor (as the case may be) received the notification.

30. The Responsible Clinician and any Social Supervisor must also, at the same time, send copies of their reports to the Secretary of State (Ministry of Justice).

31. The authors of reports should have personally met and be familiar with the patient. If an existing report is more than six weeks old, or if the status or the circumstances of the patient change after the reports have been written but before the tribunal hearing takes place (e.g. if a patient is recalled), the author of the report should then send to the tribunal an addendum addressing the up-to-date situation and, where necessary, the new applicable statutory criteria.

Responsible Clinician's Report – Conditionally Discharged Patients

32. The report must be up-to-date, specifically prepared for the tribunal and have **3-210** numbered paragraphs and pages. It should be signed and dated. The report should be written or counter-signed by the patient's Responsible Clinician. If there is no Social Supervisor, the Responsible Clinician's report should also provide the required social circumstances information. The sources of information for the events and incidents described must be made clear. This report should not be an addendum to (or reproduce extensive details from) previous reports, or recite medical records, but must briefly describe the patient's recent relevant medical history and current mental health presentation, and must include:
- a) whether there are any factors that might affect the patient's understanding or ability to cope with a hearing, and whether there are any adjustments that the tribunal may consider in order to deal with the case fairly and justly;
- b) details of the patient's index offence(s), and any other relevant forensic history;
- c) details and details of the patient's relevant forensic history;
- d) a chronology listing the patient's involvement with mental health services including any admissions to, discharge from and recall to hospital;
- e) reasons for any previous recall following a Conditional Discharge and details of any previous failure to comply with conditions;
- f) the circumstances leading up to the current Conditional Discharge;
- g) any conditions currently imposed (whether by the tribunal or the Secretary of State), and the reasons why the conditions were imposed;
- h) details of the patient's compliance with any current conditions;
- i) whether the patient is now suffering from a mental disorder and, if so, what the diagnosis is and why;
- j) whether the patient has a learning disability and, if so, whether that dis-

ability is associated with abnormally aggressive or seriously irresponsible conduct;

k) details of any legal proceedings or other arrangements relating to the patient's mental capacity, or their ability to make decisions or handle their own affairs;

l) details of any appropriate and available medical treatment prescribed, provided, offered or planned for the patient's mental disorder;

m) the strengths or positive factors relating to the patient;

n) a summary of the patient's current progress, behaviour, capacity and insight;

o) the patient's understanding of, compliance with, and likely future willingness to accept any prescribed medication or comply with any appropriate medical treatment for mental disorder;

p) details of any incidents where the patient has harmed themselves or others, or threatened harm, or damaged property, or threatened damage;

q) an assessment of the patient's prognosis, including the risk and likelihood of a recurrence or exacerbation of any mental disorder;

r) the risk and likelihood of the patient re-offending and the degree of harm to which others may be exposed if the patient does re-offend;

s) whether it is necessary for the patient's health or safety, or for the protection of others, that the patient should receive medical treatment and, if so, why;

t) whether the patient, if absolutely discharged, would be likely to act in a manner harmful to themselves or others, whether any such risks could be managed effectively in the community and, if so, how;

u) whether it continues to be appropriate for the patient to remain liable to be recalled for further medical treatment in hospital and, if so, why;

v) whether, and if so the extent to which, it is desirable to continue, vary and/or add to any conditions currently imposed;

w) any recommendations to the tribunal, with reasons.

Social Circumstances Report – Conditionally Discharged Patients

3-211 33. The report must be up-to-date, specifically prepared for the tribunal and have numbered paragraphs and pages. It should be signed and dated. The sources of information for the events and incidents described should be made clear. This report should not be an addendum to (or reproduce extensive details from) previous reports, but must briefly describe the patient's recent relevant history and current presentation, and must include:

a) the patient's full name, date of birth, and current address;

b) the full official name of the Responsible Authority;

c) whether there are any factors that might affect the patient's understanding or ability to cope with a hearing, and whether there are any adjustments that the tribunal may consider in order to deal with the case fairly and justly;

d) details of the patient's index offence(s), and any other relevant forensic history;

e) a chronology listing the patient's involvement with mental health services including any admissions to, discharge from and recall to hospital;

f) any conditions currently imposed (whether by the tribunal or the Secretary of State), and the reasons why the conditions were imposed;

g) details of the patient's compliance with any past or current conditions;

h) the patient's home and family circumstances;

[834]

i)   the housing or accommodation currently available to the patient;

j)   the patient's financial position (including benefit entitlements);

k)   any employment or available opportunities for employment;

l)   details of the community support or Section 117 after-care that is being, or could be made available to the patient, together with details of the current care plan;

m)   whether there are any issues as to funding the current or future care plan and, if so, the date by which those issues will be resolved;

n)   the current adequacy and effectiveness of the care plan;

o)   the strengths or positive factors relating to the patient;

p)   a summary of the patient's current progress, compliance, behaviour and insight;

q)   details of any incidents where the patient has harmed themselves or others, or threatened harm, or damaged property, or threatened damage;

r)   the patient's views, wishes, beliefs, opinions, hopes and concerns;

s)   the views of any partner, family member or close friend who takes a lead role in the care and support of the patient but who is not professionally involved;

t)   whether the patient is known to any Multi Agency Public Protection Arrangements (MAPPA) meeting or agency and, if so, in which area, for what reason, and at what level – together with the name of the Chair of any MAPPA meeting concerned with the patient, and the name of the representative of the lead agency;

u)   in the event that a MAPPA meeting or agency wishes to put forward evidence of its views in relation to the level and management of risk, a summary of those views (or an Executive Summary may be attached to the report); and where relevant, a copy of the Police National Computer record of previous convictions should be attached;

v)   in the case of an eligible compliant patient who lacks capacity to agree or object to their placement or treatment, whether or not deprivation of liberty under the Mental Capacity Act 2005 (as amended) would be more appropriate;

w)   whether the patient, if absolutely discharged, would be likely to act in a manner harmful to themselves or others, whether any such risks could be managed effectively in the community and, if so, how;

x)   whether it continues to be appropriate for the patient to remain liable to be recalled for further medical treatment in hospital and, if so, why;

y)   whether, and if so the extent to which, it is desirable to continue, vary and/or add to any conditions currently imposed;

z)   any recommendations to the tribunal, with reasons.

E.   Patients Under the Age of 18

34.   All the above requirements in respect of statements and reports apply, as appropriate, depending upon the type of case.   **3-212**

35.   In addition, *for all patients under the age of 18*, the *Social Circumstances Report* must also state:

a)   the names and addresses of any people with parental responsibility, and how they acquired parental responsibility;

b) which public bodies either have worked together or need to liaise in relation to after-care services that may be provided under Section 117 of the Act;

c) the outcome of any liaison that has taken place;

d) if liaison has not taken place, why not – and when liaison will take place;

e) the details of any multi-agency care plan in place or proposed;

f) whether there are any issues as to funding the care plan and, if so, the date by which those issues will be resolved;

g) the name and contact details of the patient's Care Co-ordinator, Community Psychiatric Nurse, Social Worker/AMHP or Social Supervisor;

h) whether the patient's needs have been assessed under the Children Act 1989 or the Chronically Sick and Disabled Persons Act 1970 and, if not, the reasons why such an assessment has not been carried out and whether it is proposed to carry out such an assessment;

i) if there has been such an assessment, what needs or requirements have been identified and how those needs or requirements will be met;

j) if the patient is subject to or has been the subject of a Care Order or an Interim Care Order:
   - the date and duration of any such order;
   - the identity of the relevant local authority;
   - the identity of any person(s) with whom the local authority shares parental responsibility;
   - whether there are any proceedings which have yet to conclude and, if so, the court in which proceedings are taking place and the date of the next hearing;
   - whether the patient comes under the Children (Leaving Care) Act 2000;
   - whether there has been any liaison between, on the one hand, social workers responsible for mental health services to children and adolescents and, on the other hand, those responsible for such services to adults;
   - the name of the social worker within the relevant local authority who is discharging the function of the Nearest Relative under Section 27 of the Act;

k) if the patient is subject to guardianship under Section 7 of the Act, whether any orders have been made under the Children Act 1989 in respect of the patient, and what consultation there has been with the guardian;

l) if the patient is a Ward of Court, when the patient was made a ward of court and what steps have been taken to notify the court that made the order of any significant steps taken, or to be taken, in respect of the patient;

m) whether any other orders under the Children Act 1989 are in existence in respect of the patient and, if so, the details of those orders, together with the date on which such orders were made, and whether they are final or interim orders;

n) if a patient has been or is a looked after child under Section 20 of the Children Act 1989, when the child became looked after, why the child became looked after, what steps have been taken to discharge the obligations of the local authority under Paragraph 17(1) of Schedule 2 of the Children Act 1989, and what steps are being taken (if required) to discharge the obligations of the local authority under Paragraph 10 (b) of Schedule 2 of the Children Act 1989;

o) if a patient has been treated by a local authority as a child in need (which

[836]

includes a child who has a mental disorder) under Section 17(11) of the Children Act 1989, the period or periods for which the child has been so treated, why they were considered to be a child in need, what services were or are being made available to the child by virtue of that status, and details of any assessment of the child;

p) if a patient has been the subject of a secure accommodation order under Section 25 of the Children Act 1989, the date on which the order was made, the reasons it was made, and the date it expired;

q) if a patient is a child provided with accommodation under Sections 85 and 86 of the Children Act 1989, what steps have been taken by the accommodating authority or the person carrying on the establishment in question to discharge their notification responsibilities, and what steps have been taken by the local authority to discharge their obligations under Sections 85, 86 and 86A of the Children Act 1989.

PRACTICE DIRECTION FIRST TIER AND UPPER TRIBUNAL CHILD, VULNERABLE ADULT AND SENSITIVE WITNESSES

1. In this Practice Direction: 3-213
   a. "child" means a person who has not attained the age of 18;
   b. "vulnerable adult" has the same meaning as in the Safeguarding Vulnerable Groups Act 2006;
   c. "sensitive witness" means an adult witness where the quality of evidence given by the witness is likely to be diminished by reason of fear or distress on the part of the witness in connection with giving evidence in the case.

Circumstances Under Which a Child, Vulnerable Adult or Sensitve Witness May Give Evidence

2. A child, vulnerable adult or sensitive witness will only be required to attend as   3-214
a witness and give evidence at a hearing where the Tribunal determines that the evidence is necessary to enable the fair hearing of the case and their welfare would not be prejudiced by doing so.

3. In determining whether it is necessary for a child, vulnerable adult or sensitive witness to give evidence to enable the fair hearing of a case the Tribunal should have regard to all the available evidence and any representations made by the parties.

4. In determining whether the welfare of the child, vulnerable adult or sensitive witness would be prejudiced it may be appropriate for the Tribunal to invite submissions from interested persons, such as a child's parents.

5. The Tribunal may decline to issue a witness summons under the Tribunal Procedure Rules or to permit a child, vulnerable adult or sensitive witness to give evidence where it is satisfied that the evidence is not necessary to enable the fair hearing of the case and must decline to do so where the witness's welfare would be prejudiced by them giving evidence.

Manner in Which Evidence is Given

3-215   6.   The Tribunal must consider how to facilitate the giving of any evidence by a child, vulnerable adult or sensitive witness.

7.   It may be appropriate for the Tribunal to direct that the evidence should be given by telephone, video link or other means directed by the Tribunal, or to direct that a person be appointed for the purpose of the hearing who has the appropriate skills or experience in facilitating the giving of evidence by a child, vulnerable adult or sensitive witness.

8.   This Practice Direction is made by the Senior President of Tribunals with the agreement of the Lord Chancellor. It is made in the exercise of powers conferred by the Tribunals, Courts and Enforcement Act 2007.
LORD JUSTICE CARNWATH
SENIOR PRESIDENT OF TRIBUNALS
30 October 2008

Practice Statement

PRACTICE STATEMENT DELEGATION OF FUNCTIONS TO REGISTRARS, TRIBUNAL CASE WORKERS AND AUTHORISED TRIBUNAL STAFF ON OR AFTER 8 JULY 2016

FIRST-TIER TRIBUNAL HEALTH, EDUCATION & SOCIAL CARE CHAMBER (MENTAL HEALTH)

3-216   1.   This Practice Statement replaces the previous Practice Statement for mental health cases dated 27th April 2015 in respect of authorised tribunal staff and approved Registrars.

2.   In accordance with rule 4(1) of The Tribunal Procedure (First-tier Tribunal) (Health, Education and Social Care Chamber) Rules 2008 the Senior President of Tribunals hereby approves that, in relation to mental health cases (as defined in rule 1(3)), the following specified functions of the Health, Education & Social Care Chamber of the First-tier Tribunal may be carried out by certain members of staff appointed under section 40(1) of the Tribunals, Courts and Enforcement Act 2007 where those members of staff have been jointly authorised by an Operations Manager (B and C) and a salaried tribunal judge (nominated by the relevant Deputy Chamber President) of the First-tier Tribunal (HESC – Mental Health) to exercise some or all of these functions, and in accordance with any standard operating procedures (known as "Job Cards") approved from time to time, by the relevant Deputy Chamber President:
    (a)   Under rule 5(3)(a), and unless such extension would conflict with a provision of another enactment containing a time limit), to extend the time for:
        i.   submission of reports under rule 32(4)(b) and rule 32(6); and
        ii.   complying with any other rule, practice direction or direction so long as all parties agree
    (b)   Under rule 5(3)(b), to issue an order for two or more sets of proceedings in

relation to the same patient and involving identical parties to be heard together;

(c) Under rule 5(3)(d), to issue standard directions for a party or person to provide any specified documents or information relevant to the proceedings. The directions are to be in standard form as approved, from time to time, by the relevant Deputy Chamber President;

(d) Under rule 5(3)(g), to grant permission for witnesses to give evidence by video/telephone link so long as the parties are in agreement and the Responsible Authority has confirmed the necessary equipment is available at the hearing venue;

(e) Under rule 5(3)(h), to bring hearings forward or grant postponements, so long as the change of date is agreed by the parties and the new date can be accommodated by the tribunal and is within the case listing window;

(f) Under rule 11(7), to appoint a legal representative for the patient;

(g) Under rule 15(1), to issue standard directions for a party or person to give written evidence or provide submissions relevant to the proceedings. The directions are to be in standard form as approved, from time to time, by the relevant Deputy Chamber President;

(h) Under rule 17(2), to consent to a notice of withdrawal lodged by or on behalf of a patient by a representative under rule 17(1)(a);

(i) Under rule 44, to correct a clear and obvious clerical mistake, or other clear and obvious accidental slips or omissions, in any document recording a decision or direction of the tribunal.

3. In accordance with rule 4(1) of The Tribunal Procedure (First-tier Tribunal) (Health, Education and Social Care Chamber) Rules 2008 the Senior President of Tribunals hereby approves that, in relation to mental health cases (as defined in rule 1(3)), the following functions of the Health, Education & Social Care Chamber of the First-tier Tribunal may be carried out by certain members of staff appointed under section 40(1) of the Tribunals, Courts and Enforcement Act 2007 where those members of staff have been designated by the Chamber President of the Health, Education and Social Care Chamber as either a "Registrar" or "Tribunal Case Worker", and have been authorised by the Chamber President or the relevant Deputy Chamber President (HESC) to exercise some or all of these functions:

(a) Under rule 5, to exercise any case management powers except under rule 5(3)(l);

(b) Under rule 7(2)(a) or (b), to deal with any irregularities;

(c) Under rule 8(3)(a), to strike out proceedings if the tribunal does not have jurisdiction;

(d) Under rule 9, to give directions to substitute or to add a party or parties;

(e) Under rule 11(7), to appoint a legal representative for the patient;

(f) Under rule 14, to prohibit disclosure or publication of documents or information;

(g) Under rule 15(1), to give directions in relation to the giving or oral or written evidence and submissions;

(h) Under rule 16, to summons witnesses and issue orders to persons to answer questions or produce documents;

(i) Under rule 17, to consent to the withdrawal of a case, or to direct reinstatement of a case;

(j) Under rule 33, to decide to whom notice of proceedings should be sent;

(k) Under rule 44, to correct clerical mistakes or other accidental slips or omissions in decisions or records of decisions;

(l) Under rule 4(3), to exercise the powers of a judge where an authorized member of tribunal staff has made the initial decision under the delegated powers set out in paragraph 2 of this Practice Statement;

(m) In the case of a Registrar only, under rule 4(3), to exercise the powers of a judge where a Tribunal Case Worker has made the initial decision under the delegated powers set out in paragraph 3 of this Practice Statement.

4. In accordance with rule 4(3) of the Tribunal Procedure (First Tier Tribunal) (Health Education and Social Care Chamber) Rules 2008, within 14 days after the date that the tribunal sends notice of a decision made by an authorised member of tribunal staff (pursuant to an approval under paragraph 2 above), or a Registrar or Tribunal Case Worker (pursuant to an approval under paragraph 3 above) to a party or person, that party or person may apply in writing to the tribunal for the decision to be considered afresh and, if so, it will be considered afresh by a judge or, under paragraph 3(l) or 3(m) above, by a Registrar or Tribunal Case Worker, as appropriate.

SIR ERNEST RYDER
SENIOR PRESIDENT OF TRIBUNALS
7 July 2016

FIRST-TIER TRIBUNAL HEALTH, EDUCATION & SOCIAL CARE CHAMBER (MENTAL HEALTH) ENFORCEMENT PROCEDURE, DIRECTIONS AND SUMMONSES

The Responsible Authority's duty to provide its written evidence within 3 weeks.

3-217 **1.** Except where the patient is detained for assessment under Section 2 Mental Health Act 1983, or is already subject to a Conditional Discharge, the Responsible Authority has a statutory duty to send or deliver the written evidence specified in the "Senior President's Practice Direction on the Contents of Statements and Reports in Mental Health Cases" to the tribunal office so that the documents are received by the tribunal within the period of 3 weeks after the Responsible Authority made the reference or received a copy of the application or reference.

2. Generally, the Responsible Authority will be the Hospital Managers. Thus, for an NHS hospital, this will be the relevant NHS Trust, and for a private hospital, this will be the managing or controlling company owning or running the hospital.

3. For patients who are already subject to a Conditional Discharge, it is the Responsible Clinician and any Social Supervisor named by the Secretary of State who must send or deliver the written evidence specified in the Senior President's Practice Direction to the tribunal office – again, within the period of 3 weeks after being notified by the tribunal of an application or reference being received in the tribunal office.

4. The full disclosure in writing (in advance of the hearing) of the Responsible

Authority's evidence, or the evidence of the Responsible Clinician and Social Supervisor, is essential in the interests of fairness and natural justice, and the timely and prompt submission of this written evidence (including key information about the patient) is vital, not least because the freedom of patients subject to the Mental Health Act 1983 is involved in all tribunal cases, even if the patient is not currently detained in hospital.

5. For Section 2 patients, due to the importance of a speedy and effective hearing, the specified written evidence cannot usually be made available more than a short time in advance, but it must be made available in the tribunal hearing room, and to the patient's legal representative, at least one hour before the hearing is due to start.

6. The written evidence specified in the Senior President's Practice Direction depends upon the type of case. For detained patients, the written evidence comprises a Statement of Information about the Patient (formerly known as the "Part A Statement"), the Responsible Clinician's Report, a Nursing Report, and a Social Circumstances Report.

7. If the patient is not detained in hospital, the requirement for a Nursing Report is dispensed with, and if the patient is subject to a Conditional Discharge, the requirement for a Statement of Information is dispensed with.

8. Whether or not the patient is placed out of area, the Responsible Authority must ensure that all statements and reports, including the Social Circumstances report, contain all the information listed in the relevant part of the Senior President's Practice Direction.

9. The obligation to arrange for the writing and submission of the specified statements and reports, on time, lies with the Responsible Authority and their nominated statement and report-writers including the Responsible Clinician, Key Nurse, and Social Workers or Supervisor. It is *totally unacceptable* for social circumstances reports to be delayed or missing because of negotiations with the locality team about who will prepare the social circumstances report. The Responsible Authority may ask the locality team to prepare the report, but they cannot hand over the legal duty to provide it on time.

The Responsible Authority's duty to cooperate with the tribunal, and provide the full identity and secure contact details of its statement and report writers

10. The Responsible Authority has a legal duty to cooperate with the tribunal. Where the tribunal advises the Responsible Authority that a case has been registered it also (amongst other things) asks the Responsible Authority to provide the personal secure contact details of its statement and report writers. A personal secure email address or a postal address is acceptable, but a non-secure email address is not acceptable because confidential patient details will always be included in any subsequent directions sent by the tribunal.   **3-218**

11. The tribunal directs the provision of this contact information so that, if a statement or a report is not submitted by the three-week deadline, it can *promptly* remind the person responsible for the document that their personal written evidence is urgently due, and (by Form MH5 sent personally to the named person in default) direct its immediate submission to the tribunal.

12. Most Responsible Authorities discharge their duties to the tribunal via their Mental Health Act Administrator (MHAA). Thus, except where the patient is subject to a Conditional Discharge, it usually falls to the Responsible Authority's MHAA to provide the Statement of Information about the Patient, and to identify the professionals who must provide the written and oral evidence on behalf of the Responsible Authority. The MHAA is expected to provide the names and secure contact details of the person who will prepare the Statement of Information about the Patient (usually the MHAA himself or herself), and of the report writers that the Responsible Authority has nominated to prepare the Responsible Authority's written evidence. This is because the Responsible Authority's MHAA will (or should) know the identity of the patient's Responsible Clinician, Key Nurse and Social Worker(s), and it is the Responsible Authority's MHAA that will ask for, or arrange for, the statement and reports to be prepared for the tribunal.

13. If, before the written evidence is submitted to the tribunal, the identity or personal secure contact details of the relevant witness changes, the Responsible Authority must immediately provide updated information to the tribunal.

14. If a direct secure email address cannot be provided for any named report or statement writer, a generic secure email address may be provided BUT the following undertaking must be given and complied with by the MHAA:

> "*If a generic email address is given above, I undertake that any directions or summonses addressed to the named report-writer and sent to that address WILL be forwarded direct to the named person within one working day, AND that proof of this will be retained and produced to the tribunal upon request.*"

15. Where it can, the tribunal will send notifications and directions to the relevant MHAA and to named report writers. However, due process cannot be defeated by a willful or negligent failure by the Responsible Authority, the MHAA or report-writers to provide the information and evidence that the tribunal needs, at the time that the tribunal needs it.

16. Ultimately, it is the Responsible Authority's Chief Executive that -personifies and represents the Responsible Authority. So, if the MHAA or other professionals employed by or working with the Responsible Authority do not sufficiently cooperate with the tribunal in any case, or generally, then it is likely that directions and summonses will thereafter be sent to the Chief Executive personally, and the Chief Executive will then have a personal and enforceable duty to provide the evidence, and attend the hearing.

17. Unfortunately, some Responsible Authorities (or MHAAs) do not provide the tribunal with accurate identity and contact details, or they fail to keep the tribunal up to date if the details change. This is extremely unhelpful and prevents the tribunal taking any workable steps to enforce compliance with the law. It is also inconsistent with the legal duty on the parties to cooperate with the tribunal. If the tribunal is not provided with the information required as to the identity and contact details of statement and report-writers, it will send just one reminder (Forn MHAA. Thereafter, if necessary, the tribunal will send directions an⟨ to the Responsible Authority's Chief Executive.

18. Whether or not those responsible for giving the Responsible Autho ten evidence are identified by name with contact details provided, th⟨ expects that the statements and reports will be submitted by the legally � ..cd three-week deadline.

19. If need be, and if there are good grounds for doing so, an application to extend the three-week deadline can be made to the tribunal and a judicial decision will be made as to whether (or not) to grant an extension. But the three-week deadline must not be ignored, and any extension granted *must* be adhered to without any additional delay.

The Responsible Authority's duty to arrange for the attendance of witnesses

20. Once the Responsible Authority has provided its written evidence, as speci-   **3-219** fied by law, the onus then falls upon the Responsible Authority, as a party to the proceedings, to ensure the attendance of such witnesses as it considers necessary to establish its case.

21. There is a convention and an expectation that all the report-writers will attend to give oral evidence. This is so that the report-writers can give the tribunal an update, and be questioned by or on behalf of the patient, and by the tribunal. Generally, there is no expectation that the MHAA will attend because the Statement of Information about the patient is likely to be factual, a matter of record, and uncontroversial. However, if the Statement of Information is not provided, the tribunal may have to formally direct a named MHAA to provide the Statement, and therefore the identity of the relevant MHAA is required. If the identity of the relevant MHAA is not provided, the tribunal will have to send any formal directions to the Responsible Authority's Chief Executive.

22. Despite the convention and expectation that the Responsible Authority will arrange for its report-writers to attend the tribunal hearing, *the written evidence is ultimately the Responsible Authority's evidence, and it is for the Responsible Authority (and not the tribunal) to identify the required witnesses.* It may also be necessary for a different professional to attend the hearing if the original report-writer is unavailable, and this is usually permissible to support the Responsible Authority's case so long as the alternative witness is suitable qualified and sufficiently aware of the patient's circumstances to substitute for the report-writer.

23. However, if the Responsible Authority is asked by the patient's legal representative to make a particular witness available at the hearing, then it should make arrangements to comply with the request, or advise the patient's legal representative why it will not, or cannot, do so.

The Legal Representative's Duties

24. The patient is a party to the proceedings and, as in all legal cases before courts   **3-220** and tribunals, the parties' legal representatives must be prepared to take appropriate steps ahead of the hearing to obtain the written evidence and attendance of witnesses that they consider to be necessary, in order to properly prepare and present their client's case.

25. Consequently, in relation to the provision of evidence by the Responsible Authority, there is a clear duty on the patient's legal representative to chase up any missing written evidence directly with the Responsible Authority.

26. The tribunal considers that legal representatives cannot legitimately complain about a missing statement, report or witness if they have not taken all the necessary steps to ensure that the written evidence is made available to them in advance of the hearing, and that any witness that they deem necessary will attend at the hearing.

27. If all efforts to engage directly with the Responsible Authority fail, the patient's legal representative may then ask the tribunal to issue directions or summonses. However, it will always be necessary for legal representatives to explain what efforts they have themselves made to secure compliance and the submission of the statements and reports.

28. Similarly, legal representatives *cannot* expect to be granted an adjournment at a hearing just because written evidence is missing, or because a witness has not attended, if they have not taken all necessary steps to obtain the evidence or secure the witness's attendance in advance of the hearing, or if they have failed apply for a postponement in good time, prior to the listed hearing, as soon as it became apparent that there was a problem that could not be resolved in time. Any request for a postponement (or to withdraw an application to the tribunal) must be made before 4.30pm on the working day before the hearing, otherwise it will be too late for it to be decided in the office, and the request will be left for the panel to decide after it has convened at the hearing venue.

What will the tribunal do to enforce compliance?

3-221 **29.** Although the tribunal has no duty laid down in the Act or the applicable procedure rules to chase-up the parties, it will generally try to take certain routine steps intended to advise and remind responsible professionals of their duties. However, these steps are inevitably standard procedures, require the full cooperation of the Responsible Authority and others, and do not and cannot replace the duty on all parties and their legal representatives to ensure that the required written and oral evidence is made available at the appropriate time. It is the parties' shared duty to avoid the upset and wastefulness of a panel convening – only then to be asked to adjourn because a report or witness is missing. If that happens, and all necessary steps have not been taken to secure the report or witness, the answer is likely to be a refusal to adjourn.

The MH5 direction to a named person to immediately provide written evidence

3-222 **30.** If a statement or a report is not submitted by the three-week deadline, the tribunal may remind the person responsible that their written evidence is immediately due, and (by Form MH5 sent to the person in default) direct its immediate submission to the tribunal.

[844]

31. The purpose of the MH5 direction is to remind the person responsible, or the Chief Executive of the Responsible Authority, that the law has not been complied with and that the written evidence is immediately required. The tribunal needs, by law, to be able to send the MH5 direction to a named person, requiring that person immediately to give their written evidence to the tribunal in the form of a compliant report or statement.

32. For the MH5 direction to be of practical benefit and enforceable, it must be sent to the named person who has been nominated (by the Responsible Authority) to give the written evidence in question. This is why the MHAA is asked at an early stage to provide the identity and secure contact details of the Responsible Authority's statement and report writers. A personal secure email address or a postal address is acceptable, but a non-secure email address is not acceptable because patient details are confidential.

33. An MH5 will only be sent if a statement or report is overdue, and the MH5 will, therefore, direct the *immediate* submission of the late report or statement. It is not appropriate for professionals to wait until an MH5 is received before starting to think about the required written evidence. The tribunal does not believe that failure to comply with the three-week deadline should result in (or be rewarded by) extra time being automatically given. By the time an MH5 direction is sent, the report is already late.

34. If the recipient of an MH5 direction considers that he or she has been wrongly identified by the Responsible Authority as responsible for providing a written statement or report, or if they are no longer responsible, then they must apply to have the direction set aside, and reasons for the request must be given. Thereafter, the tribunal will send directions to the Responsible Authority's Chief Executive as the tribunal cannot spend time chasing up the Responsible Authority for the correct or updated details, and cannot get involved in a dispute as to who is responsible for giving the written evidence to the tribunal.

Failure to comply with a personal MH5 Direction to give written evidence

35. Failure to give the specified written evidence when directed to do so can result in the failure being referred to the Upper Tribunal for consideration of penalty. Even if we decide not to refer the failure, we are very likely to seek both an explanation and a binding undertaking that it will not happen again. If the First-tier Tribunal does refer the default, then the Upper Tribunal has a wide range of powers to impose a punishment.   **3-223**

Summonses

36. The tribunal may issue a summons of its own volition, or on the request of a party. Following failure to comply with a direction to give written evidence, the tribunal will not issue any more directions to the person in default. It will simply move to a possible referral to the Upper Tribunal and may also issue a summons to the person in default, requiring their personal attendance at the hearing. Where it has been left with no alternative, the tribunal will summons the Responsible Authority's Chief Executive. It must be understood, however, that the issue of a summons does not mean that the outstanding report is no longer required because, obviously, the requirement remains.   **3-224**

37. Failure to comply with a summons is punishable by the Upper Tribunal as contempt. The tribunal will generally be reluctant to summons a MHAA but, if a MH5 direction addressed to the MHAA has not been complied with, the tribunal may refer the matter to the Upper Tribunal because the Statement of Information is legally required, and provides the tribunal with vital information about the patient's history and circumstances.

M Hinchliffe (Deputy Chamber President)
24/7/2017

PART 4: GOVERNMENT GUIDANCE

(FEBRUARY 2009)

Introduction

1. The recall of a conditionally discharged patient is one of the most significant **4-001** decisions taken at official level in Mental Health Casework Section (MHCS) on behalf of the Secretary of State as it deprives an individual of his or her liberty. While we issue Guidance Notes to Psychiatric Supervisors at the point of conditional discharge in every case, the statement below is a detailed explanation of our policy on recalls. This is the same statement of policy as used by officials in MHCS when determining whether to recall in a particular case. It is not, of course, possible to cover every eventuality but hopefully the guidance below will cover the major issues that regularly crop up in respect of conditionally discharged restricted patients. I should emphasis that this does not supersede or replace the Guidance Notes to Psychiatric Supervisors, but complements the guidance contained within that booklet.

The legislation

2. Section 42(3) of the Mental Health Act 1983 provides that: **4-002**

The Secretary of State may at any time during the continuance in force of a restriction order in respect of a patient who has been conditionally discharged under subsection (2) above by warrant recall the patient to such hospital as may be specified in the warrant

3. The legislation gives the Secretary of State a broad power of recall that applies to any conditionally discharged restricted patient. The parameters of how that power must be exercised have been set by case law. It follows that, while the power under the legislation is a broad one, any policy on its use formulated by Mental Health Casework Section and agreed by Ministers must be within the parameters established by case law.

The case law

4. The key case law on the use of recall powers establishes that: **4-003**
    - In order for the Justice Secretary to recall there must be evidence of mental disorder of a nature or degree warranting detention (following *Winterwerp v Netherlands* (1979) as reflected in the Mental Health Act 1983).
    - In order to justify recall and before recalling the Justice Secretary must have up to date medical evidence showing that these legal criteria for detention are met (see *R(B) v MHRT* [2002] All ER (D) 304 (Jul)), *except in an emergency* (see *K v United Kingdom* (1998)). In an emergency such evidence *must be* obtained as soon as possible following recall.
    - There is no statutory requirement for the Justice Secretary to obtain the

agreement of the hospital doctors to re-admit a recalled patient. The Justice Secretary is entitled to take a different view to that of the supervising psychiatrist, provided there are sufficient grounds/evidence to justify this and satisfy the Secretary of State that the criteria for detention under the Mental Health Act are met.

- The Justice Secretary can recall a patient where the mental disorder at time of recall is different from that at time of discharge (see *R (AL) v SSHD* [2005] EWCA Civ 02).
- There is no need for the patient's mental health to have necessarily deteriorated in order to justify recall. If a patient has a mental disorder and is presenting an elevated risk linked to that disorder that warrants detention in hospital then the patient can be recalled. In such a case the criteria for detention would be met because the disorder was of a nature (rather than degree) that warranted detention in hospital and this is necessary for the protection of other persons.
- Similarly, where the primary concern relates to a deterioration (or potential deterioration) in a patient's mental state then this will be evidence that the disorder is of a degree that warrants detention in hospital.

Mental Health Casework Section's policy on recalls

4-004 **5.** Mental Health Casework Section's policy is that patients will be recalled where it is necessary to protect the public from the actual or potential risk posed by that patient *and* that risk is linked to the patient's mental disorder. It is not possible to specify all the circumstances when recall will be appropriate but public safety will always be the most important factor.

- Decision on whether to recall largely turns on the degree of danger the patient might present. The gravity of any potential or actual risk will be relevant factors as will how imminent such a risk is. The more immediate the risk the more likely that recall will be indicated. Similarly, the more serious the risk or potential risk the more likely that recall is indicated.
- Recall does not require any evidence of deterioration in the patient's mental state. However, except in an emergency, medical evidence is required that the patient is currently mentally disordered.
- Recall will not be used to deal with anti-social or offending behaviour that is unconnected with the patient's mental disorder.
- Recall decisions always give precedence to public safety considerations. This may mean that the Justice Secretary will decide to recall on public safety grounds even though the supervising psychiatrist may be of the view that recall would be counter-therapeutic for the patient.
- Recall will be considered where it appears necessary for the protection of others from harm because of a combination of the patient's mental disorder and his behaviour. This includes potential behaviour where there is evidence that indicates the imminent likelihood of risk behaviours.
- In an emergency the Justice Secretary will recall for assessment in the absence of any fresh evidence as regards mental disorder.
- The fact that recall may not be supported by one or both the supervisors will be relevant in considering recall but not determinative. The Justice Secretary can and should recall, if his judgement is that recall is indicated on the evidence, even though the supervisors may not be recommending recall.
- Where recall is supported by at least one supervisor, then the expectation

is that the patient should be recalled unless there are compelling reasons not to recall.

Alcohol and substance abuse

6. Substance (or alcohol) misuse cannot, of itself, lead to recall, even if it is in breach of the patient's conditions of discharge. Substance (and alcohol) misuse will lead to consideration of recall if there is evidence that these are risk behaviours and/or such misuse is known to have had a detrimental effect on the patient's mental state. It is not necessary to wait for the patient's mental state to deteriorate, if there is evidence of a pattern of behaviour likely to lead to such a deterioration. What constitutes such a pattern will, of course, depend upon the circumstances of the case. **4-005**

Defaulting on medication

7. Non-compliance with medication will lead to consideration of recall. Whether recall is indicated will, of course, turn on the circumstances of the particular case. Relevant factors will include: **4-006**
- whether there is a pattern of non-compliance with medication (and a history of such non-compliance)
- is this a "one-off"?
- whether there is also evidence of a general disengagement with supervision, or other relevant factors such as substance misuse
- the inter-relationship between compliance with medication and relapse, including the likely rapidity of any deterioration in the patient's mental state
- crucially, the potential risk to others as a result of non-compliance.

Informal admissions

8. Recall must be considered where there is any admission to psychiatric hospital. As with any consideration of recall, public safety is of paramount importance. In deciding whether recall is indicated where a patient has been informally admitted to hospital, relevant factors are: **4-007**
- the likely length of admission. If an admission of more than a few weeks is likely then recall is indicated, unless there are compelling reasons against recall.
- any evidence of increased risk to others will lead to recall.
- regardless of the fact that the patient is in hospital voluntarily, would the supervising psychiatrist seek to detain the patient if he wished, or attempted to leave?

9. In answering these questions we are guided by the information provided by, and discussions with the supervisors and our knowledge of the background, history and risk factors in the case. For example, has the patient a pattern of rapid deterioration or previous non-compliance?

10. Where a decision is taken not to recall but to allow the informal admission to continue then the case must be reviewed regularly. A weekly up-date will normally be appropriate, but a longer period may be indicated depending upon the circumstances of the case.

Informal admissions and risk of self-harm/suicide

4-008 **11.** Where a patient has been informally admitted because of risk of self-harm/suicide and there is no evidence of risk to others, it may not be appropriate to recall. Again, it is not possible to cover the differing circumstances of cases but the following principles should be applied in considering the case.

12. If the medical evidence is that the patient does not meet the criteria for compulsory detention under the Mental Health Act, then recall will not normally be indicated, regardless of the likely length of admission

13. If the medical evidence is that the patient, while in hospital voluntarily, does meet the criteria for compulsory detention under the Mental Health Act, then recall may be indicated if the likely length of admission is more than about a month.

Admission under Section 2 or Section 3 of the Mental Health Act 1983

4-009 **14.** If a Restricted patient requires compulsory detention in hospital under the Mental Health Act then recall will almost invariably be appropriate.

15. The only circumstances where recall may not be indicated would be where discharge was imminent (within days rather than weeks), or where the admission is solely due to self-harm/suicide issues and the admission is likely to last less than about a month.

Conditionally discharged patients and periods of imprisonment

4-010 **16.** Where a conditionally discharged patient is sentenced to a period of imprisonment, consideration must be given to recalling that patient when the custodial part of his or her sentence expires.

17. Where the patient has been transferred to hospital while serving the sentence of imprisonment, then he or she must be recalled upon the expiration of the Section 49 restrictions.

18. If in any particular case, a supervising psychiatrist has an issue that is either causing them concern or they are unsure about I would urge them to contact the Casework Manager responsible for the case. We are always happy to discuss cases with the doctors responsible for the patient. Such contact can only help to develop and maintain effective working relationships between the Ministry of Justice and patient's care teams.

DISCHARGE CONDITIONS THAT AMOUNT TO DEPRIVATION OF LIBERTY

(JANUARY 2019)

1 Introduction

4-011 This document sets out the Secretary of State's position on the discharge of restricted patients on conditions that involve a deprivation of liberty, following the decision of the Supreme Court in *The Secretary of State for Justice v MM* [2018] UKSC 60 which was handed down on 28 November 2018.

The Supreme Court held that the Mental Health Act 1983 (MHA) does not permit either the First-tier Tribunal (Mental Health), the Mental Health Tribunal for Wales ("the Tribunal") or the Secretary of State to order a conditional discharge of a restricted patient subject to conditions which amount to detention or a deprivation of liberty.

The independent review of the MHA, published on 6 December 2018[1] included a recommendation (number 136) in relation to this issue as follows:

> "The Government should legislate to give the Tribunal the power to discharge patients with conditions that restrict their freedom in the community, potentially with a new set of safeguards."

Relevant Government leads, including the Ministry of Justice and the Department of Health and Social Care are currently considering all recommendations in the MHA review's final report.

More immediately, the Justice Secretary will implement the following operational policy in relation to patients affected by the issue of discharge conditions that amount to a deprivation of liberty.

The aim of this operational policy is to ensure that, where appropriate, restricted patients do not need to remain in hospital beds and can continue their rehabilitation in a community-based setting, while on a long-term escorted leave of absence under section 17(3) MHA. This will ensure affected patients are managed safely, detained in an appropriate setting, detained in accordance with a procedure prescribed by law and are subject to the safeguards of a detained patient.

This document sets out the Secretary of State's view and guidance for his own officials. It is not intended as any kind of guidance for the Tribunal who, as an independent judicial body, will set their own guidance on the judgment.

2 Deprivation of liberty

Conditions objectively will give rise to a deprivation of liberty within the meaning of Article 5 of the European Convention on Human Rights if the patient: **4-012**
  a) is not free to leave his placement; and
  b) is subject to continuous supervision and control (per Baroness Hale in *P v Cheshire West & Chester Council* [2014] UKSC 19, [2014] AC 896 at § 49 and 54).

The deprivation of liberty will breach Article 5 if it is not authorised in accordance with a procedure prescribed by law.

The Secretary of State recognises that there are some patients already living in the community subject to conditions amounting to a deprivation of liberty and, therefore, unlawful conditions. Our policy on how we intend to deal with those patients is set out in section 5. There are also patients living in the community whose conditions of discharge in and of themselves are not unlawful, but who are subject to a care plan that includes arrangements that amount to a deprivation of liberty.

---

[1] *http://www.gov.uk/government/publications/modernising-the-mental-health-act-final-report-from-the-independent-review*

3 Patients with capacity

4-013   Where the patient has capacity to decide whether or not s/he should be accommodated at the relevant discharge placement with a care plan that includes arrangements that amount to a deprivation of liberty (DoL), the placement cannot be authorised under provisions of the Mental Capacity Act 2005 (the MCA), and the patient cannot validly consent to the arrangements. If a patient is being considered for discharge and the responsible clinician considers that they no longer require treatment in hospital, but are not yet suitable for discharge without constant supervision, the Secretary of State can consider providing his consent to a long-term escorted leave of absence, under section 17(3) MHA. Please refer to section 6 for further details.

The Secretary of State is aware of the case of *Hertfordshire County Council v AB* [2018] EWHC 3103 (Fam) where the High Court used its inherent jurisdiction to make an order authorising the DoL that arose from the patient's care plan. The Secretary of State does not consider that this is the correct approach. Where a patient continues to present such a risk to public protection, linked to his mental disorder, the Secretary of State considers that his treatment is best managed under the provisions of the MHA so that either the Secretary of State or the Tribunal can consider the public protection aspect of detention under the MHA. If further treatment and rehabilitation could be given in a community setting for such a patient, then a section 17(3) long term escorted leave approach would be more appropriate than to conditionally discharge with a care plan that required a DoL authorisation under the inherent jurisdiction of the High Court.

4 Patients lacking capacity

4-014   The earlier Court of Appeal decision in *MM* indicated that it could be appropriate for the Tribunal to defer conditional discharge of a patient who lacks capacity and whose discharge care plan would involve constant supervision. Such a deferred conditional discharge would enable the jurisdiction of the Court of Protection to be invoked to authorise the deprivation of liberty on discharge under section 16 of the MCA. At paragraph 27 of the *MM* judgment, the Supreme Court stated:

> "Whether the Court of Protection could authorise a future deprivation, once the (Tribunal) has granted a conditional discharge, and whether the (Tribunal) could defer its decision for this purpose, are not issues which it would be appropriate for this court to decide at this stage in these proceedings."

Where the Secretary of State or the Tribunal is considering discharge from detention in hospital for treatment under the MHA and considers that it is not satisfied that it is necessary for the health or safety of the patient or for the protection of other persons that s/he should receive such treatment, then a conditional discharge decision can usually be made.

The Secretary of State's view is that there are broadly two groups of patients lacking capacity who may be subject to a proposed discharge plan which would involve a deprivation of their liberty. The first set of patients are those who lack capacity and in their best interests, it is proposed that they live in a residential care home (or similar) as they are not able to look after themselves without the support such a placement would provide. In most of these cases, the need for such a care plan is due to the patient's inability to perform Activities of Daily Living or self-care without support that would involve an objective deprivation of their liberty.

The second set of patients are those who lack capacity and the argument is made that it is in their best interests for their care plan to involve constant supervision in order to prevent them from re-offending (i.e. it is in the best interests not to suffer the trauma of being prosecuted for an offence, or face physical threats from others should they re-offend). While it is recognised that there will be some cross-over between the first and second group, it is considered that there are a specific group of patients who, but for the risks they present to others, could live independently, without the need for constant supervision. Where a patient falls into this group, the Secretary of State considers caution should be exercised when considering whether to conditionally discharge such a patient with a care plan that would require a DoL authorisation under the MCA. (See section 4.2 below)

General Note

In *MC v Sygnet Behavioural Health Ltd* [2020] UKUT 230 (AAC); [2021] M.H.L.R. 157, UT Judge Jacobs said that he was "not convinced that the division the Secretary of State makes in the Guidance between patients whose care plan is in the patients' best interests, and those where the deprivation of liberty is primarily for the purpose of managing risk to the public, is one that stands up to close scrutiny" (para.42).

4-015

4.1 Patients lacking capacity – care plan that requires Deprivation of Liberty (DoL) to be authorised under the MCA

Where the care plan requires a Deprivation of Liberty (DoL) authorisation under the MCA, that is a separate consideration and the Secretary of State considers that the Tribunal can direct a deferred conditional discharge. Once conditional discharge is deferred, the necessary arrangements to put a DoL authorisation in place can be made and the patient discharged accordingly once the Tribunal has confirmed its decision. As the Secretary of State does not have the power to defer conditional discharge, in these circumstances, he can give an *indication* that he is minded to conditionally discharge on the basis that a DoL authorisation is put in place.

4-016

If, after a Tribunal decision to defer conditional discharge with a care plan that amounts to a DoL (or a Secretary of State indication that he would be minded to conditionally discharge), the Local Authority or the Court of Protection *declines* to issue a DoL authorisation, it is likely this would mean that the proposed placement is no longer available. In those circumstances, and where the responsible clinician can no longer support conditional discharge, he should inform the Tribunal and invite it to reconsider its deferred conditional discharge decision.

This procedure was set out in the case of *R (on the application of H) v the Secretary of State for the Home Department* [2003] UKHL 59, which upheld the Court of Appeal's decision where it summarised the following:

(i) The tribunal can, at the outset, adjourn the hearing to investigate the possibility of imposing conditions.

(ii) The tribunal can make a provisional decision to make a conditional discharge on specified conditions, including submitting to psychiatric supervision, but defer directing a conditional discharge while the authorities responsible for after-care under section 117 of the Act make the necessary arrangements to enable the patient to meet those conditions.

(iii) The tribunal should meet after an appropriate interval to monitor progress in making these arrangements if they have not by then been put in place.

(iv) Once the arrangements have been made, the tribunal can direct a conditional discharge without holding a further hearing.

(v)   If problems arise with making arrangements to meet the conditions, the tribunal has a number of options, depending upon the circumstances; (a) it can defer for a further period, perhaps with suggestions as to how any problems can be overcome; (b) it can amend or vary the proposed conditions to seek to overcome the difficulties that have been encountered; (c) it can order a conditional discharge without specific conditions, thereby making the patient subject to recall; (d) it can decide that the patient must remain detained in hospital for treatment.

(vi) It will not normally be appropriate for a tribunal to direct a conditional discharge on conditions with which the patient will be unable to comply because it has not proved possible to make the necessary arrangements." (emphasis added)

4.2   Patients lacking capacity – care plan that requires Deprivation of Liberty to be authorised under the MCA where the best interests requirement under the MCA is primarily managing risk to the public

4-017   As noted above, the Secretary of State considers that there is a much smaller set of patients who lack capacity, and a care plan which amounts to a DoL is required on discharge in order to manage the risks they continue to pose to others. In those cases, the Secretary of State considers that conditional discharge would not be appropriate, but would be open to consideration of a s17(3) MHA long-term escorted leave of absence in the alternative (see section 6).

While the MCA does allow for a DoL where the best interests requirement is met on the basis of preventing the patient from re-offending, generally, the Secretary of State considers that such patients are best managed under the provisions of the MHA. This enables either the Secretary of State for Justice or the Tribunal to consider the public protection aspects of the criteria for detention under the MHA, rather than this important consideration being made under the provisions of the MCA. It also means that where such a patient can no longer be subject to a care plan with a DoL (for example if the DoL authorisation is not renewed), there is no immediate risk to the public, as the patient remains detained under the MHA.

While it is not easy to describe in general terms what characteristics such a case may have, a compelling factor will be what the care plan provides. For example, if the treatment set out in the care plan was analogous to that which would be delivered in an MHA setting (e.g. psychological/therapeutic interventions to reduce risk) and that appears to be the primary reason for the need for constant supervision, then it is likely that is the sort of patient who continues to meet the MHA detention criteria. If further treatment and rehabilitation could be given in a community setting for such a patient, then a section 17(3) long term escorted leave approach would be more appropriate than to conditionally discharge with a care plan that required a DoL authorisation under the MCA. The Secretary of State does not consider that there would be any requirement for a parallel authority under the MCA where a patient is subject to 17(3) long term escorted leave under the MHA.

5   Discharged patients on existing conditions

4-018   The Secretary of State is aware that there are a number of patients (both with and without capacity) who, prior to this decision, were discharged on conditions or a, which objectively amount to a deprivation of liberty. As these cases are identified, the Secretary of State will consider their case in the light of the Supreme Court's judgment, and will have a number of options:

a. Exercise the Secretary of State's power to revoke or amend a condition to remove the illegality, if it is considered that the public would remain adequately protected without that condition (or with an amended condition);

b. Recall the patient to hospital on the grounds that the clarification of the law constitutes a material change of circumstance. *In these circumstances, the Secretary of State will at the same point consider granting immediate consent to the use of long term escorted leave of absence under section 17(3) MHA to enable the patient to remain in the community, where this appears to be in the patient's best interests and where any risk to the public can be safely managed during the patient's period of leave.* Where this option is appropriate, the Secretary of State will generally only give consent to long-term escorted leave of absence for up to 12 months and the recall will only be a technicality (i.e. the patient should not actually be physically returned to hospital). Both considerations and decisions will be made concurrently to enable the patient to remain where they are currently placed while a decision is made. The Secretary of State could extend consent to longer-term escorted leave of absence on the application of the responsible clinician after 12 months, but it will be necessary to review the continued appropriateness of such a leave of absence before extending it;

c. Absolutely discharge the patient, if it is considered that the public would remain adequately protected without restrictions (including the power to recall to hospital at a later date);

d. Refer the case to the Tribunal to consider amending or removing the relevant condition, or to consider absolute discharge.

In most cases, once the Mental Health Casework Section (MHCS) has identified that existing conditions are unlawful, the Secretary of State will initially ask the responsible clinician whether s/he considers that a restriction of the kind imposed by the unlawful condition remains necessary in order to protect the public. In some cases, MHCS will seek further information in order to decide the best approach, which might include a request for an updated risk assessment. On consideration of the case once this information is received, the Secretary of State will decide which of the above options to take. Where the Secretary of State considers that he is unable to take any of the first three options, he will refer the case to the Tribunal. It is anticipated that this will only be necessary in cases where closer examination of the issues by the independent Tribunal is required.

Where the discharged patient's conditions of discharge do not in their own right amount to a DoL, but where the care plan does, responsible clinicians should review the care plan to ascertain whether the arrangements remain necessary and proportionate. If they do, the responsible clinician should contact the MHCS and seek advice on whether any action is necessary. If such a patient lacks capacity and there is a DoL authorisation under the MCA in place, it is unlikely any action will be required.

If you are a professional responsible for the supervision of a restricted patient and consider that their conditions or implementation of their care plan may be unlawful, please contact the MHCS for advice: https://www.gov.uk/guidance/noms-mental-health-casework-section-contact-list

6   Detained patients whose current discharge plans include a requirement for constant supervision in the community – long-term escorted leave of absence

4-019   As noted above, the Secretary of State will consent to the use of a long-term escorted leave of absence, under s17(3) MHA (i.e. leave for more than seven consecutive days) if it appears appropriate in an individual case.

The Secretary of State will always initially consider whether a restricted patient could be conditionally discharged rather than consenting to a long-term escorted leave of absence.

6.1 *Where the patient lacks capacity,* it may be possible for the Secretary of State to consent to the use of a long-term escorted leave of absence to test the suitability for a conditional discharge to a community placement if this is considered a necessary step. If the patient will need to live in a residential care home (for example) and as such their liberty would be severely restricted on discharge, the Secretary of State, at the appropriate time, would indicate his willingness to discharge to such a placement, on the basis that a DoL authorisation could be put in place under the MCA. While such a patient is on a long-term escorted leave of absence to the proposed discharge placement under s17(3) MHA, the Secretary of State considers that there is no need for an additional DoL authorisation under the MCA. A restricted patient on a long-term escorted leave of absence remains a detained patient and continues to have all the protections of the MHA, including the entitlement to apply to the Tribunal every 12 months. As paragraph 26 of the Supreme Court judgment in *MM* states, a restricted patient who is actually detained in hospital is ineligible for a DoL authorisation under the MCA. It is only at the point of conditional discharge that a DoL authorisation would be required.

6.2 *Where the patient has capacity* and the responsible clinician considers that s/he no longer needs treatment in hospital, but his risks are such that s/he could only be safely managed in the community with conditions that amount to a DoL (for example constant supervision while in the community), the Secretary of State (or the Tribunal) would not be able to conditionally discharge with such conditions.

The Secretary of State would consider consenting to a s17(3) long-term escorted leave of absence in these circumstances, with conditions that require constant supervision, if that would be a safe and appropriate way of enabling the patient to continue treatment and rehabilitation away from the hospital, while remaining a detained patient. Such a leave of absence would not be permanent, and the Secretary of State will generally only provide his consent for a maximum of 12 months at a time and would review the appropriateness of it continuing when the responsible clinician applies for an extension. Where there is a breach of leave conditions, or the responsible clinician is concerned that risks have increased, the responsible clinician may revoke the leave of absence and recall the patient to hospital without needing to apply for a recall warrant from the Secretary of State, as described in s17 MHA. Once the risks reduce such that constant supervision is no longer necessary, the responsible clinician can then apply for conditional discharge.

The Secretary of State will not generally agree to a long-term unescorted leave of absence in cases where the responsible clinician simply wishes to test a proposed discharge placement. Where there are no requirements for constant supervision and the application is simply consent for unescorted overnight leave prior to discharge, the Secretary of State's current policy of only granting up to 5 nights overnight leave remains in place. This is to ensure that s17 leave is not being used where conditional discharge is more appropriate.

> **MHCS INTERNAL GUIDANCE:**   **4-020**
>
> *IN ALL CASES, WHERE THERE IS A KEY DECISION MADE, SUCH AS RECALL, LEAVE, CONDITIONAL DISCHARGE, PLEASE ENSURE THAT VICTIM ISSUES ARE CONSIDERED AND THE VLO INFORMED IN ACCORDANCE WITH EXISTING PROCEDURES AND GUIDANCE.*
>
> *Section 1 – Conditionally discharged patients*
>
> *Case managers:*
> When reviewing CD reports, check the discharge conditions for any that could amount to a deprivation of liberty (e.g. "the patient must be escorted at all times"). If you think a condition might amount to a deprivation of liberty, refer the case to your Head of Team by creating a manual milestone allocated to the "B9 Discharge Requests and Decisions" list.
>
> *Senior managers*
> When reviewing unlawful conditions where the patient is already discharged: Ascertain whether the patient lacks capacity.
>
> 1) *If the patient lacks capacity:*
>
>   a.   Is there a DoL authorisation in place under the MCA? If there is an authorisation, consider whether removal of the unlawful discharge condition has any effect on the protection of the public.
>
>   b.   Where a patient is subject to a DoL authorisation (and therefore his liberty has been lawfully deprived under the MCA), it is likely that you can remove the unlawful condition with no practical change to how the patient is being managed or any subsequent increase in risk to the public. It is important to note, however, that were circumstances to change in the future, and the patient no longer be subject to a DoL authorisation, consideration will need to be given to whether this increases their risk and, if so, how that can be safely and appropriately managed. In the majority of cases, however, the DoL authority under the MCA will not solely be in place due to public protection concerns and there will be other reasons in the patient's best interests that it was put in place.
>
>   c.   If the conditions can be safely removed, create a "change of conditions review" in the usual way. Letters to the patient and RC should also include the following lines, to ensure MHCS is informed of any change to the DoL authorisation:
>
> > *"Further, the responsible clinician is to notify the Secretary of State within twenty-four hours of any (i) imposition, removal or variation of a Deprivation of Liberty (DoL) Safeguard concerning your supervision in the community; (ii) any application for the imposition, removal or variation of such a DoL; and (iii) any forthcoming significant procedural step in respect of any such application."*
>
>   d.   You should also create a manual milestone to ensure that the case is reviewed when the DoL authorisation is due to be renewed (usually every 12 months).

e. If the patient lacks capacity, but there is no DoL authorisation in place, discuss with the clinical and social supervisors why there is no authorisation and whether it is possible to put one in place. If none can be imposed, then treat the case as though the patient has capacity.

2) *If the patient has capacity:*

a. Consider whether removal of the unlawful condition has any effect on the protection of the public or the safety of the patient.

b. Where, on the surface, it appears that the condition was imposed in order to manage a high risk of offending, you should contact the responsible clinician and social supervisor to seek their views on the current risk presented by the patient, should the condition be removed. It may be necessary to seek an up to date clinical assessment of risk.

c. Where the condition appears to have been imposed not to manage risk to others, but due to the patient's risk to himself, you should contact the responsible clinician and social supervisor to seek their views on the current risk presented to the patient, should the condition be removed. It may be appropriate to ascertain whether the patient has capacity; if not the most appropriate way forward may be to remove the condition while ensuring that a DoL authorisation is put in place under the MCA.

d. Where the patient has progressed such that removal of the unlawful condition would not mean the public is at risk and that the patient can be safely managed in the community, then it may be appropriate to remove it. If so, create a change of conditions review in the usual way.

e. Where it is clear that removing the condition would mean the risk to the public is elevated (or that the patient would be a danger to himself if not escorted in the community), it may be appropriate to recall the patient to hospital, on the basis that there has been a material change in circumstances. If so, create a recall review in the usual way. This step should first be discussed with the responsible clinician, together with the consideration for immediate leave of absence, set out at f. below. If you are able to agree to an immediate leave of absence as set out at f. below, then the recall will be a technicality and the patient should not actually be physically returned to hospital. Both considerations and decisions should be made concurrently to enable the patient to remain where they are currently placed while a decision is made.

f. If recall does appear to be necessary, consideration should always be given to immediate consent for a long-term escorted leave of absence under section 17(3) MHA. In order to maintain public protection, the Secretary of State's consent to leave may well involve imposing conditions on the leave of absence that amount to a deprivation of liberty, which would be lawful under the MHA, as the patient is now a detained patient, having been recalled. If recall, followed by immediate consent to leave of absence under the same conditions to the current placement is appropriate, you will still need to identify a hospital for the recall warrant. You should issue the recall warrant and the leave authority together. A long-term escorted leave review should be created at the same time as the recall review. Generally, the Secretary of State will only agree to a long-term escorted leave of absence up to a period of 12 months, at which point the responsible clinician will need to request the consent is extended for a further 12 month period (or they can apply for conditional discharge).

g.   It should be noted that where the Secretary of State recalls a conditionally discharged patient (even with an immediate leave of absence) this means that:

    i.   the patient's legal status changes from being a conditionally discharged patient to a recalled detained patient;

    ii.   the patient's case will be immediately be referred to the Tribunal following recall;

    iii.   the patient thereafter has the right to apply to the Tribunal annually (and in the absence of such an application, the Secretary of State must refer the case every three years); and

    iv.   the indefinite leave of absence will only be consented to for a period of up to 12 months, which can be extended on the application of the responsible clinician.

h.   In order to ensure the leave of absence is reviewed regularly, the senior manager should decide how often progress reports are required (minimum of every six months) and create a manual milestone for 11 months' time to remind the responsible clinician that the consent for long-term leave will shortly expire.

i.   The senior manager should ensure that the Secretary of State's statement to the Tribunal makes it clear that while the patient has been recalled, due to the material change in circumstances, he is on a long-term escorted leave of absence. The statement should also explain why the Secretary of State considered that the unlawful condition could not be safely removed.

j.   When reviewing these cases, the option of lifting the restrictions (absolute discharge) must always be considered. If none of the first three options set out in section 5 above appear appropriate, then it is likely you will need to make a discretionary referral to the Tribunal. In doing so, you should explain your reasons for making the referral and the Secretary of State's formal statement to the Tribunal should set out why he did not consider he could exercise his own powers within one of the first three options.

Section 2 – Detained patients

Tribunal proceedings

Case managers:

When reviewing tribunal discharge decisions or preparing tribunal statements: Check whether the conditions imposed (or requested) could amount to a deprivation of liberty (e.g. "the patient must be escorted at all times"). If you think a condition might amount to a deprivation of liberty, refer the case to your Head of Team by creating a manual milestone allocated to the "B9 Discharge Requests and Decisions" list.

Senior managers:
When reviewing cases before the Tribunal where there is a clinical recommendation for discharge with conditions that objectively amount to a DoL:

1) Ascertain whether the patient lacks capacity;
2) If so, does the discharge plan include a DoL authorisation? If so, ensure that the Tribunal statement sets out the Secretary of State's position as above in Section 4, with regard to the imposition of conditions and potential for deferred CD to enable arrangements for a DoL authorisation. Bear in mind that where a DoL authorisation will be in place, any request for conditions that objectively amount to a DoL is likely to be superfluous (it would add nothing to the safeguard provided by the DoL authority) and such a condition would be unlawful;
3) If the patient has capacity, ensure that the Tribunal statement sets out the Secretary of State's position as above. You particularly need to consider what the implications are for public protection if a patient with capacity is discharged without such a restrictive condition, where the clinical assessment is that s/he needs constant supervision and whether it is appropriate for the Secretary of State to offer a view on suitability for discharge (e.g. in cases where the responsible clinician recommends discharge but has requested an unlawful condition which amounts to a DoL);
4) If the patient has capacity and the responsible clinician is requesting an unlawful condition, it may be appropriate to suggest that an alternative approach might be for him to seek consent for a long-term leave of absence.
5) If the unlawful conditions have already been imposed by the Tribunal (post the MM UKSC decision), seek legal advice on the best way to resolve the situation.

Applications for escorted overnight leave/long-term escorted leave of absence:
Case managers:

1) If the patient lacks capacity and the responsible clinician is requesting escorted overnight leave to a proposed discharge address, make sure it is clear whether eventual discharge is likely to involve a DoL authorisation. You may need to check with the responsible clinician. If so, escorted overnight leave is likely to be appropriate (and necessary). You should make your risk assessment as usual, but take into account the fact the overnight leave will be escorted. Bear in mind that the patient will not have had access to unescorted day leave. This is not an issue in these circumstances and not a barrier to escorted overnight leave.
2) Not all patients who lack capacity will need a long-term escorted leave of absence and may only require escorted overnight leave in the usual way (i.e. up to five nights per week). Ensure that the responsible clinician has clearly expressed what type of leave they are requesting and clarify with them if it is not clear.
3) If the patient does not lack capacity, but the responsible clinician is requesting an escorted leave of absence for the purposes of testing at a proposed discharge address, you should ask the responsible clinician to clarify why *escorted* overnight leave is being sought. It may be appropri-

ate to consent to a leave of absence with restrictive conditions for detained patients in the same way it would be considered for those already in the community after recall (see below).

4) If in doubt, consult your Head or Deputy Head of Team for advice before completing your recommendation. Please note that a long-term leave of absence will generally only be considered if such leave is to be escorted. Where the patient can take unescorted overnight leave, a long-term leave of absence will not generally be appropriate and the Secretary of State's policy remains that most patients will only require a period of testing on overnight leave for a maximum of five nights per week, prior to consideration of conditional discharge.

Senior managers:

1) Deputy Heads of Casework should ascertain whether the application is for a long-term escorted leave of absence. If so, the case should be referred to the Head of Team for a final decision. Please ensure that the correct review has been opened (i.e. the new "long term escorted leave" review) to enable MHCS to monitor volumes of such applications.

2) Where the application is for a long term leave of absence, please apply the following considerations:

a. Is the long-term leave of absence to be unescorted? If so, ascertain why the responsible clinician considers this step necessary. Generally, the Secretary of State will not agree to allow a long-term *unescorted* leave of absence and would prefer shorter periods of testing (up to five nights per week) and/or consideration of conditional discharge at the appropriate point.

b. Is the long-term leave of absence to be escorted? If so, ascertain why this is necessary. If the patient lacks capacity, is there a plan for eventual discharge that would require a DoL authority to be in place under the MCA? Is testing via a long-term escorted leave of absence necessary prior to consideration of conditional discharge?

c. You should always consider whether periods of overnight leave (up to five nights per week) or conditional discharge is more appropriate than a long-term leave of absence, before consenting to such a step.

Applications for conditional discharge where a responsible clinician has requested a condition that amounts to a deprivation of liberty
Senior managers:

1) Ascertain whether the patient lacks capacity;

2) If so, is there or will there be a DoL authorisation in place? If yes, consider whether you are content that, where relevant, the DoL authorisation is a sufficient safeguard to manage risks in the community on discharge. Bear in mind that the majority of DoL authorisations will be with regard to the patient's best interests with regard to assistance with daily living, rather than on the basis of management of risk to others. It is possible, however, to argue that a DoL authorisation is in the patient's best interests to prevent him causing harm to others due to the consequences of re-offending. If this is the case, you should satisfy yourself that it would be appropriate to conditionally discharge in these circumstances – does the patient still require treatment in hospital; can the risks be safely managed in the com-

> munity? You should continue to consider the case like any other, bearing in mind that the patient will not be able to have been tested on unescorted leave. This is not a barrier to discharge. The fact the discharge plan will involve a lawful deprivation of liberty under the MCA will be relevant to your consideration, but may not be central to the decision;
>
> 3) If not, and the responsible clinician has requested a condition that objectively amounts to a deprivation of liberty, you should not, in any circumstances, impose such a condition. You should continue to consider the case like any other. It may be appropriate to consider a long-term escorted leave of absence (subject to the appropriate conditions), rather than discharge in these circumstances.

Guidance on the High Security Psychiatric Services (Arrangements for Safety and Security) Directions 2019

(21 JUNE 2019)

1. Introduction

4-021 **1.1** This guidance accompanies the High Security Psychiatric Services (Arrangements for Safety and Security) Directions 2019, which apply to providers of high security psychiatric services.

1.2 This document contains:
(a) general information (paragraphs (2.1) to (2.2)) about the High Security Psychiatric Services (Arrangements for Safety and Security) Directions 2019;
(b) specific guidance about the implementation of certain requirements contained in the Directions (paragraph (4.1));
(c) general guidance on the way policies (including procedures and protocols) should be produced, and promulgated to staff within the high security hospitals (paragraphs (5.1) to (5.10));
(d) *annexes A & B*: protocols for the identification and management of 'high risk' patients and locking patients in their rooms at night;
(e) *attachment 1*: the decision tree for risk management of 'high risk' patients; and
(f) *attachment 2*: the management strategies supporting the decision making for the risk management of 'high risk' patients.

2. Status of the Directions and Guidance

4-022 **2.1** The Directions are issued by the Secretary of State for Health and Social Care and providers of high security psychiatric services must comply with them. This guidance is not mandatory, but providers must have regard to it. Providers must also have regard to the NHS England Clinical Security Framework. Direction 3 sets out reporting requirements where a provider is not compliant with the Directions, guidance or the NHS England Clinical Security Framework and any action it is taking to become compliant.

2.2 The High Security Psychiatric Services (Arrangements for Safety and

Security) Directions 2019 should be read alongside the High Security Psychiatric Services (Arrangements for Visits by Children) Directions 2013 (due to reference in this guidance to visits by children) and providers of high security psychiatric services must comply with them. Arrangements for visits by vulnerable adults must be included within the high security hospitals local policies and procedures.

3 Human Rights and Equalities Legislation

3.1 When implementing the Directions and guidance, providers are responsible for doing so in a way which takes human rights and equalities into consideration to ensure they comply with: **4-023**
(a) The Human Rights Act 1998; and
(b) The Equality Act 2010.

4 Guidance on the Implementation of Specific Directions

4.1 This section of the guidance is specifically about the implementation of certain requirements contained in the Directions. Only those Directions which required further detailed guidance, clarification, or pose a greater security risk have been included.   **4-024**

Direction 2: Interpretation

In addition to the interpretations as specified within Direction 2, this guidance defines the following: **4-025**
(a) "responsible clinician" - this will include any person appointed by the provider to provide cover in the absence of the "responsible clinician" (e.g. during non-working hours, annual leave etc);
(b) "visitor" - any person aged 18 or over who proposes to enter the secure area of the hospital and is not a member of staff. It will, for example, include Care Quality Commissioner personnel, Mental Health Review Tribunal personnel, the police, health professionals and solicitors;
(c) "security director" - this includes the person nominated to undertake delegated responsibilities and duties by the security director that the security director would undertake.

Direction 3: Promotion of safety and security

To comply with the requirements of paragraph (2) of this Direction each provider must have regard to this guidance and the NHS England Clinical Security Framework in addition to complying with the requirements set out in the Directions.   **4-026**

To comply with the requirements in paragraph (3) of this Direction to report non-compliance without delay, initial contact may be made by telephone by an officer of the provider delegated this authority by the Chief Executive. However, the Chief Executive of the relevant provider of high security psychiatric services must also report non-compliances in writing without delay to NHS England and NHS Improvement.

The Directions and guidance, together with the Clinical Security Framework, cover minimum physical and operational standards of safety and security. They do not focus on the therapeutic aspects of the work of the hospitals. However, by supporting a safe environment for patients and staff, the arrangements should enhance the therapeutic activities of the hospitals.

It is not the purpose of the Directions and guidance or the Clinical Security Framework to cover every aspect/area of policies which providers should have in place. Each provider should determine what other areas need to be covered by policies. In addition, some of this will be governed by legislation, for example the Mental Health Act 1983; the Human Rights Act 1998; equality, health inequalities, employment legislation, and legislation relating to drugs management and misuse.

Direction 5: Requirements for conducting a rub-down search of a patient

4-027   A rub-down search must be a search of a type at least equivalent to a rub-down search as described in the Clinical Security Framework.

The Directions state that rub-down searches must, unless there are exceptional circumstances, be carried out by members of staff who are of the same sex as the person being searched. There should always be a member of staff of the same sex present when the search is carried out.

If a search without consent is authorised, or the search is being undertaken under paragraph (2) of this Direction, a further attempt should be made to obtain the patient's consent before proceeding with a search without consent.

Where searches of patients are conducted without consent, the minimum of force needed to complete the search should be used.

It is recommended that all patients are made aware of the searching processes that affect them.

A member of staff has the authority to undertake a rub-down search of a patient if they have "reasonable grounds" to believe that the patient possess' an item which causes an immediate risk to the patient's own safety or the safety of any other person. This would include any concern about tools, improvised weapons or items, including drugs or prescribed medication, that may be used to either commit deliberate self-harm or harm another person.

"Reasonable grounds" would include situations where a patient is believed to have an improvised a weapon; a tool or implement is known to be missing and has not been accounted for; and, security intelligence provides a reasoned view that a patient has an item or items that may cause an immediate risk to themselves or others.

Direction 6: Searches of patients that involve the removal of clothing other than outer clothing

4-028   "Outer clothing" means a top coat and any other items of clothing (e.g. jacket, cardigan) that are bulky and inhibit a proper search being conducted.

Each provider should provide instructions to staff regarding the detailed arrangements for conducting a search of a patient that involves the removal of clothing. These instructions should include:

(a)   measures aimed at providing privacy and protecting the dignity of the patient;

(b)   identification of the limited circumstances where a search of this type may be used; and

(c)   the arrangements for authorising a search of this type.

If a search without consent is authorised, or the search is being undertaken under paragraph (2) of this Direction, a further attempt should be made to obtain the patient's consent before proceeding with a search without consent.

Where searches of patients are conducted without consent, the minimum of force needed to complete the search should be used.

It is recommended that all patients are made aware of the searching processes that affect them.

"Reasonable grounds" for the searching of a patient under paragraph (2) of this Direction reflects that as required for the decision-making process as set out in this guidance for Direction 5.

"Admission facility" – for the purposes of Direction 6(14) an "admission facility" should include suitable facilities to carry out a search involving the removal of clothing other than outer clothing whilst maintaining the patient's dignity and privacy.

Direction 7: Searches of patients, rooms and lockers

When developing the local hospital policy in respect of the routine searching of **4-029** patients, their rooms and lockers the provider should have regard to the standards set out in the Clinical Security Framework.

Unless circumstances dictate otherwise, a patient should be present when their room, locker, and possessions are searched. This may be clinically beneficial for the patient and witnessing thorough searches may act as a deterrent in future.

Providers should consider whether room searches are most appropriately carried out by ward staff, dedicated search teams, or both.

In the interests of protecting staff from any allegations of inappropriate action, it is advisable for room searches to be undertaken by more than one member of staff.

If items belonging to a patient are removed, the patient should be given a receipt for the items and informed why the items have been removed and where they are being kept. A receipt is not required where items of rubbish such as discarded packaging or items of food waste are removed, and if this is the case the patient should be informed.

Decisions to undertake a search of a patient's room and any locker used by that patient pursuant to Direction 7(3) should be based on reliable intelligence and reasonable suspicion that a search maybe required.

A decision to undertake a rub-down search of a patient must meet requirements of Direction 5.

It is recommended that patients be made aware of the searching processes that affect them.

Direction 8: Searches when patients move around the secure area

When developing the local hospital policy in respect of the searches of patients **4-030** who move around in the secure area the provider should have regard to the standards set out in the Clinical Security Framework.

Direction 9: Searches of ward areas and other areas

Each provider in developing their local hospital policy on the searches of ward **4-031** areas and other areas should have regard to the standards set out in the Clinical Security Framework.

The requirement to search therapy, workshop, recreation and leisure facility areas, and other non-ward areas which a patient may visit in the secure area has been set to at least once every three months. Existing arrangements for the searching and supervision of patients, checking of tools before and after sessions and controls on patients' access, should already minimise the risk of illicit items being hidden in those areas. However, searches should also be undertaken whenever a credible risk is identified.

Direction 10: Security of tools, equipment and materials

4-032   When issuing written instructions to members of staff, providers should have regard to the standards set out in the Clinical Security Framework regarding the control of tools, equipment and materials in secure areas of the hospital.

Direction 11: Searches of members of staff and key-holders

4-033   When developing the local policy for the searching of members of staff and key-holders, providers should have regard to the standards set out in the Clinical Security Framework.

What constitutes a rub-down search is contained in the guidance to Direction 5.

A member of staff who refuses to be searched or to permit his/her possessions to be searched must be denied entry to the secure area. A member of staff who refuses to be searched or to allow their possessions to be searched on the way out of the secure area cannot, however, be prevented from leaving. Providers must include within their policies arrangements for managing such refusals.

Only visitors who have had an Enhanced Disclosure Barring Service (DBS) check and completed the appropriate training detailed in Direction 43(2) can be key-holders.

Direction 12: Arrangements in respect of visitors and visiting children

4-034   What constitutes a rub-down search is contained in the guidance to Direction 5.

Bringing and sending food items into the hospital presents risks in terms of checking for concealed illicit items. It also presents potential health hazards. The restrictions on bringing and sending food into the hospital, other than in limited and carefully controlled circumstances, are intended to address these concerns. Providers should ensure a sufficiently varied range of food is available on site to cater for differing tastes and dietary requirements among patient/visitor groups.

The security director should be informed of any decision to allow a visitor to bring food into the hospital under paragraph (5)(b) of this Direction.

There is no legal power to routinely require a visitor to submit to a search but if a search is refused, the provider is entitled to refuse that person entry. Applying restrictions to visitors who refuse to submit to searches on their way out of the hospital is more problematic because visitors cannot be prevented from leaving the hospital. However, searches of visitors on entry and searches of the patient prior to the visit, if carried out thoroughly, should minimise the risk of inappropriate items being passed between the patient and the visitor. Nevertheless, if there is reason to believe that a visitor may be carrying an inappropriate item out of the hospital, and they refuse to submit to a search, consideration should be given to contacting the police about the matter or informing the visitor that entry may be refused on a future occasion.

Care should be taken with regard to obtaining consent to search visiting children of any age. Where children have the capacity to understand the implications, and make an informed decision about being searched, it would be appropriate to seek their consent in addition to, or instead of, the adult who is accompanying them. A forced search of a visiting child who is competent to understand and make a decision on the matter, even if carried out with the accompanying adult's consent, may constitute an assault.

Members of the First-Tier Tribunal (Mental Health) carrying out a judicial function who are exempt from rub-down searches under Direction 12(10), should be invited to participate in rub-down searches in the interests of their own safety and that of the safety and security of the hospital. A record should be made on each occasion a tribunal member enters the secure area of the hospital and whether or not they participated in a rub-down search.

Direction 12(13) refers to senior members of the Royal family carrying the title His or Her Majesty (HM) or His or Her Royal Highness (HRH).

Direction 13: Searches of visitors and inspection of possessions

Under normal circumstances, it is expected that both male and female staff will be available to search visitors entering the secure area, and that it will therefore be possible for searching to be carried out by a person of the same sex as the visitor. However, there may be circumstances when searching by a member of staff of the opposite sex is considered appropriate, even when staff of the same sex are available. For example, female staff searching male babies or infants. This should only be done at the request of the visitor or with appropriate consent. **4-035**

It may not be possible to X-ray all property entering the secure area with contractors and it is accepted that they will often need to take into the secure area tools and other equipment which, whilst unacceptable for other visitors, will be needed by contractors to enable them to complete the tasks which they are employed to perform within the hospital. Providers should have suitable arrangements in place for:

(a) checking contractors' tools and other equipment both on arrival and departure from the secure area; and

(b) the supervision of contractors while they are working within the secure area.

Providers must have regard to the standards set out in the Clinical Security Framework when developing their policies for the management of contractors and their property.

Direction 14: Supply of food by staff and key-holders to patients

In developing local policy and instructions to staff each provider must have regard to the standards set out in the Clinical Security Framework. **4-036**

These restrictions are intended to prevent staff and key-holders in direct contact with patients being involved in bringing food into the hospital for consumption by patients. The security director's authority detailed in paragraph (2) of this Direction may be given to groups of staff or key-holders as well as individuals. It may be a standing authority which would not have to be applied for on each occasion, that these staff bring food into the hospital for patients.

Direction 15: Checks of vehicles

Providers must have regard to the standards set out in the Clinical Security Framework when developing policies for members of staff managing and escorting vehicles, including contractor's vehicles within secure areas. **4-037**

The Direction requires any vehicle to be checked before the vehicle enters or leaves the secure area, apart from an emergency services vehicle that is attending to an emergency. It will be impracticable to carry out a detailed search of every vehicle entering and leaving the secure perimeter. It is however, expected that vehicles will be carefully checked for unauthorised persons both on arrival and departure, and that a watch will be kept for illicit or potentially dangerous items which are not required by the occupants of the vehicles for the tasks which they will be performing within the secure area.

Whilst not a requirement set out within the Directions, it is good operational practice to ensure that vehicles are not normally left in the secure area of the hospital. The security director should only give permission having considered, and approved, both the location and any necessary supervisory arrangements for the vehicle.

Direction 16: Testing for illicit substances

4-038   The provider must in developing the local policy for the testing of illicit substances have regard to the standards set out in the Clinical Security Framework.

It is recommended that patients are made aware of the requirements within the Directions for providers to carry out these tests.

It is not envisaged that patients should be physically forced to provide a sample for testing. A refusal to co-operate with a request for a sample might raise concern but it is for the provider to consider what action to take in the event of a refusal, taking into account individual circumstances and the Clinical Security Framework.

Direction 18: Written or electronic records of certain searches and tests

4-039   The provider must ensure that written and electronic records as required in Direction 18 adhere to the standards set out in the Clinical Security Framework.

Direction 19: Security information

4-040   Providers must have regard to the standards set out in the Clinical Security Framework when developing policies for the maintenance and use of security information records.

Security records should be developed and maintained to contain:

(a)   security information relating to each patient; and

(b)   other security information relating to the hospital.

Security records may comprise of written and electronic records and should form the basis of an electronic security intelligence system.

Security records and other sources of relevant information should be analysed/assessed for the purpose of developing security intelligence.

Security records and the intelligence developed from them should be used to inform risk assessment and operational practice.

Security intelligence systems should be set up with due regard to legal requirements for protecting patient confidentiality and the disclosure of information. It is recommended that clear protocols are drawn up which cover the need for security and clinical records to be kept as entirely separate entities.

The security director in discharging their duties under Direction 19(4)(d) should ensure they consider any request for disclosing security records and hold the authority for sharing security information.

Direction 20: Patients' possessions

Providers must have regard to the standards set out in the Clinical Security   **4-041**
Framework when developing policies for managing patients' property.
Providers should also have regard to the following:

(a)   If a patient is denied access to an item of property under this Direction they
should be given a reason for that refusal if they request it, and be informed
of the process for appealing that decision; and

(b)   The possessions in patients' rooms and their personal lockers should be
limited to a level and type which are compatible with the facilitation of
searching within a defined period of time outlined in both the Clinical
Security Framework and hospital policy, the maintenance of security and the
reduction of fire hazards. Providers should also manage the risk presented
by the potential to misuse technology, particularly that capable of displaying, recording, storing and distributing images and other data.

Although not a requirement of the Direction, it is good practice to ensure all access to electrical items in patients' rooms should be thoroughly risk assessed.

If patients are allowed access to electrical items in their rooms, the quantity
should be appropriately limited and exclude multiple items of the same type (e.g.
they should only have a single television, CD player etc).

Each provider should have a strategy for managing patients' access to televised
and other similar material which includes appropriate controls over access to unacceptable / clinically harmful material. The strategy should be compliant with the following guidelines:

(a)   Patients should not be able to access pay-to-view television unless this is
controlled by the provider;

(b)   Access to equipment capable of recording televised material should only be
allowed if the provider has in place effective controls and systems for checking recorded content;

(c)   Patients should not have access to equipment capable of making copies of
previously recorded video material;

(d)   Care should be exercised when considering access to new/developing
technologies which are designed for or could be used for recording/storing
images; and

(e)   Patients should not be allowed to loan or exchange recorded material
amongst themselves unless by prior agreement with a suitably qualified
member of nursing/medical staff who should ensure that any necessary
amendments are made to the property inventories of the patients concerned.

Patients may have access to electrical items that the clinical team, acting on advice
from the security department, has agreed the patient may have.

Direction 21: Items delivered or brought to hospital premises for patients and
Direction 25: Patients' incoming post

Providers should have regard to the standards set out in the Clinical Security   **4-042**
Framework when developing policies for managing items delivered or brought to
the hospital premises for patients.

Items delivered or brought to hospital premises for patients include any items of
patients' property arriving at hospital on admission, carried by patients or otherwise
and property carried by a patient on return from leave of absence.

Where multi-media devices, DVDs, videos or items in other formats intended for

[871]

/ or are capable of recording images are concerned, it is recommended that:

(a) Any item delivered or brought into the hospital premises should, on arrival in the hospital, be checked by an authorised member of staff to establish that it is what it is purported to be and then, subject to c) below, be passed to the clinical team for a decision as to whether or not it is suitable for the patient for whom it is intended. Bearing in mind that apparently innocent content may be considered inappropriate for some patients;

(b) No item should be passed to a patient if it has a classification of 18R;

(c) Patient's access to information technology equipment should be controlled in accordance with Direction 22.

Providers should have arrangements in place for managing items delivered to the hospital for patients that they are not allowed, either because they breach the Directions, the Clinical Security Framework or the provider's policy.

Direction 22: Patients' access to information technology equipment and the internet

4-043 Providers must have in place policies for controlling patient's access to, and use of, information technology equipment and the internet. Such policies must have regard to the standards set out in the Clinical Security Framework.

Policies should be underpinned by robust risk assessment to anticipate and mitigate risks associated with introducing rapidly developing technologies and their potential impact on the security of the hospital. These policies should be informed where necessary by independent expert advice.

"Direct supervision" means the patient is subject to a member of staff sitting with them and directly supervising their access;"remote supervision" means the supervising member of staff is undertaking this supervision via remote location (on another computer).

A patient's access to information technology equipment in their room should only be allowed following risk assessment of the patient.

Direction 24: Role of patients in managing or working in patients' shops and other specified employment

4-044 When identifying any suitable employment opportunities for patients in the hospital, providers should consider the risks associated with these opportunities.

Where the level of risk is considered to be similar or higher than that presented by working in a patients' shop, these work placements should be classified as 'specified employment' opportunities. It is for the provider to decide what work falls within the definition of 'specified employment'.

Referrals to the Grounds Access Committee should only be made where a patient's clinical team has undertaken a risk assessment and proposes that working in a patients' shop or in 'specified employment' should be included as part of the patient's treatment plan.

Direction 27: Internal post

4-045 Post between patients and members of their clinical team should not be opened routinely under this Direction. Post between patients and staff should only be opened in response to security or other concerns.

Direction 28: Incoming post addressed to members of staff

Postal packets addressed to staff should not be opened and inspected for security **4-046**
reasons unless the addressee is present and has given their consent.

Staff should be informed that a postal packet addressed to them is not allowed
into the secure area if they refuse to allow it to be opened and inspected.

If a postal packet is withheld the member of staff should be informed of the
following:

(a) the reasons for withholding it;

(b) that they can request that the security director review the decision to withhold it; and

(c) that they can take the postal packet when they leave the secure area.

Direction 29: mobile telephones

When developing local policies for the management of mobile telephones, the **4-047**
provider must have regard to the standards set out in the Clinical Security
Framework. The routine authorisation of mobile telephones for staff use within the
secure perimeter is not expected.

Patients are not allowed possession of, or access to mobile telephones within the
secure area. Any patient access to a mobile telephone outside of the secure area,
such as when on an extended medical leave of absence for compassionate reasons,
should be risk assessed and recorded in the Leave of Absence Management Plan
and be directly supervised by escorting staff and authorised by the security director.

Direction 30: Patients' outgoing telephone calls

Providers must have regard to the standards set out in the Clinical Security **4-048**
Framework when developing policies for managing patients' outgoing telephone
calls.

Where a provider decides to include patient contact with the Samaritans within
its policy on telephone use by patients, it should agree its policy proposals, and the
detailed arrangements, with the Samaritans prior to making the service available to
patients.

Contact with the Samaritans should be on an individual patient basis, be risk assessed and included within the patient's treatment plan.

Direction 31: Patients' incoming telephone calls

Providers should have regard to the standards set out in the Clinical Security **4-049**
Framework when developing policies for managing patients' incoming telephone
calls.

Pre-arranged incoming calls should only be authorised when the caller is not in
a position to receive a call from the patient e.g. where the caller is a patient in
another high security hospital or another establishment which restricts incoming
calls.

Direction 32: Security Risk Assessments

Providers must have regard to the standards set out in the Clinical Security **4-050**
Framework when developing policies for managing security risk assessments of
patients.

[873]

Providers must ensure that when considering leave of absence for patients, including the preparation required in advance to facilitate an emergency medical leave of absence, the security risk assessment must be reflected in the leave of absence risk management plan for each individual patient and for each individual leave of absence episode.

Direction 35(2) Grounds Access requires that providers must include security arrangements and risk assessments in accordance with Direction 32 to enable a patient to be granted grounds access as part of a treatment plan.

Direction 33: Monitoring telephone calls

4-051　The identification of telephone calls for recording under paragraph (7) of this Direction should be based on a random selection.

Where a provider decides to retain a record under paragraph (8) of this Direction it should record the reason for that decision.

Direction 34: Security at night

4-052　Each provider should have a policy on the circumstances in which a patient can be locked in their room at night.

There is a distinction between night-time confinement under these Directions and seclusion. Locking the room of a patient at night under Direction 34 is not the same as seclusion.

Paragraphs 26.103 to 26.149 of the Mental Health Act 1983 Code of Practice ('the Code of Practice') define seclusion and describe processes for its use.

By contrast, arrangements made by a hospital for patients' rooms to be locked at night (referred to as night time confinement) refers to the pre-determined locking-in of patients, and not a reaction to a patient's immediate behaviour. Night-time confinement in accordance with the Directions should be pre-determined and only permitted in accordance with Direction 34. A risk assessment must be carried out under Direction 32 and a risk management plan prepared, which must include any decision (including a date on which the decision must be reviewed) to lock the room of a patient at night in accordance with Direction 34.

Longer-term segregation as described in paragraph 26.150 of the Code of Practice is also not the same as night-time confinement under the Directions. Longer-term segregation of a patient should follow guidance in paragraphs 26.150 to 26.160 of the Code of Practice.

Annex A provides an example of a protocol to meet the requirement for an individual risk assessment of each patient. The protocol incorporates arrangements for considering whether high risk patients should or could be locked in their rooms at night as part of their risk management plan made under the Directions.

Annex B provides an example of a protocol which sets out the requirements for making decisions regarding the locking of other patients (under Direction 34) in their rooms at night.

Direction 35: Grounds Access

4-053　Grounds access is a positive activity that all patients may, following a security risk assessment, be granted by the provider's Grounds Access Committee in accordance with Direction 37 or the medical director in accordance with Direction 38.

A request for grounds access should be made by a member of the clinical team to the Grounds Access Committee and must only be refused if this will adversely affect the safety and security of patients, staff or visitors or the security of the hospital.

Further to the interpretation and definition of 'grounds access' within Direction 2, this does not include unescorted patient access into ward garden areas which are to be treated as part of the ward area if:

(a) the garden area is accessible from the patient's ward;

(b) the garden area is defined by a demarcation line which effectively separates it from adjacent areas; and

(c) access is approved by the patient's clinical team following individual documented risk assessment.

Direction 37: Functions of the Grounds Access Committee

The provider's policy for grounds access must ensure that if the Grounds Access Committee refuse a request for grounds access that the individual patient has the right to request, through their responsible clinician, a review of the decision in accordance with Direction 38.

4-054

When granting grounds access the Grounds Access Committee must identify the area or areas of the hospital premises to which the grounds access applies.

It is recommended that the Grounds Access Committee should, as part of its responsibilities, keep under review the total number, and the mix, of patients who should be permitted grounds access at any one time.

Direction 39: Leave of absence

The provider must ensure that before a patient is granted leave of absence, or for planning the arrangements to facilitate an emergency medical leave of absence, the responsible clinician, having consulted the patient's clinical team produces a risk assessment in compliance with Direction 39.

4-055

When developing policies for the management of leave of absence, providers should ensure they have regard to any relevant Ministry of Justice guidance to responsible clinicians and any guidance within the Clinical Security Framework. They should also consider the following:

(a) Child protection issues should be a central consideration in leave of absence planning. Contact between patients and named children during leave of absence must be approved following the principles outlined in the High Security Psychiatric Services (Arrangements for Visits by Children) Directions 2013;

(b) When leave of absence is used for rehabilitation purposes, it should be written into a care plan and have clear objectives;

(c) Whilst the responsible clinician has statutory power to grant leave of absence (subject to Ministry of Justice consent where necessary), the security director has a responsibility to consider and advise on safety issues and to approve all leave of absence management plans. Leave of absence should not take place unless the management arrangements are approved; and

(d) Unescorted leave of absence is only likely to be appropriate in exceptional circumstances.

Direction 40: Escorting patients

4-056   All staff including drivers involved in the escorting of patients must receive training as appropriate to their role and in accordance with the Clinical Security Framework.

When developing policies for members of staff on carrying out escorting duties, including the appropriate use of handcuffs, escorting chains and other mechanical restraints, providers must have regard to the standards set out in the Clinical Security Framework.

Direction 41: Security of keys and locks

4-057   When developing policies for members of staff and other key-holders on the security of keys and locks, providers must have regard to the standards set out in the Clinical Security Framework.

All key-holders will be subject to Enhanced DBS clearance.

Direction 43: Provision of training

4-058   All training should have due regard to the standards set out in the Clinical Security Framework.

5   General Guidance on Policies

4-059   **5.1** Providers are required by Direction 4 to cooperate with other providers for the purpose of making arrangements in respect of safety and security. However, it is for each provider to develop its policies around the Directions, guidance and the standards set out in the Clinical Security Framework. This includes deciding whether to apply more rigorous arrangements either across the hospital as a whole, in particular areas of the hospital or with regard to specific patients or patient groups.

5.2 Providers should consider the requirements of the whole hospital environment when developing organisational policies. It will often be appropriate for them to have a separate or supplementary policy framework to effectively meet all these needs. Providers should also ensure that these policies can only be changed with clearance at the highest management level.

5.3 When developing, reviewing, amending and implementing these policies providers should fulfil their responsibilities regarding human rights and equality outlined in paragraph 3.1 above.

5.4 Providers should ensure that each policy clearly states:
    (a)   the objective that it is intended to achieve;
    (b)   how that objective is to be achieved;
    (c)   the key staff group(s) to be involved in its implementation and operation;
    (d)   what, if any, scope there is for staff discretion in its operation – it being accepted that within the framework of hospital policies there may be a number of clearly defined areas where clinical units/directorates and clinical teams may exercise discretion to interpret policies to reflect the distinctive needs of a particular patient group;
    (e)   how and when the policy will be reviewed; and

[876]

(f)   who has lead responsibility for the policy.

5.5   To ensure effective implementation providers should have appropriate arrangements in place to inform, educate and train staff about the existence of, and reasons for, each policy, together with an efficient audit mechanism.

5.6   It is recommended that:
(a)   each provider ensures that all patients are informed, where appropriate, of the content of policies that affect them. The Clinical Security Framework provides further instruction to providers on policy content that must be shared with patients as well as policies that must not be shared with patients;
(b)   all hospital staff have access on request, or direct access, to the Clinical Security Framework;
(c)   an up to date record of all relevant policies is easily and readily available to all ward staff and its location and contents are known by all ward staff;
(d)   the full policy documents are clear and concise. Staff should be required to know the contents of all relevant policies and have become familiar with them before working within the secure perimeter. They should be asked to confirm that they have read them and to re-confirm this regarding any changes made to them;
(e)   any changes to policies are immediately recorded in the policies record and communicated to all staff in advance of implementation by an agreed method, such as regular team briefings;
(f)   where staff are permitted to use discretion in the exercise of a policy, the reasons for exercising that discretion are recorded;
(g)   the number of policies is maintained at a manageable level so that staff are not overwhelmed and have a realistic prospect of becoming familiar with them. A single page summary attached to each policy, highlighting key principles and instructions for staff may be useful in this respect.

5.7   It is recommended that providers share copies of their main policies with each other to encourage sharing good practice and achieving a generally consistent approach across the high security hospitals. However, it is accepted that there may be some variation in the approach of each provider to reflect their different local circumstances.

5.8   Where appropriate, NHS England and providers should consider whether common issues and policies across the hospitals should be addressed through amending and updating the Clinical Security Framework to ensure consistent best practice across all providers of high secure services.

5.9   NHS England must work with providers and through the Clinical Secure Practice Forum to regularly review and update the Clinical Security Framework to ensure it remains up to date with current best practice.

5.10   NHS England must maintain a robust governance framework for monitoring and updating the Clinical Security Framework with oversight from the National Oversight Group for High Secure Services.

6   Annex A: Risk Assessments, the Determination of 'High Risk' and Risk Management Plans

4-060   *Protocol for:*
   (a)   *risk assessment and management (Direction 32);*
   (b)   *identification and management of 'high risk' patients in high security hospitals; and*
   (c)   *locking these patients in their rooms at night (Direction 34).*

6.1   This protocol is designed to ensure that the public, patients and staff in hospitals are protected from harm by addressing systematically the risks that patients may present. It enables the identification of all patients who present high levels of risk in specific areas (see Direction 32(4)) and suggests options for the safe management of these risks. It includes consideration as to whether locking patients in their rooms at night should be included within risk management plans in accordance with Direction 34 and associated guidance.

6.2   The mental disorder which led to a patient's admission to hospital may have a profound effect on the presentation of risk, causing it to fluctuate (often frequently) over time and producing different types of risk in combination. Consideration should be given to the interdependencies of all risks within the risk management plan, and the impact of mitigating action on each risk, to ensure safety is not compromised.

6.3   This protocol should be used to assess patients at 6-monthly intervals, at least, but the frequency of assessment should be set for individual patients in the light of their clinical condition and security intelligence (see Direction 32(9)).

6.4   For reasons including, but not confined to, their mental disorder, some patients may be unwilling or unable to cooperate with arrangements for managing risks. When developing risk management plans for patients, consideration must be given to their capability of making appropriate decisions.

6.5   Good practice requires the management of patients and identified risks includes the development of a multi-disciplinary care plan, alongside a risk management plan, as a key component of risk reduction in the effective treatment of the patient's mental disorder.

6.6   *Below is a model protocol for risk assessments, the determination of 'high risk' (Direction 32) and the development of risk management plans including whether these should include locking patients in their rooms at night (Direction 34).*
   (a)   A multi-disciplinary risk assessment must be undertaken and recorded to ensure that security risks are identified (see Direction 32). This risk assessment must be used to make a judgment as to whether the patient presents a 'high risk' in either of the two main categories:
      (i)   risk of escaping or absconding; and
      (ii)   risk of subverting safety and security, or organising action to subvert safety and security.
   (b)   A management plan for each identified risk should be agreed and documented by the multi-disciplinary team (see Direction 32(5) and *Attachment 2*).

[878]

(c) Review dates should be agreed and documented for each identified risk and its associated management plan (see Direction 32(8)). In some instances, the review frequency may be determined by the policies governing the specific interventions deployed (e.g. seclusion, close observation etc).

(d) In any category, risk may range from 'no risk' to 'high risk' and this is a matter of clinical judgement. The underpinning reasons for the conclusion must be documented if the patient is assessed as 'high risk' in any of the main categories (see Direction 32(8)(a)).

(e) The clinical team should consult a member of the security department when drawing up the management plan and must do so if the patient is assessed as 'high risk' (see Direction 32(7)).

(f) A decision tree has been designed to standardise the development of risk management plans for each identified risk (see *Attachment 1*).

(g) Where the patient is identified as 'high risk' such plans could include any one or all of the procedures noted in the decision tree, determined in the light of all relevant clinical factors. Where following this protocol would suggest a patient should be locked in their room at night but this is not pursued, the reasons for not doing so should be recorded.

(h) The provider's policy should include a requirement that, before a decision is taken to include locking a patient in their room in their risk management plan, the patient's clinical team must first consider whether there are clinical or psychosocial grounds for not locking the patient up at night. For example, this may be a consideration for patients assessed as at risk of taking their own life or self-harming. These risks should be balanced with the security risks (see *Attachment 1*, and Box 1 in *Attachment 2*).

(i) The provider's policy should include arrangements for reviewing any decision to include locking a patient in their room at night as part of their risk management plan. This should include both a requirement for regular reviews, and reviews whenever assessed risk levels change (see Direction 32(9)).

(j) Locking of patients' rooms at night, where they have been assessed as 'high risk', may contribute to maintaining the safety of patients, staff, public and the overall security of the establishment.

(k) Locking a patient in their room at night must only take place if the room has integral sanitation and a staff call system, or the patient is continuously observed by a member of staff (see Direction 34(2)).

(l) Locking a patient in their room at night must be supervised containment and frequent monitoring and review of the patient will be necessary. The local seclusion procedures should be referred to as a model of good practice in this respect, thus ensuring any necessary changes in the patient's management are made in a timely manner to address changes in the patient's clinical presentation.

(m) Most patients are asleep in their rooms at night. Supervision of corridors is crucial to detecting patient movement, which may be an indication of increasing risk and hence a need to upgrade the risk management plan. Corridor supervision can be enhanced by deploying increased levels of staff. This should be considered as part of the overall risk management policy for the hospital. However, consideration should also be given to deploying technologies (e.g. CCTV monitoring of corridors, video motion detectors, infra-red detectors, bedroom door alarms) to provide technological support to clinical management and enhance risk management by ensuring the untoward movement of any patient will be identified, even when not anticipated.

7 Annex B: Protocol For Locking Non 'High Risk' Patients in Their Rooms At Night

Protocol for making decisions regarding locking patients in their rooms at night where this is not part of a risk management plan to manage 'high risk' (Direction 32)

4-061 **7.1** This protocol sets out the requirements for providers wishing to include arrangements in their policies for locking individual patients, or groups of patients, in their room(s) at night (Direction 34) where this is not part of a risk management plan to manage their 'high risk' (Direction 32), nor patients locked in their rooms as part of local seclusion policies.

7.2 Providers may include these arrangements within their policies, but these should only be put in place where it is considered that this will maximise therapeutic benefit for patients, as a whole, in the hospital.

7.3 No patient should be locked in their room at night if it is considered this would have a detrimental effect on their well-being (see paragraphs (7.5) & (7.6) below).

7.4 Groups of patients should only be locked in their rooms at night following discussion and approval at Board level. These arrangements should be reviewed on a minimum three-monthly basis.

7.5 The provider's policy should include a requirement that, before a decision is taken to lock a patient in their room at night, the patient's clinical team must consider whether there are clinical or psychosocial grounds for not taking this action.

7.6 Arrangements, reflected in the provider policies, should also be made for reviewing decisions if there are circumstances, for example the risk of suicide or self-harm, which would indicate that locking the patient in their room at night might have a detrimental effect on their well-being or be unsafe.

7.7 Locking a patient in their room at night must only take place if the room has integral sanitation and a staff call system or the patient is continuously observed by a member of staff (see Direction 34(2)).

7.8 Locking a patient in their room at night must be supervised containment and frequent monitoring and review of the patient will be necessary. This is to ensure that any necessary changes in the patient's management are made in a timely manner to address changes in the patient's clinical presentation. Locked-in patients should not be left unsupervised at night, and there must be capacity to unlock them at any time if clinically indicated.

ATTACHMENT 1: DECISION TREE FOR RISK MANAGEMENT OF HIGH RISK PATIENTS

Decision tree for risk management of 'high risk' patients, including decisions about locking them into their rooms at night to manage risk

4-062

ATTACHMENT 2: MANAGEMENT STRATEGIES

Management strategies supporting the decision making for the risk management of 'high risk' patients

Box 1

4-063

High Risk Suicide/Self Harm
Specific treatment focussed on suicide/self-harm for the individual;
reduced access to risk items;
enhanced levels of observation (refer to hospital's observation policy);
enhanced emotional support; and

occasionally a suicidal/self-harming patient is also violent and prone to assaulting others and in this situation the patient may be locked in their room at night in conjunction with enhanced levels of observation.[2]

Box 2

High risk of Escape or Absconding

locking in room for identified 'high risk' periods (e.g. night time)[3];[4]

geographical manipulation i.e. consider moving the patient to a higher staffed location, or restrict access to a more confined area of the ward;[5]

enhanced monitoring of visits (including closed visits) or temporary suspension of visits;[6]

enhanced monitoring of mail and telephone calls;[7]

enhanced precautions for leave of absence from hospital (refer to policy);[8]

enhanced escorting (to be specified precisely) for movement within hospital's secure perimeter;[9]

enhanced levels of observation (refer to the provider's observation policy);[10]

enhanced restrictions on access to risk items;

enhanced search/drug screening procedures.[11]

Box 3

High Risk of Subverting Security

---

[2] locking patients in their rooms at night should be supervised (see paragraph 6.6(1) *Annex A* & 7.8 of *Annex B*).

[3] a decision not to lock a patient in their room at night in accordance with the protocol should be clearly documented in the notes.

[4] locking patients in their rooms at night should be supervised (see paragraph 6.6(1) *Annex A* & 7.8 of *Annex B*).

[5] if these measures do not reduce the risk of escape in the view of the clinical team and security department, then locking in for 'high risk' periods may be necessary (see paragraphs (32) & (34) of the Directions).

[6] if these measures do not reduce the risk of escape in the view of the clinical team and security department, then locking in for 'high risk' periods may be necessary (see paragraphs (32) & (34) of the Directions).

[7] if these measures do not reduce the risk of escape in the view of the clinical team and security department, then locking in for 'high risk' periods may be necessary (see paragraphs (32) & (34) of the Directions).

[8] if these measures do not reduce the risk of escape in the view of the clinical team and security department, then locking in for 'high risk' periods may be necessary (see paragraphs (32) & (34) of the Directions).

[9] if these measures do not reduce the risk of escape in the view of the clinical team and security department, then locking in for 'high risk' periods may be necessary (see paragraphs (32) & (34) of the Directions).

[10] if these measures do not reduce the risk of escape in the view of the clinical team and security department, then locking in for 'high risk' periods may be necessary (see paragraphs (32) & (34) of the Directions).

[11] if these measures do not reduce the risk of escape in the view of the clinical team and security department, then locking in for 'high risk' periods may be necessary (see paragraphs (32) & (34) of the Directions).

locking in room for identified 'high risk' periods (e.g. night time)[12];[13]

geographical manipulation i.e. consider moving the patient to a higher staffed location, or restrict access to a more confined area of the ward;[14]

enhanced monitoring of visits (including closed visits) or temporary suspension of visits;[15]

enhanced monitoring of mail and telephone calls;[16]

enhanced precautions for leave of absence from hospital (refer to policy);[17]

enhanced escorting (to be specified precisely) for movement within hospital's secure perimeter;[18]

enhanced levels of observation (refer to the provider's observation policy);[19]

enhanced restrictions on access to risk items;

enhanced search/drug screening procedures.[20]

Box 4

Corridor Supervision at night
Corridor supervision can be enhanced by increasing levels of staff and this should be considered as part of risk management. Consideration should also be given to deploying technology to enhance corridor supervision. Appropriate technology would include CCTV monitoring of corridors, video motion detectors, infra-red detectors, and door alarms. These can all be used to give early warning of untoward patient movement.

---

[12] a decision not to lock a patient in their room at night in accordance with the protocol should be clearly documented in the notes.

[13] locking patients in their rooms at night should be supervised (see paragraph 6.6(1) *Annex A* & 7.8 of *Annex B*).

[14] if these measures do not reduce the risk of escape in the view of the clinical team and security department, then locking in for 'high risk' periods may be necessary (see paragraphs (32) & (34) of the Directions).

[15] if these measures do not reduce the risk of escape in the view of the clinical team and security department, then locking in for 'high risk' periods may be necessary (see paragraphs (32) & (34) of the Directions).

[16] if these measures do not reduce the risk of escape in the view of the clinical team and security department, then locking in for 'high risk' periods may be necessary (see paragraphs (32) & (34) of the Directions).

[17] if these measures do not reduce the risk of escape in the view of the clinical team and security department, then locking in for 'high risk' periods may be necessary (see paragraphs (32) & (34) of the Directions).

[18] if these measures do not reduce the risk of escape in the view of the clinical team and security department, then locking in for 'high risk' periods may be necessary (see paragraphs (32) & (34) of the Directions).

[19] if these measures do not reduce the risk of escape in the view of the clinical team and security department, then locking in for 'high risk' periods may be necessary (see paragraphs (32) & (34) of the Directions).

[20] if these measures do not reduce the risk of escape in the view of the clinical team and security department, then locking in for 'high risk' periods may be necessary (see paragraphs (32) & (34) of the Directions).

Medical Leave for Restricted Patients

(FEBRUARY 2021)

1. Introduction

4-064   This document sets out the arrangements that apply for restricted patients detained in psychiatric hospitals who are required to attend general hospitals, dentists, opticians or other designated medical facilities for appointments or procedures for their physical health.

This guidance formalises and replaces the arrangements for medical leave set out in the letter from the then Head of Mental Health Casework Section (MHCS) of 18 April 2019 to all Responsible Clinicians (RC). The 2019 letter provided RCs with general consent to exercise their power to grant leave for medical treatment under section 17 of the Mental Health Act 1983.

The guidance is subject to review or withdrawal as deemed appropriate by MHCS.

The guidance is not intended to supersede but instead to supplement the document 'Guidance: Section 17 – Leave of Absence' published in December 2020, which is available at the following link:

https://assets.publishing.service.gov.uk/government/uploads/system/uploads/attachment_data/file/946325/MHCS_Leave_Guidance.docx

The guidance should be read in conjunction with the document titled 'Mentally Disordered Offenders – The restricted patient system' which is available on the following link:

https://assets.publishing.service.gov.uk/government/uploads/system/uploads/attachment_data/file/670671/RP_Background_Brief_v1_Dec_2017.pdf

2. General Principles for Medical Leave

4-065   a.   **Authority for Medical Leave** The statutory authority to facilitate the absence of a patient from a psychiatric hospital be that secure, locked or open is set out in section 17 of the Mental Health Act 1983 (The 1983 Act). Detained patients who are subject to 'special restrictions' as set out in sections 41 and 49 of the 1983 Act require the Secretary of State's approval to take leave of absence from a hospital for any purpose.

b.   **Medical Appointments and Procedures Definition** This consent for routine day appointments or overnight medical leave applies only to situations where there is a medical need for the treatment/appointment outside the secure hospital site. The Secretary of State does not generally consider that cosmetic surgery, tattoo removal, or similar elective treatments are essential. Where the RC is of the view that such an appointment is essential, a RC must seek authority for such an appointment from the Secretary of State, by application.

c.   **Managing Risk** In all cases an appropriate risk assessment must be carried out by the RC in advance of any medical appointment and consideration must be given as to whether it is necessary to impose further security measures based on the level of risk identified.

If there are incidences of the leave being misused or evidence of behaviours which pose a risk to the public or patient, the RC must suspend the leave.

The Secretary of State's consent is given on the understanding that the granting of section 17 leave pursuant to this Guidance involves no undue risk to the patient or to others and that there is a medical need for the treatment/ appointment outside the secure hospital site.

If the patient fails to return to hospital from leave by the agreed time, the local police should be contacted at once and the Mental Health Casework Section should be informed by telephone, with a follow up written report from the RC.

Our contact details can be obtained from this link: HMPPS Mental Health Casework Section contact list - GOV.UK (*www.gov.uk*)

d. **Recording instances of Medical Leave** Details of the medical leave taken for treatment and appointments should be recorded in the Annual Statutory Reports that must be routinely submitted to MHCS.

3. High Profile Patients

High profile patients are not covered by this general authority for medical leave and the Responsible Clinician must apply for medical leave through MHCS. The application for medical leave can be found at: *https://www.gov.uk/government/ publications/leave-application-for-restricted-patients*   **4-066**

High profile patients are designated as such by MHCS either on admission to hospital or following a referral for a review of that status. Hospitals are informed of which of their patients are classed as high profile and if they are unsure they can contact MHCS. The guidance that sets out the 'Designation and Management of High Profile Restricted Patients' by MHCS can be found at the link below: *https:// assets.publishing.service.gov.uk/government/uploads/system/uploads/attachment_ data/file/845326/Guidance_-_The_Designation_and_Management_of_High_Profile_ Restricted_Patients__2_.pdf*

a. **Emergency Treatment for High Profile Patients** Where a high profile patient is required to attend hospital in an emergency, any pre-existing escorting arrangements for medical leave should be implemented as far as the hospital are able. However, any need for emergency treatment will outweigh the requirement to adhere to pre-existing arrangements. Where there are no pre-existing arrangements then the hospital should ensure that the patient has escorts within close proximity of the patient for any appointments and within eyeline for any procedures.

MHCS will expect to be notified at the earliest opportunity when a high profile patient has been removed from hospital for emergency treatment, either by email to MHCSmailbox@justice.gov.uk or by calling one of the numbers set out below:

07812 760 274
07812 760 582
07812 760 523
07812 760 356

4. High Secure Hospitals – any restricted patient

For all restricted patients who are not high profile and are detained in high security, consent to section 17 leave for the purposes of medical treatment is granted in the following terms: **4-067**

In accordance with section 41(3)(c) of the Mental Health Act 1983 ("the 1983 Act"), the Secretary of State consents to the exercise of the power in section 17 of the 1983 Act to grant a leave of absence for the purposes of attending medical appointments to any restricted patient detained in a High Secure Hospital, subject to the following conditions:

a. **Emergencies** In the case of emergency medical leave the priority is to deal with the physical health crisis. Responsible Clinicians should apply appropriate security arrangements at their discretion. Responsible Clinicians are asked to seek to ensure the usual security arrangements as set out in b, below, are in place, but the Secretary of State recognises that this will not always be possible or appropriate in an emergency situation.

There is no need to inform the Secretary of State of the emergency medical leave immediately, but an email to MHCS at MHCSmailbox@justice.gov.uk as soon as practicable is requested. Where appropriate, the Responsible Clinician should also inform the local Police. If the admission to general hospital develops into overnight leave, the arrangements at c. should be put into place and the Secretary of State should be informed.

b. **Routine Day Appointments** In the case of routine appointments, Responsible Clinicians have authority to grant leave at their discretion according to the following conditions:

- The patient must be escorted by a minimum of three (3) members of staff at all times.
- The patient must be transported in secure hospital vehicle. A driver is in addition to the three escort staff.
- Handcuffs must be used at all times, except when their removal is necessary for the purposes of a medical appointment or procedure.
- The patient must return to hospital immediately following the appointment/s.
- If any concerns arise, leave must be immediately suspended and MHCS notified.
- A check on victim location should be made in order to prevent possible inadvertent contact (through the Victim Liaison Officer if there is one)

Any request to deviate from these conditions must be agreed in writing by the Secretary of State.

Applications for deviation should be submitted via the link below: *https ://www.gov.uk/government/publications/leave-application-for-restricted-patients*

c. **Overnight Medical Leave**

- In the case of overnight medical leave appointments for one or more nights, Responsible Clinicians have authority to grant leave at their discretion according to the following conditions:
- The Responsible Clinician must inform the Secretary of State in writing in advance of the overnight leave setting out the reason for the overnight stay and the expected length of time such leave will take
- The patient must be escorted by a minimum of three (3) members of staff at all times
- They must travel in a secure hospital vehicle with a separate driver
- Handcuffs must be used at all times, except when their removal is necessary for a medical procedure
- A check on victim location should be made in order to prevent pos-

sible inadvertent contact (through the Victim Liaison Officer if there is one)

- The patient must be returned to hospital immediately following discharge from general hospital
- If any concerns arise, leave must be immediately suspended, or security arrangements increased to protect the public

Any request to deviate from these conditions must be agreed in writing by the Secretary of State.

Applications for deviation should be submitted via the link below: *https ://www.gov.uk/government/publications/leave-application-for-restricted-patients*

5. Patients transferred from prisons or subject to section 45A hospital direction and limitation directions

Terms of medical leave for all hospitals, other than high secure, for patients detained under sections 45A, 47/49, 48/49 of the 1983 Act: **4-068**

In accordance with section 41(3)(c) of the Mental Health Act 1983 ("the 1983 Act"), the Secretary of State consents to the exercise of the power in section 17 of the 1983 Act to grant a leave of absence for the purposes of attending medical appointments subject to the following conditions:

a. **Emergencies** In the case of emergency medical leave the priority is to deal with the physical health crisis. Responsible Clinicians should apply appropriate security arrangements at their discretion. Responsible Clinicians are asked to seek to ensure the usual security arrangements as set out in b, below, are in place, but the Secretary of State recognises that this will not always be possible or appropriate in an emergency situation.

There is no need to inform the Secretary of State of the emergency medical leave immediately, but an email to MHCS at MHCSmailbox@justice.gov.uk as soon as practicable is requested. Where appropriate, the Responsible Clinician should also inform the local Police. If the admission to general hospital develops into overnight leave, the arrangements at c. should be put into place and the Secretary of State should be informed.

b. **Routine Day Appointments** In the case of routine appointments, Responsible Clinicians have authority to grant leave at their discretion according to the following conditions:

- The patient must be escorted by a minimum of two (2) members of staff at all times
- They must travel in a secure vehicle with a separate driver (in addition to the 2 escorting staff)
- Handcuffs must be carried and are to be worn as necessary
- A check on victim location should be made in order to prevent possible inadvertent contact (through the Victim Liaison Officer if there is one)
- The patient must be returned to hospital immediately following the appointments
- If any concerns arise, leave must be immediately suspended

Any request to deviate from these conditions must be agreed in writing by the Secretary of State.

Applications for deviation should be submitted via the link below: *https*

[887]

://www.gov.uk/government/publications/leave-application-for-restricted-patients

  c. **Overnight Medical Leave** In the case of overnight medical leave appointments for one or more nights, Responsible Clinicians have authority to grant leave at their discretion according to the following conditions:

- The Responsible Clinician must inform the Secretary of State in writing in advance of the overnight leave setting out the reason for the overnight stay and the expected length of time such leave will take
- The patient must be escorted by a minimum of two (2) members of staff at all times
- They must travel in a secure vehicle with a separate driver (in addition to the 2 escorting staff)
- Handcuffs must carried and are to be worn as necessary
- A check on victim location should be made in order to prevent possible inadvertent contact (through the Victim Liaison Officer if there is one)
- The patient must be returned to hospital immediately following discharge from general hospital
- If any concerns arise, leave must be immediately suspended, or security arrangements increased to protect the public

Any request to deviate from these conditions must be agreed in writing by the Secretary of State.

Applications for deviation should be submitted via the link below: *https ://www.gov.uk/government/publications/leave-application-for-restricted-patients*

6. Patients Subject to section 37/41 orders

4-069   Terms of medical leave for all hospitals, other than high secure, for patients detained under sections 37/41 hospital orders (or equivalent):

In accordance with section 41(3)(c) of the Mental Health Act 1983 ("the 1983 Act"), the Secretary of State consents to the exercise of the power in section 17 of the 1983 Act to grant a leave of absence for the purposes of attending medical appointments subject to the following conditions:

  a. **Emergencies** In the case of emergency medical leave the priority is to deal with the physical health crisis. Responsible Clinicians should apply appropriate security arrangements at their discretion. Responsible Clinicians are asked to seek to ensure the usual security arrangements as set out in b below. Are in place, but the Secretary of State recognises that this will not always be possible or appropriate in an emergency situation.

There is no need to inform the Secretary of State of the emergency medical leave immediately, but an email to MHCS at MHCSmailbox@justice.gov.uk as soon as practicable is requested. Where appropriate, the Responsible Clinician should also inform the local Police. If the admission to general hospital develops into overnight leave, the arrangements at c. should be put into place and the Secretary of State should be informed.

  b. **Routine Day Appointments** In the case of routine appointments, Responsible Clinicians have authority to grant leave at their discretion according to the following conditions:

- The patient must be escorted by a minimum of two (2) members of staff at all times
- Use of handcuffs is at the Responsible Clinician's discretion
- Use of secure transport is at the Responsible Clinician's discretion
- A check on victim location should be made in order to prevent possible inadvertent contact (through the Victim Liaison Officer if there is one)
- The patient must be returned to hospital immediately following the appointments
- If any concerns arise, leave must be immediately suspended

Any request to deviate from these conditions must be agreed in writing by the Secretary of State.

Applications for deviation should be submitted via the link below: *https ://www.gov.uk/government/publications/leave-application-for-restricted-patients*

c. **Overnight Medical Leave** In the case of overnight medical leave appointments for one or more nights, Responsible Clinicians have authority to grant leave at their discretion according to the following conditions:

- The Responsible Clinician must inform the Secretary of State in writing in advance of the overnight leave setting out the reason for the overnight stay and the expected length of time such leave will take
- The patient must be escorted by a minimum of two (2) members of staff at all times
- Use of handcuffs is at the Responsible Clinician's discretion
- Use of secure transport is at the Responsible Clinician's discretion
- A check on victim location should be made in order to prevent possible inadvertent contact (through the Victim Liaison Officer if there is one)
- The patient must be returned to hospital immediately following discharge from general hospital
- If any concerns arise, leave must be immediately suspended, or security arrangements increased to protect the public

Any request to deviate from these conditions must be agreed in writing by the Secretary of State.

Applications for deviation should be submitted via the link below: *https ://www.gov.uk/government/publications/leave-application-for-restricted-patients*

7. Escorts not employed by the detaining hospital

The Secretary of State expects hospitals to use staff directly employed by that hospital when medical leave is being undertaken. However, MHCS understand occasions may arise where this will not be possible. If hospitals require staff not directly employed by them to act as escorts then the RC must submit an application to vary the conditions, stating why staff not employed by the hospital are being used as escorts. MHCS will expect that the necessary delegation of escorting responsibilities is authorised in advance by hospital managers in accordance with section 17(3) of the 1983 Act.   **4-070**

Applications for the variation can be submitted via the link below: *https:// www.gov.uk/government/publications/leave-application-for-restricted-patients*

GUIDANCE: SECTION 17 – LEAVE OF ABSENCE

(MARCH 2022)

1. Introduction

4-081   **1.1**   The Secretary of State for Justice (SoS) recognises that leave has an important part to play in the treatment and rehabilitation of restricted patients. It also provides valuable information to help ensure the safe management of restricted patients whilst detained in hospital and help prepare them for subsequent life in the community when discharged. The SoS recognises the need to balance the protection of the public with the rights of patients to receive treatment. This guidance sets out the SoS's approach to applications for community leave under section 17 of the Mental Health Act 1983 (MHA).

1.2   Mental Health Casework Section (MHCS) and NHS England (NHSE) have agreed joint performance management framework and target timescales for decisions setting out the roles and responsibilities of both parties (see: Performance Management Framework). The same principles and procedures will apply by MHCS to applications from patients under NHS Wales care.

2. Legal Provisions

4-082   **2.1**   Section 41(3)(c)(i) of the MHA requires a Responsible Clinician (RC) to obtain consent from the SoS before granting section 17 leave to a restricted patient. No such patient may leave the hospital or unit named on the detention authority (DA – see Glossary) without such consent. In practice, decisions are taken by officials from MHCS within HM Prison and Probation Service (HMPPS), an executive agency of the Ministry of Justice (MOJ), on behalf of the SoS under delegated arrangements.

3. Types of Restricted Patients

4-083   **3.1**   Restricted patients are mentally disordered offenders who are detained in hospital for treatment and who are subject to special controls by the SoS. They include offenders diverted from the Courts into the hospital system, and those transferred to secure hospitals from prison (or Immigration Centre) and made subject to a restriction direction. For full details of the types of Restricted Patient see Mentally disordered offenders - the restricted patient system.

4. Specific Categories of Patients

Patients Considered Unfit to Plead at their Trial

4-084   **4.1**   Patients identified by the Court as unfit to plead at the time of trial, and made subject to a Hospital Order made under section 5 of the Criminal Procedure (Insanity) Act 1964 (as substituted by s24 of the Domestic Violence Crime and Victims Act 2004), are subject to regular review by MHCS to establish whether they are now considered to be fit to plead (see guidance available here). In response to applications for leave on behalf of these patients, however, MHCS case managers may ask RCs again whether they think the patient is fit to plead their offence prior to making a decision. Applications are treated on their merits and decisions made following risk assessment irrespective of the patient's fitness to plead at any time but the overall context is that if the patient has recovered to the extent that they are considered suitable to have leave from hospital, then a question should also be asked about their suitability to stand trial for the offences for which they were originally considered unfit to plead.

Discharged Patients Recalled to Hospital

4.2 Restricted Patients who have previously been conditionally discharged into the community but recalled by warrant of the SoS, are detained under the terms of their original Hospital and Restriction Orders and controls on their leave in the community are resumed at the point they are admitted to hospital again. Such patients will not have any community leave and RCs will need to apply for leave in the usual way.

Transferred Prisoners

4.3 When making decisions on prisoners (and s45A patients), the SoS expects the RC to have considered whether, if the patient has recovered sufficiently well to be suitable for leave, they continue to meet the MHA detention criteria, and whether a return (remission) to prison should be sought. This is the case even if there have been previous indications that there is no intention to return the patient to prison, as remission is an option which remains open to the SoS at any time whilst the prison sentence is extant and the patient's condition subject to change at any time.

4.4 The SoS takes the view that, in general, transferred prisoners, and s45A patients, should not have unescorted leave in the community from secure hospitals where they would not be eligible to be considered for such leave from prison (under Release on Temporary Licence). However, each application will be treated on its merits and a risk assessment undertaken before a decision is made. RCs should consult with a transferred prisoner's Offender Manager prior to submitting an application to the SoS for consideration. Please refer to section 8 on victims below which also applies to applications from transferred prisoners.

High Profile Patients

4.5 There are some patients designated as 'High Profile' on, or after, entry into the system if, for example, it is considered that: they present an unusually high risk of harm; there are particularly sensitive victim issues; or they committed a noteworthy offence which has generated substantial media attention. For a full list of the criteria please see the guidance here. To help ensure public protection, senior managers within MHCS make the decisions on all applications for these patients in order to ensure that an added level of scrutiny is given. However, this does not mean that there is a different threshold or are different criteria which apply to considering applications for leave from patients designated as "high profile".

Foreign National Patients

4.6 The Home Office may have an interest in patients who are nationals of countries outside the UK particularly those who are suitable for deportation or have an outstanding deportation order against them. Leave is not automatically denied to these patients but account will be taken of their immigration status and their risk of absconding assessed.

Patients who Lack Capacity (and who may be subject to a DOLS Order following discharge)

4.7   There are a number of patients who, following assessment, are thought to lack capacity and who, if they were to be discharged into the community, would need, in their best interests, to be constantly supervised in a residential care home (or similar) under a Deprivation of Liberty Safeguards (DOLS) Order (Liberty Protection Safeguards) made under the Mental Capacity Act, as they are not able to live independently without the support such arrangements provide. When considering applications for leave for these patients the SoS will carefully consider the circumstances and assess the level of risk presented by the patient alongside the longer-term plans to discharge them into the community. Further details of the options available to patients who lack capacity can be found here.

5.   Applications for Community Leave

4-085   **5.1**   The SoS accepts that the mental health of the majority of patients will, at some stage in their treatment, improve to the point where the risk they pose is considered sufficiently low to enable their progress toward recovery to be tested out with leave in the community (usually with certain restrictions or conditions in place).

The Standard Application Form

5.2   To help ensure that the SoS receives all of the information necessary to take a decision, an application form for leave (apart from leave for medical treatment – see below) is available to RCs to use.

Risk Assessment

5.3   Officials within MHCS take decisions on applications following a risk assessment of the proposal. This system helps ensure that the SoS makes decisions which balance the need to protect the public, whilst recognising the rights of patients to receive treatment for their mental disorders under the MHA.

Leave within the Grounds of the Specified Detention Authority (DA)

5.4   The RC cannot allow the patient beyond the boundaries of the hospital or unit named on the DA without the SoS's agreement. However, it is accepted that the layout of each hospital or unit is unique and there are differences in the security arrangements at each site. RCs are free to contact MHCS to establish or discuss the practical effects of the DA on the patient at any time but should be familiar with the contents of the DA prior to allowing patients to access the grounds of their unit.

6.   Types of Leave authorised by the SoS

Leave for Medical Treatment

4-086   **6.1**   On entry into hospital either from Court, Immigration Centre or Prison (unless the patient is designated as High Profile), authority for leave outside the hospital will automatically be granted to allow patients access to either emergency treatment or to attend routine medical appointments. MHCS will set out the conditions applying to the authority in the letter sent to RCs following the imposition of the

[892]

Hospital Order or transfer direction or following recall. Only if the RC wishes to seek a derogation from the conditions set on entry need they apply to the SoS for medical leave (apart from emergency treatment). For derogations and for all High Profile patients, there is a separate medical leave guidance and application form for medical leave.

6.2 In emergency situations, prior SoS permission does not need to be sought for any patient but RCs should inform the MHCS as soon as possible via email giving brief details and expected or actual date of return to their detaining unit.

Escorted Day Leave

6.3 In most cases following treatment for their patient's disorder, the RC will wish to test the efficacy of that treatment by proposing leave in the community in order to give access to a greater range of rehabilitative activities. For many patients, this may be the first time they will experience life outside the hospital for some considerable time. The SoS recognises the importance of community leave as part of treatment but must balance the interests of public protection with any possible therapeutic benefits. Escorting the patient whilst on leave in the community is *normally* – i.e., where no concerns arise then or subsequently - the first stage in a graduated programme on the path to discharge in the longer term.

6.4 Escorts are defined as employees of the hospital Trust or those engaged on a formal contract basis or individuals authorised for this purpose by the hospital under s17(3) of the MHA. Generally, the number and ratio of escorts to patients will be left to the RC to determine but the SoS may, on occasion, specify a number and type of escort. Patients should be within a reasonable distance of escorts at all times so as to enable them to intervene quickly, if so required, to ensure public safety and security (and that of the patient).

Escorted Overnight Leave

6.5 RCs can apply for patients to have escorted leave which involves the patient spending one or more nights away from the hospital in which they are detained. Officials will give particular scrutiny to the expected therapeutic benefits of such leave, the proposed arrangements for any escorts and the availability of support for the patient should they become unwell (also see section on long-term escorted leave below).

Unescorted Day Leave

6.6 The SoS will consider applications for unescorted community leave at the point where the RC believes the patient is sufficiently fit and rehabilitated enough to be able to respect the conditions of leave, behave safely in the community and abide by the limits set for return to hospital without being escorted.

6.7 As with escorted community leave, the SoS will consider the particular circumstances of the request carefully and in particular will consider the patient's offence history, any incidents of abscond or escape, progress in hospital, the therapeutic benefit of the leave and the potential risk posed by the patient to themselves or others. As this decision involves the patient being in the community alone, perhaps for the first time since being detained in hospital, decisions are taken by senior officials within MHCS normally based on recommendations made by Case Managers thus ensuring added scrutiny is given to applications in the interests of public safety.

Unescorted Overnight Leave

6.8   As patients approach the stage of their rehabilitation where they are close to potential discharge, it is common for RCs to ask for unescorted overnight leave. As with any application for S17 leave, the SoS will only consent if satisfied the proposal does not put the public, or patient, at undue risk. The SoS will consider each application for overnight leave on its merits, but may require that the number of nights away from the detaining hospital is limited if necessary for the safe rehabilitation and testing of the patient or the appropriateness of their accommodation.

6.9   The SoS can consider applications for any period or periods of overnight leave to a named address, including those limiting the leave to a set number of nights per week or where the number of nights at the address per week are not limited (continuous leave). Overnight leave will only be agreed where there is a clear explanation from the RC outlining how the progress on leave will be managed, how it fits in the discharge plan and where it does not pose an unacceptable level of risk to the public or patient. Please note that this type of leave is differentiated from 'extended leave of absence' (see next section) in that the patient will ultimately be discharged from hospital without any restrictive conditions which may amount to a deprivation of liberty.

6.10   Continuous overnight leave will normally only be agreed for a maximum of three months with the expiration date clearly set out in the authorisation letters to the RC. At the conclusion of the three months, if required, the RC is able to apply for renewal of the authorisation by giving a brief report on its use and confirmation that the patient remains suitably placed and safe for the leave to continue. In the case of patients subject to s37/41 orders RCs should explain why an extension is being requested which would take the total authorisation to six months as this is considered to be a reasonable maximum period for such leave to take place prior to the application for discharge (to the Tribunal or the SoS). For patients under a s47/49 or s45A direction, who are subject to indeterminate sentences the release by the Parole Board will be used as the equivalent to discharge. The expiry of continuous overnight leave for patients subject to determinate sentences will be dictated by the restriction expiry date, which is the earliest date they could have been released from prison, if they had remained in prison custody. If they are not satisfied, the SoS will give consideration to either terminating the authority or (re)introducing a limitation on the number of nights per week.

6.11   Where the Tribunal has made a deferred conditional discharge and the proposed discharge address is a hostel or other placement, which insists on a minimum period of overnight assessment of the patient, the SoS will consider any request for overnight leave in the context of that decision, so as not to frustrate the proposed discharge. Nonetheless, the SoS will not grant permission for leave unless satisfied that it does not put the public, or patient, at an undue level of risk.

Long-Term Escorted Leave (Extended Leave of Absence)

6.12 There are a small number of restricted patients who it is difficult to discharge from hospital because of the risks associated with their mental disorder. In order to continue their treatment and rehabilitation, the SoS will consider applications for long-term (i.e. more than seven consecutive nights per week) escorted leave of absence in a community-based setting. Authority for such leave will be periodically reviewed at least annually and leave suspended if there is an escalation of risks presented by the patient. In considering such applications, the SoS will carefully assess what existing authority for leave exists and may rescind other types of leave in favour of this type. Further details are in section 6 of the guidance on Discharge Conditions which amount to a Deprivation of Liberty.

Compassionate Leave

6.13 Leave may sometimes be sought for compassionate reasons for patients who would not otherwise qualify, either because it does not involve any treatment or rehabilitation activity; on risk grounds; or because they have been in hospital for too short a time to have been assessed for community leave. Examples of this are to visit a terminally ill relative or to attend their funeral. The SoS will look sympathetically on such requests, but must still be satisfied with the risk control measures suggested by the hospital.

Leave to Attend Court

6.14 Where a Court directs the attendance of a patient, the SoS will rarely refuse consent to leave and for transferred prisoners remanded to prison (s48), escorted leave to attend Court in relation to the offence(s) under trial will be granted at the time of their transfer. However, applications for other types of patient should be submitted so that adequate arrangements are made to ensure the safety and security of the public. Existing leave authorisations can be used for this purpose but patients without such authority should not attend a court hearing without escort and will need the SoS's express agreement.

6.15 The SoS's permission is also required for leave to attend Court for other legal proceedings. It is recognised that some restricted patients may be required to attend Court for purposes other than criminal proceedings, for example to attend the Family Court. Where a patient's attendance is not strictly required but is voluntary or may be seen as useful to the administration of justice, the SoS will consider all applications according to the same criteria as outlined above. Again, existing leave authorisations can be used for this purpose but patients without such authority should not attend a court hearing without escort and will need the SoS's express agreement.

Leave for Restricted Patients Subject to Police Investigation

6.16 A patient who is the subject of Police interest, for example if an alleged offence has taken place while in hospital, or if earlier allegations come to light and are then to be investigated, can be arrested and taken to a Police station for questioning. The consent of the SoS is not necessary but the Police should be informed that the person is a detained patient, subject to the provisions of the MHA,

[895]

who must be returned to hospital at the conclusion of questioning. Hospitals should inform MHCS of the circumstances of the matter (in advance if possible) and advise them of the patient's return to hospital (or other conclusion). The SoS may apply additional scrutiny for requests for community leave for patients who are subject to ongoing police inquiry or who have outstanding criminal charges.

Leave outside England and Wales

Scotland

6.17 Section 17 leave to Scotland from England and Wales can be authorised subject to appropriate assessments of risk. Escorts from both Scotland and England & Wales have the necessary powers of custody in both jurisdictions. For unescorted leave, the patient may similarly be taken into lawful custody should it become necessary, with the intention of returning them to England & Wales. Explicit agreement for the period of leave will be sought from the Scottish Government at RestrictedPatient@gov.scot

Northern Ireland

6.18 Section 17 leave to Northern Ireland may also be permitted subject to appropriate assessments of risk with escorts from England & Wales having powers under the MHA to take into custody any patient who absconds or escapes. For unescorted leave, the patient may similarly be taken into lawful custody should it become necessary, with the intention of returning them to England & Wales.

Other Jurisdictions

6.19 RCs should seek MHCS advice if seeking leave to other jurisdictions within the UK (the Channel Islands and the Isle of Man). Leave will not be authorised to locations outside the UK under any circumstances.

7. Rescinding Leave Authority

4-087 **7.1** For all patients, once agreed, the SoS's consent to leave remains in operation unless the circumstances of the patient's health or other factors change the risk assessment. The RC should inform MHCS immediately should any change occur which materially affects the basis on which consent has previously been given, particularly any factor that changes a patient's risk. Based on that evidence, the SoS may rescind permission or suspend it for a period of time. The RC may also take action to suspend a patient's leave for similar reasons and should advise MHCS immediately if this occurs.

8. Victim Involvement

4-088 **8.1** When considering an application for community leave, the risk assessment will take into account any known victim considerations concerning measures which will help set the conditions of leave. If the victim(s) has engaged with the Victim Contact Scheme (VCS), MHCS will seek representations from the patient's Victim Liaison Officer (VLO) when considering an application (unless, as with a small number of applications for urgent medical or compassionate leave, time does not allow for this). It is anticipated that, where a victim has registered with the VCS, then conversations between the RC and the VLO will already have taken place and recorded on the application form. MHCS will also notify the VLO where leave is granted (although the VLO may be aware of this through contact with the clinical team). If the VLO is notified that a patient has been granted leave, it will be on the understanding that details of the timing and purpose of the leave should not be disclosed to the victim.

8.2 RCs are encouraged to develop and maintain their own contacts with the VLO and inform or consult them at important points during the patient's journey towards discharge notably any conditions the victims would wish to attach to any leave authorisation (see guidance for clinicians and The Victims Code).

8.3 If conditions requested by victims cannot be incorporated into the authority as proposed, then MHCS will explain the reasons why these have been rejected or amended to the VLO.

9. Multi-Agency Public Protection Arrangements (MAPPA)

9.1 MAPPA is the set of arrangements through which the Police, Probation and Prison Services work together with other agencies to manage the risks posed by violent and sexual offenders and other offenders deemed dangerous living in the community in order to protect the public. The arrangements for Mentally Disordered Offenders are set out in chapter 26 of the MAPPA guidance. Due to the type and nature of the offences committed by restricted patients, it is likely that almost all s37/41 and s45A patients will be MAPPA eligible though, depending on the age of the offence, they may not all be covered. It is the responsibility of the hospital to ensure their records are accurate as there is no central list of MAPPA registered offenders. Some s47/49 transferred prisoners may also be MAPPA eligible and registered. **4-089**

9.2 On some applications, MHCS may ask for RCs to obtain a view from MAPPA agencies prior to considering the proposal. This applies, in particular, to transferred prisoners including those serving indeterminate sentences; those who have committed a particularly serious crime, or those patients subject to multi-Agency management at level 2 or 3.

9.3 In all cases where leave has been granted by the SoS (apart from medical leave) the MAPPA coordinator should be notified by the hospital so they are aware of the position.

ANNEX A: – GLOSSARY OF TERMS

MHA	Mental Health Act 1983	The primary legislation appertaining to the detention and treatment of mentally disordered people. Part 3 covers mentally disordered offenders (MDOs). See Mental Health Act 1983 and its associated Code of Practice	**4-090**
RC	Responsible Clinician	The RC has overall responsibility for care and treatment for restricted patients under the MHA	

SoS	Secretary of State for Justice	The member of the Cabinet with responsibilities under part III of the MHA (transferred from the Home Secretary in 2007). Day to day decisions are delegated to officials within the MOJ (HMPPS) under the Carltona principle.
MOJ	Ministry of Justice	The MOJ is the government department responsible for the discharging the SoS's functions under the MHA. Many clinicians, social supervisors and other staff involved with patient care refer to the MOJ as shorthand for MHCS.
HMPPS	His Majesty's Prison and Probation Service	HMPPS is an Executive Agency of the MOJ.
MHCS	Mental Health Casework Section	MHCS is the section within HMPPS Public Protection Group which oversees the practical management of Restricted Patients including making decisions on behalf of the SoS
Tribunal	The First-Tier (Mental Health) Tribunal and the Mental Health Review Tribunal for Wales	The Tribunals are the independent judicial bodies charged with reviewing patients' detention in hospital.
DA	Detention Authority	The DA means the Hospital Order (set by the Court), Hospital Direction, Transfer Direction, Recall Warrant or letter agreeing to trial leave or transfer to another hospital (set by the SoS). The DA may name a complete hospital, a named unit within a hospital, or a specific level of security within a hospital. So, for example, a patient whose order states a particular unit as the DA, cannot be allowed access to the grounds of the whole hospital to which the public have access, unless an application for section 17 leave into the community has been agreed by the SoS.
VCS	Victim Contact Scheme	Under the Domestic Violence, Crime and Victims Act 2004 (DVCVA), where a restricted patient was sentenced on or after 1 July 2005, victims of serious violent and sexual offences have the right to information on key developments in a patient's progress and to make representations about discharge conditions, from the National Probation Service (NPS) under the Victim Contact Scheme (VCS). Victims do not statutorily qualify may be accepted on to the scheme on a discretionary basis.

| MCA | Mental Capacity Act | The Mental Capacity Act 2005, covering England and Wales, provides a statutory framework for people who lack capacity to make decisions for themselves, or who have capacity and want to make preparations for a time when they may lack capacity in the future. It sets out who can take decisions, in which situations, and how they should go about this. The MCA Code of Practice can be found here. |
| DOLS | Deprivation of Liberty Safeguarding (Order) | Deprivation of Liberty Safeguards is the procedure prescribed in law when it is necessary to deprive the liberty of a patient who lacks capacity to consent to their care and treatment in order to keep them safe from harm. Further information is available here |

GUIDANCE: SECTION 42 DISCHARGE

(MARCH 2022)

1. Introduction

1.1 The Secretary of State for Justice (SoS) recognises that the aim of all treatment of restricted patients is to help prepare them for their eventual discharge into the community and to help manage the risks they may continue to present to the public whilst there. The SoS recognises that his ultimate obligation is to exercise his statutory powers so as to protect the public, whilst being mindful of the rights of patients to receive treatment in the least restrictive setting commensurate with their needs and risks. This guidance sets out the SoS's approach to applications for discharge under section 42(2) of the Mental Health Act 1983 (MHA). **4-091**

1.2 The Mental Health Casework Section (MHCS) performance management framework sets out target timescales for decisions (see: Performance Management Framework). In order to meet those timescales MHCS requires applications on a standard template (see: discharge application form)

2. Legal Provisions

2.1 Section 42(1) and (2) of the MHA enables the SoS to consider applications for the discharge of a restricted patient into the community. In practice, decisions are taken by officials from MHCS within HM Prison and Probation Service (HMPPS), an executive agency of the Ministry of Justice (MOJ), on behalf of the SoS under delegated arrangements. **4-092**

2.2 Applications for confirmation of discharge under Section 23 will be considered as if they had been made under Section 42.

[899]

3. Types of Restricted Patients

4-093 **3.1** Restricted patients are mentally disordered offenders who are detained in hospital for treatment and who are subject to special controls by the SoS. They include offenders diverted from the Courts into the hospital system, and those transferred to secure hospitals from prison (or Immigration Centre) and made subject to a restriction direction. For full details of the types of Restricted Patient see Mentally disordered offenders - the restricted patient system.

4. Specific Categories of Patients

Patients Considered Unfit to Plead at their Trial

4-094 **4.1** Patients identified by the Court as unfit to plead at the time of trial, and made subject to a Hospital Order made under section 5 of the Criminal Procedure (Insanity) Act 1964 (as substituted by s24 of the Domestic Violence Crime and Victims Act 2004), are subject to regular review by MHCS to establish whether they are now considered to be fit to plead (see guidance available here). In response to applications for discharge on behalf of these patients, however, MHCS case managers may ask Responsible Clinicians (RCs) again whether they think the patient is fit to plead to their offence prior to making a decision. Applications are treated on their merits and decisions made following risk assessment irrespective of the patient's fitness to plead at any time but the overall context is that if the patient has recovered to the extent that they are considered suitable to be discharged from hospital, then a question should also be asked about their suitability to stand trial for the offences for which they were originally considered unfit to plead.

Transferred Prisoners

4.2 As a matter of policy, SoS will only consider applications from s37/41 patients. Any application from serving prisoners (transferred under s47 or subject to a s45A direction) will be considered as application to the Secretary of State for executive release and considered under procedures which apply to serving prisoners. If the RC believes that a transferred prisoner (or s45A patients), has recovered sufficiently well to be suitable for discharge, consideration must be given as to whether they continue to meet the MHA detention criteria, and whether a return (remission) to prison should be sought.

Foreign National Patients

4.3 The Home Office may have an interest in patients who are nationals of countries outside the UK particularly those who meet the criteria for deportation or have an outstanding deportation order against them. In order to assist the Home Office in discharging its statutory obligations, RCs and hospitals should coordinate the patient's discharge well in advance with the Home Office. Contact should be made with the specialist Mentally Disordered Offenders Team in the Home Office (fnorcmdoenquiries@homeoffice.gov.uk) when a patient is on a discharge pathway and an application for discharge is likely within the next 6-12 months. This allows time for the Home Office to obtain reports from the RC and to consider the case in full, and to allow for any appeal process.

4.4 The Home Office will seek to coordinate with RCs so that the patient, if deported, is supported by their care team and this is better done with deportation direct from hospital to allow RCs to prepare the patient for deportation and where appropriate to make contact with counterparts in the receiving country. Where deportation action cannot be enacted in a reasonable timescale or is not appropriate, close liaison with the Home Office team will ensure all safeguarding and contact management measures are put in place prior to the patient's discharge in the UK, including working closely with other agencies within MAPPA processes (see below).

Patients who Lack Capacity (and who may be subject to a DOLS Order following discharge)

4.5 There are a number of patients who, following assessment, are thought to lack capacity and who, if they were to be discharged into the community, would need, in their best interests, to be constantly supervised in a residential care home (or similar) under a Deprivation of Liberty Safeguards (DOLS) Order (Liberty Protection Safeguards) made under the Mental Capacity Act 2005, as they are not able to live independently without the support such arrangements provide. When considering applications for discharge for these patients the SoS will carefully consider the circumstances and assess the level of risk presented by the patient alongside the proposal to make a DOLS Order. Further details of the options available to patients who lack capacity can be found here.

Extremists

4.6 There are some restricted patients who have either been convicted of a terrorist (TACT) offence or who have come to the attention of agencies involved with the Prevent strategy or for some other reason. In these cases the RC will have been provided with a letter with a disclosable 'Form of Words' which will have outlined the nature of the concerns and will have identified the responsibilities of agencies under MAPPA and Prevent in the management of these cases. MHCS will take into account the risks presented by such offending and how it relates to the patient's mental disorder when making any decision on discharge and may notify Counter-Terrorism policing colleagues and partner agencies of the application.

5. Applications for Discharge

5.1 The SoS accepts that the mental health of the majority of patients will, at some stage in their treatment, improve to the point where the risk they pose is considered sufficiently low to enable them to be discharged safely into the community (with conditions in place).   **4-095**

The Standard Application Form

5.2 To help ensure that the SoS receives all of the information necessary to take a decision, an application form for discharge is available to RCs to use.

Risk Assessment

5.3 Officials within MHCS take decisions on applications following a risk assessment of the proposal. This system helps ensure that the SoS makes decisions which reflect the need to protect the public, whilst recognising the rights of patients to receive treatment for their mental disorders under the MHA.

6. Types of Discharge

4-096   **6.1**   The power of the Secretary of State to discharge contained in section 42 of the MHA is very broad. Section 42(2) permits discretionary absolute or conditional discharge where the SoS thinks fit. As explained above, these powers must only be exercised with regard to a range of factors which are set out in this policy, but these criteria are not exhaustive. It should initially be noted that the SoS is not bound by the criteria set out in section 72 or 73 of the MHA (Tribunal powers to discharge restricted patients) when exercising the power under section 42, however, due regard to those criteria will be given when considering applications. It should be noted that applications or referrals to the Tribunal can run in parallel but the first decision, if to discharge, will take priority and the other application will automatically lapse. The SoS will also consider other circumstances where they may think fit to discharge a patient.

Conditional

6.2   In order to agree discharge with conditions, the SoS must normally be satisfied that the patient within the last 6-12 months:
- Has presented as stable in hospital with no recent violent, aggressive or threatening conduct; consumption of alcohol or illicit drugs; sexually inappropriate behaviour; instances of self-harm; escaping from hospital or absconding whilst on community leave; criminal activity including any charges and/or subsequent, convictions sentences; trafficking of contraband items with other patients;
- Has willingly engaged with treatment and complied with the need to take any medication so as to have some level of insight into the importance of managing their disorder;
- Have completed work addressing their index offence and the part played by their disorder in it, either on this admission or on previous admissions;
- Has used leave appropriately including spells involving overnight stays in the community;
- Has not attempted to contact any registered victims and understands and appreciates conditions of discharge which may be imposed to protect their interests;
- Appreciates that any change in the nature or degree of their condition which increases their risk to others may result in them being recalled to hospital;
- Has not self-harmed or has addressed the reasons for this in treatment;
- Has, if recalled to hospital, addressed the circumstances behind that decision; and
- Understands the reasons for the proposed discharge conditions.

6.3   In addition, the SoS will need to be satisfied that the arrangements for the safe management and aftercare are in place including appointed RC and other Team members and a level of professional support commensurate with the patient's needs. This should include the level of management under MAPPA where appropriate.

6.4   In setting the conditions of discharge, the SoS will ensure that they are reasoned and proportionate and address the risk the patient still presents because of their disorder to the public including, specifically, any victims of their offending (see annex B).

Absolute

6.5 The SoS considers the restriction placed upon a conditionally discharged patient to be minimal and as such there should be no expectation that any conditionally discharged patient will eventually be absolutely discharged.

6.6 As explained above in paragraph 6.1, discretion to discharge absolutely under section 42(2) is very broad but must only be exercised having regard to all the matters outlined in this policy. The SoS will normally only grant absolute discharge under section 42(2) in circumstances where it is clear that restrictions are no longer required to ensure the patient's safe management and where the patient no longer requires the provision of recall. The below criteria are not definitive or exhaustive but will form the basis of most assessments. Other circumstances will also be considered where the SoS thinks fit.

6.7 Applications for absolute discharge normally fall into two broad categories:
  a. **Compassionate Grounds**
    (i) Applications where the patient has a terminal illness
    An application must contain evidence from a relevant medical practitioner (usually a Consultant) that the patient has a terminal illness.
    To approve an application from a patient, the SoS would need to be satisfied that the patient:
- has a short life expectancy. There is no hard and fast time frame, but by short it would generally mean a life expectancy of weeks, ie, less than 3months; and
- is highly unlikely to offend or cause serious harm in the community because they are so severely incapacitated as to be unable to cause harm taking into account that a withdrawal of medication and support intended to control and manage their mental disorder (if applicable) may lead to a relapse and to displays of aggressive behaviour which may cause distress to others.
- Whether those responsible for aftercare have the full knowledge of, and are able to manage, any risks the patient may present because of their mental disorder.
- For detained patients, that they cannot be conditionally discharged instead (the first question for the applicant would be why a conditional discharge from hospital is not being sought)

    Applications for absolute discharge based solely on a patient's wish to die 'with dignity' or 'a clear conscience' will not be approved. Such a wish be the basis for approving absolute discharge, only if the patient's risk does not need conditions to enable the RC to manage it effectively.
    (ii) Applications where the patient is suffering from another condition (often a progressive condition) which will impair their everyday functioning so seriously for the rest of their lives, that the risks associated with their mental disorder are assessed as negligible.
    An application must contain evidence from a relevant medical practitioner (usually a Consultant) that the patient has such a condition and will have it for the rest of their lives and which is considered to be 'incurable' at this time.
    To approve an application from a patient, the SoS would need to be

satisfied that the patient:

- Suffers from a level of physical or mental impairment or functioning which would prevent the patient causing significant harm to others by violent conduct or overtly aggressive behaviour;
- Will need treatment or management for the rest of their life and there is currently no known cure for the condition or may be a degenerative illness such as multiple sclerosis, Parkinson's disease, or Alzheimer's disease;
- Was not suffering from this condition, or was undiagnosed, at the time of the index offence and subsequent trial;
- Does not pose an unacceptable risk to others in spite of their illness or condition including whether they are, or will be, so severely incapacitated as to be unable to cause physical harm
- If medication intended to control their mental disorder is withdrawn (if applicable), that this will not lead to a relapse and displays of aggressive or violent behaviour which may cause distress to others;
- Whether those responsible for aftercare have the full knowledge of the risks the patient may present; and
- Cannot be conditionally discharged (see above).

b.   **Other Applications** If the Secretary of State is satisfied that the patient is no longer suffering from a mental disorder, he should discharge the patient, but the discharge can be conditional or absolute. Alongside the individual needs of the patient, the SoS will continue to give due consideration to risk and the duty of public protection.

The following is not an exhaustive list, however it is indicative of the evidence the Secretary of State will consider positively when making an assessment of an application for absolute discharge.

There must be evidence that the *discharged* patient:

- Has willingly engaged with treatment and demonstrated an ability to successfully manage the disorder (accepting that most patients remain mentally disordered to some extent) whilst in hospital and in the community;
- Accepts that s/he does not need to be subject to the (Hospital and) Restriction Order to receive treatment;
- Has not recently been disruptive because of their disorder;
- Understands how the disorder(s) affects them and the sort of risks it creates when control measures are removed;
- Understands and appreciates the seriousness of the index offence and the link between the disorder and offending;
- Understands and accepts the need to avoid future offending behaviour and has, in the past, accepted treatment designed to address the circumstances of the index offence);
- Recognises the harm they caused to victims of the crime and has shown some recognition, remorse or regret;
- Has not attempted to contact the victim(s) of their index offence, or enter exclusion zones where expressly forbidden to do so;
- Is not subject to another form of legal Order or control (SOPO, DOLS, Restraining etc) where the mental disorder featured as part of the reasoning behind its implementation; and

[904]

- Has not been recalled to hospital following conditional discharge, within the last five years.

In *addition* for a *detained patient:*

- That they cannot be conditionally discharged instead as a first consideration;
- Has used community leave without concern;
- Displays a very low risk of harming others in the future because of their disorder and appreciates what will happen when there is no longer a legal requirement for treatment, supervision and support (including the need to continue with any medication prescribed for the disorder); and
- Cannot have their Restriction Order lifted.

7. Lifting the Restriction Order (RO)

7.1   Section 42(1) permits the lifting of a RO where the SoS is satisfied the restric-   **4-097**
tion order is no longer required for the protection of the public from serious harm.
Applications to lift the s41 Restriction Order in accordance with section 42(1) will
therefore only be considered where it is clear that restrictions are no longer required
to ensure the patient's safe management and where the patient no longer requires
the provision of recall. The effect of lifting the RO for a detained patient is that they
would remain detained in hospital as if their original Order was a under s37 only.
It would remove the SoS's interest and powers over a patient. For a patient subject
to an existing conditional discharge, lifting the RO would have the effect of
absolutely discharging the patient.

8. Patient Management

8.1   In considering an application for discharge, MHCS will take into account the   **4-098**
plans for the future management and supervision of the patient in the community.
The SoS will need to be assured that, if conditionally discharged, the patient will
have an appointed multi-disciplinary team led by a RC able to effectively and safely
supervise them in the community.

9. Victim Involvement

9.1   When considering an application for conditional discharge, the risk assess-   **4-099**
ment will take into account any known victim considerations concerning measures
which will help set the conditions of discharge. If the victim(s) has engaged with
the Victim Contact Scheme (VCS), MHCS will seek representations from the
victim's Victim Liaison Officer (VLO) when considering an application. It is
anticipated that, where a victim has registered with the VCS, then conversations
between the RC and the VLO will already have taken place and recorded on the application form. MHCS will also notify the VLO where discharge is granted
(although the VLO may be aware of this through contact with the clinical team).
If the VLO is notified that a patient has been discharged, it will be on the
understanding that patient's location will not be disclosed to the victim.

9.2   When considering an application for absolute discharge or the lifting of the
Restriction Order, MHCS will notify victims through their VLO before a final decision is taken.

9.3 RCs are encouraged to develop and maintain their own contacts with the VLO and inform or consult them at important points during the patient's journey towards discharge notably any conditions the victims would wish to attach to any authorisation (see guidance for clinicians and The Victims Code).

9.4 If conditions requested by victims cannot be incorporated into the discharge as proposed, then MHCS will explain the reasons why these have been rejected or amended to the VLO.

10. Multi-Agency Public Protection Arrangements (MAPPA)

4-100   **10.1** MAPPA is the set of arrangements through which the Police, Probation and Prison Services work together with other agencies to manage the risks posed by violent and sexual offenders and other offenders deemed dangerous living in the community in order to protect the public. The arrangements for Mentally Disordered Offenders are set out in chapter 26 of the MAPPA guidance. In addition, MHCS has issued dedicated guidance on MAPPA which can be found here. Due to the type and nature of the offences committed by restricted patients, it is likely that almost all s37/41 and s45A patients will be MAPPA eligible though, depending on the age of the offence, they may not all be covered. However, offenders who have committed an offence murder or an offence under s.327(4A) or sch.15 of the Criminal Justice Act 2003 are automatically eligible for MAPPA management. Others may be referred on a discretionary basis it the level of risk and need requires multi agency panel oversight. It is the responsibility of the hospital to ensure their records are accurate as there is no central list of MAPPA registered offenders. Some s47/49 transferred prisoners may also be MAPPA eligible and registered.

10.2 In all cases where discharge has been granted by the SoS, the MAPPA coordinator should be notified by the hospital so they are aware of the position.

ANNEX A: – GLOSSARY OF TERMS

4-101

MHA	Mental Health Act 1983	The primary legislation appertaining to the detention and treatment of mentally disordered people. Part 3 covers mentally disordered offenders (MDOs). See Mental Health Act 1983 and its associated Code of Practice
RC	Responsible Clinician	The RC has overall responsibility for care and treatment for restricted patients under the MHA
SoS	Secretary of State for Justice	The member of the Cabinet with responsibilities under Part III of the MHA (transferred from the Home Secretary in 2007). Day to day decisions are delegated to officials within the MOJ (HMPPS) under the Carltona principle.
MOJ	Ministry of Justice	The MOJ is the government department responsible for the discharging the SoS's functions under the MHA. Many clinicians, social supervisors and other staff involved with

		patient care refer to the MOJ as shorthand for MHCS.
HMPPS	His Majesty's Prison and Probation Service	HMPPS is an Executive Agency of the MOJ.
MHCS	Mental Health Casework Section	MHCS is the section within HMPPS Public Protection Group which oversees the practical management of Restricted Patients including making decisions on behalf of the SoS
Tribunal	The First-Tier (Mental Health) Tribunal and the Mental Health Review Tribunal for Wales	The Tribunals are the independent judicial bodies charged with reviewing patients' detention in hospital.
DA	Detention Authority	The DA means the Hospital Order (set by the Court), Hospital Direction, Transfer Direction, Recall Warrant or letter agreeing to trial leave or transfer to another hospital (set by the SoS).
VCS	Victim Contact Scheme	Under the Domestic Violence, Crime and Victims Act 2004 (DVCVA), where a restricted patient was sentenced on or after 1 July 2005, victims of serious violent and sexual offences have the right to information on key developments in a patient's progress and to make representations about discharge conditions, from the National Probation Service (NPS) under the Victim Contact Scheme (VCS). Victims do not statutorily qualify may be accepted on to the scheme on a discretionary basis.
MCA	Mental Capacity Act	The Mental Capacity Act 2005, covering England and Wales, provides a statutory framework for people who lack capacity to make decisions for themselves, or who have capacity and want to make preparations for a time when they may lack capacity in the future. It sets out who can take decisions, in which situations, and how they should go about this. The MCA Code of Practice can be found here.
DOLS	Deprivation of Liberty Safeguarding (Order)	Deprivation of Liberty Safeguards is the procedure prescribed in law when it is necessary to deprive the liberty of a patient who lacks capacity to consent to their care and treatment in order to keep them safe from harm. Further information is available here
MAPPA	Multi Agency Public Protection Arrangements	It is the set of arrangements through which the Police, Probation and Prison Services work together with other agencies to manage the

		risks posed by violent and sexual offenders living in the community in order to protect the public

ANNEX B: – STANDARD CONDITIONS OF DISCHARGE

4-102

The following are examples of conditions which Responsible Clinicians may wish to consider when applying for conditional discharge for their patient.

• Reside at [specify address] [24 hour supported/supported/residential accommodation as directed by the RC and social supervisor] [and abide by any rules of the accommodation], and consult with the responsible clinician and social supervisor for any stay of one or more nights at a different address.

• *NB: The Secretary of State also requires a clause whereby the Ministry of Justice and MAPPA should be informed of any change of address at least 14 days prior to the move taking place*

• Allow access to the accommodation, as reasonably required by the responsible clinician and social supervisor.

• Comply with medication and other medical treatment [and with monitoring as to medication levels] [including... [Specify here any particular non-pharmacological medical treatment]], as directed by the responsible clinician and social supervisor.

• Engage with and meet the clinical team, as directed by the responsible clinician and social supervisor.

• Abstain from alcohol [save as directed by the responsible clinician and social supervisor].

• Abstain from illicit drugs.

• Submit to random drugs and alcohol testing, as directed by the responsible clinician and social supervisor.

• Not to enter the area[s] of [specify general location] as delineated by the zone[s] marked on the map[s] supplied by [specify name of person/organisation producing map] [save as agreed in advance by the responsible clinician and social supervisor].

• Not seek to contact directly or indirectly [specify names or use 'victim(s) of the index offence'].

• Disclose to the responsible clinician and social supervisor any developing intimate relationship with any other person.

• Disclose all pending and current [employment, whether paid or voluntary] [all educational activities] [all community activities] to the responsible clinician and social supervisor.

• Not leave the UK without consulting the responsible clinician and social supervisor.

PART 5: HUMAN RIGHTS ACT

HUMAN RIGHTS ACT 1998

(1998 c.42)

An Act to give further effect to rights and freedoms guaranteed under the
European Convention on Human Rights; to make provision with respect to holders of certain judicial offices who become judges of the European Court of Human Rights; and for connected purposes.

[9th November 1998]

General Note

This Part examines the Human Rights Act 1998 as it applies to the care and treatment of mentally **5-001**
disordered people.

Introduction

The Second World War and its associated horrors caused an upsurge in international concern for hu- **5-002**
man rights. The European Convention for the Protection of Human Rights and Fundamental Freedoms,
commonly known as the European Convention on Human Rights ("the Convention"), emerged out of
that concern. It was concluded under the auspices of the Council of Europe in 1950, was ratified by the
UK in 1951 and entered into force in 1953. In *Bank Mellat v Her Majesty's Treasury (No.2)* [2013]
UKSC 39, Lord Reed said that "inherent in the whole of the Convention is a search for a fair balance
between the demands of the general interest of the community and the requirements of the protection
of the individual's fundamental rights" (para.70).

The Commission and the Court

One of the most distinctive features of the Convention has been the role played by two organs, the **5-003**
European Commission on Human Rights ("the Commission") and the European Court on Human Rights
("the Court"), in building up a substantial body of case law in the course of deciding petitions brought
by individuals. In 1998 the Commission was abolished and there are now only two European institutions, the Court (which can sit in Chambers and in a Grand Chamber) and the Committee of Ministers
of the Council of Europe, that administer the Convention. Under art.35 of the Convention, the Court will
only deal with an application after all domestic remedies have been exhausted.

Human Rights Act 1998

This Act is one of the most significant pieces of constitutional legislation enacted in the UK. It "cre- **5-004**
ates domestic rights expressed in the same terms as those contained in the Convention" (*Re McKerr*
[2004] 1 W.L.R. per Lord Hoffmann at para.63). The relevant provisions of the Convention are
reproduced in Sch.1 to the Act, which is set out below. The Act is ultimately subject to the sovereignty
of Parliament, in that:

1. It does not provide the courts with a power to strike down primary legislation that is inconsistent with the Convention.
2. It leaves Parliament free, if it chooses to do so, to enact and maintain legislation that is
   incompatible with the Convention.
3. The Act is not entrenched against repeal.

Within these constraints, the Act attempts to achieve the Government's aim to "bring rights home"
(*Rights Brought Home: the Human Rights Bill*, Cm.3782 (1997)) by operating through three
mechanisms:

1. Courts and tribunals are required to construe all legislation (past and future) "so far as it is possible to do so ... in a way which is compatible with Convention rights" (s.3). When doing so
   the court or tribunal must take account of the case law of the Court and the Commission. This
   requirement means that domestic courts must search for a construction that would prevent the
   making of a "declaration of incompatibility": see point 3, below.
2. All public authorities, including all courts and tribunals, and private providers who are exercis-

[911]

ing "functions of a public nature", are required to act in accordance with the Convention, within the scope permitted by primary legislation (s.6) and to have regard to European jurisprudence (s.2). An "act" includes a failure to act (s.6(6)). Approved mental health professionals, responsible clinicians, approved clinicians and nurses are public authorities for the purposes of the Convention when they perform functions under the Mental Health Act. Decisions made by a private hospital relating to the care or treatment of detained patients are decisions of a public nature. The hospital therefore becomes a public authority for the purposes of s.6 and its decisions are susceptible to judicial review (*R. (on the application of A) v Partnership in Care Ltd* [2002] EWHC 529; [2002] M.H.L.R. 298).

3. The higher courts are able to make a "declaration of incompatibility" in respect of a provision of primary legislation, which the court considers to be incompatible with a Convention right (s.4). Such a declaration does not affect the validity, continued operation or enforcement of the provision in respect of which it is made (s.4(6)(a)) but it may lead to the correction of the legislation by Parliament making a "remedial order" which has the effect of bypassing the full legislative process (s.10).

Where it is not possible to interpret subordinate legislation so as to be compatible with the Convention, the courts have power to disapply it unless the primary legislation prevents removal of the incompatibility (s.4(4)(b)). In *RR v Secretary of State for Work and Pensions* [2019] UKSC 52, the Supreme Court said that the courts have consistently held that, where it is possible to do so, a provision of subordinate legislation which results in a breach of a Convention right must be disregarded, if it is possible to do so without affecting the statutory scheme (para.30).

SCHEDULE 1

THE ARTICLES

PART I

THE CONVENTION RIGHTS AND FREEDOMS

Article 2 Right to Life

5-005   1. Everyone's right to life shall be protected by law. No one shall be deprived of his life intentionally save in the execution of a sentence of a court following his conviction of a crime for which this penalty is provided by law.

2. Deprivation of life shall not be regarded as inflicted in contravention of this Article when it results from the use of force which is no more than absolutely necessary:
    (a) in defence of any person from unlawful violence;
    (b) in order to effect a lawful arrest or to prevent the escape of a person lawfully detained;
    (c) in action lawfully taken for the purpose of quelling a riot or insurrection.

General Note

5-006   The European Court of Human Rights has stated that this article "ranks as one of the most fundamental provisions in the Convention and, together with Article 3, enshrines one of the basic values of the democratic societies making up the Council of Europe" (*Cakici v Turkey* (2001) 31 E.H.R.R. 5 para.86). The object and purpose of the Convention requires that this article be interpreted and applied so as to make its safeguards practical and effective (*McCann v United Kingdom* (1996) 21 E.H.R.R. 97, paras 146–147).

This article is unconcerned with issues to do with the quality of living or what a person chooses to do with his or her life. It cannot be interpreted as conferring the diametrically opposite right, namely a right to die; nor can it create a right to self-determination in the sense of conferring on an individual the entitlement to choose death rather than life (*Pretty v United Kingdom* (2002) 35 E.H.R.R. 1 para.39). However, the right of an individual to decide how and when to end his life is one aspect of the right to respect for private life within the meaning of art.8: see *Haas v Switzerland* (2011) 53 E.H.R.R. 33, noted under art.8 under "private life".

In *Osman v United Kingdom* (2000) 29 E.H.R.R. 245 para.115, the Court said that it was common ground that the State's obligation under this article may "imply in certain well-defined circumstances a positive obligation on the authorities to take preventive operational measures to protect an individual whose life is at risk from the criminal acts of another individual".

The Court said that for this positive obligation to be breached it must be established to the Court's satisfaction "that the authorities knew or ought to have known at the time of the existence of a real and immediate risk to the life of an identified individual or individuals from criminal acts of a third party and that they failed to take measures within the scope of their powers which, judged reasonably, might have been expected to take to avoid that risk" (para.116). Note, however, that in *Sarjantson v The Chief Constable of Humberside Police* [2013] EWCA Civ 1252, the Court of Appeal reviewed subsequent Strasbourg authorities and held that the scope of this article is not limited to circumstances where there is a risk to *identified* individuals. In *Osman*, the Court also said that, given the reality of resource allocation and the operational choices that have to be made, not every claimed risk to life can entail for the authorities a Convention requirement to take operational measures to prevent the risk from materialising and that the positive obligation "must be interpreted in a way which does not impose an impossible or disproportionate burden on the authorities" (para.116). In *Traylor v Kent and Medway NHS Social Care Partnership Trust* [2022] EWHC 260 (QB), Johnson J. considered Osman and held that "a real risk is simply a risk that is not fanciful" (para.132) and that "an immediate risk may be one that is present and continuing" (para.134).

The positive obligation applies in the public-health sphere (*Dodov v Bulgaria* (2008) 47 E.H.R.R. 41 para.80). However, "where a Contracting State had made adequate provision for securing high professional standards among health professionals and the protection of the lives of patients, it cannot accept that matters such as error of judgment on the part of a health professional or negligent co-ordination among health professionals in the treatment of a particular patient are sufficient of themselves to call a Contracting State to account from the standpoint of its positive obligations under art.2 of the Convention to protect life" (*Powell v UK* (2000) 30 E.H.R.R. CD 362).

The *Osman* case places professionals who are performing functions under the Mental Health Act **5-007** under a positive obligation to take appropriate preventative measures in respect of patients whom they know (or ought to have known) to be so dangerous as to be a threat to the lives of others. The Osman principle has been extended to self harm by people for whose welfare the state is responsible (*Keenan v United Kingdom* (2001) 33 E.H.R.R. 38; also see *Renolde v France* [2008] M.H.L.R. 331).

The application of the positive obligation to hospital patients who are detained under the Mental Health Act was examined by the House of Lords in *Savage v South Essex Partnership NHS Foundation Trust* [2008] UKHL 74; [2009] M.H.L.R 41 where it was held that it was not necessary for a claimant alleging a breach of this article to establish either gross negligence or anything more serious. The obligations of health authorities under this article were summarised by Lord Rodger:

"68. In terms of Art 2, health authorities are under an over-arching obligation to protect the lives of patients in their hospitals. In order to fulfil that obligation, and depending on the circumstances, they may require to fulfil a number of complementary obligations.

69. In the first place, the duty to protect the lives of patients requires health authorities to ensure that the hospitals for which they are responsible employ competent staff and that they are trained to a high professional standard. In addition, the authorities must ensure that the hospitals adopt systems of work which will protect the lives of patients. Failure to perform these general obligations may result in a violation of Art 2. If, for example, a health authority fails to ensure that a hospital puts in place a proper system for supervising mentally ill patients and, as a result, a patient is able to commit suicide, the health authority will have violated the patient's right to life under Art 2.

70. Even though a health authority employed competent staff and ensured that they were trained to a high professional standard, a doctor, for example, might still treat a patient negligently and the patient might die as a result. In that situation, there would be no violation of Art 2 since the health authority would have done all that the article required of it to protect the patient's life. Nevertheless, the doctor would be personally liable in damages for the death and the health authority would be vicariously liable for her negligence. This is the situation envisaged by *Powell* [*Powell v United Kingdom* (2000) 30 E.H.R.R. CD 362].

71. The same approach would apply if a mental hospital had established an appropriate system for supervising patients and all that happened was that, on a particular occasion, a nurse negligently left his post and a patient took the opportunity to commit suicide. There would be no violation of any obligation under Art 2, since the health authority would have done all that the article required of it. But, again, the nurse would be personally liable in damages for the death and the health authority would be vicariously liable too. Again, this is just an application of *Powell*.

72. Finally, Art 2 imposes a further 'operational' obligation on health authorities and their hospital staff. This obligation is distinct from, and additional to, the authorities' more general obligations. The operational obligation arises only if members of staff know or ought to know that a particular patient presents a 'real and immediate' risk of suicide. In these circumstances Art 2 requires them to do all that can reasonably be expected to prevent the patient from committing suicide. If they fail to do this, not only will they and the health authorities be liable in negligence, but there will also be a violation of the operational obligation under art 2 to protect the patient's life. This is comparable to the position in *Osman* and *Keenan*. As the present case shows, if no other remedy is available, proceedings for an alleged breach of the obligation can be taken under the Human Rights Act 1998."

The operational duty is owed to a vulnerable person in circumstances where their death occurred in a hospital or care home, for which the state was responsible, as a result of conditions of neglect or abuse or where the state had been aware of such shortcomings, through regulatory inspections, but had failed to act on them. However, the duty does not apply to the provision of ordinary medical treatment to a vulnerable person, absent exceptional circumstances (*R. (on the application of Maguire) v Blackpool and Fylde Senior Coroner* [2020] EWCA Civ 738). When this case reached the Supreme Court ([2023] UKSC 20), the Court set out the structure of the obligations imposed by this article. The following is taken from the Press summary of the case:

"In addition to prohibiting certain conduct, article 2 imposes a positive obligation on contracting states to take 'appropriate steps to safeguard the lives of those within their jurisdiction' [9]. There are two types of substantive positive obligations: an obligation to have appropriate legal regimes and administrative systems in place to provide general protection for the lives of citizens and persons in its territory ('the systems duty') and an obligation to take operational steps to protect a specific person or persons when on notice that they are subject to a risk to life of a particularly clear and pressing kind ('the operational duty') [10].

Article 2 also imposes certain procedural positive obligations regarding the investigation of and the opportunity to call state authorities to account for potential breaches of the substantive positive obligations. The precise content of those obligations varies according to context [12].

Three different levels of the procedural obligation are identified. First, to check whether there might be any question of a potential breach of a person's right to life under article 2, state authorities should take some steps to establish whether the cause of death is from natural causes (the 'basic procedural obligation') [14]. Second, in particular contexts, a state may be required to take further steps to investigate possible breaches of the article 2 substantive obligations to ensure appropriate accountability and redress and, as appropriate, to punish persons responsible for the death (the 'enhanced procedural obligation') [15]. Third, in certain other cases where there is no relevant compelling reason giving rise to an enhanced procedural obligation, but there is still a possibility that the substantive obligations in article 2 have been breached, there is an obligation to provide means by which a person complaining of such possible breaches can make that complaint, have it investigated or obtain redress (the 'redress procedural obligation') [19]. It is only where the enhanced procedural obligation applies that there is a statutory obligation on a coroner to direct a jury at an inquest to give an expanded verdict [27]–[33]."

The "positive operational duty" under this article is also analysed in *R. (on the application of Morahan) v Her Majesty's Assistant Coroner for West London* [2021] EWHC 1603 (Admin) at paras 38–67. In this case, the court rejected a submission "that the death of a voluntary psychiatric patient whether in or away from the hospital and whatever the cause of death requires an article 2 compliant inquest" (para.45). An appeal in this case was dismissed by the Court of Appeal at [2022] EWCA Civ 1410 where the court gave a helpful account of both the investigative and operational duty under this article.

In *Rabone v Pennine Care NHS Trust* [2012] UKSC 2; [2012] M.H.L.R. 66, the Supreme Court held that the "operational obligation" identified in *Savage* also applied to an informal patient in a situation where the patient was admitted to hospital as a real and immediate suicide risk, was extremely vulnerable and the NHS Trust had assumed responsibility for her; she was under its control. If she had tried to leave the hospital voluntarily, the Trust could and should have sought her detention under the 1983 Act as a means of preventing her leaving. The difference between the patient's position and that of a hypothetical detained psychiatric patient was one of form not substance. [NB Identifying whether a person is at "real and immediate" risk of suicide is problematic: see G. Szmukler et al., "'Rabone' and four unresolved problems in mental health law", *The Psychiatrist* (2013), 37, 297–301.] In *Fernandes de Olivera v Portugal* (2019) 69 E.H.R.R. 8; [2019] M.H.L.R. 358), the Court confirmed that the duty to take reasonable measures to prevent a person from self-harm exists with respect to both voluntary and involuntary patients and said that, with regard to the latter, "the Court, in its own assessment, may apply a stricter standard of scrutiny" (para.124). In *Raznatovic v Montenegro*, September 2 2021 (App.No.14742/18) the Court held that hospital authorities had not breached this article in respect of the suicide of a voluntary mental patient where they could not have known, or been expected to know, that the patient posed a risk of suicide.

In both *Savage* and *Rabone*, the court identified close relatives of the patients as victims for the purposes of s.7(7) of the 1998 Act and awarded them damages of £10,000 (*Savage* [2012] EWHC 865 (QB)) and £5000 (*Rabone*) for non-pecuniary loss.

There is authority for the proposition that this article would only be engaged by failure of process or systemic failures on the part of a hospital and would not be engaged by one-off or "casual" acts by hospital staff: see *Powell v UK*, above, *Savage v South Essex NHS Trust*, above at paras 45 and 57–58 per Lord Rodger and para.91 per Lady Hale, and *Rabone v Pennine Care NHS Trust*, above, at paras

19 and 119 per Lord Dyson and Lord Mance. In *R. (Maguire) v HM Senior Coroner for Blackpool & Fylde & United Response* [2019] EWHC 1232 (Admin), the court said that in "the absence of either systemic dysfunction arising from a regulatory failure or a relevant assumption of responsibility in a particular case, the state will not be held accountable under article 2" (para.44).

In *R. (on the application of Antoniou) v Central and North West London NHS Foundation Trust* [2013] EWHC 3055 (Admin); [2014] M.H.L.R. 212, the Divisional Court held that where a detained patient takes their own life, the procedural obligation imposed by this article is fulfilled by a coroner's inquest and that, unlike prison or police station deaths, there is no additional requirement for an immediate and independent investigation prior to the inquest.   **5-008**

In November 2015, the Department of Health published "Article 2 of the European Convention on Human Rights and the investigation of serious incidents in mental health services". It can be accessed at: *www.gov.uk/government/publications/echr-article-2-investigations-into-mental-health-incidents*. Also see "Deaths in Mental Health Detention: An investigation framework fit for purpose?" (2015), a report by INQUEST into deaths in mental health settings where the patient is detained under the Act. The report can be accessed at INQUEST's website: *www.inquest.org.uk/site/home*.

Paragraph 1

Everyone's life shall be protected by law   Apart from the law relating to abortion, the extent to which this article can be invoked to protect the life of an unborn child is uncertain: see the note on "Human Rights Act 1998" under s.3 of the Act.   **5-009**

Intentionally   This word should be given its natural and ordinary meaning, and applies only to cases where the purpose of the prohibited action is to cause death (*Re A (Children) (Conjoined Twins: Surgical Separation)* [2004] 4 All E.R. 961 CA; also see *Association X v United Kingdom* (1978) 14 D. & R. 31).

Paragraph 2

Use of force   The force used must be strictly proportionate to the achievement of the permitted aims (*McKerr v United Kingdom* (2002) 34 E.H.R.R. 20 para.110). In *Saoud v France*, October 9, 2007 (App.No.9375/02) the Court said that the authorities had a positive obligation to protect the health of persons who were in detention or police custody or who had just been arrested. A breach of this article was found in this case where an arrested person who suffered from schizophrenia and was very dangerous died from slow asphyxia after being held on the ground by the police for 35 minutes. The Court deplored the fact that no precise instructions had been issued to the police regarding this type of immobilisation technique. Also see *Stefancic v Slovenia*, October 24, 2017 (App. No.58349/09), paras 65 and 66.   **5-010**

Article 3 Prohibition of Torture
No one shall be subjected to torture or to inhuman or degrading treatment or punishment.

General Note

In *Stanev v Bulgaria* (2012) 55 E.H.R.R.; [2012] M.H.L.R. 23, the Court summarised the approach that it takes to claims based on this article: **5-011**

"201. Article 3 enshrines one of the most fundamental values of democratic society. It prohibits in absolute terms torture or inhuman or degrading treatment or punishment, irrespective of the circumstances and the victim's behaviour (see, among other authorities, *Kudla v. Poland* [GC], no. 30210/96, § 90, ECHR 2000-XI, and *Poltoratskiy v. Ukraine*, no. 38812/97, § 130, ECHR 2003-V).
202. Ill-treatment must attain a minimum level of severity if it is to fall within the scope of Article 3. The assessment of this minimum is, in the nature of things, relative; it depends on all the circumstances of the case, such as the nature and context of the treatment, the manner and method of its execution, its duration, its physical or mental effects and, in some instances, the sex, age and state of health of the victim (see *Kudla*, cited above, § 91, and *Poltoratskiy*, cited above, § 131).
203. Treatment has been held by the Court to be "inhuman" because, inter alia, it was premeditated, was applied for hours at a stretch and caused either actual bodily injury or intense physical or mental suffering (see *Labita v. Italy* [GC], no. 26772/95, § 120, ECHR 2000-IV). Treatment has been considered "degrading" when it was such as to arouse in its victims feelings of fear, anguish and inferiority capable of humiliating and debasing them and possibly breaking their physi-

cal or moral resistance or driving them to act against their will or conscience (see *Jalloh v. Germany* [GC], no. 54810/00, § 68, ECHR 2006-IX). In this connection, the question whether such treatment was intended to humiliate or debase the victim is a factor to be taken into account, although the absence of any such purpose does not inevitably lead to a finding that there has been no violation of Article 3 (see *Peers v. Greece*, no. 28524/95, §§ 67, 68 and 74, ECHR 2001-III, and *Kalashnikov v. Russia*, no. 47095/99, § 95, ECHR 2002-VI).

204. The suffering and humiliation involved must in any event go beyond that inevitable element of suffering or humiliation connected with a given form of legitimate treatment or punishment. Measures depriving a person of his liberty may often involve such an element. Yet it cannot be said that deprivation of liberty in itself raises an issue under Article 3 of the Convention. Nevertheless, under that Article the State must ensure that a person is detained in conditions which are compatible with respect for his human dignity, that the manner and method of the execution of the measure do not subject him to distress or hardship of an intensity exceeding the unavoidable level of suffering inherent in detention and that, given the practical demands of imprisonment, his health and well-being are adequately secured by, among other things, providing him with the requisite medical assistance (see *Kudła*, cited above, §§ 92–94).

205. When assessing the conditions of a deprivation of liberty under Article 3 of the Convention, account has to be taken of their cumulative effects and the duration of the measure in question (see *Kalashnikov*, cited above, §§ 95 and 102; *Kehayov v. Bulgaria*, no. 41035/98, § 64, 18 January 2005; and *Iovchev v. Bulgaria*, no. 41211/98, § 127, 2 February 2006). In this connection an important factor to take into account, besides the material conditions, is the detention regime. In assessing whether a restrictive regime may amount to treatment contrary to Article 3 in a given case, regard must be had to the particular conditions, the stringency of the regime, its duration, the objective pursued and its effects on the person concerned (see *Kehayov*, cited above, § 65)."

In *Selmouni v France* (2000) 29 E.H.R.R. 403 at para.101, the Court said that it:

"has previously examined cases in which it concluded that there had been treatment which could only be described as torture. However, having regard to the fact that the Convention is a 'living instrument which must be interpreted in the light of present-day conditions', the Court considers that certain acts which were classified in the past as 'inhuman and degrading treatment' as opposed to 'torture' could be classified differently in future. It takes the view that the increasingly high standard being required in the area of the protection of human rights and fundamental liberties correspondingly and inevitably requires greater firmness in assessing breaches of the fundamental values in a democratic society".

This significant statement means that the concept of inhuman or degrading treatment will inevitably expand to encompass conduct that was previously outside the scope of this article. Note, however, that in *R. (on the application of DB) v Secretary of State for the Home Department* [2006] EWHC 659 (Admin) Davis J. said that over-ready assertions of reliance on this article, "if not kept under proper restraint, can only operate to debase in the public perception what ought to be regarded as one of the most fundamental of rights enshrined in the Convention" (para.45).

In assessing evidence, the Court has adopted the standard of proof "beyond reasonable doubt". However, as applied by the Court, this term has an autonomous meaning. The role of the Court is not to rule on criminal guilt or civil liability, but on the responsibility of Contracting States under the Convention (*Mathew v Netherlands* (2006) 43 E.H.R.R. 23 para.156).

Although this article admits of no exceptions, logically the prohibition of inhuman and degrading treatment ought to have the same exceptions as those contained in art.2(2). The Court has acted on the assumption that this article is subject to such exceptions as long as any force used is strictly necessary and proportionate: see, for example, *RIVAS v France*, April 1, 2004, at paras 41, 42.

Provided it is sufficiently real and immediate, a mere threat of conduct prohibited by this article may itself constitute a violation (*Campbell and Cosans v United Kingdom* (1982) 4 E.H.R.R. 293 para.26).

In *A v United Kingdom* (1999) 27 E.H.R.R. 611, the Court held that this article requires "States to take measures designed to ensure that individuals within their jurisdiction are not subjected to torture or inhuman or degrading treatment or punishment, including such ill-treatment administered by private individuals" (para.22). There is a particular need for states to take such measures in the context of psychiatric hospitals, where patients are typically in a position of inferiority and helplessness (*Wilkinson v United Kingdom* (1998) 26 E.H.R.R. CD131). In *ZH v Hungary* [2014] M.H.L.R. 1 at para.29, the Court said that any "interference with the rights of persons belonging to particularly vulnerable groups—such as those with mental disorders—is required to be subject to strict scrutiny, and only very weighty reasons could justify any restriction". A failure to take reasonably available measures which could have had a real prospect of altering the outcome or mitigating the harm is sufficient to engage the responsibility of the state (*E v United Kingdom* (2003) 36 E.H.R.R. 31 para.99). These measures "should provide effective protection, in particular, of children and other vulnerable persons and include reasonable steps to prevent ill-treatment of which the authorities had or ought to have had knowledge" (*Z v United Kingdom* (2002) 34 E.H.R.R. 3 para.73). In *Dordevic v Croatia* [2013] M.H.L.R. 89, the Court held that the failure of the Croatian State to prevent the persistent harassment of a severely disabled young man was a breach of this article.

Measures depriving a person of his liberty may often involve an inevitable element of suffering or humiliation. Nevertheless, the level of suffering and humiliation involved must not go beyond that which is inevitably connected with a given form of legitimate treatment or punishment (*Szafranski v Poland* (2017) 64 E.H.R.R. 23, para.21). For the link between this article and art.5, see *Rooman v Belgium* which is noted under art.5(1)(e).

Where an individual raised an arguable claim that, in breach of this article, he had been seriously ill-treated by state agents, this article read with art.1 required by implication that there should be an effective official investigation (*Kucheruk v Ukraine* (2011) 52 E.H.R.R. 28, para.155). The investigation "should be capable of leading to the identification and punishment of those responsible" (*Assenov v Bulgaria* (1999) 28 E.H.R.R. 652, para.102). A failure to find state agents guilty of a crime of violence against a detainee under their control cannot absolve the state of its responsibilities under the Convention (*Afanasyev v Ukraine* (2006) 42 E.H.R.R. 52 para.64). In *M.S. v Croatia (No.2)*, [2015] M.H.L.R. 294 the Court said, at para.74, that a state's domestic legal system, and in particular the criminal law applicable in the circumstances of the case, must provide practical and effective protection of the rights guaranteed by this article. In *GM v Moldova*, November 15, 2022 (App.No.44394/15), the Court held that there had been an ineffective investigation into allegations of forced abortions and forced contraception after rape by a doctor in a residential asylum, and that this article had been violated due to the State's failure to establish and apply effectively a system providing protection to intellectually disabled women in psychiatric institutions against serious breaches of their integrity.

The duration of the ill-treatment can be short. In *ZH v Metropolitan Police Commissioner* [2013] EWCA Civ 69; [2013] 3 All E.R. 113, the duration of the episode which constituted ill-treatment was 40 minutes.

In *NHS Trust A v NHS Trust B v H* [2001] 1 All E.R. 801, Butler-Sloss P. held that this Article "requires the victim to be aware of the inhuman and degrading treatment which he or she is experiencing or at least be in a state of physical or mental suffering" (para.49). This surprising finding, which has the effect of removing the protection afforded by this article from a group of extremely vulnerable citizens, i.e. insensate patients, was criticised by Munby J. in *R. (on the application of Burke) v General Medical Council* [2004] EWHC 1879 (Admin); [2004] 2 F.L.R. 1121, who said at para.149:

"In my judgment treatment is capable of being 'degrading' within the meaning of Article 3, whether or not it arouses feelings of fear, anguish or inferiority in the victim. It is enough if judged by the standard of right thinking bystanders—human rights violations obviously cannot be judged by the standards of the perpetrators—it would be viewed as humiliating or debasing the victim, showing a lack of respect for, or diminishing, his or her human dignity."

It is submitted that Munby J.'s obiter statement is to be preferred as it is consistent with Convention case law: see *Keenan v United Kingdom* (2001) 33 E.H.R.R. 913 para.112.

In *Bouyid v Belgium* (2016) 62 E.H.R.R. 32, the Court said that "it may well suffice that the victim is humiliated in his own eyes, even if not in the eyes of others" (para.87).

The assessment of whether a particular treatment or punishment is incompatible with the standards **5-012** of this article has, in the case of mentally ill persons, to take into consideration their vulnerability and their inability, in some cases, to complain coherently or at all about how they are being affected by any particular treatment (*Keenan v United Kingdom* (2001) 33 E.H.R.R. 38 para.110). In *Keenan*, the Court said at para.112 that:

"in respect of a person deprived of his liberty, recourse to physical force which has not been made strictly necessary by his own conduct diminishes human dignity and is in principle an infringement of the right set out in Article 3. Similarly, treatment of a mentally ill person may be incompatible with the standards imposed by Article 3 in the protection of fundamental human dignity, even though that person may not be able, or capable of, pointing to any specific ill-effects".

Case law on this article indicates that medical treatment only engages the article if the free and informed consent of the patient has not been forthcoming (*X v Denmark* (1983) 32 D. & R. 282). The Court has been reluctant to categorise either psychiatric treatment (no matter how disagreeable (*Naumenko v Ukraine*, February 10, 2004)) or institutional conditions as "inhuman or degrading treatment". In *Herczegfalvy v Austria* (1993) 15 E.H.R.R. 437, a mentally disordered patient had been handcuffed to a security bed with a belt placed around his ankles. The Court, in holding that medical treatment could, in principle reach a level of severity sufficient to amount to "inhuman or degrading treatment" contrary to this article, said at paras 82, 83:

"The Court considers that the position of inferiority and powerlessness which is typical of patients confined in psychiatric hospitals calls for increased vigilance in reviewing whether the Convention has been complied with. While it is for the medical authorities to decide, on the basis of recognised rules of medical science, on the therapeutic methods to be used, if necessary by force, to preserve the physical and mental health of patients who are entirely incapable of deciding for themselves and for whom they are therefore responsible, such patients nevertheless remain under the protection of Article 3, the requirements of which permit no derogation … [H]owever, the evidence before the Court is not sufficient to disprove the Government's argument that, according to the psychiatric principles generally accepted as the time, medical necessity justified the treatment in issue". [N.B. In *Koroviny v Russia* [2019] M.H.L.R. 46, the Court held that tying a patient to a bed for 24 hours breached this article.]

Although these principles were advanced in relation to a patient who lacked capacity, in *Nevmerzhitsky v Ukraine* (2006) 43 E.H.R.R. 32, the Court applied them to a mentally capable applicant, who was not mentally ill, who complained that he had been force-fed while in criminal detention and that this had infringed this article. The Court held at para.94:

"[A] measure which is of therapeutic necessity from the point of view of established principles of medicine cannot in principle be regarded as inhuman or degrading. The same can be said about force-feeding that is aimed at saving the life of a particular detainee who consciously refuses to take food. The Convention organs must nevertheless satisfy themselves that the medical necessity has been convincingly shown to exist."

The *Bolam* test (see *Bolam v Friern Barnet Hospital* [1957] 1 W.L.R. 582) does not apply to the question of "medical necessity" under this article (*R. (on the application of N) v M and others* [2002] EWHC Admin 1911). The onus of justifying medical necessity is placed on the patient's approved clinician (*Bolam* above). This approach was approved by the Court of Appeal ([2002] EWCA Civ 1789; [2003] M.H.L.R. 157 at paras 17, 18) where the court said that the phrase "convincingly shown" is easily understood. Although the standard is a high one, it does not need "elaboration or further explanation". The factors that need to be addressed when forming a judgment as to whether the proposed treatment has been convincingly shown to be a medical necessity include:

"(a) how certain is it that the patient does suffer from a treatable mental disorder; (b) how serious a disorder is it; (c) how serious a risk is presented to others; (d) how likely is it that, if the patient does suffer from such a disorder, the proposed treatment will alleviate the condition; (e) how much alleviation is there likely to be; (f) how likely is it that the treatment will have adverse consequences for the patient; and (g) how severe may they be" (para.19).

The court rejected a submission that, in a case where there is a responsible body of opinion that a patient is not suffering from a treatable condition, that the treatment is not in the patient's best interests and is not medically necessary, then it cannot be convincingly shown that the treatment proposed is in the patient's best interests or medically necessary (para.29).

5-013   The conclusion from *Herczegfalvy* is that forcible measures inflicted upon either an incapacitated or a capacitated patient which are not a medical necessity may constitute inhuman or degrading treatment. Conversely, a denial of treatment which has been found to be a medical necessity could also be claimed to be a violation of this article (*D v United Kingdom* (1997) 24 E.H.R.R. 423). *Herczegfalvy* was applied in *Bures v Czech Republic* [2013] M.H.L.R. 126, where the Court said that "using restraints is a serious measure which must always be justified by preventing imminent harm to the patient or the surroundings and must be proportionate to such an aim" (para.96).

In *M.S. v Croatia (No.2)* [2015] M.H.L.R. 294 the Court said at para.97:

"In respect of persons deprived of their liberty, recourse to physical force which has not been made strictly necessary by their own conduct diminishes human dignity and is in principle an infringement of the right set forth in Article 3 of the Convention (see *Krastanov v. Bulgaria*, no. 50222/99, § 53, 30 September 2004)."

With respect to the use of physical restraint and seclusion, the Court said:

"104. In respect of the use of measures of physical restraint on patients in psychiatric hospitals, the

Court sees no reason to disagree in principle with the Government's submission that medical standards in psychiatry allow for a recourse to such measures when no other measures could produce the desired result of calming an agitated individual down and to prevent him or her from harming himself or herself or others .... It notes, however, that the developments in contemporary legal standards on seclusion and other forms of coercive and non-consensual measures against patients with psychological or intellectual disabilities in hospitals and all other places of deprivation of liberty require that such measures be employed as a matter of last resort and when their application is the only means available to prevent immediate or imminent harm to the patient or others ....

105. Furthermore, the use of such measures must be commensurate with adequate safeguards from any abuse, providing sufficient procedural protection, and capable of demonstrating sufficient justification that the requirements of ultimate necessity and proportionality have been complied with and that all other reasonable options failed to satisfactorily contain the risk of harm to the patient or others. It must also be shown that the coercive measure at issue was not prolonged beyond the period which was strictly necessary for that purpose ...."

In *Aggerholm v Denmark* (2021) 72 E.H.R.R. 9; [2021] M.H.L.R. 176, the Court said at para.95:

"The Court observes that European and national standards ... are unanimous in declaring that physical restraints can be used only exceptionally, as a matter of last resort and when their application is the only means available to prevent immediate or imminent harm to the patient or others."

Removal from association, such as the seclusion of a mentally disordered patient, does not normally amount to inhuman or degrading treatment, but it will depend upon the conditions, duration, purpose and the effects on the person concerned (*Koskinen v Finland* (1994) 18 E.H.R.R. CD 146 and *A v United Kingdom*, App.No.6840/74).

A strip and intimate body search carried out in an appropriate manner with due respect for human dignity and for a legitimate purpose may be compatible with this article. However, where the manner in which a search is carried out has debasing elements which significantly aggravate the inevitable humiliation of the procedure, this article will be engaged. The requirement to submit to a strip search will generally constitute an interference under art.8(1) and require to be justified under art.8(2) (*Wainwright v United Kingdom* (2007) 44 E.H.R.R. 40 at paras 42, 43). Also see *Hellig v Germany* (2012) 55 E.H.R.R. 3, para.56, where it was said that depriving a person of their clothing is capable of giving rise to feelings of fear, anguish and humiliation capable of humiliating and debasing him.

A hospital must not adopt a policy on either the searching or the seclusion of patients which exposes patients to a significant risk of treatment prohibited by this article: see *BK and RH v Secretary of State for Justice* [2015] EWCA Civ 1259, para.54, and *R. (on the application of Munjaz) v Mersey Care National Health Service Trust* [2005] UKHL, para.29).

An admissibility decision of the Commission in *Grare v France* (1992) 15 E.H.R.R. CD 100, suggests that psychiatric treatment in the form of medication with unpleasant side-effects could involve a breach of this article if the side-effects were sufficiently serious: see O. Thorold, "The Implications of the European Convention on Human Rights for United Kingdom Mental Health Legislation" [1996] E.H.R.L. 619–636, at 620. If the medication is therapeutically justified, an application on this ground would have little prospect of success unless it could be shown that there was alternative medication available which was equally efficacious and gave rise to significantly less serious side effects.

Although the courts will doubtless be reluctant to interfere in matters of pure clinical judgment, the Commission, in *Tanko v Finland*, May 19, 1994 (App.No.23634/94), said that it "does not exclude that a lack of proper care in a case where someone is suffering from a serious illness could be certain circumstances amount to treatment contrary to Article 3". In *X v Denmark* (1983) 32 D. & R. 282 at 283, the Commission held that "medical treatment of an experimental character and without the consent of the person involved may under certain circumstances be prohibited by Article 3" (cited in E. Wicks, "The Right to Refuse Medical Treatment under the European Convention on Human Rights" (2001) 9 Med. L.R. 17 at 22).

Although this article cannot be interpreted as laying down a general obligation to release a detainee on health grounds or to place him in a civil hospital to enable him to receive specific medical treatment (*Kalashnikov v Russia* (2003) 36 E.H.R.R. 34 para.95), the detention of persons of unsound mind in an unsatisfactory or non-therapeutic environment could amount to a violation of this article if the ill-treatment of the patient attains a minimum level of severity (*Aerts v Belgium* (2000) 29 E.H.R.R. 50). In *Aerts* the Court held that, where the sole basis of detention is unsoundness of mind, an anti-therapeutic environment may contravene art.5(1), even if it is not severe enough to amount to inhuman and degrading treatment under this article. When assessing conditions of detention, account has to be taken of the cumulative effect of those conditions, as well as the specific allegations made by the applicant (*Dougoz v Greece* (2002) 34 E.H.R.R. 61 para.46). The effect of the decision in *Aerts* was explained by the Court in *Kudla v Poland* (2002) 35 E.H.R.R. 11 at para.94:

> "[Under Article 3] the State must ensure that a person is detained in conditions which are compatible with respect for his human dignity, that the matter and method of the execution of the measure do not subject him to distress or hardship of an intensity exceeding the unavoidable level of suffering inherent in detention and that, given the practical demands of imprisonment, his health and well-being are adequately secured by, among other things, providing him with the requisite medical assistance".

There are three particular elements to be considered in relation to the compatibility of an applicant's health with his stay in detention: (a) the medical condition of the prisoner, (b) the adequacy of the medical assistance and care provided in detention, and (c) the advisability of maintaining the detention measure in view of the state of health of an applicant (*Dybeku v Albania* [2009] 1 M.H.L.R. 1 para.42.) In this case, the Court said at para.50 that "a lack of resources cannot in principle justify detention conditions which are so poor as to reach the threshold of severity for Art.3 to apply". In *Parascineti v Romania*, March 13, 2012 (App.No.32060/05), the Court found that a combination of severe overcrowding, unhygienic conditions, and low staffing levels in a psychiatric hospital violated this article.

The lack of appropriate medical treatment for a prison detainee may amount to treatment contrary to this article (*Keenan v United Kingdom* (2001) 33 E.H.R.R. 38, para.110; also see *Murray v Netherlands* (2017) 64 E.H.R.R. 3 where the Court confirmed that the treatment concerned could be treatment for the prisoner's mental disorder (para.117), and that obligations under this article may go so far as to impose an obligation on the state to transfer prisoners (including mentally ill ones) to special facilities in order to receive adequate treatment (para.105)). Keenan was a case where the threshold of this article was reached where a serious disciplinary punishment involving segregation and additional detention was imposed on a mentally ill prisoner known to be a suicide risk without any effective monitoring or psychiatric care. A similar finding was made in *Renolde v France* (2009) 48 E.H.R.R. 42. The threshold was not reached in *Drew v United Kingdom* (2006) 43 E.H.R.R. SE2, where a prisoner was detained on a prison medical wing for eight days without access to effective psychiatric medication prior to his transfer to hospital. In *Brand v Netherlands* [2001] M.H.L.R. 275, the Court declared inadmissible an application that a lengthy detention of a mentally disordered person in prison pending a place being found in a secure psychiatric institution constituted a breach of this article on the ground that there was no evidence that the applicant's mental health or the possibilities of treatment had suffered on account of the time spent in prison. The unsuitability of psychiatric wings in prisons being used to detain people with mental disorders was emphasised by the Court in *Claes v Belgium*, April 10, 2013 (App.No.43418/09) at para.98. Where the treatment cannot be provided in the place of detention, it must be possible to transfer the detainee to hospital or to a specialised unit (*Rooman v Belgium* [2020] M.H.L.R. 1, para.148).

5-014   The principles governing the question whether art.3 prevents the extradition (or immigration removal) of an individual to a third country was summarised in para.24 of the opinion of Lord Bingham in *R. (on the application of Ullah) v Special Adjudicator* [2004] 2 A.C. 323:

> "While the Strasbourg jurisprudence does not preclude reliance on articles other than article 3 as a ground for resisting extradition or expulsion, it makes it quite clear that successful reliance demands presentation of a very strong case. In relation to article 3, it is necessary to show strong grounds for believing that the person, if returned, faces a real risk of being subjected to torture or to inhuman or degrading treatment or punishment: *Soering* para 91; *Cruz Varas* para 69 *Vilvarajah* para 103."

In *D v United Kingdom* (1997) 24 E.H.R.R. 423 the Court said, at para.54, that "aliens ... who are subject to expulsion cannot in principle claim any entitlement to remain on the territory of a contracting state in order to continue to benefit from medical, social or other forms of assistance provided by the expelling state during their stay". D was applied in *N v United Kingdom* (2008) 47 E.H.R.R. 39 where the Court said, at para.42, that the:

> "decision to remove an alien who is suffering from a serious mental or physical illness to a country where the facilities for the treatment of that illness are inferior to those available in the Contracting State may raise an issue under Article 3, but only in a very exceptional case, where the humanitarian grounds against the removal are compelling. In the D. case the very exceptional circumstances were that the applicant was critically ill and appeared to be close to death, could not be guaranteed any nursing or medical care in his country of origin and had no family there willing or able to care for him or provide him with even a basic level of food, shelter or social support".

5-015   The Court observed, at para.45:

"that, although the present application … is concerned with the expulsion of a person with an HIV and AIDS-related condition, the same principles must apply in relation to the expulsion of any person afflicted with any serious, naturally occurring physical or mental illness which may cause suffering, pain and reduced life expectancy and require specialised medical treatment which may not be so readily available in the applicant's country of origin or which may be available only at substantial cost".

In *Paposhvili v Belgium*, December 13, 2016 (App.No.41738/10), the Court sought to clarify the approach taken in N:

"The Court considers that the 'other very exceptional cases' within the meaning of the judgment in *N. v. the United Kingdom* which may raise an issue under Article 3 should be understood to refer to situations involving the removal of a seriously ill person in which substantial grounds have been shown for believing that he or she, although not at imminent risk of dying, would face a real risk, on account of the absence of appropriate treatment in the receiving country or the lack of access to such treatment, of being exposed to a serious, rapid and irreversible decline in his or her state of health resulting in intense suffering or to a significant reduction in life expectancy. The Court points out that these situations correspond to a high threshold for the application of Article 3 of the Convention in cases concerning the removal of aliens suffering from serious illness (para.183).

The case of *Savran v Denmark*, December 7, 2021 (App.No.5746/15) demonstrates the extremely high evidential threshold that is required in order satisfy the "substantial grounds" test established in *Paposhvili*.

In *AM (Zimbabwe) v Secretary of State for the Home Department* [2020] UKSC 17, the Supreme Court held that the approach taken by the Court in *Paposhvili* should be followed.

The Court's case law does not exclude that treatment which does not reach the severity of treatment under this article may nonetheless breach art.8 in its private life aspect where there are sufficiently adverse effects on physical and moral integrity (*Costello-Roberts v United Kingdom* (1995) 19 E.H.R.R. 112). However, it would be difficult, although not necessarily impossible, for a claimant who relies on health grounds to resist removal from the UK to fail under this article but succeed under art.8 (*R. (on the application of Razgar) v Secretary of State for the Home Department* [2004] UKHL 27; [2004] 3 All E.R. 821 para.59). In *SL (St Lucia) v Secretary of State for the Home Department* [2018] EWCA Civ 1894, Hickinbottom L.J. said:

"[A]rticle 8 is not art.3 with merely a lower threshold: it does not provide some sort of safety net where a medical case fails to satisfy the art.3 criteria. An absence of medical treatment in the country of return will not in itself engage art.8. The only relevance to art.8 of such an absence will be where that is an additional factor in the balance with other factors which themselves engage art.8" (para.27).

Aspects of mental health practice that could be challenged under this article include:

(a)   the placing of female patients with a history of sexual abuse by men in a mixed sex environment;

(b)   the automatic handcuffing of patients. In *Mouisel v France* [2004] 38 E.H.R.R. 34 at para.48, the Court held that handcuffing did not normally give rise to an issue under art.3 where it was imposed in connection with lawful detention and did not entail use of force or public exposure exceeding what was reasonably considered necessary. It was important to consider whether there was a risk that the person might abscond or cause injury or damage. The case law on this issue was considered in *R. (on the application of Faizovas) v Secretary of State for Justice* [2009] EWCA Civ 373, where the Court of Appeal considered *Unyan v Turkey*, January 8, 2009, and said, at para.22, that Unyan highlights the importance of separate consideration of the necessity for security measures at the treatment stage and that at that stage the authorities had to take account of not only the security risk but also the type of treatment which the prisoner had to undergo;

(c)   the unjustified use of CS spray or a Taser;

(d)   the imposition of control and restraint techniques on a patient where neither the patient's history nor a current assessment justifies their use;

(e)   forcible measures inflicted upon a patient which are not a medical necessity; and

(f)   the forced feeding of a patient: see the note on "degrading" below.

Torture

The Court has defined torture as "deliberate inhuman treatment causing very serious and cruel suffering" (*Ireland v United Kingdom* (1978) 2 E.H.R.R. 25 para.167). An overview of the Court's case law on the meaning of "torture" is provided in *Cestaro v Italy*, April 7, 2015 (App.No.6884/11) at paras 171 to 176.

Inhuman

See *Stanev v Bulgaria*, above.

Degrading

5-016   In *X v Germany* (1984) 7 E.H.R.R. 152, the Commission said that:

"the forced feeding of a person does involve degrading elements which in certain circumstances may be regarded as prohibited by Article 3 ... Under the Convention the High Contracting parties are, however, also obliged to secure to everyone the right to life as set out in Article 2. Such an obligation should in certain circumstances call for positive action on the part of the Contracting Parties, in particular an active measure to save lives when the authorities have taken the person in question into their custody. When, as in the present case, a detained person maintains a hunger strike this may inevitably lead to a conflict between an individual's right to physical integrity and the High Contracting Party's obligation under Article 2 ... a conflict which is not solved by the Convention itself".

X was applied in *Nevmerzhitsky v Ukraine* (2006) 43 E.H.R.R. 32, where the Court held, at para.94, that force-feeding that was aimed at saving the life of a detainee who consciously refused to take food could not in principle be regarded as inhuman and degrading. However, the medical necessity for such a procedure had to be convincingly shown to exist and the Court had to ascertain that the procedural guarantees for the decision to force feed had been complied with. Moreover, the manner in which an individual was subjected to force-feeding could not trespass the threshold of minimum severity envisaged by the case law on this article. Force feeding which was not a medical necessity was found to have breached this article in *Ciorap v Moldova*, June 19, 2007 (App.No.12066/02). It is clear from these cases that a State may on occasions be justified in inflicting treatment which would otherwise be in breach of this article in order to serve the ends of art.2 (*R. (on the application of Pretty) v Director of Public Prosecutions* [2001] UKHL 61; [2002] 1 All E.R. 1, per Lord Bingham at para.13).

Article 4 Prohibition of Slavery and Forced Labour

5-017   1.   No one shall be held in slavery or servitude.

2.   No one shall be required to perform forced or compulsory labour.

3.   For the purpose of this Article the term "forced or compulsory labour" shall not include:
   (a)   any work required to be done in the ordinary course of detention imposed according to the provisions of Article 5 of this Convention or during conditional release from such detention;
   (b)   any service of a military character or, in case of conscientious objectors in countries where they are recognised, service exacted instead of compulsory military service;
   (c)   any service exacted in case of an emergency or calamity threatening the life or well-being of the community;
   (d)   any work or service which forms part of normal civic obligations.

Article 5 Right to Liberty and Security

5-018   1.   Everyone has the right to liberty and security of person. No one shall be deprived of his liberty save in the following cases and in accordance with a procedure prescribed by law:
   (a)   the lawful detention of a person after conviction by a competent court;
   (b)   the lawful arrest or detention of a person for non-compliance with the lawful order of a court or in order to secure the fulfilment of any obligation prescribed by law;
   (c)   the lawful arrest of detention of a person effected for the purpose of bringing him before the competent legal authority on reasonable suspicion of having committed an offence or when it is reasonably considered necessary to prevent his committing an offence or fleeing after having done so;
   (d)   the detention of a minor by lawful order for the purpose of educational supervision or his lawful detention for the purpose of bringing him before the competent legal authority;
   (e)   the lawful detention of persons for the prevention of the spreading of infectious diseases, of persons of unsound mind, alcoholics or drug addicts or vagrants;
   (f)   the lawful arrest or detention of a person to prevent his effecting an unauthorised entry

into the country or of a person against whom action is being taken with a view to deportation or extradition.

2. Everyone who is arrested shall be informed promptly, in a language which he understands, of the reasons for his arrest and of any charge against him.

3. Everyone arrested or detained in accordance with the provisions of paragraph 1(c) of this Article shall be brought promptly before a judge or other officer authorised by law to exercise judicial power and shall be entitled to trial within a reasonable time or to release pending trial. Release may be conditioned by guarantees to appear for trial.

4. Everyone who is deprived of his liberty by arrest or detention shall be entitled to take proceedings by which the lawfulness of his detention shall be decided speedily by a court and his release ordered if the detention is not lawful.

5. Everyone who has been the victim of arrest or detention in contravention of the provisions of this Article shall have an enforceable right to compensation.

General Note

In *McKay v United Kingdom* (2007) 44 E.H.R.R. 41 at para.20, the Court said: **5-019**

"Article 5 of the Convention is, together with Articles 2, 3 and 4, in the first rank of the fundamental rights that protect the physical security of an individual and as such its importance is paramount. Its key purpose is to prevent arbitrary or unjustified deprivations of liberty."

This article, "as currently interpreted, does not contain a prohibition on detention on the basis of impairment, in contrast to what is proposed by the UN Committee on the Rights of Persons with Disabilities in points 6–9 of its 2015 Guidelines concerning Article 14 of the CRPD" (*Rooman v Belgium* [2020] M.H.L.R. 1, para.205).

The protection that art.5(1) provides against a deprivation of liberty is absolute, subject only to the cases listed in sub-paragraphs (a) to (f). The applicability of one ground does not necessarily preclude that of another; a deprivation of liberty may, depending on the circumstances, be justified under one or more sub-paragraphs (*Witold Litwa v Poland* [2000] M.H.L.R. 226, para.49). A person who is deprived of his liberty continues to enjoy all the fundamental rights and freedoms guaranteed under the Convention save for the right to liberty: see *Munjaz v United Kingdom* [2012] M.H.L.R. 351 which is noted in the General Note to art.8.

In *Storck v Germany* (2006) 43 E.H.R.R. 6; [2005] M.H.L.R. 211, the Court held that:

1. The State has a positive obligation to protect the liberty of its citizens, and the State was therefore obliged to take measures providing effective protection of vulnerable persons, including reasonable steps to prevent a deprivation of liberty of which the authorities had or ought to have had knowledge (para.100).

2. The State could not completely absolve itself from its responsibility by delegating its obligations in this sphere to private bodies or individuals. Private psychiatric institutions, in particular those able to hold persons without a court order, need not only a licence, but a competent supervision on a regular basis of the justification of the confinement and medical treatment (para.103).

3. Detention in a private institution could engage the State's responsibility under the Convention in three ways; by the direct involvement of public authorities, such as police officers, in the applicant's detention; by the courts' failure to interpret the provisions of the civil law relating to her claim in the spirit of art.5; and by the violation of its positive obligations to protect the applicant against interferences with her liberty carried out by private persons (para.89).

This Article embraces the detention and release of the mentally disordered, but not the conditions of detention or a right to treatment (*Winterwerp v Netherlands* (1979) 2 E.H.R.R. 387 at para.51 and *Ashingdane v United Kingdom* (1985) 7 E.H.R.R. 528, at para.44). These decisions, in so far as they relate to a right to treatment, need to be read in the light of the decision in *Rooman v Belgium* which is noted under para.(1)(e), below.

In *Re X (Court of Protection Practice)* [2015] EWCA Civ 599 Black L.J. said that "pressure on resources and even considerations of increased delay are not material to a determination of whether there are adequate safeguards to satisfy Article 5" (para.18).

In *IN v Ukraine*, June 20, 2016 (App.No.28472/08), the Court said that "the broad powers vested in health-care professionals are to be counterbalanced by procedures aimed at preventing indiscriminate involuntary hospitalisation" (para.81).

Paragraph 1

5-020   Detention pursuant to this paragraph inevitably brings with it a restriction for the detained person of his private and family life. The Court has held that it is essential that the detaining authority helps that person to maintain contact with his close family (*Messina v Italy (No.2)*, September 28, 2000, para.41).

Everyone   Including children (*Nielsen v Denmark* (1989) 11 E.H.R.R. 175 para.58).

Security of person   This phrase is to be understood in the context of physical liberty rather than physical safety. The inclusion of the word "security" simply serves to emphasise the requirement that detention could not be arbitrary (*Hajdouva v Slovakia* (2011) 53 E.H.R.R. 8, para.54).

Procedure prescribed by law   As this expression and the expression "in accordance with the law" in art.8(2) are to be understood as bearing the same meaning (*R. (on the application of Gillan) v Metropolitan Police Commissioner* [2006] UKHL 12; [2006] 4 All E.R. 1041 para.31) reference should be made to the note on that phrase in art.8(2).

Paragraph 1(a)

5-021   **Conviction**   A mentally disordered offender who is convicted of a criminal offence and ordered to be detained in a psychiatric hospital will be detained under both art.5(1)(a) and 5(1)(e) (*X v United Kingdom* (1982) 4 E.H.R.R. 188 para.39).

Paragraph 1(e)

5-022   In *Witold Litwa v Poland* (2001) 33 E.H.R.R. 53, the Court identified a link between all of the categories of people noted in this sub-paragraph. The link is that all those persons:

"may be deprived of their liberty either in order to be given medical treatment or because of considerations dictated by social policy, or on both medical and social grounds ... [A] predominant reason why the Convention allows the persons mentioned in paragraph 1(e) of Article 5 to be deprived of their liberty is not only that they are dangerous for public safety but also that their own interests may necessitate their detention" (para.60).

In *Zagidulina v Russia* [2015] M.H.L.R. 246, the Court said that it is "is mindful that individuals suffering from a mental illness constitute a particularly vulnerable group and therefore any interference with their rights must be subject to strict scrutiny, and only 'very weighty reasons' can justify a restriction of their rights (see *Alajos Kiss v. Hungary*, no. 38832/06, § 42, 20 May 2010)" (para.52).

In *Stanev v Bulgaria* (2012) 55 E.H.R.R.; [2012] M.H.L.R. 23 the Court summarised the principles relating to the detention of persons of unsound mind as follows:

"143. The Court reiterates that in order to comply with Article 5 § 1, the detention in issue must first of all be 'lawful', including the observance of a procedure prescribed by law; in this respect the Convention refers back essentially to national law and lays down the obligation to conform to the substantive and procedural rules thereof. It requires in addition, however, that any deprivation of liberty should be consistent with the purpose of Article 5, namely to protect individuals from arbitrariness (see *Herczegfalvy v. Austria* 24 September 1992, § 63, Series A no. 244). Furthermore, the detention of an individual is such a serious measure that it is only justified where other, less severe measures have been considered and found to be insufficient to safeguard the individual or public interest which might require that the person concerned be detained. That means that it does not suffice that the deprivation of liberty is in conformity with national law; it must also be necessary in the circumstances (see *Witold Litwa v. Poland*, no. 26629/95, § 78, ECHR 2000-III).

144. In addition, sub-paragraphs (a) to (f) of Article 5 § 1 contain an exhaustive list of permissible grounds of deprivation of liberty; such a measure will not be lawful unless it falls within one of those grounds (ibid., § 49; see also, in particular, *Saadi v. the United Kingdom* [GC], no. 13229/03, § 43, ECHR 2008, and *Jendrowiak v. Germany*, no. 30060/04, § 31, 14 April 2011).

145. As regards the deprivation of liberty of mentally disordered persons, an individual cannot be deprived of his liberty as being of 'unsound mind' unless the following three minimum conditions are satisfied: firstly, he must reliably be shown to be of unsound mind; secondly, the mental disorder must be of a kind or degree warranting compulsory confinement; thirdly, the validity of continued confinement depends upon the persistence of such a disorder (see *Winterwerp v. the*

Netherlands 24 October 1979, § 39, Series A no. 33; *Shtukaturov*, cited above, § 114; and *Varbanov*, cited above, § 45).

146. As to the second of the above conditions, the detention of a mentally disordered person may be necessary not only where the person needs therapy, medication or other clinical treatment to cure or alleviate his condition, but also where the person needs control and supervision to prevent him, for example, causing harm to himself or other persons (see *Hutchison Reid v. the United Kingdom*, no. 50272/99, § 52, ECHR 2003-IV).

147. The Court further reiterates that there must be some relationship between the ground of permitted deprivation of liberty relied on and the place and conditions of detention. In principle, the 'detention' of a person as a mental-health patient will be 'lawful' for the purposes of Article 5 § 1 (e) only if effected in a hospital, clinic or other appropriate institution authorised for that purpose (see *Ashingdane*, cited above, § 44, and *Pankiewicz v. Poland*, no. 34151/04, § 42–45, 12 February 2008). However, subject to the foregoing, Article 5 § 1 (e) is not in principle concerned with suitable treatment or conditions (see *Ashingdane*, cited above, § 44, and *Hutchison Reid*, cited above, § 49)."

Taking the three *Winterwerp* requirements in turn (i.e. the patient must reliably be shown to be of unsound mind, the mental disorder must be of a kind or degree warranting compulsory confinement and the validity of continued confinement must depend upon the persistence of the disorder):

(i)   The Court held that the term "persons of unsound mind" is "not one that can be given a definitive interpretation ... it is a term whose meaning is constantly evolving as research in psychiatry progresses, an increasing flexibility in treatment is developing and society's attitude to mental illness changes, in particular so that a greater understanding of the problems of mental patients is becoming wide-spread. In any event, Art.5(1)(e) obviously cannot be taken as permitting the detention of a person simply because his views or behaviour deviate from the norms prevailing in a particular society" (para.37). In *X v Federal Republic of Germany* 6 D. & R. 182, the Commission found that the term "unsound mind" did not just mean mental illness, but must be understood in a wider sense to include abnormal personality disorder. The test under this paragraph has been described in the domestic courts as one of "whether it can 'reliably be shown' that [the patient] suffers from a mental disorder sufficiently serious to warrant detention" (*R. (on the application of H) v Mental Health Review Tribunal, North and East London Region* [2001] EWCA Civ 415, at para.29 per Lord Phillips M.R.).

The medical assessment must be based on the actual state of mental health of the person concerned and not solely on past events. A medical opinion cannot be seen as sufficient to justify deprivation of liberty if a significant period of time has elapsed between the deprivation and the provision of the opinion (*Varbanov v Bulgaria* [2000] M.H.L.R. 263, para.47). In *Winterwerp*, the Court said that a period of emergency detention which lasted for six weeks before a medical opinion was obtained from a general practitioner did not violate this article. In *Yaikov v Russia* [2016] M.H.L.R. 108, the Court said at para.63:

"The relevant time at which a person must be established to be of unsound mind, for the purposes of Article 5 § 1 (e), is the date of adoption of the measure depriving that person of liberty as a result of that condition (see *O.H. v. Germany*, no. 4646/08, § 78 24 November 2011, with further references)."

In *Nawrot v Poland*, October 19, 2017 (App.No.77850/12), para.73, the Court said:

"[I]n order to amount to a true mental disorder for the purposes of sub-paragraph (e) of Article 5(1), the mental disorder in question must be so serious as to necessitate treatment in an institution appropriate for mental health patients .... The Court has further expressed doubts as to whether a person's dissocial personality or dissocial personality disorder alone could be considered a sufficiently serious mental disorder so as to be classified as a 'true' mental disorder for the purposes of Article 5(1) (e) ...."

In *RB v United Kingdom* (2017) 65 E.H.R.R. SE17, an admissibility decision, the Court, at paras 36 and 37, equated the effects of a person's lack of capacity with unsoundness of mind.

The national authorities have a certain margin of appreciation regarding the merits of clinical diagnoses since it is in the first place for them to evaluate the evidence in a particular case (*S v Estonia* [2011] M.H.L.R. 396, para.38). In *Ilnseher v Germany*, December 4, 2018, (App.Nos 10211/12 and 27505/14) the Court said that "in certain specific cases, it has considered it necessary for the medical experts in question to have a specific qualification, and has in particular required the assessment to be carried out by a psychiatric expert where the person confined as being 'of unsound mind' had no history of mental disorders" (para 130). In *G v E* [2010] EWCA Civ 822, para.60, the Court of Appeal said that evidence from a psychologist was appropriate if the person concerned had learning difficulties.

(ii) In *Kolanis v United Kingdom* (2006) 42 E.H.R.R. 12, para.70, the Court rejected a submission that the decision of the Mental Health Review Tribunal that the patient could be discharged subject to conditions was tantamount to a finding that the second *Winterwerp* criterion was no longer fulfilled, with the result that any subsequent undue delay in release was in breach of art.5; see further the notes on s.73(7).

(iii) The requirement relating to the persistence of the mental disorder links to the review procedure provided for under para.4 of this article. In *Johnson v United Kingdom* (1999) 27 E.H.R.R. 296, the Court rejected the submission of the applicant, a restricted patient, that once there had been a finding by an expert authority, in this case the Mental Health Review Tribunal, that the mental disorder had ceased, he should as a consequence have been immediately and unconditionally released.

In *Aerts v Belgium* (2000) 25 E.H.R.R. 50, the applicant, who was an offender patient, was placed in provisional detention in the psychiatric wing of a prison for seven months before a place became available in a psychiatric institution. The Court heard evidence that the wing was not regarded as an appropriate institution for persons of unsound mind, as there was no regular medical attention and it was not a therapeutic environment. The Court held that, in principle, the detention of a person of unsound mind will only be lawful for the purposes of this paragraph "if effected in a hospital, clinic or other appropriate institution authorised for that purpose" (para.44). In this context "for that purpose" must mean purpose of caring for the mentally disordered. The detention of the applicant violated this paragraph because the "proper relationship between the aim of the detention and the conditions in which it took place was ... deficient" (para.49). This implies that there must be some therapeutic involvement with the patient. The Court further found that the conditions in which the applicant was detained were not sufficiently severe to lead to a finding of inhuman or degrading treatment under art.3. It follows that where detention is justified under this paragraph, complaints about the conditions in the patient's place of detention are better brought under this article rather than art.3. It is likely that the Court would need evidence that standards relating to the provision of services and/or the quality of conditions in the place of detention had fallen very low for it to be satisfied that this article had been violated; also see the note on s.47 under the heading "Human Rights Act 1998".

The Court has developed its approach for the need for the detained person to receive appropriate therapy. In *Rooman v Belgium* [2020] M.H.L.R. 1, the Court held:

1. That, in the light of the developments in its case-law and the current international standards which attach significant weight to the need to provide treatment for the mental health of persons in compulsory confinement, it "is necessary to recognise explicitly that there exists an obligation on the authorities to ensure appropriate and individualised therapy, based on the specific features of the compulsory confinement, such as the conditions of the detention regime, the treatment proposed or the duration of the detention" (para.205).

2. "Any detention of mentally ill persons must have a therapeutic purpose, aimed specifically, and in so far as possible, at curing or alleviating their mental-health condition, including, where appropriate, bringing about a reduction in or control over their dangerousness." Patients are "entitled to be provided with a suitable medical environment accompanied by real therapeutic measures, with a view to preparing them for their eventual release" (para.208).

3. The level of care required must go beyond basic care. The Court said: "Mere access to health professionals, consultations and the provision of medication cannot suffice for a treatment to be considered appropriate and thus satisfactory under Article 5" (para.209).

With regard to the link between this article and art.3, the court noted that

"the question of a continued link between the purpose of detention and the conditions in which it is carried out, and the question of whether those conditions attain a particular threshold of gravity, are of differing intensity. This implies that there may be situations in which a care path may correspond to the requirements of Article 3 but be insufficient with regard to the need to maintain the purpose of the compulsory confinement, and thus lead to a finding that there has been a violation of Article 5(1). In consequence, a finding that there has been no violation of Article 3 does not automatically lead to a finding that there has been no violation of Article 5(1), although a finding of a violation of Article 3 on account of a lack of appropriate treatment may also result in a finding that there has been a violation of Article 5(1) on the same grounds" (para 213).

Lawful   This paragraph does not require the initial detention to be authorised by a court or tribunal. The lawfulness under domestic law of a person's detention is not of itself decisive: it must also be established that the detention was in conformity with para.1, which is to prevent persons from being deprived of their liberty in an arbitrary fashion (*Withold Litwa v Poland*, above, paras 72, 73). A detention will be arbitrary where, despite complying with the letter of national law, there has been an element of bad faith or deception on behalf of the authorities or where the domestic authorities neglected to attempt to apply the relevant legislation correctly or where there was an excessive delay in renewing the patient's detention (*Mooren v Germany* (2010) 50 E.H.R.R. 23, paras 78 to 81)).

A subsequent finding that a court erred under domestic law in making the order depriving a person of their liberty will not necessarily affect the validity of the intervening period of detention (*Benham v United Kingdom* (1996) 22 E.H.R.R. 293 para.42). *Benham* was applied in *R. (on the application of A) v Harrow Crown Court* [2003] EWHC 2020 (Admin) where Stanley Burton J. held that the detention of a patient on the authority of an irregular order did not infringe this article because the detention was not arbitrary. However, there will be a breach of this article if the defect in the order amounts to "a gross and irregular irregularity" (*Mooren v Germany*, above, para.75).

A significant delay in the transfer of a mentally disordered person who needs psychiatric treatment from a penal establishment to a psychiatric hospital can constitute a violation of this paragraph (*Mocarska v Poland* [2007] M.H.L.R. 228; also see *Pankiewicz v Poland* [2008] M.H.L.R. 233). In the absence of an exceptional and unforeseeable situation, a delay of six months is impermissible (*Proshkin v Russia*, February 7, 2012 (App. No.28869/03), para.81).

Detention   Whether a person's situation constitutes a "deprivation of liberty" for the purposes of para.1 is considered in Part 6.

In *Munjaz v United Kingdom* [2012] M.H.L.R. 351, the Court did not consider that there was a general rule that either solitary confinement or seclusion per se can amount to a further deprivation of the liberty of a person who was already lawfully detained. Whether or not there has been a further deprivation of liberty in respect of such a person must depend on the circumstances of case, including the type, duration, effects and manner of implementation of the measure in question (paras 65–66). The Court held that the secluded detained patient had not been the subject of a further deprivation of liberty because:

(i)   he was a long-term patient in a high security hospital: even when he was not in seclusion, he was already subjected to greater restrictions on his liberty than would normally be the case for a mental health patient;

(ii)   seclusion, though coercive, was not imposed as a punishment but to contain severely disturbed behaviour likely to cause harm to others;

(iii)   while its duration, notably of 9, 14 and 18 days, would point towards a further deprivation of liberty, duration alone was not determinative; the length of seclusion was foremost a matter of clinical judgment; and

(iv)   the manner of implementing the hospital's seclusion policy carried the greatest weight: the hospital's approach was to allow secluded patients the most liberal regime that was compatible with their presentation, and seclusion was being flexibly applied (paras 69–72).

The Convention does not guarantee "for a person who has been ordered to undergo compulsory psychiatric treatment, the right to choose the place of his detention" (*Valle v Finland* [2000] M.H.L.R. 255).

Persons of unsound mind   See the note on the first of the *Winterwerp* requirements, above.

Alcoholics   Persons who are not medically diagnosed as "alcoholics", but whose conduct and behaviour under the influence of alcohol pose a threat to public order or themselves, can be taken into custody for the protection of the public or their own interests, such as their health or personal safety (*Withold Litwa v Poland* (2001) 33 E.H.R.R. 35). This finding would equally apply to persons who were not medically diagnosed as drug addicts, but whose conduct and behaviour under the influence of drugs give rise to similar concerns.

Paragraph 2

In *Khlaifia v Italy*, December 15, 2016, (App.No.16483/12), the Court said at para.115:   **5-023**

"[This paragraph] lays down an elementary safeguard: any person who has been arrested should know why he is being deprived of his liberty. This provision is an integral part of the scheme of protection afforded by Article 5: any person who has been arrested must be told, in simple, non-technical language that he can understand, the essential legal and factual grounds for his deprivation of liberty, so as to be able to apply to a court to challenge its lawfulness in accordance with paragraph 4 ... Whilst this information must be conveyed "promptly", it need not be related in its entirety by the arresting officer at the very moment of the arrest. Whether the content and promptness of the information conveyed were sufficient is to be assessed in each case according to its special features ...."

In *LM v Slovenia*, June 12, 2014, (App.No.32863/05), the Court held that a delay of four days between the patient's detention and the giving of reasons breached this paragraph.

Paragraph 4

5-024   Article 5.4 "is first and foremost a guarantee of a fair procedure for reviewing the lawfulness of detention—an applicant is not required, as a precondition to enjoying that protection, to show that on the facts of his case he stands any particular chance of success in obtaining his release. In matters of such crucial importance as the deprivation of liberty and where questions arise involving, for example, an assessment of the applicant's character or mental state, the Court's case law indicates that it may be essential to the fairness of the proceedings that the applicant be present at an oral hearing" (*Waite v United Kingdom* (2003) 36 E.H.R.R. 54, para.59). The applicant's legal representative must meet the patient before the hearing. At the hearing he or she must not just act as a passive observer (*M.S. v Croatia (No.2)* [2015] M.H.L.R. 294, para.156).

No issue arises under this paragraph where the impugned detention is of a short duration: see *Rozhkov v Russia (No.2)* January 31, 2017, (App.No.38898/04), para.65, where the applicant's detention lasted only several hours.

The role of the reviewing body is to identify whether the reasons which initially justified the detention continue to subsist, not to review the decision to detain (*X v UK* (1992) 14 E.H.R.R. 188 para.58). This paragraph does not require the reviewing body to have any other control of the detention process, such as decisions regarding leave of absence (*Roux v UK* (1986) 48 D. & R. 263 at 268). Where a court initially orders detention, the review required by this paragraph is incorporated in that decision (*Winterwerp v Netherlands* (1979) 2 E.H.R.R. 387, para.55).

Although it is generally useful to keep detailed records of what happens at hearings, neither this article nor any other provision of the Convention contains a requirement that an official record of a hearing be kept, whether verbatim or in summary form (*Nakach v Netherlands* [2006] M.H.L.R. 22 paras 35, 36). However, a failure to draw up an official record of a hearing as required by domestic law would breach para.1 of this article (*Schenkel v Netherlands* [2006] M.H.L.R. 27).

In the *Winterwerp* case, the Commission said that the patient's lawyer had the right to examine the patient's file, but that it was not necessary for the patient to be informed of all the evidence or that he be allowed access to all of the information in his medical file. This approach was confirmed by the Court in *Nikolova v Bulgaria* [2001] E.H.R.R. 3 at para.58 where it was said that "[e]quality of arms is not ensured if counsel is denied access to those documents in the investigation file which are essential in order effectively to challenge the lawfulness of his client's detention".

This paragraph is not concerned with the details of detention, such as the place and conditions of the patient's detention (*Ashingdane v UK* (1985) 7 E.H.R.R. 528 paras 43, 49) and it cannot be invoked by a person who is lawfully released (*Stephens v Malta* (2010) 50 E.H.R.R. 8, para.102).

The principles which emerge from the Court's case law on this paragraph as they apply to the detention of person of unsound mind were summarised in *Megyeri v Germany* (1993) 15 E.H.R.R. 584, at para.22. They include the following:

(i)   A person of unsound mind who is compulsorily confined in a psychiatric institution for an indefinite or lengthy period is in principle entitled, at any rate where there is no automatic periodic review of a judicial character, to take proceedings "at reasonable intervals" before a court to put in issue the "lawfulness"—within the meaning of the Convention—of his detention (see *X v United Kingdom*, above, at para.52).

(ii)   Article 5(4) requires that the procedures followed have a judicial character and give to the individual concerned guarantees appropriate to the kind of deprivation of liberty in question; in order to determine whether a proceeding provides adequate guarantees, regard must be had to the particular nature of the circumstances in which such proceedings takes place (see *Wassink v Netherlands*, September 27, 1990, Series A, No. 185-A, p.13, para.30).

(iii)   The judicial proceedings referred to in art.5(4) need not always be attended by the same guarantees as those required under art.6(1) for civil or criminal litigation. None the less, it is essential that the person concerned should have access to a court and the opportunity to be heard either in person or, where necessary, some form of representation. Special procedural safeguards may prove called for in order to protect the interests of persons who, on account of their mental disabilities, are not fully capable of acting for themselves (see *Winterwerp v Netherlands*, above, at para.60).

(iv)   Article 5(4) does not require that persons committed to care under the head of "unsound mind" should themselves take the initiative in obtaining legal representation before having recourse to a court (*Winterwerp* above, para.60)

The Court went on to say at para.23 that it:

"follows from the foregoing that where a person is confined in a psychiatric institution on the ground of the commission of acts which constituted criminal offences but for which he could not be held responsible on account of mental illness, he should—unless there are special circumstances— receive legal assistance in subsequent proceedings relating to the continuation, suspension or termination of his detention. The importance of what is at stake for him—personal liberty—taken together with the very nature of his affliction—diminished mental capacity—compel this conclusion".

Megyeri does not establish an entitlement under this paragraph to public funding of a lawyer of the patient's choice (*R. (on the application of Brady) v Lord Chancellor* [2017] EWHC 410 (Admin); [2017] M.H.L.R 274).

In *MH v United Kingdom* (2014) 58 E.M.R.R. 35; [2014] M.H.L.R. 249 at para.77(a), the Court   **5-025** identified an additional principle arising from the Court's case law concerning persons of unsound mind:

"[A]n initial period of detention may be authorised by an administrative authority as an emergency measure provided that it is of short duration and the individual is able to bring judicial proceedings 'speedily' to challenge the lawfulness of any such detention including, where appropriate, its lawful justification as an emergency measure (*Winterwerp v Netherlands*, above, paras.57–61 and *X v. the United Kingdom*, above, para.58)".

Where a tribunal finds that a patient's detention in hospital is no longer necessary and that he is eligible for release on conditions, new issues of lawfulness may arise where detention nonetheless continues, due, for example, to difficulties in fulfilling the conditions. It follows that such patients are entitled under this paragraph to have the lawfulness of that continued detention determined by a court with requisite promptness (*Kolanis v United Kingdom* (2006) 42 E.H.R.R. 12, para.80).

Everyone   Either personally or through some form of representation (*De Wilde, Ooms and Versyp v Belgium* (1971) 1 E.H.R.R. 373, paras 73–76).

To take proceedings   Until relatively recently, the Court accepted that an automatic review of the patient's case would satisfy this paragraph; see, for example, *X v United Kingdom* [1981] 4 E.H.R.R. 188. However a study of the Strasbourg jurisdiction reveal a shift of emphasis in recent years towards a greater stress on the requirement that a detained person should be able to take the initiative himself to start proceedings to challenge the lawfulness of his detention; see, for example, *Rakevich v Russia* [2004] M.H.L.R. 37. This shift is considered by Keene L.J. in *Secretary of State for Justice v Rayner* [2008] EWCA Civ 176; [2008] M.H.L.R. 115.

Lawfulness of his detention   It is for the authorities to prove that an individual satisfies the conditions for compulsory detention, rather than the converse (*Reid v United Kingdom* (2003) 37 E.H.R.R. 9 para.70). The review must encompass the lawfulness of the detention under this article as well as its lawfulness under domestic law (*Johnson v United Kingdom* (1999) E.H.R.R. 296 para.60). Detention lasts from the time when the detention is authorised to the time when it is officially lifted, even if the patient is not physically detained during the whole of this period, i.e. it covers periods of leave of absence and absence without leave (*Van der Leer v Netherlands* (1990) 12 E.H.R.R. 567, para.35).

Decided   It is not sufficient for the court to have merely advisory functions, it must have the power to order release if it finds the detention to be unlawful (*Benjamin and Wilson v United Kingdom* (2003) 36 E.H.R.R. 1, para.34).

Speedily   Which is a less stringent requirement than arises with the tem "promptly" in para.3 (*E v Norway*, below, para.64). In the Court's view, "this concept cannot be defined in the abstract; the matter must ... be determined in the light of the circumstances of each case" (*Sanchez-Reisse v Switzerland* (1987) 9 E.H.R.R. 71 at para.55). In practice, the Court has dealt with this issue on a case-by-case basis. It is the obligation of the state to organise its legal system to enable it to comply with convention requirements (*Bezicheri v Italy* (1989) 12 E.H.R.R. 210 para.25). The "excessive workload" of the judge assigned to a particular case cannot be prayed in aid. Nor can the fact that the judge is on holiday (*E v Norway* (1990) 17 E.H.R.R. 30, para.64). There is no general principle that "administrative necessity" excuses delay (*R. (on the application of Noorkoiv) v Secretary of State for the Home Department* [2002] EWCA Civ 770; [2002] 4 All E.R. 515 para.26). Where there has been a delay in undertaking a review, the Court must determine whether the delay can be attributed to the authorities (*Luberti v Italy* (1984) 6 E.H.R.R. 440 para.34). In proceedings concerning a review of a psychiatric detention, the complexity of the medical issues involved in a case is a factor which may be taken into account when assessing compliance with the requirements of this paragraph (*Musial v Poland* (2001) 31 E.H.R.R. 29 para.47). Where there are complex issues to be determined "the primary responsibility for delays resulting from the provision of expert opinions rests ultimately with the state" (Musial at para.46).

5-026   In *Cottenham v United Kingdom* [1999] M.H.L.R. 97, the Court, in an admissibility decision, found that the tribunal could not be criticised for a delay of 10 months which had been caused by the patient's solicitor's request for an adjournment to obtain an independent psychiatric report. The Court said that it:

"does not rule out that, given the particular problems of detained patients, where it appears that the legal representatives of such a person are acting negligently or in some way causing unjustified delay in the presentation of an application to a MHRT, the tribunal would be under a duty to make enquiries and to ensure that the application is proceeded with expeditiously".

Less urgency is required when the patient makes a further application in pursuance of his right to a periodic review of his detention. However, a delay of over four months in these circumstances has been held by the Court to be incompatible with this paragraph (*Koendjbiharie v Netherlands* (1990) 13 E.H.R.R. 820). It is also the case that the standard of "speediness" is less stringent when it comes to proceedings before a court of appeal (*Dzhurayev v Russia* (2013) 57 E.H.R.R. 22, para.224).

In *R. (on the application of C) v Mental Health Review Tribunal London South and West Region* [2001] EWCA Civ 1110; [2002] M.H.L.R. 110, the Court of Appeal said that decisions of the Court such as *E v Norway*, above, where a delay of eight weeks between application and hearing was held to violate this paragraph, were not attempts to decide as of principle whether a particular practice or policy of setting a specified time for a hearing was in breach of this paragraph. What the Court made clear is that each case has to be decided upon its own particular circumstances. The Court of Appeal held that this approach was not compatible with a policy of automatically listing cases for hearing eight weeks after the application had been made: see the note on r.37 of the Tribunal Procedure (First-tier Tribunal) (Health, Education and Social Care Chamber) Rules 2008.

Court   A body can be a court if it is independent of the executive and of the parties to the case and has a judicial character (*De Wilde, Ooms and Versp* (1971) 1 E.H.R.R. 373 para.76). The court must also be impartial (*DN v Switzerland* (2003) 37 E.H.R.R. 21 para.42). In *DN*, the Court said that "impartiality must be determined by a subjective test, that is on the basis of the personal conviction of a particular judge in a given case, and also by an objective test, that is ascertaining whether the judge offered guarantees sufficient to exclude any legitimate doubt in this respect" (para.44). The Court also said that:

"any judge in respect of whom there is legitimate reason to fear a lack of impartiality must withdraw. In deciding whether in a given case there is a legitimate reason to fear that a particular judge lacks impartiality, the standpoint of the parties concerned is important but not decisive. What is decisive is whether this fear can be held to be objectively justified" (para.46).

A tribunal clearly qualifies as a court for the purposes of the Convention (*X v United Kingdom* (1982) 4 E.H.R.R. 188). Hospital managers, when exercising their power to review the detention of a patient, are not a court because the managers are a party to the review (*De Wilde, Ooms and Versp*, above).

Paragraph 5

5-027   This paragraph requires an enforceable claim for compensation before a national court if a breach of any of the other paragraphs in this article has occurred. The Court has held that "… there can be no question of 'compensation' where there is no pecuniary or non-pecuniary damage to compensate" (*Wassink v Netherlands*, September 27, 1990, para.38). In *R. (on the application of Wright) v Secretary of State for the Home Department* [2006] EWCA Civ 67; [2006] H.R.L.R. 23, the Court of Appeal held that the right under this paragraph is a domestic right and, as a matter of construction, a person could only be the victim of a detention in contravention of the provisions of this paragraph if there were a breach of paras 1 and/or 4 recognised by domestic law.

The court has awarded modest pecuniary damages where the applicant has suffered damage resulting from a deprivation of liberty that he would not have suffered had this paragraph not been violated (*Niedbala v Poland* (2001) 33 E.H.R.R. 48).

Damages under this paragraph should be calculated in accordance with the guidance given by the House of Lords in *R. (on the application of Greenfield) v Secretary of State for the Home Department* [2005] UKHL 14; [2005] 2 All E.R. 240, an art.6 case, and by the Supreme Court in *R (on the application of Faulkner) v Secretary of State for Justice* [2013] UKSC 23; [2013] 2 All E.R. 1013: see the General Note to s.6 of the Act under the heading "Damages for an unlawful detention". In *R.(on the application of Faulkner) v Director of Legal Aid Caseworker* [2016] EWHC 717, Mostyn J. said at paras 37 and 38:

"I accept that an award of damages made under Article 5 (5) of the European Convention on Human Rights is a serious matter. Detention by the State is, on any view, a very bad business. The award of damages – although they are customarily modest – should reflect the fact that it is only in Article 5 (5) of the Convention that compensation is mentioned. However I do not accept that awards of damages for State detention pursuant to the Convention are a class apart from all other types of damages. I do not accept that because they are awarded to Mr Faulkner as a victim of human rights violation that they should be subjected to a process of immunisation in the way that perhaps damages for personal injury or an award of damages for, say, the loss of an eye or a leg would not. Naturally, State detention is a bad business but the consequences of many personal injuries are far more long-enduring than temporary State detention as happened in this case by virtue of delay in convening a Parole Board hearing.

It is for these reasons that I reject the argument that there is some kind of special status or numinous quality to be attached to these damages. These damages are to be treated under the costs regime, in my judgment, in exactly the same way as any other damages."

Article 6 Right to fair trial

1. In the determination of his civil rights and obligations or of any criminal charge against him, everyone is entitled to a fair and public hearing within a reasonable time by an independent and impartial tribunal established by law. Judgment shall be pronounced publicly but the press and public may be excluded from all or part of the trial in the interest of morals, public order or national security in a democratic society, where the interests of juveniles or the protection of the private life of the parties so require, or to the extent strictly necessary in the opinion of the court in special circumstances where publicity would prejudice the interests of justice.

5-028

2. Everyone charged with a criminal offence shall be presumed innocent until proved guilty according to law.

3. Everyone charged with a criminal offence has the following minimum rights:

(a) to be informed promptly, in a language which he understands and in detail, of the nature and cause of the accusation against him;

(b) to have adequate time and facilities for the preparation of his defence;

(c) to defend himself in person or through legal assistance of his own choosing or, if he has not sufficient means to pay for legal assistance, to be given it free when the interests of justice so require;

(d) to examine or have examined witnesses against him and to obtain the attendance and examination of witnesses on his behalf under the same conditions as witnesses against him;

(e) to have the free assistance of an interpreter if he cannot understand or speak the language used in court.

General Note

This article, which provides for the right to a fair hearing in civil or criminal proceedings in domestic law, "is concerned with standards of justice, the separation of powers and the rule of law" (*Matthews v Ministry of Defence* [2003] UKHL 4; [2003] 1 All E.R. 689 at para.25 per Lord Hoffmann). The Court in *Aerts v Belgium* (1998) 29 E.H.R.R. 50, para.59, held that "the right to liberty … is a civil right". This article is therefore engaged when a tribunal reviews the detention of a patient. The Court has consistently held that the "procedural" guarantees under art.5(1) and (4) are broadly similar to those under art.6(1) of the Convention (*Stanev v Bulgaria* (2012) 55 E.H.R.R. 696, [2012] M.H.L.R. 23, para.232).The lawfulness of the detention of patients can be challenged under art.5(4) and the Court, in its interpretation of that paragraph, has been prepared to borrow some of the concepts of fairness in judicial proceedings from this article: see *Shtukaturov v Russia* (2012) 54 E.H.R.R. 27; [2008] M.H.L.R. 238 para.66.

5-029

In *AH v West London Mental Health Trust* [2010] UKUT 264 (AAC); [2010] M.H.L.R. 326 and *AR v West London NHS Trust and the Secretary of State for Justice* [2020] UKUT 273 (AAC); [2021] M.H.L.R. 168, the Upper Tribunal considered that the relevant factors in deciding whether to direct a public hearing of the First-tier Tribunal (Mental Health). These cases are noted in the General Note to r.38 of the Tribunal Rules.

Paragraph 1

5-030

The right of access to a court guaranteed by this Article is "practical and effective", not "theoretical or illusory" (*Del Sol v France* (2002) 35 E.H.R.R. 38 at para.21).

In *Ashingdane v UK* (1985) 7 E.H.R.R. 528, the Court found that the restrictions on bringing legal proceedings placed on patients by s.141 of the Mental Health Act 1959 (now see s.139 of the 1983 Act) did not transgress the patient's "right to a court" under this paragraph. The Court said at para.57:

"Certainly, the right of access to the courts is not absolute but may be subject to limitations; these are permitted by implication since the right of access 'by its very nature calls for regulation by the State, regulation which may vary in time and in place according to the needs and resources of the community and of individuals' (*Golder v UK* (1979) 1 E.H.R.R. 524, paragraph 38). In laying down such regulation, the Contracting States enjoy a certain margin of appreciation. Whilst the final decision as to observance of the Convention's requirements rests with the Court, it is no part of the Court's function to substitute for the assessment of the national authorities any other assessment of what might be the best policy in this field."

Civil rights and obligations In (*R. (on the application of Wilkinson) v The Responsible Medical Officer Broadmoor Hospital* [2001] EWCA Civ 1545; [2002] 1 W.L.R. 419 at para.35, Simon Brown L.J. said that a decision to treat a patient forcibly will inevitably determine his civil rights. However, the right to state medical treatment is not a civil right falling within this article (*L v Sweden* (App.No.10801/84)).

A decision to place a patient in seclusion does not engage this article (*R. (on the application of King) v Secretary of State for Justice* [2012] EWCA Civ 376).

Fair ... hearing Among the rights that the Court and the Commission have identified as comprising the right to a fair hearing are: the right to adversarial proceedings, the right to have a hearing within a reasonable time, the right to equality of arms, the right to know the grounds on which a decision is based and access to information necessary to bring the case effectively: see further S. Grosz et al., *Human Rights: The 1998 Act and the European Convention* (2000), pp.244 et seq.

Although a party has a right to a fair trial under this article, that does not mean that he or she necessarily has an absolute and unqualified right to see all the documents (*Doorson v Netherlands* (1996) 22 E.H.R.R. 330 para.70; also see *Re B (Disclosure to Parties)* [2001] 2 F.L.R. 1017).

Although there is no automatic right under the Convention for legal aid or legal representation to be available for an applicant who is involved in proceedings which determine his or her civil rights and obligations, this article may be engaged under two interrelated aspects. Firstly, para.(1) embodies the right of access to a court. A failure to provide the applicant with the assistance of a lawyer may breach this provision where such assistance is indispensable for effective access to court. Secondly, the key principle governed by the application of this article is fairness. In cases where an applicant appears in court notwithstanding lack of assistance of a lawyer and manages to conduct his or her case, the question may nonetheless arise as to whether the procedure was fair (*P, C and S v UK* (2002) 35 E.H.R.R. 31).

Independent and impartial tribunal The components of impartiality were identified in *Kamenos v Cyprus* (2018) 67 E.H.R.R. 11 at para.96:

"The Court reiterates that impartiality normally denotes the absence of prejudice or bias and its existence or otherwise can be tested in various ways. According to the Court's settled case-law, the existence of impartiality for the purposes of Article 6 § 1 must be determined according to a subjective test where regard must be had to the personal conviction and behaviour of a particular judge, that is, whether the judge held any personal prejudice or bias in a given case; and also according to an objective test, that is to say by ascertaining whether the tribunal itself and, among other aspects, its composition, offered sufficient guarantees to exclude any legitimate doubt in respect of its impartiality."

The House of Lords has explained that "there is now no difference between the common law test of bias and the requirements under Article 6 of the Convention of an independent and impartial tribunal" (*Lawal v Northern Spirit Ltd* [2003] I.C.R. 856 at 862 para.14 per Lord Steyn). Also see the notes on r.34 of the Tribunal Procedure (First-tier Tribunal) (Health, Education and Social Care Chamber) Rules 2008.

In *R. (on the application of PD) v West Midlands and North West London Mental Health Review Tribunal* [2004] EWCA Civ 311, the Court of Appeal made reference to *Piersack v Belgium* (1982) 5 E.H.R.R. 169 where "the Court appears to have contemplated that the practical problems of finding properly qualified members of a Tribunal may be relevant when considering whether a member is disqualified on account of bias". The Court of Appeal said, at para.11, that it "would not exclude the possibility that such considerations might be relevant in an extreme case where it was impossible, or virtually impossible, to assemble a Tribunal free of connections that might give rise to apprehension of apparent bias".

Paragraph (3)(c)

In *R. v Brown* [2015] EWCA Crim 1328; [2016] M.H.L.R 142, it was held that this provision was not breeched in a situation where a patient was handcuffed to nursing staff during a conference with his lawyers because of a real possibility that the patient would use the conference to harm himself or his lawyers.   **5-031**

Article 7 No punishment without law

1.   No one shall be held guilty of any criminal offence on account of any act or omission which did not constitute a criminal offence under national or international law at the time when it was committed. Nor shall a heavier penalty be imposed than the one that was applicable at the time the criminal offence was committed.   **5-032**

2.   This Article shall not prejudice the trial and punishment of any person for any act or omission which, at the time when it was committed, was criminal according to the general principles of law recognised by civilised nations.

Article 8 Right to respect for private and family life

1.   Everyone has the right to respect for his private and family life, his home and his correspondence.   **5-033**

2.   There shall be no interference by a public authority with the exercise of this right except such as is in accordance with the law and is necessary in a democratic society in the interests of national security, public safety or the economic well-being of the country, for the prevention of disorder or crime, for the protection of health or morals, or for the protection of the rights and freedoms of others.

General Note

The purpose of this article "is to protect the individual against intrusion by agents of the state, unless for good reason, into the private sphere within which individuals expect to be left alone to conduct their personal affairs and live their persona lives as they choose" (*R. (on the application of the Countryside Alliance) v Attorney General* [2007] UKHL 52 at para.10). It was described by Stanley Burnton J. as "the least defined and most unruly of the rights enshrined in the Convention" in *R. (on the application of Wright) v Secretary of State for Health* [2006] EWHC 2886 (Admin) at para.60. A person can consent to acts which would otherwise involve an infringement of his rights, whether at common law or under this article (*Millar v Dickson* [2001] UKPC D4).   **5-034**

In *Glaser v United Kingdom* (2001) 33 E.H.R.R. 1, the Court said at para.63:

"The essential object of Article 8 is to protect the individual against arbitrary interference by public authorities. There may however be positive obligations inherent in an effective 'respect' for family life. These obligations may involve the adoption of measures designed to secure respect for family life even in the sphere of relations between individuals, including both the provision of a regulatory framework of adjudicatory and enforcement machinery protecting individuals' rights and the implementation, where appropriate, of specific steps (see among other authorities, *X and Y v Netherlands* (1986) 8 E.H.R.R. 235, and, mutatis mutandis, *Osman v United Kingdom* (2000) 29 E.H.R.R. 245). In both the negative and positive contexts, regard must be had to the fair balance which has to be struck between the competing interests of the individual and the community, including other concerned third parties, and of the state's margin of appreciation (see, among other authorities, *Keegan v Ireland* ((1994) 18 E.H.R.R. 342)."

The reference to "relations between individuals" in *Glaser* demonstrates the link between the right to private life and the right to family life. If members of a family are prevented from sharing family life together, art.8(1) is likely to be infringed (*Anufrijeva v London Borough of Southwark* [2003] EWCA Civ 1406; [2004] 1 All E.R. 833 at para.12).

Positive obligations may exceptionally arise in the case of the handicapped in order to ensure that they are not deprived of the possibility of developing social relations with others and therefore developing their own personalities. In the case of the physically handicapped, positive obligations require appropriate measures to be taken, to the greatest extent feasible, to ensure that they have access to essential economic and social activities and to an appropriate range of recreational and cultural activities. A positive obligation will only be imposed where there is both (i) a direct and immediate link between the measures sought and the applicant's private life (*Botta v Italy* (1998) 26 E.H.R.R. 241, paras 34, 35) and (ii) a special link between the situation complained of and the particular needs of the applicant's private life (*Sentges v Netherlands* (2004) 7 C.C.L.R. 400, 405). In *Hajduová v Slovakia* [2016] M.H.L.R. 417, the Court held that a failure to detain a domestic violence victim's husband for psychiatric treatment, such that more violence was threatened, amounted to a breach of the State's positive obligations under this article to secure respect for the applicant's private life.

Positive obligations are not absolute. Before inaction can amount to a lack of respect for private and family life, there must be some ground for criticising the failure to act. There must be an element of culpability. Where the complaint is that there has been culpable delay in the administrative process necessary to determine and to give effect to an art.8 right, there will be no infringement of the article unless substantial prejudice has been caused to the applicant. In *Passannante v Italy* (1998) 26 E.H.R.R. CD 153, a case where the applicant had waited five months to see a hospital specialist, the Commission stated that:

"where the State has an obligation to provide medical care, an excessive delay of the public health service in providing a medical service to which the patient is entitled and the fact that such a delay has, or is likely to have, a serious impact on the patient's health could raise an issue under Article 8(1) of the Convention".

There is a need to have regard to resources when considering the obligations imposed by a State by this article (*Anufrijeva v London Borough of Southwark*, above, paras 45–47). In *Milicevic v Montenegro* (2019) 69 E.H.R.R. 338, the Court held that there was a breach of the positive obligation to protect against the imminent and serious risk posed by a mentally disordered person in circumstances where the State ought to have been aware of the risk faced by a particular individual.

In "Protecting the Rights of People with Mental Disabilities: The European Convention on Human Rights", Oliver Lewis states that in the psychiatric setting, this article will be engaged by issues as diverse as:

"freedom of correspondence, right not to be in a crowded living space, access to non-pharmacological therapy, access to fresh air and exercise, privacy in washing and toileting, privacy of visits, confidentiality of medical records, rights to sexuality, right to be free from unwanted sexual advances, freedom from surveillance of daily life and searches of living space and of person" (E.J.H.L. (2002) 9: 293–320, 308).

A particularly wide margin of appreciation was due where the issues involved an assessment of competing priorities for a limited state resource (*Sentges v Netherlands* (2004) 7 C.C.L.R. 400).

MacDonald J made the following remarks in *Wigan M.D.C. v W* [2021] EWHC 1982 (Fam) at para.70:

"[A]s made clear in *Botta v Italy* (1998) 26 EHRR 241, in considering the application of Art 8 a fair balance must struck between the general interest and the interests of the individual and the State has, in any event, a margin of appreciation. Within this context, and historically, the courts have stopped short of holding that there is an obligation under Art 8 to provide treatment at any specific level (see for example *Tysiac v Poland* (2007) 45 EHRR 947 and *R (A) v West Middlesex University Hospital NHS Trust* [2008] EWHC 855 (Admin)). The domestic courts have likewise been reluctant to interfere with the decision by a health authority in respect of the allocation of a limited budget, even where a child's life expectancy is in issue (see *R v Cambridgeshire District Health Authority ex p B* [1995] 2 All ER 129)."

5-035   Under this Article the authorities:

"must strike a fair balance between the interests of a person of unsound mind and the other legitimate interests concerned. However, as a rule, in such a complex matter as determining somebody's mental capacity, the authorities should enjoy a wide margin of appreciation. This is mostly explained by the fact that the national authorities have the benefit of direct contact with the persons concerned and are therefore particularly well placed to determine such issues" (*Shtukaturov v Russia* (2012) 54 E.H.R.R. 27; [2008] M.H.L.R. 238 at para.87).

The Commission recognised that public authorities might have to take particular steps to protect the mentally disordered in order to fulfil their obligations under this article:

"... The impossibility for the above category of persons [the mentally disabled] to form or express their will calls for protective measures on behalf of the authorities which go beyond what is required with regard to persons who are in full possession of their physical and mental capacities" (*X and Y v Netherlands* (1983) 6 E.H.R.R. CD311 at para.81).

In *Munjaz v United Kingdom* [2012] M.H.L.R. 351, the Court said at paras 79 and 80:

"In assessing the proper scope of private life for those who are deprived of their liberty, the Court reiterates that, under the Convention system, the presumption is that detained persons 'continue to enjoy all the fundamental rights and freedoms guaranteed under the Convention save for the right to liberty, where lawfully imposed detention expressly falls within the scope of Article 5 of the Convention' ([*Hirst v United Kingdom* (2006) 42 E.H.R.R. 41, para.69]). Any restriction on those rights must be justified in each individual case ([*Dickson v United Kingdom* (2008) 46 E.H.R.R. 41, para.68]).
In applying those principles to the present case, the Court agrees that the compulsory seclusion of the applicant interfered with his physical and psychological integrity and even a minor such interference must be regarded as an interference with the right to respect for private life under Article 8 if it is carried out against the individual's will ([*Storck v Germany* (2006) 43 E.H.R.R. 6, para.143]) Moreover, the importance of the notion of personal autonomy to Article 8 and the need for a practical and effective interpretation of private life demand that, when a person's personal autonomy is already restricted, greater scrutiny be given to measures which remove the little personal autonomy that is left."

Where a public authority commits acts which it knows are likely to cause psychiatric harm to an individual, those acts are capable of constituting an infringement of this article. Maladministration will not, however, cause such an infringement simply because it causes stress that leads to a particularly susceptible individual to suffer such harm in circumstances where this was not reasonably to be anticipated. No lack of respect for family life is manifested in such circumstances (*Anufrijeva v London Borough of Southwark*, above, para.143).

In *Ciliz v Netherlands* [2000] 2 F.L.R. 469 at 482, the Court said that whilst this article contains no explicit procedural requirements, the decision-making process leading to measures of interference must be fair and such as to afford due respect to the interests safeguarded by the article; see also *H and L v A City Council* [2011] EWCA Civ 403, per Munby L.J. at para.51. It is therefore the case that a violation of this article is likely to occur if an application is made to detain a child under the Mental Health Act in circumstances where the parents of the child have not been offered the opportunity of being involved in the decision-making process. In *Glass v United Kingdom* (2004) 39 E.H.R.R. 15, the Court held that a failure to obtain the authority of the High Court to authorise the treatment of a child in a non-emergency situation where the child's parents objected to the treatment in question constituted a violation of this article.

Treatment that does reach the level of severity required by art.3 may nevertheless breach this article in its private life aspects where there are sufficiently adverse effects on a person's physical and moral integrity (*Costello-Roberts v United Kingdom* (1995) 19 E.H.R.R. 112).

In *Storck v Germany* (2006) 43 E.H.R.R. 6; [2005] M.H.L.R. 211, the Court held that the state's obligations under this article in respect of a person who has been detained in a private psychiatric clinic arises for the same reasons to those relevant to art.5.

Paragraph 1

In *R. (on application of Bridges) v The Chief Constable of South Wales Police* [2019] EWHC 2341 (Admin), the Divisional Court said at para.98:   **5-036**

"If an interference with Article 8(1) rights is to be justified it must meet the four-part test in *Bank Mellat v Her Majesty's Treasury (No 2)* [2013] UKSC 39, namely:

(1)   whether the objective of the measure pursued is sufficiently important to justify the limitation of a fundamental right;

(2)   whether it is rationally connected to the objective;
(3)   whether a less intrusive measure could have been used without unacceptably compromising the objective; and
(4)   whether, having regard to these matters and to the severity of the consequences, a fair balance has been struck between the rights of the individual and the interests of the community."

Everyone   Including a person who lacks mental capacity (*A Local Authority v E* [2012] EWHC 1639 (COP), para.124).

Respect   ""Respect" means more than 'acknowledge' or 'take into account', it implies some positive obligations on the part of the public authorities" (*Campbell and Cosans v United Kingdom* (1982) 4 E.H.R.R. 293; *Valsamis v Greece* (1997) 24 E.H.R.R. 294)" (*Anufrijeva v Southwalk London Borough Council* [2002] EWHC 3136 (QB) at para.104). In *Sheffield and Horsham v United Kingdom* (1998) 27 E.H.R.R. 163, the Court said at para.52:

"The Court reiterates that the notion of 'respect' is not clear cut, especially as far as the positive obligations inherent in that concept are concerned: having regard to the diversity of the practices followed and the situation obtaining in the Contracting States, the notion's requirements will vary considerably from case to case."

Private ... life   In *Bensaid v United Kingdom* (2001) 33 E.H.R.R. 10, the Court said at para.47:

"Private life is a broad term not susceptible to exhaustive definition. The Court has already held that elements such as gender identification, name and sexual orientation and sexual life are important elements of the personal sphere protected by Article 8. Mental health must be regarded as a crucial part of private life associated with the aspect of moral integrity. Article 8 protects a right to identity and personal development, and the right to establish and develop relationships with other human beings and the outside world. The preservation of mental stability is in that context an indispensable precondition to effective enjoyment of the right to respect for private life."

But, not "every act or measure which adversely affects moral or physical integrity will interfere with the right to respect to private life" (*Bensaid*, above, para.46). However, even a minor interference with the physical integrity of an individual must be regarded as an interference with the right to respect for private life if it is carried out against the individual's will (*Storck v Germany* (2006) 43 E.H.R.R. 6, para.168).

In *Botta v Italy* (1998) 26 E.H.R.R. 241, the Court said that "the guarantee afforded Art.8 is primarily intended to ensure the development, without outside interference, of the personality of each individual in his relations with other human beings" (para.32). In this case, the Court's case law on the concept of private life was described as being "based on a pragmatic, common-sense approach rather than a formalistic or purely legal one" (para.27). The rights invoked must not be "too wide and indeterminate" (*Zehnalova and Zehnal v Czech Republic*, May 14, 2002). In *Niemietz v Germany* (1992) 16 E.H.R.R. 97 at para.29, the Court said that

"it would be too restrictive to limit the notion to an 'inner circle' in which the individual may live his own personal life as he chooses and to exclude therefrom entirely the outside world encompassed within that circle. Respect for private life must also comprise, to a certain degree, the right to establish and develop relationships with human beings".

The right of an individual to decide how and when to end his life, provided he was in a position to make up his own mind in that respect and to take appropriate action, is one aspect of the right to respect for private life within the meaning of this article. The state's positive obligation to take steps to allow for a dignified suicide is subject to a certain margin of appreciation which varies in accordance with the issues and the importance of the interests at stake (*Haas v Switzerland* (2011) 53 E.H.R.R. 33).

A person's private life may be concerned in measures effected outside his or her home or private property. It can include the publication of a person's photograph (*Sciacca v Italy* (2006) 43 E.H.R.R. 20). A person's reasonable expectation of privacy is a significant though not necessarily conclusive factor (*Perry v United Kingdom* (2004) 39 E.H.R.R. 3 para.37).

The "ability to conduct one's life in a manner of one's own choosing may also include the opportunity to pursue activities perceived to be of a physically or morally harmful or dangerous nature for the individual concerned" (*Pretty v United Kingdom* (2002) 35 E.H.R.R. 1, at para.62).

In *Raninen v Finland* (1998) 26 E.H.R.R. 563 para.63, the Court acknowledged that the notion of **5-037** physical and moral integrity of the person extends to situations of deprivation of liberty (which can involve the seclusion of a patient (*Munjaz v United Kingdom* [2012] M.H.L.R. 351)). It also includes information about a person's mental condition (*Gaskin v United Kingdom* (1990) 12 E.H.R.R. 36 para.37).

In *R. (on the application of H) v Ashworth Hospital Authority* [2001] EWHC Admin 872; [2001] M.H.L.R. 241, Sir Christopher Bellamy QC said, citing *Guerra v Italy* (1998) 26 E.H.R.R. 357 and *Lopez Ostra v Spain* (1995) 20 E.H.R.R. 277, that there was support for the proposition that the notion of physical integrity identified in *X and Y v Netherlands* (1986) 8 E.H.R.R. 235, extends to the protection of a person's health (para.124). In order to succeed under this article the claimant would have to show that there was a real and immediate risk to his health from which the defendant has failed to protect him, and that the defendant had not taken such steps as were reasonably to be expected of it to obviate that risk (para.128).

The "imposition of medical treatment, without consent of a mentally competent adult patient, would interfere with a person's physical integrity in a manner capable of engaging the rights protected by [this article]" (*Pretty v United Kingdom*, above, para.63; also see *Wilkinson v UK* [2006] M.H.L.R. 142). Mentally competent patients have a right to make choices about medical treatment "that accord with their own views and values, regardless of how irrational, unwise or imprudent such choices may appear to others" (*Jehovah's Witnesses of Moscow v Russia* [2011] 53 E.H.R.R. 4, para.136). This article would not be breached if forcible treatment is given to a mentally incompetent detained patient in a situation where, "according to the psychiatric principles generally accepted at the time, medical necessity justified the treatment in issue": see *Herczegfalvy v Austria* (1993) 15 E.H.R.R. 437, paras 83, 86, noted under art.3. However, in the context of the forced administration of medication, safeguards must be in place to protect all patients against arbitrary interference with their rights under this article: see *X v Finland* [2012] M.H.L.R. 318, which is considered in the note to s.63 of the Act under the heading Human Rights Act 1998. Where the patient is a child, any medical treatment (including the taking of a medical photograph) must be authorised by the person with parental responsibility for that child (*Glass v United Kingdom* (2004) 39 E.H.R.R. 15, para.75).

With regard to action taken to prevent detainees harming themselves, the authorities:

"... must discharge their duties in a manner compatible with the rights and freedoms of the individual concerned. There are general measures and precautions which will be available to diminish the opportunities for self-harm, without infringing personal autonomy. Whether any more stringent measures are necessary in respect of a prisoner and whether it is reasonable to apply them will depend on the circumstances of the case" (*Keenan v United Kingdom* (2001) 33 E.H.R.R 38, para.91).

In *R. (on the application of N) v Secretary of State for Health* [2009] EWCA Civ 795; [2009] M.H.L.R. 266, the Court of Appeal held that this article did not protect the right for patients to smoke at Rampton Hospital: the prohibition of smoking in such an institution did not have a sufficiently adverse effect on a patient's physical or moral integrity. The Court found that the hospital's policy which banned smoking on its premises, but allowed for individual exceptions on clinical grounds, was lawful. In *McCann v State Hospitals Board for Scotland* [2017] UKSC 31; [2017] M.H.L.R 306, the Supreme Court held that although a comprehensive ban on smoking at the State Hospital came within the ambit of this article, the interference was justified under paragraph (2).

Restrictions placed on a male psychiatric patient's freedom to dress as a woman and to assume the **5-038** appearance of a woman constitute an interference with his private life: see *R. (on the application of E) v Ashworth Hospital Authority* [2001] EWHC Admin 1089 para.40, where Richards J. held that the interference was justified under para.2 by virtue of therapeutic and security concerns that had been put forward in support of the hospital's approach; also see *R. (on the application of Green) v Secretary of State for Justice* [2013] EWHC 3491 (Admin). As a matter of domestic law, a hospital is entitled to give precedence to the interests of the patients as a whole over the interests of individual patients (*R. v Broadmoor Special Hospital Ex p. S, H and D* [1998] C.O.D. 199).

In *R. (on the application of DB) v Secretary of State for the Home Department* [2006] EWHC 659 (Admin); [2006] M.H.L.R. 158, the court held that the decision to detain a former prisoner who was a male to female transsexual in an all-male high security psychiatric hospital, and to keep her detained there, was justified and proportionate, and did not infringe her rights under either this article or art.3. The court further held that the Secretary of State had been justified in declining to exercise his powers under the Mental Health Act to transfer her, as there was no appropriate alternative bed for her elsewhere.

A person has a right under this article to have access to files concerning his own life. Any restriction on this right in domestic law must meet the requirements of para.2. In cases involving the disclosure of personal data, the Court has recognised that a margin of appreciation should be left to national authorities in striking a fair balance between the relevant public and private interests. The scope of this margin depends on such factors as the nature and seriousness of the interests at stake and the gravity of the interference (*Peck v United Kingdom* (2003) 36 E.H.R.R. 41 para.77). The data subject is not required to specifically justify a request to be provided with a copy of their personal files; rather, it is for the authorities to show that there existed compelling reasons for refusing that facility (*KH v Slovakia* (2009) 49 E.H.R.R. 34, para.48). If a public authority is not able to secure the consent of a person who has contributed to the file to have that material disclosed, there must be an independent authority that can decide whether the material should be disclosed (*Gaskin v United Kingdom*, above and *MG v United Kingdom* (2003) 36 E.H.R.R. 3).

In *Z v Finland* (1997) 25 E.H.R.R. 371 at paras 95–97, the Court said that:

> "the protection of personal data, not least medical data, is of fundamental importance to a person's enjoyment of his or her right to respect for private and family life … Respecting the confidentiality of health data … is crucial not only to respect the sense of privacy of a patient but also to preserve his or her confidence in the medical profession and in health services in general. [Disclosure must be justified by] an overriding requirement in the public interest".

At the same time, the Court accepted that "the interests of a patient and the community as a whole in protecting the confidentiality of medical data may be outweighed by the interest in investigation and prosecution of crime and in the publicity of court proceedings … where such interests are shown to be of even greater importance".

The confidentiality of a patient's medical records belongs to the patient. For the particular importance of confidentiality in psychiatric medical notes, see *Ashworth Hospital Authority v MGN Ltd* [2002] UKHL 29; [2002] 4 All E.R. 193 para.63; also see the note on the "rights and freedoms of others", below, and Fenella Morris, "Confidentiality and the Sharing of Information" (2003) *Journal of Mental Health Law*, 9, 38–50.

Where the report of an independent inquiry into homicides committed by a mentally disordered person contains citations from his medical and other records, a claim that the publication of the report to the world at large would breach this article in that it was not necessary in the public interest must be the subject of a "very high intensity" review by a court. It is not enough to assert that the decision to taken was a reasonable one: a compelling case needs to exist to justify publication. In such a situation art.10 also comes into play if only because of the general corresponding right of the public to be free to receive information where it is sought to be published (*R. (on the application of Stone) v South East Coast Strategic Health Authority* [2006] EWHC 1668 (Admin); [2006] M.H.L.R. 288 at paras 31–33).

An enquiry by a patient's doctor addressed to a third party which is aimed at obtaining information about the patient rather than communicating it does not infringe this article (*R. (on the application of O'Reilly) v Blenheim Healthcare Ltd* [2005] EWHC 241 (Admin)).

5-039 The searching of a mentally disordered detained patient would violate this article in the absence of a justification under para.2.

However, in *R. (on the application of Gillan) v Metropolitan Police Commissioner* [2006] UKHL 12; [2006] 4 All E.R. 1041 at para.28, Lord Bingham said that he was:

> "doubtful whether an ordinary superficial search of the person can be said to show a lack of respect for private life. It is true that 'private life' has been generously construed to embrace wide rights to personal autonomy. But it is clear Convention jurisprudence that intrusions must reach a certain level of seriousness to engage the operation of the Convention which is, after all, concerned with human rights and fundamental freedoms, and I incline to the view that an ordinary superficial search of the person and an opening of bags, of the kind which passengers uncomplainingly submit at airports, for example, can scarcely be said to reach that level".

In *Wainwright v United Kingdom* (2007) 44 E.H.R.R. 40 para.43, the Court held that the requirement to submit to a strip search will generally constitute interference under this paragraph that would require justification under para.2.

The use of surveillance techniques, such as CCTV in hospitals and care homes may well involve art.8 rights. In *Khan v UK* (2001) 31 E.H.R.R. 45, a case involving the use of a covert listening device by the police, the Court said at para.26:

"The Court recalls, with the Commission in the case of *Govell*, that the phrase 'in accordance with the law' not only requires compliance with domestic law but also relates to the quality of that law, requiring it to be compatible with the rule of law. In the context of covert surveillance by public authorities, in this instance the police, domestic law must provide protection against arbitrary interference with an individual's right under Article 8. Moreover, the law must be sufficiently clear in its terms to give individuals an adequate indication as to the circumstances in which and the conditions on which public authorities are entitled to resort to such covert measures."

Surveillance operations conducted by local authorities and NHS trusts must comply with the provisions of Pt II of the Regulations of Investigatory Powers Act 2000 which was passed partly as a result of the decision in *Khan*. The normal use of security cameras per se, whether in the public street or on premises, do not raise issues under this article as long as they serve a legitimate and foreseeable purpose (*Perry v United Kingdom* (2004) 39 E.H.R.R. 3 para.40).

Family … life   The state must act in a manner calculated to allow those concerned to lead a normal **5-040** family life (*Z and E v Austria* (1986) 49 D. & R. 67). The existence or non-existence of "family life" is essentially a question of fact depending upon the reality in practice of close personal ties (*K v Finland (No.1); T v Finland (No.1)* (2001) 31 E.H.R.R. 18 para.150). It is therefore the case that it is actual family life, rather than family life in the abstract that needs to be considered (*R. (on the application of Ahmadi) v Secretary of State for the Home Department* [2005] EWHC 687 (Admin) para.25). This article "makes no distinction between the 'legitimate and the illegitimate' family" (*Marckx v Belgium* (1979) 2 E.H.R.R. 330 para.31). The concept of family life embraces, even where there is no co-habitation, the tie between a parent and his or her child (*Boughanemi v France* (1996) 22 E.H.R.R. 228) including adoptive parent/child relationships (*X v Belgium and Netherlands* (1975) D.R. 75). When deciding whether a relationship between a couple can be said to amount to "family life", a number of factors may be relevant, including whether the couple live together, the length of their relationship and whether they have demonstrated their commitment to each other by having children together or by any other means (*Al-Nashif v Bulgaria* (2003) 36 E.H.R.R. 37 para.112). In *R. (on the application of L) v Secretary of State for Health* [2001] 1 F.L.R. 406, Scott Baker J. considered the jurisprudence on this article. He said:

"Family life it seems to me, is an elastic concept that depends very much on the facts of the individual case. In some cases the existence of family life will be immediately obvious; in others the reverse will be true. But the onus of establishing family life in each case is in my judgment on the applicant".

There must be extraordinarily compelling reasons before a baby can be physically removed from its mother, against her will, immediately after birth as a consequence of a procedure in which neither she nor her partner has been involved (*P, C and S v United Kingdom* (2002) 35 E.H.R.R. 31). In "judicial decisions where the rights under Article 8 of parents and of a child are at stake, the child's rights must be the paramount consideration" (*Yousef v Netherlands* (2003) 36 E.H.R.R. 20 at para.73).

The Court has held that it is an essential part of a prisoner's right under this Article that he be enabled to maintain contact with his close family, and that blanket bans on visiting are unlawful (*Khoroshenko v Russia*, June 30, 2015 (App.No. 4148/04), paras 106 and 126)).

There is no Convention duty to provide support to foreign nationals who are in a position freely to return home (*R. (on the application of Kimani) v Lambeth LBC* [2003] EWCA Civ 1150; [2004] 1 W.L.R. 272), and the right to family life is not infringed because it must be conducted outside the United Kingdom in a country with a lower standard of living (*R. (on the application of Mahmood) v Secretary of State for the Home Department* [2001] 1 W.L.R. 840). However, deportation cases can exceptionally raise issues under this article: see the notes on art.3.

Home   For the purposes of this article, a home is "will usually be the place, the physically defined area, **5-041** where private and family life develops" (*Gomez v Spain* (2005) 41 E.H.R.R. 40 at para.53). However, this article does not protect everything that people may want to do in their private space (*R. (on the application of Countryside Alliance v Attorney General* [2007] UKHL 52, para.116).

Neither this article nor any other provision of the Convention guarantees housing of a particular standard or at all (*Chapman v United Kingdom* (2001) 33 E.H.R.R. 399, para.99). However, a refusal of the authorities to solve a housing problem of an individual suffering from a severe disease might in certain circumstances raise an issue under this article because of the impact of such refusal on the private life of the individual (*Marzari v Italy* (1999) 28 E.H.R.R. CD 175). Although not every breach of a local authority's duty to provide residential accommodation under s.21 of the National Assistance Act 1948 [now see s.18 of the Care Act 2014] will result in a breach of this article, those entitled to care under s.21 are a particularly vulnerable group. Positive measures have to be taken, by way of community care facilities, to enable them to enjoy, so far as possible, a normal and family life. The question that needs to be asked is what was the effect of the breach in practical terms on the claimant's family and private life? (*R. (on the application of Bernard) v London Borough of Enfield* [2002] EWHC 2282 (Admin); (2002) 5 C.C.L.R. 577). In *Anufrijeva v Southwark London Borough Council* [2003] EWCA Civ 1406; [2004] 1 All E.R. 833, the Court of Appeal, in confirming the correctness of the approach adopted in *Bernard*, said at para.43:

> "We find it hard to conceive, however, of a situation in which the predicament of an individual will be such that Article 8 requires him to be provided with welfare support, where his predicament is not sufficiently severe to engage Article 3. Article 8 may more readily engaged where a family unit is involved. Where the welfare of children is at stake, Article 8 may require the provision of welfare support in a manner which enables family life to continue."

In *R. (on the application of N) v Secretary of State for Health* [2009] EWCA Civ 795, the Court of Appeal held that although Rampton Hospital was the patient's home, it was not the same as a private home in that it was a public institution operated as a hospital where supervision was intense for safety and security reasons. The degree to which a person could expect freedom to do as he pleased, and engage in personal and private activity, would vary according to the nature of the accommodation in which he lived. A patient in a high security hospital did not lose all rights to a private life but the nature of that life and the activities he may pursue were seriously restricted, and always supervised.

In *R. v North and East Devon Health Authority Ex p. Coughlan* [2000] 3 All E.R. 850, the Court of Appeal held that the enforced move of a patient by an NHS Trust from accommodation that had been promised as her home for life, a move that would be both emotionally devastating and seriously anti-therapeutic, was a breach of this article that was not justified by para.2.

Correspondence A law which allows for state interference with correspondence must not leave the authorities too much latitude. It must "indicate with reasonable clarity the scope and manner of the exercise of the relevant discretion conferred on the public authorities" (*Domenichini v Italy* (2001) 32 E.H.R.R. 4 para.33).

In *Klass v Germany* (1979) 2 E.H.R.R. 214, the Court held that this article protects telephone conversations as well as written correspondence. A similar finding would almost certainly be made on other forms of communication, such as email.

Paragraph 2

5-042   The exceptions provided for in this paragraph must be interpreted narrowly, and the need for them in any given case must be convincingly established (*Societe Colas Est v France* (2004) 39 E.H.R.R. 17 para.47). In *Re L (Care: Threshold Criteria)* [2007] 1 F.L.R. 2050 at para.51, Hedley J. said that "Art.8(2) … contemplate[s] the exceptional rather than the commonplace".

The principles which govern the court's approach in determining whether an interference with an art.8 right can be justified under this paragraph were identified by Newman J. in *R. (on the application of N) v Ashworth Special Hospital Authority and the Secretary of State for Health* [2001] EWHC Admin 339; [2001] M.H.L.R. 77 at para.9:

> "(i)   When considering whether an interference with a Convention right is proportionate the burden lies on the state to justify its actions.
> (ii)   The interference must go no further than is strictly necessary to achieve its permitted purpose.
> (iii)   The more substantial the interference the more that is required to justify it.
> (iv)   The court should anxiously scrutinise a decision of the executive which interferes with human rights and should consider applying an objective test 'whether the decision maker could reasonably have concluded that the interference was necessary to achieve one or more of the legitimate aims recognised by the Convention'.
> (v)   The mode of such objective review is more intrusive, or it could be said, more demanding than the convention *Wednesbury* test.
> (vi)   The court should give due deference or allow a margin of appreciation to the decision maker."

Where the interference is with an intimate part of an individual's private life, there must be particularly serious reasons to justify the interference (*Smith v United Kingdom* (2000) 29 E.H.R.R. 493 at para.89). However, the state is entitled to control even seemingly consensual sexual acts in private where it is necessary to "safeguard … against exploitation and corruption … those who are specially vulnerable because they are young, weak in body or mind, inexperienced, or in a state of special physical, official or economic dependence" (*Dudgeon v United Kingdom* (1982) 4 E.H.R.R. 149 at para.49).

In accordance with the law   The Court's case law on the meaning of this phrase was summarised in *Munjaz v United Kingdom* [2012] M.H.L.R. 351, at para.88:

"[T]he wording 'in accordance with the law' requires the impugned measure both to have some basis in domestic law and to be compatible with the rule of law, which is expressly mentioned in the preamble to the Convention and inherent in the object and purpose of Article 8. The law must thus be adequately accessible and foreseeable, that is, formulated with sufficient precision to enable the individual—if need be with appropriate advice—to regulate his conduct ([*S. v the United Kingdom* (2009) 48 E.H.R.R. 50, para.95]). It is also well-established in its case-law that the Court recognises the impossibility of attaining absolute certainty in the framing of laws and the risk that the search for certainty may entail excessive rigidity ([*Silver v the United Kingdom* (1983) 5 E.H.R.R. 247, para.88]). Instead, the level of precision required of the domestic legislation depends to a considerable degree on the content of the instrument considered, the field it is designed to cover and the number and status of those to whom it is addressed ([*Hasan v Bulgaria* (2002) 34 E.H.R.R. 55, para.84]). With respect to the need for foreseeability, what is required is that, where discretionary powers are conferred on authorities, the law must indicate the scope of any such discretion conferred on the competent authorities and the manner of its exercise with sufficient clarity to give the individual adequate protection against arbitrary interference" (see, among many authorities, [*Liberty v the United Kingdom* (2009) 48 E.H.R.R. 1, paras 66–69]).

In applying these requirements to the seclusion policy adopted by Ashworth Hospital, the Court held that the discretion conferred on Ashworth to depart from the guidance in the *Code of Practice* and to formulate its own seclusion policy met the requirement of foreseeability because there was sufficient indication of the scope of discretion that Ashworth enjoyed and the manner of exercise of that discretion was indicated with sufficient clarity such as to protect the applicant against arbitrary interference with his art.8 rights (paras 89–90).

Necessary in a democratic society   The: **5-043**

"notion of necessity implies that the interference corresponds to a pressing social need and, in particular, that it is proportionate to the legitimate aims pursued. In determining whether an interference was 'necessary in a democratic society' the Court will take into account that a margin of appreciation is left to Contracting States. Furthermore the Court cannot confine itself to considering the impugned facts in isolation but must apply an objective standard and look at them in the light of the case as a whole" (*Matter v Slovakia* (2001) 31 E.H.R.R. 32, para.66).

The criteria used to determine whether an interference with private or family life in an expulsion case is "necessary in a democratic society" have been summarised by the Grand Chamber in *Uner v Netherlands* (2007) 45 E.H.R.R. 14 at paras 57 and 58.

Economic well-being   A court should be slow to interfere with decisions which involve a balance of competing claims on the public purse in the allocation of economic resources (*R. v Criminal Injuries Compensation Board Ex p. P* [1995] 1 All E.R. 870 per Neill L.J. at 881). This approach has been reaffirmed in home closure cases since the coming into force of the 1998 Act. For example, in *R. (on the application of Phillips and Rowe) v Walsall MBC* [2001] EWHC 789 (Admin), Lightman J. said at para.11:

"I may add that if (contrary to my view) a move such as is presently contemplated could possibly constitute an interference with a fundamental right under Article 8, it could surely be justified as required for the economic well-being of the Council and of those in need of its services. Resources of public authorities are notoriously limited and it must be a matter for elected authorities such as the Council to have leeway in how they are husbanded and applied."

Protection of health   Although the Court declined to decide in *A, B and C v Ireland* (2011) 53 EHRR   **5-044**
13 whether "others" within this paragraph includes unborn children, a State can invoke as a legitimate aim the moral values of the State, including the right to life of the unborn: see paras 227–228.
    The Court has not developed an equivalent test of "medical necessity" in relation to this article, as it has in the context of art.3.
    In *R. (on the application of Razgar) v Secretary of State for the Home Department* [2004] UKHL

27; [2004] 3 All E.R. 821 at para.59, Lady Hale made the following comments in a case where the applicant's health needs were being properly or at least adequately met in this country and the complaint was that they would not be adequately met in the county to which he is to be expelled:

"Although the possibility cannot be excluded, it is not easy to think of a foreign health care case which would fail under Art.3 but succeed under Art.8. There clearly must be a strong case before the Article is even engaged and then a fair balance must be struck under Art.8(2). In striking that balance, only the most compelling humanitarian -considerations are likely to prevail over the legitimate aims of immigration control or public safety."

Rights and freedom of others   "Article 8.2 could have been, but is not, expressly limited to Convention rights and liberties"; per Stanley Burnton J. in *Craven v Secretary of State for the Home Department and the Parole Board* [2001] EWHC Admin 850 at para.35. In this case an exclusion zone attached to a prisoner's parole was upheld partly because "the respect for private life protected by Article 8 should include a victim's family right to go about their business with a minimum of anxiety, and without undue restriction on their own movements". Also note the statement of Hale L.J. in *Re W & B (Children)* [2001] EWCA Civ 757 at para.54, that the rights of the child to be taken into account in this paragraph are not confined to his Convention rights, and include his interests.

In *TV v Finland* (1994) 18 E.H.R.R. CD 179, the Commission held that the disclosure that a prisoner was HIV positive to prison staff directly involved in his custody and who themselves were subject to obligations of confidentiality was justified as being necessary "for the protection of the rights and freedoms of others". Similar considerations would apply to a patient who had been assessed as being a danger to other patients or to staff.

Article 9 Freedom of thought, conscience and religion

5-045   **1.**   Everyone has the right to freedom of thought, conscience and religion; this right includes freedom to change his religion or belief and freedom, either alone or in community with others and in public or private, to manifest his religion or belief, in worship, teaching, practice and observance.

2.   Freedom to manifest one's religion or beliefs shall be subject only to such limitations as are prescribed by law and are necessary in a democratic society in the interests of public safety, for the protection of public order, health or morals, or for the protection of the rights and freedoms of others.

General Note

5-046   In *JP v South London and Maudsley NHS Foundation Trust* [2012] UKUT 486 (AAC); [2013] M.H.L.R. 148, UT Judge Lane said at para.46:

"Detention under s.2 of the Mental Health Act 1983 is not aimed at controlling political, religious or other thoughts or beliefs but at ensuring that any underlying mental disorder of the appropriate degree is assessed and (if possible) treated (inter alia) for the safety or health of the patient or others. To those ends alone, he may be detained. But that is the subject matter of Article 5 of the ECHR. The jurisprudence of the European Court of Human Rights on art 9 shows that the 'Strasbourg institutions have resisted the attempts of applicants to raise issues under article 9 when they may be considered as falling under some other article of the Convention' (Lester & Pannick, *Human Rights Law and Practice* [4.9.2], LexisNexus 2009). It would, therefore, be surprising if Article 9 was engaged in relation to a decision that a patient had a mental disorder which warranted detention for assessment for a limited period justified in the interests of his own health, where such detention is lawful under Article 5."

Article 10 Freedom of expression

5-047   **1.**   Everyone has the right to freedom of expression. This right shall include freedom to hold opinions and to receive and impart information and ideas without interference by public authority and regardless of frontiers. This Article shall not prevent States from requiring the licensing of broadcasting, television or cinema enterprises.

2.   The exercise of these freedoms, since it carries with it duties and responsibilities, may be subject to such formalities, conditions, restrictions or penalties as are prescribed by law and are necessary in a democratic society, in the interests of national security, territorial integrity or public safety, for the prevention of disorder or crime, for the protection of health or morals, for the protection of the reputation or rights of others, for preventing the disclosure of information received in confidence, or for maintaining the authority and impartiality of the judiciary.

General Note

The courts "have frequently stated that in the field of freedom of speech there is no difference in principle between English law and [this Article]" (*Ashworth Security Hospital v MGN Ltd* [2001] 1 All E.R. 991 at para.71 CA, per Lord Phillips M.R.). Paragraph 1 of this article guarantees the right to freedom of expression. An interference with this right entails a violation of the article if it does not fall within one of the exceptions provided for in para.2.   **5-048**

This Article will often overlap with an art.8 claim, especially with regard to a claim concerning access to information.

Paragraph 2

In *Kelly v BBC* [2001] 1 All E.R. 323, Munby J. said at 335:   **5-049**

"Well-known jurisprudence of the European Court on Human Rights establishes: (i) that the exceptions in paragraph 2 must be narrowly interpreted; (ii) that if a restraint is to be justified under paragraph 2 it must be 'necessary in a democratic society'—that is to say, the necessity for any such restriction must be 'convincingly established' by reference to the existence of a 'pressing social need', and the restriction must be 'proportionate to the legitimate aim pursued'; and (iii) that the restriction must be 'prescribed by law'—that is, the law must be 'adequately accessible to the citizen' and must be 'formulated with sufficient precision to enable a citizen to regulate his conduct': see *Rantzen v Mirror Group Newspapers (1986) Ltd* [1993] 4 All E.R. 975 at 990, citing *Sunday Times v United Kingdom (No.1)* (1979) 2 E.H.R.R. 245 and *Sunday Times v United Kingdom (No.2)* (1992) 14 E.H.R.R. 229".

With regard to the question whether a detained patient should be allowed to have in his possession hardcore pornographic magazines, it is likely that the courts will adopt the reasoning of Scott Baker L.J. in *R. (on the application of Morton) v The Governor of Long Lartin Prison* [2003] EWCA Civ 644, in respect of hospitals that detain patients whose mental disorder might be adversely affected if they had access to such material. His Lordship said at para.22:

"Because the prisoner lives in a small and enclosed community, the interests of others are concerned as well as those of the prisoner himself. That is why Article 10(2) bites in this case. It seems to me obvious that once material of the kind prohibited in this case is allowed in the hands of a prisoner, there is an obvious risk that it will reach the eyes and hands of others, with the consequential risk of abuse, exploitation, assault and so forth".

The interviewing of detained patients by journalists can be monitored without contravening this article. Permission for the interview need not be forthcoming if it would place the patient's well-being at risk or would have an adverse effect on other patients or on good order or security in the hospital. Where national security is involved, the interview can take place within the earshot of an official and tape-recorded (*R. (on the application of A) v Home Secretary* [2003] EWHC 2846 (Admin)).

Article 11 Freedom of assembly and association   **5-050**

1. Everyone has the right to freedom of peaceful assembly and to freedom of association with others, including the right to form and to join trade unions for the protection of his interests.

2. No restrictions shall be placed on the exercise of these rights other than such as are prescribed by law and are necessary in a democratic society in the interests of national security or public safety, for the prevention of disorder or crime, for the protection of health or morals or for the protection of the rights and freedoms of others. This Article shall not prevent the imposition of lawful restrictions on the exercise of these rights by members of the armed forces, of the police or of the administration of the State.

Article 12 Right to marry   **5-051**

Men and women of marriageable age have the right to marry and to found a family, according to the national laws governing the exercise of this right.

General Note

This article "secures the fundamental right of a man and a woman to marry and to found a family. The second aspect is not however a condition of the first and the inability of any couple to conceive or   **5-052** parent a child cannot be regarded as per se removing their right to enjoy the first limb of this provision" (*Goodwin v United Kingdom* (2002) 35 E.H.R.R. 18 at para.98).

While this article is confined to legally formalised heterosexual relationships (as defined by gender, see *Goodwin*, above), art.8 is far broader in its scope. An interference with family life which is justified under art.8(2) cannot at the same time constitute a violation of this article (*X & Y v Switzerland* (1978) 13 D. & R. 105).

The Marriage Act 1983 places no restrictions on mentally disordered patients, whether detained or not, from marrying as long as they have sufficient mental capacity to contract a marriage (see the General Note to the Act under the heading "Marriage"). Any substantial interference with this right would violate this article. However, the Commission in *Hamer v United Kingdom* ((1982) 4 E.H.R.R. 139) left open whether it might, exceptionally, be possible to prohibit a patient's marriage on the grounds of special dangerousness, and the consequential risk posed to the partner: see O. Thorold, "The Implications of the European Convention on Human Rights for United Kingdom Mental Health Legislation" [1996] E.H.R.L.R. 619–636 at 634.

Although the Court has declined to require the provision of conjugal visits to prisoners by their partners, it has left open the possibility that the position might change. In *Aliev v Ukraine*, July 29, 2003 (App.No.41220/98), para.188, the Court said:

"Whilst noting with approval the reform movements in several European countries to improve prison conditions by facilitating conjugal visits, the Court considers that the refusal of such visits may for the present time be regarded as justified for the prevention of disorder and crime within the meaning of the second paragraph of Article 8 of the Convention ...."

Different considerations would apply to the position of mentally disordered detained patients because the justification of the "prevention of disorder and crime" will not be applicable in the majority of cases. Thorold argues that conjugal visits:

"can help to preserve a patient's marital relationship and thereby improve longer-term mental health prognosis. Any limitation on sexual relationships between patients, or a patient and a spouse, would have to be strictly justified. A prohibition which was expressed in general terms would be in grave danger of breaching Art.12. It may therefore be necessary for a policy to be formulated which permits sexual relations subject to well-defined exceptions, of which danger to another person would clearly be one" (op. cit., at 635).

In *Secretary of State for the Home Department Ex p. Mellor* [2001] EWCA Civ 472, the Court of Appeal concluded that the qualifications on the right to respect for family life that are recognised by art.8(2) apply equally to rights under this article (per Lord Phillips M.R. at para.39). This means that justification for the exceptions referred to by Thorold must be found in art.8(2).

Right to marry

Even if there is no prospect of cohabitation (*Hamer v United Kingdom*, above).

Article 14 Prohibition of discrimination
5-053 The enjoyment of the rights and freedoms set forth in this Convention shall be secured without discrimination on any ground such as sex, race, colour, language, religion, political or other opinion, national or social origin, association with a national minority, property, birth or other status.

General Note

5-054 In *Botta v Italy* (1998) 26 E.H.R.R. 241, the Court said at para.39:

"Article 14 complements the other substantive provisions of the Convention and its protocols. It has no independent existence, since it has effect solely in relation to 'the enjoyment of the rights and freedoms' safeguarded by those provisions. Although the application of Article 14 does not presuppose a breach of one or more of those provisions—and to this extent it is autonomous—there can be no room for its application unless the facts of the case fall within the ambit of one or more of the latter."

The general approach to issues which arise under this article was summarised by Lord Reed in *R. (on the application of SC, CB and 8 children) v Secretary of State for Work and Pensions* [2021] UKSC 26, at para.37, as follows:

"The general approach adopted to article 14 by the European court has been stated in similar terms on many occasions, and was summarised by the Grand Chamber in the case of *Carson v United Kingdom* (2010) 51 EHRR 13(2010) 51, para 61. For the sake of clarity, it is worth breaking down that paragraph into four propositions:

(1) 'The court has established in its case law that only differences in treatment based on an identifiable characteristic, or "status", are capable of amounting to discrimination within the meaning of article 14.'

(2) 'Moreover, in order for an issue to arise under article 14 there must be a difference in the treatment of persons in analogous, or relevantly similar, situations.'

(3) 'Such a difference of treatment is discriminatory if it has no objective and reasonable justification; in other words, if it does not pursue a legitimate aim or if there is not a reasonable relationship of proportionality between the means employed and the aim sought to be realised.'

(4) 'The contracting state enjoys a margin of appreciation in assessing whether and to what extent differences in otherwise similar situations justify a different treatment. The scope of this margin will vary according to the circumstances, the subject matter and the background.'"

Any ground such as

The list is illustrative, not exhaustive. In *R. (on the application of Pretty) v Director of Public Prosecutions* [2001] UKHL 61; [2002] 1 All E.R. 1 at para.105, Lord Hope held this article is capable of extending to discrimination in the enjoyment of Convention rights on the grounds of physical or mental capacity. Also note that in *B v Secretary of State for Work and Pensions* [2005] EWCA Civ 929 at para.25, Sedley L.J. said that mental capacity, "although not listed in [this article], is arguably at least as sensitive a personal characteristic, in relation to discrimination, as race or sex".

Sex

Very weighty reasons are generally required for differences of treatment based solely on gender (*Abdulaziz, Cabales and Balkandali v United Kingdom* (1985) 7 E.H.R.R. 471 at para.78).

Other status

Which could include the status of a patient detained under the 1983 Act and a prisoner (*R (on the application of N) v Secretary of State for Health* [2009] EWCA Civ 795). The scope of "other status" was examined by Leggatt L.J. in *JT v First-tier Tribunal* [2018] EWCA Civ 1735 at paras 71 to 75.

Article 16 Restrictions on political activity of aliens
Nothing in Article 10, 11 and 14 shall be regarded as preventing the High Contracting Parties from imposing restrictions on the political activity of aliens. **5-055**

Article 17 Prohibition of abuse of rights
Nothing in this Convention may be interpreted as implying for any State, group or person any right to engage in any activity or perform any act aimed at the destruction of any of the rights and freedoms set forth herein or at their limitation to a greater extent than is provided for in the Convention. **5-056**

Article 18 Limitation of use of restrictions on rights
The restrictions permitted under this Convention to the said rights and freedoms shall not be applied for any purpose other than those for which they have been prescribed. **5-057**

PART II

THE FIRST PROTOCOL

Article 1 Protection of property
Every natural or legal person is entitled to the peaceful enjoyment of his possessions. No one shall be deprived of his possessions except in the public interest and subject to the conditions provided for by law and by the general principles of international law. **5-058**

The preceding provisions shall not, however, in any way impair the right of a State to enforce such laws as it deems necessary to control the use of property in accordance with the general interest or to secure the payment of taxes or other contributions or penalties.

Article 2 Right to education

5-059 No person shall be denied the right to education. In the exercise of any functions which it assumes in relation to education and to teaching, the State shall respect the right of parents to ensure such education and teaching in conformity with their own religious and philosophical convictions.

Article 3 Right to free elections

5-060 The High Contracting Parties undertake to hold free elections at reasonable intervals by secret ballot, under conditions which will ensure the free expression of the opinion of the people in the choice of the legislature.

General Note

5-061 While this article is phrased in terms of the obligation to hold elections, the case law of the Court establishes that it guarantees individual rights, including the right to vote and to stand for election. In *Hirst v United Kingdom (No.2)* (2006) 42 E.H.R.R. 41, the Court held that although states enjoy a wide margin of appreciation in determining whether restrictions on prisoners' right to vote can be justified, it could not accept that s.3 of the Representation of the People Act 1983, which provides for absolute bar on voting by any serving prisoner in any circumstances, falls within an acceptable margin of appreciation. The Court said, at para.71, that there must be a discernable link "between the sanction and the conduct and circumstances of the individual concerned". This ruling required the Government to review the position of patients who are detained under the Mental Health Act and who are disenfranchised by virtue of the operation of s.3A of the 1983 Act: see the General Note to the Act under the heading *Voting*.

PART III

THE SIXTH PROTOCOL

Article 1 Abolition of the death penalty

5-062 The death penalty shall be abolished. No one shall be condemned to such penalty or executed.

Article 2 Death penalty in time of war

5-063 A state may make provision in its law for the death penalty in respect of acts committed in time of war or of imminent threat of war; such penalty shall be applied only in the instances laid down in the law and in accordance with its provisions. The State shall communicate to the Secretary General of the Council of Europe the relevant provisions of that law.

PART 6: DEPRIVATIONS OF LIBERTY

DEPRIVATIONS OF LIBERTY—MENTAL HEALTH ACT 1983 OR MENTAL CAPACITY ACT 2005?

This Part considers the following question: if action taken, or about to be taken, **6-001** with respect to a mentally incapacitated person constitutes a deprivation of that person's liberty which Act should be invoked, the Mental Health Act ("the 1983 Act") or the Mental Capacity Act ("the 2005 Act")? This choice exists as a result of the Government's response to the finding of the European Court of Human Rights ("the ECtHR") in *HL v United Kingdom* (2005) 40 E.H.R.R. 32.

HL v United Kingdom (the "Bournewood case")

In *HL*, Mr L alleged that he had been detained at the Bournewood Hospital as **6-002** an informal patient in violation of art.5(1) of the European Convention on Human Rights ("the Convention") which is designed to ensure that no one should be arbitrarily deprived of his liberty. He also claimed that the procedures available to him for a review of the legality of his detention did not satisfy the requirements of art.5(4), which provides a person who has been deprived of his liberty with a right to a speedy independent legal review of the detention.

The decision of the ECtHR focused on the finding of the House of Lords ([1998] 3 All E.R. 289) that the detention of a compliant mentally incapacitated patient could be justified under the common law doctrine of necessity. The ECtHR held that HL's detention contravened both arts 5(1) and 5(4) of the Convention. In particular, the Court found "striking the lack of any fixed procedural rules by which the admission and detention of compliant incapacitated patients is conducted" when contrasted with "the extensive network of safeguards applicable to psychiatric committals covered by the 1983 Act" (para.120).

In order to remedy the breaches of art.5 identified by the ECtHR, the Government undertook to provide additional procedural safeguards for incapacitated people who were not subject to the 1983 Act, but whose care and treatment involved a deprivation of liberty. Accordingly, a consultative document ("'Bournewood' Consultation: The approach to be taken in response to the judgment of the European Court of Human Rights in the 'Bournewood' case" (March 2005)) was issued by the Government. The following options were identified:

1. A new form of "protective care" which would consist of a new system to govern admission/detention procedures, reviews of detention and appeals.
2. Extending the use of detention under the 1983 Act to the *Bournewood* group of patients.
3. Using existing arrangements for guardianship under the 1983 Act (modified as necessary).

A report of the outcome of the consultation was published in June 2006. At the same time the Government announced its decision to proceed with the protective care option, which had been favoured by the majority of respondents to the consultation, with a view to new deprivation of liberty safeguards (DoLs) being introduced into the Mental Capacity Act 2005. The Mental Health Bill (now the Mental Health Act 2007) was identified as a suitable vehicle through which to amend the 2005 Act for this purpose.

What constitutes a "deprivation of liberty"?

6-003   The Supreme Court addressed this question in *P v Cheshire West and Chester Council; P and Q v Surrey County Council* [2014] UKSC 19; [2014] M.H.L.R. 394 ("Cheshire West") which are cases about the criteria for judging whether the living arrangements made for a mentally incapacitated person amount to a deprivation of liberty. If they do, then the deprivation has to be authorised, either by the Court of Protection or by the deprivation of liberty safeguards.

Lord Kerr defined liberty at para.76:

> "Liberty means the state or condition of being free from external constraint. It is predominantly an objective state. It does not depend on one's disposition to exploit one's freedom. Nor is it diminished by one's lack of capacity."

Lady Hale examined the relevant case law of the ECtHR to identify the essential character of a deprivation of liberty. Three components were identified:

(i)   the objective component of confinement in a particular restricted place for a not negligible length of time;

(ii)   the subjective component of lack of valid consent; and

(iii)   the attribution of responsibility to the state.

With regard to component (i), Lady Hale said at para.38:

> "Simply asking whether a person is 'confined' is not enough except in obvious cases. The 'starting point' is always upon the 'concrete situation' of the particular person concerned and 'account must be taken of a whole range of criteria such as the type, duration, effects and manner of implementation of the measures in question'. The presence or absence of coercion is also relevant. Thus there is no single 'touchstone' of what constitutes a deprivation of liberty in this or any other context."

With regard to component (ii), it should be noted that consent to what would otherwise be a deprivation of liberty can be given in advance in cases where valid consent has been given when the person had the relevant capacity.

Rather than attempt to lay down a prescriptive list of criteria for a deprivation of liberty, Lady Hale identified, at para.50, the factors that are *not* relevant to the determination. They are:

(i)   the person's compliance or lack of objection;

(ii)   the relative normality of the placement (whatever the comparison made); and

(iii)   the reason or purpose behind a particular placement.

The "acid test"

6-004   Lady Hale identified the "acid test" for a deprivation of liberty as being the fact that the person concerned "was under continuous supervision and control and was not free to leave" (para.49). This formula can be found in the decision of the ECtHR in *HL v United Kingdom*, above, at para.91. It is important to appreciate that to be deprived of his liberty the person must be under continuous supervision and control and must not be free to leave. With regard to the period of confinement, in *Storck v Germany* (2006) 43 E.H.R.R. 6 at para.74, the ECtHR held that will be no deprivation of liberty if the confinement in question is for a negligible length of time. Neither is there a deprivation of liberty if the deprivation is required for a short period in order to respond to an emergency (*X v United Kingdom* (1982) 4 E.H.R.R. 188, para.41). However, cases are very fact sensitive and in *ZH v Commissioner of the Police for the Metropolis* [2013] EWCA Civ 69 a deprivation of liberty was found to have occurred in a situation where P had been subjected to intense restraint for approximately 40 minutes.

Lady Hale said the supervision and control is not relevant only insofar as it demonstrates that the person is not free to leave as a "person might be under constant supervision and control but still be free to leave should he express the desire so to do. Conversely, it is possible to imagine situations in which a person is not free to leave but is not under such continuous supervision and control as to lead to the conclusion that he was deprived of his liberty". For an example of the latter situation, see *W City Council v Mrs L* [2015] EWCOP 20 where, although Mrs L was prevented from leaving her home, the restrictions placed on her were not "continuous or complete" (para.26).

In a perceptive article, Anselm Eldergill states that it is "problematic" that the "acid test" has been interpreted "without reference to whether there is or has been any actual coercion or interference with the individual's freedom to do what they are able to do and choose to do": see Eldergill, A. ERA Forum (2019) 19: 511. *https ://doi.org/10.1007/s12027-018-0541-4* at p.526.

Continuous supervision and control

What constitutes continuous supervision and control? Although it is clearly **6-005** something more substantial that occasional supervision and control, no guidance was provided by the court on the nature or extent of the supervision and control that must be present. In *Guzzardi v Italy* (1981) 3 E.H.R.R. 333 at para.95, the ECtHR said that the supervision was carried out "strictly and on an almost constant basis". Lady Hale used the phrase "constant monitoring and control" at para.46 of her judgment. In *Northumberland County Council v MD* [2018] EWFC 47, Cobb J. took the view "that 'complete' or 'constant' defines 'supervision' and 'control' as indicating something like 'total', 'unremitting', 'thorough', and/or 'unqualified'" (para.31). The case law of the ECtHR has confirmed that "a person may be considered to have been 'detained' for the purposes of art.5(1) of the ECHR even during a period when he or she was allowed to make certain journeys or was in an open ward with regular unescorted access to unsecured hospital grounds and the possibility of unescorted leave outside the hospital": see *Atudorei v Romania* [2018] M.H.L.R. 1, para.129.

It is important to recognise that control, which involves the exercise of power to ensure that something happens to a person even if he does not want it to happen, is not the same as support, which is to help and/or encourage a person to do something for himself.

It is not entirely clear what "supervision" means in this context. It probably involves both the monitoring and observation of individuals. It is submitted that all mentally incapacitated patients should be subject to continuous supervision, but that not all such patients would be the subject of continuous control. The point at which "supervision" becomes "control" was not addressed by the court.

It is important for those who are assessing whether a deprivation of liberty exists to take account of the cumulative effect of the restrictions imposed on a person (*Guzzardi v Italy*, above, para.95), bearing in mind that the exercise of restraint which does not constitute a deprivation of liberty is authorised under s.6 of the 2005 Act.

Not free to leave

6-006   No analysis of this component of the "acid test" was provided, although in the cases before the court not free to leave meant "not free to go anywhere without permission and close supervision" (per Lady Hale at para.48). It is not a precondition of the test that the person must have expressed a desire to leave; it is sufficient for those in control to have formed the opinion that the person would be prevented from leaving if he made an attempt to leave. The vast majority of people who have a significant degree of mental incapacity are likely to come into this category. The Department of Health's Guidance on the *Cheshire West* judgment dated October 22, 2015, states at para.32:

> "[I]t may be useful to bear in mind that, just because an individual is physically unable to leave their place of care/ treatment, this does not necessarily mean the individual is 'not free to leave' under the acid test. Rather, the question is, would they be allowed to leave if they were assisted to do so e.g. by family/ friends? If the provider would facilitate the person leaving, then the individual is not deprived of their liberty."

In *Northumberland County Council v MD*, above, Cobb J. said:

> "'Free to leave' does not mean leaving for the purpose of some trip or outing approved by those managing the institution; it means leaving in the sense of removing herself permanently in order to live where and with whom she chooses. It is accepted wisdom that a typical fourteen or fifteen-year old is not free to leave her home" (para.29).

It seems that the absence of an alternative place of residence for P is not a relevant factor.

Deprivation of liberty of patients receiving treatment for physical disorders in hospital settings

6-007   In *R. (on the application of Ferreira) v HM Senior Coroner for Inner South London* [2017] EWCA Civ 31; [2017] M.H.L.R 258, the Court of Appeal distinguished *Cheshire West* by holding that the administration of life-saving treatment to a patient of either sound or unsound mind in an intensive care unit did not come within the scope of art.5 of the ECHR (para.88). The only judgment of substance was given by Arden L.J. who accepted "the submission that Cheshire West is distinguishable since it is directed to a different situation, namely that of living arrangements for persons of unsound mind" (para.91). Her Ladyship said that there is in general no need in the case of physical illness for a person of unsound mind to have the benefit of safeguards against the deprivation of liberty where the treatment is given in good faith and is materially the same treatment as would be given to a person of sound mind with the same physical illness. The treatment is neither arbitrary nor the consequence of her impairment" (para.93). In addition, her Ladyship said that in her judgment "Article 5(1)(e) is directed to the treatment of persons of unsound mind because of their mental impairment. The purpose of Article 5(1)(e) is to protect persons of unsound mind. This does not apply where a person of unsound mind is receiving materially the same medical treatment as a person of sound mind. Article 5(1)(e) is thus not concerned with the treatment of the physical illness of a person of unsound mind. That is a matter for Article 8" (para.95).

Her Ladyship summarised her conclusions by stating that the patient "was not deprived of her liberty at the date of her death because she was being treated for a physical illness and her treatment was that which it appeared to all intents would have been administered to a person who did not have her mental impairment. She was physically restricted in her movements by her physical infirmities and by the treatment she received (which for example included sedation) but the root cause of any loss of liberty was her physical condition, not any restrictions imposed by the hospital" (para.10).

The effect of the decision in *Ferreira* is that a deprivation of liberty will not occur in cases where medical treatment for a physical disorder is being provided to a mentally incapacitated person in any setting which is materially the same as that provided to a person without a mental disorder.

Deprivations of Liberty under the Mental Capacity Act 2005

Section 4A of the 2005 Act prohibits the deprivation of the liberty of a person **6-008** under that Act other than in the following situations:

(i)   where, in an order made under s.16(2)(a), the Court of Protection has authorised the deprivation;

(ii)   where the deprivation is authorised for life-sustaining or other emergency treatment while a decision is awaited from the Court (s.4B); or

(iii)   where the deprivation is authorised by Sch.A1.

As an authorisation under Sch.A1 can only apply to the deprivation of a person's liberty in a hospital or a care home, an application must be made to the Court of Protection if the deprivation takes place elsewhere. A deprivation of liberty authorised under the 2005 Act does not entitle the institution to do anything other than detain the patient or resident for the purposes of the order or authorisation.

The authorisation procedures, which are set out in Sch.A1 (and the associated Sch.1A), are considered in Pt 2 of the author's *Mental Capacity Act Manual* (2018). There are two types of authorisation: standard and urgent. A "managing authority" must request a standard authorisation when it appears likely that at some time during the next 28 days someone will be accommodated in its hospital or care home in circumstances that amount to a deprivation of liberty within the meaning of art.5. The request must be made to the "supervisory body". Whenever possible, authorisation should be obtained in advance of the deprivation occurring. Where this is not possible, and the managing authority believes it is necessary to deprive someone of their liberty in their best interests before the standard authorisation process can be completed, the managing authority must itself give an urgent authorisation and then apply for a standard authorisation.

Schedule 1A—persons ineligible to be deprived of liberty by the Mental Capacity Act

In the following notes, "P" is used to denote a person who would otherwise **6-009** satisfy the authorisation eligibility criteria set out in Sch.A1, and references to paragraph numbers are references to the paragraphs in Sch.1A.

The 2005 Act cannot be used to deprive P of his liberty if P is "ineligible": see s.16A of the 2005 Act for the Court of Protection and Sch.A1 paras 12(e) and 17 for the authorisation procedure. P is ineligible if he falls within Cases A to E of Sch.1A.

Case A (Patients detained under the Mental Health Act 1983)

6-010   P is ineligible if he is subject to the "hospital treatment regime" and is detained under that regime in either an independent or NHS hospital by virtue of being subject to a "hospital treatment obligation", i.e. he is detained under ss.2, 4, 3, 35, 36, 37, 38, 44, 45A, 47, 48 or 51 of the 1983 Act or under "another England and Wales enactment which has the same effect as a hospital treatment obligation", such as the Criminal Procedure (Insanity) Act 1964 (paras 2, 8). The consequence of this is that if P is detained in hospital under the 1983 Act he is ineligible for detention under the 2005 Act for any purpose (*A NHS Trust v Dr A* [2013] EWHC 2442 (COP)).

Case B (Patients on Leave of Absence or Conditional Discharge)

6-011   This Case applies if P is subject to the "hospital treatment regime" (i.e. he is subject to a "hospital treatment obligation": see above) but is not detained in hospital under that regime. This covers patients who have been granted leave of absence under s.17 of the 1983 Act or who have been granted a conditional discharge under either s.42 or s.73 of that Act. P will be ineligible if:

(i)   the proposed course of action under the 2005 Act is "not in accordance with a requirement" which the 1983 Act imposes, such as a requirement as to where P is, or is not, to reside (para.3). This means that P would be ineligible if, for example, there is a conflict between where P is required to reside under the conditions of a conditional discharge and where he would be required to reside under a standard authorisation; or

(ii)   the proposed care and treatment to be administered under the 2005 Act "consists in whole or in part of medical treatment for mental disorder in a hospital" (para.4). In *A Hospital Trust v CD* [2015] EWCOP 74, Mostyn J. held that if P is detained under the 1983 Act and is granted leave of absence to be treated in another hospital for a physical disorder, then P will be eligible.

Case C (Patients on a Community Treatment Order)

6-012   P is ineligible if:

(i)   he is subject to a "community treatment regime", i.e. a community treatment order under s.17A of the 1983 Act, or "an obligation under another England and Wales enactment which has the same effect as a community treatment order" (para.9); and

(ii)   either of the situations set out in paras (i) or (ii) of Case B, above, apply.

Case D (Patients subject to Guardianship)

6-013   If P is subject to a guardianship application under s.7 of the 1983 Act, a guardianship order under s.37 of that Act, or an obligation under another England and Wales enactment which has similar effect (para.10), he will be ineligible if:

(i)   the proposed course of action under the 2005 Act is not in accordance with a requirement imposed by the guardian, including any requirement where P is to reside (para.3). This means that P would be ineligible if, for example, there is a conflict between where P is required to reside by the guardian and where he would be required to reside under a standard authorisation; or

(ii) the standard authorisation would authorise P to be a mental health patient (i.e. a person accommodated in a hospital for the purpose of being given medical treatment for mental disorder (para.16)), P objects (or would be likely to object if he was in a position to do so) to being a mental patient or to being given some or all of the mental health treatment, and no valid consent has been given by a donee of a lasting power of attorney or a court deputy to each matter to which P objects: see the notes on Case E. If such consent is forthcoming, P becomes eligible. The donee and the deputy will be required to act in P's best interests when making their decision (s.4 of the 2005 Act). In determining whether P would be likely to object, regard must be had to all the circumstances, including P's behaviour, his wishes and feelings and his views values and beliefs, although circumstances from the past only need to be considered insofar as it is appropriate to consider them (para.5).

Case E (Patients who are "within the scope" of the 1983 Act but are not subject to it)

This Case does not refer to a person who is accommodated in a care home (*W* **6-014** *Primary Care Trust v TB* [2009] EWHC 1737 (Fam)).

Having considered the case law and the statutory provision, Hayden J. said that "it is clear that the magnetic north when contemplating the deprivation of liberty of those who fall within Case E is and is likely to remain the Mental Health Act" (*Northampton Healthcare NHS Foundation Trust v ML* [2014] EWCOP 2, para.76).

P is "within the scope" of the 1983 Act if an application under s.2 or s.3 of that Act "could be made in respect of him" and P could be detained in a hospital in pursuance of such an application, were one made (para.12(1)). This is an objective test; whether the assessor would have made an application in the circumstances of the case is not relevant. Note that the reference is to "a hospital"; the assessor cannot restrict his or her consideration to the hospital where the patient might be receiving treatment for a physical condition.

When assessing whether P comes within the scope of the 1983 Act, it is to be assumed that the necessary medical recommendations are in place (para.12(3),(4)) and that the treatment referred to in s.3(2)(c) of that Act cannot be provided under the 2005 Act (para.12(5)). In *GJ v Foundation Trust* [2009] EWHC 2972 (Fam); [2010] M.H.L.R. 13, Charles J. said that "the assessor under the MCA should also proceed on the assumption that assessment and treatment under s.2 MHA 1983 cannot be provided under the MCA" (para.44).

Manchester University Hospitals NHS Foundation Trust v JS and Manchester City Council [2023] EWCOP 12, is a case about "a young person [JS] with complex mental health needs that leave her in danger by her own hand as well as at the hands of others. Her presentation can be dramatic and disturbing. The various organs of the state whose duty it is to provide care and safety to JS are seemingly unable to do so. This is due to a combination of the challenges presented by her condition and behaviour, a lack of readily available resources and ... a fundamental difficulty in understanding and applying the law" (para.3). No Tier 4 provision was available to JS and the hospital where she was being treated was ill equipped environmentally and in terms of its lack of specialist CAMHS psychiatric expertise to care for her (para.28). JS, who was objecting to her treatment, was assessed as "not being detainable under s.3 MHA. The reason for this is because a Tier 4 admission would (they say) further increase Jane's 'risk level' in the context of neurodevelopmental disorder rather than a treatable mental illness because of the increasing incidents of self-harm and verbal aggression" (para.33). There was no immediately effective plan for JS to be cared for in the community. The issue before HHJ Burrows (sitting as a nominated Judge of the Court of Protection and as a Judge of the High Court) was whether JS came within the scope of Case E. His Honour held that she was and that an application could and should have been made under the 1983 Act in respect of her. JS was receiving treatment for "the manifestations of her mental disorder" even though "the treatment was not optimal and was not aimed at the 'core disorder' from which she suffers which is likely to be addressed only by psychological and other therapies over a long period of time" (paras 70, 71, 102).

His Honour rejected the following submissions that were made in support of the contention that JS was not within the scope of the MHA:

"90. Firstly, that she was accommodated at the Hospital as a place of safety because there was nowhere else for her to go and, once the physical damage caused by her overdose was successfully treated, she needed no inpatient medical treatment. The answer to that is: of course, she did. She was a danger to herself. She needed to be nursed safely and medicated to address the effects of her mental disorder (viz. to injure herself and abscond away for safety).

91. It was submitted that although Jane suffers from a mental disorder it was not of a nature or degree to make it appropriate for her to receive medical treatment for that disorder in a hospital. This is clearly wrong. The medical treatment she did receive as a detained patient in hospital was necessary to keep her safe and to prevent her from absconding or harming herself. There was no readily available alternative when she was receiving it.

92. It is submitted that the outcome of the MHA Assessments was that inpatient care for Jane's condition was neither available nor desirable because she could be treated in the community under the MCA. This too is plainly wrong. She could only be treated in the community once a suitable package of care was available for her. Until then she could not safely leave hospital. That was the situation with which I was confronted at the first hearing. At that point hospital was the only option."

Speaking more generally, His Honour said:

"96. There seems to be a belief, not just in this case but in others which I have heard recently, that the decision to use the MHA should be viewed in isolation from what is available elsewhere at the time the decision to detain or not detain is taken. Ideally, a 17-year-old vulnerable young person would not be detained in a psychiatric facility, let alone a mixed adult general ward. However, where there is literally no option in which that young person will be safe, or as safe as possible in the circumstances, I cannot see how the MHA decision maker can avoid the decision I have had to make in this judgment. If the patient has to be detained for treatment for their mental disorder, and there is no alternative outside the hospital setting, and no other treatment plan available, then it seems clear to me the patient should not be detained under the MCA but rather under the MHA."

An appeal against the decision of HHJ Burrows was dismissed by Theis J. at [2023] EWCOP 33. Her Ladyship agreed, at paras 48 and 49, that the following questions provide a useful structure to aid practitioners and judges who must navigate Case E:

(1)   Is P a 'mental health patient'?
(2)   Is P an 'objecting' mental health patient?
(3)   Could P be detained under s.3 of the 1983 Act?

With regard to point 3 (which, it is submitted, should also encompass s.2 of the Act) her Ladyship agreed with Charles J.'s construction of the meaning of "could" in *GJ*, above, at para.80, namely that the decision maker should "ask himself whether in his view the criteria set by, or the grounds in, s.2 or s.3 MHA 1983 are met (and if an application was made under them a hospital would detain P)".

Where there is a dispute between the decision maker under the Mental Health Act and Mental Capacity Act, Theis J. endorsed, at para.118, the following "practical suggestions" put forward by the Secretary of State for Health and Social Care:

"(1)   The MHA and MCA decision-makers should arrange for discussions between the relevant professionals. They should be undertaken in what Ms Kelly describes as 'the spirit of cooperation and appropriate urgency'. This will ensure the relevant professionals have reviewed and considered relevant evidence and if required further inquiries can be made.

(2)   If these discussions do not result in a detention being authorised under the MCA the hospital has a number of choices:

(i)   It can seek the person's admission under the MHA 1983 to authorise the deprivation of liberty, including on a short-term basis while it seeks to advance the person's discharge.

(ii)   It can seek for the person to be detained in an alternative setting, such as a care home, in which Case E has no application, with consideration being given to what can be put in place to support the person in the community under s 117 MHA 1983 and/or Care Act 2014 duties.

(iii) It can stop depriving the person of their liberty if it considers the person should not be detained under MHA 1983, even with the knowledge that the person will not be detained under the MCA 2005.

(iv)   If the hospital does not consider that an application for assessment or treatment under MHA 1983 is warranted but does consider it is in the person's best interests to be detained in hospital for treatment of a mental disorder, it should consider carefully its reasons for drawing this distinction. The hospital could apply to the Court of Protection for a determination of whether the person is eligible for detention under the MCA 2005."

A patient will not come within the scope of the 1983 Act if it is not possible to make an application under either s.2 or 3 in respect of him by virtue of the ruling in *R. v East London and The City Mental Health Trust Ex p. Brandenburg* [2003] UKHL 58 where it was held that a patient who had been discharged from the 1983 Act by a Mental Health Review Tribunal could not be re-detained under that Act in the absence of a "new information" test being satisfied. In *South Staffordshire and Shropshire Healthcare NHS Foundation Trust v The Hospital Managers of St George's Hospital* [2016] EWHC 1196 (Admin), Cranston J. held that the principle established in *Brandenburg* also applies to a decision of a panel of the hospital managers exercising their power to discharge a patient under s.23 of the 1983 Act. In *R. (on the application of Worcestershire C.C.) v Secretary of State for Health and Social Care* [2021] EWHC 682 (Admin), para.14, a patient who had been discharged from detention under s.3 by a tribunal remained in the hospital as a detained patient by virtue of her being made subject to a deprivation of liberty authorisation.

If P comes within the scope of the 1983 Act, he would be ineligible for a deprivation of liberty authorisation if the situation set out in para.(ii) of Case D, above, applies, i.e. he objects (or would be likely to object if he was in a position to do so) to being admitted to hospital or to being treated for his mental disorder there and no valid consent has been given by a donee or a deputy. If a donee or deputy consents, P will be eligible. In determining whether P would be likely to object, regard must be had to all the circumstances, including P's behaviour, his wishes and feelings and his views, values and beliefs, although circumstances from the past only need to be considered insofar as it is appropriate to consider them (para.5, and see below).

The overall effect of Case E is that:

1. If P is within the scope of the 1983 Act and is objecting to being in hospital or to being treated there, he cannot be made subject to a deprivation of liberty authorisation.
2. If P is within the scope of the 1983 Act and is not objecting to being in hospital or to being treated there, he can be made subject to a deprivation of liberty authorisation.
3. If P is not within the scope of the 1983 Act and is objecting to being in hospital or to being treated there, he can be made subject to a deprivation of liberty authorisation.

This confusing situation is the consequence of Parliament's decision to legislate for two parallel routes to authorise the civil detention of mentally disordered patients in hospital.

In determining whether the first condition of the objection test (see below) is satisfied i.e. the relevant instrument "authorises P to be a mental health patient", Charles J. held in *GJ*, above, that the decision maker should adopt a "but for" test if P suffers from both a mental and a physical disorder (para.87). This means that the decision maker should ask (i) what treatment would P receive for his physical disorder which is unconnected to his mental disorder, and (ii) what treatment would P receive for his mental disorder (including treatment for a physical disorder or illness that is connected to his mental disorder and/or which is likely to directly affect his mental disorder). The decision maker should then ask whether, "but for" the need for P to have treatment for his physical disorder, should P be detained in hospital. If the answer is in the negative, P does not satisfy the test. Put another way, the test is not satisfied if the need for treatment for his physical disorder is "the only effective reason" for P's detention (para.89).

His Lordship said that the "objection" condition has to be looked at "without taking any fine distinctions between the potential reasons for the objection to treatment of different types, or to simply being in a hospital. As is recognised and provided for by para.5(6), this is because it is often going to be the case that the relevant person (P) does not have the capacity to make a properly informed and balanced decision. So what matters, applying the approach set out in paragraph 5(6), is whether P will or does object to what is proposed" (para.83). This statement establishes a low threshold for establishing whether P objects in that any non compliant behaviour by P is likely to constitute evidence of an objection.

The Code of Practice on the Deprivation of Liberty Safeguards, para.4.46, states that if there is reason to think that P would object if able to do so, then P "should be assumed to be objecting". It is not the role of the assessor to consider whether an objection is reasonable.

Paragraph 5 of Sch.1A reads:

"P objects to being a mental health patient etc

5.—(1)   This paragraph applies in cases D and E in the table in paragraph 2.

(2)   P is ineligible if the following conditions are met.

(3)   The first condition is that the relevant instrument authorises P to be a mental health patient.

(4)   The second condition is that P objects—

    (a)   to being a mental health patient, or

    (b)   to being given some or all of the mental health treatment.

(5)   The third condition is that a donee or deputy has not made a valid decision to consent to each matter to which P objects.

(6)   In determining whether or not P objects to something, regard must be had to all the circumstances (so far as they are reasonably ascertainable), including the following—

    (a)   P's behaviour;

    (b)   P's wishes and feelings;

    (c)   P's views, beliefs and values.

(7)   But regard is to be had to circumstances from the past only so far as it is still appropriate to have regard to them."

In order for P to be ineligible, all conditions in this paragraph must be met (*BHCC v KD* [2016] EWCOP B2, HHJ Farquar). This conclusion was followed by HHJ Burrows in *Manchester University Hospitals NHS Foundation Trust v Manchester City Council* [2023] EWCOP 12.

The 1983 Act or the 2005 Act?

Deprivations of liberty in hospitals

Paragraph 13.69 of the *Code of Practice* on the Mental Health Act states: **6-015**

"In the rare cases where neither the Act nor a DoLS authorisation nor a Court of Protection order is appropriate, then to avoid an unlawful deprivation of liberty it may be necessary to make an application to the High Court to use its inherent jurisdiction to authorise the deprivation of liberty."

Schedule 1A sets out the circumstances that prevent a person who is being deprived of his liberty from being the subject of a standard authorisation under the 2005 Act. If Sch.1A applies, the 1983 Act must be used. In circumstances where a choice has to be made between the two regimes, Charles J. said in *AM v South London & Maudsley NHS Foundation Trust* [2013] UKUT 365 (AAC); [2014] M.H.L.R. 181 at para.75 that the following approach should be adopted:

    "(i)   the First-tier Tribunal (and earlier decision makers under the MHA) have to apply the statutory tests imposed by the MHA and the possible application of the MCA and its DOLS are relevant to that exercise,

    (ii)   the First-tier Tribunal (and the earlier decision makers under the MHA) have to assess whether as a result of the identified risks the relevant person ought to be detained, or kept in hospital in circumstances which on a objective assessment give rise to a risk that cannot be ignored that they amount to a deprivation of liberty (see for example paragraph 22 of Upper Tribunal Judge Jacobs decision in *DN v Northumberland & Wear NHS Foundation Trust* [see below]),

    (iii)   if the answer is 'yes', this triggers a value judgment applying the 'necessity test' as between the choices that are or will or may become available,

    (iv)   the search applying the MHA 'necessity test' is for the alternative that best achieves the objective of assessment or treatment of the type described in ss. 2 and 3 MHA in the least restrictive way. This potentially introduces tensions and so a need to balance the impact of detention under the MCA and an authorisa-

(v)   tion under the DOLS as the means of ensuring that a deprivation of liberty to best achieve the desired objective is lawful and governed by a statutory regime, and the theoretical and practical availability of the MCA regime and its DOLS is one of the factors that needs to be considered by the MHA decision maker in carrying out that search, as are their overall impact in best achieving the desired objective when compared with other available choices and so detention under ss. 2 or 3 MHA".

Among the factors that must be considered when applying the "necessity test" are: "consideration of what is in the best interests of the incapacitated person in line with the best interests assessment in the DOLS process, and so for example conditions that can be imposed under the DOLS, fluctuating capacity and the comparative impact of both the independent scrutiny and review and the enforcement provisions relating to the MHA scheme on the one hand and the MCA scheme and its DOLS on the other, and possibly ... a consideration of the likelihood of continued compliance and triggers to possible non-compliance and their effect on the suitability of the regimes ..." (para.73).

It is likely that the practical effect of Charles J.'s analysis will be largely confined to the situation of an incapacitated patient who, subsequent to being detained under the 1983 Act becomes compliant to both detention and treatment but who continues to be detained because he satisfies the "acid test" established by the Supreme Court in *Cheshire West*. The question of whether compliant mentally incapable patients should be detained under the 1983 Act or be made the subject of a DOL authorisation is considered in the General Note to Part 2 of the 1983 Act under the heading *The detention of compliant mentally incapable patients*.

If the patient has been discharged from detention under the 1983 Act by the tribunal in anticipation of an authorisation being granted under the 2005 Act but the DOL assessor concludes that the patient is ineligible for an authorisation, a fresh application for the detention of the patient under the 1983 Act might have to be made. The justification for making such an application would be that the decision of the assessor satisfies the new information test established by the House of Lords in *R. v East London and The City Mental Health Trust Ex p. Brandenburg* [2003] UKHL 58. The *Brandenburg* case is discussed in the General note to s.3 of the Act under the heading *The re-sectioning of a patient subsequent to a discharge by the First-tier Tribunal (Mental Health), the Mental Health Review Tribunal for Wales or a Hospital Managers' Panel*.

A request for a standard authorisation under Sch.A1 of the 2005 Act can be made in respect of a patient who is detained under the 1983 Act in anticipation of the patient being discharged from detention and being placed in a care home if (i) he would be subject to a deprivation of liberty in the care home and (ii) the provisions of para.12 of Sch.A1 would be satisfied: see *DN v Northumberland Tyne and Wear NHS Foundation Trust* [2011] UKHT 327 (AAC); [2011] M.H.L.R. 249, para.22. Note that in *Hertfordshire CC v NK* [2020] EWHC 139 (Fam), MacDonald J. said that before making an anticipatory order "the court will need cogent evidence that the regime proposed will be the regime that will be applied to the child if the DOL order is granted, rather than the far more speculative situation that pertains in this case" (para.42). The decision in the *DN* case follows the approach set out by the Department of Health in a letter to the tribunal about the relationship between the two Acts. The letter is reproduced in Pt 2 of the author's *Mental Capacity Act Manual* (2018) at para.2–058.

Deprivations of liberty in care homes

In the *Cheshire West* case, the Supreme Court held that in order to be deprived   **6-016**
of his liberty for the purposes of the 2005 Act a mentally incapacitated person must
be under "continuous supervision and control and ... not free to leave". It follows
that although the guardianship provisions of the 1983 Act provide authority to
convey P to a care home, to require him to remain there, and to return him if he
absconds, an authorisation under Sch.A1 will be required if P is subject to a continuous supervision and control within the care home and is assessed as meeting the
qualifying requirements (*C v Blackburn and Darwen Borough Council* [2011]
EWHC 3321; [2012] M.H.L.R. 202, para.30, where Peter Jackson J. incorrectly
stated that guardianship does not provide a power to prevent the person from
leaving: see *KD v A Borough Council*, noted under s.8(1)(a)).

APPENDICES

FURTHER POWERS TO RESTRAIN AND/OR DETAIN MENTALLY DISORDERED PATIENTS

A-001   Where a patient has been detained under the Mental Health Act (the Act), there is an implied power for staff to exercise a degree of control over the activities of the patient: see the note on "the power to control the activities of detained patients" in s.139. Both statute and the common law provide further powers that can be used to restrain and/or detain patients. They are:

1.   In *R. (on the application of Munjaz) v Mersey Care NHS Trust* [2003] EWCA Civ 1036; [2003] M.H.L.R. 362 at para.46 Hale L.J. said:

> "There is a general [common law] power to take such steps as are reasonably necessary and proportionate to protect others from the immediate risk of significant harm. This applies whether or not the patient lacks the capacity to make decisions for himself".

It is submitted that this power extends to the use of sedation on a person in an emergency if the sedation is used to restrain that person from causing harm to others.

2.   If the patient is mentally incapacitated, s.6 of the Mental Capacity Act 2005 enables the patient to be restrained when: (1) the person using the restraint reasonably believes that its use is necessary to prevent harm to the patient; and (2) its use is proportionate both to the likelihood and seriousness of the harm and is in the patient's best interests; see further, the author's *Mental Capacity Act Manual* (2018), pp.80–83.

3.   Under s.3(1) of the Criminal Law Act 1967 "a person may use such force as is reasonable in the circumstances in the prevention of crime, or in effecting or assisting the lawful arrest of offenders or suspected offenders or persons unlawfully at large". This provision, which could apply to any patient, enables a member of staff to use reasonable force to either restrain the patient or to place him in seclusion in self-defence or in the defence of others or to protect property. It does not apply where the patient is insane because such a person is deemed not capable of committing a crime. The test of insanity established by the House of Lords in the *M'Naghten case [1843–60] All E.R. 229*, is that:

> "it must be clearly proved that, at the time of the committing of the act, the party accused was labouring under such a defect of reason, from disease of the mind, as not to know the nature and quality of the act he was doing was wrong, or, if he did know it, that he did not know he was doing what was wrong".

The components of the test of insanity were analysed by the Court of Appeal in *R. v Keal* [2022] EWCA Crim 341 where it was held that:

(i)   in order to establish the defence of insanity within the *M'Naghten* Rules on the ground of not knowing the act was "wrong", the defendant must establish both that (a) he did not know that his act was unlawful and (b) he did not know that his act was "morally" wrong by the standards of ordinary reasonable people (para.41); and

(ii)   the defence of insanity is not available to a defendant who, although he knew what he was doing was wrong, he believed that he had no choice but to commit the act in question (para.48).

4. The common law power to prevent a breach of the peace was summarised by Lord Bingham in *R. (on the application of the Laporte) v Chief Constable of Gloucestershire Constabulary* [2006] UKHL 55; [2007] 2 All E.R. 529 at para.29:

> "Every constable, and also every citizen, enjoys the power and is subject to the duty to seek to prevent, by arrest or other action short of arrest, any breach of the peace occuring in his presence, or any breach of the peace which (having oc- curred) is likely to be renewed, or any breach of the peace which is about to occur."

A breach, which can take place in public or on private property, involves "actual harm done either to a person or to a person's property in his pres- ence or some other form of violent disorder or disturbance and itself neces- sarily involves a criminal offence" (ibid., per Lord Brown at para.111). Harm to property will constitute a breach only if done or threatened in the owner's presence because the natural consequence of such harm is likely to be a violent retaliation (*Percy v Director of Public Prosecutions* [1995] 3 All E.R. 124 DC). The power to prevent a breach of the peace would en- able a nurse physically to restrain a patient whose words or behaviour are such that imminent violence is expected on a hospital ward. Detention under this power can only be justified for a short period. Prolonged detention must be authorised either by the Act or by arresting the person concerned and bringing him or her before a magistrate. With regard to the use of this power, the Court of Appeal has held that: (i) there has to be a sufficiently real and present threat to the peace to justify the extreme step of depriving a citizen of his liberty when that citizen is not at that time acting unlawfully (*Foulkes v Chief Constable of Merseyside Police* [1998] 3 All E.R. 705); and (ii) a breach can occur on private premises even if the only persons likely to be affected by the breach are inside the premises and no member of the public outside the premises is involved (*McConnell v Chief Constable of the Greater Manchester Police* [1990] 1 All E.R. 423).

5. In *Black v Forsey*, 1988 S.L.T. 57, a case under the Mental Health (Scotland) Act 1984, the House of Lords held that although the powers of detention conferred on hospital authorities by the 1984 Act were exhaus- tive and that any common law power of detention which a hospital author- ity might otherwise have possessed had been impliedly removed, the com- mon law continues to confer upon a private individual power to detain, in a situation of necessity, a person of unsound mind who is a danger to him or herself or others. A person exercising the power must be able to justify his or her action, if challenged, by proving the mental disorder of the detainee and the necessity of detention. In the opinion of Lord Griffiths, the power is:

> "confined to imposing temporary restraint on a lunatic who has run amok and is a manifest danger either to himself or to others—a state of affairs as obvious to a layman as to a doctor. Such a common law power is confined to the short period of confinement necessary before the lunatic can be handed over to a proper authority".

The existence of this power was confirmed by Lord Goff in *R. v Bournewood NHS Trust, Ex p. L* [1998] 3 All E.R. 289, at 302:

> "[T]he common law permit[s] the detention of those who were a danger, or potential danger, to themselves or others, in so far as this was shown to be necessary."

A-002   The combination of powers set out above provide sufficient authority for a mental health professional or member of the public to act swiftly to prevent a mentally disordered person from causing harm to himself, to another person or to property as long as the force used is both necessary and proportionate to the harm threatened. They cannot be used as an alternative to the powers of detention contained in the Act: if the Act provides for the detention of a person in a particular situation, neither the common law nor the Mental Capacity Act 2005 apply (*R. (on the application of Sessay) v South London and Maudsley NHS Foundation Trust* [2011] EWHC 2617 (QB); [2012] M.H.L.R. 94). However, the powers can be invoked for a short period in emergency situations where the persons who have the authority to invoke the appropriate Mental Health Act power are not immediately available. This was implicitly accepted in *Sessay* where Supperstone J. said at para.39:

> "[I]f a patient evidences an intention to leave the hospital before the s.4 application is completed, hospital staff may contact the police who have the power to detain the patient under s.136. We do not accept that there should be any problem with the use of s.136 in these circumstances."

The detention of a patient by staff while awaiting the attendance of the police is governed by the common law. A similar justification obtains if a patient needs to be restrained during the course of an assessment under the Mental Health Act. Supperstone J. said at para.57:

> "[I]n our view it is unlikely in the ordinary case that there will be a false imprisonment at common law or deprivation of liberty for the purposes of Article 5(1) ECHR if there is no undue delay during the processing of an application under ss.2 or 4 MHA for admission."

The European Court of Human Rights has confirmed that the detention of a person for a short period in an emergency does not involve a violation of art.5 of the European Convention on Human Rights (*Winterwerp v Netherlands* (1979–80) 2 E.H.R.R. 387, para.39 and *X v United Kingdom* (1982) 4 E.H.R.R. 188, para.45).

Apart from the powers noted above, the extent to which common law powers enable informal patients to be subject to the control of staff is unclear. In *Pountney v Griffiths* [1976] A.C. 314, the House of Lords noted that it had been conceded by counsel for a Broadmoor Hospital patient that hospital staff have "powers of control over all mentally disordered patients, whether admitted voluntarily or compulsorily, though the nature and duration of control varies with the category to which the patient belongs". The Report of the Committee of Inquiry into Complaints about Ashworth Hospital (Cm. 2028–1) considered that this statement "would be likely to receive the endorsement of the courts today ... see *R. v Deputy Governor of Parkhurst Prison and others Ex p. Hague; sub nom. Hague v Deputy Governor of Parkhurst Prison; Weldon v Home Office* [1992] 1 A.C. 58" (para.196). The powers to control informal patients are clearly far less extensive that those that apply to detained patients. If a mentally capable informal patient is unable to accept the control and discipline that is considered by staff to be in his best interests and/or conducive to the good administration of the hospital, he should either be asked to leave or consideration given to using the powers of detention under the Act.

THE HIGH SECURITY PSYCHIATRIC SERVICES (ARRANGEMENTS FOR VISITS BY CHILDREN) DIRECTIONS 2013

General Note

B-001   A previous version of these Directions was found to be lawful and not in breach of the European Convention on Human Rights in *R. (on the application of L) v Secretary of State for Health* [2001] 1 F.L.R. 406 where Scott Baker J. said:

> "If there are special circumstances in which the patient has good reason for being visited by a child who is not within the permitted category relationship the remedy is to apply to the court for an order under the Children Act 1989."

Guidance

B-002   Guidance on these Directions, which was published by the Department of Health in December, 2013, can be accessed at: *https://assets.publishing.service.gov.uk/ government/uploads/system/uploads/attachment_data/file/268548/Visits_by_ Children_Guidance.pdf.*

The Secretary of State gives the following Directions in exercise of the powers conferred by ss.4(3A)(a), 8 and 273(1) and (4) of the National Health Service Act 2006.

Citation, commencement and interpretation

B-003   **1.—**   These Directions may be cited as the High Security Psychiatric Services (Arrangements for Visits by Children) Directions 2013 and come into force on 15th July 2013.

(2)   In these Directions—

"the 1983 Act" means the Mental Health Act 1983;
"the 2006 Act" means the National Health Service Act 2006;
"chief executive" means, in relation to a hospital, the chief executive of the Trust which is responsible for that hospital or that person's deputy;
"child" means a person under the age of eighteen;
"clinical team" means the multi-disciplinary team responsible for a patient's treatment, including the responsible clinician;
"executive director" means a member of the provider's senior management team with executive responsibilities for a hospital at which high security psychiatric services are provided;
"hospital" means a hospital or any part of a hospital which is treated as a separate unit as covered by the definition of "hospital premises" in section 4(4) of the 2006 Act;
"nominated officer" means the officer nominated pursuant to paragraph 3(1)(a) of these Directions;
"parental responsibility" has the same meaning as in the Children Act 1989;
"patient" means a patient liable to be detained at a hospital under—
  (a)   the 1983 Act;

(b) an order of the Crown Court under section 5 of the Criminal Procedure (Insanity) Act 1964; or

(c) an order of the Court of Appeal under section 6 or 14 of the Criminal Appeal Act 1968;

"provider" means any person who is approved to provide high security psychiatric services under section 4(3)(b) of the 2006 Act;

"relevant local authority" means the local authority in which the child resides;

"responsible clinician" has the meaning given in sections 34 and 55 of the 1983 Act;

"Trust" means an NHS trust established under section 25 of the 2006 Act or an NHS foundation trust authorised under section 35 of the 2006 Act;

"ward area" means the day rooms, patients' bedrooms, corridors, toilets, bathrooms, ward kitchens and any other rooms or garden area in the residential parts of the hospital to which the patients have access as a matter of course.

Visits by children

2.— A provider must only permit a patient in a hospital to receive a visit from a child in accordance with these Directions.   **B-004**

(2) Subject to paragraph (4), a hospital must not permit a patient to receive a visit from a child unless—

    (a) the nominated officer has approved the child's visit in accordance with these Directions; and

    (b) in the case of a patient who is assessed as posing a risk or potential risk of harm to the child, that patient—

      (i) is the parent or relative of that child; or

      (ii) has parental responsibility of that child; or

      (iii) was cohabiting with the parent of that child immediately prior to their detention under the 1983 Act and the child was treated as a member of their household.

(3) In paragraph (2) "parent" means the mother or father, the adoptive mother or father or the stepmother or stepfather of the child, and"relative" means a grandparent, brother, sister, uncle or aunt or cousin related to the child by blood (including half-blood), marriage or adoption.

(4) Paragraph (2) does not apply where an order made under the Children Act 1989 specifies that the child may visit the patient in the hospital.

Procedure for deciding on requests for visits

3.— A hospital must—   **B-005**

(a) nominate a senior manager to act as the nominated officer to be responsible for overseeing the process of dealing with any request for permission for a child to visit a patient and for deciding whether to approve the visit;

(b) set up a multi-disciplinary panel to assist and advise the nominated officer in carrying out their responsibilities and reaching decisions on applications; and

(c) ensure that the nominated officer discharges their responsibilities in accordance with these Directions.

(2) Any request for permission for a child to visit a patient in a hospital must be made in writing by the patient and must be forwarded to the nominated officer.

(3) Except in a case to which paragraphs (11) to (14) or direction 6 applies, the procedure set out in paragraphs (4) to (10) will apply.

(4) The nominated officer must arrange for the patient's clinical team to carry out the assessment—

    (a) as to whether, in their view, it would be appropriate for the visit to take place having regard to the patient's offending history (if any), their clinical history and present mental state; and

    (b) in the event that a visit is recommended, of any particular arrangements which would need to be made for a visit by that child to take place.

(5) Where following the assessment referred to in paragraph (4)—

    (a) the nominated officer is satisfied that it would not be appropriate for the child to visit the patient, they must refuse the request for a visit, or

    (b) in any other case, the nominated officer must seek the advice of the relevant local authority as to whether it is in the best interests of the child to visit the patient and must send with that request for advice, a copy of the assessment referred to in paragraph (4).

(6) Subject to paragraph (8), on receipt of the advice from the relevant local authority, the nominated officer must decide whether to approve the visit having regard to—

    (a) that advice;

    (b) the assessment referred to in paragraph (4); and

    (c) any other relevant information.

(7) When deciding whether to approve the visit, if the advice from the relevant local authority has been received within the last 12 months, the nominated officer does not need to seek advice again, but should obtain confirmation from the local authority that there has not been any new contact with or concerns raised with the local authority which may affect the nominated officer's decision.

(8) The nominated officer must not approve a visit in any case where the advice from the relevant local authority is that it is not or may not be in the best interests of the child to visit the patient.

(9) If no decision has been reached within eight weeks of the date on which a request for a visit is received from a patient the nominated officer must inform the patient in writing of the reasons for the delay and refer the matter to the executive director of the hospital.

(10) The nominated officer must notify—

    (a) the patient;

    (b) the parent of the child and any other person with parental responsibility for the child or caring for the child;

    (c) the child if they are of sufficient age and understanding; and

    (d) any relevant local authority,

of the decision and the reasons for that decision in writing.

(11) Subject to paragraph (14), where the patient is assessed as posing a risk or potential risk of harm to the child and that child is not within the categories of relationship set out in direction 2(2)(b), paragraphs (4) to (10) shall not

apply and the nominated officer must refuse the request for a visit and notify the patient accordingly.

(12) Subject to paragraphs (13) and (14), where the person with parental responsibility for the child, or in the case of a child subject to a care order the designated local authority in whose care the child is placed under section 31(1)(a) of the Children Act 1989, has not agreed the child may visit the patient, paragraphs (4) to (10) shall not apply and the nominated officer must refuse the request for the visit and notify the patient accordingly.

(13) Save in the case of a child subject to a care order, where there is more than one person with parental responsibility for the child, it is the person with parental responsibility with whom the child is living who must agree to the visit.

(14) In any case where an order made under the Children Act 1989 specifies that the child may visit the patient in the hospital the nominated officer must allow the visit to take place.

Validity of approval of visit and withdrawal of such approval

4.— Subject to paragraph (3), any approval for the child to visit the patient must **B-006** be valid for a period of 12 months from the date on which it is given and may only be withdrawn in that period if the nominated officer is satisfied that there has been a relevant change of circumstances.

(2) If, after that period of 12 months referred to in paragraph (1) has elapsed, the patient wishes to continue to have visits from the child, the nominated officer must—

   (a) review the permission in accordance with paragraphs (3) to (9) of direction 3; and

   (b) must notify the persons mentioned in paragraph (9) of direction 3 of their decision and the reasons for that decision in writing.

(3) Notwithstanding paragraph (1), the nominated officer may at any time refuse to allow a visit to take place if there are concerns about the patient's mental state at the time of the proposed visit.

Complaints

5. A provider must set up a procedure to enable a patient to make representa- **B-007** tions against any decision of the nominated officer not to approve a visit other than a refusal on the grounds set on in direction 3, paragraphs (10) or (11).

Visits in exceptional circumstances

6.— In exceptional circumstances and subject to any guidance given by the **B-008** Secretary of State, the chief executive or the executive director may give their written authority for a patient to receive a visit from a child without an assessment in accordance with direction 3.

(2) The chief executive or the executive director must consult the nominated officer before approving a visit in such circumstances.

(3) Paragraph (1) does not apply where the patient is a person described in sub-paragraph (2)(b) of direction 2 and the child is not within the permitted categories of relationship set out in that sub-paragraph.

Arrangements to be put in place for visits

B-009 7.— A hospital must ensure that—

(a) during a visit the child has direct contact only with the patient for whom permission has been given for that child to visit,

(b) subject to paragraph (2), the child is accompanied by—

  (i) a person with parental responsibility for that child and with whom the child is living, or

  (ii) another person who is caring for the child,

(c) a visit takes place in an appropriate setting designated for visits by children and not in the ward area,

(d) if in exceptional circumstances, a visit takes place in an area or place other than an appropriate setting designated for visits by children as set out in sub-paragraph (c), it must be appropriate, not be detrimental to the child and approved by the nominated officer, and

(e) that there are sufficient staff of any appropriate grade and with requisite knowledge and understanding present to supervise a child's visit at all times.

(2) Sub-paragraph (1)(b) does not apply in the case of a child aged 16 or 17 where the nominated officer, having regard to the information they have received under direction 3, is satisfied that an unaccompanied visit is unlikely to prejudice the child's welfare.

Annual report to the Provider's Board of Directors

B-010 8. The chief executive must submit an annual report to the provider's board at the end of each financial year providing details of—

(a) the number of patients visited by children in that year;

(b) any special arrangements put in place to ensure that safety of those children whilst visiting patients, together with the chief executive's assessment of the appropriateness of such arrangements; and

(c) the chief executive's assessment of the continuing adequacy of the arrangements put in place by the hospital to ensure the safety of children whilst visiting patients.

Revocation

B-011 9. The Visits by Children to Ashworth, Broadmoor and Rampton Hospitals Directions that came into force on 1st September 1999 are revoked.

THE HIGH SECURITY PSYCHIATRIC SERVICES (ARRANGEMENTS FOR SAFETY AND SECURITY) DIRECTIONS 2019

General Note

In *Buck v Nottinghamshire Healthcare NHS Trust* [2006] EWCA Civ 1576, the **C-001** Court of Appeal held that the existence of a previous version of these Directions and the failure to implement them could inform the court as to the content of the duty of care owned by Rampton Hospital to its nursing staff. *Buck* was applied in *Watson v Nottinghamshire NHS Trust*, Lincoln County Court, September 26, 2008, a case where a nurse at Rampton Hospital was subjected to a prolonged and violent attack by a patient. In a trial on the issue of liability under, inter alia, the 2013 version of these Directions, Recorder Beale held that the hospital was under a duty, in considering whether some precaution needed to be taken against a foreseeable risk, to weigh, on the one hand, the magnitude of the risk, the likelihood of an accident happening and the possible serious consequences if an accident were to happen, and, on the other hand, the difficulty and expense and any other disadvantage of taking the precaution.

Guidance

Guidance on these Directions is reproduced in Part 4. **C-002**

Coronavirus Pandemic

"*Legal guidance for mental health, learning disability and autism, and* **C-003** *specialised commissioning services supporting people of all ages during the coronavirus pandemic*", NHS England (January 21, 2021) states at p.19:

- "It may be necessary due to the implications of COVID for high secure services to derogate from the Safety and Security Directions. Where this is required, the issues identified should be considered by the high secure provider along with potential solutions and mitigations. Any outstanding risks associated with taking these actions should also identified.
- The position should then be shared with the relevant NHS England and NHS Improvement regional specialised commissioner and the head of mental health for specialised commissioning nationally for their consideration and onward support.
- The chief officer, or their nominated deputy, in each provider will need to authorise the actual derogation from the Directions.
- This will need to be reported to the relevant commissioners by the agreed SitRep report and a weekly summary provided to a core group from the High Secure National Oversight Group (NOG) to ensure oversight.
- Where any significant changes are enacted during this time, these will be discussed 'by exception' with NOG members, with the potential to also communicate these changes as required to the Secretary of State".

The Secretary of State gives the following Directions in exercise of the powers conferred by ss.4(3A)(a), 8 and 273(1) and (4) of the National Health Service Act 2006.

Application, citation and commencement

C-004 **1.**—(1) These Directions apply to any person who is approved by the Secretary of State for the purposes of section 4(3)(b) of the 2006 Act to provide high security psychiatric services.

(2) These Directions may be cited as the High Security Psychiatric Services (Arrangements for Safety and Security) Directions 2019.

(3) These Directions come into force on 28th May 2019.

Interpretation

C-005 **2.** In these Directions—

"escape" means where a patient unlawfully gains liberty by breaching the secure perimeter of the hospital;

"abscond" means where a patient unlawfully gains liberty outside of the secure perimeter of the hospital by breaking away from the custody and supervision of staff;

"authorised member of staff" means a person appointed under section 134(7) of the 1983 Act;

"the 1983 Act" means the Mental Health Act 1983;

"the 2006 Act" means the National Health Service Act 2006;

"the 2008 Regulations" means the Mental Health (Hospital, Guardianship and Treatment) (England) Regulations 2008;

"the Additional Functions Regulations 2011" means the Care Quality Commission (Additional Functions) Regulations 2011;

"chief executive" means, in relation to a hospital, the chief executive of the NHS Trust or NHS Foundation Trust which is responsible for that hospital, or that person's deputy;

"Clinical Security Framework" means the document of the same title issued by the Board;

"clinical team" means the multi-disciplinary team responsible for a patient's treatment, including the responsible clinician;

"contractor" means a person, other than a member of staff or a member of the emergency services, who provides services to a hospital;

"grounds access" means unescorted access to areas of a hospital other than the ward area;

"hospital" means a hospital or any part of a hospital which is treated as a separate unit as covered by the definition of "hospital premises" in section 4(4) of the 2006 Act;

"illicit substance" means—

(a) any drug which is a controlled drug for the purposes of the Misuse of Drugs Act 1971;

(b) alcohol; or

(c) a psychoactive substance as defined by section 2 of the Psychoactive Substances Act 2016;

"key-holder" means, in relation to a hospital, a person who is authorised by the provider to hold keys to the secure area of the hospital;

"leave of absence" means leave granted under section 17 of the 1983 Act;

"medical director" means, in relation to a hospital, the medical director, chief medical officer or clinical director of the hospital appointed by the provider which is responsible for that hospital, or that person's deputy;

"member of staff" means, in relation to a hospital—
    (a) any person employed by the provider responsible for the hospital in connection with the provision of high security psychiatric services at the hospital, or any other person who provides services under contract and is treated as being an employee by the provider; and
    (b) the chairman and any non-executive director of the provider;
"patient" means a patient liable to be detained at a hospital under—
    (a) the 1983 Act;
    (b) an order of the Crown Court under section 5 of the Criminal Procedure (Insanity) Act 1964; or
    (c) an order of the Court of Appeal under section 6 or 14 of the Criminal Appeal Act 1968;
"postal packet" has the same meaning as in the Postal Services Act 2000;
"provider" means any person who is approved to provide high security psychiatric services for the purposes of section 4(3)(b) of the 2006 Act;
"responsible clinician" has the meaning given in sections 34 and 55 of the 1983 Act;
"rub-down search" means a search of a person, and the contents of that person's pockets, but does not include a search that involves the removal of any item of clothing other than an outer layer of clothing;
"secure area" means the part of the hospital that is inside the secure perimeter;
"security department" means the members of staff of a hospital responsible for advising on, monitoring and, where relevant, implementing security policy at that hospital;
"security director" means, in relation to a hospital, the member of staff with responsibility for the security department at the hospital;
"security information" means any information held by a hospital about its safety and security;
"secure perimeter of the hospital" means the outside wall, fence, reception or declared boundary of the hospital;
"senior member of the Royal Family" means those carrying the style His or Her Majesty (HM) or His or Her Royal Highness (HRH);
"visiting child" means any person visiting a hospital who is under the age of 18;
"visitor" means any person, other than a member of staff, visiting a hospital who is 18 or over;
"ward area" means the day rooms, patients' bedrooms, corridors, toilets, bathrooms, ward kitchens and any other rooms or garden area in the residential parts of the hospital to which patients have access as a matter of course.

Promotion of safety and security

3.—(1) For the purpose of promoting safety and security in the hospital for which it is responsible, each provider must exercise its functions in connection with the provision of high security psychiatric services in accordance with these Directions.   **C-006**

(2) In exercising those functions, each provider must have regard to any guidance issued by the Secretary of State on arrangements for safety and security at the hospital and to the Clinical Security Framework.

(3) If a provider intends to perform its functions other than in accordance with guidance referred to in paragraph (2) or the Clinical Security Framework, it

must notify without delay:

(a) the Board;

(b) the NHS Trust Development Authority; and

(c) where the provider is a NHS Foundation Trust, Monitor,

and give reasons for the decision or act, as well as setting out action being taken to become compliant.

Duty to co-operate

C-007 **4.** Each provider must co-operate with other providers for the purpose of making arrangements in respect of safety and security in the hospital for which it is responsible.

Requirements for conducting a rub-down search of a patient

C-008 **5.**—(1) Each provider must ensure in respect of the hospital for which it is responsible that any rub-down search of a patient in the hospital is carried out in accordance with this direction.

(2) This direction does not apply to the search of a patient if a member of staff has reasonable grounds to believe that the patient possesses an item which causes an immediate risk to the patient's own safety, the safety of any other person, or the safety of the hospital.

(3) Subject to paragraph (2), a rub-down search may only be carried out—

(a) with the patient's consent; or

(b) where authorised by the responsible clinician or the medical director in accordance with the provisions of this direction.

(4) If a patient does not consent to a rub-down search, the matter must be referred to the patient's responsible clinician.

(5) The responsible clinician may authorise a rub-down search if the responsible clinician considers that the proposed search would not be detrimental to the patient's wellbeing.

(6) If the responsible clinician considers that the proposed search would be detrimental to the patient's wellbeing, that clinician must consult a member of the security department.

(7) Following consultation with a member of the security department, the responsible clinician may authorise, or refuse to authorise, a rub-down search.

(8) In making a decision under paragraph (7) the responsible clinician must take into account—

(a) interests of the patient;

(b) the opinion of the member of the security department consulted under paragraph (6);

(c) the safety of staff, patients, visitors and visiting children; and

(d) the security of the hospital.

(9) If the responsible clinician refuses to authorise a search under paragraph (7), the member of the security department consulted under paragraph (6) may refer the matter to the medical director.

(10) Where a matter is referred under paragraph (9), the medical director may authorise, or refuse to authorise, the search.

(11) In making a decision under paragraph (10), the medical director must take into account—

(a) the interests of the patient;

   (b) the opinion of the responsible clinician;

   (c) the opinion of the member of the security department consulted under paragraph (6);

   (d) the safety of staff, patients, visitors and visiting children to the hospital; and

   (e) the security of the hospital.

(12) Any patient who has refused to consent to a rub-down search must be—

   (a) kept under observation;

   (b) isolated from other patients; and

   (c) kept informed of what is happening and why in terms appropriate to their understanding,

until such time as a search has been authorised, or refused, under paragraph (5), (7) or (10).

(13) In all cases a rub-down search must be carried out with due regard for the patient's dignity and privacy.

(14) Unless there are exceptional circumstances, a rub-down search must be carried out by members of staff who are of the same sex as the patient.

Searches of patients that involve the removal of clothing other than outer clothing

6.—(1) Each provider must ensure in respect of the hospital for which it is responsible that any search of a patient in the hospital, other than a rub down search under direction 5, is carried out in accordance with this direction.   **C-009**

(2) This direction does not apply to the search of a patient if a member of staff has reasonable grounds to believe that the patient possesses an item which causes an immediate risk to the patient's own safety, the safety of any other person, or the safety of the hospital.

(3) A search that involves the removal of clothing may only be carried out—

   (a) on the patient's admission to the hospital;

   (b) if, before that patient goes on leave of absence, the provider requires a search to be carried out;

   (c) where there is reason to believe that the patient may be in possession of—

      (i) illicit substances, or

      (ii) a weapon; or

   (d) if the patient is considered by a member of staff to pose a risk—

      (i) of harm to themselves,

      (ii) to the safety of any person, or

      (iii) to the security of the hospital.

(4) A search involving the removal of clothing may only be carried out—

   (a) with the patient's consent; or

   (b) where authorised by the responsible clinician or the medical director in accordance with this direction.

(5) If a patient does not consent to a search involving the removal of clothing, the matter must be referred to the patient's responsible clinician.

(6) The responsible clinician may authorise the search if the responsible clinician considers that the proposed search would not be detrimental to the patient's wellbeing.

(7) If the responsible clinician considers that the proposed search would be

detrimental to the patient's wellbeing, that clinician must consult a member of the security department.

(8) Following consultation with a member of the security department, the responsible clinician may authorise, or refuse to authorise, the search.

(9) In making a decision under paragraph (8), the responsible clinician must take into account—

    (a) the interests of the patient;

    (b) the opinion of the member of the security department consulted under paragraph (7);

    (c) the safety of staff, patients, visitors and visiting children; and

    (d) the security of the hospital.

(10) If the responsible clinician refuses to authorise a search under paragraph (8), the member of the security department consulted under paragraph (7) may refer the matter to the medical director.

(11) Where a matter is referred under paragraph (10), the medical director may authorise, or refuse to authorise, the search.

(12) In making a decision under paragraph (11), the medical director must take into account—

    (a) the interests of the patient;

    (b) the opinion of the responsible clinician;

    (c) the opinion of the member of the security department consulted under paragraph (7);

    (d) the safety of staff, patients, visitors and visiting children to the hospital; and

    (e) the security of the hospital.

(13) Any patient who has refused to consent to a search involving the removal of clothing must be—

    (a) kept under observation;

    (b) isolated from other patients; and

    (c) kept informed of what is happening and why in terms appropriate to their understanding, until such time as a search has been authorised, or refused, under paragraph (6), (8) or (11).

(14) A search under this direction must take place on the patient's ward or in the hospital's admission facility which is a facility designed for carrying out administrative and security checks associated with the admission of patients.

(15) A search under this direction must be carried out by two members of staff, at least one of whom must be a registered nurse.

(16) Unless there are exceptional circumstances, a search under this direction may only be undertaken by members of staff who are the same sex as the patient.

(17) In all cases a search under this direction must be carried out with due regard for the patient's dignity and privacy.

(18) Nothing in this direction is to be taken as allowing an intimate body search of a patient.

(19) In this direction "intimate body search" means a search which consists of the physical examination of a person's body orifices other than the mouth.

Searches of patients, rooms and lockers

C-010   7.—(1) Each provider must in respect of the hospital for which it is responsible make arrangements for the routine searching of patients, their rooms and their lockers, in accordance with the Clinical Security Framework, and this direction.

(2) Each patient's room, its contents and any locker used by that patient must be searched at least once each calendar month on any day and at any time on a random basis.

(3) Each provider must also make arrangements for searching a patient's room and any locker used by that patient whenever there is reliable intelligence or reasonable suspicion that a search may be required.

(4) Subject to paragraph (5), each patient's locker located on a ward must be searched on one further occasion each month at any day or time on a random basis.

(5) Paragraph (4) does not apply where there is more than one search of that locker under paragraph (2) in any calendar month.

Searches when patients move around in the secure area

8. Each provider must in respect of the hospital for which it is responsible make arrangements in accordance with the Clinical Security Framework for searching patients who move between different parts of the hospital. **C-011**

Searches of ward areas and other areas

9. Each provider must in respect of the hospital for which it is responsible make arrangements to ensure that— **C-012**
  (a) all ward areas of the hospital, other than patients' rooms, are searched at least once a week; and
  (b) all therapy, workshop, recreation and leisure facility areas, and any other areas (other than ward areas) of that hospital which a patient may visit within the secure area, are searched at least once every three months.

Security of tools, equipment and materials

10.—(1) Each provider must issue written instructions to members of staff at the hospital for which it is responsible on the control of tools, equipment and materials in the secure area of the hospital. **C-013**

(2) Each provider must make arrangements to ensure that where, prior to the end of an activity or session, a patient leaves an area in which a tool or other equipment is or has been in use, that patient is subject to a rub-down search before leaving that area if the requirements for carrying out such a search set out in direction 5 are met.

Searches of members of staff and key-holders

11.—(1) Each provider must, in respect of the hospital for which it is responsible, make arrangements to ensure that— **C-014**
  (a) at least 10% of occasions when members of staff or key-holders enter the secure area, and 5% of times when members of staff leave the secure area, will result in a rub-down search of members of staff or key-holders who are chosen randomly;
  (b) members of staff and key-holders pass through a staffed metal detection portal immediately prior to entry into the secure area except where medical or other extenuating reasons make this impracticable;

(c) all bags, packages or similar in possession of members of staff or key-holders are x-rayed and (where appropriate) physically inspected prior to entry into the secure area;

(d) any member of staff or key-holder escorting a patient on leave of absence is subject to a rub-down search on entry to or departure from the secure area; and

(e) where a member of staff or key-holder is escorting a patient on leave of absence, any bags, packages or similar possessions of that individual are x-rayed and, where appropriate, physically inspected on entry to or departure from the secure area.

(2) The provider must x-ray and, where appropriate, physically inspect any bags, packages or similar possessions of a member of staff or key-holder who is subject to a rub-down search under paragraph (1)(a) on leaving the secure area.

(3) A rub-down search under paragraphs (1)(a) and (d) must be carried out—

(a) by a person of the same sex as the member of staff or key-holder, unless there are exceptional circumstances or with permission from the member of staff; and

(b) with due regard for the dignity of the person.

Arrangements in respect of visitors and visiting children

C-015   12.—(1) Each provider must in respect of the hospital for which it is responsible make arrangements in respect of any visitor or visiting children in accordance with this direction.

(2) All patient visits must be arranged with the provider in advance.

(3) Tobacco, tobacco products, and electronic cigarettes must not be brought into the secure area.

(4) The provider must provide facilities within the secure area for the purpose of enabling visitors to acquire, in accordance with such rules as the provider may determine from time to time, food for consumption by themselves, by any visiting child accompanying them or by a patient whom they are visiting.

(5) Visitors and visiting children must not bring food into the secure area unless—

(a) that food is being supplied to the hospital under contract with the provider; or

(b) following consultation with the patient's clinical team and the medical director, the responsible clinician gives permission for the visitor to bring food into the secure area and for the patient to consume that food during the visit as part of the patient's care treatment plan.

(6) Subject to paragraphs (9) to (11), a visitor or a visiting child must—

(a) be subject to a rub-down search; and

(b) have their possessions inspected,

before they are permitted to enter the secure area.

(7) Subject to paragraphs (9) to (11), a visitor must be refused entry to the secure area unless the visitor—

(a) consents to a rub-down search and an inspection of their possessions; and

(b) in the case where a visitor is accompanied by a visiting child for whom the visitor is responsible, consents to a rub-down search of that child and an inspection of that child's possessions.

(8) Subject to paragraphs (9) and (11), any visiting child must not be permitted

to enter the secure area unless—

(a) the visitor responsible for that child consents to a rub-down search of that child and an inspection of the child's possessions; or

(b) if the child is of sufficient understanding to make an informed decision about any search or inspection, that child consents to a rub-down search of that child and an inspection of their possessions.

(9) A visiting child must be permitted access to the secure area if a child arrangements order has been made under section 10 of the Children Act 1989 in respect of that child and a patient in that hospital.

(10) Where a visitor is a member of the First-tier Tribunal (Mental Health) and needs to enter the secure area in connection with performing their judicial function, they must not be subject to a rub-down search on entering or leaving the secure area on that occasion unless—

(a) they will be carrying out an examination of a patient in accordance with Rule 34 of the Tribunal Procedure (First-tier Tribunal) (Health, Education and Social Care Chamber) Rules 2008(c) whilst in the secure area;

(b) they activate the metal detection portal on passing through it and the reason for the activation cannot be established by other means; or

(c) the chief executive considers that there is an exceptional reason why they should be subject to a rub-down search.

(11) Where a visitor, or a visiting child, is not permitted access to the secure area, the chief executive shall, if so requested, review that decision and may permit entry subject to such conditions as the chief executive may require.

(12) Where there is a child arrangements order in place in respect of a visiting child and the child and any accompanying visitor is permitted to enter the secure area without being searched or their possessions being inspected, entry to the secure area may be subject to such conditions as the director of security may require.

(13) Paragraphs (6) to (12) do not apply to—

(a) a senior member of the Royal Family; or

(b) a member of the emergency services who is attending to an emergency.

(14) This direction does not apply to any visitor who is a key-holder.

(15) In this direction—

"tobacco product" means a product consisting wholly or partly of tobacco and intended to be smoked, sniffed, sucked or chewed; and

"electronic cigarette" means a product that—

(a) can be used for the consumption of nicotine-containing vapour via a mouth piece, or any component of that product, including a cartridge, a tank and the device without cartridge or tank (regardless of whether the product is disposable or refillable by means of a refill container and a tank, or rechargeable with single use cartridges); and

(b) is not a medicinal product or medical device.

Searches of visitors and inspection of possessions

13.—(1) Each provider must ensure that in respect of the hospital for which it is responsible, any search of any visitor, or visiting child, and the inspection of any possessions of that person, is carried out in accordance with this direction. **C-016**

(2) Any rub-down search must be carried out—

(a) subject to paragraph (5)—
    (i) with the consent of the person being searched or, in the case of a visiting child, the consent of the responsible adult in respect of that child, and
    (ii) by a person of the same sex as the person being searched, unless there are exceptional circumstances and the person to be searched, or the responsible adult in respect of any visiting child, consents to the search on that basis; and
(b) with due regard for the dignity of the person being searched.

(3) All visitors must pass through a metal detection portal on entry to the secure area except where medical or other extenuating reasons make this impracticable.

(4) All bags, packages and other possessions to be taken into the secure area—
    (a) must, where possible, be inspected by x-ray equipment;
    (b) may, following x-ray, be physically inspected; and
    (c) must be physically inspected if inspection by x-ray is not possible.

(5) Where a visiting child is of sufficient understanding to make an informed decision about any search, that child must consent to the search, before it takes place.

(6) Paragraphs (3) and (4) do not apply to—
    (a) a senior member of the Royal Family; or
    (b) a member of the emergency services who is attending to an emergency.

(7) This direction does not apply to any visitor who is a key-holder.

Supply of food by staff and key-holders to patients

C-017   **14.**—(1) Subject to paragraph (2), each provider must ensure that in respect of the hospital for which it is responsible, no member of staff or key-holder brings food into the secure area for consumption by a patient.

(2) The security director may authorise any member of staff (including a member of catering staff or a porter) or key-holder to bring food for a patient into the secure area of the hospital where it is not practicable for a contractor to do so.

Checks of vehicles

C-018   **15.**—(1) Subject to paragraph (2), each provider must, in respect of the hospital for which it is responsible, have arrangements in place for the search of any vehicle which enters or leaves the secure area, and for the management of vehicles in the secure area, in accordance with the Clinical Security Framework.

(2) Paragraph (1) does not apply in relation to any emergency services vehicle that is attending to an emergency.

Testing for illicit substances

C-019   **16.**—(1) Each provider must, in respect of the hospital for which it is responsible, make arrangements for testing patients for the use of illicit substances in accordance with this direction.

(2) Provided that the patient consents, samples must be collected from—
    (a) each patient on admission to the hospital;
    (b) any patient suspected of using or possessing illicit substances; and

    (c)   at least 5% of the total number of patients at the hospital each month, selected randomly.

(3)   Any patient required to provide a sample must be afforded such privacy as is compatible with the need to prevent or detect adulteration or falsification of the sample.

(4)   In no circumstances must a patient be required to provide a sample of urine in the sight of a person of the opposite sex.

(5)   In this direction "sample" means—

    (a)   a sample of urine;

    (b)   a breath test for alcohol;

    (c)   a swab taken from a patient's mouth; or

    (d)   a sample of hair, other than pubic hair.

Control of prescribed drugs

17.—(1)   Each provider must, in respect of the hospital for which it is responsible, issue written instructions to members of staff on the control of prescribed drugs.   **C-020**

(2)   Instructions issued under paragraph (1) must include instructions on—

    (a)   the transportation of prescribed drugs between the hospital pharmacy and a ward area;

    (b)   the security of medication storage and the location of those units;

    (c)   arrangements for distributing prescribed drugs to patients; and

    (d)   arrangements for ensuring that patients take prescribed drugs at the point at which they are dispensed, or at such other times as may be authorised by the clinical team.

Written or electronic records of certain searches and tests

18.   Each provider must, in respect of the hospital for which it is responsible, make arrangements to ensure that a written or electronic record is kept of—   **C-021**

    (a)   any search of persons or possessions undertaken under these Directions;

    (b)   any refusal to consent to a search;

    (c)   any refusal of entry under direction 12 (arrangements in respect of visitors and visiting children);

    (d)   any test undertaken in accordance with arrangements made under direction 16 (testing for illicit substances), and the outcome of that test; and

    (e)   any refusal by a patient to give a sample in accordance with arrangements made under direction 16.

Security information

19.—(1)   Each provider must ensure that, in respect of the hospital for which it is responsible, it has arrangements in place with regard to the gathering and maintenance of security information.   **C-022**

(2)   The security director for the hospital must establish and maintain written or electronic security records having regard to any relevant guidance issued by the Secretary of State.

(3)   For the purposes of this direction "security records" means records concerning possible threats to safety or security and includes information on—

    (a)   plans for escape;

    (b) plans to abscond;

    (c) potential disturbances at the hospital;

    (d) attempts to bring unauthorised items into the hospital; and

    (e) any other matters which could threaten the well-being of a patient, visitor, visiting child or a member of staff.

(4) The security director must ensure that—

    (a) security reports are given to members of the patients' clinical teams and the board of directors of the provider on a regular basis;

    (b) instructions are given to the security department on the collection, collation, evaluation, and assessment of the reliability of security information;

    (c) instructions are given to members of staff on what, and how, security information should be reported to the security department; and

    (d) instructions are given to members of staff on sharing security information and on data protection.

Patients' possessions

C-023   **20.**—(1) Each provider must, in respect of the hospital for which it is responsible, have written policies in relation to patients' possessions which are consistent with the requirements of safety and security in the hospital and, in particular, the policies must cover—

    (a) the identification of patients' possessions in an inventory;

    (b) arrangements to ensure that the inventory is signed and dated on each occasion when it is compiled or updated by—

       (i) the patient and a member of staff, or

       (ii) if the patient does not agree to sign, by two members of staff; and

    (c) in what circumstances patients' access to their possessions must be granted and in what circumstances such access may be refused.

(2) Where a patient request for access to their possessions is granted, the provider must aim to provide access to those possessions—

    (a) within 24 hours of the request being granted if the possessions are stored in a ward area; or

    (b) within 48 hours of the request being granted, not including weekends and public holidays, if the possessions are stored elsewhere.

Items delivered or brought to hospital premises for patients

C-024   **21.**—(1) Each provider must make arrangements in respect of the hospital for which it is responsible, to ensure that any item which is delivered or brought to the hospital for delivery to a patient is examined in accordance with the provisions of this direction.

(2) The item must be—

    (a) x-rayed; and

    (b) opened and inspected,

by a member of staff.

(3) Any item brought to the hospital for a patient may be withheld on the grounds that the item—

    (a) is one which the patient has asked to be withheld;

    (b) is likely to cause distress to the person to whom it is addressed or to any other person;

   (c) may cause a danger to any person;

   (d) may prejudice the safety of any person; or

   (e) may prejudice security in the hospital.

(4) Where an item is withheld—

   (a) that decision must be recorded;

   (b) the patient must be given notice of the decision and told why the item has been withheld; and

   (c) the patient must be given notice that the decision may be reviewed by the Care Quality Commission if a written application for review is made within six months beginning with the day on which the information set out in this sub-paragraph is received.

(5) The provider must comply with any direction given by the Care Quality Commission under regulation 2(2) of the Additional Functions Regulations 2011.

(6) This direction does not apply to incoming postal packets addressed to a patient provided for under directions 25 and 27.

General Note

Paragraph (3)

Regulation 2 of the Care Quality Commission (Additional Functions) Regulations 2011 (SI 2011/1551) (as amended) reads: **C-025**

"Review of decision to withhold an item delivered or brought to a high security hospital for a patient

   2.—(1) The Care Quality Commission shall review a decision made under [direction 21(3) of the 2019 Directions] (items delivered or brought to hospital premises for patients) to withhold an item if an application to review that decision is made by the intended recipient of the item within six months beginning with the day on which that person receives the information set out in [direction 21(4)(c)] of those Directions.

   (2) On an application under paragraph (1) the Care Quality Commission may direct that the item which is the subject of the application shall not be withheld."

Patients' access to information technology equipment and the internet

22.—(1) Each provider must, in respect of the hospital for which it is responsible, make arrangements for the control of patients' access to, and use of, information technology equipment and the internet.   **C-026**

(2) The arrangements must ensure that—

   (a) patients' access to and use of information technology equipment and the internet is robustly risk assessed to mitigate any security risks;

   (b) there are clear governance processes for auditing any information technology equipment that is used by patients; and

   (c) there are clear governance processes for monitoring patients' use of information technology equipment and the internet.

(3) Any arrangement for risk assessment under paragraph (2)(a) must—

   (a) take into account the safety and protection of all patients and staff;

   (b) consider any impact or potential impact on any relevant victim; and

   (c) determine whether or not a patient's use of information technology equipment or the internet should be supervised, either directly or remotely.

(4) Each provider must ensure that the arrangements referred to in paragraph (1)

are reviewed annually and on each occasion when its scope is extended to a new technology.

(5) Arrangements under paragraph (1) must ensure that patients do not have—

(a) unsupervised access to live internet content, except to internet hosted applications and services which have been approved by the security director;

(b) access to any social media or other communication platforms that enable communication with other persons unless approved by the security director; and

(c) access to any information technology equipment or the internet unless approved by the provider.

(6) In this direction, "information technology equipment" includes any laptop or notebook computer, desktop computer, gaming console, handheld computing device, personal organiser or any electronic device containing a computer processor and capable of connecting to the internet, and any reference to information technology equipment includes a reference to—

(a) a component part of a device of that description; or

(b) any article designed or adapted for use with any information technology equipment (including any disk, film or other separate article on which images, sounds, computer code or other information may be stored or recorded).

Location of patients' shops

C-027   **23.**—(1) Subject to paragraph (2), each provider must ensure that a patients' shop is not located in a ward area of a hospital for which it is responsible.

(2) Subject to the prior approval of the security director, a mobile patients' shop may visit a ward area from time to time.

Role of patients in managing or working in patients' shops and other specified employment

C-028   **24.**—(1) Each provider must ensure that, in respect of the hospital for which it is responsible, a patient is not allowed to—

(a) manage a patients' shop; or

(b) work in a patients' shop or in other specified employment unless—

(i)   the Grounds Access Committee has given permission under direction 36 or the medical director has given permission under direction 38, and

(ii) a member of staff monitors and supervises any such work at all times.

(2) In paragraph (1) "other specified employment" means employment where the nature or location of the work, or the proposed level of supervision, generates a significant level of risk.

Patients' incoming post

C-029   **25.**—(1) Each provider must make arrangements in respect of the hospital for which it is responsible for incoming postal packets addressed to a patient to be x-rayed.

(2) Subject to—

(a) sections 134 (correspondence of patients) and 134A (review of decisions to withhold correspondence) of the 1983 Act; and

(b) regulations 29 and 30 of the 2008 Regulations (inspection and opening of postal packets: review of decisions to withhold),

each provider must make arrangements for incoming postal packets addressed to a patient at a hospital for which it is responsible to be opened and inspected by an authorised member of staff in accordance with this direction.

(3) Paragraphs (1) and (2) do not apply where a postal packet has been sent by or on behalf of any person or body identified in section 134(3) of the 1983 Act.

(4) Where paragraph (3) applies the postal packet may only be opened and inspected by an authorised member of staff in so far as it is necessary to confirm its origin.

(5) A postal packet opened and inspected in accordance with paragraph (4) must be delivered to the patient without further inspection if the packet has been sent by a person or body listed in section 134(3) of the 1983 Act.

Patients' outgoing post

26.—(1) Subject to—   **C-030**

(a) section 134 and 134A(1) to (3) of the 1983 Act; and

(b) regulations 29 and 30 of the 2008 Regulations,

each provider must make arrangements for the inspection of patients' outgoing postal packets at a hospital for which it is responsible in accordance with this direction.

(2) Any outgoing postal packet from a patient, other than a letter or card, must be packaged and sealed by the patient on their ward and in the presence of an authorised member of staff.

(3) Subject to paragraph (4) an authorised member of staff may open and inspect any outgoing letter or card.

(4) Where a letter or card is addressed to any person or body identified in section 134(3) of the 1983 Act, the letter or card may only be opened where it is necessary to confirm its destination and must not be further inspected if the intended recipient is a person or body identified in that section.

Internal post

27.—(1) Each provider must make arrangements, in respect of the hospital for **C-031** which it is responsible, for the inspection and withholding of internal post.

(2) An authorised member of staff may open and inspect any item of internal post.

(3) A provider may withhold delivery of internal post, or an item included in such post, in accordance with its arrangements under paragraph (1).

(4) If any post, or an item included in such post, is withheld under paragraph (3), the provider must ensure that—

(a) a record is made of the decision; and

(b) both the sender and the intended recipient are informed—

(i) that the post or item has been withheld;

(ii) the reason why; and

(iii) that they have a right to a review of that decision by the Care Quality Commission if a written application is made within six months beginning with the day on which the information set out in this subparagraph is received.

(5) For the purposes of this direction "internal post" means post—
  (a) between patients within the same hospital; or
  (b) from a patient to a member of staff of the hospital where the patient is detained.

(6) The provider must comply with any direction given by the Care Quality Commission under regulation 3(2) of the Additional Functions Regulations 2011 (review of decision to withhold internal post in high security hospitals).

General Note

Paragraph (3)

C-032   Regulation 3 of the Care Quality Commission (Additional Functions) Regulations 2011 (SI 2011/1551) (as amended) reads:

"Review of decision to withhold internal post in high security hospitals

3.—(1)   The Care Quality Commission shall review a decision made under direction 27(3) of the [2019 Directions] (internal post) to withhold internal post, or an item included in such post, if an application to review that decision is made by the sender or the intended recipient of the post or item within six months beginning with the day on which that person receives the information set out in direction 27(4)(b) of those Directions.
(2)   On an application under paragraph (1) the Care Quality Commission may direct that the post or item which is the subject of the application shall not be withheld."

Incoming post addressed to members of staff

C-033   **28.**—(1)   Each provider must make arrangements in accordance with this direction, in respect of the hospital for which it is responsible, for the examination of postal packets addressed to a member of staff.

(2) A postal packet addressed to a member of staff must be x-rayed before delivery of it to that person within the secure area.

(3) An authorised member of staff may open and inspect a postal packet under paragraph (1) with the consent of the member of staff to whom it is addressed.

(4) A postal packet must not be delivered to a member of staff within the secure area if, following a request, that person refuses to allow it to be opened and inspected.

Mobile telephones

C-034   **29.**—(1)   Each provider must make arrangements in accordance with this direction, in respect of the hospital for which it is responsible, for the control of mobile telephones.

(2) Patients must not have possession of, or access to, a mobile telephone in the secure area.

(3) Subject to paragraph (5), visitors and visiting children must not have possession of, or access to, a mobile telephone in the secure area.

(4) Members of staff and key-holders must not have possession of a mobile telephone in the secure area unless—
  (a) that telephone is owned, or hired, by the provider; and
  (b) the security director has authorised possession.

(5) Members of the emergency services may carry mobile telephones where—
  (a) they are responding to an emergency; or
  (b) the security director has so authorised.

(6) Contractors may carry a mobile telephone only with the approval of the security director.

Patients' outgoing telephone calls

30.—(1) Each provider must make arrangements in accordance with this direction, in respect of the hospital for which it is responsible, for the control of patients' outgoing telephone calls.   **C-035**

(2) If the provider allows a patient to telephone the Samaritans, it must provide a telephone dedicated solely for that purpose.

(3) A patient may not make a telephone call to another patient in the same hospital.

(4) Subject to paragraph (2), a patient may only make a telephone call—
- (a) to a telephone number pre-programmed by a member of staff using the pre-programmed system; or
- (b) if access to the pre-programmed system is temporarily unavailable, to any number that has been pre-programmed in accordance with paragraph (7) of this direction.

(5) For the purposes of paragraph (4), pre-programmed telephone numbers must—
- (a) include the telephone number of any person or organisation identified in section 134(3) of the 1983 Act where the patient has asked for that number to be pre-programmed; or
- (b) otherwise be approved by the responsible clinician, having consulted with the clinical team.

(6) Except for a dedicated telephone provided under paragraph (2), a patient may only have access to a telephone in any area where the patient normally has access, including a ward or therapeutic area—
- (a) at such times as the provider may determine between 8.00am and 10.00pm; and
- (b) at other times, where access is specifically authorised by a member of staff.

(7) Where paragraph (4)(b) applies, a member of staff—
- (a) must dial the telephone number and establish the identity of the person or organisation called; and
- (b) observe the patient at all times during the call.

Patients' incoming telephone calls

31.—(1) Each provider must make arrangements in accordance with this direction, in respect of the hospital for which it is responsible, for the control of patients' incoming telephone calls.   **C-036**

(2) Subject to paragraph (4), a patient may not receive an incoming telephone call.

(3) Where a member of staff answers a telephone call for a patient, other than one to which paragraph (4) applies, they must inform the patient that a call has been received and the main points of the conversation between the caller and the member of staff.

(4) A patient may receive a telephone call, other than a call from a patient in the same hospital, where—
- (a) the call has been pre-arranged by a member of staff and authorised by the security director; or
- (b) in the opinion of a member of staff—

         (i)   the urgency of the case is such that the patient should receive the call, or

        (ii) there are compassionate grounds for allowing the patient to receive the call.

(5)   Where a patient receives a telephone call under paragraph (4), a member of staff—

    (a) must observe the patient at all times during the telephone call; and

    (b) may monitor the telephone call in accordance with direction 33 (monitoring telephone calls).

Security risk assessments

C-037   **32.**—(1) Each provider must make arrangements in accordance with this direction, in relation to the hospital for which it is responsible, for security risk assessments of each patient to be carried out.

(2)   Subject to paragraph (3), a security risk assessment must be carried out by the clinical team prior to the admission of a patient.

(3)   Where it is not practicable to carry out a security risk assessment prior to the admission of a patient, that assessment must be carried out within 6 hours of admission of the patient.

(4)   The security risk assessment must include an assessment of whether a patient presents a high risk of—

    (a) escaping or absconding; or

    (b) subverting safety and security, or organising action to subvert safety or security.

(5)   Following a security risk assessment the clinical team must prepare a risk management plan.

(6)   Any risk management plan must include details of any decision to—

    (a) monitor the patient's telephone calls in accordance with direction 33;

    (b) lock the room of a patient at night in accordance with direction 34.

(7)   Where there is a high risk of the patient undertaking one or more of the actions identified in paragraph (4), the clinical team must consult a member of the security department before finalising the risk management plan.

(8)   The risk management plan must—

    (a) record the reasons for a decision of the clinical team that a patient presents a high risk in accordance with paragraph (4);

    (b) specify the date on which any decision to—

        (i)   monitor the telephone calls of the patient, or

        (ii) lock the patient's room at night,

      must be reviewed; and

    (c) specify when the risk management plan must be reviewed.

(9)   The clinical team must review each security risk assessment, and each risk management plan—

    (a) following any significant incident or change of circumstances which could impact on a patient's security risk assessment, including—

        (i)   any act, or the receipt of any intelligence, relating to escape or unauthorised absence of the patient, or related attempts, or

        (ii) any action, or threat of action, by the patient which has or could subvert security;

(b)   in relation to a risk management plan, by the dates specified in the plan; and
(c)   at least once every six months.

Monitoring telephone calls

33.—(1)   Each provider must make arrangements in accordance with this direc-   **C-038**
tion, in respect of the hospital for which it is responsible, for the monitoring
of patients' telephone calls.

(2)   A telephone call between a patient and any person or body identified in section 134(3) of the 1983 Act (persons or bodies to whom section 134(1)(b) or (2) do not apply) may not be monitored or recorded.

(3)   A telephone call between a patient and the Samaritans may not be monitored or recorded.

(4)   Before an incoming or outgoing telephone call is monitored or recorded in accordance with this direction the patient and any other person making or receiving the call must be informed if the call—
(a)   is being monitored or recorded; or
(b)   may be monitored or recorded.

(5)   Subject to paragraphs (2) and (3) if, following a security risk assessment, the patient's clinical team decide that—
(a)   a patient presents a high risk of escaping or organising action to subvert safety and security; or
(b)   there is a need to protect the safety and security of the patient or of others,
it must consider including in the risk management plan for that patient arrangements for an authorised member of staff to monitor and record the patient's incoming and outgoing telephone calls.

(6)   Where the risk management plan requires a patient's telephone calls to be monitored and recorded—
(a)   each telephone call must be monitored and recorded at the time at which it is made or received; and
(b)   that patient must be informed of the reasons for the decision to monitor and record telephone calls and of the right to have that decision reviewed by the Care Quality Commission, if a written application for review is made within six months beginning with the day on which the information set out in this sub-paragraph is received.

(7)   In addition to any recording made under arrangements included in a risk assessment plan under paragraph (5), an authorised member of staff—
(a)   may record up to 10 per cent of incoming or outgoing patient telephone calls over a seven day period; and
(b)   must listen to any recording made under sub-paragraph (a).

(8)   A recording of a telephone conversation made under this direction—
(a)   may be retained for such initial period and such subsequent extension of that period as the provider considers necessary;
(b)   at the end of that period, including any extension where relevant, must be destroyed.

(9)   The provider must comply with any direction given by the Care Quality Commission under regulation 4(2) of the Additional Functions Regulations 2011.

General Note

Paragraph (5)

C-039   Regulation 4 of the Care Quality Commission (Additional Functions) Regulations 2011 (SI 2011/1551) (as amended) reads:

"Review of decisions to record and monitor telephone calls in high security hospitals

> **4.**—(1)   The Care Quality Commission shall review a decision made in accordance with [direction 33(5) of the 2019 Directions] (monitoring telephone calls) that a patient's telephone calls will be monitored and recorded if an application to review that decision is made by the patient within six months beginning with the day on which that person receives the information set out in [direction 33(6)(b) of those Directions].
>
> (2)   On an application under paragraph (1) the Care Quality Commission may direct that the recording and monitoring of the patient's telephone calls pursuant to [direction 33(5) and (6) of the 2019 Directions] shall cease."

Paragraph (7)

C-040   In *R. (on the application of N) v Ashworth Special Hospital Authority* [2001] EWHC 339 (Admin); [2001] M.H.L.R 77, a patient challenged the legality of the equivalent to para.(7) in the High Security Psychiatric Services (Arrangements for Safety and Security at Ashworth, Broadmoor and Rampton Hospitals) Directions 2011. In dismissing the application for judicial review, Newman J. held that the provision of random monitoring of telephone calls, whilst constituting an interference with patient's rights under art.8 of the European Convention on Human Rights, is directed at a legitimate aim, namely the Secretary of State's duty under s.4 of the National Health Service Act 1977 (now the NHS Act 2006), and that the direction was a proportionate response to the permitted purpose of reducing the security risks at high security hospitals.

Security at night

C-041   **34.**—(1)   Each provider may in accordance with this direction, in respect of the hospital for which it is responsible, and having regard to any guidance issued by the Secretary of State, make arrangements for patients' rooms to be locked at night.

(2)   The provider may only lock a patient's room at night if—

(a)   the room has integral sanitation facilities and a staff call system; or

(b)   the patient is subject to continuous observation by a member of staff.

Grounds Access

C-042   **35.**—(1)   Each provider must ensure, in accordance with this direction and in respect of the hospital for which it is responsible, that it makes arrangements on the granting of patient access to grounds at the hospital.

(2)   The arrangements referred to in paragraph (1) must include security arrangements and risk assessments in accordance with direction 32 (security risk assessments) that enable a patient to be granted grounds access as part of a treatment plan.

(3)   Grounds access may be granted only by the provider's Grounds Access Committee in accordance with direction 37 or by the medical director in accordance with direction 38.

Grounds Access Committee

C-043   **36.**—(1)   Each provider must continue to maintain a Grounds Access Committee at the hospital for which it is responsible.

(2) A Grounds Access Committee must be chaired by—
   (a) the security director; or
   (b) a person nominated by the security director.

Functions of the Grounds Access Committee

37.—(1) Each provider must ensure that the Grounds Access Committee for the hospital for which it is responsible performs its functions in accordance with this direction.   **C-044**

(2) The Grounds Access Committee must—
   (a) consider any request by a member of the clinical team for a patient to be granted grounds access; and
   (b) consider any proposal by a member of the clinical team concerning the proposed employment of a patient under direction 24 (role of patients in managing or working in patients' shops and other specified employment).

(3) When considering a proposal referred to in paragraph (2)(b), the Grounds Access Committee must consider any recommendations made by a member of the patient's clinical team.

(4) The Grounds Access Committee may—
   (a) grant grounds access or a request concerning the employment of a patient unconditionally;
   (b) grant such access or such a request with conditions; or
   (c) refuse such access or such a request.

(5) Where the Grounds Access Committee refuses a request, each provider must, for the hospital for which it is responsible, have a policy in place for a patient to request, through the patient's responsible clinician, a review of the decision in accordance with direction 38.

(6) Where the Grounds Access Committee grants grounds access, it must specify the areas of the hospital to which access is granted.

(7) In performing its functions the Grounds Access Committee must take into account the clinical and therapeutic needs of any patient in relation to whom a request or proposal has been made under paragraph (2).

(8) A request or proposal for grounds access must only be refused if this will adversely affect—
   (a) the safety and security of patients, staff or visitors; or
   (b) the security of the hospital.

Review of decision of the Grounds Access Committee

38.—(1) Each provider must ensure that, where a patient's responsible clinician considers that a decision made by the Grounds Access Committee under direction 37 would impede the treatment of a patient, the decision is referred to the medical director for review.   **C-045**

(2) In reviewing a decision the medical director must consult the security director and take into account—
   (a) the views of the responsible clinician;
   (b) the safety and security of the patients, staff, visitors and visiting children; and
   (c) the security of the hospital.

(3) The medical director must—
   (a) confirm the decision of the Grounds Access Committee;

(b) vary the decision of the Grounds Access Committee; or

(c) overturn the decision of the Grounds Access Committee.

(4) Where the medical director grants grounds access, they must specify the areas of the hospital to which access is granted.

Leave of absence

C-046 **39.**—(1) Each provider must ensure that, before a patient in a hospital for which it is responsible is granted leave of absence—

(a) the responsible clinician, having consulted the patient's clinical team, produces a risk assessment;

(b) the clinical team develop a management plan addressing any risks that are identified in that assessment; and

(c) the security director, or a member of the security department who is authorised by the security director to act on his behalf, considers and approves that management plan.

(2) For the purposes of paragraph (1) the clinical team must include a member of the security department.

(3) The risk assessment prepared in accordance with paragraph (1)(a) must include an assessment of whether, if the patient was granted leave of absence, the patient would present a high risk of—

(a) escaping or absconding; or

(b) subverting safety and security, or organising action to subvert safety or security.

(4) The risk management plan prepared in accordance with paragraph (1)(b) must—

(a) record the reasons for a decision of the clinical team that a patient presents a high risk in accordance with paragraph (3);

(b) specify when the risk management plan for a patient's leave of absence must be reviewed; and

(c) specify when the risk management plan for the purpose of emergency medical leave of absences must be reviewed.

(5) The clinical team must review each risk assessment, and each risk management plan—

(a) following any significant incident or change of circumstances which could impact on a patient's risk assessment, including—

(i) any act, or the receipt of any intelligence, relating to escape or unauthorised absence of the patient, or related attempts, or

(ii) any action, or threat of action, by the patient which has or could subvert security;

(b) in relation to a risk management plan, by the dates specified in the plan; and

(c) at least once every six months.

Escorting patients

C-047 **40.** Each provider must—

(a) provide training for members of staff who are responsible for escorting patients outside the secure area of the hospital for which it is responsible; and

(b) issue written instructions to those members of staff on escorting patients outside the secure area, including instructions on the use of handcuffs and escorting chains.

Security of keys and locks

41. Each provider must ensure that the security director of the hospital for which it is responsible issues written instructions to—   **C-048**
(a) members of staff; and
(b) any other key-holders,
on the use and control of locks and keys.

Security audits

42. Each provider must provide such assistance as is necessary for the purpose of any assessment of the compliance with these Directions.   **C-049**

Provision of training

43.—(1) Each provider must make arrangements for the provision of safety and security training on a regular basis, to—   **C-050**
(a) all members of staff at the hospital for which it is responsible; and
(b) any other key holders at that hospital.
(2) Each provider must ensure that any person at the hospital for which it is responsible to whom keys are to be allocated receives—
(a) security induction training;
(b) training on the control of keys and locks; and
(c) such other training as the provider considers appropriate,
before keys are allocated.
(3) Each provider must ensure that any person at the hospital for which it is responsible to whom keys have been allocated receives security update training at least once in every 12 month period.

Perimeter security

44. Each provider in respect of the hospital for which it is responsible must implement perimeter security arrangements with the aim of, as far as is practically possible, preventing subversion and/or the escape by patients having due regard to the High Secure Building Design Guide.   **C-051**

Revocation

45. The High Security Psychiatric Services (Arrangements for Safety and Security) Directions 2013 are revoked.   **C-052**

REPRESENTATION BEFORE MENTAL HEALTH TRIBUNALS

Appendix D is reproduced with kind permission of The Law Society and may also be found at the Society's website.

Last updated August 31, 2022

1 Introduction

1.1 Who should read this practice note?

D-001 All practitioners who represent clients before the First-Tier Tribunal (Mental Health) in England and the Mental Health Review Tribunal for Wales.

Unless otherwise specified, references to 'the tribunal' include both tribunals.

2 The right to legal advice and representation before the tribunal

D-002 The right of access to a court is a fundamental right at common law under the European Convention on Human Rights (ECHR) and is guaranteed by Article 6 of the convention.

Article 5(4) of the convention further guarantees the right to legal representation.

When an individual is detained on the grounds of mental disorder, Article 5(4) requires that effective legal representation is provided by the state, free of charge, unless there are 'special circumstances'.

To comply with the state's obligations under Article 5(4), any legal representation that is provided must be 'effective'. That means the legal representative must:

- be suitably qualified and experienced (although not necessarily a qualified lawyer), and
- have adequate time and facilities to prepare the case, including sufficient opportunity to visit the client and take instructions.

'Special circumstances' do not include the fact that the detainee's prospects of release are poor or that the detainee has the means to instruct their own lawyers. Even if representation is available (whether at the detainee's or the state's expense) the state must still ensure the detainee is represented unless satisfied that they have capacity and have made an informed choice not to be represented. See for example *Megyeri v Germany* (1992) 15 EHRR 584.

In England and Wales, public authorities have duties under the Human Rights Act to ensure that detained patients are represented. In practical terms, this will mean that a tribunal should consider appointing a legal representative for an unrepresented patient under rule 11(7) of the First-Tier Tribunal rules in England or rule 13 in Wales, even where the detainee has chosen not to be represented, unless satisfied that the individual has capacity to make that choice.

See 8.1 Legal and other requirements for further details.

2.1 The role of the hospital

D-003 Under the English and Welsh codes of practice, hospital managers must ensure that patients are told how to contact a suitably experienced representative (paragraph 12.6 and paragraph 26.5, respectively). The way in which hospitals assist clients to obtain legal representation varies widely.

Under Section 132 of the Mental Health Act 1983 (MHA 18983), hospital managers must ensure that a patient understands 'what rights of applying to a tribunal are available to him in respect of his detention', which would include advice on the right to be legally represented. This information is contained in a leaflet which should be given to patients upon admission.

A list of mental health legal practitioners can be provided by the ward or the mental health act administrator to patients. The tribunals in both England and Wales also hold a list of accredited practitioners, as does the Law Society.

You are advised to contact the mental health act administrator at hospitals to check if you or your firm have been included in the list of representatives available to represent detained patients. Details of firms that employ a qualified practitioner in England and Wales can be found using our Find a Solicitor service.

2.2 Independent mental health advocates

The role of an independent mental health advocate (IMHA) is to help qualify- **D-004** ing patients understand the legal provisions to which they are subject under the MHA 1983), and the rights and safeguards to which they are entitled. IMHAs can accompany patients to tribunal and hospital managers' hearings and may speak on their behalf (with the prior permission of the deputy chamber president) if they are not legally represented. The IMHA may also assist patients to exercise their rights (for example, helping them complete an application to the tribunal).

IMHAs are not the same as legal representatives and are not expected to take over duties currently undertaken by solicitors or other legal practitioners. The following patients are entitled to have access to an IMHA:
- patients detained under the MHA 1983, even if they are currently on leave of absence from hospital, apart from those patients detained under sections 4, 5(2), 5(4), 135 or 136
- patients subject to guardianship under the act
- a community patient.

A patient will also qualify for the assistance of an IMHA if:
- they discuss with a registered medical practitioner or approved clinician the possibility of being given a form of treatment to which section 57 applies
- not having attained the age of 18 years and not being a qualifying patient they discuss with a registered medical practitioner or approved clinician the possibility of being given a form of treatment to which section 58A applies.

In England the tribunal has issued guidance on the role of IMHAs.

You should note that in Wales, all psychiatric in-patients have the right of access to an IMHA following implementation of the Mental Health (Wales) Measure 2010, part 4. Additional guidance to the measure is available under the code of practice to parts 2 and 3 of the Mental Health (Wales) Measure 2010.

2.3 Receiving referrals

You must comply with the seven SRA principles when seeking to obtain new **D-005** instructions. You should also read and abide by any code of conduct issued by the relevant trust or hospital.

If you are a member of the Mental Health Lawyers Association (MHLA) you should look at clause 3 of the MHLA Code of Conduct, which deals with making appointments.

You may:

- contact the mental health act administrator of the hospitals in your area to express willingness to accept referrals for tribunal representation
- contact IMHA service providers in your area to express willingness to accept referrals for tribunal representation.

You must not approach clients on hospital wards without prior appointments to obtain referrals. You should also be mindful of the potential for a conflict of interest to arise should you provide gifts or incentives to members of hospital staff.

If you are in doubt as to how to resolve any issue relating to referrals or gifts, you should contact the SRA professional ethics helpline on 0370 606 2577.

If a patient approaches you on a ward seeking representation then you should check with the mental health act administrator to ascertain whether that patient is already legally represented.

If the patient is not already represented, or the mental health act administrator does not know whether or not the patient is legally represented, you can leave your details and invite the patient to contact you for an appointment.

You can take instructions immediately in emergency situations after first checking with the mental health act administrator as to whether the patient is legally represented. Examples of emergency situations include section 2 patients where a date has already been set for a hearing or the time limit for appealing is very close.

2.4 Change of solicitor

D-006 Under the regulation 23(4) of the Civil Legal Aid (Procedure) Regulations 2012, you must not provide legal help to a client who has received legal help for the same matter from another supplier within the preceding six months.

The exceptions to this are:

- there has been a material change in relevant circumstances since the initial determination
- the individual has reasonable cause to be dissatisfied with the services provided under the initial determination
- the individual's usual residence has changed since the initial determination and, as a result, effective communication between the individual and the provider is not practicable
- the provider named in the initial determination has confirmed in writing that no remuneration will be claimed under arrangements made by the lord chancellor under section 2(1) of the act in respect of any services provided under the initial determination.

Where a patient requests a change of solicitor, you should record brief reasons in a file note as to why the patient is seeking to change their legal representative to you. You should write to the firm currently instructed and ask if they object to the change of solicitor.

2.5 Appointing a representative

D-007 The tribunal can exercise its power to appoint a representative:

- in England under Rule 11(7) of the Tribunal Procedure (First-tier Tribunal) (Health, Education and Social Care Chamber) Rules 2008 (the FTT Procedure Rules 2008)
- in Wales under Rule 13(5) of the Mental Health Review Tribunal for Wales Rules 2008 (the Tribunal (Wales) Rules 2008).

See 8.1 Legal and other requirements.

The tribunal may exercise this power when a patient either:

- states they want to be represented or does not want to conduct their own case
- lacks the capacity to appoint a representative but the tribunal believes that being represented is in the patient's best interests.

A refusal of representation from a client with capacity to make that decision cannot be overridden. See 4.1 Clients with capacity.

The upper tribunal has the power to appoint a representative for the patient under rule 11(7) of the Tribunal Procedure (Upper Tribunal) Rules 2008 (UT Rules 2008) in the same circumstances as the tribunal.

The MHA 1983 does not provide for a litigation friend to be appointed for a person who lacks capacity to give instructions to a representative.

For more information, see 4.2 Clients without capacity.

3   Communication with the client

Tailoring the way in which you communicate with clients who have mental **D-008** health problems is crucial in providing effective representation. The tribunal process can be a daunting process for patients who will often require increased levels of client care, including attendance time, well ahead of significant milestones in their case.

A report by the Administrative Justice and Tribunals Council provides useful analysis and information for you to consider when preparing for and undertaking hearings before the tribunal.

You should:

- be alert to, and seek to overcome, communication challenges which the client faces, including those arising from:
  — lack of capacity or use of medication
  — hearing difficulties
  — learning difficulties
  — language barriers or other cross-cultural issues.
- present information in a clear and straightforward manner, avoiding complicated forms and overly legalistic language
- allow extra time to explain issues in the case to clients and, if necessary, attend clients well ahead of a hearing to minimise confusion on the day of the hearing
- ensure clients have timely access to necessary information on their case, for example, expert reports where necessary.

3.1   Initial contact with the client

You should make initial contact with the client in a timely manner, to take instruc- **D-009** tions and give initial advice. You should advise clients on:

- their rights as a detained patient
- the issue of consent to treatment
- entitlement to legal aid
- the strengths and weaknesses of their case
- hearing procedures
- tribunal powers
- timescales
- their right to independent advocacy assistance.

You should also consider whether or not to request that the secretary of state exercise their discretion to refer the case to the tribunal if the patient has not applied to the tribunal within the relevant period. You may not be able to communicate all the information above in one meeting—it depends on the unique circumstances of each client. You should refer a client to another specialist legal adviser if you lack expertise on other significant issues for which they might need legal advice. Importantly, this is a requirement of legal aid contracts (see the 2015 Standard Civil Contract specification general rules). Examples of common significant issues include:

- family
- welfare benefits
- debt
- housing
- crime
- public law
- discrimination
- human rights
- community care
- clinical negligence
- immigration.

Legal aid changes have severely restricted or terminated funding in many of these areas. In some cases it may be appropriate to refer clients to Citizens Advice.

You should maintain regular contact with the client, and be willing to adjust the level of contact depending on the client's mental health condition. The client's clarity may change during the case as a result of changing mental health or medication.

You should aim to make contact with clients in person as much as possible, rather than relying on telephone or written communication. If your first referral is from a member of staff at the hospital or an IMHA you should try and speak to the client before your first attendance to reassure them that you will be coming to see them.

If your client is not detained but lives in the community then you should offer them an appointment at your office. If they are unable to attend your office you should consider what arrangements can be made to meet your client in private at a venue that is appropriate to your client's needs and is safe for you both.

You should be aware that your correspondence, although addressed to the client, may find its way on to the client's medical notes, thereby breaching solicitor/client confidentiality. It will sometimes be appropriate to visit the client rather than send correspondence by post. If you do so, you should read out the correspondence, offer the client a copy to keep and make a note on your file accordingly. If you find that your correspondence has been put into your client's records, you should check with your client whether they object to this and if so raise it with staff on the ward.

You must not disclose to the client any documents sent to you by the Tribunal Service or the Tribunal Secretariat in Wales which is marked 'not for disclosure'. You may only disclose such documents to your client if the tribunal authorises you to do so. See 5.3 Duty of confidentiality, which provides more information on disclosure issues.

3.2   Client care letters

D-010   Client care letters are especially important when working with clients who have mental health problems. The general rules (set out below) apply but special care and attention may be required.

Paragraphs 3.1 to 3.6 of the SRA Code of Conduct for Solicitors, RELs and RFLs outline client care requirements with regards to service and competence. These paragraphs state that solicitors must provide a proper standard of service, which takes into account the individual needs and circumstances of each client.

Paragraphs 8.6 to 8.11 of the Code of Conduct for Solicitors outline client care requirements with regards to client information and publicity. This includes providing clients with the information they need to make informed decisions about the services they need, how these will be delivered and how much they will cost.

These paragraphs should be interpreted with reference to the seven mandatory SRA principles of the SRA Standards and Regulations 2019.

Your initial letter to the client explaining terms of business is often called the client care letter. It acts as:

- a clear record for you and the client of the instructions given and what will happen next
- a useful guide for your client on your role and responsibilities
- evidence against complaints of insufficient information or inadequate professional service.

You should tailor client care letters to the individual needs of the client, reflecting their communication needs. You should use clear, simple and jargon-free language.

In some cases it may be inappropriate to send a letter, for example if the likelihood of distress to your client is significant. If for any reason you consider it inappropriate to send the client a client care letter, you should retain the letter on file and go through the letter in person with the client when appropriate and as far as their comprehension allows.

You should always record the reason for taking this approach. If an IMHA or independent mental capacity advocate (IMCA) is involved, you may wish to make them aware of the contents of the letter, subject to client confidentiality (see below).

For more information see the practice note on client care letters.

4 Taking instructions

4.1 Clients with capacity

The following guidance applies where: **D-011**
- a patient with capacity has instructed you directly
- you have been appointed to represent them under r 11(7) (a) FTT Rules 2008 or rule 13(5) (a) of the Tribunal (Wales) Rules or r 11(7) (a) Upper Tribunal Rules 2008; namely where the patient 'states they want to be represented or does not want to conduct their own case'.

You must assume that your client has capacity unless the contrary is established (section 1(2) MCA).

The test of litigation capacity is set out in *Masterman-Lister v Brutton & Co* [2003] 1 WLR 1511, namely 'whether the party to legal proceedings is capable of understanding, with the assistance of proper explanation from legal advisers and experts in other disciplines as the case may require, the issues on which his consent or decision is likely to be necessary in the course of those proceedings'. This is sometimes referred to as the client having capacity to instruct a solicitor. It is important to note, as the Supreme Court made clear in *Dunhill v Burgin* [2014] 1 WLR 933, that the test must be applied to the claim that the party in fact has, not to the claim as formulated by their lawyers.

The information that a patient is required to understand to instruct a solicitor in the context of an application to a tribunal is not complex and people severely affected by a mental disorder may still be able to provide instructions if you explain matters simply and clearly.

The question of whether the person is able to provide instructions is a judgment that in many cases an experienced mental health advocate will be able to make themselves. In the rare cases where you are unable to form an opinion you should obtain the opinion of the responsible clinician (RC)—either directly or via the mental health act administrator—as to the client's litigation capacity by reference to the test in *Masterman-Lister*. You should also ask the RC for their opinion of the client's capacity to appoint you.

If you are instructed at a point when the patient is considering whether to make an application, you should be aware that the capacity to make an application to the tribunal is set out in *VS v St Andrew's Healthcare* [2018] UKUT 250 (AAC).

This was confirmed in *SM v Livewell Southwest CIC* [2020] UKUT 191 (AAC), paragraph 87, "...the applicant must have sufficient understanding that she is detained and that the tribunal has the power to release her from that detention".

If you form the view that your client does not have capacity to make an application, but it is clear that they wish to leave the hospital, you should invite the hospital managers to consider asking the secretary of state to refer the case to the tribunal.

If you conclude that your client has the capacity to instruct you, you must take instructions from them and must act in accordance with those instructions, even where they are inconsistent, unhelpful to the case or vary during the preparation of the case, or during the hearing itself. However, the fact that the client's instructions are contrary to their best interests may be evidence that they lack capacity.

During the course of an application to the tribunal, you must refuse to advance an argument which is not 'properly arguable', despite instructions to do so, see *Buxton v Mills-Owen* [2010] EWCA Civ 122, para 45. However, a submission may be 'properly arguable' even if it has few, if any, prospects of success (para 43). It will depend upon the context and your judgment. It is highly unlikely that to seek a client's discharge in accordance with his or her express wishes would not be 'properly arguable', even if it is unlikely to succeed.

If you consider that an argument that your client instructs you to advance is properly arguable, you must advance it without reservation. In other words, you should not advance a submission at the same time as signalling to the judge that you may think that it is weak or hopeless, for example by using coded language such as 'I am instructed that'. Such coded language is well understood as conveying that the advocate expects it to be rejected (*Buxton v Mills-Owen* at paragraph 44).

Where you believe your client's instructions are unrealistic or contrary to their interests you should discuss with the client an alternative and more realistic line of challenge.

You may pursue this alternative line only if the client agrees. Your duty to act in accordance with the client's instructions takes precedence over your duty to act in what you perceive to be their best clinical interests. Therefore if your client wishes you to argue for their discharge you should do this, even if in your view your client needs hospital treatment.

Paragraph 3.1 of the SRA Code of Conduct for Solicitors states that "if you have reason to suspect that the instructions do not represent your client's wishes, you do not act unless you have satisfied yourself that they do. However, in circumstances where you have legal authority to act notwithstanding that it is not possible to obtain or ascertain the instructions of your client, then you are subject to the overriding obligation to protect your client's best interests."

In those circumstances you must not act on those instructions until you have satisfied yourself that they represent the client's wishes.

As an advocate, you are responsible for decisions about the manner in which you put your client's case to the tribunal, and you must bear in mind your professional responsibilities to the court—in this case the tribunal—as well as to the client. See *R v Farooqi and others* [2013] EWCA Crim 1649.

4.2 Clients without capacity

You must assume that your client has capacity to give you instructions unless the contrary is established. Nevertheless, there will be occasions on which you will not be able to accept instructions directly, or by way of a referral, because the client lacks capacity to instruct you. You may form this view if, for example, the client is profoundly learning disabled and cannot appreciate that they are detained under the MHA 1983.

D-012

If you think that your client lacks capacity to instruct you then you cannot act for this client unless either:

- you are instructed by a properly authorised third party, such as a court-appointed deputy or the donee of a power of property and affairs power of attorney
- the relevant tribunal has appointed you to act under the First-Tier Tribunal Rules, Tribunal (Wales) Rules or the Upper Tribunal Rules.

See above: 2.5 Appointing a representative.

As set out at paragraph 2.5, the tribunal can appoint a solicitor for a patient if satisfied that the patient lacks capacity to appoint a representative. In *YA v Central and NW London NHS Trust and others* [2015] UKUT 0037 (AAC), Charles J held that to have capacity to appoint a representative a patient must be able to appreciate their ability to conduct the proceedings unaided. The appointment by the tribunal operates as a retainer for the client.

An appointment by the tribunal does not mean that you are also appointed to act as the client's litigation friend. You should not automatically assume that guidance that may have been prepared for the use of a litigation friend in other court proceedings applies to you as a representative.

Although there is some overlap between capacity to appoint a representative and capacity to litigate, you should not assume when you are appointed that the patient will lack capacity to give instructions on all matters which relate to the application.

Once appointed by the tribunal, you have a heightened responsibility to identify and then to act in the interests of the client. The duty to act in the client's best interests is set out in principle 1 of the SRA Code of Conduct 2011 and applies to clients with or without litigation capacity.

In *YA v CNWL* (above) at paragraphs 13-16, Charles J considered the responsibilities of a representative who has been appointed by the tribunal. He said:

- the representative must promote the best interests of the patient
- in respect of matters where the patient has capacity to instruct the representative, the representative should follow those instructions
- where the patient lacks capacity to give instructions in relation to some matters the representative must ascertain the patient's views and wishes
- once the representative has ascertained the patient's views and wishes, then if the representative does not consider that the argument the patient wishes to put forward is in the patient's best interests, or where the patient wishes to put forward an unarguable point, the representative should:

— explain the patient's views and wishes to the tribunal, alerting the tribunal to the fact that there is a divergence between the representative and the patient
— invite the Tribunal to hear from the patient
— advance such arguments as they properly can in support of the patient's wishes.

- where there is no divergence between what the patient wishes to argue and what the representative considers to be in his or her best interests, then the representative should advance all arguable points to test the basis for detention in hospital.

Where the client lacks the ability to express their wishes, you should:

- ensure that the tribunal receives all relevant material so that it can determine whether the criteria for continued detention are satisfied
- test the criteria for continued detention
- remember your client's right to treatment in the least restrictive setting and alert the tribunal to possible alternatives to detention under the MHA 1983, such as community treatment Orders (CTOs) and guardianship
- In the case of a patient who is aged 18 and over and unable to consent to be detained for purposes of assessment or treatment in hospital but appears to be compliant, you may wish to consider whether the Deprivation of Liberty Safeguards (DoLS) regime under schedule A1 to the Mental Capacity Act 2005 (MCA 2005) might provide a better and less restrictive way of ensuring that your client receives treatment or assessment in hospital (see *AM v SLAM NHS Foundation Trust* [2013] UKUT 365 (AAC)).

You should not automatically argue for discharge if you are unable to ascertain the patient's wishes, but you are obliged to test the criteria for detention.

Separate considerations arise if the client is adamant that they do not wish to be represented by you, notwithstanding your appointment by the tribunal under rule 11(7) (b), the tribunal having assessed the client as lacking capacity to appoint a representative.

If on meeting the client you think that he or she has capacity to appoint you, then you should alert the tribunal and ask for the appointment to be discharged. It is then the client's decision whether to instruct you or not.

If you consider that the client lacks capacity to instruct you but think the client is hostile to being represented by you, then in some cases you should consider informing the tribunal and requesting the appointment to be discharged. This may be appropriate where:

- attempting to represent the client would cause them distress or interfere with their ability to participate in proceedings
- the client's hostility is such that you cannot fulfil your professional obligations to them
- continuing to attempt to represent the client puts your safety at risk and the risk cannot be managed using local policies at the unit where the client is detained.

For further guidance on obtaining copies of the medical records of a client lacking capacity see section 6.2 Access to medical records.

Note, finally, that it is possible that the tribunal will take the view that the client lacked the capacity to bring the application in the first place.

If this happens at a point when you have been appointed, and are therefore in a position to make representations, you should note to the tribunal that the proper course of action is likely to be for the tribunal to adjourn and to invite the secretary of state to make a reference to it to consider the client's case: se *Southwest CIC* [2020] UKUT 191 (AAC).

5 Your duties towards your client

5.1 Duty to act in the best interests of clients

Solicitors must act in the best interests of the client under principle 7 o. ...e SRA principles. This duty arises whether the client has litigation capacity or not. It is important to note that the term 'best interests' here does not necessarily mean the same as 'best interests' for the purposes of the MCA 2005.   **D-013**

See Professional conduct in the Legal status box below and 8.1 Legal and other requirements Aspects of the duty to act in the client's best interests will include:

* advising clients of the likelihood of being discharged
* advising clients on possible steps towards discharge
* advising clients in respect of disclosure issues
* following the instructions of a client with capacity to instruct you or communicating the views or wishes of a client without capacity to instruct you
* advising on aftercare
* advising on other related issues, for example, compulsory treatment provisions, alternatives to detention such as CTOs and guardianship
* advising on the possibility and consequences of the patient withdrawing the application to the tribunal.

5.2 Where conflicts may arise

Conflicts may arise because of the nature of the information that you have access to as a representative (regardless of your client's capacity to give you instructions). For example, in *RM v St. Andrew's Healthcare* [2010] UKUT 119 (AAC), the Upper Tier Tribunal ruled that documents revealing the patient was being covertly medicated should be disclosed to the patient because their fair trial rights (which the tribunal referred to as their best legal interests) required it, even though it was accepted it was likely to affect their health adversely (which the tribunal referred to as the patient's best clinical interests).   **D-014**

There may be other situations not covered by this practice note. If you are in doubt you should seek guidance from the SRA's professional ethics helpline.

5.3 Duty of confidentiality

5.3 Confidential information

This duty is covered in paragraph 6.3 of the SRA Code of Conduct for Solicitors, stating "you keep the affairs of current and former clients confidential unless disclosure is required or permitted by law or the client consents".   **D-015**

The SRA have released useful further guidance on the disclosure of client's confidential information which you should read. You must achieve outcome 4.1 which requires solicitors to keep the affairs of clients and former clients confidential, except where disclosure is required or permitted by law or the client consents.

For more specific guidance as to how you should approach particular situations you may encounter you should contact the SRA professional ethics helpline.

Privileged information

D-016   You should not disclose information passed to you in circumstances giving rise to a duty of legal professional privilege, which is absolute (see *R v Derby Magistrates ex p B* [1996] AC 487, *L (a minor)* [1997] AC 17 (see 24B-G) and *B v Auckland Law Society* [2003] 2 A.C. 736).

If you find yourself in this situation—for example, if disclosure of privileged information has been made mistakenly—you should contact the SRA's professional ethics helpline for advice on 0370 606 2577.

Duties of disclosure and circumstances where non-disclosure may be appropriate

D-017   Paragraph 6.4 of the SRA Code of Conduct for Solicitors deals with the issue of disclosure:

> "Where you are acting for a client on a matter, you make the client aware of all information material to the matter of which you have knowledge, except when:
> - the disclosure of the information is prohibited by legal restrictions imposed in the interests of national security of the prevention of crime;
> - your client gives informed consent, given or evidenced in writing, to the information not being disclosed to them;
> - you have reason to believe that serious physical or mental injury will be caused to your client or another if the information is disclosed; or
> - the information is contained in a privileged document that you have knowledge of only because it has been mistakenly disclosed."

The tribunal can withhold disclosure of documents from a patient if disclosure is likely to cause serious harm to the patient or another person and it is proportionate to do so. In England, this is possible under rule 14, Tribunal Procedure (First-Tier Tribunal) (Health, Education and Social Care Chamber) Rules 2008. In Wales, this is possible under rule 17, Mental Health Review Tribunal for Wales Rules 2008.

Under these rules, the information can be disclosed to the solicitor on the basis that they do not disclose it to anyone else, including the client. Rule 14 (6) (England) and rule 17 (5) (Wales) prohibits the representative from disclosing documents or the information they contain either directly or indirectly to anyone else.

The rule does not prohibit the representative from informing the client that the representative has a document or information that cannot be disclosed to the client, provided that the representative does not thereby indirectly disclose to the client the information which is being withheld.

If the tribunal has made such a direction then your duty to disclose the information to the client is over-ridden by this legal restriction (see IB4.4). This can be a difficult situation for you to manage. If documents are disclosed to you on this basis you should either:

- consider requesting an earlier hearing which the client does not attend
- consider dealing with disclosure as a preliminary issue without the client on the day of the hearing
- consider making an application for the issue to be considered by a salaried tribunal judge on the papers before the hearing.

Dorset Healthcare NHS Foundation Trust v MHRT (2009) UKUT 4 (AAC) gives guidance on when a responsible authority can resist disclosure of confidential third-party information or when a solicitor wishes to disclose such information to their client.

If you request full access to your client's medical records, the responsible authority should disclose all documents to you subject to an undertaking, if necessary, not to disclose certain specific third-party documents to the patient.

If in 'exceptional circumstances' the responsible authority refuses even to disclose documents to the solicitor, they must show that it is appropriate to do so by serving a skeleton argument to the tribunal office and the tribunal must make a ruling.

You should seek permission from the tribunal to disclose to your client any documents disclosed to you if you consider that it may improve the prospects of a successful outcome. In other words, if the documents are 'material to the client's matter'.

You should set out your reasons for disclosure by way of a skeleton argument. In *RM v St Andrew's Healthcare* [2010] UKUT 119 (AAC), also referred to in paragraph 5.2.1 above, the Upper Tribunal ruled that in deciding whether disclosure should be ordered the overriding consideration must be to ensure that the patient has a fair hearing, and that this must take precedence over any concerns that disclosure will harm the patient's health. It would follow that the requirement of a fair hearing can often override considerations of third-party confidentiality.

Where a request or refusal of request is not resolved, either party can apply to the tribunal for an order under rule 5 (d). This can be heard as a preliminary issue on the day of the hearing or a decision can be taken before the hearing following written or oral submissions.

The Upper Tribunal has stressed the desirability of dealing with disclosure issues between the parties without the need to involve the tribunal.

The guidance above with regard to disclosure, which arises from the Dorset case, is limited to those cases where there are ongoing proceedings in the tribunal. In other circumstances, if a trust or other body holding data on your client provides you with material that is relevant to your client's case then you must disclose it to the client unless any of the circumstances in paragraph 6.4 of the SRA Code of Conduct for Solicitors apply.

6 Representing children and young people before the tribunal

The tribunal has established a Child and Adolescent Mental Health Service (CAMHS) panel. **D-018**

The purpose of a CAMHS panel is to ensure that at least one of the tribunal members has special expertise in dealing with cases where a child is either detained under the MHA 1983 or subject to another order under the act.

For the purposes of the CAMHS panel, a child is treated as any person under the age of 18 at the time of the application or reference.

Although the tribunal rules do not make any specific provision in relation to child patients, the child's legal representative should always consider the following:

- the wishes and feelings of the child
- the need to ensure that the child is able to participate fully in the proceedings by, for example, requesting that the proceedings are dealt with in as informal manner as appropriate.

In relation to under 18s' capacity to instruct, although as noted in paragraph 4.1 above there is a presumption of capacity under section 1 of the MCA 2005 that this only applies to people aged 16 years and over.

While younger children may be able to give instructions if the issues are explained to them clearly and in an age-appropriate language, there is no presumption of capacity for under 16s.

Accordingly where your client is aged 15 and under, you may find it helpful to record that you have assessed the child's capacity to instruct you and (where this is the case) you are satisfied that the child is able to do so.

Where under 18s lack the capacity to instruct, as noted in paragraph 4.2, the tribunal can appoint a legal representative to act on their behalf.

You should also be familiar with legislation and policy specific to the child, for example the impact of the Children Act 1989 on decision making in relation to the child and the need to identify the child's entitlement to aftercare services under children's legislation and mental health legislation.

Relevant legislation is noted in Annex E of the 2013 Practice Direction (England) and 2019 Practice Direction (Wales).

Additional key legislation and policy issued since the Practice Direction for England include the Children and Families Act 2014 (relevant to under 18s with special educational needs), the Care Act 2014 (which includes 'transition assessments' for those likely to need support on becoming an adult) and Care, Education and Treatment Reviews (see 7.3 Care and Treatment Reviews).

The Royal College of Psychiatrists have produced a *Guide to Mental Health Tribunals for Young People* which may be a helpful tool in advising younger clients on the tribunal process.

7 Good tribunal practice

7.1 Avoiding delay

D-019   The tribunal's overriding objective is to deal with cases fairly and justly. This includes avoiding delay, so far as compatible with proper consideration of the issues.

Often delay can be caused by late reports from the responsible authority. In this situation it is the responsibility of the mental health act administrator to secure reports and submit them to the tribunal within the time limit. The tribunal in turn is responsible for issuing directions where reports are late. You should keep an eye on time limits for the submission of reports and ensure that the tribunal issue appropriate directions when it is necessary.

Once statutory reports are received you should ensure they comply with the

President's Practice Direction. In Wales you need to ensure that they comply with the requirements set out in the schedule to the Mental Health Review Tribunal for Wales Rules 2008.

These objectives are stated in rule 2 of the Tribunal Procedure (First-Tier Tribunal) (Health, Education and Social Care Chamber) Rules 2008 and rule 3 of the Mental Health Review Tribunal for Wales Rules 2008. This is also the case in the Upper Tribunal as stated in rule 2 of the Tribunal Procedure (Upper Tribunal) Rules 2008.

See 8.1 Legal and other requirements.

You should take all appropriate steps to ensure that tribunal hearings are not delayed.

7.2 Access to medical records

You should examine the section papers as soon as possible after your appointment as this will enable you to scrutinise the legality of your client's detention. **D-020**

The detention paperwork should be made available to the patient as soon as practicable and as a priority unless the hospital managers are of the opinion that the information would adversely affect the health or wellbeing of the patient or others (paragraph 4.16 *Mental Health Act 1983: Code of Practice* and paragraph 4.14 *Mental Health Act 1983: Code of Practice for Wales Review*).

The provision of detention papers being made available extends to the patient's representative and a signed form of authority should not be required.

You must read your client's medical records. These include documents such as:

- progress notes
- prescription charts
- minutes of ward or Care Programme Approach (CPA) meetings
- records held in the community

Again, the means by which you can obtain access will vary across hospitals.

If your client lacks capacity to consent to your access to their section papers or records then you should ask the RC to agree to disclosure on the basis that it is in their best interests to have their case properly prepared. If you cannot resolve this issue with the RC you should apply to the tribunal using the CMR1 form for an order for disclosure under rule 5 (d). In Wales you should apply for an order under rule 5 (c).

If your client lacks capacity to instruct you and you have been appointed by the relevant tribunal to act in the patient's best legal interests, then the tribunal appointment will serve as suitable authority to access the patient's records.

In March 2020, the First-tier Tribunal issued a direction providing for the disclosure of medical records to legal representatives.

Upon receipt of the CNL1 form, the responsible authority (RA) must allow the legal representative immediate access to the patient's medical and nursing notes without a written form of consent signed by the patient. There is no equivalent practice direction in Wales.

On request from the patient's legal representative specifying the notes they require, the RA shall ensure the records are sent without delay by secure email to the patient's legal representative.

If the RA has information in the notes that they do not want disclosed to the patient, they shall highlight this in the notes and the legal representative shall not disclose this information without further order of the tribunal.

7.3 Care and Treatment Reviews

D-021   If you are providing advice or representation to a client with a learning disability who is detained in a hospital or other setting you should be aware of the introduction of care and treatment reviews (CTRs) in England (but not in Wales).

CTRs are an independent review of an individual's care and treatment aimed at improving their care and reducing admissions and unnecessarily lengthy stays in hospitals. CTRs are reviews led by the responsible commissioner working together with an individual or family member with experience of learning disability services ('expert by experience'), an independent clinical expert and the care service provider.

The review should focus on four specific areas of care:
1.   the person's safety,
2.   the quality of their care,
3.   whether a forward looking care plan is in place and,
4.   importantly, whether care and treatment could be provided in a community setting.

CTRs should be carried out either:
- in the community when hospital admission is being actively considered
- within 10 working days of admission if no community CTR has been possible
- at six-monthly intervals for those who remain in specialist mental health and learning disability hospitals.

Reports and notes detailing the CTR and its recommendations may provide valuable information for use by you and/or the tribunal for the purposes of testing the criteria for continued detention or improving the care received by your client. If your client appears to you to be eligible for a CTR and one has not taken place you may request that a review is undertaken with your client's consent. If your client lacks capacity, a best interests decision-making process should be initiated unless you have the power to request one under the authority of a health and welfare lasting power of attorney (LPA).

Requests for a CTR should be made to your client's responsible commissioner, care co-ordinator or responsible clinician. Where you consider it necessary or helpful you may seek to attend the CTR, although this is a matter for your professional judgment.

7.4 Independent reports

D-022   You should always consider whether it is appropriate to obtain independent evidence. Expert evidence may cover a range of issues such as diagnosis, treatment, placement and activities of daily living. You should also maintain an approved list of experts. Prompt instruction of an expert may reduce the need for adjournments and will ensure that your client has a fair hearing. Further guidance is available in the Mental Health Peer Review guidance.

You should request independent reports as soon as possible and, in restricted cases, send them to the tribunal office and the Ministry of Justice no later than 21 days before the hearing so that the secretary of state can comment on the report.

7.5 Witnesses

D-023   You should confirm in advance the availability of all witnesses, including experts, who are expected to attend the tribunal. You should not appear as an advocate if you or anyone in your firm will be called as a witness or in any other instant where there is an own interest conflict or a significant risk of such a conflict (see paragraph 6.1 of the SRA Code of Conduct for Solicitors).

7.6 Interpreters

In England, form T110 (application to the First-Tier Tribunal (Mental Health)) **D-024** and the listing form HO1, must indicate whether your client will require an interpreter. If you need an interpreter, you should notify the tribunal as early as possible in proceedings. In Wales you should notify the tribunal by email or letter.

7.7 Documents

You should send all relevant documents to the tribunal office no later than seven **D-025** days before the hearing.

7.8 Pre-hearing medical examination

A pre-hearing examination is indicated in all section 2 cases. In all other cases **D-026** you should always consider whether it is appropriate to request a pre-hearing medical examination by the medical member of the tribunal. You must make such a request on form CMR1 (if in England) within the prescribed period (i.e. 14 days before the date fixed for the hearing).

If your client lacks capacity to make the decision you must consider whether or not it would benefit your client's case for there to be such an examination. However, if your case is before the Welsh tribunal, the default position is that the tribunal will carry out a preliminary examination.

In Wales, it remains the case that PHEs are indicated in every case. However there remain practical post-COVID difficulties with access to the patient either in person or remotely at most venues, so further guidance should be sought from the tribunal office.

7.9 Applications for postponements

You should avoid applications for postponements wherever possible. These are **D-027** frequently postponed in both the English and Welsh Tribunal, especially those made at the last minute. Any application for a postponement should be made to the tribunal.

If the tribunal is in England you must use form CMR1 where a request is made for any of the following:
- directions
- postponement
- prohibition of disclosure of information
- wasted costs
- permission to withdraw an application
- other applications.

If you consider that a postponement is in the interests of the client, you should advise the client accordingly, but leave the final decision to the client if the client has capacity to litigate.

If a postponement appears unavoidable, you should apply as early as possible, setting out the reasons.

Where delay is caused by late reports from the responsible authority, if the tribunal has not already issued directions, solicitors should request directions immediately after the breach of the time limits on submission of statutory reports.

7.10 Withdrawing an application to the tribunal

D-028 An application can be withdrawn at any time by the client if the tribunal accepts the withdrawal. A reference cannot be withdrawn.

If the client wants to withdraw the application, you should notify the tribunal office using form CMR1 (in England) giving the reasons.

Early notification allows for other cases to be rescheduled and maximises the use of the tribunal's time.

Where the withdrawal is received directly from the patient and that patient is represented, the solicitor will be approached by the tribunal and encouraged to make contact with the client to discuss the request to ensure the patient has not been put under pressure to withdraw.

The patient may make a fresh application for a tribunal within the same period of eligibility.

A welfare deputy, appointed by the Court of Protection, has no power to withdraw a patient's application to the tribunal unless the order expressly provides for that person to act as the patient's representative in mental health proceedings. See *AMA v Greater Manchester West Mental Health NHS Foundation Trust & Others* [2015] UKUT 36 (AAC).

7.11 Other codes of conduct

Mental Health Lawyers Association (MHLA) code of conduct

D-029 The MHLA has adopted a code of conduct. It covers:
- quality of service
- making appointments
- behaviour on the wards
- disputes over representation
- seeking clients
- gifts
- hospital procedures
- dress code.

NHS mental health trusts—codes of conduct

D-030 Some NHS mental health trusts and private hospitals have developed voluntary codes of conduct for solicitors. These codes ask solicitors to:
- contact the ward in advance to inform them of their intention to visit
- produce identification when visiting
- report to the ward office when visiting
- inform a member of staff if they wish to hold an informal meeting with another client whom they are visiting
- respect the operational needs of the unit/ward
- leave the ward following the completion of their appointment with a client.

Solicitors are asked not to:
- make unsolicited visits or telephone calls

- talk to or approach other patients
- hand out publicity materials
- offer gifts or money to service users other than existing clients
- offer gifts to staff.

You should find out whether there is such a code in place at the relevant hospital. If you have any concerns about the code, you should contact the relevant trust.

8 More information

8.1 Legal and other requirements

- The Mental Health Act 1983 as amended by Mental Health Act 2007 **D-031**
- The Tribunal Procedure (First-Tier Tribunal) (Health, Education and Social Care Chamber) Rules 2008
- The practice direction issued 30/10/08 (for England)
- The Mental Health Review Tribunal for Wales Rules 2008 (for Wales)
- The MHA codes of practice (different for England and Wales)
- Mental Capacity Act 2005
- Tribunal Procedure (Upper Tribunal) Rules 2008
- The Equality Act 2010
- Mental Health (Wales) Measure 2010

8.2 Mental Health Accreditation Scheme

The Law Society operates the Mental Health Accreditation Scheme. **D-032**
If you are a member of the scheme you are authorised to advise and represent clients who have been detained under the MHA 1983, before the relevant tribunal.

Since 1 August 2014, membership of the scheme is mandatory for advocates appearing before the tribunal, other than self-employed counsel, and all legal aid providers must comply with this (see 7.6(b) Category Specific Rules, 2014 Standard Civil Contract Mental Health Specification). Requirements for membership of the scheme include a good working knowledge of this practice note.

The provisions of the MHA 1983 have been qualified by the following legislation, statutory instruments and codes of practice:

- The Mental Health Act 2007
- The Tribunal Procedure (First-tier Tribunal) (Health, Education and Social Care Chamber) Rules 2008 (for England)
- The Mental Health Review Tribunal for Wales Rules 2008 (for Wales)
- The Mental Health Act codes of practice (different for England and Wales)
- Mental Health (Wales) Measure 2010
- Code of practice to parts 2 and 3 of Mental Health (Wales) Measure 2010.

You should familiarise yourself with all of the above and know which provisions apply, depending on whether you practise in England or Wales.

You should also have knowledge of:

- 2018 Standard Civil Contract Mental Health Specification
- Improving your Quality - Mental Health (Peer Review Guidance) – 6th Edition, February 2021.

Read copies of the relevant practice directions and updates, which all practitioners should be familiar with.

See 8.1 Legal and other requirements for further details.

Find out more about eligibility and membership

8.3 Other products and services

Practice Advice Service

D-033 The Law Society's Practice Advice Service can be contacted on 020 7320 5675 from 09:00 to 17:00 on weekdays.

Solicitors Regulation Authority's Professional Ethics Helpline

D-034 Solicitors may obtain further help on matters relating to professional ethics from the Solicitors Regulation Authority's professional ethics helpline on 0370 606 2577 from 09:00 to 17:00 on weekdays.

Law Society publications

- Assessment of Mental Capacity, 4th edition
- Guidance on meeting the needs of vulnerable clients
- Guidance on working with clients who may lack mental capacity

Other publications
- Easy read mental health tribunal information

8.4 Acknowledgements

D-036 This practice note has been prepared and updated by the Law Society's Mental Health and Disability Committee.

INDEX

LEGAL TAXONOMY
FROM SWEET & MAXWELL

This index has been prepared using Sweet & Maxwell's Legal Taxonomy. Main index entries conform to keywords provided by the Legal Taxonomy except where references to specific documents or non-standard terms (denoted by quotation marks) have been included. These keywords provide a means of identifying similar concepts in other Sweet & Maxwell publications and online services to which keywords from the Legal Taxonomy have been applied. Readers may find some minor differences between terms used in the text and those which appear in the index. Suggestions to *sweetandmaxwell.taxonomy@tr.com*.

definition, 1-1466
emergency treatment en route to named
  hospital, 1-118
emergency treatment en route to place of
  safety, 1-1411
general hospital, in, 1-119
generally, 1-1468
guardians powers, 1-147
informal admissions, 1-1337
leave for, 4-086
patient engagement, 1-076
remands to hospital for treatment
  Act provisions, 1-532
  applications, 1-536
  further remands, 1-542
  generally, 1-532—1-544
  introduction, 1-532
  orders made in other proceedings, 1-537
  transport to and from court, 1-538
Medical treatment (community patients)
adult community patients
  certificates, 1-900—1-906
  certified in writing, 1-864
  conditions, 1-864
  emergency treatment, 1-891—1-899
  generally, 1-852—1-859
  patients lacking capacity, 1-870—1-876
  withdrawal of consent, 1-888—1-890
certificates, 1-900—1-906
child community patients
  certificates, 1-900—1-906
  Code of Practice, 1-880
  emergency treatment, 1-891—1-899
  generally, 1-877—1-882
  patients lacking competence, 1-883—1-887
  withdrawal of consent, 1-888—1-890
Code of Practice, 1-847, 1-848
community patients
  adults, 1-852—1-876
  children, 1-883—1-887
  emergency treatment, 1-891—1-899
  withdrawal of consent, 1-888—1-890
definitions, 1-912
introduction, 1-847
liability for negligence, 1-907
objection to treatment, 1-908—1-910
Part 4A certificates, 1-900—1-906
patients lacking capacity
  adults, 1-870—1-876
  children, 1-883—1-887
  emergency treatment, 1-891—1-899
  withdrawal of consent, 1-888—1-890
relevant treatment, 1-849—1-851
withdrawal of consent, 1-888—1-890
Medical treatment (compulsory admissions)
Act provisions, 1-058
applications, 1-068, 1-070
appropriate treatment, 1-074—1-075
classification of mental disorder, 1-072
Code of Practice, 1-069
deterioration of patient's condition, 1-065
discharge
  generally, 1-059

readmission, 1-059—1-064
discretion to admit, 1-066
health of patients, 1-074—1-075
human rights, 1-067
in-patient treatment, 1-060
introduction, 1-059
medical recommendations, 1-074—1-075
out-patient treatment, 1-060
patient engagement, 1-076
protection of others, 1-074—1-075
readmission, 1-059—1-064
risk assessment, 1-074—1-075
safety of patients, 1-074—1-075
time limits, 1-070
treatability, 1-073
Tribunal applications, 1-922—1-926
Members of Parliament
mental illness, 1-1453—1-1454
Mental Capacity Act 2005
Code of Practice, 1-009
consent to treatment, 1-756
"nearest relative", 1-436
"relative", 1-436
Mental disorder
abnormally aggressive conduct, 1-036
Act provisions, 1-029
alcohol dependency, 1-037
arrested development of mind, 1-035
behaviour, 1-035
Code of Practice, 1-032
compulsory admissions
  assessment, 1-054
  treatment, 1-074—1-075
definition, 1-035
disability of mind, 1-035
disorder of the mind, 1-035
drug dependency, 1-037
generally, 1-035—1-038
human rights, 1-033
incomplete development of mind, 1-038
introduction, 1-031
learning disabilities
  definition, 1-038
  generally, 1-036
mental illness, 1-035
mental impairment, 1-035
neuroses, 1-035
paraphilias, 1-035
psychopathic disorders
  generally, 1-035
  persistent psychopathic disorders, 1-037
remands to hospital for reports, 1-511
seriously irresponsible conduct, 1-036
severe mental impairment, 1-035
sexual deviancy, 1-035
transient mental disturbances, 1-035
treatment without consent, 1-840
Mental Health Act 1983
abbreviations, 1-028
allocation of resources to detained patients,
  1-007
amendments
  consequential, 1-490

restriction orders, 1-954—1-959
Refugees
see also Asylum seekers
after-care, 1-1178
"Registered establishments"
definition, 1-495
human rights, 1-498
Registered medical practitioners
see Doctors
Regulations
generally, 1-487—1-490
guardianship, 1-156—1-158
Regulatory authority
see Care Quality Commission
Relatives
see also Nearest relatives
definition, 1-433—1-445
Release from custody
absence without leave, 1-724
Act provisions, 1-715, 1-725
generally, 1-715—1-724
human rights, 1-718
introduction, 1-717
life imprisonment, 1-720—1-721
treatability, 1-719
Remand
custody
magistrates' courts, 1-733—1-737
Remands to hospital
consent to treatment, 1-516
contempt of court, 1-520
conveyance to hospital, 1-530
evidence of mental disorder, 1-525
family law orders, 1-520
further remands, 1-527
generally, 1-514—1-531
insanity, 1-518
introduction, 1-516
offences punishable with imprisonment,
1-523
orders made in other proceedings, 1-520
time limits, 1-528
transport to and from court, 1-521
medical treatment, for
Act provisions, 1-532
applications, 1-536
further remands, 1-542
generally, 1-532—1-544
introduction, 1-532
orders made in other proceedings, 1-537
procedure, 1-517, 1-535
transport to and from court, 1-538
reports on condition, for
Act provisions, 1-514
applications, 1-519
Removal
see also Transfer (patients)
place of safety, to
guardianship orders, 1-568
hospital orders, 1-568
police powers and duties, 1-1416
warrants, 1-1389—1-1406

Removal of patients
see Transfer (patients)
Removal to hospital
see Transfer directions
Remuneration
mentally disordered persons, 1-1455—1-1457
registered medical practitioners,
1-1230—1-1233
Repatriation
patients, of, 1-1116, 1-1119, 1-1120
Reports
compulsory admission of in-patients, 1-100
consent to treatment, 1-516
contempt of court, 1-520
conveyance to hospital, 1-530
evidence of mental disorder, 1-525
family law orders, 1-520
further remands, 1-527
generally, 1-514—1-531
insanity, 1-518
introduction, 1-516
offences punishable with imprisonment,
1-523
orders made in other proceedings, 1-520
time limits, 1-528
transport to and from court, 1-521
remands to hospital
Act provisions, 1-514
applications, 1-519
restriction orders, 1-621
Residence
carers, 1-442
designated place of residence, 1-148
nearest relatives, 1-445
Residential accommodation
children, 1-1349—1-1352
informal admissions, 1-1349—1-1352
Residential care
nearest relatives, 1-445
"Responsible authority"
duties to tribunals
duty to arrange attendance of witnesses,
3-219
duty to co-operate with tribunals, 3-218
duty to provide written evidence, 3-217
use of force policy
Act provisions, 1-1517
introduction, 1-1519
Responsible clinicians
administration of medication, 1-793
background, 1-495
definition, 1-495, 1-749
generally, 1-499
human rights, 1-498
Responsible medical officers
see Responsible clinicians
Restitution
after-care, 1-1185, 1-1187
Restraint
see also Use of force
additional powers, A-001—A-002
administering treatment, 1-763
treatment without consent, 1-841